90£

# HISTORY OF CANADIAN CHILDHOOD AND YOUTH

# HISTORY OF CANADIAN CHILDHOOD AND YOUTH

/

## A BIBLIOGRAPHY

COMPILED BY
NEIL SUTHERLAND,
JEAN BARMAN, AND LINDA L. HALE

*TECHNICAL CONSULTANT: W. G. BRIAN OWEN*

Bibliographies and Indexes in World History,
Number 28

**Greenwood Press**
Westport, Connecticut • London

**Library of Congress Cataloging-in-Publication Data**

Sutherland, Neil.
    History of Canadian childhood and youth : a bibliography /
compiled by Neil Sutherland, Jean Barman, and Linda L. Hale ; technical
consultant, W. G. Brian Owen.
        p.    cm.—(Bibliographies and indexes in world history, ISSN
0742-6852 ; no. 28)
    Includes bibliographical references and index.
    ISBN 0-313-28585-3 (alk. paper)
    1. Children—Canada—History—Bibliography.  2. Youth—Canada—
History—Bibliography.  I. Barman, Jean, 1939-  .  II. Hale,
Linda Louise, 1949-  .  III. Title.  IV. Series.
Z7164.C5S94   1992
[HQ792.C2]
016.30523'0971—dc20        92-27767

British Library Cataloguing in Publication Data is available.

Library of Congress Catalog Card Number: 92-27767
ISBN: 0-313-28585-3
ISSN: 0742-6852

First published in 1992

Greenwood Press, 88 Post Road West, Westport, CT 06881
An imprint of Greenwood Publishing Group, Inc.

Printed in the United States of America

The paper used in this book complies with the
Permanent Paper Standard issued by the National
Information Standards Organization (Z39.48-1984).

10  9  8  7  6  5  4  3  2  1

# Contents

# Introduction

This volume and its companion one, *Contemporary Canadian Child-hood and Youth: A Bibliography*, are unique. Together they include virtually every serious piece of writing about Canadian children that has appeared in English. They are an essential tool for those conducting research into any aspect of the history of childhood in Canada.

The bibliography includes books, monographs, reports of government commissions, scholarly and professional articles and magistral and doctoral theses. To ensure that the bibliography was as complete as possible, project staff made a systematic and in-depth search of the major research libraries in Canada. They identified 144 journals that were likely to contain articles on Canadian children and reviewed each from its first issue to the last issue of 1990, or until the journal ceased publication if it did so before the end of 1990. These journals are listed below. To locate theses project members surveyed standard thesis listings, consulted regional and topic bibliographies and carried out on-site examinations of the principal university library collections across Canada. Canadian Thesis in Microform numbers are provided for as many as could be located. Most Ph.D. theses completed at universities in the United States are available from University Microfilm International, Ann Arbor, Michigan. Since articles published in anthologies are particularly difficult for researchers to find, project staff made a careful effort to locate and examine over 270 of these sources. In addition, staff found relevant articles in another 170 Canadian and international journals. The bibliography can be approached by region, by subject, and by author. The main listing in the bibliography is sub-divided by region under the geographical headings of Canada, British Columbia, the Prairie provinces, Central Canada, Atlantic Canada, and the North. Each item has been given a full bibliographic citation, including title, sub-title, author(s), and imprint information.

The bibliography has two indexes. The subject index, which is based on a natural language thesaurus developed especially for the bibliography, provides the most flexible approach to the bibliography. Composed of concepts and personal and institutional names, it gives access to the intellectual content of the materials listed. The author index lists all authors, including each name on a multi-authored work, and the names of persons with whom commissions are commonly identified.

## Acknowledgments

The Canadian Childhood History Project, which prepared this bibliography, gratefully acknowledges three research grants awarded by the Social Sciences and Humanities Research Council of Canada, under its Family and Socialization of Children and Canadian Studies Research Tools programs. The University of British Columbia's Faculty of Education, Department of Social and Educational Studies, and University Library provided essential support. The National Library of Canada and university libraries from coast to coast participated in the project by generously and competently assisting project staff visiting their collections and by lending items. Margaret Friesen and her staff in the Interlibrary Loans Division of the University Library provided invaluable support. Their cooperation made it possible to compile a bibliography that is truly national in scope.

An outstanding group of undergraduate and graduate students undertook the arduous task of locating, reading, and assessing each of the items in the bibliography. Our warm and grateful thanks are therefore due to Don Appleby, Brian Bain, Patrick Burden, Leon Chik, Sandra Cox, Elizabeth Crissman, Terry Groat, Celia Haig-Brown, Jeff Hasenaur, Robert Hunter, Maria Jacobs, Cathy James, Richard Jerome, Leslie-Ann Kealty, Elizabeth Lees, Bill Maciejko, Eileen Mak, Indiana Matters, Kathryn McPherson, Emilie Montgomery, Alison· Morham, Barbara Murdoch, Donna Penney, Katherine Pewsey, Kenneth Pite, Leanne Purkis, Theresa Richardson, Rosemary Speakman, Penny Crabtree Stephenson, Tony Varga, Elizabeth Wojciechowicz, and Susan Woods.

## Journals Systematically Searched

Acadiensis; Adolescence; Advocate; Alberta Historical Review; Alberta History; Alberta Journal of Educational Research; Alberta Law Review; Archivaria; Arctic Anthropology; Atlantis; B.C. Historical News; B.C. Journal of Special Education; BC Studies; Beaver; Branching Out; British Columbia Historical News; British Columbia Historical Quarterly; British Columbia Police Journal; Bulletin of the Canadian Psychological Association; Bulletin of the Institute of Child Study; Canadian Child Welfare News; Canadian Community Law Journal; Canadian Education; Canadian Education and Research Digest; Canadian Ethnic Studies; Canadian Historical Association. Historical Papers; Canadian Historical Review; Canadian Journal of Anthropology; Canadian Journal of Behavioural Science; Canadian Journal of Corrections; Canadian Journal of Criminology; Canadian Journal of Criminology and Corrections; Canadian Journal of Education; Canadian Journal of Family Law; Canadian Journal of History of Sport; Canadian Journal of History of Sport and Physical Education; Canadian Journal of Law and Jurisprudence; Canadian Journal of Mental Hygiene; Canadian Journal of Native Education; Canadian Journal of Native Studies; Canadian Journal of Psychiatry; Canadian Journal of Psychology;

Canadian Journal of Public Health; Canadian Journal of Sociology; Canadian Medical Association Journal; Canadian Native Law Reporter; Canadian Newsletter of Research on Women; Canadian Nurse; Canadian Psychiatric Association Journal; Canadian Psychological Review; Canadian Psychologist; Canadian Public Health Journal; Canadian Review of Sociology and Anthropology; Canadian Welfare; Canadian Welfare Summary; Canadian Woman Studies; Canadian Women's Studies; Child and Family Welfare; Child Development; Child Welfare News; Collections of the Nova Scotia Historical Society; Coordinator; Dalhousie Law Journal; Dalhousie Review; Education Bulletin of the Faculty and College of Education: Vancouver and Victoria; Education Canada; Etudes Inuit Studies; Family Coordinator; Family Law Review; Family Life Coordinator; Family Relations; Health Law in Canada; Histoire sociale/ Social History; Historical and Scientific Society of Manitoba Transactions. Series 3; Historical Studies in Education; Indian Ed.; Indian Ed.: Canadian Journal of Native Education; Interchange; International Journal of Women's Studies; Journal of Anthropology at McMaster; Journal of Broadcasting and Electronic Media; Journal of Canadian Culture; Journal of Canadian Studies; Journal of Comparative Family Studies; Journal of Consumer Research; Journal of Education of the Faculty and College of Education: Vancouver and Victoria; Journal of Education of the Faculty of Education, Vancouver; Journal of Educational Thought; Journal of Leisurability; Journal of the Canadian Church Historical Society; Journal of Youth and Adolescence; Labour/Le travail; Law Society Gazette; Law Society of Upper Canada Gazette; Legal Medical Quarterly; McGill Journal of Education; McGill Law Journal; Manitoba History; Manitoba Journal of Education; Manitoba Journal of Educational Research; Manitoba Law Journal; Manitoba Law School Journal; Manitoba Pageant; Material History Bulletin; Nova Scotia Historical Quarterly; Nova Scotia Historical Review; Okanagan Historical Society Report; Okanagan History; Ontario Education; Ontario Historical Society, Papers and Records; Ontario History; Osgoode Hall Law Journal; Ottawa Law Review; Perception: A Canadian Journal of Social Comment; Prairie Forum; Public Health Journal; Public Health Nurses Bulletin; Queen's Law Quarterly; Queen's Quarterly; Raincoast Chronicles; Reports of Family Law; Reports of Family Law. Second Series; Reports of Family Law. Third Series; Resources for Feminist Research; Royal Society of Canada Proceedings and Transactions; Saskatchewan Bar Review; Saskatchewan History; Saskatchewan Law Review; Sound Heritage; Supreme Court Law Review; University of British Columbia Law Review; University of New Brunswick Law Journal; University of Toronto. Faculty of Law. Faculty of Law Review; University of Toronto Law Journal; University of Western Ontario Law Review; Urban History Review; Vancouver; Vancouver Historical Society Newsletter; Waterloo Historical Society Annual Report; Waterloo Historical Society Report; Western Canadian Journal of Anthropology; Western Law Review; Western Ontario Law Review.

# HISTORY OF CANADIAN CHILDHOOD AND YOUTH

# General

1. **Abbott, John S.C.** *"The Management of Boys by Mothers."* John S.C. Abbott. Canadian Temperance Advocate 15(16 July 1849).

2. **Abella, Irving** *A Coat of Many Colours: Two Centuries of Jewish Life in Canada.* Irving Abella.

3. **Abella, Irving** *None Is too Many: Canada and the Jews of Europe, 1933-1948.* Irving Abella and Harold Troper. Toronto: Lester and Orpen Dennys, c1982.

4. **Abella, Irving, ed.** *The Canadian Worker in the Twentieth Century.* Irving Abella and David Millar, eds. Toronto: Oxford University Press, 1978.

5. **Abella, Rosalie Silberman** *"The Critical Century: the Rights of Women and Children from 1882-1982."* Rosalie Silberman Abella. Law Society Gazette 18, 1(Mar. 1984): 40-53.

6. **Abrahamson, Una** *God Bless Our Home: Domestic Life in Nineteenth Century Canada.* Una Abrahamson. Don Mills, Ont.: Burns and MacEachern, c1966.

7. **Abu-Laban, Baha** *"The Canadian Muslim Community: the Need for a New Survival Strategy."* Baha Abu-Laban. Edmonton: University of Alberta Press, c1983. In The Muslim Community in North America, pp. 75-92. Edited by Earle H. Waugh, Baha Abu-Laban, and Regula B. Qureshi.

8. **Adam, Ettie** *"A Backward Glance."* Ettie Adam. Okanagan Historical Society Report 46(1982): 124-128.

9. **Adamczyk, Mary Madeleine** *The Effectiveness of a Multi-level Reading Program at the Intermediate Grade Level.* Sister Mary Madeleine Adamczyk. Ottawa: University of Ottawa, 1959.
Thesis (Ph.D.)--University of Ottawa, 1959.

10. **Adams, Gerald R.** *"Historical-Cultural Change in the Expression of Vocational Preference and Expectation by Preschool and Elementary School Age Children."* Gerald R. Adams and Mandy Hicken. Family Relations 33, 2(Apr. 1984): 301-307.

11. **Adams, Ian** *The Real Poverty Report.* Ian Adams, William Cameron, Brian Hill and Peter Penz. Edmonton: M.G. Hurtig, 1971.

12. **Adams, Peter** *Early Loggers and the Sawmill.* Peter Adams. Toronto: Crabtree Pub., c1981.

13. **Adaskin, Eleanor J.** *"Janie: a Disturbed Child."* Eleanor J. Adaskin. Canadian Nurse 61, 9(Sept. 1965): 734-736.

14. **Adaskin, Harry** *A Fiddler's World: Memoirs to 1938.* Harry Adaskin. Vancouver: November House, 1977.

15. **Ages, Sandra Elizabeth Mendelson** *The Effects of Overt Verbalization on a Recognition Task with Six-year-old Children.* Sandra Elizabeth Mendelson Ages. Toronto: University of Toronto, 1971.

Thesis (M.A.)—University of Toronto, 1971.

16. **Aggarwal, Usha Rani** *Feasibility of Teaching Probability at Grade Five Level.* Usha Rani Aggarwal. Edmonton: University of Calgary, 1971. Thesis (M.Ed.)—University of Calgary, 1971.

17. **Ahitt, Bruce John** *Computer Assistance For Individualized Instruction.* Bruce John Ahitt. Calgary: University of Calgary, 1971. Thesis (M.Ed.)—University of Calgary, 1971.

18. **Ahlawat, Kapur Singh** *Evaluation of the Effects of Differential Modes of Television Presentation on Children's Looking Time.* Kapur Singh Ahlawat. Toronto: University of Toronto, 1971. Thesis (M.A.)—University of Toronto, 1971.

19. **Aichinger, Peter** *Earle Birney.* Peter Aichinger. Boston: Twayne, c1979.

20. **Albert, S. James** *The Incorrigible Juvenile - Who is He?* S. James Albert. Toronto: University of Toronto, 1958. Thesis (M.S.W.)—University of Toronto, 1958.

21. **Albridge, Marg** *"A Barnardo Family History: Esther and Elizabeth Dawson."* Marg Albridge. Canadian Genealogist 2(June 1983): 83-101.

22. **Alderton, Harvey R.** *"The Children's Pathology Index as a Predictor of Follow-up Adjustment."* Harvey R. Alderton. Canadian Psychiatric Association Journal/Revue de l'Association canadienne de psychiatrie 15, 3(June 1970): 289-294.

23. **Alderton, Harvey R.** *"Communication, Learning and Therapeutic Process in a Children's Psychiatric Hospital."* Harvey R. Alderton. Canadian Psychiatric Association Journal/Revue de l'Association canadienne de psychiatrie 10, 5(Oct. 1965): 338-349.

24. **Alderton, Harvey R.** *"A Contracted Study of the Use of Thioridazine in the Treatment of Hyperactive Children and Aggressive Children in a Children's Psychiatric Hospital."* Harvey R. Alderton and B.A. Hoddinott. Canadian Psychiatric Association Journal/Revue de l'Association canadienne de psychiatrie 9, 3(June 1964): 239-247.

25. **Alderton, Harvey R.** *"Imipramine in the Treatment of Nocturnal Enuresis of Childhood."* Harvey R. Alderton. Canadian Psychiatric Association Journal/Revue de l'Association canadienne de psychiatrie 10, 2(Apr. 1965): 141-151.

26. **Alderton, Harvey R.** *"Reactive Psychosis in Adolescence."* Harvey R. Alderton. Canadian Psychiatric Association Journal/Revue de l'Association canadienne de psychiatrie 8, 4(Aug. 1963): 256-266.

27. **Alderton, Harvey R.** *"A Review of Schizophrenia in Childhood."* Harvey R. Alderton. Canadian Psychiatric Association Journal/Revue de l'Association canadienne de psychiatrie 11, 4(Aug. 1966): 276-285.

28. **Alexander, E.R.** *"Tort Responsibility of Parents and Teachers for Damage Caused By Children."* E.R. Alexander. University of Toronto Law Journal 16, 1(1965-1966): 165-172.

29. **Alexander, William Hardy** *"Likewise Also the Cup."* William Hardy Alexander. Queen's Quarterly 52, 4(Winter 1945/1946): 408-413.

30. **Alexandris, Athina** *"Effect of Thioridazine, Amphetamine and Placebo on the Hyperkinetic Syndrome and Cognitive Area in Mentally Deficient Children."* Athina Alexandris and Frederick W. Lundell. Canadian Medical Association Journal/Journal de l'Association medicale canadienne 98, 2(Jan. 13, 1968): 92-96.

31. **Alexiade, Helen** *A Comparative Study of the Behaviour of Children of Greek Immigrant Parents and Those of Canadian-born Parents.* Helen Alexiade. Toronto: University of Toronto, 1962. Thesis (M.S.W.)—University of Toronto, 1962.

32. **Allard, Herbert A.** *"What Do We Want From Our Juvenile and Family Courts?"* Herbert A. Allard. Canadian Welfare 44, 1(Jan.-Feb. 1968): 18-23.

33. **Allen, Charlotte Vale** *Daddy's Girl.* Charlotte Vale Allen. Toronto: McClelland and Stewart Ltd., c1980.

34. **Allinson, Alec Arnison** *An Examination of the Concept "Creative Language" with Reference to Grades Four, Five and Six.* Alec Arnison Allinson. Toronto: University of Toronto, 1971. Thesis (M.A.)—University of Toronto, 1971.

35. **Alton, J.A.** *"Cyanosis in Infants Due to High Nitrate Content in Water."* J.A. Alton. Canadian Medical Association Journal 60, 3(Mar. 1949): 288-289.

36. *American Family History: a Historical Bibliography.* Santa Barbara, Calif.: ABC-Clio Information Services, 1984.

37. **Ames, V.N.,** ed. *The Canadian Superintendent, 1967.* V.N. Ames, ed. Toronto: The Ryerson Press, c1967.
Published as the Centennial of Confederation Yearbook of the Canadian Association of School Superintendants and Inspectors 1867 1967.

38. **Ammerman, B.E.** *"Industrial Scholarships."* Miss B.E. Ammerman. Canadian Nurse 11, 9(Sept. 1915): 534-535.

39. **Amyot, G.F.** *"School Health Services: a Panel Discussion."* G.F. Amyot, C.B. Routley, H.L. Logan, J.M. Hershey, C.E. Phillips, I.M. Cleghorn, Jules Gilbert, Elizabeth Smith and G.M. Wheatley. Canadian Journal of Public Health 38, 8(Aug. 1947): 361-375.

40. **Amyot, J.A.** *"Child Welfare."* J.A. Amyot. In Proceedings of Sixth Annual Canadian Conference on Child Welfare 1927, pp. 45-47.

41. **Anderson, Allan** *Remembering the Farm: Memories of Farming, Ranching and Rural Life in Canada, Past and Present.* Allan Anderson. Toronto: MacMillan of Canada, c1977.

42. **Anderson, Grace M.** *A Future to Inherit: Portuguese Communities in Canada.* Grace M. Anderson and David Higgs. Toronto: McClelland and Stewart Ltd., 1976.

43. **Anderson, J.F.C.** *"Management of the Diabetic Child."* J.F.C. Anderson. Canadian Nurse 57, 4(Apr. 1961): 342-347.

44. **Anderson, J.T.M.** *The Education of the New-Canadians: a Treatise on Canada's Greatest Educational Problem.* J.T.M. Anderson. Toronto: J.M. Dent & Sons, c1918.
Text is the published version of the author's D.Paed. dissertation presented at the University of Toronto in 1918.

45. **Anderson, Sadie Bernice** *Development of the Concept of a Function in Secondary School Students.* Sadie Bernice Anderson. Calgary: University of Calgary, 1971. Thesis (M.Ed.)–University of Calgary, 1971.

46. **Andrews, Eva** *"Autism and Schizophrenia in a Child Guidance Clinic."* Eva Andrews and Daniel Cappon. Canadian Psychiatric Association Journal/Revue de l'Association canadienne de psychiatrie 2, 1(Jan. 1957): 1-25.

47. **Anglican Young People's Association** *The Anglican Young People's Association Golden Jubilee 1902-1952, Fifty Years "For Christ and the Church".* Anglican Young People's Association. Toronto: The Association, 1951.

48. **Angrave, James** *"Team Teaching and Nongrading: a Case for Individual Timetabling in Canadian Schools."* James Angrave. Canadian Education and Research Digest 5, 1(Mar. 1965): 48-59.

49. **Angus, H.F.,** ed. *Canada and Her Great Neighbor: Sociological Surveys of Opinions and Attitudes in Canada Concerning the United States.* H.F. Angus, ed. Toronto: Ryerson Press, 1938.

50. **Anisfeld, Moshe** *"English Pluralization Rules of Six-year-old Children."* Moshe Anisfeld and G. Richard Tucker. Child Development 38, 4(Dec. 1967): 1201-1217.

51. **Anonymous** *Baby's Health and Record: a Practical Book for Mothers of Canada.* Winnipeg: Merton Corporation Ltd., 1948. First printed 1922.

52. **Anonymous** *"Dora."* Canadian Nurse 10, 1(Jan. 1914): 23-24.

53. **Anonymous** *"Featuring Bonnie Babies."* Beaver 1, 5(Feb. 1921): 17-19.

54. **Anonymous** *"The Health of the Child."* Canadian Medical Association Journal 2, 8(Aug. 1912): 704-705.

55. **Anonymous** *"Human Sacrifice."* Public Health Journal 4, 2(Feb. 1913): 95-96.

56. **Anonymous** *"In the Children's Ward."* Canadian Nurse 5, 4(Apr. 1909): 175-179.

57. **Anonymous** *"The Juvenile Delinquent."* Canadian Nurse 12, 9(Sept. 1916): 492-499.

58. **Anonymous** *"Medical Inspection of Schools."* Public Health Journal 5, 11(Nov. 1914): 683.

59. **Anonymous** *"A True Story."* Canadian Nurse 25, 10(Oct. 1929): 628-629.

60. **Ansley, H.A.** *"State of Health of People of Canada in 1945."* H.A. Ansley and J.T. Marshall. Canadian Journal of Public Health 38, 6(Jun. 1947): 269-278.

61. **Argles, Paul** *Teachers' Views of the Problem of Mental Health in the Schools.* Paul Argles. Montreal: McGill University, 1958.
Thesis (M.S.W.)–McGill University, 1958.

**62. Armour, R.D.** *"The Legitimation and Adoption Act."* R.D. Armour. Canadian Bar Review 5, 3(Mar. 1927): 186-189.

**63. Armstrong, Audrey** *Sulphur and Molasses: Home Remedies and Other Echoes of the Canadian Past.* Audrey Armstrong. Don Mills: Musson Book Co., c1977.

**64. Armstrong, Rinaldo William** *The Salt of the Earth: a Study in Rural Life and Social Progress.* Rinaldo William Armstrong. Ottawa: Graphic Publishers Press, 1930.

**65. Arrell, H.C.** *"Judicial and Welfare Aspects of the Family Court."* H.C. Arrell. Canadian Journal of Corrections/Revue canadienne de criminologie 3, 3(July 1961): 278-282.

**66. Arvello, Hector Antonio Puig** *A Study of Students' Opinions Regarding Teaching Practices.* Hector Antonio Puig Arvello. Toronto: University of Toronto, 1954.
Thesis (M.Ed.)--University of Toronto, 1954.

**67. Asher, Julie** *Maternal Child Rearing Attitudes and Adolescent Adjustment: a Comparison of the Child Rearing Attitudes of 20 Mothers of Emotionally Disturbed Adolescents and 28 Mothers of Normal Adolescents.* Julie Asher, Gayle McLachlan and Sylvia Nathanson. Montreal: McGill University, 1966.
Thesis (M.S.W.)--McGill University, 1966.

**68. Ashworth, Mary** *Blessed With Bilingual Brains: Education of Immigrant Children With English as a Second Language.* Mary Ashworth. Vancouver: Pacific Educational Press, University of British Columbia, c1988.

**69. Asmer, Michael** *The Prediction of Academic Success in High School.* Michael Asner. Toronto: University of Toronto, 1968.
Thesis (M.A.)--University of Toronto, 1968.

**70. Astburg, John S.** *Examinations with Particular Reference to Their Place in Secondary Schools.* John S. Astburg. Montreal: McGill University, 1938.
Thesis (M.A.)--McGill University, 1938.

**71. Atkinson, Harry K.** *"Boys in Trouble."* Harry K. Atkinson. Child and Family Welfare 7, 6(Mar. 1932): 1-22.

**72. Atkinson, Harry K.** *"Corporal Punishment for Young Offenders."* Harry K. Atkinson. Canadian Welfare Summary 14, 4(Nov. 1938): 51-59.

**73. Atkinson, Harry K.** *"Debatable Points in Industrial School Treatment, Part 1."* Harry k. Atkinson. Canadian Welfare 17, 8(Feb. 1942): 26.

**74. Atkinson, Harry K.** *"Debatable Points in Industrial School Treatment, Part 2."* Harry K. Atkinson. Canadian Welfare 18, 1(Apr. 1942): 33-36.

**75. Atkinson, Harry K.** *"Facts From the Annual Report of Juvenile Delinquents in Canada, 1935."* Harry K. Atkinson. Child and Family Welfare 12, 5(Jan. 1937): 59-61.

**76. Atkinson, Harry K.** *"Next Step in the Delinquency Programme."* Harry K. Atkinson. Child and Family Welfare 6, 2(May 1930): 25-27.

**77. Atkinson, Harry K.** *"What Several Hundred Delinquents Think of the Police."* Harry K. Atkinson. Canadian Welfare Summary 15, 2(July 1939): 45-55.

**78. Auden, George A.** *"School Inspection and the Public Health Service."* George A. Auden. Public Health Journal 2, 5(May 1911): 207-210.

**79. Aun, Karl** *The Political Refugees: a History of the Estonians in Canada.* Karl Aun. Toronto: McClelland and Stewart Ltd., 1985.

**80. Awan, Sadiq N.** *The People of Pakistani Origin in Canada: the First Quarter Century.* Sadiq Noor Alam Awan. Abr. ed. Ottawa-Hull: Canada-Pakistan Assoc., c1976.

**81. Awan, Sadiq N.** *"The People of Pakistani Origin in Canada: Their First Twenty-five Years."* Sadiq N. Awan. Toronto: Butterworth and Co. (Canada) Ltd., 1980. In Visible Minorities and Multiculturalism: Asians in Canada, pp. 243-246. Edited by K. Victor Ujimoto and Gordon Hirabayashi, with the assistance of P.A. Saram.

**82. Axelrod, Paul** *"The Student Movement of the 1930s."* Paul Axelrod. Kingston: McGill-Queen's University Press, 1989. In Youth, University and Canadian Society: Essays in the Social History of Higher Education, pp. 216-246. Edited by Paul Axelrod and John G. Reid.

83. **Ayoade, Emmanuel Folorunsho Peter** *Some Relationships Between the Level of Naturalistic Thinking and Achievement on an Elementary Science Demonstration Lesson among Grade Six Pupils from Four Cultural Backgrounds.* Emmanuel Folorunsho Peter Ayoade. Toronto: University of Toronto, 1970. Thesis (M.A.)–University of Toronto, 1970.

84. **Bacher, John C.** *"Keeping Warm and Dry: the Policy Response to the Struggle for Shelter Among Canada's Homeless, 1900-1960."* John C. Bacher and J. David Hulchanski. Urban History Review/Revue d'histoire urbaine 26, 2(Oct. 1987): 147-163.

85. **Backhouse, Constance B.** *"Desperate Women and Compassionate Courts: Infanticide in Nineteenth Century Canada."* Constance B. Backhouse. University of Toronto Law Journal 34(1984): 447-478.

86. **Backhouse, Constance B.** *"Involuntary Motherhood: Abortion, Birth Control and the Law in Nineteenth Century Canada."* Constance B. Backhouse. Windsor Yearbook of Access to Justice/Recueil annuel de Windsor d'access a la justice 3(1983): 61-130.

87. **Backhouse, Constance B.** *"Nineteenth Century Canadian Rape Law: 1800-92."* Constance B. Backhouse. Toronto: For the Osgoode Society by University of Toronto Press, c1983. In Essays in the History of Canadian Law, v.2, pp. 200-247. Edited by David H. Flaherty.

88. **Backhouse, Constance B.** *"Shifting Patterns in Nineteenth Century Canadian Custody Law."* Constance B. Backhouse. Toronto: Published for Osgoode Society by University of Toronto Press, c1981. In Essays in the History of Canadian Law, v.1, pp. 212-248. Edited by David H. Flaherty.

89. **Backhouse, Constance B.** *"The Tort of Seduction: Fathers and Daughters in Nineteenth Century Canada."* Constance Backhouse. Dalhousie Law Journal 10, 1(June 1986): 45-80.

90. **Bagnell, Kenneth** *"Britain's Children Who Came to Stay."* Kenneth Bagnell. Ontario Education 13, 1(Jan.-Feb. 1981): 4-9.

91. **Bagnell, Kenneth** *The Little Immigrants: the Orphans Who Came to Canada.* Kenneth Bagnell. Toronto: Macmillan of Canada, c1980, 1987.

92. **Bain, David Alexander** *Self Preference in Relation to Other Sociometric Variables in a Group of Eight Fourth Grade Children over a School Year.* David Alexander Bain. Toronto: University of Toronto, 1956. Thesis (M.A.)–University of Toronto, 1956.

93. **Baird, Agnes B.** *"Problems in Infant Hygiene and What Statistics Reveal."* Agnes B. Baird. Canadian Public Health Journal 25, 4(Apr. 1934): 167-170.

94. **Baird, Agnes B.** *"Statistical Indications in Some Problems in Maternal and Child Hygiene."* Agnes B. Baird. Child and Family Welfare 9, 3(Sept. 1933): 6-11.

95. **Baird, Marjorie** *"The Mother and Big Sister in the Home."* Marjorie Baird. Canadian Nurse 24, 9(Sept. 1928): 483-485.

96. **Baker, G. Blaine** *"The Juvenile Advocate Society, 1821-1826: Self-proclaimed Schoolroom for Upper Canada's Governing Class."* G. Blaine Baker. Canadian Historical Association, Historical Papers/Communications historiques (1985): 74-101.

97. **Baker, Harry** *"Paroxysmal Tachycardia in Childhood."* H. Baker. Canadian Medical Association Journal 45, 5(Nov. 1941): 426-430.

98. **Baker, Nancy Elizabeth** *The Influence of Some Task and Organismic Variables in the Manifestation of Conservation of Number.* Nancy Elizabeth Baker. Toronto: University of Toronto, 1967. Thesis (M.A.)–University of Toronto, 1967.

99. **Baker, Walter** *The Place of the Private Agency in the Administration of Government Policies: a Case Study: the Ontario Children's Aid System, 1893-1965.* Walter Baker. Kingston: Queen's University, 1966. (CTM no. 268) Thesis (Ph.D.)–Queen's University, 1966.

100. **Ballance, Karoline E.** *Report on Legislation and Services for Exceptional Children in Canada.* Karoline E. Ballance and David C. Kendall. [Toronto]: Council for Exceptional Children, Canadian Committee, 1969.

101. **Banister, Philip** *"Congenital Malformations: Preliminary Report of an Investigation of Reduction Deformities of the Limbs, Triggered by a Pilot Surveillance System."* Philip Banister. Canadian Medical Association Journal/Journal de l'Association medicale canadienne 103, 5(Sept. 12, 1970): 466-472.

102. **Barbeau, Gerard L.** *"Mental Deficiency."* Gerard L. Barbeau. Canadian Welfare 27, 7(Feb. 1952): 5-9.

103. **Bargen, Peter Frank** *The Legal Status of the Canadian Public School Pupil.* Peter Frank Bargen. Toronto: MacMillan, 1961.

104. **Barker, Lillian** *The Quints Have a Family.* Lillian Barker. New York: Sheed and Ward, 1941.

105. **Barkman, David** *Parental Role Performance in Families Where Children Are Neglected.* David Barkman Myrna C. Caswell, Jean Elliott, Elinor R. Haythorne, Nancy E. Opdecam and Mary Elaine Sweet. Toronto: University of Toronto, 1965.
    Thesis (M.S.W.)--University of Toronto, 1965.

106. **Barman, Jean** *"Comment on Cookson: the Boarding School in a Canadian Context."* Jean Barman. Journal of Educational Thought 16, 2(Aug. 1982): 98-100.

107. **Barman, Jean** *"The Legacy of the Past: an Overview."* Jean Barman. Vancouver: University of British Columbia Press, 1986. In Indian Education in Canada, Volume 1: the Legacy, pp. 1-22. Edited by Jean Barman, Yvonne Hebert and Don McCaskill.

108. **Barman, Jean, ed.** *Indian Education in Canada: Volume I: the Legacy.* Jean Barman, Yvonne Hebert and Don McCaskill, eds. Vancouver: University of British Columbia Press, c1986.

109. **Barnstead, Elinor G.** *"Youth, Marriage, and the Family."* Elinor G. Barnstead. Canadian Welfare 23, 8(Mar. 1948): 10-12.

110. **Barr, Helen, ed.** *Early Education in West Vancouver, 1911-1981: the First Seventy Years.* Helen Barr, ed. [West Vancouver]: West Vancouver University Women's Club, Local History Group, [1981?].

111. **Barraclough, W.W.** *"The Convulsive Child in the Community."* W.W. Barraclough. Canadian Public Health Journal 31, 4(Apr. 1940): 188

112. **Barrow, Patricia (Jeffers)** *A Study of Families Who Foster Children with Special Needs.* Patricia (Jeffers) Barrow. Toronto: University of Toronto, 1966. Thesis (M.S.W.)--University of Toronto, 1966.

113. **Bartlett, George W.** *"The Boy and the Boy Scout Programme."* G.W. Bartlett. In Proceedings and Papers Fourth Annual Canadian Conference on Child Welfare 1923, pp. 131-135.

114. **Bate, Clive** *"The Humane Limits of Therapy."* Clive Bate. Canadian Welfare 46, 2(Mar.-Apr. 1970): 8-10.

115. **Bate, William P.** *Aspiration, a Study of the Effect of Unemployment for the Education and Occupation of the Eldest Public School Child.* William P. Bate. Toronto: University of Toronto, 1963. Thesis (M.S.W.)--University of Toronto, 1963.

116. **Bates, Gordon** *"The Need for Social Hygiene."* Gordon Bates. In Proceedings and Papers Fifth Annual Canadian Conference on Child Welfare 1925, pp. 125-130.

117. **Batten, Jack** *Robinette: the Dean of Canadian Lawyers.* Jack Batten. Toronto: Macmillan of Canada, c1984.

118. **Battiste, Marie** *"Micmac Literacy and Cognitive Assimilation."* Marie Battiste. Vancouver: University of British Columbia Press, 1986. In Indian Education in Canada, Volume 1: the Legacy, pp. 23-44. Edited by Jean Barman, Yvonne Hebert and Don McCaskill.

119. **Baudouin, J.A.** *"Vaccination Against Tuberculosis with the B.C.G. Vaccine."* J.A. Baudouin. Canadian Public Health Journal 27, 1(Jan. 1936): 20-26.

120. **Baudouin, J.A.** *"War Against Infant Mortality."* J.A. Bauduin. Public Health Journal 5, 5(May 1914): 305-309.

121. **Baumanis, Debora** *"Both Sides of the Coin: the Retarded Child and His Family."* Debora Baumanis. Canada's Mental Health 18, 3&4(May/Aug. 1970): 23-28.

122. **Baumgartel, Bernd W.** *A Study of Some Aspects of Juvenile Delinquency among Children of Immigrants.* Bernd W. Baumgartel. Toronto: University of Toronto, 1955. Thesis (M.S.W.)--University of Toronto, 1955.

123. **Baxter, Donna M.** *"What Should Tommy Eat?"* Donna M. Baxter. Canadian Nurse 48, 12(Dec. 1952): 986-991.

124. **Baxter, Hamilton** *"Plastic Connection of Protruding Ears in Children."* Hamilton Baxter. Canadian Medical Association Journal 45, 3(Sept. 1941): 217-220.

**125. Baxter, Ian F.G.** *"Recognition of Status in Family Law: a Proposal for Simplification."* Baxter, Ian F.G. Canadian Bar Review/Revue du Barreau Canadien 39, 3(Sept. 1961): 301-350.

**126. Bayley, Susan Nancy** *The Teaching of French in English Primary Schools, 1960-1982: a Philosophical and Institutional Approach to its Emergence and Decline.* Susan Nancy Bayley. Montreal: McGill University, 1982.
Thesis (M.A.)–McGill University, 1982.

**127. Bayrakal, Sadi** *"The Significance of Electroencephalographic Abnormality in Behavior-problem Children."* Sadi Bayrakal. Canadian Psychiatric Association Journal/Revue de l'Association canadienne de psychiatrie 10, 5(Oct. 1965): 387.

**128. Beattie, C., comp.** *Sociology Canada: Readings.* Christopher Beattie and Stewart Crysdale, compilers. Scarborough; Butterworths, 1974.

**129. Beattie, H.R.** *"Special Education: Responsibilities and Provisions."* H.R. Beattie. Canadian Education and Research Digest 1, 4(Dec. 1961): 47-60.

**130. Beattie, Jessie L.** *Black Sheep Folklore of Canada.* Jessie L. Beattie. Hamilton: Fleming Press, 1981.

**131. Beattie, Jessie L.** *A Season Past: Reminiscences of a Rural Canadian Childhood.* Jessie Louise Beattie. Toronto: McClelland and Stewart Ltd., 1968.

**132. Beattie, Kathleen L.** *"Suggestibility in Delinquents."* Kathleen L. Beattie and F.R. Wake. Canadian Journal of Corrections/Revue canadienne de criminologie 7, 2(Apr. 1965): 157-172.

**133. Beattie, Lewis S.** *"The Development of Student Potential."* Lewis S. Beattie and Edward F. Sheffield. Ottawa: The Conference, 1961. In Canadian Conference on Education, Conference Studies, no pagination.
Papers individually published in 1961 for the 1962 Conference.

**134. Bell, Bernice** *Successful Foster Homes for Mildly Retarded Children.* Bernice Bell. Toronto: University of Toronto, 1964.
Thesis (M.S.W.)–University of Toronto, 1964.

**135. Bell, Bess** *"Nursery Education and the Child with Special Needs."* Bess Bell. Canada's Mental Health 16, 6(Nov./Dec. 1968): 3-10.

**136. Bell, Sara Leslie** *"The Emotional Development of the Preschool Child."* Sara Leslie Bell. Canadian Nurse 25, 1(Jan. 1929): 25-28.

**137. Belmonte, Mimi M.** *"Diabetes in Childhood."* Mimi M. Belmonte. Canadian Nurse 58, 11(Nov. 1962): 988-990.

**138. Belmonte, Mimi M.** *"Diabetes in Childhood."* Mimi M. Belmonte. Canadian Nurse 59, 2(Feb. 1963): 143-145.

**139. Benedict, Elsie Graves** *"The Contribution of the Junior Red Cross to Public Health."* Elsie Graves Benedict. Canadian Public Health Journal 17, 7(July 1927): 322-330.

**140. Benham, Mary Lile** *Nellie McClung.* Mary Lile Benham. Don Mills: Fitzhenry and Whiteside, c1975.

**141. Benham, Mary Lile** *Paul Kane.* Mary Lile Benham. Don Mills: Fitzhenry & Whiteside, 1977.

**142. Bennet, Beverly** *A Group Program of Infant Stimulation Stressing Maternal Participation.* Beverly Bennet. Toronto: University of Toronto, 1971.
Thesis (M.A.)–University of Toronto, 1971.

**143. Berkeley, Heather** *"Children's Rights in the Canadian Context."* Heather Berkeley, Chad Gaffield and Gordon West. Interchange 8, 1-2(1977-1978): 1-4.
Extended version of the paper is published in Children's Rights: Legal and Educational Issues, pp. 3-14. Edited by Heather Berkeley, Chad Gaffield and W. Gordon West.
Heather Berkeley is not named as an author of the extended version of the paper.

**144. Berkeley, Heather, ed.** *Children's Rights: Legal and Educational Issues.* Heather Berkeley, Chad Gaffield and W. Gordon West, eds. Toronto: OISE, c1978.
Original versions of the papers in this volume appeared in Interchange 8, 1-2(1977-78).

**145. Bernard, Harold W.** *Mental Hygiene for Classroom Teachers.* Harold W. Bernard. Toronto: McGraw-Hill Book Company, 1952.

**146. Bernhardt, Karl S.** *Being a Parent: Unchanging Values in a Changing World.* Karl S. Bernhardt and David K. Bernhardt, ed. Toronto: University of Toronto Press, c1970.

147. **Bernhardt, Karl S.** *"By Way of Introduction."* Karl S. Bernhardt. Bulletin of the Institute of Child Study 23, 3(Sept.-Dec. 1961): 1-2.

148. **Bernhardt, Karl S.** *Discipline and Child Guidance.* Karl S. Bernhardt. New York: McGraw-Hill, [c1964].

149. **Bernhardt, Karl S.** *"The Effect of Added Thiamine on Intelligence and Learning with Identical Twins."* Karl S. Bernhardt, Mary Northway and Catherine M. Tatham. Canadian Journal of Psychology 2, 2(June 1948): 58-61.

150. **Berton, Pierre** *Adventures of a Columnist.* Pierre Berton. [Toronto]: McClelland and Stewart, c1960.

151. **Berton, Pierre** *The Smug Minority.* Pierre Berton. Toronto: McClelland and Stewart Ltd., c1968.

152. **Berton, Pierre** *"Universities: Pastures for the Privileged."* Pierre Berton. Toronto: McClelland & Stewart, c1972. In Making It: the Canadian Dream, pp. 95-106. Edited by Bryan Finnigan and Cy Gonick. Reprinted from The Smug Minority by Pierre Berton.

153. **Besier, Dorothy Phillips** *Cognitive Dissonance, Self-esteem and Interpersonal Attraction.* Dorothy Phillips Besier. Edmonton: University of Alberta, 1971. Thesis (M.A.)--University of Alberta, 1971.

154. **Beyea, John B.** *Self Concept and Academic Achievement.* John B. Beyea. Fredericton: University of New Brunswick, c1969.
Thesis (M.Ed.)--University of New Brunswick, 1969.
National Library of Canada MIC TC-5629.

155. **Biggar, J.L.** *"An Adequate Program for the Treatment of Crippled Children."* J.L. Biggar. In Proceedings of Sixth Annual Canadian Conference on Child Welfare 1927, pp. 36-39.

156. **Biggar, J.L.** *"A Survey of Crippled Children."* J.L. Biggar. Child and Family Welfare 6, 7(Mar. 1931): 14-16.

157. **Bilson, Geoffrey** *The Guest Children.* Geoffrey Bilson. Saskatoon: Fifth House, c1988.

158. **Birt, Arthur R.** *"Some Thoughts on Infantile Eczema."* Arthur R. Birt. Canadian Medical Association Journal 61, 6(Dec. 1949): 589-592.

159. **Birt, Lillian M.** *The Children's Home-finder: the Story of Annie MacPherson and Louisa Birt.* Lillian M. Birt. London, Eng.: Lisbet, 1913.

160. **Bissell, Claude T.** *"Canadian Education Today."* Claude T. Bissell. Durham: Duke University Press, 1967. In Contemporary Canada, pp. 177-190. Edited by Richard Leach.

161. **Bissell, Claude T.** *Ernest Buckler Remembered.* Claude Bissell. Toronto: University of Toronto Press, 1989.

162. **Black, Norman Fergus** *English for the Non-english.* Norman Fergus Black. Regina: Regina Book Shop Limited, 1913. Thesis (D.Paed.)--University of Toronto, 1913.
Thesis published as monograph.

163. **Blackader, A.D.** *"The More Important Causes Underlying the Heavy Infantile Death Rate in Large Cities and the Benefits to be Derived from the Establishment of Milk Depots."* A.D. Blackader. Public Health Journal 3, 7(July 1912): 369-370.

164. **Blair, Ella L.** *"A Plea for Help in the Prevention of Blindness."* Ella L. Blair and Carolyn C. Van Blarcom. Canadian Nurse 11, 9(Sept. 1915): 493-497.

165. **Blais, Gabrielle** *"The Complete Feminine Personality": Female Adolescence in the Canadian Girls in Training 1915-1955.* Gabrielle Blais. Ottawa: University of Ottawa, 1986. (CTM no. 30992)
Thesis (M.A.)--University of Ottawa, 1986.

166. **Blanchard, Vaughn S.** *"School Health Problems."* Vaughn S. Blanchard. Canadian Journal of Public Health 36, 6(June 1945): 217-225.

167. **Blatz, William E.** *"Abstracts of Studies on the Development of the Dionne Quintuplets."* W.E. Blatz. Canadian Medical Association Journal 37, 5(Nov. 1937): 424-433.

168. **Blatz, William E.** *Collected Studies on the Dionne Quintuplets.* W.E. Blatz, N. Chant, M.W. Charles, M.I. Fletcher, N.H.C. Ford, A.L. Harris, J.W. MacArthur, M. Mason and D.A. Millichamp. Toronto: University of Toronto, c1937.
Item consists of 6 separately titled and authored studies in the University of Toronto Studies, Child Development Series. No. 11 A Biological Study of the Dionne Quintuplets--an Identical Set by J.W. MacArthur and N.H.C. Ford; No. 12 The Mental Growth of the Dionne

Quintuplets by W.E. Blatz and D.A. Millichamp; No. 13 The Early Social Development of the Dionne Quintuplets by W.E. Blatz, D.A. Millichamp and M.W. Charles; No. 14 The Development of Self-discipline in the Dionne Quintuplets by W.E. Blatz, D.A. Millichamp and N. Chant; No. 15 Routine Training of the Dionne Quintuplets by W.E. Blatz, D.A. Millichamp and A.L. Harris; No. 16 Early Development in Spoken Language of the Dionne Quintuplets by W.E. Blatz, M.I. Fletcher and M. Mason.

**169. Blatz, William E.** *Emotional Episodes in the Child of School Age.* W.E. Blatz, S.N.F. Chant and M.D. Salter. Toronto: University of Toronto Press, 1937.

**170. Blatz, William E.** *The Management of Young Children.* William E. Blatz and Helen Bott. Toronto: McClelland and Stewart, 1930.

**171. Blatz, William E.** *Nursery Education: Theory and Practice.* William E. Blatz, Dorothy Millichamp and Margaret Fletcher. New York: William Morrow and Company, 1936.

**172. Blatz, William E.** *Parents and the Pre-school Child.* William E. Blatz and Helen McM. Bott. Toronto: J.M. Dent & Sons Ltd., 1928.

**173. Blatz, William E.** *Understanding the Young Child.* William E. Blatz. Toronto: Clarke, Irwin & Company Ltd., c1944.

**174. Blishen, Bernard R., ed.** *Canadian Society: Sociological Perspectives.* Bernard R. Blishen, Frank E. Jones, Kasper D. Naegele and John Porter, eds. 1st ed. Toronto: Macmillan Company of Canada Limited, 1961.

**175. Blishen, Bernard R., ed.** *Canadian Society: Sociological Perspectives.* Bernard R. Blishen, Frank E. Jones, Kasper D. Naegele and John Porter, eds. 2nd ed. Toronto: Macmillan of Canada Limited, 1964.

**176. Blishen, Bernard R., ed.** *Canadian Society: Sociological Perspectives.* Bernard R. Blishen, Frank E. Jones, Kasper D. Naegele and John Porter, eds. 3rd ed. Toronto: Macmillan of Canada, 1968.

**177. Blishen, Bernard R., ed.** *Canadian Society: Sociological Perspectives.* Bernard R. Blishen, Frank E. Jones, Kasper D. Naegele and John Porter, eds. Abr. 3rd ed. Toronto: Macmillan of Canada Limited, 1971.

**178. Bliss, Michael** *""Pure Books on Avoided Subjects": Pre-Freudian Sexual Ideas in Canada."* Michael Bliss. Canadian Historical Association, Historical Papers/Communications historiques (1970): 88-108.
Reprinted in Studies in Canadian Social History, pp. 326-346. Edited by Michiel Horn and Ronald Sabourin.

**179. Blue, M.T.** *"The Battered Child Syndrome from a Social Work Viewpoint."* M.T. Blue. Canadian Journal of Public Health 56, 5(May 1965): 197-198.

**180. Bocher, Bonocho** *"Work with the Children's Voices in the "Bodra Smyana" Chorus."* Bonocho Bocher. Journal of Education of the Faculty of Education, Vancouver 14(Apr. 1968): 56-68.

**181. Boggs, Stephen Taylor** *Ojibwa Socialization: Some Aspects of Parent-Child Interaction in a Changing Culture.* Stephen Taylor Boggs. St. Louis, Missouri: Washington University, 1955.
Thesis (Ph.D.)--Washington University, 1955.

**182. Bolaria, B. Singh** *Racial Oppression in Canada.* B. Singh Bolaria and Peter S. Li. Toronto: Garamond Press, c1985.

**183. Bolt, Richard Arthur** *"The Education of the Medical Student in Relation to Child Welfare."* Richard Arthur Bolt. Public Health Journal 9, 7(July 1918): 302-309.

**184. Bonaccorsi, M.T.** *"Psychotherapy with a Blind Child."* M.T. Bonaccorsi and Hyman Caplan. Canadian Psychiatric Association Journal/Revue de l'Association canadienne de psychiatrie 10, 5(Oct. 1965): 393-398.

**185. Booth, John H.** *"Elective Induction of Labour: a Controlled Study."* John H. Booth and Victor B. Kurdyak. Canadian Medical Association Journal/Journal de l'Association medicale canadienne 103, 3(Aug. 14, 1970): 245-248.

**186. Borra, Sonia** *"Long-term Home Hemodialysis in Children."* Sonia Borra and Michael Kaye. Canadian Medical Association Journal/Journal de l'Association medicale canadienne 105, 9(Nov. 2, 1971): 927-929.

**187. Bostwick, Colleen** *"All Work and No Play: Children in the New Industries."* Colleen Bostwick. Labour History 2, 4(Spring 1981): 2-6.
Article followed by excerpts from the Royal Commission on the Relations of Labour and Capital, 1889, pp. 7-15.

**188. Boswell, David M.** *A Study of the Recently Established Provincial Government Youth Departments and Agencies in Seven Provinces of Canada.* David H. Boswell. Ann Arbor: University Microfilms International, 1978.
Thesis (Ed.D.)–Brigham Young University, 1971.

**189. Botler, Susan Ruth** *A Comparative Study of the Identification, Treatment and Training of the Mentally Retarded Child (With Special Reference to Canada, England and Wales, Holland, Japan, Scotland and the United States, and with Recommendations for Quebec).* Susan Ruth Botler. Montreal: McGill University, 1963.
Thesis (M.A.)–McGill University, 1963.

**190. Boudreau, A.J.** *"French Canadian Society."* A.J. Boudreau and Rachel Paradis-Richard. Ottawa: L'Association canadienne des educateurs de langue francaise, c1967. In Facets of French Canada, pp. 357-388.

**191. Boulanger, J.B.** *"Depression in Childhood."* J.B. Boulanger. Canadian Psychiatric Association Journal/Revue de l'Association canadienne de psychiatrie 11, Supplement(1966): s309-s312.

**192. Boulanger, J.B.** *"Group Psychoanalysis Therapy in Child Psychiatry."* Boulanger, J.B. Canadian Psychiatric Association Journal/Revue de l'Association canadienne de psychiatrie 6, 5(Oct. 1961): 272-275.

**193. Bourque, Guy** *Effects of Direction of Attention on Reading Speed and Reading Comprehension of High Anxious and Low Anxious Students.* Guy Bourque. Toronto: University of Toronto, 1971.
Thesis (M.A.)–University of Toronto, 1971.

**194. Bouschard, Phyllis Lou** *Parent-Child Relationships and Alcoholism.* Phyllis Lou Bouschard. Toronto: University of Toronto, 1959.
Thesis (M.S.W.)–University of Toronto, 1959.

**195. Bovey, Wilfrid** *The French Canadians To-day: a People on the March.* Wilfrid Bovey. Toronto: J.M. Dent & Sons (Canada) Ltd., 1938.

**196. Bowd, Alan D.** *"Practical Abilities of Indians and Eskimos."* Alan D. Bowd. Canadian Psychologist/Psychologie canadienne 15, 3(July 1974): 281-290.

**197. Bowers, Joan E.** *Exceptional Children in Home, School, and Community.* Joan E. Bowers, Josie Clement, Marion I. Francis and Marion Campbell Johnston. Rev ed. Toronto: J.M. Dent & Sons (Canada) Ltd., c1967.

**198. Bowers, Sithun** *"Child Welfare, 1954."* Sithun Bowers. Canadian Welfare 30, 5(Nov. 1954): 5-9.

**199. Bowie, William** *"Recreation in Children's Institutions."* William Bowie. Child and Family Welfare 6, 2(May 1930): 14-15.

**200. Bown, E.F.** *The Natural Virtues in Adolescence.* E.F. Bown. Ottawa: University of Ottawa, 1952.
Thesis (M.A.)–University of Ottawa, 1952.

**201. Boy Scouts Association in Canada. Canadian General Council** *Handbook for Canada.* Boy Scouts Association in Canada, Canadian General Council. Toronto: McClelland and Stewart, 1919.

**202. Boy Scouts Association in Canada. Canadian General Council** *Handbook for Canada.* Boy Scouts Association in Canada, Canadian General Council. Rev. ed. Toronto: McClelland and Stewart, 1930.

**203. Boy Scouts Association in Canada. Canadian General Council** *Policy, Organization and Rules.* The Canadian General Council. Rev. ed. S.l.: Boy Scouts Association, 1957.

**204. Boy Scouts Association in Canada. Canadian General Council** *Policy Organization and Rules for Canada.* Boy Scouts Association in Canada, Canadian General Council. Toronto: McClelland and Stewart, 1925.

**205. Boyd, Gladys** *"Medulloblastoma of the Cerebellum Simulating Tuberculous Meningitis."* Gladys Boyd. Canadian Medical Association Journal 77, 9(Nov. 1, 1957): 871-872.

**206. Boyd, Susan B.** *"Child Custody Law and the Invisibility of Women's Work."* Susan B. Boyd. Queen's Quarterly 96, 4(Winter 1989): 831-858.

**207. Boyle, Harry J.** *Memories of a Catholic Boyhood.* Harry J. Boyle. Don Mills: PaperJacks, 1973.

**208. Bradbrook, Adrian J.** *"The Relevance of Psychological and Psychiatric Studies to the Future Development of the Laws Governing the Settlement of Inter-parental Child Custody Disputes."* Adrian J. Bradbrook. Journal of Family Law 11, 3(1971-1972): 557-587.

**209. Braddock, John** *"Strife on Campus."* John Braddock. Vancouver: Copp Clark Publishing Co., c1970. In Social and Cultural Change in Canada v.2, pp. 210-215. Edited by W.E. Mann.
Reprinted from The Atlantic Advocate 59, 9(May 1969).

**210. Brady, Paul Richard** *The Relationship of Introversion-Extraversion to Physical Persistence.* Paul Richard Joseph Brady. Edmonton: University of Alberta, 1966.
Thesis (M.A.)--University of Alberta, 1966.

**211. Brant, Marlene J.** *Parental Neglect in Indian Families: a Descriptive Study of Twenty Case Records of Indian Families Whose Children Became Permanent Wards of the Children's Aid Society of Metropolitan Toronto.* Marlene J. Brant. Toronto: University of Toronto, 1959.
Thesis (M.S.W.)--University of Toronto, 1959.

**212. Braun, Carl** *"The Efficacy of Selected Stimulus Modalities in Acquisition and Retention of Sex-typed Textual Responses in Kindergarten Children."* Carl Braun. Manitoba Journal of Educational Research 3, 1(Dec. 1967): 5-23.

**213. Braun, Peter Hans** *Subjective and Psychometric Non-cognitive Scales in Relation to Over- and Under-achievement.* Peter Hans Braun. Edmonton: University of Alberta, 1970.
Thesis (M.Sc.)--University of Alberta, 1970.

**214. Brechin, Mary** *"Blind Alleys or Tools for the Job."* Mary Brechin. Canadian Welfare 21, 5(Oct. 1945): 21-24.

**215. Breeze, Elizabeth G.** *"The Metropolitan Health Committee of Greater Vancouver."* Elizabeth G. Breeze. Canadian Nurse 34, 5(May 1938): 233-238.

**216. Brennan, Wendy Margaret** *Age Differences in Infants' Attention to Stimuli Varying in Complexity.* Wendy Margaret Brennan. Vancouver: University of British Columbia, 1965.
Thesis (M.A.)--University of British Columbia, 1965.

**217. Breton, Raymond** *"Academic Stratification in Secondary Schools and Educational Plans of Students."* Raymond Breton. Canadian Review of Sociology and Anthropology/Revue canadienne de sociologie et d'anthropologie 7, 1(Jan. 1970): 17-24.

**218. Breton, Raymond** *"Aspects of Parent-Adolescent Relationships: the Perceptions of Secondary School Students."* Raymond Breton and John C. McDonald. Toronto: Rinehart and Winston of Canada Ltd., c1971. In The Canadian Family, pp. 151-168. Edited by K. Ishwaran.
Reprinted in The Canadian Family Revised, pp. 182-199. Edited by K. Ishwaran.

**219. Breton, Raymond** *Career Decisions of Canadian Youth: a Compilation of Basic Data.* Raymond Breton and John C. McDonald. Ottawa: Department of Manpower and Immigration, 1967.
Volume one of Career Decisions Project, 1967.

**220. Breton, Raymond** *"Occupational Preference of Canadian High School Students."* Raymond Breton and John C. McDonald. In Canadian Society: Sociological Perspectives, 3rd ed., 1968, pp. 269-294 and abr. 3rd ed., 1971, pp. 185-210. Edited by Bernard R. Blishen, Frank E. Jones, Kasper D. Naegele and John Porter.

**221. Breul, Frank R.** *Family Allowances in Canada: a Discussion of the Social, Economic, and Political Considerations Which Led to the Family Allowances Act of 1944 and a Description and Analysis of its Administration.* Frank R. Breul. Montreal: McGill University, 1951.
Thesis (Ph.D)--McGill University, 1951.

**222. Broadfoot, Barry** *The Immigrant Years: from Britain and Europe to Canada 1945-1967.* Barry Broadfoot. Vancouver: Douglas and McIntyre, 1986.

**223. Broadfoot, Barry** *Six War Years 1939-1945: Memories of Canadians at Home and Abroad.* Barry Broadfoot. 1st ed. Toronto: Doubleday Canada Ltd., c1974.

**224. Broadfoot, Barry** *Ten Lost Years 1929-1939: Memories of Canadians Who Survived the Depression.* Barry Broadfoot. Toronto: Doubleday Canada Ltd., 1973.

**225. Brodeur, Ruth** *A Study of Parental Values Towards Children's Behaviour.* Ruth Brodeur. Montreal: McGill University, 1955.
Thesis (M.S.W.)--McGill University, 1955.

**226. Brown, Alan** *"The Ability of Mothers to Nurse Their Infants."* Alan Brown. Canadian Medical Association Journal 7, 3(Mar. 1917): 241-247.

227. **Brown, Alan** *"The Deficiency Diseases of Infancy and Childhood."* Alan Brown. Canadian Medical Association Journal 7, 10(Oct. 1917): 911-924.

228. **Brown, Alan** *The Normal Child: Its Care and Feeding.* Alan Gowans Brown. New York: Century Co., 1923.

229. **Brown, Alan** *"Some Common Mistakes in the Diagnosis and Therapy of Diseases of Children."* Alan Brown. Canadian Medical Association Journal 19, 3(Sept. 1928): 313-318.

230. **Brown, Alan** *"Some Factors Concerning the Care of the Newborn."* Alan Brown. Canadian Public Health Journal 29, 7(July 1938): 337-344.

231. **Brown, David William** *Athleticism in Selected Canadian Schools for Boys to 1918.* David William Brown. Edmonton: University of Alberta, 1984. Thesis (Ph.D.)--University of Alberta, 1984.

232. **Brown, G. Gordon** *"The Family in a Divided Society."* G. Gordon Brown. Canadian Welfare 25, 7(Jan. 1950): 17-20.

233. **Brown, Isabel** *An Exploratory Study of Teasing.* Isabel Brown. Toronto: University of Toronto, 1938. Thesis (M.A.)--University of Toronto, 1938.

234. **Brown, Jennifer S.H.** *"Changing Views of Fur Trade Marriage and Domesticity: James Hargrave, His Colleagues and "The Sex"."* Jennifer S.H. Brown. Western Canadian Journal of Anthropology 6, 3(1976): 92-105.

235. **Brown, Jennifer S.H.** *"Children of the Early Fur Trades."* Jennifer S.H. Brown. Toronto: McClelland and Stewart, c1982. In Childhood and Family in Canadian History, pp. 44-68. Edited by Joy Parr.

236. **Brown, Jennifer S.H.** *Company Men and Native Families: Fur Trade Social and Domestic Relations in Canada's Old Northwest.* Jennifer S.H. Brown. Chicago: University of Chicago, 1976. Thesis (Ph.D.) --University of Chicago, 1976.

237. **Brown, Jennifer S.H.** *Strangers in Blood: Fur Trade Company Families in Indian Country.* Jennifer S.H. Brown. Vancouver: University of British Columbia Press, c1980.

238. **Brown, Jennifer S.H.** *"Ultimate Respectability: Fur-trade Children in the "Civilized World"."* Jennifer S.H. Brown. Beaver 308, 3(Winter 1977): 4-10.

239. **Brown, Jennifer S.H.** *"Ultimate Respectability: Fur-trade Children in the "Civilized World", Second of Two Parts."* Jennifer S.H. Brown. Beaver 308, 4(Spring 1978): 48-55.

240. **Brown, Julia** *The Schizophrenic Child in the School System.* Julia Brown. Toronto: University of Toronto, 1956. Thesis (M.S.W.)--University of Toronto, 1956.

241. **Brown, Marguerite W.** *It Takes Time to Grow.* Marguerite W. Brown. [Toronto]: United Church of Canada, 1953, 1956.

242. **Brown, Susan E.** *"Rational Creatures and Free Citizens: the Language of Politics in the Eighteenth Century Debate on Women."* Susan E. Brown. Canadian Historical Association, Historical Papers/Communications historiques (1988): 35-47.

243. **Brown, W. David** *"Militarism and Canadian Private Education: Ideal and Practice, 1861-1918."* W. David Brown. Canadian Journal of History of Sport/Revue canadienne de l'histoire des sports 17, 1(May 1986): 46-59.

244. **Brown, W. David** *"Sport, Darwinism and Canadian Private Schooling to 1918."* W. David Brown. Canadian Journal of History of Sport/Revue canadienne de l'histoire des sports 16, 1(May 1985): 27-37.

245. **Brown, William Gordon** *Novel and Familiar Stimuli as Reinforcement for Preschool Children.* William Gordon Brown. London: University of Western Ontario, 1968. Thesis (M.A.)--University of Western Ontario, c1968.

246. **Brown, William Lorne** *The Sunday School Movement in the Methodist Church of Canada, 1875-1925.* W.L. Brown. Toronto: University of Toronto, 1959. Thesis (M.Theo.)--University of Toronto, 1959.

247. **Browne, Jean E.** *"Contributions of the Junior Red Cross to Public Health."* Jean E. Browne. Canadian Public Health Journal 30, 1(Jan. 1939): 20-23.

248. **Browne, Jean E.** *"The Junior Red Cross: "An Idea Whose Time Has Come ."* Jean E. Browne. Canadian Public Health Journal 30, 1(Jan. 1939): 20-23

249. **Browne, Jean E.** *"The Programme of the Junior Red Cross."* Jean Browne. In Proceedings and Papers Fourth Annual Canadian Conference on Child Welfare 1923, pp. 72-77.

250. **Bruce, Jean, comp.** *After the War.* Jean Bruce, comp. Toronto: Fitzhenry and Whiteside, 1982.

251. **Brundage, Donald H.** *Y.M.C.A. Work with the Family in Canada.* Donald Hazen Brundage. New York: Columbia University, 1968.
Thesis (Ed.D.)--Teachers' College, Columbia University, 1968.

252. **Bruneau, W.A.** *"Opportunism and Altruism in Official Moral Education, 1880-1939: the Examples of France and Canada."* William Bruneau. History of Education Review 14, 1(1985): 25-39.

253. **Bryans, Fred E.** *"Some Problems in Paediatric Gynaecology."* Fred E. Bryans. Canadian Medical Association Journal 76, 2(Jan. 15, 1957): 150-155.

254. **Bryce, Peter H.** *"The History of American Indians in Relation to Health."* Peter H. Bryce. Ontario Historical Society, Papers and Records 12(1914): 128-141.

255. **Brydgen, R.L.** *"Socialization of the Public Schools."* Rev. R.L. Brydges. Toronto: Social Services Council of Canada, c1914. In Social Services Congress, Ottawa, 1914: Report of Addresses and Proceedings, pp. 137-141.

256. **Buchanan, M.F.** *"The Management of the Sick Child in the Hospital."* M.F. Buchanan. Canadian Nurse 35, 1(Jan. 1939): 23-26.

257. **Buchignani, Norman** *Continuous Journey: a Social History of South Asians in Canada.* Norman Buchignani and Doreen M. Indra, with Ram Srivastiva. Toronto: McClelland and Stewart Ltd., c1985.

258. **Buckler, Agnes Gladup** *A Study of Behavioral Patterns Associated with Creative Ability at the High School Level.* Agnes Gladup Buckler. Edmonton: University of Alberta, 1968.
Thesis (M.Ed.)--University of Alberta, 1968.

259. **Buckley, Suzann** *"Efforts to Reduce Infant Maternity Morality in Canada Between the Two World Wars."* Suzann Buckley. Atlantis 2, 2(Spring 1977): 76-84.

260. **Buckley, Suzann** *"Ladies or Midwives?: Efforts to Reduce Infant and Maternal Mortality."* Suzann Buckley. Toronto: Women's Educational Press, c1979. In A Not Unreasonable Claim: Women and Reform in Canada, 1880's-1920's, pp. 131-149. Edited by Linda Kealey.

261. **Bullen, John** *"Orphans, Lunatics and Historians: Recent Approaches to the History of Child Welfare in Canada."* John Bullen. Histoire sociale/Social History 18, 35(May 1985): 133-145.

262. **Bullen, John** *"Recent Views of Family and Child in Early Industrial Society."* John Bullen. Register (McGill History Journal) 2, 2(Sept. 1981): 62-72.

263. **Bumsted, J.M.** *The People's Clearance: Highland Emigration to British North America, 1770-1815.* J.M. Bumsted. Winnipeg: University of Manitoba Press, 1982.

264. **Bumsted, J.M.** *"The Victorian Family in Canada in Historical Perspective: the Ross Family of Red River and the Jarvis Family of Prince Edward Island."* J.M. Bumsted and Wendy Owen. Manitoba History 13(Spring 1987): 12-18.

265. **Burch, Thomas K.** *Family History Survey: Preliminary Findings.* Thomas K. Burch. Ottawa: Statistics Canada, 1985.

266. **Burchill, John** *Attention and Its Development.* John Burchill. Toronto: University of Toronto, 1898.
Thesis (M.A.)--University of Toronto, 1898.

267. **Burgers, Donald A.** *"The Past Went That-a-Way."* Donald A. Burgers. McGill Journal of Education 14, 1(Winter 1979): 163-172.

268. **Burnet, Jean** *"Coming Canadians": an Introduction to a History of Canada's Peoples.* Jean R. Burnet, with Howard Palmer. Toronto: McClelland and Stewart, c1988.

269. **Burns, Anne Y.** *"The Child and Maternal Health Division of the Department of National Health and Welfare."* Anne Y. Burns. Medical Services Journal of Canada 23, 4(Apr. 1967): 678-702.

270. **Burns, K. Phyllis** *"Group Care of Children: a Challenge to the Community."* K. Phyllis Burns. Canadian Welfare 29, 1(May 1953): 8-14.

271. **Burns, K. Phyllis** *"Institutional Resources in Canada for Dependent Children."* K. Phyllis Burns. Canadian Welfare 28, 5(Nov. 1952): 31-34.

272. **Burns, K. Phyllis** *"What's Happening to Canada's Children."* K. Phyllis Burns. Canadian Welfare 31, 2(May 1955): 114-119.

273. **Burns, Richard** *Immediate Memory Span and Logical Levels.* Richard Burns. Edmonton: University of Alberta, 1971. Thesis (M.Ed.)--University of Alberta, 1971.

274. **Burrell, Martin** *"The "Children"s Aid' and Child Protection."* Martin Burrell. Child and Family Welfare 7, 6(Mar. 1932): 30-35.

275. **Burshtyn, Roslyn** *"New Directions in Day Care."* Roslyn Burshtyn. Ottawa: Vanier Institute of the Family, c1970. In Day Care, a Resource for the Contemporary Family, pp. 63-72. Edited by Roslyn Burshtyn.

276. **Burt, Heather R.** *An Investigation of Grade 5 Students Reading Understanding of Similies.* Heather R. Burt. Edmonton: University of Alberta, 1971. Thesis (M.Ed.)--University of Alberta, 1971.

277. **Bussard, L.H.** *A Comparative Study of Social Studies Achievement of Canadian Grade 11 Students.* L.H. Bussard. Edmonton: University of Alberta, 1945. Thesis (M.Ed.)--University of Alberta, 1945.

278. **Busterd, Irene** *"What Do They Read?: Books for Canadian Children."* Irene Busterd. Queen's Quarterly 61, 3(Autumn 1954): 367-380.

279. **Butler, Ethelyn** *"From Little Acorns..."* Ethelyn Butler. Canadian Nurse 52, 1(Jan. 1956): 31-37.

280. **Butler, Rick** *Vanishing Canada.* Rick Butler. Toronto: Clarke, Irwin & Co. Ltd., c1980.

281. **Caldwell, George** *"An Island Between Two Cultures: the Residential Indian School."* George Caldwell. Canadian Welfare 43, 4(July-Aug. 1967): 12-17.

282. **Callwood, June** *"June Callwood Talks to Women About Hippies."* June Callwood. Canadian Welfare 44, 5(Sept.-Oct. 1968): 17-18.

283. **Cameron, Hector Charles** *"Sleep and Its Disorders in Childhood."* Hector Charles Cameron. Canadian Medical Association Journal 24, 2(Feb. 1931): 239-244.

284. **Cameron, Wendy** *"Selecting Peter Robinson's Irish Emigrants."* Wendy Cameron. Histoire sociale/Social History 9, 17(May 1976): 29-46.

285. **Campbell, Doreen Evelyn** *Decisions of Removal or Retention in Child Neglect Cases: an Analysis of the Reasons for Decision in the Cases of Twenty Disturbed Children Known to Family and Children's Agencies in Vancouver.* Vancouver: University of British Columbia, 1951. Thesis (M.S.W.)--University of British Columbia, 1951.

286. **Campbell, Ross M.** *"The Spastic Child."* Ross M. Campbell. Canadian Nurse 42, 6(June 1946): 469-473.

287. **Camu, Pierre** *"The People: the Components of Canadian Population Growth."* Pierre Camu, E.P. Weeks and Z.W. Sametz. In Economic Geography of Canada, pp. 55-86. Edited by Pierre Camu, E.P. Weeks and Z.W. Sametz. Reprinted in abridged form in Canadian Society: Sociological Perspectives, 3rd ed., 1968, pp. 22-51 and abr. 3rd ed., 1971, pp. 21-50. Edited by Bernard R. Blishen, Frank E. Jones, Kasper D. Naegele and John Porter.

288. **Canada. Commission of Inquiry into the Non-Medical Use of Drugs** *Interim Report: of the Commission of Inquiry into the Non-Medical Use of Drugs.* The Commission. Ottawa: Queen's Printer, c1970. Chairman: Gerald Le Dain.

289. **Canada. Committee on Juvenile Delinquency** *Juvenile Delinquency in Canada: the Report of the Department of Justice Committee on Juvenile Delinquency.* Committee on Juvenile Delinquency. Ottawa: Queen's Printer, c1965.

290. **Canada. Department of Health** *Handbook of Child Welfare in Canada.* Department of Health and Helen MacMurchy, ed. Ottawa: F.A. Acland, King's Printer, 1923.

291. **Canada. Department of Health and Welfare** *Up the Years From One to Six.* The Department. Ottawa: King's Printer, 1950.

292. **Canada. Department of Health and Welfare** *Up the Years From One to Six.* Rev. ed. Ottawa: Information Canada, 1971.

293. **Canada. Department of Health and Welfare. Information Services Division** *You and Your Family: Your Family Allowance, Spending the Family Income, Children and Their Problems.* Prepared by Information Services Division. Ottawa: King's Printer, 1949.

294. **Canada. Department of Indian Affairs and Northern Development. Education Branch** *5,000 Little Indians Went to School: a Survey of the First Four Critical Growth Years of School Starters Enrolled in Federal Schools in 1964.* The Branch. Ottawa: The Department, 1971.

295. **Canada. Department of Labour** *The Employment of Children and Young Persons in Canada.* Department of Labour. Ottawa: King's Printer, 1930.

296. **Canada. Department of Labour** *Training Canada's Young Unemployed: Facts, Figures and Objectives of the Dominion-Provincial Youth Training Programme.* The Department. Ottawa: The Department, 1938.

297. **Canada. Department of Labour. Director of Technical Education** *Proceedings of the First National Conference on Technical Education.* Department of Labour, Director of Technical Education. Ottawa: Thomas Mulvey, King's Printer, 1921.
    Proceedings of the National Conference on Technical Education (1st: 1920: Ottawa).

298. **Canada. Department of Labour. Vocational Training Branch** *Apprenticeship in Manufacturing: a Look at Current Practices in a Selected Number of Canadian Companies.* The Branch. Ottawa: Queen's Printer, 1960.

299. **Canada. Department of National Health and Welfare** *The Application of the Principles of Medical Asepsis to Maternity and Newborn Care: a Guide for Nurses.* Department of National Health and Welfare. Ottawa: Queen's Printer, 1960.

300. **Canada. Department of National Health and Welfare** *Mental Retardation in Canada: Report, Federal-Provincial Conference, Ottawa, Ontario, October 19-22, 1964.* The Department. Ottawa: Information Services, Department of National Health and Welfare, 1965.
    Chairman: K.C. Charron.

301. **Canada. Department of National Health and Welfare** *Mothers' Allowances Legislation In Canada.* The Department. Rev. ed. Ottawa: Department of National Health and Welfare, Research and Statistics Division, 1960.

302. **Canada. Department of National Health and Welfare. Child and Maternal Health Division** *The Canadian Mother and Child.* The Division. 2nd ed. Ottawa: Queen's Printer, 1953.

303. **Canada. Department of National Health and Welfare. Child and Maternal Health Division** *Recommended Standards for Maternity and Newborn Care.* The Division. [Ottawa: Queen's Printer, 1968].

304. **Canada. Department of National Health and Welfare. Health Programs Branch** *The Canadian Mother and Child.* The Branch. 3rd ed. Ottawa: Queen's Printer, 1967.

305. **Canada. Department of National Health and Welfare. Information Services Division** *You and Your Family.* The Division. Ottawa: King's Printer, 1949.

306. **Canada. Department of National Health and Welfare. Mental Health Division** *Residential Treatment Services in Canada for Emotionally Disturbed Children.* The Division. Ottawa: Department of National Health and Welfare, 1960.

307. **Canada. Department of National Health and Welfare. Research and Statistics Directorate** *Survey of Residential and In-patient Treatment Centres for Emotionally Disturbed Children, Canada, 1968.* The Directorate. Ottawa: The Department, 1970.

308. **Canada. Department of the Secretary of State** *Speaking Together: Canada's Native Women.* Canada. Department of the Secretary of State. Ottawa: Secretary of State, 1975.

309. **Canada. Dominion Bureau of Statistics** *Canadian Conference on Children, 1965 = Conference canadienne de l'enfance, 1965: Selected Statistics on Children = Statistiques choisies chez les enfants.* The Bureau. Ottawa: Dominion Bureau of Statistics, c1965.

310. **Canada. Dominion Bureau of Statistics** *Illiteracy and School Attendance in Canada: a Study of the Census of 1921 with Supplementary Data.* Dominion Bureau of Statistics. Ottawa: F.A. Acland, 1926.

311. **Canada. Dominion Bureau of
Statistics** *A Study in Maternal, Infant
and Neo-Natal Mortality in Canada.*
Prepared by Dominion Bureau of
Statistics. Ottawa: [s.n.], 1942.

312. **Canada. Dominion Bureau of
Statistics. Demography Branch** *Children
in Gainful Occupations.* Dominion Bureau
of Statistics, Demography Branch. Ottawa:
King's Printer, 1929.
Bilingual.

313. **Canada. Dominion Bureau of
Statistics. Education Division** *Census
and Other Data for Vocational Counsellors:
1961 Census.* Dominion Bureau of
Statistics, Education Division. Ottawa:
Queen's Printer, 1968.

314. **Canada. Dominion Bureau of
Statistics. Health and Welfare Division**
*Infant Mortality, 1950-1964 = Mortalite
infantile, 1950-1964.* Dominion Bureau of
Statistics, Health and Welfare Division.
Ottawa: Queen's Printer, 1967.

315. **Canada. Parliament. Senate. Special
Senate Committee on Mass Media**
*Good, Bad or Simply Inevitable?* The
Committee. v. 3. Ottawa: Queen's Printer,
1970.

316. **Canada. Parliament. Senate. Special
Senate Committee on Poverty**
*Highlights from the Report of the Special
Senate Committee on Poverty.* The
Committee. Ottawa: Information Canada,
c1971.
Chairman: David A. Croll.

317. **Canada. Royal Commission on
Bilingualism and Biculturalism** *Report
of the Royal Commission on Bilingualism
and Biculturalism: Book II - Education.*
The Commission. Ottawa: Queen's Printer,
c1968.
Chairmen: Andre Laurendeau and
Arnold Davison Dunton.

318. **Canada. Royal Commission on
Bilingualism and Biculturalism** *Report
of the Royal Commission on Bilingualism
and Biculturalism: Book V - The Federal
Capital; Book VI - Voluntary Associations.*
The Commission. Ottawa: Queen's Printer,
c1970.
Chairmen: Andre Laurendeau and
Arnold Davidson Dunton.

319. **Canada. Royal Commission on
Bilingualism and Biculturalism** *Report
of the Royal Commission on Bilingualism
and Biculturalism: Book IV - The Cultural
Contributions of the Other Ethnic Groups.*
The Commission. Ottawa: Queen's Printer,
c1970.
Chairmen: Andre Laurendeau and
Arnold Davidson Dunton.

320. **Canada. Royal Commission on
Health Services** *Report.* The Commission.
Ottawa: Queen's Printer, 1964.
Chairman: Emmett Matthew Hall.

321. **Canada. Royal Commission on
Industrial Training and Technical
Education** *Report of the Commissioners,
Parts I - IV.* The Commission. Ottawa:
King's Printer, 1913.
Chairman: James W. Robertson.

322. **Canada. Royal Commission on the
Criminal Law Relating to Criminal
Sexual Psychopaths** *Report of the Royal
Commission on the Criminal Law Relating
to Criminal Sexual Psychopaths.* The
Commission. Ottawa: Queen's Printer,
1958.
Chairman: James Chalmers McRuer.

323. **Canada. Royal Commission on the
Relations of Labour and Capital** *Report
of the Royal Commission on the Relations
of Labour and Capital in Canada:
Evidence, New Brunswick.* Ottawa: Queen's
Printer, 1889.
Chairmen: James Armstrong 1886-1888
and Augustus Toplady Freed 1888-1889.

324. **Canada. Royal Commission on the
Relations of Labour and Capital** *Report
of the Royal Commission on the Relations
of Labour and Capital in Canada.* The
Commission. Ottawa: Queen's Printer,
1889.
First report dated February 23, 1889
issued as Sessional Paper Letter A-1889,
pp. 7-75.
Second report, undated, issued as
Sessional Paper Letter A-1889, pp.
7b-195, also issued separately as this
item.
Chairmen: James Armstrong 1886-1888
and Augustus Toplady Freed 1888-1889.

325. **Canada. Royal Commission on the
Status of Women in Canada** *Report of
the Royal Commission on the Status of
Women in Canada.* The Commission.
Ottawa: [s.n.], 1970.
Chairman: Florence Bird.

326. **Canada. Royal Commission to
Investigate the Penal System of
Canada** *Report of the Royal Commission
to Investigate the Penal System of Canada.*
The Commission. Ottawa: J.O. Patenaude,
King's Printer, 1938.
Chairman: Joseph Archambault.

327. **Canada. Secretary of State** *Support
to Education by the Government of
Canada.* Canada. Secretary of State.
[Ottawa: The Secretary], c1983.

**328. Canada. Secretary of State.**
**Committee on Youth** *It's Your Turn...: a*
*Report to the Secretary of State by the*
*Committee on Youth.* Committee on Youth.
Ottawa: Information Canada, c1971.

**329. Canadian Association for Health,**
**Physical Education, and Recreation**
*The CAHPER Fitness-performance Test*
*Manual for Boys and Girls 7 to 17 Years*
*of Age.* Canadian Association for Health,
Physical Education. and Recreation.
Toronto: CAHPER, c1966.

**330. Canadian Association of Child**
**Protection Officers** *Proceedings of the*
*Canadian Association of Child Protection*
*Officers: Fourth Annual Meeting Held in*
*Toronto, Ontario, June 24-25. 1924.*
Canadian Association of Child Protection
Officiers. Ottawa: Department of Health,
1925.

**331. Canadian Conference on Child**
**Welfare (4th: 1923: Winnipeg)**
*Proceedings and Papers.* Ottawa: King's
Printer, 1924.

**332. Canadian Conference on Child**
**Welfare (5th: 1925: Ottawa)** *Proceedings*
*and Papers.* Ottawa: King's Printer, 1926.

**333. Canadian Conference on Child**
**Welfare (6th: 1927: Vancouver and**
**Victoria)** *Proceedings.* Ottawa: King's
Printer, 1928.

**334. Canadian Conference on Children**
**(1st: 1960: Ste. Adele and Ste.**
**Marguerite)** *Canadian Conference on*
*Children, 1960: Proceedings of the April*
*Planning Conference, 1958.* The
Conference. [Ottawa]: The Conference,
1960.

**335. Canadian Conference on Children**
**(1st: 1960: Ste. Adele and Ste.**
**Marguerite)** *Proceedings of the April*
*Planning Conference 1958.* Reva Gerstein
and Keith S. Armstrong. [S.l.: s.n.], 1958.

**336. Canadian Conference on Children**
**(1st: 1960: Ste. Adele and Ste.**
**Marguerite)** *Proceedings of the September*
*Planning Conference, 1958.* The
Conference. Ottawa: The Conference, 1958.
Planning Conference for the first
Canadian Conference on Children held in
1960.

**337. Canadian Conference on Children**
**(2nd: 1965: Montreal)** *Canadian*
*Conference on Children 1965: Reports*
*From Our Provincial Committees.* The
Conference. Ottawa: The Conference, 1965.

**338. Canadian Conference on Children**
**(2nd: 1965: Montreal)** *Roads to Maturity*
*= Vers la maturite.* The Conference,
Margery King, ed. Toronto: University of
Toronto Press, c1967.
Proceedings of the Second Canadian
Conference on Children, Oct. 31 to Nov.
4, 1965.

**339. Canadian Conference on Education**
**(1st: 1958: Ottawa)** *Addresses and*
*Proceedings of the Canadian Conference on*
*Education, Ottawa, February 16-20, 1958.*
Edited by George G. Croskery and Gerald
Nason. Ottawa: The Conference, c1958.

**340. Canadian Conference on Education**
**(2nd: 1962: Montreal)** *The Second*
*Canadian Conference on Education: a*
*Report.* Edited by Fred W. Price.
[Toronto]: University of Toronto Press,
c1962.

**341. Canadian Conference on the**
**Family (1st: 1964: Ottawa)** *"The Gap*
*Between the Generations: Commentary and*
*the Views of Six Young People."* The
Conference. Ottawa: Vanier Institute of
the Family, 1965. In The Canadian
Conference on the Family: Proceedings of
the Sessions, pp. 105-117.

**342. Canadian Corrections Association**
*The Child Offender and the Law: a Brief*
*Presented to the Department of Justice*
*Committee on Juvenile Delinquency.* The
Association. Ottawa: Canadian Welfare
Council, 1963.

**343. Canadian Corrections Association**
*The Family Court in Canada.* The
Association. Ottawa: Canadian Welfare
Council, 1960.

**344. Canadian Corrections Association**
*Proceedings of the Canadian Congress of*
*Corrections, Montreal, May 26-29, 1957.*
Canadian Corrections Association. Ottawa
The Association, 1957.
Bilingual.

**345. Canadian Corrections Association**
*Report of the Committee Established to*
*Consider Child Welfare and Related*
*Implications Arising from the Department*
*of Justice Report on Juvenile Delinquency.*
Canadian Corrections Association. Ottawa
The Association, 1967.

**346. Canadian Corrections Association**
*"Report of the Committee Established to*
*Consider Child Welfare and Related*
*Implications Arising from the Department*
*of Justice Report on Juvenile Delinquency."*
Canadian Corrections Association.
Canadian Journal of Corrections/Revue
canadienne de criminologie 10, 3(July
1968): 480-484.

347. **Canadian Corrections Association** *A Survey of Juvenile Delinquency Services in Canada.* Canadian Corrections Association. Ottawa: The Association, 1957.

348. **Canadian Council on Child and Family Welfare** *"Amendment, Juvenile Delinquents' Act of Canada."* Canadian Council on Child and Family Welfare. Child and Family Welfare 7, 6(Mar. 1932): 35-36.

349. **Canadian Council on Child and Family Welfare** *"The Blind Child."* Canadian Council on Child and Family Welfare. Child and Family Welfare 6, 3 (July 1930): 30-32.

350. **Canadian Council on Child and Family Welfare** *"Canada to Emulate Borstal System."* Canadian Council on Child and Family Welfare. Child and Family Welfare 11, 3(Sept. 1935): 39-43.

351. **Canadian Council on Child and Family Welfare** *"Canadian Calvalcade, 1920-1935."* Canadian Council on Child and Family Welfare. Child and Family Welfare 11, 1(May 1935) Supplement: 1-48.

352. **Canadian Council on Child and Family Welfare** *"Canadian Council on Child and Family Welfare: Progress Report."* Canadian Council on Child and Family Welfare. Child and Family Welfare 6, 2(May 1930): 1-7.

353. **Canadian Council on Child and Family Welfare** *"The Canadian Welfare Council."* Canadian Council on Child and Family Welfare. Child and Family Welfare 11, 3(Sept. 1935): 1-2.

354. **Canadian Council on Child and Family Welf. re** *"The Child Hygiene Section."* Canadian Council on Child and Family Welfare. Child and Family Welfare 6, 6(Jan. 1931): 19-30.

355. **Canadian Council on Child and Family Welfare** *"Child Protection in Four Great Cities."* Canadian Council on Child and Family Welfare. Child and Family Welfare 6, 7(Mar. 1931): 23-32.

356. **Canadian Council on Child and Family Welfare** *"Child Welfare Problems Seen by a School Inspector."* Canadian Council on Child and Family Welfare. Child and Family Welfare 6, 3(July 1930): 37-39.

357. **Canadian Council on Child and Family Welfare** *"Council Notes."* Canadian Council on Child and Family Welfare. Child and Family Welfare 6, 4(Sept. 1930): 1-3.

358. **Canadian Council on Child and Family Welfare** *"Crippled Children: Resolutions of the International Society."* Canadian Council on Child and Family Welfare. Child and Family Welfare 8, 1(May 1932): 32-34.

359. **Canadian Council on Child and Family Welfare** *"Cruelty to Children."* Canadian Council on Child and Family Welfare. Child and Family Welfare 9, 2(July 1933): 17-18.

360. **Canadian Council on Child and Family Welfare** *"Delinquency and Preventive Service."* Canadian Council on Child and Family Welfare. Child and Family Welfare 8, 6(Mar. 1933): 51-56.

361. **Canadian Council on Child and Family Welfare** *"The Formation of Provincial Committees for Work on Behalf of Crippled Children."* Canadian Council on Child and Family Welfare. Child and Family Welfare 6, 4(Sept. 1930): 36-39.

362. **Canadian Council on Child and Family Welfare** *"Girls' Work."* Canadian Council on Child and Family Welfare. Child and Family Welfare 9, 6(Mar. 1934): 53.

363. **Canadian Council on Child and Family Welfare** *"The Illegitimate Child and the Adopted Child."* Canadian Council on Child and Family Welfare. Child and Family Welfare 10, 1(May 1934): 22-23.

364. **Canadian Council on Child and Family Welfare** *"Immunization Conquers "The Strangler"."* Canadian Council on Child and Family Welfare. Child and Family Welfare 10, 4(Nov. 1934): 4.

365. **Canadian Council on Child and Family Welfare** *"Imperial Baby Week Challenge Shield."* Canadian Council on Child and Family Welfare. Child and Family Welfare 6, 6(Jan. 1931): 18.

366. **Canadian Council on Child and Family Welfare** *"The Importance of Prenatal Care."* Canadian Council on Child and Family Welfare. Child and Family Welfare 10, 2(July 1934): 10-12.

367. **Canadian Council on Child and Family Welfare** *"The Interpretation of Section 33, Juvenile Delinquents' Act."* Canadian Council on Child and Family Welfare. Child and Family Welfare 9, 3(Sept. 1933): 15-18.

368. **Canadian Council on Child and Family Welfare** *"The League and Child Welfare 1934."* Canadian Council on Child and Family Welfare. Child and Family Welfare 10, 3(Sept. 1934): 1-12.

369. **Canadian Council on Child and Family Welfare** *"Legislation 1932 in Canada and Her Provinces Affecting Social Welfare."* Canadian Council on Child and Family Welfare. Child and Family Welfare 8, 4(Nov. 1932): 1-39.

370. **Canadian Council on Child and Family Welfare** *"Legislation in Canada and Her Provinces (1929-1930) Affecting Social Welfare."* Canadian Council on Child and Family Welfare. Child and Family Welfare 6, 5(Nov. 1930): 1-40.

371. **Canadian Council on Child and Family Welfare** *"Legislation in Canada and her Provinces (1930-1931) Affecting Social Welfare."* Canadian Council on Child and Family Welfare. Child and Family Welfare 7, 3(Sept. 1931): 3-32.

372. **Canadian Council on Child and Family Welfare** *"Maternal and Child Health: the Work of the Child Hygiene Section."* Canadian Council on Child and Family Welfare. Child and Family Welfare 8, 5(Jan. 1933): 33-36.

373. **Canadian Council on Child and Family Welfare** *"Maternal and Child Hygiene."* Canadian Council on Child and Family Welfare. Child and Family Welfare 10, 1(May 1934): 14-19.

374. **Canadian Council on Child and Family Welfare** *"Maternal and Infant Mortality."* Canadian Council on Child and Family Welfare. Child and Family Welfare 10, 6(Mar. 1935): 28.

375. **Canadian Council on Child and Family Welfare** *"The Migration of Juveniles to Canada."* Canadian Council on Child and Family Welfare. Child and Family Welfare 6, 6(Jan. 1931): 59-60, 67.

376. **Canadian Council on Child and Family Welfare** *"Preschool Letters Have Kindergarten Section."* Canadian Council on Child and Family Welfare. Child and Family Welfare 13, 3(Sept. 1937): 57-59.

377. **Canadian Council on Child and Family Welfare** *"Progress Report: the Canadian Council on Child and Family Welfare."* Canadian Council on Child and Family Welfare. Child and Family Welfare 6, 6(Jan. 1931): 3-12.

378. **Canadian Council on Child and Family Welfare** *"Progress Report of the Council, April 1st, Sept. 30th, 1931."* Canadian Council on Child and Family Welfare. Child and Family Welfare 7, 4(Nov. 1931): 3-21.

379. **Canadian Council on Child and Family Welfare** *The Relationship Between Public and Private Agencies in the Family Field: the Experience of Twelve Canadian Cities from the Angle of the Private Agency.* Canadian Council on Child and Family Welfare. Ottawa: The Council, 1930.

380. **Canadian Council on Child and Family Welfare** *"The Second Conference of the National Committee on Work for Crippled Children in Canada."* Canadian Council on Child and Family Welfare. Child and Family Welfare 6, 7(Mar. 1931): 11-13.

381. **Canadian Council on Child and Family Welfare** *"Social Work in the Church of England in Canada, 1933-4."* Canadian Council on Child and Family Welfare. Child and Family Welfare 10, 4(Nov. 1934): 33-34.

382. **Canadian Council on Child and Family Welfare** *Suggestions for the Organization of Community Welfare and Relief Services: the Actual Provision of Relief, (Food, Clothing, Fuel, Shelter, etc.).* Canadian Council on Child and Family Welfare. Ottawa: The Council, 1932.

383. **Canadian Council on Child and Family Welfare** *"Unemployment Insurance."* Canadian Council on Child and Family Welfare. Child and Family Welfare 10, 6(Mar. 1935): 7-18.

384. **Canadian Council on Child and Family Welfare. Delinquency Section. Special Committee** *Youth in Revolt: a Study of Youthful Offenders in Canadian Penitentiaries.* The Council. Ottawa: The Council, 1931.
Chairman: Frank T. Sharpe.

385. **Canadian Council on Child Welfare** *"Assisted Migration."* Canadian Council on Child Welfare. Canadian Child Welfare News 4, 2(May 15, 1928): 3-7.

386. **Canadian Council on Child Welfare** *"Canada's Largest Children's Aid Societies."* Canadian Council on Child Welfare. Canadian Child Welfare News 4, 1(Feb. 15, 1928): 24-26.

387. **Canadian Council on Child Welfare** *"The Canadian Council on Child Welfare: Progress Report, 1928."* Canadian Council on Child Welfare. Canadian Child Welfare News 4, 3(Aug. 15, 1928): 1-2.

388. **Canadian Council on Child Welfare** *"The Canadian Council on Child Welfare: Progress Report, 1929."* Canadian Council on Child Welfare. Child Welfare News 5, 2(May 1929): 1-5.

**389. Canadian Council on Child Welfare**
*"The Canadian National Institute for the
Blind and Child Welfare."* Canadian
Council on Child Welfare. Canadian Child
Welfare News 4, 1(Feb. 15, 1928): 17.

**390. Canadian Council on Child Welfare**
*"Child Hygiene."* Canadian Council on
Child Welfare. Child Welfare News 6,
1(Feb. 1930): 18-26.

**391. Canadian Council on Child Welfare**
*"Child Welfare Legislation, 1928."*
Canadian Council on Child Welfare.
Canadian Child Welfare News 4, 3(Aug.
15, 1928): 5-15.

**392. Canadian Council on Child Welfare**
*"Child Welfare Legislation in Canada,
1929."* Canadian Council on Child
Welfare. Child Welfare News 5, 2(Feb.
1929): 7-17.

**393. Canadian Council on Child Welfare**
*Child Welfare Leglislation in Canada,
1926-1927.* Canadian Council on Child
Welfare. [Ottawa]: Canadian Council on
Child Welfare, [1927].

**394. Canadian Council on Child Welfare**
*"Child Welfare with Canadian National
Organizations."* Canadian Council on Child
Welfare. Canadian Child Welfare News 4,
3(Aug. 15, 1928): 42-55.

**395. Canadian Council on Child Welfare**
*"Children's Section: Canadian Conference
on Social Work."* Canadian Council on
Child Welfare. Canadian Child Welfare
News 4, 2(May 15, 1928): 11-14.

**396. Canadian Council on Child Welfare**
*"Crippled Children in Canada."* Canadian
Council on Child Welfare. Child Welfare
News 5, 2(May 1929): 35-38.

**397. Canadian Council on Child Welfare**
*"Development of Breast-fed and
Artificially-fed Children."* Canadian Council
on Child Welfare. Child Welfare News 5,
2(May 1929): 40-41.

**398. Canadian Council on Child Welfare**
*"Diarrhoea as a Factor in Infant
Mortality."* Canadian Council on Child
Welfare. Canadian Welfare Summary 15,
2(July 1939): 31-33.

**399. Canadian Council on Child Welfare**
*"Five Canadian Provinces Endorse
Placing-out."* Canadian Council on Child
Welfare. Canadian Child Welfare News 4,
1(Feb. 15, 1928): 21-24.

**400. Canadian Council on Child Welfare**
*"Good Night and Good Morning."*
Canadian Council on Child Welfare. Child
Welfare News 6, 1(Feb. 1930): 1.

**401. Canadian Council on Child Welfare**
*Housing and Care of the Dependent Child.*
The Council. Ottawa: The Council, 1924.

**402. Canadian Council on Child Welfare**
*"Imperial Baby Week Challenge Shield
Competition."* Canadian Council on Child
Welfare. Child Welfare News 5, 1(Feb.
1929): 57.

**403. Canadian Council on Child Welfare**
*"Institute on Problems of Unmarried
Parenthood."* Canadian Council on Child
Welfare. Canadian Welfare 18, 1(Apr.
1942): 31-32.

**404. Canadian Council on Child Welfare**
*"International Child Welfare Loses an
Inspirational Leader."* Canadian Council on
Child Welfare. Child Welfare News 5,
1(Feb. 1929): 44-45.

**405. Canadian Council on Child Welfare**
*"International Definitions of Deficiency."*
Canadian Council on Child Welfare. Child
Welfare News 6, 1(Feb. 1930): 42-43.

**406. Canadian Council on Child Welfare**
*"Juvenile Immigration Development."*
Canadian Council on Child Welfare. Child
Welfare News 5, 1(Feb. 1929): 41-43.

**407. Canadian Council on Child Welfare**
*Juvenile Immigration Report No. 2: Being
a Summary of Representative Canadian
Opinion, the British Government's Oversea
Settlement Committee Report, and Recent
Progressive Developments in the Canadian
Government Policy.* Canadian Council on
Child Welfare. Ottawa: Canadian Council
on Child Welfare, 1925.

**408. Canadian Council on Child Welfare**
*"The Juvenile Immigration Survey."*
Canadian Council on Child Welfare.
Canadian Child Welfare News 4, 3(Aug.
15, 1928): 19-32.

**409. Canadian Council on Child Welfare**
*Legislation (as of Date, January 1, 1929),
Canada and Her Provinces: Affecting the
Status and Protection of the Child of
Unmarried Parents.* Canadian Council on
Child Welfare, Charlotte Whitton and
Kathleen Snowdon. Ottawa: The Council,
[1929].

**410. Canadian Council on Child Welfare**
*"The Maternal Mortality Study."* Canadian
Council on Child Welfare. Canadian Child
Welfare News 4, 2(May 15, 1928): 14-19.

411. **Canadian Council on Child Welfare**
*"The Montreal Theatre Fire."* Canadian
Council on Child Welfare. Canadian Child
Welfare News 4, 1(Feb. 15, 1928): 27-32.

412. **Canadian Council on Child Welfare**
*"Public Liability in the Provinces of
Canada for the Care and Treatment of
Crippled Children."* Canadian Council on
Child Welfare. Canadian Child Welfare
News 4, 2(May 15, 1928): 29-36.

413. **Canadian Council on Child Welfare**
*Some Angles of Discussion on the Juvenile
Immigration Problem of Canada.* The
Council. Ottawa: The Council, 1924.

414. **Canadian Council on Child Welfare**
*"The Utilization of Workers' Spare Time in
its Relation to Child Welfare."* Canadian
Council on Child Welfare. Canadian Child
Welfare News 4, 3(Aug. 15, 1928): 33-40.

415. **Canadian Council on Child Welfare**
*"Why Our Babies Die."* Canadian Council
on Child Welfare. Canadian Nurse 23,
1(Jan. 1927): 33.

416. **Canadian Council on Child Welfare**
*"With the Houses of Parliament."* Canadian
Council on Child Welfare. Canadian Child
Welfare News 4, 2(May 15, 1928): 48-50.

417. **Canadian Council on Child Welfare
(9th: 1928: Ottawa)** *"Proceedings of the
Ninth Annual Meeting of the Canadian
Council on Child Welfare, Ottawa, October
22, 1928."* Canadian Council on Child
Welfare. Child Welfare News 4, 4(Nov.
15, 1928): 1-62.

418. **Canadian Council on Child Welfare
(10th: 1929: Ottawa)** *"Proceedings of the
Tenth Annual Meeting of the Canadian
Council on Child Welfare, Ottawa, Nov. 25
& 26, 1929."* Canadian Council on Child
Welfare. Child Welfare News 5, 4(Nov.
1929): 1-100.

419. **Canadian Council on Children and
Youth** *Prevention in the Pre-school Years:
Report of the Board of Directors' Seminar,
Toronto, April 20-21, 1967.* Canadian
Council on Children and Youth. [Toronto:
The Council, 1967].

420. **Canadian Council on Social
Development** *Day Care: Report of a
National Study by the Canadian Council
on Social Development.* The Council.
Ottawa: The Council, 1972.
  Chairman: John Weir.

421. **Canadian Council on Social
Development** *The One Parent Family:
Report of an Inquiry on One Parent
Families in Canada.* Canadian Council on
Social Development. Ottawa: Canadian
Council on Social Development, c1971.

422. **Canadian Council on Social
Development** *Transient Youth 70-71:
Report of an Inquiry About Programs in
1970, and Plans for 1971.* Canadian
Council on Social Development. Rev ed.
Ottawa: The Council, 1971.

423. **Canadian Council on Social
Development** *Youth '71: an Inquiry by
the Canadian Council on Social
Development into the Transient Youth and
Opportunities for Youth Programs in the
Summer of 1971.* Canadian Council on
Social Development. Ottawa: The Council,
1971.

424. **Canadian Criminology and
Corrections Association** *Brief on the
Young Offenders Act, (Bill C-192): an
Official Statement of Policy.* Canadian
Criminology and Corrections Association.
Ottawa: Canadian Council on Social
Development, 1971.

425. **Canadian Dental Association** *Dental
Conditions Adversely Affecting the Health
of Children: a Report to the Canadian
Conference on Children.* The Association.
Ottawa: The Association, 1960.

426. **Canadian Education Association.
Research and Information Division** *The
Present Status of Sex Education in
Canadian Schools.* Research Information
Division, Canadian Education Association.
Toronto: The Association, 1964.

427. **Canadian Medical Association.
Special Committee on Medical
Inspection of Schools** *"Special Committee
on Medical Inspection of Schools: Report
1910-1911."* Canadian Medical Association.
Special Committee on Medical Inspection
of Schools. Canadian Medical Association
Journal 1, 9(Sept. 1911): 896-902.

428. **Canadian Mental Health
Association** *The Legal Rights of Children.*
Canadian Mental Health Association and
the World Federation for Mental Health.
Montreal: The Association, [1970?].

429. **Canadian National Institute for the
Blind** *"Report on Blind Children in
Canada."* Canadian National Institute for
the Blind and the Canadian Council on
Child Welfare. Canadian Child Welfare
News 4, 1(Feb. 15, 1938): 9-16.

430. **Canadian Nurses Association** *A
Statement to the Canadian Conference on
Children.* Canadian Nurses Association.
Ottawa: The Association, 1960.

**431. Canadian Ophthalmological Society**
*Ophthalmia Neonatorum: (Babies' Sore
Eyes).* Canadian Ophthalmological Society.
Ottawa: Canadian Welfare Council, 1942.

**432. Canadian Public Health Association**
*Report of the Study Committee on Public
Health Practice in Canada.* Canadian
Public Health Association. Toronto: The
Association, 1950.

**433. Canadian Red Cross Society** *"The
Role of One Voluntary Organization in
Canada's Health Service: a Brief Presented
to the Royal Commission on Health
Services on Behalf of the Central Council
of the Canadian Red Cross Society."*
Canadian Red Cross Society. Toronto:
National Office, Canadian Red Cross
Society, 1962.

**434. Canadian Research Committee on
Practical Education** *"Two Years After
School: a Report of the Canadian Research
Committee on Practical Education."*
Canadian Research Committee on
Practical Education. Canadian Education
6, 2(Mar. 1951): 1-147.

**435. Canadian Research Committee on
Practical Education** *Your Child Leaves
School: a Study of 12124 Graduates and
14219 Dropouts From Canadian Schools
During 1948.* Canadian Research
Committee on Practical Education.
[Toronto: The Committee], 1950.
Report no. 2 of the Committee.

**436. Canadian Teachers' Federation**
*Rankings of the Provinces on Various
Aspects of Canadian Education.* Canadian
Teachers' Federation. Ottawa: The
Federation, 1967.

**437. Canadian Welfare Council** *"Action
by the Y.W.C.A."* Canadian Welfare
Council. Canadian Welfare 20, 1(Apr.
1944): 25.

**438. Canadian Welfare Council** *The
Adoption Laws of the Canadian Provinces:
Comparative Analysis as of Feb. 1st, 1946.*
Canadian Welfare Council. Rev. ed.
Ottawa: The Council, 1947.

**439. Canadian Welfare Council** *"The
Adoption Situation."* Canadian Welfare
Council. Canadian Welfare 31, 5(Dec.
1955): 221-223.

**440. Canadian Welfare Council** *Analysis
of Mothers' Allowances Legislation in
Canada.* Canadian Welfare Council. Rev
ed. Ottawa: The Council, 1944.

**441. Canadian Welfare Council** *"British
Money for Our War Guests."* Canadian
Welfare Council. Canadian Welfare 17,
8(Feb. 1942): 9, 14.

**442. Canadian Welfare Council** *"Canada
and the Child Refugees."* Canadian
Welfare Council. Canadian Welfare
Summary 15, 5(Jan. 1940): 50-52.

**443. Canadian Welfare Council** *"The
Canadian Youth Commission."* Canadian
Welfare Council. Canadian Welfare 19,
3(July 1943): 12-13.

**444. Canadian Welfare Council** *"Child
Labour and the War."* Canadian Welfare
Council. Canadian Welfare 17, 8(Feb.
1942): 17-21.

**445. Canadian Welfare Council** *"Child
Placing in Canada."* Canadian Welfare
Council. Child and Family Welfare 11,
6(Mar. 1936): 23-38.

**446. Canadian Welfare Council** *Child
Protection in Canada.* Canadian Welfare
Council. Ottawa: The Council, 1954.

**447. Canadian Welfare Council** *Child
Protection in Canada.* Canadian Welfare
Council Ottawa: The Council, 1961.

**448. Canadian Welfare Council**
*"Children's Allowances: Pro or Con?"*
Canadian Welfare Council. Canadian
Welfare 19, 5(Oct. 1943): 1.

**449. Canadian Welfare Council** *"Company
of Young Canadians."* Canadian Welfare
Council. Canadian Welfare 41, 4(July-Aug.
1965): 184-185.

**450. Canadian Welfare Council**
*"Conference on Children Held."* Canadian
Welfare Council. Canadian Welfare 41,
6(Nov.-Dec. 1965): 295.

**451. Canadian Welfare Council** *"CWC
Reports on Transient Youth."* Canadian
Welfare Council. Canadian Welfare 46,
2(Mar.-Apr. 1970): 19-20.

**452. Canadian Welfare Council** *Day Care
of Children in Wartime.* Canadian Welfare
Council. Ottawa: The Council, 1942.

**453. Canadian Welfare Council**
*"Delinquency Shows Downward Trend."*
Canadian Welfare Council. Canadian
Welfare 20, 3(July 1944): 1.

**454. Canadian Welfare Council** *"Dominion
Will Not Appeal Judgement Affecting
Juvenile and Family Courts."* Canadian
Welfare Council. Canadian Welfare
Summary 14, 3(Sept. 1938): 1.

455. **Canadian Welfare Council** *Essentials in Adoption Service: I. Basic Principles in Adoption, II. Social Treatment of the Unmarried Mother, III. Supervision in Adoption, IV. Requisites in Adoption Leglislation.* Canadian Welfare Council. Ottawa: The Council, 1944.

456. **Canadian Welfare Council** *"Essentials in Adoption Services: Part I: Basic Principles in Adoption."* Canadian Welfare Council. Canadian Welfare 19, 5(Oct. 1943): 8-13.

457. **Canadian Welfare Council** *"Essentials in Adoption Services: Part II: Requisites in Adoption Legislation."* Canadian Welfare Council. Canadian Welfare 19, 6(Dec. 1943): 24-26.

458. **Canadian Welfare Council** *"Faith and Adoption."* Canadian Welfare Council. Canadian Welfare 38, 1(Jan.-Feb. 1962): 3.

459. **Canadian Welfare Council** *"Geneva Standards in Child Placing."* Canadian Welfare Council. Canadian Welfare Summary 14, 2(July 1938): 27-33.

460. **Canadian Welfare Council** *The In Between Years: a Series of Seven Letters to Canadian Parents on the Development and Occupations of their Children from Ten to Twelve Years of Age.* Canadian Welfare Council, Public Health and Nursing Services. 3rd ed. Ottawa: the Canadian Welfare Council, 1942.

461. **Canadian Welfare Council** *"Jobless Youth Gets a Break in Canada's Training Project."* Canadian Welfare Council. Canadian Welfare 16, 1(Apr. 1940): 11-14.

462. **Canadian Welfare Council** *The Juvenile Court in Law.* Canadian Welfare Council. 4th ed. Ottawa: The Council, 1952.

463. **Canadian Welfare Council** *Juvenile Courts in Canada.* Canadian Welfare Council. [Ottawa]: The Council, [1941].

464. **Canadian Welfare Council** *Juvenile Courts in Canada: Being a Brief Description of Juvenile Court Organization in the Provinces.* Canadian Welfare Council. Ottawa: The Council, 1943.

465. **Canadian Welfare Council** *"The Next Adults."* Canadian Welfare Council. Canadian Welfare 45, 5(Sept.-Oct. 1969): 4-6, 30.

466. **Canadian Welfare Council** *"Pneumonia as a Factor in Infant Mortality."* Canadian Welfare Council. Canadian Welfare Summary 15, 3(Sept. 1939): 40-42.

467. **Canadian Welfare Council** *A Preliminary Report on Rural Poverty in Four Selected Areas: Highlights of a Study Prepared for the ARDA.* Canadian Welfare Council. [Ottawa]: Canada, Department of Forestry, 1965.

468. **Canadian Welfare Council** *"Prematurity Factor in Infant Mortality."* Canadian Welfare Council. Canadian Welfare Summary 15, 1(May 1939): 28-29.

469. **Canadian Welfare Council** *"Presenting a C.W.C. Division and its Chairman."* Canadian Welfare Council. Canadian Welfare 26, 2(June 1950): 8-10.

470. **Canadian Welfare Council** *Private Home Care for Children in Need.* Canadian Welfare Council. 3rd ed. Ottawa: The Council, 1936.

471. **Canadian Welfare Council** *Probation and Related Services with Special Reference to Older Girls and Young Women.* Canadian Welfare Council. Ottawa: The Council, 1942.

472. **Canadian Welfare Council** *"Protecting Kin in Our Care."* Canadian Welfare Council. Canadian Welfare 17, 2(May 1941): 10-12.

473. **Canadian Welfare Council** *"The Protection of the Child Refugee."* Canadian Welfare Council. Canadian Welfare Summary 15, 6(Mar. 1940): 53-56.

474. **Canadian Welfare Council** *"Sanctuary for Children in Need."* Canadian Welfare Council. Canadian Welfare 16, 3(July 1940): 4-8.

475. **Canadian Welfare Council** *"School Performance of Children."* Canadian Welfare Council. Canadian Welfare 42, 5(Sept.-Oct. 1966): 214-217.

476. **Canadian Welfare Council** *Summary of the Laws of Canada and Her Provinces as Affecting Children.* Canadian Welfare Council. Ottawa: The Council, [1947].

477. **Canadian Welfare Council** *"Teenage Mothers: YWCA Study."* Canadian Welfare Council. Canadian Welfare 40, 3(May-June 1964): 140-141.

478. **Canadian Welfare Council** *Transient Youth: Report of an Inquiry in the Summer of 1969.* Canadian Welfare Council. Ottawa: The Council, 1970.

479. **Canadian Welfare Council** *"Trends in Canadian Family Size."* Canadian Welfare Council. Canadian Welfare 21, 3(July 1945): 16-18.

480. **Canadian Welfare Council** *"Trends in Maternal and Infant Mortality."* Canadian Welfare Council. Canadian Welfare Summary 15, 5(Jan. 1940): 53-56.

481. **Canadian Welfare Council** *"United Church Board of Evangelism and Social Service."* Canadian Welfare Council. Canadian Welfare Summary 14, 3(Sept. 1938): 5-7.

482. **Canadian Welfare Council** *"War's Shadow in the Classroom."* Canadian Welfare Council. Canadian Welfare 16, 6(Nov. 1940): 45-48.

483. **Canadian Welfare Council** *Welfare Legislation in Canada and the Provinces, 1942-1943.* Canadian Welfare Council. Ottawa: The Council, [1943].

484. **Canadian Welfare Council** *"What the Council is Doing: Memo to CYC."* Canadian Welfare Council. Canadian Welfare 41, 6(Nov.-Dec. 1965): 302.

485. **Canadian Welfare Council** *"Working Mothers and Their Children."* Canadian Welfare Council. Canadian Welfare 18, 1(Apr. 1942): 13-17.

486. **Canadian Welfare Council** *"Young Volunteers at Home for the Aged."* Canadian Welfare Council. Canadian Welfare 40, 5(Sept.-Oct. 1964): 230-231.

487. **Canadian Welfare Council** *Your Town Against Delinquency.* Canadian Welfare Council. Ottawa: The Council, 1948.

488. **Canadian Welfare Council. Committee on Child Refugees** *The Protection of Child Refugees: the Report of the Committee on Child Refugees of the Canadian Welfare Council.* The Committee. Ottawa: The Council, 1940.
   Chairman: Robert E. Mills.

489. **Canadian Welfare Council. Division of Maternal and Child Hygiene** *Good Posture Means: Good Health, Efficiency, Confidence and Grace.* Canadian Welfare Council, Division of Maternal and Child Hygiene. Ottawa: The Council, [1936].

490. **Canadian Welfare Council. Division of Maternal and Child Hygiene** *Need Our Mothers Die?: a Study Made by a Special Committee of the Division on Maternal and Child Hygiene.* Canadian Welfare Council, Division on Maternal and Child Hygiene. Ottawa: Canadian Welfare Council, 1935.

491. **Canadian Youth Commission** *Young Canada and Religion.* The Commission. Toronto: Ryerson Press, c1945.

492. **Canadian Youth Commission** *Youth and Health: a Positive Health Programme for Canada.* The Commission. Toronto: Ryerson Press, c1946.

493. **Canadian Youth Commission** *Youth and Jobs in Canada.* The Commission. Toronto: Ryerson Press, c1945.

494. **Canadian Youth Commission** *Youth and Recreation: New Plans for New Times.* The Commission. Toronto: Ryerson Press, c1946.

495. **Canadian Youth Commission** *Youth Challenges the Educators.* The Commission. Toronto: Ryerson Press, c1946.

496. **Canadian Youth Commission** *Youth, Marriage and the Family.* The Commission. Toronto: Ryerson Press, c1948.

497. **Canadian Youth Commission** *Youth Speaks Out on Citizenship.* The Commission. Toronto: Ryerson Press, c1947.

498. **Canadian Youth Commission. Subcommittee on Education** *What Canadian Youth Thinks of Its Education: a Report of the Subcommittee on Education of the Canadian Youth Commission.* The Commission. [S.l.The Subcommittee, 1945?].

499. **Canning-Dew, Joanna, ed.** *Hastings and Main: Stories From an Inner City Neighbourhood.* Joanna Canning-Dew, ed. with Laurel Kimbly, interviewer and comp. Vancouver: New Star Books, c1987.

500. **Capell, Jeannette** *""Johnny Was Sick This Morning.""* Jeannette Capell. Canadian Welfare 36, 6(Nov. 1960): 257-258.

501. **Cappon, Daniel** *"Perceptual Organization in Infancy and Childhood."* Daniel Cappon. Canadian Psychiatric Association Journal/Revue de l'Association canadienne de psychiatrie 6, 5(Oct. 1961): 247-251.

**502. Carder, E.D.** *"Neonatal Mortality and Ante-natal Care."* E.D. Carder. In Proceedings of Sixth Annual Canadian Conference on Child Welfare 1927, pp. 13-15.

**503. Cardinal, Douglas** *""Educators, Your Systems Have Failed!""* Douglas Cardinal. Education Canada 10, 4(Dec. 1970): 22-24.

**504. Cardinal, Harold** *"The Unjust Society: the Tragedy of Canada's Indians."* Harold Cardinal. Scarborough, Ont.: Prentice-Hall, 1971. In Native Peoples, pp. 134-149. Edited by Jean Leonard Elliott.

**505. Cargill, Isabel Agnes** *An Investigation of Cognitive Development among Infants on a Canadian Indian Reservation.* Isabel Agnes Cargill. Toronto: University of Toronto, 1970.
Thesis (M.A.)--University of Toronto, 1970.

**506. Carnine, June Audrey Mavis** *An Investigation of the Effect of Transformational and Structure Grammar on the Writing of Grade 7 Students.* June Audrey Mavis Carnine. Edmonton: University of Alberta, 1968.
Thesis (M.Ed.)--University of Alberta, 1968.

**507. Carniol, Benjamin** *Attitudes Towards Selected Adolescent Characteristics.* Benjamin Carniol. Montreal: McGill University, 1964.
Thesis (M.S.W.)--McGill University, 1964.

**508. Carr, Robert** *Family Law.* Robert Carr. 2 v. [Winnipeg]: University of Manitoba, Faculty of Law, 1976.
Second revision June 1976.

**509. Carran, Ethel Georgina** *A Study of Auditory Blending Ability and Its Relationship to Reading Achievement in Grade Two.* Ethel Georgina Carran. Edmonton: University of Alberta, 1968.
Thesis (M.Ed.)--University of Alberta, 1968.

**510. Carriere, Gabrielle** *Careers for Women in Canada.* Gabrielle Carriere. Toronto: J.M. Dent & Sons, 1946.

**511. Carrothers, W.A.** *Emigration from the British Isles: with Special Reference to the Development of the Overseas Dominions.* W.A. Carrothers. London, Eng.: P.S. King, 1929.
Reprinted by Frank Cass & Co., 1965.

**512. Carruthers, Eileen M.** *"Getting the Preschool Child Ready."* Eileen M. Carruthers. Public Health Nurses' Bulletin 1, 9(Mar. 1932): 19-20.

**513. Carstens, C.C.** *"Social Background: Child Protection and Home Finding."* C.C. Carstens. Public Health Journal 12, 4(Apr. 1921): 169-174.

**514. Carter, G. Emmett** *"The Adolescent."* Very Reverend G. Emmett Canon Carter. Toronto: W.J. Gage and Co., 1956. In Education: a Collection of Essays on Canadian Education, v.1, 1954-1956, pp. 73-76.

**515. Carter, Robert Richard** *An Investigation of the Ability of Grade Six Students to Read Selected Social Studies Material.* Robert Richard Carter. Edmonton: University of Alberta, 1969.
Thesis (M.Ed.)--University of Alberta, 1969.

**516. Case, Thomas Robert** *An Analysis of Difficulties Encountered by Disadvantaged Children in Solving a Visually Represented Problem.* Thomas Robert Case. Toronto: University of Toronto, 1968.
Thesis (M.A.)--University of Toronto, 1968.

**517. Cassel, Jay** *The Secret Plague: Venereal Disease in Canada, 1838-1939.* Jay Cassel. Toronto: University of Toronto Press, c1987.

**518. Cassidy, H.M.** *The Rowell-Sirois Report and the Social Services in Summary.* H.M. Cassidy. Ottawa: Canadian Welfare Council, [1940?].

**519. Cathcart, W. George** *"Values of High School Students and Their Teachers."* W. George Cathcart. Manitoba Journal of Educational Research 3, 2(June 1968): 33-41.

**520. Cayley, David** *The World of the Child.* David Cayley. Toronto: CBC Transcripts, c1983.

**521. Chabassol, David J.** *"Prejudice and Personality in Adolescents."* David Chabassol. Alberta Journal of Educational Research 16, 1(Mar. 1970): 3-12.

**522. Chabassol, David J.** *"A Theory of Underachievement."* David J. Chabassol. Canadian Education and Research Digest 3, 3(Sept. 1963): 216-220.

**523. Chalmers, Hal** *Student Perception of the Teacher Image.* Hal Chalmers. Edmonton: University of Alberta, 1968.
Thesis (M.Ed.)--University of Alberta, 1968.

**524. Chalmers, John West** *Education Behind the Buckskin Curtain: a History of Native Education in Canada.* John West Chalmers. Edmonton: University of Alberta Bookstore, 1974.

**525. Chambers, Juanita** *"The Triumph of Adoption."* Juanita Chambers. Canadian Welfare 35, 3(May 1959): 104-105.

**526. Chandler, A.B.** *"Breast Feeding in Health Centres."* A.B. Chandler. Canadian Nurse 25, 11(Nov. 1929): 663-670.

**527. Chandler, A.B.** *"Problems in Child Development."* A.B. Chandler. Canadian Medical Association Journal 24, 3(May 1931): 404-407.

**528. Chapel, James L.** *"Behaviour Modification Techniques with Children and Adolescents."* James L. Chapel. Canadian Psychiatric Association Journal/Revue de l'Association canadienne de psychiatrie 15, 3(June 1970): 315-322.

**529. Chapman, P.B.** *"The Lawyer in Juvenile Court: a Gulliver Among Lilliputians."* P.B. Chapman. Western Ontario Law Review 10(1971): 88-107.

**530. Chapman, Terry L.** *"Sex Crimes in the West: 1890-1920."* Terry L. Chapman. Alberta History 35, 4(Autumn 1987): 6-18.

**531. Chapman, Terry L.** *"Women, Sex and Marriage in Western Canada 1890-1920."* Terry L. Chapman. Alberta History 33, 4(Autumn 1985): 1-12.

**532. Charles, Enid** *The Changing Size of the Family in Canada.* Enid Charles. Ottawa: King's Printer, 1948.

**533. Charlton, P.** *"The Public Health Nurse."* P. Charlton. Public Health Nurses' Bulletin 1, 6(Apr. 1929): 6-7.

**534. Charon, Milly, ed.** *Between Two Worlds: the Canadian Immigrant Experience.* Milly Charon, ed. Toronto: Quadrant Editions, 1983.

**535. Cheal, John E.** *Investment in Canadian Youth: an Analysis of Input-Output Differences Among Canadian Provincial School Systems.* John E. Cheal. Toronto: Macmillan Company of Canada, c1963.

**536. Cherwinski, W.J.C.** *"Wooden Horses and Rubber Cows: Training British Agricultural Labour for the Canadian Prairies, 1890-1930."* W.J.C. Cherwinski. Canadian Historical Association, Historical Papers/Communications historiques (1980): 133-154.

**537. Chesley, Joan P.** *The Significance of Paternal Deprivation among Delinquent Boys.* Joan P. Chesley. Toronto: University of Toronto, 1964.
Thesis (M.S.W.)--University of Toronto, 1964.

**538. Chetkow, Harold** *"Discipline and the Art of Punishment."* Harold Chetkow. Canadian Welfare 41, 3(May-June 1965): 130-132.

**539. Cheung, Donald P.K.** *A Longitudinal Study of the Anterior Gum-pact Relationships of Infants from Birth to 8 Months.* Donald P.K. Cheung. Edmonton: University of Alberta, 1971.
Thesis (M.Sc.)--University of Alberta, 1971.

**540. Children's Psychiatric Research Institute Annual Symposium (10th: 1971: London, Ont.)** *Sexuality.* Children's Psychiatric Research Institute, London, Ontario. London: The Institute, 1971.

**541. Chimbos, Peter D.** *The Canadian Odyssey: the Greek Experience in Canada.* Peter D. Chimbos. Toronto: McClelland and Stewart Ltd., 1980.

**542. Chipman, W.W.** *"The Infant Soldier."* W.W. Chipman. Canadian Nurse 14, 12(Dec. 1918): 1453-1463.

**543. Chisholm, Barbara A.** *"Children's Rights."* Barbara A. Chisholm. Perception: a Canadian Journal of Social Comment/Un journal canadien de critique sociale 1, 2(Nov.-Dec. 1977): 22-27.

**544. Chisholm, Barbara A.** *"A Report on All the Questions About Day Care."* Barbara A. Chisholm. Canadian Welfare 43, 6(Nov.-Dec. 1967): 30-36.

**545. Chisholm, Brock** *"The Family: Basic Unit of Social Learning."* Brock Chisholm. Coordinator 4, 4(June 1956): 2-15.

**546. Chisholm, Brock** *"On Being a Mature Parent."* Brock Chisholm. Coordinator 5, 2(Dec. 1956): 32-45.

**547. Chisholm, Brock** *"Social Change is Everybody's Business."* Brock Chisholm. Family Life Coordinator 9, 4(Oct. 1962): 75-82.

**548. Chunn, Dorothy E.** *"Regulating the Poor in Ontario: From Public Courts to Family Courts."* Dorothy E. Chunn. Canadian Journal of Family Law/Revue canadienne de droit familial 6, 1(Summer 1987): 85-102.

**549. Church, E.J.M.** *An Evaluation of Preschool Education in Canada.* E.J.M. Church. Toronto: University of Toronto, 1950.
Thesis (Ph.D.)–University of Toronto, 1950.

**550. Church, E.J.M.** *"An Evaluation of Preschool Institutions in Canada."* E.J.M. Church. Canadian Education 5, 3(June 1950): 14-46.

**551. Cipywnyk, Sonia** *"Multiculturalism and the Child in Western Canada: Then and Now."* Sonia Cipywnyk. Saskatchewan Teachers of Ukrainian in Saskatoon 10, 1(Mar. 1979): 1-12.

**552. Clark, Donna** *The Social Background and Development of Children Who Experienced Institutional Living in Their Infant Years.* Donna Clark. Toronto: University of Toronto, 1961.
Thesis (M.S.W.)–University of Toronto, 1961.

**553. Clark, Earl Arthur** *Value Indicators in Three Canadian Adolescent Subcultures.* Earl Arthur Clark. Edmonton: University of Alberta, 1969.
Thesis (M.Ed.)–University of Alberta, 1969.

**554. Clark, James W.** *"Individual Differences in Pain Thresholds."* James W. Clark and Dalbir Bindra. Canadian Journal of Psychology 10, 2(June 1956): 69-76.

**555. Clark, Ruth** *"Physical Education."* Ruth Clark. Queen's Quarterly 27, 3(Jan.-Mar. 1920): 234-239.

**556. Clark, Samuel Delbert** *The Social Development of Canada: an Introductory Study with Select Documents.* Samuel Delbert Clark. New York: AMS Press, c1976.

**557. Clarke, C.K.** *"The Evolution of Imbecility."* C.K. Clarke. Queen's Quarterly 6, 4(Apr. 1899): 297-314.

**558. Clarke, C.K.** *"Juvenile Delinquency and Mental Defect."* C.K. Clarke. Canadian Journal of Mental Hygiene 2, 3(Oct. 1920): 228-232.

**559. Clarke, Emma deV.** *"Mental Health in the School."* E. deV. Clarke. Canadian Nurse 25, 8(Aug. 1929): 422-425.

**560. Clarke, Emma deV.** *"The Problem Child and the School Nurse."* Emma deV. Clarke. Canadian Nurse 24, 1(Jan. 1928): 28-34.

**561. Clarke, S.C.T.** *Youth and Tomorrow: a Guide to Personal Development in the Early and Middle Teens.* S.C.T. Clarke and J.G. Woodsworth. Toronto: McClelland, 1956.

**562. Clarke, Sandra** *"Education in the Mother Tongue: Tokenism Versus Cultural Autonomy in Canadian Indian Schools."* Sandra Clarke and Marguerite Mackenzie. Canadian Journal of Anthropology 1, 2(Winter 1980): 205-217.

**563. Cleland, C.A.** *"Schizoid Trends in Children."* C.A. Cleland. Canadian Medical Association Journal 34, 5(May 1936): 514-518.

**564. Clerk, Gabrielle** *"Reflections on the Role of the Mother in the Development of Language in the Schizophrenic Child."* Gabrielle Clerk. Canadian Psychiatric Association Journal/Revue de l'Association canadienne de psychiatrie 6, 5(Oct. 1961): 252-256.

**565. Clifford, Howard** *"Debunking the Day Care Mythology."* Howard Clifford. Canadian Welfare 47, 5(Sept.-Oct. 1971): 13-15, 30.

**566. Clifford, Howard** *"Neighborhood Need: a Day Care Centre."* Howard Clifford. Canadian Welfare 44, 2(Mar.-Apr. 1968): 28-32.

**567. Clifford, Howard** *"An Overview of Canadian Day Care Services."* Howard Clifford. Ottawa: Vanier Institute of the Family, c1970. In Day Care, a Resource for the Contemporary Family, pp. 56-62. Edited by Roslyn Burshtyn.

**568. Coady, Mary Frances** *Champion on Wheels: a Biography of Jocelyn Lovell.* Mary Frances Coady. Richard Hill, Ont.: c1987.

**569. Coburn, John** *I Kept My Powder Dry.* Rev. John Coburn. Toronto: Ryerson Press, c1950.

**570. Cochrane, Jean** *The One-room School in Canada.* Jean Cochrane. Toronto: Fitzhenry and Whiteside Limited, 1981.

**571. Cochrane, Jessie** *"A Noiseless Tonsillectomy Morning."* Jessie Cochrane. Canadian Nurse 42, 3(Mar. 1946): 219-221.

**572. Cochrane, W.A.** *"Nutritional Excess in Infancy and Childhood."* W.A. Cochrane. Canadian Medical Association Journal/Journal de l'Association medicale canadienne 81, 6(Sept. 15, 1959): 454-456.

573. Cohen, J.L. *Mothers' Allowance Legislation in Canada: a Legislative Review and Analysis With a Proposed Standard Act.* J.L. Cohen. Toronto: Macmillan Company of Canada, 1927.

574. Cohen, Zvi *"Jewish Education in Canada."* Zvi Cohen. Toronto: Canadian Jewish Historical Publishing Co., 1933. In Canadian Jewry: Prominent Jews of Canada, pp. 12-14. Edited by Zvi Cohen.

575. Cohen, Zvi, ed. *Canadian Jewry: Prominent Jews of Canada.* Zvi Cohen, ed. Toronto: Canadian Jewish Historical Publishing Co., 1933.

576. Cohn, Jeri *Parent-Child Relationships of Early Adolescent Female Offenders.* Jeri Cohn. Toronto: University of Toronto, 1964.
    Thesis (M.S.W.)--University of Toronto, 1964.

577. Coleman, H.T.J. *"Training for the New Citizenship."* H.T.J. Coleman. Queen's Quarterly 27, 1(July-Sept. 1919): 12-21.

578. Collins-Williams, C. *"Accidents in Children."* C. Collins-Williams. Canadian Medical Association Journal 65, 6(Dec. 1951): 531-535.

579. Collins-Williams, C. *"The Prognosis of Asthma in Children."* C. Collins-Williams. Canadian Medical Association Journal/Journal de l'Association medicale canadienne 82, 1(Jan. 2, 1960): 33-37.

580. Commission on Emotional and Learning Disorders in Children *One Million Children [the CELDIC Report]: a National Study of Canadian Children with Emotional and Learning Disorders.* The Commission. Toronto: Crainford, for the Commission, 1970.
    Chairmen: Denis Lazure and C.A. Roberts.

581. Comparative and International Education Society of Canada (1969: Toronto) *Papers, 1969.* Edited by M. Braham, J. Gagne, S.L. Kong and A.F. Skinner. [S.l.]: The Society, [1969].

582. Conference on the Canadian High School (1st: 1963: Banff) *The Canadian Secondary School: an Appraisal and a Forecast.* Edited by Lawrence W. Downey and L. Ruth Godwin. Toronto: W.J. Gage Limited and Macmillan Company of Canada Limited, c1963.

583. Conference on the Canadian High School (2nd: 1964: Banff) *Educational Change: Problems and Prospects.* Edited by R. Wardhaugh and J.W.G. Ivany. [Edmonton]: Department of Secondary Education, University of Alberta, 1964.

584. Conklin, Rodney Craig *A Psychometric Instrument for the Early Identification of Underachievers.* Rodney Craig Conklin. Edmonton: University of Alberta, 1965.
    Thesis (M.Ed.)--University of Alberta, 1965.

585. Conrad. R. *"The Decay Theory of Immediate Memory and Recall."* R. Conrad and Barbara A. Hille. Canadian Journal of Psychology 12, 1(Mar. 1958): 1-6.

586. Cook, Ramsay, ed. *Minorities, Schools, and Politics.* Ramsay Cook, Craig Brown and Carl Berger, eds. Toronto: University of Toronto Press, c1960.

587. Cook, Ramsay, ed. *The Proper Sphere: Women's Place in Canadian Society.* Ramsay Cook and Wendy Mitchinson, eds. Toronto: Oxford University Press, c1976.

588. Cook, William R. *"Getting Down to Brass Tacks in Community Planning for Leisure Time."* William R. Cook. Child and Family Welfare 13, 6(Mar. 1938): 8-17.

589. Coombe, Dorothy Louise *Rehabilitation Services for the Chronically Dependent Family: a Sample Survey, (Vancouver, 1959) and a Review of the Coordinated Community Approach.* Dorothy Louise Coombe. Vancouver: University of British Columbia, 1961.
    Thesis (M.S.W.)--University of British Columbia, 1961.

590. Cooper, Barry *"Alexander Kennedy Ibister, a Respectable Victorian."* Barry Cooper. Canadian Ethnic Studies/Etudes ethniques au Canada 17, 2(1985): 44-63.

591. Cooper, Marilyn *"Cirrhosis of the Liver."* Marilyn Cooper. Canadian Nurse 53, 12(Dec. 1957): 1106-1114.

592. Cooper, R.M. *Beatlemania: an Adolescent Contraculture.* R.M. Cooper. Montreal: McGill University, 1968.
    Thesis (M.A.)--McGill University, 1968.

593. Cooper, Vera E. *"What Happens in Child Protection."* Vera E. Cooper. Canadian Welfare 38, 2(Mar.-Apr. 1962): 66-69.

**594. Corbett, Gail H.** *Barnardo Children in Canada.* Gail H. Corbett. Peterborough, Ont.: Woodland Pub., 1981.

**595. Cormier, Bruno M.** *"The Black Sheep."* Bruno M. Cormier, Miriam Kennedy, Anton Obert, Jadwiga Sangowicz, Michael Sendbuehler and Andre Thiffault. Canadian Journal of Corrections/Revue canadienne de criminologie 3, 4(Oct. 1961): 456-462.

**596. Cormier, Bruno M.** *The Family and Delinquency.* Bruno M. Cormier, Anton Obert, Miriam Kennedy, Jadwiga Sangowicz, Andre Thiffault and Raymond Boyer. Montreal: Centre de Recherches en Relations Humaines, 1965.

**597. Corrective Collective** *Never Done: Three Centuries of Women's Work in Canada.* The Corrective Collective. Toronto: Canadian Women's Educational Press, c1974.

**598. Corrigan, Philip** *"Education, Inspection and State Formation: a Preliminary Statement."* Philip Corrigan and Bruce Curtis. Canadian Historical Association, Historical Papers/Communications historiques (1985): 156-171.

**599. Cosentino, Frank** *A History of Physical Education in Canada.* Frank Cosentino and Maxwell L. Howell. Don Mills: General Publishing, c1971.

**600. Cosentino, Frank** *Winter Gold: Canada's Winners in the Winter Olympic Games.* Frank Cosentino and Glynn Leyshon. Markham: Fitzhenry & Whiteside, 1987.

**601. Cossitt, Mary** *A Study of Reading Achievement of Twins in Grade One.* Mary Cossitt. Edmonton: University of Alberta, 1966.
    Thesis (M.Ed.)--University of Alberta, 1966.

**602. Costello, C.G.** *"Behavior Modification with Children."* C.G. Costello. Canadian Psychologist/Psychologie canadienne 8a, 2(Apr. 1967): 73-75.

**603. Coughlin, Mrs. Graham Watt** *The Central Bureau in the Catholic Welfare Programme.* Mrs. Graham Watt Coughlin. Ottawa: Canadian Council on Child and Family Welfare, [1932].

**604. Coulter, Rebecca** *""The Dear Little Ones": Canada's Changing Childhood, 1880-1920."* Rebecca Coulter. ATA Magazine 59, 2(Jan. 1979): 4-8.

**605. Coulter, Rebecca** *"Young Women and Unemployment in the 1930's: the Home Service Solution."* Rebecca Coulter. Canadian Woman Studies/Cahiers de la femme 7, 4(Winter 1986): 77-80.

**606. Coulter, Rebecca** *"Youth Unemployment in Canada 1920-1950."* Rebecca Coulter. Canadian History of Education Association Bulletin 5, 2(May 1988): 71-74.

**607. Cousens, William L.** *Personality Characteristics as Achievement Predictors of Basic Skills in the Junior High School.* William L. Cousens. Edmonton: University of Alberta, 1971.
    Thesis (M.Ed.)--University of Alberta, 1971.

**608. Couture, Ernest** *The Canadian Mother and Child.* Ernest Couture. 1st ed. Ottawa: King's Printer, 1940.

**609. Couture, Ernest** *"Some Aspects of the Child Health Program in Canada."* Ernest Couture. Canadian Public Health Journal 30, 12(Dec. 1939): 580-584.

**610. Couture, Ernest** *"What of the Child?"* Ernest Couture. Canadian Public Health Journal 31, 11(Nov. 1940): 531-538.

**611. Cowan, Douglas James** *Educating the Educable Mentally Retarded: Parent and Teacher Perception of the Task.* Douglas James Cowan. Edmonton: University of Alberta, 1969.
    Thesis (M.Ed.)--University of Alberta, 1969.

**612. Coward, N. Barrie** *"The Nervous Child."* N. Barrie Coward. Canadian Nurse 31, 3(Mar. 1935): 117-119.
    Continued, under the same title, in Canadian Nurse 31, 4(Apr. 1935): 165-166 and 31, 6(June 1935): 263-266.

**613. Cowley, R.H.** *"The Macdonald School Gardens."* R.H. Cowley. Queen's Quarterly 12, 4(Apr. 1905): 391-419.

**614. Cox, F.N.** *"Young Children in a New Situation With and Without Their Mothers."* F.N. Cox and Dugal Campbell. Child Development 39, 1(Mar. 1968): 123-131.

**615. Craig, James Munn** *An Investigation into the Relationship between Mental Abilities, Reading Abilities and Knowledge of Some Basic Concepts in Social Studies.* James Munn Craig. Edmonton: University of Alberta, 1950.
    Thesis (M.Ed.)--University of Alberta, 1950.

616. **Crane, Denis** *John Bull's Surplus Children: a Plea for Giving Them a Fairer Chance.* Denis Crane. London, Eng.: Horace Marshall and Son, 1915.

617. **Crawford, A.W.** *"Linking Learning and Labour."* A.W. Crawford. In Proceedings of Sixth Annual Canadian Conference on Child Welfare 1927, pp. 51-57.

618. **Crean, John F.** *"Forgone Earnings and the Demand for Education: Some Empirical Evidence."* John F. Crean. Canadian Journal of Economics 6, 1(Feb. 1973): 23-42.

619. **Critchley, David** *"The Disturbed Child - and the Disturbed Professional."* David Critchley. Canadian Welfare 43, 6(Nov.-Dec. 1967): 24-28.

620. **Critchley, David** *"Mothers Who Stay at Home."* David Critchley. Canadian Welfare 37, 2(Mar. 1961): 57-61.

621. **Critchley, David** *"No Place for Youth."* David Critchley. Canadian Welfare 42, 1(Jan.-Feb. 1966): 15-18.

622. **Crooks, Roland C.** *"The Effects of an Interracial Preschool Program Upon Racial Preference, Knowledge of Racial Differences and Racial Identification."* Roland C. Crooks. Journal of Social Issues 26, 4(Autumn 1970): 137-144.
    Reprinted in Readings in Social Psychology: Focus on Canada, pp. 127-134. Edited by David Koulak and Daniel Perlman.

623. **Crosbie, Diana Margaret** *The Effect of Organization, Both Grouping and Superordinate Classification, on the Development of Memory in Young Children.* Diana Margaret Crosbie. Toronto: University of Toronto, 1969.
    Thesis (M.A.)–University of Toronto, 1969.

624. **Crosbie, Jean** *"Child Welfare."* Jean Crosbie. Canadian Nurse 17, 6(June 1921): 341-344.

625. **Crosby, John F.** *"The Effect of Family Life Education on the Values and Attitudes of Adolescents."* John F. Crosby. Family Coordinator 20, 2(Apr. 1971): 137-140.

626. **Crosland, Margaret Ruth** *Administrative Programming for Crippled Children in Six Canadian Special Schools.* Margaret Ruth Crosland. Toronto: University of Toronto, 1966.
    Thesis (Ed.D.)–University of Toronto, 1966.

627. **Crowley, Ruth Holt** *Your Contented Baby.* Ruth Holt Crowley. [Toronto: Carnation Company Ltd., 194-?].

628. **Crozier, Kathleen** *"Care of Baby."* Kathleen Crozier. Public Health Nurses' Bulletin 1, 6(Apr. 1929): 7-8.

629. **Crozier, L. Richard** *Teaching Receptive Vocabulary to Young Mongoloid Children: a Behavior Modification Study.* L. Richard Crozier. Edmonton: University of Alberta, 1970.
    Thesis (M.Ed.)–University of Alberta, 1970.

630. **Cruikshank, H.C.** *"The Basis of Future Child Welfare Work."* H.C. Cruikshank. Canadian Nurse 21, 12(Dec. 1925): 633-635.

631. **Cumming, Gordon R.** *"Failure of School Physical Education to Improve Cardiorespiratory Fitness."* Gordon R. Cumming, David Goulding and Gil Baggley. Canadian Medical Association Journal/Journal de l'Association medicale canadienne 101, 2(July 26, 1969): 69-73.

632. **Cunningham, Rowena** *"The Young Offenders Act: Walking the Tightrope Between Public Protection and Due Process."* Rowena Cunningham. Rights and Freedoms/Droits et libertes 57(Mar. 1986): 1-4.

633. **Currie, A.B.** *A Study of Some Factors Relating to Success and Failure in an Exam at a Commercial High School.* A.B. Currie. Edmonton: University of Alberta, 1932.
    Thesis (M.A.)–University of Alberta, 1932.

634. **Curry, Mary** *"Consumer Education."* Mary Curry. Education Canada 10, 4(Dec. 1970): 10-13.

635. **Curtis, Henry S.** *"The Playground Attendance and the Playground Director."* Henry S. Curtis. Public Health Journal 6, 8(Aug. 1915): 389-393.

636. **Curtis, James** *Understanding Canadian Society.* James Curtis and Lorne Tepperman. Toronto: McGraw-Hill Ryerson, 1988.

637. **D'Oyley, Vincent R.** *"Schooling and Ethnic Rights."* Vincent R. D'Oyley. Toronto: OISE, c1978. In Children's Rights: Legal and Educational Issues, pp. 137-144. Edited by Heather Berkeley, Chad Gaffield and W. Gordon West. Original version published in Interchange 8, 1-2(1977-78): 101-108.

**638. Dafoe, Allan Roy** *"The Physical Welfare of the Dionne Quintuplets."* Allan Roy Dafoe and William A. Dafoe. Canadian Medical Association Journal 37, 5(Nov. 1937): 415-423.

**639. Dale, Ernest A.** *Twenty-one Years A-Building: a Short Account of the Student Christian Movement of Canada, 1920-1941.* Ernest A. Dale. [S.l.]: Student Christian Movement, [194-?].

**640. Dallaire, Louis** *"Autoimmunity and Chromosomal Aberrations: Serological Studies in Mothers of Children With Down's Syndrome."* Louis Dallaire, Diana Kingsmill-Flynn and Giles Leboeuf. Canadian Medical Association Journal/Journal de l'Association medicale canadienne 100, 1(Jan. 4, 1969): 1-4.

**641. Danaher, Mary Alice** *Discovery and Rule-example Task Presentation to Students of High and Low Curiosity.* Mary Alice Danaher. Toronto: University of Toronto, 1971.
Thesis (M.A.)--University of Toronto, 1971.

**642. Dantow, M.** *"The Preschool Years: Prevention of Disease."* M. Dantow. Canadian Nurse 57, 4(Apr. 1961): 339-342.

**643. Darrah, Edwin** *Nonverbal Communication Between Mother and Preschool Child.* Edwin Darrah. Edmonton: University of Alberta, 1971.
Thesis (M.Ed.)--University of Alberta, 1971.

**644. Darroch, A. Gordon** *"Family and Household in Nineteenth Century Canada: Regional Patterns and Regional Economies."* A. Gordon Darroch and Michael D. Ornstein. Journal of Family History 9, 2(Summer 1984): 158-177.

**645. Darroch, A. Gordon** *"Family Coresidence in Canada in 1871: Family Life-cycles, Occupations and Networks of Mutual Aid."* A. Gordon Darroch. and Michael D. Ornstein. Canadian Historical Association, Historical Papers/Communications historiques (1983): 30-55.

**646. Davey, Frank** *Earle Birney.* Frank Davey. [S.l.]: Copp Clark, c1971.

**647. Davey, Helen Isabel** *The Effect of Monetary Reward upon the Figure-ground Perception and Attributive Judgements of Children.* Helen Isabel Davey Toronto: University of Toronto, 1960.
Thesis (M.A.)--University of Toronto, 1960.

**648. Davey, R.F.** *"Education of Indians in Canada."* R.F. Davey. Canadian Education 10, 3(June 1955): 25-38.

**649. Davidson, George F.** *"Family Allowances: an Instalment on Social Security. Part I."* George F. Davidson. Canadian Welfare 20, 3(July 1944): 2-6.

**650. Davidson, George F.** *"Family Allowances: an Instalment on Social Security. Part II."* George F. Davidson. Canadian Welfare, 20 4(Sept. 1944): 6-11.

**651. Davidson, George F.** *"Family Allowances: an Instalment on Social Security. Part III."* George F. Davidson. Canadian Welfare 20, 5(Oct. 1944): 11-17.

**652. Davidson, George F.** *"Family Allowances: a Children's Charter for Canada."* George F. Davidson. Canadian Nurse 41, 4(Apr. 1945): 271-274.

**653. Davidson, Joyce** *"Mental Health in the Nursery School."* Joyce Davidson. Canadian Nurse 25, 8(Aug. 1929): 425-426.

**654. Davie, G.H.** *An Investigation into the Relationship between the Reading Ability of Grade 9 Students and Their Achievement in Each of Two Content Fields.* G.H. Davie. Edmonton: University of Alberta, 1952.
Thesis (M.Ed.)--University of Alberta, 1952.

**655. Davies, Blodwen** *Youth Speaks Its Mind.* Blodwen Davies. Toronto: Ryerson Press, c1948.

**656. Davies, J.W.** *"Experience With Measles in Canada and the United States."* J.W. Davies, A.E. Acreas and P.V. Varughese. Canadian Medical Association Journal/Journal de l'Association medicale canadienne 126, 2(Jan. 15, 1982): 123-125.

**657. Davis, Deborah Lynn** *The Impact of Residential Mobility Upon School Children: a Case Study.* Deborah Lynn Davis. Toronto: University of Toronto, 1971.
Thesis (M.A.)--University of Toronto, 1971.

**658. Davis, John E.** *The Political Socialization of Children in Remote Areas of Canada.* John E. Davis. Toronto: University of Toronto, 1971.
Thesis (Ph.D.)--University of Toronto, 1971.

**659. Davis, Marianne K.** *"The Problem Reader in the Classroom."* Marianne K. Davis. Canadian Psychologist/Psychologie canadienne 9, 2(Apr. 1968): 162-173.

**660. Davison, Nancy Elizabeth** *Children's Reading Comprehension of Connectives and Personal Pronouns in Social Studies.* Nancy Elizabeth Davison. Edmonton: University of Alberta, 1968.
Thesis (M.Ed.)--University of Alberta, 1968.

**661. Dawson, Leo Shirey** *A Follow-up Study of High School Shorthand Students.* Leo Shirey Dawson. Edmonton: University of Alberta, 1966.
Thesis (M.Ed.)--University of Alberta, 1966.

**662. Day, H.I.** *"The Importance of Arousal as a Motivational Factor in Learning to Read."* H.I. Day. Canadian Psychologist/Psychologie canadienne 9, 2(Apr. 1968): 154-161.

**663. Day, Michael George** *A Re-Examination of the Social Action Process in the Light of the C.Y.C. Experience, 1970.* Michael George Day. Calgary: University of Calgary, 1970. (CTM no. 7654)
Thesis (M.S.W.)--University of Calgary, 1970.

**664. de Kiriline, Louise** *The Quintuplet's First Year: the Survival of the Famous Five Dionne Babies and Its Significance for All Mothers.* Louise de Kiriline. Toronto: Macmillan Company of Canada Ltd., 1936.

**665. de Vries, John** *Explorations in the Demography of Language and Ethnicity: the Case of Ukrainians in Canada.* John de Vries. Ottawa: Department of Sociology and Anthropology, Carleton University, [1983].

**666. Deadman, William J.** *"Infanticide."* William J. Deadman. Canadian Medical Association Journal/Journal de l'Association medicale canadienne 91, 11(Sept. 5, 1964): 558-560.

**667. Deehy, Patrick** *"The Impact of Parole Upon the Family."* Patrick Deehy. Canadian Journal of Corrections/Revue canadienne de criminologie 3, 3(July 1961): 291-297.

**668. DeGraaf, Rosemary** *Twilight of a Dancer: a Biography of Catherine Collingwood.* Rosemary DeGraaf. Winnipeg: Peguis Publishing, 1987.

**669. Deith, Esther M.** *"Child Health in Wartime."* Esther M. Deith. Canadian Welfare 18, 8(Mar. 1943): 6-9.

**670. Demers, P.** *"An Epidemiological Study of Infantile Scurvy in Canada: 1961-63."* P. Demers, D. Fraser, R. Goldbloom, R. MacLean, H. Medovy, A. Morrison, J. Webb and W. Cochrane. Canadian Medical Association Journal/Journal de l'Association medicale canadienne 93, 11(Sept. 11, 1965): 573-576.

**671. Denney, W.L.** *"The Nervous Child."* W.L. Denney. Canadian Medical Association Journal 18, 5(May 1928): 555-556.

**672. Denning, Lord** *"The Family Story."* Lord Denning. Queen's Law Journal 7, 1(Fall 1981): 174-179.

**673. Denton, Frank T.** *Historical Estimates of the Canadian Labour Force.* Frank T. Denton and Sylvia Ostry. Ottawa: Bureau of Statistics, 1967.

**674. Denton, Ronald L.** *"Blood Groups and Disputed Parentage."* Ronald L. Denton. Canadian Bar Review 27, 5(May 1949): 537-549.

**675. Deverell, A. Fred** *"Specific Dyslexia: Nature and Treatment."* A. Fred Deverell. Canadian Education and Research Digest 4, 4(Dec. 1964): 279-290.

**676. Deverell, Jessie Marion** *The Ukrainian Teacher as an Agent of Cultural Assimilation.* Jessie Marion Deverell. Toronto: University of Toronto, 1941
Thesis (M.A.)--University of Toronto, 1941.

**677. DeVries, Robert Eric** *Evaluation of the Effects of Differential Techniques of Television Presentations on Children's Performance on Concrete vs. Abstract and Familiar vs. Unfamiliar Concept Tasks.* Robert Eric DeVries. Toronto: University of Toronto, 1970.
Thesis (M.A.)--University of Toronto, 1970.

**678. Dickenson, Victoria** *Canada's Multicultural Heritage: a Brief History of Immigration.* Victoria Dickenson. Ottawa: National Museum of Man, National Museums of Canada, 1975.

**679. Dickins, March** *"Permament Wardship ... for Better or Worse."* March Dickins. Canadian Welfare 35, 1(Jan. 1959): 22-27.

**680. Dickinson, George A.** *The Country Boy.* George A. Dickinson. Toronto: William Briggs, 1907.

**681. Dimock, Hedley** *The Child in Hospital: a Study of His Emotional and Social Well-Being.* Hedley Dimock. Toronto: MacMillan Co. of Canada, 1959.

**682. Dingman, Jocelyn** *"Preschool Education."* Jocelyn Dingman. Ontario Education 3, 2(Mar.-Apr. 1971): 28-30.

**683. Dixon, Richard C.** *"Constitutional Issues of Educational Television."* Richard C. Dixon. Manitoba Law Journal 3, 1(1968): 75-86.

**684. Dobransky, Eugene** *Evaluation of Partially Integrated Classes for Low-achievers.* Eugene Dobransky. Edmonton: University of Alberta, 1970.
   Thesis (M.Ed.)--University of Alberta, 1970.

**685. Dobson, Hugh** *"The Juvenile Immigrant in the Canadian Community."* Hugh Dobson. In Proceedings and Papers Fifth Annual Canadian Conference on Child Welfare 1925, pp. 172-175.

**686. Dobson, Hugh** *"Whither, the Canadian Family."* Hugh Dobson. Canadian Welfare 16, 6(Nov. 1940): 2-6.

**687. Dockrell, W.B.** *"Special Education for Gifted Children."* W.B. Dockrell. Canadian Education and Research Digest 2, 1(Mar. 1962): 37-45.

**688. Dodd, Diane** *"The Canadian Birth Control Movement on Trial, 1936-1937."* Diane Dodd. Histoire sociale/Social History 16, 32(Nov. 1983): 411-428.

**689. Doerksen, John G.** *History of the Education of the Mennonite Bretheren of Canada.* John G. Doerksen. Winnipeg: University of Manitoba, 1963.
   Thesis (M.Ed.)--University of Manitoba, 1963.

**690. Donohue, William B.** *"Abnormalities in the Growth and Eruption of the Teeth."* William B. Donohue. Canadian Nurse 58, 12(Dec. 1962): 1095-1097.

**691. Donovan, A.L.** *"Heart Disease in Children."* A.L. Donovan. Canadian Nurse 42, 10(Oct. 1946): 851-855.

**692. Douglas, Virginia I.** *"Developmental Changes in the Attribution of Blame."* Virginia I. Douglas and H.B. Shaffer. Canadian Psychologist/Psychologie canadienne 12, 2(Apr. 1971): 248-253.

**693. Doust, John W. Lovett** *"Studies on the Physiology of Awareness: an Oximetrically Monitored Controlled Stress Test."* John W. Lovett Doust and Robert A. Schneider. Canadian Journal of Psychology 9, 2(June 1955): 67-78.

**694. Doyle, Andrew** *Emigration of Pauper Children to Canada.* Andrew Doyle. [London, Eng.]: House of Commons, 1875.

**695. Doyle, Hortense** *The Self Concept Studied in Relation to the Culture of Teen-age Boys and Girls in Canada, England and the United States.* Mother Hortense Doyle. St. Louis, Mo.: St. Louis University, c1960.
   Thesis (Ph.D.)--St. Louis University, 1960.

**696. Doyle, Mary Patricia** *A Study of Drop-in Centres with References to the Special Needs of Girls Who Attend the Centres.* Mary Patricia Doyle. Toronto: University of Toronto, 1967.
   Thesis (M.S.W.)--University of Toronto, 1967.

**697. Doyon, Rita** *"Nurse-Teacher Cooperation."* Rita Doyon. Canadian Nurse 49, 8(Aug. 1953): 631-636.

**698. Drainie, Bronwyn** *Living the Part: John Drainie and the Dilemma of Canadian Stardom.* Bronwyn Drainie. Toronto: MacMillan of Canada, c1988.

**699. Dreisziger, N.F.** *"Immigrant Lives and Lifestyles in Canada, 1924-1939."* N.F. Dreisziger. Hungarian Studies Review 8, 1(Spring 1981): 61-84.

**700. Drost, Helmar** *"Is Youth Unemployment a Temporary Problem?"* Herman Drost. Atkinson Review of Canadian Studies 3, 2(Spring-Summer 1986): 9-18.

**701. Drummond, Keith N.** *"Cyclophosphamide in the Nephrotic Syndrome of Childhood: Its Use in Two Groups of Patients Defined by Clinical, Light Microscopic and Immunopathologic Findings."* Keith N. Drummond, Donald A. Hillman, J.H. Victor Marchessault and William Feldman. Canadian Medical Association Journal/Journal de l'Association medicale canadienne 98, 11(Mar. 16, 1968): 524-531.

**702. Ducharme, Jacques Charles** *"Burns and Pediatrics."* Jacques Charles Ducharme. Canadian Nurse 57, 9(Sept. 1961): 851-853.

703. **Duff, Patricia Barbara Elliott** *A Comparative Study of the Background, Recreational Activities, School Achievement and Personality of Superior and Normal Children.* Patricia Barbara Elliott Duff. Toronto: University of Toronto, 1940. Thesis (M.A.)–University of Toronto, 1940.

704. **Duncan, A.G.** *"Milkers' Nodules."* A.G. Duncan. Canadian Medical Association Journal 77, 4(Aug. 15, 1957): 339-342.

705. **Dunham, Elda Y.** *"Hyaline Membrane Disease."* Elda Y. Dunham. Canadian Nurse 56, 7(July 1960): 645-648.

706. **Dunlop, J. Bruce** *"Torts Relating to Infants."* J.Bruce Dunlop. Western Law Review 5(1966): 116-125.

707. **Dunn, H.G.** *"The Canadian Association for Retarded Children."* H.G. Dunn. Canadian Medical Association Journal 79, 8(Oct. 15, 1958): 661-664.

708. **Dunsworth, F.A.** *"Mental Health and Children."* Frank Dunsworth. Canadian Nurse 57, 10(Oct. 1961): 969-973.

709. **Dunsworth, F.A.** *"Phobias in Children."* F.A. Dunsworth. Canadian Psychiatric Association Journal/Revue de l'Association canadienne de psychiatrie 6, 5(Oct. 1961): 291-294.

710. **Dunsworth, F.A.** *"School Phobias."* F.A. Dunsworth. Canadian Medical Association Journal 79, 11(Dec. 1, 1958): 932-935.

711. **Duthie, Eric** *"Canada, an Illiterate Nation II: English in Ashelon."* Eric Duthie. Queen's Quarterly 43, 1(Spring 1936): 43-50.

712. **Dutton, Joan M.** *An Exploratory Study of Children's Reasons for Painting Preferences.* Joan M. Dutton. Edmonton: University of Alberta, 1971. Thesis (M.Ed.)–University of Alberta, 1971.

713. **Duvall, Evelyn Millis** *"Family Dilemmas with Teenagers."* Evelyn Millis Duvall. Family Life Coordinator 14, 2(Apr. 1965): 25-35.

714. **Dyde, W.F.** *Public Secondary Education in Canada.* W.F. Dyde. New York: Bureau of Publications, Teachers' College, Columbia University, c1929.

715. **Eadie, Susan Jane** *The Adjustment of Educable Mentally Handicapped Children in Special and Regular Classes: a Classroom Observation Study.* Susan Jane Eadie. Toronto: University of Toronto, 1971. Thesis (M.A.)–University of Toronto, 1971.

716. **Eastman, Sheila Jane** *Barbara Pentland: a Biography.* Sheila Jane Eastman. Vancouver: University of British Columbia, 1974. Thesis (M.Mus.)–University of British Columbia, 1974.

717. **Eastman, Sheila Jane** *Barbara Pentland.* Sheila Eastman and Timothy J. McGee. Toronto: University of Toronto, 1983.

718. **Ebbs, J.H.** *"Summer Diarrhoea."* J.H. Ebbs. Canadian Medical Association Journal 76, 10(May 15, 1957): 869-871.

719. **Ede, William John** *The Identification of Future School Dropouts by the Analysis of Elementary School Records.* William John Ede. Edmonton: University of Alberta, 1967. Thesis (M.Ed.)–University of Alberta, 1967.

720. **Edmonds, Alan** *The Years of Protest 1960-1970.* Alan Edmonds. Toronto: Natural Science of Canada Ltd., 1979.

721. **Edmund, Mary** *"Acute Rheumatic Fever."* Mary Edmund. Canadian Nurse 51, 11(Nov. 1955): 877-880.

722. *Education: a Collection of Essays on Canadian Education, Volume 1, 1954-1956.* Toronto: W.J. Gage Limited, 1956.

723. *Education: a Collection of Essays on Canadian Education, Volume 2, 1956-1968.* Toronto: W.J. Gage Limited, 1959.

724. *Education: a Collection of Essays on Canadian Education, Volume 3, 1958-1960.* Toronto: W.J. Gage Limited, 1960.

725. *Education: a Collection of Essays on Canadian Education, Volume 4, 1960-1962.* Toronto: W.J. Gage Limited, c1962.

726. *Education: a Collection of Essays on Canadian Education, Volume 5, 1962-1964.* Toronto: W.J. Gage Limited, c1965.

727. *Education: a Collection of Essays on Canadian Education, Volume 6, 1964-1967.* Toronto: W.J. Gage Limited, c1967.

728. **Eekelaar, John M.** *"Family Law and Social Problems."* John M. Eekelaar. University of Toronto Law Journal 34(1984): 236-244.

729. **Eichler, Margrit** *Families in Canada: an Introduction.* Margrit Eichler and Mary Bullen. Toronto: OISE, c1986.

730. **Einarsson, Magnus, comp.** *Nothing But Stars: Leaves from the Immigrant Saga.* Compiled by Magnus Einarsson. Ottawa: National Museum of Man, National Museums of Canada, 1984.

731. **Eisenhardt, Ian** *"Building a Better and Nobler Canadian Youth."* Ian Eisenhardt. Child and Family Welfare 13, 3(Sept. 1937): 18-20.

732. **Elder, David Murdoch** *The Learning of French Words in Vocabulary and Context.* David Murdoch Elder. Toronto: University of Toronto, 1957.
Thesis (M.Ed.)--University of Toronto, 1957.

733. **Elkin, Frederick** *The Family in Canada: an Account of Present Knowledge and Gaps in Knowledge about Canadian Families.* Frederick Elkin. Ottawa: Canadian Conference on the Family, 1964.
Printed twice in 1964, with changes.

734. **Elkin, Frederick** *"Family Life Education and the Mass Media."* Frederick Elkin. Toronto: Holt, Rinehart and Winston of Canada Ltd., c1971. In The Canadian Family, pp. 282-296. Edited by K. Ishwaran.
Reprinted in The Canadian Family Revised, pp. 341-373. Edited by K. Ishwaran.

735. **Elliot, G. Gordon** *An Investigation of Possible Correlates of Abnormal Abstract Thinking Capacity in a Group of High School Students.* G. Gordon Elliot. Toronto: University of Toronto, 1948.
Thesis (M.A.)--University of Toronto, 1948.

736. **Elliot, J.H.** *"Tuberculosis in the Child: Preventative Role of the Open Air School, the Summer Camp, the Preventorium."* J.H. Elliot. Canadian Medical Association Journal 15, 8(Aug. 1925): 796-799.

737. **Elliott, J.H.** *"Shall We Have Pure Milk in Canada."* J.H. Elliott. Public Health Journal 2, 8(Aug. 1911): 353-357.

738. **Elliott, Jean Leonard, ed.** *Minority Canadians Volume 2: Immigrant Groups.* Jean Leonard Elliott. Scarborough: Prentice-Hall, 1971.

739. **Elliott, Jean Leonard, ed.** *Native Peoples.* Jean Leonard Elliott, ed. Scarborough, Ont.: Prentice-Hall, 1971.

740. **Elliott, John C.** *Children Advertised for Adoption.* John C. Elliott. Toronto: University of Toronto, 1964.
Thesis (M.S.W.)--University of Toronto, 1964.

741. **Elwood, Sandra** *"The Response of Canadian Elementary Schools to the Problems of Juvenile Delinquents."* Sandra Elwood. Canadian Education and Research Digest 6, 2(June 1966): 113-126.

742. **Emerson, Blanche** *"Child Welfare."* Blanche Emerson. Canadian Nurse 26, 4(Apr. 1930): 199-201.

743. **Emerson, William Robie Patten** *Nutrition and Growth in Children.* William R.P. Emerson. New York: D. Appleton and Co., 1923.

744. **Emery, Edward C.** *A Study of the Out-of-school Activities of a Group of First Form High School Boys and Girls.* Edward C. Emery. Toronto: University of Toronto, 1955.
Thesis (M.S.W.)--University of Toronto, 1955.

745. **Emery, J.W.** *The Library, the School, and the Child.* J.W. Emery. Toronto: MacMillan Company of Canada Limited, 1917.
Thesis (D.Paed.)--University of Toronto, 1917.
Thesis published as a monograph.

746. **England, Robert** *Central European Immigrant in Canada.* Robert England. Toronto: Macmillan Company of Canada, 1929.

747. **Englander, Rhoda** *Change in Children as Perceived by Parents in Groups Led by Trained Workers and in Groups Led by Volunteer Workers.* Rhoda Englander. Toronto: University of Toronto, 1954.
Thesis (M.S.W.)--University of Toronto, 1954.

748. **Engstad, Peter** *"The Impact of Alienation on Delinquency Rates."* Peter Engstad and Jim Hackler. Canadian Journal of Criminology and Corrections/Revue canadienne de criminologie 13, 2(Apr. 1971): 147-154.

749. **Enns, David Stanley** *Technical Education and Industrial Training in Early Twentieth Century Canada: the Royal Commission of 1910.* David Stanley Enns. Halifax: Dalhousie University, 1982. (CTM no. 57940)
Thesis (M.A.)--Dalhousie University,

1982.

**750. Epp, Frank H.** *Mennonites in Canada, 1786-1920: the History of a Separate People.* Frank H. Epp. Toronto: Macmillan of Canada, c1974.

**751. Epp, Frank H.** *Mennonites in Canada, 1920-1940: a People's Struggle for Survival.* Frank H. Epp. Toronto: Macmillan of Canada, c1982.

**752. Erwin, Renee** *Adoption of Older Children.* Renee Erwin. Toronto: University of Toronto, 1959.
Thesis (M.S.W.)--University of Toronto, 1959.

**753. Esperanca, M.** *"Nocturnal Enuresis: Comparison of the Effect of Imipramine and Dietary Restriction on Bladder Capacity."* M. Esperanca and J.W. Gerrard. Canadian Medical Association Journal/Journal de l'Association medicale canadienne 101, 12(Dec. 13, 1969): 721-724.

**754. Esperanca, M.** *"Nocturnal Enuresis: Studies in Bladder Function in Normal Children and Enuretics."* M. Esperanca and J.W. Gerrard. Canadian Medical Association Journal/Journal de l'Association medicale canadienne 101, 6(Sept. 20, 1969): 324-327.

**755. Evans, Keith Leland** *The Academic History of the 1945 Grade 9 Class in Their Subsequent High School Careers.* Keith Leland Evans. Edmonton: University of Alberta, 1953.
Thesis (M.Ed.)--University of Alberta, 1953.

**756. Evans, Lindsay A.** *Young A.Y. Jackson: Lindsay A. Evans Memories 1902-1906.* Lindsay A. Evans. Ottawa: EDAHL Productions, 1982.

**757. Ewart, M.** *"Home Visiting in Connection With School Nursing."* M. Ewart. Canadian Nurse 12, 6(June 1916): 307-308.

**758. Fahlman, Lila** *Opinions of Students, Businessmen, and Educational Administrators Toward a Course in Interior Decorating in a Vocational Composite High School.* Lila Fahlman. Edmonton: University of Alberta, 1971.
Thesis (M.Ed.)--University of Alberta, 1971.

**759. Fair, Donald Clarence** *The Relationship of the California Psychological Inventory to Academic Achievement.* Donald Clarence Fair. Edmonton: University of Alberta, 1959.
Thesis (M.A.)--University of Alberta, 1959.

**760. Farewell, John Stanley** *An Investigation of the Standard of Achievement at the Lower Limit of the B Group in Grade 9 Social Studies in June 1948.* John Stanley Farewell. Edmonton: University of Alberta, 1949.
Thesis (M.Ed.)--University of Alberta, 1949.

**761. Faries, Richard** *"Autobiography of Richard Faries."* Richard Faries. Journal of the Canadian Church Historical Society 15, 1(Mar. 1973): 14-19.

**762. Farmer, A.W.** *"Timing in Children's Surgery."* A.W. Farmer. Canadian Nurse 45, 4(Apr. 1949): 257-262.

**763. Farquharson, C.D.** *"Conservation of Hearing in Children."* C.D. Farquharson. Canadian Journal of Public Health 51, 4(Apr. 1960): 165-166.

**764. Farquharson, R.F.** *"Anorexia Nervosa: the Course of 15 Patients Treated From 20 to 30 Years Previously."* R.F. Farquharson and H.H. Hyland. Canadian Medical Association Journal/Journal de l'Association medicale canadienne 94, 9(Feb. 26, 1966): 409-419.

**765. Fast, Vera** *Missionary on Wheels: Eva Hasell and the Sunday School Caravan Missions.* Vera Fast. Toronto: Anglican Book Centre, c1979.

**766. Faughnan, Jeanne E.** *"The Child in Hospital."* Jeanne E. Faughnan. Canadian Nurse 52, 12(Dec. 1956): 956-959.

**767. Featherby, Elizabeth A.** *"The Effect of Isoproterenol on Airway Obstruction in Cystic Fibrosis."* Elizabeth A. Featherby, Tzong-Ruey Weng and Henry Levison. Canadian Medical Association Journal/Journal de l'Association medicale canadienne 102, 8(Apr. 25, 1970): 835-838.

**768. Federation of Kindergarten, Nursery School, and Kindergarten-Primary Teachers** *"The Hamilton Conference."* Federation of Kindergarten, Nursery School, and Kindergarten-Primary Teachers. Child and Family Welfare 13, 4(Nov. 1937): 68-69.

**769. Feinberg, Abraham L.** *"Recent Jewish Immigration Projects."* Abraham L. Feinberg. Canadian Welfare 25, 8(Mar. 1950): 2-13.

**770. Feist, Margaret Elizabeth** *An Investigation of Predominant Para-linguistic Features of Language Involved in Communication Process.* Margaret Elizabeth Feist. Edmonton: University of Alberta, 1968.
Thesis (M.Ed.)--University of Alberta,

1968.

771. **Felty, Isabel K.** *Parental Assessment of Apparent Values of a Camp Experience for Diabetic Children.* Isabel K. Felty. Toronto: University of Toronto, 1961. Thesis (M.S.W.)--University of Toronto, 1961.

772. **Ferguson, Robert G.** *"The Child in the Tuberculous Home."* R.G. Ferguson. In Proceedings and Papers Fourth Annual Canadian Conference on Child Welfare 1923, pp. 81-84.

773. **Ferguson, Robert G.** *"Medical Examination of School Children."* Robert G. Ferguson. Canadian Medical Association Journal 15, 4(Apr. 1925): 397-399.

774. **Ferns, Henry Stanley** *Reading From Left to Right: One Man's Political History.* Henry Stanley Ferns. Toronto: University of Toronto Press, c1983.

775. **Ferrier, Thompson** *Indian Education in the Northwest.* Rev. Thompson Ferrier. Toronto: Department of Missionary Literature of the Methodist Church, [1906].

776. **Fingard, Judith** *"The Poor in Winter: Seasonality and Society in Pre-industrial Canada."* Judith Fingard. Toronto: McClelland and Stewart, 1982. In Pre-industrial Canada 1760-1849. pp. 62-78. Edited by Michael S. Cross and Gregory S. Kealey.

777. **Fingard, Judith** *"The Winter's Tale: Contours of Pre-industrial Poverty in British North America, 1815-1860."* Judith Fingard. Canadian Historical Association, Historical Papers/Communications historiques (1974): 65-94.

778. **Finley, E. Gault** *Education in Canada: a Bibliography.* E.G. Finley. Toronto: Dundurn Press, 1989.

779. **Finnigan, Bryan, ed.** *Making It: the Canadian Dream.* Bryan Finnigan and Cy Gonick, eds. Toronto: McClelland and Stewart Ltd., c1972.

780. **Fisk, Sylvia** *"A Case Study in Lead Poisoning in a Child."* Sylvia Fisk. Canadian Nurse 28, 6(June 1932): 293-295.

781. **Fitzpatrick, Wilfred James** *The Nature of Sex Differences in Spelling as Evidenced by Canadian Children's Free Writing.* Wilfred James Fitzpatrick. Edmonton: University of Alberta, 1960. Thesis (M.Ed.)--University of Alberta, 1960.

782. **Fitzpatrick, Wilfred James** *"Sex Differences in Spelling in Canadian Children's Free Writing."* W.J. Fitzpatrick and Harvey W. Zingle. Alberta Journal of Educational Research 6, 4(Dec. 1960): 200-210.

783. **Flander, Madeleine** *"The Nursing Care of Children with Acute Rheumatic Fever."* Madeleine Flander. Canadian Nurse 48, 6(June 1952): 461-463.

784. **Fleming, A. Grant** *"A Public Health Programme for the Preschool Child."* Grant Fleming. Canadian Nurse 20, 9(Sept. 1924): 569-574.

785. **Fleming, A. Grant** *"The Value of Periodic Health Examinations."* A. Grant Fleming. Canadian Nurse 25, 6(June 1929): 283-286.

786. **Fleming, Mae** *Child Care Within the Institution: a Mental Hygiene Approach.* Mae Fleming. Ottawa: Canadian Welfare Council, 1935.

787. **Fleming, W.G.** *Educational Opportunity: the Pursuit of Equality.* W.G. Fleming. Scarborough, Ontario: Prentice-Hall of Canada Limited, c1974.

788. **Fleming, W.G.** *"In Defence of Objective Testing."* W.G. Fleming. Canadian Education and Research Digest 1, 4(Dec. 1961): 40-46.

789. **Fleming, W.G.** *A Study of the Leisure-time Reading Habits of Senior High School Students with Low Sociometric Status.* William Gerald Fleming. Toronto: University of Toronto, 1953. Thesis (M.Ed.)--University of Toronto, 1953.

790. **Fletcher, Carolyn** *"Meningitis."* Carolyn Fletcher. Canadian Nurse 58, 6(June 1962): 540-542.

791. **Fletcher, Margaret I.** *A Guide to Nursery Education for Nursery Assistants.* Margaret Fletcher, Dorothy Millichamp and Karl Bernhardt. Toronto: Institute of Child Study University of Toronto, 1952.

792. **Flint, Betty M.** *The Security of Infants.* Betty Margaret Flint. [Toronto]: University of Toronto Press, c1959.

793. **Flower, George E.** *"Education."* George E. Flower. Toronto: MacMillan of Canada, [1967?]. In The Canadians 1867-1967, pp. 568-585. Edited by J.M.S. Careless and R. Craig Brown.

794. **Follet, Elvie** *"No Time for Fear."* Elvie Follet. Canadian Nurse 66, 1(Jan. 1970): 39-40.

795. **Foran, Maxwell** *Roland Gissing: the People's Painter.* Maxwell Foran and Nonie Houlton. Calgary: University of Calgary Press, 1988.

796. **Ford, William George** *Communication of Information in Children's Language.* William George Ford. Toronto: University of Toronto, 1971. Thesis (M.A.)--University of Toronto, 1971.

797. **Fornataro. J.V.** *"It's Time to Abolish the Notion of Pre-delinquency."* J.V. Fornataro. Canadian Journal of Corrections/Revue canadienne de criminologie 7, 2(Apr. 1965): 189-191.

798. **Forsey, Eugene** *"A Note on the Dominion Factory Bills of the Eighteen-eighties."* Eugene Forsey. Canadian Journal of Economics and Political Science 13, 4(Nov. 1947): 580-583.

799. **Forster, Harvey G.** *The Church in the City Streets.* Harvey G. Forster. Toronto: United Church of Canada, 1942.

800. **Forster, Mattie Louise** *"Sex Education? By Whom?"* Mattie Louise Forster. Public Health Journal 9, 5(May 1918): 229-230.

801. **Foster, Ann E.** *Common-law Unions and Child Welfare.* Ann E. Foster. Toronto: University of Toronto, 1957. Thesis (M.S.W.)--University of Toronto, 1957.

802. **Foster, Jack Donald** *"Juvenile Court Referrals to Voluntary Agencies."* Jack Donald Foster. Canadian Journal of Corrections/Revue canadienne de criminologie 12, 2(Apr. 1970): 129-131.

803. **Foster, Mrs. John** *"Foster Home Programmes."* Mrs. John Foster. Child and Family Welfare 12, 5(Jan. 1937): 44-49.

804. **Fotheringham, J.T.** *"Primary Pyelitis in Infants."* J.T. Fotheringham. Canadian Medical Association Journal 1, 12(Dec. 1911): 1155-1161.

805. **Fox, Elsworth Eugene** *The Effect of Verbal Experience on Written Language Development.* Elsworth Eugene Fox. Edmonton: University of Alberta, 1968. Thesis (M.Ed)--University of Alberta, 1968.

806. **Fox, William H.** *"Confessions by Juveniles."* William H. Fox. Western Law Review 2, 1(1962-63): 121-129.

807. **Fox, William H.** *"Sentencing the Juvenile Offender."* William H. Fox. Western Law Review 5(1966): 109-115.

808. **Fraser, Charles G.** *"Feeble Minded and the Public Schools."* Chas. G. Fraser. Public Health Journal 7, 5(May 1916): 237-238.

809. **Fraser, David** *"Sources in Manuscripts for the History of Canadian Youth."* David Fraser. Archivist/Archiviste 12, 3(May-June 1985): 8-9.

810. **Frayne, Trent** *The Best of Times: Fifty Years of Canadian Sport.* Trent Frayne. Toronto: Key Porter Books, 1988.

811. **French, G.E.** *"Toxoplasmosis."* G.E. French. Canadian Medical Association Journal/Journal de l'Association medicale canadienne 80, 11(June 1, 1959): 910-912.

812. **Friesen, David** *"Profile of the Potential Dropout."* David Friesen. Alberta Journal of Educational Research 13, 4(Dec. 1967): 299-309.

813. **Friesen, David** *A Study of the Subculture of Students in Eight Selected Western Canadian High Schools.* David Friesen. Grand Forks: University of North Dakota, 1966. Thesis (Ph.D.)--University of North Dakota, 1966.

814. **Friesen, John W.** *Schools With a Purpose.* John W. Friesen. Calgary: Detselig Enterprises, 1983.

815. **Fritze, Otto Francis** *An Examination of the Relationship of Oral and Written Reasoning Ability in Elementary School Children.* Otto Francis Fritze. Edmonton: University of Alberta, 1959. Thesis (Ph.D.)--University of Alberta, 1959.

816. **Frommer, Frances D.** *An Investigation of Children's Questions.* Frances Deborah Frommer. Toronto: University of Toronto, 1965. Thesis (M.A.)--University of Toronto, 1965.

817. **Fudge, David G.** *Family Courts: an Assessment.* David G. Fudge. Ottawa: Vanier Institute of the Family, 1970.

818. **Fuller, Jerry B.** *Factors Influencing Rotation on the Bender-Gestalt Performance of Children.* Jerry B. Fuller. Ottawa: University of Ottawa, 1960.
Thesis (Ph.D.)–University of Ottawa, 1960.

819. **Fyfe, W H.** *"The Incurable Malady of Listening."* W.H. Fyfe. Queen's Quarterly 43, 2(Summer 1936): 175-181.

820. **Gaetez, Edwin Linton** *Perceived Childrearing Practices in Relation to Intelligence.* Edwin Linton Gaetez. Calgary: University of Calgary, 1970.
Thesis (M.Ed.)–University of Calgary, 1970.

821. **Gaffield, Chad** *"Demography, Social Structure and the History of Schooling."* Chad M. Gaffield. Winnipeg: University of Manitoba, 1981. In Approaches to Educational History, pp. 85-111. Edited by David C. Jones, Nancy M. Sheehan, Robert M. Stamp and Neil G. McDonald.

822. **Gallay, Grace** *"Interracial Adoptions."* Grace Gallay. Canadian Welfare 39, 6(Nov.-Dec. 1963): 248-250.

823. **Gandy, John M.** *"Rehabilitation and Treatment Programs in the Juvenile Court: Opportunities for Change and Innovation."* John M. Gandy. Canadian Journal of Criminology and Corrections/Revue canadienne de criminologie 13, 1(Jan. 1971): 9-23.

824. **Ganzevoort, H.** *A Bittersweet Land: the Dutch Experience in Canada, 1890-1980.* H. Ganzevoort. Toronto: McClelland and Stewart, 1988.

825. **Gardner, Ethel B.** *"Recognition and Legitimization of First Nations Languages: B.C. Challenge."* Ethel B. Gardner and Mandy Jimmie. Canadian Journal of Native Education 16, 2(Fall 1989): 3-24.

826. **Gardner, Robert C.** *"Ethnic Stereotypes: Attitudes or Beliefs?"* Robert C. Gardner, Henry J. Feenstra and D.M. Taylor. Canadian Journal of Psychology/Revue canadienne de psychologie 25, 5(Oct. 1970): 321-334.

827. **Gareau, Urban J.** *"Nutrition in Childhood. Part 2."* Urban J. Gareau. Canadian Nurse 23, 7(July 1927): 347-350, 354.

828. **Garrett, Hugh D.** *"Criminal Responsibility of Infants."* Hugh D. Garrett. Western Law Review 5(1966): 97-108.

829. **Garrood, Olive M.** *"Sir Truby King: a Tribute."* Olive M. Garrood. Public Health Nurses' Bulletin 2, 5(Mar. 1938): 10-12.

830. **Garton, Lorraine E.** *Jewish Youth and the Community with Specific Reference to the Association between Adolescent Jewish Identity and Agreement with Parents' Jewish Identity.* Lorraine E. Garton. Toronto: University of Toronto, 1968.
Thesis (M.S.W.)–University of Toronto, 1968.

831. **Gaskell, Jane S.** *"Equal Opportunity for Women."* Jane Gaskell. Calgary: Detselig Enterprises Limited, c1981. In Canadian Education in the 1980's, pp. 173-193. Edited by J. Donald Wilson.

832. **Gattinger, F.G.** *"The Prevention of Mental Retardation."* F.G. Gattinger. Canadian Nurse 59, 6(June 1963): 544-547.

833. **Gauthier, Yvon** *"The Mourning Reaction of a Ten-year-old Boy."* Yvon Gauthier. Canadian Psychiatric Association Journal/Revue de l'Association canadienne de psychiatrie 11, Supplement(1966): s307-s308.

834. **Gavinchuk, Michael Nicholas** *A Comparative Study of the Relation of Academic Achievement and Certain Intelligence Tests at the Junior High School Level.* Michael Nicholas Gavinchuk. Edmonton: University of Alberta, 1954.
Thesis (M.Ed.)–University of Alberta, 1954.

835. **Geddes, James W.** *The Social Functioning of Boys Separated from Their Fathers.* James W. Geddes. Toronto: University of Toronto, 1968.
Thesis (M.S.W.)–University of Toronto, 1968.

836. **Gee, Arthur M.** *"Personality Development of the Preschool Child."* Arthur M. Gee. Canadian Nurse 34, 12(Dec. 1938): 706-709.

837. **Genkind, Ethel Ostry** *"Children from Europe."* Ethel Ostry Genkind. Canadian Welfare 25, 4(Sept. 1949): 31-34.

838. **George, John D.** *Relation of Selected Aptitudes to the Verbal and Diagrammatic Content of Physics Tests.* John D. George. Edmonton: University of Alberta, 1971.
Thesis (M.Ed.)–University of Alberta, 1971.

839. **Gerrard. John W.** *"Milk Allergy: Clinical Picture and Familial Incidence."* J.W. Gerrard, M.C. Lubos, L.W. Hardy, B.A. Holmlund and D. Webster. Canadian Medical Association Journal/Journal de l'Association medicale canadienne 97, 13(Sept. 23, 1967): 780-785.

840. **Gerstein, Reva Appleby** *"An Analysis of Infant Behavioural Development."* Reva Appleby Gerstein. Bulletin of the Canadian Psychological Association 5, 3(Oct. 1945): 73-75.
Author presented a thesis with the same title at the University of Toronto, 1945.

841. **Gibbon, John Murray** *Canadian Mosaic: the Making of a Northern Nation.* John Murray Gibbon. Toronto: McClelland and Stewart, 1938.

842. **Gibbon, John Murray** *"The Foreign Born."* J. Murray Gibbon. Queen's Quarterly 27, 4(Apr.-June 1920): 331-351.

843. **Giberson, Patricia** *Psychosocial Aspects of Congenital Heart Diseases in Children.* Patricia Giberson. Montreal: McGill University, 1954.
Thesis (M.S.W.)--McGill University, 1954.

844. **Gibson, David** *"Early Infantile Autism Symptom and Syndrome."* David Gibson. Canadian Psychologist/Psychologie canadienne 9, 1(Jan. 1968): 36-39.

845. **Gibson, David** *"Public Mental Retardation Services in Canada: Evolution and Trends."* David Gibson. Canadian Psychiatric Association Journal/Revue de l'Association canadienne de psychiatrie 8, 5(Oct. 1963): 337-343.

846. **Gibson, J.W.** *"Agricultural Training in Elementary and Secondary Schools."* J.W. Gibson. In Proceedings of Sixth Annual Canadian Conference on Child Welfare 1927, pp. 57-61.

847. **Gibson, Robert** *"Dietary Treatment of Phenylketonuria."* Robert Gibson. Canadian Medical Association Journal 78, 10(May 15, 1958): 788-789.

848. **Gibson, Robert** *"The Widening Etiology of Mental Defect."* R. Gibson. Canadian Medical Association Journal 75, 8(Oct. 15, 1956): 685-690.

849. **Giffen, Jean** *"A Corner in the Children's Memorial Hospital."* Jean Giffen. Canadian Nurse 14, 12(Dec. 1918): 1464-1467.

850. **Giffen, P.J.** *"Official Rates of Crime and Delinquency."* P.J. Giffen. 2nd ed. Toronto: Macmillan of Canada, c1976. In Crime and Its Treatment in Canada, pp. 66-110. Edited By W.T. McGrath.

851. **Giffen, P.J.** *"Rates of Crime and Delinquency."* P.J. Giffen. In Crime and Its Treatment in Canada, pp. 66-110. Edited by W.T. McGrath.
Reprinted in Critical Issues in Canadian Society, pp. 444-479. Edited by Craig L. Boydell, Carl F. Grindstaff and Paul C. Whitehead.

852. **Gifford, Elizabeth Violet** *Schizophrenic Performance of the 1937 Revision of the Stanford-Binet (Form L).* Elizabeth Violet Gifford. Toronto: University of Toronto, 1939.
Thesis (M.A.)--University of Toronto, 1939.

853. **Gigeroff, Alexander K.** *Sexual Offences in Relation to Homosexual, Exhibitionistic and Pedophilic Acts, with Particular Reference to Canadian Legislation and Case Law.* Alexander K. Gigeroff. Toronto: University of Toronto, 1966.
Thesis (LL.M.)--University of Toronto, 1966.

854. **Gilbert, Jules** *"Health Teaching in the Primary School."* Jules Gilbert. Canadian Public Health Journal 33, 2(Feb. 1942): 79-81.

855. **Gilbert, Sid** *"Differentiation and Stratification: the Issue of Inequality."* Sid Gilbert and Hugh A. McRoberts. Scarborough: Prentice-Hall of Canada Ltd., c1975. In Issues in Canadian Society: an Introduction to Sociology, pp. 91-136. Edited by Dennis Forcese and Stephen Richer.

856. **Giles, T.E.** *Educational Administration in Canada.* T.E. Giles and A.J. Proudfoot. 3rd ed. Calgary: Detselig Enterprises, c1984.

857. **Gillett, Margaret** *"The Becoming of Caroline."* Margaret Gillett. McGill Journal of Education 6, 1(Spring 1971): 119-124.
Reprinted in Mother Was Not a Person, pp. 38-43. Edited by Margaret Anderson.

858. **Gillett, Margaret, ed.** *A Fair Shake: Autobiographical Essays by McGill Women.* Margaret Gillett and Kay Sibbald, eds. Montreal: Eden Press, c1984.

859. **Girl Guides of Canada** *Organization, Policy and Rules.* Girl Guides Association, Canadian Council. Toronto: The Association, 1925, 1929, 1943.

860. **Glennon, Mary Bernadette** *An Investigation of the Relationships Between Two Speeded Tests of Visual Motor Skills and a Measure of Reading Achievement.* Mary Bernadette Glennon. Edmonton: University of Alberta, 1961.
  Thesis (M.Ed.)--University of Alberta, 1961.

861. **Glicken, Morley D.** *"A Candid Look at "Play Therapy"."* Morley D. Glicken. Canadian Welfare 45, 2(Mar.-Apr. 1969): 17-18.

862. **Godard, W.V.** *"A Comparison of Health Service in Elementary and Secondary Schools."* W.V. Godard. Canadian Nurse 38, 11(Nov. 1942): 859-863.

863. **Goddard, Peter** *Shakin' All Over: the Rock 'N' Roll Years in Canada.* Peter Goddard and Philip Kamin. Toronto: McGraw-Hill Ryerson, 1989.

864. **Godfrey, Ray** *Child Welfare Services: Winding Paths to Maturity.* Ray Godfrey and Benjamin Schlesinger. Toronto: Canadian Conference on Children, 1965.

865. **Godwin, Ruth** *"Studies Related to the Teaching of Written Composition."* Ruth Godwin. Canadian Education and Research Digest 3, 1(Mar. 1963): 35-47.

866. **Goffman, Irving J.** *"Canadian Social Welfare Policy."* Irving J. Goffman. Durham: Duke University Press, 1967. In Contemporary Canada, pp. 191-224. Edited by Richard Leach.

867. **Goldberg, Benjamin** *"Family Psychiatry and the Retarded Child."* Benjamin Goldberg. Canadian Journal of Psychiatry/Revue canadienne de psychiatrie 27, 3(June 1982): 140-146.

868. **Goldbloom, Alton** *"A Twenty-five Year Retrospective of Infant Feeding."* Alton Goldbloom. Canadian Nurse 44, 4(Apr. 1945): 279-284.

869. **Goldenberg, Leah** *The Influence of Cultural Values in Child-rearing.* Leah Goldenberg. Toronto: University of Toronto, 1965.
  Thesis (M.S.W.)--University of Toronto, 1965.

870. **Goldfarb, William** *"Corrective Socialization: a Rationale for the Treatment of Schizophrenic Children."* William Goldfarb. Canadian Psychiatric Association Journal/Revue de l'Association canadienne de psychiatrie 10, 6(Dec. 1965): 481-496.

871. **Goldring, Cecil Charles** *"Today's Secondary School Students."* C.C. Goldring. Toronto: W.J. Gage Ltd., 1959. In Education: a Collection of Essays on Canadian Education, v.2, 1956-1958, pp. 9-12.

872. **Golombek, Harvey** *"The Therapeutic Contact with Adolescents."* Harvey Golombek. Canadian Psychiatric Association Journal/Revue de l'Association canadienne de psychiatrie 14, 5(Oct. 1969): 457-502.

873. **Goodfellow, H.D.L.** *"Training Defectives in Institutions."* H.D.L. Goodfellow. Canadian Nurse 41, 10(Oct. 1945): 787-792.

874. **Goodwin, Winifred** *A Study of Withdrawals from Six Public Day Nurseries.* Winifred Goodwin. Toronto: University of Toronto, 1955.
  Thesis (M.S.W.)--University of Toronto, 1955.

875. **Goodykoontz, Bess** *"Pressures on Young Children."* Bess Goodykoontz. Journal of Education of the Faculty of Education, Vancouver 12(Jan. 1966): 23-28.

876. **Gordon, Charles W.** *Postscript to Adventure: the Autobiography of Ralph Connor.* Charles W. Gordon. New York: Farrar and Rinehart, c1938.

877. **Gordon, Diana Marie** *"Questioning of Judgements by Infant Litigants."* D.M. Gordon. Canadian Bar Review 21, 1(Jan. 1943): 23-31.

878. **Gordon, Karl Aston** *Visual Conditioners of Oral Response: a Psycholinguistic Approach to the Testing of Second-language Learning.* Karl Aston Gordon. Edmonton: University of Alberta, 1968.
  Thesis (M.Ed.)--University of Alberta, 1968.

879. **Gorham, Deborah** *"Children and the Family."* Deborah Gorham. Queen's Quarterly 84, 3(Autumn 1977): 385-393.

880. **Gormely, Sheila** *Drugs and the Canadian Scene.* Sheila Gormely. Toronto: Pagurian Press Ltd., c1970.

881. **Gosse, Richard** *Family Law: a Collection of Selected Statutory Materials.* Richard Fraser Gosse. Rev. ed. [Vancouver]: U.B.C. Faculty of Law, 1971.

**882. Gould, Allan** *The New Entrepreneurs: 80 Canadian Success Stories.* Allan Gould. Toronto: McClelland and Stewart-Bantam, 1986.

**883. Gould, Dulce Eva** *An Investigation into the Relationship of Rhythmic Ability and Reading Achievement.* Dulce Eva Gould. Edmonton: University of Alberta, 1966.
Thesis (M.Ed.)–University of Alberta, 1966.

**884. Gould, Margaret S.** *The Day Nursery in the Programme of Child Care.* Margaret S. Gould and the Canadian Council on Child and Family Welfare. Ottawa: Canadian Council on Child and Family Welfare, 1933.

**885. Gould, Margaret S.** *"The Day Nursery is the Programme of Child Care."* Margaret S. Gould. Child and Family Welfare 9, 2(July 1933): 2-12.

**886. Govan, Elizabeth** *"Institutions for Children and Others."* Elizabeth Govan. Canadian Welfare 33, 5(Dec. 1957): 211-218.

**887. Goyecke, John R.M.** *The Development of Children's Reaction Time Set: the Significance of Time Estimation and Cardiac Activity.* John R.M. Goyecke. London: University of Waterloo, 1969.
Thesis (Ph.D.)–University of Waterloo, 1969.

**888. Gracey, Helen** *"Asphyxia Neonatorum and Resusitation Methods."* Helen Gracey and Norma Morasutti. . Canadian Nurse 50, 4(Apr. 1954): 265-267.

**889. Graham-Cumming, G.** *"Prenatal Care and Infant Mortality among Canadian Indians."* G. Graham-Cumming. Canadian Nurse 63, 9(Sept. 1967): 29-31.

**890. Grant, Anne** *"Methods and Materials in School Health Education."* Anne Grant. Canadian Journal of Public Health 40, 1(Jan. 1949): 13-19.

**891. Grant, James** *"Brain Power: How to Preserve It."* James Grant. Royal Society of Canada Proceedings and Transactions Series 2, 9, appendix A(May 1903): xlix-lvii.

**892. Gratton, L.** *"Group Psychoanalytic Work with Children."* L. Gratton, C. LaFontaine and J. Guibeault. Canadian Psychiatric Association Journal/Revue de l'Association canadienne de psychiatrie 11, 5(Oct. 1966): 430-442.

**893. Grauer, Albert Edward** *Labour Legislation: a Study Prepared for the Royal Commission on Dominion-Provincial Relations.* A.E. Grauer. Ottawa: [s.n.], 1939.

**894. Grauer, Albert Edward** *Public Health: a Study Prepared for the Royal Commission on Dominion-Provincial Relations.* Albert Edward Grauer. Ottawa: [s.n.], 1939.

**895. Gray, Charlotte** *"Dr. Thomas Barnardo's Orphans Were Shipped 5000 km to Save Body and Soul."* Charlotte Gray. Canadian Medical Association Journal/Journal de l'Association medicale canadienne 121, 7(Oct. 6, 1979): 981-987.

**896. Gray, Margaret** *Charles Comfort.* Margaret Gray, Margaret Rand and Lois Steen. Agincourt, Ont.: Gage Publishing, 1976.

**897. Gray, Reta** *Queer Questions Quaintly Answered, or, Creative Mysteries Made Plain to Children.* Reta Gray. Toronto: J.L. Nichols, [1899?].

**898. Gray, Stanley** *"New Left, Old Left."* Stanley Gray. [S.l.]: Canadian Dimension Magazine, 1970. In Canadian Dimension Kit No. 2: Youth Revolt and the New Left, pp. 17-19.
Reprinted from Canadian Dimension (Nov. 1965).

**899. Grayson, L.M., ed.** *The Wretched of Canada: Letters to R.B. Bennett, 1930-1935.* L.M. Grayson and Michael Bliss, eds. Toronto: University of Toronto Press, 1971.

**900. Greene, Adam** *"Canadian Education: a Utopian Approach."* Adam Greene. Toronto: University of Toronto Press, c1961. In Social Purpose for Canada, pp. 86-102. Edited by Michael Oliver.

**901. Greenfield, Thomas Barr** *Teacher Leader Behaviour and its Relation to Effectiveness as Measured by Pupil Growth.* Thomas Barr Greenfield. Edmonton: University of Alberta, 1961.
Thesis (M.Ed.)–University of Alberta, 1961.

**902. Greenlee, James Grant Christopher** *Sir Robert Falconer: a Biography.* James Grant Christopher Greenlee. Toronto: University of Toronto Press, 1988.

**903. Greer, Rosamond Fiddy** *The Girls of the King's Navy.* Rosamond "Fiddy" Greer. Victoria: Sono Nis Press, c1983.

904. **Grescoe, Paul** *The Money Rustlers: Self-Made Millionaires of the New West.* Paul Grescoe and David Cruise. Markham, Ontario: Viking, 1985.

905. **Grewar, David A.I.** *"Breast Feeding."* D. Grewar. Canadian Medical Association Journal/Journal de l'Association medicale canadienne 81, 10(Nov. 15, 1959): 844-845.

906. **Grewar, David A.I.** *"Nutritional Disturbance in Infancy."* David Grewar and Grace Linney. Canadian Nurse 50, 4(Apr. 1954): 268-273.

907. **Griffin, A.W.** *"Problems of the Gifted Child."* A.W. Griffin. Canadian Education and Research Digest 1, 2(June 1961): 37-42.

908. **Griffin, J.D.M.** *"The Contribution of Child Psychiatry to Mental Hygiene."* J.D.M. Griffin. Canadian Public Health Journal 29, 11(Nov. 1938): 550-553.

909. **Griffin, J.D.M.** *A Guide for the Taking of Psychiatric Histories and the Examination of Children.* J.D.M. Griffin. Toronto: University of Toronto, 1933. Thesis (M.A.)--University of Toronto, 1933.

910. **Griffin, John D.** *"What "Discipline" is Justified?"* John D. Griffin. Canadian Welfare 44, 6(Nov.-Dec. 1968): 7.

911. **Griffith, Gwyneth** *The Meaning of Wardship to a Child.* Gwyneth Griffith. Toronto: University of Toronto, 1956. Thesis (M.S.W.)--University of Toronto, 1956.

912. **Griffiths, Margaret** *The Child Faces Placement.* Margaret H. Griffiths. Ottawa: Canadian Welfare Council, 1946.

913. **Griffiths, Margaret** *"Essentials in Adoption Services: Part III: Supervision in Adoption."* Margaret Griffiths. Canadian Welfare 19, 7(Jan. 1944): 27-30.

914. **Grigg, David H.** *From One to Seventy.* David H. Grigg. Vancouver: Mitchell Printing and Publishing Co. Ltd., c1953.

915. **Gripton, James** *Education and Occupational Training of Children's Aid Society's Wards.* James Gripton. Toronto: University of Toronto, 1958. Thesis (M.S.W.)--University of Toronto, 1958.

916. **Grodecki, G.** *"Polish Language Schools in Canada."* G. Grodecki. Ottawa: Inter-University Committee on Canadian Slavs, [1970?]. In Slavs in Canada, v.3 pp. 185-190. Edited by Cornelius J. Jaenen.

917. **Grout, W. Wallace** *"A Preschool Child Development Clinic."* W. Wallace Grout. Canadian Psychiatric Association Journal/Revue de l'Association canadienne de psychiatrie 8, 2(Apr. 1963): 79-86.

918. **Grunau, Ruth V.** *Developmental Changes in the Use of Facial Expression as a Basis of Classification.* Ruth V. Grunau. Vancouver: University of British Columbia, 1969. Thesis (M.A.)--University of British Columbia, 1969.

919. **Guest, Harry H.** *"Family Life Education."* Harry H. Guest. Medical Services Journal of Canada 23, 4(Apr. 1967): 621-628.

920. **Guest, L. Haden** *"Poverty and School Clinics."* L. Haden Guest. Public Health Journal 2, 7(July 1911): 317-319.

921. **Guild, Dorothy J.** *"The Promotion of Safety: the Role of the Public Health Nurse."* Dorothy J. Guild. Canadian Nurse 51, 6(June 1955): 456-459.

922. **Gunby, Lise** *Early Farm Life.* Lise Gunby. Toronto: Crabtree Pub., c1983.

923. **Gunn, Angus M.** *Inequalities Within Canada.* Angus M. Gunn. Toronto: Oxford University Press, 1974.

924. **Guppy, L. Neil** *"Changing Patterns of Educational Inequality in Canada."* Neil Guppy, Paulina D. Mikicich, and Ravi Pendakur. Canadian Journal of Sociology 9, 3(Summer 1984): 319-332.

925. **Gussack, Anne** *The Construction of a Group Intelligence Test.* Anne Gussack. Toronto: University of Toronto, 1933. Thesis (M.A.)--University of Toronto, 1933.

926. **Gustafson, Ralph** *"Snow."* Ralph Gustafson. Journal of Canadian Studies/Revue d'etudes canadiennes 4, 1(Feb. 1969): 3-6.

927. **Hackney, I. Marcy** *"Schizoid Characteristics in Learning Disabilities."* I. Marcy Hackney. Canadian Psychiatric Association Journal/Revue de l'Association canadienne de psychiatrie 15, 3(June 1970): 309-310.

928. **Haig, G.T.** *"Suppose Tommy Won't Eat."* G.T. Haig. Canadian Nurse 49, 1(Jan. 1953): 38-40.

929. **Haley, Bernice** *"Chorea."* Bernice Haley. Canadian Nurse 48, 6(June 1952): 467-468.

930. **Haley, Joseph** *"Child Dependency and Family Relief."* Josephy Haley. In Proceedings and Papers Fifth Annual Canadian Conference on Child Welfare 1925, pp. 155-159.

931. **Hall, Bertha E.** *"Provision for Infant Care in a Small Community."* Bertha E. Hall. In Proceedings of Sixth Annual Canadian Conference on Child Welfare 1927, pp. 27-31.

932. **Hall, Oswald** *"The Girls' and Boys' World."* Oswald Hall and Bruce McFarlane. In Canadian Society: Sociological Perspectives, 2nd ed., 1964, pp. 200-202, 3rd ed., 1968, pp. 215-217 and abr. 3rd ed., pp. 1971, pp. 150-152. Edited by Bernard R. Blishen, Frank E. Jones, Kasper D. Naegele and John Porter.

933. **Hall, Oswald** *Transition from School to Work.* Oswald Hall and Bruce McFarlane. Ottawa: Roger Duhamel, Queen's Printer, 1963.

934. **Halliday, Claire** *"Boracic Acid: the Wolf in Sheep's Clothing."* Claire Halliday. Canadian Nurse 55, 12(Dec. 1959): 1093-1094.

935. **Halliday, Claire** *"New Safety Container Prevents Poisoning Accidents."* Claire Halliday. Canadian Nurse 49, 11(Nov. 1953): 852-854.

936. **Hally, Daisy** *"Understanding the Reactions of Children."* Daisy Hally. Canadian Nurse 30, 7(July 1934): 318-320.

937. **Halpern, Esther** *"Mental Health Consultations and the School Psychologist."* Esther Halpern. Canadian Psychologist/Psychologie canadienne 6a 1(Jan. 1965): 38-60.

938. **Hamaluk, Orest John** *The Effectiveness of the Illinois Test of Psycholinguistic Abilities in Predicting Reading Ability.* Orest John Hamaluk. Edmonton: University of Alberta, 1967. Thesis (M.Ed.)--University of Alberta, 1967.

939. **Hambleton, Ronald Kenneth** *The Effects of Item Order and Anxiety on Test Performance and Stress.* Ronald Kenneth Hambleton. Toronto: University of Toronto, 1968. Thesis (M.A.)--University of Toronto, 1968.

940. **Hamilton, Frank A.E.** *"The Court at Work."* Frank A.E. Hamilton. In Proceedings of Sixth Annual Canadian Conference on Child Welfare 1927, pp. 94-100.

941. **Hamilton, Ian** *The Children's Crusade: the Story of the Company of Young Canadians.* Ian Hamilton. Toronto: Peter Martin Associates Limited, 1970.

942. **Hamilton, L.A.** *"Educational Possibilities: Sex Education."* L.A. Hamilton. Public Health Journal 12, 2(Feb. 1921): 59-65.

943. **Hamilton, Lorne D.** *"Drugs: What Can the Schools Do About the Problem?"* Lorne D. Hamilton. Education Canada 10, 4(Dec. 1970): 30-36.

944. **Hammond, Sam** *"Role and Place of Youth in Our Society."* Sam Hammond. Communist Viewpoint 3, 4(July-Aug. 1971): 35-40.

945. **Han, Po-Lin** *A Study of the Psycho-social Problems Posed for the Widows and Their Dependent Children.* Po-lin Han. Montreal: McGill University, 1968. Thesis (M.S.W.)--McGill University, 1968.

946. **Hancock, Carol L.** *No Small Legacy.* Carol L. Hancock. 1st ed. Winfield, B.C.: Wood Lake Books Inc., c1979.

947. **Hancock, Mary R.** *A Study of Wardship Applications By the Children's Aid Society of Metro Toronto in Which There Was Opposition to the Society's Application by the Parent Guardian or Person in Whose Charge the Child Was.* Mary R. Hancock. Toronto: University of Toronto, 1964. Thesis (M.S.W.)--University of Toronto, 1964.

948. **Hani, Frances** *"Grandmother."* Frances Hani. Queen's Quarterly 89, 4(Winter 1982): 710-721.

949. **Hansen, Rick** *Rick Hansen: Man in Motion.* Rick Hansen and Jim Taylor. Vancouver: Douglas & McIntyre, c1987.

**950. Harasym, Peter Humphrey** *Effects of Three Cognitive Levels of Questions on Achievement.* Peter Humphrey Harasym. Edmonton: University of Alberta, 1970. Thesis (M.Ed.)--University of Alberta, 1970.

**951. Hardie, A.D.** *"Parental Responsibility."* A.D. Hardie. In Proceedings and Papers Fifth Annual Canadian Conference on Child Welfare 1925, pp. 130-134.

**952. Harding, Madeline Isobel** *Auditory Blending as a Factor in the Reading and Spelling Achievement of Grade Four Pupils with Reading Disabilities.* Madeline Isobel Harding. Toronto: University of Toronto, 1966.
Thesis (M.Ed.)--University of Toronto, 1966.

**953. Hardwick, Francis C., ed.** *To The Promised Land: Contributions of Ukrainian Immigrants and Their Descendants to Canadian Society.* Edited by Francis C. Hardwick in co-operation with Philip Moir. Research by Alan Kozak. Vancouver: Tantalus Research Ltd., 1973.

**954. Hare, Robert Douglas** *An Investigation of the Relationship of the Level of Abstraction in Written Expression to Intellectual Ability and Academic Achievement.* Robert Douglas Hare. Edmonton: University of Alberta, 1960. Thesis (M.A.)--University of Alberta, 1960.

**955. Hariton, Nicolas** *"The Kinetic Test of Hostility."* Nicolas Hariton. Canadian Psychiatric Association Journal/Revue de l'Association canadienne de psychiatrie 7, 3(June 1962): 174-177.

**956. Harkness, D.B.** *Courts of Domestic Relations: Duties, Methods and Services of Such Courts: Are They Needed in Canada?* D.B. Harkness. Ottawa: Canadian Council on Child Welfare, 1924.

**957. Harrington, Martha Jane** *The Relevance of Verbal Cues to the Behaviors of Educable Mentally Retarded and Non-retarded Children.* Martha Jane Harrington. Edmonton: University of Alberta, 1969.
Thesis (M.Ed.)--University of Alberta, 1969.

**958. Harris, Robert Clayton** *A Comparison of the Effect of Two Guidance Programs on the Learning of Grade Eight History and English.* Robert Clayton Harris. Montreal: McGill University, 1964. Thesis (M.A.)--McGill University, 1964.

**959. Harrison, D.B.** *"Piaget, Bruner, and the Teacher."* D.B. Harrison. Manitoba Journal of Education 4, 1(Nov. 1968): 7-19.

**960. Harrison, Lee** *"Spina Bifida."* Lee Harrison. Canadian Nurse 50, 4(Apr. 1954): 277-278.

**961. Harrison, Phyllis, ed.** *The Home Children: Their Personal Stories.* Phyllis Harrison, ed. Winnipeg: Watson & Dwyer Pub. Ltd., c1979.

**962. Harshaw, Josephine Perfect** *When Women Work Together: a History of the Young Women's Christian Association in Canada.* Josephine Perfect Harshaw. Toronto: Ryerson Press, c1966.

**963. Hart, Alfred P.** *"Nutrition: a Health Food in Relation to the Preschool Child."* Alfred P. Hart. Canadian Public Health Journal 20, 3(Mar. 1929): 151-154.

**964. Hart, Margaret E.** *"Community Aspects of Care and Control of Pneumonia in Children."* Margaret E. Hart. Canadian Nurse 45, 1(Jan. 1949): 20-25.

**965. Haslam, Phyllis** *"The Damaged Girl in a Distorted Society."* Phyllis Haslam. Canadian Welfare 37, 2(Mar. 1961): 81-85.

**966. Hastings, C.J.** *"The Value of Heliotherapy."* C.J. Hastings. Child Welfare News 5, 1(Feb. 1929): 43.

**967. Hastings, John E.F.** *Organized Community Health Services.* John E.F. Hastings and William Mosley. Ottawa: Queen's Printer, 1966.

**968. Hawke, William A.** *"Impact of Cerebral Palsy on Patient and Family."* William A. Hawke. Canadian Nurse 63, 1(Jan. 1967): 29-31.

**969. Hawkins, Mary E.** *"Epilepsy as a School Health Problem."* Mary E. Hawkins. Canadian Nurse 46, 3(Mar. 1950): 182-183.

**970. Hayward, Myrtle** *An Investment in Health: Hot Lunches for Schools in Rural Districts.* Myrtle Hayward. Ottawa: Canadian Council on Child Welfare, 1929.

**971. Headon, Christopher** *"Women and Organized Religion in Mid- and Late-nineteenth Century Canada."* Christopher Headon. Journal of the Canadian Church Historical Society 20, 1-2(Mar.-June 1978): 3-18.

**972. Heffernan, Helen** *"A Vital Curriculum for Today's Child."* Helen Heffernan. Journal of Education of the Faculty of Education, Vancouver 12(Jan. 1966): 3-9.

**973. Heinemann, L.** *"Dependency Factors in Delinquent Behaviour."* L. Heinemann. Canadian Journal of Corrections/Revue canadienne de criminologie 6, 3(July 1964): 296-307.

**974. Heise, B.W.** *"Let's Talk Children's Aid."* B.W. Heise. Canadian Welfare 18, 2(June 1942): 15-18.

**975. Heise, B.W., ed..** *New Horizons For Canada's Children: Proceedings.* B.W. Heise, ed. [Toronto]: University of Toronto Press, c1961.

**976. Henderson, Edmund H.** *"Self-Other Orientations of French- and English-Canadian Adolescents."* Edmund H. Henderson, Barbara N. Long and Helene Gantcheff. Canadian Journal of Psychology/Revue canadienne de psychologie 24, 3(June 1970): 142-152.

**977. Henderson, Selena** *"The Value of Mental Hygiene in the School."* Selena Henderson. Canadian Nurse 41, 2(Feb. 1945): 109-112.

**978. Hendry, Charles E.** *"The Home and the School: Their Place in Society and Education."* Charles E. Hendry. Ottawa: Mutual Press, 1958. In Addresses and Proceedings of the Canadian Conference on Education, Ottawa, February 16-20, 1958, pp. 371-385. Edited by George G. Croskery and Gerald Nason.

**979. Henig, Harry** *Elusive Summit: the Biography of Sheila Henig.* Harry Henig and Madeline Thompson. Toronto: Williams-Wallace International, 1981.

**980. Henniger, Polly Johnson** *Infant Problem Solving.* Polly Johnson Henniger. Toronto: University of Toronto, 1968. Thesis (M.A.)–University of Toronto, 1968.

**981. Henrichon, Marthe** *"Posture and the School Age Child."* Marthe Henrichon. Canadian Nurse 55, 9(Sept. 1959): 826-828.

**982. Henry, Arthur M.** *Neogenetic Abstraction as an Essential Principle of Learning and Intelligence, with Particular Reference to Teaching Mathematics, Science, Language and Other Subjects, with a View to Creating an Active Method of Teaching Pupils to Think.* Arthur M. Henry. Montreal: McGill University, 1938. Thesis (M.A.)–McGill University, 1938.

**983. Henry, Lorne J.** *Canadians: a Book of Biographies.* Lorne J. Henry. Toronto: Longmans, Green and Company, 1952.

**984. Herberg, Edward N.** *Ethnic Groups in Canada: Adaptations and Transitions.* Edward N. Herberg. Scarborough: Nelson Canada, c1989.

**985. Herder, Dale M.** *"American Values and Popular Culture in the Twenties: the Little Blue Books."* Dale M. Herder. Canadian Historical Association, Historical Papers/Communications historiques (1971): 289-299.

**986. Herman, Albert** *"Effects of High School Program Choice on Self Concept."* A.B. Herman. Alberta Journal of Educational Research 17, 1(Mar. 1971): 13-31.

**987. Herman, Kathleen** *"The Junior Red Cross."* Kathleen Herman. Canadian Education 11, 3(June 1956): 3-17.

**988. Heron, Alastair** *"Personality and Occupational Adjustment: a Cross Validation Study."* Alastair Heron. Canadian Journal of Psychology 9, 1(Mar. 1955): 15-20.

**989. Heron, W. Craig** *"Saving the Children."* Craig Heron. Acadiensis 13, 1(Autumn 1983): 168-175.

**990. Hersak, G.A.** *Immigration of Children as a Response to Demographic Concerns.* G.A. Hersak and S. Francolini. Ottawa: Employment and Immigration, 1987.

**991. Hershfield, Leible** *The Jewish Athlete: a Nostalgic View.* Leible Hershfield. [S.l.: s.n.], 1980.

**992. Hewitt, Adlynn Miskew** *"Guardianship, Wills: the Infant Mother Who Has Never Been Married and Wishes to Provide for Her Illegitimate Child."* Adlynn Miskew Hewitt. Alberta Law Review 7(1969): 318-320.

**993. Hewitt, Elva M.** *"The Care of the Premature Baby."* Elva M. Hewitt. Canadian Nurse 42, 2(Feb. 1946): 127-130.

**994. Hewitt, Molly** *Sixty Years of CGIT: 1915-75.* Molly Hewitt. Toronto: National CGIT Committee Anniversary Task Force, [1975?].

**995. Hewson, John Cecil** *The History of Commercial Education in Canada.* John Cecil Hewson. Edmonton: University of Alberta, 1940. Thesis (M.A.)–University of Alberta, 1940.

**996. Heydenkorn, Benedykt** *"Through a Prism of Memoirs."* Benedykt Heydenkorn. Toronto: Canadian Polish Research Institute, 1985. In A Community in Transition: the Polish Group in Canada, pp. 249-256. Edited by Benedykt Heydenkorn.

**997. Heydenkorn, Benedykt, ed.** *A Community in Transition: the Polish Group in Canada.* Benedykt Heydenkorn, ed. Toronto: Canadian Polish Research Institute, 1985.

**998. Higgs, Nora** *"The Value of Preschool Work."* Nora Higgs. Public Health Nurses' Bulletin 1, 6(Apr. 1929): 23-24.

**999. Hilditch, Rochelle L.** *Middle-class Families' Needs and Uses of Services for Children.* Rochelle Hilditch. Toronto: University of Toronto, 1963. Thesis (M.S.W.)--University of Toronto, 1963.

**1000. Hill, Daniel G.** *The Freedom-seekers: Blacks in Early Canada.* Daniel G. Hill. Agincourt: Book Society of Canada, c1981.

**1001. Hill, Dorothy J.** *"Cleft Lips and Palates."* Dorothy J. Hill. Canadian Nurse 55, 5(May 1959): 439-441.

**1002. Hill, Dorothy Lillian** *A Study of Sex and Grade Differences in the Relationship between School Achievement and Sociometric Status in an Elementary School.* Dorothy Lillian Hill. Toronto: University of Toronto, 1959. Thesis (M.A.)--University of Toronto, 1959.

**1003. Hill, Florence Marguerite** *A Comparative Study of the Psychometric Performance, School Achievement, Family Background, Interests and Activities of Shy and Normal Children.* Florence Marguerite Hill. Toronto: University of Toronto, 1941. Thesis (M.A.)--University of Toronto, 1941.

**1004. Hill, Polly** *Children and Space.* Polly Hill. [S.l.: s.n., 1971]. Reprinted from Habitat, Central Mortgage and Housing Corporation.

**1005. Hincks, C.M.** *"An Adequate Mental Hygiene Program."* C.M. Hincks. In Proceedings of Sixth Annual Canadian Conference on Child Welfare 1927, pp. 90-93.

**1006. Hincks, C.M.** *"Mental Hygiene of Childhood."* C.M. Hincks. Canadian Public Health Journal 21, 1(Jan. 1930): 26-29.

**1007. Hirsch, Morris** *A Clarification of the Concept of Security in the Academic Area and its Relationship to Feeling Tone of a Group of Grade 10 Students.* Morris Hirsch. Toronto: University of Toronto, 1952. Thesis (M.A.)--University of Toronto, 1952.

**1008. Hirschbach, Ernest** *Group Homes For Children.* Ernest Hirshbach. Rev. ed. Ottawa: Family and Child Welfare Division, Canadian Welfare Council, 1967. First issued in 1965.

**1009. Hirst, Linda J.** *The Young Offenders Act: Focus, the Right to Counsel.* Linda J. Hirst. Toronto: University of Toronto, 1985. Thesis (LL.M.)--University of Toronto, 1985.

**1010. Hirtle, Dorothy V.** *A Study of Personality Characteristics of Children with Psychosomatic Disorders.* Dorothy V. Hirtle. Toronto: University of Toronto, 1950. Thesis (M.A.)--University of Toronto, 1950.

**1011. Hoare, Harold John** *The Relationship of Personality Rigidity to the Scholastic Achievement of Matriculated Students.* Harold John Hoare. Edmonton: University of Alberta, 1968. Thesis (M.Ed.)--University of Alberta, 1968.

**1012. Hobart, Charles W.** *"Changing Orientations to Courtship: a Study of Young Canadians."* Charles W. Hobart. Toronto: Copp Clark Publishing Co., c1970. In Social and Cultural Change in Canada v.2, pp. 272-295. Edited by W.E. Mann.

**1013. Hobart, Charles W.** *""Growing Up Absurd": Youth and the Changing Moral Structure."* Charles W. Hobart. Toronto: MacMillan of Canada, 1968. In Trends and Change in Canadian Society: Their Challenge to Youth, pp. 147-162. Edited by B.Y. Card.

**1014. Hobart, Charles W.** *"The Implications of Student Power for High Schools."* Charles Hobart. Education Canada 9, 2(June 1969): 21-32.

**1015. Hodgetts, A.B.** *What Culture? What Heritage?* A.B. Hodgetts. Toronto: Ontario Institute for Studies in Education, 1968.

**1016. Hodgetts, Charles A.** *"Infantile Mortality in Canada."* C.A. Hodgetts. Canadian Medical Association Journal 1, 8(Aug. 1911): 720-729.

**1017. Hodgetts, Charles A.** *"The Statistics of Infantile Paralysis."* C.A. Hodgetts. Canadian Medical Association Journal 1, 11(Nov. 1911): 1036-1039.

**1018. Hohol, Albert** *A Review of the Evidence on the Problem of Why Youth Leave School.* Albert Edward Hohol. Edmonton: University of Alberta, 1954. Thesis (M.Ed.)--University of Alberta, 1954.

**1019. Holmes, Janet** *"Deck the Halls: Toys for a Canadian Christmas."* Janet Holmes. Rotunda 11, 4(Winter 1978/1979): 4-11.

**1020. Holmes, Louise** *Child Care Plans Made by Families During a Mother's Hospitalization with a Psychiatric Illness.* Louise Holmes. Toronto: University of Toronto, 1955. Thesis (M.S.W.)--University of Toronto, 1955.

**1021. Holt, K.A.** *"The Future Offenders in Canada: Nature and Extent."* K.A. Holt. Canadian Journal of Corrections/Revue canadienne de criminologie 12, 4(Oct. 1970): 360-378.

**1022. Holt, L. Emmett** *"Health Education of Children."* L. Emmett Holt. Canadian Public Health Journal 13, 3(Mar. 1922): 106-113.

**1023. Holt, Simma** *Sex and the Teenage Revolution.* Simma Holt. Toronto: McClelland and Stewart Ltd., c1967.

**1024. Hopper, R.W.** *"Conservation of Life: the Crippled Child."* R.W. Hopper. Canadian Welfare 16, 4(Aug. 1940): 31-34.

**1025. Hopper, R.W.** *"Cooperation Between the Family Agency and the Children's Agencies."* R.W. Hopper. In Proceedings of Sixth Annual Canadian Conference on Child Welfare 1927, pp. 129-134.

**1026. Hopper, R.W.** *"The Lame Walk."* R.W. Hopper. Canadian Welfare 21, 1(Apr. 1945): 9-11.

**1027. Horn, Mildred A., ed.** *Mother and Daughter: a Digest for Women and Growing Girls, Which Completely Covers the Field of Sex Hygiene.* Edited by Mildred A. Horn. Toronto: Hygienic Productions, 1946.

**1028. Horn, Ruth** *Behaviour Modification and Perceptual-motor Performance.* Ruth Horn. Edmonton: University of Alberta, 1971. Thesis (M.A.)--University of Alberta, 1971.

**1029. Horne, James** *"R.M. Bucke: Pioneer Psychiatrist, Practical Mystic."* James Horne. Ontario History 59, 3(Sept. 1967): 197-208.

**1030. Horowitz, Aron** *Striking Roots: Reflections on Five Decades of Jewish Life.* Aron Horowitz. Oakville: Mosaic Press, 1979.

**1031. Howell, David** *"Social Gospel and the Young Boy Problem, 1895-1925."* David Howell and Peter Lindsey. Canadian Journal of History of Sport/Revue canadienne de l'histoire des sports 17, 1(May 1986): 75-87.

**1032. Howland, N.A.** *"The Indian Youth and a Grizzly Bear."* N.A. Howland. Beaver 1, 6(Mar. 1921): 14-15.

**1033. Howse, Ernest Marshall** *Roses in December: the Autobiography of Ernest Marshall Howse.* Ernest Marshall Howse. Winfield, B.C.: Wood Lake Books, 1982.

**1034. Hubbard, H. Albert** *"Marriage Prohibitions, Adoption and Private Acts of Parliament: the Need for Reform."* H. Albert Hubbard. McGill Law Journal 28, 2(Mar. 1983): 177-227.

**1035. Huber, Mary Wehe** *"Speech Correction for Cleft Palate Patients."* Mary Wehe Huber. Canadian Nurse 38, 7(July 1942): 479-482.

**1036. Hughes, James L.** *Mistakes in Teaching and Training.* James Laughlin Hughes. Toronto: W.J. Gage & Co., 1928.

**1037. Hughes, Margaret E.** *"Family Law."* Margaret E. Hughes. Ottawa Law Review 5, 1(1971): 176-195.

**1038. Hume, William E.** *Trouble in the School: Educators Cheat Your Child and the Nation.* William E. Hume and Harold F. Taylor. Bracebridge, Ont.: Bracebridge Books, [1958].

**1039. Humphreys, Darlene Marie** *Denial of Anxiety and Educational Achievement.* Darlene Marie Humphreys. Calgary: University of Calgary, 1970. Thesis (M.Ed.)--University of Calgary, 1970.

**1040. Hunka, Stephen M.** *The Effects of Bus Transportation on Pupil Achievement.* Stephen M. Hunka. Edmonton: University of Alberta, 1958. Thesis (M.Ed.)--University of Alberta, 1958.

1041. **Hunter, Alfred A.** *Class Tells: On Social Inequality in Canada.* Alfred A. Hunter. 1st ed. Toronto: Butterworths, c1981.

1042. **Hunter, Alfred A.** *Class Tells: On Social Inequality in Canada.* Alfred A. Hunter. 2nd ed. Toronto: Butterworths, c1986.

1043. **Hunter, Donald William** *The Effects of Stating Level of Aspiration According to Hope, Expect and Encouragement Instructions upon Performance of a Motor Task.* Donald William Hunter. Edmonton: University of Alberta, 1970.
Thesis (M.A.)–University of Alberta, 1970.

1044. **Hunter, Robert** *The Storming of the Mind.* Robert Hunter. Toronto: McClelland and Stewart, 1971.

1045. **Hurley, Edith B.** *"What the Public Health Nurse Can Do for the Tuberculous Child."* Edith B. Hurley. In Proceedings and Papers Fifth Annual Canadian Conference on Child Welfare 1925, pp. 113-116.

1046. **Hurley, J.R.** *The Teaching of and Teaching in a Language Other Than English in the Five Western Provinces.* J.R. Hurley and W.T.R. Wilson.

1047. **Hurt, Everett F.** *Bases of Rural Community Education.* Everett F. Hurt. Edmonton: University of Alberta, 1937.
Thesis (M.A.)–University of Alberta, 1937.

1048. **Hutton, D.V.** *"The Pathway of Life."* D.V. Hutton. Canadian Welfare 24, 8(Mar. 1949): 33-35.

1049. **Hutton, Edward** *Extracurricular Activities in St. Joseph's Boys' High School.* Edward Hutton. Edmonton: University of Alberta, 1960.
Thesis (M.Ed.)–University of Alberta, 1960.

1050. **Ignatieff, Michael** *"The Family Album."* Michael Ignatieff. Queen's Quarterly 89, 1(Spring 1982): 54-70.

1051. **Ilg, Frances L.** *"The Child's Idea of What and How to Eat."* Frances L. Ilg. Canadian Nurse 45, 7(July 1949): 513-516.

1052. **Ingram, John** *Social Class Based Educational Deficit and the Social Environment of the School.* John Ingram. Edmonton: University of Alberta, 1971.
Thesis (M.Ed.)–University of Alberta, 1971.

1053. **Innis, Mary Quayle** *"Travellers West."* Mary Quale Innis. Queen's Quarterly 52, 1(Spring 1945): 31-35.

1054. **Innis, Mary Quayle** *Unfold the Years: a History of the Young Women's Christian Association in Canada.* Mary Quayle Innis. Toronto: McClelland & Stewart Ltd., c1949.

1055. **Innis, Mary Quayle, ed.** *The Clear Spirit: Twenty Canadian Women and Their Times.* Mary Quayle Innis, ed. Toronto: University of Toronto Press, c1966.

1056. **International Conference on Mixed Race Adoptions (1st: 1969: Montreal)** *First International Conference on Mixed Race Adoptions (May 30, 31, Jun. 1, 1969).* The Conference. Montreal: Open Door Society, 1970.

1057. **Ireland, Joyce** *"By Air from Hong Kong."* Joyce Ireland. Canadian Welfare 39, 4(July-Aug. 1963): 152-156.

1058. **Isbister, Ruth** *"One in a Thousand Gets Day Care."* Ruth Isbister. Canadian Welfare 43, 3(May-June 1967): 10-12.

1059. **Ishwaran, K.** *"The Canadian Family: Variations and Uniformities."* K. Ishwaran. Toronto: Holt, Rinehart and Winston of Canada, 1971. In Social Process and Institution: the Canadian Case, pp. 372-395. Edited by James E. Gallagher and Ronald D. Lambert. Reprinted in Social Space: Canadian Perspectives, pp. 22-33. Edited by D.I. Davies and Kathleen Herman.

1060. **Ishwaran, K.** *"The Rural Family."* K. Ishwaran. Agincourt: Gage Publishing Ltd., c1983. In The Canadian Family, pp. 84-96. Edited by K. Ishwaran.

1061. **Ishwaran, K., ed.** *The Canadian Family.* K. Ishwaran, ed. Toronto: Holt, Rinehart and Winston of Canada, c1971. Revised in 1976 as The Canadian Family Revised.

1062. **Israels, Belle Linder** *The Child.* Belle Linder Israels. [S.l.]: Metropolitan Life Insurance Co., 1916.

1063. **Ivory, Carol** *"A Student Teacher's Diary."* Carol Ivory. Toronto: W.J. Gage Ltd., 1969. In Education: a Collection of Essays on Canadian Education, v.7, 1968-1969, pp. 83-121.

1064. **Iwasaki, Elsie M.** *The Emotional Problems of a Sibling Relationship When One Child Is Mentally Subnormal.* Elsie M. Iwasaki. Toronto: University of Toronto, 1957.
Thesis (M.S.W.)–University of Toronto,

1957.

**1065. Jackson, Michael** *Cases and Materials on Family Law.* Michael Jackson. 15 v. [Vancouver]: Faculty of Law, University of British Columbia, 1971-1981.

**1066. Jacobson, Edith** *"The Return of a Lost Parent."* Edith Jacobson. Canadian Psychiatric Association Journal/Revue de l'Association canadienne de psychiatrie 11, Supplement(1966): S259-S266.

**1067. Jaenen, Cornelius J.** *"Canadian Education and Minority Rights."* Cornelius J. Jaenen. Toronto: Inter-University Committee on Canadian Slavs, [1970]. In Slavs in Canada, v.3 pp. 191-208. Edited by Cornelius J. Jaenen.

**1068. Jaenen, Cornelius J.** *"Cultural Diversity and Education."* C.J. Jaenen. Toronto: McClelland and Stewart, 1972. In Must Schools Fail?: the Growing Debate in Canadian Education, pp. 199-217. Edited by Niall Byrne and Jack Quarter.

**1069. Jaenen, Cornelius J.** *"Ruthenian Schools in Western Canada 1897-1919."* Cornelius J. Jaenen. Paedagogica Historica 10, 3(1970): 517-541.
Reprinted in Shaping the Schools of the Canadian West, pp. 39-58, edited by David C. Jones, Nancy M. Sheehan and Robert M. Stamp.

**1070. James, Christina F.** *"Social and Emotional Factors Associated with Heart Disease in Children."* Christina F. James. Canadian Nurse 48, 6(June 1952): 464-466.

**1071. Jamieson, Laura** *"Sex Eduation in the Child Welfre Program."* Laura E. Jamieson. In Proceedings of Sixth Annual Canadian Conference on Child Welfare 1927, pp. 77-80.

**1072. Jan, James E.** *"Nitrazepam in the Treatment of Epilepsy in Childhood."* J.E. Jan, J.A. Reigl, J.U. Crichton and H.G. Dunn. Canadian Medical Association Journal/Journal de l'Association medicale canadienne 104, 7(Apr. 3, 1971): 571-575.

**1073. Japanese Canadian Centennial Project** *A Dream of Riches: the Japanese Canadians, 1877-1977.* Japanese Canadian Centennial Project. Toronto: Japanese Canadian Centennial Project, c1978.

**1074. Jeffrey, Fred W.** *"Death from Plastic Film."* Fred W. Jeffrey. Canadian Nurse 55, 12(Dec. 1959): 1096-1097.

**1075. Jegard, Suzanne** *"A Study of Some Determinants of Aggression in Young Children."* Suzanne Jegard and Richard H. Walters. Child Development 31, 4(Dec. 1960): 739-747.

**1076. Jennison, Mary** *"Community Centres: Schools for Citizenship."* Mary Jennison. Canadian Welfare 21, 8(Mar. 1946): 8-13.

**1077. Jensen, Forest Deane** *A Study of the Relationship Between Personality Test Scores of Dropouts and Non-dropouts in Junior and Senior High School Music Students.* Forest Deane Jensen. Edmonton: University of Alberta, 1970.
Thesis (M.Ed.)—University of Alberta, 1970.

**1078. Jeune, Susanne L.** *Three Approaches to the Writing of Fiction and Historical Literature for Children in Canada: an Examination of the Work of Roderick L. Haig-Brown, John F. Hayes, and Richard Stanton Lambert.* Susanne L. Jeune. Ottawa: Carlton University, 1974.

**1079. Jobin, Albert** *"Heat and Infant Mortality."* Albert Jobin. Canadian Medical Association Journal 10, 7(July 1920): 661-664.

**1080. John Howard Society** *"The Use of Marijuana."* John Howard Society. Canadian Welfare 45, 1(Jan.-Feb. 1969): 14-16.

**1081. Johnson, Ellen** *"Infantile Eczema."* Ellen Johnson. Canadian Nurse 56, 1(Jan. 1960): 62-68.

**1082. Johnson, F. Henry** *A Brief History of Canadian Education.* F. Henry Johnson. Toronto: McGraw-Hill Company of Canada Limited, c1968.

**1083. Johnson, F. Henry** *"Changing Conceptions of Discipline and Pupil-Teacher Relations in Canadian Schools."* F. Henry Johnson. Canadian Education 7, 3(June 1952): 26-36.

**1084. Johnson, F. Henry** *Changing Conceptions of Discipline and Pupil-Teacher Relations in Canadian Schools.* F. Henry Johnson. Toronto: University of Toronto, 1952.
Thesis (D.Paed.)—University of Toronto, 1952.

**1085. Johnson, George** *Crime in Canada: a Monograph.* George Johnson. Ottawa: Queen's Printer, 1893.

1086. **Johnson, James A.** *The Legal Drinking Age and the Demand for Beverage Alcohol in Canada.* James A. Johnson, Ernst H. Oksanen, Michael R. Veall and Debra A. Fretz. Hamilton: Program for Quantitative Studies in Economics and Population Faculty of Social Science, McMaster University, [1980's].

1087. **Johnson, Ruby Mary** *Understanding of Spatial Prepositions by Children in Kindergarten, Grades One and Two.* Ruby Mary Johnson. Edmonton: University of Alberta, 1970.
Thesis (M.Ed.)--University of Alberta, 1970.

1088. **Johnson, Stanley C.** *A History of Emigration: from the United Kingdom to North America 1763-1912.* Stanley C. Johnson. London, Eng.: Routledge & Kegan Paul, 1913.
Reprinted by Frank Cass & Co., 1966

1089. **Johnston, Greg** *"The Function of Counsel in Juvenile Court."* Jeffrey S. Leon. Osgoode Hall Law Journal 7, 2(1969): 199-212.

1090. **Johnstone, John C.** *Young People's Images of Canadian Society: an Opinion Survey of Canadian Youth 13 to 20 Years of Age.* John C. Johnstone with the assistance of Jean-Claude Willig and Joseph M. Spina. Ottawa: Queen's Printer, c1969.

1091. **Jolliffe, Penny** *"Today's Dropouts, Tomorrow's Unemployed."* Penny Jolliffe. Canadian Welfare 37, 1(Jan. 1961): 23-26.

1092. **Joncas, J.** *"Studies on Infectious Mononucleosis: 3. Clinical Data, Serologic and Epidemiologic Findings."* J. Joncas, J.P. Chiasson, J. Turcotte and P. Quennec. Canadian Medical Association Journal/Journal de l'Association medicale canadienne 98, 18(May 4, 1968): 848-854.

1093. **Jones, David** *"Family Service Units in 1964."* David Jones. Canadian Welfare 40, 3(May-June 1964): 124-128.

1094. **Jones, David C., ed.** *Approaches to Educational History.* David C. Jones, Nancy M. Sheehan, Robert M. Stamp and Neil G. McDonald, eds. Winnipeg: University of Manitoba, c1981.

1095. **Jones, Edward Austin** *An Investigation of the Relationship Between Written Composition and Reading Ability and Reading Habits.* Edward Austin Jones. Edmonton: University of Alberta, 1966.
Thesis (M.Ed.)--University of Alberta, 1966.

1096. **Jones, Lorraine** *A Study of Fifth Grade Children's Concept of God.* Lorraine Jones. Edmonton: University of Alberta, 1971.
Thesis (M.Ed.)--University of Alberta, 1971.

1097. **Jones, Pauline A.** *An Investigation of the Relationship of Integration Setting to Need for Achievement.* Pauline A. Jones. Edmonton: University of Alberta, 1965.
Thesis (M.Ed.)--University of Alberta, 1965.

1098. **Jones, Ronald A.** *"About Face in Special Education."* Ronald A. Jones. Education Canada 11, 4(Dec. 1971): 14-18.

1099. **Jordan, Gerald H.S.** *"Popular Literature and Imperial Sentiment: Changing Attitudes, 1870-1890."* Gerald H.S. Jordan. Canadian Historical Association, Historical Papers (1967): 148-155.

1100. **Jost, A.C.** *"The Conservation of Child Life."* A.C. Jost. Public Health Journal 11, 11(Nov. 1920): 503-512.

1101. **Joynt, Judith** *Conflict of Values Between Children and Staff in Boys' and Girls' Training Schools.* Judith Joynt. Toronto: University of Toronto, 1964.
Thesis (M.S.W.)--University of Toronto, 1964.

1102. **Judd, W.W.** *"The Vision and the Dream: the Council of Social Services, Fifty Years."* W.W. Judd. Journal of the Canadian Church Historical Society 7, 4(Dec. 1965): 96-97.

1103. **Juschka, Barbara Ellen** *Toward Identification of Artistically Gifted Children.* Barbara Ellen Juschka. Calgary: University of Calgary, 1984. (CTM no. 22342)
Thesis (M.A.)--University of Calgary, 1984.

1104. **Kach, Nick** *"The Ukrainian-Canadian Child, 1890's to 1970's: From a Deprived Minority to a Cultural Elite."* N. Kach and P. Pundy. Edmonton: University of Alberta, 1980. In The Child and Stress in Contemporary Society, pp. 33-44. Edited by Nick Kach.

1105. **Kach, Nick, ed.** *Essays on Canadian Education.* Nick Kach, Kas Mazurek, Robert S. Patterson and Ivan DeFaveri, eds. Calgary: Detselig Enterprises Limited, c1986.

**1106. Kage, Joseph** *"Immigration and Social Service."* Joseph Kage. Canadian Welfare 24, 8(Mar. 1949): 3-8.

**1107. Kaill, Robert Cecil** *An Enquiry into the Relationship between the Occupational Level of Parents, Their Attitude Toward Education and the Educational Achievement of the Child.* Robert Cecil Kaill. Toronto: University of Toronto, 1963.
Thesis (M.S.A.)--University of Toronto, 1963.

**1108. Kalbach, Warren E.** *"Canada: a Demographic Analysis."* Warren E. Kalbach. Toronto: MacMillan Co. of Canada Ltd., c1976. In Introduction to Canadian Society: Sociological Analysis, pp. 11-76. Edited by G.N. Ramu and Stuart D. Johnson.

**1109. Kalbach, Warren E.** *The Impact on Immigration on Canada's Population.* Warren E. Kalbach. Ottawa: Dominion Bureau of Statistics, 1970.

**1110. Kallal, Signe Gertrude** *Word and Meaning Retrieval in Grade One Reading.* Signe Gertrude Kallal. Edmonton: University of Alberta, 1968.
Thesis (M.Ed.)--University of Alberta, 1968.

**1111. Kalman, Bobbie** *Early Christmas.* Bobbie Kalman. Toronto: Crabtree Publishing, c1981.

**1112. Kalman, Bobbie** *The Early Family Home.* Bobbie Kalman. Toronto: Crabtree Publishing Company, 1982.

**1113. Kalman, Bobbie** *Early Health and Medicine.* Bobbie Kalman. Toronto: Crabtree Publishing, 1983.

**1114. Kalman, Bobbie** *Early Pleasures and Pastimes.* Bobbie Kalman. Toronto: Crabtree, c1983.

**1115. Kalman, Bobbie** *Early Settler Children.* Bobbie Kalman. Toronto: Crabtree Publishing Co., c1982.

**1116. Kalman, Bobbie** *Early Village Life.* Bobbie Kalman. Toronto: Crabtree Publishing Co., c1981.

**1117. Kalmus, Herbert T.** *"Personality and the Child."* Herbert T. Kalmus. Queen's Quarterly 19, 2(Oct.-Dec. 1911): 162-169.

**1118. Kamin, Leon J.** *"The Interrelations Among Some Behavioural Measures of Anxiety."* Leon J. Kamin, Dalbir Bindra, James W. Clark and Helene Waksberg. Canadian Journal of Psychology 9, 2(June 1955): 79-83.

**1119. Kardash, Sidney** *"Efficacy of Imipramine in Childhood Enuresis: a Double-blind Control Study With Placebo."* Sidney Kardash, Elizabeth S. Hillman and John Werry. Canadian Medical Association Journal/Journal de l'Association medicale canadienne 99, 6(Aug. 10, 1968): 263-265.

**1120. Karnauchow, P.N.** *"Fatal Disseminated Histoplasmosis."* P.N. Karnauchow and J.L. Marciniak. Canadian Medical Association Journal 75, 11(Dec. 1, 1956): 929-931.

**1121. Karrys, Eva** *A Comparison of Delinquents and Non-delinquents on Their Feelings of Security and Insecurity in the Familial Area.* Eva Karrys. Toronto: University of Toronto, 1951.
Thesis (M.A.)--University of Toronto, 1951.

**1122. Katz, Joseph** *Canadian Education Today: a Symposium.* Joseph Katz. Toronto: McGraw-Hill Company of Canada Limited, [1956].

**1123. Katz, Joseph** *Education in Canada.* Joseph Katz. Vancouver: Douglas, David and Charles, 1974.

**1124. Katz, Joseph** *Society, Schools and Progress in Canada.* Joseph Katz. 1st ed. Toronto: Pergamon Press, 1969.

**1125. Katz, Joseph, ed.** *Elementary Education in Canada.* Joseph Katz, ed. Toronto: McGraw-Hill Company of Canada Limited, c1961.

**1126. Katz, Teresa** *Effects of the Presence of Typewriters on Performance of Grade One Pupils.* Teresa Katz. Toronto: University of Toronto, 1971.
Thesis (M.A.)--University of Toronto, 1971.

**1127. Kaufman, Max** *"The Challenge to the Community in Child Welfare."* Max Kaufman nd David Weiss. Canadian Welfare 31, 4(Nov. 1955): 186-189.

**1128. Kavanagh, Oliver Finran** *An Evaluation of the Montessori "Prepared Environment" in the Light of Evidence for Curiosity as an Agent in Learning in Early Childhood.* Oliver Finran Kavanagh. Toronto: University of Toronto, 1969.
Thesis (M.A.)--University of Toronto, 1969.

**1129. Kay, Marion** *Parental Problems in the Home Care of a Schizophrenic Child.* Marion Kay. Toronto: University of Toronto, 1958.
Thesis (M.S.W.)--University of Toronto, 1958.

**1130. Kaye, Elaine** *A Follow-up Study of Children Discharged As Improved.* Elaine Kaye. Toronto: University of Toronto, 1956.
Thesis (M.S.W.)--University of Toronto, 1956.

**1131. Kealey, Gregory S., ed.** *Canada Investigates Industrialization: the Royal Commission on the Relations of Labour and Capital.* Greg Kealey, ed. Toronto: University of Toronto Press, 1973.

**1132. Kehoe, Constance Clara** *School Subcultures and Peer Group Pressures in Adolescent Deviance.* Constance Clara Kehoe. Toronto: University of Toronto, 1971.
Thesis (M.A.)--University of Toronto, 1971.

**1133. Kehoe, John W.** *A Measure of the Interest of Adolescents in the Social Studies.* John William Kehoe. Toronto: University of Toronto, 1970.
Thesis (M.A.)--University of Toronto, 1970.

**1134. Keilson, Eva** *"The Case of Little Walti."* Eva Keilson. Canadian Nurse 37, 11(Nov. 1941): 775-777.

**1135. Keith, John D.** *"Some Observations on the Prevelence of Rheumatic Heart Disease in Canada."* John D. Keith and L.A. Pequegnat. Canadian Journal of Public Health 38, 3(Mar. 1947): 111-117.

**1136. Kelly, Laurence A.** *Family Allowances and the Tax System.* Laurence A. Kelly. Kingston: Industrial Relations Centre, Queen's University, c1971.

**1137. Kelner, Merrijoy** *"Emerging Patterns of Adolescence and Youth."* Merrijoy Kelner and Evelyn Latowsky. Toronto: Holt, Rinehart and Winston of Canada Ltd., c1971. In The Canadian Family, pp. 169-185. Edited by K. Ishwaran.
Reprinted in The Canadian Family Revised, pp. 213-226. Edited by K. Ishwaran.
Evelyn Latowsky subsequently named Evelyn Kallen.

**1138. Kelso, J.J.** *"Importance of Child Welfare."* J.J. Kelso. Toronto: Social Services Council of Canada, c1914. In Social Service Congress-Ottawa-1914: Report of Addresses and Proceedings, pp. 91-93.

**1139. Kelso, J.J.** *"Neglected and Friendless Children."* J.J. Kelso. Toronto: University of Toronto Press, c1974. In Saving the Canadian City, pp. 113-118. Edited by Paul Rutherford.
Reprinted from Canadian Magazine 2(Jan. 1895): 213-216.

**1140. Kelso, J.J.** *"Reforming Delinquent Children."* J.J. Kelso. In Proceedings of the National Conference of Charities and Correction, 1903, pp. 230-237.
Also issued as a pamphlet.

**1141. Kendall, David C.** *"Learning Problems: a Note on Biological and Cultural Factors."* David C. Kendall. Journal of Education of the Faculty of Education, Vancouver 13(May 1967): 12-23.

**1142. Kendall, David C.** *"Some Thoughts about the Integration of Educable Mentally Retarded (EMR) Children in Regular Classes."* David C. Kendall. Journal of Education of the Faculty of Education, Vancouver 15(Apr. 1969): 26-36.

**1143. Kennedy, Gilbert D.** *"Adoption in the Conflict of Laws."* Gilbert D. Kennedy. Canadian Bar Review 34, 5(May 1956): 507-563.

**1144. Kennedy, Gilbert D.** *"The Legal Effects of Adoption."* Gilbert D. Kennedy. Canadian Bar Review 33, 7(Aug.-Sept. 1955): 751-875.

**1145. Kerr, Illingworth** *Paint and Circumstances.* Illingworth Kerr. Calgary: Jules and Maureen Poscents, Ralph Hedlin, Heidi Redekop and Wm. H. Hopper, 1987.

**1146. Kettle, John** *The Big Generation.* John Kettle. Toronto: McClelland and Stewart, 1980.

**1147. Keyfitz, Nathan** *"Population and Ecology: Population Problems."* Nathan Keyfitz. Toronto: McClelland and Stewart Ltd., c1964. In French Canadian Society, v.1, pp. 216-244. Edited by Marcel Rioux and Yves Martin.
Reprinted from Essais sur le Quebec contemporain = Essays on Contemporary Quebec, pp 67-95. Edited by Jean C. Falardeau.

**1148. Kidd, John P.** *"Time on Their Hands."* John P. Kidd. Canadian Welfare 22, 6(Dec. 1946): 30-34.

**1149. King, Margery R.** *"Mothers Working Outside the Home."* Margery R. King. Canadian Welfare 37, 2(Mar. 1961): 63-65.

**1150. King, Richard E.** *A Study of Computer Use in a Grade 11 Mathematics Program.* Richard E. King. Calgary: University of Calgary, 1971. (CTM no. 10098)
Thesis (M.Ed.)--University of Calgary, 1971.

1151. **King, Robert John** *Teacher Expectations, Students' Performance and the Self Concept of the Student.* Robert John King. Toronto: University of Toronto, 1971.
Thesis (M.A.)–University of Toronto, 1971.

1152. **Kinney, B.D.** *"Child Neglect."* B.D. Kinney. Manitoba Law Review 3, 1(1968): 31-46.

1153. **Kinsman, R.P.** *"Mental Hygiene and Its Relation to Infants and Children."* R.P. Kinsman. Canadian Medical Association Journal 35, 5(Nov. 1936): 540-542.

1154. **Kinzie, David M.** *Parental Assessment of Change in Handicapped Children Resulting from a Camping Experience.* David M. Kinzie. Toronto: University of Toronto, 1958.
Thesis (M.S.W.)–University of Toronto, 1958.

1155. **Kirkpatrick, Margaret** *Feeding the Preschool Child.* Margaret Kirkpatrick. Vancouver: Copp Clark Publishing Co., c1963.

1156. **Kit, Grace Lo Wai** *Some Emotional and Social Aspects of Epilepsy During Childhood: a Descriptive Study of the Psycho-social and Environmental Aspects of Epilepsy in Children, and their Implications for the Rehabilitation of Young Seizure Patients.* Grace Lo Wai Kit. Montreal: McGill University, 1967.
Thesis (M.S.W.)–McGill University, 1967.

1157. **Kitchen, A.J.** *"Toward a Better Understanding of Our Juvenile Delinquents."* A.J. Kitchen. Canadian Journal of Corrections/Revue canadienne de criminologie 1, 2(Apr. 1958): 30-39.

1158. **Klassen, Peter George** *A History of Mennonite Education in Canada, 1786-1960.* Peter George Klassen. Toronto: University of Toronto, 1970.
Thesis (Ed.D.)–University of Toronto, 1970.

1159. **Klein, Joel Perry** *The Risk Taking Behaviour of Underachievers.* Joel Perry Klein. Toronto: University of Toronto, 1967.
Thesis (M.A.)–University of Toronto, 1967.

1160. **Klempay, Mary Janet** *The Effectiveness of Various Responses to Students' Expressed Need of Counselling on Measures of Self Concept.* Mary Janet Klempay. Ottawa: University of Ottawa, 1964.
Thesis (Ph.D.)–University of Ottawa, 1964.

1161. **Knight, A.P.** *"The Teeth: an Address to Young People."* Knight, A.P. Queen's Quarterly 15, 3(Jan.-Mar. 1908): 187-190.

1162. **Knight, Bryan M.** *Voices of Canadian Jews: Thirty-Six Accomplished Men and Women Speak Out on Politics, Patriotism, Religion and Sex.* Bryan M. Knight and Rachel Alkallay. Montreal: Chestnut Press, 1988.

1163. **Kniseley, Mabel** *"The Unmarried Mother."* Mabel Kniseley. Canadian Nurse 14, 2(Feb. 1918): 845-850.

1164. **Kopf, Kathryn E.** *"Family Variables and School Adjustments of Eighth Grade Father-absent Boys."* Kathryn E. Kopf. Family Coordinator 19, 2(Apr. 1970): 145-150.

1165. **Kosa, John** *"Marriage and Family Among Hungarians in Canada."* John Kosa. In Land of Choice: the Hungarians in Canada, pp. 44-60. By John Kosa. Reprinted in Canadian Society: Sociological Perspectives, 1st ed., 1961, pp. 177-193, 2nd ed., 1964, pp. 155-171 and 3rd ed., 1968, pp. 167-183. Edited by Bernard R. Blishen, Frank E. Jones, Kasper D. Naegele and John Porter.

1166. **Kosachova, N.G.** *"The Doukhobors."* N.G. Kosachova. Ottawa: Borealis Press, 1983. In Russian Canadians: Their Past and Present [Collected Essays], pp. 11-47. Edited by T.F. Jeletzky, V.I. Grebenschikov, N. Gridgeman, and I. Gryndahl.

1167. **Kostash, Myrna** *Long Way From Home: the Stories of the Sixties Generation in Canada.* Myrna Kostash. Toronto: James Lorimer & Co. Publisher, c1980.

1168. **Krashinsky, Gertrude** *Volunteers in a Preschool Enrichment Project.* Gertrude Krashinsky. Montreal: McGill University, 1968.
Thesis (M.S.W.)–McGill University, 1968.

1169. **Krasner, Leonard** *"Growth of Behaviour Therapies with Children."* Leonard Krasner. Canadian Psychologist/Psychologie canadienne 8a, 2(Apr. 1967): 71-72.

1170. **Kreisel, Henry** *"Diary of an Internment."* Henry Kreisel. Edmonton: NeWest Press, c1985. In Another Country: Writings By and About Henry Kreisel, pp. 19-44. Edited by Shirley Neuman.

1171. **Krivy, Gary Joseph Paul** *Counselling the Elementary School Child: an Experimental Study.* Gary Joseph Paul Krivy. Edmonton: University of Alberta, 1968.
Thesis (M.Ed.)–University of Alberta,

1968.

**1172. Krysowaty, Joyce Bernice**
*Children's Perceptions of the Reality or
Unreality of Selected Phenomena.* Joyce
Bernice Krysowaty. Edmonton: University
of Alberta, 1969.
Thesis (M.Ed.)--University of Alberta,
1969.

**1173. Kubryk, D.** *"Paralytic Poliomyelitis in
Canada, 1960."* D. Kubryk. Canadian
Medical Association Journal/Journal de
l'Association medicale canadienne 86,
24(June 16, 1962): 1099-1106.
Incudes tables and statistics.

**1174. Kubryk, D.** *"Paralytic Poliomyelitis
Trends, Canada, 1958."* D. Kubryk.
Canadian Medical Association
Journal/Journal de l'Association medicale
canadienne 81, 4(Aug. 15, 1959): 228-231.

**1175. Kuplowsky, Olga** *French-English
Bilingual Education for Ethnic Minorities.*
Olga Kuplowsky. Toronto: University of
Toronto, 1971.
Thesis (M.A.)--University of Toronto,
1971.

**1176. Kurelek, William** *Jewish Life in
Canada.* William Kurelek and Abraham
Arnold. Edmonton: Hurtig Publishers,
1976.

**1177. Kurelek, William** *A Northern
Nativity: Christmas Dreams of a Prairie
Boy.* William Kurelek. Montreal: Tundra
Books, 1976.

**1178. Kurelek, William** *A Prairie Boy's
Summer.* William Kurelek. Montreal:
Tundra Books, 1975, 1979, 1984.

**1179. Kurelek, William** *A Prairie Boy's
Winter.* William Kurelek. Montreal: Tundra
Books, 1973.

**1180. Kyba, Patrick** *Alvin: a Biography of
the Honourable Alvin Hamilton, P.C.*
Patrick Kyba. Regina: Canadian Plains
Research Centre, 1989.

**1181. L'Esperance, Jeanne** *"The Mystery
of Miss MacKenzie."* Jeanne L'Esperance.
Archivist/Archiviste 12, 5(Sept.-Oct. 1985):
18.

**1182. Labenson, Dorothy Roslyn** *The
Effects of Socioeconomic Status on
Recognition and Recall Vocabularies of
Grade One Children.* Dorothy Roslyn
Labenson. Edmonton: University of
Alberta, 1967.
Thesis (M.Ed.)--University of Alberta,
1967.

**1183. Lacelle, Claudette** *Urban Domestic
Servants in 19th-century Canada.*
Claudette Lacelle. Ottawa: Environment
Canada, Parks Division, 1987.
Original in French.

**1184. Laing, Hamilton M.** *Allan Brooks:
Artist Naturalist.* Hamilton M. Laing.
Victoria: British Columbia Provincial
Museum, 1979.

**1185. Lamb, A.S.** *Posture Body Mechanics.*
A.S. Lamb. Ottawa: Canadian Welfare
Council, Division on Maternal and Child
Care, 1936.
Reprint.

**1186. Lamb, Silvia** *The Social Behaviour
Surrounding Children's Health Problems.*
Silvia Lamb and David N. Solomon.
Toronto: Canadian Conference on Children,
[1965].

**1187. Lambert, Ronald D.** *Sex-role
Imagery in Children: Social Origins of
Mind.* Ronald D. Lambert. Ottawa:
Information Canada, c1971.

**1188. Lamont, G.A.** *"Fatigue in Children."*
G.A. Lamont. Canadian Medical
Association Journal 36, 1(Jan. 1937):
47-51.

**1189. Lamont, G.A.** *"The Preschool Child."*
G.A. Lamont. Canadian Nurse 25, 12(Dec.
1929): 709-714.

**1190. Landis, Judson T.** *"A Comparison
of Children from Divorced and Non
Divorced Unhappy Marriages."* Judson T.
Landis. Family Life Coordinator 11, 3(July
1962): 61-65.

**1191. Landry, Pauline L.** *"Home Visiting
by the Children's Aid Society."* Pauline L.
Landry. Child and Family Welfare 8,
3(Sept. 1932): 6-10.

**1192. Lane,. Russella J.** *A Study of
Children's Drawings of the Human Figure.*
Russella J. Lane. London, Ont.: University
of Western Ontario, 1950.
Thesis (M.A.) – University of Western
Ontario, 1950.

**1193. Lane, W.F.** *"Juvenile Courts and
Juvenile Delinquency."* W.F. Lane.
University of New Brunswick Law Journal
7(Apr. 1954): 17-23.

**1194. Langstaff, Anne Louise** *Development
of Visual Perception and Its Relation to
Specific Intellectual Abilities in a Group of
Preschool Children.* Anne Louise Langstaff.
Toronto: University of Toronto, 1967.
Thesis (M.A.)--University of Toronto,
1967.

**1195. Langstaff, Carroll** *A Study of the Learning Curves of Preschool Children in Problem-solving Situations with Reference to the Concept of Insight.* Carroll Langstaff. Toronto: University of Toronto. 1929.
Thesis (M.A.)–University of Toronto, [1929].
No bibliography.

**1196. Langworth, Jane T.** *"Sudden Unexpected Death in Infancy."* Jane T. Langworth and Robert Steele. Canadian Nurse 62, 9(Sept. 1966): 41-45.

**1197. Lansdell, Clyde Edison** *Moral Education in Ontario - Past, Present and Future: an Example of How Social Change is Effected.* Clyde Edison Lansdell. Toronto: University of Toronto, 1976.
Thesis (M.A.)–University of Toronto, 1976.

**1198. Lapointe, Jean-L.** *"Child Psychiatry Across Canada: an Outline of Current Facilities and Resources."* Jean-L. Lapointe. Canadian Psychiatric Association Journal/Revue de l'Association canadienne de psychiatrie 6, 5(Oct. 1961): 241-246.

**1199. Lappin, Ben** *The Redeemed Children: the Story of the Rescue of War Orphans by the Jewish Community of Canada.* Ben Lappin. Toronto: University of Toronto, 1963.

**1200. Laurence, Mary Wright** *Studies on the Concept of Security, a Clarification of the Concept in the Familial Area.* Mary Wright Laurence. Toronto: University of Toronto, 1949.
Thesis (M.A.)–University of Toronto, 1949.

**1201. LaViolette, Forrest E.** *The Canadian Japanese and World War II: a Sociological and Psychological Account.* Forrest E. LaViolette. Toronto: University of Toronto Press, c1948.

**1202. Lawr, Douglas A., ed.** *Educating Canadians: a Documentary History of Public Education.* Douglas A. Lawr and Robert D. Gidney, eds. Toronto: Van Nostrand Reinhold Limited, c1973.

**1203. Lawson, Clifford A.** *"Children in Need: a Community Responsibility."* Clifford A. Lawson. Canadian Welfare 47, 6(Nov.-Dec. 1971): 13-15, 29.

**1204. Laxer, James** *"The Student Movement and Canadian Independence."* James Laxer. [S.l.]: Canadian Dimension Magazine, 1970. In Canadian Dimension Kit No. 2: Youth Revolt and the New Left, pp. 1-9.
Reprinted from Canadian Dimension 6, 3-4(Sept-[Oct.], 1969).

**1205. Laycock, Joseph E.** *"Juvenile Courts in Canada."* Joseph E. Laycock. Canadian Bar Review 21, 1(Jan. 1943): 1-22.

**1206. Laycock, Joseph E.** *"War and Youth Employment."* J.E. Laycock. Canadian Welfare 17, 1(Apr. 1941): 20-22.

**1207. Laycock, Samuel R.** *Education for a Post-war World.* Samuel R. Laycock. Toronto: Ontario Education Association, 1944.

**1208. Laycock, Samuel R.** *"The Educational Needs of Handicapped Children."* Samuel R. Laycock. Canadian Nurse 58, 8(Aug. 1962): 683-690.

**1209. Laycock, Samuel R.** *Educational Psychology.* S.R. Laycock and B.C. Munro. Toronto : Copp Clark, c1966.

**1210. Laycock, Samuel R.** *"The Gifted Child in the Rural School."* Samuel R. Laycock. Canadian Education 10, 4(Sept. 1955): 80-93.

**1211. Laycock, Samuel R.** *"Helping the Emotionally Disturbed Child in the School Setting."* Samuel R. Laycock. Journal of Education of the Faculty and College of Education: Vancouver and Victoria 5(Mar. 1961): 10-16.

**1212. Laycock, Samuel R.** *Links With Life.* S.R. Laycock. Toronto: Ryerson Press, c1951.

**1213. Laycock, Samuel R.** *""A Look, a Touch, a Tone of Voice..."*" Samuel R. Laycock. Education Canada 11, 1(Mar. 1971): 22-26.

**1214. Laycock, Samuel R.** *Mental Hygiene in the School.* Samuel R. Laycock. Toronto: Copp Clark, 1960.

**1215. Laycock, Samuel R.** *Special Educational Facilities for Children.* Samuel R. Laycock. [S.l.: s.n.], 1961.

**1216. Laycock, Samuel R.** *Teaching and Learning: a Textbook in Educational Psychology.* S.R. Laycock. Toronto: Copp Clark, c1954.

**1217. Laycock, Samuel R.** *"Understanding Pupils' Self Concepts."* Samuel R. Laycock. Toronto: W.J. Gage Ltd., 1965. In Education: a Collection of Essays on Canadian Education, v.5, 1962-1964, pp. 83-87.

**1218. Lazarevich, Gordana** *The Musical World of Frances James and Murray Adaskin.* Gordana Lazarevich. Toronto: University of Toronto Press, 1988.

**1219. Lazerson, Marvin** *"Schools and the Work Crisis: Vocationalism in Canadian Education."* Marvin Lazerson and Timothy Dunn. London, Ont.: Alexander, Blake Associates, c1977. In Precepts Policy and Process: Perspectives on Contemporary Canadian Education, pp. 285-303. Compiled and edited by Hugh A. Stevenson and J. Donald Wilson.

**1220. Lazure, Denis** *"Psychotherapy of Adolescents: Some Considerations on Technique."* Denis Lazure. Canadian Psychiatric Association Journal/Revue de l'Association canadienne de psychiatrie 6, 5(Oct. 1961): 286-292.

**1221. Le Bas, Margaret Gertrude** *The Validity of Items of Preschool Tests.* Margaret Gertrude Le Bas. Toronto: University of Toronto, 1938.
Thesis (M.A.)–University of Toronto, 1938.

**1222. Le Riche, Harding** *"1000 Cases of Tonsillectomy in a Prepayment Plan: Preoperative and Postoperative History."* Harding Le Riche and W.B. Stiver. Canadian Medical Association Journal 77, 2(July 15, 1957): 109-116.

**1223. Lea, Nora** *"Child Care and Protection in the Community."* Nora Lea. Child and Family Welfare 12, 4(Nov. 1936): 33-40.

**1224. Leacock, Eleanor** *"Montagne Marriage and the Jesuits of the Seventeenth Century: Incidents from the Relations of Paul Le Jeune."* Eleanor Leacock and Jacqueline Goodman. Western Canadian Journal of Anthropology 6, 3(1976): 77-91.

**1225. Leah, Ronnie** *"Women's Labour Force Participation and Day Care Cutbacks in Ontario."* Ronnie Leah. Atlantis 7, 1(Fall 1981): 36-44.

**1226. Leake, Albert H.** *Means and Methods of Agricultural Education.* Albert H. Leake. Boston: Houghton Mifflin Co., 1915.

**1227. Lechelt, Eugene Carl** *Effects of Motivational Factors on a Child's Discrimination of Number.* Eugene Carl Lechelt. Edmonton: University of Alberta, 1966.
Thesis (M.Sc.)–University of Alberta, 1966.

**1228. Lecker, Sidney** *"Adolescence: a Cultural Dilemma."* Sidney Lecker. McGill Journal of Education 5, 1(Spring 1970): 47-55.

**1229. Lee, Albert O.** *"The Pied Pipers of England."* Albert O. Lee. Toronto: Quadrant Editions, 1983. In Between Two Worlds: the Canadian Immigrant Experience, pp. 58-76. Edited by Milly Charon.

**1230. Lee, Emily Mee-Lee** *The Correlates of Reading Underachievers.* Emily Mee-Lee Lee. Edmonton: University of Alberta, 1964.
Thesis (M.Ed.)–University of Alberta, 1964.

**1231. Lee, Thomas Chun-Yon** *The Influence of Continuous Employment on the Family and the Community with Emphasis on the Incidence of Juvenile Delinquency and Other Behaviour Problems.* Thomas Chun-Yon Lee. Toronto: University of Toronto, 1967.
Thesis (M.S.W.)–University of Toronto, 1967.

**1232. Lefrancois, Guy** *"A Treatment Hierarchy for the Acceleration of Conservation of Substance."* Guy Lefrancois. Canadian Journal of Psychology/Revue canadienne de psychologie 22, 4(Dec. 1968): 277-284.

**1233. Lehmann, Heinz** *The German Canadians 1750-1937: Immigration, Settlement and Culture.* Heinz Lehmann. Translated, edited and introduced by Gerhard P. Bassler. St. John's: Jesperson Press, 1986.

**1234. Lemay-Warren, Jeanne d'Arc** *Juvenile Delinquency in Canada = La Delinquance juvenile au Canada.* Jeanne d'Arc Lemay-Warren. [Montreal]: Canadian Conference on Children, [1960].

**1235. Lemby, G.F.** *Family Law.* G.F. Lemby. 2nd. ed. North Vancouver: International Self-Counsel Press Ltd, 1974.

**1236. Lenskyj, Helen** *"Common Sense and Physiology: North American Medical Views on Women and Sport 1890-1930."* Helen Lenskyj. Canadian Journal of History of Sport/Revue canadienne de l'histoire des sports 20, 1(May 1990): 49-65.

**1237. Leon, Jeffrey S.** *"The Development of Canadian Juvenile Justice: a Background for Reform."* Jeffrey S. Leon. Osgoode Hall Law Journal 15, 1(1977): 71-106.

**1238. Leon, Jeffrey S.** *"New and Old Themes in Canadian Juvenile Justice: the Origins of Delinquency Programs and the Prospects for Recognition of Children's Rights."* Jeffrey S. Leon. Interchange 8, 1-2(1977-1978): 151-175.
Reprinted in Children's Rights: Legal and Educational Issues, pp. 35-58. Edited by Heather Berkeley, Chad Gaffield and W. Gordon West.

**1239. Lester, Eva P.** *"Cognitive Structure and Achievement in the Young Child."* Eva P. Lester, R. Muir and Stephanie Z. Dubek. Canadian Psychiatric Association Journal/Revue de l'Association canadienne de psychiatrie 15, 3(June 1970): 279-289.

**1240. Lester, Eva P.** *"Recent Trends in Child Psychiatry."* Eva P. Lester. Canadian Psychiatric Association Journal/Revue de l'Association canadienne de psychiatrie 15, 6(Dec. 1970): 599-604.

**1241. Lewis, E.P.** *"Foster-home Placement of Problem Children."* E.P. Lewis. Canadian Public Health Journal 31, 3(Mar. 1940): 127-132.

**1242. Lewis, Norah Lillian** *"Goose Grease and Turpentine: Mother Treats the Family's Illnesses."* Norah L. Lewis. Prairie Forum 15, 1(Spring 1990): 67-84.

**1243. Lewis, Ruth** *"The Psychological Approach to the Preschool Stutterer."* Ruth Lewis. Canadian Medical Association Journal 60, 5(May 1949): 497-500.

**1244. Lewko, John H.** *The Relationship of Self Concept and Physical Performance in Children with Learning Disabilities.* John Henry Lewko. London: University of Western Ontario, 1970.
Thesis (M.A.)--University of Western Ontario, 1970.

**1245. Li, Janet Wai-ling** *A Comparison of Written Work Performance by Chinese Bilingual and Canadian Monolingual Children of Grades Five and Six.* Janet Wai-ling Li. Toronto: University of Toronto, 1970.
Thesis (M.A.)--University of Toronto, 1970.

**1246. Li, Peter S.** *"The Chinese-Canadian Family."* Peter S. Li. Toronto: Garamond Press, c1983. In Racial Minorities in Multicultural Canada, pp. 86-96. Edited by Peter S. Li and B. Singh Bolaria.

**1247. Li, Peter S.** *The Chinese in Canada.* Peter S. Li. Toronto: Oxford University Press, c1988.

**1248. Liedtke, Werner W.** *Linear Measurement Concepts of Bilingual and Monolingual Children.* Werner Walter Liedtke Edmonton: University of Alberta, 1968.
Thesis (M.Ed.)--University of Alberta, 1968.

**1249. Light, Beth, ed.** *Canadian Women on the Move, 1867-1920.* Beth Light and Joy Parr, eds. Toronto: New Hogtown Press and OISE, c1983.

**1250. Light, Beth, ed.** *Pioneer and Gentlewomen of British North America, 1713-1867.* Beth Light and Alison Prentice, eds. Toronto: New Hogtown Press, c1980.

**1251. Lindan, Rosemary** *"Accidental Poisoning in Childhood."* Rosemary Lindan. Canadian Medical Association Journal 75, 3(Aug. 1, 1956): 227-228.

**1252. Lindenburgh, Marion** *"Teaching of Health in High Schools."* Marion Lindenburgh. Canadian Public Health Journal 20, 6(June 1929): 294-298.

**1253. Lindsay, Lionel M.** *"The Overweight Child."* Lionel M. Lindsay. Canadian Medical Association Journal 44, 5(May 1941): 504-506.

**1254. Lipman, Margaret R.** *A Follow-up Study of Adopted Children with a Familial Background of Mental Illness.* Margaret R. Lipman. Toronto: University of Toronto, 1963.
Thesis (M.S.W.)--University of Toronto, 1963.

**1255. Liss, Howard** *Hockey's Greatest All-stars.* Howard Liss. New York: Hawthorn Books, c1972.

**1256. Lissak, David** *"Reading Difficulties in Children: Proceedings of the Douglas Hospital Conference."* David Lissak. Canadian Psychologist/Psychologie canadienne 9, 2(Apr. 1968): 115-210.

**1257. Litsky, Herman** *"Child Abuse, Some Perspectives."* Herman Litsky. Canadian Welfare 44, 4(July-Aug. 1968): 13-14.

**1258. Litsky, Herman** *"The Cult of the Juvenile Court."* Herman Litsky. Canadian Welfare 46, 4(July-Aug. 1970): 16-17, 25.

**1259. Litsky, Herman** *"The Take-over from the Juvenile Courts."* Herman Litsky. Canadian Welfare 45, 6(Nov.-Dec. 1969): 8, 15.

**1260. Lloyd-Smith, Mrs. W.** *"Dilemmas Faced by Inter-racial Families."* Mrs. W. Lloyd-Smith, Mr. D.G. Cowan and Mrs. J. Burrows. Montreal: Open Door Society, c1970. In Mixed Race Adoptions, pp. 45-47. Edited by The Open Door Society.

**1261. Locke, John C.** *"The Prevention of Retrolental Fibroplasia."* John C. Locke. Canadian Medical Association Journal 73, 6(Sept. 15, 1955): 480-481.

**1262. Lockwood, Barbara Lois** *Family Relations Test Patterns in a Deviant Group.* Barbara Lois Lockwood. Calgary: University of Calgary, 1971. Thesis (M.Ed.)--University of Calgary, 1971.

**1263. Loken, Gulbrand** *From Fjord to Frontier: a History of the Norwegians in Canada.* Gulbrand Loken. Toronto: McClelland and Stewart Ltd., c1980.

**1264. Long, Eleanor Ruth** *A Study of Children's Appreciation of Consequences.* Eleanor Ruth Long. Toronto: University of Toronto, 1938. Thesis (Ph.D.)--University of Toronto, 1938.

**1265. Long, J.A.** *"The Problem of the Gifted Child."* J.A. Long. Canadian Education 8, 2(Mar. 1953): 17-24.

**1266. Loosley, Elizabeth W.** *"Early Canadian Costume."* Elizabeth W. Loosley. Canadian Historical Review 23, 4(Dec. 1942): 349-362.

**1267. Lopez, Rafael** *"Hyperactivity in Twins."* Rafael Lopez. Canadian Psychiatric Association Journal/Revue de l'Association canadienne de psychiatrie 10, 5(Oct. 1965): 421-426.

**1268. Lorenz, Kenneth Lio Joseph** *Study of Scientific Attitudes of High School Students Comparison of Rural and Urban Areas.* Kenneth Lio Joseph Lorenz. Calgary: University of Calgary, 1971. Thesis (M.Ed.)--University of Calgary, 1971.

**1269. Louie, Alan D.** *Domestic Relations: (Family Law).* Alan D. Louie. Vancouver: Coast Legal Publications, c1970.

**1270. Lowery, Robert** *"Student at the Centre."* Robert Lowery and J.G. Enns. Education Canada 11, 4(Dec. 1971): 4-13.

**1271. Lowry, Horace Vernon** *A Study of the Effects of Certain Home Practices on Reading Achievement of Second Grade Children.* Horace Vernon Lowry. Edmonton: University of Alberta, 1968. Thesis (M.Ed.)--University of Alberta, 1968.

**1272. Luboff, Charlene G.** *Stressor Events Precipitating Child Placement.* Charlene G. Luboff. [Vancouver]: University of British Columbia, 1969. Thesis (M.SW.)--University of British Columbia, 1969.

**1273. Lucas, Jane I.** *A Study of Girls Charged under the Female Refugees Act.* Jane I. Lucas. Toronto: University of Toronto, 1958. Thesis (M.S.W.)--University of Toronto, 1958.

**1274. Lucow, William H.** *"School Marks and Professional Integrity."* William H. Lucow. McGill Journal of Education 3, 1(Spring 1968): 34-39.

**1275. Luke, Brother** *"Research on the Vocabulary of Children."* Brother Luke. Canadian Education 8, 1(Dec. 1952): 44-47.

**1276. Lupul, Manoly R.** *"Business and Education: the Ever-growing Chasm."* Manoly R. Lupel. McGill Journal of Education 5, 1(Spring 1970): 38-43.

**1277. Lupul, Manoly R.** *"Educational Crises in the New Dominion to 1917."* Manoly R. Lupul. Scarborough: Prentice-Hall of Canada, c1970. In Canadian Education: a History, pp. 266-289. Edited by J. Donald Wilson, Robert M. Stamp and Louis-Philippe Audet.

**1278. Lurie, Sh.** *"Jewish Youth in Canada."* Sh. Lurie. Toronto: Canadian Jewish Historical Publishing Co., 1933. In Canadian Jewry: Prominent Jews of Canada, pp. 23-25. Edited by Zvi Cohen.

**1279. Lynch, Charles** *First Aid In the Home.* Charles Lynch. [S.l.]: Metropolitan Life Insurance Co., c1914. Printed in Canada.

**1280. Lyons, John Edward** *A History of Doukhobor Schooling in Saskatchewan and British Columbia, 1899-1939.* John Edward Lyons. Calgary: University of Calgary, 1973. (CTM no. 15590) Thesis (M.A.)--University of Calgary, 1973.

**1281. McAllister, Claire** *"The Immigrant Children."* Claire McAllister. Canadian Welfare 39, 1(Jan.-Feb. 1963): 22-26.

**1282. McAlpine, K.L.** *"Management of the Nutritional Anaemia of Infancy."* K.L. McAlpine. Canadian Medical Association Journal 44, 4(Apr. 1941): 386-390.

**1283. McBuer, J.C.** *"Punishment of Juveniles and Young Persons."* J.C. McBuer, W.B. Common and Eileen Mitchell. Canadian Bar Review 22, 7(Aug.-Sept. 1944): 585-597.

**1284. McCaldon, R.J.** *"Rape."* R.J. McCaldon. Canadian Journal of Criminology and Corrections/Revue canadienne de criminologie 9, 1(Jan. 1967): 37-58.
Reprinted in Deviant Behaviour and Societal Reaction, pp. 546-565. Edited by Craig L. Boydell, Carl F. Grindstaff and Paul C. Whitehead.

**1285. McCallum, Helen** *"Teaching the Diabetic Child."* Helen McCallum. Canadian Nurse 39, 4(Apr. 1943): 272-274.

**1286. McCarthy, Annabel** *"Acute Anterior Poliomyelitis."* Annabel McCarthy. Canadian Nurse 46, 10(Oct. 1950): 793-798.

**1287. McClachy, Mary Craig** *"The Effect Upon Young People of the Economic Depression and Unemployment."* Mary Craig McClachy. Child and Family Welfare 11, 4(Nov. 1935): 1-9.

**1288. McConney, Douglas M.** *The Eleven-year-old Boy: a Study of Dropouts from the Boy Scouts Association.* Douglas M. McConney. Toronto: University of Toronto, 1957.
Thesis (M.S.W.)--University of Toronto, 1957.

**1289. McConville, Brian J.** *"Mourning Processes in Children of Varying Ages."* Brian J. McConville, L.C. Boag and A.P. Purohit. Canadian Psychiatric Association Journal/Revue de l'Association canadienne de psychiatrie 15, 3(June 1970): 253-255.

**1290. McCormack, A. Ross** *"Networks Among British Immigrants and Accomodation to Canadian Society: Winnipeg, 1900-1914."* A. Ross McCormack. Histoire sociale/Social History 17, 34(Nov. 1984): 357-74.

**1291. McCormack, Marilyn Jean** *The Influence of Classification and Seriation Ability on the Mathematical Achievement of First Graders.* Marilyn Jean McCormack. Edmonton: University of Alberta, 1969.
Thesis (M.Ed.)--University of Alberta, 1969.

**1292. McCormack, Thelma** *"Television and the Changing Cultures of Childhood."* Thelma McCormack. Toronto: McGraw-Hill Ryerson, c1979. In Childhood and Adolescence in Canada, pp. 302-321. Edited by K. Ishwaran.

**1293. McCormick, Mary Frances Judith** *The Development of Attachment in Early Infancy: Affective and Cognitive Aspects of Attachment Behaviour.* Mary Frances Judith McCormick. Toronto: University of Toronto, 1968.
Thesis (M.A.)--University of Toronto, 1968.

**1294. McCormick, W.J.** *"Public Health Aspects of Wading Pools for Children."* W.J. McCormick. Canadian Public Health Journal 26, 1(Jan. 1935): 26-32.

**1295. McCreary, John F.** *Evaluation of Prenatal Programmes, Well Baby Clinics, Preschool Clinics, School Health Services, Mental Health Programmes and Special Hospital Facilities for Children.* John Ferguson McCreary. [S.l.: s.n.], 1960.

**1296. McCreary-Juhasz, Anne** *Adolescents in Society: Selected Sources in Personal and Social Relationships.* Anne McCreary-Juhasz and George Szasz. Toronto: McClelland and Stewart Ltd., c1969.

**1297. MacCrimmon, Jean** *"Twenty-ninth Annual Meeting and Conference of the Canadian Welfare Council, Montreal, June 1-4, 1949: Some Highlights in Digest Form."* Jean MacCrimmon. Canadian Welfare 25, 3(July 1949): 3-16.

**1298. McDaniel, Susan A.** *Towards Family Policies in Canada With Women in Mind.* Susan A. McDaniel. Ottawa: Canadian Research Institute for the Advancement of Women, 1990.

**1299. McDermott, Joseph** *Rebellious Youth in Conflict With the Law: a Study of Juvenile Delinquency.* Joseph McDermott. Toronto: University of Toronto, 1932.
Thesis (M.A.)--University of Toronto, 1932.

**1300. MacDonald, A.L.** *"Child Trespassers."* A.L. MacDonald. Canadian Bar Review 8, 1(Jan. 1930): 8-25.

**1301. McDonald, David** *For the Record: Canada's Greatest Women Athletes.* David McDonald, Lauren Drewery, Jeffrey Hume and Mary Keyes. Toronto: Mesa Associates, c1981.

**1302. MacDonald, Ervin Austin** *The Rainbow Chasers.* Ervin Austin MacDonald. Vancouver: Douglas and MacIntyre, c1982.

**1303. MacDonald, John A.** *"A Critique of Bill C-192, The Young Offenders Act."* John A. MacDonald. Canadian Journal of Criminology and Corrections/Revue canadienne de criminologie 13, 2(Apr. 1971): 166-180.

**1304. MacDonald, Lynn** *"Crime and Punishment in Canada: a Statistical Test of the "Conventional Wisdom"."* Lynn MacDonald. Canadian Review of Sociology and Anthropology/Revue canadienne de sociologie et d'anthropologie 6, 4(Nov. 1969): 212-236.

**1305. McDonald, Neil G., ed.** *Egerton Ryerson and His Times.* Neil McDonald and Alf Chaiton, eds. Toronto: Macmillan Company of Canada Limited, c1978.

**1306. Macdonnell, G.M.** *"The Treatment of Crime by the State."* G.M. Mcdonnell. Queen's Quarterly 4, 4(Apr. 1897): 257-268.

**1307. McDonnell, Malcolm Whitney** *The Prediction of Academic Achievement of Superior Grade Three Pupils.* Malcolm Whitney McDonnell. Edmonton: University of Alberta, 1959.
Thesis (M.Ed.)--University of Alberta, 1959.
Author published an article with the same title in Alberta Journal of Educational Research 8, 2(June 1962): 111-118.

**1308. MacDougall, Charles S.** *"Malnutrition in School Children."* Charles S. MacDougall. Public Health Journal 12, 10(Oct. 1921): 451-454.

**1309. MacDougall, Donald J.** *"The Constitution and Ancillary Belief Under the Divorce Act."* Donald J. MacDougall. Advocate 27, 5(Oct.-Nov. 1969): 260-263.

**1310. MacDougall, John** *Rural Life in Canada: Its Trends and Tasks.* John MacDougall. Toronto: Westminster Co. Ltd., c1913.
Reprinted in 1973 by University of Toronto Press.

**1311. McDougall, William Dewar** *An Evaluation of Pupil Progress in the Skill Subjects in Enterprise and Conventional Schools.* William Dewar McDougall. Edmonton: University of Alberta, 1939.
Thesis (M.A.)--University of Alberta, 1939.

**1312. McEachern, Melville Duncan** *An Investigation into the Growth of Language Concepts in History of Bellevue Intermediate and High School Students.* Melville Duncan McEachern. Edmonton: University of Alberta, 1937.
Thesis (M.A.)--University of Alberta, 1937.

**1313. McEwan, Ernest R.** *"Youth in Your Town."* Ernest R. McEwan. Canadian Welfare 26, 1(Apr. 1950): 28-32.

**1314. McEwan, Robert Charles** *Children's Reactions to Failure as a Function of Instructions and Goal Distance.* Robert Charles McEwan. London: University of Western Ontario, 1967.
Thesis (M.A.)--University of Western Ontario, 1967.

**1315. McFarland, E.** *"The Development of Supervised Playgrounds."* E. McFarland. Ottawa: Carleton University Press, 1982. In Recreational Land Use: Perspectives on its Evolution in Canada, pp. 272-298. Edited by G. Wall and J.S. March.

**1316. MacFarland, Mary P.** *"The Child and the Radio."* Mary MacFarland. Canadian Welfare Summary 14, 6(Mar. 1939): 60-62.

**1317. MacFarlane, Phyllis Osborne** *Factors Affecting the Capacity of Adolescents to Utilize Psychiatric Outpatient Treatment.* Phyllis Osborne MacFarlane. Toronto: University of Toronto, 1961.
Thesis (M.S.W.)--University of Toronto, 1961.

**1318. McGann, David** *"Three Villages: a View of Congregate Living for Children in Care."* David McGann. Canadian Welfare 43, 3(May-June 1967): 14-18.

**1319. McGee, Joan Elizabeth** *Effects on Adolescent Children When Mothers Are Employed or Involved in Education.* Joan Elizabeth McGee. Toronto: University of Toronto, 1966.
Thesis (M.S.W.)--University of Toronto, 1966.

**1320. MacGill, Elsie Gregory** *My Mother the Judge: a Biography of Helen Gregory MacGill.* Elsie Gregory MacGill. Toronto: Ryerson Press, c1955.
Republished, with an introduction by Naomi Black, by PMA Books, 1981.

**1321. MacGill, Helen Gregory** *"The Child in Industry."* Helen Gregory MacGill. Labour Gazette 25, 10(Oct. 1925): 983-991.

**1322. MacGill, Helen Gregory** *"Conditions Governing the Issuance of Marriage Licences and Discussion."* Helen Gregory MacGill. In Proceedings of Sixth Annual Canadian Conference on Child Welfare 1927, pp. 85-89.

**1323. MacGill, Helen Gregory** *"A Constructive Programme for the Prevention of Juvenile Delinquency."* Helen MacGill. In Proceedings and Papers Fourth Annual Canadian Conference on Child Welfare 1923, pp. 153-156.

**1324. MacGill, Helen Gregory** *The Juvenile Court in Canada: Origin, Underlying Principles, Governing Legislation and Practice.* Helen Gregory MacGill. Ottawa: Canadian Council on Child Welfare, 1925.

**1325. MacGill, Helen Gregory** *"The Relation of the Juvenile Court to the Community."* Helen Gregory MacGill. Canadian Journal of Mental Hygiene 1, 3(Oct. 1919): 232-236.

**1326. McGrath, Thomas Joseph** *Extracurricular Participation in Three Urban High Schools: Selected Determinants and Outcomes.* Thomas Joseph McGrath. Edmonton: University of Alberta, 1971. Thesis (M.Ed.)--University of Alberta, 1971.

**1327. McGrath, W.T.** *"Delinquency: Predicting it in the Bud."* W.T. McGrath. Canadian Welfare 38, 1(Jan.-Feb. 1962): 15-19.

**1328. McGrath, W.T.** *Youth and the Law.* William Thomas McGrath. Toronto: W.J. Gage Ltd., c1964.

**1329. McGregor, J.B.** *"The Care of the Child Who is Different."* J.B. McGregor. In Proceedings of Sixth Annual Canadian Conference on Child Welfare 1927, pp. 119-120.

**1330. MacGregor, Mary E.** *Day Care as a Service in the Community.* Mary E. MacGregor. Toronto: University of Toronto, 1965. Thesis (M.S.W.)--University of Toronto, 1965.

**1331. McGregor, Mrs. J. Breckenridge** *"Several Years After": an Analysis of the Histories of a Selected Group of Juvenile Immigrants Brought to Canada in 1910, and in 1920, By British Emigration Societies.* Mrs. J. Breckenridge McGregor. Ottawa: Canadian Council on Child Welfare, 1928.

**1332. McGuire, Joan** *The Age Factor in Unmarried Motherhood.* Joan McGuire. Toronto: University of Toronto, 1954. Thesis (M.S.W.)--University of Toronto, 1954.

**1333. MacHaffie, Lloyd P.** *"The Artificial Feeding of Young Babies."* Lloyd P. MacHaffie. Canadian Nurse 23, 12(Dec. 1927): 635-640.

**1334. MacHaffie, Lloyd P.** *"Health Pitfalls and Tragedies of the Preschool Child."* Lloyd P. MacHaffie. Child and Family Welfare 12, 1(May 1936): 7-12.

**1335. MacHaffie, Lloyd P.** *Infantile Paralysis: a Message to Parents.* Lloyd P. MacHaffie and the Canadian Welfare Council. Ottawa: Canadian Welfare Council, 1937.

**1336. MacHaffie, Lloyd P.** *"Preventative Paediatrics as Seen by the School Medical Officer."* L.P. MacHaffie. Canadian Public Health Journal 28, 10(Oct. 1937): 498-504.

**1337. MacHaffie, Lloyd P.** *Respiratory Diseases in Young Children.* Lloyd P. MacHaffie. Ottawa: Canadian Welfare Council, Division on Maternal and Child Hygiene, 1938. Reprint.

**1338. McHenry, E.W.** *"Nutrition and Child Health."* E.W. McHenry. Canadian Public Health Journal 33, 4(Apr, 1942): 152-156.

**1339. MacInnes, B. Orlo** *"The Care of the Cardiac Child."* B. Orlo MacInnes. Canadian Nurse 36, 1(Jan. 1940): 17-20.

**1340. McIntosh, Robert** *"Canada's Boy Miners."* Robert McIntosh. Beaver 67, 5(Dec. 1987-Jan. 1988): 34-38.

**1341. McIntyre, Walter G.** *"The Relationship of Family Functioning to School Achievement."* Walter G. McIntyre and David C. Payne. Family Coordinator 20, 3(July 1971): 265-268.

**1342. McIver, Allen Gordon** *Student Opinions and Attitudes in Second Language Learning.* Allen Gordon McIver. Edmonton: University of Alberta, 1970. Thesis (M.Ed.)--University of Alberta, 1970.

**1343. McKay, Doreen P.** *A Study of the Spelling Achievement of Rural High School Pupils.* Doreen P. McKay. Edmonton: University of Alberta, 1959. Thesis (M.Ed.)--University of Alberta, 1959. Author published an article with the same title in Alberta Journal of Educational Research 8, 1(Mar. 1962): 45-53.

**1344. McKay, Jean** *Gone To Grass.* Jean McKay. Toronto: Coach House Press, c1983.

**1345. MacKay, Judith** *"Twins."* Judith MacKay. Canadian Nurse 59, 10(Oct. 1963): 968-970.

**1346. McKenzie, Angus L.** *"Statutes Affecting Infants and Infants' Rights."* Angus L. McKenzie. Western Law Review 5(1966): 153-159.

**1347. McKenzie, Edwin** *"Reading Interests of Intermediate Grade Pupils."* Edwin McKenzie. Alberta Journal of Educational Research 8, 1(Mar. 1962): 33-38.

**1348. McKerlie, E.** *"The Psychological Impact of and on the New Arrival."* E. McKerlie and Laura Einarson. Canadian Nurse 50, 4(Apr. 1954): 262-264.

**1349. McKerracher, Dorothy M.** *"The Public Health Aspect of Cerebral Palsy."* Dorothy M. McKerracher and Leora R. Wright. Canadian Nurse 42, 6(June 1946): 475-477.

**1350. Mackie, Marlene** *"Socialization: Changing Views of Child Rearing and Adolescence."* Marlene Mackie. Toronto: McGraw-Hill Ryerson Ltd., c1984. In The Family: Changing Trends in Canada, pp. 35-62. Edited by Maureen Baker.

**1351. Mackie, Richard** *Hamilton Mack Laing, Hunter Naturalist.* Richard Mackie. Victoria: Sono Nis Press, 1985.

**1352. McKim, J.S.** *"Child Health Related to a Children's Hospital."* J.S. McKim. Canadian Medical Association Journal/Journal de l'Association medicale canadienne 105, 7(Oct. 9, 1971): 726-730.

**1353. MacKinnon, Archibald Roderick** *How Do Children Learn to Read?: an Experimental Investigation of Children's Early Growth in Awareness of the Meanings of Printed Symbols.* Archie Roderick MacKinnon. [Toronto]: Copp Clark Publishing Company, 1959.

**1354. MacKinnon, Fred R.** *Foster Home Care and Group Care of Children Pending Adoption.* Fred R. MacKinnon. [Ottawa]: Canadian Conference on Children, 1960.

**1355. McKinnon, N.E.** *"Heart Disease Mortality: the Public Health Problem in Ontario."* N.E. McKinnon. Canadian Public Health Journal 30, 6(June 1939): 288-296.

**1356. Mackintosh, Margaret** *The Social Significance of Child Labour in Agriculture and Industry.* Margaret Mackintosh. Ottawa: Canadian Committee on Child Welfare, 1924.

**1357. MacLachlan, Ethel** *"The Delinquent Child."* Ethel MacLachlan. In Proceedings and Papers Fifth Annual Canadian Conference on Child Welfare 1925, pp. 168-171.

**1358. McLaren, Angus** *""What Has This to do With Working Class Women?": Birth Control and the Canadian Left, 1900-1939."* Angus McLaren. Histoire sociale/Social History 14, 28(Nov. 1981): 435-454.

**1359. Maclaughlin, Anne K.** *"Familial Infantile Corticile Hyperostosis in a Large Canadian Family."* Anne K. Maclauglin, John W. Gerrard, C. Stuart Houston and Elizabeth J. Ives. Canadian Medical Association Journal/Journal de l'Association medicale canadienne 130, 9(May 1, 1984): 1172-1174.

**1360. MacLean, Annie Marion** *"Factory Legislation for Women in Canada."* Annie Marion MacLean. American Journal of Sociology 5, 2(Sept. 1899): 172-181.

**1361. McLean, D.M.** *"Coxsackie B5 Virus in Association with Pericarditis and Pleurodynia."* D.M. McLean, Selma J. Walker and H.W. Bain. Canadian Medical Association Journal 79, 10(Nov. 15, 1958): 789-793.

**1362. McLean, Elizabeth M.** *"Prisoners of the Indians."* Elizabeth M. McLean. Beaver 278, 1(June 1947): 14-17.

**1363. McLean, James Henry** *An Investigation into the Growth of Language Concepts in Science of Bellevue Intermediate and High School Students.* James Henry McLean. Edmonton: University of Alberta, 1937.
Thesis (M.A.)–University of Alberta, 1937.

**1364. MacLean, M.C.** *Illiteracy and School Attendance.* M.C. MacLean [and] Dominion Bureau of Statistics. Ottawa: King's Printer, 1942.

**1365. MacLean, M.C.** *A Statistical Review of Canadian Schools.* M.C. MacLean. Ottawa: Canadian Council on Child Welfare, 1923.

**1366. McLeish, John** *A Canadian For All Seasons: the John E. Robbins Story.* John A.B. McLeish. Toronto: Lester and Orpen, c1978.

1367. McLennan, T.A. "Plastic Helmet for Head Protection in Children." T.A. McLennan. Canadian Medical Association Journal 73, 11(Dec. 1, 1955): 809.

1368. McLeod, A. "Ecclesiasticism in the Public School." A. McLeod. Queen's Quarterly 4, 2(Oct. 1896): 82-92.

1369. MacLeod, A.J. "The Juvenile Delinquency Committee." A.J. McLeod. Canadian Journal of Corrections/Revue canadienne de criminologie 6, 1(Jan. 1964): 43-49.

1370. MacLeod, Adrienne A Study of Factors Involved in Telling a Child about His Adoption. Adrienne MacLeod. Toronto: University of Toronto, 1957.
Thesis (M.S.W.)–University of Toronto, 1957.

1371. MacLeod, Alan J. "Echo 9 Virus Infections in Eastern Canada: Clinical and Laboratory Studies." Alan J. MacLeod, Ruth S. Faulkner and C.E. van Rooyen. Canadian Medical Association Journal 78, 9(May 1, 1958): 661-665.

1372. MacLeod, Alastair "What Are Canada's Special Needs in Education?" Alastair MacLeod. Ottawa: Mutal Press, 1958. In Addresses and Proceedings of the Canadian Conference on Education, Ottawa, February 16-20, 1958, pp. 423-426. Edited by George G. Croskery and Gerald Nason.

1373. McLeod, Carol Legendary Canadian Women: Studies of Famous Canadian Women. Carol McLeod. Hantsport, N.S.: Lancelot Press, 1983.

1374. MacLeod, D.R.E. "Poliomyelitis Antibody Response After Various Vaccination Schedules and at Different Ages." D.R.E. MacLeod, C.W.J. Armstrong, G.W.O. Moss, F.C. Potter and R.J. Wilson. Canadian Medical Association Journal/Journal de l'Association medicale canadienne 81, 6(Sept. 15, 1959): 443-449.

1375. Macleod, David "A Live Vaccine: the YMCA and Male Adolescence in the United States and Canada, 1870-1920." David MacLeod. Histoire sociale/Social History 11, 21(May 1978): 5-25.

1376. McLeod, Jill L. "Doli Incapax: the Forgotten Presumption in Juvenile Court Trials." Jill L. McLeod. Canadian Journal of Family Law/Revue canadienne de droit familial 3, 2 and 3(Apr.-July 1980): 251-280.

1377. McLeod, Marguerite "Osteogenic Carcinoma." Marguerite McLeod. Canadian Nurse 60, 1(Jan. 1964): 49-52.

1378. McLeod, Miriam "The Mental Health Program." Miriam McLeod. Canadian Nurse 45, 8(Aug. 1949): 595-596.

1379. McMillan, Floyd Walter An Investigation of Retention in Physics by Grade 11 Students Determined on the Basis of the Categories of Bloom's Taxonomy of Educational Objectives. Floyd Walter McMillan. Edmonton, University of Alberta, 1968.
Thesis (M.Ed.)–University of Alberta, 1968.

1380. McMorrow, Kevin Henry Moral Development and the Acquisition of Conservation in Montessori Children. Kevin Henry McMorrow. Toronto: University of Toronto, 1970.
Thesis (M.A.)–University of Toronto, 1970.

1381. MacMurchy, Helen Be Prepared to Prevent Infantile Paralysis. Helen MacMurchy. Ottawa: Department of Pensions and Maternal Health, 1930.

1382. MacMurchy, Helen "Canada's Maternal Mortality." Helen MacMurchy. Canadian Nurse 24, 4(Apr. 1928): 180-181.

1383. MacMurchy, Helen The Canadian Mother's Book. Helen MacMurchy. Ottawa: King's Printer, 1921.

1384. MacMurchy, Helen The Canadian Mother's Book. Helen MacMurchy. Ottawa: King's Printer, 1923.

1385. MacMurchy, Helen The Canadian Mother's Book: Supplement. Helen MacMurchy. Ottawa: King's Printer, 1923.

1386. MacMurchy, Helen The Canadian Mother's Book. Helen MacMurchy. Confederation Diamond Jubilee ed. Ottawa: King's Printer, 1927.

1387. MacMurchy, Helen The Canadian Mother's Book. Helen MacMurchy. Ottawa: King's Printer, 1932.

1388. MacMurchy, Helen The Canadian Mother's Book. [Helen MacMurchy]. Ottawa: King's Printer, 1934.

1389. MacMurchy, Helen "Child Welfare in Canada." Helen MacMurchy. Annals 105(Jan. 1923): 267-276.

**1390. MacMurchy, Helen** *"Defective Children."* Helen MacMurchy. Toronto: Social Services Council of Canada, c1914. In Social Services Congress, Ottawa, 1914: Report of Addresses and Proceedings, pp. 98-101.

**1391. MacMurchy, Helen** *"The Division of Child Welfare, Department of Pensions and National Health."* Helen MacMurchy. Canadian Public Health Journal 19, 11(Nov. 1928): 514-521.

**1392. MacMurchy, Helen** *How to Avoid Accidents and Give First Aid.* Helen MacMurchy. Ottawa: King's Printer, 1928.

**1393. MacMurchy, Helen** *How to Take Care of the Baby.* Helen MacMurchy. Ottawa: King's Printer, 1922.

**1394. MacMurchy, Helen** *How to Take Care of the Baby.* Helen MacMurchy. Ottawa: King's Printer, 1923.

**1395. MacMurchy, Helen** *How to Take Care of the Children.* Helen MacMurchy. Ottawa: King's Printer, 1922.

**1396. MacMurchy, Helen** *How to Take Care of the Children.* Helen MacMurchy. Ottawa: King's Printer, 1923.

**1397. MacMurchy, Helen** *"Infant Mortality."* Helen MacMurchy. Public Health Journal 2, 10(Oct. 1911): 490.

**1398. MacMurchy, Helen** *"Neo-natal Mortality."* Helen MacMurchy. Public Health Journal 17, 9(Sept. 1926): 442-447.

**1399. MacMurchy, Helen** *"The Relation Between Maternal Mortality and Infant Mortality."* Helen MacMurchy. Public Health Journal 16, 8(Aug. 1925): 379-382.

**1400. MacMurchy, Helen** *Rickets: Prevention and Care.* Helen MacMurchy. Ottawa: King's Printer, 1929.

**1401. MacMurchy, Helen, ed.** *Handbook of Child Welfare Work in Canada for the Year Ended March 31, 1922.* Helen MacMurchy, ed. Ottawa: King's Printer, 1923.

**1402. MacMurchy, Marjory** *The Canadian Girl At Work.* Marjory MacMurchy. Toronto: A.T. Wilgress, 1919.

**1403. McMurrich, Helen M.** *"The Deaf Are Calling."* Helen M. McMurrich. Canadian Nurse 37, 4(Apr. 1941): 242-244.

**1404. McNeil, Bill** *Bill McNeil Presents Voice of the Pioneer.* Bill McNeil. Toronto: Doubleday Canada Ltd., c1988.

**1405. McNeil, Bill** *Voice of the Pioneer: Volume One.* Bill McNeil. Toronto: Macmillan of Canada, c1978.

**1406. McNeil, Bill** *Voice of the Pioneer: Volume Two.* Bill McNeil. Toronto: Macmillan of Canada, c1984.

**1407. MacPhail, E.S.** *"Scope for Improvement in Canadian Stillbirth Statistics."* E.S. MacPhail. Canadian Public Health Journal 27, 1(Jan. 1936): 27-31

**1408. McPhedran, Harris** *"The Preschool Child."* Harris McPhedran and Alphonse Pelletier. Canadian Medical Association Journal 20, 6(June 1929): 659-661.

**1409. MacPhee, Earle Douglas** *Footsteps: an Autobiography.* Earle Douglas MacPhee. Vancouver: Versatile Publishing Co., 1978.

**1410. McTaggart, A.N.** *"The Psychiatric Care of Children in a Teaching Hospital."* A.N. McTaggart. Canadian Psychiatric Association Journal/Revue de l'Association canadienne de psychiatrie 10, 5(Oct. 1965): 332-337.

**1411. Mailloux, Noel** *"Delinquency and Repetition Compulsion."* Noel Mailloux. Canadian Journal of Corrections/Revue canadienne de criminologie 6, 1(Jan. 1964): 139-147.

**1412. Mailloux, Noel** *"Healing the Delinquent."* Noel Mailloux. Canadian Welfare 37, 3(May 1961): 123-125.

**1413. Mailloux, Noel** *"Our Lawless Youth."* Noel Mailloux. Canadian Journal of Corrections/Revue canadienne de criminologie 4, 2(April 1962): 152-159.

**1414. Makowski, William** *The Polish People in Canada: a Visual History.* William Makowski. Montreal: Tundra Books, c1987.

**1415. Malcolmson, Mrs. A.H.** *"Normal Activities: Guiding."* Mrs. A.H. Malcolmson. In Proceedings and Papers Fifth Annual Canadian Conference on Child Welfare 1925, pp. 252-253.

**1416. Malik, Mukhtar A.** *School Performance of Children in Families Receiving Public Assistance in Canada.* Mukhtar A. Malik. Ottawa: Canadian Welfare Council, 1966.

**1417. Malik, Mukhtar A.** *"Welfare Children in School."* Mukhtar Malik. Canadian Welfare 44, 2(Mar.-Apr. 1968): 20-23.

**1418. Malzberg, Benjamin** *Mental Disease Among Foreign-born in Canada 1950-1952 in Relation to Period of Immigration.* Benjamin Malzberg. Albany, N.Y.: Research Foundation for Mental Hygiene, 1964.

**1419. Mandell, Nancy** *"The Child Question: Links Between Women and Children in the Family."* Nancy Mandell. Toronto: Butterworths, c1988. In Reconstructing the Canadian Family: Feminist Perspectives, pp. 49-81. Edited by Nancy Mandell and Ann Duffy.

**1420. Mander, Christine** *Emily Murphy, Rebel: First Female Magistrate in the British Empire.* Christine Mander. Toronto: Simon & Pierre, c1985.

**1421. Manke, Ruth Elizabeth** *The Vocational Adjustment of Former Students of a Vocational School.* Ruth Elizabeth Manke. Toronto: University of Toronto, 1966.
Thesis (M.S.W.)–University of Toronto, 1966.

**1422. Mann, William Edward** *Canada: the Way It Is and Could Be.* William E. Mann. Willowdale: Willowdale Enterprise Ltd., 1968.

**1423. Mann, William Edward** *Canadian Trends in Premarital Behavior: Some Preliminary Studies of Youth in High School and University.* W.E. Mann. Toronto: Anglican Church of Canada, 1967.

**1424. Mann, William Edward** *"Nonconformist Sexual Behaviour on the Canadian Campus."* W.E. Mann. Toronto: Social Science Publishers, c1968. In Deviant Behaviour in Canada, pp. 300-309. Edited by W.E. Mann.

**1425. Mann, William Edward** *"Socialization in a Medium Security Reformatory."* W.E. Mann. Canadian Review of Sociology and Anthropology/Revue canadienne de sociologie et d'anthropologie 1, 3(Aug. 1964): 138-155.
Reprinted in Canadian Society: Sociological Perspectives, 3rd ed., 1968, pp. 782-801 and abr. 3rd ed., 1971, pp. 522-541. Edited by Bernard R. Blishen, Frank E. Jones, Kasper D. Naegele and John Porter.

**1426. Mann, William Edward, ed.** *Deviant Behaviour in Canada.* W.E. Mann, ed. Toronto: Social Science Publishers, c1968.

**1427. Mann, William Edward, ed.** *Poverty and Social Policy in Canada.* W.E. Mann, ed. Toronto: Copp Clark, c1969.

**1428. Mannarino, Anthony P.** *"The Development of Children's Friendships."* Anthony P. Mannarino. Chichester, Eng.: John Wiley & Sons Ltd., c1980. In Friendship and Social Relationships in Children, pp. 45-61. Edited by Hugh C. Foot, Anthony J. Chapman and Jean R. Smith.

**1429. Manning, Sarah J.** *Young People and Missions.* Sarah J. Manning. [S.l.: s.n., 189-?].

**1430. Maracle, Lee** *Bobbi Lee, Indian Rebel.* Lee Maracle. New ed. Toronto: Women's Press, 1990.
The first edition of this book was published in 1975 under the author's former name Bobbie Lee.

**1431. Marshall, Dorothy B.** *"The Teacher-Nurse Team."* Dorothy B. Marshall. Canadian Nurse 46, 11(Nov. 1950): 895-898.

**1432. Marshall, William Edson** *The Effects of Anxiety and Isolation on the Autokinetic Judgements of Adolescent Boys.* William Edson Marshall. Toronto: University of Toronto, 1960.
Thesis (M.A.)–University of Toronto, 1960.

**1433. Martens, Bruno** *"The Relationship of Intelligence, Attitudes and Study Habits to Academic Achievement."* Bruno Martens. Canadian Education and Research Digest 4, 4(Dec. 1964): 268-272.

**1434. Martin, Glenn M.** *"Pulmonary Hyaline Disease of Infants."* Glenn M. Martin and Robert H. More. Canadian Medical Association Journal 73, 4(Aug. 15, 1955): 273-277.

**1435. Martin, J.K.** *Chronic Disabilities in Children = L'importance des handicaps chroniques chez les enfants.* J.K. Martin. [S.l.: s.n.], 1960.

**1436. Martin, John** *"The Married Woman in Industry."* John Martin. Public Health Journal 7, 6(June 1916): 303-306.

**1437. Martin, John** *"The Mother in Industry."* John Martin. Public Health Journal 7, 7(July 1916): 347-350.

**1438. Martynowych, Orest T.**
*""Canadianizing the Foreigner":*
*Presbyterian Missionaries and Ukrainian*
*Immigrants."* Orest T. Martynowych.
Winnipeg: Ukrainian Academy of Arts
and Sciences in Canada, c1983. In New
Soil - Old Roots: the Ukrainian
Experience in Canada, pp. 33-57. Edited
by Jaroslav Rozumnyj, with the assistance
of Oleh W. Gerus and Mykhailo H.
Marunchak.

**1439. Marunchak, Mykhailo H.** *The*
*Ukrainian Canadians: a History.* Michael
H. Marunchak. 2nd ed. Winnipeg:
Ukrainian Academy of Arts and Sciences
(UVAN) in Canada, 1982.
    Originally published: Winnipeg:
    Ukrainian Free Academy of Sciences,
    1970.

**1440. Mary Perpetual Help, Sister** *"Child*
*Art and Personality."* Sister Mary
Perpetual Help. Toronto: W.J. Gage Ltd.,
1959. In Education: a Collection of
Essays on. Canadian Education, v.2,
1956-1958, pp. 73-76.

**1441. Mason, Jean** *"Why Girls Don't Go*
*In Training."* Jean Mason. Canadian
Nurse 41, 9(Sept. 1945): 696-700.

**1442. Mason, M.** *A Study of the Influence*
*of Instruction on the Learning of Preschool*
*and Elementary School Children.* Molly
Mason. Toronto: University of Toronto,
1935.
    Thesis (M.A.)--University of Toronto,
    1935.

**1443. Matejko, Alexander** *"Polish Peasants*
*in the Canadian Prairies."* Alexander and
Joanna Matejko. Toronto: Canadian-Polish
Research Institute, 1975. In From Prairies
to Cities: Papers on the Poles in Canada
at the VIII World Congress of Sociology,
pp. 9-31. Edited by Benedykt Heydenkorn.

**1444. Matejko, Alexander** *"The Slavic*
*Influx."* Aleksander Matejko. Toronto:
Canadian-Polish Research Institute, 1974.
In Past and Present: Selected Topics on
the Polish Group in Canada, pp. 73-79.
Edited by Benedykt Heydenkorn.

**1445. Matheson, Shirlee Smith**
*Youngblood of the Peace: the Authorized*
*Biography of Father Emile Jungbluth,*
*O.M.I.* Shirlee Smith Matheson. Edmonton:
Lone Pine Publishing, c1986.

**1446. Matwe, Marie Anne** *Intensive Study*
*of the Services of a High School Couselling*
*Program.* Marie Anne Matwe. Calgary:
University of Calgary, 1971.
    Thesis (M.Ed.)--University of Calgary,
    1971.

**1447. Maxim, Paul Stefan** *Some Trends*
*in Juvenile Delinquency in Canada:*
*1958-1973.* Paul Stefan Maxim. Ann
Arbor: University Microfilms International,
1980.
    Thesis (Ph.D.)--University of
    Pennsylvania, 1980.

**1448. Maxse, Marjorie** *"Children of the*
*Motherland."* Marjorie Maxse. Canadian
Welfare 20, 4(Sept. 1944): 32-35.

**1449. Maxwell, Mary Percival** *"Boarding*
*School: Social Control, Space and*
*Identity."* Mary Percival Maxwell and
James D. Maxwell. Toronto: New Press,
1971. In Social Space: Canadian
Perspectives. pp. 157-164. Edited by D.I.
Davies and Kathleen Herman.

**1450. Maynard, Fredelle Bruser** *Raisins*
*and Almonds.* Fredelle Bruser Maynard.
Toronto: Doubleday Canada Ltd., c1972.

**1451. Mayo, Eileen J.** *"Upper Extremity*
*Prostheses for Children."* Eileen J. Mayo.
Canadian Nurse 58, 2(Feb. 1962):
145-148.

**1452. Medjuck, Sheva** *"The Importance of*
*Boarding for the Structure of the*
*Household in the Nineteenth Century:*
*Moncton, New Brunswick and Hamilton,*
*Canada West."* Sheva Medjuck. Histoire
sociale/Social History 13, 25(May 1980):
207-213.

**1453. Medovy, H.** *"Adolescents: Past,*
*Present and Future."* Harry Medovy.
Canadian Journal of Public Health 62,
3(May-June 1971): 199-204.

**1454. Medovy, H.** *"Paediatric News."*
Harry Medovy. Canadian Medical
Association Journal 77, 1(July 1, 1957):
54-58.

**1455. Meichenbaum, Donald**
*"Reflection-Impulsivity and Verbal Control*
*of Motor Behavior."* Donald Meichenbaum
and Joseph Goodman. Child Development
40, 3(Sept. 1969): 785-797.

**1456. Meigs, Mary** *Lily Briscoe, a*
*Self-portrait: an Autobiography.* Mary
Meigs. Vancouver: Talonbooks, 1981.

**1457. Meikle, S.** *"Changes in Perceptual,*
*Motor, and Reading Test Scores in a*
*Remedial Reading Group."* S. Meikle and
Doreen L. Kilpatrick. Canadian
Psychologist/Psychologie canadienne 12,
2(Apr. 1971): 254-269.

**1458. Meiklejohn, Phyllis J.** *The Family: Selected Sources.* Phyllis J. Meiklejohn. Toronto: McClelland and Stewart Ltd., c1969.

**1459. Melhuish, Martin** *Heart of Gold: 30 Years of Canadian Pop Music.* Martin Melhuish. Toronto: CBC Enterprises, c1983.

**1460. Melicherick, John** *"Child Welfare Policy."* John Melicherick. 2nd ed. Waterloo: Wilfrid Laurier University Press, c1981. In Canadian Social Policy, pp. 195-223. Edited by Shankar A. Yelaja. Originally published 1978.

**1461. Melvyn, Carla** *"A Psychiatric Ward in a Children's Hospital: the Social Worker's Contribution."* Carla Melvyn. Canadian Psychiatric Association Journal/Revue de l'Association canadienne de psychiatrie 6, 5(Oct. 1961): 299-301.

**1462. Menear, David William** *Parent Opinion and Pupil Achievement.* David William Menear. Edmonton: University of Alberta, 1961. Thesis (M.Ed.)--University of Alberta, 1961.

**1463. Menzies, M. Albert** *"The Angry Parent in Family Oriented Therapy."* M. Albert Menzies. Canadian Psychiatric Association Journal/Revue de l'Association canadienne de psychiatrie 10, 5(Oct. 1965): 405-410.

**1464. Menzies, M. Albert** *"An Intensive Approach to Brief Family Diagnosis in a Child Guidance Clinic."* M. Albert Menzies, S. Bodlak and O. McRae. Canadian Psychiatric Association Journal/Revue de l'Association canadienne de psychiatrie 6, 5(Oct. 1961): 295-298.

**1465. Meredith, Howard V.** *"Body Size of Contemporary Groups of Preschool Children Studied in Different Parts of the World."* Howard V. Meredith. Child Development 39, 2(June 1968): 335-377.

**1466. Messner, Joseph A.** *"Day Care, Right or Remedy?"* Joseph A. Messner. Canadian Welfare 42, 2(Mar.-Apr. 1966): 63-67.

**1467. Metcalf, Vicky** *Catherine Schubert.* Vicky Metcalf. Don Mills, Ont.: Fitzhenry & Whiteside, c1978.

**1468. Metropolitan Life Insurance Co.** *"A Friend in Need Is a Friend Indeed": Health Hints for the Home.* New York: Metropolitan Life Insurance Co., 1898.

**1469. Metropolitan Life Insurance Co.** *Your Baby.* [New York?]: Metropolitan Life Insurance Co., [194-?]. Widely distributed in Canada.

**1470. Metson, Graham** *Alex Colville: Diary of a War Artist.* Graham Metson and Cheryl Lean. Halifax: Nimbus Publishing, 1981.

**1471. Meyers, Leonard** *Twenty-three Skidoo.* Leonard Meyers. Toronto: Kingswood House, 1958.

**1472. Migus, Paul M.** *Ukrainian Canadian Youth: a History of Organizational Life in Canada, 1907-1953.* Paul Michael Migus. Ottawa: University of Ottawa, 1975. Thesis (M.A.)--University of Ottawa, 1975.

**1473. Mikulicic, Elsa** *"Poliomyelitis."* Elsa Mikulicic. Canadian Nurse 49, 7(July 1953): 565-566.

**1474. Miles, Hazel** *A Study of Responsibility in a Nursery School Setting.* Hazel Miles. Toronto: University of Toronto, 1939. Thesis (M.A.)--University of Toronto, 1939.

**1475. Millar, Mary Aileen** *A Study of Common Stories Told by Nursery School Children on the Children's Apperception Test.* Mary Aileen Millar. Edmonton: University of Edmonton, 1952. Thesis (M.A.)--University of Edmonton, 1952.

**1476. Millar, T.P.** *"Peptic Ulcers in Children."* T.P. Millar. Canadian Psychiatric Association Journal/Revue de l'Association canadienne de psychiatrie 10, 1(Feb. 1965): 43-50.

**1477. Millard, Peggy** *"Company Wife."* Peggy Millard. Beaver 315, 4(May 1985): 30-39.

**1478. Miller, J.R.** *"The Irony of Residential Schooling."* J.R. Miller. Canadian Journal of Native Education 14, 2(Winter 1987): 3-14.

**1479. Miller, Leonard G.** *The Relationship of Socioeconomic Status to Grade Six Children's Reading of Proverbs.* Leonard G. Miller. Edmonton: University of Alberta, 1970. Thesis (M.Ed.)--University of Alberta, 1970.

**1480. Miller, Muriel** *Famous Canadian Artists.* Muriel Miller. Peterborough, Ont.: Woodland Pub., 1983.

**1481. Miller, Orlo** *Twenty Mortal Murders: Bizarre Murder Cases from Canada's Past.* Hanson Orlo Miller. Toronto: Macmillan of Canada, c1978.

**1482. Millichamp, Dorothy A.** *"Day Nurseries and the Community."* Dorothy A. Millichamp. Canadian Welfare 28, 1(May 1952): 39-42.

**1483. Millichamp, Dorothy A.** *"Intelligence: its Guidance in Kindergarten and Nursery School."* Dorothy A. Millichamp. Canadian Welfare 16, 3(July 1940): 42-43.

**1484. Millichamp, Dorothy A.** *"Report of the Nursery Schools."* Dorothy A. Millichamp. Child and Family Welfare 13, 4(Nov. 1937): 71-72.

**1485. Mills, Robert E.** *"The Child and the Institution."* Robert E. Mills. Canadian Welfare Summary 15, 3(Sept. 1939): 43-48.

**1486. Mills, Robert E.** *"The Child Protection Society."* Robert E. Mills. Child and Family Welfare 8, 3(Sept. 1932): 11-15.

**1487. Mills, Robert E.** *The Placing of Children in Families.* Robert E. Mills. Ottawa: Canadian Welfare Council, 1938. Reprinted from the Canadian Welfare Summary, 1938.

**1488. Mills, Robert E.** *"The Placing of Children in Families, Part One."* Robert E. Mills. Canadian Welfare Summary 14, 1(May 1938): 33-38.

**1489. Mills, Robert E.** *"The Placing of Children in Families, Part Three."* Robert E. Mills. Canadian Welfare Summary 14, 3(Sept. 1938): 14-34.

**1490. Mills, Robert E.** *"The Placing of Children in Families, Part Two."* Robert E. Mills. Canadian Welfare Summary 14, 2(July 1938): 44-54.

**1491. Mills, Robert E.** *"Progress in the Care of Children."* Robert E. Mills. Canadian Welfare 24, 7(Jan. 1949): 70-73.

**1492. Milner, Wayne M.** *Comparison of the Galvanic Skin Response to Non-signal and Signal Stimuli in Normal and Retarded Children.* Wayne M. Milner. Edmonton: University of Alberta, 1971. Thesis (M.Ed.)--University of Alberta, 1971.

**1493. Minkler, Frederick** *A Study of the Voluntary Reading Interests of Children in Canadian Elementary Schools.* Frederick Minkler. Toronto: University of Toronto, 1946. Thesis (D.Paed.)--University of Toronto, 1946.

**1494. Minkler, Frederick** *Voluntary Reading Interests in Canadian Elementary Schools.* Frederick Minkler. Toronto: Macmillan Company of Canada Limited and The Ryerson Press, 1948.

**1495. Minor, Democritus** *"Some Notes on Education for Mental Health."* Democritus Minor. Queen's Quarterly 68, 3(Autumn 1961): 496-503.

**1496. Mitcham, Allison** *Gray Owl's Favorite Wilderness.* Allison Mitcham. Moonbeam, Ont.: Penumbra Press, c1981.

**1497. Mitchell, Eileen** *"Young Offenders."* Eileen Mitchell. Canadian Welfare 21, 5(Oct. 1945): 32-38.

**1498. Mitchell, H.S.** *"Lead Poisoning in Children."* H.S. Mitchell. Canadian Nurse 28, 6(June 1932): 290-292.

**1499. Mitchell, Liz** *"The Clinical/Judicial Interface in Legal Representation for Children."* Liz Mitchell. Canadian Community Law Journal/Revue canadienne de droit communautaire 7(1984): 75-108.

**1500. Mitchell, W.T.B.** *"Child Training in the Child-caring Agency."* W.T.B. Mitchell. Child and Family Welfare 6, 2(May 1930): 16-18.

**1501. Mitchell, W.T.B.** *"Letting Our Children Grow Up."* W.T.B. Mitchell. Canadian Nurse 29, 2(Feb. 1933): 83-86.

**1502. Mitchinson, Wendy** *"The YWCA and Reform in the Nineteenth Century."* Wendy Mitchinson. Histoire sociale/Social History 12, 24(Nov. 1979): 368-384.

**1503. Moberly, J.V.** *"Children Born Out of Wedlock."* J.V. Moberly. In Proceedings of Sixth Annual Canadian Conference on Child Welfare 1927, pp. 120-125.

**1504. Moffatt, John Gordon** *The Ability of Kindergarten Children to Discriminate Selected Vowel and Semivowel Speech Sounds.* John Gordon Moffatt. Edmonton: University of Alberta, 1970. Thesis (M.Ed.)--University of Alberta, 1970.

1505. **Mohr, Johann W.** *"The Pedophilias: their Clinical, Social and Legal Implications."* Johann W. Mohr. Canadian Psychiatric Association Journal/Revue de l'Association canadienne de psychiatrie 7, 5(Oct. 1962): 255-260.

1506. **Moilliet, Melrose** *Sketches: an Introduction to Emily Carr and the Fine Art of Sketching.* Melrose Moilliet. Victoria: M.R. Publishing, 1981.

1507. **Momryk, Myron** *"Ukrainian Canadian Youth."* Myron Momryk. Archivist/Archiviste 12, 3(May-June 1985): 6-7.

1508. **Mongeau, Estelle** *"Nutrition in Adolescence."* Estelle Mongeau. Canadian Journal of Public Health 62, 4 (July-Aug. 1971): 330-332.

1509. **Montague, Joll** *"Impressions of Some Canadian Medical Institutions in 1837: Extracts from the Diary of Dr. James MacDonald."* Joll Montague and Shahnaz Montague. Canadian Psychiatric Association Journal/Revue de l'Association canadienne de psychiatrie 21, 3(Apr. 1976): 181-182.

1510. **Montgomery, Jacqueline** *"A Junior Kindergarten Programme."* Jacqueline Montgomery. Bulletin of the Institute of Child Study 30, 1(Spring 1968): 32-35.

1511. **Moore, Nora** *"Child Welfare Work."* Nora Moore. Canadian Nurse 12, 11(Nov. 1916): 634-635.

1512. **Moore, William Henry** *The Clash!: a Study in Nationalities.* William Henry Moore. Toronto: J.M. Dent & Sons Ltd., 1918.

1513. **Morgan, A. Lloyd** *"Surgical Treatment of Strabimus."* A. Lloyd Morgan. Canadian Medical Association Journal 45, 6(Dec. 1941): 500-504.

1514. **Morgan, John S.** *"The Welfare Aspects of Civil Defence."* John S. Morgan. Canadian Welfare 26, 6(Dec. 1950): 10-16.

1515. **Morlock, Maud** *"Chosen Children."* Maud Morlock. Canadian Welfare 21, 1(Apr. 1945): 3-8.

1516. **Morrison, M.E.** *"Opportunities of the School Nurse."* M.E. Morrison. Canadian Nurse 17, 8(Aug. 1921): 277-285.

1517. **Morrison, M. Flora** *"So Much to Learn."* M. Flora Morrison. Bulletin of the Institute of Child Study 28, 1(Spring 1966): 35-37.

1518. **Morrison, Patricia** *Family Play: a Study of the Family Recreation Carried on by 132 Families Represented in the Iverly Community Centre in Montreal.* Patricia Morrison. Montreal: McGill University, 1953.
Thesis (M.S.W.)--McGill University, 1953.

1519. **Morrison, William A.** *"Group Work Plays Its Part."* William A. Morrison. Canadian Welfare 16, 6(Nov. 1940): 27-31.

1520. **Morton, Desmond** *"The Cadet Movement in the Moment of Canadian Militarism, 1909-1914."* Desmond Morton. Journal of Canadian Studies/Revue d'etudes canadiennes 13, 2(Summer 1978): 56-68.

1521. **Mosher, Clayton James** *The Twentieth Century Marihuana Phenomenon in Canada.* Clayton James Mosher. Burnaby: Simon Fraser University, 1985.
Thesis (M.A.)--Simon Fraser University, 1985.

1522. **Mott, H.S.** *"The Juvenile Court in Crime Prevention."* H.S. Mott. Child and Family Welfare 9, 4(Nov. 1933): 45-46.

1523. **Moyes, Peter D.** *"Subdural Effusions in Infants."* Peter D. Moyes. Canadian Medical Association Journal/Journal de l'Association medicale canadienne 100, 5(Feb. 1, 1969): 231-324.

1524. **Moyle, H.B.** *"Mental Disturbances of Childhood."* H.B. Moyle. Canadian Journal of Mental Hygiene 3, 3(Oct. 1921): 249-258.

1525. **Muir, Donna June** *A Study of the Social Structure of the Training School: an Organization or a Community.* Donna June Muir. Toronto: University of Toronto, 1964.
Thesis (M.S.W.)--University of Toronto, 1964.

1526. **Muir, Walter** *Looking Behaviour in Normal and Retarded Children During Directed Search Tasks and Discrimination Learning.* Walter Muir. Edmonton: University of Alberta, 1971.
Thesis (Ph.D.)--University of Alberta, 1971.

1527. **Mullin, J. Heurner** *"Child Welfare in a Democracy."* J. Heurner Mullin. Public Health Journal 9, 10(Oct. 1918): 445-456.

1528. **Muncaster, Eric** *"Strengthening Family Ties Through Recreation."* Eric Muncaster. Child and Family Welfare 9, 4(Nov. 1933): 47-49.

**1529. Mundie, Gordon S.** *"Child Guidance Clinics."* Gordon S. Mundie. Canadian Medical Association Journal 14, 6(June 1924): 508-511.

**1530. Mundie, Gordon S.** *"Feeble-minded and Backward Children."* Gordon S. Mundie. Public Health Journal 5, 3(Mar. 1914): 166-167.

**1531. Mundie, Gordon S.** *"Juvenile Courts in Canada."* Gordon S. Mundie. Canadian Journal of Mental Hygiene 3, 3(Oct. 1921): 275-279.

**1532. Munro, Iain R.** *Immigration.* Iain R. Munro. Toronto: Wiley Publishers of Canada Ltd., c1978.

**1533. Murphy, Emily** *"The Prevention of Delinquency."* Emily Murphy. In Proceedings and Papers Fifth Annual Canadian Conference on Child Welfare 1925, pp. 211-217.

**1534. Murphy, Emily** *"The Supervision of a Case in Court."* Emily F. Murphy. In Proceedings of Sixth Annual Canadian Conference on Child Welfare 1927, pp. 98-100.

**1535. Murray, J. Lovell** *Nation Builders.* J. Lovell Murray. Toronto: Ryerson Press, 1925.

**1536. Murray, John Wilson** *Further Adventures of the Great Detective: Incidents in the Life of John Wilson Murray.* John Wilson Murray. Toronto: Collins, c1904. Selections from the original: Memoirs of a Great Detective. London: W. Heinemenn, 1904.

**1537. Musclow, C. Elizabeth** *"Glue Sniffing: Report of a Fatal Case."* C. Elizabeth Musclow and C.F. Awen. Canadian Medical Association Journal/Journal de l'Association medicale canadienne 104, 6(Feb. 20, 1971): 315-319.

**1538. Musgrove, W.M.** *"Some Problems of Childhood."* W.M. Musgrove. Canadian Medical Association Journal 17, 4(Apr. 1927): 438- 441.

**1539. Myhre, Harold Kenneth** *Computer-assisted Instruction in the Presentation of Calculus Using a Small Computer.* Harold Kenneth Myhre. Calgary: University of Calgary, 1971. Thesis (M.Ed.)–University of Calgary, 1971.

**1540. Nakaneshny, Maurice Robert** *Study of the Relationship Between Counsellor Empathy and Student Perception of the Counsellor Role.* Maurice Robert Nakaneshny. Calgary: University of Calgary, 1971. Thesis (M.Ed.)–University of Calgary, 1971.

**1541. Nash, Paul** *"The Assumptions and Consequences of Objective Examinations."* Paul Nash. Canadian Education and Research Digest 1, 1(Mar. 1961): 42-50.

**1542. Nash, Paul** *"Objective Examinations and the Process of Education."* Paul Nash. Canadian Education and Research Digest 2, 2(June 1962): 99-109.

**1543. National Committee for School Health Research** *Absenteeism in Canadian Schools.* The National Committee for School Health Research. Toronto: The Committee, 1948.

**1544. National Committee for School Health Research** *A Health Survey of Canadian Schools, 1945-1946: a Survey of Existing Conditions in the Elementary and Secondary Schools of Canada.* The National Committee for School Health Research. Toronto: The Committee, 1947.

**1545. National Consultation on Transient Youth (1970: Sainte-Adele, Que.)** *More About Transient Youth: Report of a National Consultation on Transient Youth, Convened by the Canadian Welfare Council as a Follow up to the Transient Youth Inquiry.* National Consultation on Transient Youth. Ottawa: Canadian Welfare Council, 1970. Chairman: William Zimmerman.

**1546. National Council of Women of Canada** *The International Congress of Women, 1909.* The National Council of Women of Canada. Toronto: Geo. Parker and Sons, 1910.

**1547. National Federation of Kindergarten Nursery School and Kindergarten-Primary Teachers** *"The Kindergarten-Primary."* National Federation of Kindergarten Nursery School and Kindergarten-Primary Teachers. Child and Family Welfare 11, 4(Nov. 1935): 52.

**1548. Neatby, Hilda** *So Little for the Mind.* Hilda Neatby. 2nd ed. Toronto: Clarke, Irwin and Company Limited, 1953. Annotated bibliography pp. 373-376.

**1549. Neatby, Hilda** *So Much to Do, So Little Time: the Writings of Hilda Neatby.* Hilda Neatby. Vancouver: University of British Columbia Press, c1983.

**1550. Nelson, Winnifred** *"Mongolism."* Winnifred Nelson. Canadian Nurse 55, 5(May 1959): 452-456.

**1551. Nesset, Inez** *"The Story of Joey."* Inez Nesset. Canadian Nurse 41, 11(Nov. 1945): 875-876.
  Case study.

**1552. Nett, Emily M.** *Canadian Families: Past and Present.* Emily M. Nett. Toronto: Butterworths, c1988.

**1553. Nett, Emily M.** *"The Changing Forms and Functions of the Canadian Family: a Demographic View."* E.M. Nett. Toronto: Holt, Rinehart and Winston of Canada Ltd., c1976. In The Canadian Family Revised, pp. 46-76. Edited by K. Ishwaran.

**1554. Neutzling, Bernadine Elaine** *Effects of Subject Motivation on Composition in Printing at the Kindergarten Level.* Bernadine Elaine Neutzling. Calgary: University of Calgary, 1971.
  Thesis (M.Ed.)--University of Calgary, 1971.

**1555. Newark, Michael** *"Blood Tests and Paternity."* Michael Newark and Alec Samuels. University of Toronto Law Journal 19, 4(1969): 605-614.

**1556. Newman, James Edward** *The Relationships Among Physical Work Capacity, Physical Fitness Index and Performance Time in Swimmers throughout a Season of Training.* James Edward Newman. Edmonton: University of Alberta, 1968.
  Thesis (M.Sc.)--University of Alberta, 1968.

**1557. Newman, Warren Oscar** *Children's Understanding of Time Duration.* Warren Oscar Newman. Edmonton: University of Alberta, 1967.
  Thesis (M.Ed.)--University of Alberta, 1967.

**1558. Newsholme, Arthur** *"Report Adopted and Presented to the Conference by the Section of Child Welfare."* Arthur Newsholme. Public Health Journal 11, 4(Apr. 1920): 170-175.

**1559. Nichol, Hamish** *"Death of a Parent."* Hamish Nichol. Canadian Psychiatric Association Journal/Revue de l'Association canadienne de psychiatrie 9, 3(June 1964): 262-271.

**1560. Nicholls, John V.V.** *"The Office Management of Patients with Reading Difficulties."* John V.V. Nicholls. Canadian Medical Association Journal/Journal de l'Association medicale canadienne 81, 5(Sept. 1, 1959): 356-360.

**1561. Nicholls, John V.V.** *"Reading Disorders in School Children."* John V.V. Nicholls. Canadian Journal of Public Health 60, 9(Sept. 1969): 337-343.

**1562. Noel, E.E.** *"The Young Adult Offender."* Warden E.E. Noel. Canadian Journal of Corrections/Revue canadienne de criminologie 12, 3(July 1970): 296-300.

**1563. Norcross, Rene** *"The Little Brother."* Rene Norcross. Canadian Nurse 11, 2(Feb. 1915): 112-114.

**1564. Nordly, Frederick Torgeir** *Effect of Certain Sequence Variations and Methods of Information and Concept Consolidations on the Effectiveness of a Multi-activity Learning Technique.* Frederick Torgeir Nordly. Calgary: University of Calgary, 1971.
  Thesis (M.Ed.)--University of Calgary, 1971.

**1565. Norine, Beatrice Irene** *Spontaneous Verbalization and Displacement Behaviour During Problem-solving in Subnormal Children.* Beatrice Irene Norine. Calgary: University of Calgary, 1970.
  Thesis (M.Ed.)--University of Calgary, 1970.

**1566. Northway, Mary L.** *"Appraisal of the Social Development of Children at a Summer Camp."* Mary L. Northway. Toronto: University of Toronto Press, 1940. In University of Toronto Studies, Psychology Series, v.5, no.1, pp. 5-62.

**1567. Northway, Mary L.** *Difficulty of the Task and the Ability of the Subject as Factors in "Whole-part" Learning.* Mary L. Northway. Toronto: University of Toronto, 1934.
  Thesis (M.A.)--University of Toronto, 1934.

**1568. Northway, Mary L., ed.** *The Camp Counselor's Book.* Mary L. Northway and Barry G. Lowes. Toronto: Longmans Canada, c1963.

**1569. Northway, Mary L., ed.** *Well Children: a Progress Report on the Research Conducted at the Institute of Child Study University of Toronto July 1953 to December 1955 by the Director and Staff of the Institute, under Federal Health Grant 605-5-147.* Mary L. Northway, ed. Toronto: University of Toronto Press, 1956.

1570. **Nowlan, Nadine M.** *A Study of the Relationship Between the "Prescriptiveness of the Pattern of Constituent Performances" of Art and Crafts Projects and the Participation of a Group of Disturbed Girls.* Nadine M. Nowlan. Toronto: University of Toronto, 1962.
Thesis (M.S.W.)—University of Toronto, 1962.

1571. **Nye, F. Ivan** *"Some Family Attitudes and Psychosomatic Illness in Adolescents."* F. Ivan Nye. Coordinator 6, 2(Dec. 1957): 26-30.

1572. **Nyrose, Garry Wayne** *Grade One Math Achievement and the Individually Prescribed Instruction Programs.* Garry Wayne Nyrose. Calgary: University of Calgary, 1971.
Thesis (M.Ed.)—University of Calgary, 1971.

1573. **O'Bryan, Maureen Hazel** *Attitudes of Males Toward Selected Aspects of Physical Education.* Maureen Hazel O'Bryan. Edmonton: University of Alberta, 1967.
Thesis (M.A.)—University of Alberta, 1967.

1574. **O'Conner, W.F.** *"Liability of an Infant Upon His Contracts for Service."* W.F. O'Conner. Canadian Bar Review 4, 4(Apr. 1926): 365-373.

1575. **O'Heir, Judith** *Infant Feeding in North America 1880-1920: the Physician-Nurse Relationship.* Judith O'Heir. Edmonton: University of Alberta, 1984.
Thesis (M.N.)--University of Alberta, 1984.

1576. **Olson, David R.** *The Role of Verbal Rules in the Cognitive Processes of Children.* David Richard Olson. Edmonton: University of Alberta, 1963.
Thesis (Ph.D.)—University of Alberta, 1963.

1577. **O'Malley, Martin** *Doctors.* Martin O'Malley. Toronto: Macmillan of Canada, 1983.

1578. **Orlikow, Lionel** *Report on Second Language Teaching in the Western Provinces and in Ontario.* Lionel Orlikow. Report consists of five separate studies on second-language teaching in Canada.

1579. **Ormsby, Margaret A.** *"An Appreciation."* Margaret A. Ormsby. British Columbia Historical News 23, 2(Spring 1990): 8-9.

1580. **Osborne, Robert F.** *"Can School Physical Education Be Justified?"* Robert F. Osborne. Journal of Education of the Faculty and College of Education: Vancouver and Victoria 3(Mar. 1959): 51-60.

1581. **Ostry, Ethel** *"Children and Hospital Care."* Ethel Ostry. Canadian Welfare 35, 4(July 1959): 158-162.

1582. **Ouellet, Francoise Miller** *"Play Therapy and the Nurse."* Francoise Miller Ouellet. Canadian Nurse 56, 4 and 5(Apr. and May 1960): 342-350 and 444-446.

1583. **Oughton, Libby** *"Two Things I'd Change."* Libby Oughton and Muriel Smith. Canadian Women's Studies 2, 1(Autumn 1980): 106-107.

1584. **Pacey, Desmond** *Ten Canadian Poets: a Group of Biographical and Critical Essays.* Desmond Pacey. Toronto: Ryerson Press, c1958.

1585. **Pady, Cecil A.** *A Study of Jewish Adolescent Religious Conviction and Behaviour.* Cecil A. Pady. Toronto: University of Toronto, 1968.
Thesis (M.S.W.)—University of Toronto, 1968.

1586. **Paget, A.P.** *"The Juvenile Immigrant."* A.P. Paget. In Proceedings and Papers Fifth Annual Canadian Conference on Child Welfare 1925, pp. 159-162.

1587. **Pannekoek, Frits** *"Protestant Agricultural Zions for the Western Indians."* Frits Pannekoek. Journal of the Canadian Church Historical Society 14, 3(Sept. 1972): 55-66.

1588. **Park, E. Louise** *"Health Needs of High School Students."* E. Louise Park and Alice G. Nicolle. Canadian Nurse 50, 12(Dec. 1954): 979-982.

1589. **Park, Edwards A.** *"The Preservation of the Ideal in a University Children's Clinic."* Edwards A. Park. Canadian Medical Association Journal 66, 6(June 1952): 478-485.

1590. **Parker, Alfred J.** *Give Your Child Its Inheritance: a Study of Child and Parent Problems.* Alfred J. Parker. New York: Exposition Press, c1957.

1591. **Parker, Edwin B.** *"Changes in the Function of Radio with the Adoption of Television."* Edwin B. Parker. Journal of Broadcasting 5, 1(Winter 1960-1961): 39-48.

1592. **Parker, Edwin B.** *The Impact of U.S. Media on Canadian Children.* Edwin B. Parker. [S.l.: s.n., 1961].

1593. **Parker, Graham** *"The Appellate Court View of the Juvenile Court."* Graham Parker. Osgoode Hall Law Journal 7, 2(1969): 155-175.

1594. **Parker, Graham** *"The Century of the Child."* Graham Parker. Canadian Bar Review/Revue du Barreau Canadien 45, 4(Dec. 1967): 741-763.

1595. **Parker, Graham** *"Juvenile Delinquency, Transfer of Juvenile Cases to Adult Courts, Factors to be Considered Under the Juvenile Delinquents Act."* Graham Parker. Canadian Bar Review/Revue du Barreau Canadien 48, 2(May 1970): 336-346.

1596. **Parker, Margaret** *"Behind the Sateen Curtain."* Margaret Parker. Saskatoon: Western Producer Prairie Books, c1982. In Christmas in the West, pp. 141-144. Edited by Hugh A. Dempsey.

1597. **Parlee, Mary Julia** *Adolescent Unmarried Mothers.* Mary Julia Parlee. Toronto: University of Toronto, 1959. Thesis (M.S.W.)–University of Toronto, 1959.

1598. **Parr, Joy** *"Case Records as Sources for Social History."* G.J. Parr. Archivaria 1, 4(1977): 122-136.

1599. **Parr, Joy** *The Home Children: British Juvenile Immigrants to Canada 1868-1924.* Gwyenth Joy Parr. New Haven, Conn.: Yale University, 1977. Thesis (Ph.D.)–Yale University, 1977. Note on sources leaves 292-302.

1600. **Parr, Joy** *Labouring Children: British Immigrant Apprentices to Canada, 1869-1924.* Joy Parr. London: Croom Helm; Montreal: McGill-Queen's University Press, c1980.

1601. **Parr, Joy** *"Nature and Hierarchy: Reflections on Writing the History of Women and Children."* Joy Parr. Atlantis 11, 1(Fall 1985): 39-44.

1602. **Parr, Joy** *""Transplanting from Dens of Iniquity": Theology and Child Emigration."* Joy Parr. Toronto: Women's Educational Press, c1979. In A Not Unreasonable Claim: Women and Reform in Canada, 1880's-1920's, pp. 169-183. Edited by Linda Kealey.

1603. **Parr, Joy, ed.** *Childhood and Family in Canadian History.* Joy Parr, ed. Toronto: McClelland and Stewart, c1982.

1604. **Parr, Joy, ed.** *Still Running...: Personal Stories by Queen's Women Celebrating the Fifieth Anniversary of the Marty Scholarship.* Joy Parr, ed. Kingston, Ont.: Queen's University Alumnae Association, c1987.

1605. **Parry, R.Y.** *"Keeping Babies Well."* R.Y. Parry. In Canadian Conference on Charities and Correction Proceedings 1911, pp. 65-70.

1606. **Parry, Robert S.** *The Relational Value-Orientations of Grade 10 Students and of Their Fathers.* Robert S. Parry. Calgary: University of Calgary, 1967. Thesis (M.Ed.)–University of Calgary, 1967.

1607. **Paton, James M.** *Examinations in English: a Critical Survey of Examination Philosophy and Practice in High School English of British, American and Canadian Schools, with Particular Reference to Canadian Conditions at the High School Leaving Level.* James M. Paton. Toronto: University of Toronto, 1948. Thesis (D.Paed.)–University of Toronto, 1948.

1608. **Paton, Richard Thurston** *"The Influence of Three Reinforcement Modifications on Perseveration in Psychotic Children."* Richard T. Paton and Gerald J.S. Wilde. Canadian Psychologist/Psychologie canadienne 11, 3(July 1970): 261-268. Author presented a dissertation with the same title at Queen's University, 1969.

1609. **Paton, Richard Thurston** *"Token Reinforcements in the Shaping of Children's Mealtime Behaviour."* Richard T. Paton. Canadian Psychologist/Psychologie canadienne 9, 1(Jan. 1968): 22-27.

1610. **Patsula, Philip James** *Felt Powerlessness as Related to Perceived Parental Behaviour.* Philip J. Patsula. Edmonton: University of Alberta, 1969. Thesis (Ph.D.)–University of Alberta, 1969.

1611. **Patsula, Philip James** *Relation of Alienation and Introversion to Academic Achievement Among Grade Ten Students.* Philip James Patsula. Edmonton: University of Alberta, 1968. Thesis (M.Ed.)–University of Alberta, 1968.

**1612. Patterson, L.P.** *"What Specific Provisions Will Answer the Needs of the Handicapped?"* L.P. Patterson. Ottawa: Mutal Press, 1958. In Addresses and Proceedings of the Canadian Conference on Education, Ottawa, February 16-20, 1958, pp. 427-432. Edited by George G. Croskery and Gerald Nason.

**1613. Patterson, Robert S.** *"Society and Education During the Wars and Their Interlude: 1914-1945."* Robert S. Patterson. Scarborough: Prentice-Hall of Canada, c1970. In Canadian Education: a History, pp. 360-384. Edited by J. Donald Wilson, Robert M. Stamp and Louis-Philippe Audet.

**1614. Payne, Audrey B.** *"Public Health Nursing in Montreal and Saanich."* Audrey B. Payne. Public Health Nurses' Bulletin 1, 8(Mar. 1931): 15-17.

**1615. Payne, Julien D.** *"Contracts Relating to Infants."* Julien D. Payne. Western Law Review 5(1966): 136-152.

**1616. Pearse, J.D.** *"Meeting the Needs of Youth."* J.D. Pearse. Ottawa: Mutal Press, 1958. In Addresses and Proceedings of the Canadian Conference on Education, Ottawa, February 16-20, 1958, pp. 168-172. Edited by George G. Croskery and Gerald Nason.

**1617. Pedde, Mervyn Leroy** *Children's Concepts of Base Area Symbols.* Mervyn Leroy Pedde. Edmonton: University of Alberta, 1966.
Thesis (M.Ed.)--University of Alberta, 1966.

**1618. Pedersen, Diana L.** *""Building Today for the Womanhood of Tormorrow": Businessmen, Boosters, and the YWCA 1890-1930."* Diana Pedersen. Urban History Review/Revue d'histoire urbaine 25, 3(Feb. 1987): 225-242.

**1619. Pedersen, Diana L.** *""The Call to Service": the YWCA and the Canadian College Woman, 1886-1920."* Diana Pedersen. Kingston: McGill-Queen's University Press, 1989. In Youth, University and Canadian Society: Essays in the Social History of Higher Education, pp. 187-215. Edited by Paul Axelrod and John G. Reid.

**1620. Pedersen, Diana L.** *"Keeping Our Good Girls Good": the Young Women's Christian Association of Canada, 1870-1920.* Diana L. Pedersen. Ottawa: Carelton University, 1981. (CTM no. 55626)
Thesis (M.A.)--Carleton University, 1981.

**1621. Pedersen, Diana L.** *""Keeping Our Good Girls Good": the YWCA and the "Girl Problem," 1870-1930."* Diana Pedersen. Canadian Woman Studies/Cahiers de la femme 7, 4(Winter 1986): 20-24.

**1622. Peel, Paul** *Time Effects on the Creative Writing of Sixth Grade Children.* Paul Peel. Edmonton: University of Alberta, 1968.
Thesis (M.Ed.)--University of Alberta, 1968.

**1623. Pelletier, Alphonse J.** *The Canadian Family.* A.J. Pelletier, F.D. Thompson and A. Rochon. Ottawa: King's Printer, 1942.

**1624. Penfield, Wilder** *Man and His Family.* Wilder Penfield. Toronto: McClelland and Stewart, c1967.

**1625. Penman, James T.** *"Some Mental Health Problems Affecting the Bright Child of School Age."* James T. Penman. Canadian Journal of Public Health 54, 7(July 1963): 309-913.

**1626. Pepler, E.** *"The Juvenile Delinquents Act, 1929."* E. Pepler. Canadian Bar Review 30, 8(Oct. 1952): 819-830.

**1627. Pequegnat, L.A.** *"Health Services in the Secondary Schools."* L.A. Pequegnat. Canadian Public Health Journal 33, 9(Sept. 1942): 427-437.

**1628. Perchal, Wladyslaw** *"Sins of the Father."* Wladyslaw Perchal. Toronto: Canadian Polish Research Institute, 1985. In A Community in Transition: the Polish Group in Canada, pp. 243-248. Edited by Benedykt Heydenkorn.

**1629. Percy, David R.** *"The Present Law of Infants' Contracts."* David R. Percy. Canadian Bar Review/Revue du Barreau Canadien 53, 1(Mar. 1975): 1-55.

**1630. Perreault, J. Georges** *"Dentition in Childhood."* J. Georges Perreault. Canadian Nurse 58, 12(Dec. 1962): 1090-1094.

**1631. Perry, Lloyd W.** *"Sales of an Infant's Interest in Land: the Responsibilities of the Office of the Official Guardian."* Lloyd W. Perry. Western Law Review 5(1966): 170-176.

**1632. Petryshyn, Jaroslav** *Peasants in the Promised Land: Canada and the Ukrainians, 1891-1914.* Jaroslav Petryshyn, with L. Dzubak. Toronto: James Lorimer & Company, 1985.

**1633. Pett, L.B.** *"Malnutrition in Canada."*
L.B. Pett. Canadian Medical Association
Journal 50, 1(Jan. 1944): 9-14.

**1634. Pett, L.B.** *"A Nutrition Survey
Among School Children in British
Columbia and Saskatchewan."* L.B. Pett
and F.W. Hanley. Canadian Medical
Association Journal 56, 2(Feb. 1947):
187-192.

**1635. Pettifor, Jean L.** *"The Role of
Language in the Development of Abstract
Thinking: a Comparison of Hard-of-hearing
and Normal Hearing Children on Levels of
Conceptual Thinking."* Jean L. Pettifor.
Canadian Journal of Psychology/Revue
canadienne de psychologie 22, 3(Jun.
1968): 139-156.

**1636. Phair, J.T.** *"Child Hygiene: the
Eating of Candy."* J.T. Phair and H.E.
Young. Canadian Public Health Journal
20, 6(June 1929): 310-311.

**1637. Phair, J.T.** *"Rural School Hygiene."*
J.T. Phair. Canadian Public Health
Journal 20, 6(June 1929): 277-281.

**1638. Phair, J.T.** *"Symposium on Anterior
Poliomyelitis: Present Incidence of
Poliomyelitis in Ontario."* J.T. Phair.
Canadian Public Health Journal 28,
9(Sept. 1937): 417-441.

**1639. Phillips, A.J.** *"Final Report of the
National Committee for School Health
Research, Sponsored by the Canadian
Education Association and the Canadian
Public Health Association: a Five Year
Program in School Health Research."* A.J.
Phillips. Canadian Journal of Public
Health 41, 9(Sept. 1950): 341-348.

**1640. Phillips, A.J.** *"Some Data on Mental
Health Problems in Canadian Schools."*
A.J. Phillips. Canadian Education 3,
2(Mar. 1948): 11-51.

**1641. Phillips, Charles E.** *Public
Secondary Education in Canada.* Charles
E. Phillips. Toronto: W.J. Gage and
Company Limited, 1955.

**1642. Philpott, N.W.** *"Care of the
Unmarried Mother and Her Child."* N.W.
Philpott and Christina F. Goodwin.
Canadian Medical Association Journal 55,
3(Sept. 1946): 293-295.
   Reprinted in Canadian Nurse 43, 5(May
1947): 357-359.

**1643. Pidzamecky, Taras** *"Ukrainian
National Youth Federation of Canada: Five
Decades of Youth Leadership."* Taras
Pidzamecky. Forum: a Ukrainian Review
58(Spring 1984): 12-17 and 25.

**1644. Pigott, Arthur** *"Education and
Employment."* Arthur Pigott. Ottawa: The
Conference, 1961. In Canadian Conference
on Education, Conference Studies, no
pagination.
   Papers individually published in 1961 for
the 1962 Conference.

**1645. Pike, Robert M.** *"Social Class as a
Factor in Selection for Higher Education."*
Robert Pike. In Who Doesn't Get to
University - and Why: a Study on
Accessibility to Higher Education in
Canada, pp. 53-70. By Robert Pike.
Reprinted in Social Space: Canadian
Perspectives, pp. 94-104. Edited by D.I.
Davies and Kathleen Herman.

**1646. Pike, Robert M.** *Who Doesn't Get to
University , and Why: a Study on
Accessibility to Higher Education in
Canada.* Robert Pike. Ottawa: Association
of Universities and Colleges of Canada,
1970.

**1647. Pinckney, W.G.** *"The Use of Blood
Tests in Cases of Disputed Paternity."*
W.G. Pinckney. Saskatchewan Law Review
34, 2(1969-70): 142-156.

**1648. Pinkerton, Patricia A.** *"The
Pediatric Nurse and Play Therapy."*
Patricia A. Pinkerton. Canadian Nurse
55, 1(Jan. 1959): 28-29.

**1649. Plant, G.F.** *Overseas Settlement:
Migration from the United Kingdom to the
Dominions.* G.F. Plant. London: Oxford
University Press, 1951.

**1650. Plewes, Doris W.** *"Play for
Preschoolers."* Doris W. Plewes. Canadian
Nurse 50, 1(Jan. 1954): 27-29.

**1651. Poffenberger, Thomas** *"Sex-courting
Concerns of a Class of Twelfth Grade
Girls."* Thomas Poffenberger. Family Life
Coordinator 10, 4(Oct. 1961): 75-81.

**1652. Polk, James** *Wilderness Writers:
Ernest Thompson Seton, Charles G. D.
Roberts, Grey Owl.* James Polk. Toronto:
Clarke, Irwin, c1972.

**1653. Porter, Eric Ronald** *The Anglican
Church and Native Education: Residential
Schools and Assimilation.* Eric Ronald
Porter. Toronto: University of Toronto,
1981. (CTM no. 53139)
   Thesis (Ed.D.)—University of Toronto,
1981.

**1654. Porter, John A.** *"Social Class and
Education."* John Porter. In Social Purpose
for Canada, pp. 103-129. Edited by
Michael Oliver.
   Later verions of the text are published.
   1. In The Vertical Mosaic: an Analysis
of Social Class and Power in Canada,

pp. 165-198. By John Porter. 2. In
Canadian Society: Sociological
Perspectives, 2nd ed., 1964, pp. 482-495,
3rd ed., 1968, pp. 242-264 and abr. 3rd
ed., 1971, pp. 158-182. Edited by
Bernard R. Blishen, Frank E. Jones,
Kasper D. Naegele and John Porter.
Not in 1st ed. of Canadian Society:
Sociological Perspectives.

**1655. Porter, John A.** *The Vertical
Mosaic: an Analysis of Social Class and
Power in Canada.* John Porter. Toronto:
University of Toronto Press, c1965.

**1656. Post, Shirley** *"Hospitalization of
Children Under Five."* Shirley Post.
Canadian Nurse 62, 7(July 1966): 34-37.

**1657. Potter, Donald** *An Analysis of
Perceptions and Expectations of Teachers
and Students.* Donald Potter. Edmonton:
University of Alberta, 1969.
   Thesis (M.Ed.)–University of Alberta,
1969.

**1658. Potts, Florence** *"The Nursing of
Children."* F. Potts. Canadian Nurse 4,
11(Nov. 1908): 531-534.

**1659. Pound, Allan Nathanael Courtie**
*The Family.* Allan Nathanael Courtie
Pound. Toronto: University of Toronto,
1914.
   Thesis (M.A.)–University of Toronto,
1914.

**1660. Powles, William E.** *"Group
Management of Emotionally Ill Adolescents
in a Canadian Mental Hospital."* William
E. Powles. Canadian Psychiatric
Association Journal/Revue de l'Association
canadienne de psychiatrie 4, 1(Jan. 1959):
77-89.

**1661. Pozsonyi, Joseph** *"Growth Hormone
Investigation in Patients With Mental
Dysfunction."* J. Pozsonyi and H. Friesen.
Canadian Medical Association
Journal/Journal de l'Association medicale
canadienne 104, 1(Jan. 9, 1971): 26-29.

**1662. Prang, Margaret** *""The Girl God
Would Have Me Be": the Canadian Girls
In Training, 1915-1939."* Margaret Prang.
Canadian Historical Review 66, 2(June
1985): 154-184.

**1663. Prentice, Alison** *Canadian Women:
a History.* Alison Prentice, Paula Bourne,
Gail Cuthbert Brandt, Beth Light, Wendy
Mitchinson and Naomi Black. Toronto:
Harcourt, Brace Jovanovich, c1988.

**1664. Prentice, Alison** *"The Feminization
of Teaching in British North America and
Canada 1845-1875."* Alison Prentice.
Histoire sociale/Social History 8, 15(May
1975): 5-20.

**1665. Prentice, Alison** *"Towards a
Feminist History of Women and
Education."* Alison Prentice. Winnipeg:
University of Manitoba, 1981. In
Approaches to Educational History, pp.
39-64. Edited by David C. Jones, Nancy
M. Sheehan, Robert M. Stamp and Neil
G. McDonald.

**1666. Prentice, Alison, ed.** *Family, School
and Society in Nineteenth-century Canada.*
Alison L. Prentice and Susan E. Houston,
eds. Toronto: Oxford University Press,
c1975.

**1667. Prentice, Alison, ed.** *"Places for
Girls and Women."* Alison Prentice and
Susan Houston, eds. Toronto: Oxford
University Press, 1975. In Family, School
and Society in 19th Century Canada, pp.
224-269. Edited by Alison Prentice and
Susan Houston.

**1668. Prentice, Susan** *""Kids are Not for
Profit": the Politics of Child Care."* Susan
Prentice. Toronto: Between the Lines,
c1988. In Social Movement, Social
Change: the Politics and Practice of
Organizing, pp. 98-128. Edited by Frank
Cunningham, Sue Findlay, Marlene Kadar,
Alan Lennon and Ed Silva.

**1669. Prescott, Daniel A.** *"The Role of
Love in the Education of Preschool
Children."* Daniel A. Prescott. Journal of
Education of the Faculty of Education,
Vancouver 12(Jan. 1966): 10-20.

**1670. Preston, Paul J. L.** *Life Experiences
of Drug Users.* Paul John Louis Preston.
Edmonton: University of Alberta, 1987.
(CTM no. 40882)
   Thesis (M.Ed.)–University of Alberta,
1987.

**1671. Preston, Sarah** *"Individual
Awareness as Expressed in a Life History."*
Sarah Preston. Ottawa: National Museums
of Canada, 1981. In Canadian
Ethnological Society Papers from the
Sixth Annual Congress, 1979, pp.
206-212.

**1672. Price, Frederick W.** *The Use of
Radio in the School.* Frederick W. Price.
Montreal: McGill University, 1942.
   Thesis (M.A.)–McGill University, 1942.

**1673. Prisoners' Aid Association of Canada** *The Dominion Government and Prison Reform.* [The Association?]. [Toronto?: s.n., 1894?].

**1674. Pritz, Alexandra** *"Ukrainian Dance in Canada: the First Fifty Years, 1924-1974."* Alexandra Pritz. Winnipeg: Ukrainian Academy of Arts and Sciences in Canada, c1983. In New Soil - Old Roots: the Ukrainian Experience in Canada, pp. 124-154. Edited by Jaroslav Rozumnyj, with the assistance of Oleh W. Gerus and Mykhailo H. Marunchak.

**1675. Puffer, Gordon Percival** *Giant Among Pioneers.* Gordon Percival Puffer. Edmonton: The Author, 1976.

**1676. Pumphrey, Avis** *"The Adolescent Patient."* Avis Pumphrey. Canadian Nurse 47, 1(Jan. 1951): 30-32.

**1677. Purdy, Phyllis M.** *Growth and Movement in Adolescent Girls.* Phyllis M. Purdy. Toronto: University of Toronto, 1955.
   Thesis (M.S.W.)--University of Toronto, 1955.

**1678. Putman, J.H.** *"Shortening the Elementary School Course."* J.H. Putman. Queen's Quarterly 27, 4(Apr.-June 1920): 398-408.

**1679. Quance, Francis Melville** *The Present Situation in Elementary Education.* Francis Melville Quance. Edmonton: University of Alberta, 1915.
   Thesis (M.A.)--University of Alberta, 1915.

**1680. Quarrington, Mary Ormiston Lewis** *Developmental Aspects of Sociometric Ratings of Nursery School Children.* Mary Ormiston Lewis Quarrington. Toronto: University of Toronto, 1953.
   Thesis (M.A.)--University of Toronto, 1953.

**1681. Quarter, Jack** *"The Teacher's Role in the Classroom: the Primary Source of Teacher Frustration and Discontent."* Jack Quarter. In Must Schools Fail?: the Growing Debate in Canadian Education, pp. 47-68. Edited by Niall Byrne and Jack Quarter.

**1682. Quiggan, Betty** *"Run Mother Run, See Mother Run."* Betty Quiggan. Canadian Welfare 43, 3(May-June 1967): 4-6.

**1683. Quinlan, Patrick Joseph** *The Evaluation of Transition Classes for Low-achievers.* Patrick Joseph Quinlan. Edmonton: University of Alberta, 1964.
   Thesis (M.Ed.)--University of Alberta, 1964.

**1684. Quinn, Carol** *"Tom: a Patient with Schizophrenia."* Carol Quinn. Canadian Nurse 60, 2(Feb. 1964): 129-132.

**1685. Rabinovitch, M. Sam** *"Sequelae of Prematurity: Psychological Test Findings."* M. Sam Rabinovitch, R. Bibace and H. Caplan. Canadian Medical Association Journal/Journal de l'Association medicale canadienne 84, 15(Apr. 15, 1961): 822-824.

**1686. Rabinowitch, Dorothy** *The Effects of Success and Failure on Learning.* Dorothy Rabinowitch. Toronto: University of Toronto, 1936.
   Thesis (M.A.)--University of Toronto, 1936.
   No bibliography.

**1687. Radecki, Henry** *Ethnic Organizational Dynamics: the Polish Group in Canada.* Henry Radecki. Waterloo, Ont: Wilfrid Laurier University Press, c1979.

**1688. Radecki, Henry** *"How Relevant are the Polish Part-time Schools?"* Henry Radecki. Toronto: Canadian-Polish Research Institute, 1974. In Past and Present: Selected Topics on the Polish Group in Canada, pp. 61-72. Edited by Benedykt Heydenkorn.

**1689. Radecki, Henry** *A Member of a Distinguished Family: the Polish Group in Canada.* Henry Radecki, with Benedykt Heydenkorn. Toronto: McClelland and Stewart, c1976.

**1690. Rae-Grant, Quentin** *Children in Canada [sic] Residential Care.* Quentin Rae-Grant and Patricia J. Moffat. [Toronto: Leonard Crainford for Canadian Mental Health Association, 1971].

**1691. Rafferty, Pat** *An Exploratory Study of Kindergarten and Elementary School Age Children's Verbal Responses to Paintings.* Pat Rafferty. Edmonton: University of Alberta, 1971.
   Thesis (M.Ed.)--University of Alberta, 1971.

**1692. Rainsberry, F.B.** *Children and TV: the Moral Concern.* F.B. Rainsberry. [S.l.]: Canadian Broadcasting Corporation, [1965].

**1693. Ramirez, Bruno** *"French Canadian Immigrants in the New England Cotton Industry: a Socioeconomic Profile."* Bruno Ramirez. Labour/Le Travailleur 11(Spring 1983): 125-142.

**1694. Ramu, G.N.** *"The Family and Marriage in Canada."* G.N. Ramu. Toronto: MacMillan Co. of Canada Ltd., c1976. In Introduction to Canadian Society: Sociological Analysis, pp. 295-348. Edited by G.N. Ramu and Stuart D. Johnson.

**1695. Rancier, Gordon James** *Ten Case Studies of High School Dropouts in the Acadia School Division.* Gordon James Rancier. Edmonton: University of Alberta, 1962.
Thesis (M.Ed.)--University of Alberta, 1962.

**1696. Randall, Reuben** *"Memoirs of the Early 1900's."* Reuben Randall. Okanagan Historical Society Report 33(1969): 106-112.

**1697. Ratte, Marie Christine** *"Rescue Work for Girls."* Marie Christine Ratte. Toronto: Social Services Council of Canada, c1914. In Social Services Congress-Ottawa-1914: Report of Addresses and Proceedings, pp. 222-224.

**1698. Ravenhill, Alice** *"The Health of Public School Children in British Columbia."* Alice Ravenhill. Child 4, 9(June 1914): 697-699.

**1699. Rawson, Hildred I.** *Piaget's Conception of Logical Development and Its Relation to Comprehension in Reading.* Hildred I. Rawson. Edmonton: University of Alberta, 1965.
Thesis (M.Ed.)--University of Alberta, 1965.

**1700. Ray, G.R.** *"Open Letters Addressed to Maria by a Friend: No. 3, Parents and Children."* Edited by G.R. Ray. Beaver 4, 2(Nov. 1923): 56-57.

**1701. Read, Frederick** *"The Legal Position of the Child of Unmarried Parents."* Frederick Read. Canadian Bar Review 9, 9 and 10(Nov. and Dec. 1931): 609-618 and 729-736.

**1702. Read, John H.** *"Preventive Pediatrics in Medical Education: 1. Child Health and the Organization of Preventive Pediatrics in Canada."* John H. Read. Canadian Medical Association Journal/Journal de l'Association medicale canadienne 88, 14(Apr. 6, 1963): 721-726.

**1703. Read, Stanley E.** *Tommy Bradshaw: the Ardent Angler-Artist.* Stanley E. Bradshaw. Vancouver: University of British Columbia Press, 1977.

**1704. Reagh, Fred** *"The Need for a Comprehensive Family Court System."* Fred Reagh. University of British Columbia Law Review 5, 1(June 1970): 13-42.

**1705. Reckless, John B.** *"Enforced Outpatient Treatment of Advantaged Pseudosociopathic Neurotically Disturbed Young Women."* John B. Reckless. Canadian Psychiatric Association Journal/Revue de l'Association canadienne de psychiatrie 15, 4(Aug. 1970): 335-345.

**1706. Reed, Howard** *"Squint or Strabismus."* Howard Reed. Canadian Nurse 55, 1(Jan. 1959): 16-20.

**1707. Regan, Helen Gail** *An Action Theory Analysis of Some Classroom Social Processes and Learning Outcomes.* Helen Gail Regan. Toronto: University of Toronto, 1969.
Thesis (M.A.)--University of Toronto, 1969.

**1708. Reid, Dennis** *Edwin Holgate.* Dennis Reid. Ottawa: National Gallery of Canada, 1976.

**1709. Reid, John** *"Political Education Through Youth Programs."* John Reid. Halifax: Institute for Research on Public Policy, 1988. In Political Education in Canada, pp. 141-145. Edited by Jon H. Pammett and Jean-Luc Pepin.

**1710. Reid, Timothy E.** *"Automation and Its Impact on Education."* Timothy E. Reid. Canadian Education and Research Digest 5, 3(Sept. 1965): 190-200.

**1711. Reimer, Abram John** *First Grade Mathematics Achievement and Conservation.* Abram John Reimer. Edmonton: University of Alberta, 1968.
Thesis (M.Ed.)--University of Alberta, 1968.

**1712. Renne, Thomas** *The Effect of Verbalizers on the Achievement of Non-verbalizers in an Enquiring Classroom.* Thomas Renne. Edmonton: University of Alberta, 1970.
Thesis (M.Ed.)--University of Alberta, 1970.

**1713. Rhodes, A.J.** *"Recent Advances in Poliomyelitis and Other Virus Diseases."* A.J. Rhodes. Canadian Nurse 51, 7(July 1955): 527-532.

**1714. Rice, Marnie E.** *Modeling and Information: Effects on Children's Performance of Altruistic, Neutral and Aggressive Behaviours.* Marnie Elizabeth McKee Rice. Toronto: University of Toronto, 1971.
Thesis (M.A.)--University of Toronto, 1971.

**1715. Richardson, Theresa R.** *The Century of the Child: the Mental Hygiene Movement and Social Policy in the United States and Canada.* Theresa Marianne Rupke Richardson. Vancouver: University of British Columbia, 1987. (CTM no. 419911)
Thesis (Ph.D.)--University of British Columbia, 1987.

**1716. Richardson, Theresa R.** *The Century of the Child: the Mental Hygiene Movement and Social Policy in the United States and Canada.* Theresa R. Richardson. Albany, N.Y.: State University of New York Press, 1989.

**1717. Richer, Stephen** *"Equality to Benefit from Schooling: the Issue of Educational Opportunity."* Stephen Richer and Dennis Forcese, ed. 2nd. Scarborough, Ont.: Prentice-Hall Canada, 1988. In Social Issues: Sociological Views of Canada, pp. 262-286. Edited by Dennis Forcese and Stephen Richer.
Also in Social Issues: Sociological Views of Canada, 1st edition, 1982, pp. 336-374.

**1718. Richer, Stephen** *Programme Grouping and Educational Plans: a Study of Canadian High School Students.* Stephen Irwin Richer. Baltimore: Johns Hopkins University, 1968.
Thesis (Ph.D.)--Johns Hopkins University, 1968.

**1719. Richman, Alex** *Psychiatric Care in Canada: Extent and Results.* Alex Richman. [Ottawa: R. Duhamel, Queen's Printer, 1966].

**1720. Ricou, Laurence** *Everyday Magic: Child Languages in Canadian Literature.* Laurie Ricou. Vancouver: University of British Columbia Press, 1987.

**1721. Riddell, R.A.** *"The Special Needs of the Gifted."* R.A. Riddell. Ottawa: Mutual Press, 1958. In Addresses and Proceedings of the Canadian Conference on Education, Ottawa, February 16-20, 1958, pp. 433-437. Edited by George G. Croskery and Gerald Nason.

**1722. Rideout, Marjorie** *"Care of the Infant With Pneumonia."* Marjorie Rideout. Canadian Nurse 45, 1(Jan. 1949): 17-19.

**1723. Rifka, Ruth** *"Maureen O'Hara with Pimples."* Ruth Rifka. Branching Out 4, 1(Mar.-Apr. 1977): 20-22.

**1724. Riggs, D. Elaine** *Students and Drug Use: a Study of Personality Characteristics and Extent of Drug Using Behaviour.* D. Elaine Riggs. Edmonton: University of Alberta, 1971.
Thesis (M.Ed.)--University of Alberta, 1971.

**1725. Rivera, Margo** *"Multiple Personality: an Outcome of Child Abuse."* Margo Rivera. Canadian Woman Studies/Cahiers de la femme 8, 4(Winter 1987): 18-23.

**1726. Robbins, John E.** *Dependency of Youth.* J.E. Robbins [and] Dominion Bureau of Statistics. Ottawa: King's Printer, 1942.

**1727. Robbins, John E.** *Youth Figured Out: a Statistical Study of Canadian Youth.* John E. Robbins. Ottawa: Canadian Youth Commission, [1947]

**1728. Roberts, Barbara Ann** *"Daughters of the Empire and Mothers of the Race: Caroline Chisholm and Female Emigration in the British Empire."* Barbara Roberts. Atlantis 1, 1(Fall 1975): 106-127.

**1729. Roberts, Dennis M.** *"An Empirical Investigation of Ferguson's Theory of Human Abilities."* Dennis W. Roberts, F.J. King and Russell P. Kropp. Canadian Journal of Psychology/Revue canadienne de psychologie 23, 4(Aug. 1969): 254-267.

**1730. Roberts, Percy** *"Child Immigration: Barnardo's Contribution to Ontario."* Percy Roberts. In Proceedings and Papers Fifth Annual Canadian Conference on Child Welfare 1925, pp. 175-195.

**1731. Roberts, W.H.** *"The Reconstruction of the Adolescent Period of Our Canadian Girl."* W.H. Roberts. Public Health Journal 10, 11(Nov. 1919): 489-496.

**1732. Robertson, Caroline** *"Nursing an Adolescent With Seizures."* Caroline Robertson and Patricia Murray. Canadian Nurse 61, 3(Mar. 1965): 177-184.

**1733. Robertson, Elizabeth Chant** *"Diarrhoea and Typhoid Infections."* Elizabeth Chant Robertson. Canadian Public Health Journal 27, 1(Jan. 1936): 37-41

**1734. Robertson, Elizabeth Chant** *Today's Child: a Modern Guide to Baby Care and Child Training.* Elizabeth Chant Robertson and Margaret I. Wood. Toronto: Pagurian Press, 1971.

**1735. Robertson, Esther J.** *"Mental Health and Maternity Care."* Esther J. Robertson. Canadian Nurse 56, 3(Mar. 1960): 219-223.

**1736. Robertson, Ina V.** *The Influence of the Peer Group on the Educational Attitudes of Teenage Girls.* Ina V. Robertson. Toronto: University of Toronto, 1961.
Thesis (M.A.)--University of Toronto, 1961.

**1737. Robertson, Irene M.** *"Get Down to Brass Tacks, Prevent Home Accidents."* Irene M. Robertson. Canadian Nurse 55, 12(Dec. 1959): 1097-1100.

**1738. Robertson, Jean Elizabeth** *An Investigation of Pupil Understanding of Connectives in Reading.* Jean Elizabeth Robertson. Edmonton: University of Alberta, 1966.
Thesis (Ph.D.)--University of Alberta, 1966.

**1739. Robertson, Linda** *"Children in Hospital."* Linda Robertson. Canadian Nurse 41, 6(June 1945): 441-443.

**1740. Robinson, H. Lukin** *"Rates of Stillbirth in Canada."* H. Lukin Robinson. Canadian Journal of Public Health 38, 4(Apr. 1947): 168-181.

**1741. Robinson, H. Lukin** *"Symposium on Population: 3. Mortality Trends and Public Health in Canada."* H. Lukin Robinson. Canadian Journal of Public Health 39, 2(Feb. 1948): 60-70.

**1742. Robinson, Marita Irenee Ensio** *Celebration: 75 Years of Challenge and Change.* Marita Irenee Ensio Robinson. Toronto: Grosvenor House, 1984.

**1743. Robson, Bonnie** *"Children of Parental Divorce: Vulnerable or Invulnerable."* B.E. Robson. Canadian Journal of Psychiatry/Revue canadienne de psychiatrie 30, 4(June 1985): 239.

**1744. Rock, Ursula** *Instruction in the Use of Self-guiding Speech and the Performance of the Five-year-old Child.* Ursula Rock. Calgary: University of Calgary, 1971.
Thesis (M.Ed.)--University of Calgary, 1971.

**1745. Rodenburg, Martin** *"Child Murder by a Depressed Mother: a Case Report."* Martin Rodenburg. Canadian Psychiatric Association Journal/Revue de l'Association canadienne de psychiatrie 16, 1(Feb. 1971): 49-53.

**1746. Rodenburg, Martin** *"Child Murder by Depressed Parents."* Martin Rodenburg. Canadian Psychiatric Association Journal/Revue de l'Association canadienne de psychiatrie 16, 1(Feb. 1971): 41-48.

**1747. Rodger, Andrew** *"Youth and Sport."* Andrew Rodger. Archivist/Archiviste 12, 3(May-June 1985): 10-11.

**1748. Rodgers, Denis Cyril** *Reading Retardation, Auditory Memory, and Motivation, in Grade 4, 5, and 6 Boys.* Denis Cyril Rodgers. Edmonton: University of Alberta, 1966.
Thesis (M.Ed.)--University of Alberta, 1966.

**1749. Roe, Michael** *Drugs and the Schools: Report of a Seminar Convened by the Canadian Education Association, June 15 and 16, 1970, Royal York Hotel, Toronto.* Michael Roe. Toronto: Canadian Education Association, [1970].

**1750. Rogers, Kenneth H.** *"A Comparison of "Good" and "Bad" Foster Homes."* Kenneth H. Rogers. Child and Family Welfare 10, 2(July 1934): 14-21.

**1751. Rogers, Kenneth H.** *"Reducing Juvenile Delinquency."* Kenneth H. Rogers. Canadian Nurse 40, 11(Nov. 1944): 839-841.

**1752. Rogers, Kenneth H.** *"To Neutralize the Swing to Lawlessness."* Kenneth H. Rogers. Canadian Welfare 21, 7(Jan. 1946): 26-28.

**1753. Rogers, Walter B.** *The Rural Church, the Farm Family.* Walter B. Rogers and George E. Buckmire. Edmonton: Department of Agriculture Economics, University of Alberta, 1967.

**1754. Roland Charles G.** *Clarence Hincks: Mental Health Crusader.* Charles G. Roland. Toronto: Dundurn Press, 1990.

**1755. Rooke, Patricia T.** *"The 'Child-institutionalized' in Canada, Britain and the U.S.A.: a Trans-Atlantic Perspective."* Patricia T. Rooke. Journal of Educational Thought 11, 2(Aug. 1977): 156-171.

**1756. Rooke, Patricia T.** *"Child Welfare in English Canada, 1920-1948."* Patricia T. Rooke and R.L. Schnell. Social Service Review 55, 3(Sept. 1981): 484-506.

**1757. Rooke, Patricia T.** *"Childhood and Charity in 19th Century British North America."* Patricia T. Rooke and R.L. Schnell. Histoire sociale/Social History 15, 29(May 1982): 157-179.

**1758. Rooke, Patricia T.** *Discarding the Asylum: From Child Rescue to the Welfare State in English Canada (1800-1950).* Patricia T. Rooke and R.L. Schnell. Lanham: University Press of America Inc., 1983.

**1759. Rooke, Patricia T.** *"Imperial Philanthropy and Colonial Response: British Juvenile Emigration to Canada, 1896-1930."* Patricia T. Rooke and R.L. Schnell. Historian 46, 1(Nov. 1983): 56-77.

**1760. Rooke, Patricia T.** *"The "King's Children" in English Canada: a Psychohistorical Study of Abandonment, Rejection and Colonial Response (1869-1930)."* Patricia T. Rooke and R.L. Schnell. Journal of Psychohistory 8, 4(Spring 1981): 387-420.

**1761. Rooke, Patricia T.** *""Making the Way More Comfortable": Charlotte Whitton's Child Welfare Career, 1920-48."* Patricia T. Rooke and R.L. Schnell. Journal of Canadian Studies/Revue d'etudes canadiennes 17, 4(Winter 1982-1983): 33-45.

**1762. Rooke, Patricia T.** *No Bleeding Heart: Charlotte Whitton, a Feminist on the Right.* P.T. Rooke and R.L. Schnell. Vancouver: University of British Columbia Press, 1987.

**1763. Rooke, Patricia T.** *"The Rise and Decline of British North American Protestant Orphans' Homes as Woman's Domain, 1850-1930."* Patricia T. Rooke and R.L. Schnell. Atlantis 7, 2(Spring 1982): 21-35.

**1764. Rooke, Patricia T., ed.** *Studies in Childhood History: a Canadian Perspective.* Patricia T. Rooke and R.L. Schnell, eds. Calgary: Detselig Enterprises Ltd., c1982.

**1765. Rorke, Robert F.** *"Infant Feeding."* Robert F. Rorke. Canadian Nurse 12, 2(Feb. 1916): 67-70.

**1766. Rose, Albert** *"The Jewish Community in Canada."* Albert Rose. Canadian Welfare 30, 7(Feb. 1955): 31-35.

**1767. Rose, C.D.** *"Modern Trends in the Education of Children With Impaired Hearing."* C.D. Rose. Canadian Journal of Public Health 59, 9(Sept. 1968): 345-348.

**1768. Rosen, Theodora Nadine** *A Comparison of the Figural-cognitive Abilities of Eleven and Twelve Year Old Average and Disabled Readers.* Theodora Nadine Rosen. Toronto: University of Toronto, 1970.
Thesis (M.A.)–University of Toronto, 1970.

**1769. Rosenberg, Louis** *Canada's Jewish Community: a Brief Survey of its History, Growth and Characteristics.* Louis Rosenberg. Montreal: Canadian Jewish Congress, [1954].

**1770. Ross, Alan** *"Children in Hospital."* Alan Ross. Canadian Welfare 33, 1(May 1957): 25-29.

**1771. Ross, Alexander** *The Booming Fifties 1950-1960.* Alexander Ross. Toronto: Natural Science of Canada Ltd., 1977.

**1772. Ross, Betty** *Activity Preferences of Adolescent Girls.* Betty Ross. Toronto: University of Toronto, 1940.
Thesis (M.A.)–University of Toronto, 1940.

**1773. Ross, David P.** *The Working Poor: Wage Earners and the Failure of Income Security Policies.* David P. Ross. Toronto: James Lorimer and Company, 1981.

**1774. Ross, Douglas Heber** *A Comparative Study of Intra-class Grouping and Non-grouping in Grade Seven Achievement.* Douglas Heber Ross. Edmonton: University of Alberta, 1965.
Thesis (M.Ed.)–University of Alberta, 1965.

**1775. Ross, Murray G.** *The Y.M.C.A. in Canada: the Chronicle of a Century.* Murray G. Ross. Toronto: Ryerson Press, c1951.

**1776. Ross, Norman L.** *The Interpersonal Relationships of Troubled School Children.* Norman L. Ross. Toronto: University of Toronto, 1961.
Thesis (M.S.W.)–University of Toronto, 1961.

**1777. Routley, F.W.** *"The Responsibility of the Voluntary Health Agency to the Mother and Child in the Outpost."* F.W. Routley. In Proceedings and Papers Fifth Annual Canadian Conference on Child Welfare 1925, pp. 92-94.

**1778. Royer, Albert** *"Cerebral Palsy."* Albert Royer. Canadian Nurse 58, 11(Nov. 1962): 1012-1014.

**1779. Royer, Albert** *"Problems in Infant Feeding."* Albert Royer. Canadian Nurse 58, 11(Nov. 1962): 991-993.

**1780. Royer, B. Franklin** *"Child Welfare."* B. Franklin Royer. Public Health Journal 12, 7(July 1921): 289-293.

**1781. Rudominer, Rayna** *Self-reliance, Initiative, and Mastery of Montessori and Non-Montessori Trained Preschool Children.* Rayna Rudominer. Toronto: University of Toronto, 1970.
Thesis (M.A.)–University of Toronto, 1970.

1782. Ruggles, Richard I. "Hospital Boys of the Bay." Richard I. Ruggles. Beaver 308, 2(Autumn 1977): 4-11.

1783. Russell, David H. Implications of Research for Canadian Classroom Practices. David H. Russell. Toronto: W.J. Gage and Company Limited, 1953.

1784. Russell, H. Howard "Gifted Students in Junior High School." H. Howard Russell. Toronto: W.J. Gage and Co., 1960. In Education: a Collection of Essays on Canadian Education, v.3, 1958-1960, pp. 49-53.

1785. Rusynyk, Constance Elizabeth Simple Classification and Its Relation to Free Recall Tasks in Young Children. Constance Elizabeth Rusynyk. Toronto: University of Toronto, 1969. Thesis (M.A.)--University of Toronto, 1969.

1786. Rutman, Leonard "Importation of British Waifs into Canada 1868 to 1916." Leonard Rutman. Child Welfare 52, 2(Mar. 1973): 158-166.

1787. Rutman, Leonard "J.J. Kelso and the Development of Social Welfare." Leonard Rutman. Toronto: Garamond Press, 1987. In The Benevolent State: the Growth of Welfare in Canada, pp. 68-76. Edited by Allan Moscovitch and Jim Albert.

1788. Ruzicka, Robert L. A Study of Some Physiologic Responses of Children to Their Initial Dental Experience. Robert L. Ruzicka. Edmonton: University of Alberta, 1971. Thesis (M.Sc.)--University of Alberta, 1971.

1789. Ryan, Thomas. J. "Poverty and Early Education in Canada." Thomas J. Ryan. Interchange 2, 2(1971): 1-11.

1790. Sabey, Ralph Harris A Comparison of the Achievement of Grade 9 Pupils in Various School Organizations. Ralph Harris Sabey. Edmonton: University of Alberta, 1966. Thesis (M.Ed.)--University of Alberta, 1966.

1791. Saint-Denis, Henri "French-Canadian Ideals in Education." Henri Saint-Denis. Toronto: Ryerson Press, 1940. In French Canadian Backgrounds: a Symposium, pp. 21-40.

1792. Salama, Abd Elaziz A. "Multiple Personality: a Case Study." Abd Elaziz A. Salama. Canadian Journal of Psychiatry/Revue canadienne de psychiatrie 25, 7(Nov. 1980): 569-572.

1793. Salisbury, D.E. "The Use of Blood Test Evidence in Paternity Suits: a Scientific and Legal Analysis." D.E. Salisbury. University of Toronto Faculty of Law Review 30(Aug. 1972): 47-74.

1794. Sanche, Robert P. Self Concept and Beliefs of Educationally Retarded Youth. Robert Paul Sanche. Edmonton: University of Alberta, 1968. Thesis (M.Ed.)--University of Alberta, 1968.

1795. Sanders, Douglas Esmond Family Law and Native People. Douglas Esmond Sanders. Ottawa: Law Reform Commission of Canada, 1975.

1796. Sandiford, Peter "The School Program and Sex Education." Peter Sandiford. Public Health Journal 13, 2(Feb. 1922): 59-62.

1797. Sandiford, Peter "Subnormal Intelligence as an Educational Problem." Peter Sandiford. Canadian Journal of Mental Hygiene 1, 1(Apr. 1919): 65-69.

1798. Sargeant, Sybil Ulrica Educational Achievement within the Poverty Matrix. Sybil Ulrica Sargeant. Edmonton: University of Alberta, 1971. Thesis (M.Ed.)--University of Alberta, 1971.

1799. Saucier, Jean-Francois Psychiatric Problems of Children Born from Biethnic Marriages. Jean-Francois Saucier. Montreal: Allan Memorial Institute, 1967.

1800. Saunders, S.A. "Educating the Blind in Canada." S.A. Saunders. Toronto: W.J. Gage and Co., 1960. In Education: a Collection of Essays on Canadian Education, v.3, 1958-1960, pp. 127-131.

1801. Saunders, S.A. "Nature and Extent of Unemployment in Canada." S.A. Saunders. Toronto: MacMillan of Canada, 1939. In Canada's Unemployment Problem, pp. 1-58. Edited by L. Richter.

1802. Savage, Candace Our Nell: a Scrapbook Biography of Nellie L. McClung. Candace Savage. Saskatoon: Western Producer Prairie Books, c1979.

1803. Savage, Leslie A.E. Infanticide, Illegitimacy and the Origins and Evolution of the Role of the Misericordia Sisters, Montreal and Edmonton 1848-1906: a Study in Child Rescue and Female Reform. Leslie A.E. Savage. Edmonton: University of Alberta, 1982. (CTM no. 60379) Thesis (M.Ed.)--University of Alberta, 1982.

**1804. Scagliola, Marie Louise** *Pupil Interests and French Text Content.* Marie Louise Scagliola. Edmonton: University of Alberta, 1971.
Thesis (M.Ed.)–University of Alberta, 1971.

**1805. Scaldwell, William Arnold** *A Study of Personality Concepts in Children with Reading Problems, Using the Q-technique.* William Arnold Scaldwell. Toronto: University of Toronto, 1965.
Thesis (M.Ed.)–University of Toronto, 1965.

**1806. Scarfe, Neville** *"Understanding Children's Play."* Neville Scarfe. Journal of Education of the Faculty of Education, Vancouver 12(Jan. 1966): 21-22.

**1807. Schlesinger, Benjamin** *"Adoption Fees: Sales or Service?"* Benjamin Schlesinger. Canadian Welfare 37, 6(Nov. 1961): 265-267.

**1808. Schlesinger, Benjamin** *The Multi-problem Family: a Review and Annotated Bibliography.* Benjamin Schlesinger. Toronto: University of Toronto Press, 1965.

**1809. Schlesinger, Benjamin** *"The One-parent Family in Perspective."* Benjamin Schlesinger. Updated ed. [Toronto]: University of Toronto Press, c1970. In The One-Parent Family: Perspectives and Annotated Bibliography, pp. 3-12. Edited by Benjamin Schlesinger and Florence Strakhovsky.

**1810. Schlesinger, Benjamin** *Poverty in Canada and the United States: Overview and Annotated Bibliography.* Benjamin Schlesinger. Toronto: University of Toronto Press, 1966.

**1811. Schlesinger, Benjamin, ed.** *The Multi-problem Family: a Review and Annotated Bibliography.* Benjamin Schlesinger and Florence Strakhovsky, eds. 3rd ed. Toronto: University of Toronto Press, c1970.

**1812. Schlosser, M. Joyce** *"Third Party Child-centred Disputes: Parental Rights v. Best Interest of the Child."* M. Joyce Schlosser. Alberta Law Review 22, 3(1984): 394-416.

**1813. Schmeiser, Douglas A.** *Civil Liberties in Canada.* D.A. Schmeiser. London: Oxford University Press, c1964.

**1814. Schmidt, Herminio** *"Die Deutschen Sonnabendschulen in Kanada = The Saturday Morning German Schools After World War II in Canada: Entwick und Prognose = Development and Prognosis."* Herminio Schmidt. Toronto: Historical

Society of Mecklenburg Upper Canada Inc., 1981. German Canadian Yearbook/Deutschkanadisches Jahrbuch, v.6, pp. 183-198. Edited by Hartmut Froeschle.

**1815. Schnee, Bernice** *"A Child With Phenylketonuria."* Bernice Schnee. Canadian Nurse 60, 7(July 1964): 665-667.

**1816. Schnell, R.L.** *"A Children's Bureau for Canada: the Origins of the Canadian Council on Child Welfare, 1913-1921."* R.L. Schnell. Toronto: Garamond Press, 1987. In The Benevolent State: the Growth of Welfare in Canada, pp. 95-110. Edited by Allan Moscovitch and Jim Albert.

**1817. Schnell, R.L.** *"History of Childhood as History of Education: a Review of Approaches and Sources."* R.L. Schnell. Alberta Journal of Educational Research 25, 3(Sept. 1979): 192-203.

**1818. Schnell, R.L.** *"The Institutional Society: Childhood, Family and Schooling."* R.L. Schnell and Patricia T. Rooke. Winnipeg: University of Manitoba, 1981. In Approaches to Educational History, pp. 113-130. Edited by David C. Jones, Nancy M. Sheehan, Robert M. Stamp and Neil G. McDonald.

**1819. Schoemperlen, Diane** *Double Exposures.* Diane Schoemperlen. Toronto: Coach House Press, c1984.

**1820. Scholes, Alex G.** *Education for Empire Settlement: a Study of Juvenile Migration.* Alex G. Scholes. London, Eng.: Longmans Green, 1932.
Originally presented as a Ph.D. dissertation, University of Edinburgh.

**1821. Schreiber, J.R.G.** *"Comments Upon Indictable Offences in the Juvenile Delinquents Act."* J.R.G. Schreiber. Canadian Bar Review 35, 9(Nov. 1957): 1073-1085.

**1822. Schulman, Perry D.** *"Confessions by Juveniles."* Perry D. Schulman. Manitoba Law School Journal 1, 3(1964-65): 291-296.

**1823. Schuman, Elsie** *"Preventing Infancy Ailments."* Elsie Schuman. Canadian Nurse 45, 7(July 1949): 501-503.

**1824. Scott, Francis Reginald** *"Areas of Conflict in the Field of Public Law and Policy."* F.R. Scott. Toronto: University of Toronto Press, 1960. In Canadian Dualism: Studies of French-English Relations, pp. 81-105. Edited by Mason Wade.

**1825. Scott, Joseph W.** *"A Perspective on Middle-class Delinquency."* Joseph W. Scott and Edmund W. Vaz. Canadian Journal of Economics and Political Science 29, 3(Aug. 1963): 324-335.

**1826. Scott, Lorraine M.** *A Follow-up Study of the Experiences after Discharge of a Number of Girls Who Have Lived in Warrendale, a Residential Treatment Centre.* Lorraine M. Scott. Toronto: University of Toronto, 1959.
Thesis (M.S.W.)--University of Toronto, 1959.

**1827. Scott, R.L.** *"The Rights of the Child."* R.L. Scott. Toronto: Social Services Council of Canada, c1914. In Social Service Congress-Ottawa-1914: Report of Addresses and Proceedings, pp. 94-97.

**1828. Scott, W.C.M.** *"Differences Between the Playroom Used in Child Psychiatric Treatment and in Child Analysis."* W.C.M. Scott. Canadian Psychiatric Association Journal/Revue de l'Association canadienne de psychiatrie 6, 5(Oct. 1961): 281-285.

**1829. Scott, W.L.** *The Canadian Juvenile Delinquent Act: an Address Before the American Prison Association.* W.L. Scott. Ottawa: [s.n.], 1914.

**1830. Scott, W.L.** *The Dominion Acts Relating to Neglected and Delinquent Children.* W.L. Scott. Ottawa: [s.n.], 1921.

**1831. Scott, W.L.** *An Explanation of the Need for a Dominion Act Dealing With Juvenile Delinquency.* W.L. Scott. Toronto: Ontario Department of the Provincial Secretary, [1908].

**1832. Scott, W.L.** *Suggested Amendments to the Juvenile Delinquents Act.* W.L. Scott. Ottawa: [s.n.], 1922.

**1833. Scriver, Jessie Boyd** *"The Use of Banana as a Food for Young Children."* Jessie Boyd Scriver and S.G. Ross. Canadian Nurse 27, 7(July 1931): 352-354.

**1834. Seeley, John R.** *"Family and Socialization in an Upper Class Community."* John R. Seeley, R. Alexander Sim and Elizabeth W. Loosley. In Crestwood Heights: a North American Suburb, pp. 159-223. By John R. Seeley, R. Alexander Sim and Elizabeth W. Loosley.
Reprinted in abridged form in Canadian Society: Sociological Perspectives, 1st ed., 1961, pp. 117-168, 2nd ed., 1964, pp. 103-134, 3rd ed., 1968, pp. 109-139 and abr. 3rd ed., 1971, pp. 84-114. Edited by Bernard R. Blishen, Frank E. Jones, Kasper D. Naegele and John Porter.

**1835. Seelye, Margaret** *Spatial Representation in Children's Drawings.* Margaret Seelye. Edmonton: University of Alberta, 1971.
Thesis (M.Ed.)--University of Alberta, 1971.

**1836. Segal, John J.** *"Effects of Paternal Exposure to Prolonged Stress in the Mental Health of the Spouse and Children: Families of Canadian Army Servicemen of the Japanese World War II Camp."* John J. Segal. Canadian Psychiatric Association Journal/Revue de l'Association canadienne de psychiatrie 21, 3(Apr. 1976): 169-172.

**1837. Selby, Mary E.** *Emotional and Behavioral Disturbances of Adopted Children.* Mary E. Selby. Toronto: University of Toronto, 1963.
Thesis (M.S.W.)--University of Toronto, 1963.

**1838. Sellers, A. Hardisty** *"Accidents and the Public Health: With Particular Reference to Automobile Accidents."* A. Hardisty Sellers. Canadian Public Health Journal 27, 3(Mar. 1936): 125-137.

**1839. Sellers, A. Hardisty** *"Report of the Association's Work During 1937: Report of the Subcommittee on Stillbirth Registration and Certification."* (Committee on the Certification of Causes of Death) H.A. Ansley, Eugene Gagnon, A.P. Paget, Donald Mackie, Paul Parot, Ed Picton and A. H. Sellers, chairman. Canadian Public Health Journal 29, 11(Nov. 1938): 558-570.

**1840. Sellers, A. Hardisty** *"Report of the Association's Work During 1938-1939: Report of the Subcommittee on Stillbirth Registration and Certification."* A.H. Sellers. Canadian Public Health Journal 30, 9(Sept. 1939): 457-465.

**1841. Semple, Neil** *""The Nurture and Admonition of the Lord": Nineteenth Century Canadian Methodism's Response to Childhood."* Neil Semple. Histoire sociale/Social History 14, 27(May 1981): 157-175.

**1842. Sen, Joya** *Unemployment of Youth: the Importance of Education for Their Adjustment in the Canadian Labor Market.* Joya Sen. Toronto: Ontario Institute for Studies in Education, 1982.

**1843. Sen, Joya** *Youth Unemployment: the Importance of Education in Canadian Labour Market Adjustment.* Joyasree Sen. Toronto: University of Toronto, 1981.
Thesis (M.A.)--University of Toronto, 1981.

**1844. Shamsie, S. Jalal** *"Disturbed Adolescents: a Suggested Community Approach to Treatment."* S. Jalal Shamsie and E. Ellick. Canadian Psychiatric Association Journal/Revue de l'Association canadienne de psychiatrie 10, 5(Oct. 1965): 399-404.

**1845. Shamsie, S. Jalal** *"Reading Difficulties as a Cause of Behaviour Problems in Adolescence."* Jalal S. Shamsie. Canadian Psychologist/Psychologie canadienne 9, 2(Apr. 1968): 196-200.

**1846. Shanks, Connie** *"The Orphans' Odyssey."* Connie Shanks. Atlantic Advocate 80, 3(Nov. 1989): 36-38.

**1847. Sharpe, Frank T.** *"The Recidivist Group [and Discussion]."* Frank T. Sharpe. In Proceedings of Sixth Annual Canadian Conference on Child Welfare 1927, pp. 100-109.

**1848. Shaw, Margaret Mason** *Geologists and Prospectors: Tyrell, Camsell, Cross and LaBine.* Margaret Mason Shaw. Toronto: Clarke Irwin, c1958.

**1849. Shaw, Robert C.** *Boys Needing Institutional Care.* Robert C. Shaw. Toronto: University of Toronto, 1959. Thesis (M.S.W.)--University of Toronto, 1959.

**1850. Sheehan, Nancy M.** *"The IODE, the Schools and World War I."* Nancy M. Sheehan. History of Education Review 13, 1(Spring 1984): 29-44.

**1851. Sheridan, Robert** *"Exploration: Concepts Within the Child's Grasp."* Robert Sheridan. Bulletin of the Institute of Child Study 28, 1(Spring 1966): 12-16.

**1852. Sherritt, Norman Albert** *An Evaluation of the Contribution of Extra-curricular Activities to the Accomplishment of Educational Objectives.* Norman Albert Sherritt. Edmonton: University of Alberta, 1964. Thesis (M.Ed.)--University of Alberta, 1964.

**1853. Sherwood, Herbert Francis** *Children of the Land: the Story of the Macdonald Movement in Canada.* Herbert Francis Sherwood. [S.l.: s.n., 191?]. Reprinted from The Outlook, 23 April 1910.

**1854. Sherwood, Mary** *"Some Problems of Child Hygiene."* Mary Sherwood. Public Health Journal 11, 2(Feb. 1920): 54-61.

**1855. Shewell, Anne** *"In the Children's Ward."* Anne Shewell. Canadian Welfare 38, 3(May-June 1962): 108-110.

**1856. Shook, Vernon Phray** *Some Aspects of Child Care and Protection. a Comparative Study of Six Phases of Care and Protection of Children in Canada, Denmark, Greece, Italy and the United States.* Vernon Phray Shook. Vancouver: University of British Columbia, 1949. Thesis (M.S.W.)--University of British Columbia, 1949.

**1857. Shostak, Peter** *Informal Teacher Pupil Interaction and Learning of Art Concepts at the Third Grade Level.* Peter Shostak. Edmonton: University of Alberta, 1970. Thesis (M.Ed.)--University of Alberta, 1970.

**1858. Shostak, Peter** *Saturday Came But Once a Week.* Peter Shostak. Victoria: Yalenka Enterprises, 1984.

**1859. Silcox, C.E.** *The Revenge of the Cradles.* C.E. Silcox. Toronto: Ryerson Press, c1945.

**1860. Silverman, Barruch** *"Some Aspects of the Mental Hygiene of Childhood."* Barruch Silverman. Canadian Public Health Journal 20, 8(Aug. 1929): 398-406.

**1861. Silverthorne, Nelles** *"Meningitis in Childhood."* Nelles Silverthorne. Canadian Medical Association Journal 48, 3(Mar. 1943): 218-223.

**1862. Silverthorne, Nelles** *"Present Status of Whooping Cough."* Nelles Silverthorne. Canadian Medical Association Journal 75, 1(July 1, 1956): 54.

**1863. Sim, R. Alexander** *"Indian Schools for Indian Children."* R. Alex Sim. Canadian Welfare 45, 2(Mar./Apr. 1969): 11-13, 16.

**1864. Sinclair, Donald** *"Training Schools in Canada."* Donald Sinclair. Toronto: Macmillan of Canada, c1965. In Crime and Its Treatment in Canada, pp. 244-278. Edited by W.T. McGrath.

**1865. Sinclair, Marise Elaine Graham** *The Relationship Between Word Fluency and Reading Comprehension.* Marise Elaine Graham Sinclair. Edmonton: University of Alberta, 1966. Thesis (M.Ed.)--University of Alberta, 1966.

**1866. Sinclair, Robert Archibald** *The Deaf and Hard-of-hearing Child in British Columbia.* Robert Archibald Sinclair. Vancouver: University of British Columbia, 1963.
Thesis (M.A.)–University of British Columbia, 1963.

**1867. Sinclair, Samuel Bower** *First Year at School, or, Blending of Kindergarten With Public School Work: a Manual for Primary Teachers.* Samuel Bower Sinclair. Toronto: University of Toronto, 1889.
Thesis (M.A.)–University of Toronto, 1889.
Thesis published by the University of Toronto, 1892.

**1868. Slinn, Peter Easter** *Teacher Influence and Pupil Achievement in Elementary Science.* Peter Easter Slinn. Edmonton: University of Alberta, 1969.
Thesis (M.Ed.)–University of Alberta, 1969.

**1869. Sloman, Leon** *"A Psychiatric Approach to School Achievement."* Leon Sloman. McGill Journal of Education 2, 1(Spring 1967): 108-118.

**1870. Small, Gerald Albert** *An Experiment in Teaching Critical Thinking in Grade Six Social Studies.* Gerald Albert Small.
Thesis (M.Ed.)–University of Alberta, 1969.

**1871. Smart, G. Bogue** *"Juvenile Immigration."* G. Bogue Smart. In Proceedings and Papers Fourth Annual Canadian Conference on Child Welfare 1923, pp. 191-205.

**1872. Smart, Reginald G.** *"The Extent of Illicit Drug Use in Canada: a Review of Current Epidemiology."* Reginald G. Smart and Dianne Fejer. Toronto: Holt, Rinehart and Winston of Canada, [1971]. In Critical Issues in Canadian Society, pp. 508-520. Edited by Craig L. Boydell, Carl F. Grindstaff and Paul C. Whitehead.

**1873. Smart, Reginald G.** *"The Prevention of Drug Abuse by Young People: an Argument Based on the Distribution of Drug Use."* Reginald G. Smart, Paul C. Whitehead and Lucien Laforest. Toronto: Holt, Rinehart and Winston of Canada, [1971]. In Critical Issues in Canadian Society, pp. 534-540. Edited by Craig L. Boydell, Carl F. Grindstaff and Paul C. Whitehead.
Reprinted in Bulletin on Narcotics 23, 2(Apr.-June 1971): 11-15.

**1874. Smit, Eric I.** *"Reflections After Ste. Adele."* Eric I. Smit. Canadian Welfare 36, 6(Nov. 1960): 258-259.

**1875. Smith, Anne Briar** *The Development of Connotative and Denotative Meaning in Middle and Lower Class Children.* Anne Briar Smith. Edmonton: University of Alberta, 1969.
Thesis (M.Ed.)–University of Alberta, 1969.

**1876. Smith, C. Ebble White** *A Study of the Validity of Intelligence Test Items Relative to "G" as Criterion.* C. Ebble White Smith. Toronto: University of Toronto, 1935.
Thesis (D.Paed.)–University of Toronto, 1935.

**1877. Smith, Colin M.** *"Family Size, Birth Rank, and Ordinal Position in Psychiatric Illness."* Colin M. Smith and Sharon McIntyre. Canadian Psychiatric Association Journal/Revue de l'Association canadienne de psychiatrie 8, 4(Aug. 1963): 244-246.

**1878. Smith, D.D.** *"Abilities and Interests: a Factorial Study."* D.D. Smith. Canadian Journal of Psychology 12, 3(Sept. 1958): 191-201.

**1879. Smith, David Geoffrey** *Historical Perspectives on Foundations of Western Childhood.* David Geoffrey Smith. Vancouver: University of British Columbia, 1978.
Thesis (M.A.)–University of British Columbia, 1978.

**1880. Smith, Dorothy** *"Household Space and Family Organization."* Dorothy Smith. Pacific Sociological Review 14, 1(Jan. 1971): 53-78.
Reprinted in Social Space: Canadian Perspectives, pp. 62-69. Edited by D.I. Davies and Kathleen Herman.

**1881. Smith, Helen** *"Keeping Babies Well."* Helen Smith. In Canadian Conference on Charities and Correction Proceedings 1911, pp. 70-74.

**1882. Smith, Joan M.** *"Service for the Child With Defective Hearing."* Joan M. Smith. Canadian Nurse 45, 2(Feb. 1949): 105-108.

**1883. Smith, Leslie** *"Learning for Earning."* Leslie Smith. Beaver 291, 2(Autumn 1960): 39-44.

**1884. Smith, Robin N.** *"The Use of Vocational Interest Inventories in Secondary Schools."* Robin N. Smith. Education Bulletin of the Faculty and College of Education: Vancouver and Victoria 2(Mar. 1958): 83-90.

**1885. Smith, Stuart L.** *"School Refusal with Anxiety: a Review of Sixty-three Cases."* Stuart L. Smith. Canadian Psychiatric Association Journal/Revue de l'Association canadienne de psychiatrie 15, 3(June 1970): 257-264.

**1886. Smith, W.G.** *A Study in Canadian Immigration.* William George Smith. Toronto: Ryerson Press, 1920.

**1887. Snell, Blanche Edgington** *Standards of Measurement in Art for Elementary and Secondary Schools.* Blanche Edgington Snell. Toronto: University of Toronto, 1943.
Thesis (M.A.)--University of Toronto, 1943.

**1888. Snell, James G.** *""The White Life for Two": the Defence of Marriage and Sexual Morality in Canada, 1890-1914."* James G. Snell. Histoire sociale/Social History 16, 31(May 1983): 111-129.

**1889. Sneyd, Marie Laura Hill** *Reading Retardation and Psycholinguistic Skills.* Marie Laura Hill Sneyd. Toronto: University of Toronto, 1968.
Thesis (M.A.)--University of Toronto, 1968.

**1890. Solway, Sidney H.** *Blissful Devotion to the Anatomy of Love.* Sidney H. Solway. Toronto: Solway, c1966.

**1891. Sookman, Bella** *The Childhood Schizophrenic in Remission During Adolescence: Implications for the Practice and Role of Social Work.* Bella Sookman. Montreal: McGill University, 1965.
Thesis (M.S.W.)--McGill University, 1965.

**1892. Sorenson, Marlene Mae** *Self Perception of Orthopedically Handicapped Children and Normal Children.* Marlene Mae Sorenson. Edmonton: University of Alberta, 1970.
Thesis (M.Ed.)--University of Alberta, 1970.

**1893. Spears, W.C.** *"An Investigation of Different Instructional Methods on Number-concept Understanding and Arithmetic Learning."* W.C. Spears and P.C. Dodwell. Canadian Journal of Behavioural Science/Revue canadienne de sciences du comportement 2, 2(Apr. 1970): 136-147.

**1894. Spencer, John C.** *"Social Workers, the Social Services and the Juvenile Court: the Relevance for Canada of Recent Scottish Proposals."* John C. Spencer. Canadian Journal of Corrections/Revue canadienne de criminologie 9, 1(Jan. 1967): 1-10.

**1895. Spencer, John C.** *"Work With the Hard-to-reach Youth."* John C. Spencer. Canadian Welfare 36, 4(July 1960): 165-170.

**1896. Spencer, Mark Craig** *The Effect of the School Attended on the Development of Students' Study Habits and Attitudes.* Mark Craig Spencer. Edmonton: University of Alberta, 1968.
Thesis (M.Ed.)--University of Alberta, 1968.

**1897. Splane, Richard B.** *Child Welfare in Canada.* Richard B. Splane and Flora Hurst. Ottawa: Research and Statistics Division, Department of National Health and Welfare, 1959.

**1898. Splane, Richard B.** *"The Evolution and Application in Canada of Rights Relating to Motherhood and Children."* Richard B. Splane. Labour Gazette 58, 11(Nov. 1958): 1236-1240.

**1899. Splane, Richard B.** *"The Legal Effects of Adoption."* Richard B. Splane. Canadian Welfare 32, 6(Feb. 1957): 273-275.

**1900. Splane, Richard B.** *"Towards a History of Social Welfare."* Richard B. Splane. Canadian Welfare 41, 2(Mar.-Apr. 1965): 56-59.

**1901. Spohn, Peter H.** *"The Adequate Care of the Premature Infant."* Peter H. Spohn. Canadian Medical Association Journal 62, 4(Apr. 1950): 317-323.

**1902. Spragge, George W.** *Monitorial Schools in the Canadas, 1810-1845.* George W. Spragge. Toronto: University of Toronto, 1935.
Thesis (D.Paed.)--University of Toronto, 1935.

**1903. St. John, J. Bascom** *Spotlight on Canadian Education.* J. Bascom St. John. Toronto: W.J. Gage Limited, 1959.

**1904. Staebler, Edna** *Whatever Happened to Maggie: and Other People I've Known?* Edna Staebler. Toronto: McClelland and Stewart, c1983.

**1905. Stamp, Robert M.** *"Canadian High Schools in the 1920's and 1930's: the Social Challenge to the Academic Tradition."* Robert M. Stamp. Canadian Historical Association, Historical Papers/Communications historiques (1978): 76-93.

1906. **Stamp, Robert M.** *"Education and the Social and Economic Milieu: the English-Canadian Scene From the 1870's to 1914."* Robert M. Stamp. Scarborough: Prentice-Hall of Canada, c1970. In Canadian Education: a History, pp. 290-313. Edited by J. Donald Wilson, Robert M. Stamp and Louis-Philippe Audet.

1907. **Stamp, Robert M.** *"Evolving Patterns of Education: English-Canada From the 1870's to 1914."* Robert M. Stamp. Scarborough: Prentice-Hall of Canada, c1970. In Canadian Education: a History, pp. 314-336. Edited by J. Donald Wilson, Robert M. Stamp and Louis-Philippe Audet.

1908. **Stamp, Robert M.** *"Government and Education in Post-war Canada."* Robert M. Stamp. Scarborough: Prentice-Hall of Canada, c1970. In Canadian Education: a History, pp. 444-470. Edited by J. Donald Wilson, Robert M. Stamp and Louis-Philippe Audet.

1909. **Stamp, Robert M.** *"Teaching Girls Their "God Given Place in Life": the Introduction of Home Economics in the Schools."* Robert M. Stamp. Atlantis 2, 2(Spring 1977): 18-34.

1910. **Stanley, George F.G.** *"French and English in Western Canada."* George F.G. Stanley. Toronto: University of Toronto Press, 1960. In Canadian Dualism: Studies of French-English Relations, pp. 311-350. Edited by Mason Wade.

1911. **Stanley, Wilma L.** *Frictions in a Children's Institution.* Wilma L. Stanley. Toronto: University of Toronto, 1954. Thesis (M.S.W.)--University of Toronto, 1954.

1912. **Stasiuk, Eugene S.** *Remarriage as Family Reorganization, with Special Emphasis on Children.* Eugene S. Stasiuk. Toronto: University of Toronto, 1968. Thesis (M.S.W.)--University of Toronto, 1968.

1913. **Statistics Canada** *Canada's Lone Parent Families.* Statistics Canada. Ottawa: Statistics Canada, 1984.

1914. **Statistics Canada** *Schooling in Canada.* Ottawa: Statistics Canada, 1984.

1915. **Statistics Canada. Education, Science and Culture Division** *Enrolment in Elementary and Secondary Schools in Canada = Clientele scolaire aux ecoles elementaires et secondaires au Canada.* The Division. Ottawa: Information Canada, 1971/72-1977/78.

1916. **Statten, Taylor** *"Depressive Anxieties and Their Defences in Childhood."* Taylor Statten. Canadian Medical Association Journal/Journal de l'Association medicale canadienne 84, 15(Apr. 15, 1961): 824-827.

1917. **Steinson, S.W.** *"They Are the Forgotten."* S.W. Steinson. Toronto: W.J. Gage and Co., 1956. In Education: a Collection of Essays on Canadian Education, v.1, 1954-1956, pp. 69-72.

1918. **Stephen, C.R.** *"Basic Principles of Paediatric Anaesthesia."* C.R. Stephen and H.M. Slater. Canadian Medical Association Journal 60, 6(June 1949): 566-572.

1919. **Stern, Phyllis Rash** *"An Eclectic Approach to Education for the Emotionally Disturbed."* Phyllis Rash Stern. McGill Journal of Education 2, 1(Spring 1967): 119-126.

1920. **Sterrett, Joyce E.** *"Factors Related to Adolescents' Expectations of Marital Roles."* Joyce E. Sterrett and Stephan R. Bollman. Family Coordinator 19, 4(Oct. 1970): 353-356.

1921. **Steven, Edward Miller** *Medical Supervision in Schools: Being an Account of the Systems at Work in Great Britain, Canada, the United States, Germany and Switzerland.* Edward Miller Steven. London, Eng.: Balliere, Tindall & Cox, 1910.

1922. **Stevenson, Hugh A.** *"Crisis and Continuum: Public Education in the Sixties."* Hugh A. Stevenson. Scarborough: Prentice-Hall of Canada, c1970. In Canadian Education: a History, pp. 471-508. Edited by J. Donald Wilson, Robert M. Stamp and Louis-Philippe Audet.

1923. **Stevenson, Hugh A.** *"Developing Public Education in Post-war Canada to 1960."* Hugh A. Stevenson. Scarborough: Prentice-Hall of Canada, c1970. In Canadian Education: a History, pp. 386-415. Edited by J. Donald Wilson, Robert M. Stamp and Louis-Philippe Audet.

1924. **Stevenson, Margaret Theresa** *The Reading Interests of Grade Five Pupils.* Margaret Theresa Stevenson. Edmonton: University of Alberta, 1969. Thesis (M.Ed.)--University of Alberta, 1969.

1925. **Stewart, Ann** *"Schizophrenia."* Ann Stewart. Canadian Nurse 52, 2(Feb. 1956): 114-120.

**1926. Stewart, J.H.** *Young Canada Goes to Work.* J.H. Stewart. Toronto: Ryerson Press, 1946.

**1927. Stewart, John** *"Medical Inspection of Schools: Report to the Canadian Medical Association."* John Stewart. Canadian Medical Association Journal 1, 5(May 1911): 425-439.

**1928. Stewart, Margaret A.** *The Stress of Unemployment as Reflected in Parent-Child Interaction.* Margaret A. Stewart. Toronto: University of Toronto, 1963. Thesis (M.S.W.)--University of Toronto, 1963.

**1929. Stewart, R. Cameron** *"Whooping Cough."* R. Cameron Stewart. Canadian Nurse 34, 3(Mar. 1938): 124-127.

**1930. Stewart, V. Lorne** *The Development of Juvenile Justice in Canada.* V. Lorne Stewart. Philadelphia: University of Pennsylvania, Center for Studies in Criminology and Criminal Law, 1974.

**1931. Stewart, V. Lorne** *"Three and a Half Steps Toward Juvenile Justice in Canada."* V. Lorne Stewart. Interchange 8, 1-2(1977-1978): 203-209.

**1932. Stoddart, Jennifer** *""...And Things Were Going Wrong at Home.""* Jennifer Stoddart and Veronica Strong-Boag. Atlantis 1, 1(Fall 1975): 38-44.

**1933. Stogdill, C.** *"Problem Children, Their Parents and Teachers."* C. Stogdill. Canadian Public Health Journal 27, 2(Feb. 1936): 73-76.

**1934. Stone, Olive M.** *"The Importance of Children in Family Law."* Olive M. Stone. Western Ontario Law Review 6(1967): 21-38.

**1935. Storey, Arthur G.** *"The Self Image and Wish Patterns of the Underachiever."* Arthur G. Storey and Ronald B. Clark. McGill Journal of Education 3, 1(Spring 1968): 56-62.

**1936. Storie, A. Lynn** *"Legg-Perthes' Disease."* A. Lynn Storie. Canadian Nurse 60, 1(Jan. 1964): 39-41.

**1937. Stortz, Gerald J.** *"Nineteenth Century Child Immigration to Canada."* Gerald J. Stortz. Immigration History Newsletter 14, 1(May 1982): 8-9.

**1938. Stothers, C.E.** *"Some Effects of the Mirror Reading Technique in Individual Programs of Remedial Reading."* C.E. Stothers. Canadian Education and Research Digest 3, 1(Mar. 1963): 17-27.

**1939. Strandberg, Lloyd Allan** *The Relation of Pupil Achievement in Science to Teacher Characteristics and Certain Environmental Conditions.* Lloyd Allan Strandberg. Edmonton: University of Alberta, 1966. Thesis (M.Ed.)--University of Alberta, 1966.

**1940. Strangeland, Melvin Richard** *Teacher Ratings of Maladjustment.* Melvin Richard Strangeland. Calgary: University of Calgary, 1970. Thesis (M.Ed.)--University of Calgary, 1970.

**1941. Stratton, Taylor** *"The Early Stages of Psychoanalysis of a 4 1/2-year-old Girl."* Taylor Stratton. Canadian Psychiatric Association Journal/Revue de l'Association canadienne de psychiatrie 6, 5(Oct. 1961): 276-280.

**1942. Street, Margaret M.** *Watch-fires on the Mountains: ·the Life and Writings of Ethel Johns.* Margaret M. Street. Toronto: University of Toronto Press, 1973.

**1943. Strong-Boag, Veronica** *"Canada's Early Experience with Income Supplements: the Introduction of Mothers' Allowances."* Veronica Strong-Boag. Atlantis 4, 2, Part 2(Spring 1979): 35-43.

**1944. Strong-Boag, Veronica** *The New Day Recalled: Lives of Girls and Women in English Canada, 1919-1939.* Veronica Strong-Boag. Markham: Penguin Books, 1988.

**1945. Strong-Boag, Veronica** *""Wages for Housework": Mothers' Allowances and the Beginnings of Social Security in Canada."* Veronica Strong-Boag. Journal of Canadian Studies/Revue d'etudes canadiennes 14, 1(Spring 1979): 24-34.

**1946. Strong, Margaret K.** *Mothers' Allowances: an Investigation.* [Compiled and written ... by Miss Margaret K. Strong]. Toronto: Ryerson Press, 1920. Prepared for the Ontario Department of Labour.

**1947. Struthers, R.R.** *"Parent Training."* R.R. Struthers. Canadian Nurse 27, 11(Nov. 1931): 573-578.

**1948. Struthers, R.R.** *"Recent Advances in Child Hygiene."* R.R. Struthers. Canadian Journal of Public Health 35, 3(Mar. 1944): 113-119.

**1949. Stuewe, Paul** *The Storms Below: the Turbulent Life and Times of Hugh Garner.* Paul Stuewe. Toronto: James Lorimer and Company, c1988.

**1950. Sussmann, F.B.** *"Brief on Young Offenders Act Bill C-192."* F.B. Sussmann and W.T. McGrath. Canadian Journal of Criminology and Corrections/Revue canadienne de criminologie 13, 4(Oct. 1971): 307-318.

**1951. Sutherland, D.F.** *"Medical Evidence of Rape."* D.F. Sutherland. Canadian Medical Association Journal/Journal de l'Association medicale canadienne 81, 5(Sept. 1, 1959): 407-408.

**1952. Sutherland, Neil** *Children in English Canadian Society: Framing the Twentieth Century Consensus.* Neil Sutherland. Minneapolis: University of Minnesota, 1973
    Thesis (Ph.D.)--University of Minnesota, 1973.

**1953. Sutherland, Neil** *Children in English Canadian Society: Framing the Twentieth Century Consensus.* Neil Sutherland. Toronto: University of Toronto Press, c1976.

**1954. Sutherland, Neil** *"The History of Canadian Children: Some Notes for the International Year of the Child."* Neil Sutherland. CSSE News/Nouvelles scee 6, 2(Nov. 1979): 3-8.
    An earlier version of the article appeared in the Canadian Home Economics Journal 29, 1(Apr. 1979): 57-61.

**1955. Sutherland, Neil** *"The History of Childhood: Some Notes on the Canadian Experience."* Neil Sutherland. Canadian Home Economics Journal 29, 1(Apr. 1979): 57-61.

**1956. Sutherland, Neil** *"Listening to the Winds of Childhood: the Role of Memory in the History of Education."* Neil Sutherland. Canadian History of Education Association Bulletin 5, 1(Feb. 1988): 5-32.

**1957. Sutherland, Neil** *""To Create a Strong and Healthy Race": School Children in the Public Health Movement, 1880-1914."* Neil Sutherland. History of Education Quarterly 12, 3(Fall 1972): 304-333.
    Reprinted in Medicine in Canadian Society: Historical Perspectives, pp. 361-393. Edited by S.E.D. Shortt. Reprinted in Education and Social Change: Themes From Ontario's Past, pp. 131-161. Edited by Michael B. Katz and Paul H. Mattingly.

**1958. Sutherland, Neil** *"Towards a History of English-Canadian Youngsters."* Neil Sutherland. New York: New York University Press, 1975. In Education and Social Change: Themes from Ontario's Past, pp. xi-xxxi. Edited by Michael B.

Katz and Paul H. Mattingly.

**1959. Sutherland, Neil** *"The Urban Child."* Neil Sutherland. History of Education Quarterly 9, 3(Fall 1969): 305-311.

**1960. Sutherland, Neil** *""We Always Had Things to Do": the Paid and Unpaid Work of Anglophone Children Between the 1920s and the 1960s."* Neil Sutherland. Labour/Le Travail 25(Spring 1990): 105-141.

**1961. Sutton, N.H.** *"The Value of the Immune Serum in Poliomyelitis."* N.H. Sutton. Canadian Public Health Journal 24, 8(Aug. 1933): 360-367.

**1962. Suzuki, David T.** *Metamorphosis: Stages in a Life.* David Suzuki. Toronto: Stoddart Pub. Co., c1987.

**1963. Swainson, Donald** *"Franklin Walker, Separate Schools and the Question of Canadian Identity."* Donald Swainson. Queen's Quarterly 96, 1(Spring 1989): 14-21.

**1964. Swampy, Grace Marie** *"The Role of the Native Woman in the Native Society."* Grace Marie Swampy. Canadian Journal of Native Education 9, 2(Winter 1982): 2-20.

**1965. Swanson, Cecil** *The Days of My Sojourning: a Reminiscence.* Cecil Swanson. Calgary: Glenbow-Alberta Institute, c1977.

**1966. Swayze, Carolyn** *Hard Choices: a Life of Tom Berger.* Carolyn Swayze. Vancouver: Douglas and McIntyre, c1987.

**1967. Sweeney, John Roland** *A Comparative Study of the Use of the Cuisenaire Method and Materials and a Non-Cuisenaire Approach and Materials on a Grade One Mathematics Program.* John Roland Sweeney. Toronto: University of Toronto, 1969.
    Thesis (M.Ed.)--University of Toronto, 1969.

**1968. Swyer, Paul R.** *"The First Breath: Natural and Induced."* Paul Swyer. Canadian Medical Association Journal 78, 6(Mar. 15, 1958): 428-429.

**1969. Swyripa, Frances** *"The Ukrainians and Private Education."* Frances Swyripa. Toronto: McClelland and Stewart Ltd., 1982. In A Heritage in Transition: Essays in the History of Ukrainians in Canada, pp. 244-262. Edited by Manoly R. Lupul.

1970. Sylvestre, J. Ernest *"Nutrition and School Children."* J. Ernest Sylvestre. Canadian Journal of Public Health 38, 4(Apr. 1947): 82-86.

1971. Symons, Harry *Playthings of Yesterday.* Harry Symons. Toronto: Ryerson Press, 1963.

1972. Synge, Jane *"The Sociology of Canadian Education."* Jane Synge. Toronto: MacMillan of Canada, 1976. In Introduction to Canadian Society: Sociological Analysis, pp. 401-437. Edited by G.N. Ramu and Stuart D. Johnson.

1973. Szasz, George *"Adolescent Sexual Activity."* George Szasz. Canadian Nurse 67, 10(Oct. 1971): 39-43.

1974. Szyrynski, Victor *"Psychotherapy with Parents of Maladjusted Children."* Victor Szyrynski. Canadian Psychiatric Association Journal/Revue de l'Association canadienne de psychiatrie 10, 5(Oct. 1965): 350-357.

1975. Tadman, Martin *"A Critical Analysis of Bill C-192: the Young Offenders Act."* Martin Tadman. Manitoba Law Journal 4, 2(1971): 371-380.

1976. Tait, Margaret *"Care of Premature Babies."* Margaret Tait. Canadian Nurse 28, 7(July 1922): 397-398.

1977. Tait, William D. *"The Exceptional Child."* William D. Tait. Public Health Journal 5, 9(Sept. 1914): 563-573.

1978. Tait, William D. *"The Gifted Child."* William D. Tait. Canadian Journal of Mental Hygiene 3, 3(Oct. 1921): 265-273.

1979. Takata, Toyo *Nikkei Legacy: the Story of Japanese Canadians from Settlement to Today.* Toyo Takata. Toronto: NC Press Ltd., 1983.

1980. Tannock, Rosemary *Communication Patterns Between Mothers and Preschool-aged Children.* Rosemary Tannock. Toronto: University of Toronto, 1980.
    Thesis (M.A.)—University of Toronto, 1980.

1981. Tarasoff, Koozma J. *Traditional Doukhobor Folkways: an Ethnographic and Biographic Record of Prescribed Behaviour.* Koozma J. Tarasoff. Ottawa: National Museums of Canada, 1977.

1982. Tate, Dorothy E. *"The Problem of Teeth in Children."* Dorothy E. Tate. Public Health Nurses' Bulletin 2, 2(Apr. 1935): 26.

1983. Taylor, Charles *Six Journeys: a Canadian Pattern.* Charles Taylor. Toronto: Anansi, c1977.

1984. Teed, Eric L. *"The Incapacity of a Married Woman to be Next Friend or Guardian Ad Litom."* Eric L. Teed. University of New Brunswick Law Journal 7(Apr. 1954): 29-31.

1985. Temins, Irving D. *Law of Divorce in Canada.* Irving D. Temins. Toronto: Primrose Publishing Co., [1969].

1986. Tetley, Dorothy Fern *The Relationship of Certain Teacher Characteristics to Pupil Achievement in Reading.* Dorothy Fern Tetley. Edmonton: University of Alberta, 1964.
    Thesis (M.Ed.)--University of Alberta, 1964.

1987. Therrien, Susan Alice *Self Concept: Implications for Early Childhood Education.* Susan Alice Therrien. Edmonton: University of Alberta, 1969.
    Thesis (M.Ed.)--University of Alberta, 1969.

1988. Thom, Evalene *Sensory Integration and Initial Reading.* Evalene Thom. Toronto: University of Toronto, 1970.
    Thesis (Ph.D.)--University of Toronto, 1970.

1989. Thompson, Laura A. *Laws Relating to Mothers' Pensions in the U.S., Canada, Denmark and New Zealand.* Laura A. Thompson. Washington: Government Printing Office, 1919.

1990. Thompson, Murray *"Social Diseases and Child Life."* Murray Thompson. In Proceedings of Sixth Annual Canadian Conference on Child Welfare 1927, pp. 80-85.

1991. Thompson, Ronald T.F. *Origins and Development of the Wolf Cub Movement in Canada, 1914-1940: a "Pilot Project" Collection of Source Material (Beginning with Particular References to Manitoba).* Ronald T.F. Thompson. Victoria: University of Victoria Press, 1971.

1992. Tibbits, Ethel Burnett *On to the Sunset.* Ethel Burnett Tibbits. Toronto: Ryerson Press, c1953.

**1993. Tischer, Selma** *"Psycho-motor Re-education for Children with Reading Difficulties."* Selma Tischer. Canadian Psychologist/Psychologie canadienne 9, 2(Apr. 1968): 187-195.

**1994. Tisdall, F.F.** *"Care of the Infant and Child During the Summer Months."* F.F. Tisdall. Canadian Public Health Journal 20, 7(July 1919): 357-360.

**1995. Titley, E. Brian** *"Indian Industrial Schools in Western Canada."* E. Brian Titley. Calgary: Detselig Enterprises, 1986. In Schools in the West: Essays in Canadian Educational History, pp. 133-153. Edited by Nancy M. Sheehan, J. Donald Wilson and David C. Jones.

**1996. Titus, Dorothy A.** *"The Public Health Nurse and the Cardiac Child."* Dorothy A. Titus. Canadian Nurse 42, 10(Oct. 1946): 858-859.

**1997. Tobias, Ruth Charlotte** *The Development of a Counselling Program in a Private School.* Ruth Charlotte Tobias. Toronto: University of Toronto, 1945.
Thesis (M.A.)--University of Toronto, 1945.

**1998. Tomander, Beata** *"Harelip."* Beata Tomander. Canadian Nurse 49, 12(Dec. 1953): 956-957.

**1999. Tomko, Tony Mike** *Personality Correlates of Home Disruption.* Tony Mike Tomko. Edmonton: University of Alberta, 1969.
Thesis (M.Ed.)--University of Alberta, 1969.

**2000. Tompkins, M. Gregory** *"Clinical Aspects of High Risk Pregnancy."* M. Gregory Tompkins. Medical Services Journal of Canada 23, 4(Apr. 1967): 500-511.

**2001. Topping, Wesley** *The Family and Modern Marriage.* Wesley Topping. Toronto: Ryerson Press, [1953].

**2002. Towler, John Orchard** *Spatial Concepts of Elementary School Children.* John Orchard Towler. Edmonton: University of Alberta, 1965.
Thesis (M.Ed.)--University of Alberta, 1965.
Co-authored with Nelson Doyal article with same title in Alberta Journal of Educational Research 13, 1(Mar. 1967): 34-50.

**2003. Towler, John Orchard** *Training Effects and Concept Development: a Study of the Conservation of Continuous Quantity in Children.* John Orchard Towler. Edmonton: University of Alberta, 1967.
Thesis (Ph.D.)--University of Alberta, 1967.

**2004. Tremblay, Adrien W.** *The Development of Scales from a Pupil Biographical Inventory and Their Usefulness as Predictors of Academic Achievement.* Adrien W. Tremblay. Edmonton: University of Alberta, 1970.
Thesis (M.Ed.)--University of Alberta, 1970.

**2005. Tremble, G. Edward** *"The Conservative Treatment of Sinusitis in Children."* G. Edward Tremble. Canadian Medical Association Journal 49, 6(Dec. 1943): 497-501.

**2006. Trost, Fred J.** *"Group Dynamics, the School and Delinquency."* Fred J. Trost. Family Life Coordinator 10, 4(Oct. 1961): 82-84.

**2007. Trottier, Monique** *Survey of Facilities for Emotionally Disturbed Children in Canada: [Report to] the Canadian Conference on Children.* Monique Trottier and John Stanley. [S.l.: s.n., 1961?].

**2008. Truss, Donald** *Teaching Values in High School Literature and Science.* Donald Truss. Calgary: University of Calgary, 1968.
Thesis (M.Ed.)--University of Calgary, 1968.

**2009. Truszka, Mary Gregory** *A Survey of the Reading Interests of Catholic High School Girls With Implications for Guidance Practices.* Mary Gregory Truszka. Ottawa: University of Ottawa, 1961.
Thesis (Ph.D.)--University of Ottawa, 1961.

**2010. Tsao, Fei** *Is AQ or F Score the Last Word in Determining Individual Effort?* Fei Tsao. Toronto: University of Toronto, 1941.
Thesis (M.A.)--University of Toronto, 1941.

**2011. Tuck, Gerald Stuart** *"A Separation of Church and State in Ontario Adoption Procedure."* Gerald Stuart Tuck and Robert Burnside Burgess. Osgoode Hall Law Journal 2, 2(Apr. 1961): 216-230.

**2012. Tucker, Muriel** *Family Relief in Canada and the United States.* Muriel Tucker. Ottawa: Canadian Welfare Council, 1936.

**2013. Tulloch, John** *How to Succeed in Life: a Book for Young People.* John Tulloch. New ed. Toronto: Belfords, Clarke, 1879.

**2014. Turner, Alec M.** *"What Specific Provisions Will Answer the Needs of the Gifted?"* Alec M. Turner. Ottawa: Mutal Press, 1958. In Addresses and Proceedings of the Canadian Conference on Education, Ottawa, February 16-20, 1958, pp. 438-445. Edited by George G. Croskery and Gerald Nason.

**2015. Turner, Kathleen** *An Analysis of Imitative Behavior in Relation to Learning.* Kathleen Turner. Toronto: University of Toronto, 1940.
Thesis (M.A.)--University of Toronto, 1940.

**2016. Turner, Keith** *"Children in Court."* Keith Turner. Manitoba Law School Journal 1, 1(1962): 23-29.

**2017. Turner, Wesley B.** *""80 Stout and Healthy Looking Girls.""* Wesley B. Turner. Canada: An Historical Magazine 3, 2(Dec. 1975): 36-49.

**2018. Tuttle, George** *Youth Organizations in Canada: a Reference Manual.* George Tuttle. Toronto: Ryerson Press, c1946.

**2019. Tymchuk, Alexander J.** *EEG and Psychological Test Performance in Children.* Alexander J. Tymchuk. London, Ont.: University of Western Ontario, 1968.
Thesis (M.A.)--University of Western Ontario, 1968.

**2020. Underhill, Harold Fabian** *Labor Legislation in British Columbia.* Harold Fabian Underhill. Berkeley: University of California, 1936.
Thesis (Ph.D.)--University of California, 1936.
bibliography.

**2021. Uniat, Philip** *Analysis of Speed and Accuracy on Timed Writings.* Philip Uniat. Edmonton: University of Alberta, 1966.
Thesis (M.Ed.)--University of Alberta, 1966.

**2022. Unwin, J. Robertson** *"Depression in Alienated Youth."* J. Robertson Unwin. Canadian Psychiatric Association Journal/Revue de l'Association canadienne de psychiatrie 15, 1(Feb. 1970): 83-86.

**2023. Urquhart, M.C., ed.** *Historical Statistics of Canada.* M.C. Urquhart, ed. and K.A.H. Buckley, assistant ed. Toronto: MacMillan Company of Canada Limited, 1965.

**2024. Usher, Saul J.** *"The Development, Management and Care of the Normal Child."* S.J. Usher. Canadian Nurse 28, 1(Jan. 1932): 19-23.

**2025. Valiquet, L.P.** *French Language Proficiency at University Entrance: a Survey of Bilingualism Among Freshmen at Twenty-Five English Canadian Universities and Colleges.* L.P. Valiquet.

**2026. Vallieres, Pierre** *"From Working Class Slum to the FLQ: the Life Story of Pierre Vallieres."* Pierre Vallieres. Toronto: McClelland and Stewart Ltd., c1972. In Making It: the Canadian Dream, pp. 360-368. Edited by Bryan Finnigan and Cy Gonick.
Excerpts from Les Negres blanc d'Amerique by Pierre Vallieres.

**2027. Valois, Jocelyne** *Families and Socioeconomic Changes.* Jocelyne Valois and Denise Lemieux. Ottawa: Ministry of Forestry and Rural Development, 1967.

**2028. Van Brummelen, Harro Walter** *Molding God's Children: the History of Curriculum in Christian Schools Rooted in Dutch Calvanism.* Harro Walter Van Brummelen. Vancouver: University of British Columbia, 1984. (CTM no. 206217) Thesis (Ph.D.)--University of British Columbia, 1984.

**2029. VanderMey, Albert** *To All Our Children: the Story of the Postwar Dutch Immigration to Canada.* Albert VanderMey. Jordan Station, Ont.: Paideia Press, c1983.

**2030. Van Die, Marguerite** *An Evangelical Mind: Nathanael Burwash and the Methodist Tradition in Canada, 1839-1918.* Marguerite Van Die. Ontario: McGill-Queen's University Press, 1989.

**2031. Van Die, Marguerite** *Nathanile Burwash: a Study in Revivalism and Canadian Culture, 1839-1918.* Marguerite Van Die. London, Ont.: University of Western Ontario, 1987. (CTM no. 40805) Thesis (Ph.D.)--University of Western Ontario, 1987.

**2032. Vanier Institute of the Family** *Milieu 70: Report of the National Conference held at the Fort Garry Hotel, Winnipeg, October 25-29, 1970.* Vanier Institute of the Family and The Canadian Council on Children and Youth. [S.l.: s.n., 1970].

**2033. Van Kirk, Sylvia** *"Fur Trade Social History: Some Recent Trends."* Sylvia Van Kirk. Edmonton: Pica Pica Press, c1985. In The Prairie West: Historical Readings, pp. 71-82. Edited by R. Douglas Francis and Howard Palmer.

**2034. Van Kirk, Sylvia** *Many Tender Ties: Women in Fur-Trade Society in Western Canada, 1670-1870.* Sylvia Van Kirk. Winnipeg: Watson & Dwyer Pub. Ltd., 1980.

**2035. Van Kirk, Sylvia** *""Women in Between": Indian Women in Fur Trade Society in Western Canada."* Sylvia Van Kirk. Canadian Historical Association, Historical Papers/Communications historiques (1977): 31-46.

**2036. van Vliet, Maurice L., ed.** *Physical Education in Canada.* M.L. van Vliet, ed. Scarborough: Prentice-Hall, c1965.

**2037. Varamis, J.** *"Manic Depressive Disease in Childhood: a Case Report."* J. Varamis and S.M. MacDonald. Canadian Psychiatric Association Journal/Revue de l'Association canadienne de psychiatrie 17, 4(Aug. 1972): 279-281.
Gives a chronology of events.

**2038. Vaughn, J.B.** *The Wandering Years: an Odyssey of the Dirty Thirties, the Hobo Jungles, the Logging Camps and the Trapper's Wilderness.* J.B. Vaughn. Saanichton, B.C.: Hancock House Pub. Ltd., c1975.

**2039. Vaz, Edmund W.** *"Delinquency and Youth Culture: Upper- and Middle-class Boys."* Edmund W. Vaz. Journal of Criminal Law, Criminology and Police Sciences 60, 1(Mar. 1969): 33-46.
Reprinted in Deviant Behaviour and Societal Reaction, pp. 212-231. Edited by Craig L. Boydell, Carl F. Grindstaff and Paul C. Whitehead.

**2040. Vaz, Edmund W.** *"Juvenile Delinquency in the Middle Class Youth Culture."* Edmund W. Vaz. New York: Harper & Row, [1967]. In Middle Class Juvenile Delinquency, pp. 131-147. Edited by Edmund W. Vaz.
Reprinted in Critical Issues in Canadian Society, pp. 479-490. Edited by Craig L. Boydell, Carl F. Grindstaff and Paul C. Whitehead.

**2041. Vaz, Edmund W.** *"Middle Class Adolescents: Self-reported Delinquency and Youth Culture Activities."* Edmund W. Vaz. Canadian Review of Sociology and Anthropology/Revue canadienne de sociologie et d'anthropologie 2, 1(Feb. 1965): 52-70.
Reprinted in Canada: a Sociological Profile, pp. 106-120. Edited by W.E. Mann.

**2042. Vaz, Edmund W.** *"Middle Class Adolescents: Youth Culture Activities."* Edmund W. Vaz. In Canadian Society: Sociological Perspectives, 3rd ed., 1968, pp. 223-233. Edited by Bernard R. Blishen, Frank E. Jones, Kasper D. Naegele and John Porter.

**2043. Vaz, Edmund W.** *"Self-reported Juvenile Delinquency and Socioeconomic Status."* Edmund W. Vaz. Canadian Journal of Corrections/Revue canadienne de criminologie 8, 1(Jan. 1966): 20-27.

**2044. Vaz, Edmund W.** *"The "Straight" World of Middle-class High School Kids."* Edmund W. Vaz. Toronto: Holt, Rinehart and Winston, 1971. In Social Process and Institution: the Canadian Case, pp. 174-186. Edited by James E. Gallagher.

**2045. Vernon, C.W.** *"Child Labour in the Country."* C.W. Vernon. In Proceedings and Papers Fourth Annual Canadian Conference on Child Welfare 1923, pp. 115-121.

**2046. Vince, Dennis J.** *"Banding of the Pulmonary Artery in Infancy: Selection of Patients and Results of Main Pulmonary Artery Banding in the Treatment of Congenital Heart Disease."* Dennis J. Vince. Canadian Medical Association Journal/Journal de l'Association medicale canadienne 97, 1(July 1, 1967): 1-8.

**2047. Vine, William George** *The Child, the Court, and the Training School.* William George Vine. Toronto: University of Toronto, 1962.
Thesis (M.S.W.)--University of Toronto, 1962.

**2048. Vineberg, Sima Gafter** *A Pilot Study of Children's Reactions to Visual Illusions and the Relation of Illusion to Tolerance for Ambiguity.* Sima Gafter Vineberg. Montreal: Sir George Williams University, 1970.
Thesis (M.A.)--Sir George Williams University, 1970.

**2049. Vines, T.** *"Therapy for Hearing-impaired Children."* T. Vines. Canadian Nurse 62, 8(Aug. 1966): 42-44.

**2050. Voice, Brian Hugh** *A Study of the Awareness of Fifth Grade Students of Context Clues in Selected Basal Reading Material.* Brian Hugh Voice. Edmonton: University of Alberta, 1968.
Thesis (M.Ed.)--University of Alberta, 1968.

2051. **Von Baeyer, Renate** *"The Strong One."* Renate Von Baeyer. Canadian Welfare 35, 4(July 1959): 155-157.

2052. **von Schilling, Karin C.** *"Needed: a Positive Approach to the Mentally Retarded."* Karin C. von Schilling. Canadian Nurse 66, 6(June 1970): 30-32.

2053. **Vulpe, Shirley German** *Home Care and Management of the Mentally Retarded Child.* Shirley German Vulpe. Toronto: National Institute on Mental Retardation, 1969.

2054. **Wade, Mark Sweeten** *The Overlanders of '62.* Mark Sweeten Wade. Surrey, B.C.: Frontier Books, 1981, c1931.

2055. **Wade, Mason** *The French Canadians: 1760-1967.* Mason Wade. 2 v. Toronto: Macmillan of Canada, 1968.

2056. **Wade, Mason, ed.** *Canadian Dualism: Studies of French-English Relations.* Mason Wade, ed. Toronto: University of Toronto Press, 1960.

2057. **Wagner, Gillian** *Barnardo.* Gillian Wagner. London: Weidenfeld and Nicolson, 1979.

2058. **Wagner, Gillian** *Children of the Empire.* Gillian Wagner. London, Eng.: Weidenfield and Nicolson, c1982.

2059. **Wai-man, Lee** *Portraits of a Challenge: an Illustrated History of the Chinese Canadians.* Lee Wai-man. Toronto: Council of Chinese Canadians in Ontario, c1984.

2060. **Wakabayashi, Akiko** *Long-term Boarding Home Care for Children.* Akiko Wakabayashi. Toronto: University of Toronto, 1959.
Thesis (M.S.W.)--University of Toronto, 1959.

2061. **Wake, F.R.** *"Changing Sex Roles: Implications for Education."* F.R. Wake. McGill Journal of Education 3, 3(Fall 1968): 154-160.

2062. **Wake, F.R.** *"Normal Aggression and Delinquency."* F.R. Wake. Canadian Journal of Corrections/Revue canadienne de criminologie 2, 2(Apr. 1960): 175-183.

2063. **Walker, J.** *"The Process of Juvenile Detention: the Training School Act, the Child Welfare Act."* J. Walker and A. Glasner. Osgoode Hall Law Journal 3, 2(Apr. 1965): 343-361.

2064. **Walker, James W. St.G.** *A History of Blacks in Canada: a Study Guide for Teachers and Students.* James W. St.G. Walker. [Hull]: Ministry of Supply and Services Canada, c1980.

2065. **Walker, Laurence** *A Comparison of Definite and Indefinite Time Expressions as Factors of Difficulty in Reading Comprehension in Grade 7 Social Studies.* Laurence Walker. Edmonton: University of Alberta, 1968.
Thesis (M.Ed.)--University of Alberta, 1968.

2066. **Wall, Vincent H.** *A Study of School Dropouts in the Grads' Club.* Vincent H. Wall. Toronto: University of Toronto, 1963.
Thesis (M.S.W.)--University of Toronto, 1963.

2067. **Wallace, H. Ross** *Behaviour Problems of Boys Separated from Their Fathers.* H. Ross Wallace. Toronto: University of Toronto, 1959.
Thesis (M.S.W.)--University of Toronto, 1959.

2068. **Walsh, H., ed.** *Stewards of a Goodly Heritage: a Survey of the Church's Mission Fields in Canada.* H. Walsh, ed. [S.l.]: Joint Committee on Summer Schools and Institutes of the Church of England in Canada, 1934.

2069. **Wankowicz, Melchior** *Three Generations.* Melchior Wankowicz. Toronto: Canadian Polish Research Institute in Canada, 1973.

2070. **Ward, Bonnie M.** *A New Resource for the Hard-to-place Child.* Bonnie M. Ward. Toronto: University of Toronto, 1957.
Thesis (M.S.W.)--University of Toronto, 1957.

2071. **Ward, T.G.** *"A Study of Childhood Schizophrenia and Early Infantile Autism: Part I: Description of the Sample; Part II: Selection of a Group for In-patient Treatment."* T.G. Ward. Canadian Psychiatric Association Journal/Revue de l'Association canadienne de psychiatrie 10, 5(Oct. 1965): 377-388.

2072. **Warescha, Blaine Eugene** *Comparison of American, Indian, Eskimo, Spanish-American, and Anglo Youthful Offenders on the Minnesota Counselling Inventory.* Blaine Eugene Warescha. Salt Lake City, Ut.: Utah University, c1971.
Thesis (Ph.D.)--Utah University, 1971.

2073. **Wargon, Sylvia T.** *Canadian Households and Families: Recent Demographic Trends.* Sylvia T. Wargon. Ottawa: Statistics Canada, 1979.

2074. **Warner, Elizabeth** *"A Survey of Mongolism, With a Review of One Hundred Cases."* Elizabeth Warner. Canadian Medical Association Journal 33, 5(Nov. 1935): 495-500.

2075. **Warner, Francis** *The Study of Children: and Their School Training.* Francis Warner. Toronto: George N. Morang, 1898.

2076. **Warner, R.I.** *"School Care of Girls During Puberty."* R.I. Warner. Public Health Journal 7, 6(June 1916): 311.

2077. **Warren, Olive B.** *"Rheumatic Fever: Scourge of Early Childhood."* Olive B. Warren. Canadian Nurse 45, 11(Nov. 1949): 857-858.

2078. **Waterman, Nairn** *"Disclosure of Social and Psychological Reports at Disposition."* Nairn Waterman. Osgoode Hall Law Journal 7, 2(1969): 214-233.

2079. **Watkin, J.F.** *Achievement in Grade 9 Social Studies.* J.F. Watkin. Edmonton: University of Alberta, 1941.
    Thesis (M.Ed.)--University of Alberta, 1941.

2080. **Watson, Robert** *A Boy of the Great North West: the Rousing Experience of a Young Canadian among Cowboys, Hunters, Trappers, Fur Traders, Fishermen and Indians.* Robert Watson. Ottawa: Graphic Publishers Ltd., 1930.

2081. **Watson, Robert** *"Souvenirs Presented to the Right Honourable Stanley Baldwin and Mrs. Baldwin."* Robert Watson. Beaver 258, 2(Sept. 1927): 60-62.

2082. **Watson, S.B.** *"A Layman's View of the Teaching of History."* S.B. Watson. Canadian Historical Review 15, 2(June 1934): 155-170.

2083. **Watters, Jessie** *"A Challenge to the Nation."* Jessie Watters. Canadian Welfare 26, 1(Apr. 1950): 9-12.

2084. **Watts, Gertrude M.** *"Occupations for the Sick Child."* Gertrude M. Watts. Canadian Nurse 41, 7(July 1945): 527-532.

2085. **Webb, Jean F.** *"Canadian Thalidomide Experience."* Jean F. Webb. Canadian Medical Association Journal/Journal de l'Association medicale canadienne 89, 19(Nov. 9, 1963): 987-992.

2086. **Webber, Alika** *"The Naskapi Child."* Alika Webber and Ray Webber. Beaver 294, 3(Winter 1963): 14-16.

2087. **Weber, Jack L.** *"The Speech and Language Abilities of Emotionally Disturbed Children."* Jack L. Weber. Canadian Psychiatric Association Journal/Revue de l'Association canadienne de psychiatrie 10, 5(Oct. 1965): 417-420.

2088. **Weiler, Karen M.** *"The Exercise of Jurisdiction in Custody Disputes."* Karen M. Weiler. Canadian Journal of Family Law/Revue canadienne de droit familial 3, 2 and 3(Apr.-July 1980): 281-302.

2089. **Weiner, Roberta Wilson** *"Children, Comics and Television."* Roberta Wilson Weiner. Canadian Welfare 33, 4(Nov. 1957): 157-162.

2090. **Weinstein, Edwin Lawrence** *Development of Persuasive Skills in Children.* Edwin Lawrence Weinstein. Toronto: University of Toronto, 1971.
    Thesis (M.A.)--University of Toronto, 1971.

2091. **Weir, H.A.** *"Unemployed Youth."* H.A. Weir. Toronto: MacMillan of Canada, 1939. In Canada's Unemployment Problem, pp. 111-171. Edited by L. Richter.

2092. **Weld, Lindsay Ann** *Children's Predictions of the Sociometric Choices of Those They Choose Highly.* Lindsay Ann Weld. Toronto: University of Toronto, 1956.
    Thesis (M.A.)--University of Toronto, 1956.

2093. **Weldon, Richard Chapman** *A Comparison of French-speaking and Non-French-speaking Students in High School French.* Weldon, Richard Chapman. Edmonton: University of Alberta, 1947.
    Thesis (M.Ed.)--University of Alberta, 1947.

2094. **Wells, Anna E.** *"The Provincial Programme for Infant Care."* Anna E. Wells. Canadian Nurse 24, 1(Jan. 1928): 8-13.

2095. **Wells, Anna E.** *"Provincial Programs for Infant Care."* A.E. Wells. In Proceedings of Sixth Annual Canadian Conference on Child Welfare 1927, pp. 16-27.

2096. **Welp, Herman H.** *Families and Household, 1951-1961.* Herman H. Welp. Montreal: City Planning Department, 1964.

**2097. Westermark, Tory I.** *A Comparative Study of Selected Canadian and American Sixth Grade Students' Knowledge of Certain Basic Concepts About Canada and the United States.* Tory I. Westermark. Corvalis: University of Oregon, 1962. Thesis (Ph.D.)--University of Oregon, 1962.

**2098. Westman, A.G.** *"Trends in the Care of Delinquent Girls."* A.G. Westman. Child and Family Welfare 6, 3(July 1930): 33-36.

**2099. Weston, W.A.** *"A Community Program in Child Protection."* W.A. Weston. In Proceedings of Sixth Annual Canadian Conference on Child Welfare 1927, pp. 126-129.

**2100. Wetmore, F.H.** *"Fecal Infection with Special Reference to Medical Inspection of Schools."* F.H. Wetmore. Canadian Medical Association Journal 11, 1(Jan. 1921): 43-45.

**2101. Wheatley, George M.** *"Rheumatic Fever and the School Child."* George M. Wheatley. Canadian Nurse 45, 10(Oct. 1949): 758-760.

**2102. Wherrett, George Jasper** *The Miracle of the Empty Beds: a History of Tuberculosis in Canada.* George Jasper Wherrett. Toronto: University of Toronto Press, c1977.

**2103. Wherrett, George Jasper** *Tuberculosis in Canada.* George Jasper Wherrett. Ottawa: Queen's Printer, 1965. Alternate title: Tuberculosis in Canada: Royal Commission on Health Services.

**2104. White, Orville E.** *The History of the Practical Education Courses in Canadian Secondary Schools.* Orville E. White. Montreal: McGill University, 1951. Thesis (M.A.)--McGill University, 1951.

**2105. White, Walter G.W.** *"A Comparison of Some Parental and Guardian 'Rights."* Walter G.W. White. Canadian Journal of Family Law/Revue canadienne de droit familial 3, 2 and 3(Apr.-July 1980): 219-250.

**2106. Whitelaw, Jean** *"The Preschool Blind Child."* Jean Whitelaw. Canadian Welfare 26, 1(Apr. 1950): 25-27.

**2107. Whitlam, Valerie** *"The Autistic Child."* Valerie Whitlam. Canadian Nurse 66, 11(Nov. 1970): 44-47.

**2108. Whitton, Charlotte** *"A Baker's Dozen Principles in Child Protection."* Charlotte Whitton. Canadian Welfare 24, 3(July 1948): 28-29.

**2109. Whitton, Charlotte** *The Bewildered Community To-day: Canada, 1934.* Charlotte Whitton. Ottawa: Canadian Council on Child and Family Welfare, 1934.

**2110. Whitton, Charlotte** *Canada and the World's Child Welfare Work: a Commentary on Canadian Child Welfare Work in the Light of International Discussion of Child Welfare Problems.* Charlotte Whitton. Ottawa: Canadian Council on Child Welfare, 1927.

**2111. Whitton, Charlotte** *"Handicapped Children and the Junior Red Cross."* Charlotte Whitton. Canadian Nurse 23, 1(Jan. 1927): 8-11.

**2112. Whitton, Charlotte** *"The King's Words From Over. the Sea."* Charlotte Whitton. Canadian Welfare 16, 4(Aug. 1940): 13-18.

**2113. Whitton, Charlotte** *"The Problem of the Juvenile and Youthful Offender."* Charlotte Whitton. Child and Family Welfare 13, 5(Jan. 1938): 49-56.

**2114. Whitton, Charlotte** *"Progress 1920-5 and Recommendations 1925-30 in Child Welfare Legislation."* Charlotte Whitton. Reprinted as a pamphlet by the Canadian Council on Child Welfare, Publication no. 26.

**2115. Whitton, Charlotte** *"Report on Placement of Crippled Children."* Charlotte Whitton. Child and Family Welfare 6, 7(Mar. 1931): 19-22.

**2116. Whitton, Charlotte** *"Shades of the Prison House."* Charlotte Whitton. Canadian Welfare 17, 6(Nov. 1941): 21.

**2117. Whitton, Charlotte** *"Welfare Services for Dependents of Enlisted Men."* Charlotte Whitton. Canadian Welfare Summary 14, 4(Nov. 1939): 19-21.

**2118. Whyte, M.B.** *"The Hard-of-hearing Child."* M.B. Whyte. Canadian Nurse 29, 7(July 1933): 371-373.

**2119. Wickberg, Edgar ed.** *From China to Canada: a History of the Chinese Communities in Canada.* Harry Con, Ronald J. Con, Graham Johnson, Edgar Wickberg [and] William E. Willmott. Toronto: Published by McClelland and Stewart Ltd. in association with the Multiculturalism Directorate, Department of the Secretary of State, and the Canadian Government Publishing Centre,

Supply and Services Canada, 1982.

**2120. Wiebe, Russell Gordon** *Cognitive Preferences of Students in Two High School Chemistry Programs.* Russell Gordon Wiebe. Calgary: University of Calgary, 1970.
Thesis (M.Ed.)--University of Calgary, 1970.

**2121. Wiener, Judith** *The Child's Use of Sentence Structure to Organize and Learn Verbal Material.* Judith Wiener. Edmonton: University of Alberta, 1971.
Thesis (M.Ed.)--University of Alberta, 1971.

**2122. Wiggins, Reginald H.** *"The Management of Posture in Children."* Reginald Wiggins. Canadian Medical Association Journal 27, 1(July 1932): 47-51

**2123. Wiggins, Reginald H.** *"Posture in Children."* Reginald H. Wiggins. Canadian Medical Association Journal 24, 6(June 1931): 820-825.

**2124. Wigod, Annette** *"Let's Ask the Middle Class."* Annette Wigod. Canadian Welfare 44, 6(Nov.-Dec. 1968): 14-15, 18-19.

**2125. Wigod, Annette** *"What Are We Doing to Foster Babies?"* Annette Wigod. Canadian Welfare 44, 3(May-June 1968): 17-18, 24.

**2126. Wile, Ira S.** *The Child.* Ira S. Wile. [S.l.]: Metropolitan Life Insurance Co., 1924.

**2127. Wilkins, Russell** *Health Status in Canada, 1926-1976: Rising Life Expectancy, Diminishing Regional Differences, Persistent Social Disparities.* Russell Wilkins. Montreal: Institute for Research on Public Policy, 1980, c1979.

**2128. Williams, C.V.** *"Report of the Subcommittee on Dependency of the Children's Committee of the National Conference on Social Work."* C.V. Williams. Public Health Journal 10, 12(Dec. 1919): 563-569.

**2129. Williams, D.C.** *"Crime and the Comics."* D.C. Williams. Queen's Quarterly 61, 4(Winter 1955): 522-533.

**2130. Williams, Donald Harry** *The Effect of an Organized Swimming Program on Motor Fitness.* Donald Harry Williams. Edmonton: University of Alberta, 1970.
Thesis (M.Ed.)--University of Alberta, 1970.

**2131. Williams, Nancy** *Peer Group Participation of Hemophilic Boys in Adolescence.* Nancy Williams. Toronto: University of Toronto, 1965.
Thesis (M.S.W.)--University of Toronto, 1965.

**2132. Williams, P.E.** *"A Few Common Problems in Infancy."* P.E. Williams. Canadian Medical Association Journal 44, 3(Mar. 1941): 275-279.

**2133. Williamson, Paul** *"Behaviour Problems in Children."* Paul Williamson. Canadian Medical Association Journal 69, 4(Oct. 1953): 412-415.

**2134. Willits, Reba E.** *"The Impact of the School on the Health of the Child."* Reba E. Willits. Journal of Education of the Faculty and College of Education: Vancouver and Victoria 6(Dec. 1961): 95-100.

**2135. Wilson, Bertha** *"Children: the Casualties of a Failed Marriage."* Bertha Wilson. University of British Columbia Law Review 19, 2(1985): 245-270.

**2136. Wilson, Bessie** *"School Nursing."* Bessie Wilson. Canadian Nurse 32, 11(Nov. 1936): 513-516.

**2137. Wilson, Elizabeth A.** *The Effect of Father Separation or Faulty Father Image on Juvenile Delinquent Behaviour in Girls.* Elizabeth A. Wilson. Toronto: University of Toronto, 1962.
Thesis (M.S.W.)--University of Toronto, 1962.

**2138. Wilson, Graham Beech** *Assessment of Some Effects of the Availability of Computer-prepared Test Performance Data on Student Achievement.* Graham Beech Wilson. Calgary: University of Calgary, 1970.
Thesis (M.Ed.)--University of Calgary, 1970.

**2139. Wilson, H.J.** *"The Problem of Juvenile Crime and Penal Reform."* H.J. Wilson. Canadian Bar Review 24, 4(Apr. 1946): 276-283.

**2140. Wilson, J. Donald** *"From Social Control to Family Strategies: Some Observations on Recent Trends in Canadian Educational History."* J. Donald Wilson. History of Education Review 13, 1(Spring 1984): 1-13.

**2141. Wilson, J. Donald, ed.** *Canadian Education: a History.* J. Donald Wilson, Robert M. Stamp and Louis-Philippe Audet, eds. Scarborough: Prentice-Hall of Canada Limited, c1970.

2142. **Wilson, J. Donald,** ed. *An Imperfect Past: Education and Society in Canadian History.* J. Donald Wilson, ed. Vancouver: Centre for the Study of Curriculum and Instruction, University of British Columbia, 1984.

2143. **Wilson, Keith** *George Simpson and the Hudson's Bay Company.* Keith Wilson. Agincourt: Book Society of Canada, c1977.

2144. **Wilson, Larry C.** *"Changes to Federal Jurisdiction Over Young Offenders: the Provincial Response."* Larry C. Wilson. Canadian Journal of Family Law/Revue canadienne de droit familial 8, 2(Spring 1990): 303-343.

2145. **Wilson, Mary** *"Accident Prevention in Infants and Preschool Children."* Mary Wilson. Canadian Nurse 50, 4(Apr. 1954): 287-291.

2146. **Wilt, J.C.** *"Live Oral Poliovirus Vaccine After DPT Polio Vaccine."* J.C. Wilt, W.L. Parker, W. Stackiw and P.A. Hutchison. Canadian Medical Association Journal/Journal de l'Association medicale canadienne 85, 10(Sept. 2, 1961): 575-578.

2147. **Winks, Robin W.** *The Blacks in Canada: a History.* Robin W. Winks. Montreal: McGill-Queen's University Press, 1971.

2148. **Winks, Robin W.** *"Negro School Segregation in Ontario and Nova Scotia."* Robin W. Winks. Canadian Historical Review 50, 2(June 1969): 164-191.

2149. **Winn, Bertha** *"The Feeble Minded."* Bertha Winn. Canadian Nurse 12, 12(Dec. 1916): 664-667 and 13, 2 and 13, 2(Feb. and Mar. 1917): 80-82 and 122-125.

2150. **Wipper, Kirk Albert Walter** *A Study of the Influence of Two Types of Physical Education Programmes on the Physical Fitness of Participants.* Kirk Albert Walter Wipper. Toronto: University of Toronto, 1959. Thesis (M.A.)–University of Toronto, 1959.

2151. **Wise, S.F.** *Canada's Sporting Heroes.* S.F. Wise and Douglas Fisher. Don Mills: General Publishing Company, c1974.

2152. **Wishart, D.E.S.** *"The Problem of the Deaf Child."* D.E.S. Wishart. Canadian Medical Association Journal 38, 3(Mar. 1938): 254-260.

2153. **Wiswell, G.B.** *"The Sturge-Weber Syndrome."* G.B. Wiswell, C.S. Marshall and D.C. Metcalfe. Canadian Medical Association Journal 61, 6(Dec. 1949): 623.

2154. **Witcomb, Bill** *"Girl Guides Mark 75th Anniversary."* Bill Witcomb. Atlantic Advocate 75, 5(Jan. 1985): 8-11.

2155. **Wodehouse, Robert E.** *"The Child and Tuberculosis."* R.E. Wodehouse. In Proceedings and Papers Fifth Annual Canadian Conference on Child Welfare 1925, pp. 121-124.

2156. **Wodehouse, Robert E.** *"The Preventorium."* R.E. Wodehouse. Child and Family Welfare 8, 3(Sept. 1932): 28-30.

2157. **Wodehouse, Robert E.** *"Vital Statistics Pertaining to Infant Mortality."* Robert E. Wodehouse. Public Health Journal 2, 8(Aug. 1911): 363.

2158. **Wohlstein, Ronald Theodore** *Premarital Sexual Permissiveness: a Replication.* Ronald Theodore Wohlstein. Edmonton: University of Alberta, 1970. Thesis (M.A.)–University of Alberta, 1970.

2159. **Wold, David A.** *"The Adjustment of Siblings to Childhood Leukemia."* David A. Wold and Brenda D. Townes. Family Coordinator 18, 2(Apr. 1969): 155-160.

2160. **Wolfe, Gordon S.** *A Study of the Jewish Upper-middle Class Adolescent Girl Through Her Use of Time.* Gordon S. Wolfe. Toronto: University of Toronto, 1961. Thesis (M.S.W.)–University of Toronto, 1961.

2161. **Wolfe, S. Herbert** *Care of Dependents of Enlisted Men in Canada.* S. Herbert Wolfe. Washington, D.C.: Government Printing Office, 1917. Study of the Canadian situation undertaken by the United States Department of Labor Children's Bureau, Miscellaneous Series no. 10 and Bureau Publication no. 25.

2162. **Wong, Paul T.P.** *Infantile Stimulation and the Generalized Persistence Effect.* Paul Tsai-Pao Wong. Toronto: University of Toronto, 1968. Thesis (M.A.)–University of Toronto, 1968.

2163. **Woodcock, George** *The Doukhobors.* George Woodcock and Ivan Avakumovic. Toronto: Oxford University Press (Canadian Branch), 1968.

2164. **Woodhouse, Fraser** *"Boys' Clubs of Canada: a Scholarship Plan."* Fraser Woodhouse. Canadian Welfare 37, 4(July 1961): 191-193.

2165. **Woods, Jessie M.** *"The Public Health Nurse and Infant Care."* Jessie M. Woods. In Proceedings and Papers Fifth Annual Canadian Conference on Child Welfare 1925, pp. 99-102.

2166. **Woodsworth, J.S.** *My Neighbour: a Study of City Conditions, a Plea for Social Service.* J.S. Woodsworth. [Toronto]: University of Toronto Press, [c1972]. First published by the Missionary Society of the Methodist Church in 1911 at Toronto.

2167. **Woodsworth, J.S.** *Strangers Within Our Gates: or Coming Canadians.* James S. Woodsworth; intro. by Marilyn Barber. [Toronto]: University of Toronto Press, [1972]. Originally published in 1909.

2168. **Workshop on Education and Career Planning for Children With Impaired Vision (1st: 1966: Vancouver)** *Proceedings of the Workshop on Education and Career Planning for Children with Visual Impairments, March 11-12, 1966.* Vancouver: University of British Columbia, 1966.

2169. **Wormith, J. Stephen** *A Survey of Dangerous Sexual Offenders in Canada: 1948-1977.* J.S. Wormith and Monika Ruhl. [Ottawa]: Ministry of the Solicitor General, Secretariat, 1986.

2170. **Worthington, Peter** *Looking for Trouble: a Journalist's Life.* Peter Worthington. Toronto: Key Porter, c1984.

2171. **Woycenko, Ol'ha** *"Community Organizations."* Ol'ha Woycenko. Toronto: McClelland and Stewart Ltd., 1982. In A Heritage in Transition: Essays in the History of Ukrainians in Canada, pp. 173-194. Edited by Manoly R. Lupul.

2172. **Wright, Helen K.** *Nellie McClung and Women's Rights.* Helen K. Wright. Agincourt: Book Society of Canada, c1980.

2173. **Wyllie, John C.** *"Sex Differences in Infant Mortality."* J. Wyllie. Canadian Public Health Journal 24, 4(Apr. 1933): 177-185.

2174. **Wyllie, John C.** *"Sex Differences in the Mortalities of Childhood and Adult Life."* J. Wyllie. Canadian Public Health Journal 24, 11(Nov. 1933): 530-542.

2175. **Yorke, Elizabeth Ann** *A Study of Youth in the Jewish Community with Reference to the Relationship between Sex and Affiliation with the Jewish Community.* Elizabeth Ann Yorke. Toronto: University of Toronto, 1968. Thesis (M.S.W.)--University of Toronto, 1968.

2176. **Young, H.E.** *"Child Hygiene: Defective Vision in Children."* H.E. Young and J.T. Phair. Canadian Public Health Journal 20, 3(Mar. 1929): 155-157.

2177. **Young, John E.M.** *A Study in the Measurement of the Expressed Attitude of English-Speaking Canadian High School Seniors Toward Americans.* John Ernest McKern Young. Toronto: University of Toronto, 1952. Thesis (Ph.D.)--University of Toronto, 1952.

2178. **Young Men's Christian Association. Study Committee** *The Years Ahead: a Plan for the Canadian YMCA in the Next Decade.* The Committee. 2nd ed. Toronto: National Council of Y.M.C.A.'s of Canada, 1945. Joint publication with the Canadian Youth Commission. Chairman: K.E. Norris.

2179. **Young, Scott** *Neil and Me.* Scott Young. Toronto: McClelland and Stewart, c1984.

2180. **Younghusband, Eileen** *"Is All Well With the Child?"* Eileen Younghusband. Canadian Welfare 27, 5(Nov. 1951): 3-14.

2181. **Zay, Nicolas** *"Gaps in Available Statistics on Crime and Delinquency in Canada."* Nicolas Zay. Canadian Journal of Economics and Political Science 29, 1(Feb. 1963): 75-89. Reprinted in Deviant Behaviour and Societal Reaction, pp. 78-92. Edited by Craig L. Boydell, Carl F. Grindstaff and Paul C. Whitehead.

2182. **Zeman, Brenda** *To Run With Longboat: Twelve Stories of Indian Athletes in Canada.* Brenda Zeman; edited by David Williams. Edmonton: GMS2 Ventures Incorporated, c1988.

2183. **Zingle, Harvey W.** *"Experimental Tests of Two Hypotheses Concerning Normalization of Form Perception."* Harvey W. Zingle and Roland A. Lambert. Alberta Journal of Educational Research 9, 3(Sept. 1963): 147-156.

2184. **Zlotkin, Norman K.** *"Judicial Recognition of Aboriginal Customary Law in Canada: Selected Marriage and Adoption Cases."* Norman K. Zlotkin. Canadian Native Law Reporter 4(1984): 1-12.

# British Columbia

2185. **Ackery, Ivan** *Fifty Years on Theatre Row*. Ivan Ackery. North Vancouver: Hancock House, c1980.

2186. **Adachi, Ken** *The Enemy That Never Was: a History of the Japanese Canadians*. Ken Adachi. Toronto: McClelland and Stewart, 1976.

2187. **Adams, Joan** *Frozen Schools and Frozen Inkwells: the One-Room Schools of British Columbia*. Joan Adams and Becky Thomas. Madeira Park, B.C.: Harbour Publishing, 1985.

2188. **Adams, Robert L.** *Utilization of Manpower at Children's Aid Society of Vancouver, B.C.* Robert L. Adams, Dianne G. Bunting, Olga M. Dekler, Linda R. Korbin, John C. Snyder and Francis W. Winters. Vancouver: University of British Columbia, 1967.
Thesis (M.S.W.)--University of British Columbia, 1967.

2189. **Ahrendt, Kenneth Martin** *An Analysis of the Effects of an Experimental Remedial Reading Program on the Comprehension Skills of Potential School Dropouts*. Kenneth Martin Ahrendt. Vancouver: University of British Columbia, 1969.
Thesis (Ph.D.)--University of British Columbia, 1969.

2190. **Aitken, E.** *"Early Records of Salmon Valley and Glenemma Schools."* E. Aitken. Okanagan Historical Society Report 29(1965): 49-53.

2191. **Akin, Clifford K.** *Follow-up Study of Family Group Therapy*. Clifford K. Akin, Rhetta Dlin, Corraine A.J. Forst, Kenneth L. Levitt, Carol A. Smith and Jack S. Yee. Vancouver: University of British Columbia, 1966.
Thesis (M.S.W.)--University of British Columbia, 1966.

2192. **Allen, Emily G.** *"Ladysmith and District."* Emily G. Allen. Public Health Nurses' Bulletin 2, 2(Apr. 1935): 7-8.

2193. **Allen, Emily G.** *"The Neglected Age."* E.G. Allen. Public Health Nurses' Bulletin 2, 4(Mar. 1937): 5.

2194. **Allen, Emily G.** *"Public Health, Ladysmith and District."* E.G. Allen. Public Health Nurses' Bulletin 2, 3(June 1936): 4-5.

2195. **Allen, Emily G.** *"Thoughts on Taking Over a District."* Emily G. Allen. Public Health Nurses' Bulletin 1, 9(Mar. 1932): 21-22.

2196. **Allison, Susan** *A Pioneer Gentlewoman in British Columbia: the Recollections of Susan Allison*. Susan Allison and Margaret A. Ormsby, ed. Vancouver: University of British Columbia Press, c1976.

2197. **Alvarez, A.F.** *"Meconium Peritonitis Following Perforation of the Duodenum in the Newborn."* A.F. Alvarez, J.D. Hare and H.A. Unruh. Canadian Medical Association Journal 72, 2(Jan. 15, 1955): 120-122.

**2198. American Psychiatric Association** *Survey of Mental Health Needs and Resources of British Columbia.* American Psychiatric Association, Mathew Ross, ed. [Washington, D.C.: s.n., 1961].

**2199. Anastasi, Anne** *"A Study of Animal Drawings by Indian Children of the North Pacific Coast."* Anne Anastasi and John P. Foley, Jr. Journal of Social Psychology 9, 3(Aug. 1938): 363-374.

**2200. Anderson, Donald O.** *"The Incidence of Illness Among Young Children in Two Communities of Different Air Quality: a Pilot Study."* Donald O. Anderson and A.A. Larson. Canadian Medical Association Journal/Journal de l'Association medicale canadienne 95, 18(Oct. 29, 1966): 893-904.

**2201. Anderson, M. Doris** *"A Mother Breast Feeds Her Baby."* M. Doris Anderson. Canadian Nurse 46, 12(Dec. 1950): 972-973.

**2202. Anderson, W.F.** *"Blighted Twin."* W.F. Anderson. Canadian Medical Association Journal 76, 3(Feb. 1, 1957): 216-218.

**2203. Andrade, Teresa Manalad** *Growth Patterns in Reading Achievement.* Teresa Manalad Andrade. Vancouver: University of British Columbia, 1969.
　　Thesis (Ed.D.)--University of British Columbia, 1969.

**2204. Andrews, Gerry** *"Beyond the Rugged Mountains."* Gerry Andrews. Alberta History 36, 1(Winter 1988): 11-18.

**2205. Andrews, Gerry** *"Beyond Those Rugged Mountains."* Gerry Andrews. British Columbia Historical News 20, 4(Fall 1987): 12-14.

**2206. Andrews, Gerry** *Metis Outpost: Memoirs of the First Schoolmaster at the Metis Settlement of Kelly Lake, B.C., 1923-1925.* Gerry Andrews. Victoria: G. Smedley Andrews, c1985.

**2207. Andrews, Leslie G.** *"Spina Bifida Cystica: a Follow-up Survey."* Leslie G. Andrews. Canadian Medical Association Journal/Journal de l'Association medicale canadienne 97, 6(Aug. 5, 1967): 280-285.

**2208. Andrews, Margaret W.** *"Epidemic and Public Health: Influenza in Vancouver, 1918-1919."* Margaret W. Andrews. BC Studies 34(Summer 1977): 21-44.

**2209. Anglican Young People's Association** *Historical Sketch of the Anglican Young People's Association in British Columbia Up to 1945.* Anglican Young People's Association, edited by Rev. L.D. Dixon. Rev. ed. [Victoria: Victoria Printing and Publishing, 1945].

**2210. Angus, Anne Margaret** *Children's Aid Society of Vancouver, B.C., 1901-1951.* Anne Margaret Angus. [Vancouver: Allied Printing Trades Council, 1951].

**2211. Anonymous** *"A Dental Clinic in a Rural District."* Public Health Nurses' Bulletin 1, 8(Mar. 1931): 19-23.

**2212. Anonymous** *"The Faceless Ones."* Vancouver Historical Society Newsletter 14, 8(Feb. 1975): 3-6.

**2213. Anonymous** *"Medical Inspection of Schools in British Columbia."* Public Health Journal 5, 3(Mar. 1914): 147-154.

**2214. Archibald, Jo-Ann** *"Locally Developed Native Studies Curriculum: an Historical and Philosophical Rationale."* Jo-Ann Archibald. Vancouver: Mokakit Indian Education Research Association, 1986. In Establishing Pathways to Excellence in Indian Education: Selected Papers from the First Mokakit Conference, July 25-27, 1984, pp. 1-21. Edited by Harvey A. McCue.

**2215. Arima, E.Y.** *The West Coast (Nootka) People.* E.Y. Arima. Victoria: British Columbia Provincial Museum, 1983.

**2216. Armstrong, Norah E.** *"Cooperation."* Norah E. Armstrong. Public Health Nurses' Bulletin 1, 6(Apr. 1929): 32.

**2217. Armstrong, Norah E.** *"The Duncan Consolidated School District."* N. Armstrong. Public Health Nurses' Bulletin 1, 4(Apr. 1927): 30-31.

**2218. Armstrong, Norah E.** *"Nanaimo Schools."* Norah E. Armstrong. Public Health Nurses' Bulletin 1, 7(May 1930): 32-33.

**2219. Armstrong, Norah E.** *"North Vancouver Eye Clinic."* N.E. Armstrong. Public Health Nurses' Bulletin 2, 5(Mar. 1938): 5-6.

**2220. Armstrong, Norah E.** *"The North Vancouver Health Unit."* Norah E. Armstrong. Public Health Nurses' Bulletin 1, 8(Mar. 1931): 49-51.

**2221. Armstrong, Shirley** *"Endicott Centre."* Shirley Armstrong. British Columbia Historical News 24, 1(Winter 1990-91): 26-28.

**2222. Arnell, George Charles** *An Experimental Study of the Relationship Between Selected Stimuli and the Quality of Student Expository Writing.* George Charles Arnell. Burnaby: Simon Fraser University, 1970.
Thesis (M.A.)--Simon Fraser University, 1970.

**2223. Arnould, J.M.** *"Matsqui-Sumas-Abbotsford Demonstration Area."* J. Maryon Arnould. Public Health Nurses' Bulletin 2, 4(Mar. 1937): 5-7.

**2224. Arnould, J.M.** *"Public Health Work in a Demonstration Area."* J.M. Arnould. Public Health Nurses' Bulletin 2, 3(June 1936): 5-7.

**2225. Arnould, J.M.** *"Water Problems in a Rural Area."* J.M. Arnould. Public Health Nurses' Bulletin 2, 5(Mar. 1938): 6-7.

**2226. Ashlee, Ted** *Gabby, Ernie and Me: a Vancouver Boyhood.* Ted Ashlee. Vancouver: J.J. Douglas, c1976.

**2227. Ashworth, Mary** *The Forces Which Shaped Them: a History of the Education of Minority Group Children in British Columbia.* Mary Ashworth [and] Rosemary Brown, intro. Vancouver: New Star Books, c1979.

**2228. Association for Retarded Children of B.C.** *Let's Help Them, Not Hide Them: a Brief on Behalf of British Columbia's Retarded Children.* Association for Retarded Children of B.C. [Vancouver: The Association, 1959?]

**2229. Assu, Harry** *Assu of Cape Mudge: Recollections of a Coastal Indian Chief.* Harry Assu and Joy Inglis. Vancouver: University of British Columbia Press, 1989.

**2230. Atkinson, Raymond Gareth** *The Battered Child Syndrome: Medical, Legal and Social Work Machinery for Dealing With the Battered Child Syndrome.* Raymond Gareth Atkinson, Mary Nora Clark, Marjorie-Guy Lukas and Gary Steeves Wright Wickeet. Vancouver: University of British Columbia, 1965.
Thesis (M.S.W.)--University of British Columbia, 1965.

**2231. Audain, James** *From Coalmine to Castle: the Story of the Dunsmuirs of Vancouver Island.* James Audain. New York: Pageant Press, c1955.

**2232. B.C. Indian Arts Society** *Mungo Martin: Man of Two Cultures.* B.C. Indian Arts Society. Sidney, British Columbia: Gray's Publishing Limited, c1982.

**2233. Bach, Frank** *Vocational Problems of the Adolescent Offender: Some Applications to New Haven and B.C. Borstal Association Groups.* Frank Bach. Vancouver: University of British Columbia, 1961.
Thesis (M.S.W.)--University of British Columbia, 1961.

**2234. Baher, Mathias** *The Life and Times of the Elk Valley Sourdough.* Mathias Baher. Sparwood, B.C.: M. Baher, [1984], c1983.

**2235. Baity, Earl Shaw** *I Remember Chilako.* Earl Shaw Baity. Prince George: Prince George Printers, c1978.

**2236. Baker, Harry** *"Five Years Experience with a High Humidity Room."* Harry Baker. Canadian Medical Association Journal 72, 12(June 15, 1955): 914-917.

**2237. Baker, John W.B.** *"Into the North."* John W.B. Baker. Alberta History 33, 2(Spring 1985): 19-27.

**2238. Barker, Ken** *"Home Port: Vancouver."* Ken Barker. Vancouver: New Star Books Ltd., c1980. In Along the No. 20 Line: Reminiscences of the Vancouver Waterfront, pp. 175-189. By Rolf Knight.

**2239. Barman, Jean** *"Growing Up British in British Columbia: the Vernon Preparatory School, 1914-1946."* Jean Barman. Calgary: Detselig Enterprises Ltd., 1980. In Schooling and Society in 20th Century British Columbia, pp. 119-138. Edited by J. Donald Wilson and David C. Jones.

**2240. Barman, Jean** *Growing Up British in British Columbia: Boys in Private School, 1900-1950.* Jean Alice Barman. Vancouver: University of British Columbia, 1982. (CTM no. 59157)
Thesis (Ed.D.)--University of British Columbia, 1982.

**2241. Barman, Jean** *Growing Up British in British Columbia: Boys in Private School.* Jean Barman. Vancouver: University of British Columbia Press, 1984.

**2242. Barman, Jean** *""Knowledge is Essential for Universal Progress But Fatal to Class Privilege": Working People and the Schools in Vancouver During the 1920s."* Jean Barman. Labour/Le Travail 22(Fall 1988): 9-66.

**2243. Barman, Jean** *"Lost Opportunity: All Hallows School for Indians and White Girls, 1884-1920."* Jean Barman. British Columbia Historical News 22, 2(Spring 1989): 6-9.

**2244. Barman, Jean** *"Marching to Different Drummers: Public Education and Private Schools in British Columbia."* Jean Barman. B.C. Historical News 14, 1(Fall 1980): 2-11.

**2245. Barman, Jean** *"Separate and Unequal: Indian and White Girls at All Hallows School, 1884-1920."* Jean Barman. Vancouver: University of British Columbia Press, 1986. In Indian Education in Canada, Volume 1: the Legacy, pp. 110-131. Edited by Jean Barman, Yvonne Hebert and Don McCaskill.

**2246. Barman, Jean** *"Skimming Off the Cream: the Social Impact of Private Education in British Columbia, 1900-1950."* Jean Barman. History of Education Review 16, 1(1987): 51-60.

**2247. Barr, Frances** *"Teen Canteens."* Frances Barr. Canadian Welfare 20, 3(July 1944): 15-16.

**2248. Barton, Hilda E.** *"Summary of a Year's Work."* Hilda E. Barton. Public Health Nurses' Bulletin 1, 9(Mar. 1932): 12-13.

**2249. Barton, Hilda E.** *"Westbank, Peachland, and Indian Reservation."* Hilda E. Barton. Public Health Nurses' Bulletin 1, 8(Mar. 1931): 6-7.

**2250. Bartsch, Maxine Mae** *The Reservation of Children From Adoption: a Survey of the Determining Factors for Older Children (Aged 6-10 Years) in the Care of the Children's Aid Society, Vancouver, 1949.* Maxine Mae Bartsch. Vancouver: University of British Columbia, 1951.
    Thesis (M.S.W.)--University of British Columbia, 1951.

**2251. Bateman, Lillian Lamont** *"Fire Up Above, Fire Down Below."* Lillian Lamont Bateman. Raincoast Chronicles 12(1990): 32-37.

**2252. Batten, Jack** *Nancy: an Affectionate Look in Pictures at the World's Greatest Woman Skier and One of its Most Charming Girls.* Jack Batten and Peter Gzowski. Toronto: Star Reader Service, c1968.

**2253. Bauman, Adin Martin** *Education for Family Living Through Co-Operative Preschool Groups: a Study of Teacher, Parent, and Child Experience, Greater Vancouver, 1962-1963.* Adin Martin Bauman. Vancouver: University of British Columbia, 1963.
    Thesis (M.S.W.)--University of British Columbia, 1963.

**2254. Baxter, E.H.** *"The Learning of the Occupational Hierarchy."* E.H. Baxter and T.A. Nosanchuk. Toronto: McClelland and Stewart, c1975. In Socialization and Values in Canadian Society, v.2, pp. 28-50. Edited by Robert M. Pike and Elia Zureik.

**2255. Baxter, Sheila** *No Way to Live: Poor Women Speak Out.* Sheila Baxter. Vancouver: New Star Books, 1988.

**2256. Beattie, Jessie L.** *Goofy Willie Nye of the Cariboo Country.* Jessie L. Beattie. Hamilton: Flemming Press, c1983.

**2257. Beck, Dorothy Joan** *Resistance of the Adolescent to Casework Services: Relationship of Emancipatory Efforts and Psychosexual Conflicts of Adolescence to Resistance Shown in Treatment at the Child Guidance Clinic, Vancouver.* Dorothy Joan Beck. Vancouver: University of British Columbia, 1954.
    Thesis (M.S.W.)--University of British Columbia, 1954.

**2258. Beckett, C.H.** *"The Alexandra Home Activities."* C.H. Beckett. Canadian Welfare Summary 14, 6(Mar. 1939): 30-33.

**2259. Beckley, A. Verna** *"Public Health in Nanaimo."* A. Verna Beckley. Public Health Nurses' Bulletin 1, 5(Apr. 1928): 18.

**2260. Beckley, A. Verna** *"Public Health in Nanaimo."* A. Verna Beckley. Public Health Nurses' Bulletin 1, 6(Apr. 1929): 22.

**2261. Begg, Sheila C.** *The Relationship of Social Factors of the Female Juvenile Offender to the Disposition of Her Case in the Juvenile Court.* Sheila C. Begg, Susan L. Gellatly, Dorothy J. Lamont, Anna K. Luckyj, Judith A. Nenzel, Carole H. Sloan and Lieselotte Wolf. Vancouver: University of British Columbia, 1967.
    Thesis (M.S.W.)--University of British Columbia, 1967.

**2262. Beiber, Benjamin Arnold** *Search and Leadership Training in Probation: a Pre-Evaluative Study of an Experiment in the Treatment of Delinquency in British Columbia.* Benjamin Arnold Beiber, Sheridan Brind, Anthony Kendall, Hugh David Campbell, Robert Noel Doupe, Lyle

Edward Garinger and Frederick Mazie. Vancouver: University of British Columbia, 1967. Thesis (M.S.W.)--University of British Columbia, 1967.

**2263. Bell, Ann** *"Youth in Our Town."* Ann Bell. Canadian Welfare 39, 2(Mar.-Apr. 1963): 50-53.

**2264. Bell, Betty** *The Fair Land: Saanich.* Betty Bell. Victoria: Sono Nis Press, c1982.

**2265. Bell-Irving, Elizabeth** *Crofton House School, the First Ninety Years 1898-1988.* Elizabeth Bell-Irving. Vancouver: The School, c1988.

**2266. Bell, Kenneth Edward** *The Recognition and Treatment of Emotionally Disturbed Children in Grades One to Four of a Public School System: a Sample Survey of the Children From Twelve Burnaby Schools Reported by Their Teachers as Maladjusted, With Further Study of the Children From Three Schools and the Help Presently Given Such Children to Overcome Their Emotional Disturbance.* Kenneth Edward Bell. Vancouver: University of British Columbia, 1951. Thesis (M.S.W.)--University of British Columbia, 1951.

**2267. Bene, Eva Mary** *Mothers' Attitudes and Nursery School Children's Adjustments.* Eva Mary Bene. Vancouver: University of British Columbia, 1948. Thesis (M.A.)--University of British Columbia, 1948.

**2268. Benger, Basil Charles** *A Study of the Relationships of Perception and Personality to Achievement of Grade One Pupils.* Basil Charles Benger. Burnaby: Simon Fraser University, 1969. Thesis (M.A.)--Simon Fraser University, 1969.

**2269. Bennest, Jean** *"Development of Social Services in the Okanagan, 1930-1980."* Jean Bennest. Okanagan Historical Society Report 45(1981): 18-23.

**2270. Bennett, V.E.** *"All Hallows School, Yale, B.C."* V.E. Bennett. Okanagan Historical Society Report 24(1960): 101-104.

**2271. Billington, Alan Roy** *Group Work Practice in a Receiving Home for Boys: an Analysis of an Experimental Project in Boys' Receiving Home of the Children's Aid Society of Vancouver, British Columbia, 1952-53.* Alan Roy Billington. Vancouver: University of British Columbia, 1953. Thesis (M.S.W.)--University of British

Columbia, 1953.

**2272. Bimbi-Kovacs, Agnes E.** *"Potter's Facies Associated with Polycystic Kidney with Laurence-Biedl-Moon Syndrome in Siblings."* Agnes E. Bimbi-Kovacs and A.F. Hardyment. Canadian Medical Association Journal 74, 7(Apr. 1, 1956): 549-551.

**2273. Bingham, T.D.** *Address of the Superintendent of Child Welfare, Mr. T.D. Bingham: to a Joint Meeting of the Children's Aid Society and Catholic Children's Aid Society in Vancouver, on February 24th, 1966.* [Vancouver: s.n., 1966].

**2274. Birch, George David** *"She Came Before the Railway: Mabel McLarty Petersen, a Pioneer of Prince George."* George David Birch. British Columbia Historical News 18, 2(Spring 1984): 16-20.

**2275. Birkett, Geraldine** *"Trends and Problems in British Columbia's Present Reading Program."* Geraldine Birkett. Journal of Education of the Faculty and College of Education: Vancouver and Victoria 6(Dec. 1961): 19-24.

**2276. Bjerring, Barbara Frances** *Factors in the Early Termination of Family Day Care Service: a Survey of Agency Experience in Family Day Care Service in Greater Vancouver, 1966-1967, with Special Reference to the Department of Day Care Services, the Family Service Centre of Vancouver.* Barbara Frances Bjerring, Sheena Dalton Brown, Emery Charles Gardiner and Janet Ayre Murphy. Vancouver: University of British Columbia, 1967. Thesis (M.S.W.)--University of British Columbia, 1967.

**2277. Blacklock, Donald John** *The Juvenile Court in British Columbia: an Evaluation of the Juvenile Courts, the Probation Services and Other Associated Facilities in British Columbia, 1960.* Donald John Blacklock. Vancouver: University of British Columbia, 1960. Thesis (M.S.W.)--University of British Columbia, 1960.

**2278. Blackman, Margaret B.** *During My Time: Florence Edenshaw Davidson, a Haida Woman.* Margaret B. Blackman. Seattle: University of Washington Press, c1982.

**2279. Blake, Don** *Blakeburn, From Dust to Dust: the Rise and Fall of a Coal Mining Town.* Don Blake. Penticton, B.C.: Skookum Publications, c1985.

**2280. Blanchard, Paula** *The Life of Emily Carr.* Paula Blanchard. Seattle: University of Washington Press, 1987.

**2281. Blank, Lillian** *"A Rural Baby Clinic."* Lillian Blank. Public Health Nurses' Bulletin 2, 5(Mar. 1938): 7-8.

**2282. Blinder, Rose** *"In Search of Foster Homes."* Rose Blinder. Canadian Welfare 33, 2(June 1957): 65.

**2283. Blinder, Rose** *Treatment for Emotionally Disturbed Wards of Children's Aid Society.* Rose Blinder. Vancouver: University of British Columbia, 1954. Thesis (M.S.W.)--University of British Columbia, 1954.

**2284. Boggis, Steve** *A History of the Public Schools in Richmond 1877-1979.* Steve Boggis. Richmond, British Columbia: Richmond School Board, [1979].

**2285. Bolt, Clarence R.** *"The Conversion of the Port Simpson Tsimshian: Indian Control or Missionary Manipulation?"* Clarence R. Bolt. BC Studies 57(Spring 1983): 38-56.

**2286. Bonham, G.H.** *"Fluid Intake Patterns of 6-year-old Children in a Northern Fluoridated Community."* G.H. Bonham, A.S. Gray and M. Luttrell. Canadian Medical Association Journal/Journal de l'Association medicale canadienne 91, 14(Oct. 3, 1964): 749-751.

**2287. Bouchie Lake Women's Institute** *Pioneers of Bouchie Lake.* Bouchie Lake Women's Institute and Marion Booth, ed. [S.l.: s.n.], 1975.

**2288. Bourgon, Nan** *Rubber Boots for Dancing: and Other Memories of Pioneer Life in the Bulkley Valley.* Nan Bourgon and Marjorie Rosberg, ed. Smithers, B.C.: T. and J. Hetherington, c1979.

**2289. Bowd, Alan D.** *A Cross Cultural Study of Environmental Influences and Mechanical Aptitude in Several Indian Groups.* Alan Douglas Bowd. Calgary: University of Calgary, 1971. Thesis (Ph.D.)--University of Calgary, 1971.

**2290. Bowen, Lynne** *Boss Whistle: the Coal Miners of Vancouver Island Remember.* Lynne Bowen. Lantzville: Oolichan Books, 1982.

**2291. Bowmer, E.J.** *"Typhoid Fever: Where There's a Case, There's a Carrier."* E.J. Bowmer, Vivienne J. Hudson and W.F. Sunderland. Canadian Medical Association Journal 80, 3(Feb. 1, 1959): 179-186.

**2292. Boyd, Denny** *"An Unforgettable Cop."* Denny Boyd. British Columbia Police Journal 5, 1(Autumn 1982): 10-11.

**2293. Boyer, Cedric M.** *"Fun in Twenty-one: Memories of a Boyhood in Kelowna."* Cedric M. Boyer. Okanagan Historical Society Report 47(1983): 138-142.

**2294. Braithwaite, John William** *An Approach to Evaluative Research in a Correctional Setting: an Examination of the Research Resources Available for the Study of the New Haven Open Borstal Program in British Columbia.* John William Braithwaite. Vancouver: University of British Columbia, 1956. Thesis (M.S.W.)--University of British Columbia, 1956.

**2295. Brander, Lorraine** *"Dolls, Roller Skates and Dockyards."* Lorraine Brander. Vancouver: New Star Books, c1980. In Along the No. 20 Line: Reminiscences of the Vancouver Waterfront, pp. 190-201. By Rolf Knight.

**2296. Bredin, Grace** *"The Child Study Centre of the University of British Columbia: Its History and Development."* Grace Bredin. Journal of Education of the Faculty of Education, Vancouver 12(Jan. 1966): 39-47.

**2297. Breeze, Elizabeth G.** *"Little Mothers' League."* Elizabeth G. Breeze. Canadian Nurse 22, 4(Apr. 1926): 199-200.

**2298. Breeze, Elizabeth G.** *"School Nursing."* Elizabeth Breeze. Public Health Nurses' Bulletin 1, 6(Apr. 1929): 4-5.

**2299. Bristowe, Elizabeth Anne** *How Dropouts Experience Schooling.* Elizabeth Anne Bristowe. Victoria: University of Victoria, 1971. Thesis (M.A.)--University of Victoria, 1971.

**2300. British Columbia. Advisory Committee on Juvenile Delinquency** *Report of the Advisory Committee on Juvenile Delinquency, 1936.* B.C. Advisory Committee on Juvenile Delinquency. Victoria: King's Printer, 1937.

**2301. British Columbia Child Welfare Survey Committee** *Report of the British Columbia Child Welfare Survey.* British Columbia Child Welfare Survey Committee and the Service Clubs of Vancouver City. Vancouver: The Committee, 1927.

**2302. British Columbia Civil Liberties
Association** *A Handbook on Youth and
the Law.* British Columbia Civil Liberties
Association. Vancouver: British Columbia
Civil Liberties Association, c1971.

**2303. British Columbia Civil Liberties
Association** *Youth and the Law.* British
Columbia Civil Liberties Association.
Vancouver: B.C. Civil Liberties
Association, c1971.

**2304. British Columbia. Commission
Appointed to Inquire Into Certain
Matters Connected With the Provincial
Lunatic Asylum at New Westminster**
*"Report of the Commission to Inquire Into
Certain Matters Connected With the
Provincial Lunatic Asylum at New
Westminster: Return to an Address of the
Legislative Assembly Requesting His Honour
the Lieutenant-Governor to Cause to be
Laid Before the House All the Papers in
Connection With the Late Enquiry Into the
Management of the Provincial Lunatic
Asylum Together With the Letter of
Instructions to the Commissioners Appointed
to Make the Enquiry."* The Commission. In
British Columbia Legislative Assembly
Sessional Papers, 7th Parliament, 1st
Session, Session 1894-95 pp. 503-574.
Chairman: Edward Hasell.

**2305. British Columbia. Commission to
Enquire As to the Laws Relating to
the Subjects of Mothers' Pensions,
Maternity Insurance, Health Insurance
and Public Health Nursing Which Are
in Force in Other Countries** *Report on
Mothers' Pensions With Appendix.* The
Commission. Victoria: King's Printer,
1920.
Chairman: E.S.H. Winn.

**2306. British Columbia. Department of
Education** *Public Elementary and
Secondary Education in British Columbia.*
The Department. Victoria: The
Department, 1955.

**2307. British Columbia. Department of
Education** *Survey of the Schools of the
Greater Victoria Area.* The Department.
Victoria: Charles F. Banfield, King's
Printer, 1938.

**2308. British Columbia. Department of
Education. Division of Alcohol
Education** *Alcohol Education: Subject
Integration in Grades 7 to 12.* The
Division. Victoria: The Department, 1947.

**2309. British Columbia Federation of
Athletic Associations** *A Brief to the
Provincial Legislature Supporting a Request
for the Establishment of a Legislative
Commission to Undertake a Comprehensive
Inquiry into the Special Needs of the
Youth of British Columbia.* British

Columbia Federation of Athletic
Associations and The British Columbia
Teachers' Association. [S.l.: s.n.], 1969.

**2310. British Columbia. Inquiry Into the
Administration of Mount View High
School** *Report of John Owen Wilson,
Commissioner re Mount View High School,
Saanich.* The Commission. [Vancouver:
s.n., 1944].
Commissioner: John Owen Wilson.

**2311. British Columbia. Juvenile
Delinquency Inquiry Board** *Report of
the Juvenile Delinquency Inquiry Board,
1960.* The Board. Victoria: The Board,
1960.
Chairman: Eric C.F. Martin.

**2312. British Columbia [Laws, Statutes,
Etc.]** *Protection of Children Act.* British
Columbia. Victoria, B.C.: Queen's Printer,
1974.
Original act passed in 1960,
consolidated for convenience July 19,
1974.

**2313. British Columbia Protestant
Orphans Home** *Constitution.* British
Columbia Protestant Orphans Home.
Victoria: The Association, 1893.

**2314. British Columbia Protestant
Orphans Home** *Constitution and By-laws.*
British Columbia Protestant Orphans
Home. Victoria: The Association, 1893.

**2315. British Columbia. Public Inquiry
Into the Circumstances of the
Disturbance Which Occurred on a
Saturday Night, August 7, 1971, in
that Part of the City of Vancouver
Known as Gastown** *Report of the
Gastown Inquiry.* The Commission.
Vancouver: The Commission, 1971.
Chairman/Commissioner: Thomas A.
Dohm.

**2316. British Columbia. Royal
Commission on Education (1960)** *A
Precis of the Report of the Royal
Commission on Education.* The
Commission. Victoria: [s.n.], 1960.
Chairman: S.N.F. Chant.

**2317. British Columbia. Royal
Commission on Education (1960)** *Report
of the Royal Commission on Education.*
The Commission. [Victoria: Queen's
Printer, 1960].
Chairman: S.N.F. Chant.

**2318. British Columbia. Royal
Commission on Labour, 1912** *Report of
the Royal Commission on Labour
Appointed on the 4th Day of December
1912 Under the Public Inquiries Act.* The
Commission. Victoria: King's Printer,
1914.

Chairman: H.G. Parson.

**2319. British Columbia. Royal Commission on Mental Hygiene** *Final Report of the Royal Commission on Mental Hygiene.* The Commission. Victoria: King's Printer, 1928.
Chairman: P.P. Harrison.

**2320. British Columbia. Royal Commission on Mental Hygiene** *Report of the Royal Commission on Mental Hygiene.* The Commission. Victoria: King's Printer, 1927.
Chairman: E.J. Rothwell.

**2321. British Columbia Teachers' Federation** *Brief Presented to the Royal Commission on Education.* British Columbia Teachers' Federation. Vancouver: The Federation, 1959.

**2322. Brock, David** *"The Innocent Mind, or, My Days as a Juvenile Delinquent."* David Brock. Canadian Journal of Corrections/Revue canadienne de criminologie 2, 1(Jan. 1960): 25-35.

**2323. Brown, Irene** *"In and Around South Vancouver."* Irene Brown. Vancouver Historical Society Newsletter 14, 6(Dec. 1974): 3-4.
Life in South Vancouver around 1930.

**2324. Brown, Joanne Victoria** *Family Contributions in Treatment of the Hearing Handicapped Child of School Age: an Exploratory Survey of Parents of Jericho Hill School Pupils.* Joanne Victoria Brown. Vancouver: University of British Columbia, 1960.
Thesis (M.S.W.)--University of British Columbia, 1960.

**2325. Brunador, Imelda Beetz** *"A Child with Post-Rubella Encephalitis."* Imelda Beetz Brunador. Canadian Nurse 53, 7(July 1957): 610-615.

**2326. Bryenton, Joy Gertrude** *Communication with Children: an Aspect of Foster Home Placement with Social Work with Children.* Joy Gertrude Bryenton. Vancouver: University of British Columbia,1958.
Thesis (M.S.W.)--University of British Columbia, 1958.

**2327. Buckley, Geoffrey John** *Reading Achievement in Grade Five and Its Relationship to Potential Occupation, Verbal Intelligence and Certain Environmental Factors.* Geoffrey John Buckley. Vancouver: University of British Columbia, 1967.
Thesis (Ed.D.)--University of British Columbia, 1967.

**2328. Bulman, T. Alex** *Kamloops Cattlemen: One Hundred Years of Trail Dust!* T. Alex Bulman. Sydney B.C.: Gray's Publishing Ltd., c1972..

**2329. Burton Book Committee** *Whistle Stops Along the Columbia River Narrows: a History of Burton and Surrounding Area.* [Burton Book Committee].

**2330. Butterworth, Paul** *The Effects of Material and Non-material Reinforcement on the Perseverance Behaviour of Indian Children.* Paul Butterworth. Victoria: University of Victoria, 1969.
Thesis (M.A.)--University of Victoria, 1969.

**2331. Calam, John** *British Columbia Schools and Society.* John Calam and Thomas Fleming. Victoria: Queen's Printer, c1988.

**2332. Cambon, Kenneth G.** *"Middle Ear Disease in Indians of the Mount Currie Reservation, British Columbia."* Kenneth Cambon, J.D. Galbraith and G. Kong. Canadian Medical Association Journal/Journal de l'Association medicale canadienne 93, 25(Dec. 18, 1965): 1301-1305.

**2333. Cameron, Maxwell A.** *The Small High School in British Columbia.* Maxwell A. Cameron. Vancouver: University of British Columbia, 1932.
Thesis (M.A.)--University of British Columbia, 1932.

**2334. Cameron, Silver Donald** *Seasons in the Rain: an Expatriate's Notes on British Columbia.* Silver Donald Cameron. Toronto: McClelland and Stewart, 1978.

**2335. Campbell, Janet** *"Kamloops."* J. Campbell. Public Health Nurses' Bulletin 1, 3(Apr. 1926): 14-16.

**2336. Campbell, Janet** *"Public Health Work in Kamloops."* Janet Campbell. Public Health Nurses' Bulletin 1, 4(Apr. 1927): 23-24.

**2337. Campbell, M.A.** *"Public Health."* M.A. Campbell. Public Health Nurses' Bulletin 2, 4(Mar. 1937): 9-10.

**2338. Canada. Department of Labour** *Report on the Administration of Japanese Affairs in Canada, 1942-1944.* The Department. [S.l.: s.n., 1944].
Mimeographed.

**2339. Canada. Department of Labour. British Columbia Security Commission** *Report of the British Columbia Security Commission: March 4, 1942 to October 31, 1942.* The Commission. Vancouver: British Columbia Security Commission, [1942].

2340. **Canadian Council on Child and Family Welfare** *"British Columbia's Departure."* Canadian Council on Child and Family Welfare. Child and Family Welfare 10, 5(Jan. 1935): 43-45.

2341. **Canadian Council on Child and Family Welfare** *"An Experiment in Day Nursery Foster Home Interest Groups."* Canadian Council on Child and Family Welfare. Child and Family Welfare 13, 1(May 1937): 32.

2342. **Canadian Council on Child and Family Welfare** *"Foster Care in Day Nursery Work."* Canadian Council on Child and Family Welfare. Child and Family Welfare 9, 3(Sept. 1933): 18-19.

2343. **Canadian Council on Child and Family Welfare** *"Grist to British Columbia Mill."* Canadian Council on Child and Family Welfare. Child and Family Welfare 13, 6(Mar. 1938): 47-50.

2344. **Canadian Council on Child and Family Welfare** *Report on the Administration of Mothers' Pensions in British Columbia, 1920-1 to 1930-1.* Canadian Council on Child and Family Welfare and S.L. Howe. [S.l.: s.n.], 1932. Supplement to "Child and Family Welfare" - May 1932.

2345. **Canadian Council on Child and Family Welfare** *"A Sikh Well-baby Clinic in British Columbia."* Canadian Council on Child and Family Welfare. Child and Family Welfare 11, 6(Mar. 1936): 17-19.

2346. **Canadian Council on Child and Family Welfare** *"A Tribute to Miss Lexa Denne."* Canadian Council on Child and Family Welfare. Child and Family Welfare 6, 2(May 1930): 27-28.

2347. **Canadian Council on Child and Family Welfare** *"A Year's Experiment in Private Home Care."* Canadian Council on Child and Family Welfare. Child and Family Welfare 10, 6(Mar. 1935): 35-36.

2348. **Canadian Council on Child Welfare** *"Child Welfare in British Columbia."* Canadian Council on Child Welfare. Canadian Child Welfare News 4, 1(Feb. 15, 1928): 46.

2349. **Canadian Council on Child Welfare** *"Vancouver: the Grand Jury and Child Welfare."* Canadian Council on Child Welfare. Child Welfare News 5, 1(Feb. 1929): 54.

2350. **Canadian Council on Child Welfare** *"Vancouver Children's Aid Society: Annual Meeting."* Canadian Council on Child Welfare. Canadian Child Welfare News 4, 2(May 15, 1928): 25-28.

2351. **Canadian Council on Child Welfare** *"Vancouver Children's Aid Society."* Canadian Council on Child Welfare. Child Welfare News 5, 2(May 1929): 34-35.

2352. **Canadian Council on Child Welfare** *"Vancouver Presbytery, the United Church of Canada, Endorses B.C. Survey Findings."* Canadian Council on Child Welfare. Canadian Child Welfare News 4, 1(Feb. 15, 1928): 45.

2353. **Canadian Japanese Association** *The Japanese Contribution to Canada.* Canadian Japanese Association. Vancouver: Canadian Japanese Association, 1940.

2354. **Canadian Mental Health Association. British Columbia Division. Scientific Planning Committee** *The Mental Health of Children in British Columbia.* Scientific Planning Committee of the Canadian Mental Health Association, British Columbia Division. Vancouver: [The Committee], 1966.

2355. **Canadian Mental Health Association. British Columbia Division. Scientific Planning Committee** *The Mental Health of Children in British Columbia: Final Report.* The Committee. Vancouver: [s.n.], 1966.

2356. **Canadian National Committee for Mental Hygiene** *"Mental Hygiene Survey of the Province of British Columbia."* Canadian National Committee for Mental Hygiene. Canadian Journal of Mental Hygiene 2, 1(Apr. 1920): 3-59.

2357. **Canadian National Committee for Mental Hygiene** *Mental Hygiene Survey of the Province of British Columbia.* The Committee.

2358. **Canadian Welfare Council** *"Delinquency Study in Victoria."* Canadian Welfare Council. Canadian Welfare 41, 2(Mar.-Apr. 1965): 81-82.

2359. **Canadian Welfare Council** *"Vancouver Children's Aid Society, 1901-1951."* Canadian Welfare Council. Canadian Welfare 27, 1(Apr. 1951): 20-24.

2360. Caple, Kenneth Percy "A Small Boy's West End." Kenneth P. Caple. Vancouver Historical Society Newsletter 16, 7(Apr. 1977): 4-9.

2361. Cardwell, Marion Torrence "A Day Spent in the Mennonite Settlement at Yarrow." Marion Torrence Cardwell. Public Health Nurses' Bulletin 1, 9(Mar. 1932): 45-47.

2362. Carlisle, Sheila Jane Case Work Referrals in Camping: a Study of Co-operative Services and Essential Procedures in Referring Children From Case Work Agencies to Summer Camps, Vancouver, British Columbia. Sheila Jane Carlisle. Vancouver: University of British Columbia, 1950.
Thesis (M.S.W.)–University of British Columbia, 1950.

2363. Carr, Emily The Book of Small. Emily Carr. Toronto: Clarke, Irwin and Company, c1942.

2364. Carr, Emily Growing Pains. Emily Carr. Toronto: Oxford University Press, c1946.

2365. Carr, Emily The Heart of a Peacock. Emily Carr. Toronto: Oxford Press, 1953.

2366. Carroll, Leila Wild Roses and Rail Fences. Leila Carroll. [S.l: s.n.], 1975.

2367. Carter, Norman R. "Dental Clinic for Rural Schools of Arrow Lakes District." Norman R. Carter. Public Health Nurses' Bulletin 1, 3(Apr. 1926): 16-17.

2368. Carter, Norman R. "Dental Clinic in Oliver District." Norman R. Carter. Public Health Nurses' Bulletin 1, 5(Apr. 1928): 17-18.

2369. Carter, Norman R. "Dental Clinics." Norman R. Carter. Public Health Nurses' Bulletin 1, 4(Apr. 1927): 18.

2370. Carter, Norman R. "Dental Service in the Arrow Lakes District." Norman R. Carter. Public Health Nurses' Bulletin 1, 4(Apr. 1927): 30.

2371. Carter, Norman R. "Problem of Mouth Health Among Children in Rural Districts of British Columbia in Relation to the Public Health Nurses." Norman R. Carter. Public Health Nurses' Bulletin 1, 3(Apr. 1926): 12-14.

2372. Cecilia, Mary Ann "A Child with Laryngotracheo Bronchitis." Mary Ann Cecilia. Canadian Nurse 52, 5(May 1956): 351-356.

2373. Chadney, James Gaylord The Vancouver Sikhs: an Ethnic Community in Canada. James Gaylord Chadney. Ann Arbor, Mich.: University Microfilms International, 1977.
Thesis (Ph.D.)–Michigan State University, 1976.

2374. Charlton, P. "Health Progress in the Armstrong Schools." P. Charlton. Public Health Nurses' Bulletin 1, 7(May 1930): 10-11.

2375. Charlton, P. "Health-teaching in Armstrong Consolidated School." P. Charlton. Public Health Nurses' Bulletin 1, 4(Apr. 1927): 12-13.

2376. Charlton, P. "Health-work in Armstrong." P. Charlton. Public Health Nurses' Bulletin 1, 9(Mar. 1932): 36-37.

2377. Charlton, P. "Mental Health in Our Schools." P. Charlton. Public Health Nurses' Bulletin 2, 2(Apr. 1935): 34-35.

2378. Charlton, P. "Progress in Health Work in Armstrong." P.A. Charlton. Public Health Nurses' Bulletin 1, 5(Apr. 1928): 5-7.

2379. Charlton, P. "Public Health in Armstrong." P. Charlton. Public Health Nurses' Bulletin 1, 8(Mar. 1931): 52-53.

2380. Charlton, P. "School Work in Armstrong." P. Charlton. Public Health Nurses' Bulletin 1, 3(Apr. 1926): 8.

2381. Chave, Estelle Christine The Pre-clinical Conference as a Diagnostic Screen in the Child Guidance Setting: a Preliminary Survey of the Use of the Procedure in Canadian Clinical Practice, and an Analysis of Selected Cases in the Child Guidance Clinic at Vancouver. Estelle Christine Chave. Vancouver: University of British Columbia, 1952.
Thesis (M.S.W.)–University of British Columbia, 1952.

2382. Cheng Tien-Fang Oriental Immigration in Canada. Cheng Tien-Fang. Rpt. ed. Ann Arbor: University Microfilms International, 1980.
Facsimile reprint, originally published under same title, 1931, Shanghai, Commercial Press.

2383. Child, Alan H. "A Little Tempest: Public Reaction to the Formation of a Large Educational Unit in the Peace River District of British Columbia." Alan H. Child. BC Studies 16(Winter 1972-1973): 57-70.

**2384. Child Welfare Association of British Columbia Annual Convention (1st: 1918: Vancouver)** *Report of the First Annual Convention of the Child Welfare Association of British Columbia, Held in Vancouver, Dec. 12, 13, and 14, 1918.* The Association. Vancouver: Grandview Printers, [1918?].

**2385. Child Welfare Association of British Columbia Annual Convention (2nd: 1919: Vancouver)** *Child Welfare Association of British Columbia: Second Annual Convention, October 29, 30, 31, 1919.* The Association. [S.l.: s.n., 1919].

**2386. Children's Aid Society of British Columbia** *Twenty-first Anniversary of the Children's Aid Society of British Columbia.* Children's Aid Society of British Columbia. [Vancouver: The Society, 1923].

**2387. Children's Aid Society of Vancouver** *The Role and Services of the Children's Aid Society of Vancouver.* Children's Aid Society of Vancouver. Vancouver: The Society, 1969.

**2388. Children's Aid Society of Vancouver** *Sixtieth Anniversary 1901-1961.* Children's Aid Society of Vancovuer. [Vancouver: The Society, 1961].

**2389. Chodat, I.** *"Coombs and District."* I. Chodat. Public Health Nurses' Bulletin 2, 3(June 1936): 7-9.

**2390. Christensen, Rolf Buschardt** *"Multiculturalism: the Foundation of Canadian Society."* Rolf Buschardt Christensen. Toronto: Quadrant Editions, 1983. In Between Two Worlds: the Canadian Immigrant Experience, pp. 240-247. Edited by Milly Charon.

**2391. Claman, A. David** *"Reaction of Unmarried Girls to Pregnancy."* A. David Claman, Barry J. Williams and L. Wogan. Canadian Medical Association Journal/Journal de l'Association medicale canadienne 101, 6(Sept. 20, 1969): 328-334.

**2392. Clark, Cecil** *"A Side Glance at History: Juvenile Delinquency."* Cecil Clark. British Columbia Police Journal 1, 1(Autumn 1978): 17-19.

**2393. Claxton, M.** *"Cowichan Health Centre: Starting Work at Bamberton."* M. Claxton. Public Health Nurses' Bulletin 1, 5(Apr. 1928): 15-16.

**2394. Claxton, M.** *"Cowichan Health Centre."* M. Claxton. Public Health Nurses' Bulletin 1, 6(Apr. 1929): 13-14.

**2395. Claxton, M.** *"North of the Peace River."* M. Claxton. Public Health Nurses' Bulletin 1, 9(Mar. 1932): 3-5.

**2396. Clyne, Dorothy** *Sharps and Flats in the Okanagan Valley.* Dorothy Cline. Kelowna, B.C.: [D. Cline]: c1977.

**2397. Cobbin, Jack Macdonald** *Treatment of Emotionally Disturbed Teenage Boys in (a Group Living) Residence: an Examination of Children's Aid Society Wards, With Special Reference to Movement Shown After a Period in a Group Living Institution.* Jack Macdonald Cobbin. Vancouver: University of British Columbia, 1955.
Thesis (M.S.W.)–University of British Columbia, 1955.

**2398. Cocks, A.W.** *The Pedagogical Value of the True-False Examination.* A.W. Cocks. Baltimore: Warwick and York, Incorporated, 1929.
Thesis (D.Paed.)--University of Toronto, 1929.

**2399. Cole, Douglas** *"Sigismund Bacstrom's Northwest Coast Drawings and an Account of His Curious Career."* Douglas Cole. BC Studies 46(Summer 1980): 61-86.

**2400. Collier, Eric** *Three Against the Wilderness.* Eric Collier. New York: E.P. Dutton & Co. Inc., c1959.

**2401. Collier, H.W.** *"Probation Services vs. Custodial Care."* H.W. Collier. In Proceedings and Papers Fourth Annual Canadian Conference on Child Welfare 1923, pp. 156-160.

**2402. Collins, David L.** *"Neonatal Hepatitis: Including a Case Associated with Maternal Hepatitis during Pregnancy."* David L. Collins. Canadian Medical Association Journal 75, 10(Nov. 15, 1956): 828-832.

**2403. Collins, Joan Manon** *An Exploration of the Role of Opposition in Cognitive Processes of Kindergarten Children.* Joan Manon Collins. Burnaby: Simon Fraser University, 1969.
Thesis (M.A.)–Simon Fraser University, 1969.

**2404. Colman, Mary Elizabeth** *"Schoolboy at Fort Victoria."* Mary Elizabeth Colman. Beaver 282, 3(Dec. 1951): 19-22.

**2405. Community Centres Conference (1946: Vancouver)** *Report of the Community Centres Conference, June 24-27, 1946 at the University of British Columbia.* Community Centres Conference. Vancouver: Department of University Extension, [1946].

**2406. Community Chest and Council of Greater Vancouver. Family and Child Welfare Division. Working Boys' Home Committee** *Senior Boys' Residences.* [The Committee]. [Vancouver: The Committee, 1954].

**2407. Community Chest and Councils of the Greater Vancouver Area. Welfare and Recreation Council** *Juvenile Delinquency Prevention, City of Vancouver: Report of Committee to Assess Juvenile Delinquency and Prevention Programs in the Greater Vancouver Area.* Welfare and Recreation Council, Community Chest and Councils of the Greater Vancouver Area. [Vancouver: The Council], 1965.

**2408. Community Chest and Councils of the Greater Vancouver Area. Welfare and Recreation Council. Committee to Study Day Care Needs in the Greater Vancouver Area** *The Report of the Committee to Study Day Care Needs in the Greater Vancouver Area.* [The Committee]. [Vancouver: The Committee, 1965].

**2409. Conroy, J.J.** *"Boyhood Recollections."* J.J. Conroy. Okanagan Historical Society Report 33(1973): 33-37.

**2410. Conway, Clifford B.** *A Study of Public and Private Kindergarten and Non-kindergarten Children in the Primary Grades [of] School Districts 39 and 61, Vancouver and Victoria.* C.B. Conway and other members of the Department of Education, Victoria, B.C. [Vancouver: Educational Research Institute of B.C.], 1968.

**2411. Coppock, Audrey Mary** *Children in Group Homes: a Survey of Wards of the Children's Aid Society Living in these Units, Vancouver 1954.* Audrey Mary Coppock. Vancouver: University of British Columbia, 1955.
Thesis (M.S.W.)--University of British Columbia, 1955.

**2412. Cornwall, Charlotte Elizabeth** *Use of Professional Time in Relation to Case Content and Services Rendered: an Exploratory Analysis Based on a Representative Group of Cases Carried by the Children's Aid Society of Vancouver and the Agency Time Study of June 1955.* Charlotte Elizabeth Cornwall. Vancouver: University of British Columbia, 1956.
Thesis (M.S.W.)--University of British

Columbia, 1956.

**2413. Cosgrove-Smith, Patricia** *Innovations for a Changing Time: Willie Seaweed, a Master Kwakiutl Artist.* Patricia Cosgrove-Smith. [Seattle: Pacific Science Center], c1983.

**2414. Cote, Maurice Norbert** *Children's Aid Society of the Catholic Archdiocese of Vancouver: Its Origins and Development, 1905 to 1932.* Maurice Norbert Cote. Vancouver: University of British Columbia, 1953.
Thesis (M.S.W.)--University of British Columbia, 1953.

**2415. Cox, David** *Why Do Young People Go on Welfare?: a Study of 166 Single 18-25 Year Olds on Welfare in Vancouver.* David Cox, George Garbutt, Russell Petch, Jack D. Rudd and Elsie Widdowson. [Burnaby]: British Columbia Institute of Technology, [1971].

**2416. Crafter, Lucy** *"Communicable-disease Control."* Lucy Crafter. Public Health Nurses' Bulletin 2, 5(Mar. 1938): 8.

**2417. Crafter, Lucy** *"Victorian Order of Nurses."* L.W.V. Crafter. Public Health Nurses' Bulletin 2, 4(Mar. 1937): 10-11.

**2418. Craig, Glen Horace** *The Means and Modes of Living on the Pioneer Fringe of Land Settlement With Special Reference to the Peace River Area.* Glen Horace Craig. Montreal: McGill University, 1933.
Thesis (M.A.)--McGill University, 1933.

**2419. Craig, Isabella** *"Health and Happiness for the Rural Families."* Isabella Craig. Public Health Nurses' Bulletin 1, 9(Mar. 1932): 20-21.

**2420. Crawford, Margaret Ruth** *A Study of Some Psycho-sociological Factors Influencing the Occupational Interests of High School Girls.* Margaret Ruth Crawford. Vancouver: University of British Columbia, 1963.
Thesis (M.A.)--University of British Columbia, 1963.

**2421. Crawford, Robert Neil** *A Research Inventory of Community Welfare Services (British Columbia and Vancouver, 1959).* Robert Neil Crawford, Lloyd Woodrow Dewalt, Ellen Isobelle Esau and Glenda Elaine Gentleman. Vancouver: University of British Columbia, 1959.
Thesis (M.S.W.)--University of British Columbia, 1959.

**2422. Creelman, Lyle** *"Revelstoke Reflections."* Lyle Creelman. Public Health Nurses' Bulletin 2, 4(Mar. 1937): 11-14.

**2423. Csapo, Marg** *"Secondary Special Education in British Columbia: an Historical Perspective."* Marg Csapo. B.C. Journal of Special Education 1, 1(Winter 1977): 27-38.

**2424. Cull, J.S.** *"Health Services Under the Larger Unit of Administration."* J.S. Cull. Public Health Nurses' Bulletin 2, 3(June 1936): 56-61.

**2425. Cunningham, Nora** *"Baby-Welfare, Fort St. John."* Nora Cunningham. Public Health Nurses' Bulletin 2, 3(June 1936): 10-12.

**2426. Daggett, Jessie Catherine** *Housing Condition in Relation to Child Protection: a Descriptive Examination of Significant Family Cases from the Children's Aid Society and the City Social Service Department, Vancouver, 1956.* Jessie Catherine Daggett. Vancouver: University of British Columbia, 1957.
Thesis (M.S.W.)--University of British Columbia, 1957.

**2427. Dahlie, Jorgen** *"The Japanese in B.C. Lost Opportunity? Some Aspects of the Education of Minorities."* Jorgen Dahlie. BC Studies 8(Winter 1970-1971): 3-16.

**2428. Daniells, Roy** *"Plymouth Brother."* Roy Daniells. Canadian Literature 90(Autumn 1981): 25-37.

**2429. Dauphinee, A. Josephine** *"Vancouver's Sub-normal Problem."* A. Josephine Dauphinee. Canadian Journal of Mental Hygiene 3, 1(Apr. 1921): 117-124.

**2430. Davenport, Harold T.** *"Day Surgery for Children."* Harold T. Davenport, Chandrakant P. Shah and Geoffrey C. Robinson. Canadian Medical Association Journal/Journal de l'Association medicale canadienne 105, 5(Sept. 4, 1971): 498-500.

**2431. Davidson, Allan H.** *"Westbank Schools."* Allan H. Davidson. Okanagan Historical Society Report 15(1951): 132-136.

**2432. Davison, Robert J.** *"Turning a Blind Eye: the Historian's Use of Photographs."* Robert J. Davison. BC Studies 52(Winter 1981-1982): 16-35.

**2433. Dawson, C.A.** *The Settlement of the Peace River Country: a Study of a Pioneer Area.* C.A. Dawson [and] R.W. Murchie. Toronto: MacMillan of Canada, St. Martin's House, 1934.

**2434. de Rimanoczy, Magda Elizabeth** *Some Aspects of Adoption Probation: an Illustrative Study of a Sample of Wards of the Vancouver Children's Aid Society Placed on a Boarding Basis With a View to Adoption.* Magda Elizabeth de Rimanoczy. Vancouver: University of British Columbia, 1956.
Thesis (M.S.W.)--University of British Columbia, 1956.

**2435. Decker, Frances** *Pemberton: the History of a Settlement.* Frances Decker, Margaret Fougberg and May Ronayne with Gordon R. Elliott, ed. Pemberton, B.C.: Pemberton Pioneer Women, c1977.

**2436. Dickie, Grace** *"The Hunter Family of Thetis Island, B.C."* Grace Dickie. British Columbia Historical News 23, 1(Winter 1990): 24-25.

**2437. Dickinson, Christine F.** *"Mining Camp School."* Christine F. Dickinson. British Columbia Historical News 22, 2(Spring 1989): 4-5.

**2438. Dodd, Kerry Mason** *Sunlight in the Shadows: the Landscape of Emily Carr.* Kerry Mason Dodd. Toronto: Oxford University Press Canada, 1984.

**2439. Dodd, Paul W.** *Factors Precipitating Agency Care of Children.* Paul W. Dodd, Joan Konon, Shirley Langstaff, Pam Manson, Donna Moroz, Miriam Schachner, Thomas Williams. Vancouver: University of British Columbia, 1967.
Thesis (M.S.W.)--University of British Columbia, 1967.

**2440. Doherty, Charles E.** *"The Care of the Mentally Defective."* Chas. E. Doherty. Canadian Journal of Mental Hygiene 2, 3(Oct. 1920): 207-218.

**2441. Dolman, C.L. Aszkanazy** *"Acute Pancreatitis in Pregnancy Complicated by Renal Cortical Necrosis and Cerebral Mucormycosis."* C.L. Aszkanazy Dolman and J.A. Herd. Canadian Medical Association Journal/Journal de l'Association medicale canadienne 81, 7(Oct. 1, 1959): 562-564.

**2442. Dorosh, Andrew Ivan** *Trends in Apprehension Policies: a Comparative Analysis of Committals of Children by the Children's Aid Society of Vancouver, British Columbia, in the Years 1938 and 1952.* Andrew Ivan Dorosh. Vancouver: University of British Columbia, 1954.
Thesis (M.S.W.)--University of British Columbia, 1954.

**2443. Doughty, J.** *"Some Observations from a Preliminary Study of Infant Mortality in British Columbia."* J. Doughty. Canadian Journal of Public Health 40, 7(July 1949): 302-305.

**2444. Douglas, Lawrence Fitzroy** *"Quiet Rebellion": a Study of Youth.* Lawrence Fitzroy Douglas. Vancouver: University of British Columbia, 1962.
Thesis (M.A.)–University of British Columbia, 1962.

**2445. Douglas, May G.** *"Organizing a Well Baby Clinic."* May G. Douglas. Canadian Nurse 43, 1(Jan. 1947): 36.

**2446. Down, Mary Margaret** *Century of Service: a History of the Sisters of Saint Ann and Their Contributions to Education in British Columbia and Alaska.* Sister Mary Margaret Down. Victoria: Morriss Printing Co. Ltd., c1966.

**2447. Down, Mary Margaret.** *The Sisters of St. Ann: Their Contribution to Education in the Pacific Northwest 1858-1958.* Edith Emily Down. Vancouver: University of British Columbia, 1962.
Thesis (M.A.)–University of British Columbia, 1962.

**2448. Dunae, Patrick A.** *"Waifs: the Fairbridge Society in British Columbia, 1931-1951."* Patrick A. Dunae. Histoire sociale/Social History 21, 42(Nov. 1988): 224-250.

**2449. Dunbar, Jean A.** *"The Public Health Nurse in Fernie."* Jean A. Dunbar. Public Health Nurses' Bulletin 1, 4(Apr. 1927): 17-18.

**2450. Dunbar, Jean A.** *"Public Health Work in Qualicum District."* J.A. Dunbar. Public Health Nurses' Bulletin 1, 5(Apr. 1928): 16-17.

**2451. Dunbar, Jean A.** *"School Nursing in a Mining Town."* Jean A. Dunbar. Public Health Nurses' Bulletin 1, 3(Apr. 1926): 17-18.

**2452. Dunn, Nancy E.** *"Consolidation of Schools: From a Nurse's Point of View."* N.E. Dunn. Public Health Nurses' Bulletin 2, 4(Mar. 1937): 14-16.

**2453. Dunn, Nancy E.** *"On Organizing Dental Clinics in the Peace River Block."* N.E. Dunn. Public Health Nurses' Bulletin 2, 3(June 1936): 12-14.

**2454. Dunn, Nancy E.** *"Public Health Service South of the Peace River, B.C."* Nancy E. Dunn. Public Health Nurses' Bulletin 1, 9(Mar. 1932): 34-35.

**2455. Dunn, Nancy E.** *"The Tuberculin Testing in Nelson Schools."* Nancy E. Dunn. Public Health Nurses' Bulletin 2, 5(Mar. 1938): 9-10.

**2456. Dunn, Timothy A.** *"The Rise of Mass Public Schooling in British Columbia, 1900-1929."* Timothy A. Dunn. Calgary: Detselig Enterprises Ltd., 1980. In Schooling and Society in 20th Century British Columbia, pp. 23-51. Edited by J. Donald Wilson and David C. Jones.

**2457. Dunn, Timothy A.** *"Teaching the Meaning of Work: Vocational Education in British Columbia, 1900-1929."* Timothy A. Dunn. Calgary: Detselig Enterprises, 1979. In Shaping the Schools of the Canadian West, pp. 236-256. Edited by David C. Jones, Nancy M. Sheehan and Robert M. Stamp.

**2458. Dunn, Timothy A.** *"Vocationalism and Its Promoters in British Columbia, 1900-1929."* Timothy A. Dunn. Journal of Educational Thought 14, 2(Aug. 1980): 92-107.

**2459. Dunn, Timothy A.** *Work, Class and Education: Vocationalism in British Columbia's Public Schools, 1900-1929.* Timothy Allan Dunn. Vancouver: University of British Columbia, 1978.
Thesis (M.A.)–University of British Columbia, 1978.

**2460. Duxbury, James H.** *"Bilateral Agenesis of the Kidneys."* James H. Duxbury. Canadian Medical Association Journal 78, 2(Jan. 15, 1958): 123.

**2461. Dyer, Harold** *"Rheumatism in the Children of Vancouver and District."* Harold Dyer. Canadian Medical Association Journal 2, 6(June 1912): 494-501.

**2462. East, Patricia** *"School and District Nurse, Keremeos."* Patricia East. Public Health Nurses' Bulletin 1, 4(Apr. 1927): 29-30.

**2463. Ellis, E.N.** *"An Evaluation of Cuisenaire Materials in Primary Numberwork."* E.N. Ellis. Journal of Education of the Faculty and College of Education: Vancouver and Victoria 6(Dec. 1961): 60-69.

**2464. Ellis, E.N.** *Trends in Graduation From Secondary Schools in British Columbia and Vancouver, 1952 to 1974: an Analysis of Data From Educational Data Services and Research and Standards Branch, Department of Education.* E.N. Ellis and L. Murdoch. Vancouver: Board of School Trustees, 1975.

**2465. Ellis, Vivian Mauretta** *Multiple Placement of Foster Children: a Preliminary Study of Causes and Effects, Based Upon a Sample of Fifty Foster Children in Vancouver.* Vivian Mauretta Ellis. Vancouver: University of British Columbia, 1949.
Thesis (M.S.W.)–University of British Columbia, 1949.

**2466. Elliston, Graham** *"Bamfield Memories, School Days."* Graham Elliston. Barkley Sounder 5, 9(Sept. 1987): 33-37.

**2467. Endicott, Marion** *Emily Carr: the Story of an Artist.* Marion Endicott. Toronto: Women's Educational Press, 1981.

**2468. English, John Frederick Kerr** *The Combined Junior-Senior High School and Its General Adaptibility to the Small Centres of British Columbia.* John Frederick Kerr English. Vancouver: University of British Columbia, 1933.
Thesis (M.A.)–University of British Columbia, 1933.

**2469. Ewing, John M.** *An Experimental Study of Two School Procedures as Applied to Superior Children.* John M. Ewing. Toronto: University of Toronto, 1931.
Thesis (M.A.)–University of Toronto, 1931.

**2470. Fairbank, John Keith** *Juvenile Vandalism in the City of Vancouver: an Exploratory Study of Juvenile Vandalism as Found in the City of Vancouver, British Columbia, Canada.* John Keith Fairbank, Sophia Ming Ren Leung, Robert Graham Pittman and Madlyn Gertrude Wills. Vancouver: University of British Columbia, 1965.
Thesis (M.S.W.)–University of British Columbia, 1965.

**2471. Fawcett, Hetty E.** *"Mission and Maple Ridge."* H.E. Fawcett. Public Health Nurses' Bulletin 1, 8(Mar. 1931): 28-31.

**2472. Fawcett, Hetty E.** *"Public Health Nursing, Maple Ridge and Mission Municipalities."* Hetty E. Fawcett. Public Health Nurses' Bulletin 1, 7(May 1930): 45-48.

**2473. Fell, Fay** *"The C.B. Harris Family."* Fay Fell. Okanagan History 52(1988): 28-32.

**2474. Finlayson, Helen M.** *Play Therapy Techniques: an Examination of a Children's Aid Society Experimental Project For Disturbed Children, 1948 to 1951.* Helen M. Finlayson. Vancouver: University of British Columbia, 1951.

Thesis (M.S.W.)–University of British Columbia, 1951.

**2475. Fisher, Jack** *"When I Was a Sickly Six Year Old."* Jack Fisher. Vancouver Historical Society Newsletter 13, 11(Mar. 1974): 5-7.

**2476. Fisher, Marion** *"Kamloops."* Marion Fisher. Public Health Nurses' Bulletin 1, 2(Apr. 1925): 10-12.

**2477. Fiske, Jo-Anne** *And Then We Played Again: Carrier Women, Colonialism and Mission Schools.* Jo-Anne Fiske. Vancouver: University of British Columbia, 1981.
Thesis (M.A.)–University of British Columbia, 1981.

**2478. Fister, W.P.** *"The Treatment of Hepatonticular Degeneration with Penicillamine, with Report of Two Cases."* W.P. Fister, J.E. Boulding and R.A. Baker. Canadian Medical Association Journal 78, 2(Jan. 15, 1958): 99-102.

**2479. Fleming, Thomas** *"A Century in the Lives of Three Students: Some Historical Reflections on Schooling for the Normal, Subnormal and Gifted Child in British Columbia, 1872-1972."* Thomas Fleming. B.C. Journal of Special Education 14, 2(Summer 1990): 101-109.

**2480. Fletcher, Arthur Robert** *A Study to Compare Grade 7 Achievement in the British Columbia Peace River Area with Selected Factors.* Arthur Robert Fletcher. Edmonton: University of Alberta, 1966.
Thesis (M.Ed.)–University of Alberta, 1966.

**2481. Flynn, Bethine** *Flynn's Cove.* Bethine Flynn. Sidney, B.C.: Porthole Press, c1986.

**2482. Fogarty, Patrick James** *Relation of Children's Disorders to Limiting Parental Influences: an Essay in Classification and Analysis, Concerning a Certain Group of Children Who Were Referred Privately to the Vancouver Child Guidance Clinic Between 1948-1951.* Patrick James Fogarty. Vancouver: University of British Columbia, 1952.
Thesis (M.S.W.)–University of British Columbia, 1952.

**2483. Foner, S. Philip** *"The Coloured Inhabitants of Vancouver Island."* S. Philip Foner. BC Studies 8(Winter 1970-1971): 29-33.

**2484. Foord, Esme N.** *Special Education in British Columbia*. Esme N. Foord. Toronto, University of Toronto. 1959. Thesis (Ed.D.)--University of Toronto, 1959.

**2485. Forshaw, Jessie** *"How Child Welfare Work Can Be Assisted in the Rural Districts of British Columbia."* Jessie Forshaw. Public Health Journal 12, 6(June 1921): 283-288.

**2486. Forteath, Ruby Sidney** *"East Princeton, My School 1917-19."* Ruby Sidney Forteath. British Columbia Historical News 23, 3(Summer 1990): 11-16.

**2487. Foster, John Keith** *Education and Work in a Changing Society: British Columbia, 1870-1930*. John Keith Foster. Vancouver: University of British Columbia, 1970. Thesis (M.A.)--University of British Columbia, 1970.

**2488. Fraser, Douglas P.** *"Early School Days in Osoyoos."* Douglas P. Fraser and Margaret A. Driver. Okanagan Historical Society Report 50(1986): 81-87.

**2489. Fraser, H.A.** *"Reminiscences of the Old Days."* H.A. Fraser. Okanagan Historical Society Report 14(1950): 129-133.

**2490. Freedman, Myer** *"Growing Up in Vancouver's East End."* Myer Freedman. Scribe 11, 2(Fall 1989): 4-7.

**2491. Freer, Nell Wilson** *Brief Service in a Child Guidance Clinic: a Preliminary Survey: a Descriptive Study Based on Child Guidance Clinic Cases, Burnaby, 1954-1957*. Nell Wilson Freer. Vancouver: University of British Columbia, 1957. Thesis (M.S.W.)--University of British Columbia, 1957.

**2492. Friesen, Elaine Cornelia** *Usefulness of the Marianne Frostig Developmental Test of Visual Perception and the Frostig Program for the Development of Visual Perception at the First Grade Level*. Elaine Cornelia Friesen. Vancouver: University of British Columbia, 1969. Thesis (M.A.)--University of British Columbia, 1969.

**2493. Frith, Monica M.** *"Home Nursing Services in B.C."* Monica M. Frith. Canadian Welfare 38, 3(May-June 1962): 119-122.

**2494. Fry, Alan** *The Ranch on the Cariboo*. Alan Fry. Garden City, N.Y.: Doubleday & Co. Inc., c1962.

**2495. Furness, Anne-Marie** *Summer Day Camping: an Evaluation of Current Vancouver Experience in Relation to Accepted Standards in Day Camping*. Anne-Marie Furness. Vancouver: University of British Columbia, 1951. Thesis (M.S.W.)--University of British Columbia, 1951.

**2496. Gaddes, W.H.** *"The Problem of the Emotionally Disturbed Child in Our Public Schools."* W.H. Gaddes. Journal of Education of the Faculty and College of Education: Vancouver and Victoria 5(Mar. 1961): 3-9.

**2497. Gaitskell, Charles Dudley** *An Experiment in Art Motivation in the Peace River Educational Area*. Charles Dudley Gaitskell. Vancouver: University of British Columbia, 1939. Thesis (M.A.)--University of British Columbia, 1939.

**2498. Galbraith, J.D.** *"Tuberculosis in Indian Children: Primary Pulmonary Tuberculosis."* J.D. Galbraith, S. Grzybowski, C.L. Law and J. Rowe. Canadian Medical Association Journal/Journal de l'Association medicale canadienne 100, 11(Mar. 15, 1969): 497-502.

**2499. Garner, Joe** *Never a Time to Trust: a Story of British Columbia, Her Pioneers, Predators and Problems*. Joe Garner. Nanaino: Cinnabar Press, c1984.

**2500. Garner, Joe** *Never Fly Over an Eagle's Nest*. Joe Garner. 2nd Rev. ed. Nanaimo, B.C.: Cinnabar Press, c1982. First published Lantzville: Oolichan Books, c1980.

**2501. Garr, Allen** *Tough Guy: Bill Bennett and the Taking of British Columbia*. Allan Garr. Toronto: Key Porter Books, c1985.

**2502. Garrood, Olive M.** *"Health News from Kamloops."* Olive M. Garrood. Public Health Nurses' Bulletin 1, 8(Mar. 1931): 43.

**2503. Garrood, Olive M.** *"Progress of Public Health in Kamloops, 1925-1935."* Olive M. Garrood. Public Health Nurses' Bulletin 2, 2(Apr. 1935): 38-41.

**2504. Garrood, Olive M.** *"Public Health in Kamloops."* Olive M. Garrood. Public Health Nurses' Bulletin 1, 7(May 1930): 26-29.

2505. **Garrood, Olive M.** *"Public Health in Kamloops, B.C."* Olive M. Garrood. Public Health Nurses' Bulletin 1, 9(Mar. 1932): 32-34.

2506. **Garrood, Olive M.** *"Public Health Nurses and Education."* Olive M. Garrood. Public Health Nurses' Bulletin 2, 4(Mar. 1937): 17-18.

2507. **Garrood, Olive M.** *"Public Health Work in Kamloops."* Olive M. Garrood. Public Health Nurses' Bulletin 1, 6(Apr. 1929): 29-31.

2508. **Garrood, Olive M.** *"Public Health Work on the Kootenay Lake."* Olive M. Garrood. Public Health Nurses' Bulletin 1, 4(Apr. 1927): 13-14.

2509. **Garrood, Olive M.** *"Some Ways and Means of Correcting Physical Defects Among the School Children of Kamloops."* Olive M. Garrood. Public Health Nurses' Bulletin 2, 3(June 1936): 14-16.

2510. **Garrood, Olive M.** *"Teaching Public Health in Kamloops."* Olive M. Garrood. Public Health Nurses' Bulletin 1, 5(Apr. 1928): 21-23.

2511. **Gatien, A.** *"First White Girl Born in Okanagan."* A. Gatien. Okanagan Historical Society Report 18(1954): 66-68.

2512. **Gelley, Maurine Ellen** *Social Case Work in Foster Home Finding.* Maurine Ellen Gelley. Vancouver: University of British Columbia, 1954.
Thesis (M.S.W.)--University of British Columbia, 1954.

2513. **Genn, Robert** *Robert Genn: in Praise of Painting.* Robert Genn. Toronto: Merritt Publishing Company, 1981.

2514. **Gerard, Bernice** *Converted in the Country: the Life Story of Bernice Gerard as Told by Herself.* Jacksonville, Fla.: McColl-Gerard Pubs., 1956.

2515. **Gibson, Donna Lee** *Retinopathy of Prematurity in British Columbia.* Donna Lee Gibson. Vancouver: University of British Columbia, 1987.
Thesis (M.Sc.)--University of British Columbia, 1987.

2516. **Gibson, Gordon** *Bull of the Woods: the Gordon Gibson Story.* Gordon Gibson with Carol Renison. Vancouver: Douglas & McIntyre, 1980.

2517. **Gibson, James R.** *"Smallpox on the Northwest Coast, 1835-1838."* James R. Gibson. BC Studies 56(Winter 1982-1983): 61-81.

2518. **Gibson, Wilma Mary** *The Social Worker in Adoption Practice: an Exploratory Study of 28 Adopted Children Who Were Referred Privately to the Vancouver Child Guidance Clinic, 1953-55.* Wilma Mary Gibson. Vancouver: University of British Columbia, 1944.
Thesis (M.S.W.)--University of British Columbia, 1955.

2519. **Glenesk, Alfred H.** *"A Study of Three Programs of Continuing Education."* Alfred H. Glenesk and Coolie Verner. Canadian Education and Research Digest 5, 1(Mar. 1965): 31-39.

2520. **Glover, Ernest Geoffrey** *Case Work Interviewing Methods in a Child Guidance Setting: an Analysis Based on Records of Privately Referred Cases for 1948-1950 in the Child Guidance Clinic at Vancouver.* Ernest Geoffrey Glover. Vancouver: University of British Columbia, 1951.
Thesis (M.S.W.)--University of British Columbia, 1951.

2521. **Golden and District Historical Society, ed.** *"Schools: School Days in Early Golden."* Golden, B.C.: Golden Historical Society, c1982. In Golden Memories-Golden City 1982, pp. 30-39. Edited by Golden and District Historical Society.

2522. **Golden and District Historical Society, ed.** *"Social Events."* Golden, B.C.: Golden and District Historical Society, c1982. In Golden Memories-Golden City 1982, pp. 142-149. Edited by the Golden and District Historical Society.

2523. **Goodall, Trevor** *Trevor Goodall's Memories of the Alberni Valley.* Trevor Goodall. [Port Alberni, B.C.]: Trevor Goodall, c1983.

2524. **Goodfellow, Florence Agassiz** *Memories of Pioneer Life in British Columbia: a Short History of the Agassiz Family.* Florence Agassiz Goodfellow. Wenatchee, Wash.: [s.n.], 1945.

2525. **Gorby, C.W.** *An Interim Report and Recommendations on Co-ordination of Government and Community Resources in the Treatment of Juvenile Delinquency for Rural British Columbia.* C.W. Gorby. [Victoria]: A. Sutton, 1963.

**2526. Gorby, C.W.** *A Report and Recommendations on Co-ordination of Youth Services in Greater Vancouver and Greater Victoria.* C.W. ' Gorby. [Victoria]: A. Sutton, 1965.

**2527. Gordon, Kathleen M.** *"Community Organization in the Development of a Health Unit."* Kathleen Gordon. Public Health Nurses' Bulletin 2, 1(May 1933): 12-14.

**2528. Gordon, Kathleen M.** *"An Impossibility Becomes a Reality."* Kathleen Gordon. Public Health Nurses' Bulletin 2, 3(June 1936): 16-17.

**2529. Gordon, Kathleen M.** *"An Impossibility Becomes a Success."* Kathleen M. Gordon. Public Health Nurses' Bulletin 2, 4(Mar. 1937): 18-20.

**2530. Gordon, Kathleen M.** *"Nelson's Health Problem."* Kathleen Gordon. Public Health Nurses' Bulletin 2, 2(Apr. 1935): 28-30.

**2531. Gordon, Roth Garthley** *Secondary Education in Rural British Columbia.* Roth Garthley Gordon. Vancouver: University of British Columbia, 1935.
Thesis (M.A.)--University of British Columbia, 1935.

**2532. Gosbee, Chuck, ed.** *"Glancing Back": Reflections and Anecdotes on Vancouver Public Schools.* Chuck Gosbee and Leslie Dyson, eds. Vancouver: Vancouver School Board, c1988.

**2533. Gould, Ed** *Ralph Edwards of Lonesome Lake.* Ed Gould. Saanichton, B.C.: Hancock House Publishers Inc., c1979.

**2534. Gould, Jan** *Women of British Columbia.* Jan Gould. Saanichton, B.C.: Hancock House Publishers, c1975.

**2535. Gourlay, Robert H.** *"Staphylococcal Pneumonia and Empyema in Infants and Children:"* Robert H. Gourlay. Canadian Medical Association Journal/Journal de l'Association medicale canadienne 87, 21(Nov. 24, 1962): 1101-1105.

**2536. Gowan, Mary** *"Peachland-Westbank."* Mary Gowan. Public Health Nurses' Bulletin 2, 3(June 1936): 18-19.

**2537. Gowan, Mary** *"Peachland-Westbank District Committee."* M. Gowan. Public Health Nurses' Bulletin 2, 5(Mar. 1938): 12-13.

**2538. Gowers, Ruth** *Emily Carr.* Ruth Gowers. New York: St. Martin's Press, 1987.

**2539. Grace, Alice Mary** *Probation Services for the Girl Delinquent: an Evaluation of Case Work Treatment in an Involuntary Setting Based on a Representative Group of Cases Appearing Before the Vancouver Juvenile Court.* Alice Mary Grace. Vancouver: University of British Columbia, 1951.
Thesis (M.S.W.)--University of British Columbia, 1951.

**2540. Graham, Clara** *"Journey to Yesterday."* Clara Graham. Vancouver: Alexander Nicolls Press, 1976. In Kootenay Yesterdays, pp. 1-86. Edited by Edward L. Affleck.

**2541. Grant, J.H.B.** *"Immunization in Children."* J.H.B. Grant. Canadian Medical Association Journal 55, 5(Nov. 1946): 493-497.

**2542. Grant, Mike** *"Teenagers in Foster Care."* Mike Grant. Canadian Welfare 45, 1(Jan.-Feb. 1969): 12, 21.

**2543. Green, Winifred E.** *"Public Health Work in Chilliwack Municipality."* Winifred E. Green. Public Health Nurses' Bulletin 1, 7(May 1930): 16-17.

**2544. Greene, Nancy** *Nancy Greene: an Autobiography.* Nancy Greene with Jack Batten. Don Mills: General Publishing, c1968.

**2545. Gresko, Jacqueline** *"Creating Little Dominions Within the Dominion: Early Catholic Indian Schools in Saskatchewan and British Columbia."* Jacqueline Gresko. Vancouver: University of British Columbia Press, 1986. In Indian Education in Canada, Volume 1: the Legacy, pp. 88-109. Edited by Jean Barman, Yvonne Hebert and Don McCaskill.

**2546. Gresko, Jacqueline** *"The View From the Centre of the Earth."* Jacqueline Gresko. Vancouver Historical Society Newsletter 14, 5(Nov. 1974): 3-4.

**2547. Grierson, Mary E.** *"Advancement Along Preventive Lines."* Mary E. Grierson. Public Health Nurses' Bulletin 1, 9(Mar. 1932): 23-24.

**2548. Grierson, Mary E.** *"An Attempt at Stock-Taking."* Mary E. Grierson. Public Health Nurses' Bulletin 2, 2(Apr. 1935): 14-15.

**2549. Grierson, Mary E.** *"Dewdney Health District."* Mary E. Grierson. Public Health Nurses' Bulletin 2, 5(Mar. 1938): 13-14.

**2550. Grierson, Mary E.** *"Health-work in Port Alberni."* Mary E. Grierson. Public Health Nurses' Bulletin 1, 6(Apr. 1929): 24-25.

**2551. Grierson, Mary E.** *"Immunization."* Mary E. Grierson. Public Health Nurses' Bulletin 2, 1(May 1933): 4-5.

**2552. Grierson, Mary E.** *"Maple Ridge and Missions Districts."* Mary E. Grierson. Public Health Nurses' Bulletin 2, 4(Mar. 1937): 20-21.

**2553. Grierson, Mary E.** *"Mission and Maple Ridge Districts."* E. Grierson. Public Health Nurses' Bulletin 2, 3(June 1936): 19-20.

**2554. Grierson, Mary E.** *"Port Alberni."* Mary E. Grierson. Public Health Nurses' Bulletin 1, 7(May 1930): 33-34.

**2555. Grierson, Mary E.** *"Port Alberni."* Mary E. Grierson. Public Health Nurses' Bulletin 1, 8(Mar. 1931): 40-41.

**2556. Grierson, Mary E.** *"Public Health Work in Port Alberni."* Mary E. Grierson. Public Health Nurses' Bulletin 1, 5(Apr. 1928): 10.

**2557. Grieve, Tarrance** *The Relationship of Cognitive Style and Method of Instruction to Performance in Grade Nine Geography.* Tarrance Don Grieve. Victoria: University of Victoria, 1969.
Thesis (M.A.)--University of Victoria, 1969.

**2558. Griffin, Margaret M.** *"Breast-feeding for the Infants of Saanich Municipality."* Margaret M. Griffin. Public Health Nurses' Bulletin 1, 4(Apr. 1927): 24-27.

**2559. Griffin, Margaret M.** *"French Creek and District."* Margaret M. Griffin. Public Health Nurses' Bulletin 1, 7(May 1930): 22-23.

**2560. Griffin, Margaret M.** *"French Creek and District."* Margaret M. Griffin. Public Health Nurses' Bulletin 1, 8(Mar. 1931): 7-9.

**2561. Griffin, Margaret M.** *"Qualicum and District Public Health Association: Class Instruction."* Margaret M. Griffin. Public Health Nurses' Bulletin 1, 6(Apr. 1929): 12-13.

**2562. Grindon, Anne F.** *"The Development of Public Health Nursing in Kelowna Rural Districts."* Anne F. Grindon. Public Health Nurses' Bulletin 1, 7(May 1930): 37-41.

**2563. Grindon, Anne F.** *"The Kelowna Rural Schools Health Association."* Anne Frances Grindon. Public Health Nurses' Bulletin 1, 8(Mar. 1931): 31-33.

**2564. Grindon, Anne F.** *"The Organization of a Dental Clinic in the Kelowna Rural Districts."* Anne F. Grindon. Public Health Nurses' Bulletin 2, 5(Mar. 1938): 15-17.

**2565. Grindon, Anne F.** *"The Organization of Public Health Work in the Kelowna Rural District."* Anne F. Grindon. Public Health Nurses' Bulletin 1, 6(Apr. 1929): 17-19.

**2566. Grindon, Anne F.** *""Selling Public Health" in the Kelowna Rural Districts."* Anne F. Grindon. Public Health Nurses' Bulletin 2, 3(June 1936): 20-22.

**2567. Grindon, Anne F.** *"The Value of an Annual School Health Cup Competition."* Anne F. Grindon. Public Health Nurses' Bulletin 2, 4(Mar. 1937): 21-24.

**2568. Gundry, C.H.** *"Mental Health and School Health Work."* C.H. Gundry. Canadian Public Health Journal 31, 10(Oct. 1940): 482-486.

**2569. Gundry, C.H.** *"The Mental Hygiene Division."* C.H. Gundry and Lara Thordarson. Canadian Nurse 49, 7(July 1953): 551-553.

**2570. Gustafson, Lillian, comp.** *Memories of the Chemainus Valley: a History of the People.* Lillian Gustafson and Gordon Elliott, ed. Victoria: The Society, c1978.

**2571. Gutman, Gloria** *Balance and Agreement in Children's Social Perception.* Gloria Margaret Gutman. Vancouver: University of British Columbia, 1970.
Thesis (Ph.D.)--University of British Columbia, 1970.

**2572. Haegert, Dorothy** *Children of the First People.* Dorothy Haegert. Vancouver: Tillacum Library, c1983.

**2573. Haig-Brown, Celia** *Resistance and Renewal: Surviving the Indian Residential School.* Celia Haig-Brown. Vancouver: Tillicum Library, 1988.

**2574. Hall, I. Proctor** *"Moulds in the Alimentary Canal."* I. Proctor Hall. Canadian Medical Association Journal 1, 12(Dec. 1911): 1162-1164.

**2575. Hallett, Evelyn** *"Those Early Days."* Evelyn Hallett. Okanagan History 52(1988): 27-28.

**2576. Hamilton, Bea** *Salt Spring Island.* Bea Hamilton. Vancouver: Mitchell Press, c1969.

**2577. Hamilton, Glen Francis** *The Teenage Gang and the Community: a Study and Treatment of a Teenage Delinquent Gang With Implications for Community Services and Recommendations for Social Action.* Glen Francis Hamilton. Vancouver: University of British Columbia, 1949.
Thesis (M.S.W.)--University of British Columbia, 1949.

**2578. Haralson, Doris Neely** *Northland Echoes.* Doris Neely Haralson. Yarrow, B.C.: Doris Neely Haralson, c1981.

**2579. Harder, Ilse Martha** *Social Work Services for the Putative Father: a Review of Administration Under the Children of Unmarried Parents Act and Vancouver Social Welfare Branch Experience, June 1950-May 1955.* Martha Ilse Harder. Vancouver: University of British Columbia, 1956.
Thesis (M.S.W.)--University of British Columbia, 1956.

**2580. Hardy, W.** *"Control of Communicable Diseases."* W. Hardy. Public Health Nurses' Bulletin 2, 3(June 1936): 22-23.

**2581. Hardyment, A.F.** *"The Control of Infections in the Newborn."* A.F. Hardyment. Canadian Medical Association Journal 70, 4(Apr. 1954): 379-382.

**2582. Hare, Allan Cecil** *Kerrisdale Youth.* Allan Cecil Hare. Vancouver: University of British Columbia, 1954.
Thesis (M.A.)--University of British Columbia, 1954.

**2583. Harford, H.** *"The First Fairview School."* H. Harford. Okanagan Historical Society Report 23(1959): 63-69.

**2584. Harker, Douglas E.** *Saints: the Story of St. George's School for Boys, Vancouver.* Douglas E. Harker. Vancouver: Mitchell Press, c1979.

**2585. Harker, Douglas E.** *"Some Early Schools of British Columbia."* Douglas Harker. British Columbia Historical News 22, 2(Spring 1989): 18-20.

**2586. Harold, T.C.** *"School Medical Services."* T.C. Harold and J.M. Hershey. Canadian Journal of Public Health 36, 9(Sept. 1945): 349-354.

**2587. Harris, Ernest A.** *Spokeshute: Skeena River Memory.* Ernest A. Harris. Victoria: Orca Book Publishers, 1990.

**2588. Harris, Nan** *Nan: a Child's Eye View of Early Okanagan Settlement.* Nan Harris. [Kelowna: Nan Harris, c1981]. Originally published as Lake Water Laughing.

**2589. Harvey, Myrtle E.** *"Depression and Community Health."* Myrtle E. Harvey. Public Health Nurses' Bulletin 2, 1(May 1933): 2-4.

**2590. Harvey, Myrtle E.** *"School Attendance in Saanich."* Myrtle E. Harvey. Public Health Nurses' Bulletin 1, 7(May 1930): 14-15.

**2591. Hassen, Mat** *"Farm Youth Clubs in the Armstrong Spallumcheen District."* Douglas Scott. Okanagan Historical Society Report 46(1982): 97-102.

**2592. Hastings, Margaret Lang** *Along the Way: an Account of Pioneering White Rock and Surrounding District in British Columbia.* Margaret Lang Hastings. Rev. ed. Cloverdale, B.C.: The Author, c1981. Revised edition of 1967 edition of Along the Way by Margaret Lang.

**2593. Hatcher, Frank Sydney** *Social and Cultural Factors in Casework Practice: an Examination of the Recognition of Social and Cultural Factors in the Problems of Children From Particular Ethnic Backgrounds, Based on a Sample of Cases From the Vancouver Child Guidance Clinic, 1955.* Frank Sydney Hatcher. Vancouver: University of British Columbia, 1955.
Thesis (M.S.W.)--University of British Columbia, 1955.

**2594. Haugen, Maureen** *Attitudes Toward Indian Education: Implications for Counselling.* Maureen Haugen. Victoria: University of Victoria, 1971.
Thesis (M.A.)--University of Victoria, 1971.

**2595. Hawley, Constance Margaret** *Role, Stress and Social Casework Practice: an Assessment of the Concepts of Role and Stress in Relation to a Sample of Social Casework Practice.* Constance Margaret Hawley. Vancouver: University of British Columbia, 1961.
Thesis (M.S.W.)--University of British Columbia, 1961.

**2596. Hawthorne, Dan Robert** *Patterns of 20th Century Attendance: a Systematic Study of Victoria Public Schools, 1910 and 1921.* Dan Robert Hawthorne. Victoria: University of Victoria, 1985. (CTM no. 242418)
Thesis (M.A.)--University of Victoria, 1985.

**2597. Hayball, Gwen** *"Agnes Deans Cameron, 1863-1912."* Gwen Hayball. B.C. Historical News 7, 4(June 1974): 18-19.

**2598. Heady, Eleanor M.** *"The Public Health Nurse and Mental Hygiene."* Eleanor M. Heady. Canadian Nurse 47, 1(Jan. 1951): 37-43.

**2599. Helgesen, Marion I., ed.** *Footprints: Pioneer Families of the Metchosin District, Southern Vancouver Island, 1851-1900.* Marion I. Helgeson, comp. and ed. [S.l.]: Metchosin School Museum Society, c1983.

**2600. Hembroff-Schleicher, Edythe** *Emily Carr: the Untold Story.* Edythe Hembroff-Schleicher. Saanichton, B.C.: Hancock House, 1978.

**2601. Henry, Robert** *Factors That Impede the Anti-social Teenage Gang in the Use of Organized Community Programs: an Analysis of the East End Boys Project as an Attempt to Redirect Anti-social Behavior.* Robert Henry. Vancouver: University of British Columbia, 1955.
Thesis (M.S.W.)--University of British Columbia, 1955.

**2602. Heritage Club Project** *Bulkley Valley Stories: Collected from the Old Timers Who Remember.* Heritage Club Project, Marjorie Roseberg, ed. [S.l: s.n.], c1973.

**2603. Hershey, J.M.** *"A Child Health Program."* J.M. Hershey. Canadian Journal of Public Health 36, 11(Nov. 1945): 413-418.

**2604. Hershey, J.M.** *"An Outbreak of Acute Poliomyelitis in the Okanagan Valley, British Columbia."* J.M. Hershey. Canadian Public Health Journal 33, 9(Sept. 1942): 452-460.

**2605. Hertzman, V.O.** *"Patent Ductus Arteriosus."* V.O. Hertzman and G.F. Strong. Canadian Medical Association Journal 61, 5(Nov. 1949): 495-501.

**2606. Hewertson, S.** *"Ladysmith."* S. Hewertson. Public Health Nurses' Bulletin 1, 4(Apr. 1927): 12.

**2607. Hewertson, S.** *"Saanich Health Centre."* S. Hewertson. Public Health Nurses' Bulletin 1, 5(Apr. 1928): 13-14.

**2608. Hiebert, A.** *"Assisting the Mentally Handicapped in the Vernon Area: the First 25 Years."* A. Hiebert and Dorothy Alexander. Okanagan Historical Society Report 49(1985): 70-78.

**2609. Higgs, Nora** *"Child Welfare Work in Saanich."* N. Higgs. Public Health Nurses' Bulletin 1, 5(Apr. 1928): 14-15.

**2610. Hill, Grace** *"Public Health in Westbank."* Grace Hill. Public Health Nurses' Bulletin 2, 2(Apr. 1935): 32.

**2611. Hill, H.W.** *"Nonrelation of Malnutrition in School Children to Infection."* H.W. Hill and Elizabeth Breeze. Public Health Journal 17, 9(Sept. 1926): 421-432.

**2612. Hill, H.W.** *"Nonrelation of Malnutrition in School Children to Infection."* H.W. Hill. In Proceedings of Sixth Annual Canadian Conference on Child Welfare 1927, pp. 31-36.

**2613. Hill, Margaret** *"The Detention of Freedomite Children, 1953-1959."* Margaret Hill. Canadian Ethnic Studies/Etudes ethniques au Canada 18, 3(1986): 47-60.

**2614. Hill, Robert H.** *"Juvenile Dermatomyositis."* Robert H. Hill and William S. Wood. Canadian Medical Association Journal/Journal de l'Association medicale canadienne 103, 11(Nov. 21, 1970): 1152-1156.

**2615. Hill, Robert H.** *"Juvenile Rheumatoid Arthritis: a Medical and Social Profile of Non-Indian and Indian Children."* Robert H. Hill and K. Walters. Canadian Medical Association Journal/Journal de l'Association medicale canadienne 100, 10(Mar. 8, 1969): 458-464.

**2616. Hillas, H.** *"The Public Health Attitude."* H. Hillas. Public Health Nurses' Bulletin 1, 9(Mar. 1932): 45.

**2617. Hindle, George** *The Educational System of British Columbia: an Appreciative and Critical Estimate of the Educational System of the Mountain Province.* George Hindle. Trail, B.C.: Trail Printing and Publishing Co., Ltd, 1918.
Thesis (D. Paed.)--University of Toronto, [1918].

2618. **Hodge, Meta** *"A Visit to Queen Alexandra Solarium."* Meta Hodge. Canadian Nurse 23, 5(May 1927): 242-243.

2619. **Hodgson, M.** *"Okanagan Landing School Days."* M. Hodgson. Okanagan Historical Society Report 34(1970): 116-119.

2620. **Hogg, Robert Stephen** *The Demographic History of Two British Columbian Native Reserve Populations.* Robert Stephen Hogg. Victoria: University of Victoria, 1987.
　　Thesis (M.A.)--University of Victoria, 1987.

2621. **Holloway, Shirley Kathleen** *Emotional Responses of Young Children to Hospital and Surgery: a Comparative Study of Procedures in the Vancouver General Hospital, 1953-58.* Shirley Kathleen Holloway. Vancouver: University of British Columbia, 1958.
　　Thesis (M.S.W.)--University of British Columbia, 1958.

2622. **Holt, Simma** *Terror in the Name of God: the Story of the Sons of Freedom Doukhobors.* Simma Holt. Toronto: McClelland and Stewart, 1964.

2623. **Homer, Donald Garth** *A Survey of Wards Not in Foster Homes: a Study of the Group Who Severed Contact With the Agency (Children's Aid Society, Vancouver).* Donald Garth Homer. Vancouver: University of British Columbia, 1956.
　　Thesis (M.S.W.)--University of British Columbia, 1956.

2624. **Homfray, Geraldine E.** *"The Possibilities in a Well-coordinated Plan of Development."* Geraldine E. Homfray. Public Health Nurses' Bulletin 1, 9(Mar. 1932): 27-29.

2625. **Homfray, Geraldine E.** *"A Publicity Campaign."* Geraldine Homfray and Marion Cardwell. Public Health Nurses' Bulletin 2, 1(May 1933): 10-12.

2626. **Hops, Zona Joyce** *The Effects of Models of Perceived Similarity on Two Types of Altruistic Behavior in Fifth Grade Children.* Zona Joyce Hops. Vancouver: University of British Columbia, 1969.
　　Thesis (D.Ed.)--University of British Columbia, 1969.

2627. **Howard, Irene** *"First Memories of Vancouver."* Irene Howard. Vancouver Historical Society Newsletter 13, 5(Sept. 1973).

2628. **Howay, Frederick William** *"The Negro Immigration into Vancouver Island in 1858."* Frederick W. Howay. British Columbia Historical Quarterly 3, 2(Apr. 1939): 101-114.

2629. **Hughes, Mary Louise** *Standard for Day Care Programs: a Creative Approach to the Care of Pre-School Children Outside the Home, Based on a Review of Day Care Facilities in Greater Vancouver, 1962-1963.* Mary Louise Hughes. Vancouver: University of Vancouver, 1963.
　　Thesis (M.S.W.)--University of Vancouver, 1963.

2630. **Hundleby, Glenn Daryll** *Effectiveness of Benton Right-Left Discrimination Test in Identifying Children with Reading Disabilities.* Glenn Daryll Hundleby. Victoria: University of Victoria, 1969.
　　Thesis (M.A.)--University of Victoria, 1969.

2631. **Hundleby, Sigrid Anne** *Reading Achievement of Boys and Girls in Their Third Year of School.* Sigrid Anne Hundleby. Victoria: University of Victoria, 1969.
　　Thesis (M.A.)--University of Victoria, 1969.

2632. **Hunkin, Arthur Thomas** *A Remedial Reading Project in a British Columbia Junior High School.* Arthur Thomas Hunkin. [Seattle]: University of Washington, 1940.
　　Thesis (M.A.)--University of Washington, 1940.

2633. **Hunt, Edmund Arthur** *History of Physical Education in the Public Schools of British Columbia from 1918 to 1967.* Edmund Arthur Hunt. Seattle: University of Washington, 1967.
　　Thesis (M.A.)--University of Washington, 1967.

2634. **Hunter, Trenna G.** *"School Health Practices: Ritualistic or Purposeful?"* Trenna G. Hunter and C.H. Gundry. Canadian Journal of Public Health 46, 1(Jan. 1955): 9-14.

2635. **Hutcheson, Sydney** *Depression Stories.* Sydney Hutcheson. Vancouver: New Star Books, c1980.

2636. **Hutchinson, Harold Keith** *Dimensions of Ethnic Education: the Japanese in British Columbia, 1880-1940.* Harold Keith Hutchinson. Vancouver: University of British Columbia, 1973.
　　Thesis (M.A.)--University of British Columbia, 1973.

**2637. Hutchison, Bruce** *Far Side of the Street: a Personal Record.* Bruce Hutchison. Toronto: McMillan of Canada, c1976.

**2638. Hutchison, Bruce** *Western Windows.* Bruce Hutchison. Don Mills: Longmans Canada, c1967.

**2639. Huxley, Gigi** *"The Role of St. Mary's Mission School in Settlement."* Gigi Huxley. British Columbia Historical News 17, 2(Spring 1983): 16-17.

**2640. Ing, Rosalyn N.** *The Effects of Residential Schools on Native Child-rearing Patterns.* Rosalyn N. Ing. Vancouver: University of British Columbia, 1990. Thesis (M.Ed.)--University of British Columbia, 1990.

**2641. Ingeborg, Paulus** *Psychedelic Drug Use in Vancouver: Notes on the New Drug Scene.* Paulus Ingeborg. Vancouver: Narcotic Addiction Foundation of British Columbia, c1967.

**2642. Inglis, A.M.** *"Common Foot Problems in Young Children."* A.M. Inglis. Canadian Medical Association Journal/Journal de l'Association medicale canadienne 84, 7(Feb. 18, 1961): 363-370.

**2643. Inglis, B.D.** *"Adoption, the Marshall Case, and the Conflict of Laws."* B.D. Ingliss. Canadian Bar Review 35, 9(Nov. 1957): 1027-1045.

**2644. Ings, Olive** *"First Impressions."* Olive Ings. Public Health Nurses' Bulletin 1, 9(Mar. 1932): 42-43.

**2645. Innis, Hattie B.** *"The Rotary Fresh Air Camp at Vancouver, B.C."* Hattie B. Innis. Canadian Nurse 23, 12(Dec. 1927): 624-625.

**2646. Isbister, Winnifred** *My Ain Folk.* Winnifred Isbister. Comox Valley, B.C.: E.W. Bickle Ltd., 1977.

**2647. Jack, Joan** *"Store Promotion That Went Over No. 2., The Kiddies' Revue."* Joan Jack. Beaver 262, 4(Mar. 1932): 424-426.

**2648. Jan, James E.** *"Cerebral Complications in Juvenile Rheumatoid Arthritis."* James E. Jan, Robert H. Hill and Morton D. Low. Canadian Medical Association Journal/Journal de l'Association medicale canadienne 107, 7(Oct. 7, 1972): 623-625.

**2649. Jeffares, Isabelle M.** *"A Clinic Babies' Christmas Party."* Isabelle M. Jeffares. Public Health Nurses' Bulletin 1, 4(Apr. 1927): 14-17.

**2650. Jeffares, Isabelle M.** *"Generalized Public Health Nursing on Vancouver Island."* Isabelle Jeffares. Canadian Nurse 23, 2(Feb. 1927): 70-71.

**2651. Jeffares, Isabelle M.** *"Queen Alexandra Solarium for Crippled Children."* Isabelle M. Jeffares. Public Health Nurses' Bulletin 1, 4(Apr. 1927): 5.

**2652. Jenkins, Bertha** *"Health-teaching in Schools: a New Idea."* Bertha Jenkins. Public Health Nurses' Bulletin 1, 8(Mar. 1931): 53-54.

**2653. Jenkinson, Joanna** *"Hydrocephalus."* Joanna Jenkinson. Canadian Nurse 52, 11(Nov. 1956): 885-890.

**2654. Johnson, F. Henry** *"The Doukhobors of British Columbia: the History of a Sectarian Problem in Education."* F. Henry Johnson. Queen's Quarterly 70, 4(Winter 1963/64): 528-541.

**2655. Johnson, F. Henry** *A History of Public Education in British Columbia.* F. Henry Johnson. Vancouver: University of British Columbia, Publications Centre, c1964.

**2656. Johnson, F. Henry** *John Jessop: Goldseeker and Educator: Founder of the British Columbia School System.* F. Henry Johnson. Vancouver: Mitchell Press Limited, [1971].

**2657. Johnson, F. Henry** *"The Ryersonian Influence on the Public School System of British Columbia."* F. Henry Johnson. BC Studies 10(Summer 1971): 26-34.

**2658. Johnson, Gordon Kempton** *An Analysis of Six Theories As to the Origin of Delinquent Behavior.* Gordon Kempton Johnson. Vancouver: University of British Columbia, 1952. Thesis (M.A.)--University of British Columbia, 1952.

**2659. Johnson, Graham E.** *"Chinese Family and Community in Canada: Tradition and Change."* Graham E. Johnson. Scarborough, Ont.: Prentice-Hall of Canada Ltd., c1979. In Two Nations, Many Cultures: Ethnic Groups in Canada, pp. 358-371. Edited by Jean Leonard Elliott.

**2660. Johnson, Terry Dawson** *The Relationship Between Connotative Meaning and Reading Achievement of Boys and Girls in the Second Grade.* Terry Dawson Johnson. Vancouver: University of British Columbia, 1969.
Thesis (Ph.D.)–University of British Columbia, 1969.

**2661. Johnston, Mabel** *"Saanich Dental Clinics."* Mabel Johnston. Public Health Nurses' Bulletin 1, 7(May 1930): 18-19.

**2662. Jones, Charles** *Queesto: Pacheenaht Chief by Birthright.* Charles Jones with Stephen Bosustow. Nanaimo: Theytus Books, 1981.

**2663. Jones, David C.** *Agriculture, the Land, and Education: British Columbia, 1914-1929.* David Charles Jones. Vancouver: University of British Columbia, 1978.
Thesis (D.Ed.)–University of British Columbia, 1978.

**2664. Jones, David C.** *""We Cannot Allow It To Be Run By Those Who Do Not Understand Education": Agricultural Schooling in the Twenties."* David C. Jones. BC Studies 39(Autumn 1978): 30-60.

**2665. Jupp, Ursula** *From Cordwood to Campus in Gordon Head, 1852-1959: the Story of a District From its Days as Primeval Forest to the Establishment of a University.* Ursula Jupp. Victoria: Ursula Jupp, c1975.

**2666. Juvenile Delinquency Study Committee** *Juvenile Delinquency in Greater Victoria.* Juvenile Delinquency Study Committee and D.H. Nelson, Chairman. [Victoria]: Community Welfare Council of Greater Victoria, 1964.

**2667. Kanee, B.** *"BAL in the Successful Treatment of Mercury Poisoning from Gray Powder."* B. Kanee and I. Stoffman. Canadian Medical Association Journal 60, 3(Mar. 1949): 292-294.

**2668. Katz, Sidney** *"The Lost Children of British Columbia."* Sidney Katz. Toronto: Macmillan of Canada, c1978. In Canada from the Newstands, pp. 89-100. Edited by Val Clery.

**2669. Kaufmann, Theresa** *Child Mothers: Social Circumstances and Treatment Problems of Unmarried Mothers of School Age.* Theresa Kaufmann. Vancouver: University of British Columbia, 1962.
Thesis (M.S.W.)–University of British Columbia, 1962.

**2670. Kean, Alex** *"Lost in the Forest."* Alex Kean. Raincoast Chronicles 6(1976): 18-21.

**2671. Keate, Stuart** *Paper Boy: the Memoirs of Stuart Keate.* Stuart Keate. Toronto: Clarke, Irwin and Company, c1980.

**2672. Kee, Herbert William** *Reversal and Nonreversal Shifts in Indian and White Children.* Herbert William Kee. Vancouver: University of British Columbia, 1966.
Thesis (M.A.)–University of British Columbia, 1966.

**2673. Keenan, Verne** *"Presentation Method and Learning-time Consistency in Serial Learning."* Verne Keenan. Canadian Journal of Psychology/Revue canadienne de psychologie 24, 5(Oct. 1970): 311-320.

**2674. Keenleyside, Hugh L.** *Memoirs of Hugh L. Keenleyside: Hammer the Golden Day.* Hugh L. Keenleyside. Vol. 1. Toronto: McClelland and Stewart, c1981.

**2675. Keenleyside, Violet B.** *They Also Came.* Violet B. Keenleyside. Duncan, B.C.: Vibook Committee, Duncan United Church, c1987.

**2676. Kellerman, William Mathias** *Financing Child Care and Preventative Services: an Analysis of the Per-Diem Formula and Assisted Financing as Applied to the Catholic Children's Aid Society, Vancouver 1953 to 1960.* William Mathias Kellerman. Vancouver: University of British Columbia, 1960.
Thesis (M.S.W.)–University of British Columbia, 1960.

**2677. Kelly, Helen** *"Colwood."* Helen Kelly. Public Health Nurses' Bulletin 1, 1(Oct. 1924): 2-4.

**2678. Kelly, Helen** *"Esquimalt Rural Nursing Service."* H. Kelly. Public Health Nurses' Bulletin 1, 3(Apr. 1926): 9-11.

**2679. Kelly, Helen** *"Esquimalt Rural Nursing Service: Report of Progress."* Helen Kelly. Public Health Nurses' Bulletin 1, 4(Apr. 1927): 6-7.

**2680. Kelly, Helen** *"Esquimalt Rural Nursing Service."* Helen Kelly. Public Health Nurses' Bulletin 1, 5(Apr. 1928): 11-13.

**2681. Kelly, Helen** *"Esquimalt Rural Nursing Service."* Helen Kelly. Public Health Nurses' Bulletin 1, 6(Apr. 1929): 19-21.

**2682. Kelly, Helen** *"Esquimalt Rural Nursing Service."* Helen Kelly. Public Health Nurses' Bulletin 1, 7(May 1930): 6-8.

**2683. Kelly, Helen** *"Esquimalt Rural Nursing Service."* Helen Kelly. Public Health Nurses' Bulletin 1, 8(Mar. 1931): 26-28.

**2684. Kelly, Helen** *""Health Must Come First.""* Helen Kelly. Public Health Nurses' Bulletin 1, 9(Mar. 1932): 16-17.

**2685. Kelly, Helen** *"Problems of the Public Health Nurse."* H. Kelly. Public Health Nurses' Bulletin 1, 2(Apr. 1925): 7-8.

**2686. Kelso, Jack** *"Ocean Falls, B.C., Canada's Reservoir of Outstanding Competitive Swimmers: 1948-1974."* Jack Kelso. [Vancouver]: School of Physical Education and Recreation, University of British Columbia, 1979. In 4th Canadian Symposium on the History of Sport and Physical Education, no. 11, no pagination. Edited by Barbara Schrodt, Eric Broom, and Robert Morford.

**2687. Kennedy, Gilbert D.** *"British Columbia's New Adoption Legislation."* Gilbert D. Kennedy. University of Toronto Law Journal 12, 2(1957-1958): 296-300.

**2688. Kennedy, Gilbert D.** *"New British Columbia Legitimacy Legislation."* Gilbert D. Kennedy. University of Toronto Law Journal 14, 1(1961-1962): 122-125.

**2689. Kennedy, Liv** *Vancouver, Once Upon a Time: a Collection of Stories.* Liv Kennedy, Lorraine Harris [and] Elva Oglanby. [Vancouver: Radio Station CJOR, 1974].

**2690. Kenney, Mart** *Mart Kenney and His Western Gentlemen.* Mart Kenney. Saskatoon: Western Producer Prairie Books, 1981.

**2691. Kent, Dennis E.** *Report on Juvenile Services.* Dennis E. Kent. [Victoria: Corrections Branch, Department of the Attorney General, 1975].

**2692. Kenyon, Eva** *School Referrals to a Family Agency: a Study of Non-Voluntary Referrals of School Children With Family Problems to the Family Welfare Bureau of Greater Vancouver.* Eva Kenyon. Vancouver: University of British Columbia, 1950. Thesis (M.S.W.)--University of British Columbia, 1950.

**2693. Kerr, Margaret E.** *"Curious Superstitions and Beliefs."* Margaret E. Kerr. Public Health Nurses' Bulletin 2, 4(Mar. 1937): 27-29.

**2694. Kerr, Margaret E.** *"The Public Health Nurse and Child-study Groups."* Margaret E. Kerr. Public Health Nurses' Bulletin 1, 9(Mar. 1932): 10-12.

**2695. Kerr, Margaret E.** *"School Nursing in Nanaimo."* Margaret E. Kerr. Public Health Nurses' Bulletin 1, 4(Apr. 1927): 27-29.

**2696. Kerr, Margaret E.** *"School Nursing in Nanaimo."* Margaret E. Kerr. Public Health Nurses' Bulletin 1, 5(Apr. 1928): 9-10.

**2697. Kerr, Ruby A.** *"Special Class Work in Vancouver."* Ruby A. Kerr. Canadian Nurse 19, 3(Mar. 1923): 156-159.

**2698.** *The Kerrisdale Story.* [Vancouver]: Kerrisdale Courier, [1955?].

**2699. Khairat, Lara** *An Exploratory Study of the Effectiveness of the Parent Education Conference Method on Child Health.* Lara Khairat. Vancouver: University of British Columbia, 1970. Thesis (M.Ed.)--University of British Columbia, 1970.

**2700. Kilpatrick, Doreen L.** *A Revision of the Intermediate Version of the Halstead Category Test.* Doreen L. Kilpatrick. Victoria: University of Victoria, 1969. Thesis (M.A.)--University of Victoria, 1969.

**2701. Kilpatrick, Heather** *"A Day in a Logging Camp."* Heather Kilpatrick. Public Health Nurses' Bulletin 2, 3(June 1936): 26-29.

**2702. Kilpatrick, Heather** *"How Impetigo can Travel!"* Heather Kilpatrick. Public Health Nurses' Bulletin 1, 9(Mar. 1932): 29-30.

**2703. Kilpatrick, Heather** *"What Do You Really Do?"* H. Kilpatrick. Public Health Nurses' Bulletin 2, 4(Mar. 1937): 29-31.

**2704. King, Fred** *"A Kaleden Boyhood."* Fred King. Okanagan Historical Society Report 50(1986): 158-162.

**2705. Kitagawa, Muriel** *This is My Own: Letters to Wes and Other Writings on Japanese Canadians, 1941-1948.* Muriel Kitagawa, edited by Roy Miki. Vancouver: Talonbooks, 1985.

**2706. Kitteringham, G.M.** *"The Osoyoos Testalinda, Oliver, Fairview, and Falls Districts."* G.M. Kitteringham. Public Health Nurses' Bulletin 1, 8(Mar. 1931): 35-36.

**2707. Klonoff, Harry** *"Epidemiology of Head Injuries in Children: a Pilot Study."* Harry Klonoff and Geoffrey C. Robinson. Canadian Medical Association Journal/Journal de l'Association medicale canadienne 96, 19(May 13, 1967): 1308-1311.

**2708. Kloppenborg, Anne, ed.** *Vancouver's First Century: a City Album, 1860-1965.* Anne Kloppenborg, Alice Niwinski, Eve Johnson and Robert Gruetter, eds. Vancouver: Douglas and McIntyre, c1985.

**2709. Knight, Phyllis** *A Very Ordinary Life: as Told to Rolf Knight.* Phyllis Knight. Vancouver: New Star Books, c1974.

**2710. Knight, Rolf** *Along the No. 20 Line: Reminiscences of the Vancouver Waterfront.* Rolf Knight. Vancouver: New Star Books Ltd., c1980.

**2711. Knight, Rolf** *Stump Ranch Chronicles and Other Narratives.* Rolf Knight. Vancouver: New Star Books, 1977.

**2712. Knowles, Bill** *"My Early Days in Kelowna."* Bill Knowles. Okanagan Historical Society Report 47(1983): 143-147.

**2713. Kolodinski, Elsie** *Planning Non-Ward Care for Children of Mentally Ill Parents: an Analysis of Decisions Made at the Children's Aid Society of Vancouver in the Years 1957 to 1959.* Elsie Kolodinski. Vancouver: University of British Columbia, 1961.
Thesis (M.S.W.)–University of British Columbia, 1961.

**2714. Koopman, Peggy R.** *"Infants' Preferences for Facial Arrangements: a Failure to Replicate."* Peggy R. Koopman and Elinor W. Ames. Child Development 39, 2(June 1968): 481-487.

**2715. Koopman, Peggy R.** *Input-Output Modes and Short-term Memory for Object Sequences in Grade 1 Children.* Peggy Rae Koopman. Vancouver: University of British Columbia, 1968.
Thesis (Ed.D.)–University of British Columbia, 1968.

**2716. Kootenay Lake Historical Society** *Pioneer Families of Kaslo.* Kootenay Lake Historical Society. Kaslo, B.C.: The Society, c1980.

**2717. Koppenaal, R.J.** *"Postremity in Human Maze Learning."* R.J. Koppenaal and D.T. Kenny. Canadian Journal of Psychology 14,2 (June 1960): 121-130.

**2718. Kyle, John** *"Carrying Education to the Frontier Child."* John Kyle. In Proceedings of Sixth Annual Canadian Conference on Child Welfare 1927, pp. 61-63.

**2719. Ladner, Leon Johnson** *The Ladners of Ladner: By Covered Wagon to the Welfare State.* Leon J. Ladner. Vancouver: Mitchell Press Ltd., c1972.

**2720. Ladner, T. Ellis** *Above the Sand Heads: Firsthand Accounts of Pioneering in the Area Which in 1877, Became the Municipality of Delta, British Columbia.* Ellis T. Ladner and Edna G. Ladner.

**2721. Lai, Chuen-yan David** *Chinatowns: Towns Within Cities in Canada.* Chuen-yan David Lai. Vancouver: University of British Columbia Press, 1988.

**2722. Lai, Chuen-yan David** *"The Issue of Discrimination in Education in Victoria, 1901-1923."* Chuen-yan David Lai. Canadian Ethnic Studies/Etudes ethniques au Canada 19, 3(1987): 47-67.

**2723. Laidman, Leslie Warde** *Premature Withdrawal from Treatment in a Child Guidance Clinic: Exploratory Study of the Factors Which Underlie Clients' Decision to Withdraw from Social Work Treatment at the Provincial Child Guidance Clinic, North Burnaby, British Columbia.* Leslie Warde Laidlaw. Vancouver: University of British Columbia, 1957.
Thesis (M.S.W.)–University of British Columbia, 1957.

**2724. Lamb, W. Kaye** *"Robie Lewis Reid (1866-1945): a Memoir."* W. Kaye Lamb. British Columbia Historical Quarterly 9, 2(Apr. 1945): 79-88.

**2725. Lamb, W. Kaye** *"Some Notes on the Douglas Family."* W. Kaye Lamb. British Columbia Historical Quarterly 17, 3(July-Oct. 1953): 41-52.

**2726. Landsdowne, Rosemary** *The Concept of Non-Adoptability: a Study of the Concept of Non-Adoptability on Case Work Services to the Unmarried Mother, and an Examination of the Validity of this Concept.* Rosemary Landsdowne. Vancouver: University of British Columbia, 1949.

Thesis (M.S.W.)–University of British Columbia, 1949.

**2727. Lang, Margaret** *Along the Way: Book 1.* Margaret Lang. White Rock, B.C.: The Author, c1967.
Reprinted as Along the Way: an Account of Pioneering White Rock and Surrounding District in British Columbia, c1981, under author's married name Margaret Lang Hastings.

**2728. Langdale, Arthur Leslie** *How Foster Children Turn Out: a Follow-Up Study of Former Foster Children Over Twenty-One, and the Effects of Foster Home Care.* Arthur Leslie Langdale. Vancouver: University of British Columbia, 1951.
Thesis (M.S.W.)–University of British Columbia, 1951.

**2729. Langlois, William J.** *"Francis Williams, Haida Artist."* W.J. Langlois and Francis Williams. Victoria: Provincial Archives, 1976. Sound Heritage 4, 3-4(1976): 76-80.

**2730. Lappage, Ronald S.** *"British Columbia's Contribution to the Dominion-Provincial Youth Training Programme Through the Provincial-Recreation Programme."* Ronald S. Lappage. Canadian Journal of History of Sport and Physical Education 9, 1(Dec. 1978): 86-92.

**2731. Laturnus, Elizabeth** *"Infectious Mononucleosis."* Elizabeth Laturnus. Canadian Nurse 53, 12(Dec. 1957): 1100-1103.

**2732. Lavington, Dude** *Born to Be Hung.* H. "Dude" Lavington. Victoria, B.C.: Sono Nis Press, c1983.

**2733. Lavington, Dude** *Nine Lives of a Cowboy.* H. "Dude" Lavington. Victoria, B.C.: Sono Nis Press, c1982.

**2734. Law, Annie S.** *"Public Health Nursing in the Peace River and in Cowichan: a Comparison."* Annie S. Law. Public Health Nurses' Bulletin 2, 6(Mar. 1939): 9-13.

**2735. Law, Annie S.** *"A Sikh Well-baby Clinic."* Annie S. Law. Public Health Nurses' Bulletin 2, 2(Apr. 1935): 21-23.

**2736. Lay, Jackie** *"To Columbia on the Tynemouth: the Emigration of Single Women and Girls in 1862."* Jackie Lay. Victoria: Camousun College, c1980. In In Her Own Right: Selected Essays on Women's History in B.C., pp. 19-41. Edited by Barbara Latham and Cathy Kess.

**2737. Laycock, Samuel R.** *Study of Educational Provision For and Needs of Emotionally Disturbed Children in the Elementary and Secondary Schools of British Columbia.* S.R. Laycock; with the assistance of J.A. Findlay. Vancouver: Educational Research Institute of British Columbia, 1969.

**2738. Leach, W.B.** *"Calcific Arteriosclerosis of Infancy."* W.B. Leach. Canadian Medical Association Journal 73, 9(Nov. 1, 1955): 733-735.

**2739. Ledoux, Marguerite M.** *"Cystic Fibrosis of the Pancreas."* Marguerite M. Ledoux. Canadian Nurse 47, 3(Mar. 1951): 173-176.

**2740. Lee, Amy A.** *"Public Health Nursing in Nanaimo."* A.A. Lee and M.J. Woods. Public Health Nurses' Bulletin 1, 2(Apr. 1925): 9-10.

**2741. Lee, Amy A.** *"School Nursing in Revelstoke."* Amy A. Lee. Public Health Nurses' Bulletin 1, 9(Mar. 1932): 9-10.

**2742. Leeson, Lavell H.** *"Hearing Defects in Children."* Lavell H. Leeson. Canadian Medical Association Journal 62, 2(Feb. 1950): 167-169.

**2743. Lehmann, Eric C.H.** *"Neonatal Screening in Vancouver for Congenital Dislocation of the Hip."* Eric C.H. Lehmann and Donald G. Street. Canadian Medical Association Journal/Journal de l'Association medicale canadienne 124, 8(Apr. 15, 1981): 1003-1008.

**2744. Leslie, Joyce** *"The Rebirth of a Public Health Service."* Joyce Leslie. Public Health Nurses' Bulletin 2, 6(Mar. 1939): 14-17.

**2745. Leslie, Perry Thorold** *Comparison of Deaf Children's Performance on Tasks Related to Reading Skills.* Perry Thorold Leslie. Vancouver: University of British Columbia, 1970.
Thesis (M.A.)–University of British Columbia, 1970.

**2746. Levirs, F.P.** *"Promotional Policies in Theory and Practice in British Columbia."* F.P. Levirs. Journal of Education of the Faculty and College of Education: Vancouver and Victoria 6(Dec. 1961): 113-121.

**2747. Lewis, Claudia** *"Doukhobor Childhood and Family Life."* Claudia Lewis. Vancouver: University of British Columbia Press, 1952. In Report of the Doukhobor Research Committee, pp. 108-135. Edited by Harry B. Hawthorn.
Reprinted in abridged form in Canadian Society: Sociological Perspectives, 1st ed.,

1961, pp. 193-209, 2nd ed., 1964, pp. 172-188 and 3rd ed., 1968, pp. 184-200. Edited by Bernard R. Blishen, Frank E. Jones, Kapser D. Naegele and John Porter.

2748. **Lewis, Claudia** *Indian Families of the Northwest Coast: the Impact of Change.* Claudia Lewis. Chicago: University of Chicago Press, c1970.

2749. **Lewis, Claudia** *A Study of the Impact of Modern Life on a Canadian Indian Band.* Claudia Lewis. New York: Columbia University, 1959.
Thesis (Ph.D.) -- Columbia University, 1959.

2750. **Lewis, Norah Lillian** *Advising the Parents: Child Rearing in British Columbia During the Interwar Years.* Norah Lillian Lewis. [Vancouver]: University of British Columbia, 1980. (CTM no. 51737)
Thesis (D.Ed.)--University of British Columbia, 1980.

2751. **Lewis, Norah Lillian** *"Creating the Little Machine: Child Rearing in British Columbia, 1919-1939."* Norah L. Lewis. BC Studies 56(Winter 1982-1983): 44-60.

2752. **Lewis, Norah Lillian** *"Physical Perfection for Spiritual Welfare: Health Care for the Urban Child, 1900-1939."* Norah Lewis. Calgary: Detselig Enterprises Ltd., 1982. In Studies in Childhood History: a Canadian Perspective, pp. 135-166. Edited by Patricia T. Rooke and R.L. Schnell.

2753. **Lidster, Norman** *No Time For Why.* Norman Lidster. Vancouver: Versatile Publishing Co., c1972.

2754. **Lim, Sing** *West Coast Chinese Boy.* Sing Lim. Montreal: Tundra Books, c1979.

2755. **Lindberg, Wayne Charles** *An Exploratory Study in Conceptualizing Children's Investigatory Activities of Natural Phenomena by Utilizing Thomas S. Kuhn's View of Science as a Theoretical Framework.* Wayne Charles Lindberg. Vancouver: University of British Columbia, 1969.
Thesis (M.A.)--University of British Columbia, 1969.

2756. **Lindenfeld, Elda** *"Emotionally Disturbed Children."* Elda Lindenfeld. Canadian Medical Association Journal 78, 4(Feb. 15, 1958): 287.

2757. **Lindo, Millicent A., ed.** *Making History: an Anthology of British Columbia.* Millicent A. Lindo. [S.l.] : The Author, 1974.

2758. **Liqournik, Isreal** *The Strategy of Delinquency Control: a Critical Survey of Recent Developments and a Proposal for Some Local Applications.* Isreal Liqournik, David Michael Stolee and Marie Irene Varnam. Vancouver: University of British Columbia, 1963.
Thesis (M.S.W.)--University of British Columbia, 1963.

2759. **Lirenman, D.S.** *"Urinary Tract Infections in the Newborn: Diagnosis from Mid-stream Urine Specimens."* D.S. Lirenman. Canadian Medical Association Journal/Journal de l'Association medicale canadienne 101, 11(Nov. 29, 1969): 664-666.

2760. **Little, Margaret** *"A Vaccination Clinic."* Margaret Little. Public Health Nurses' Bulletin 2, 6(Mar. 1939): 17-21.

2761. **Little, Margaret** *"What We Are Doing at Revelstoke."* Margaret Little. Public Health Nurses' Bulletin 2, 5(Mar. 1938): 18-22.

2762. **Livingston, Philip** *Fringe of the Clouds.* Sir Philip Livingston. London, Eng.: Johnson Pub., [1962].

2763. **Logan, Harry T.** *"The Fairbridge Farm School."* Harry T. Logan. London: The Times, 1939. In Canada, pp. 71-72. Reprinted from the Canada Number of The Times, May 15, 1939.

2764. **Loggins, Olive Spencer** *Tenderfoot Trail: Greenhorns in the Cariboo.* Olive Spencer Loggins. Victoria: Sono Nis Press, c1983.

2765. **Logie, Ted** *Ted Tells (Okanagan) Tales: True Stories from Our Okanagan Pioneers.* Ted Logie. Penticton, B.C.: Penticton Herald, [1967?].

2766. **Longley, Dorothy** *"The Care of Cerebral Palsy."* Dorothy Longley. Canadian Nurse 42, 6(June 1946): 473-474.

2767. **Lothian, George** *Flight Deck: Memoirs of an Airline Pilot.* George Lothian. Toronto: McGraw-Hill Ryerson, 1979.

2768. **Lowry, R. Brian** *"Birth Prevalance of Cleft Lip and Palate in British Columbia Between 1952 and 1986: Stability of Rates."* R. Brian Lowry, Nancy Y. Thunem and Soo Hong. Canadian Medical Association Journal/Journal de l'Association medicale canadienne 140,

10(May 1989): 1167-1170.

**2769. Lowther, Elizabeth** *"Chicken-pox."* Elizabeth Lowther. Public Health Nurses' Bulletin 1, 8(Mar. 1931): 12-13.

**2770. Lowther, Elizabeth** *"The Generalized Public Health Nurse."* Elizabeth Lowther. Public Health Nurses' Bulletin 2, 2(Apr. 1935): 27-28.

**2771. Lowther, Elizabeth** *"Measles."* Elizabeth Lowther. Public Health Nurses' Bulletin 1, 9(Mar. 1932): 30-31.

**2772. Loyal Protestant Association of New Westminster** *Souvenir of Formal Opening September 15th 1928 of the Loyal Protestant Home for Children, New Westminster.* Loyal Protestant Association. Vancouver: Lionel Ward & Co., [1928].

**2773. Luboff, Charlene G.** *Differential Patterns of Family Life Education in Neighbourhood-based Programs.* Charlene G. Luboff. Vancouver: Family Service Centres of Greater Vancouver Area, 1971.

**2774. Lucas, Celia A.** *"Little Mothers' League Classes as Conducted in Saanich Over a Period of Five Years."* C.A. Lucas. Public Health Nurses' Bulletin 1, 4(Apr. 1927): 8-10.

**2775. Lucas, Celia A.** *"Some Experiences in the University Health Service."* Celia A. Lucas. Public Health Nurses' Bulletin 1, 9(Mar. 1932): 48-52.

**2776. Lucas, Celia A.** *"University Hill School."* C.A. Lucas. Public Health Nurses' Bulletin 1, 8(Mar. 1931): 10-11.

**2777. Lugtig, Donald Joseph** *The Psychological Factors Which May Intensify the Adolescent Foster Child's Concern About His Unknown Parents: an Exploratory Study of Seven Adolescent Wards of the Vancouver Children's Aid Society.* Donald Joseph Lugtig. Vancouver: University of British Columbia, 1956. Thesis (M.S.W.)--University of British Columbia, 1956.

**2778. Luke, Allan** *Theory, Practice, Policy, Research: Concepts and Criteria for Literacy in British Columbia 1920-1940.* Allan Luke. Burnaby: Simon Fraser University, 1980. (CTM no. 825224) Thesis (M.A.-Ed.)--Simon Fraser University, 1980.

**2779. Lupton, Nora** *"Notes on the British Columbia Protestant Orphan's Home."* Nora Lupton. Victoria: Camousun College, c1980. In In Her Own Right: Selected Essays on Women's History in B.C., pp. 43-54. Edited by Barbara Latham and Cathy Kess.

**2780. Lyne, Frances** *"School Nursing in Kelowna City Schools."* Frances Lyne. Public Health Nurses' Bulletin 1, 6(Apr. 1929): 26-29.

**2781. Lyons, Elma Fairweather** *"Oliver's First School."* Elma Fairweather Lyons. Okanagan History 54(1990): 128-129.

**2782. McAllister, Claire** *"The Doll House that Travelled."* Claire McAllister. B.C. Historical News 7, 2(Feb. 1974): 14-15.

**2783. McAllister, Claire** *"Getting Dressed."* Claire McAllister. B.C. Historical News 8, 1(Nov. 1974): 23-26.

**2784. McAllister, Claire** *"Women of the West Kootenay."* Claire McAllister. B.C. Historical News 10, 3(Mar. 1977): 13-17.

**2785. McAlpine, Mary** *The Other Side of Silence: a Life of Ethel Wilson.* Mary McAlpine. Madeira Park: Harbour Pub., c1988.

**2786. McCallum, Mary Freck** *Family Differentials in the Habilitation of Children with a Brain Injury.* Mary Freck McCallum. Vancouver: University of British Columbia, 1961. Thesis (M.S.W.)--University of British Columbia, 1961.

**2787. McClung, M.R.** *"Kelowna Fall Fair."* M.R. McClung. Public Health Nurses' Bulletin 1, 2(Apr. 1925): 7.

**2788. McCormick, Lucy Hill** *"Early Rural Schools of Vernon and White Valley."* Lucy Hill McCormick. Okanagan Historical Society Report 46(1982): 38-44.

**2789. McCracken, Merle Diane** *The Regulation of Behaviour by Speech in Preschool Children.* Merle Diane McCracken. Vancouver: University of British Columbia, 1968. Thesis (M.A.)--University of British Columbia, 1968.

**2790. McCubbin, Frances Amy** *Counselling Services at the Junior High School Level: a Study of Counselling Problems in a Vancouver Sample School and Social Work Implications.* Frances Amy McCubbin. Vancouver: University of British Columbia, 1953. Thesis (M.S.W.)--University of British Columbia, 1953.

**2791. MacDermot, M. Dorothea** *"School Work in Nanaimo."* M. Dorothea MacDermot. Public Health Nurses' Bulletin 1, 8(Mar. 1931): 37-38.

**2792. MacDonald, John A.** *The Spallumcheen Indian Band and Its Impact on Child Welfare Policy in British Columbia.* John A. MacDonald. [Vancouver]: School of Social Work, University of British Columbia, 1981.

**2793. MacDonald, John A.** *"The Spallumcheen Indian Band By-law and Its Potential Impact on Native Indian Child Welfare Policy in British Columbia."* John A. MacDonald. Canadian Journal of Family Law/Revue canadienne de droit familial 4, 1(Jan. 1983): 75-96.

**2794. McDonald, Robert A.J.** *""Holy Retreat" or "Practical Breathing Spot"?: Class perceptions of Vancouver's Stanley Park, 1910-1913."* Robert A.J. McDonald. Canadian Historical Review 65, 2(June 1984): 127-153.

**2795. Macdonald, William Balfour** *At Sea and By Land: the Reminiscences of William Balfour, R.N.* William Balfour Macdonald. Victoria, B.C.: Sono Nis Press, 1983.

**2796. Macdougall, John Innes** *A Survey of Richmond Municipality Relative to the Establishment of a Junior High School.* John Innes Macdougall. Vancouver: University of British Columbia, 1937. Thesis (M.A.)–University of British Columbia, 1937.

**2797. McFarlane, Mary Frank** *A Survey of Preschool Centres in Vancouver.* Mary Frank McFarlane. Vancouver: University of British Columbia, 1949. Thesis (M.S.W.)–University of British Columbia, 1949.

**2798. McGann, David** *"More in Sorrow: Social Action and the Indian Boarding Home Program."* David McGann. Canadian Welfare 43, 4(July-Aug. 1967): 24-29.

**2799. McGeachie, Pixie** *"Intrepid in the Name of God."* Pixie McGeachie. British Columbia Historical News 23, 3(Summer 1990): 28-31.

**2800. McGeer, Ada** *"Agnes Deans Cameron...A Memory."* Ada McGeer. B.C. Historical News 8, 1(Nov. 1974): 16-17.

**2801. McGeer, Ada** *"Oh Call Back Yesterday, Bid Time Return".* Ada McGeer. Vancouver: Versatile, 1981.

**2802. MacGill, Helen Gregory** *"The Oriental Delinquent in the Vancouver Juvenile Court."* Helen Gregory MacGill. Sociology and Social Research 22, 5(May/June 1938): 428-438.

**2803. MacGill, Helen Gregory** *The Story of Vancouver Social Service.* Helen Gregory MacGill.

**2804. MacGill, Helen Gregory, comp.** *Daughters, Wives and Mothers in British Columbia: Some Laws Regarding Them.* Compiled by Helen Gregory MacGill. 2nd ed. Vancouver: Moore Printing Co., 1913.

**2805. MacGill, Helen Gregory, comp.** *Daughters, Wives and Mothers in British Columbia: Some Laws Regarding Them.* Helen Gregory MacGill, compiler. 1st ed. Vancouver: Moore Printing Co., 1913.

**2806. MacGill, Helen Gregory, comp.** *Daughters, Wives and Mothers in British Columbia: Some Laws Regarding Them.* Compiled by Helen Gregory MacGill. Vancouver: Moore Printing Co., 1914.

**2807. MacGill, Helen Gregory, comp.** *Laws for Women and Children in British Columbia.* Compiled by Helen Gregory MacGill. Vancouver: Evans and Hastings, 1925.

**2808. MacGill, Helen Gregory, comp.** *Laws for Women and Children in British Columbia.* Compiled by Helen Gregory MacGill. Vancouver: McBeath-Campbell, 1928.

**2809. MacGill, Helen Gregory, comp.** *Laws for Women and Children in British Columbia.* Compiled by Helen Gregory MacGill. Vancouver: McBeath-Campbell, 1935.

**2810. MacGill, Helen Gregory, comp.** *Laws for Women and Children in British Columbia.* Compiled by Helen Gregory MacGill. Vancouver: [s.n.], 1939.

**2811. MacGill, Helen Gregory, comp.** *Supplement to Daughters, Wives and Mothers in British Columbia.* Compiled by Helen Gregory MacGill. Vancouver: [s.n., 1915].

**2812. McIntosh, J.W.** *"The Vancouver Outbreak of Haemorrhagic Smallpox: 2. Lessons Learned From the Outbreak."* J.W. McIntosh. Canadian Public Health Journal 24, 3(Mar. 1933): 112-119.

**2813. McKay, Alvin** *"Education as a Total Way of Life: the Nisga'a Experience."* Alvin McKay and Bert McKay. Vancouver: University of British Columbia Press, 1987. In Indian Education in Canada, Volume 2: the Challenge, pp. 64-85. Edited by Jean Barman, Yvonne Hebert and Don McCaskill.

2814. McKeever, J. Larry "Hazards of the Horse and Buggy Days." J. Larry McKeever. Okanagan Historical Society Report 46(1982): 92-96.

2815. Mackenzie, Budd Cumming The Play Interview as a Social Work Technique in a Child Guidance Setting: an Analysis of Five Individual Play Interviews with Children with Adjustment Problems Conducted by Social Workers in the Provincial Child Guidance Clinic of Vancouver. Budd Cumming Mackenzie. Vancouver: University of British Columbia, 1956.
Thesis (M.S.W.)--University of British Columbia, 1956.

2816. MacKenzie, D.B. "Providing for Individual Differences in Secondary Education in British Columbia." D.B. MacKenzie. Toronto: W.J. Gage, 1956. In Education: a Collection of Essays on Canadian Education, v.1, 1954-1956, pp. [33]-36.

2817. MacKenzie, Dorothy E. "Health Insurance and Public Health." Dorothy E. MacKenzie. Public Health Nurses' Bulletin 1, 9(Mar. 1932): 52-53.

2818. Mackie, H.F. "The Polio Epidemic of 1927." H.F. Mackie. Okanagan Historical Society Report 29(1965): 43-48.

2819. MacKinnon, George Watson The Evolution of the School System of British Columbia. George Watson MacKinnon. Seattle: University of Washington, 1920.
Thesis (M.A.)--University of Washington, 1920.

2820. MacLachlan, T.B. "Hydramnios: Review and Report of 81 Cases." T.B. MacLachlan and A.D. Claman. Canadian Medical Association Journal/Journal de l'Association medicale canadienne 86, 3(Jan. 20, 1962): 106-109.

2821. McLaren, Angus "The Creation of a Haven for 'Human Thoroughbreds': the Sterilization of the Feeble-Minded and the Mentally Ill in British Columbia." Angus McLaren. Canadian Historical Review 67, 1(Mar. 1986): 127-150.

2822. McLaren, Henry Moncrieff Adjustment of the Adolescent in Rural Foster Homes: a Pioneer Study of the Problems in Giving Service to Adolescent Boys and Girls, and the Difficulty This Age Group Has in Adjustment to Foster Homes in Rural Communities. Henry Moncrieff McLaren. Vancouver: University of British Columbia, 1954.
Thesis (M.S.W.)--University of British Columbia, 1954.

2823. McLarty, Stanley D. The Story of Strathcona School. Stanley D. McLarty. Vancouver: [s.n.], 1961.

2824. MacLaughlin, Mrs. V.S. "Child Health Programme in British Columbia." Mrs. V.S. MacLaughlin. Public Health Journal 14, 3(Mar. 1923): 119-126.

2825. MacLaurin, Donald Leslie The History of Education in the Crown Colonies of Vancouver Island and British Columbia and in the Province of British Columbia. Donald Leslie MacLaurin. Seattle: University of Washington, 1936.
Thesis (Ph.D.)--University of Washington, 1936.

2826. McLean, Alan The Detached Work Program of the Boys Clubs of Vancouver: an Analysis of the Detached Work Programs, its Initiation and Progress From May 1964 - September 1967. Alan McLean, Douglas Purdy and Barry Worsfold. Vancouver: University of British Columbia, 1967.
Thesis (M.S.W.)--University of British Columbia, 1967.

2827. McLean, D.M. "Atypical Measles Following Immunization With Killed Measles Vaccine." D.M. McLean, G.D.M. Kettyls, J. Hingston, P.S. Moore, R.P. Paris and J.M. Rigg. Canadian Medical Association Journal/Journal de l'Association medicale canadienne 103, 7(Oct. 10, 1970): 743-744.

2828. McLellan, Marney "Rheumatic Heart Disease." Marney McLellan. Canadian Nurse 47, 7(July 1951): 513-519.

2829. McLeod, Joan, ed. We Are Their Children: Ethnic Portraits of British Columbia. Joan McLeod, ed., Trisha Mason and Janis Fisher. Vancouver, B.C.: CommCept Publishers Ltd., c1977.

2830. McMillan, Isabel "Day Before Christmas." I. McMillan. Public Health Nurses' Bulletin 2, 4(Mar. 1937): 43-45.

2831. McMillan, Isabel "Emancipation of Children's Play-clothes." Isabel McMillan. Public Health Nurses' Bulletin 2, 3(June 1936): 37-38.

2832. McNab, J.A. "Obstetrical Analgesia and Anaesthesia." J.A. McNab. Canadian Medical Association Journal 72, 9(May 1, 1955): 681-686.

2833. McNamara, Jeannette Beaubien Wilderness Dream: Glimpses of Pioneer Life in British Columbia. Jeannette Beaubien McNamara. Victoria: Braemar Books Ltd., c1986.

**2834. McPhee, Malcolm** *"Skookumchuk Soliloquy."* Malcolm McPhee. British Columbia Historical News 22, 2(Spring 1989): 20-21.

**2835. McRae, B.C.** *The Effect of a Course in Indian History on the Attitudes of Elementary Pupils Towards Five Selected Concepts.* B.C. McRae. Vancouver: Board of School Trustees, 1970.

**2836. Maddison, Doris** *"Infectious Mononucleosis."* Doris Maddison. Canadian Nurse 50, 3(Mar. 1954): 208-215.

**2837. Magnussen, Karen** *Karen: the Karen Magnussen Story.* Karen Magnussen and Jeff Cross. Don Mills, Ont.: Collier-Macmillan, 1973.

**2838. Maguire, Evelyn** *"The Mennonite in British Columbia."* Evelyn Maguire. Public Health Nurses' Bulletin 2, 5(Mar. 1938): 22-24.

**2839. Mahon, Rita M.** *"Inkaneep Indian Reserve, Oliver District."* Rita M. Mahon. Public Health Nurses' Bulletin 2, 2(Apr. 1935): 11-14.

**2840. Mahon, Rita M.** *"Problems of Disease Prevention."* Rita M. Mahon. Public Health Nurses' Bulletin 2, 4(Mar. 1937): 32-34.

**2841. Malkin, L.** *"Another Dental Clinic."* L. Malkin. Public Health Nurses' Bulletin 2, 6(Mar. 1939): 21-27.

**2842. Malkin, L.** *"Justification for the Appointment of a Social Worker to Complete the Health and Education Programme in the Peace River District, B.C."* L. Malkin. Public Health Nurses' Bulletin 2, 4(Mar. 1937): 34-36.

**2843. Malkin, L.** *"Sex Education."* L. Malkin. Public Health Nurses' Bulletin 2, 5(Mar. 1938): 25-26.

**2844. Mallek, Howard** *"On the Comparative Use of Silver Nitrate and Penicillin in the Eyes of the Newborn."* Howard Mallek, Peter Spohn and Josephine Mallek. Canadian Medical Association Journal 68, 2(Feb. 1953): 117-119.

**2845. Malloff, Marjorie, comp.** *Toil and Peaceful Life: Portraits of Doukhobors.* Marjorie Malloff and Peter Ogloff, comps. Victoria, B.C.: Aural History, Provincial Archives, 1977.

**2846. Mann, Jean Simpson** *Progressive Education and the Depression in British Columbia.* Jean Simpson Mann. Vancouver: University of British Columbia, 1978.
Thesis (M.A.)--University of British Columbia, 1978.

**2847. Marcus, Robert J.** *"Youth Services Can Be Relevant."* Robert J. Marcus. Canadian Welfare 45, 5(Sept.-Oct. 1969): 13-14, 16.

**2848. Marcuse, Berthold** *Long Term Dependancy and Malajustment: Cases in the Family Service Agency.* Berthold Marcuse. Vancouver: University of British Columbia, 1956.
Thesis (M.S.W.)--University of British Columbia, 1956.

**2849. Marlatt, Daphne, ed.** *Opening Doors: Vancouver's East End.* Compiled and edited by Daphne Marlatt and Carole Itter. Victoria: PABC, 1979.

**2850. Marson, Gervase** *Learning Modalities and Reading in Kindergarten.* Gervase Marson. Victoria: University of Victoria, 1971.
Thesis (M.A.)--University of Victoria, 1971.

**2851. Martin, Elizabeth E.** *"Dental Work in Vernon Schools."* Elizabeth E. Martin. Public Health Nurses' Bulletin 2, 3(June 1936): 31-33.

**2852. Martin, Elizabeth E.** *"Our Responsibility for the Health of the School Children."* Elizabeth E. Martin. Public Health Nurses' Bulletin 1, 9(Mar. 1932): 6-8.

**2853. Martin, Elizabeth E.** *"School Nursing in the Vernon Consolidated Schools."* Elizabeth E. Martin. Public Health Nurses' Bulletin 1, 7(May 1930): 12-14.

**2854. Martin, Elizabeth E.** *"Vernon."* E. Martin. Public Health Nurses' Bulletin 1, 6(Apr. 1929): 21-22.

**2855. Martin, Elizabeth E.** *"Vernon."* E. Martin. Public Health Nurses' Bulletin 2, 4(Mar. 1937): 36-37.

**2856. Martin, Elizabeth E.** *"Vernon."* Elizabeth E. Martin. Public Health Nurses' Bulletin 2, 5(Mar. 1938): 26-27.

**2857. Martin, Elizabeth E.** *"Vernon Consolidated School District."* Elizabeth E. Martin. Public Health Nurses' Bulletin 1, 8(Mar. 1931): 47-48.

**2858. Martin, S.** *"School Work in Vernon."* S. Martin. Public Health Nurses' Bulletin 1, 5(Apr. 1928): 10-11.

**2859. Mason, Elda Copely** *Lasquiti Island: History and Memory.* Elda Copely Mason. South Wellington: [s.n.], c1976.

**2860. Mason, Ruth** *Torn Between Two Passions.* Ruth Mason. Vancouver: Standard Press, c1986.

**2861. Massy, Patricia Graham** *Foster Home Planning for the Indian Child: a Casework Study of Foster Children, Parents, Foster Parents, and Agency Service: Children's Aid Society of Vancouver, 1959-61.* Patricia Graham Massy. Vancouver: University of British Columbia, 1962.
  Thesis (M.S.W.)--University of British Columbia, 1962.

**2862. Massy, Patricia Graham** *"Frances and the Vancouver Children's Aid Society."* Patricia G. Massy [Vancouver]: University of British Columbia, Department of Extension, 1963. In The Indians of British Columbia: a Study-Discussion Text, pp. 221-224. Edited by Jill A. Willmott.

**2863. Matheson, Hugh Naismith** *A Study of Errors Made in Paragraphs Written by Grade 12 Students on the June, 1953, English 40 (Language) University Entrance Examination, British Columbia Department of Education.* Hugh Naismith Matheson. Vancouver: University of British Columbia, 1960.
  Thesis (M.A.)--University of British Columbia, 1960.

**2864. Matheson, K. Douglas** *Child Separation in British Columbia: an Epidemiological Analysis.* K. Douglas Matheson and Davis C. Neave. Vancouver: University of British Columbia, School of Social Work, 1971.

**2865. Matheson, K. Douglas** *Epidemiological Survey of Children Admitted to Care in the Province of British Columbia.* Kenneth Douglas Matheson and Davis Colden Neave. Vancouver: University of British Columbia, 1967.
  Thesis (M.S.W.)--University of British Columbia, 1967.

**2866. Matheson, K. Douglas** *Survey of the Numbers and Needs of Children in British Columbia With Special Placement Problems.* K. Douglas Matheson and D. Neave. [British Columbia: s.n., 1967].

**2867. Matheson, Malcolm A.** *"Search and Leadership Training for Young Offenders at Lakeview Forest Camp."* Malcolm A. Matheson. Canadian Journal of Corrections/Revue canadienne de criminologie 8, 4(Oct. 1966): 237-245.

**2868. Matison, Sonja Constance** *Child Neglect Situations: a Comparative Case Analysis of Two Neglect Cases from Vancouver Agencies, 1955.* Sonja Constance Matison. Vancouver: University of British Columbia, 1955.
  Thesis (M.S.W.)--University of British Columbia, 1955.

**2869. Matters, Diane L.** *"The Boys' Industrial School: Education for Juvenile Offenders."* Diane L. Matters. Calgary: Detselig Enterprises Ltd., 1980. In Schooling and Society in 20th Century British Columbia, pp. 53-70. Edited by J. Donald Wilson and David C. Jones.

**2870. Matters, Diane L.** *A Chance To Make Good: Juvenile Males and the Law in Vancouver, B.C., 1910-1915.* Diane Louise Janowski Matters. Vancouver: University of British Columbia, 1978.
  Thesis (M.A.)--University of British Columbia, 1978.
  Author subsequently changed her name to Indianna Matters.

**2871. Matters, Diane L.** *"Public Welfare Vancouver Style, 1910-1920."* Dianne L. Matters. Journal of Canadian Studies/Revue d'etudes canadiennes 14, 1(Spring 1979): 3-15.

**2872. Maunders, Thomas Fulton** *A Casework Study of Parents Requesting the Adoption Placement of Legitimate Children: a Study of Cases from Greater Vancouver Social Agencies, 1951.* Thomas Fulton Maunders. Vancouver: University of British Columbia, 1953.
  Thesis (M.S.W.)--University of British Columbia, 1953.

**2873. Mess, A.L.** *"The Story of a Children's Aid Society on the Pacific Coast."* A.L. Mess. Child and Family Welfare 12, 4(Nov. 1936): 41-47.

**2874. Metropolitan Hospital Planning Council** *A Study of Paediatric Bed Use in the Province of British Columbia, 1961: Prepared for the Professional Subcommittee of the Metropolitan Hospital Planning Council.* The Council. Vancouver: The Council, [1962].
  Chairman: Bruce D. Graham.

**2875. Mett, Judd** *Pioneers: Book 2.* Judd Mett. [Vancouver, B.C.: The Author], c1983.

**2876. Mickelson, Norma I.** *Meaningfulness in Children's Verbal Learning.* Norma I. Mickelson. Victoria: University of Victoria, 1968.
Thesis (M.A.)--University of Victoria, 1968.

**2877. Miles, Marion C.** *"The Organization of a Rural Health Unit."* Marion Miles. Public Health Nurses'· Bulletin 2, 6(Mar. 1939): 27-30.

**2878. Miles, Marion C.** *"The School Dental Clinic."* Marion C. Miles. Public Health Nurses' Bulletin 2, 5(Mar. 1938): 27-28.

**2879. Miles, Marion C.** *"Time is Money: Absentees."* Marion C. Miles. Public Health Nurses' Bulletin 2, 4(Mar. 1937): 37-41.

**2880. Miles, Marion C.** *"Tuberculin Tests in a City School."* Marion Miles. Public Health Nurses' Bulletin 2, 3(June 1936): 33-35.

**2881. Miller, Charles A.** *Valley of the Stave.* Charles A. Miller. Surrey, B.C.: Hancock House, c1981

**2882. Miller, Velma** *"A Day at Bamberton."* Velma Miller. Public Health Nurses' Bulletin 1, 8(Mar. 1931): 44-46.

**2883. Mitchell, Beverley Joan** *Ethel Wilson and Her Works.* Beverley Mitchell. Toronto: ECW Press, [1984].

**2884. Mitchell, Blanche** *"Cowichan Health Centre."* Blanche Mitchell. Public Health Nurses' Bulletin 1, 7(May 1930): 21-22.

**2885. Mitchell, Helen** *Diamond in the Rough: the Campbell River Story.* Helen Mitchell. Aldergrove, B.C.: Frontier Publishing Ltd, c1975.
First published in 1966.

**2886. Mitchell, Margaret F.** *"The Irwins, Amber Ski Hill and the Olympics."* Margaret F. Mitchell and Marjorie Yerburg. Okanagan Historical Society Report 48(1984): 114-115.

**2887. Mitchell, Robert James Gordon** *The Family Welfare Bureau of Greater Vancouver: its Origins and Development, 1927 to 1952.* Robert James Gordon Mitchell. Vancouver: University of British Columbia, 1952.
Thesis (M.S.W.)--University of British Columbia, 1952.

**2888. Miyazaki, M.** *My Sixty Years in Canada.* M. Miyazaki. [Vancouver, B.C.: The Author, 1973].

**2889. Moody, Eva** *"Chilliwack."* Eva Moody. Public Health Nurses' Bulletin 2, 4(Mar. 1937): 41-42.

**2890. Moody, Eva** *"Chilliwack Municipality at a Glance."* Eva Moody. Public Health Nurses' Bulletin 2, 5(Mar. 1938): 36-38.

**2891. Moore, Catherine Jean** *Recreational Projects Sponsored by Service Clubs: a Survey of a Representative Group of Recreational Projects Sponsored by Service Clubs in Greater Vancouver.* Catherine Jean Moore. Vancouver: University of British Columbia, 1949.
Thesis (M.S.W.)--University of British Columbia, 1949.

**2892. Moore, Emily Josephine Leighton** *The Reliability of the British Columbia Test in the Fundamentals of Arithmetic.* Emily Josephine Leighton Moore. Toronto: University of Toronto, 1930.
Thesis (M.A.)--University of Toronto, 1930.

**2893. Moore, O.M.** *"Peptic Ulcer in Children."* O.M. Moore. Canadian Medical Association Journal 44, 5(May 1941): 462-466.

**2894. Morales, Dolores Averna** *Casework in the Return of Non-ward Care Cases to the Parental Home: a Descriptive and Analytical Study of Social Welfare Branch (British Columbia) Cases, 1953-1956.* Dolores Averna Morales. Vancouver: University of British Columbia, 1957.
Thesis (M.S.W.)--University of British Columbia, 1957.

**2895. Moran, Bridget** *Stoney Creek Woman: the Story of Mary John.* Bridget Moran. Vancouver: Tillicum Library, 1988.

**2896. More, Arthur J.** *"An Approach to Non-discriminatory Assessment of Native Indian Children."* Arthur J. More and Buff Oldridge. B.C. Journal of Special Education 4, 1(Spring 1980): 51-59.

**2897. Morley, Alan** *Roar of the Breakers: a Biography of Peter Kelly.* Alan Morley. Toronto: Ryerson Press, c1967.

**2898. Morris, Maxine** *"The Child-guidance Clinic."* Maxine Morris. Public Health Nurses' Bulletin 2, 3(June 1936): 35-37.

**2899. Morris, Maxine** *"Generalized Nursing System."* Maxine Morris. Public Health Nurses' Bulletin 2, 4(Mar. 1937): 42-43.

**2900. Morrow, D.F.** *"Fatal Myocarditis Complicating Interstitial Pneumonitis: a Report of Three Cases."* D.F. Morrow and C.J. Coady. Canadian Medical Association Journal/Journal de l'Association medicale canadienne 80, 12(June 15, 1959): 980-982.

**2901. Morton, James** *The Dusty Road From Perth.* James Morton. Vancouver: Douglas & McIntyre, c1981.

**2902. Moslin, Ralph Sidney** *Differential Treatment in Child Guidance Case Work: an Analysis of Case Work Treatment Methods in Work with 40 Mothers of Preschool Children with Behavior Problems, Vancouver Child Guidance Clinic, 1950.* Ralph Sidney Moslin. Vancouver: University of British Columbia, 1952.
Thesis (M.S.W.)–University of British Columbia, 1952.

**2903. Mould, Jack** *Stump Farms and Broadaxes.* Jack Mould. Saanichton, B.C.: Hancock House, c1976.

**2904. Mozzanini, John S.** *An Evaluation of the Facilities and Services of the Vancouver B.C. Juvenile Detention Home.* John S. Mozzanini. Vancouver: University of British Columbia, 1950.
Thesis (M.S.W.)–University of British Columbia, 1950.

**2905. Mulloy, Florence Stuart** *Counselling Problems of the Junior High School Girl.* Florence Stuart Mulloy. Vancouver: University of British Columbia, 1949.
Thesis (M.A.)–University of British Columbia, 1949.

**2906. Munro, Marjory Helen** *A General Survey and Evaluation of an Institution for the Observation and Treatment of Problem Children.* Marjory Helen Munro. Vancouver: University of British Columbia, 1946.
Thesis (M.A.)–University of British Columbia, 1946.

**2907. Murray, Andrew B.** *"A Survey of Hearing Loss in Vancouver School Children: Part 2. The Association Between Secretory Otitis Media and Enlarged Adenoids, Infection and Nasal Allergy."* Andrew B. Murray, Donald O. Anderson, Kenneth G. Cambon, Hossein K. Moghadam and Geoffrey C. Robinson. Canadian Medical Association Journal/Journal de l'Association medicale canadienne 98, 21(May 25, 1968): 995-1001.

**2908. Murray, Hilda** *"Vitalizing Statistics in Saanich."* Hilda Murray. Public Health Nurses' Bulletin 1, 4(Apr. 1927): 19-20.

**2909. Myers, Gerald George** *Predelinquency: its Recognition in School.* Gerald George Myers. Vancouver: University of British Columbia, 1949.
Thesis (M.S.W.)–University of British Columbia, 1949.

**2910. Naden, Esther** *"The Home School Visit, Saanich."* Esther Naden. Public Health Nurses' Bulletin 1, 6(Apr. 1929): 14-16.

**2911. Naden, Esther** *"The Saanich Health Centre."* Esther S. Naden. Public Health Nurses' Bulletin 1, 8(Mar. 1931): 9.

**2912. Nahm, Tilman E.** *"Boyhood Memories of the Upper Bankhead Water User's Community."* Tilman E. Nahm. Okanagan Historical Society Report 50(1986): 35-38.

**2913. Nahm, Tilman E.** *"Memories of a Telegraph Messenger."* Tilman E. Nahm. Okanagan Historical Society Report 51(1987): 7-12.

**2914. Nakayama, Timothy M.** *"Anglican Missions to the Japanese in Canada."* Timothy M. Nakayama. Journal of the Canadian Church Historical Society 8, 2(June 1966): 26-45.

**2915. Narcotic Addiction Foundation of British Columbia** *Drug Use Among Vancouver Secondary Students.* Narcotic Addiction Foundation of British Columbia. Vancouver: Narcotic Addiction Foundation of British Columbia, 1971.

**2916. Neave, Davis C.** *"Directions in Research: Questions About Politics and Practice in Parent-Child Separation."* Davis C. Neave and K. Douglas Matheson. Canadian Welfare 46, 6(Nov.-Dec. 1970): 15-17, 22.

**2917. Nechako Valley Historical Society** *Vanderhoof: the Town That Wouldn't Wait.* Nechako Valley Historical Society, with Lyn Hancock, ed. Vanderhoof, B.C.: The Society, c1979.

**2918. Neering, Rosemary** *Emily Carr.* Rosemary Neering. Don Mills: Fitzhenry & Whiteside, 1975.

**2919. Neilson, Kathryn Elizabeth** *Delinquency of Indian Girls in British Columbia: a Study in Socialization.* Kathryn Elizabeth Neilson. Vancouver: University of British Columbia, 1971.
Thesis (M.A.)–University of British Columbia, 1971.

**2920. Nesbitt, James K.** *"The Diary of Martha Cheney Ella, 1853-1856: Part I and Part II."* Nesbitt, James K., ed. British Columbia Historical Quarterly 13, 2(Apr./June 1949): 91-112; 13, 3/4(July-Oct. 1949): 257-270.

**2921. Newcombe, Howard B.** *"Risks to Siblings of Stillborn Children."* Howard B. Newcombe. Canadian Medical Association Journal/Journal de l'Association medicale canadienne 98, 4(Jan. 27, 1968): 189-193.

**2922. Newitt, Angela** *"Some Childhood Memories of Clo'oose."* Angela Newitt. Raincoast Chronicles 11(1987): 16-24.

**2923. Nicholls, M.** *"Jane Klyne McDonald: 1810-1879."* M. Nicholls. British Columbia Historical News 21, 4(Fall 1988): 2-5.

**2924. Norcross, Elizabeth Blanche** *"1918-1928: the Decade of Social Legislation."* E.B. Norcross. British Columbia Historical News 17, 1(Winter 1983): 13-16.

**2925. Norcross, Elizabeth Blanche** *The Warm Land: a History of Cowichan.* Elizabeth Blanche Norcross. Duncan, B.C.: Island Books, 1959.

**2926. Norfolk, Eric** *Cooney and His Clan.* Eric Norfolk. Prince George, B.C.: Noreen DeLisle, c1979.

**2927. Norman, Viollete** *"The Nursery."* Viollete Norman. Public Health Nurses' Bulletin 1, 4(Apr. 1927): 10-11.

**2928. Norris, John** *Wo Lee Stories: Memories of a Childhood in Nelson, B.C.* John Norris. New Denver, B.C.: John Norris, c1986.

**2929. North, Lionel E.** *"The Norths of Armstrong."* Lionel E. North. Okanagan Historical Society Report 48(1984): 125-129.

**2930. Nuttall-Smith, J.** *"Pulmonary Histoplasmosis Accompanied by Erythema Nodosum."* J. Nuttall-Smith. Canadian Medical Association Journal 74, 1(Jan. 1, 1956): 59-60.

**2931. O'Brian, H.** *"The Vernon Commonage School."* H. O'Brian. Okanagan Historical Society Report 36(1972): 61-64.

**2932. Ochs, Elizabeth** *"Vaccination in a Rural Area."* Elizabeth Ochs. Public Health Nurses' Bulletin 2, 5(Mar. 1938): 39-40.

**2933. Olds, Charles H.** *Far Pastures.* C.H. Olds. [Prince George?: The Olds Family, 1989].

**2934. O'Neail, Hazel** *Doukhobor Daze.* Hazel O'Neail. Sidney: Gray's Publishing Ltd., 1962.

**2935. Orchard, Imbert, ed.** *Floodland and Forest: Memories of the Chilliwack Valley.* Imbert Orchard. Victoria: PABC, 1983.

**2936. Orchard, Imbert, ed.** *Growing Up In the Valley: Pioneer Childhood In the Lower Fraser Valley.* Imbert Orchard. Victoria: PABC, 1983.

**2937. Osborne, Robert F.** *"Leadership in Recreation in British Columbia."* Robert F. Osborne. Canadian Welfare 32, 2(June 1956): 83-88.

**2938. Packford, B. Levitz** *"Foster Parents Help Each Other."* B. Levitz Packford. Canadian Welfare 44, 3(May-June 1968): 14-16.

**2939. Page, Shirley** *"The Murphys Pioneers of the Okanagan."* Shirley Page. Okanagan History 52(1988): 46-61.

**2940. Palmer, Hugh** *Circumnavigating Father.* Hugh Palmer. Surrey: Hancock House Publishers Ltd., 1990.

**2941. Parker, Mrs. G. Cameron** *Problems in Family Welfare, Relief and Child Protection in Greater Victoria: Being a Summary of a Report Made Under the Auspices of the Victoria Survey Committee 1931-1932.* Mrs. G. Cameron Parker. [S.l.]: Canadian Council on Children and Family Welfare, [1932].

**2942. Paternaude, Branwen C.** *Because of Gold.* Branwen C. Paternaude. Quesnel: Branwen C. Paternaude, c1981.

**2943. Paterson, Donald** *"Health Services for the Handicapped Child in British Columbia."* Donald Paterson. Canadian Medical Association Journal 76, 6(Mar. 15, 1957): 483-485.

**2944. Patillo, Roger** *Alienated, Transient and Runaway Youth.* Roger Patillo. Vancouver: United Community Services of Greater Vancouver, 1970.

**2945. Patillo, Roger** *Summary, Transient, Alienated and Runaway Youth.* Roger Patillo. [Vancouver: s.n.], 1970.

2946. **Pattinson, Ann** *"Tick Paralysis with Bulbar Involvement."* Ann Pattinson. Canadian Nurse 51, 2(Feb. 1955): 134-140.

2947. **Pazdro, Roberta J.** *"Agnes Deans Cameron: Against the Current."* Roberta J. Pazdro. Victoria: Camousun College, c1980. In In Her Own Right: Selected Essays on Women's History in B.C., pp. 101-123. Edited by Barbara Latham and Cathy Kess.

2948. **Peachland Historical Society** *Peachland Memories: a History of the Peachland and Trepanier Districts in the Beautiful Okanagan Valley.* Peachland Historical Society, comps. 2 v. Peachland, B.C.: The Society, c1987.

2949. **Peake, Frank A.** *The Anglican Church in British Columbia.* Frank A. Peake. Vancouver: Mitchell Press, 1959.

2950. **Pease, E.** *"Some Aspects of Tuberculosis Work in the Okanagan."* E. Pease. Public Health Nurses' Bulletin 2, 6(Mar. 1939): 30-32.

2951. **Pelton, Terrance Ronald** *Motor Performance of Correctional Institution Inmates.* Terrance Ronald Pelton. Vancouver: University of British Columbia, 1965.
Thesis (M.P.E.)--University of British Columbia, 1965.

2952. **Pennington, Gary** *Education Through Challenge and Adventure: a Report on Physical Education in British Columbia.* Gary Pennington, Jack Stevens, Barbara Kallus, and Peter Moody. [Vancouver: Educational Research Institute of B.C.], 1971.

2953. **Peters, Hilda** *"Chilliwack."* Hilda Peters. Public Health Nurses' Bulletin 1, 8(Mar. 1931): 33-35.

2954. **Peters, Hilda** *"Ladysmith."* H. Peters. Public Health Nurses' Bulletin 1, 6(Apr. 1929): 25-26.

2955. **Peters, Hilda** *"Ladysmith."* Hilda Peters. Public Health Nurses' Bulletin 1, 7(May 1930): 19-20.

2956. **Peterson, Lester Ray** *Indian Education in British Columbia.* Lester Ray Peterson. Vancouver: University of British Columbia, 1959.
Thesis (M.A.)--University of British Columbia, 1959.

2957. **Phillips, Cecilie Anne Bannatyne** *Coping Skills of Incest and Sexual Abuse Victims.* Cecilie Anne Bannatyne Phillips. Vancouver: University of British Columbia, 1985.
Thesis (M.A.)--University of British Columbia, 1985.

2958. **Piersdorff, Kay Hartley** *"The Hartley Road."* Kay Hartley Piersdorff. British Columbia Historical News 17, 3(Summer 1984): 11-16.

2959. **Pioneer Researchers, comp.** *Memories Never Lost: Stories of the Pioneer Women of the Cowichan Valley and a Brief History of the Valley, 1850-1920.* Pioneer Researchers, comp. [Cowichan Bay]: Pioneer Researchers, c1986.

2960. **Pleas, Roy Thomas** *Services for Adoptive Families: an Exploratory Study of Needs and Attitudes, Vancouver, 1961.* Roy Thomas Pleas. Vancouver: University of British Columbia, 1961.
Thesis (M.S.W.)--University of British Columbia, 1961.

2961. **Plenderleith, Eileen Mavis** *A Study of British Columbia Teachers Attitudes to Students Behaviour Problems.* Eileen Mavis Plenderleith. Vancouver: University of British Columbia, 1948.
Thesis (M.A.)--University of British Columbia, 1948.

2962. **Pollard, Juliet Thelma** *The Making of the Metis in the Pacific Northwest Fur Trade Children: Race, Class and Gender.* Juliet Thelma Pollard. Vancouver: University of British Columbia, 1990
Thesis (Ph.D.)--University of British Columbia, 1990.

2963. **Porteous, Aileen** *"The Osborne-Smith Story."* Aileen Porteous. Okanagan Historical Society Report 48(1984): 110-113.

2964. **Porteous, Aileen** *"St. Michael's School."* Aileen Porteous. Okanagan Historical Society Report 35(1971): 149-151.

2965. **Posener, L.J.** *"An Epidermoid Cyst of the Spleen."* L.J. Posener and O.K. Litherland. Canadian Medical Association Journal 75, 6(Sept. 15, 1956): 510-512.

2966. **Priestly, E. Dorothy** *"Our First Year."* E. Dorothy Priestly. Public Health Nurses' Bulletin 2, 5(Mar. 1938): 40-41.

**2967. Priestly, E. Dorothy** *"The Reactions on the Opening of a New Health Centre."* E. Dorothy Priestly. Public Health Nurses' Bulletin 2, 6(Mar. 1939): 33-36.

**2968. Pritchard, H.D.** *"Story of the Vernon Schools."* H.D. Pritchard and Clarence Fulton. Okanagan Historical Society Report 15(1951): 137-143.

**2969. Pryce, Elizabeth** *"The Findlays of Kaleden."* Elizabeth Pryce. Okanagan History 52(1988): 128-132.

**2970. Pryce, Elizabeth** *"Leo Fuhr: "Mr. Beekeeper" of the Okanagan."* Elizabeth Pryce. Okanagan History 53(1989): 107-114.

**2971. Purdy, Al** *No Other Country.* Al Purdy. Toronto: McClelland and Stewart, c1977.

**2972. Putman, J.H.** *Survey of the School System.* J.H. Putman and G.M. Weir. Victoria: King's Printer, 1925.

**2973. Putnam, Madeleine** *"Public Health Activities, Nanaimo Indian Reservation."* Madeleine Putnam. Public Health Nurses' Bulletin 2, 4(Mar. 1937): 45-46.

**2974. Queen Margaret's School. History Committee** *Beyond All Dreams: a History of Queen Margaret's School, Duncan, British Columbia: an Independent School for Girls.* The Committee. Duncan: The Committee, 1975.

**2975. Radcliffe, Roland W.** *"The Social Problems of Epileptics with Special Reference to Canada."* Roland W. Radcliffe. Canadian Medical Association Journal 72, 9(May 1, 1955): 647-654.

**2976. Rands, Marian** *"Getting to School in the Good Old Days."* Marian Rands. Okanagan Historical Society Report 49(1985): 165-166.

**2977. Ravenhill, Alice** *"The Tale of the Nativity as Told by the Children of Inkaneep, British Columbia."* Alice Ravenhill. British Columbia Historical Quarterly 5, 1(Jan. 1941): 84-85.

**2978. Read, John H.** *"The Epidemiology and Prevention of Traffic Accidents Involving Child Pedestrians."* John H. Read, Eleanor J. Bradley, Joan D. Morison, David Lewall and David A. Clarke. Canadian Medical Association Journal/Journal de l'Association medicale canadienne 89, 14(Oct. 5, 1963): 687-701.

**2979. Read, John H.** *"A University Centre for Children with Handicaps."* John H. Read. Journal of Education of the Faculty and College of Education: Vancouver and Victoria 5(Mar. 1961): 89-99.

**2980. Redford, James** *"Attendance at Indian Residential Schools in British Columbia, 1890-1920."* James Redford. BC Studies 44(Winter 1979-1980): 41-56.

**2981. Reed, Patricia** *Maintenance Collections from Putative Fathers: an Evaluation of the Administration of the Children of Unmarried Parents Act in the Province of British Columbia with Special Reference to the Relative Merits of Settlements and Continued Monthly Payment.* Patricia Reed. Vancouver: University of British Columbia, 1950. Thesis (M.S.W.)--University of British Columbia, 1950.

**2982. Reid, Marilyn J.** *A Review of the Provisions in Vancouver Schools for New Canadians at the Primary Level.* Marilyn J. Reid and Lynne Guinet. Vancouver: Board of School Trustees, 1971.

**2983. Reid, Robie Lewis** *"How One Slave Became Free: an Episode of the Old Days of Victoria."* Robie L. Reid. British Columbia Historical Quarterly 6, 4(Oct. 1942): 251-256.

**2984. Reimer, Derek, ed.** *"The Gulf Islanders."* Derek Reimer, ed. Victoria: Provincial Archives, 1976. Sound Heritage 5, 4(1976).

**2985. Renwick, D.H.G.** *"Estimates of Incidence and Prevalence of Mongolism and of Congenital Heart Disease in British Columbia."* D.H.G. Renwick, J.R. Miller and Donald Paterson. Canadian Medical Association Journal/Journal de l'Association medicale canadienne 91, 8(Aug. 22, 1964): 365-371.

**2986. Rhodes, H. Cecil** *"Venereal Disease Education in the High School: British Columbia's Experiment."* H. Cecil Rhodes and Pauline M.C. Capelle. Canadian Journal of Public Health 35, 5(May 1944): 181-189.

**2987. Rice, Cora** *"Cora's Memoirs."* Cora Rice. Okanagan Historical Society Report 43(1979): 82-83.

**2988. Richmond, Hector Allan** *Forever Green: the Story of One Of Canada's Foremost Foresters.* Hector Allan Richmond. Lantzville, B.C.: Oolichan Books, 1983.

**2989. Ridout, Katherine** "A Woman of Mission: the Religious and Cultural Odyssey of Agnes Wintemute Coates." Katherine Ridout. Canadian Historical Review 71, 2(June 1990): 208-244.

**2990. Rienhart, Edith M.** "One Oliver Pioneer Family." Edith M. Rienhart. Okanagan History 53(1989): 94-96.

**2991. Roberts, A.M.** "Opening Up a New Service in the Peace River." A.M. Roberts. Public Health Nurses' Bulletin 1, 8(Mar. 1931): 5-6.

**2992. Roberts, Evelyn Marie** Mental Health Clinical Services: a Study of the Children Between 6 and 12 Years of Age Examined by Mental Health Clinics in Vancouver from 1945 to 1947 Inclusive. Evelyn Marie Roberts. Vancouver: University of British Columbia, 1949. Thesis (M.S.W.)–University of British Columbia, 1949.

**2993. Robertson, A. Marion W.** "S.S. Moyie: the Last of the Stern Wheelers." A. Marian W. Robertson. British Columbia Historical News 21, 2(Spring 1988): 25-26.

**2994. Robillard, Richard H.** Earle Birney. Richard H. Robillard. Toronto: McClelland and Stewart, c1971.

**2995. Robinson, Geoffrey C.** "Hospital Emergency Services for Children and Adolescents: a One Year Review at the Vancouver General Hospital." Geoffrey C. Robinson and Harry Klonoff. Canadian Medical Association Journal/Journal de l'Association medicale canadienne 96, 19(May 13, 1967): 1304-1308.

**2996. Robinson, Geoffrey C.** "A Study of Congenital Blindness in British Columbia: Methodology and Medical Findings." Geoffrey C. Robinson, James A. Watt and Eileen Scott. Canadian Medical Association Journal/Journal de l'Association medicale canadienne 99, 17(Nov. 2, 1968): 831-836.

**2997. Robinson, Geoffrey C.** "A Survey of Hearing Loss in Vancouver School Children: Part 1. Methodology and Prevalence." Geoffrey C. Robinson, Donald O. Anderson, Hossein K. Moghadam, Kenneth G. Cambon and Andrew B. Murray. Canadian Medical Association Journal/Journal de l'Association medicale canadienne 97, 20(Nov. 11, 1967): 1199-1207.

**2998. Robinson, Geoffrey C.** "Use of a Hospital Emergency Service by Children and Adolescents for Primary Care." Geoffrey C. Robinson, Claire Kinnis, Donald O. Anderson, Corinne Argue and Hugh S. Miller. Canadian Medical Association Journal/Journal de l'Association medicale canadienne 101, 9(Nov. 1, 1969): 543-547.

**2999. Robinson, Michael** "Rose Skuki." Michael Robinson. B.C. Historical News 3, 1(Feb. 1970): 10-12.

**3000. Roddan, Sam** Batter My Heart. Sam Roddan. Vancouver: United Church of Canada, B.C. Conference, c1975.

**3001. Rogers, Mary** M.I. Rogers: 1869-1965. Mary Rogers and Michael Kluckner, comp. and ed. [Victoria, B.C.: J. Gudewill, 1987].

**3002. Rogow, Sally M.** An Investigation of Delayed Language Development of a Withdrawn Blind Child. Sally M. Rogow. Vancouver: University of British Columbia, 1971. Thesis (D.Ed.)–University of British Columbia, 1971.

**3003. Rohner, Ronald P.** "The Kwakiutl: Indians of British Columbia." Ronald P. Rohner and Evelyn C. Rohner. Scarborough: Prentice-Hall, 1971. In Native Peoples, pp. 116-133. Edited by Jean Leonard Elliott.

**3004. Rolston, Joyce Fairchild** Clinical Treatment of Adolescents With Behaviour Disorders: an Evaluative Survey of Patients Admitted to Crease Clinic, (British Columbia), 1956-1958. Joyce Fairchild Rolston. Vancouver: University of British Columbia, 1959. Thesis (M.S.W.)–University of British Columbia, 1959.

**3005. Rose, C.** "The Preschool Visit." C. Rose. Public Health Nurses' Bulletin 1, 8(Mar. 1931): 39-40.

**3006. Roy, Patricia E.** "British Columbia's Fear of Asians, 1900-1950." Patricia Roy. Histoire sociale/Social History 13, 25(May 1980): 161-172.

**3007. Roy, Patricia E.** "The Illusion of Toleration: White Opinions of Asians in British Columbia, 1929-37." Patricia E. Roy. Toronto: Butterworth and Co. (Canada) Ltd., 1980. In Visible Minorities and Multiculturalism: Asians in Canada, pp. 81-91. Edited by K. Victor Ujimoto and Gordon Hirabayashi, with the assistance of P.A. Saram.

**3008. Roy, Patricia E.** A White Man's Province: British Columbia Politicians and Chinese and Japanese Immigrants, 1858-1914. Patricia E. Roy. Vancouver: University of British Columbia Press, 1989.

**3009. Ruhmann, William** *"Soldiers of the Soil: Recollections, the Activities of Vernon Boys 1914-1918."* William Ruhmann. Okanagan Historical Society Report 47(1983): 68-76.

**3010. Ruhmann, William** *"Soldiers of the Soil 1914-1919."* William Ruhmann. British Columbia Historical News 23, 2(Spring 1990): 11-13.

**3011. Runnalls, F.E.** *"Boom Days in Prince George."* F.E. Runnalls. British Columbia Historical Quarterly 8, 4(Oct. 1944): 281-306.

**3012. Rush, Gary B.** *North Vancouver Adolescent Study.* G.B. Rush, F.B. Collinge and R.W. Wyllie. [Burnaby?: Simon Fraser University?], 1969.

**3013. Russell, John S.** *Drug Use Among Young Adults.* John S. Russell [and] George S. Tuxford. [Vancouver]: Narcotic Addiction Foundation of British Columbia, 1971.

**3014. Russell, John S.** *Survey of Drug Use in Selected British Columbia School Districts.* John Russell. Vancouver: Narcotic Addiction Foundation of British Columbia, c1970.

**3015. Sager, Edward** *The Bootlegger's Lady.* Ed Sage and Mike Frye. Surrey, B.C.: Hancock House, c1984

**3016. Sale, T. Don** *"Education in the Cariboo Fifty Years Ago."* T. Don Sale. British Columbia Historical News 22, 2(Spring 1989): 16-18.

**3017. Sale, T. Don** *"One Room Schools of Fifty Years Ago."* T.D. Sale. B.C. Historical News 14, 1(Fall 1980): 16-17.

**3018. Sandiford, Peter** *"Inheritance of Talent Among Canadians."* Peter Sandiford. Queen's Quarterly 35, 1(July-Sept. 1927): 2-19.

**3019. Sandison, James M.** *"City Bush."* James M. Sandison. Vancouver Historical Society Newsletter 13, 10(Feb. 1974): 5-7.

**3020. Sandison, James M., ed.** *Schools of Old Vancouver.* James M. Sandison, ed. Vancouver: Vancouver Historical Society, 1971.

**3021. Sapir, Edward** *"A Girl's Puberty Ceremony among the Nootka Indians."* Edward Sapir. Royal Society of Canada Proceedings and Transactions Series 3, 7, 2(May 1913): 67-80.

**3022. Sapir, Edward** *"Life of a Nootka Indian."* Edward Sapir. Queen's Quarterly 28, 3 and 4(Jan.-Mar. and Apr.-June 1921): 232-243.

**3023. Schinbein, J.E.** *"Testicular Tumours."* J.E. Schinbein. Canadian Medical Association Journal 78, 2(Jan. 15, 1958): 126-127.

**3024. Schreck, Cynthia Ann Nagel** *An Analysis of Number Conservation Ability.* Cynthia Ann Nagel Schreck. Vancouver: University of British Columbia, 1971. Thesis (M.A.)--University of British Columbia, 1971.

**3025. Schriver, Joanne** *"Harrison Indian Childhood."* Joanne Schriver and Eleanor B. Leacock. New York: Columbia University Press, 1949. In Indians of the Urban Northwest, pp. 195-242. Edited by Marian W. Smith. Shorter version of the article is published in The Indians of British Columbia: a Study-Discussion Text, pp. 74-84. Edited by Jill A. Willmott.

**3026. Schwesinger, Gladys C.** *Recollections of Early Vancouver in My Childhood, 1893-1912.* Gladys C. Schwesinger. Vancouver, B.C.: Brock Webber Print Co., c1960.

**3027. Scott, Douglas** *"The First Okanagan College."* Douglas Scott. Okanagan Historical Society Report 46(1982): 55-67.

**3028. Scott, Eileen** *Preschool Blind Child and His Parents.* Eileen Scott. [Vancouver]: University of British Columbia, 1955.

**3029. Scott, Ian** *"Mystery of Little Bay Still Unsolved."* Ian Scott. Islander (July 25, 1971): 7.

**3030. Scrivener, Leslie** *Terry Fox: His Story.* Leslie Scrivener. Toronto: McClelland and Stewart, c1981.

**3031. Sedgewick, G.G.** *"On Disillusionment in Freshmen."* G.G. Sedgewick. Queen's Quarterly 39, 4(Nov. 1932): 704-709.

**3032. Servos, Ledwina H.** *"Impressions."* Ledwina H. Servos. Public Health Nurses' Bulletin 1, 8(Mar. 1931): 25-26.

**3033. Seymour, Winifred E.** *"Fernie."* Winifred Seymour. Public Health Nurses' Bulletin 2, 5(Mar. 1938): 41-42.

**3034. Seymour, Winifred E.** *"Public Health Nursing in Fernie."* Winifred Seymour. Public Health Nurses' Bulletin 1, 8(Mar. 1931): 24-25.

**3035. Seymour, Winifred E.** *"Public Health Work in Fernie."* Winifred E. Seymour. Public Health Nurses' Bulletin 1, 7(May 1930): 7-9.

**3036. Seymour, Winifred E.** *"Remarks from Fernie."* Winifred E. Seymour. Public Health Nurses' Bulletin 2, 2(Apr. 1935): 5.

**3037. Seymour, Winifred E.** *"School Work in Fernie."* Winifred E. Seymour. Public Health Nurses' Bulletin 1, 5(Apr. 1928): 20.

**3038. Seymour, Winifred E.** *"School Work in Fernie."* Winifred Seymour. Public Health Nurses' Bulletin 1, 6(Apr. 1929): 34-35.

**3039. Seymour, Winifred E.** *"Views Upon Education."* Winifred E. Seymour. Public Health Nurses' Bulletin 1, 9(Mar. 1932): 38.

**3040. Shadbolt, Doris** *The Art of Emily Carr.* Doris Shadbolt. Toronto: Clarke, Irwin; Vancouver: Douglas & McIntyre, 1979.

**3041. Shadbolt, Doris** *Bill Reid.* Doris Shadbolt. Vancouver: Douglas & McIntyre, 1986.

**3042. Sharp, Robert F.** *An Objective Study of the Junior High School in Vancouver.* Robert F. Sharp. Toronto: University of Toronto, 1940. Thesis (D.Paed.)--University of Toronto, 1940.

**3043. Shelford, Arthur** *We Pioneered.* Arthur Shelford and Cyril Shelford. Victoria: Orca Book Publishers, c1988.

**3044. Shelford, Cyril** *"From Snowshoes to Politics."* Cyril Shelford. Victoria: Orca Book Publishers, 1987.

**3045. Sheppard, Kathleen** *"Tonsil Clinic in the Peace River Block."* Kathleen Sheppard. Public Health Nurses' Bulletin 2, 5(Mar. 1938): 42-44.

**3046. Shibata, Yuko** *The Forgotten History of the Japanese-Canadians: the Role of Japanese Canadians in the Early Fishing Industry in B.C.* Yuko Shibata, Shoji Matsumoto, Rintaro Hayashi and Shotaro Iida. Vancouver: New Star Books, c1977.

**3047. Shilvock, Winston** *"Florence Baker Warren Waterman Willson."* Winston Shilvock. British Columbia Historical News 21, 4(Fall 1988): 6.

**3048. Shilvock, Winston** *"King Edward High School."* Winston Shilvock. British Columbia Historical News 22, 2(Spring 1989): 2-3.

**3049. Shilvock, Winston** *"Private Schools in the Okanagan."* Winston Shilvock. British Columbia Historical News 23, 2(Spring 1990): 25-26.

**3050. Siddoo, J.K.** *"Mediterranean Anaemia in Chinese Canadians."* J.K. Siddoo, C.J. Coady, L. Morgan-Dean and W.H. Perry. Canadian Medical Association Journal 74, 2(Jan. 15, 1956): 124-130.

**3051. Sieben, Gerald Alexander** *Cognitive Style and Children's Performance on Measures of Elementary Science Competencies.* Gerald Alexander Sieben. Vancouver: University of British Columbia, 1971. Thesis (M.A.)--University of British Columbia, 1971.

**3052. Signori, E.I.** *Statistical Data Re: Pupil Enrolment; Pupil/Teacher Ratio; Enrolment by Subject and Programme; Graduation Rates and Ability of Pupils; Educational Retardation and Acceleration; Retention of Pupils.* E.I. Signori, Lee R. Leedham, P.W. Easton, M. Ferr and J. Meuldijk. [Vancouver: U.B.C.?], 1960.

**3053. Signori, E.I.** *Statistical Data Re: B.C. Population; Teachers; Private Schools; Costs of Education. B.C. Population; Teachers; Private Schools; Costs of Education.* E.I. Signori, Lee R. Leedham, P.W. Easton, M. Ferr, J. Meuldijk and Barbara Scott. [Vancouver: U.B.C.?], 1960.

**3054. Signori, E.I.** *A Study of First Year University Students' Opinions of Grade 11 and 12 Training.* E.I. Signori, Lee R. Leedham and M. Ferr. [Vancouver: U.B.C.?], 1959.

**3055. Signori, E.I.** *A Study of the Subsequent School Performance of Grade Six Failures in the Vancouver School System.* E.I. Signori and Lee R. Leedham. [Vancouver: U.B.C.?], 1960.

**3056. Singleton, Anna Genevieve** *Child Welfare Administration Under Protection Acts in British Columbia: its History and Development.* Anna Genevieve Singleton. Vancouver: University of British Columbia, 1950. Thesis (M.S.W.)--University of British Columbia, 1950.

**3057. Sirotnik, Gareth** *Running Tough:*
*the Story of Vancouver's Jack Diamond.*
Gareth Serotnik. Vancouver: The Diamond
Family, c1988.

**3058. Skinner, James Maxwell**
**Richardson** *Indian Education on Gilford*
*Island: the Factor of Anxiety.* James
Maxwell Richardson Skinner. Montreal:
McGill University, 1959.
Thesis (M.A. in Education)--McGill
University, 1959.

**3059. Smith, Dorothy Blakey** *"Early*
*Memories of Vancouver."* Dorothy Blakey
Smith. Vancouver Historical Society
Newsletter 13, 7(Nov. 1973): 3-6.

**3060. Smith, Dorothy Blakey** *"Early*
*Memories of Vancouver."* Dorothy Blakey
Smith. British Columbia Historical News
17, 3(Summer 1984): 21-24.

**3061. Smith, M.R.** *"Toxoid."* M.R. Smith.
Public Health Nurses' Bulletin 2, 2(Apr.
1935): 35-36.

**3062. Smith, M.R.** *""Why Nurses Go*
*Grey"."* M.R. Smith. Public Health Nurses'
Bulletin 2, 3(June 1936): 39-40.

**3063. Smith, Peter L.** *Come Give a Cheer:*
*One Hundred Years of Victoria High*
*School 1876-1976.* Peter L. Smith.
Victoria, B.C.: Victoria High School
Centennial Celebrations Committee, 1976.

**3064. Smith, S. Rocksborough** *"New*
*Haven."* S. Rocksborough Smith. Canadian
Welfare 24, 3(July 1948): 13-15.

**3065. Smith, St.J. Brock** *"Children's*
*Promotion Features, Vancouver Store."* St.J.
Brock Smith. Beaver 262, 3(Dec. 1931):
361-362.

**3066. Smyser, Martha Marbury** *Protective*
*Services for Children: Changing Patterns*
*in Children's Protective Services· in the*
*United States and Canada, 1874-1954,*
*and in ˙the Children's Aid Society of*
*Vancouver, British Columbia, 1901-1954.*
Martha Marbury Smyser. Vancouver:
University of British Columbia, 1954.
Thesis (M.S.W.)--University of British
Columbia, 1954.

**3067. Snowdon, Kathleen** *"Public Health*
*Nursing in Keremeos."* Kathleen Snowdon.
Public Health Nurses' Bulletin 1, 6(Apr.
1929): 31-32.

**3068. Snowdon-Proetsch, Milenia** *Bayview*
*Community School 1914-1989.* Milenia
Snowdon-Proetsch. [Vancouver: s.n., 1989].

**3069. Snowsell, Frank** *"Reminiscences of*
*Kelowna."* Frank Snowsell. Okanagan
History 52(1988): 15-18.

**3070. Sone, Michael, ed.** *Pioneer Tales of*
*Burnaby: Early Burnaby as Recalled by*
*the Settlers....* Michael Sone, ed. Burnaby,
B.C.: Corporation of the District of
Burnaby, c1987.

**3071. Speare, Jean E., ed.** *The Days of*
*Augusta.* Jean E. Speare, ed. Vancouver:
J.J. Douglas, c1973.

**3072. Splane, Richard B.** *"Adoption in the*
*Conflict of Laws."* Richard B. Splane.
Canadian Welfare 33, 6(Feb. 1958):
277-278.

**3073. Spohn, Howard** *"The Healthy Child:*
*Our Greatest National Asset."* Howard
Spohn. Public Health Journal 12, 8(Aug.
1921): 352-359.

**3074. Spradley, James P.** *Guests Never*
*Leave Hungry: the Autobiography of James*
*Sewid, a Kwakiutl Indian.* James P.
Spradley. New Haven, Connecticut: Yale
University Press, c1969.

**3075. Spreen, Otfried** *"WISC Information*
*Subtest in a Canadian Population."* Otfried
Spreen and H. Howard Tryk. Canadian
Journal of Behavioural Science/Revue
canadienne de sciences du comportement
2, 4(Oct. 1970): 294-298.

**3076. Stanbury, W.T.** *"Urban Indians in*
*British Columbia."* W.T. Stanbury.
Scarborough: Prentice-Hall of Canada Ltd.,
c1979. In Two Nations, Many Cultures:
Ethnic Groups in Canada, pp. 33-43.
Edited by Jean Leonard Elliott.

**3077. Stanley, Timothy J.** *"White*
*Supremacy, Chinese Schooling and School*
*Segregation in Victoria: the Case of the*
*Chinese Students' Strike, 1922-1923."*
Timothy J. Stanley. Historical Studies in
Education/Revue d'histoire de l'education 2,
2(Fall 1990): 287-306.

**3078. Steeves, Dorothy G.** *The*
*Compassionate Rebel: Ernest Winch and*
*the Growth of Socialism in Western*
*Canada.* Dorothy G. Steeves. Vancouver:
J.J. Douglas, 1977.

**3079. Stephenson, P. Susan** *"Factors*
*Affecting Psychiatric Referral of Juvenile*
*Delinquents."* P. Susan Stephenson.
Canadian Journal of Criminology and
Corrections/Revue canadienne de
criminologie 13, 3(July 1971): 274-282.

**3080. Stewart, Donald Granville**
*Strathcona Nursery School: its
Contributions for Working Mothers.* Donald
Granville Stewart. Vancouver: University
of British Columbia, 1956.
Thesis (M.S.W.)–University of British
Columbia, 1956.

**3081. Stirling, G.F.** *"Dry Valley School."*
G.F. Stirling. Okanagan Historical Society
Report 19(1955): 85-86.

**3082. Stoochnoff, John Philip** *Men of
Goodwill.* John Philip Stoochnoff. Calgary:
MacLeod Printing and Mailing Ltd., 1976.

**3083. Storrs, Monica** *God's Galloping Girl:
Storrs, Monica* Monica Storrs and W.L.
Morton, ed. Vancouver: University of
British Columbia Press, c1979.

**3084. Stortz, Paul James** *The Rural
School Problem in British Columbia in the
1920's.* Paul James Stortz. Vancouver:
University of British Columbia, 1988.
Thesis (M.A.)–University of British
Columbia, 1988.

**3085. Strayer, Janet** *Stimulus Orientation
as a Factor in the Development Lag
Between Perception and Performance.* Janet
Strayer. Burnaby: Simon Fraser
University, 1970.
Thesis (M.A.)–Simon Fraser University,
1970.

**3086. Strong-Boag, Veronica** *"The
Confinement of Women: Childbirth and
Hospitalization in Vancouver, 1919-1939."*
Veronica Strong-Boag and Kathryn
McPherson. BC Studies
69-70(Spring-Summer 1986): 142-174.

**3087. Sunahara, Ann Gomer** *Politics of
Racism: the Uprooting of Japanese
Canadians during the Second World War.*
Ann Gomer Sunahara. Toronto: James
Lorimer & Co., 1981.

**3088. Sunrise-Two Rivers Women's
Institute** *Pioneers of Sunrise - Two
Rivers.* Frances Bennett. [S.l.]: The
Institute, 1981.

**3089. Surkes, Steven** *Accelerating
Children's Question-Asking Performance.*
Steven Surkes. Victoria: University of
Victoria, 1971.
Thesis (M.A.)–University of Victoria,
1971.

**3090. Sutherland, Dorothy** *"A Visit to
Vancouver."* Dorothy Sutherland.
Vancouver Historical Society Newsletter
14, 9(Mar. 1975): 5-6.

**3091. Sutherland, Neil** *""Everyone Seemed
Happy in Those Days": the Culture of
Childhood in Vancouver Between the
1920's and the 1960's."* Neil Sutherland.
History of Education Review 15, 2(1986):
37-51.

**3092. Sutherland, Neil** *""One, Two, Three,
Alary": Vancouver School Grounds Between
the 1920's and the 1960's."* Neil
Sutherland. British Columbia Historical
News 22, 2(Spring 1989): 23-24.

**3093. Sutherland, Neil** *"Social Policy,
"Deviant" Children, and the Public Health
Apparatus in British Columbia Between the
Wars."* Neil Sutherland. Journal of
Educational Thought 14, 2(Aug. 1980):
80-91.

**3094. Sutherland, Neil** *"The Triumph of
Formalism: Elementary Schooling in
Vancouver from the 1920's to the 1960's."*
Neil Sutherland. BC Studies
69-70(Spring-Summer 1986): 175-210.

**3095. Suttie, Gwen** *"With the Nisei in
New Denver."* Gwen Suttie, edited by
Dorothy Blakey Smith. B.C. Historical
News 5, 2(Feb. 1972): 15-25.

**3096. Swalwell, Eliza Jane** *"Girlhood
Days in Okanagan."* Eliza Jane Swalwell.
Okanagan Historical Society Report
8(1939): 34-40.

**3097. Symons, Kyrle C.** *That Amazing
Institution: the Story of St. Michael's
School, Victoria B.C. from 1910-1948.*
Kyrle C. Symons. [S.l.: s.n., 1949?].

**3098. Szychter, Gwen** *"Women's Role in
Early Farming in British Columbia."* Gwen
Szychter. British Columbia Historical
News 24, 1(Winter 1990-91): 22-25.

**3099. Tait, Claire** *"The Chilliwack Rotary
Dental Clinic."* Claire Tait. Public Health
Nurses' Bulletin 2, 3(June 1936): 40-42.

**3100. Tait, Claire** *"The Kin Kiddy Camp."*
Claire Tait. Public Health Nurses'
Bulletin 2, 4(Mar. 1937): 47-49.

**3101. Tait, Claire** *"What of Eyes and
Ears?"* Claire Tait. Public Health Nurses'
Bulletin 2, 5(Mar. 1938): 45-46.

**3102. Takashima, Shizuye** *A Child in
Prison Camp.* Shizuye Takashima.
Montreal: Tundra Books, 1971.

**3103. Tate, Dorothy E.** *""An Open
Letter"."* Dorothy Tate. Public Health
Nurses' Bulletin 2, 3(June 1936): 42-44.

3104. Taylor, John "Relief from Relief: the Cities' Answer to Depression Dependency." John Taylor. Journal of Canadian Studies/Revue d'etudes canadiennes 14, 1(Spring 1979): 16-23.

3105. Telford, Douglas "Congenital Anomalies of the Anorectum." Douglas Telford. Canadian Medical Association Journal 77, 5(Sept. 1, 1957): 492-494.

3106. Temple, June Bush Teacher in B.C. June Temple. Burlington, Ont.: Welch Publishing Company Inc., c1985.

3107. Thatcher, Margaret A. "First Impressions of School Nursing: Duncan." Margaret A. Thatcher. Public Health Nurses' Bulletin 1, 5(Apr. 1928): 8.

3108. Thiessen, Katie "Subjects, But Not Citizens." Katie Thiessen. B.C. Teacher 15, 10(June 1936): 13-15.

3109. Thom, Agnes "First Impressions in Revelstoke." Agnes Thom. Public Health Nurses' Bulletin 2, 2(Apr. 1935): 18-21.

3110. Thom, Agnes "Health Pursuits in Revelstoke." Agnes Thom. Public Health Nurses' Bulletin 2, 3(June 1936): 44-46.

3111. Thomas, Gregory Edward Gwynne British Columbia Ranching Frontier: 1858-1896. Gregory Edward Gwynne Thomas. Vancouver: University of British Columbia, 1976.
Thesis (M.A.)–University of British Columbia, 1976.

3112. Thomas, J.W. "The Haemophilic Syndrome." J.W. Thomas, D.M. Whitelaw and W.H. Perry. Canadian Medical Association Journal 79, 2(July 15, 1958): 100-103.

3113. Thomas, W.D.S. "Maternal Mortality in Native British Columbia Indians, a High Risk Group." W.D.S. Thomas. Canadian Medical Association Journal/Journal de l'Association medicale canadienne 99, 2(July 13, 1968): 64-67.

3114. Thomson, B. "Contrasts." B. Thomson. Public Health Nurses' Bulletin 2, 5(Mar. 1938): 49.

3115. Thomson, B. "Keeping a New Year's Resolution." B. Thomson. Public Health Nurses' Bulletin 1, 9(Mar. 1932): 25-27.

3116. Thomson, B. "Keremeos, Cawston, and Upper and Lower Similkameen." Bertha Thomson. Public Health Nurses' Bulletin 1, 7(May 1930): 17-18.

3117. Thomson, B. "Keremeos, Cawston, Upper and Lower Similkameen Reserve." B. Thomson. Public Health Nurses' Bulletin 1, 8(Mar. 1931): 17-19.

3118. Thomson, B. "News Letter From Keremeos." B. Thomson. Public Health Nurses' Bulletin 2, 4(Mar. 1937): 49.

3119. Thomson, B. "The Story of Five Years at Keremeos." B. Thomson. Public Health Nurses' Bulletin 2, 2(Apr. 1935): 6-7.

3120. Thomson, George A Survey of Academic Programmes and Requirements Prescribed for the Secondary Schools of British Columbia, 1876-1972. George Alexander Victor Thomson. Victoria: University of Victoria, 1972. (CTM no. 23535)
Thesis (M.A.)--University of Victoria, 1972.

3121. Thomson, Mary The Social Worker in the School: an Experimental Study of the Liaison and Service Functions of the Social Worker in a Vancouver Elementary School. Mary Thomson. Vancouver: University of British Columbia, 1948.
Thesis (M.S.W.)–University of British Columbia, 1948.

3122. Thores, O.A. "Down's Syndrome in British Columbia Indians." O.A. Theres and J. Philion. Canadian Medical Association Journal/Journal de l'Association medicale canadienne 109, 11(Dec. 1, 1973): 1108-1109.

3123. Tippett, Maria Emily Carr: a Biography. Maria Tippett. Toronto: Oxford University Press, 1979.

3124. Tisdall, Edith W. "Active Immunization Against Diphtheria, Kelowna." Edith W. Tisdall. Public Health Nurses' Bulletin 1, 8(Mar. 1931): 23-24.

3125. Tisdall, Edith W. "Hurrah for a Bowl of Soup!" Edith W. Tisdall. Public Health Nurses' Bulletin 1, 9(Mar. 1932): 31-32.

3126. Tisdall, Edith W. "Kelowna School Nursing." Edith W. Tisdall. Public Health Nurses' Bulletin 1, 7(May 1930): 23-26.

3127. Tisdall, Edith W. "New Developments in the Kelowna City Schools." Edith W. Tisdall. Public Health Nurses' Bulletin 1, 8(Mar. 1931): 38-39.

3128. Todd, John L. "Tick Bite in British Columbia." John L. Todd. Canadian Medical Association Journal 2, 12(Dec. 1912): 1118-1119.

**3129. Toren, Cyril Kirby** *Indian Housing and Welfare: a Study of the Housing Conditions and Welfare Needs of the Mission Reserve Indians.* Cyril Kirby Toren. Vancouver: University of British Columbia, 1957.
Thesis (M.S.W.)–University of British Columbia, 1957.

**3130. Trebett, Jean** *"In The Plate Shop."* Jean Trebett. Vancouver: New Star Books Ltd., c1980. In Along the No. 20 Line: Reminiscences of the Vancouver Waterfront, pp. 148-160. By Rolf Knight.

**3131. Trebett, Margaret** *"Folk Within the Sound of Big Ole."* Margaret Trebett. B.C. Historical News 5, 4(June 1972): 16-20.

**3132. Trites, A.E.W.** *"Benign Cystic Ovarian Teratomas of Childhood or "Ovarian Hydrocephalus"."* A.E.W. Trites. Canadian Medical Association Journal/Journal de l'Association medicale canadienne 84, 11(Mar. 18, 1961): 606-607.

**3133. Trower, Peter** *"Pulptown Childhood."* Peter Trower. Vancouver 12, 3(Mar. 1979): 42-47, 90-92.

**3134. Tuckey, Elizabeth Ursula Townsend** *Family Influence on Child Protection Cases at the Point of Apprehension and in Later Foster Care: an Exploratory Study of a Group of Wards (of the Children's Aid Society, Vancouver) in Foster Care More Than Two Years (1958).* Elizabeth Ursula Townsend Tuckey. Vancouver: University of British Columbia, 1958.
Thesis (M.S.W.)–University of British Columbia, 1958.

**3135. Turnbull, Elsie G.** *"A Little Girl in Trail Ninety Years Ago."* Elsie G. Turnbull. British Columbia Historical News 17, 4(Fall 1984): 11-18.

**3136. Twiddy, M.A.** *"A Child Study Group."* M.A. Twiddy. Public Health Nurses' Bulletin 2, 5(Mar. 1938): 49-50.

**3137. Twiddy, M.A.** *"Dental Problems of the Day."* M.A. Twiddy. Public Health Nurses' Bulletin 2, 2(Apr. 1935): 8-9.

**3138. Twiddy, M.A.** *"Health-teaching."* M.A. Twiddy. Public Health Nurses' Bulletin 1, 9(Mar. 1932): 17-19.

**3139. Twiddy, M.A.** *"Oliver, Okanagan Falls, and Osoyoos."* M.A. Twiddy. Public Health Nurses' Bulletin 1, 7(May 1930): 5-6.

**3140. Twiddy, M.A.** *"Preventive Medicine."* M.A. Twiddy. Public Health Nurses' Bulletin 2, 4(Mar. 1937): 50-51.

**3141. Twiddy, M.A.** *"Progress."* M.A. Twiddy. Public Health Nurses' Bulletin 2, 3(June 1936): 47-48.

**3142. Twiddy, M.A.** *"Then and Now."* M.A. Twiddy. Public Health Nurses' Bulletin 1, 8(Mar. 1931): 13-14.

**3143. Twigg, Alan** *Vander Zalm: From Immigrant to Premier.* Alan Twigg. Madeira Park, B.C.: Harbour Pub. Co., c1986.

**3144. Upshall, Muriel** *""Mighty Oaks From Little Acorns Grow"."* Muriel Upshall. Public Health Nurses' Bulletin 2, 3(June 1936): 48-52.

**3145. Upshall, Muriel** *"Nanaimo."* Muriel Upshall. Public Health Nurses' Bulletin 1, 8(Mar. 1931): 41-42.

**3146. Upshall, Muriel** *"New Developments in Health-teaching and Clinics in Nanaimo."* Muriel Upshall. Public Health Nurses' Bulletin 1, 9(Mar. 1932): 24-25.

**3147. Upshall, Muriel** *"Public Health in Nanaimo."* Muriel Upshall. Public Health Nurses' Bulletin 1, 7(May 1930): 35-36.

**3148. Upshall, Muriel** *"Rain or Shine?"* Muriel Upshall. Public Health Nurses' Bulletin 2, 2(Apr. 1935): 33-34.

**3149. Usukawa, Saeko, ed.** *Sound Heritage: Voices from British Columbia.* Saeko Usukawa, ed. Vancouver: Douglas and MacIntyre, c1984.

**3150. Vaitmaa, Erna** *A Case Study of C.A.S. Wards Not in Foster Homes: Being a Study of Eighteen Cases of Children in Correctional Institutions as of October 31, 1954.* Erna Vaitmaa. Vancouver: University of British Columbia, 1955.
Thesis (M.S.W.)–University of British Columbia, 1955.

**3151. Van Campen, Jacqueline** *A Study of the French Vocabulary of School Children in Maillardville, B.C.* Jacqueline Van Campen. Burnaby: Simon Fraser University, 1970.
Thesis (M.A.)–Simon Fraser University, 1970.

**3152. Vancouver Association for Children with Learning Disabilities** *A Brief on Children with Learning Disabilities for Presentation to the Vancouver School Board.* Vancouver Association for Children with Learning Disabilities. Vancouver: The Association,

1971.

**3153. Vancouver, B.C. School Board**
*Lucky to Live in Cedar Cottage: Memories of Lord Selkirk Elementary School and Cedar Cottage Neighbourhood, 1911-1963.* The Board. Vancouver: Vancouver School Board, 1986.

**3154. Van Norden, H.J.** *"Pectus Carinatum."* H.J. Van Norden and J.E. Musgrove. Canadian Medical Association Journal 71, 4(Oct. 1954): 378.

**3155. Varley, Elizabeth Anderson** *Kitimat: My Valley.* Elizabeth Anderson Varley. Terrace, B.C.: Northern Times Press, c1981.

**3156. Varley, Peter** *Frederick H. Varley.* Peter Varley. Toronto: Key Porter Books, 1983.

**3157. Varwig, Renate** *Family Contibutions in Preschool Treatment of the Hearing-handicapped Child: an Analytical Survey of Children in the Speech and Hearing Clinic, Health Centre for Children, Vancouver General Hospital 1955-59.* Renate Varwig. Vancouver: University of British Columbia, 1960.
Thesis (M.S.W.)–University of British Columbia, 1960.

**3158. Ventress, Cora A., comp.** *The Peacemakers of the North Peace.* Cora A. Ventress, Marguerite Davies and Edith Kyllo, comps. [S.l.]: Davies, Ventress and Kyllo, c1973.

**3159. Vince, Dennis J.** *"Cardiac Catheterization in the First Year of Life: an Assessment of Risk."* Dennis J. Vince. Canadian Medical Association Journal/Journal de l'Association medicale canadienne 98, 8(Feb. 24, 1968): 386-391.

**3160. Vince, Dennis J.** *"The Hospital Incidence and Clinical Significance of Congenital Heart Malformations Resulting From Rubella Embryopathy."* Dennis J. Vince. Canadian Medical Association Journal/Journal de l'Association medicale canadienne 102, 4(Feb. 28, 1970): 374-376.

**3161. Vince, Dennis J.** *"Medical Radiation to Children With Congenital Heart Disease."* Dennis J. Vince. Canadian Medical Association Journal/Journal de l'Association medicale canadienne 91, 26(Dec. 26, 1964): 1345-1349.

**3162. Vince, Dennis J.** *"The QRS Vectorcardiogram of the Normal Newborn Human."* Dennis J. Vince and Lambertus C. de Groot. Canadian Medical Association Journal/Journal de l'Association medicale canadienne 92,

3(Jan. 16, 1965): 108-111.

**3163. Virgin, Victor Ernest** *History of North and South Saanich: Pioneers and District.* Victor E. Virgin. 3rd ed. Saanichton, B.C.: Saanich Pioneer Society, 1959.

**3164. Wace, C.** *"Queen Alexandra Solarium."* C. Wace. Canadian Nurse 23, 5(May 1927): 241-242.

**3165. Wachtel, Eleanor** *"The Invention of Jack Hodgins."* Eleanor Wachtel. Books in Canada 16, 6(Aug.-Sept. 1987): 6-10.

**3166. Wade, Susan** *"Helena Gutteridge: Votes for Women and Trade Unions."* Susan Wade. Victoria: Camousun College, c1980. In In Her Own Right: Selected Essays on Women's History in B.C., pp. 187-203. Edited by Barbara Latham and Cathy Kess.

**3167. Waites, K.A., ed.** *The First Fifty Years: Vancouver High Schools 1890-1940.* K.A. Waites, ed. [Vancouver: s.n., 1940?].

**3168. Walls, Edith M.** *"Carrying the Message of Health to Sayward, B.C."* Edith M. Walls. Public Health Nurses' Bulletin 1, 9(Mar. 1932): 5-6.

**3169. Walls, Edith M.** *"Greetings from Sayward."* Edith M. Walls. Public Health Nurses' Bulletin 1, 5(Apr. 1928):7.

**3170. Walls, Edith M.** *"Pioneer Nursing on Vancouver Island."* M. Walls. Public Health Nurses' Bulletin 1, 2(Apr. 1925): 5-7.

**3171. Walls, Edith M.** *"Public Health Work at Sayward."* Edith M. Walls. Public Health Nurses' Bulletin 1, 7(May 1930): 11-12.

**3172. Walls, Edith M.** *"Sayward, Vancouver Island."* Edith M. Walls. Public Health Nurses' Bulletin 1, 6(Apr. 1929): 11-12.

**3173. Walls, Edith M.** *"Work in Sayward."* Edith M. Walls. Public Health Nurses' Bulletin 2, 2(Apr. 1935): 23.

**3174. Walsh, A.** *"The Inkaneep Indian School."* A. Walsh. Okanagan Historical Society Report 38(1974): 14-19.

**3175. Wanden, June** *Working With the Delinquent.* June Wanden. Vancouver: University of British Columbia, 1947.
Thesis (M.S.W.)–University of British Columbia, 1947.

3176. **Ward, Arthur** *"Growing Up in Glenmore."* A. Ward. Okanagan Historical Society Report 44(1980): 101-105.

3177. **Ward, Arthur** *"Saturday Night in Kelowna (1920)."* Arthur Ward. Okanagan Historical Society Report 46(1982): 136-138.

3178. **Watson, Edwin Francis** *A Summary and Discussion of the History and Problem of Child Welfare Services in Vancouver with Particular Reference to Temporary Foster Home (Non-Ward) Care and Its Costs.* E.F. Watson. [Vancouver]: Family and Child Welfare Division, Community Chest and Councils of the Greater Vancouver Area, 1960.

3179. **Watson, Edwin Francis** *What Happens to Children in Latter Adolescence?: a Study and Evaluation of the Adjustment of Thirty-One Wards of the Superintendent of Child Welfare for the Province of British Columbia, Who Have Been in Foster Care, and Who Reached Eighteen Years of Age During the Year January 1, 1954-December 31, 1954.* Edwin Francis Watson. Vancouver: University of British Columbia, 1955. Thesis (M.S.W.)–University of British Columbia, 1955.

3180. **Watson, Eunice Lenore** *Social Services in the Greater Vancouver Public School System: a Comparative Survey of the Administration of Social Services to Pupils: Mental Hygiene Division (Metropolitan Health Committee), Special Counsellors and Other Relevant Teaching Personnel, Vancouver, 1959.* Eunice Lenore Watson. Vancouver: University of British Columbia, 1959. Thesis (M.S.W.)–University of British Columbia, 1959.

3181. **Watson, John** *"Twenty Miles to Paradise: Gower Point 1917-1925."* John Watson. Raincoast Chronicles 12(1990): 38-51.

3182. **Wayman, Sara Gertrude** *High School Dropouts: a Reconnaissance Survey of Some of the Personal and Social Factors, with Special Reference to Superior Students, Vancouver, 1959-1960.* Sara Gertrude Wayman. Vancouver: University of British Columbia, 1961. Thesis (M.S.W.)–University of British Columbia, 1961.

3183. **Webber, Jean** *"Okanagan Summer School of Fine Arts."* Jean Webber. Okanagan Historical Society Report 46(1982): 139-160.

3184. **Webber, Jean** *"Okanagan Summer School of the Arts, Part 2."* Jean Webber. Okanagan Historical Society Report 47(1983): 154-176.

3185. **Webster, Peter S.** *As Far as I Know: Reminiscences of an Ahousat Elder.* Peter S. Webster. Campbell River: Campbell River Museum and Archives, c1983.

3186. **Weightman, Barbara Ann** *The Musqueam Reserve: a Case Study of the Indian Social Milieu in an Urban Environment.* Barbara Ann Weightman. Seattle: University of Washington, 1972. Thesis (Ph.D.)–University of Washington, 1972.

3187. **Weir, G.M.** *"The School Serves the Family."* George M. Weir. [S.l.: s.n., 1946]. In Proceedings of Eighth Annual Meeting, Pacific Northwest Conference of Family Relations, pp. 7-10.

3188. **Weir, Joan S.** *The Caledonians: a History of the Scots in Kamloops.* Joan S. Weir. Kamloops, B.C.: Peerless Printers Ltd., c1977.

3189. **Weir, Winnifred Ariel** *"Pioneer Women in the Windermere Valley."* Winnifred Ariel Weir. British Columbia Historical News 21, 4(Fall 1988): 7-11.

3190. **Weiss, Gillian M.** *The Development of Public School Kindergartens in British Columbia.* Gillian M. Weiss. Vancouver: University of British Columbia, 1979. Thesis (M.A.)–University of British Columbia, 1979.

3191. **Weiss, Gillian M.** *"An Essential Year for the Child: the Kindergarten in British Columbia."* Gillian Weiss. Calgary: Detselig Enterprises Ltd., 1980. In Schooling and Society in 20th Century British Columbia, pp. 139-161. Edited by J. Donald Wilson and David C. Jones.

3192. **Wejr, Stan** *"Memories of Trinity Creek Area in the 1920's."* Stan Wejr. Okanagan Historical Society Report 50(1986): 78-79.

3193. **Welfare Council of Greater Vancouver. Children's Division. Child Welfare Legislation Committee** *Summary of the Laws of British Columbia Affecting Children: as in Force Up to and Including All Enactments of the Session of the Legislature 1943.* The Committee and Elizabeth King, ed. [Vancouver: The Council, 1944].
The 1947 edition can be found in Summary of the Laws of Canada and Her Provinces as Affecting Children.

3194. **Wells, Richard E.** *There's a Landing Today.* R.E. Wells. Victoria: Sono Nis Press, c1988.

3195. **West, Donald James** *Understanding Sexual Attacks: a Study Based Upon a Group of Rapists Undergoing Psychotherapy.* D.J. West, C. Roy and Florence L. Nichols. London: Heinemann Educational Books Ltd., c1978.

3196. **Wetstein-Kroft, Susan Beth** *The Early Identification and Relative Incidence of Academic Underachievement: a Follow-up Study of Average, Bright and Intellectually Superior Kindergarten Children.* Susan Beth Wetstein-Kroft. Vancouver: University of British Columbia, 1982. (CTM no. 62947)
Thesis (M.A.-Ed.)--University of British Columbia, 1982.
Reprinted by the Educational Research Institute of British Columbia, 1982.

3197. **Wharf, Brian** *Toward First Nation Control of Child Welfare: a Review of Emerging Developments in B.C.* Brian Wharf. [Victoria]: University of Victoria, 1987.

3198. **Wheeler, Marilyn J., comp. and ed.** *The Robson Valley Story.* Marilyn J. Wheeler, comp. and ed. [S.l.]: McBride Robson Valley Story Group, c1979.

3199. **Wheeler, Michael** *A Report on Needed Research in Welfare in British Columbia: a Survey Undertaken for the Community Chest and Councils of the Greater Vancouver Area.* Michael Wheeler. Vancouver: The Community Chest, 1961.

3200. **Wheeler, Michael** *A Summary of A Report on Needed Research in Welfare in British Columbia: (The Wheeler Report).* Michael Wheeler. Vancouver: The Community Chest, 1961.

3201. **Whelan, Gloria** *"Maria Grant, 1854-1937: the Life and Times of an Early Twentieth Century Christian."* Gloria Whelan. Victoria: Camousun College, c1980. In *In Her Own Right: Selected Essays on Women's History in B.C.,* pp. 125-146. Edited by Barbara Latham and Cathy Kess.

3202. **White, George Brooks** *"Development of the Eastern Fraser Valley."* George B. White. British Columbia Historical Quarterly 12, 4(Oct. 1948): 259-291.

3203. **White, Harold** *"School Medical Services, City of Vancouver."* Harold White. Public Health Journal 19, 5(May 1928): 222-229.

3204. **White, Howard** *"The Bomb That Mooed: Memories of a Logging Camp Childhood."* Howard White. Raincoast Chronicles 10(1980): 22-27.

3205. **White, Howard** *"Duchaume: Anatomy of a Legend."* Howard White. Raincoast Chronicles 9(1979): 51-57.

3206. **Whitehead, Margaret** *Missionaries and Indians in Cariboo: a History of St. Joseph's Mission, Williams Lake, British Columbia.* Margaret Mary Whitehead. Victoria: University of Victoria, 1979. Thesis (M.A.)--University of Victoria, 1979.

3207. **Whitehead, Ursula** *"A Suggested Programme for Venereal Disease Control in a Community of Five to Ten Thousand."* Ursula Whitehead. Public Health Nurses' Bulletin 2, 6(Mar. 1939): 36-46.

3208. **Whitton, Charlotte** *"Realizing Juvenile Delinquency Services."* Charlotte Whitton. Child and Family Welfare 13, 6(Mar. 1938): 36-38.

3209. **Whitton, Charlotte** *"Vocational Training and Unemployed Youth."* Charlotte Whitton. Child and Family Welfare 13, 6(Mar. 1938): 65.

3210. **Wick, Lawrence B.** *Children in Commercial Boarding Homes: a Survey of Wards of the Children's Aid Society of Vancouver Living in These Units in October 1954.* Lawrence B. Wick. Vancouver: University of British Columbia, 1956. Thesis (M.S.W.)--University of British Columbia, 1956.

3211. **Wicks, Walter** *Memories of the Skeena.* Walter Wicks. Saanichton, B.C.: Hancock House, c1976.

3212. **Wilcox, Jack** *"William James Wilcox of Salmon Arm."* Jack Wilcox. Okanagan Historical Society Report 50(1986): 142-146.

3213. **Wilkie, Dora W.** *"Esquimalt Rural Nursing Service."* Dora W. Wilkie. Public Health Nurses' Bulletin 2, 3(June 1936): 52-53.

3214. **Wilkie, Dora W.** *"Growing Up."* D. Wilkie. Public Health Nurses' Bulletin 2, 5(Mar. 1938): 50-51.

3215. **Wilkie, Dora W.** *"Notes of an Esquimalt Rural Nurse."* Dora Wilkie. Public Health Nurses' Bulletin 2, 4(Mar. 1937): 51-53.

3216. **Williamson, Richard John** *A Comparison of Reading Achievement Between Students Enrolled in Graded and Nongraded Reading Programs.* Richard John Williamson. Victoria: University of Victoria, 1971.
Thesis (M.A.)–University of Victoria, 1971.

3217. **Willis, Grant** *"Second Lower Similkameen School."* Grant Willis. Okanagan Historical Society Report 37(1973): 117-119.

3218. **Willis, Marjorie** *"Family Service in a Generalized Health Agency."* Marjorie Willis. Canadian Nurse 46, 2(Feb. 1950): 122-127.

3219. **Willmott, Jill A., ed.** *The Indians of British Columbia: a Study Discussion Text.* Jill A. Willmott. [Vancouver]: University of British Columbia, Department of University Extension, 1963.

3220. **Wilson, Ethel** *"Young Vancouver Seen By the Eyes of Youth."* Ethel Wilson. British Columbia Historical News 19, 4(Fall 1986): 14.

3221. **Wilson, J. Donald** *""May the Lord Have Mercy on You": the Rural School Problem in British Columbia in the 1920s."* J. Donald Wilson and Paul J. Stortz. BC Studies 79(Autumn 1988): 24-58.

3222. **Wilson, J. Donald** *"Negroes, Finns, Sikhs: Education and Community Experience in British Columbia."* J. Donald Wilson and Jorgen Dahlie. Toronto: Peter Martin Associates, 1975. In Sounds Canadian: Languages and Cultures in Multi-Ethnic Society, pp. 76-92. Edited by Paul M. Migus.

3223. **Wilson, J. Donald, ed.** *Schooling and Society in 20th Century British Columbia.* J. Donald Wilson and David C. Jones, ed. Calgary: Detselig Enterprises Ltd., 1980.

3224. **Wilson, Lolita** *A Comparison of the Raven Progressive Matrices (1947) and the Performance Scale of the Wechsler Intelligence Scale for Children for Assessing the Intelligence of Indian Children.* Lolita Wilson. Vancouver: University of British Columbia, 1952.
Thesis (M.A.)–University of British Columbia, 1952.

3225. **Wilson, Margaret** *"Child Welfare Activities in Nanaimo."* Margaret Wilson. Public Health Nurses' Bulletin 1, 4(Apr. 1927): 22-23.

3226. **Wilson, Reginald** *"Paradoxical Diarrhoea in Childhood."* Reginald Wilson and C.H. Gundry. Canadian Medical Association Journal 72, 5(Mar. 1, 1955): 362-368.

3227. **Winch, Guy C.** *"Prolapse of the Cord."* Guy C. Winch and A.D. Claman. Canadian Medical Association Journal/Journal de l'Association medicale canadienne 84, 24(June 17, 1961): 1369-1373.

3228. **Winterbottom, Doris** *"Of Boats and Ships."* Doris Winterbottom. Vancouver Historical Society Newsletter 13, 8(Dec. 1973): 5-8.
Maiden name, Manson.

3229. **Wise, Bert** *Tales of a B.C. Trucker.* Bert Wise. Burnaby: The Author, 1987.

3230. **Wolcott, Harry F.** *A Kwakiutl Village and School.* Harry F. Wolcott. Toronto: Holt, Rinehart and Winston, c1967.

3231. **Wolfenden, Madge** *"John Tod: Career of a Scotch Boy."* Madge Wolfenden. British Columbia Historical Quarterly 18, 3-4(Oct.-Dec. 1954): 133-238.

3232. **Wood, Viola** *"Roses in December."* Viola Wood. Raincoast Chronicles 6(1976): 4-10.

3233. **Wooding, Lillian A.** *"Gibsons Landing."* Lillian A. Wooding. Public Health Nurses' Bulletin 2, 5(Mar. 1938): 52.

3234. **Woods, M.J.** *"Speaking of Results."* M.J. Woods. Public Health Nurses' Bulletin 1, 1(Oct. 1924): 1-2.

3235. **Woodward, Frances M.** *"Childhood Memories of "The Coast"."* Frances Woodward. Vancouver Historical Society Newsletter 15, 1(Apr. 1975): 3-4.

3236. **Woodward, Mary Twigg Wynn** *Juvenile Delinquency Among Indian Girls: an Examination of the Causes and Treatment of a Sample Group and the Resulting Social Implications.* Mary Twigg Wynn Woodward. Vancouver: University of British Columbia, 1949.
Thesis (M.S.W.)–University of British Columbia, 1949.

3237. **Wormsbecker, John H.** *The Development of Secondary Education in Vancouver.* John Henry Wormsbecker. Toronto: University of Toronto, 1961.
Thesis (Ed.D.)–University of Toronto, 1961.

**3238. Wormsbecker, John H.** *"Organizing and Programming to Accommodate All Students in the Secondary School."* John H. Wormsbecker. Toronto: W.J. Gage, 1965. In Education: a Collection of Essays on Canadian Education, v.5, 1962-1964, pp. [95]-100.

**3239. Worthington, J.** *"Ladysmith."* J. Worthington. Public Health Nurses' Bulletin 1, 8(Mar. 1931): 14-15.

**3240. Wright, Joanna R.** *"Indian Affairs in British Columbia."* Joanna R. Wright. Canadian Welfare 30, 8(Mar. 1955): 13-16.

**3241. Wright, Kenneth William Thomas** *A Survey of Male Juvenile Delinquency in British Columbia From 1920 to 1941.* Kenneth William Thomas Wright. Vancouver: University of British Columbia, 1941.
Thesis (M.A.)–University of British Columbia, 1941.

**3242. Wright, Mildred May** *Social and Family Backgrounds as an Aspect of Recidivism Among Juvenile Delinquents: a Compilation and Review for a Group of Juvenile Delinquents Who Failed to Respond to Programmes Provided for Their Rehabilitation.* Mildred May Wright. Vancouver: University of British Columbia, 1957.
Thesis (M.S.W.)–University of British Columbia, 1957.

**3243. Wright, Vera Lawson** *"Early Memories of Kelowna, 1907-1910."* Vera Lawson Wright. Okanagan Historical Society Report 45(1981): 122-123.

**3244. Wycherley, Kathleen** *A Brief History of the Pre-school Movement in Vancouver Written in This Centennial Year 1958 for the British Columbia Pre-school Education Association.* Kathleen Wycherley. Vancouver: British Columbia Pre-school Education Association, 1958.

**3245. Yaholnitsky, Pauline** *""The District Nurse's 'Soft Job'"."* Pauline Yaholnitsky. Public Health Nurses' Bulletin 2, 3(June 1936): 53-55.

**3246. Yaholnitsky, Pauline** *"On Regular Yearly Dental Clinics in the Peace River Health Unit."* Pauline Yaholnitsky. Public Health Nurses' Bulletin 2, 5(Mar. 1938): 53.

**3247. Yaholnitsky, Pauline** *"Toxoid and Vaccination Clinics in West District of Peace River Block."* Pauline Yaholnitsky. Public Health Nurses' Bulletin 2, 4(Mar. 1937): 53-54.

**3248. Yates, Anne** *"Child Welfare Work in the Cowichan District."* Anne Yates. Public Health Nurses' Bulletin 1, 7(May 1930): 29-32.

**3249. Yates, Anne** *"The Cowichan Dental Clinic."* A. Yates. Public Health Nurses' Bulletin 1, 6(Apr. 1929): 16-17.

**3250. Yee, Paul Richard** *Saltwater City: an Illustrated History of the Chinese in Vancouver.* Paul Yee. Vancouver: Douglas & McIntyre, 1988.

**3251. Yeo, Douglas J.** *"Dental Health."* Douglas J.Yeo. Canadian Nurse 49, 3(Mar. 1953): 182-184.

**3252. York, Lillian C., ed.** *Lure of the South Peace: Tales of the Early Pioneers to 1945.* Lillian York, ed. Dawson Creek: South Peace Historical Book Committee, c1981.

**3253. York, Lillian C., ed.** *Petticoat Pioneers of the South Peace: the Life Stories of Fifteen Pioneer Women of the South Peace.* Lillian C. York, comp., ed., and illustrator. [Dawson Creek?]: Northern Lights College Women's Advisory Committee to Community Education, 1979.

**3254. Young, Charles H.** *The Japanese Canadians: with a Second Part on Oriental Standards of Living.* Charles H. Young, Helen R.Y. Reid and W.A. Carrothers. Toronto: University of Toronto Press, 1938.

**3255. Young, Fyvie** *"How Far is it Safe for a Health Organization to Undertake Relief Work?"* Fyvie Young. Public Health Nurses' Bulletin 2, 1(May 1933): 9-10.

**3256. Young, Fyvie** *""Out of the Mouths of Babes..."*" Fyvie Young. Public Health Nurses' Bulletin 1, 9(Mar. 1932): 43-44.

**3257. Young, H.E.** *"Queen Alexandra Solarium."* H.E. Young. Public Health Journal 19, 8(Aug. 1928): 374-377.

**3258. Young Women's Christian Association** *50th Anniversary of the Y.W.C.A., May 1947, Vancouver, B.C.* Young Womens Christian Association. Vancouver: The Association, 1947.

**3259. Zubeck, John P.** *A Study of the Local Attitudes of High School Students and Adults Towards the Doukhobors of Southern British Columbia.* John Peter Zubeck. Toronto: University of Toronto, 1948.
Thesis (M.A.)–University of Toronto, 1948.

3260. **Zureik, Elia T.** *"Children and Political Socialization."* Elia T. Zureik. Toronto: Holt, Rinehart and Winston of Canada Ltd., c1971. In The Canadian Family, pp. 186-199. Edited by K. Ishwaran.
Reprinted in The Canadian Family Revised, pp. 227-240. Edited by K. Ishwaran.

3261. **Zureik, Elia T.** *Political Socialization of Elementary School Children: an Empirical Study.* Elia T. Zureik. Burnaby: Simon Fraser University, 1968.
Thesis (M.A.)–Simon Fraser University, 1968.

# The Prairies

3262. *1905-1980 Leipzig*. [S.l.: s.n., 1980].

3263. **Abu-Laban, Baha** *"In-group Orientation and Self-conceptions of Indian and Non-Indian Students in an Integrated School."* Baha Abu-Laban. Alberta Journal of Educational Research 11, 3(Sept. 1965): 188-194.

3264. **Acadia Valley Community Club** *Times to Remember*. Acadia Valley Community Club. Acadia Valley, Alta.: Acadia Valley Community Club, 1981.

3265. **Acheson, John B.** *Relationships Between Maternal Interference and the Reflective-Impulsive Response Style of the Preschool Child*. John B. Acheson. Edmonton: University of Alberta, 1969.
Thesis (M.Ed.)–University of Alberta, 1969.

3266. **Acme and District Historical Society** *Acme Memories*. Acme and District Historical Society. Acme, Alta.: Acme and District Historical Society, 1979.

3267. **Adamchuk, Jean** *Tent Town, 1898-1979: a History of Minitonas and District*. Jean Adamchuk, Ruth Iwanchuk [and] Minitonas Community Centre Committee. Minitonas, Man.: Community Centre Committee, [1979].

3268. **Adames, John** *Productive Society: a Study of Junior High School Student Opinion*. John Adames. Calgary: University of Alberta, 1971.
Thesis (M.Ed.)--University of Alberta, 1971.

3269. **Adams, Howard** *"Canada from the Native Point of View."* Howard Adams. Scarborough: Prentice-Hall of Canada Ltd., c1979. In Two Nations, Many Cultures: Ethnic Groups in Canada, pp. 23-32. Edited by Jean Leonard Elliott.
Reprinted from Prison of Grass: Canada From the Native Point of View.

3270. **Adams, Irene** *Walk Back Through Time: a History of Langenburg and District*. Irene Adams, Gilbert Johnson and Langenburg History Book Committee. Langenburg, Sask.: The Authors, 1980.

3271. **Adamson, Georgina** *Study of the Concurrent Validity of the Frost-Safran School Situations Test*. Georgina Adamson. Calgary: University of Calgary, 1970. (CTM no. 7636)
Thesis (M.Ed.)–University of Calgary, 1971.

3272. **Adamson, Leslie** *An Examination of One Factor of Socioeconomic Status, Father's Occupation, and its Relationship to Dropout from Secondary Schools and to Failure to Enter University*. Leslie Adamson. Montreal: McGill University, 1967.
Thesis (M.A.)–McGill University, 1967.

3273. **Admiral History Book Club** *Admiral: Prairie to Wheatfields*. Admiral History Book Club. [S.l.]: Admiral History Book Club, 1978.

**3274. Alberta Beach and Districts Pioneers and Archives Society** *Spirit and Trails of Lac Ste. Anne.* Alberta Beach and Districts Pioneers and Archives Society. Alberta Beach, Alta.: Alberta Beach and Districts Pioneers and Archives Society, 1982.

**3275. Alberta. Commission Appointed to Investigate the Provincial Training School at Red Deer, Provincial Mental Institute at Oliver, Provincial Mental Hospital at Ponoka** *Report of the Commission to Investigate the Provincial Training School at Red Deer, Provincial Mental Institute at Oliver, Provincial Mental Hospital at Ponoka.* The Commission. [Edmonton: s.n., 1928].
Commissioners: C.M. Hincks and C.B. Farrar.

**3276. Alberta. Commission of Inquiry to Investigate Charges, Allegations and Reports Relating to the Child Welfare Branch of the Department of Public Welfare** *Report of the Commission to Investigate Charges, Allegations and Reports Relating to the Child Welfare Branch of the Department of Public Welfare.* The Commission. [Edmonton: s.n., 1948].
Chairman: W.R. Howson.

**3277. Alberta. Department of Education. Special Services Branch** *The Hard-of-Hearing Child in the Regular Classroom.* Special Services Department of the Department of Education. [Edmonton: The Department, 1964].

**3278. Alberta. Enquiry Into and Concerning the Problems of Health, Education and General Welfare of the Half-breed Population of the Province** *Report of the Enquiry Into and Concerning the Problems of Health, Education and General Welfare of the Half-breed Population of the Province.* The Commission. [Edmonton: s.n., 1934].

**3279. Alberta. Royal Commission on Education, 1959** *Report of the Royal Commission on Education in Alberta, 1959.* The Commission. [Edmonton]: Queen's Printer, 1959.
Chairman: Donald Cameron.

**3280. Alberta. Royal Commission on Juvenile Delinquency** *Report of the Alberta Royal Commission on Juvenile Delinquency.* The Commission. [Edmonton: s.n.], 1967.
Chairman: F.H. Quigley.

**3281. Alberts, Pauline E.** *A Comparison of Kinesthetic Effect of Two Different Kinds of Dance Instruction Given to Elementary School Children.* Pauline E. Alberts. Calgary: University of Calgary, 1971. (CTM no. 10029)
Thesis (M.Ed.)–University of Calgary, 1971.

**3282. Alcock, A.J.W.** *"Respiratory Poliomyelitis: a Follow-up Study."* A.J.W. Alcock, J.A. Hildes, P.A. Kaufert, J.M. Kaufert and J. Bickford. Canadian Medical Association Journal/Journal de l'Association medicale canadienne 130, 10(May 15, 1984): 1305-1310.

**3283. Alexander, J.F.** *"A Case of Mercury Poisoning: Acrodynia in a Child of 8."* J.F. Alexander and Rosa Rosario. Canadian Medical Association Journal/Journal de l'Association medicale canadienne 104, 10(May 22, 1971): 929-930.

**3284. Alhambra and District Reunion and Historical Society** *Our Priceless Heritage: History of Alhambra, Arbutus, Beaver Flat, Bingley, Horseguard, Oras, Sleepy Valley and Taimi.* Alhambra and District Reunion and Historical Society. Alhambra, Alta.: Alhambra and District Reunion and Historical Society, 1980.

**3285. Alix Clive Historical Club** *Gleanings: After Pioneers and Progress.* Alix Clive Historical Club. Alix, Alta.: Alix Clive Historical Club, 1981.

**3286. Alix Clive Historical Club** *Pioneers and Progress.* Alix Clive Historical Club. Alix, Alta.: Alix Clive Historical Club, 1974.

**3287. Allan and District History Book Committee** *Times Past to Present.* Allan and District History Book Committee. Allan, Sask.: Allan and District History Book Committee, 1981.

**3288. Allan, Billie Lamb** *Dew Upon the Grass.* Billie Lamb Allan. 1st ed. Saskatoon: Modern Press, 1963.

**3289. Allan, Iris** *Mother and Her Family.* Iris Allan. Cobalt, Ont.: The Author, 1977.

**3290. Allison, Charles John** *"Characteristics of Students Who Failed Grade Seven."* C.J. Allison. Alberta Journal of Educational Research 8, 1(Mar. 1962): 11-23.

**3291. Allison, Charles John**
*Characteristics of Students Who Failed Grade Seven in Edmonton Junior High Schools, 1951-1952.* Charles John Allison. Edmonton: University of Alberta, 1959. Thesis (M.Ed.)–University of Alberta, 1959.

**3292. Alsask History Book Committee**
*Captured Memories: a History of Alsask and Surrounding School Districts.* Alsask History Book Committee. Alsask, Sask: Alsask History Book Committee, 1983.

**3293. Alvi, Abdul W.** *"Primary Peptic Ulcer in Children: Report of 14 Cases and Review of Literature."* Abdul W. Alvi and Arnold G. Rogers. Canadian Medical Association Journal/Journal de l'Association medicale canadienne 80, 5(Mar. 1, 1959): 352-359.

**3294. Anderson, Alan B.** *"Ukrainian Ethnicity: Generations and Change in Rural Saskatchewan."* Alan B. Anderson. Scarborough: Prentice-Hall of Canada Ltd., c1979. In Two Nations, Many Cultures: Ethnic Groups in Canada, pp. 250-269. Edited by Jean Leonard Elliott.

**3295. Anderson, Alvin L.** *The Comparative Effects Of Presentation Mode on Success in Arithmetic Problem Solving.* Alvin L. Anderson. Edmonton: University of Alberta, 1970. Thesis (M.Ed.)–University of Alberta, 1970.

**3296. Anderson, Anne** *The First Metis, a New Nation.* Anne Anderson. Edmonton: UVISCO Press, 1985.

**3297. Anderson, Charles C.** *"Further Evidence on Cognitive Function Fluctuation."* Charles C. Anderson. Alberta Journal of Educational Research 4, 1(Mar. 1958): 40-49.

**3298. Anderson, Charles C.** *"The Many Voices: a Preliminary Investigation into the Consistency of the Self Concept."* Charles C. Anderson. Alberta Journal of Educational Research 5, 1(Mar. 1959): 7-15.

**3299. Anderson, Charles C.** *"Responses of Adolescents to American Tests of Value and Character."* C.C. Anderson. Canadian Education and Research Digest 1, 4(Dec. 1961): 71-77.

**3300. Anderson, Dale G.** *"The Use of Expectancy Tables in Educational Guidance."* Dale G. Anderson and Herbert E. Stiles. Alberta Journal of Educational Research 14, 2(June 1968): 129-135.

**3301. Anderson, Francis Garfield**
*Personal Contact Affecting City Children's Knowledge of and Attitudes Toward Alberta Indians.* Francis Garfield Anderson. Calgary: University of Calgary, 1969. Thesis (M.Ed.)–University of Calgary, 1969.

**3302. Anderson, George Renwick** *A Statistical Procedure for Rating Pupils in Arithmetic.* George Renwick Anderson. Toronto: University of Toronto, [1929]. Thesis (D.Paed.)–University of Toronto, [1929].

**3303. Anderson, H.J.** *"A Study of 345 Family Contacts with Tuberculosis Lesions."* H.J. Anderson. Canadian Public Health Journal 32, 12(Dec. 1941): 594-600.

**3304. Andrew Historical Society** *Dreams and Destinies: Andrew and District.* Andrew Historical Society. Andrew, Alta.: Andrew Historical Society, 1980.

**3305. Andrews, Lorna** *"The Young Historians: 4-H."* Lorna Andrews. Manitoba History 2(1981): 26-28.

**3306. Andrews, W.R.** *Behavioral and Client Centered Counselling of High School Underachievers.* W.R. Andrews. Edmonton: University of Alberta, 1969. Thesis (Ph.D.)–University of Alberta, 1969.

**3307. Annand, Bessie May** *An Investigation of Lateral Dominance, Left-Right Discrimination and Reading Achievement of Children in the Second Year of School.* Bessie May Annand. Edmonton: University of Alberta, 1971. Thesis (M.Ed)–University of Alberta, 1971.

**3308. Anonymous** *"Infant Welfare Work in Regina."* Public Health Journal 4, 6(June 1913): 391-392.

**3309. Anonymous** *"Medical Inspection of Schools in the Middle West."* Public Health Journal 5, 1(Jan. 1914): 89-95.

**3310. Anonymous** *"Resume of the Report on the Poliomyelitis Epidemic in Manitoba, 1928."* Canadian Public Health Journal 20, 5(May 1929): 225-234.

**3311. Anonymous** *"School Hygiene in Saskatchewan."* Public Health Journal 15, 9(Sept. 1924): 404-408.

**3312. Anthony, Geraldine** *Gwen Pharis Ringwood.* Geraldine Anthony. Boston: Twayne, c1981.

3313. **Aoki, Tetsuo** *The Development of the Lethbridge School District Number 51 to 1960*. Tetsuo Aoki. Edmonton: University of Alberta, 1963.
Thesis (M.Ed.)--University of Alberta, 1963.

3314. **Arbeau, Arthur Melbourne** *A Survey of Pupil Grouping Practices in Grade 1 to 12 in Alberta Schools*. Arthur Melbourne Arbeau. Edmonton: University of Alberta, 1963.
Thesis (M.Ed.)--University of Alberta, 1963.

3315. **Arborfield History Book Committee** *Echoes from the Past: a History of Arborfield and District*. Arborfield History Book Committee. [S.l.] : Arborfield History Book Committee, 1981.

3316. **Archerwill and District Historical Society** *The Past to the Present*. Archerwill and District Historical Society. Archerwill, Sask.: Archerwill and District Historical Society, 1984.

3317. **Arelee and District Historical Association** *Reflections: a History of Arelee and Districts*. Arelee and District Historical Association. Arelee, Sask.: Arelee and District Historical Association, 1982.

3318. **Argamaso, Ravelo V.** "*Pathology, Mortality and Prognosis of Burns: a Review of 54 Critical and Fatal Cases.*" Ravelo V. Argamaso. Canadian Medical Association Journal/Journal de l'Association medicale canadienne 97, 9(Aug. 26, 1967): 445-449.

3319. **Armstrong, E.J.** *Attitude Adjustment as the Result of a Single Lecture on the Implications of Drug Abuse*. E.J. Armstrong. Edmonton: University of Alberta, 1970.
Thesis (M.Ed.)--University of Alberta, 1970.

3320. **Armstrong, F.B.** "*Intracranial Tuberculoma in Native Races of Canada: With Special Reference to Symptomatic Epilepsy and Neurologic Features.*" F.B. Armstrong and A.M. Edwards. Canadian Medical Association Journal/Journal de l'Association medicale canadienne 89, 2(July 13, 1963): 56-65.

3321. **Armstrong, J.G.** *Development of Selected Science Concepts Through Secondary School Grades Being A Study Of Grade Growth of, (1) Scientific Vocabulary; (2) Ability to Relate Science to Mathematics; (3) Use of Scientific Knowledge; (4) Scientific Attitude*. J.G. Armstrong. Edmonton: University of Alberta, 1936.
Thesis (M.A.)--University of Alberta, 1936.

3322. **Armstrong, Jerrold** *Kinistino: the Story of a Parkland Community in Central Saskatchewan in Two Parts*. Jerrold Armstrong and Kinistino and District Historical Organization. Melfort, Sask.: Kinistino and District Historical Organization, 1980.

3323. **Armstrong, Miss** "*Child Welfare Work.*" Miss Armstrong. Canadian Nurse 17, 8(Aug. 1921): 282-285.

3324. **Armstrong, Robert D.** *An Experiment in Teaching Work-Study Skills by Television to Grades Five and Six*. Robert D. Armstrong. Edmonton: University of Alberta, 1960.
Thesis (M.Ed.)--University of Alberta, 1960.

3325. **Arnason, David, ed.** *The Icelanders*. David Arnason, ed. and Michael Olito, ed. Winnipeg: Turnstone Press, 1981.

3326. **Arnaud Historical Committee** *Arnaud: Through the Years*. Arnaud Historical Committee. [S.l.] : Arnaud Historical Committee, 1974.

3327. **Arrowwood-Mossleigh Historical Society** *Furrows of Time: a History of Arrowwood, Shouldice, Mossleigh and Farrow, 1883-1982*. Arrowwood-Mossleigh Historical Society. [S.l.]: Arrowwood-Mossleigh Historical Society, 1982.

3328. **Artibise, Alan F.J.** "*Patterns of Population Growth and Ethnic Relationships in Winnipeg, 1874-1974.*" Alan F.J. Artibise. Histoire sociale/Social History 9, 18(Nov. 1976): 297-335.

3329. **Artibise, Alan F.J.** *Winnipeg: a Social History of Urban Growth, 1874-1914*. Alan F.J. Artibise. Montreal: McGill-Queen's University Press, 1975.

3330. **Artibise, Alan F.J.** *Winnipeg: an Illustrated History*. Alan F.J. Artibise. Toronto: James Lorimer & Co. and National Museums of Canada, 1977.

3331. **Ashern Historical Society** *Taming a Wilderness: a History of Ashern and District*. Ashern Historical Society. Ashern, Man.: Ashern Historical Society, 1976.

3332. **Asquith and District Historical Society** *The Asquith Record*. Asquith and District Historical Society. Asquith, Sask.: Asquith and District Historical Society, [1982].

**3333. Asselstine, J.L.** *"A Child Guidance Clinic for School Children."* J.L. Asselstine. Canadian Medical Association Journal 73, 12(Dec. 15, 1955): 969-971.

**3334. Asselstine, J. L.** *"Child Guidance, the Exceptional Child, and the School System."* J. Asselstine. Canadian Psychiatric Association Journal/Revue de l'Association canadienne de psychiatrie 4, 3(July 1959): 198-208.

**3335.** *At Your Service.* Accounts by Calgary authors. [Calgary]: Century Calgary Publications, 1975.

**3336. Atherton, John F.** *"The Pioneer Child."* John F. Atherton. Alberta History 27, 4(Autumn 1979): 15-22.

**3337. Atkinson, Harry K.** *Boys in Trouble: a Review of the Work of the Manitoba Industrial Training School for Boys Over a Five-Year Period from July 15, 1926 - July 5, 1931.* Harry Atkinson and the Canadian Council on Child and Family Welfare. Ottawa: Canadian Council on Child and Family Welfare, 1931.

**3338. Atwater Historical Society** *The Atwater Afterglow: Fond Memories of the Past.* Atwater Historical Society. [Atwater, Sask.: Atwater Historical Society, 1980].

**3339. Atwell, Phyllis Harryette** *Kinship and Migration Among Calgarian Residents of Indian Origin.* Phyllis Harryette Atwell. Calgary: University of Calgary, 1969. (CTM no. 4603)
Thesis (M.A.)--University of Calgary, 1969.

**3340. Avonlea Historical Committee** *Arrowheads to Wheatfields: Avonlea, Hearne and Districts.* Avonlea Historical Committee. Avonlea, Sask.: Avonlea Historical Committee, 1983.

**3341. Bachman, Mary Baptista** *Pattern of Errors in Reading Comprehension of Grade 9 Underachieving Students.* Sister Mary Baptista Bachman. Edmonton: University of Alberta, 1965.
Thesis (M.Ed.)--University of Alberta, 1965.

**3342. Backstrom, Elvira** *"Pioneer Parents."* Elvira Backstrom. Alberta Historical Review 9, 4(Autumn 1961): 14-21.

**3343. Badger, William Lloyd** *A Study of the Handling of Controversial Issues in Social Studies Classes of Edmonton: Public High Schools.* William Lloyd Badger. Edmonton: University of Alberta, 1967.
Thesis (M.Ed.)--University of Alberta, 1967.

**3344. Bagley, Ray** *"Lacombe in the Nineties."* Ray Bagley. Alberta Historical Review 10, 3(Summer 1962): 18-27.

**3345. Bailey, Charles Anthony** *A School Counsellor, a Blind Child and the Sighted School.* Charles Anthony Bailey. Edmonton: University of Alberta, 1971.
Thesis (M.Ed.)--University of Alberta, 1971.

**3346. Bain, Bruce** *Form Copying and Reading Ability.* Bruce Campbell Bain. Edmonton: University of Alberta, 1968.
Thesis (M.Ed.)--University of Alberta, 1968.

**3347. Baker, A.H.** *"Tuberculosis Survey of School Children in Alberta, 1924."* A.H. Baker. Canadian Medical Association Journal 15, 8(Aug. 1925): 816-817.

**3348. Baker, Esme M.** *"Enuresis."* Esme M. Baker. Canadian Nurse 51, 9(Sept. 1955): 709-714.

**3349. Baker, Laura Doris** *The Development of Special Educational Provisions for Exceptional Children in the City of Winnipeg.* Laura Doris Baker. Toronto: University of Toronto, 1967.
Thesis (Ed.D.)--University of Toronto, 1967.

**3350. Baker, Laura Doris** *A Study of Under-functioning Pupils in Grades 4, 5 and 6 in One of Winnipeg's Schools.* L.D. Baker. Winnipeg: University of Manitoba, 1950.
Thesis (M.Ed.)--University of Manitoba, 1950.

**3351. Baker, Robert Leonard Cecil** *A Comparison of Techniques Used to Implement a Study of Current Events.* Robert Leonard Cecil Baker. Elementary: University of Alberta, 1963.
Thesis (M.Ed.)--University of Alberta, 1963.

**3352. Bakerspigel, A.** *"Ringworm in Saskatchewan Caused by Trichophyton Verrucosum."* A. Bakerspigel and R. Bremner. Canadian Medical Association Journal 73, 8(Oct. 15, 1955): 665-667.

**3353. Bakken, Melvin Rudolph** *Money Management Understanding of Tenth Grade Students.* Melvin Rudolph Bakken. Edmonton: University of Alberta, 1966.
Thesis (M.Ed.)--University of Alberta, 1966.

**3354. Bale, David Joseph** *A Comparison of Programmed and Conventional Mathematics Enrichment Materials over Two Grade Seven Mathematics Achievement Levels.* David Joseph Bale. Edmonton: University of Alberta, 1966.

Thesis (M.Ed.)–University of Alberta, 1966.

**3355. Bale, Gordon** *"Law, Politics and the Manitoba School Question: Supreme Court and Privy Council."* Gordon Bale. Canadian Bar Review/Reuve du Barreau Canadien 63, 3(Sept. 1985): 461-518.

**3356. Balfour, G.S.** *"The Inheritance of Diabetes Mellitus."* G.S. Balfour. Canadian Medical Association Journal/Journal de l'Association medicale canadienne 80, 11(June 1, 1959): 891-893.

**3357. Ball, Geraldine F.** *Some Extracts and Reminiscences of a Lifetime.* Geraldine F. Ball. Regina: Leader Publishing Co., 1922.

**3358. Banmen, John** *An Exploratory Study of Guidance Services in the High Schools of Manitoba.* John Banmen. Laramie, Wy.: University of Wyoming, c1970. Thesis (Ph.D.)–University of Wyoming, 1970.

**3359. Banting, Meredith Black** *Prairie Pioneers.* Meredith Black Banting. Centennial ed. [S.l.: s.n.], 1966.

**3360. Barber, Marilyn** *"Canadianization Through the Schools of the Prairie Provinces Before World War I: the Attitudes and Aims of the English-speaking Majority."* Marilyn Barber. Regina: Canadian Plains Research Center, 1978. In Ethnic Canadians: Culture and Education, pp. 281-294. Edited by Martin L. Kovacs.

**3361. Barilko, Olga Louise** *A Study of the Incidence of Juvenile Delinquency and Its Treatment in Edmonton in 1944.* Olga Louise Barilko. Edmonton: University of Alberta, 1955. Thesis (M.A.)–University of Alberta, 1955.

**3362. Barker, George** *Forty Years a Chief.* George Barker. Winnipeg: Peguis Publishers Limited, c1979.

**3363. Barkman, Alma** *"Free Home Deliveries."* Alma Barkman. Winnipeg: Centennial Publications, 1977. In Mennonite Memories: Settling in Western Canada, pp. 235-239. Edited by Lawrence Klippenstein and Julius G. Toews.

**3364. Barkman, Peter T.** *"Building the Reserves: Steinbach Mills."* Peter T. Barkman. Winnipeg: Centennial Publications, 1977. In Mennonite Memories: Settling in Western Canada, pp. 58-63. Edited by Lawrence Klippenstein and Julius G. Toews.

**3365. Barnett, Don C.** *The Efficiency with Which Children of Grades Seven, Eight, and Nine are Able to Read and Interpret Vertical Aerial Photographs.* Don C. Barnett. Calgary: University of Calgary, 1969. Thesis (M.Ed.)–University of Calgary, 1969.

**3366. Barnett, Don C.** *The Hutterite People: a Religious Community.* Don C. Barnett and Lowry R. Knight. Saskatoon: Western Extension College, 1977.

**3367. Baron, Robert B.D.** *A Comparative Analysis of Grade 12 Answer Papers in Social Studies of July 1944.* Robert B.D. Baron. Edmonton: University of Alberta, 1946. Thesis (M.Ed.)–University of Alberta, 1946.

**3368. Barrett, Kevin A.** *"High School Students' Smoking Habits."* Kevin A. Barrett. Canadian Journal of Public Health 53, 12(Dec. 1962): 500-510.

**3369. Barrhead History Book Committee** *The Golden Years.* Barrhead History Book Committee. Barrhead, Alta.: Barrhead History Book Committee, 1978.

**3370. Barrowcliffe, Wayne T.** *Target Authoritarianism as a Correlate of Self-disclosure of Adolescents.* Wayne T. Barrowcliffe. Calgary: University of Calgary, 1971. Thesis (M.Ed.)–University of Calgary, 1971.

**3371. Barry, Walter W.** *Anecdotal History of Calgary Separate Schools.* Walter W. Barry, Mary Inamasu and Albert Standell. Calgary: [s.n.], 1967.

**3372. Barsky, Percy** *"The Management of Poliomyelitis."* Percy Barsky. Canadian Medical Association Journal 70, 5(May 1954): 517-520.

**3373. Barsky, Percy** *"Seven Recurrent Attacks of Pneumococcic Meningitis with Recovery."* Percy Barsky. Canadian Medical Association Journal 72, 3(Feb. 1, 1955): 210-212.

**3374. Bartlett, George W.** *The Child of Canada's Hinterlands.* George W. Bartlett. Ottawa: Canadian Council on Child Welfare, 1924.

**3375. Bate, John Peter** *Retention of Gains in Critical Thinking Effected by a Fenton Inquiry Sequence.* John Peter Bate. Calgary: University of Calgary, 1969. Thesis (M.Ed.)–University of Calgary, 1969. bibliography leaves 39-41.

3376. Bate, W. Richard *An Investigation into the Relation Between Aggression and Educational Achievement.* W. Richard Bate. Calgary: University of Calgary, 1968. Thesis (M.Ed.)–University of Calgary, 1968.

3377. Battel, Mildred E. *Children Shall Be First: Child Welfare Saskatchewan, 1944-46.* Mildred E. Battel and the Local History Program, Saskatchewan Department of Culture and Youth. [Regina: s.n., 1980?].

3378. Bayly, Archer George *An Evaluation of an Originally Organized System of Teaching Primary Reading Under Ordinary Classroom Conditions.* Archer George Bayly. Edmonton: University of Alberta, 1948. Thesis (M.Ed.)–University of Alberta, 1948.

3379. Beaton, Mary Anne *The Effects of Acceleration on the Academic Progress and on the Personal and Social Development of Calgary and Edmonton Grade 10 Students.* Mary Anne Beaton. Edmonton: University of Alberta, 1956. Thesis (M.Ed.)–University of Alberta, 1956.

3380. Beaton, Mary Anne *A Study of Underachievers in Mathematics at Tenth Grade Level in Three Calgary High Schools.* Mary Anne Beaton. Evanston, Ill.: Northwestern University, c1966. Thesis (Ph.D.)–Northwestern University, 1966.

3381. Beattie, Keith N. *The Comparative Effectiveness of Four Matriculation Mathematices Programs in Alberta High Schools.* Keith N. Beattie. Calgary: University of Calgary, 1967. Thesis (M.Ed.)–University of Calgary, 1967.

3382. Beatty and District Historical Society *Memory Lane: Beatty and District.* Beatty and District Historical Society. Beatty, Sask.: Beatty and District Historical Society, 1983.

3383. Beaugrand, Helen *Heaven Via Little New York.* Helen Beaugrand. Aldergrove, B.C.: Valcraft Printing Ltd., [1979].

3384. Bechard, Riceton, Gray and Estlin History *"The Ties That Bind": Estlin, Gray, Riceton, Bechard.* Bechard, Riceton, Gray and Estlin History. Riceton, Sask.: Bechard, Riceton, Gray and Estlin History, 1984.

3385. Becker, A. *"The Story of Frieden School District No. 613."* A. Becker. Saskatchewan History 38, 1(Winter 1985): 20-25.

3386. Becker, Florence Muriel *A Description of Observed Oral Reading Phenomena of Grade Four Children.* Florence Muriel Becker. Edmonton: University of Alberta, 1970. Thesis (M.Ed.)–University of Alberta, 1970.

3387. Beddie, Alastair *"Mothers, Mongols and Mores."* Alastair Beddie and Humphry Osmond. Canadian Medical Association Journal 73, 3(Aug. 1, 1955): 167-170.

3388. Belbutte-Bapaume History Committee *Links with the Past: Belbutte-Bapaume.* Belbutte-Bapaume History Committee. Spiritwood, Sask.: Belbutte-Bapaume History Committee, 1980.

3389. Belisle, Olga *Children of the Homesteaders [and the Kinship Between the Canadian and American Peoples].* Olga Belisle. Vernon, B.C.: Canho Enterprises, 1981.

3390. Bell, D.A. *"Ten Year Follow-up of Low-birth-weight Infants: Intellectual Functioning."* D.A. Bell, W.C. Taylor and W.B. Dockrell. Alberta Journal of Educational Research 11, 4(Dec. 1965): 220-225.

3391. Bellan, Ruth *"Growing Up in a Small Saskatchewan Town."* Ruth Bellan. Winnipeg: Jewish Historical Society of Western Canada, c1983. In Jewish Life and Times: a Collection of Essays, pp. 115-122.

3392. Belle *"Documents."* Belle. Manitoba History 1(1979): 33-34. Excerpts from the "Letters from Elkhorn" collection submitted to the Manitoba Historical Society in 1979.

3393. Bench History Hustlers *Rippling Memories: Aldag, Bench, Golden Sheaf, Twin Buttes, String Butte.* Bench History Hustlers. Gull Lake, Sask.: Bench History Hustlers, 1980.

3394. Bender, Urie A. *Stumbling Heavenward: the Extraordinary Life of an Ordinary Man.* Urie A. Bender. Winnipeg: Hyperion Press, 1984.

3395. Benger, Kathlyn *A Study of the Relationships Between Perception, Personality, Intelligence and Grade One Reading Achievement.* Kathlyn Benger. Edmonton: University of Alberta, 1966. Thesis (M.Ed.)–University of Alberta,

1966.

**3396. Bennett, John W.** *"A Cree Indian Reserve."* John W. Bennett. Scarborough, Ont.: Prentice-Hall, 1971. In Native Peoples, pp. 99-115. Edited by Jean Leonard Elliott.

**3397. Bennett, Michael G.** *The Indian Child in School: an Examination of the Socio-Cultural Factors Influencing the Development of the Occupational Aspirations of Canadian Indian Children Attending Indian Residential Schools in Saskatchewan.* Michael G. Bennett and Anita M. Thelander. Montreal: McGill University, 1967.
Thesis (M.S.W.)--McGill University, 1967.

**3398. Benoit, Lionel Charles** *An Analysis of Political Attitudes of High School Students.* Lionel Charles Benoit. Edmonton: University of Alberta, 1967.
Thesis (M.Ed.)--University of Alberta, 1967.

**3399. Benson Historical Society** *Toil, Tears and Thanksgiving: Rural Municipality of Benson, No. 35.* Benson Historical Society. Benson, Sask.: Benson Historical Society, 1981.

**3400. Bergen, Elizabeth** *"A Pioneer Mother."* Elizabeth Bergen. Winnipeg: Centennial Publications, 1977. In Mennonite Memories: Settling in Western Canada, pp. 233-234. Edited by Lawrence Klippenstein and Julius G. Toews.

**3401. Berkner, Melvin** *"Homesteading in the Floral District."* Melvin Berkner. Saskatchewan History 39, 1(Winter 1986): 32-38.

**3402. Bernadette, Sister** *"Recreation in an Institution."* Sister Bernadette. Canadian Welfare 27, 6(Dec. 1951): 22-27.

**3403. Berry, Lois Minerva** *The Readiness Centre: a Case Study.* Lois Minerva Berry. Calgary: University of Calgary, 1971. (CTM no. 10039)
Thesis (M.S.W.)--University of Calgary, 1971.

**3404. Berrymoor-Carnwood Historical Society** *Forests to Grainfields.* Berrymoor-Carnwood Historical Society. Berrymoor, Alta.: Berrymoor-Carnwood Historical Society, 1977.

**3405. Bert, Arthur R.** *"Troublesome Skin Diseases in Infancy and Childhood."* Arthur R. Bert. Canadian Medical Association Journal 46, 2(Feb. 1942): 132-136.

**3406. Best, S.C.** *"Pine House (Saskatchewan) Nutrition Project."* S.C. Best and J.W. Gerrard. Canadian Medical Association Journal/Journal de l'Association medicale canadienne 81, 11(Dec. 1, 1959): 915-917.

**3407. Bethune and District Historical Society** *Wagon Trails to Blacktop.* Bethune and District Historical Society. Bethune, Sask.: Bethune and District Historical Society, 1983.

**3408. Betke, Carl** *"The Social Significance of Sport in the City: Edmonton in the 1920s."* Carl Betke. Ottawa: National Museums of Canada, 1975. In Cities in the West, pp. 211-235. Edited by A. Ross McCormack and Ian MacPherson.

**3409. Bevan, George Henry** *An Empirical Study of the Need for Independence in High School Students.* George Henry Bevan. Edmonton: University of Alberta, 1970.
Thesis (Ph.D.)--University of Alberta, 1970.

**3410. Bevington, Wilbert George** *Effect of Age at Time of Entrance into Grade 1 on Subsequent Achievement.* Wilbert George Bevington. Edmonton: University of Alberta, 1957.
Thesis (M.Ed.)--University of Alberta, 1957.

**3411. Bevington, Wilbert George** *"Effect of Age at Time of Entrance into Grade 1 on Subsequent Achievement."* W.G. Bevington. Alberta Journal of Educational Research 4, 1(Mar. 1958): 6-16.

**3412. Big Beaver Historical Society** *Happy Valley Happenings: Big Beaver and District.* Big Beaver Historical Society. Big Beaver, Sask.: Big Beaver Historical Society, 1983.

**3413. Big River History Book Committee** *Timber Trails: History of Big River and District.* Big River History Book Committee. Big River, Sask.: Big River History Book Committee, 1979.

**3414. Binder, Alfred** *Instruments to Measure and Compare the Knowledge of and Attitude toward the City Among Indian and Non-Indian Pupils.* Alfred Binder. Calgary: University of Calgary, 1969.
Thesis (M.Ed.)--University of Calgary, 1969.

**3415. Binning, Griffith** *"Adequate School Examination."* Griffith Binning. Canadian Public Health Journal 29, 1(Jan. 1938): 13-18.

**3416. Binning, Griffith** *"Earlier Physical and Mental Maturity Among Saskatoon Public School Children."* Griffith Binning. Canadian Journal of Public Health 49, 1(Jan. 1958): 9-17.

**3417. Binning, Griffith** *"The Incidence of Goitre Amongst Saskatoon School Children."* Griffith Binning. Canadian Medical Association Journal 32, 5(May 1935): 533-537.

**3418. Binning, Griffith** *"The Influence of the Perturbations of Childhood Life upon the Occurrence of Appendectomy."* Griffith Binning. Canadian Medical Association Journal 63, 5(Nov. 1950): 461-467.

**3419. Binning, Griffith** *"A Study of Goitre in Saskatoon, 1938."* Griffith Binning. Canadian Public Health Journal 30, 8(Aug. 1939): 393-399.

**3420. Binscarth History Committee** *Binscarth Memories.* Binscarth History Committee. Binscarth, Man: Binscarth History Committee, 1984.

**3421. Birch Hills Historical Society** *Grooming the Grizzly: a History of Wanham and Area.* Birch Hills Historical Society. Wanham, Alta.: Birch Hills Historical Society, 1982.

**3422. Birdsall, Elliot Henry** *A Questionnaire Investigation of the Reactions of School Children to Moving Picture Shows.* Elliott Henry Birdsall. Edmonton: University of Alberta, 1933.
Thesis (M.A.)--University of Alberta, 1933.

**3423. Birney, Earle** *"Child Addict in Alberta."* Earle Birney. Canadian Literature 90(Autumn 1981): 6-12.

**3424. Birt, Arthur R.** *"Griseofulvin in the Oral Treatment of Tinea Capitis."* A.R. Birt, J. Hoogstraten and M. Norris. Canadian Medical Association Journal/Journal de l'Association medicale canadienne 81, 3(Aug. 1, 1959): 165-167.

**3425. Birt, Arthur R.** *"An Outbreak of Tinea Capitis and Tinea Corporis Due to Microsporum Lanosum."* Arthur R. Birt. Canadian Medical Association Journal 78, 8(Apr. 15, 1958): 579-583.

**3426. Bishop, Robert Francis** *A Historical Survey of the Learning Experience of Northern Cree People of Manitoba.* Robert Francis Bishop. Winnipeg: University of Manitoba, 1979.
Thesis (M.Ed.)--University of Manitoba, 1979.

**3427. Bittern Lake-Sifton History Book Association** *The Bitter 'N Sweet: the History of the Bittern Lake-Sifton District.* Bittern Lake-Sifton History Book Association and Bittern Lake Community Association. Bittern Lake, Alta.: Bittern Lake-Sifton History Book Association and Bittern Lake Community Association, 1983.

**3428. Bjorkdale History Committee** *A Season or So: a History of the People of Bjorkdale and Surrounding Districts.* Bjorkdale Historical Committee. Bjorkdale, Sask.: Bjorkdale Historical Committee, 1983.

**3429. Black, Donald B.** *"A Comparison of the Performance on Selected Standardized Tests to that on the Alberta Grade 12 Departmental Examination of a Select Group of University of Alberta Freshmen."* Donald B. Black. Alberta Journal of Educational Research 5, 3(Sept. 1959): 180-190.

**3430. Black, Donald B.** *"The Prediction of University Freshman Success Using Grade 9 Departmental Examination Scores."* Donald B. Black. Alberta Journal of Educational Research 5, 4(Dec. 1959): 229-239.

**3431. Black, Donald B.** *Pupil Personnel in Alberta Secondary Schools.* D.B. Black, R.S. MacArthur and J.G. Paterson. Edmonton: Alberta Advisory Committee on Educational Research, 1961.

**3432. Black, Donald B.** *"A Three Year Academic History of Eight Hundred and Thirty-Three Superior Alberta Grade 9 Students."* Donald B. Black. Alberta Journal of Educational Research 7, 1(Apr. 1961): 50-61.

**3433. Black, Elinor F.E.** *"Vaginal Occlusion and Cryptomenorrhea."* Elinor F.E. Black. Canadian Medical Association Journal 78, 9(May 1, 1958): 699-701.

**3434. Black, Errol** *"The Making of the East End Community Club."* Errol Black and Tom Black. Labour/Le Travailleur 12(Fall 1983): 155-172.

**3435. Blackburn, Cecil R.** *The Development of Sports in Alberta, 1900-1918.* Cecil R. Blackburn. Edmonton: University of Alberta, 1974. (CTM no. 20970)
Thesis (M.A.)--University of Alberta, 1974.

**3436. Blackford, Charles Douglas** *The Classification Abilities of Elementary School Students.* Charles Douglas Blackford. Edmonton: University of Alberta, 1970. Thesis (M.Ed.)--University of Alberta, 1970.

**3437. Blackley, Gardenvilla and Hilmaurs History** *Memories of Rural Saskatoon, 1890-1982.* Blackley, Gardenvilla and Kilmaurs History. Saskatoon: Blackley, Gardenvilla and Kilmaurs History, 1982.

**3438. Blackmore, David E.** *A Latent Trait Study of Item Bias and Achievement Differences.* David E. Blackmore. Edmonton: University of Alberta, 1980. Thesis (Ph.D.)--University of Alberta, 1980.

**3439. Blaine Lake (Municipality)** *Bridging the Years: Era of Blaine Lake and District, 1790-1980.* Town and R.M. of Blaine Lake. Blaine Lake, Sask.: Town and R.M. of Blaine Lake, 1984.

**3440. Blair, Mancell John** *Familism and Style of Participation in the Christian Family Movement in Canada, 1968.* John Mancell Blair. Notre Dame, Indiana: Notre Dame University, 1968. Thesis (Ph.D.)--University of Notre Dame, 1968.

**3441. Blake, Victor** *An Application of Social-Psychological Theory in the Analysis of the Choice of a Scientific Career.* Victor Blake. Edmonton: University of Alberta, 1965. Thesis (Ph.D.)--University of Alberta, 1965.

**3442. Blanshard Rural Municipality** *History of the R.M. of Blanshard.* The Municipality. [Blanshard, Man.: s.n., 1960].

**3443. Blowers, Elizabeth A.** *Barriers to the Education of Economically Disadvantaged Students as Seen by their Parents, their Teachers and by School Principals.* Elizabeth Anne Blowers. Edmonton: University of Alberta, 1969. Thesis (M.Ed.)--University of Alberta, 1969.

**3444. Blucher Historical Society** *Blucher Builders: Blucher Community, 1900-1982.* Blucher Historical Society. Saskatoon, Sask.: Blucher Historical Society, 1982.

**3445. Bociurkiw, Bohdan R.** *"Ethnic Identification and Attitudes of University Students of Ukrainian Descent: the University of Alberta Case Study."* Bohdan R. Bociurkiw. Toronto: Inter-University Committee on Canadian Slavs, [1970]. In Slavs in Canada, v.3 pp. 15-110. Edited

by Cornelius J. Jaenen.

**3446. Boissevain History Committee** *Beckoning Hills Revisited: Ours is a Goodly Heritage, Morton-Boissevain, 1881-1981.* Boissevain History Committee. Boissevain, Man.: Boissevain History Committee, 1981.

**3447. Boldt, Edward D.** *Conformity and Deviance: the Hutterites of Alberta.* Edward D. Boldt. Edmonton: University of Alberta, 1966. Thesis (M.A.)--University of Alberta, 1966.

**3448. Borden History Book Committee** *Our Treasured Heritage: Borden and District.* Borden History Book Committee. Borden, Sask.: Borden History Book Committee, 1980.

**3449. Borthwick-Leslie, K.** *"Preoperative Sedation in Children."* K. Borthwick-Leslie. Canadian Medical Association Journal 46, 4(Apr. 1942): 345-347.

**3450. Botsford, Brenda** *Physical Education Programs in Alberta Schools for Trainable Mentally Retarded Children.* Brenda Botsford. Edmonton: University of Alberta, 1970. Thesis (M.A.)--University of Alberta, 1970.

**3451. Bow, Malcolm R.** *"Public Health and Welfare in Alberta."* Malcolm R. Bow. Canadian Welfare Summary 15, 5(Jan. 1940): 38-44.

**3452. Bowker, Marjorie Montgomery** *"Juvenile Court in Retrospect: Seven Decades of History in Alberta (1913-1984)."* Marjorie Montgomery Bowker. Alberta Law Review 24, 2(1986): 234-274.

**3453. Bowman, Maxwell** *"An Epidemic of Typhoid Fever Due to Infected Cheese: Manitoba, December 1939-March 1940."* Maxwell Bowman. Canadian Public Health Journal 33, 10(Oct. 1942): 541-547.

**3454. Bowman, Pauline** *"Child Welfare Clinic."* Pauline Bowman. Canadian Nurse 22, 9(Sept. 1926): 484-485.

**3455. Bowsfield, Hartwell** *Louis Riel: the Rebel and the Hero.* Hartwell Bowsfield. Toronto: Oxford University Press, c1971.

**3456. Bowtell, Fred** *"Trails of Yesteryear."* Fred Bowtell. Alberta Historical Review 4, 3(Summer 1956): 8-11.

3457. Boyd, Helen, ed. *"Growing Up Privileged in Edmonton."* Helen Boyd and T.A. Crowley, eds. Alberta History 30, 1(Winter 1982): 1-10.

3458. Boyko, Steve *Current Practices in Extracurricular Activities in Alberta Centralized Schools.* Steve Boyko. Edmonton: University of Alberta, 1959. Thesis (M.Ed.)--University of Alberta, 1959.

3459. Brace, Alec T. *The Preschool Child's Concept of Number.* Alec T. Brace. Edmonton: University of Alberta, 1963. Thesis (M.Ed.)--University of Alberta, 1963.

3460. Bradshaw, A.K. *"Acute Laryngotracheo Bronchitis."* A.K. Bradshaw. Canadian Medical Association Journal 70, 4(Apr. 1954): 447-449.

3461. Bradshaw, Elsie *Patterns of Perceptual Performance in Children Who Are Severely Retarded in Reading.* Elsie Bradshaw. Edmonton: University of Alberta, 1963. Thesis (M.Ed.)--University of Alberta, 1963.

3462. Brady, Paul Richard *Relationships Between Maternal Control, Communication and Cognitive Behaviour of the Preschool Child.* Paul Richard Brady. Edmonton: University of Alberta, 1969. Thesis (Ph.D.)--University of Alberta, 1969.

3463. Bragg, Lloyd E. *A Study of the Effects of Two Corrective Reading Programs on Selected Reading Skills of High School Students.* Lloyd E. Bragg. Calgary: University of Calgary, 1970. Thesis (M.Ed.)--University of Calgary, 1970.

3464. Brailsford, Eugene Gerald *The Use of the Trail Making Test with Brain-damaged and Normal Children.* Eugene Gerald Brailsford. Edmonton: University of Alberta, 1962. Thesis (M.A.)--University of Alberta, 1962.

3465. Brass, Eleanor *"The File Hills Ex-pupil Colony."* Eleanor Brass. Saskatchewan History 6, 2(Spring 1953): 66-69.

3466. Braun, Carl *"A Transformational Analysis of Oral Syntactic Structures of Children Representing Varying Ethnolinguistic Communities."* Carl Braun and Bernard Klassen. Child Development 42, 5(Nov. 1971): 1859-1871.

3467. Braver, Jorn Heinz *Mental Practice in Relation to the Learning of Rapid Reading Skills.* Jorn Heinz Braver. Edmonton: University of Alberta, 1970. Thesis (M.Ed.)--University of Alberta, 1970.

3468. Brick, A.L. *"Reverend J. Gough Brick and His Shaftesbury Mission Farm."* A.L. Brick. Alberta Historical Review 3, 2(Spring 1955): 3-12.

3469. Briggs, E.J.N. *"Staphylococcic Pneumonia in Infants and Young Children."* J.N. Briggs. Canadian Medical Association Journal 76, 4(Feb. 15, 1957): 269-272.

3470. Briggs, James W. *"A Comparison of Client-centered vs Directed Group Counselling with High School Students."* James W. Briggs. Alberta Journal of Educational Research 14, 3(Sept. 1968): 193-201.

3471. Britton. Edward Chester *A Study of the Organized Community Life of Junior High School Students.* Edward Chester Britton. Edmonton: University of Alberta, 1946. Thesis (M.A.)--University of Alberta, 1946.

3472. Broadview Pioneer History Society *Centennial Tribute: Oakshela, Broadview, Percival, 1882-1982.* Broadview Pioneer History Society. Broadview, Sask.: Broadview Pioneer History Society, 1982.

3473. Brockman, Mary Annata *"Relationship Between Transiency and Test Achievement."* Mary Annata Brockman and A.W. Reeves. Alberta Journal of Educational Research 13, 4(Dec. 1967): 319-330.

3474. Brockman, Mary Annata *Relationship Between Transiency and Test Achievement of Grade 6 Students.* Mary Annata Brockman. Edmonton: University of Alberta, 1965. Thesis (M.Ed.)--University of Alberta, 1965.

3475. Brooks, Martha *A Hill for Looking.* Martha Brooks. Winnipeg: Queenston House, c1982.

3476. Brosseau, John Francis *Factors Influencing Second Language Learning.* John Francis Brosseau. Edmonton: University of Alberta, 1965. Thesis (M.Ed.)--University of Alberta, 1965.

**3477. Brown, Alan F.** *The Differential Effect of Stress-inducing Supervision on Classroom Teaching Behaviour.* Alan Fergus Brown. Edmonton: University of Alberta, 1961.
Thesis (Ph.D.)--University of Alberta, 1961.

**3478. Brown, Alan F.** *"The Self in Interpersonal Theory."* Alan F. Brown. Alberta Journal of Educational Research 3. 3(Sept. 1957): 138-148.

**3479. Brown, Annora** *Sketches From Life.* Annora Brown. Edmonton: Hurtig Publishers, 1981.

**3480. Brown, Chesley Kenneth** *Pupil Personality, Teaching Style and Achievement.* Kenneth Chesley Brown. Edmonton: University of Alberta, 1967. Thesis (Ph.D.)--University of Alberta, 1967.

**3481. Brown, Dorine, ed.** *Pembina Country.* Dorine Brown, ed. [and] Miami Museum. Miami, Man.: Miami Museum, 1974.

**3482. Brown, Frank** *A History of the Town of Winkler, Manitoba.* Frank Brown. Winkler, Man.: The Author, 1973.

**3483. Brown, Kenneth Gordon** *The Relation Between Intelligence and Achievement Using Computer-assisted Instruction.* Kenneth Gordon Brown. Edmonton: University of Alberta, 1969. (CTM no. 4920)
Thesis (Ph.D.)--University of Alberta, 1969.

**3484. Brown, Violet** *"Over the Red Deer: Life of a Homestead Missionary."* Violet Brown. Alberta History 33, 3(Summer 1985): 9-18.

**3485. Browne, Jean E.** *"Health Education in Rural Schools."* Jean E. Browne. Public Health Journal 11, 12(Dec. 1920): 533-541.

**3486. Browne, Jean E.** *"The School Nurse."* Jean E. Browne. Canadian Nurse 7, 10(Oct. 1911): 505.

**3487. Browne, Jean E.** *"School Nursing in Regina."* Jean E. Browne. Canadian Nurse 7, 9(Sept. 1911): 445-447.

**3488. Browne, Jean E.** *"School Nursing in Regina."* Jean Browne. Canadian Nurse 9, 12(Dec. 1913): 794-797.

**3489. Browne, Jean E.** *"School Nursing in Regina."* Jean Browne. Public Health Journal 5, 2(Feb. 1914): 91-92.

**3490. Browne, Margaret Patricia Jane** *An Exploratory Study of Teacher-Pupil Verbal Interaction in Primary Reading Program.* Margaret Patricia Jane Browne. Edmonton: University of Alberta, 1971. Thesis (Ph.D.)--University of Alberta, 1971.

**3491. Bruce, Jean** *The Last Best West.* Jean Bruce. Toronto: Fitzhenry and Whiteside, 1976.

**3492. Bruce, Margaret A.** *Generalized Imitative Affection: Relationship to Prior Kinds of Imitation Training.* Margaret A. Bruce. Calgary: University of Calgary, 1970. (CTM no. 7649)
Thesis (M.Sc.)--University of Calgary, 1970.

**3493. Bryans, David Garth** *Education and Acculturation: the School in a Multicultural Setting.* David Garth Bryans Edmonton: University of Alberta, 1971. Thesis (Ph.D.)--University of Alberta, 1971.

**3494. Bryans, David Garth** *A Study of Some Environmental Influences on the Level of Educational Aspiration of Urban Grade 9 Students.* David Garth Bryans. Edmonton: University of Alberta, 1969. Thesis (M.Ed.)--University of Alberta, 1969.

**3495. Bryce, Mrs. George** *"Historical Sketch of the Charitable Institutions of Winnipeg."* Mrs. George Bryce. Historical and Scientific Society of Manitoba Transactions 54(Feb. 21, 1899): [2]-31.

**3496. Bublitz, Dorothea E.** *Life on the Dotted Line.* Dorothea E. Bublitz. New York: Vantage Press, 1960.

**3497. Buchanan, Carl J.** *"A Winterday on the Homestead."* Carl J. Buchanan. Beaver 307, 3(Winter 1976): 6-9.

**3498. Buck, Carl E.** *Public Health in Manitoba: a Report of a Study Made by the American Public Health Association.* Carl E. Buck. [S.l.]: American Public Health Association, 1941.

**3499. Buck Lake History** *Packhorse to Pavement.* Buck Lake History. Buck Lake, Alta.: Buck Lake History, 1981.

**3500. Buckland History Book Committee** *Buckland's Heritage.* Buckland History Book Committee. [S.l.]: Buckland History Book Committee, 1980.

3501. **Buckwold, A.E.** *"Acute Neonatal Neutropenia in Siblings."* A.E. Buckwold and H.E. Emson. Canadian Medical Association Journal 80, 2(Jan. 15, 1959): 116-119.

3502. **Burfield, Fred A.** *"Day of a Thousand Suns."* Fred A. Burfield. Alberta History 31, 2(Spring 1983): 33-35.

3503. **Burnside, Edith, ed.** *Legacies of Lansdowne: a Sequel.* Edith Burnside, ed. [and] Lansdowne History Book Committee. Arden, Man.: Rural Municipality of Lansdowne History Committee, 1984.

3504. **Burstall History Book Committee** *Treasured Memories: a History of Burstall and District.* Burstall History Book Committee. [S.l.: s.n., 1983].

3505. **Burt, David L.** *"A Comparative Study of Different Modes of Presentation on Efficiency of Learning and Retention."* David L. Burt amd W.D. Knill. Alberta Journal of Educational Research 16, 3(Sept. 1970): 149-156.

3506. **Byemoor History Committee** *Still God's Country: the Early History of Byemoor and Area.* Byemoor History Committee. Byemoor, Alta.: Byemoor History Committee, 1975.

3507. **Cadham, R.G.** *"Poliomyelitis in Winnipeg, 1958: Epidemiological Study, Including the Evaluation of Artificial Immunization."* R.G. Cadham and J.E. Davies. Canadian Medical Association Journal/Journal de l'Association medicale canadienne 80, 6(Mar. 15, 1959): 436-439.

3508. **Cahill, Cyril** *"Outline of a School Psychiatric Service in Manitoba."* Cyril Cahill and Dorothy M. Sokolyk. Canadian Psychiatric Association Journal/Revue de l'Association canadienne de psychiatrie 10, 5(Oct. 1965): 411.

3509. **Cairns, Phyllis Helen** *The Alberta Child Welfare Client System and the Decision-making Process.* Phyllis Helen Cairns. Calgary: University of Calgary, 1969. (CTM no. 4614)
Thesis (M.S.W.)--University of Calgary, 1969.

3510. **Calder, James** *"Aplastic Anaemia Following Sulfonamide Therapy."* James Calder, Samuel Hanson, Leslie Kovacs and Matthew Matas. Canadian Medical Association Journal 74, 7(Apr. 1, 1956): 548.

3511. **Calder School Reunion Association** *Early History of Calder School and District.* The Association. Edmonton: The Association, 1977.

3512. **Caldwell, George** *Indian Residential Schools: a Research Study of the Child Care Programs of Nine Residential Schools in Saskatchewan.* George Caldwell. Ottawa: Canadian Welfare Council, 1967. Prepared for the Department of Indian Affairs and Northern Development, Government of Canada, 1967.

3513. **Calf Robe, Ben** *Siksika: a Blackfoot Legacy.* Ben Calf Rob with Adolf and Beverly Hungry Wolf. Invermere: Good Medicine Books, 1979.

3514. **Calgary Association for Retarded Children** *Proposed School for Calgary's Retarded Children.* The Association. Calgary: The Association, 1955.

3515. **Callwood, June** *Emma.* June Callwood. Toronto: Stoddart, 1984.

3516. **Cam, Elizabeth** *"The Four Corners of Dufferin and King."* Elizabeth Cam. Manitoba Pageant 18, 1(Spring 1972): 14-19.

3517. **Cameron, Bruce** *"Animism and Artificialism in the Thinking of Grade 1 Children."* Bruce Cameron and Geoffrey Smith. Alberta Journal of Educational Research 11, 3(Sept.1965): 154-166.

3518. **Cameron, Hugh F.** *"A Case of Fracture of the Skull Complicated By Extradural Hemorrhage in an Infant Ten Months of Age."* Hugh F. Cameron. Canadian Medical Association Journal 45, 5(Nov. 1941): 442-443.

3519. **Campbell, Charles Scott H.** *"Leisure Reading in the Senior High Schools of Alberta."* C.H.S. Campbell. Alberta Journal of Educational Research 10, 1(Mar. 1964): 46-55.

3520. **Campbell, Charles Scott H.** *A Survey of Leisure Reading in the Senior High Schools of Alberta.* Charles Scott H. Campbell. Edmonton: University of Alberta, 1962.
Thesis (M.Ed.)--University of Alberta, 1962.

3521. **Campbell, Lochlan MacLean** *"Ability Grouping and Grade Nine Achievement."* L.M. Bell and W.D. Knill. Alberta Journal of Educational Research 11, 4(Dec 1965): 226-232.

3522. Campbell, Lochlan MacLean *A Study of the Relationship Between Ability Grouping and the Achievement of Grade 9 Pupils From 1956-1964.* Lochlan MacLean Campbell. Edmonton: University of Alberta, 1965.
Thesis (M.Ed.)--University of Alberta, 1965.

3523. Campbell, Maria *Halfbreed.* Maria Campbell. Toronto: McClelland and Stewart Ltd., c1973.

3524. Campbell, Morris Wilfred *Measurement of Economic Understanding of Grade 12 Students.* Morris Wilfred Campbell. Edmonton: University of Alberta, 1964.
Thesis (M.Ed.)--University of Alberta, 1964.

3525. Canada. Department of Citizenship and Immigration. Indian Affairs Branch *"Rehabilitation Services for Indians."* The Branch. Canadian Welfare 31, 7(Mar. 1956): 332-333.

3526. Canada. Department of Labour. Vocational Training Branch *A Modern Concept of Apprenticeship: the Story of Apprenticeship in Alberta.* The Branch. Ottawa: Queen's Printer, 1957.

3527. Canadian Council on Child and Family Welfare *"The Blind in Manitoba."* Canadian Council on Child and Family Welfare. Child and Family Welfare 6, 7(Mar. 1931): 63-64.

3528. Canadian Council on Child and Family Welfare *"Calgary Council on Child and Family Welfare."* Canadian Council on Child and Family Welfare. Child and Family Welfare 6, 3(July 1930): 42-43.

3529. Canadian Council on Child and Family Welfare *"Child Care, Winnipeg."* Canadian Council on Child and Family Welfare. Child and Family Welfare 10, 5(Jan. 1935): 15.

3530. Canadian Council on Child and Family Welfare *"Child Protection in Saskatchewan."* Canadian Council on Child and Family Welfare. Child and Family Welfare 7, 4(Nov. 1931): 39-42.

3531. Canadian Council on Child and Family Welfare *"The Children's Aid, Brandon, Manitoba."* Canadian Council on Child and Family Welfare. Child and Family Welfare 7, 4(Nov. 1931): 42-43.

3532. Canadian Council on Child and Family Welfare *"An Important Alberta Judgement Re The Juvenile Delinquents' Act, Canada, 1929."* Canadian Council on Child and Family Welfare. Child and Family Welfare 7, 6(Mar. 1932): 39-40.

3533. Canadian Council on Child and Family Welfare *"More County Health Units."* Canadian Council on Child and Family Welfare. Child and Family Welfare 6, 2(May 1930): 13.

3534. Canadian Council on Child and Family Welfare *"One Hundred Training School Boys."* Canadian Council on Child and Family Welfare. Child and Family Welfare 6, 6(Jan. 1931): 42-44.

3535. Canadian Council on Child and Family Welfare *"The Winnipeg Children's Aid Society."* Canadian Council on Child and Family Welfare. Child and Family Welfare 8, 1(May 1932): 24.

3536. Canadian Council on Child Welfare *"Calgary Comes Second in Empire-wide Competition."* Canadian Council on Child Welfare. Canadian Child Welfare News 4, 1(Feb. 15, 1928): 39.

3537. Canadian Council on Child Welfare *"The Manitoba Child Welfare Inquiry."* Canadian Council on Child Welfare. Child Welfare News 5, 1(Feb. 1929): 31.

3538. Canadian Council on Child Welfare *"News from the Front: Alberta."* Canadian Council on Child Welfare, Child Welfare News 6, 1(Feb. 1930): 9-10.

3539. Canadian Council on Child Welfare *"The Prairie Conference."* Canadian Council on Child Welfare. Child Welfare News 5, 3(Aug. 1929): 59-75.

3540. Canadian Council on Child Welfare *"Summary of Report of the Royal Commission of Inquiry into the Child Welfare Act of Manitoba and its Administration, 1928."* Canadian Council on Child Welfare. Child Welfare News 5, 3(Aug. 1929): 2-53.

3541. Canadian Council on Child Welfare *"The Winnipeg Children's Aid Society."* Canadian Council on Child Welfare. Child Welfare News 5, 1(Feb. 1929): 39-40.

3542. Canadian National Committee for Mental Hygiene *"Mental Hygiene Survey of the Province of Saskatchewan."* The Committee. Canadian Journal of Mental Hygiene 3, 4(Jan. 1922): 314-399.

**3543. Canadian National Committee for Mental Hygiene** *"Survey of the Province of Manitoba."* Canadian National Committee for Mental Hygiene. Canadian Journal of Mental Hygiene 1, 1(Apr. 1919): 77-82.

**3544. Canadian Welfare Council** *"Across Canada: Tuberculosis."* Canadian Welfare Council. Canadian Welfare 24, 2(June 1948): 32.

**3545. Canadian Welfare Council** *"Child Welfare Survey in Winnipeg."* Canadian Welfare Council. Canadian Welfare 18, 7(Jan. 1943): 9-11.

**3546. Canadian Welfare Council** *"The New Child Welfare Act of Manitoba."* Canadian Welfare Council. Child and Family Welfare 12, 2(July 1936): 42-44.

**3547. Canadian Welfare Council** *"Standards for Saskatchewan."* Canadian Welfare Council. Canadian Welfare 18, 1(Apr. 1942): 30.

**3548. Cando and Area History Club** *"Can do": the Pioneer's Echo.* Cando and Area History Club. Cando, Sask.: Cando and Area History Club, 1982.

**3549. Cantlon, F.M.** *Oatmeal Porridge and Green Poplar Poles: a Story of a Pioneer Family on the Prairies in the Early Years.* F.M. Cantlon. Sedgewick: Community Press, 1976.

**3550. Canwood History Book Committee** *Chronicles of Canwood and Districts.* Canwood History Book Committee. Canwood, Sask.: Canwood History Book Committee, 1981.

**3551. Carberry History Committee** *Carberry Plains: Century One, 1882-1982.* Carberry History Committee. Carberry, Man.: Carberry History Committee, 1982.

**3552. Card, B.Y.** *Metis in Alberta Society: with Special Reference to Social, Economic and Cultural Factors Associated With Persistently High Tuberculosis Incidence.* Brigham Young Card, Gordon K. Hirabayashi and Cecil L. French. Edmonton: University of Alberta Bookstore, 1963.

**3553. Card, B.Y.** *School Achievement in Rural Alberta: an Exploratory Study of Social and Psychological Factors.* B.Y. Card and W.B. Dockrell. Edmonton: Alberta Teachers' Association, 1966.

**3554. Card, B.Y.** *"Teachers' Perception of Language Factors in the Achievement of Western Canadian Rural School Pupils."* B.Y. Card. McGill Journal of Education 1, 1(Spring 1966): 134-138.

**3555. Cardale Reunion Book Committee** *Footprints & Chalk Dust.* Cardale Reunion Book Committee. [S.l.]: Cardale Reunion Book Committee, [1981].

**3556. Carlson, James Eugene** *The MAC as a Culture-reduced Measure of Intellectual Potential.* James Eugene Carlson. Edmonton: University of Alberta, 1966.
Thesis (M.Ed.)--University of Alberta, 1966.

**3557. Carmichael, Anne** *"A Survey of Reading Achievement in Alberta Schools."* Anne Carmichael. Alberta Journal of Educational Research 1, 1(Mar. 1955): 18-33.

**3558. Carmichael, Anne** *A Survey of the Achievement of Alberta School Children in Reading.* Anne Carmichael. Edmonton: University of Alberta, 1954.
Thesis (M.Ed.)--University of Alberta, 1954.

**3559. Caron, George Alfred** *The Physician and Physical Child Abuse: Management and Control in the Province of Alberta.* George Alfred Caron. Calgary: University of Calgary, 1971. (CTM no. 10047)
Thesis (M.S.W.)--University of Calgary, 1971.

**3560. Caron History Book Committee** *From Buffalo Trails to Blacktop: a History of the R.M. of Caron no. 162.* Caron History Book Committee. Caron, Sask.: Caron History Book Committee, 1982.

**3561. Carpenter, Jock** *Fifty Dollar Bride: Marie Rose Smith, a Chronicle of Metis Life in the 19th Century.* Jock Carpenter. Sidney: Gray's Publishing Ltd., 1977.

**3562. Carr, Kevin James** *A Historical Survey of Education in Early Blackfoot Indian Culture and Its Implications for Indian Schools.* Kevin James Carr. Edmonton: University of Alberta, 1968.
Thesis (M.Ed.)--University of Alberta, 1968.

**3563. Carran, Raymond Clarence** *A Study of Student and Adult Attitudes Towards the Technical Electives Program in Edmonton Composite High Schools.* Raymond Clarence Carran. Edmonton: University of Alberta, 1961.
Thesis (M.Ed.)--University of Alberta, 1961.

**3564. Carter, D.J.** *"The Railway Mission: Regina."* D.J. Carter. Journal of the Canadian Church Historical Society 10, 4(Dec. 1968): 202-216.

**3565. Carter, William A.** *"Ingestion of Open Safety Pin in Infant."* Wm. A. Carter. Canadian Medical Association Journal 60, 3(Mar. 1949): 292.

**3566. Carver, Clifford** *Aural and Visual Factors in Word Recognition.* Clifford Carver. Calgary: University of Calgary, 1971.
Thesis (Ph.D.)--University of Calgary, 1971.

**3567. Cassell, Wilfred A.** *"Brief Communications and Clinical Notes: Psychiatric Services in Saskatchewan Under Medicare."* Wilfred A. Cassell, Colin M. Smith and Maggie Rankin. Canadian Psychiatric Association Journal/Revue de l'Association canadienne de psychiatrie 15, 1(Feb. 1970): 63-71.

**3568. Caswell, Maryanne** *"Dear Grandma."* Maryanne Caswell. Saskatoon: Western Producer Prairie Books, c1982. In Christmas in the West, p. 81. Edited by Hugh A. Dempsey.

**3569. Caswell, Maryanne** *Pioneer Girl.* Maryanne Caswell. Toronto: McGraw-Hill Company of Canada, c1964.

**3570. Cathcart, W. George** *An Investigation of Some of the Values Held by High School Students and their Teachers.* William George Cathcart. Edmonton: University of Alberta, 1967.
Thesis (M.Ed.)--University of Alberta, 1967.

**3571. Cathcart, W. George** *The Relationship Between Primary Students' Rationalization of Conservation and Their Mathematical Ability and Achievement.* William George Cathcart. Edmonton: University of Alberta, 1969.
Thesis (Ph.D.)--University of Alberta, 1969.

**3572. Cayford, Elmer H.** *Barefoot Days.* Elmer H. Cayford. Saskatoon: Western Producer, 1974.

**3573. Celebrate Saskatchewan 1980 History Book Committee** *R.M. 318 Herschel, Stranraer: From Then Until Now.* Celebrate Saskatchewan 1980 History Book Committee. [S.l.]: Celebrate Saskatchewan 1980 History Book Committee, 1981.

**3574. Chabassol, David J.** *"Correlates of Academic Underachievement in Male Adolescents."* D.J. Chabassol. Alberta Journal of Educational Research 5, 2(June 1959): 130-146.

**3575. Chabassol, David J.** *Correlates of Academic Underachievement in Male Adolescents.* David Johnstone Chabassol. Edmonton: University of Alberta, 1959.
Thesis (Ph.D.)--University of Alberta, 1959.

**3576. Chafe. J.W.** *An Apple for the Teacher: a Centennial History of the Winnipeg School Division.* J.W. Chafe. Winnipeg: Winnipeg School Division No. 1, c1967.
Illustrations by Edward Phillips.

**3577. Chalmers, James McNish** *An Analysis of Results Obtained on the WISC by Mentally Superior Subjects.* James McNish Chalmers. Edmonton: University of Alberta, 1953.
Thesis (M.Ed.)--University of Alberta, 1953.

**3578. Chalmers, John Watt** *A Study of the Relationship Between Ability in Formal Grammar and Ability in Literary and Linguistic Fields.* John Watt Chalmers. Edmonton: University of Alberta, 1941.
Thesis (M.Ed.)--University of Alberta, 1941.

**3579. Chalmers, John West** *"A Cooperative Study of High School Extra-curricular Activities."* J.W. Chalmers and R.E. Rees. Alberta Journal of Educational Research 4, 2(June 1958): 84-99.

**3580. Chalmers, John West** *"The School Superintendant: a Memoir."* John W. Chalmers. Alberta History 38, 3(Summer 1990): 12-15.

**3581. Chalmers, John West** *Schools of the Foothills Province: the Story of Public Education in Alberta.* John W. Chalmers. [Toronto]: University of Toronto Press, c1967.

**3582. Chalmers, John West** *A Study of the Effective and Recognized Vocabularies of Alberta Students in Grades 7 to 12.* John West Chalmers. Edmonton: University of Alberta, 1935.
Thesis (M.A.)--University of Alberta, 1935.

**3583. Chapman, Robert Stanley** *"Achievement and Underachievement in English Language 10 in an Alberta Composite High School."* Robert Stanley Chapman. Alberta Journal of Educational Research 5, 1(Mar. 1959): 41-49.

3584. **Chapman, Robert Stanley** *A Study of Achievement and Underachievement in English Language 10 in an Alberta Composite High School.* Robert Stanley Chapman. Edmonton: University of Alberta, 1958.
Thesis (M.Ed.)--University of Alberta, 1958.

3585. **Chapman, Terry L.** *"Film Censorship in Lethbridge, 1918-1920."* Terry L. Chapman. Alberta History 33, 1(Winter 1985): 1-8.

3586. **Chapman, Terry L.** *"Sex Crimes in the West, 1890-1920: an Overview."* Terry L. Chapman. [Ottawa: Carleton University, 1987]. In Papers Presented at the 1987 Canadian Law in History Conference, vol. 2, pp. 1-46.

3587. **Chapman, Terry L.** *Sex Crimes in Western Canada, 1890-1920.* Terry L. Chapman. Edmonton: University of Alberta, 1984. (CTM no. 67279)
Thesis (Ph.D.)--University of Alberta, 1984.

3588. **Charette, Anne-Louise** *Personality and Study-habits Correlates of Achievement Among Lower Socioeconomic Class Boys.* Anne-Louise Charette. Edmonton: University of Alberta, 1968.
Thesis (M.Ed.)--University of Alberta, 1968.

3589. **Charette, Guillaume** *Vanishing Spaces: (Memoirs of a Prairie Metis).* Guillaume Charette. Winnipeg: Editions Bois-Brules, 1980.
Translated by Ray Ellenwood.

3590. **Charlebois, Peter** *The Life of Louis Riel.* Peter Charlebois. Toronto: N.C. Press Ltd., c1975.

3591. **Charlton, Mabel, comp.** *More Griffin Prairie Wool.* Mabel Charlton, comp. [S.l.: s.n., 1970].

3592. **Charuk, Dorothy J.** *Group Counselling With Upper-elementary School Students: an Experimental Study.* Dorothy J. Charuk. Edmonton: University of Alberta, 1970.
Thesis (M.Ed.)-- University of Alberta, 1970.

3593. **Charyk, John C.** *The Biggest Day of the Year: the Old-time School Christmas Concert.* John C. Charyk. Saskatoon: Western Producer Prairie Books, c1985.

3594. **Charyk, John C.** *The Little White Schoolhouse.* John C. Charyk. Saskatoon: Prairie Books, The Western Producer, c1968.

3595. **Charyk, John C.** *Pulse of the Community.* John C. Charyk. Saskatoon: Prairie Books, The Western Producer, c1972.

3596. **Charyk, John C.** *Syrup Pails and Gopher Tails: Memories of the One-Room School House.* John C. Charyk. Saskatoon: Western Producer Prairie Books, 1983.

3597. **Charyk, John C.** *Those Bittersweet Schooldays.* John C. Charyk. Saskatoon: Western Producer Prairie Books, c1977.

3598. **Charyk, John C.** *When the School Horse Was King: a Tribute to Faithful Friends and Companions.* John C. Charyk. Saskatoon: Western Producer Prairie Books, c1988.

3599. **Chase, Lillian, A.** *"Diabetes Mellitus: Problem of Its Control."* Lillian A. Chase. Canadian Medical Association Journal 44, 3(Mar. 1941): 250-255.

3600. **Chater Centennial History Committee** *Memoirs of an Era: Chater, 1881-1981.* Chater Centennial History Committee. [S.l.: Chater Centennial History Committee, 1981].

3601. **Chatwin, A.E.** *The Motion Picture Film in the Teaching of Geography: an Experimental Study.* A.E. Chatwin. Toronto: University of Toronto, 1938.
Thesis (D.Paed.)--University of Toronto, 1938.

3602. **Cherry Grove History Committee** *Memories Past to Present: a History of Beaver Crossing and Surrounding District.* Cherry Grove History Committee. Cherry Grove, Alta.: Cherry Grove History Committee, 1981.

3603. **Chester, Sheila J.** *An Experimental Study of the Effects of Perceptual Training on the Art Work of Children with an Indefinite Painting Style.* Sheila J. Chester. Calgary: University of Calgary, 1967.
Thesis (M.Ed.)--University of Calgary, 1967.

3604. **Chestermere Historical Society** *The Changing Scene: a Supplement to Saddles, Sleighs and Sadirons.* Chestermere Historical Society. [Chestermere, Alta.: Chestermere Historical Society], 1978.

3605. **Chestermere Historical Society** *Saddles, Sleighs and Sadirons.* Chestermere Historical Society. [S.l.]: Chestermere Historical Society, c1971.

**3606. Chidley, Nadine** *"The Program For Gifted Children in the Winnipeg School Division."* Nadine Chidley. Canadian Education and Research Digest 2, 1(Mar. 1962): 46-54.

**3607. Chidley, Nadine** *"Special Education for the Slow Learner."* Nadine Chidley. Canadian Education and Research Digest 3, 3(Sept. 1963): 204-215.

**3608. Childs, Gertrude** *"Child Placing and Supervision on a Provincial Basis."* Gertrude Childs. In Proceedings of Sixth Annual Canadian Conference on Child Welfare 1927, pp. 116-118.

**3609. Chislett, Bernice Yvonne** *Sequence Perception, Finger Differentiation Ability and Reading Achievement in Achieving and Non-Achieving Readers.* Bernice Yvonne Chislett. Edmonton: University of Alberta, 1970.
Thesis (M.Ed.)–University of Alberta, 1970.

**3610. Chown, Bruce** *"The Place of Early Induction in the Management of Erythroblastosis Fetalis."* Bruce Chown. Canadian Medical Association Journal 78, 4(Feb. 15, 1958): 252-256.

**3611. Chown, Bruce** *"Severe Haemolytic Disease of the Newborn Due Probably to the Combined Action of Anti-A and Anti-S."* Bruce Chown, Marion Lewis and Brian Best. Canadian Medical Association Journal 77, 1(July 1, 1957): 31-34.

**3612. Chown, Bruce** *"Transfusion of Girls and Women Can Kill Their Babies: a Note Addressed More to Surgeons and Anaesthetists But Applicable to Others."* Bruce Chown. Canadian Medical Association Journal 78, 3(Feb. 1, 1958): 208.

**3613. Cipywnyk, Sonia** *Educational Implications for Ukrainian-English Childhood Bilingualism in Saskatchewan.* Sonia V. Cipywnyk. Saskatoon: University of Saskatchewan, 1968.
Thesis (M.Ed.)–University of Saskatchewan, 1968.

**3614. Clark, James Boyd** *A History of Vocational Education in the Calgary Public School System, 1900-1982.* James Boyd Clark. Edmonton: University of Alberta, 1982. (CTM no. 60351)
Thesis (M.Ed.)–University of Alberta, 1982.

**3615. Clarke, G.B.** *"Domestic Relations and Problems of Child Dependency: a Study of Broken Homes."* G.B. Clarke. In Proceedings and Papers Fourth Annual Conference on Canadian Child Welfare 1923, pp. 183-190.

**3616. Clarke, S.C.T.** *"The Effect of Grouping on Variability in Achievement at the Grade 3 Level."* S.C.T. Clarke. Alberta Journal of Educational Research 4, 3(Sept. 1958): 162-171.

**3617. Clifton, Rodney A.** *Self Concept and Attitudes Towards Education of Indian and Non-Indian Students Enrolled in an Integrated School.* Rodney A. Clifton. Edmonton: University Of Alberta, 1971.
Thesis (M.Ed.)–University of Alberta, 1971.

**3618. Climenhaga, Clarence Eugena** *A Survey of Arithmetical Achievement of Grade 8 Pupils in Alberta Schools.* Clarence Eugena Climenhaga. Edmonton: University of Alberta, 1955.
Thesis (M.Ed.)–University of Alberta, 1955.
Author published article with same title in Alberta Journal of Educational Research 1, 4(Dec. 1955): 35-47.

**3619. Coaldale Historical Society** *Coaldale: Gem of the West 1900-1983.* Coaldale Historical Society. Coaldale, Alta.: Coaldale Historical Society, 1983.

**3620. Coalhurst History Society** *Our Treasured Heritage: a History of Coalhurst and District.* Coalhurst History Society. Lethbridge, Alta.: Coalhurst History Society, 1984.

**3621. Coats, Douglas** *"Calgary: the Private Schools, 1900-16."* Douglas Coats. Calgary: University of Calgary, McClelland and Stewart West, 1975. In Frontier Calgary: Town, City and Region 1875-1914, pp. 141-152. Edited by Anthony W. Rasporich and Henry C. Klassen.

**3622. Colbeck, J.C.** *"An Extensive Outbreak of Staphylococcal Infections in Maternity Units: the Use of Bacteriophage Typing in Investigation and Control."* J.C. Colbeck. Canadian Medical Association Journal 61, 6(Dec. 1949): 557-568.

**3623. Cole, P.J.E.** *"Family Courts: Their Nature and Function."* P.J.E. Cole. Manitoba Law Journal 4, 2(1971): 317-346.

**3624. Collins, Robert** *Butter Down the Well: Reflections of a Canadian Childhood.* Robert Collins. Saskatoon: Western Producer Prairie Books, c1980.

**3625. Colonsay History Book Committee** *Milestones and Memories: Colonsay and Meacham Districts, 1905-1980.* Colonsay History Book Committee. Colonsay, Sask.: RM 342 Celebrate Saskatchewan 1980 Committees, 1980.

3626. **Conn, Gertrude Mary** *Vocabulary Proficiency of Bilingual Grade 9 Students in Beaver County of Alberta.* Gertrude Mary Conn. Edmonton: University of Alberta, 1964.
Thesis (M.Ed.)--University of Alberta, 1964.

3627. **Conquest, George Rionzi** *A Survey of English Language Achievement in Grades Four and Seven in Selected Alberta Schools.* George Rionzi Conquest. Edmonton: University of Alberta, 1954.
Thesis (M.Ed.)--University of Alberta, 1954.

3628. **Cook, Dean** *A History of Educational Institutions in Mormon Communities of Southern Alberta.* Dean Cook. Edmonton: University of Alberta, 1958.
Thesis (M.Ed.)--University of Alberta, 1958.

3629. **Cook, G.R.** *"Church, Schools and Politics in Manitoba, 1903-12."* G.R. Cook. Canadian Historical Review 39, 1(Mar. 1958): 1-23.

3630. **Cooke, Stuart Wesley** *A Study of the Relationship Between Selected Teacher Characteristics and Student Achievement in Traditional and Modern Mathematics.* Stuart Wesley Cooke. Calgary: University of Calgary, 1966.
Thesis (M.Ed.)--University of Calgary, 1966.

3631. **Cooper, Barry** *Alexander Kennedy Isbister: a Respectable Critic of the Honourable Company.* Barry Cooper. Ottawa: Carleton University Press, 1988.

3632. **Cormack, Barbara** *Landmarks: a History of the Girl Guides of Alberta.* Barbara Cormack. Edmonton: Girl Guides of Canada, Alberta Council, 1968.

3633. **Coronach Historical Committee** *From the Turning of the Sod: the Story of the Early Settlers in the R.M. of Hart Butte no. 11.* Coronach Historical Committee. Winnipeg: Intercollegiate Press, 1980.

3634. **Coronation T and C Gold Age Club** *In the Beginning: a History of Coronation, Throne, Federal and Fleet Districts.* Coronation T and C Golden Age Club. Coronation, Alta.: Coronation T and C Golden Age Club, 1979.

3635. **Corrigan, Cameron** *"Infantile Cortical Hyperostosis: Report of a Case in an Indian Infant."* Cameron Corrigan and R.B. Lynn. Canadian Medical Association Journal 79, 1(July 1, 1958): 41-43.

3636. **Cosens, Grace V.** *An Experimental Study of the Effect of Training in Auditory Discrimination on Reading Achievement in Grade One.* Grace Velina Cosens. Edmonton: University of Alberta, 1968.
Thesis (M.Ed.)--University of Alberta, 1968.

3637. **Coull, William H.** *"A Normative Survey of Reading Achievement of Alberta Children in Relation to Intelligence, Sex, Bilingualism and Grade Placement."* William H. Coull. Alberta Journal of Educational Research 2, 1(Mar. 1956): 18-29.

3638. **Coull, William H.** *A Normative Survey of Reading Achievement of Alberta Children in Relation to Intelligence, Sex, Bilingualism and Grade Placement.* William Henry Coull. Edmonton: University of Alberta, 1956.
Thesis (M.Ed.)--University of Alberta, 1956.

3639. **Coulson, Robert Joseph** *Educational and Occupational Aspirations and Expectations of Grade Eleven Business Education Students in Edmonton.* Robert Joseph Coulson. Edmonton: University of Alberta, 1969.
Thesis (M.Ed.)--University of Alberta, 1969.

3640. **Coulter, Rebecca** *Alberta's Department of Neglected Children, 1909-1929: a Case Study in Child Saving.* Rebecca Coulter. Edmonton: University of Alberta, 1977. (CTM no. 34321)
Thesis (M.Ed.)--University of Alberta, 1977.

3641. **Coulter, Rebecca** *"Between School and Marriage: a Case Study Approach to Young Women's Work in Early Twentieth-century Canada."* Rebecca Priegert Coulter. History of Education Review 18, 2(1989): 21-31.

3642. **Coulter, Rebecca** *""Not to Punish But to Reform": Juvenile Delinquency and Children's Protection Act in Alberta, 1909-1929."* Rebecca Coulter. Calgary: Detselig Enterprises Ltd., 1982. In Studies in Childhood History: a Canadian Perspective, pp. 167-184. Edited by Patricia T. Rooke and R.L. Schnell.

3643. **Coulter, Rebecca** *Teenagers in Edmonton, 1921-1931: Experiences of Gender and Class.* Rebecca Priegert Coulter. Edmonton: University of Alberta, 1987. (CTM no. 37610)
Thesis (Ph.D.)--University of Alberta, 1987.

**3644. Coulter, Rebecca** *"The Working Young of Edmonton. 1921-1931."* Rebecca Coulter. Toronto: McClelland and Stewart, c1982. In Childhood and Family in Canadian History, pp. 143-159. Edited by Joy Parr.

**3645. Coutts, H.T.** *The Relation Between the Reading Competence of Alberta's Ninth Grade Pupils in Four Content Fields and Their Achievement in Those Fields.* Herbert Thomas Coutts. Duluth, Min.: University of Minnesota, [1952].
Thesis (Ph.D.)--University of Minnesota, 1951.

**3646. Coutts, H.T.** *"A Study of the Written Composition of a Representative Sample of Alberta Grade Four and Grade Seven Pupils."* H.T. Coutts. Alberta Journal of Educational Research 1, 2(June 1955): 5-18.

**3647. Cowan, W.D.** *"Dental Caries in School Children and Dental Inspection."* W.D. Cowan. Public Health Journal 4, 11(Nov. 1913): 602-605.

**3648. Cox, Barbara J.** *Summer of Childhood.* Barbara J. Cox. [S.l.]: The Author, 1978.

**3649. Craig, Greta** *"Prairie Life: an Oral History of Greta Craig."* Greta Craig and Marney Allen. Atlantis 7, 2(Spring 1982): 89-102.

**3650. Creamer, David Gordon** *Moral Education: a Critical Evaluation of a Jesuit High School Values Program.* David G. Creamer. Toronto: University of Toronto, 1982.
Thesis (Ed.D.)--University of Toronto, 1982.

**3651. Crescent Heights School** *Crescent Heights High School, 50th Anniversary, 1915-1965.* Crescent Heights School. Calgary: [s.n.], 1965.

**3652. Cronin, Mary** *Construct Validity and the Assessment of Reading Processes.* Mary Christina Cronin. Edmonton: University of Alberta, 1982. (CTM no. 60368)
Thesis (Ph.D.)--University of Alberta, 1982.

**3653. Cropley, A.J.** *"Creativity, Intelligence and Achievement."* A.J. Cropley. Alberta Journal of Educational Research 13, 1(Mar. 1967): 51-58.

**3654. Cropley, A.J.** *Originality, Intelligence and Personality.* Arthur John Cropley. Edmonton: University of Alberta, 1965.
Thesis (Ph.D.)--University of Alberta, 1965.

**3655. Cropley, A.J.** *"The Relatedness of Divergent and Convergent Thinking."* A.J. Cropley. Alberta Journal of Educational Research 11, 3(Sept. 1965): 176-181.

**3656. Cropley, A.J.** *Socioeconomic Status and the Development of Intelligence.* Arthur John Cropley. Edmonton: University of Alberta, 1963.
Thesis (M.Ed.)--University of Alberta, 1963.

**3657. Crossley, H.** *"Malaria in a Saskatchewan-born Infant."* H. Crossley. Canadian Medical Association Journal 77, 3(Aug. 1, 1957): 225-226.

**3658. Cumming, Gordon R.** *"A Fitness Performance Test for School Children and Its Correlation With Physical Working Capacity and Maximal Oxygen Uptake."* Gordon R. Cumming and Rhoda Keynes. Canadian Medical Association Journal/Journal de l'Association medicale canadienne 96, 18(May 6, 1967): 1262-1269.

**3659. Cumming, Gordon R.** *"Working Capacity of Normal Children Tested on a Bicycle Ergometer."* Gordon R. Cumming and P.M. Cumming. Canadian Medical Association Journal/Journal de l'Association medicale canadienne 88, 7(Feb. 16, 1963): 351-355.

**3660. Cunnings, T.A.J.** *The Saga of Doctor Thor: Paul H.T. Thorlakson, C.C., M.D., a Biography.* T.A.J. Cunnings. Winnipeg: University of Manitoba, 1986.

**3661. Cupar Historical Committee** *Cupar District: Taking Root and Growing.* Cupar Historical Committee. [S.l.]: Cupar Historical Committee, [1981].

**3662. Curnisky, Savelia** *"How to Teach a Ukrainian."* Savelia Curnisky. Regina: Canadian Plains Research Center, 1978. In Ethnic Canadians: Culture and Education, pp. 359-369. Edited by Martin L. Kovacs.

**3663. Czuboka, Michael** *Ukrainian Canadian, Eh?: the Ukrainians of Canada and Elsewhere as Perceived by Themselves and Others.* Michael Czuboka. Winnipeg: Communigraphics/Printers Aid Group, 1983.

**3664. Czumer, William A.** *Recollections About the Life of the First Ukrainian Settlers in Canada.* William A. Czumer. Louis T. Laychuck, trans. Edmonton: Canadian Institute of Ukrainian Studies, c1981.

**3665. D'Aoust, Bernard Rene** *Concept Attainment as a Function of Stress, Personality and Sex.* Bernard Rene D'Aoust. Edmonton: University of Alberta, 1964.
Thesis (M.Ed.)--University of Alberta, 1964.

**3666. D.M.C.S. History Book Committee** *A Homesteader's Dream: History of Deer Ridge, Lone Spruce, Mayview, Cookson, Sturgeon River.* D.M.C.S. History Book. Mayview, Sask.: D.M.C.S. History Book Committee, 1981.

**3667. Dahl, Carl Bjarnason** *"A Boy's Winnipeg Decade, 1910-1920."* Carl Bjarnason Dahl. Icelandic Canadian 39, 1(Autumn 1980): 12-16.

**3668. Dahlie, Jorgen** *"Learning on the Frontier: Scandinavian Immigrants and Education in Western Canada."* Jorgen Dahlie. Canadian and International Education/Education canadienne et internationale 1, 2(Dec. 1972): 56-66.

**3669. Dahlie, Jorgen** *"Scandinavian Experiences on the Prairies, 1890-1920: the Frederiksens of Nokomis."* Jorgen Dahlie. Calgary: Comprint Pub. Co., University of Calgary, c1977. In The Settlement of the West, pp. 102-113. Edited by Howard Palmer.

**3670. Dales, Alice H.** *"Closing a Children's Institution in Saskatchewan."* Alice H. Dales. Canadian Welfare 30, 6(Dec. 1954): 39-43.

**3671. Dalgleish, H.D.** *"Wound of Penis."* H.A. Dalgleish. Canadian Medical Association Journal 60, 3(Mar. 1949): 307.

**3672. Dansom, Diane** *""The Saskatchewan Lily": a Biography of Ethel Catherwood."* Diane Dansom. Saskatchewan History 41, 3(Autumn 1988): 81-98.

**3673. Darby, G.C.** *"Saskatchewan Recreational Movement."* G.C. Darby. Canadian Welfare 21, 5(Oct. 1945): 25-30.

**3674. Davey, P.W.** *"So-Called Eosinophilic Granuloma of Bone."* P.W. Davey, G.M. Martin and C.F. Hyndman. Canadian Medical Association Journal 76, 8(Apr. 15, 1957): 623-627.

**3675. Davidson and District Historical Society** *Prairie Tapestry: Davidson, Girvin and District.* Davidson and District Historical Society. Davidson, Sask.: Davidson and District Historical Society, 1983.

**3676. Davies, Colin** *Louis Riel and the New Nation.* Colin Davies. Agincourt: Book Society of Canada, 1980.

**3677. Davis, May** *"A Pinafored Printer."* M. Davis. Saskatchewan History 9, 2(Spring 1956): 63-69.

**3678. Davis, Teresa** *Imitation and Social Reinforcement in a Classroom Setting for Institutionalized Delinquents.* Teresa Davis. Edmonton: University of Alberta, 1971.
Thesis (M.Ed.)--University of Alberta, 1971.

**3679. Davison, R.O.** *"Encephalomyelitis in Saskatchewan, 1941: Preliminary Report."* R.O. Davison. Canadian Public Health Journal 33, 8(Aug. 1942): 388-398.

**3680. Daysland History Book Society** *Along the Crocus Trail: a History of Daysland and District.* Daysland History Book Society. Daysland, Alta.: Daysland History Book Society, 1982.

**3681. de Groot, H.B.S.** *"Myiasis in Canada."* H.B.S. de Groot. Canadian Medical Association Journal 75, 8(Oct. 15, 1956): 673-674.

**3682. DeBrincat, Josephine** *"The Nurse's Responsibility in School Health Services: Rural Aspects."* Josephine DeBrincat. Canadian Nurse 48, 4(Apr. 1952): 295-297.

**3683. Defresne, L.W.** *A Study of the Incidence, Nature and Cause of Football Injuries in the City of Edmonton During 1969.* L.W. Defresne. Edmonton: University of Alberta, 1971.
Thesis (M.Ed.)--University of Alberta, 1971.

**3684. Del Bonita Historical Society** *Heritage of the High Country: a History of Del Bonita and Surrounding Districts.* Del Bonita Historical Society. Del Bonita, Alta.: Del Bonita Historical Society, 1981.

**3685. Delaney, John Oliver** *Structure of Intellectual and Divergent Production Abilities in the Lower Intellectual Range.* John Oliver Delaney. Edmonton: University of Alberta, 1970. (CTM no. 6700)
Thesis (Ph.D.)--University of Alberta, 1970.

**3686. Deloraine History Book Committee** *Deloraine Scans a Century: a History of Deloraine and District, 1880-1980.* Deloraine History Book Committee. Deloraine, Man: Deloraine History Book Committee, 1980.

**3687. Dempsey, Hugh A.** *"Games Native Children Played: How Native Children Made the Most of Winter."* Hugh A. Dempsey. Glenbow 7, 1(Jan./Feb. 1987): 10-11.

**3688. Dempsey, Hugh A.** *""Tis the Season..."*" Hugh A. Dempsey. Saskatoon: Western Producer Prairie Books, c1982. In Christmas in the West, pp. 167-172. Edited by Hugh A. Dempsey.

**3689. Dempsey, Lotta** *No Life for a Lady.* Lotta Dempsey. Don Mills: Musson Book Company, c1976.

**3690. Denny, James D.** *The Organization of Public Education in Saskatchewan.* James D. Denny. Toronto: University of Toronto, 1929.
Thesis (D.Paed.)--University of Toronto, 1929.

**3691. DePape, A.J.** *"Moniliasis Associated with Staphylococcal Infection after Antibiotic Therapy."* A.J. DePape. Canadian Medical Association Journal 80, 3(Feb. 1, 1959): 205-207.

**3692. DePape, A.J.** *"Staphylococcal Pneumonia and Pyoderma in Infancy."* A.J. De Pape and D.S. McEwen. Canadian Medical Association Journal 65, 5(Nov. 1951): 439-447.

**3693. Deverell, A. Fred** *"A Study of the Effects of the "Unified Phonics Method" in Teaching Reading in Grade 1."* A. Fred Deverell. Alberta Journal of Educational Research 9, 4(Dec. 1963): 195-224.

**3694. Dewar, John** *"Saskatchewan's Basketball Beginnings (1891-1922)."* John Dewar. Saskatchewan History 41, 3(Autumn 1988): 99-112.

**3695. Dewitt, Winnifred Anne** *A Study of Value Orientations and Academic Achievement.* Winnifred Anne Dewitt. Calgary: University of Calgary, 1970.
Thesis (M.Ed.)--University of Calgary, 1970.

**3696. Dick, Cornelius Lorne** *A Study of Social Class Differences in Language Expression: an Analysis of Some Written Samples.* Cornelius Lorne Dick. Calgary: University of Calgary, 1968.
Thesis (M.Ed.)--University of Calgary, 1968.

**3697. Dickason, Olive Patricia** *"From "One Nation" in the Northeast to "New Nation" in the Northwest: a Look at the Emergence of the Metis."* Olive Patricia Dickason. Winnipeg: University of Manitoba Press, c1985. In The New Peoples: Being and Becoming Metis in North America, pp. 19-36. Edited by

Jacqueline Peterson and Jennifer S.H. Brown.

**3698. Dickinson, Mary Ruth** *Use of Free Time by Grades Nine to Twelve Students in Two Small Roman Catholic Separate Schools.* Sister Mary Ruth Dickinson. Edmonton: University of Alberta, 1965.
Thesis (M.Ed.)--University of Alberta, 1965.

**3699. Dickson, L.M.** *"I Went Home Again."* L.M. Dickson. Queen's Quarterly 78, 2(Summer 1971): 268-273.

**3700. Dickson, Sharon Lorane** *Recognition and Application of Vowel Generalizations by Grade Four Children.* Sharon Lorane Dickson. Edmonton: University of Alberta, 1970.
Thesis (M.Ed.)--University of Alberta, 1970.

**3701. Dinmore Historical Committee** *Dynamic Dinsmore, 1979.* Dinsmore Historical Committee. Dinsmore, Sask.: Dinsmore Historical Committee, 1979.

**3702. Dixon, J.M.S.** *"Diphtheria Bacilli Isolated in Alberta in 1967 From the Throat, Nose, Ears and Skin."* J.M.S. Dixon and Shirley Thorsteinson. Canadian Medical Association Journal/Journal de l'Association medicale canadienne 101, 4(Aug. 23, 1969): 204-207.

**3703. Dockrell, W.B.** *"The Correlates of Second Language Learning by Young Children."* W.B. Dockrell and J.F. Brosseau. Alberta Journal of Educational Research 13, 4(Dec. 1967): 295-298.

**3704. Dockrell, W.B.** *"The Use of Wechsler Intelligence Scale for Children in the Diagnosis of Retarded Readers."* W.B. Dockrell. Alberta Journal of Educational Research 6, 2(June 1960): 86-91.

**3705. Domain Women's Institute, comp.** *Down Memory Lane: a History of the Domain Community, 1876-1967.* Domain Women's Institute. [S.l.]: Domain Women's Institute, 1967.

**3706. Dominique-de-Marie, Sister** *An Investigation of the Teaching of French to English Speaking Pupils of Grades 1 to 8 of Alberta and Saskatchewan Schools.* Sister Dominique-de-Marie. Edmonton: University of Alberta, 1962.
Thesis (M.Ed.)--University of Alberta, 1962.

**3707. Donovan, C.R.** *"Some Epidemiological Features of Poliomyelitis and Encephalitis, Manitoba, 1941."* C.R. Donovan and Maxwell Bowman. Canadian Public Health Journal 33, 6(June 1942): 246-257.

**3708. Dooley, Lily Bernadette** *Self Concept of English- and French-speaking High School Canadians: a Comparative Study.* Lily Bernadette Dooley. Calgary: University of Calgary, 1969. (CTM no. 4015)
Thesis (M.Ed.)--University of Calgary, 1969.

**3709. Douglas, Molly** *Going West with Annabelle.* Molly Douglas. Toronto: Nelson, Foster & Scott Ltd., c1976.

**3710. Downey, Evelyn** *"The Child Guidance Clinic of Greater Winnipeg."* Evelyn Downey. Icelandic Canadian 35, 2(Winter 1976): 10-14.

**3711. Downey, Lawrence W.** *The Small High School in Alberta: a Report of an Investigation.* Lawrence William Lorne Downey. Edmonton: Alberta School Trustees' Association, 1965.

**3712. Dreisziger, N.F.** *Struggle and Hope: the Hungarian-Canadian Experience.* N.F. Dreisziger, with M.L. Kovacs, Paul Body, and Bennett Kovig. Toronto: McClelland and Stewart Ltd., 1982.

**3713. Drewe, Fred Harold** *A Comparative Survey of the Provision of Public Education for Slow-Learning and Mentally Handicapped Children in North Dakota and Manitoba from 1900 to 1940.* Fred Harold Drewe. Ann Arbor, Mi.: Michigan State University, 1976.
Thesis (Ph.D.) -- Michigan State University, 1976.

**3714. Driben, Paul** *We Are Metis: the Ethnography of a Halfbreed Community in Northern Alberta.* Paul Driben. New York: AMS Press, 1985.
Photoreproduction of the author's Ph.D. thesis presented at the University of Minnesota in 1975.

**3715. Driver and District History Book Committee** *Along the Buffalo Coulee: History of Driver, Victory, Teo Lake.* Driver and District History Book Committee. Kindersley, Sask.: Driver and District History Book Committee, [1978].

**3716. Dryden, Murray** *With God Nothing is Impossible: a Canadian Life.* Murray Dryden. Markham: Fitzhenry and Whiteside, c1985.

**3717. Duddridge, Lew** *The Best 70 Years of My Life: It's All Downhill From Here.* Lew Duddridge. Victoria: Orca Book Publishers, c1988.

**3718. Dueck, Susan Elaine** *The Methodist Indian Day School and Indian Communities in Northern Manitoba 1890-1925.* Susan Elaine Dueck. Winnipeg: University of Manitoba, 1986. (CTM no. 33590)
Thesis (M.A.)--University of Manitoba, 1986.

**3719. Dumont, Fred J.** *Some Factors which Distinguish Early School Leavers from High School Graduates in the High Prairie School Division No. 48.* Fred J. Dumont. Edmonton: University of Alberta, 1971.
Thesis (M.Ed.)--University of Alberta, 1971.

**3720. Duncan, Chester** *Wanna Fight, Kid?* Chester Duncan. Winnipeg: Queenston House, c1975.

**3721. Duncan, Neil F.** *"Accidents in Childhood."* Neil F. Duncan. Canadian Medical Association Journal 78, 8(Apr. 15, 1958): 575-579.

**3722. Dundas, Howard** *Wrinkled Arrows: Good Old Days in Winnipeg.* Howard Dundas. Winnipeg: Queenston House, c1980.

**3723. Dundurn and District Historical Committee** *Dundurn Memories.* Dundurn and District Historical Committee. Dundurn, Sask.: Dundurn and District Historical Committee, 1982.

**3724. Dunlop, G.M.** *"Further Evidence on the Control of Individual Differences in the Classroom."* G.M. Dunlop. Alberta Journal of Educational Research 3, 2(June 1959): 104-111.

**3725. Dunlop, G.M.** *"The Influence of Time Spent in School Buses upon Achievement and Attendance of Pupils in Alberta Consolidated Schools."* G.M. Dunlop, R.J.C. Harper and S. Hanka. Alberta Journal of Educational Research 3, 4(Dec. 1957): 170-179.

**3726. Dunn, D.J.** *"Medical Inspection of School Children."* D.J. Dunn. Canadian Medical Association Journal 8, 10(Oct. 1918): 925-932.

**3727. Dunn, D.J.** *"Mental Hygiene Activities in the Public Schools."* D.J. Dunn. Public Health Journal 15, 2(Feb. 1924): 55-67.

**3728. Durieux, Marcel** *Ordinary Heros: the Journal of a French Pioneer in Alberta.* Marcel Durieux. Edmonton: University of Alberta Press, c1980.
Translated and edited by Roger Motut and Maurice Legris, with an introduction by L.G. Thomas.

**3729. Dutz, Werner** *"Appendicitis in Infancy."* Werner Dutz and Samuel Hanson. Canadian Medical Association Journal 75, 10(Nov. 15, 1956): 832-834.

**3730. Eagan, Ruth Louise** *The Relationship Between Auditory Discrimination and Auditory Memory Span in Children from Kindergarten to Grade Three.* Sister Ruth Louise Eagan. Edmonton: University of Alberta, 1970. Thesis (M.Ed.)--University of Alberta, 1970.

**3731. Eagle Valley Book Club** *Wagon Trails Plowed Under: a History of Eagle Valley, Sundre East and Sangro.* Eagle Valley Book Club. Sundre, Alta.: Eagle Valley Book Club, 1977.

**3732. Ears History Committee** *Prairie Profiles.* The Ears History Committee. [S.l.]: Ears History Committee, 1979.

**3733. East Cut Knife and Districts Historical Society** *Where the Cut Knife Waters Flow.* East Cut Knife and Districts Historical Society. [S.l.]: East Cut Knife and Districts Historical Society, 1980.

**3734.** *East Prairie Metis: 1939-1979, 40 Years of Determination.* [S.l.: s.n., 1979].

**3735. Eaton, Amaryllis** *"Right Lobar Pneumonia."* Amaryllis Eaton. Canadian Nurse 55, 12(Dec. 1959): 1108-1111.

**3736. Eatonia History Book Committee** *A Past to Cherish: a History of Royal Canadian. Newcombe, Eatonia and LaPorte.* Eatonia History Book Committee. Eatonia, Sask.: Eatonia History Book Committee, 1980.

**3737. Eckert, Helen Margaret** *The Development of Organized Recreation and Physical Education in Alberta.* Helen Margaret Eckert. Edmonton: University of Alberta, 1953. Thesis (M.Ed.)--University of Alberta, 1953.

**3738. Eddystone and District Historical Society** *Patience, Pride and Progress.* Eddystone and District Historical Society. Eddystone, Man.: Eddystone and District Historical Society, 1983.

**3739. Eden-Birnie History Book Committee** *East of the Mountains: Eden-Birnie Story, 1877-1984.* Eden-Birnie History Book Committee. Neepawa, Man.: Eden-Birnie History Book Committee, 1984.

**3740. Edenwold Anniversary Committee** *Where Aspens Whisper: Edenwold.* Edenwold Anniversary Committee. Edenwold, Sask.: Edenwold Anniversary Committee, 1981.

**3741. Edgeller, Evelyn** *Mary Belle Barclay, Founder of Canadian Hostelling.* Evelyn Edgeller. Calgary: Detselig, 1988.

**3742. Edmonton Public School Board. Drug Survey Committee** *Drug Report.* The Committee. Edmonton: The Board, 1971.
   Chairman: K.M. Grierson.

**3743. Edwardh, M.O.** *"The Enterprise as a Teaching Technique."* M.O. Edwardh. Toronto: W.J. Gage, 1956. In Education: a Collection of Essays on Canadian Education, v.1, 1954-1956, pp. [41]-44.

**3744. Eggleston, Wilfrid** *Homestead on the Range.* Wilfrid Eggleston. Ottawa: Borealis Press, 1982.

**3745. Eggleston, Wilfrid** *Literary Friends.* Wilfrid Eggleston. Ottawa: Borealis Press, c1980.

**3746. Eggleston, Wilfrid** *"The Old Homestead: Romance and Reality."* Wilfrid Eggleston. Calgary: Comprint Pub. Co., University of Calgary, c1977. In The Settlement of the West, pp. 114-129. Edited by Howard Palmer.

**3747. Eggleston, Wilfrid** *While I Still Remember: a Personal Record.* Wilfrid Eggleston. Toronto: Ryerson Press, 1968.

**3748. Eighty Year History Society** *A Harvest of Memories: a History of Rural Wilkie.* Eighty Year History Society. Wilkie, Sask.: Eighty Year History Society, 1984.

**3749. Einarsson, Helgi** *Helgi Einarsson, a Manitoba Fisherman.* Helgi Einarsson. Winnipeg: Queenston House, c1982. Translated from Icelandic by George Houser.

**3750. Elaschuk, Larry Clifford** *Educational and Occupational Aspirations and Expectations of Secondary Students in a Rural-Urban Fringe.* Larry Clifford Elaschuk. Calgary: University of Calgary, 1970. Thesis (M.Ed.)--University of Calgary, 1970.

**3751. Eley, Malcolm Gordon** *Socioeconomic Differences in Children's Discrimination Learning as a Function of the Reward and Information Factors of Reinforcement.* Malcolm Gordon Eley. Edmonton: University of Alberta, 1971 Thesis (M.Ed.)--University of Alberta,

1971.

**3752. Elkhorn and District Historical Society** *Steel and Grass Roots, 1882-1982.* Elkhorn and District Historical Society. Elkhorn, Man.: Elkhorn and District Historical Society, 1982.

**3753. Elley, W.B.** *"The Standard Progressive Matrices as a Culture-reduced Measure of General Intellectual Ability."* W.B. Elley and R.S. MacArthur. Alberta Journal of Educational Research 8, 1(Mar. 1962): 54-65.

**3754. Ellice Centennial Book Committee** *Rural Municipality of Ellice, 1883-1983.* R.M. of Ellice Centennial Book Committee. St. Lazare, Man.: Ellice Centennial Book Committee, 1983.

**3755. Elrose School Reunion Committee** *Memories of Elrose Schooldays: Tuum Este.* Elrose School Reunion Committee. Elrose: [s.n.], 1965.

**3756. Elstow and District History Book** *Memories Forever: Elstow and District 1900-1983.* Elstow and District History Book. Elstow, Sask.: Elstow and District History Book, 1983.

**3757. England, Robert** *"Ethnic Settlers in Western Canada: Reminiscences of a Pioneer."* Robert England. Canadian Ethnic Studies/Etudes ethniques au Canada 8, 2(1976): 18-33.

**3758. Ens, Gerhard** *"Dispossession or Adaptation?: Migration and Persistence of the Red River Metis, 1835-1890."* Gerhard Ens. Canadian Historical Association, Historical Papers/Communications historiques (1988): 120-144.

**3759. Ens, Gerhard** *"Heinrich H. Ewert and Mennonite Education."* Gerhard Ens. Mennonite Historian 9, 1(Mar. 1983): 1-2.

**3760. Epp-Tiessen, Esther** *Altona: the Story of a Prairie Town.* Esther Epp-Tiessen. Altona, Man.: D.W. Friesen and Sons, 1982.

**3761. Erasmus, Peter** *Buffalo Days and Nights.* Peter Erasmus as told to Henry Thompson. Calgary: Glenbow-Alberta Institute, 1976.

**3762. Ernfold Senior Citizens' Association** *From Hoofprints to Highways: Leslieville and Districts Commemorate Alberta's Seventy-Fifth Anniversary.* Leslieville and Districts Historical Society. 2 vol. Leslieville, Alta.: Leslieville and Districts Historical Society, 1980.

**3763. Ernfold Senior Citizens' Association** *From Prairie Sod to Golden Grain 1904-1974: a History of the People of Ernfold and Community.* Ernfold Senior Citizens' Association. Ernfold, Sask.: Ernfold Senior Citizens' Association, 1975.

**3764. Eskow, Elaine Doreen** *A Study of Hospital In-patient and Follow-up Procedures with Respect to Youth Drug Abuse.* Elaine Doreen Eskow. University of Calgary, 1971. (CTM no. 10073) Thesis (M.S.W.)--University of Calgary, 1971.

**3765. Estevan History Book Committee** *A Tale That is Told: Estevan, 1890-1980.* Estevan History Book Committee. 2 v. Estevan, Sask.: Estevan History Book Committee, 1981.

**3766. Evanechko, Peter O.** *Context and Connotative Meaning in Grade Five.* Peter O. Evanechko. Edmonton: University of Alberta, 1968. Thesis (M.Ed.)--University of Alberta, 1968.

**3767. Evanechko, Peter O.** *The Dimensions of Children's Meaning Space.* Peter O. Evanechko. Edmonton: University of Alberta, 1970. Thesis (Ph.D.)--University of Alberta, 1970.

**3768. Evans, Harold S.** *"Complications Arising from Meckel's Diverticulum."* Harold S. Evans and G.B. Elliott. Canadian Medical Association Journal 69, 5(Nov. 1953): 527-529.

**3769. Everett, Lorene** *"Responses of Young Children to Two Modes of Representation."* Lorene Everett and Robert D. Armstrong. Alberta Journal of Educational Research 14, 4(Dec. 1968): 217-224.

**3770. Everett, Lorene** *Responses of Young Children to Two Modes of Representation.* Lorene Mildred Everett. Edmonton: University of Alberta, 1968. Thesis (M.Ed.)--University of Alberta, 1968.

**3771. Ewanchuk, Michael** *Spruce, Swamp and Stone: a History of the Pioneer Ukrainian Settlement in the Gimli Area.* Michael Ewanchuk. Winnipeg: The Author, 1977.

**3772. Fadum, Oscar** *A Diagnosis of the Achievement of a Sample of Alberta Grade Eight Pupils in Solving Arithmetic Problems.* Oscar Fadum. Edmonton: University of Alberta, 1956. Thesis (M.Ed.)--University of Alberta, 1956.

3773. **Fairbanks. Carol** *"Lives of Girls and Women of the Canadian and American Prairies."* Carol Fairbanks. International Journal of Women's Studies 2, 5(Sept.-Oct. 1979): 452-472.

3774. **Fairley, Lilian** *Guidelines: a Story of the Girl Guides in Saskatchewan.* Lilian Fairley. Saskatchewan: Saskatchewan Council, Girl Guides of Canada, 1970.

3775. **Falun Historical Society** *Freeway West.* Falun Historical Society. Falun, Alta.: Falun Historical Society, 1974.

3776. **Fast, Dolores Joan** *The Effect of Socioeconomic Status on the Development of Auditory Discrimination as It Relates to Reading Achievement.* Dolores Joan Fast. Edmonton: University of Alberta, 1968.
Thesis (M.Ed.)--University of Alberta, 1968.

3777. **Faulknor. Cliff** *Turn Him Loose!.' Herman Linder, Canada's Mr. Rodeo.* Cliff Faulknor. Saskatoon: Western Producer Prairie Books, 1977.

3778. **Fehlberg, Dieter August** *Student Achievement Under Alberta's Semester System.* Dieter August Fehlberg. Edmonton: University of Alberta, 1968.
Thesis (M.Ed.)--University of Alberta, 1968.

3779. **Ferguson, Colin C.** *"Optimal Ages for Elective Surgery in Infants and Children."* Colin C. Ferguson. Canadian Medical Association Journal 69, 4(Oct. 1953): 381-386.

3780. **Ferguson, Colin C.** *"The Results of Open-heart Operations Performed on Children."* Colin C. Ferguson. Canadian Medical Association Journal/Journal de l'Association medicale canadienne 92, 24(June 12, 1965): 1253-1257.

3781. **Ferguson, Colin C.** *"Surgical Emergencies in the Newborn."* Colin C. Ferguson. Canadian Medical Association Journal 72, 2(Jan. 15, 1955): 75-82.

3782. **Ferguson, Colin C.** *"Surgical Emphysema Complicating Tonsillectomy and Dental Extraction."* Colin C. Ferguson, Patrick M.F. McGarry, I.H. Beckman, and Morris Broder. Canadian Medical Association Journal 72, 11(June 1, 1955): 847-848.

3783. **Ferguson, Colin C.** *"The Surgical Treatment of Transposition of the Great Vessels: Report of Two Clinical Cases."* Colin C. Ferguson. Canadian Medical Association Journal 79, 7(Oct. 1, 1958): 551-554.

3784. **Ferguson, Robert G.** *"A Pure Milk Supply for the Farm Home."* R.G. Ferguson. Public Health Journal 18, 4(Apr. 1927): 151-155.

3785. **Ferguson, Robert G.** *"Reducing Tuberculosis Among School Children in Saskatchewan."* R.G. Ferguson. Canadian Public Health Journal 27, 10(Oct. 1936): 497.
Reprint from The Valley Echo, 17, 3(1936).

3786. **Ferguson, Robert G.** *"A Tuberculosis Survey of 1346 School Children in Saskatchewan."* Robert G. Ferguson. Canadian Medical Association Journal 12, 6(June 1922): 381-383.

3787. **Fife Lake History Book Committee** *Gathering of Memories: Fife Lake, Constance, Little Woody and Area.* Fife Lake History Book Committee. Fife Lake, Sask.: Fife Lake History Book Committee, .1981.

3788. **Fifty and Over Club** *Our Prairie Heritage: Cambria 1902-1977.* Fifty and Over Club. Torquay, Sask.: Fifty and Over Club, 1978.

3789. **Figur, Berthold** *An Historical Survey of Certain Concepts Basic to Progressive Education with Particular Attention to the Alberta Scene.* Berthold Figur. Edmonton: University of Alberta, 1950.
Thesis (M.Ed.)--University of Alberta, 1950.

3790. **Finkel, K.C.** *"Pediatric Home Care Program: Review of Two and a Half Years' Experience at the Children's Hospital of Winnipeg."* K.C. Finkel and Shirley E. Pitt. Canadian Medical Association Journal/Journal de l'Association medicale canadienne 98, 3(Jan. 20, 1968): 157-164.

3791. **Fischler, Stan** *Gordie Howe.* Stan Fischler. New York: Grosset and Dunlap, c1967.

3792. **Fisher, A.D.** *"A Colonial Educational System: Historical Changes and Schooling in Fort Chipewyan."* A.D. Fisher. Canadian Journal of Anthropology 2, 1(Spring 1981): 37-44.

3793. **Fisk, Robert Ritchie** *"Leisure Reading in Alberta."* Robert Fisk. Alberta Journal of Educational Research 7, 3(Sept. 1961): 134-139.

3794. **Fisk, Robert Ritchie** *A Survey of Leisure Reading in the Junior High Schools of Alberta.* Robert Ritchie Fisk. Edmonton: University of Alberta, 1961.
Thesis (M.Ed.)--University of Alberta, 1961.

**3795. Fleischer, Leonore** *Joni Mitchell.* Leonore Fleischer. [S.l.]: Flash Books, 1976.

**3796. Flynn, P.A.** *A Statistical Survey of the Academic Progress of Manitoba High School Students Beyond Grade 11: Report 5.* P.A. Flynn, A.J. Darling, P. Olin and T.J. Scott. [Manitoba: University of Manitoba, 1961].

**3797. Foam Lake Historical Society** *They Came From Many Lands: a History of Foam Lake and Area.* Foam Lake Historical Society. Foam Lake, Sask.: Foam Lake Historical Society, 1985.

**3798. Foght, Harold W.** *A Survey of Education in the Province of Saskatchewan: a Report to the Government of the Province of Saskatchewan.* Harold W. Foght. Regina: J.W. Reid, King's Printer, 1918.

**3799. Foothills Historical Society** *Chaps and Chinooks: a History West of Calgary.* Foothills Historical Society. [S.l.]: Foothills Historical Society, 1976.

**3800. Forbes, Doris** *"The Tale of Mickey the Beaver."* Doris Forbes. Beaver 272, 3(Dec. 1941): 42-45.

**3801. Forchner, Gisela** *Growing Up Canadian: Twelve Case Studies of German Immigrant Families in Alberta.* Gisela Forchner. Edmonton: University of Alberta, 1983. (CTM no. 63857)
Thesis (Ph.D.)--University of Alberta, 1983.

**3802. Ford, Blake** *"Differential Perceptions of the School Counsellor's Role."* Blake Ford. Alberta Journal of Educational Research 15, 4(Dec. 1969): 245-253.

**3803. Foremost Historical Society** *Shortgrass Country: a History of Foremost and Nemiskam.* Foremost Historical Society. Foremost, Alta.: Foremost Historical Society, 1975.

**3804. Fornataro, J.V.** *"Treatment of the Offender in Saskatchewan."* J.V. Fornataro. Canadian Welfare 29, 8(Mar. 1954): 19-25.

**3805. Fort Assiniboine Friendship Club Book Committee** *Echoes of Fort Assiniboine and Districts.* Fort Assiniboine Friendship Club Book Committee. Fort Assiniboine, Alta.: Fort Assiniboine Friendship Club Book Committee, 1982.

**3806. Foster, John E.** *"The Origins of the Mixed Bloods in the Canadian West."* John E. Foster. Edmonton: Pica Pica Press, c1985. In The Prairie West: Historical Readings, pp. 86-99. Edited by R. Douglas Francis and Howard Palmer.

**3807. Foster, John E.** *"Some Questions and Perspectives on the Problem of Metis Roots."* John E. Foster. Winnipeg: University of Manitoba Press, c1985. In The New Peoples: Being and Becoming Metis in North America, pp. 73-91. Edited by Jacqueline Peterson and Jennifer S.H. Brown.

**3808. Foster, Marion Elizabeth** *A Comparative Study of the Reading Achievement Between Comparable Groups of Pupils in Christchurch, New Zealand and Edmonton, Alberta.* Marion Elizabeth Foster. Edmonton: University of Alberta, 1961.
Thesis (M.Ed.)--University of Alberta, 1961.

**3809. Foster, Moira** *"Children's Essay Competition: My New Home in Canada."* Moira Foster. Beaver 261, 3(Dec. 1930): 129.

**3810. Fox, J.G.** *"Newborn Screening for Hereditary Metabolic Disorders in Manitoba, 1965-1970."* J.G. Fox, D.L. Hall, J.C. Haworth, A. Maniar and L. Sekla. Canadian Medical Association Journal/Journal de l'Association medicale canadienne 104, 12(June 19, 1971): 1085-1088.

**3811. Fraser, Charles R.** *"Public Relations, Community Organization and Dollar Raising."* Charles R. Fraser. Canadian Welfare 31, 7(Mar. 1956): 337-340.

**3812. Fraser, Esther** *Wheeler.* Esther Fraser. Banff: Summerthought, 1978.

**3813. Fraser, Robert S.** *"Isolated Ventricular Septal Defect: a Review of 239 Cases."* Robert S. Fraser, Noall E. Wolff and Neil F. Duncan. Canadian Medical Association Journal/Journal de l'Association medicale canadienne 100, 20(May 24 & 31, 1969): 931-937.

**3814. Fricke, Benno Gerry Herman** *Are the Grade 11 Students in Edmonton Making Vocational Plans with Their Mental Ability?* Benno Gerry Herman Fricke. Edmonton: University of Alberta, 1950.
Thesis (M.Ed.)--University of Alberta, 1950.

3815. Friesen, Anna *The Mulberry Tree.* Anna Friesen [and] Victor Carl Friesen. Winnipeg: Queenston House, 1985.

3816. Friesen, David *"Academic-athletic-popularity Syndrome in the Canadian High School Society."* David Friesen. Adolescence 3, 9(Spring 1968): 39-52.

3817. Friesen, David *"The Adolescent Society in the Western Canadian High School."* David Friesen. Manitoba Journal of Educational Research 2, 1(Nov. 1966): 5-14.

3818. Friesen, Doris Tamara *A Comparative Study of Kindergarten Readers and Non-readers.* Doris Tamara Friesen. Calgary: University of Calgary, 1969. Thesis (M.Ed.)--University of Calgary, 1969.

3819. Friesen, Isaac I. *The Mennonites of Western Canada with Special Reference to Education.* Isaac I. Friesen. Saskatoon: University of Saskatchewan, 1934. Thesis (M.A.)--University of Saskatchewan, 1934.

3820. Friesen, John W. *A Comparison of Value Preferences and Concepts of Indian Culture of Four Groups: Indian and Non-Indian Pupils, Indian Parents and Teachers of Indian Pupils.* John W. Friesen. Calgary: University of Calgary, 1970.

3821. Friesen, John W. *"John McDougall: Educator of Indians."* J.W. Friesen [Toronto]: D.C. Heath Canada Ltd., c1974. In Profiles of Canadian Educators, pp. 57-76. Edited by Robert S. Patterson, John W. Chalmers and John W. Friesen.

3822. Friesen, John W. *"Some Philosophical Bases of Indian Educational Wants."* John W. Friesen. Journal of Education of the Faculty of Education, Vancouver 17(Apr. 1971): 56-70.

3823. Friesen, John W. *When Cultures Clash: Case Studies in Multiculturalism.* John W. Friesen. Calgary: Detselig Enterprises Ltd., c1985.

3824. Friesen, Rhinehart F. *A Mennonite Odyssey.* Rhinehart Friesen. Winnipeg: Hyperion Press Ltd., c1988.

3825. Frith, Joan *Treatise of a Society: Prince Albert Exhibition Association Centennial 1883-1983.* Joan Frith. Prince Albert, Sask.: Prince Albert Exhibition Association, 1983.

3826. Frobisher Happy Gang History Book Committee *Frobyshire to Frobisher.* Frobisher Happy Gang History Book Committee. Frobisher, Sask.: Frobisher Happy Gang, 1979.

3827. Frost, Barry P. *"Intelligence, Manifest Anxiety and Scholastic Achievement."* Barry P. Frost. Alberta Journal of Educational Research 11, 3(Sept. 1965): 167-175.

3828. Frost, Barry P. *"The Porteus Maze Test and Manual Proficiency."* Barry P. Frost. Alberta Journal of Educational Research 11, 1(Mar. 1965): 17-20.

3829. Fry, P.S. *A Study of the Utilization of Student Resources: an Investigation of the Barriers to the Completion of High School in the Calgary School District.* P.S. Fry. Calgary: Alberta Human Resources Council, 1969.

3830. Gabriel Dumont Institute of Native Studies and Applied Research, Inc. Curriculum Unit *Gabriel Dumont.* Curriculum Unit, Gabriel Dumont Institute of Native Studies and Joanne Pelletier. Regina: The Institute, c1985.

3831. Gadsby Pioneer Association *From the Bigknife to the Battle: Gadsby and Area.* Gadsby Pioneer Association. Gadsby, Alta.: Gadsby Pioneer Association, 1979.

3832. Gagnon, Anne *"The Pensionnat Assomption: Religious Nationalism in a Franco-Albertan Boarding School for Girls 1926-1960."* Anne Gagnon. Historical Studies in Education/Revue d'histoire de l'education 1, 1(Spring 1989): 95-117.

3833. Gahagan, Alvine Cyr *Yes Father: Pioneer Nursing in Alberta.* Alvine Cyr Gahagan. Manchester, N.H.: Hammer Publications, 1979.

3834. Gainsborough and District Historical Society *Yesterday's Prairie Wind 1883-1980.* Gainsborough and District Historical Society. Gainsborough, Sask.: Gainsborough and District Historical Society, 1980.

3835. Gajadharsingh, Joel Lancelot *A Study of the Effects of Instruction in the Rhetoric of the Sentence on the Written Composition of Junior High School Students.* Joel Lancelot Gajadharsingh. Edmonton: University of Alberta, 1970. Thesis (Ph.D)--University of Alberta, 1970.

3836. **Galloway, Margaret A.** *I Lived in Paradise.* Margaret A. Galloway. Winnipeg: Bulman Bros., 1941.

3837. **Gardiner, Mary** *"Toys: the Tools of Play."* Mary Gardiner. Canadian Nurse 50, 2(Feb. 1954): 104-106.

3838. **Gardner, Alison F.** *Grant McConachie.* Alison F. Gardner. Don Mills, Ont.: Fitzhenry & Whiteside, 1979.

3839. **Gareau, Urban J.** *"Nutrition in Childhood. Part 1."* Urban J. Gareau. Canadian Nurse 23, 6(June 1927): 292-298.

3840. **Garreau, Urban** *"Clinical Aspects of an Epidemic of Human Encephalomyelitis in Saskatchewan in 1938."* Urban Garreau. Canadian Public Health Journal 32, 1(Jan. 1941): 1-5.

3841. **Gavinchuk, Kay** *Academic Careers of Students Related to Ability, Choice of Program and Size of High School.* Kay Gavinchuk. Edmonton: University of Alberta, 1966. Thesis (M.Ed.)--University of Alberta, 1966.

3842. **Geddes, Catherine Mackie** *"Children's Essay Competition: My New Home in Canada."* Catherine Mackie Geddes. Beaver 261, 3(Dec. 1930): 129-130.

3843. **George, Ernest S.** *"An Old Time Winter."* Ernest S. George. Alberta Historical Review 16, 4(Autumn 1968): 27-28.

3844. **Gerrard, John W.** *"Interstitial Plasma Cellular Pneumonia due to Pneumocystis Carinii."* J.W. Gerrard and D.F. Moore. Canadian Medical Association Journal 76, 4(Feb. 15, 1957): 299-302.

3845. **Getty, Ian Allison Ludlow** *The Church Missionary Society Among the Blackfoot Indians of Southern Alberta, 1880-1895.* Ian Allison Ludlow Getty. Calgary: University of Calgary, 1970. Thesis (M.A.)--University of Calgary, 1970.

3846. **Geysir Historical Society** *Faith and Fortitude: a History of the Geysir District, 1880's-1980's.* Geysir Historical Society. Arborg, Man.: Geysir Historical Society, 1983.

3847. **Gibault, Joseph Leon** *The Effect of Instruction in French Upon the Mastery of the English Language in English-French Schools of the St. Paul Inspectorate.* Joseph Leon Gibault. Edmonton: University of Alberta, 1939. Thesis (M.A.)--University of Alberta,

1939.

3848. **Gibbons History Committee** *Our Treasured Roots: a History of Gibbons and Surrounding Areas.* Gibbons History Committee. Gibbons, Alta.: Gibbons History Committee, 1982.

3849. **Gibson, A.** *"Congenital Dysplasia of the Hip-joint."* A. Gibson. Canadian Medical Association Journal 74, 3(Feb. 1, 1956): 204-207.

3850. **Gibson, R.L.** *"A Winter in the Lost Horse Hills."* R.L. Gibson. Saskatchewan History 3, 1(Winter 1950): 28-29.

3851. **Gibson, Robert** *"Dementia Infantilis."* Robert Gibson. Canadian Medical Association Journal 80, 2(Jan. 15, 1959): 114-116.

3852. **Gibson, Robert** *"The Incidence of Arachnodactyly in an Institutional Population."* Robert Gibson. Canadian Medical Association Journal 75, 6(Sept. 15, 1956): 501-503.

3853. **Gibson, W.W.** *"The Bird Man of Balgonie."* W.W. Gibson. Saskatchewan History 12, 3(Autumn 1959): 100-106.

3854. **Giesbrecht, John H.** *"Mr. Ewert."* John H. Giesbrecht. Winnipeg: Centennial Publications, 1977. In Mennonite Memories: Settling in Western Canada, pp. 151-162. Edited by Lawrence Klippenstein and Julius G. Toews.

3855. **Gilead, Heather** *The Maple Leaf for Quite a While.* Heather Gilead. London: J.M. Dent and Sons, 1967.

3856. **Gimli Women's Institute** *Gimli Saga: the History of Gimli, Manitoba.* Gimli Women's Institute. [S.l.]: Gimli Women's Institute, 1975.

3857. **Gladstone, James** *"Indian School Days."* James Gladstone. Alberta Historical Review 15, 1(Winter 1967): 18-24.

3858. **Glenboro and Area Historical Society** *Beneath the Long Grass.* Glenboro and Area Historical Society. [S.l.]: Glenboro and Area Historical Society, 1979.

3859. **Glengarry Elementary School** *Glengarry Golden Anniversary, 1920-1970.* Glengarry Elementary School. Calgary: [s.n.], 1970.

**3860. Glenora Community Boosters History Book Committee** *Gleanings of the Past.* Glenora Community Boosters History Book Committee. [S.l.]: Glenora Community Boosters History Book Committee, [1980?].

**3861. Glover, Elwood** *Elwood Glover's Luncheon Dates.* Elwood Glover. Scarborough: Prentice Hall, 1975.

**3862. Godwin, Ruth** *"Interest Patterns of Senior High School Students: the Relation to Low Achievement in English."* Ruth Godwin. Canadian Education and Research Digest 1, 4(Dec. 1961): 61-70.

**3863. Goedicke, Rita Margaret** *The Relationship of Personality Variables to Academic Success.* Rita Margaret Goedicke. Edmonton: University of Alberta, 1968. Thesis (M.Ed.)--University of Alberta, 1968.

**3864. Gokiert, J. Guy** *"Altered Reactivity to Measles Virus in Previously Vaccinated Children."* J. Guy Gokiert and W.E. Beamish. Canadian Medical Association Journal/Journal de l'Association medicale canadienne 103, 7(Oct. 10, 1970): 724-727.

**3865. Goluboff, Nathan** *"Infantile Cortical Hyperostosis: (Caffey-Smith Syndrome)."* Nathan Goluboff. Canadian Medical Association Journal 62, 2(Feb. 1950): 189-190.

**3866. Gooderham, George H.** *"Teddy Yellow Fly."* George H. Gooderham. Alberta History 33, 1(Winter 1985): 10-13.

**3867. Gordon, Christine J.** *A Comparative Study of the Word Skills of Good and Poor Readers at the Seventh Grade Level.* Christine J. Gordon. Calgary: University of Calgary, 1970. Thesis (M.Ed.)--University of Calgary, 1970.

**3868. Gordon, J. King** *"The World of Helen Gordon."* J. King Gordon. Manitoba Pageant 24, 1(Autumn 1978): 1-14.

**3869. Gorman, Jack** *Pere Murray and the Hounds: the Story of Saskatchewan's Notre Dame College.* Jack Gorman. Sidney: Gray's Publishing, 1977.

**3870. Goroniuk, Andrew** *A Survey of Ability and Achievement of Grade Nine Students in Three Alberta Counties.* Andrew Goroniuk. Edmonton: University of Alberta, 1969. Thesis (M.Ed.)--University of Alberta, 1969.

**3871. Gosnell, Hilda C., ed.** *Echoes of the Past: a History of the Rural Municipality of Louise and Its People.* Hilda C. Gosnell, Mrs. H. Gilmour, Mrs. H. Hammond [and] Rural Municipality of Louise. [S.l.]: Rural Municipality of Louise, 1968.

**3872. Govan and District Local History Association** *Last Mountain Echoes: a Family and School History of Govan and District.* Govan and District Local History Association. Govan, Sask.: Govan and District Local History Association, 1980.

**3873. Grant, Mary Anastasia** *A Qualitative Analysis of the Vocabulary Responses of Good Readers and Poor Readers.* Mary Anastasia Grant. Edmonton: University of Alberta, 1965. Thesis (M.Ed.)--University of Alberta, 1965.

**3874. Grant, W. Wallace** *"Observations on Sleep Disturbances in Preschool Children."* W. Wallace Grant. Canadian Medical Association Journal 77, 5(Sept. 1, 1957): 444-450.

**3875. Granum History Committee** *Leavings by Trail, Granum by Rail.* Granum History Committee. Granum, Alta.: Granum History Committee, 1977.

**3876. Grapko, Michael F.** *A Study to Estimate the Degree of Relationship between Certain Personality Traits and Social Status at a Boys' Summer Camp.* Michael F. Grapko. Toronto: University of Toronto, 1947. Thesis (M.A.)--University of Toronto, 1947.

**3877. Grassy Lake Historical Society** *Faded Trails: Grassy Lake, Purple Springs.* Grassy Lake Historical Society. [Grassy Lake, Alta.]: Grassy Lake Historical Society, 1982.

**3878. Grauer, Leslie W.** *The Effects of a Changing Stimulus on the Orientating Response in Normal and Children with Learning Problems.* Leslie W. Grauer. Calgary: University of Calgary, 1971. (CTM no. 10081) Thesis (M.Sc.)--University of Calgary, 1971.

**3879. Gray, J.W.** *"Regina Has Four Civic Community Centres."* J.W. Gray. Child and Family Welfare 13, 5(Jan. 1938): 23, 41.

**3880. Gray, James H.** *Boomtime: Peopling the Canadian Prairies.* James H. Gray. Saskatoon: Western Producer Prairie Books, c1979.

**3881. Gray, James H.** *The Boy from Winnipeg.* James H. Gray. Toronto: Macmillan, c1970.
Paperback edition published in 1977 by Macmillan (Laurentian Library no. 52)

**3882. Gray, James H.** *The Roar of the Twenties.* James Henry Gray. Toronto: MacMillan of Canada, 1978.

**3883. Gray, Mary** *"An Analysis of Language Themes in Grade Five, Grade Eight, and Grade Eleven."* Mary Gray. Alberta Journal of Educational Research 7, 4(Dec. 1961): 209-216.

**3884. Great Britain. Board of Education** *Special Reports on the Systems of Education in Manitoba, North-west Territories and British Columbia.* The Board. London, Eng.: H.M. Stationery Office, 1901.
Text is a sectional reprint, numbers A5, 6 and 7, of volume four of "Special Reports on Educational Subjects."

**3885. Greenstein, Michael** *Adele Wiseman and Her Works.* Michael Greenstein. Toronto: ECW Press, [1984].

**3886. Gregor, Alexander** *The Development of Education in Manitoba: II. 1897-1982.* Alexander Gregor and Keith Wilson. [Winnipeg]: University of Manitoba, c1983.

**3887. Gregor, Alexander** *History of Education in Manitoba: I. Red River to 1879.* Alexander Gregor and Keith Wilson. [Winnipeg]: University of Manitoba, c1983.

**3888. Gresko, Jacqueline** *"White "Rites" and Indian "Rites": Indian Education and Native Responses in the West, 1870-1910."* Jacqueline Gresko. Calgary: Detselig Enterprises, 1979. In Shaping the Schools of the Canadian West, pp. 84-106. Edited by David C. Jones, Nancy M. Sheehan and Robert M. Stamp.

**3889. Grewar, David A.I.** *"The Fate of the Ex-premature: Prognosis of Prematurity."* D.A.I. Grewar, H. Medovy and K.O. Wylie. Canadian Medical Association Journal/Journal de l'Association medicale canadienne 86, 22(June 2, 1962): 1008-1013.

**3890. Grewar, David A.I.** *"Infantile Scurvy in Manitoba."* David Grewar. Canadian Medical Association Journal 78, 9(May 1, 1958): 675-680.

**3891. Grewar, David A.I.** *"Scurvy and its Prevention by Vitamin C Fortified Evaporated Milk."* David Grewar. Canadian Medical Association Journal/Journal de l'Association medicale canadienne 80, 12(June 15, 1959): 977-979.

**3892. Griesbach, William Antrobus** *I Remember.* William Antrobus Griesbach. Toronto: Ryerson Press, 1946.

**3893. Grimshaw and District Historical Society** *Land of Hope and Dreams: a History of Grimshaw and Districts.* Grimshaw and District Historical Society. Grimshaw, Alta.: Grimshaw and District Historical Society, 1980.

**3894. Grisdale, Lloyd C.** *"The Alberta Perinatal Mortality Study."* Lloyd C. Grisdale. Canadian Medical Association Journal 78, 4(Feb. 15, 1958): 256-259.

**3895. Groome, Agnes Jean** *The Working Mother: a Problem for the School?* Agnes Jean Groome. Vancouver: University of British Columbia, 1958.
Thesis (M.A.)--University of British Columbia, 1958.

**3896. Grosswerder and Districts New Horizons Heritage Group** *Prairie Legacy: Grosswerder and Surrounding Districts.* Grosswerder and Districts New Horizons Heritage Group. [S.l.:s.n.], 1980.

**3897. Gue, Leslie R.** *"Value Orientations in an Indian Community."* Leslie R. Gue. Alberta Journal of Educational Research 17, 1(Mar. 1971); 19-31.

**3898. Guenter, J.G.** *Men of Steele.* Jacob G. Guenter. Saskatoon: J.G. Guenter, c1981.

**3899. Guest, Harry H.** *Correlates of Readiness for Various Aspects of Family Life Education Among Secondary School Students of Winnipeg, Manitoba.* Henry Hewson Guest. Tallahassee, Fl.: Florida State University, c1971.
Thesis (Ph.D.)--Florida State University, 1971.

**3900. Gulutsan, Metro** *"Some Effects of Mental Health Instruction on Children's Manifest Anxiety Scale Scores."* Metro Gulutsan. Alberta Journal of Educational Research 10, 4(Dec. 1964): 209-218.

**3901. Gushaty, M.** *An Analysis of the Causes of High School Dropouts in Southern Alberta from 1947 to 1951.* M. Gushaty. Edmonton: University of Alberta, 1952.
Thesis (M.Ed.)--University of Alberta, 1952.

**3902. Gutkin, Harry** *The Worst of Times, the Best of Times.* Harry Gutkin [and] Mildred Gutkin. Markham, Ont.: Fitzhenry and Whiteside, 1987.

**3903. Haas, Maara** *"On the Street Where I Live."* Maara Haas. Historical and Scientific Society of Manitoba Transactions, Series 3, 31(1974-1975): 21-28.

**3904. Hafford History Book Committee** *A Walk Down Memory Lane: Hafford and District.* Hafford History Book Committee. Hafford, Sask.: Hafford History Book Committee, 1983.

**3905. Hagen History Book Committee** *Reflections on the Past: a History of Hagen and District.* Hagen History Book Committee. [Hagen, Sask.: Hagen History Book Committee, 1980].

**3906. Hagerman, E.M.** *"The Saskatoon Health Centre."* E.M. Hagerman. Canadian Nurse 19, 12(Dec. 1923): 720-722.

**3907. Halkirk Historical Society** *Halkirk Home Fires and Area.* Halkirk Historical Society. Halkirk, Alta.: Halkirk Historical Society, 1985.

**3908. Hall, Robert Alexander** *A Semantic Differential Study of Attitudes of a Sample of High School Students.* Robert Alexander Hall. Calgary: University of Calgary, 1970. (CTM no. 7679)
Thesis (M.Ed.)--University of Calgary, 1970.

**3909. Hambley, George H.** *The Golden Thread or the Last of the Pioneers: a Story of the Districts of Basswood and Minnedosa, Manitoba from Community Beginning to Our Present Day.* George H. Hambley. Altona, Man.: D.W. Friesen and Sons, 1971.

**3910. Hambly, J.R. Stan, ed.** *Battle River Country: the History of Duhamel and Area.* Duhamel Historical Society and J.R. Stan Hambly, ed. New Norway, Alta.: Duhamel Historical Society, 1974.

**3911. Hamilton, T. Glen** *"Some Studies on the Incidence of Goitre Among School Children in Manitoba."* T. Glen Hamilton. Canadian Medical Association Journal 15, 10(Oct. 1925): 1017-1021.

**3912. Hamiota Centennial History Committee** *Hamiota: Grains of the Century, 1884-1984.* Hamiota Centennial History Committee. Hamiota, Man.: Hamiota Centennial History Committee, 1984.

**3913. Hancock, G.R.** *"Gangrene as a Complication of Malrotation with Volvulus."* G.R. Hancock. Canadian Medical Association Journal 79, 8(Oct. 15, 1958): 660-661.

**3914. Hansen, Harry Benjamin** *The Hansens: a History of the Hansen Family from 1863-1969.* Harry Benjamin Hansen. Bentley: The Author, 1969.

**3915. Hanson, Alice** *"Helping Marjory to Get Well."* Alice Hanson. Canadian Nurse 33, 1(Jan. 1937): 16-18.

**3916. Harasym, Carolyn R.** *Cultural Orientation of Rural Ukrainian High School Students.* Carolyn R. Harasym. Calgary: University of Calgary, 1969. (CTM no. 4635).
Thesis (M.Ed.) – University of Calgary, 1969.

**3917. Harasym, Carolyn R.** *"Semantic Differential Analysis of Relational Terms Used in Conservation."* Carolyn R. Harasym, Frederic J. Boersma and Thomas O. Maguire. Child Development 42, 3(Sept. 1971): 767-779.

**3918. Hargrave, Letitia** *The Letters of Letitia Hargrave.* Letitia Hargrave. Toronto: Champlain Society Pub., 1947.

**3919. Harkness, D.B.** *"Classification of Problem Children and the Services Suited to Their Care."* D.B. Harkness. In Proceedings and Papers Fourth Annual Canadian Conference on Child Welfare 1923, pp. 160-167.

**3920. Harper, R.J.C.** *"Reading and Arithmetic Reasoning: a Partial Correlation and Multiple Regression Analysis."* R.J.C. Harper. Alberta Journal of Educational Research 3, 2(June 1957): 81-86.

**3921. Harris, Ardell** *Modification of Childrens' Classificatory Abilities.* Ardell Harris. Calgary: University of Calgary, 1971. (CTM no. 10084)
Thesis (M.Ed.)--University of Calgary, 1971.

**3922. Hart, E.J.** *Ambition and Reality: the French-Speaking Community of Edmonton, 1795-1935.* Edward John Hart. Edmonton, Alta.: Le Salon d'histoire de la francophonie albertaine, 1980.

**3923. Harvie, Beverley Jean** *Factors Associated with Student Withdrawal.* Beverley Jean Harvie. Edmonton: University of Alberta, 1969.
Thesis (M.Ed.)--University of Alberta, 1969.

**3924. Hatt, Judith Keever** *"History, Social Structure, and Life Cycle of Beaver Metis Colony."* Judy K. Hatt. Western Canadian Journal of Anthropology 1, 1(1969): 19-32.

**3925. Hatt, Judith Keever** *The Rights and Duties of the Metis Preschool Child.* Judith Keever Hatt. Edmonton: University of Alberta, 1969.
  Thesis (M.A.)–University of Alberta, 1969.

**3926. Haworth, J.C.** *"Idiopathic Hypercalcaemia of Infancy."* J.C. Haworth. Canadian Medical Association Journal/Journal de l'Association medicale canadienne 80, 6(Mar. 15, 1959): 452-455.

**3927. Haworth, J.C.** *"The Neurological and Developmental Effects of Neonatal Hypoglycemia: a Follow-up of 22 Cases."* J.C. Haworth and K.N. McRae. Canadian Medical Association Journal/Journal de l'Association medicale canadienne 92, 16(Apr. 17, 1965): 861-865.

**3928. Hawrelko, John** *An Investigation to Determine the Relationship of Certain Factors Other than Intelligence to Student Achievement in Literature 20.* John Hawrelko. Edmonton: University of Alberta, 1962.
  Thesis (M.Ed.)–University of Alberta, 1962.

**3929. Hawrelko, John** *"Some Factors and Achievement in Literature 20."* John Hawrelko. Alberta Journal of Educational Research 9, 4(Dec. 1963): 238-246.

**3930. Hays 25th Book Committee** *Hays 1952-1977: From Sod to Silver.* Hays 25th Book Committee. [S.l.: s.n.], 1977.

**3931. Hazelzet, Joseph Peter** *Achievement in Mathematics in Grade One Children Studying AAAS and Conceptual Science.* Joseph Peter Hazelzet. Calgary: University of Calgary, 1971. (CTM no. 8856)
  Thesis (M.Ed.)–University of Calgary, 1971.

**3932. Head, P.W.** *"Gastro-intestinal Cancer in a 14-year-old Boy."* P.W. Head. Canadian Medical Association Journal/Journal de l'Association medicale canadienne 80, 10(May 15, 1959): 819-821.

**3933. Healey, W.J.** *Women of Red River: Being a Book Written from the Recollections of Women Surviving from the Red River Era.* W.J. Healey [and] The Women's Canadian Club, Winnipeg. Centennial ed. Winnipeg: Pegius Publishers, 1967.
  First edition, 1923.

**3934. Hearts Hill Historical Society** *From the Hill to the Border.* Hearts Hill Historical Society. Luseland, Sask.: Hearts Hill Historical Society, 1981.

**3935. Heath, Terrence** *Uprooted: the Life and Art of Ernest Lindner.* Terrence Heath. Saskatoon: Fifth House, 1983.

**3936. Hebert, Annette Dubuc** *"Alexander Desmutals Dit Lapointe: Oldest St. Boniface College Student."* Annette Dubuc Hebert. Manitoba Pageant 4, 1(Sept. 1958): 9-12.

**3937. Hedley, R.L.** *"Student Attitude and Achievement in Science Courses in Manitoba Secondary Schools."* R.L. Hedley. Manitoba Journal of Educational Research 2, 1(Nov. 1966): 15-27.

**3938. Heisler Historical Society** *Wagon Trails in the Sod: a History of the Heisler Area.* Heisler Historical Society. Heisler, Alta.: Heisler Historical Society, 1982.
  Include photographs.

**3939. Helgason, Robert F.** *"Obstetrics at Cook County Hospital."* Robert F. Helgason. Canadian Medical Association Journal 78, 1(Jan. 1, 1958): 53-55.

**3940. Hendon and District Historical Association** *Hendon Highlights, Oxen Ways to Now-a-days: the History of Hendon and District.* Hendon and District Historical Association. [S.l.]: Hendon and District Historical Association, 1982.

**3941. Hendry, James** *"Pneumocystis Carinii Pneumonia: Report of a Case Diagnosed During Life."* J. Hendry and R.F. Myers. Canadian Medical Association Journal/Journal de l'Association medicale canadienne 81, 10(Nov. 15, 1959): 831-834.

**3942. Hepworth, R. Gordon** *"Renal Failure Treated by Peritoneal Dialysis."* R. Gordon Hepworth. Canadian Medical Association Journal/Journal de l'Association medicale canadienne 80, 5(Mar. 1, 1959): 368-370.

**3943. Herbert, F.A.** *"Pneumonia in Indian and Eskimo Infants and Children: Part 1. A Clinical Study."* F.A. Herbert, W.A. Mahon, D. Wilkinson, O. Morgante, E.C. Burchak and L.B. Costopoulos. Canadian Medical Association Journal/Journal de l'Association medicale canadienne 96, 5(Feb. 4, 1967): 257-265.

**3944. Herbert, F.A.** *"Tuberculosis in Indian and Eskimo Children."* F.A. Herbert and E.C. Burchak. Medical Services Journal of Canada 23, 12(Dec. 1967): 1293-1304.

**3945. Herman. Albert** *A Comparison of the Self Concepts and the Ideal Self Concepts of Grade Ten Matriculation and Non-matriculation Students in the County of Lacombe, Alberta.* Albert Herman. Missoula: University of Montana, 1968. Thesis (Ed.D.)--University of Montana, 1968.

**3946. Herstein, Harvey H.** *"The Evolution of Jewish Schools in Winnipeg."* Harvey Herstein. Winnipeg: Jewish Historical Society of Western Canada, c1983. In Jewish Life and Times: a Collection of Essays, pp. 7-21.

**3947. Herstein, Harvey H.** *"The Growth of the Winnipeg Jewish Community and the Evolution of its Educational Institutions."* Harvey H. Herstein. Historical and Scientific Society of Manitoba Transactions, Series 3, 22(1965-1966): 27-66.

**3948. Hetherington, Melvin Ross** *Trainability and Generality/Specificity Ratios of the Ability of Grade Five Boys to Develop Torque.* Melvin Ross Hetherington. Edmonton: University of Alberta, 1971. (CTM no. 8079)
Thesis (Ph.D.)--University of Alberta, 1971.

**3949. Heyn, Asnath** *"Esophageal Lye Burns."* Asnath Heyn. Canadian Nurse 50, 12(Dec. 1954): 997-1002.

**3950. Hicks, Myrtle E.J.** *The Bridges I Have Crossed: Reminiscences of a Manitoba Farm Girl.* Myrtle E.J. Hicks. Brandon: The Author, [1972?].

**3951. Hiemstra, Mary Pinder** *Gully Farm.* Mary Pinder Hiemstra with drawings by Stephen Andrews. London, Ont.: J.M. Dent, [1955].

**3952. Hills of Hope Historical Committee** *Hills of Hope.* Hills of Hope Historical Committee. Spruce Grove, Alta.: Carvel Unifarm, 1976.

**3953. Hirsch, John** *"How I Discovered My Roots."* John Hirsch. Winnipeg: Jewish Historical Society of Western Canada, c1983. In Jewish Life and Times: a Collection of Essays, pp. 81-83.

**3954. Hislop, Margaret J.** *A Study of the Application of Selected Phonic Generalizations by Beginning Readers.* Margaret J. Hislop. Calgary: University of Calgary, 1969.
Thesis (M.Ed.)--University of Calgary, 1969.

**3955. History Committee of the Rural Municipality of The Gap No. 39** *Builders of a Great Land: History of R.M. of The Gap No. 39, Ceylon and Hardy.* The Committee. Ceylon, Sask.: History Committee of R.M. of The Gap No. 39, 1980.

**3956. Hjartarson, Freida Amelia** *Survey of Child Care Arrangements in Edmonton.* Freida Amelia Hjartarson. Edmonton: University of Alberta, 1971.
Thesis (M.Ed.)--University of Alberta, 1971.

**3957. Ho, Kwai-yiu** *Exploring the Social-psychological Aspects of Delinquency Using Community Data.* Kwai-yiu Ho. Edmonton: University of Alberta, 1971. Thesis (M.A.)--University of Alberta, 1971.

**3958. Hobart, Charles W.** *"Changing Family Patterns Among Ukrainian Canadians in Alberta."* Charles W. Hobart. Scarborough: Prentice-Hall of Canada Ltd., c1976. In The Canadian Family in Comparative Perspective, pp. 352-365. Edited by Lyle E. Larson.

**3959. Hobart, Charles W.** *Persistence and Change: a Study of Ukrainians in Alberta.* Charles W. Hobart, Warren E. Kalbach, J.T. Borhek and A.P. Jacoby. [S.l.: s.n., 196?].
Sponsored by the Ukrainian Canadian Research Foundation.

**3960. Hobbs, A.W.** *"Juvenile Murderers."* A.W. Hobbs. Canadian Bar Review 22; 4(Apr. 1944): 377-379.

**3961. Hochstein, Lucille Agatha** *Roman Catholic Separate and Public Schools in Alberta.* Lucille Agatha Hochstein. Edmonton: University of Alberta, 1954. Thesis (M.Ed.)--University of Alberta, 1954.

**3962. Hodgeville Celebrate Saskatchewan Committee** *Hodgeville: Prairie, Pioneers, Progress.* Hodgeville Celebrate Saskatchewan Committee. Hodgeville, Sask.: Hodgeville Celebrate Saskatchewan Committee, 1980.

**3963. Hodgkins, Benjamin J.** *"Educational and Occupational Aspirations Among Rural and Urban Male Adolescents in Alberta."* Benjamin J. Hodgkins and Arnold R. Parr. Alberta Journal of Educational Research 11, 4(Dec. 1965): 255-262.

**3964. Hodgson, Ernest Daniel** *The Nature and Purposes of the Public School in the North West Territories 1885-1905 and Alberta 1905-1963.* Ernest Daniel Hodgson. [Edmonton]: University of Alberta, 1964. Thesis (Ph.D.)--University of Alberta,

1964.

**3965. Hoffman, Gordon** *A Survey of the Senior High School Student Satisfaction-Dissatisfaction in an Albertan Community.* Gordon Hoffman. Calgary: University of Calgary, 1971.
Thesis (M.Ed.)--University of Calgary, 1971.

**3966. Hogg, Georgina R.** *"Myelogenous Leukaemia in a Stillborn Infant."* Georgina R. Hogg and Otto A. Schmidt. Canadian Medical Association Journal 78, 6(Mar. 15, 1958): 421-423.

**3967. Hohol, Albert** *"Factors Associated With School Dropouts."* Albert Hohol. Alberta Journal of Educational Research 1, 1(Mar. 1955): 7-17.

**3968. Holden Historical Society** *Hemstitches and Hackamores: a History of Holden and District.* Holden Historical Society. Holden, Alta.: Holden Historical Society, 1984.

**3969. Holden, Muriel** *"The Normans Come to Calgary."* Muriel Holden. Alberta History 28, 3(Summer 1980): 26-30.

**3970. Hollenberg, C.** *"The Late Effects of Spinal Poliomyelitis."* C. Hollenberg, M.H.L. Desmarais, Lloyd Frihagen and Allan Dale. Canadian Medical Association Journal/Journal de l'Association medicale canadienne 81, 5(Sept. 1, 1959): 343-347.

**3971. Hollos, Marida** *"Families Through Three Generations in Bekevar."* Marida Hollos. Ottawa: National Museums of Canada, 1979. In Bekevar: Working Papers on a Canadian Prairie Community, pp. 65-126. Edited by Robert Blumstock.

**3972. Holman, Marion** *A Study of Attendance and Achievement in Arithmetic, Reading and Language of Vanned and Unvanned Pupils in Certain Centralized Schools of Alberta.* Marion Holman. Edmonton: University of Alberta, 1959.
Thesis (M.Ed.)--University of Alberta, 1959.

**3973. Holmgren, Donald Henry** *Experiences of Indian Students Undergoing Acculturation in Urban High Schools: an Exploratory Study.* Donald Henry Holmgren. Edmonton: University of Alberta, 1971.
Thesis (M.Ed.)--University of Alberta, 1971.

**3974. Holowach-Amiot, Elaine** *Ukranian Canadians and Education in the Province of Saskatchewan, 1905-1930.* Elaine Holowach-Amiot. Montreal: McGill University, 1979.
Thesis (M.A.)--McGill University, 1979.

**3975. Hoole, Arthur Herbert** *The Development of a Family Agency: a Historical Review of the Calgary Family Bureau.* Arthur Herbert Hoole. Vancouver: University of British Columbia, 1954.
Thesis (M.S.W.)--University of British Columbia, 1954.

**3976. Hope, Dennis Jay** *The Development of Private Schools in Alberta.* Dennis Jay Hope. Calgary: University of Calgary, 1982. (CTM no. 60860)
Thesis (M.A.)--University of Calgary, 1982.

**3977. Hopkins, Doris Mae** *A Study of the Relationship Between Linguistic Competence and Reading Achievement.* Doris Mae Hopkins. Edmonton: University of Alberta, 1970.
Thesis (M.Ed.)--University of Alberta, 1970.

**3978. Horch, Esther** *C.N. Hiebert Was My Father.* Esther Horch. Winnipeg: Christian Press, 1979.

**3979. Hore, Terrance** *Social Class Differences in Some Aspects of Verbal and Nonverbal Communication Between Mother and Preschool Child.* Terrance Hore. Edmonton: University of Alberta, 1968. (CTM no. 3387)
Thesis (Ph.D.)--University of Alberta, 1968.

**3980. Hosie, Inez B.** *"Little White School House."* Inez B. Hosie. Alberta Historical Review 15, 4(Autumn 1967): 26-28.

**3981. Hotetler, John A.** *"Education and Assimilation in Three Ethnic Groups."* John A. Hotetler and Calvin Redekop. Alberta Journal of Educational Research 8, 4(Dec. 1962): 189-203.

**3982. Houghton, John Reginald** *The Calgary Public School System 1939-1969: a History of Growth and Development.* John Reginald Houghton. Calgary: University of Calgary, 1971. (CTM no. 10090)
Thesis (M.Ed.)--University of Calgary, 1971.

**3983. Housego, Ian E.** *Alberta Composite High Schools and Gifted Youth.* Ian Edward Housego. Edmonton: University of Alberta, 1958.
Thesis (M.Ed.)--University of Alberta, 1958.

**3984. Housego, Ian E.** *"Alberta Composite High Schools and Gifted Youth."* Ian E. Housego and Gordon L. Mowat. Alberta Journal of Educational Research 5, 1(Mar. 1959): 23-30.

**3985. Howsam, Robert Basil** *A Comparative Sociometric Study of Children Attending Special Classes for the Mentally Gifted and Those Attending Ordinary Classes in the Public Elementary Schools of Saskatoon.* Robert Basil Howsam. Saskatoon: University of Saskatchewan, 1950.
Thesis (M.Ed.)--University of Saskatchewan, 1950.

**3986. Hrabi, James S.** *A Comparative Study of Male Discipline and Male Non-discipline Cases in a Selected Composite High School.* James S. Hrabi. Edmonton: University of Alberta, 1958.
Thesis (M.Ed.)--University of Alberta, 1958.

**3987. Hryniuk, Stella M.** *"The Schooling Experience of Ukrainians in Manitoba, 1896-1916."* Stella M. Hryniuk and Neil G. McDonald. Calgary: Detselig Enterprises, 1986. In Schools in the West: Essays in Canadian Educational History, pp. 155-173. Edited by Nancy M. Sheehan, J. Donald Wilson and David C. Jones.

**3988. Hubert, Kenneth W.** *A Study of the Attitudes of Non-Indian Children Toward Indian Children in an Integrated Urban Elementary School.* Kenneth W. Hubert. Calgary: University of Calgary, 1969.
Thesis (M.Ed.)--University of Calgary, 1969.

**3989. Hudson, Derrel Everett** *Student, Parent and Teacher Attitudes Toward the Pre-employment Classes in the Edmonton Public School System, 1964-65.* Derrel Everett Hudson. Edmonton: University of Alberta, 1966.
Thesis (M.Ed.)--University of Alberta, 1966.

**3990. Hughes, Kenneth James** *"Jackson Beardy: Life and Art."* Kenneth James Hughes. Canadian Dimension 14, 2(Feb. 1979): 3-49.

**3991. Hughes, Robert** *A Study of High School Dropouts in Alberta.* Robert Hughes. Edmonton: Alberta Department of Youth, 1968.

**3992. Hughes, Ronald Charles** *Reinforcement Group Counselling of Volunteering and Non-Volunteering Underachievers.* Ronald Charles Hughes. Calgary: University of Calgary, 1969.
Thesis (M.Ed.)--University of Calgary, 1969.

**3993. Hunt, Dennis** *The Comparative Performance of a Ten-year-old Group of Children on the Wechsler Intelligence Scale for Children and the Revised Stanford-Binet Scale of Intelligence, Form L.M.* Dennis Hunt. Saskatoon: University of Saskatchewan, 1961.
Thesis (M.Ed.)--University of Saskatchewan, 1961.

**3994. Hunt, Valerie Ruth** *Physical and Motor Ability Correlates of Extreme Socioeconomic Groups, Grade One Boys, Edmonton, Alberta.* Valerie Ruth Hunt. Edmonton: University of Alberta, 1970.
Thesis (M.A.)--University of Alberta, 1970.

**3995. Hurl, Lorna F.** *"The Politics of Child Welfare in Manitoba, 1922-1924."* Lorna Hurl. Manitoba History 7(Spring 1984): 2-9.

**3996. Hurl, Lorna F.** *The Welfare Bargain: Nongovernmental Organizations and the Delivery of Manitoba Child Welfare Services, 1929-1953.* Lorna Hurl. Toronto: University of Toronto, 1985.
Thesis (Ph.D.)--University of Toronto, 1985.

**3997. Hustak, Alan** *They Were Hanged.* Alan Hustak. Toronto: J. Lorimer & Co., 1987.

**3998. Hutcheson, Betty** *"Rickets."* Betty Hutcheson, Kathryn Gordon and Flora Morrison. Canadian Nurse 50, 4(Apr. 1954): 307-312.

**3999. Hutchison, Patricia A.** *"Live Attenuated Rubella Vaccine (Cendehill Strain) in School Children."* Patricia A. Hutchison, W. George Davidson, H.C. Grocott and Hulda M. Martin. Canadian Medical Association Journal/Journal de l'Association medicale canadienne 103, 7(Oct. 10, 1970): 728-731.

**4000. Hutchison, Patricia A.** *"The Sequelae of Acute Purulent Meningitis in Childhood."* Patricia A. Hutchison and Michael C. Kovacs. Canadian Medical Association Journal/Journal de l'Association medicale canadienne 89, 4(July 27, 1963): 158-166.

**4001. Hutton, Margaret M.** *"A Study of Social Factors Affecting Teenage Married Multiparae."* Margaret M. Hutton. Canadian Journal of Public Health 59, 1(Jan. 1968): 10-14.

**4002. Idylwild Women's Institute** *Pioneers and Followers of Idylwild and Witchekan Districts.* Idylwild Women's Institute. Idylwild, Sask.: Idylwild Women's Institute, 1976.

**4003. Iftody, Elizabeth Eleanor** *Labelling of Emotions and Cross-modal Coding by Deaf and Hearing Children.* Elizabeth Eleanor Iftody. Edmonton: University of Alberta, 1970.
Thesis (M.Ed.)--University of Alberta, 1970.

**4004. Imperial History Book Committee** *The Imperial Review.* Imperial History Book Committee. Imperial, Sask.: Imperial History Book Committee, 1983.

**4005. Ingle, Robert A.** *A Comparative Study of Male Teacher Influence on Elementary School Boys.* Robert A. Ingle. Calgary: University of Calgary, 1970.
Thesis (M.Ed.)--University of Calgary, 1970.

**4006. Iron River-La Corey History Committee** *Coal Oil to Crude: Iron River-La Corey and Surrounding Areas.* Iron River-La Corey History Committee. Iron River, Alta.: Iron River-La Corey History Committee, 1980.

**4007. Irvine, James William** *Correlates of Grade One Achievement.* James William Irvine. Edmonton: University of Alberta, 1968.
Thesis (M.Ed.)--University of Alberta, 1968.

**4008. Irwin, Joan M.** *An Analysis of the Miscues in the Oral Reading of Indian Children in Selected Grades.* Joan M. Irwin. Calgary: University of Calgary, 1969.
Thesis (M.Ed.)--Unversity of Calgary, 1969.

**4009. Isabella History Book Committee** *Rural Reflections, Volume 2, 1879-1982: a History of Isabella and Blaris.* Isabella History Book Committee. Isabella, Man.: Isabella History Book Committee, 1982.

**4010. Ishii, Masatatsu** *"Clinical Findings and Vaccination Status in 98 Victims of Paralytic Poliomyelitis."* Masatatsu Ishii and Brian J. Sproule. Canadian Medical Association Journal/Journal de l'Association medicale canadienne 86, 7(Feb. 17, 1962): 309-313.

**4011. Israels, A. Montague** *"Reminiscences."* A. Montague Israels. Winnipeg: Jewish Historical Society of Western Canada, c1983. In Jewish Life and Times: a Collection of Essays, pp. 1-6.

**4012. Israils, S.** *"The Dangerous Hypodermoclysis in Infancy."* S. Israils and K. Wylie. Canadian Medical Association Journal 80, 1(Jan. 1, 1959): 31-32.

**4013. Ivan, Leslie P.** *"Surgical Treatment of Infantile Hydrocephalus: Ten Year's Experience in the Use of Ventriculoatrial Shunts With the Holter Valve."* Leslie P. Ivan, Joseph G. Stratford, John W. Gerrard and Carman H. Weder. Canadian Medical Association Journal/Journal de l'Association medicale canadienne 98, 7(Feb. 17, 1968): 337-343.

**4014. Jackson, F.W.** *"The 1936 Epidemic of Poliomyelitis in Manitoba: Control Measures, Epidemiological Features."* F.W. Jackson and C.R. Donovan. Canadian Public Health Journal 28, 8(Aug. 1937): 368-375.

**4015. Jackson, F.W.** *"Health Studies in Manitoba."* F.W. Jackson. Canadian Welfare Summary 14, 5(Jan. 1939): 35-37.

**4016. Jackson, G.R.** *"School Grounds and Supervised Playgrounds."* G.R. Jackson. Public Health Journal 4, 11(Nov. 1913): 606-609.

**4017. Jackson, John J.** *Mr. 5BX, Canada Fitness Pioneer: a Biography of William A.R. Orban.* John J. Jackson. Victoria: Sono Nis Press, c1982.

**4018. Jackson, Kathleen M.** *"Alberta's Children."* Kathleen M. Jackson. Canadian Welfare 24, 8(Mar. 1949): 9-13.

**4019. Jackson, Robert Keith** *An Examination of the Role of Memory Processes in Reading Comprehension.* Robert Keith Jackson. Edmonton: University of Alberta, 1970. (CTM no. 6719)
Thesis (Ph.D.)--University of Alberta, 1970.

**4020. Jaenen, Cornelius J.** *"French Roots in the Prairies: Three Phases in French Canadian History Prior to the Present Era."* Cornelius J. Jaenen. Scarborough: Prentice-Hall of Canada Ltd., c1979. In Two Nations, Many Cultures: Ethnic Groups in Canada, pp. 136-152. Edited by Jean Leonard Elliott.

**4021. Jaenen, Cornelius J.** *"Ruthenian Schools in Western Canada 1897-1919."* Cornelius J. Jaenen. Calgary: Detselig Enterprises, 1979. In Shaping the Schools of the Canadian West, pp. 39-58. Edited by David C. Jones, Nancy M. Sheehan and Robert M. Stamp.
Originally published in Paedagogica Historica 10, 3(1970): 517-541.

**4022. Jaffary, Stuart K.** *"Welfare in Alberta."* Stuart Jaffary. Canadian Welfare 23, 6(Dec. 1947): 11-19.

**4023. Jamault, Marcel** *The Effects of Language Background and Socioeconomic Status on Second-Language Learning in Manitoba Secondary Schools.* Marcel Jamault. Winnipeg: University of Manitoba, 1972. (CTM no. 12173)
Thesis (M.Ed.) -- University of Manitoba, 1972.

**4024. James, Edward Llewellyn** *An Historical Survey of Education in the Strathmore Area of Alberta, 1900-1958.* Edward Llewellyn James. Edmonton: University of Alberta, 1963.
Thesis (M.Ed.)–University of Alberta, 1963.

**4025. Janzen, Helen** *"Father's Memoirs."* Helen Janzen. Winnipeg: Centennial Publications, 1977. In Mennonite Memories: Settling in Western Canada, pp. 78-92. Edited by Lawrence Klippenstein and Julius G. Toews.

**4026. Janzen, Helen** *"Our Family."* Helen Janzen. Winnipeg: Centennial Publications, 1977. In Mennonite Memories: Settling in Western Canada, pp. 248-256. Edited by Lawrence Klippenstein and Julius G. Toews.

**4027. Jeffares, Dolores J.** *"Effect of Socioeconomic Status and Auditory Discrimination Training on First-grade Reading Achievement and Auditory Discrimination."* Dolores J. Jeffares and Grace V. Cosens. Alberta Journal of Educational Research 16, 3(Sept. 1970): 165-178.

**4028. Jenkins, R.B.** *"Some Findings in the Epidemic of Poliomyelitis in Alberta, 1927."* R.B. Jenkins. Canadian Public Health Journal 20, 5(May 1929): 219-224.

**4029. Jenkinson, Marion D.** *"Problem Solving and Achievement."* Marion D. Jenkinson and Dorothy M. Lampard. Alberta Journal of Educational Research 5, 3(Sept. 1959): 166-172.

**4030. Jensen, Norma J.** *An Experimental Study of the Effects of Different Kinds of Visual-Motor Discrimination Training on Learning to Read a Word List.* Norma J. Jensen. Calgary: University of Calgary, 1967. (CTM no. 1688)
Thesis (M.Ed.)–University of Calgary, 1967.

**4031. Jewish Historical Society of Western Canada** *Jewish Life and Times: a Collection of Essays.* Jewish Historical Society of Western Canada. Winnipeg: Jewish Historical Society of Western Canada, c1983.

**4032. Johns, David Paul** *The Role of Play Activities Among the Kwakiutl Indian.* David Paul Johns. Edmonton: University of Alberta, 1971.
Thesis (M.A.)–University of Alberta, 1971.

**4033. Johnson, Helen Louise** *The Development of the Public Child Welfare Program in Saskatchewan.* Helen Louise Johnson. Vancouver: University of British Columbia, 1952.
Thesis (M.S.W.)–University of British Columbia, 1952.

**4034. Johnson, Morgan** *A Study of the Relationship Between Selected Activities for Teacher Preparation and Student Achievement in Grade Nine Mathematics.* Morgan Johnson. Calgary: University of Calgary, 1968.
Thesis (M.Ed.)–University of Calgary, 1968.

**4035. Johnstone, Chris** *"Little Britain."* Chris Johnstone. Manitoba Pageant 23, 2(Winter 1978): 1-4.

**4036. Jones, David C.** *"Better School Days in Saskatchewan and the Perils of Educational Reform."* David C. Jones. Journal of Educational Thought 14, 2(Aug. 1980): 125-137.

**4037. Jones, David C.** *"So Petty, So Middle Europe, So Foreign: Ruthenians and Canadianization."* David C. Jones. History of Education Review 16, 1(Spring 1987): 13-30.

**4038. Jones, David C.** *"A Strange Heartland: the Alberta Dry Belt and the Schools in the Depression."* David C. Jones. Vancouver: Tantalus Research Ltd., c1980. In The Dirty Thirties in Prairie Canada, pp. 89-109. Edited by R.D. Francis and H. Ganzevoort.

**4039. Jones, David C.** *""We Can't Live On Air All the Time": Country Life and the Prairie Child."* David C. Jones. Calgary: Detselig Enterprises Ltd., 1982. In Studies in Childhood History: a Canadian Perspective, pp. 185-202. Edited by Patricia T. Rooke and R.L. Schnell.

**4040. Jones, David C., ed.** *Shaping the Schools of the Canadian West.* David C. Jones, Nancy M. Sheehan and Robert M. Stamp, eds. Calgary: Detselig Enterprises Limited, c1979.

**4041. Jones, Pauline A.** *Person-Situation Congruence Relative to Sex Differences in Elementary School Achievement.* Pauline A. Jones. Edmonton: University of Alberta, 1969.
Thesis (Ph.D.)--University of Alberta, 1969.

**4042. Jonker, Peter** *The Song and the Silence: Sitting Wind, the Life of Stoney Indian Chief, Frank Kaquitts.* Peter Jonker. Edmonton: Lone Pine Publishing, c1988.

**4043. Jordbro, Fanny** *Along a Prairie Trail.* Fanny Jordbro. Lucky Lake, Sask.: The Author, 1981.

**4044. Josephburg History Committee** *South of the North Saskatchewan.* Josephburg History Committee. Fort Saskatchewan, Alta.: Josephburg History Committee, 1984.

**4045. K.I.K. Historical Committee** *K.I.K. Country.* K.I.K. Historical Committee. Keoma, Alta.: K.I.K. Historical Committee, 1974.

**4046. Karpoff, John Theodore** *Aptitudes for Achievement in the Vocational Programs of One Composite High School in Alberta.* John Theodore Karpoff. Edmonton: University of Alberta, 1967.
Thesis (M.Ed.)--University of Alberta, 1967.

**4047. Katz, Philip** *"Behaviour Problems in Juvenile Diabetics."* P. Katz. Canadian Medical Association Journal 76, 9(May 1, 1957): 738-743.

**4048. Kelfield History Book Committee** *Portrait of a Community: Kelfield, Saskatchewan, Canada.* Kelfield History Book Committee. [S.l.]: Kelfield History Book Committee, 1982.

**4049. Kelly, Francis J.** *"The Relation of the Broken Home to Subsequent School Behaviours."* Francis J. Kelly, Joseph North and Harvey Zingle. Alberta Journal of Educational Research 11, 4(Dec. 1965): 215-219.

**4050. Kelly, Russell** *Pattison: Portrait of a Capitalist Superstar.* Russell Kelly. Vancouver: New Star Books, 1986.

**4051. Kelvington Historical Society** *Tears, Toil and Truimph: Story of Kelvington and District.* Kelvington Historical Society. Kelvington, Sask.: Kelvington Historical Society, 1980.

**4052. Kenaston History Committee** *Kith'n Kin: the History of Kenaston and District.* Kenaston History Committee. Kenaston, Sask.: Kenaston History Committee, 1980.

**4053. Kendal History Book Committee** *Kendal Then and Now: Memories That Linger.* Kendal History Book Committee. Kendal, Sask.: Kendal History Book Committee, 1982.

**4054. Kennedy, F.W.** *Physical Education and Recreation in Manitoba.* F.W. Kennedy, E.J. Tyler, Mrs. Arva Shewchuk, J.G. Nick and Andrew Currie. Winnipeg: Ministry of Education, 1958.

**4055. Kennedy, J.J.** *Qu'Appelle Industrial School: White "Rites" for the Indians of the Old North-west.* J.J. Kennedy. Ottawa: Carleton University, 1970.
Thesis (M.A.)--Carleton University, 1970.

**4056. Kennett, Keith Franklin** *Intelligence, Family Size and Socioeconomic Status.* Keith Franklin Kennett. Regina: University of Saskatchewan, 1969. (CTM no. 4317)
Thesis (M.A.)--University of Saskatchewan (Regina Campus), 1969.

**4057. Kenyon, Gerald S.** *Values Held for Physical Activity by Selected Urban Secondary School Students in Canada, Australia, England and the United States.* Gerald S. Kenyon. Washington, D.C.: United States Office of Education, 1970.

**4058. Key, Joan** *The Third Radford: a Pioneer Adventure.* Joan Key. Victoria: Martel Publications, c1988.

**4059. Keywan, Zonia** *Greater Than Kings: Ukrainian Pioneer Settlement in Canada.* Zonia Keywan. Montreal: Harvest House Ltd., c1977.

**4060. Khattab, Abdelmoneim M.** *The Assimilation of Arab Muslims in Alberta.* Abdelmoneim M. Khattab. Edmonton: University of Alberta, 1969.
Thesis (M.A.)--University of Alberta, 1969.

**4061. Kibblewhite, Edward James** *Mental Hygiene Clinics in Alberta, With a Study of Selected Clinic Cases of School Age.* Edward James Kibblewhite. Edmonton: University of Alberta, 1937.
Thesis (M.Ed.)--University of Alberta, 1937.

**4062. Kim, Yong C.** *A Study of Drug Use for Non-medical Purposes Among Young Adults.* Yong C. Kim. Regina: Research Division, Alcoholism Commission of Saskatchewan, 1970.

**4063. Kim, Yong C.** *Survey of Attitude and Knowledge Concerning Marijuana and Its Uses Among High School Students.* Yong C. Kim. Regina: Research Division, the Alcoholism Commission of Saskatchewan, 1971.

**4064. Kincaid History Book Committee** *Trails to Crossroads 1909-1980: the History of Kincaid, Saskatchewan, and Area.* Kincaid History Book Committee. [S.l.: s.n., 1981].

**4065. Kindrachuk, Michael John** *Retardation Among Saskatoon Public School Children 1958-1959.* Michael John Kindrachuk. Saskatoon: University of Saskatchewan, 1963.
Thesis (M.Ed.)--University of Saskatchewan, 1963.

**4066. King, Dennis** *Joseph Norbert Provencher.* Dennis King. Winnipeg: Peguis Publishers Ltd., c1981.

**4067. King, Ethel M.** *"Effects of Visual Discrimination Training on Immediate and Delayed Word Recognition in Kindergarten Children."* Ethel M. King and Siegmar Muehl. Alberta Journal of Educational Research 17, 2(June 1971): 77-88.

**4068. King, Hermin Lewis** *A Study of 400 Juvenile Delinquent Recidivists Convicted in the Province of Alberta During the Years 1920-1930.* Hermin Lewis King. Edmonton: University of Alberta, 1932.
Thesis (M.A.)--University of Alberta, 1932.

**4069. King, Hermin Lewis** *A Study of the Principles Involved in Dealing with Juvenile Delinquency and Their Application in the City of Edmonton.* Hermin Lewis King. Edmonton: University of Alberta, 1934.
Thesis (M.Ed.)--University of Alberta, 1934.

**4070. Kinley, Donald Albert** *Sex-role Learning of Grade One Students.* Donald Albert Kinley. Edmonton: University of Alberta, 1966.
Thesis (M.Ed.)--University of Alberta, 1966.

**4071. Klassen, David J.** *"Acute Leukemia in Children in the Province of Saskatchewan, 1961-66."* David J. Klassen. Canadian Medical Association Journal/Journal de l'Association medicale canadienne 101, 7(Oct. 4, 1969): 414-417.

**4072. Klassen, Henry C.** *"In Search of Neglected and Delinquent Children: the Calgary Children's Aid Society, 1909-1920."* Henry C. Klassen. Regina: Canadian Plains Research Centre, University of Regina, 1981. In Town and City: Aspects of Western Canadian Urban Development, pp. 375-391. Edited by Alan F.J. Artibise.

**4073. Klassen, Peter George** *A History of Mennonite Education in Manitoba.* Peter George Klassen. Winnipeg: University of Manitoba, 1958.
Thesis (M.Ed.)--University of Manitoba, 1958.

**4074. Klippenstein, LaVerna** *"A Tribute: the Diary of Tina Schulz."* LaVerna Klippenstein. Winnipeg: Centennial Publications, 1977. In Mennonite Memories: Settling in Western Canada, pp. 219-232. Edited by Lawrence Klippenstein and Julius G. Toews.

**4075. Klippenstein, Lawrence, ed.** *Mennonite Memories: Settling in Western Canada.* Lawrence Klippenstein and Julius G. Toews, eds. Winnipeg: Centennial Publications, 1977.

**4076. Knill, William D.** *"The Adolescent Society of the High School."* William D. Knill. In The Canadian Secondary School: an Appraisal and a Forecast, pp. 56-63. Edited by Lawrence W. Downey and Ruth Godwin.
Reprinted in abridged form in Canadian Society: Sociological Perspectives, 3rd ed., 1968, pp. 218-222 and abr. 3rd ed., 1971, pp. 153-157. Edited by Bernard R. Blishen, Frank E. Jones, Kasper D. Naegele and John Porter.

**4077. Knill, William D.** *"The Hutterites: Cultural Transmission in a Closed Society."* William D. Knill. Alberta Historical Review 16, 3(Summer 1968): 1-10.

**4078. Knill, William D.** *"Occupational Aspirations of Northern Saskatchewan Students."* William D. Knill. Alberta Journal of Educational Research 10, 1(Mar. 1964): 3-16.

**4079. Knill, William D.** *Saskatchewan Public Education North of 53: a Preliminary Survey of the Provincial School System, Northern Areas Branch, 1962.* William D. Knill and Arthur K. Davis. Saskatoon: Centre for Community Studies, 1963.

**4080. Knowles, Donald W.** *A Comparative Study of Mediational-Task Performance of Indian and Middle-Class Children.* Donald W. Knowles. Edmonton: University of Alberta, 1968. Thesis (Ph.D.) -- University of Alberta, 1968.

**4081. Knowles, Donald W.** *"A Comparison of Optional Shift Performance and Language Skills in Middle Class and Canadian-Indian Children."* Donald W. Knowles and Frederic J. Boersma. Canadian Journal of Behavioural Science/Revue canadienne de sciences du comportement 3, 3(July 1971): 246-258.

**4082. Knowles, Donald W.** *"Optional Shift Performance of Culturally-different Children to Concrete and Abstract Stimuli."* Donald W. Knowles. Alberta Journal of Educational Research 14, 1(Mar. 1968): 165-177.

**4083. Koester, Mavis Addie** *"Childhood Recollections of Lundbreck."* Mavis Addie Koester. Alberta History 26, 4(Autumn 1978): 23-30.

**4084. Kohl, Seena** *"The Family in a Postfrontier Society."* Seena Kohl. Toronto: Holt, Rinehart and Winston of Canada Ltd., c1971. In The Canadian Family, pp. 79-93. Edited by K. Ishwaran.

**4085. Kohl, Seena** *Working Together: Women and Family in Southwestern Saskatchewan.* Seena Kohl. Toronto: Holt, Rinehart and Winston of Canada Ltd., c1976.

**4086. Kojder, Apolonja** *"Slavic Immigrant Women in Northwestern Saskatchewan During the Depression."* Apolonja Kojder. Canadian Woman Studies/Cahiers de la femme 4, 2(Winter 1982): 82-85.

**4087. Kostash, Myrna** *All of Baba's Children.* Myrna Kostash. Edmonton: Hurtig, 1977.

**4088. Kovacs, Leslie** *"Acute Disseminated Lupus Erythematosus in a North American Indian Girl."* Leslie Kovacs, James Calder, Matthew Matas and Samuel Hanson. Canadian Medical Association Journal 74, 7(Apr. 1, 1956): 552-556.

**4089. Kovacs, Martin L.** *Peace and Strife: Some Facets of the History of an Early Prairie Community.* Martin L. Kovacs. Regina: Department of History, University of Regina, 1980.

**4090. Kozak, Kathryn** *Education and the Blackfoot: 1870-1900.* Kathryn Kozak. Edmonton: University of Alberta, 1971. Thesis (M.A.)--University of Alberta, 1971.

**4091. Kratzman, Arthur** *"A Descriptive Survey of the Extracurricular Programs of the Composite High Schools of Alberta."* Arthur Kratzman and J.H. Brauer. Alberta Journal of Educational Research 5, 3(Sept. 1959): 177-179.

**4092. Krepps, Rex G.** *As Sparks Fly Upwards.* Rex G. Krepps. Oliver, B.C.: The Author, [1990?].

**4093. Kresz, Maria** *"Bekevar, Children, Clothing, Crafts."* Maria Kresz and Robert Blumstock, ed. Ottawa: National Museums of Canada, 1979. In Bekevar: Working Papers on a Canadian Prairie Community, pp. 127-166. Edited by Robert Blumstock.

**4094. Kreutz, Norma B.** *The Realizability of Vocational Plans of Grade Twelve Students in Alberta.* Norma B. Kreutz. Edmonton: University of Alberta. 1968. Thesis (M.Ed.)--University of Alberta, 1968.

**4095. Kristjanson, G. Albert** *An Analysis of Relationships Between Selected Factors and Level of Occupational Aspirations of Some Manitoba High School Youth.* G. Albert Kristjanson. Madison, Wis.: Wisconsin University, c1967. Thesis (Ph.D.)--Wisconsin University, 1967.

**4096. Krupa, George Joseph** *An Investigation of Student Perceptions of the Junior High School Semester System.* George Joseph Krupa. Calgary: University of Calgary, 1971. Thesis (M.Ed.)--University of Calgary, 1971.

**4097. Kupfer, George** *Middle Class Delinquency in a Canadian City.* George Kupfer. Seattle: University of Washington, 1966. Thesis (Ph.D.)--University of Washington, 1966.

**4098. Kyle District History Committee** *From Basket to Bridge 1905-1980.* Kyle District History Committee. [Kyle, Sask.: Kyle District History Committee, 1980].

**4099. L.I.F.E. History Committee** *Ten Dollars and a Dream.* L.I.F.E. History Committee. Dixonville, Alta.: L.I.F.E. History Committee, 1978.

**4100. Labercane, George D.**
*"Socioeconomic Status and the Meaning Vocabularies of Children."* G.D. Labercane and Robert D. Armstrong. Edmonton: University of Alberta, 1968. Alberta Journal of Educational Research 15, 4(Dec. 1969): 225-233.

**4101. Lacombe and District Chamber of Commerce** *Lacombe: the First Century.* Lacombe and District Chamber of Commerce. Lacombe, Alta.: Lacombe and District Chamber of Commerce, 1982.

**4102. Laforce, Marguerite Marie** *Moral Judgements Among Indian and White Children.* Sister Marguerite Marie Laforce. Edmonton: University of Alberta, 1967. Thesis (M.Ed.)--University of Alberta, 1967.

**4103. Lake Alma Over 50 Club** *Settlers of the Hills.* Lake Alma Over 50 Club. Lake Alma, Sask.: Over 50 Club, 1975.

**4104. Lambert, Roland A.** *Cognition and Achievement: an Examination of Differences Among Grade Ten Students.* Roland Aimo Lambert. Edmonton: University of Alberta, 1962. Thesis (Ph.D.)--University of Alberta, 1962.

**4105. Lamont and District Historian** *Lamont and Districts: Along Victoria Trail.* Lamont and District Historian. Edmonton, Alta.: Lamont and District Historian, 1978.

**4106. Lamontagne, Myrna L.** *D'Amour: an Era of Change.* Myrna L. Lamontagne. Leask, Sask.: The Author, 1983.

**4107. Lampman and District History Book Committee** *Poet's Corner: a History of Lampman and District and the R.M. of Browning.* Lampman and District History Book Committee. Lampman, Sask.: Lampman and District History Book Committee, 1982.

**4108. Landis History Book Committee** *The Landis Record.* Landis History Book Committee. Landis, Sask.: Landis History Book Committee, 1980.

**4109. Lang Syne History Book Committee** *Lang Syne: a History of Lang, Saskatchewan.* Lang Syne History Book Committee. Lang, Sask.: Lang Syne History Book Committee, 1980.

**4110. Langley, Gerald James** *Saskatchewan's Separate School Systems: a Study of One Pattern of Adjustment to the Problem of Education in a Multireligion Democratic Society.* Gerald James Langley. New York: Columbia University, 1952. Thesis (Ph.D.)--Columbia University,

[1952].

**4111. Langrell, Opal** *Yesteryears: Woodlands Municipal Memoirs.* Opal Langrell. Stonewall, Man.: Interlake Publishing, 1978.

**4112. Langruth Historical Society Book Committee** *Langruth Along the Crocus Trail.* Langruth Historical Society Book Committee Brandon, Man.: Langruth Historical Society, [1984].

**4113. Lapointe, Richard** *The Francophones of Saskatchewan: a History.* Richard Lapointe and Lucille Tessier. Regina: Campion College, University of Regina, 1988.

**4114. Lapp, Eula G.** *"When Ontario Girls Were Going West."* Eula G. Lapp. Ontario History 60, 2(June 1968): 71-79.

**4115. LaRiviere Historical Book Society** *Turning Leaves: a History of LaRiviere and District.* LaRiviere Historical Book Society. LaRiviere, Man.: LaRiviere Historical Book Society, 1979.

**4116. Larson, H.L.** *"The Five School Project Dropout Study."* H.L. Larson. Alberta Journal of Educational Research 4, 4(Dec. 1958): 212-215. Reprinted in Education: a Collection of Essays on Canadian Education, Volume 3, 1958-1960, pp. [45]-48.

**4117. Larson, Lyle E.** *The Family in Alberta.* Lyle E. Larson. Edmonton: Human Resources Council of Alberta, 1971.

**4118. Lashburn and District History Book Committee** *Lashburn and District History 1906-1983.* Lashburn and District History Book Committee. [Lashburn, Sask.]: Lashburn and District History Book Committee, 1983.

**4119. Laurence, Margaret** *Dance on the Earth: a Memoir.* Margaret Laurence and Jocelyn Laurence. Toronto: McClelland and Stewart, 1989.

**4120. Lavers, James Frederick** *An Investigation of Some of the Values Held by High School Students and Their Teachers in a Rural County in Alberta.* James Frederick Lavers. Edmonton: University of Alberta, 1970. Thesis (M.Ed.)--University of Alberta, 1970.

**4121. Law, Patricia** *"Play, an Essential of Every Child's Life."* Patricia Law. Canadian Nurse 51, 12(Dec. 1955): 949.

**4122. Lawler, Robert H.** *"Psychological Implications of Cystic Fibrosis."* Robert H. Lawler, Wladyslaw Nakielny and Nancy A. Wright. Canadian Medical Association Journal/Journal de l'Association medicale canadienne 94, 20(May 14, 1966): 1043-1046.

**4123. Lawler, Robert H.** *"Suicidal Attempts in Children."* Robert H. Lawler, Wladyslaw Nakielny and Nancy A. Wright. Canadian Medical Association Journal/Journal de l'Association medicale canadienne 89, 15(Oct. 12, 1963): 751-754.

**4124. Lawlor, S.D.** *"Social Class and Achievement and Orientation."* S.D. Lawlor. Canadian Review of Sociology and Anthropology/Revue canadienne de sociologie et d'anthropolgie 7, 2(May 1970): 148-153.

**4125. Lawson, Elsie** *"Public Welfare in Manitoba."* Elsie Lawson. Canadian Welfare Summary 15, 3(Sept. 1939): 14-23.

**4126. Laxdal, Oliver E.** *"Acute Respiratory Infections in Children: Part 1. An Intensive Study of Etiology in an Open Community."* Oliver E. Laxdal, H.E. Robertson, Virgil Braaten and W. Alan Walker. Canadian Medical Association Journal/Journal de l'Association medicale canadienne 88, 21(May 25, 1963): 1049-1054.

**4127. Laxdal, Oliver E.** *"Acute Respiratory Infections in Children: Part 2. A Trial of Polyvalent Virus Vaccine."* O.E. Laxdal, G.E. Evans, V. Braaten and H.E. Robertson. Canadian Medical Association Journal/Journal de l'Association medicale canadienne 90, 1(Jan. 4, 1964): 15-19.

**4128. Laxdal, Oliver E.** *"Etiology of Acute Otitis Media in Infants and Children."* Oliver E. Laxdal, Roy M. Blake, Thomas Cartmill and H.E. Robertson. Canadian Medical Association Journal/Journal de l'Association medicale canadienne 94, 4(Jan. 22, 1966): 159-163.

**4129. Laxdal, Oliver E.** *"Treatment of Acute Otitis Media: a Controlled Study of 142 Children."* Oliver E. Laxdal, Joaquin Merida and R.H. Trefor Jones. Canadian Medical Association Journal/Journal de l'Association medicale canadienne 102, 3(Feb. 14, 1970): 263-268.

**4130. Lazarenko, Joseph M., ed.** *The Ukrainian Pioneers in Alberta, Canada.* Joseph M. Lazarenko, ed. Edmonton: Ukrainian Pioneers Association in Edmonton, 1970.

**4131. Le Vann, L.J.** *"Congenital Abnormalities in Children Born in Alberta During 1961: a Survey and a Hypothesis."* L.J. Le Vann. Canadian Medical Association Journal/Journal de l'Association medicale canadienne 89, 3(July 20, 1963): 120-126.

**4132. Le Vann, L.J.** *"Trifluoperazine Dihydrochloride: an Effective Tranquillizing Agent for Behavioural Abnormalities in Defective Children."* L.J. Le Vann. Canadian Medical Association Journal 80, 2(Jan. 15, 1959): 123-124.

**4133. LeBlanc, Darrell Robert** *A Measure of Understanding of Certain Aspects of Alberta Industry.* Darrell Robert LeBlanc. Edmonton: University of Alberta, 1968. Thesis (M.Ed.)--University of Alberta, 1968.

**4134. Lecker, Robert** *Robert Kroetsch.* Robert Lecker. Boston: Twayne, c1986.

**4135. Leeck, Ernie E.** *A Follow-up Study of High School Grads and Dropouts.* Ernie E. Leeck. Edmonton: University of Alberta, 1971. Thesis (M.Ed.)--University of Alberta, 1971.

**4136. Lenoski, Edward F.** *"Single Umbilical Artery: Incidence, Clinical Significance and Relation to Autosomal Trisomy."* Edward F. Lenoski and H. Medovy. Canadian Medical Association Journal/Journal de l'Association medicale canadienne 87, 23(Dec. 8, 1962): 1229-1231.

**4137. Lent, Ada** *"A Survey of the Problems of Adolescent High School Girls Fourteen to Eighteen Years of Age."* Ada Lent. Alberta Journal of Educational Research 3, 3(Sept. 1957): 127-137.

**4138. Lent, Ada** *A Survey of the Problems of Adolescent High School Girls Fourteen to Eighteen Years of Age.* Ada Alberta Lent. Edmonton: University of Alberta, 1957. Thesis (M.Ed.)--University of Alberta, 1957.

**4139. Leonoff, Cyril Edel** *"Wapella Farm Settlement: the First Successful Jewish Farm Settlement in Canada."* Cyril Edel Leonoff. Historical and Scientific Society of Manitoba Transactions, Series 3, 27(1970-1971): 25-59.

**4140. Levesque, Marcel Paul** *The Hutterites, a Survey of Their History, Their Beliefs and Their School Systems.* Marcel Paul Levesque. Saskatoon: University of Saskatchewan, 1987. Thesis (M.Ed.)--University of Saskatchewan, 1987.

4141. Levy, Joanne "In Search of Isolation: the Holdeman Mennonites of Linden, Alberta and Their School." Joanne Levy. Canadian Ethnic Studies/Etudes ethniques au Canada 11, 1(1979): 115-130.

4142. Liberty Optimist Club Early Days to Modern Ways: History of Liberty and District. Liberty Optimist Club. Liberty, Sask.: Liberty Optimist Club, 1982.

4143. Liedtke, Werner W. "Mathematics Learning and Pupil Characteristics." Werner W. Liedtke. Alberta Journal of Educational Research 17, 3(Sept. 1971): 143-153.
   Author presented Ph.D. dissertation with same title at the University of Alberta, 1970.

4144. Limerick Historical Society Prairie Trails and Pioneer Tales: R.M. of Stonehenge, no. 73. Limerick Historical Society. Limerick, Sask.: Limerick Historical Society, 1982.

4145. Linden, Eric William Affective Ties and Delinquency. Eric William Linden. Edmonton: University of Alberta, 1970. Thesis (M.A.)--University of Alberta, 1970.
   Bibiliography leaves 60-65.

4146. Lintlaw Historical Society Echoes of the Past: a History of Lintlaw and District. Lintlaw Historical Society. Lintlaw, Sask.: Lintlaw Historical Society, [1978].

4147. Linton, Thomas E. "The C.P.I. As A Predictor of Academic Success." Thomas E. Linton. Alberta Journal of Educational Research 13, 1(Mar. 1967): 59-64.

4148. Linton, Thomas E. "Dogmatism, Authoritarianism and Academic Achievement." Thomas E. Linton. Alberta Journal of Educational Research 14, 1(Mar. 1968): 49-53.

4149. Linton, Thomas E. "Social Class and Ninth Grade Educational Achievement in Calgary." Thomas E. Linton and Donald L. Swift. Alberta Journal of Educational Research 9, 3(Sept. 1963): 157-167.

4150. Lismer, Marjorie "Adoption Practices of the Blood Indians of Alberta, Canada." Marjorie Lismer. Plains Anthropologist 19, 63(Feb. 1974): 25-33.

4151. Little, G.M. "Child Hygiene: Hyperopia and School Examination." G.M. Little. Canadian Public Health Journal 26, 8(Aug. 1935): 414-415.

4152. Liu, Yuan Hsiung The Effect of Industrial Arts on Mathematics Achievement. Yuan Hsiung Liu. Edmonton: University of Alberta, 1970. Thesis (M.Ed.)--University of Alberta, 1970.

4153. Livelong Historical Society Livelong Legacies. Livelong Historical Society. Livelong, Sask.: Livelong Historical Society, 1981.

4154. Locke, Keith James The Social Context of Educational Aspirations and Expectations: an Exploratory Study of Edmonton Junior High School Students. Keith James Locke. Edmonton: University of Alberta, 1969. Thesis (M.A.)--University of Alberta, 1969.

4155. Loewen, John I. "My Pilgrimage in Darkness." John I. Loewen. Winnipeg: Centennial Publications, 1977. In Mennonite Memories: Settling in Western Canada, pp. 289-299. Edited by Lawrence Klippenstein and Julius G. Toews.

4156. Loewen, Royden Blumenort: a Mennonite Community in Transition, 1874-1982. Royden Loewen, Betty Plett [and] Blumenort Mennonite Historical Society. [S.l.]: Blumenort Mennonite Historical Society, 1983.

4157. Lohrenz, Gerhard The Mennonites of Western Canada. Gerhard Lohrenz. Winnipeg: [s.n.], 1974.

4158. Lomond Historical Society Prairie Gold: R.M. of Lomond no. 37. Lomond Historical Society. Goodwater, Sask.: Lomond Historical Society, 1980.

4159. Love, Ken "The Coming of Age Act." Ken Love. Saskatchewan Law Review 35, 1(1970-71): 94-99.

4160. Loverna New Horizon Borderline Memories: a History of the Town of Loverna and the School Districts of Antelope, Claremont, Grattle, Pizarro, Rock Plains, Saskalta, Springville, South Loverna and Stratton. Loverna New Horizon 1980. Loverna, Sask.: Loverna New Horizon, 1980.

4161. Lowes, Warren Gophers and Tumbleweed: Tales of a Saskatchewan Boyhood. Warren Lowes. Toronto: Abraham Tanaka Assoc. Ltd., c1987.

4162. Lubeck Merrymakers Society Our Bend in the Peace: the Story of Royce and Lubeck. Lubeck Merrymakers Society. Hines Creek, Alta.: Lubeck Merrymakers Society, 1979.

**4163. Lucas, Helen** *"Growing Up Greek."* Helen Lucas. Canadian Woman Studies/Cahiers de la femme 4, 2(Winter 1982): 74-76.

**4164. Lucas, William Geoffrey** *Strength of Edmonton School Children.* William Geoffrey Lucas. Edmonton: University of Alberta, 1966. Thesis (M.A.)–University of Alberta, 1966.

**4165. Lunan, Esther** *As the Roots Grow: the History of Spruce Grove and District.* Esther Lunan. [Spruce Grove, Alta.]: Spruce Grove Public Library, [1979].

**4166. Lupul, Manoly R.** *"The Campaign for a French Catholic School Inspector in the Northwest Territories 1893-1903."* Manoly R. Lupul. Canadian Historical Review 48, 4(Dec. 1967): 332-352.

**4167. Lupul, Manoly R.** *"Education in Western Canada Before 1873."* Manoly R. Lupul. Scarborough: Prentice-Hall of Canada, c1970. In Canadian Education: a History, pp. 241-264. Edited by J. Donald Wilson, Robert M. Stamp and Louis-Philippe Audet.

**4168. Lupul, Manoly R.** *"The Portrayal of Canada's "Other Peoples" in Senior High School History and Social Studies Textbooks in Alberta, 1905 to the Present."* Manoly R. Lupul. Alberta Journal of Educational Research 22, 1(Mar. 1976): 1-33.

**4169. Lupul, Manoly R.** *The Roman Catholic Church and the North-West School Question: a Study in Church-State Relations in Western Canada, 1875-1905.* Manoly R. Lupul. Toronto: University of Toronto Press, c1974.

**4170. Lupul, Manoly R.** *"Ukrainian Language Education in Canada's Public Schools."* Manoly R. Lupul. Toronto: McClelland and Stewart Ltd., 1982. In A Heritage in Transition: Essays in the History of Ukrainians in Canada, pp. 215-243. Edited by Manoly R. Lupul.

**4171. Lupul, Manoly R. ed.** *A Heritage in Transition: Essays in the History of Ukrainians in Canada.* Edited by Manoly R. Lupul. Toronto: McClelland and Stewart Ltd., 1982.

**4172. Luseland Historical Society** *Luseland Hub and Spokes: a History of Luseland, Saskatchewan, 1905-1983.* Luseland Hub and Spokes Committee. 2 v. [Luseland, Sask.: Luseland Historical Society, 1984].

**4173. Lust, Albert** *Academic Achievement of Slow Learners in the Edmonton Continuous Progress Plan.* Albert Lust. Edmonton: University of Alberta, 1966. Thesis (M.Ed.)–University of Alberta, 1966.

**4174. Luxton, Meg** *"Motherwork: More than a Labour of Love."* Meg Luxton. Canadian Women's Studies 2, 1(Autumn 1980): 31-35.

**4175. Luxton, Meg** *Why Women's Work is Never Done: a Case Study From Flin Flon, Manitoba, of Domestic Labour in Industrial Capitalist Society.* Margaret Joan Luxton. Toronto: University of Toronto, 1978. Thesis (Ph.D.)--University of Toronto, 1978.

**4176. Lyle, Guy** *Beyond My Expectation: a Personal Chronicle.* Guy Lyle. Metuchen, N.J.: Scarecrow Press, 1981.

**4177. Lynch, M.J.** *"Fanconi's Anaemia (Aplastic Anaemia with Congenital Abnormalities)."* M.J. Lynch, L. Sherman and F.G. Elliott. Canadian Medical Association Journal 71, 3(Sept. 1954): 273-276.

**4178. Lyon, Louise C.** *Culture Change and Education: a Study of Indian and Non-Indian Views in Southern Alberta.* Louise C. Lyon and John W. Friesen. New York: Associated Educational Services, 1969.

**4179. Lyons, John Edward** *"The Almost Quiet Revolution: Doukhobor Schooling in Saskatchewan."* John Lyons. Canadian Ethnic Studies/Etudes ethniques au Canada 8, 1(1976): 25-37.

**4180. Lysne, David Edgar** *Welfare in Alberta, 1905-1936.* David Edgar Lysne. Edmonton: University of Alberta, 1966. Thesis (M.A.)–University of Alberta, 1966.

**4181. M.I.P. History Book Society** *Spurs and Shovels Along the Royal Line.* M.I.P. History Book Society. Patricia, Alta.: M.I.P. History Book Society, 1979.

**4182. McAlister, J.M.** *The Rural School as a Community Centre: a Discussion Dealing with the Problem of Assimilation of New Canadians in Western Canada.* J.M. McAlister. Edmonton: University of Alberta, 1925. Thesis (M.Sc.)–University of Alberta, 1925. No bibliography.

**4183. McArthur, C.V.** *"Pioneer Children's Aid Society Celebrates Fortieth Anniversary."* C.V. McArthur. Canadian Welfare Summary 14, 5(Jan. 1939): 40-42.

**4184. MacArthur, Russell S.** *"The Coloured Progressive Matrices as a Measure of General Intellectual Ability for Edmonton Grade 3 Boys."* R.S. MacArthur. Alberta Journal of Educational Research 6, 2(June 1960): 67-75.

**4185. McArton, Dorothy** *"75 Years in Winnipeg's Social History."* Dorothy McArton. Canadian Welfare 25, 5(Oct. 1949): 11-19.

**4186. McArton, Sidney** *"Child Welfare Services in Manitoba: Public-Private Relationships."* Sidney McArton. Canadian Welfare 25, 3(July 1949): 32-36.

**4187. McBride, Billie Eleanor Jean** *A Factorial Study of Student Assessments of Teacher Performance.* Billie Eleanor Jean McBride. Edmonton: University of Alberta, 1963.
Thesis (Ph.D.)--University of Alberta, 1963.

**4188. McBride, Billie Eleanor Jean** *The Parental Identification of Adolescents.* Billie Eleanor Jean McBride. Edmonton: University of Alberta, 1961.
Thesis (M.Ed.)--University of Alberta, 1961.

**4189. McBride, Billie Eleanor Jean** *"A Study of Student Assessment of Teacher Performance."* B.E.J. McBride. Alberta Journal of Educational Research 10, 2(June 1964): 79-89.

**4190. McCall, Ralph Lewis** *A History of the Rural High School in Alberta.* Ralph Lewis McCall. Edmonton: University of Alberta, 1956.
Thesis (M.Ed.)--University of Alberta, 1956.

**4191. McCarthy, William Charles** *Indian Dropouts and Graduates in Northern Alberta.* William Charles McCarthy. Edmonton: University of Alberta, 1971.
Thesis (M.Ed.)--University of Alberta, 1971.

**4192. McCarty, Tom** *As We Remember Big Valley.* Tom McCarty. Big Valley, Alta.: The Author, 1974.

**4193. McClung, Nellie L.** *Clearing in the West: My Own Story.* Nellie L. McClung. Toronto: Thomas Allen, [1935].

**4194. McClung, Nellie L.** *"A Homestead Christmas."* Nellie L. McClung. Saskatoon: Western Producer Prairie Books, c1982. In Christmas in the West, pp. 77-79. Edited by Hugh A. Dempsey.

**4195. McClung, Nellie L.** *Tea With the Queen.* Nellie McClung. Vancouver: Intermedia Press, c1979.

**4196. McColl, M. Lorena** *"The Rehabilitation Team."* M. Lorena McColl. Canadian Nurse 55, 3(Mar. 1959): 210-213.

**4197. McCracken, Melinda** *Memories Are Made of This: What It Was Like to Grow Up in the Fifties.* Melinda McCracken. Toronto: James Lorimer & Company, c1975.

**4198. Macdonald, Cathy** *The Edmonton Grads, Canada's Most Successful Team: a History and Analysis of Their Success.* Cathy Macdonald. Windsor: University of Windsor, 1977. (CTM no. 33206)
Thesis (M.H.K.)--University of Windsor, 1977.

**4199. MacDonald, Christine** *"Pioneer Church Life in Saskatchewan."* Christine MacDonald. Saskatchewan History 13, 1(Winter 1960): 1-18.

**4200. Macdonald, Elizabeth** *Japanese Canadians in Edmonton, 1969: an Exploratory Search for Patterns of Assimilation.* Elizabeth Macdonald. Edmonton: University of Alberta, 1970.
Thesis (M.A.)--University of Alberta, 1970.

**4201. McDonald, Neil G.** *The School as an Agent of Nationalism in the North-West Territories, 1884-1905.* Neil Gerald McDonald. Edmonton: University of Alberta, 1971.
Thesis (M.Ed.)--University of Alberta, 1971.

**4202. Macdonald, R.H.** *Grant MacEwan: No Ordinary Man.* R.H. Macdonald. Saskatoon: Western Producer Prairie Books, 1979.

**4203. Macdonald, Robert James** *"Hutterite Education in Alberta: a Test Case in Assimilation, 1920-1970."* Robert James Macdonald. Canadian Ethnic Studies/Etudes ethniques au Canada 8, 1(1976): 9-22.

**4204. Macdonald, Robert James** *"The Hutterites in Alberta."* Robert James Macdonald. Saskatoon: Western Producer Prairie Books, 1985. In Peoples of Alberta: Portraits of Cultural Diversity, pp. 348-365. Edited by Howard and Tamara Palmer.

**4205. McDonnell, Malcolm Whitney** *"The Prediction of Academic Achievement of Superior Grade Three Pupils."* M.W. McDonnell. Alberta Journal of Educational Research 8, 2(June 1962): 111-118.
Author presented a thesis with the same title at the University of Alberta, 1959.

**4206. McDougall, Eliza** *"At the Mission."* Eliza McDougall. Saskatoon: Western Producer Prairie Books, c1982. In Christmas in the West, pp. 28-31. Edited by Hugh A. Dempsey.

**4207. McDowell, Linda** *"Harriet Dick: a Lady Ahead of Her Time."* Linda McDowell. Manitoba Pageant 20, 4(Summer 1975): 11-13.

**4208. MacEwan, Grant** *The Rhyming Horseman of the Qu'Appelle Valley.* Grant MacEwan. Saskatoon: Western Producer Prairie Books, c1978.

**4209. McFaul, Arthur George** *An Analysis of the Calgary Laggard Policy.* Arthur George McFaul. Edmonton: University of Alberta, 1960.
Thesis (M.Ed.)–University of Alberta, 1960.

**4210. McFee, Janice, ed.** *Famous Manitoba Metis.* Janice McFee, project editor, and Bruce Sealey, general editor. Winnipeg: Manitoba Metis Federation Press, c1974.

**4211. McGillivray, James** *"Orthoptic Treatment of Strabismus."* James McGillivray. Canadian Medical Association Journal 46, 3(Mar. 1941): 265-267.

**4212. McGrath, W.D.** *"Pupils and Teachers Learn Together."* W.D. McGrath. Alberta Journal of Educational Research 3, 4(Dec. 1957): 193-198.

**4213. McGrath, W.T.** *Report of the Alberta Penology Study.* W.T. McGrath. [Edmonton: Executive Council, Province of Alberta], 1968.

**4214. MacGregor, James G.** *North-West of 16.* James Grierson MacGregor. Toronto: McClelland and Stewart, 1958.

**4215. MacGregor, James G.** *"North-West of Sixteen."* James G. MacGregor. Saskatoon: Western Producer Prairie Books, c1982. In Christmas in the West, pp. 101-109. Edited by Hugh A. Dempsey.

**4216. MacGregor, John Ross** *A Study of Self Concepts and Ideal Concepts of a Group of Adolescent Students.* John Ross MacGregor. Edmonton: University of Alberta, 1955.
Thesis (M.Ed.)–University of Alberta, 1955.

**4217. McGregor, John Ross** *"A Study of the Self Concept and Ideal Concept in Adolescence."* J.R. McGregor. Alberta Journal of Educational Research 1, 3(Sept. 1955): 5-16.

**4218. McGuckin, Helen Mildred** *Analysis of Adolescent Group Exposure: a Study of Some Former C.G.I.T. Members.* Helen Mildred McGuckin. Calgary: University of Calgary, 1971. (CTM no. 10118)
Thesis (M.S.W.)–University of Calgary, 1971.

**4219. McGugan, A.C.** *"Acute Anterior Poliomyelitis in Alberta in 1941."* A.C. McGugan. Canadian Public Health Journal 32, 11(Nov. 1941): 559-561.

**4220. McGugan, A.C.** *"Anterior Poliomyelitis in Alberta in 1930."* A.C. McGugan. Canadian Public Health Journal 22, 12(Dec. 1931): 595-599.

**4221. McGugan, A.C.** *"Equine Encephalomyelitis (Western Type) in Humans in Alberta, 1941."* A.C. McGugan. Canadian Public Health Journal 33, 4(Apr. 1942): 148-151.

**4222. McGugan, A.C.** *"An Outbreak of Acute Anterior Poliomyelitis in Alberta During the Winter Season."* A.C. McGugan. Canadian Public Health Journal 30, 9(Sept. 1939): 495-499.

**4223. McGuinness, F.G.** *"An Epidemic of Puerperal Mastitis: Associated with Nasopharyngeal and Skin Infection in the Newborn."* F.G. McGuinness and G.S. Musgrove. Canadian Medical Association Journal 61, 4(Oct. 1949): 356-361.

**4224. Maciejko, Bill** *"Ethnicity, Myth and History in Western Canada: the Case of David C. Jones and the "Ruthenians"."* Bill Maciejko. History of Education Review 18, 2(1989): 57-63.

**4225. MacInnis, Grace** *"J.S. Woodsworth: Personal Recollections."* Grace MacInnes. Historical and Scientific Society of Manitoba Transactions, Series 3, 24(1967-1968): 17-26.

**4226. Mack, Benjamin Josef** *A Follow-up Study of the 1967 and 1968 Graduates of the Edmonton Public School Pre-employment Program.* Benjamin Josef Mack. Edmonton: University of Alberta, 1969.
Thesis (M.Ed.)–University of Alberta,

1969.

**4227. McKague, Ormond** *"The Saskatchewan CCF: Educational Policy and the Rejection of Socialism, 1942-1948."* Ormond McKague. Journal of Educational Thought 14, 2(Aug. 1980): 138-159.

**4228. McKay, Doreen P.** *Forty Years On: the Story of Kathryn High School, 1927-1967.* Doreen P. McKay. [S.l.]: Kathryn High School, 1968.

**4229. McKay, Doreen P.** *"A Study of the Spelling Achievement of Rural High School Pupils."* Doreen P. McKay. Alberta Journal of Educational Research 8, 1(Mar. 1962): 45-53.
    Author presented a thesis with the same title at the University of Alberta, 1959.

**4230. MacKay, Ivan Leland** *The Legal Rights, Privileges and Responsibilities of Pupils in the Publicly Supported Schools of Saskatchewan.* Ivan Leland MacKay. Saskatoon: University of Saskatchewan, 1964.
    Thesis (M.Ed.)–University of Saskatchewan, 1964.

**4231. McKee, W.J.** *"A Study of the Incidence and Educational Opportunities of Partially Sighted and Hard-of-hearing Children in Manitoba."* W.J. McKee. Manitoba Journal of Educational Research 1, 1(Nov. 1965): 39-57.

**4232. McKenzie, Charles H.** *"Growing Up in Alberta [Part One]."* Charles H. McKenzie [prepared by Diane McKenzie]. Alberta History 37, 3(Summer 1989): 14-23.

**4233. McKenzie, Charles H.** *"Growing Up in Alberta [Part Two]."* Charles H. McKenzie [prepared by Diane McKenzie]. Alberta History 37, 4(Autumn 1989): 17-27.

**4234. McKenzie, Diane** *"Reminiscences of Dr. Charles McKenzie."* Diane McKenzie. Saskatchewan History 38, 2(Spring 1985): 53-65.

**4235. McKenzie, Mrs. M.I.** *"School Memories."* Mrs. M.I. McKenzie. Alberta Historical Review 7, 1(Winter 1959): 14-17.

**4236. MacKenzie, Rosalind Rosemary** *Visual Perception in Cerebral Palsied Children.* Rosalind Rosemary MacKenzie. Edmonton: University of Alberta, 1963.
    Thesis (M.A.)–University of Alberta, 1963.

**4237. McKenzie, Tully** *It's Time to Remember, 1874-1974: a Hundred Years of Progress, Tremaine-Hunterville Area.* Tully McKenzie, Ethel McKenzie [and] Tremaine Activity Group. Steinbach, Man.: Carillon Press, 1975.

**4238. McKerracher, D.G.** *"Development of a Mental Hygiene Program in Saskatchewan."* D.H. McKerracher. Canadian Welfare 23, 5(Oct. 1947): 33-36.

**4239. McKie, Florence Irene** *"An Analysis of Free-writing in Grade 4, 5 and 6."* Florence I. McKie and Marion D. Jenkinson. Alberta Journal of Educational Research 9, 4(Dec. 1963): 225-237.

**4240. McKie, Florence Irene** *An Analysis of the Characteristics of Free-writing by Grades Four, Five and Six Students.* Florence Irene McKie. Edmonton: University of Alberta, 1963.
    Thesis (M.Ed.)–University of Alberta, 1963.

**4241. Mackie, Marlene** *The Defector from the Hutterite Colony: a Pilot Study.* Marlene Marie Mackie. Calgary: University of Alberta at Calgary, 1965. (CTM no. 8433)
    Thesis (M.A.)–University of Alberta at Calgary, 1965.

**4242. MacKinnon, F.A.** *"Speech Correction Services in the Saskatoon Public Schools."* F.A. MacKinnon. Canadian Education and Research Digest 7, 3(Sept. 1967): 238-251

**4243. McKittrick, Edith Patricia** *Attitudes of High School Students in Manitoba Toward the Use of Alcoholic Beverages.* Sister Edith Patricia McKittrick. Ottawa: University of Ottawa, 1966.
    Thesis (Ph.D.)–University of Ottawa, 1966.

**4244. Mackley, Reginald Harold** *The Role of Prestige, Aptitude, and School Achievement in the Selection of High School Programs and Occupational Preferences by Selected Grade Nine Alberta Students.* Reginald Harold Mackley. Edmonton: University of Alberta, 1970.
    Thesis (M.Ed.)–University of Alberta, 1970.

**4245. McLean, Marjorie Jean** *A Study of the Bender Visual-Motor Gestalt Test in Relation to Reading Difficulties.* Marjorie Jean McLean. Winnipeg: University of Manitoba, 1961.
    Thesis (M.Ed.)–University of Manitoba, 1961.

4246. Maclennan, Gordon W. *"A Contribution to the Ethnohistory of Saskatchewan's Patagonian Welsh Settlement."* Gordon W. Maclennan. Canadian Ethnic Studies/Etudes ethniques au Canada 7, 2(1975): 57-72.

4247. MacLeod, Alan Ross *"Student's Council Leadership."* A.R. MacLeod and William D. Knill. Alberta Journal of Educational Research 14, 3(Sept. 1968): 203.

4248. MacLeod, Alan Ross *Student's Union Power and Influence Structures.* Alan Ross MacLeod. Edmonton: University of Alberta, 1971.
Thesis (Ph.D.)--University of Alberta, 1971.

4249. MacLeod, Allan Ross *Factors Related to Election to a Students Council Executive.* Allan Ross MacLeod. Edmonton: University of Alberta, 1966.
Thesis (M.Ed.)--University of Alberta, 1966.

4250. McLeod, Edna Myrtle *Kindergarten Children's Understanding of Prepositions of Spatial Positions.* Edna Myrtle McLeod. Edmonton: University of Alberta, 1969.
Thesis (M.Ed.)--University of Alberta, 1969.

4251. McLeod, K.C. *"Temporary Care in Reducing Commitments of Neglected, Dependent and Delinquent Children [and Discussion]."* K.C. McLeod. In Proceedings of Sixth Annual Canadian Conference on Child Welfare 1927, pp. 110-113.

4252. McLeod, Keith A. *Education and the Assimilation of the New Canadians in the Northwest Territories and Saskatchewan 1885-1934.* Keith Alwyn McLeod. Toronto: University of Toronto, 1975. (CTM no. 31373)
Thesis (Ph.D.)--University of Toronto, 1975.

4253. McLetchie, N.G.B. *"Essential Brown Induration of the Lungs: Idiopathic Pulmonary Haemosiderosis."* N.G.B. McLetchie and Grant Colpitts. Canadian Medical Association Journal 61, 2(Aug. 1949): 129-133.

4254. McLetchie, N.G.B. *"Nitrate Poisoning from Well-Water."* N.G.B. McLetchie and H.E. Robertson. Canadian Medical Association Journal 60, 3(Mar. 1949): 230-233.

4255. McLetchie, N.G.B. *"Staphylococcal Pneumonia in Childhood."* N.G.B. McLetchie. Canadian Medical Association Journal 60, 4(Apr. 1949): 352-356.

4256. McManus, Thomas M. *A Survey of Pupil Progress in Edmonton City Schools.* Thomas M. McManus. Edmonton: University of Alberta, 1950.
Thesis (M.Ed.)--University of Alberta, 1950.

4257. McMullen, Lorraine *Sinclair Ross.* Lorraine McMullen. Boston: Twayne, c1979.

4258. McMurray, Gordon A. *"Meaning Associated With the Phonetic Structure of Unfamiliar Foreign Words."* Gordon A. McMurray. Canadian Journal of Psychology 14, 3(Sept. 1960): 166-174.

4259. MacNeil, F.A. *"Intranasal Encephalomeningocele."* F.A. MacNeil. Canadian Medical Association Journal 74, 1(Jan. 1, 1956): 63-64.

4260. MacPherson, F.S. *"An Interesting Case of Diptheria."* F.S. MacPherson. Canadian Nurse 25, 5(May 1929): 248-249.

4261. MacRae, John Allan *A Study of Adolescents' Response to the Novel "Lord of the Flies".* John Allan MacRae. Calgary: University of Calgary, 1968.
Thesis (M.Ed.)--University of Calgary, 1968.

4262. McRae, John D. *An Investigation into the Relationship of the Inductive Cognitive Operation and Modes of Presentation.* John D. McRae. Edmonton: University of Alberta, 1971.
Thesis (M.Ed.)--University of Alberta, 1971.

4263. McRae, Kenneth N. *"The Battered Child Syndrome."* Kenneth N. McRae, Charles A. Ferguson and R.S. Lederman. Canadian Medical Association Journal/Journal de l'Association medicale canadienne 108, 7(Apr. 7, 1973): 859-866.

4264. Macrorie History Book Committee *Prairie Progress: Commemorating the Macrorie District.* Macrorie History Book Committee. Macrorie, Sask.: Macrorie History Book Committee, 1983.

4265. McShane, Damian *"Ojibwa World View: a Re-examination."* Damian McShane and Arthur W. Blue. Canadian Journal of Native Studies 5, 1(1985): 115-134.

4266. McSheffrey, J.B. *"Acute Leukemia in Children: Experience in Saskatchewan in 1966-1972."* J.B. McSheffrey, A. Naidoo and W.E.O. Hirte. Canadian Medical Association Journal/Journal de l'Association medicale canadienne 113, 3(Aug. 23, 1975): 295-298.

**4267. McTaggart, A.N.** *"Emotionally Disturbed Children."* A.N. McTaggart. Canadian Nurse 61, 4(Apr. 1965): 294-296.

**4268. Madill, Anita Ruth** *Discriminating Poor Readers in Grade One.* Anita Ruth Madill. Calgary: University of Calgary, 1971. (CTM no. 10124)
Thesis (M.Ed.)--University of Calgary, 1971.
Biliography leaves 32-34.

**4269. Maerz, Leslie R.** *Religious Education in Alberta Public Schools.* Leslie R. Maerz. Calgary: University of Calgary, 1974.
Thesis (M.A.)--University of Calgary, 1974.

**4270. Mahon, Elma** *The Children's Home of Winnipeg: a Review of Recent Developments: from Orphanage to Treatment Centre, 1950-1953.* Elma Mahon. Vancouver: University of British Columbia, 1959.
Thesis (M.S.W.)--University of British Columbia, 1959.
Bibiliography leaves 105-108.

**4271. Mahon, W.A.** *"Pneumonia in Indian and Eskimo Infants and Children: Part 2. A Controlled Clinical Trial of Antibiotics."* W.A. Mahon, F.A. Herbert, D. Wilkinson, O. Morgante, E.C. Burchak and L.R. Costopoulos. Canadian Medical Association Journal/Journal de l'Association medicale canadienne 96, 5(Feb. 4, 1967): 265-268.

**4272. Mahoney, Kent Fletcher** *WISC Pattern Analysis and Teacher Referral Categories.* Kent Fletcher Mahoney. Calgary: University of Calgary, 1970.
Thesis (M.Ed.)--University of Calgary, 1970.

**4273. Mahood, C.I.** *"Morbidity in Diphtheria."* C.I. Mahood. Public Health Journal 15, 2(Feb. 1924): 49-54.

**4274. Malaher, Gerald** *The North I Love.* Gerald Malaher. Winnipeg: Hyperion Press, 1984.

**4275. Mallett, Ivan Burdett** *A Study of Factors Associated With Failure in Selected Subject Areas of Grades 10 and 11.* Ivan Burdett Mallett. Edmonton: University of Alberta, 1963.
Thesis (M.Ed.)--University of Alberta, 1963.

**4276. Manitoba Bar Association. Committee on Continuing Legal Education** *Isaac Pitblado Lectures on Continuing Legal Education: 1970, The Law and the Minor.* Committee on Continuing Legal Education. [Winnipeg: The Committee, 1970].

**4277. Manitoba. Burwalde School District** *Diamond Jubilee Year Book of the Burwalde School at Winkler, Manitoba, 1888-1948.* The District. [Winkler, Man.: s.n.], 1948.

**4278. Manitoba. Educational Commission** *Report of the Educational Commission.* Manitoba. Educational Commission. Winnipeg: P. Purcell, King's Printer, 1924.

**4279. Manitoba. Public Welfare Commission of Manitoba** *Second Interim Report of the Public Welfare Commission of Manitoba.* The Commission. Winnipeg: King's Printer, 1919.
Chairman: T.H. Johnson.
First Interim Report, a 7 leaf typescript, released in 1918.

**4280. Manitoba. Public Welfare Commission of Manitoba** *Third and Final Interim Report.* The Commission. Winnipeg: King's Printer, 1920.
Chairman: T.H. Johnson.

**4281. Manitoba. Royal Commission on Education, 1959** *Report of the Manitoba Royal Commission on Education 1959.* The Commission. [Winnipeg: s.n.], 1959.
Chairman: R.O. MacFarlane.
Interim report, a typescript, released in 1958.

**4282. Manitoba. Royal Commission on Technical Education and Industrial Training** *Report of the Commission on Technical Education and Industrial Training.* The Commission. Winnipeg: King's Printer, 1912.
Chairman: G.R. Coldwell.

**4283. Manitoba. Royal Commission to Inquire Into All Matters Appertaining to the Welfare of Blind Persons Within the Provinces of Manitoba and Saskatchewan** *Report of the Royal Commission to Inquire Into All Matters Appertaining to the Welfare of Blind Persons Withing the Provinces of Manitoba and Saskatchewan.* The Commission. [Winnipeg]: The Commission, 1931.
Commissioner: O.H. Burritt.

**4284. Manitoba. Royal Commission to Inquire Into Child Welfare** *Manitoba Child Welfare Inquiry: Comparative Analysis, Canadian Provinces, Mothers' Allowances.* The Commission. [Winnipeg?: The Commission, 1928].
Also known as Royal Commission Appointed by Order in Council No. 747-28 to Inquire Into the Administration of the Child Welfare Division of the Department of Health and Public Welfare.
Chairman: Charlotte Whitton.

**4285. Manor History Book Committee** *Memories are Forever.* Manor History Book Committee. Manor, Sask.: Manor History Book Committee, 1982.

**4286. Margeau, Annette** *Effects of Group Counselling on Underachiever's Attitudes Toward Self and Others.* Annette Margeau. Edmonton: University of Alberta, 1971.
Thesis (M.Ed.)--University of Alberta, 1971.

**4287. Marles, John D.** *Extracurricular Activities in Edmonton Junior High Schools.* John D. Marles. Edmonton: University of Alberta, 1963.
Thesis (M.Ed.)--University of Alberta, 1963.

**4288. Marquis History Book Group** *Marquis Memories.* Marquis History Book Group. Marquis, Sask.: Marquis History Book Group, 1983.

**4289. Marsh, William Leon** *Teacher and Student Perceptions of School Climate.* William Leon Marsh. Edmonton: University of Alberta, 1970.
Thesis (M.Ed.)--University of Alberta, 1970.

**4290. Marston, E.** *"Hygiene in Winnipeg in the Early Seventies."* E. Marston. Public Health Journal 7, 7(July 1916): 366-369.

**4291. Martin, J.K.** *"The Ataxic Child."* J.K. Martin. Canadian Medical Association Journal 69, 6(Dec. 1953): 601-605.

**4292. Martin, J.K.** *"Cerebral Palsy in Manitoba."* J.K. Martin. Canadian Medical Association Journal/Journal de l'Association medicale canadienne 82, 8(Feb. 20, 1960): 411-417.

**4293. Martin, J.K.** *"An Outbreak of Nephritis at Treherne, Manitoba."* J.K. Martin and W. Bowie. Canadian Medical Association Journal 77, 8(Oct. 15, 1957): 769-772.

**4294. Martin, John** *"Prairie Reminiscences."* John Martin. Alberta Historical Review 10, 2(Spring 1962): 5-19.

**4295. Martin, John Julius** *The History of Seven Creek School No. 852 Established June 9th, 1903.* John Julius Martin. Rosebud: John Julius Martin, 1974.

**4296. Martin, Kenneth Harold** *The Effect of Religious Education on Moral Development.* Kenneth Harold Martin. Edmonton: University of Alberta, 1971.
Thesis (M.A.)--University of Alberta, 1971.

**4297. Martin, M.G.** *"Examination of the Disturbed Child in General Practice."* M.G. Martin. Canadian Medical Association Journal 79, 6(Sept. 15, 1958): 499-502.

**4298. Maryfield and District Historical Society** *Across Border and Valley: the Story of Maryfield and Fairlight and Surrounding Districts.* Maryfield and District Historical Society. 2 v. Maryfield, Sask.: Maryfield and District Historical Society, 1984.

**4299. Masinasin Historical Society** *From Sandstone to Settlers: Writing on Stone District History 1900-1983.* Masinasin Historical Society and Masinasin New Horizon's Society. Milk River, Alta.: Masinasin Historical Society and Masinasin New Horizon Society, [1983].

**4300. Mason, L.H.** *"A Case of Fatal Shock Following Oral Penicillin."* L.H. Mason. Canadian Medical Association Journal 76, 11(June 1, 1957): 958-959.

**4301. Masson, Louis I.** *"The Influence of Developmental Level on the Learning of a Second Language Among Children of Anglo-Saxon Origin."* Louis I. Masson. Canadian Education and Research Digest 4, 3(Sept. 1964): 188-192.

**4302. Matejko, Joanna** *Polish Settlers in Alberta: Reminiscences and Biographies.* Joanna Matejko. Toronto: Polish Alliance Press, 1979.

**4303. Mather History Committee** *Crocus Country: a History of Mather and Surrounding Districts.* Mather History Committee. Mather, Man.: Mather History Committee, 1981.

**4304. Matheson, William John** *Listening and Reading in Primary Grades.* William John Matheson. Calgary: University of Calgary, 1971.
Thesis (M.Ed.)--University of Calgary, 1971.

**4305. Matthiasson, John S.** *"The Icelandic Canadians: the Paradox of an Assimilated Ethnic Group."* John S. Matthiasson. Scarborough: Prentice-Hall of Canada Ltd., c1979. In Two Nations, Many Cultures: Ethnic Groups in Canada, pp. 195-205. Edited by Jean Leonard Elliott.

**4306. Maurice, Louis J.** *An Analysis of Semiotic Factors in Cartoon Visuals and Their Effect on Conveying Meaning in Second Language Teaching.* Louis J. Maurice. Edmonton: University of Alberta, 1970. (CTM no. 6741)
Thesis (Ph.D.)--University of Alberta, 1970.
Bibliogrpahy leaves 109-118.

**4307. Maxstone Historical Society** *Faith, Hope and a Homestead: History of Maxstone and Surrounding School Districts.* Maxstone Historical Society. Assiniboia, Sask.: Maxstone Historical Society, 1982.

**4308. Maymont Library Board** *From Sod to Solar: Fielding, Lilac, Maymont, Ruddell.* Maymont Library Board. Maymont, Sask.: Maymont Library Board, 1980.

**4309. Maynard, Fredelle Bruser** *The Tree of Life.* Fredelle Bruser Maynard. Markham, Ont.: Viking, c1988.

**4310. Mazur, Michael J.** *"The Higher Horizons Program in Winnipeg Schools."* Michael J. Mazur. Manitoba Journal of Educational Research 1, 2(June 1966): 37-47.

**4311. Mazzone, Perry A.** *"An Immigrant Family in Saskatchewan, 1903-1943."* Perry A. Mazzone. Canadian Ethnic Studies/Etudes ethniques au Canada 12, 3(1980): 131-139.

**4312. Medovy, H.** *"Acute Intussusception in Infancy."* Harry Medovy, Arthur E. Childe, C.W. Clarke and Evelyn Turner. Canadian Nurse 50, 4(Apr. 1954): 274-277.

**4313. Medovy, H.** *A Vision Fulfilled: the Story of the Children's Hospital of Winnipeg, 1909-1973.* Harry Medovy. Winnipeg: Peguis Publishers, c1979.

**4314. Medovy, H.** *"Well Water Methaemoglobinaemia in Infants."* Harry Medovy. Canadian Medical Association Journal 62, 3(Mar. 1950): 228-230.

**4315. Medovy, H.** *"Western Equine Encephalomyelitis in Infants."* Harry Medovy. Canadian Public Health Journal 33, 6(June 1942): 307-312.

**4316. Medstead and District History Book Committee** *Trails of Promise.* Medstead and District History Book Committee. Medstead, Sask.: Medstead and District History Book Committee, 1980.

**4317. Meikle, Stewart** *Teenage Sexuality.* Stewart Meikle, Jacquelyn A. Peitchinis and Keith Pearce. San Diego: College-Hill Press, c1985.

**4318. Melita-Arthur History Committee** *Our First Century, 1884-1984.* Melita-Arthur History Committee. Melita, Man.: Melita-Arthur History Committee, 1983.

**4319. Melnychuk, Rudolph S.** *Academic Achievement of Pupils in the Edmonton Continuous Progress Plan.* Rudolph Steve Melnychuk. Edmonton: University of Alberta, 1964. Thesis (M.Ed.)--University of Alberta, 1964.

**4320. Melnychuk, Rudolph S.** *"An Assessment of the Academic Achievement of Average and Accelerated Pupils in Edmonton's Continuous Progress Plan."* Rudolph S. Melnychuk and John H.M. Andrews. Alberta Journal of Educational Research 11, 2(June 1965): 111-115.

**4321. Meloff, William Alan** *An Investigation of the Self-images of Jewish Children Attending Summer Camp.* William Alan Meloff. Edmonton: University of Alberta, 1963. Thesis (M.A.)--University of Alberta, 1963.

**4322. Mendryk, Stephen W.** *An Analysis of Play, Physical Education and Athletic Injuries Which Occurred in the Edmonton Public and Separate School Systems During the 1967-68 School Year.* S.W. Mendryk and P.G. King. Edmonton: University of Alberta, 1969.

**4323. Mendryk, Stephen W.** *The Incidence of Injury in Athletic and Physical Education Activities in the Edmonton Public School System.* S.W. Mendryk and G.W. Dickau. Edmonton: University of Alberta, 1968.

**4324. Meota History Book Committee** *Footsteps in Time.* Meota History Book Committee. Meota, Sask.: Meota History Book Committee, 1980.

**4325. Mercier, Pauline, comp.** *Historical Notes on the Parish of St. Laurent.* Pauline Mercier, comp. [and] White Horse Plain School Division. Elie, Man.: White Horse Plain School Division, 1974. Bilingual.

**4326. Michasiw, Barbara** *"Pioneering Young."* Barbara Michasiw. Canadian Children's Literature/Litterature canadienne pour la jeunesse 35/36(1984): 50-63.

**4327. Migus, Paul M.** *"Ukrainian Nationalism and the Student Movement in Canada."* Paul M. Migus. Winnipeg: UVAN, 1976. In Jubilee Collection of the Ukrainian Free Academy of Sciences in Canada, pp. 443-466. Edited by A. Baran, O.W. Gerus and J. Rozumnyj.

**4328. Miles, Walter H.** *The History of the Wanakena School District, no. 4461, 1922-1978.* Walter H. Miles. [Debden, Sask.: The Author, 1980].

**4329. Millarville Historical Society** *Foothills Echoes.* Millarville Historical Society. Millarville, Alta.: Millarville Historical Society, 1979.

**4330. Millarville, Kew, Priddis and Bragg Creek Historical Society** *Our Foothills.* Millarville, Kew, Priddis and Bragg Creek Historical Society. Calgary, Alta.: Millarville, Kew, Priddis and Bragg Creek Historical Society, 1975.

**4331. Miller, Andrew P.** *"Nonfatal Cutaneous Anthrax of Obscure Origin."* Andrew P. Miller. Canadian Medical Association Journal/Journal de l'Association medicale canadienne 81, 1(July 1, 1959): 35-36.

**4332. Miller, Laura** *A Backward Glance: Glenavon and District.* Laura Miller [and] Walter Dawson. Kipling, Sask.: South East Press, 1980.

**4333. Miller, Philip Gordon** *A Brief History of the Seventh-day Adventist Educational Program in Canada With Special Reference to Alberta.* Philip Gordon Miller. Edmonton: University of Alberta, 1957.
Thesis (M.Ed.)--University of Alberta, 1957.

**4334. Miller, Robert Edward** *An Investigation into the Treatment of Visual Information Through the Television Medium.* Robert Edward Miller. Calgary: University of Calgary, 1971. (CTM no. 10133)
Thesis (Ph.D.)--University of Calgary, 1971.

**4335. Millet and District Historical Society** *Tales and Trails of Millet.* Millet and District Historical Society. 2 v. Millet, Alta.: Millet and District Historical Society, 1978.

**4336. Minburn Golden Age Society** *Miles to Minburn: a History of Minburn and Surrounding Areas.* Minburn Golden Age Society. Minburn, Alta.: Minburn Golden Age Society, 1980.

**4337. Minifie, James M.** *Homesteader: a Prairie Boyhood Recalled.* James M. Minifie. Toronto: MacMillan of Canada, 1972.

**4338. Minnehaha Co-op Women's Auxiliary** *Tales and Trials, 1893-1979: a Community History.* Minnehaha Co-op Women's Auxiliary. [S.l.]: Minnehaha Co-op Women's Auxiliary, 1979.

**4339. Minton 1980 Book Committee** *Golden Leaves.* Minton "1980" Book Committee. Winnipeg: Intercollegiate Press, 1980.

**4340. Minton, R.J.** *Golden Memories of Bissett.* R. John Minton. [S.l.: The Author], 1982.

**4341. Misanchuk, Earl Russell** *An Investigation of Effects of Auditory and Social Isolation on Listening Comprehension.* Earl Russell Misanchuk. Edmonton: University of Alberta, 1969.
Thesis (M.Ed.)--University of Alberta, 1969.

**4342. Mitchell, James R.** *"An Analysis of the Causes of Perinatal Death."* James R. Mitchell, Georgina Hogg, A.J. DePape, E.J.N. Briggs and Harry Medovy. Canadian Medical Association Journal/Journal de l'Association medicale canadienne 80, 10(May 15, 1959): 796-799.

**4343. Mitchell, Ross** *Medicine in Manitoba: the Story of its Beginnings.* Ross Mitchell. Winnipeg: Stovel-Advocate Press, 1954.

**4344. Mitchell, Tom** *"Forging a New Protestant Ontario on the Agricultural Frontier: Public Schools in Brandon and the Origin of the Manitoba School Question 1881-1890."* T.S. Mitchell. Prairie Forum 11, 1(Spring 1986): 33-48.

**4345. Mitchell, Tom** *"In the Image of Ontario: Public Schools in Brandon, 1881-1890."* Tom Mitchell. Manitoba History 12(Autumn 1986): 25-34.

**4346. Moore, Percy Harold** *A Country Boy.* Percy H. Moore. [Sayward, B.C.: P.H. Moore], c1983.

**4347. Moorhouse, John A.** *"Familial Haemolytic Anaemia: Concurrent Crisis in Three Members of a Family."* John A. Moorhouse and Francis A.L. Mathewson. Canadian Medical Association Journal 75, 2(July 15, 1956): 133-135.

**4348. Moosomin History Book Committee** *Moosomin Century One: Town and Country.* Moosomin History Book Committee. Moosomin, Sask.: Moosomin History Book Committee, 1981.

**4349. Morgan, E.C.** *"Pioneer Recreation and Social Life."* E.C. Morgan. Saskatchewan History 18, 2(Spring 1965): 41-54.

**4350. Morison, James B.** *"Health Education and Cigarette Smoking: a Report on a Three Year Program in the Winnipeg School Division, 1960-1963."* James B. Morison, Harry Medovy and Gordon T. MacDonell. Canadian Medical Association Journal/Journal de l'Association medicale canadienne 91, 2(July 11, 1964): 49-56.

**4351. Morison, James B.** *"Report on Smoking Habits of Winnipeg School Children: 1960-1968."* James B. Morison. Canadian Medical Association Journal/Journal de l'Association medicale canadienne 108, 9(May 5, 1973): 1138-1143.

**4352. Morison, James B.** *"Smoking Habits of Winnipeg School Children."* James B. Morison and H. Medovy. Canadian Medical Association Journal/Journal de l'Association medicale canadienne 84, 18(May 6, 1961): 1006-1012.

**4353. Morison, James B.** *"Smoking Habits of Winnipeg School Students, 1960-80."* James B. Morison. Canadian Medical Association Journal/Journal de l'Association medicale canadienne 126, 2(Jan. 15, 1982): 153-154.
Incluees tables and graphs.

**4354. Morisset, Jean, ed.** *Ted Trindell: Metis Witness to the North.* Edited by Jean Morisset and Rose-Marie Pelletier. Vancouver: Tillacum Library, 1986.

**4355. Morley, Patricia** *Kurelek: a Biography.* Patricia Morley. Toronto: MacMillan, 1986.

**4356. Morris, William Reginald** *An Analysis of the Effects of Counselling and Group Guidance on Realism of Educational and Vocational Choice at the Grade 9 Level.* William Reginald Morris. Edmonton: University of Alberta, 1960.
Thesis (M.Ed.)--University of Alberta, 1960.

**4357. Morris, William Reginald** *"Realism of Educational and Vocational Choices at Grade Nine."* W.R. Morris. Alberta Journal of Educational Research 8, 2(June 1962): 103-110.

**4358. Morton, W.L.** *"Manitoba Schools and Canadian Nationalism, 1890-1923."* W.L. Morton. Canadian Historical Association, Historical Papers (1951): 51-59.

**4359. Mosychuk, Harry** *Differential Home Environments and Mental Ability Patterns.* Harry Mosychuk. Edmonton: University of Alberta, 1969. (CTM no. 4960)
Thesis (Ph.D.)--University of Alberta, 1969.

**4360. Mosychuk, Harry** *Longitudinal Prediction of Grade 9 Exam Success for Different Urban Socioeconomic Groups.* Harry Mosychuk. Edmonton: University of Alberta, 1965.
Thesis (M.Ed.)--University of Alberta, 1965.

**4361. Mott, Morris** *"One Town's Team: Souris and Its Lacrosse Club, 1887-1906."* Morris Mott. Manitoba History 1(1979): 10-16.

**4362. Mountain Horse, Mike** *"Christmas Day."* Mike Mountain Horse. Saskatoon: Western Producer Prairie Books, c1982. In Christmas in the West, pp. 67-71. Edited by Hugh A. Dempsey.

**4363. Muir, Norman Deans** *A Comparison of Competence in Algebra of the Grade 9 Students of the Edmonton Public Schools in 1938-1959.* Norman Deans Muir. Edmonton: University of Alberta, 1960.
Thesis (M.Ed.)--University of Alberta, 1960.

**4364. Muir, Norman Deans** *"A Comparison of Competence in Algebra of the Grade 9 Students of the Edmonton Public Schools in 1938 and 1959."* Norman D. Muir. Alberta Journal of Educational Research 7, 4(Dec. 1961): 175-184.

**4365. Mullin, Evelyn, ed.** *Living Gold: a History of the Rural Municipality of Roland, Manitoba, 1876-1976.* Evelyn Mullin, ed. [and] Myrtle-Roland History Book Committee. [S.l.]: Myrtle-Roland History Book Committee, 1978.

**4366. Munro, Barry C.** *"Meaning and Learning."* Barry C. Munro. Alberta Journal of Educational Research 5, 4(Dec. 1959): 268-281.

**4367. Munro, Barry C.** *"The Structure and Motivation of an Adolescent Peer Group."* Barry C. Munro. Alberta Journal of Educational Research 3, 3(Sept. 1957): 149-161.

**4368. Munro, Barry C.** *The Structure and Motivation of an Adolescent Peer Group.* Barry Cartwright Munro. Edmonton: University of Alberta, 1957.
Thesis (M.Ed.)--University of Alberta, 1957.

**4369. Munro, Jack** *Union Jack: Labour Leader Jack Munro.* Jack Munro and Jane O'Hara. Vancouver: Douglas and McIntyre, c1988.

**4370. Murphy Jr., J.N.** *"Clinical Cases of Diptheria Occuring in Patients Who Had Previously Received One Injection of Alum Precipitated Diphtheria Toxoid."* J.N. Murphy, Jr., E.B. Cook and S.W. Bohls. Canadian Public Health Journal 31, 6(June 1940): 276-279.

**4371. Murray, D.J.** *"Spontaneous Rupture of the Spleen in an Erythroblastotic Infant."* D.J. Murray, P.W. Davey and G.M. Martin. Canadian Medical Association Journal 77, 1(July 1, 1957): 37-39.

**4372. Murray, Stuart, ed.** *Arizona, 1882-1982.* Stuart Murray, ed. [and] Arizona Women's Organization. Sidney, Man.: Arizona, Manitoba Community History, 1982.

**4373. Mutchler, Agnes Knox** *"Artists and Artisans in the Making."* Agnes Knox Mutchler. Canadian Welfare 19, 6(Dec. 1943): 19-23.

**4374. Muttart, David Garth** *The Social Climate of the Classroom: Its Description and Its Relationship to the Achievement of Low and High Ability Students in Mathematics.* David Garth Muttart. Calgary: University of Calgary, 1969. Thesis (M.Ed.)--University of Calgary, 1969.

**4375. Myles, Eugenie Louise** *The Emperor of Peace River.* Eugenie Louise Myles. Saskatoon, Sask.: Western Producer Prairie Books, 1978.

**4376. Naicam Heritage Book Committee** *Gleanings Along the Way: a History of Naicam, Lac Vert and Surrounding Districts.* Naicam Heritage Book Committee. Winnipeg: Inter-Collegiate Press, 1980.

**4377. Nanton and District Historical Society** *Mosquito Creek Roundup: Nanton-Parkland.* Nanton and District Historical Society. Nanton, Alta.: Nanton and District Historical Society, 1975.

**4378. Navalkowski, Anna** *"Shandro School."* Anna Navalkowski. Alberta Historical Review 18, 4(Autumn 1970): 8-14.

**4379. Nazeravich, William** *The Influence of Purulent Meningitis on Mental Development of Children as Determined by Psychological Tests and School Adjustment.* William Nazeravich. Winnipeg: University of Manitoba, 1961.

Thesis (M.Ed.)–University of Manitoba, 1961.

**4380. Neander, Wendy Lee** *"Tradition and Change in the Northern Alberta Woodland Cree: Implications for Infant Feeding Practices."* Wendy L. Neander and Janice M. Morse. Canadian Journal of Public Health/Revue canadienne de sante publique 80, 3(May-June 1989): 190-194.

**4381. Nearing, John Joseph** *A Study of the Academic Careers of Selected Non-academically Gifted Students in Alberta Composite High Schools.* John Joseph Nearing. Edmonton: University of Alberta, 1959. Thesis (M.Ed.)–University of Alberta, 1959. Bibliography.

**4382. Neatby, Leslie H.** *Chronicle of a Pioneer Prairie Family.* Leslie H. Neatby. Saskatoon: Western Producer Prairie Books, c1979.

**4383. Nebel, Mabel Ruttle** *"Rev. Thomas Johnson and the Insinger Experiment."* Mabel Ruttle Nebel. Saskatchewan History 11, 1(Winter 1958): 1-17.

**4384. Neepawa History Book Committee** *Heritage: a History of the Town of Neepawa and District as Told and Recorded by Its People, 1883-1983.* Neepawa History Book Committee. Neepawa, Man.: Neepawa History Book Committee, 1983.

**4385. Neering, Rosemary** *Louis Riel.* Rosemary Neering. Don Mills: Fitzhenry and Whiteside, c1977.

**4386. Nelson, Ferne** *Barefoot on the Prairie: Memories of Life on a Prairie Homestead.* Ferne Nelson. Saskatoon: Western Producer Prairie Books, 1989.

**4387. Nelson, Jean Clyne** *Supplementary Report on Juvenile Delinquency.* Jean Clyne Nelson. Edmonton: [s.n.], 1967. Supplementary Report to the Alberta Royal Commission on Juvenile Delinquency. Chairman: F.H. Quigley.

**4388. Neufeld, Peter A.** *"New Bergthal S.D."* Peter A. Neufeld. Winnipeg: Centennial Publications, 1977. In Mennonite Memories: Settling in Western Canada, pp. 211-218. Edited by Lawrence Klippenstein and Julius G. Toews.

**4389. Neville, Mary H.** *"Differential Achievement in Reading and Arithmetic."* Mary H. Neville and Barry P. Frost. Alberta Journal of Educational Research 10, 4(Dec. 1964): 192-200.

**4390. Neville, Mary H.** *The Effect of Silent Reading, Oral Reading and Listening on Accuracy and Comprehension in Beginning Reading.* Mary H. Neville. Calgary: University of Calgary, 1965. Thesis (M.Ed.)–University of Calgary, 1965.

**4391. Neville, Mary H.** *The Effects of Oral and Echoic Responses in Beginning Reading.* Mary H. Neville. Calgary: University of Calgary, 1967. Thesis (Ph.D.)–University of Calgary, 1967.

**4392. Neville, Mary H.** *"Factors Affecting the Listening Comprehension."* Mary H. Neville. Alberta Journal of Educational Research 13, 3(Sept. 1967): 201-209.

**4393. Neville, Mary H.** *"Understanding Between Children of the Same Age."* Mary H. Neville. Alberta Journal of Educational Research 13, 3(Sept. 1967): 221-229.

**4394. New F Historical Club** *Memories We Share North of Birch Hills: a History of the School Districts of New England, Winton and Fisher.* New F Historical Club. Birch Hills, Sask.: New F Historical Club, 1980.

**4395. New Finland Historical and Heritage Society** *Life in the New Finland Woods: a History of New Finland, Saskatchewan.* New Finland Historical and Heritage Society. Rocanville, Sask.: New Finland Historical and Heritage Society, 1982.

**4396. New Osgoode Restoration Club** *Preserving Our Heritage: New Osgoode and District, 1904-1983.* New Osgoode Restoration Club. Tisdale, Sask.: New Osgoode Restoration Club, 1984.

**4397. Ney, Elizabeth Aikins** *"A Girlhood in Government House."* Elizabeth Aikins Ney. Beaver 70, 2(Apr.-May 1990): 14-21.

**4398. Niddrie, John G.** *"Pioneering in Eagle Valley."* John G. Niddrie. Alberta Historical Review 9, 2(Spring 1961): 8-11.

**4399. Nielsen, James Kristian** *Case Studies of Socially Isolated Males in a High School.* James Kristian Nielsen. Edmonton: University of Alberta, 1962. Thesis (M.Ed.)–University of Alberta, 1962.

**4400. Nielsen, James Kristian** *"Case Studies of Socially Isolated Males in Senior High School."* J.K. Nielsen. Alberta Journal of Educational Research 9, 4(Dec. 1963): 247-253.

**4401. Nikkel, Abraham** *A Comparison of Problem Solving Abilities of Students Using Computer Programming Techniques with Those Using Conventional Techniques in a Grade Ten Mathematics Programme.* Abraham Nikkel. Calgary: University of Calgary, 1970. Thesis (M.Ed.)–University of Calgary, 1970.

**4402. Njaa, Lloyd Johan** *An Investigation of the Extent to Which Welfare Effects the Achievement Motivation, School Achievement, Value Orientation and Level of Aspiration of Children in the Edmomton Separate School System.* Lloyd Johan Njaa. Edmonton: University of Alberta, 1966. Thesis (M.Ed.)–University of Alberta, 1966.

**4403. Nobleford Monarch History Book Club** *Sons of Wind and Soil.* Nobleford, Monarch History Book Club. Nobleford, Alta.: Nobleford, Monarch History Book Club, 1976.

**4404. Nolan, Shelagh** *"A Young Girl in the Old West."* Shelagh Nolan. Beaver 66, 4(Aug.-Sept. 1986): 49-55.

**4405. North Battleford New Horizons Committee** *Oxen to Oil: Diamond Memories.* New Horizons Committee. North Battleford, Sask.: McIntosh Publishing, 1982.

**4406. North Gull Lake Historical Association** *From Prairie Trails to Pavement.* North Gull Lake Historical Association. Gull Lake, Sask.: North Gull Lake Historical Association, 1982.

**4407. North, Joseph** *The Relationship of Broken Homes to the Performance of School Children.* Joseph North. Edmonton: University of Alberta, 1965. Thesis (M.Ed.)–University of Alberta, 1965.

**4408. North of the Gully History Book Committee** *North of the Gully.* North of the Gully History Book Committee. Maidstone, Sask.: North of the Gully History Book Committee, 1981.

**4409. Norton Rural Municipality Historical Committee** *From the Roughbark to the Buttes: R.M. Norton, No. 69, Villages of Amulet, Forward, Khedive, Moreland and Pangman.* R.M. of Norton History Committee. Pangman, Sask.: R.M. of Norton History Committee, 1981.

**4410. Notukeu History Club** *Next Year Country.* Notukeu History Club. Notukeu, Sask.: Notukeu History Club, 1980.

**4411. Nuffield, E.W.** *With the West in Her Eyes: Nellie Hislop's Story.* Edward W. Nuffield. Winnipeg: Hyperion Press Ltd., c1987.

**4412. Nyberg, Verner Richard** *"A Longitudinal Study of Grade 3 Achievement in Edmonton Public Schools."* V.R. Nyberg and D.E. Blackmore. Alberta Journal of Educational Research 27, 2(June 1981): 154-159.

**4413. Oak Lake History Committee** *Ox Trails to Blacktop.* Oak Lake History Committee. Oak Lake, Man.: Oak Lake History Committee, 1982.

**4414. Oberg, Alaire Gwen** *Auditory Discrimination Ability of Children in Kindergarten, Grades One, Two and Three.* Alaire Gwen Oberg. Edmonton: University of Alberta, 1970.
Thesis (M.Ed.)--University of Alberta, 1970.

**4415. O'Bryan, K.G.** *Reversibility, Intelligence and Creativity.* K.G. O'Bryan. Edmonton: University of Alberta, 1967.
Thesis (M.Ed.)--University of Alberta, 1967.

**4416. O'Bryan, K.G.** *"Reversibility, Intelligence and Creativity in Nine-year-old Boys."* K.G. O'Bryan and R.S. MacArthur. Child Development 40, 1(Mar. 1969): 33-45.

**4417. O'Callaghan, William J.** *How I Flew the Forties.* William J. O'Callaghan. Edmonton: Newest Publishers, 1984.

**4418. Oder, Aileen, ed.** *Logs and Lines from the Winnipeg River: a History of the Lac du Bonnet Area.* Aileen Oder, ed. [and] Lac du Bonnet History Book Committee. [S.l.]: Senior Citizen's Historical Society, 1980.

**4419. Ogema and District Historical Society** *Prairie Grass to Golden Grain: R.M. no. 70, Ogema and Surrounding Areas.* Ogema and District Historical Society. Ogema, Sask.: Ogema and District Historical Society, 1982.

**4420. Ogilvie, Warren Louis** *A Longitudinal Study of the Effects on Achievement of Promotion and Non-promotion at the Grade 3 Level.* Warren Louis Ogilvie. Edmonton: University of Alberta, 1961.
Thesis (M.Ed.)--University of Alberta, 1961.

**4421. Ogle, Bob** *North-South Calling.* Bob Ogle Saskatoon: Fifth House in association with Novalis, c1987.

**4422. Okotoks and District Historical Society** *A Century of Memories 1883-1983: Okotoks and District.* Okotoks and District Historical Society. Okotoks, Alta.: Okotoks and District Historical Society, 1983.

**4423. Olds History Committee** *Olds: a History of Olds and Area.* Olds History Committee. Olds, Alta.: Olds History Committee, 1980.

**4424. Oliver, Edmund Henry** *The Country School in Non-English Speaking Communities in Saskatchewan.* Edmund Henry Oliver. Regina: Public Education League, 1915.

**4425. Olsen, Mildred Isabelle** *The Development of Play Schools and Kindergartens and an Analysis of a Sampling of These Institutions in Alberta.* Mildred Isabelle Olsen. Edmonton: University of Alberta, 1955.
Thesis (M.Ed.)--University of Alberta, 1955.

**4426. Olson, David R.** *"The Effect of Foreign Language Background on Intelligence Test Performance."* David R. Olson and R.S. MacArthur. Alberta Journal of Educational Research 8, 3(Sept. 1962): 157-167.

**4427. Olson, David R.** *"The Role of Stimulus Affect on Concept Attainment."* David R. Olson. and R.J.C. Harper. Alberta Journal of Educational Research 9, 3(Sept. 1963): 125-131.

**4428. Olson, Oscar** *The Invermay Story.* Oscar Olson. Ottawa: Heirs of History, 1978.

**4429. O'Neil, Agnes Eagles** *"The Measles Epidemic in Calgary 1969-1970: the Protective Effect of Vaccination for the Individual and the Community."* Agnes Eagles O'Neil. Canadian Medical Association Journal/Journal de l'Association medicale canadienne 105, 8(Oct. 23, 1971): 819-825.

**4430. Onoway and District Historical Society** *The Pathfinders, 1978: a History of Onoway, Billy, Brookdale, Glenford, Goldthorpe, Heatherdown, Hillcrest, Nakamun, Rich Valley, Speldhurst, Stettin and Sturgeon River.* Onoway and District Historical Society. Onoway, Alta.: Onoway Branch, Women's Institute, 1978.

**4431. Orange Benevolent Society of Saskatchewan** *25 Years of Guarding Canada's Greatest Asset.* Orange Benevolent Society of Saskatchewan. [Regina: Orange Benevolent Society of Saskatchewan, 1948].

**4432. Orange Benevolent Society of Saskatchewan** *The Protestant Home for Children, Indian Head, Saskatchewan: Questions and Answers.* Orange Benevolent Society of Saskatchewan. Regina, Sask.: Orange Benevolent Society of Saskatchewan, [1955?].

**4433. Orcutt, E. Roy** *"Caroline via the Mule Express."* E. Roy Orcutt. Alberta Historical Review 19, 3(Summer 1971): 22-26.

**4434. Orn, Donald Elroy** *Intelligence, Socioeconomic Status and Short-term Memory.* Donald Elroy Orn. Edmonton: University of Alberta, 1970. (CTM no. 6744)
Thesis (Ph.D.)--University of Alberta, 1970.

**4435. Ottewell, A.E.** *"Recreation Possibilities in the Small Community."* A.E. Ottewell. In Proceedings and Papers Fourth Annual Conference on Child Welfare 1923, pp. 126-131.

**4436. Oxbow-Glen Ewen History Book Committee** *Furrow to the Future.* Oxbow-Glen Ewen History Book Committee. 2 v. Oxbow, Sask.: Oxbow-Glen Ewen History Book Committee, 1984.

**4437. Oyen and District Historical Society** *Many Trails Crossed Here: a Story of Oyen, Alberta and the Surrounding Districts.* Oyen and District Historical Society. Oyen, Alta: Oyen and District Historical Society, 1981.

**4438. Pakes, Fraser** *""Skill To Do Comes of Doing": Purpose in Traditional Indian Winter Games and Pastimes."* Fraser Pakes. Calgary: Historical Society of Alberta, 1990. In Winter Sports in the West, pp. [26]-37. Edited by Elise A. Corbet and Anthony W. Rasporich.

**4439. Palate, Elizabeth Leon** *The Measurement of Sentence Structure of Deaf Children.* Elizabeth Leon Palate. Edmonton: University of Alberta, 1960. Thesis (M.Ed.)--University of Alberta, 1960.

**4440. Palate, Elizabeth Leon** *"The Measurement of Sentence Structure of Deaf Children."* E.L. Palate. Alberta Journal of Educational Research 8, 1(Mar. 1962): 39-44.

**4441. Palmer, Gwen** *"Camperville and Duck Bay."* Gwen Palmer. Manitoba Pageant 18, 2(Winter 1973): 11-17.

**4442. Palmer, Howard** *"Patterns of Racism: Attitudes Towards Chinese and Japanese in Alberta, 1920-1950."* Howard Palmer. Histoire sociale/Social History 13, 25(May 1980): 137-160.

**4443. Panabaken, Harold Edward** *The Relationship of the Laycock Mental Ability Test to Success in High School.* Harold Edward Panabaken. Edmonton: University of Alberta, 1954.
Thesis (M.A.)--University of Alberta, 1954.

**4444. Pannekoek, Frits** *"The Anglican Church and the Disintegration of Red River Society, 1818-1870."* Frits Pannekoek. Edmonton: Pica Pica Press, c1985. In The Prairie West: Historical Readings, pp. 100-115. Edited by R. Douglas Francis and Howard Palmer.

**4445. Parker, William L.** *"Pneumatosis Cystoides Intestinalis: a Report of Two Cases in Infants."* William L. Parker and James Hendry. Canadian Medical Association Journal/Journal de l'Association medicale canadienne 80, 11(June 1, 1959): 893-896.

**4446. Parr, Arnold R.** *Social Status in the High School: a Sociological Study of Education.* Arnold Richard Parr. Calgary: University of Calgary, 1967. (CTM no. 1701)
Thesis (M.A.)--University of Calgary, 1967.

**4447. Parr, John, ed.** *Speaking of Winnipeg.* John Parr, ed. Winnipeg: Queenston House, 1974.

**4448. Pass, Lawrence Eugene** *Effects of Stress Response Class Complexity Task Orientation Anxiety and Sex on Verbal Conditioning.* Lawrence Eugene Pass. Edmonton: University of Alberta, 1965.
Thesis (Ph.D.)-- University of Alberta, 1965.

**4449. Paswegin History Committee** *Pages From the Past: a History of Paswegin and School Districts Harrow, North Quill, Quill City, Tiger Lily and Wooler.* Paswegin History Committee. Wadena, Sask.: Paswegin History Committee, 1982.

**4450. Paterson, Donald** *"The Family Doctor and the Handicapped Child and Young Adult."* Donald Paterson. Canadian Medical Association Journal 80, 4(Feb. 15, 1959): 286-291.

**4451. Paterson, Sydney Bruce** *A Study of the Relationship Between Denial and Educational Achievement.* Sydney Bruce Paterson. Calgary: University of Calgary, 1969.
Thesis (M.Ed.)--University of Calgary, 1969.

**4452. Pathlow History Book** *Pathways to Pathlow.* Pathlow History Book. Pathlow, Sask.: Pathlow History Book, 1983.

**4453. Paton, Elva, ed.** *Terrell 101: Faith and Freedom.* Elva Paton, ed. and Terrell Historical Committee. Spring Valley, Sask.: Terrell Historical Committee, 1981.

**4454. Patterson, Florence W.** *A Comparison of Pupil's Reading Achievement with the Readability Levels of Social Studies Books and Basic Readers Used in Selected Intermediate Grade Classrooms.* Florence W. Patterson. Calgary: University of Calgary, 1968.
Thesis (M.Ed.)--University of Calgary, 1968.

**4455. Pattison, Jimmy** *Jimmy, an Autobiography.* Jimmy Pattison and Paul Grescoe. Toronto: Seal Books, 1987.

**4456. Paulson, Morris James** *An Investigation of the Standard of Achievement in the Lower Limits of the B Group in Grade 9 Mathematics in June, 1948.* Morris James Paulson. Edmonton: University of Alberta, 1949.
Thesis (M.Ed.)--University of Alberta, 1949.

**4457. Payne, Julien D.** *"Legislative Amelioration of the Condition of the Common Law Illegitimate: the Legitimacy Act (Saskatchewan), 1961."* Julien D. Payne. Saskatchewan Bar Review 26, 3(Sept. 1961): 78-89.

**4458. Payne, Michael B.** *Daily Life on Western Hudson Bay, 1714-1870: a Social History of York Factory and Churchill.* Ottawa: Carleton University, 1989. (CTM no. 51150)
Thesis (Ph.D.)--Carleton University, 1989.

**4459. Payne, Michael B.** *The Most Respectable Place in the Territory: Everyday Life in Hudson's Bay Company Service York Factory, 1788 to 1870.* Michael Payne. Ottawa: National Historic Parks and Sites, Canadian Parks Service, Environment Canada, 1989.
Bibliographical references.

**4460. Peach, John Whitmore** *Achievement Expectations and Student Attitudes in Ten Selected Manitoba Senior High Schools.* John Whitmore Peach. Edmonton: University of Alberta, 1970. (CTM no. 6232)

Thesis (M.A.)--University of Alberta, 1970.

**4461. Pearsall, Blanche** *Scattered Leaves.* Blanche Pearsall. Maple Ridge, B.C.: Blanche Pearsall, c1978.

**4462. Pelletier, J.D.M.** *"A Study of Grade One Children's Concepts of Linear Measurement."* J.D.M. Pelletier and L.D. Nelson. Manitoba Journal of Educational Research 1, 2(June 1966): 28-36.

**4463. Pelletier, Joanne** *Louis Riel.* Joanne Pelletier and the Curriculum Unit, Gabriel Dumont Institute of Native Studies and Applied Research, Inc. Regina: Gabriel Dumont Institute of Native Studies and Applied Research, Inc., c1985.

**4464. Pembina Lobstick Historical Society** *Foley Trail: a History of Entwhistle, Evansburg and the Surrounding Districts.* Pembina Lobstick Historical Society. 2 v. Edmonton, Alta.: UVISCO Press, 1984.

**4465. Penner, Henry P.** *Factors, Frequency and Consequences of Students Who Dropped Out of the Valleyview Junior and Senior High Schools.* Henry P. Penner. Edmonton: University of Alberta, 1970.
Thesis (M.Ed.)--University of Alberta, 1970.

**4466. Penner, Wesley Jerry** *Some Comparisons of Life Style Reflected in the Dress and Behaviour of High School Students.* Wesley Jerry Penner. Edmonton: University of Alberta, 1971.
Thesis (Ph.D.)--University of Alberta, 1971.

**4467. Pense Historical Committee** *Pense Community 1882 to 1982.* Pense Historical Committee. [S.l.]: Pense Historical Committee, [1982].

**4468. Penzance Historical Society** *Penzance Prairie Profiles.* Penzance Historical Society. Penzance, Sask.: Penzance Historical Society, 1982.

**4469. Perkins, Stanley A.** *"Learning Spelling Through the Use of Electric Typewriters."* Stanley A. Perkins. Alberta Journal of Educational Research 17, 3(Sept. 1971): 173-177.

**4470. Persson, Diane Iona** *Blue Quills: a Case Study of Indian Residential Schooling.* Diane Iona Persson. Edmonton: University of Alberta, 1980. (CTM no. 49072)
Thesis (Ph.D.)--University of Alberta, 1980.

**4471. Persson, Diane Iona** *"The Changing Experience of Indian Residential Schooling: Blue Quills, 1931-1970."* Diane Persson. Vancouver: University of British Columbia Press, 1986. In Indian Education in Canada, Volume 1: the Legacy, pp. 150-168. Edited by Jean Barman, Yvonne Hebert and Don McCaskill.

**4472. Peter, Karl A.** *"The Hutterite Family."* Karl Peter. Toronto: Rinehart and Winston of Canada Ltd., c1971. In The Canadian Family, pp. 248-262. Edited by K. Ishwaran.
Reprinted in The Canadian Family Revised, pp. 289-303. Edited by K. Ishwaran.

**4473. Peters, Tina H.** *"Remedies."* Tina H. Peters. Winnipeg: Centennial Publications, 1977. In Mennonite Memories: Settling in Western Canada, pp. 240-247. Edited by Lawrence Klippenstein and Julius G. Toews.

**4474. Peterson, Jacqueline** *"Many Roads to Red River: Metis Genesis in the Great Lakes Region, 1680-1815."* Jacqueline Peterson. Winnipeg: University of Manitoba Press, c1985. In The New Peoples: Being and Becoming Metis in North America, pp. 37-71. Edited by Jacqueline Peterson and Jennifer S.H. Brown.
Ethnic Relationships

**4475. Peterson, Jacqueline, ed.** *The New Peoples: Being and Becoming Metis in North America.* Jacqueline Peterson and Jennifer S.H. Brown., eds. Winnipeg: University of Manitoba Press, c1985.

**4476. Petkau, Irene Friesen** *Blumenfeld: Where Land and People Meet.* Irene Friesen Petkau, Peter A. Petkau [and] Blumenfeld Historical Committee. Winkler, Man.: Blumenfeld Historical Committee, 1981.

**4477. Petley-Jones, Evan** *"Memories of Rossdale."* Evan Petley-Jones. Alberta History 29, 3(Summer 1981): 32-36.

**4478. Philip, Catherine Rose** *The Crosses of Alberta.* Catherine Rose Philip. Toronto: Maclean-Hunter Pub., 1965.

**4479. Phillips, A.F.** *"Eye Tumours in Children: a Series of 15 Cases from Alberta Cancer Clinics."* A.F. Phillips. Canadian Medical Association Journal/Journal de l'Association medicale canadienne 86, 22(June 2, 1962): 1019-1022.

**4480. Phillips, Charles E.** *"Schools in Alberta."* Charles E. Phillips. Canadian Education 1, 4(July-Sept. 1946): 156-181.

**4481. Pike Lake Women's Institute** *Reflections: Pike Lake Valley Park.* Pike Lake Women's Institute. Saskatoon, Sask.: Pike Lake Women's Institute, 1981.

**4482. Pilcher, Frederick** *"The Treatment of Hypospadias."* Frederick Pilcher. Canadian Medical Association Journal 72, 3(Feb. 1, 1955): 195-199.

**4483. Pine River History Committee** *Hardships to Happiness: History Flows from Pine River and District.* Pine River History Committee. Pine River, Man.: Pine River History Committee, 1982.

**4484. Piniuta, Harry** *Land of Pain, Land of Promise: First Person Accounts by Ukrainian Pioneers, 1891-1914.* Harry Piniuta. Saskatoon: Western Producer Prairie Books, c1978.

**4485. Pinkham, Jean** *"Reminiscences of an Old Timer."* Jean Pinkham. Manitoba History 20(Autumn 1990): 16-20.
Reminiscences continue in 21(Spring 1991).

**4486. Pinkham, Mrs. W.C.** *"Selections From the Unpublished Recollections of Mrs. W.C. Pinkham, an Early Manitoban."* Mrs. W.C. Pinkham. Winnipeg: Historical and Scientific Society of Manitoba, 1974. Manitoba Pageant, vol. 19, no. 2 & 3 (Winter-Spring 1974), pp. 21-23; 19-22.

**4487. Pinwherry Community Club** *History of Pinwherry and Bushville.* Pinwherry Community Club. [S.l.]: Pinwherry Community, 1981.

**4488. Pitsula, James M.** *Let the Family Flourish: a History of the Family Service Bureau of Regina, 1913-1982.* James M. Pitsula. Regina: Family Service Bureau of Regina, c1982.

**4489. Pitsula, James M.** *"Student Life at Regina College in the 1920s."* James M. Pitsula. Kingston: McGill-Queen's University Press, 1989. In Youth, University and Canadian Society: Essays in the Social History of Higher Education, pp. 122-139. Edited by Paul Axelrod and John G. Reid.

**4490. Piwowar, Deanna G.** *A Comparison of the Performance of Kindergarten and Non Kindergarten Children on Selected Pre-Reading Tests.* Deanna G. Piwowar. Calgary: University of Calgary, 1969. Thesis (M.Ed.)–University of Calgary, 1969.

4491. **Piwowar, Roman** *An Investigation of Senior Students' Perceptions of the Semester System.* Roman Piwowar. Calgary: University of Calgary, 1970. Thesis (M.Ed.)--University of Calgary, 1970.

4492. **Pleasant Valley Community Club** *Pleasant Valley Memories, 1883-1980.* Pleasant Valley Community Club. [S.l.]: Pleasant Valley Community Club, c1981.

4493. **Pleasantdale and District History Book Committee** *Memories of the Past: History of Pleasantdale, Silver Park, Chagoness and Kinistino Indian Band, no. 91.* Pleasantdale and District History Book Committee. Pleasantdale, Sask.: Pleasantdale and District History Book Committee, 1981.

4494. **Plunkett History Committee** *Through the Fields of Time: Plunkett and District.* Plunkett History Committee. Plunkett, Sask.: Plunkett History Committee, 1982.

4495. **Pohorecky, Zenon** *"The Changing Role of Ethnocultural Organizations in Saskatchewan: Case Studies with Statistical Data Cast in Historical Perspective."* Zenon Pohorecky. Regina: Canadian Plains Research Center, 1978. In Ethnic Canadians: Culture and Education, pp. 189-228. Edited by Martin L. Kovacs.

4496. **Poirier, R.** *"Infantile Spinal Progressive Muscular Atrophy in Twins."* R. Poirier, R.C.B. Corbet, and A.E. Buckwold. Canadian Medical Association Journal 65, 4(Oct. 1951): 342-343.

4497. **Poplar Ridge Historical Committee** *The Districts' Diary: 95 Years of History of the Crossroads, Poplar Ridge, Norma and Durham Districts.* Poplar Ridge Historical Committee. Red Deer, Alta.: Poplar Ridge Historical Committee, 1981.

4498. **Potrebenko, Helen** *No Streets of Gold: a Social History of Ukrainians in Alberta.* Helen Potrebenko. Vancouver: New Star Books, 1977.

4499. **Potrebenko, Helen** *"Women and the Politics of Culture: Growing Up Ethnic."* Helen Potrebenko. Resources for Feminist Research/Documentation sur la recherche feministe 7, 3(Nov. 1979): 11-12.

4500. **Powell, Arthur Joseph Howson** *Vocational Opportunities for Boys in Alberta.* Arthur Joseph Howson Powell. Edmonton: University of Alberta, 1931. Thesis (M.A.)--University of Alberta, 1931.

4501. **Power, Marianita** *An Investigation Into Some Moral Concepts and Moral Judgements of Grade Five Children.* Marianita Power. Edmonton: University of Alberta, 1968. Thesis (M.Ed.)--University of Alberta, 1968.

4502. **Preeceville Historical Society** *Lines of the Past.* Preeceville Historical Society. Preeceville, Sask.: Preeceville Historical Society, 1982.

4503. **Prentice, J. Stuart** *"History in a Prairie School."* J. Stuart Prentice. Beaver 303, 2(Autumn 1972): 20-25.

4504. **Prevey, Esther Elizabeth** *A Study of the Mental Growth of the Preschool Child.* Esther Elizabeth Prevey. Edmonton: University of Alberta, 1934. Thesis (M.A.)--University of Alberta, 1934.

4505. **Price, Harold W.** *"Convulsions in Childhood."* Harold W. Price. Canadian Medical Association Journal 48, 5(May 1943): 433-437.

4506. **Price, Harold W.** *"Infectious Diarrhoea of Infancy."* H.W. Price. Canadian Medical Association Journal 62, 4(Apr. 1950): 351-354.

4507. **Prince Albert, Sask. Child Welfare Advisory Committee** *A Study of North Prince Albert.* The Committee. [Saskatchewan: s.n., 1951].

4508. **Pritchard, E.C.R.** *An Old Timer's Recollection of the Red River Colony: the Social and Domestic Life [and] Outstanding Personalities.* E.C.R. Pritchard. [White Rock, B.C.: White Rock Printers and Publishers, 1963].

4509. **Prokop, Manfred** *"Canadianization of Immigrant Children: Role of the Rural Elementary School in Alberta, 1900-1930."* Manfred Prokop. Alberta History 37, 2(Spring 1989): 1-10.

4510. **Proudfoot, Alexander J.** *Intercultural Education: a Study of the Effects of the Employment of Native Teacher Aides as Cross Culture Bridges Between Indian Students and Non-Indian Teachers.* Alexander J. Proudfoot, I.F. Kilpatrick, E.L. Koch and L.C. Lyon. Calgary: Faculty of Education, University of Alberta, 1971.

4511. **Prudhomme History Committee** *Life as It Was: Prud'homme, Saskatchewan, 1897-1918.* Prudhomme History Committee. Prudhomme, Sask.: Prudhomme History Committee, 1981.

**4512. Punnichy and Districts History Book Committee** *Between the Touchwoods: a History of Punnichy and Districts.* Punnichy and Districts History Book Committee. Punnichy, Sask.: Punnichy and Districts History Book Committee, 1983.

**4513. Purvis, Stuart S.** *"Rationale for a Family Court."* Stuart S. Purvis. Reports of Family Law 1(1971): 402-412.

**4514. Pusey, V.A.** *"Pulmonary Fibroplasia Following Prolonged Artificial Ventilation of Newborn Infants."* V.A. Pusey, R.I. MacPherson and V. Chernick. Canadian Medical Association Journal/Journal de l'Association medicale canadienne 100, 10(Mar. 8, 1969): 451-457.

**4515. Pusey, V.A.** *"The Relation Between Birth Weight and Gestational Age for a Winnipeg Hospital Population."* V.A. Pusey and J.C. Haworth. Canadian Medical Association Journal/Journal de l'Association medicale canadienne 100, 18(May 10, 1969): 842-845.

**4516. Pylypow, Henry** *"Two First Days."* Henry Pylypow. Alberta History 27, 3(Summer 1979): 31-34.

**4517. Qu'Appelle Historical Society** *Qu'Appelle Footprints to Progress: a History of Qu'Appelle and District.* Qu'Appelle Historical Society. Qu'Appelle, Sask.: Qu'Appelle Historical Society, 1980.

**4518. Quill Lake Historical Society** *With Quill in Hand: Quill Lake and District, 1903-1983.* Quill Lake Historical Society. Quill Lake, Sask.: Quill Lake Historical Society, 1984.

**4519. Quinn, Jean, ed.** *Sodbusters: a History of Kinuso and Swan River Settlement.* Jean Quinn, ed. [S.l.: s.n., 1979].

**4520. Raber, Jessie Brown** *Pioneering in Alberta.* Jessie Brown Raber. New York: Exposition Press, 1951.

**4521. Race, Cecil L.** *Compulsory Schooling in Alberta, 1888-1942.* Cecil L. Race. Edmonton: University of Alberta, 1978. (CTM no. 40286)
Thesis (M.A.)–University of Alberta, 1978.

**4522. Radisson and District Historical Society** *Reflections of Radisson, 1902-1982.* Radisson and District Historical Society. Radisson, Sask.: Radisson and District Historical Society, 1982.

**4523. Radomsky, Ronald Marshal** *Relationships Between Organization Climate, Student Achievement and Staff Dogmatism.* Ronald Marshal Radomsky. Calgary: University of Calgary, 1966.
Thesis (M.Ed.)–University of Calgary, 1966.

**4524. Radville Laurier Historical Society** *Radville, Laurier: the Yesteryears.* Radville Laurier Historical Society. Radville, Sask.: Radville Laurier Historical Society, 1983.

**4525. Rainier-Bow City History Book Club** *Settlers Along the Bow: a History of Rainier, Bow City.* Rainier-Bow City History Book Club. Bow City, Alta.: Rainier-Bow City History Book Club, 1975.

**4526. Ramsay, Helen** *"Citizenship in the Kindergarten."* Helen Ramsay. Canadian Welfare 16, 8(Feb. 1941): 46-47.

**4527. Rancier, Gordon James** *"Case Studies of High School Dropouts."* Gordon J. Rancier. Alberta Journal of Educational Research 9, 1(Mar. 1963): 13-21.

**4528. Rapid City Historical Book Society** *Our Past for the Future: Rapid City and District.* Rapid City Historical Book Society. Rapid City, Man.: Rapid City Historical Book Society, 1978.

**4529. Rasmussen, Linda** *A Harvest Yet to Reap: a History of Prairie Women.* Linda Rasmussen, Lorna Rasmussen, Candace Savage and Anne Wheeler. Toronto: Women's Press, c1976.

**4530. Rattan, Mohindar Singh** *"Longitudinal Prediction of School Achievement for Metis and Eskimo Pupils."* M.S. Rattan and R.S. MacArthur. Alberta Journal of Educational Research 14, 1(Mar. 1968): 37-41.

**4531. Rattan, Mohindar Singh** *Predictive Validity and Stability of Measures of Intellectual Potential for Two Samples of Indian-Metis and Eskimo Children.* Mohindar Singh Rattan. Edmonton: University of Alberta, 1966.
Thesis (M.Ed.)–University of Alberta, 1966.

**4532. Rattan, Mohindar Singh** *The Role of Language, Manipulation and Demonstration in the Acquisition, Retention and Transfer of Conservation.* Mohindar Singh Rattan. Edmonton: University of Alberta, 1970.
Thesis (Ph.D.)–University of Alberta, 1970.
Author published article with the same title in Alberta Journal of Educational Research 20, 3(Sept. 1974): 217-225.

**4533. Ravenscrag History Book Committee** *Between and Beyond the Benches: Ravenscrag.* Ravenscrag History Book Committee: Ravenscrag, Sask.: Ravenscrag History Book Committee, 1982.

**4534. Rawson, Hildred I.** *A Study of the Relationships and Development of Reading and Cognition.* Hildred I. Rawson. Edmonton: University of Alberta, 1969. (CTM no. 3932)
   Thesis (Ph.D.)--University of Alberta, 1969.

**4535. Raymore and District Historical Society** *From Prairie Wool to Golden Grain: Raymore and District 1904-1979.* Raymore and District Historical Society. Raymore, Sask.: Raymore and District Historical Society, 1980.

**4536. Rea, J.E.** *""My Main Line is the Kiddies . . . Make Them Good Christians and Good Canadians, Which is the Same Thing".* J.E. Rea. Toronto: Peter Martin Associates Ltd., c1977. In Identities: the Impact of Ethnicity on Canadian Society, pp. 3-10. Edited by .Wsevolod Isajiw.
   With a commentary by Marian McKenna, pp. 11-14.

**4537. Read, J. Don** *"Remember Dick and Jane?: Memories for Elementary Readers."* J. Don Read and Roger H. Barnsley. Canadian Journal of Behavioural Science/Revue canadienne de sciences du comportement 9, 4(Oct. 1977): 361-370.

**4538. Red Deer District Local No. 24, A.T.A. Centennial Committee** *Schools of the Parkland.* The Committee. Red Deer: The Committee, [1967].

**4539. Red Deer East Historical Society** *Mingling Memories.* Red Deer East Historical Society. Red Deer, Alta.: Red Deer East Historical Society, 1979.

**4540. Red Lake and District History Society** *Warm Prairie Winds.* Red Lake and District History Society. Moose Jaw, Sask.: Red Lake and District History Society, 1983.

**4541. Rediger, Donna Betty** *Verbal Hierarchical Classification in Disabled and Able Male Readers.* Donna Betty Rediger. Edmonton: University of Alberta, 1970.
   Thesis (M.Ed.)--University of Alberta, 1970.

**4542. Redvers Golden Age Centre** *Redvers: 75 Years Live.* Golden Age Centre and Celebrate Saskatchewan Committee. Redvers, Sask.: Golden Age Centre and Celebrate Saskatchewan Committee, [1980].

**4543. Reed, Leila** *"Pioneer Courage on the Prairie."* Leila Reed. Saskatchewan History 39, 3(Autumn 1986): 107-113.

**4544. Reeves, J.S.H.** *Hockey Injury Study.* J.S.H. Reeves and S.W. Mendryk. Edmonton: University of Alberta, 1971.

**4545. Regina Public Library** *Writing Yesterday: Living History.* Regina Public Library. [Regina]: Regina Public Library, 1984.

**4546. Reid, John Edmund** *Sports and Games in Alberta Before 1900.* John Edmund Reid. Edmonton: University of Alberta, 1970.
   Thesis (M.A.)--University of Alberta, 1970.

**4547. Reid, Thomas James** *A Survey of the Language Achievement of Alberta School Children in Relation to Bilingualism, Sex and Intelligence.* Thomas James Reid. Edmonton: University of Alberta, 1954.
   Thesis (M.Ed.)--University of Alberta, 1954.

**4548. Reimer, Peter J.B.** *"The Church School."* Peter J.B. Reimer. Winnipeg: Centennial Publications, 1977. In Mennonite Memories: Settling in Western Canada, pp. 124-127. Edited by Lawrence Klippenstein and Julius G. Toews.

**4549. Renaud, Andre** *Education and the First Canadians.* Andre Renaud. Toronto: Gage Educational Publishers, 1971.

**4550. Renpenning, H.** *"Familial Sex-linked Mental Retardation."* H. Renpenning, J.W. Gerrard, W.A. Zaleski and T. Tabata. Canadian Medical Association Journal/Journal de l'Association medicale canadienne 87, 18(Nov. 3, 1962): 954-956.

**4551. Reynolds, F.J.** *"Home Finding For Children on a Provincial Basis."* F.J. Reynolds. In Proceedings of Sixth Annual Canadian Conference on Child Welfare 1927, pp. 114-116.

**4552. Richard, Isabel** *"Children's Speech."* Isabel Richard. Journal of Education of the Faculty of Education, Vancouver 12(Jan. 1966): 59-66.

**4553. Richard Women's Institute, comp.** *Richard Remembers: a History of Richard and Surrounding Districts.* Richard Women's Institute, comp. [Richard, Sask.: Richard Women's Institute], 1980.

**4554. Richardson, T.A.** *"Cerebral Palsy."* T.A. Richardson. Canadian Nurse 51, 5(May 1955): 351-353.

**4555. Richie, Hugh** *"Special Service in Learning Disabilities."* Hugh Richie. Education Canada 9, 1(Mar. 1969): 52-53.

**4556. Richmound Historical Society** *Richmound's Heritage: a History of Richmound and District, 1910-1978.* Richmound Historical Society. Richmound, Sask.: Richmound Historical Society, 1978.

**4557. Riding Mountain and Area History Book Committee** *History of Riding Mountain and Area, 1885-1984.* Riding Mountain and Area History Book Committee. [S.l.]: Riding Mountain and Area History Book Committee, 1984.

**4558. Riegert, Paul W.** *2005 Memories: a History of the Hamburg School District No. 2005 Laird, Saskatchewan.* Paul W. Riegert. Regina: The Author, 1979.

**4559. Riggs, Frank** *Verbal and Nonverbal Conversation and Mathematics Achievement.* Frank Riggs. Edmonton: University of Alberta, 1970.
Thesis (M.Ed.)--University of Alberta, 1970.

**4560. Ringrose, C.A. Douglas** *"Abruptio Placentae: Perinatal Aspects and Current Management."* C.A. Douglas Ringrose. Canadian Medical Association Journal/Journal de l'Association medicale canadienne 84, 16(Apr. 22, 1961): 905-907.

**4561. Ritchie, D.C.** *"Maternal and Perinatal Mortality Associated with Cesarean Section in Alberta (1955-1959)."* D.C. Ritchie. Canadian Medical Association Journal/Journal de l'Association medicale canadienne 88, 13(Mar. 30, 1963): 649-654.

**4562. Robert, George Rene** *Political Orientations of Calgary Children from Grades Four to Eight.* George Rene Robert. Calgary: University of Calgary, 1969. (CTM no. 4682)
Thesis (M.Ed.)--University of Calgary, 1969.

**4563. Roberts, Carol B.** *Mrs. Minister.* Carol B. Roberts. Winfield, B.C.: Wood Lake Books, c1987.

**4564. Roberts, Sarah Ellen** *Of Us and the Oxen.* Sarah Ellen Roberts. Saskatoon: Modern Press, 1968.
Published in 1971 under the title Alberta Homestead: Chronicles of an Alberta Pioneer Family by the University of Texas Press, Austin, Texas.

**4565. Robertson, H.E.** *"Cyanosis of Infants Produced by High Nitrate Concentration in Rural Waters of Saskatchewan."* H.E. Robertson and W.A. Riddell. Canadian Journal of Public Health 40, 2(Feb. 1949): 72-77.

**4566. Robertson, John** *High Times with Stewart MacPherson.* John Robertson. Winnipeg: Prairie Publishing Company, c1980.

**4567. Robinson, Idell** *"Family Values in the Nursery School."* Idell Robinson. Canadian Welfare 16, 7(Jan. 1941): 42-44.

**4568. Robinson, Reva Leah** *The Children of Opasquia: a Study of Socialization and Society on a Contemporary Indian Reserve.* Reva Leah Robinson. Vancouver: University of British Columbia, 1970.
Thesis (M.A.)--University of British Columbia, 1970.

**4569. Rockglen 50th Anniversary Committee** *The Rolling Hills of Home: Gleanings from Rockglen and Area.* Rockglen 50th Anniversary Committee. Rockglen, Sask.: Rockglen 50th Anniversary Committee, 1978.

**4570. Rodney, William** *Kootenai Brown, His Life and Times, 1839-1916.* William Rodney. British Columbia: Gray's Publishing Ltd., 1969.

**4571. Rodnunsky, Sidney** *Change in Critical Thinking Scores Effected by a Fenton Inquiry Sequence.* Sidney Rodnunsky. Calgary: University of Calgary, 1969.
Thesis (M.Ed.)--University of Calgary, 1969.

**4572. Rodrigues, Ivo Joseph** *An Analysis of the Comparative Effectiveness of Two Mathematics Programmes for Low Achievers in Grade Ten.* Ivo Joseph Rodrigues. Calgary : University of Calgary, 1966.
Thesis (M.Ed.)--University of Calgary, 1966.

**4573. Rogers, Edith Blanche** *History Made in Edmonton.* Edith Blanche Rogers. Edmonton: The Author, 1975.

**4574. Rohac, Walter J.** *"Regina's Juvenile Bicycle Safety Court."* Walter J. Rohac. Canadian Journal of Corrections/Revue canadienne de criminologie 6, 3(July 1964): 375-376.

**4575. Rolfes, Herman Harold** *A Study of the Achievement and Self-esteem of Accelerate and Non-accelerate in the Saskatoon Separate School System.* Herman Harold Rolfes. Saskatoon: University of Saskatchewan, 1971.
Thesis (M.Ed.)--University of

Saskatchewan, 1971.

**4576. Ronaghan, Allen, ed.**
*Earnest-minded Men: an Account of Local
Government in the County of Vermilion
River.* Allen Ronaghan, ed. [Vermilion,
Alberta]: County of Vermilion River,
Kitscoty, Alberta, c1973.

**4577. Ronning, Chester A.** *A Study of an
Alberta Protestant Private School, the
Camrose Lutheran College, a Residential
High School.* Chester A. Ronning.
Edmonton: University of Alberta, 1942.
Thesis (M.A.)--University of Alberta,
1942.

**4578. Rooke, Patricia T.** *"Charlotte
Whitton and the "Babies for Export"
Controversy, 1947-1948."* Patricia T. Rooke
and R.L. Schnell. Alberta History 30,
1(Winter 1982): 11-16.

**4579. Rooke, Patricia T.** *"Charlotte
Whitton Meets "The Last Best West": the
Politics of Child Welfare in Alberta,
1929-1949."* Patricia T. Rooke and R.L.
Schnell. Prairie Forum 6, 2(Fall 1981):
143-162.

**4580. Rose Valley and District
Historical Society** *A Tribute to Our
Pioneers.* Rose Valley and District
Historical Society. Rose Valley, Sask.:
Rose Valley and District Historical
Society, 1981.

**4581. Rosebut Historical Society**
*Akokiniskway: "By the River of Many
Roses".* Rosebud Historical Society. [S.l.]:
Rosebud Historical Society, 1983.

**4582. Ross, Sinclair** *"Just Wind and
Horses."* Sinclair Ross. Toronto: Macmillan
of Canada, c1988. In The Macmillan
Anthology, v.1, pp. 83-97. Edited by John
Metcalf and Leon Rooke.

**4583. Routledge, Robert Henry** *A Study
to Establish Norms, for Edmonton
Secondary School Boys, of the Youth
Fitness Tests of the American Association
for Health, Physical Fitness, and
Recreation.* Robert Henry Routledge.
Edmonton: University of Alberta, 1961.
Thesis (M.Ed.)--University of Alberta,
1961.

**4584. Rowell, Gladys M.** *"Memories of an
English Settler."* Gladys M. Rowell.
Alberta History 30, 2(Spring 1982): 30-36.

**4585. Roy, Gabrielle** *Enchantment and
Sorrow: the Autobiography of Gabrielle
Roy.* Gabrielle Roy, translated by Patricia
Claxton. Toronto: Lester and Orpen
Dennys, c1987.

**4586. Rozumnyj, Jaroslav, ed.** *New Soil,
Old Roots: the Ukrainian Experience in
Canada.* Edited by Jaroslav Rozumnyj,
with the assistance of Oleh W. Gerus
and Mykhailo Marunchak. Winnipeg:
Ukrainian Academy of Arts and Sciences
in Canada, 1983.

**4587. Rubin, Jack A.** *"Deafness in
Children."* Jack A. Rubin. Canadian
Medical Association Journal 78, 1(Jan. 1,
1958): 51-58.

**4588. Ruest, Agnes M.** *A Pictorial History
of the Metis and Non-Status Indian in
Saskatchewan.* Agnes M. Ruest. Prince
Albert: Saskatchewan Human Rights
Commission, 1976.

**4589. Rupp, Anne Neufeld** *"Childhood
Memories in Manitoba."* Anne Neufeld
Rupp. Mennonite Life 42, 4(Dec. 1987):
22-24.

**4590. Rural Municipality of Albert
History Book Committee** *Reflections of
Time: a History of the R.M. of Albert.*
R.M. of Albert History Book Committee.
Tilston, Man.: R.M. of Albert History
Book, 1984.

**4591. Rural Municipality of Wolverine
History Committee** *R.M. of Wolverine
Memory Album.* R.M. of Wolverine History
Committee. Plunkett, Sask.: R.M. of
Wolverine History Committee, 1981.

**4592. Rush Lake History Book
Committee** *Excelsior Echoes.* Rush Lake
History Book Committee. [S.l.]: Rush Lake
History Book Committee, 1982.

**4593. Russell, Andy** *Trails of a
Wilderness Wanderer.* Andy Russell. 1st
ed. New York: Knopf, 1971.

**4594. Russell, Peter A.** *"The
Saskatchewan Conservatives, Separate
Schools and the 1929 Election."* Peter A.
Russell. Prairie Forum 8, 2(Fall 1983):
211-224.

**4595. Russon, Gordon W.** *"A Paddle for
Juvenile Delinquents."* Gordon W. Russon.
Canadian Welfare 34, 1(May 1958): 24-26.

**4596. Ruth, Jean** *Achievement Motivation:
a Follow-up Study of Cerebral Palsy in
Northern Alberta.* Jean Ruth. Edmonton:
University of Alberta, 1970. (CTM no.
6755)
Thesis (Ph.D.)--University of Alberta,
1970.

**4597. Ruth, Roy H.** *Educational Echoes: a History of Education of the Icelandic-Canadians in Manitoba.* Roy H. Ruth. Winnipeg: Columbia Printers Limited, 1964.

**4598. Rutherford School** *Rutherford School, 1910-1967, Centennial Open House.* Rutherford School. Edmonton: Rutherford School, 1967.

**4599. Rutledge, E.** *"Erythroblastosis Fetalis."* E. Rutledge. Canadian Nurse 55, 11(Nov. 1959): 1022-1024.

**4600. Ryan, Doreen** *"The Development of Speed Skating in Western Canada from a Personal Perspective."* Doreen Ryan. Calgary: Historical Society of Alberta, 1990. In Winter Sports in the West, pp. 124-131. Edited by Elise A. Corbet and Anthony W. Rasporich.

**4601. Rycroft History Book Committee** *Wheatfields and Wildflowers: a History of Rycroft and Surrounding School Districts.* Rycroft History Book Committee. Rycroft, Alta.: Rycroft History Book Committee, 1984.

**4602. Sacher, Jerry Leo** *A Study of the Effects of Environment on Indian Students' Attitudes.* Jerry Leo Sacher. Edmonton: University of Alberta, 1968.
Thesis (M.Ed.)--University of Alberta, 1968.

**4603. Safran, C.** *"The Construction and Use of a Guidance Attitude Scale."* C. Safran. Alberta Journal of Educational Research 9, 3(Sept. 1963): 140-146.

**4604. Sainte-Theresa, Sister** *An Experimental Study of Achievement in French Language by Non-French Pupils of Grade Four and Grade Seven in Selected Alberta Schools.* Sister Sainte-Theresa. Edmonton: University of Alberta, 1963.
Thesis (M.Ed.)--University of Alberta, 1963.

**4605. Saklofske, D.H.** *The Measurement of the Direction of Aggression via State and Trait Techniques.* Donald Harold Saklofske. Calgary: University of Calgary, 1970.
Thesis (M.Ed.)--University of Calgary, 1970.

**4606. Salloum, Habeeb** *"Reminiscence of an Arab Family Homesteading in Southern Saskatchewan."* Habeeb Salloum. Canadian Ethnic Studies/Etudes ethniques au Canada 15, 2(1983): 130-138.

**4607. Salloum, Habeeb** *"The Urbanization of an Arab Homesteading Family."* Habeeb Salloum. Saskatchewan History 42, 2(Spring 1989): 79-84.

**4608. Saltcoats and District Historical Society** *Saltcoats Roots and Branches.* Saltcoats and District Historical Society. Saltcoats, Sask.: Saltcoats and District Historical Society, 1982.

**4609. Salverson, Laura Goodman** *Confessions of an Immigrant's Daughter.* Laura Goodman Salverson. Toronto: University of Toronto Press, c1981.

**4610. Sanderson, M.** *"Reminiscences of St. Paul's Industrial School."* M. Sanderson. Manitoba Pageant 4, 1(Sept. 1958): 17-19.

**4611. Sanford-Ferndale History Committee** *Sanford-Ferndale, 1871-1987.* The Committee. Altona, Man.: The Committee, c1989.

**4612. Sanford, Robert M.** *An Investigation of the Response of High School Students to Poetic Language.* Robert M. Sanford. Edmonton: University of Alberta, 1971.
Thesis (Ph.D.)--University of Alberta, 1971.

**4613. Saruk, Alec** *"Academic Performance of Students and the Cultural Orientation of their Parents."* Alec Saruk and Metro Gulutsan. Alberta Journal of Educational Research 16, 3(Sept. 1970): 189-195.

**4614. Saruk, Alec** *Academic Performance of Students of Ukrainian Descent and the Cultural Orientation of Their Parents.* Alec Saruk. Edmonton: University of Alberta, 1966.
Thesis (M.Ed.)--University of Alberta, 1966.

**4615. Saskatchewan. Bureau of Publications** *Women's and Children's Rights in Saskatchewan.* Bureau of Publications. [Regina, Sask.]: Bureau of Publications, 1949.

**4616. Saskatchewan. Commission to Investigate the Penal System of Saskatchewan** *Commission to Investigate the Penal System of Saskatchewan.* The Commission. [Regina: The Commission, 1946].
Chairman: Samuel R. Laycock; Commissioners: Clarence Halliday and William H. Holman.
Chairman: Samuel R. Laycock.

**4617. Saskatchewan. Department of Education** *From Polish Peasant to Canadian Citizen: a True Story of What Saskatchewan Schools are Doing for the New Canadians.* The Department. Regina: King's Printer, 1920.

**4618. Saskatchewan Human Rights Commission.** *Education Equity.* Saskatchewan Human Rights Commission. [Saskatoon]: The Commission, 1985.

**4619. Saskatchewan. Royal Commission on Immigration and Settlement, 1930** *Report of the Saskatchewan Royal Commission on Immigration and Settlement, 1930.* The Commission. Regina: Roland S. Garrett, King's Printer, 1930. Chairman: W.W. Swanson.

**4620. Saskatoon School District No. 13** *A Visit to Our Public Schools.* Saskatoon School District No. 13. [Saskatoon, Sask.]: Saskatoon Public School Board, 1949.

**4621. Savage, Leslie A.E.** *"Perspectives on Illegitimacy: the Changing Role of the Sisters of Misericordia in Edmonton, 1900-1906."* Leslie Savage. Calgary: Detselig Enterprises Ltd., 1982. In Studies in Childhood History: a Canadian Perspective, pp. 105-133. Edited by Patricia T. Rooke and R.L. Schnell.

**4622. Sawada, Daiyo** *"Conservation of Length: Methodological Considerations."* Daiyo Sawada and L. Doyal Nelson. Alberta Journal of Educational Research 14, 1(Mar. 1968): 23-35.

**4623. Sawada, Daiyo** *Transformation and Concept Attainment: a Study of Length of Conversation in Children.* Daiyo Sawada. Edmonton: University of Alberta, 1966. Thesis (M.Ed.)--University of Alberta, 1966.

**4624. Sawchuk, Patricia** *"The Isolated Communities of Northern Alberta."* Patricia Sawchuk and Jarvis Gray. [S.l.]: Metis Association of Alberta, c1980. In The Metis and the Land in Alberta: Land Claims Research Project, pp. 270-328.

**4625. Sawchuk, T.J.** *"The Influence of Homogeneous Grouping on Teacher Marks in the High School."* T.J. Sawchuck and Donald B. Black. Alberta Journal of Educational Research 7, 3(Sept. 1961): 156-170.

**4626. Sawkey, John Andrew** *Those Were the Days: the History of MacNutt, Calder, Dropmore and the Surrounding Districts "Pioneer to Present".* John Andrew Sawkey. [S.l.]: The Author, [1972].

**4627. Scandia Historical Committee** *Scandia Since Seventeen.* Scandia Historical Committee. Scandia, Alta.: Scandia Historical Committee, 1978.

**4628. Scarrow, Mary, comp.** *Griffin Prairie Wool.* Mary Scarrow and Mabel Charlton, comps. [S.l.: s.n.], 1967.

**4629. Schalm, Philip** *School Administrators' Perceptions of Problems Arising from the Integration of Indian and Non-Indian Children in Publicly Supported Schools in Saskatchewan.* Philip Schalm. Saskatoon: University of Saskatchewan, 1968. Thesis (M.Ed.)--University of Saskatchewan, 1968.

**4630. Schmidt, Anita E.** *On the Banks of the Assiniboine: a History of the Parish of St. James.* Anita E. Schmidt. Winnipeg: Lawrence F. Schmidt, 1975.

**4631. Schonfield, David** *"Changes in Immediate Memory as a Function of Age and Meaning."* David Schonfield. Alberta Journal of Educational Research 5, 2(June 1959): 112-118.

**4632. Schulz, Henry** *A New Frontier: the Canadian Chronicles of Henry Schulz.* Henry Schulz. Campbell River, B.C.: Ptarmigin Press, 1984.

**4633. Scott-Brown, Joan** *"The Short Life of St. Dunstan's Calgary Indian Industrial School, 1896-1907."* Joan Scott-Brown. Canadian Journal of Native Education 14, 1(Fall 1987): 41-49.

**4634. Scott, Eileen M.** *Porridge and Old Clothes.* Eileen M. Scott. Victoria, B.C.: Plume Publications, 1982.

**4635. Scraba, Evangeline** *A Comparison of HTP Drawings of Normal and Emotionally Disturbed Children.* Evangeline Scraba. Toronto: University of Toronto, 1962. Thesis (M.A.)--University of Toronto, 1962.

**4636. Scragg, Edward Spencer** *A Survey of Dropouts from Alberta Schools, 1963-1968.* Edward Spencer Scragg. Edmonton: University of Alberta, 1968. Thesis (M.Ed.)--University of Alberta, 1968.

**4637. Sealey, D. Bruce** *Cuthbert Grant and the Metis.* D. Bruce Sealey. Agincourt: Book Society of Canada, c[1976].

**4638. Sealey, D. Bruce** *The Education of Native Peoples in Manitoba.* D. Bruce Sealey. [Winnipeg]: University of Manitoba, c1980.

**4639. Sealey, D. Bruce** *Education of the Manitoba Metis: an Historical Sketch.* D. Bruce Sealey. [Winnipeg: Department of Education, Native Education Branch, 1977].

**4640. Sealey, D. Bruce** *"Education of the Manitoba Metis."* D. Bruce Sealey. Winnipeg: Manitoba Metis Federation Press, c1980. In The Other Natives: the Metis, pp. 1-37. Edited by Antoine S. Lussier and D. Bruce Sealey.

**4641. Sealey, D. Bruce** *Thomas George Prince.* D. Bruce Sealey and Peter Van de Vyvere. Winnipeg: Peguis Publishers Limited, 1981.

**4642. Sealey, D. Bruce, ed.** *Stories of the Metis.* Bruce Sealey, ed. Winnipeg: Manitoba Metis Federation Press, 1975.

**4643. Semans and District Historical Society** *Always a Hometown: Semans and District History.* Semans and District Historical Society. Semans, Sask.: Semans and District Historical Society, 1982.

**4644. Semotiuk, Darwin Michael** *The Attitudes Toward and Interests in Physical Activity of Edmonton Secondary School Students.* Darwin Michael Semotiuk. Edmonton: University of Alberta, 1967. Thesis (M.Sc.)–University of Alberta, 1967.

**4645. Seunath, Oswald H.M.** *The Effect of Novel Stimuli on Attention in Children with Learning Disorders.* Oswald H.M. Seunath. Calgary: University of Calgary, 1971. (CTM no. 10165) Thesis (M.Sc.)–University of Calgary, 1971.

**4646. Shack, Sybil** *"The Education of the Immigrant Child in Manitoba Schools in the Early Twentieth Century."* Sybil Shack. Winnipeg: Jewish Historical Society of Western Canada, c1983. In Jewish Life and Times: a Collection of Essays, pp. 90-98.

**4647. Shandling, Rebecca** *A Clinical Study of Auditory Perceptual and Oral Reading Patterns in a Group of Dyslexic Boys.* Rebecca Shandling. Edmonton: University of Alberta, 1970. Thesis (M.Ed.)–University of Alberta, 1970.

**4648. Shanks, J.A.** *"Acute Interstitial Pancreatitis in a Ten Year Old Girl."* J.A. Shanks, W.C. Acton and J.D. Cottrell. Canadian Medical Association Journal 70, 6(June 1954): 682.

**4649. Shanks, J.A.** *"Acute Intestinal Obstruction in a Newborn Infant."* J.A. Shanks, J.D. Cottrell and W.C. Acton. Canadian Medical Association Journal 73, 7(Oct. 1, 1955): 562.

**4650. Sharma, Kundan L.** *A Rational Group Therapy Approach to Counselling Anxious Underachievers.* Kundan L. Sharma. Edmonton: University of Alberta, 1970. (CTM no. 6757) Thesis (Ph.D.)–University of Alberta, 1970.

**4651. Sharp, Emmit Frederick** *Manitoba High School Students and Drop-outs.* Emmit Frederick Sharp and G. Albert Kristjanson. [Winnipeg?: Department of Agriculture, 1967].

**4652. Shaw, Betty G.R.** *"Childhood Memories."* Betty G.R. Shaw. Alberta History 35, 2(Spring 1987): 25-28.

**4653. Shaw, Eva** *An Experimental Study of the Effects of Different Methods of Teaching Word Recognition.* Eva Shaw. Calgary: University of Calgary, 1971. Thesis (M.Ed.)–University of Calgary, 1971.

**4654. Sheehan, Nancy M.** *"Indoctrination: Moral Education in the Early Prairie School House."* Nancy M. Sheehan. Calgary: Detselig Enterprises, 1979. In Shaping the Schools of the Canadian West, pp. 222-235. Edited by David C. Jones, Nancy M. Sheehan and Robert M. Stamp.

**4655. Sheehan, Nancy M.** *"The Junior Red Cross Movement in Saskatchewan, 1919-1929: Rural Improvement Through the Schools."* Nancy M. Sheehan. Calgary: University of Calgary Press, c1985. In Building Beyond the Homestead: Rural History on the Prairies, pp. 67-88. Edited by David C. Jones and Ian MacPherson.

**4656. Sheehan, Nancy M.** *"Temperance, Education and the WCTU in Alberta, 1905-1930."* Nancy M. Sheehan. Journal of Educational Thought 14, 2(Aug. 1980): 108-124.

**4657. Sheehan, Nancy M.** *"The WCTU and Educational Strategies on the Canadian Prairie, 1886-1930."* Nancy M. Sheehan. History of Education Quarterly 24, 1(Spring 1984): 101-119.

**4658. Sheehan, Nancy M.** *"The WCTU on the Prairies: an Alberta-Saskatchewan Comparison."* Nancy M. Sheehan. Prairie Forum 6, 1(Summer 1981): 17-33.

**4659. Sheehan, Nancy M.,** ed. *Schools in the West: Essays in Canadian Educational History.* Nancy M. Sheehan, J. Donald Wilson and David C. Jones, eds. Calgary: Detselig Enterprises Limited, c1986.

**4660. Sheep River Historical Society** *In the Light of the Flares: History of Turner Valley Oilfields.* Sheep River Historical Society. Turner Valley, Alta.: Sheep River Historical Society, 1979.

**4661. Shell River North Book Committee** *Our Harvest of Memories.* Shell River North Book Committee. Shellbrook, Sask.: Shell River North Book Committee, 1983.

**4662. Shepard, R. Bruce** *"The Little "White" Schoolhouse: Racism in a Saskatchewan Rural School."* R. Bruce Shepard. Saskatchewan History 39, 3(Autumn 1986): 81-93.

**4663. Sheppard, R.S.** *Sex Differences.* R.S. Sheppard. Edmonton: University of Alberta, 1924.
Thesis (M.Ed.)–University of Alberta, 1924.

**4664. Sheps, Cecil G.** *"A Health Survey of Rural Manitoba Youth."* Cecil G. Sheps. Canadian Public Health Journal 32, 7(July 1941): 350-356.

**4665. Shiels, Leonard A.** *From Buffalo Grass to Wheat: a History of Long Lake District.* Leonard A. Shiels. Craven, Sask.: The Author, 1980.

**4666. Shillington, C. Howard** *Return to Avondale.* C. Howard Shillington. West Vancouver: Evvard Publications, 1990.

**4667. Short Grass Historical Society** *Long Shadows: a History of Shortgrass Country.* Short Grass Historical Society. Foremost, Alta.: Short Grass Historical Society, 1974.

**4668. Short, Roger** *"Winnipeg Last Summer."* Roger Short. Canadian Welfare 45, 5(Sept.-Oct. 1969): 7-10.

**4669. Shostak, Peter** *When Nights Were Long.* Peter Shostak. Victoria: Yalenka Books, 1982.

**4670. Siemens, H.** *"Mental Hygiene in a Health Unit."* H. Siemens. Canadian Medical Association Journal 68, 3(Mar. 1953): 205-209.

**4671. Siemens, Leonard** *Education Plans and Their Fulfillment: a Study of Selected High School Students in Manitoba.* Leonard Siemens and Winston Jackson. Winnipeg: University of Manitoba, 1965.

**4672. Siemens, Leonard** *The Influence of Selected Family Factors on the Educational and Occupational Aspiration Levels of High School-aged Youth.* Leonard Bernard Siemens. Vancouver: University of British Columbia, 1965.
Thesis (M.A.)–University of British Columbia, 1965.
Also issued by the Faculty of Agriculture and Home Economics, University of Manitoba, study no. 1.

**4673. Siemens, Leonard** *School Related Factors and the Aspiration Levels of Manitoba Senior High School Students.* Leonard Siemens and Dennis Forcese. Winnipeg: University of Manitoba, 1965.

**4674. Siemens, Leonard** *Some Rural-Urban Differences Between Manitoba High School Students.* Leonard Siemens and Leo Driedger. Winnipeg: University of Manitoba, 1965.

**4675. Siggins, Maggie** *A Canadian Tragedy: JoAnn and Colin Thatcher, a Story of Love and Hate.* Maggie Siggins. Toronto: Macmillan of Canada, c1985.

**4676. Silverman, Eliane Leslau** *"In Their Own Words: Mothers and Daughters on the Alberta Frontier, 1890-1929."* Eliane Silverman. Frontiers 2, 2(1979): 30-35.

**4677. Silverman, Eliane Leslau** *The Last Best West: Women on the Alberta Frontier 1880-1930.* Eliane Leslau Silverman. 1st ed. Montreal: Eden Press, c1984.

**4678. Simmie and District History Book Club** *Simmie Saga.* Simmie and District History Book Club. [S.l.]: Simmie and District History Book Club, 1981.

**4679. Simon, Maurice** *Bridgeland Riverside Memories: a History of Langevin and St. Angela Schools.* Calgary: [s.n.], 1977.

**4680. Simpson, Ruby M.** *"Protecting and Improving the Health of School Children."* Ruby M. Simpson. Canadian Nurse 21, 12(Dec. 1925): 621-626.

**4681. Simpson, Ruby M.** *"Protecting and Improving the Health of School Children."* R.M. Simpson. In Proceedings and Papers Fifth Annual Canadian Conference on Child Welfare 1925, pp. 102-106.

4682. Simpson, Ruby M. "The School Health Program." Ruby Simpson. In Proceedings of Sixth Annual Canadian Conference on Child Welfare 1927, pp. 67-71.

4683. Sinclair, Virginia Golden Memories of Taber Central School, Taber, Alberta, 1910-1971. Virginia Sinclair. Taber: Taber School Divison, 1971.

4684. Siperko, Gloria M. Burima The Relationship of Neighbourhood and Parental Social Controls to Teenage Misbehaviour. Gloria M. Burima Siperko. Edmonton: University of Alberta, 1970. Thesis (M.A.)–University of Alberta, 1970.

4685. Skogstad, Grace Darlene Adolescent Political Alienation. Grace Darlene Skogstad. Edmonton: University of Alberta, 1971. Thesis (M.A.)–University of Alberta, 1971. Author published an article with the same title in Socialization and Values in Canadian Society, v. 1 (1975), pp. 185-208.

4686. Skogstad, Grace Darlene "Adolescent Political Alienation." Grace D. Skogstad. Toronto: McClelland and Stewart, c1975. In Socialization and Values in Canadian Society, v.1, pp. 185-208. Edited by Elia Zureik and Robert M. Pike. Author presented a thesis with the same title at the University of Alberta, 1971.

4687. Skuba, Michael Population Density and Pupil Transportation Costs in Alberta. Michael Skuba. Edmonton: University of Alberta, 1964. Thesis (Ph.D.)--University of Alberta, 1964.

4688. Skwarok, J. The Ukrainian Settlers in Canada and Their Schools. J. Skwarok. Toronto: Basilian Press, 1959.

4689. Slager, Frances "Bronchopneumonia." Frances Slager. Canadian Nurse 54, 1(Jan. 1958): 49-52.

4690. Slater McLeod, Evelyn "Restless Pioneers." Evelyn Slater McLeod. Beaver 307, 1(Summer 1976): 34-41.

4691. Slater McLeod, Evelyn "School Days at Willow Brook." Evelyn Slater McLeod. Beaver 312, 2(Autumn 1981): 40-46.

4692. Slonim, Reuben Grand to be an Orphan. Reuben Slonim. Toronto: Clarke, Irwin & Co. Ltd., c1983.

4693. Sluman, Norma John Tootoosis: a Biography of a Cree Leader. Norma Sluman and Jean Goodwill. Ottawa: Golden Dog Press, c1982.

4694. Sly, Hildreth Francis An Analysis of Sex Differences in an Alberta School Population. Hildreth Francis Sly. Edmonton: University of Alberta, 1960. Thesis (Ed.D.)--University of Alberta, 1960.

4695. Smith, Colin M. "Childhood Emotional Disorder: an Unknown Quantity." Colin M. Smith. Canada's Mental Health 14, 4(July-Aug. 1966): 12-18. Reprinted in Deviant Behaviour and Societal Reaction, pp. 443-449. Edited by Craig L. Boydell, Carl F. Grindstaff and Paul C. Whitehead. Also reprinted in Deviant Behaviour in Canada, pp. 292-299. Edited by W.E. Mann.

4696. Smith, Denis Malcolm An Investigation of the Relationships Between Certain Factors of Self Concept and Achievement in Mathematics. Denis Malcolm Smith. Calgary: University of Calgary, 1967. Thesis (M.Ed.)--University of Calgary, 1967.

4697. Smith, Donald B. "A History of French-Speaking Albertans." Donald B. Smith. Saskatoon: Western Producer Prairie Books, 1985. In Peoples of Alberta: Portraits of Cultural Diversity, pp. 84-108. Edited by Howard and Tamara Palmer.

4698. Smith, Donald B. "The Original Peoples of Alberta." Donald B. Smith. Saskatoon: Western Producer Prairie Books, 1985. In Peoples of Alberta: Portraits of Cultural Diversity, pp. 50-83. Edited by Howard and Tamara Palmer.

4699. Smith, Hubert Melville An Investigation of the Standard of Achievement at the Lower Limit of the "B" Group in Grade Twelve English in June 1948. Hubert Melville Smith. Edmonton: University of Alberta, 1950. Thesis (M.Ed.)--University of Alberta, 1950.

4700. Smith, John William Alexander Left-Right Discrimination, Lateral Dominance and Reading Achievement in Grade 1 Children. John William Alexander Smith. Edmonton: University of Alberta, 1970. Thesis (M.Ed.)--University of Alberta,

1970.

**4701. Smoky Lake and District Cultural and Heritage Society** *Our Legacy: History of Smoky Lake and Area.* Smoky Lake and District Cultural and Heritage Society. Smoky Lake, Alta: Smoky Lake and District Cultural and Heritage Society, c1983.

**4702. Snider, Doreen** *Called to a Place: the Story of Guernsey and Surrounding School Districts.* Doreen Snider. Guernsey, Sask.: Celebrate Saskatchewan Committee, 1980.

**4703. Snider, Howard Mervin** *Variables Affecting Immigrant Adjustment: a Study of Italians in Edmonton.* Howard Mervin Snider. Edmonton: University of Alberta, 1966.
Thesis (M.A.)--University of Alberta, 1966.

**4704. Snider, James G.** *"A Comparison of All-inclusive Conceptualization in the Delinquent and the Non-delinquent."* James G. Snider. Canadian Journal of Corrections/Revue canadienne de criminologie 7, 3(July 1965): 411-413.

**4705. Snider, James G.** *"Profiles of Some Stereotypes Held by Ninth Grade Pupils."* James G. Snider. Alberta Journal of Educational Research 8, 3(Sept. 1962): 147-156.

**4706. Snow, John** *These Mountains Are Our Sacred Places: the Story of the Stoney Indians.* Chief John Snow. Toronto: Samuel Stevens, 1977.

**4707. Sodhi, Surender Singh** *Rigidity and Set in Second Language Acquisition.* Surender Singh Sodhi. Edmonton: University of Alberta, 1968. (CTM no. 3412)
Thesis (Ph.D.)--University of Alberta, 1968.

**4708. Soiseth, Len** *Community Care: a Northern Experience.* Len Soiseth. [Regina?: Dept. of Welfare for the Province of Saskatchewan?], 1970.

**4709. Soiseth, Len** *"A Community That Cares for Children."* Len Soiseth. Canadian Welfare 46, 3(May-June 1970): 8-10, 26.

**4710. Sokumapi** *"From a Blackfoot Boy."* Sokumapi. Saskatoon: Western Producer Prairie Books, c1982. In Christmas in the West, pp. 65-66. Edited by Hugh A. Dempsey.

**4711. Sommerville, Asbury** *"A Localized Outbreak of Poliomyelitis."* Asbury Sommerville. Canadian Public Health Journal 29, 11(Nov. 1938): 554-556.

**4712. South of the Gully History Committee** *South of the Gully: Banana Belt, Burke, Garvoch, Gully, Wirral.* South of the Gully History Committee. [S.l.]: South of the Gully History Committee, 1981.

**4713. South Shaunavon History Club** *Quarter Stake Echoes: Area South of Shaunavon.* South Shaunavon History Club. Shaunavon, Sask.: South Shaunavon History Club, 1981.

**4714. Sovereign Historical Group** *Mileposts to Memories.* Sovereign Historical Group. Sovereign, Sask.: Sovereign Historical Group, 1981.

**4715. Spalding and District Historical Society** *Spalding: Roots and Branches.* Spalding and District Historical Society. Spalding, Sask.: Spalding and District Historical Society, 1981.

**4716. Sparby, Harry Theodore** *A History of the Alberta School System to 1925.* Harry Theodore Sparby. Palo Alto, Calif.: Stanford University, 1958.
Thesis (Ph.D)--Stanford University, 1958.

**4717. Spiritwood, Mildred, Norbury History Society** *A Tapestry of Time: a History of Spiritwood, Mildred and Norbury Districts.* Spiritwood, Mildred, Norbury History Society. [S.l.]: Spiritwood, Mildred, Norbury History Society, 1984.

**4718. Spondin and Area History Book Society** *Prairie Rose Country: 75 Years of History 1906-1981, Spondin, Coronation South, Richdale, Stanmore, Scotfield.* Spondin and Area History Book Society. Winnipeg, Man.: Inter-Collegiate Press, 1982.

**4719. Sprague, D.N.** *The Genealogy of the First Metis Nation: the Development and Dispersal of the Red River Settlement 1820-1900.* D.N. Sprague and R.P. Frye. Winnipeg: Pemmican Publications Inc., 1983.

**4720. Springett, Evelyn Cartier Galt** *For My Children's Children.* Evelyn Cartier (Galt) Springett. Montreal: The Author, c1937.

**4721. Springside Historical Committee** *Springside and District Memories.* Springside Historical Committee. [S.l.]: Springside Historical Committee, [1982].

4722. Spruce Avenue School *A Historical Publication, Spruce Avenue School, 1918-1978.* Spruce Avenue School. Edmonton: Spruce Avenue School Reunion Committee, 1978.

4723. Spry, Irene M. *"The Metis and Mixed-Bloods of Rupert's Land Before 1870."* Irene M. Spry. Winnipeg: University of Manitoba Press, c1985. In The New Peoples: Being and Becoming Metis in North America, pp. 95-118. Edited by Jacqueline Peterson and Jennifer S.H. Brown.

4724. Spry, Irene M., ed. *"The "Memories" of George William Sanderson 1846-1936."* Irene M. Spry, editor. Canadian Ethnic Studies/Etudes ethniques au Canada 17, 2(1985): 115-134.

4725. St. Andrews (Municipality) *Beyond the Gates of Lower Fort Garry: Rural Municipality of St. Andrews.* Municipality of St. Andrews. Clandeboye, Man.: Municipality of St. Andrews, 1982.

4726. St. Clements Historical Committee *The East Side of the Red: a Centennial Project of the Rural Municipality of St. Clements, 1884-1984.* St. Clements Historical Committee. East Selkirk, Man.: St. Clements Historical Committee, [1984].

4727. St. Front History Book Committee *St. Front and Districts Memoirs, 1910-1981.* St. Front History Book Committee. St. Front, Sask.: St. Front History Book Committee, 1982. Bilingual.

4728. St. Laszlo Historical Committee *With Faith and Hope: St. Laszlo, Our Heritage.* St. Laszlo Historical Committee. St. Laszlo, Sask.: St. Laszlo Historical Committee, [1979].

4729. St. Lina History Book Club *St. Lina and Surrounding Area.* St. Lina History Book Club. St. Lina, Alta.: St. Lina History Book Club, 1978.

4730. St. Louis Local History Committee *I Remember: a History of St. Louis and Surrounding Areas.* St. Louis Local History Committee. St.Louis, Sask.: St. Louis Local History Committee, 1980.

4731. Stacey, Ann *"Initiation of a Northern Teacher."* Ann Stacey. Beaver 293, 3(Winter 1962): 37-39.

4732. Stafford, James Dale *The Stereotype of the Male High School Teacher Held by Grade Twelve Students in Alberta.* James Dale Stafford. Edmonton: University of Alberta, 1969. Thesis (M.Ed.)–University of Alberta, 1969.

4733. Stamp, Robert M. *"The Response to Urban Growth: Bureaucratization of Public Education in Calgary, 1884-1914."* Robert M. Stamp. Calgary: University of Calgary, McClelland and Stewart West, 1975. In Frontier Calgary: Town, City and Region 1875-1914, pp. 153-168. Edited by Anthony W. Rasporich and Henry C. Klassen.

4734. Stamp, Robert M. *School Days: a Century of Memories.* Robert M. Stamp. Calgary: McClelland and Stewart West for Calgary Board of Education, 1975.

4735. Standard Historical Book Society *From Danaview to Standard.* Standard Historical Book Society. Standard, Alta.: Standard Historical Book Society, 1979.

4736. Stanley, George F.G. *Alberta's Half Breed Reserve: Saint Paul des Metis 1896-1909.* George F.G. Stanley. [S.l.: Alberta Department of Education, Native Education Branch, 1978].

4737. Stanley, George F.G. *Louis Riel.* George F. G. Stanley. 2nd ed. Scarborough: McGraw-Hill Ryerson, 1985.

4738. Stanley, George F.G. *Louis Riel.* George F.G. Stanley. 1st ed. Toronto: Ryerson Press, c1963.

4739. Stanley, George F.G. *"One Man Looks Back: School Days! School Days!"* George F.G. Stanley. [S.l.]: The Historical Society of Alberta, Chinook Country Chapter, 1987. In Citymakers: Calgarians After the Frontier, pp. 1-31. Edited by Max Foran and Sheilagh Jameson.

4740. Star City Heritage Society *I Remember When...: Star City.* Star City Heritage Society. [Star City, Sask.: Star City Heritage Society], 1980.

4741. Stechishin, O. *"Neuromuscular Paralysis and Respiratory Arrest Caused by Intrapleural Neomycin."* O. Stechishin, P.C. Voloshin and C.A. Allard. Canadian Medical Association Journal/Journal de l'Association medicale canadienne 81, 1(July 1, 1959): 32-33.

4742. Steele, Jean R.G. *"Educational Work Among Crippled Children."* Jean Steele. Canadian Nurse 26, 5(May 1930): 227-230.

4743. Steele, Jean R.G. *"An Experiment in Modern Education and its Results."* Jean R.G. Steele. Canadian Nurse 27, 11(Nov. 1931): 625-628.

**4744. Steele, Phyllis L.** *The Woman Doctor of Balcarres: the Story of One Woman's Struggle, Through an Era of Inequality, to Become Successful in a Male-dominated Profession.* Phyllis L. Steele. Hamilton: Pathway Publications, 1984.

**4745. Stegner, Wallace** *"Quiet Earth, Big Sky."* Wallace Stegner. Saskatchewan History 9, 3(Fall 1956): 102-109.

**4746. Stevenson, Winona** *The Church Missionary Society Red River Mission and the Emergence of a Native Ministry 1820-1860, with a Case Study of Charles Pratt of Touchwood Hills.* Winona Stevenson. Vancouver: University of British Columbia, 1988.
Thesis (M.A.)–University of British Columbia, 1988.

**4747. Stevenson, Winona** *"The Red River Indian Mission School and John West's "Little Charges", 1820-1833."* Winona Stevenson. Native Studies Review 4, 1 & 2(1988); 129-165.

**4748. Stewart, Alistair McLeod** *The Youth Problem in Manitoba.* Alistair McLeod Stewart. Wimmipeg, Man.: Economic Survey Board, 1939.

**4749. Stewart, Edith C.** *Dad and His Six Women.* Edith Carolyn Stewart. Regina: Caxton Press, 1971.

**4750. Stewart, Edith C.** *"Pioneer Days in the Graytown District."* Edith C. Stewart. Saskatchewan History 10, 2(Spring 1957): 71-76.

**4751. Stewart, Kathleen** *"At Work in an Indian School."* Kathleen Stewart. Canadian Nurse 38, 2(Feb. 1942): 115-116.

**4752. Stewart, Norman** *Children of the Pioneers.* Norman Stewart. Calgary: Foothills Printers, 1962.

**4753. Stone, Sharon D.** *"Emelia's Story: a Ukrainian Grandmother."* Sharon D. Stone. Canadian Woman Studies/Cahiers de la femme 7, 4(Winter 1986): 10-12.

**4754. Stonehenge-Lakenheath Women's Institute** *Along the North Shore of the Twelve Mile: a History of Lakenheath, Stonehenge and Twelve Mile Lake School Districts.* Stonehenge-Lakenheath Women's Institute. Stonehenge, Sask.: Stonehenge-Lakenheath Women's Institute, 1981.

**4755. Storey, Arthur G.** *"Acceleration, Deceleration and Self Concepts."* Arthur G. Storey. Alberta Journal of Educational Research 13, 2(June 1967): 135-142.

**4756. Storey, Arthur G.** *An Exploration and Evaluation of the SRA Primary Mental Abilities Test as an Instrument for Measuring the Intelligence of First Grade Beginners.* Arthur G. Storey. Edmonton: University of Alberta, 1952.
Thesis (M.Ed.)–University of Alberta, 1952.

**4757. Storey, Arthur G.** *"Spelling Skill and Preference in Central Alberta."* Arthur G. Storey and Lorne W. Bunyan. Alberta Journal of Educational Research 11, 1(Mar. 1965): 32-44.

**4758. Storey, Arthur G.** *"What Profit Failure?"* Arthur G. Storey and B. Patterson. Alberta Journal of Educational Research 14, 3(Sept. 1968): 179-184.

**4759. Stowe, Leland** *The Last Great Frontiersman.* Leland Stowe. Toronto: Stoddart, 1982.

**4760. Strayer, B.L.** *"Bintner v. Regina Public School Board and the Constitutional Right to Segregate."* B.L. Strayer. Saskatchewan Bar Review 31, 4(Dec. 1966): 225-231.

**4761. Strohschein, Paul Longin** *Student-Parent Postsecondary Educational Aspirations in the Vermilion Area.* Paul Longin Strohschein. Edmonton: University of Alberta, 1971.
Thesis (M.Ed.)–University of Alberta, 1971.

**4762. Strong, Mary Symons** *Social Class and Levels of Aspiration Among Selected Alberta High School Students.* Mary Symons Strong. Edmonton: University of Alberta, 1963.
Thesis (M.A.)–University of Alberta, 1963.

**4763. Strutz, Peter George** *A Study of Choice Behaviour of Three Age Groups Under Three Different Treatments of a Probability Learning Task.* Peter George Strutz. Edmonton: University of Alberta, 1966.
Thesis (Ph.D.)–University of Alberta, 1966.

**4764. Stuart, J.A.D.** *The Prairie W.A.S.P.: a History of the Rural Municipality of Oakland, Manitoba.* J.A.D. Stuart. Winnipeg: Prairie Publishing Company, 1969.

**4765. Stubbs, Roy St. George** *"The First Juvenile Court Judge: the Honourable Thomas Mayne Daly, K.C."* Roy St. George Stubbs. Historical and Scientific Society of Manitoba Transactions, Series 3, 34(1979): 49-66.

**4766. Stubbs, Roy St. George** *"The First Juvenile Judge: Hon. T. Mayne Daly, K.C."* Roy St. George Stubbs. Manitoba Law Journal 10, 1(1979): 1-21.

**4767. Stubbs, Roy St. George** *"A View of the Family Court."* Roy St. George Stubbs. Manitoba Law Journal 5, 2(1973): 333-357.

**4768. Stubbs, Roy St. George** *"The Young Offender."* Roy St. George Stubbs. Manitoba Law Journal 5, 1(1972): 19-39.

**4769. Sullivan, David M.** *An Investigation of the English Disabilities of Ukrainian and Polish Students in Grade 9, 10, 11, 12 of Alberta Schools.* David M. Sullivan. Edmonton: University of Alberta, 1946.
Thesis (M.Ed.)–University of Alberta, 1946.

**4770. Sunde, Audrey Kathleen** *Individualized Instruction in Grade Seven Mathematics: Pupil Achievement and Grouping Procedures.* Audrey Kathleen Sunde. Edmonton: University of Alberta, 1970.
Thesis (M.Ed.)–University of Alberta, 1970.

**4771. Superb and District History Committee** *Prairie Tapestry, a Superb Story: a History of Superb, Patrick, Somme, Kintail, Nichol, Ethmuir and Ruby Lake.* Superb and District History Committee. Kerrobert, Sask.: Superb and District History Committee, 1981.

**4772. Surerus, Viola** *"Acute Laryngotracheo Bronchitis."* Viola Surerus. Canadian Nurse 53, 7(July 1957): 603-606.

**4773. Swallow, Gordon E.** *"Anorexia."* Gordon E. Swallow. Canadian Medical Association Journal 49, 1(July 1943): 43-46.

**4774. Swan River Valley History Book Committee** *80 Years in Swan River Valley.* Swan River Valley History Book Committee. Swan River, Man.: Swan River Valley History Book Committee, 1978.

**4775. Swanson, Ruth** *The First Hundred Years: Around Churchbridge, 1880-1980.* Ruth Swanson [and] Churchbridge History Committee. Churchbridge, Sask.: Churchbridge History Committee, 1980.

**4776. Swarthmore Book Committee** *Golden Threads: the Tapestry of Swarthmore, 1905-1980.* Swarthmore Book Committee. [S.l.]: Swarthmore Book Committee, [1980].

**4777. Swenarchuk, Janet, ed.** *From Dreams to Reality: a History of the Ukrainian Senior Citizens of Regina and District, 1896-1976.* Janet Swenarchuk, ed. [and] Ukrainian Senior Citizens Association of Regina. [Regina: Ukrainian Senior Citizens Association of Regina], c1977.

**4778. Swindlehurst, Edward B.** *4-H in Alberta, 1918-1967.* Edward B. Swindlehurst. Edmonton: 4-H and Alberta Department of Youth, 1968.

**4779. Swyripa, Frances** *Ukrainian Canadians: a Survey of their Portrayal in English-Language Works.* Frances Swyripa. Edmonton: University of Alberta Press, c1978.

**4780. Sydiaha, D.** *"Aspects of Northern Student Motivation: a Preliminary Statement."* D. Sydiaha and J. Rempel. In Saskatchewan Public Education North of 53: a Preliminary Survey of the Provincial School System, Northern Areas Branch, 1962, pp. 171-179. Written by William D. Knill and Arthur K. Davis.

**4781. Tagashira, K.** *"A Preliminary Report on Ethnicity and University Education in Saskatchewan, 1910-1962."* K. Takashira and Y.W. Lozowchuk. Toronto: Inter-University Committee on Canadian Slavs, [1970]. In Slavs in Canada, v.3 pp. 217-246. Edited by Cornelius J. Jaenen.

**4782. Talbot, Percy R.** *"Pioneering on Strawberry Plain: Early Days at Lacombe."* Percy R. Talbot. Alberta Historical Review 3, 3(Spring 1955): 14-33.

**4783. Tandy, James D.** *The Curriculum of the Morley Indian Residential School, 1923-1958.* James D. Tandy. Calgary: University of Calgary, 1980. (CTM no. 49360)
Thesis (M.A.)–University of Calgary, 1980.

**4784. Tanner, Harold** *The Relation Between Problem Solving Ability in Grade Five Arithmetic and Each of the Variables, Sex, Chronological Age and Mental Age.* Harold Tanner. Edmonton: University of Alberta, 1932.
Theseis (M.A.)–University of Alberta, 1932.

**4785. Targett, Reginald Bryan** *The Education of Exceptional Children in the Calgary Public School System.* Reginald Bryan Targett. Calgary: University of Calgary, 1965. (CTM no. 8492) Thesis (M.Ed.)–University of Calgary, 1965.

**4786. Tari, Andor Joseph** *Affect and Cognition in School Readiness: an Experimental Study in Compensatory Programs for the Disadvantaged Child.* Andor Joseph Tari. Edmonton: University of Alberta, 1968. Thesis (M.Ed.)–University of Alberta, 1968.

**4787. Tari, Andor Joseph** *The Quality of Fathering and Its Relation to the Achievement Motives of the Preschool Child.* Andor Joseph Tari. Edmonton: University of Alberta, 1971. Thesis (Ph.D.)–University of Alberta, 1971.

**4788. Taschuk, W.A.** *"An Analysis of the Self Concept of Grade Nine Students."* W.A. Taschuk. Alberta Journal of Educational Research 3, 2(June 1957): 94-103.

**4789. Taylor, Derek Richard** *A Study of the Teaching of Sight Words to Poor Readers in Grade One Through Their Preferred Modes of Learning.* Derek Richard Taylor. Edmonton: University of Alberta, 1969. Thesis (M.Ed.)–University of Alberta, 1969.

**4790. Taylor, Donald M.** *"Bicultural Communication: a Study of Communicational Efficiency and Person Perception."* Donald M. Taylor and Robert C. Gardner. Canadian Journal of Behavioural Science/Revue canadienne de sciences du comportement 2, 1(Jan. 1970): 67-81.

**4791. Taylor, Jeffrey M.** *"Professionalism, Intellectual Practice and the Educational State Structure in Manitoba Agriculture, 1890-1925."* Jeffrey M. Taylor. Manitoba History 18(Autumn 1989): 36-45.

**4792. Taylor-Pearce, J. Modupe** *Measuring Inventiveness in Senior High School Mathematics.* J. Modupe Taylor-Pearce. Edmonton: University of Alberta, 1971. (CTM no. 8129) Thesis (Ph.D.)–University of Alberta, 1971.

**4793. Taylor, W.C.** *"Accidental Poisoning with Pagitane in a Young Child."* W.C. Taylor. Canadian Medical Association Journal 72, 7(Apr. 1, 1955): 524-525.

**4794. Taylor, W.C.** *"Respiratory Rate Patterns in the Newborn Infant."* W.C. Taylor and G.M. Watkins. Canadian Medical Association Journal/Journal de l'Association medicale canadienne 83, 25(Dec. 17, 1960): 1292-1295.

**4795. Taylor, W.C.** *"A Study of Infantile Colic."* William C. Taylor. Canadian Medical Association Journal 76, 6(Mar. 15, 1957): 458-461.

**4796. Telford, Gertrude S.** *"The First Child Welfare Conferences in Saskatchewan."* Gertrude S. Telford. Saskatchewan History 4, 2(Spring 1951): 57-61.

**4797. Tessier Celebrate Saskatchewan Book Committee** *Tales and Trails of Tessier.* Tessier Celebrate Saskatchewan Book Committee. Tessier, Sask.: Tessier Celebrate Saskatchewan Book Committee, 1981.

**4798. Thatch Creek Historical Society** *Tales and Trails of Thatch Creek, 1905-1980.* Thatch Creek Historical Society. Melfort, Sask.: Thatch Creek Historical Society, [1983].

**4799. The Pas Historical Society** *The Pas: Gateway to Northern Manitoba.* The Pas Historical Society. The Pas, Man.: The Pas Historical Society, 1983.

**4800. Thomas, Jean McCorkindale** *"Homesteading at Indian Head."* Jean McCorkindale Thomas. Saskatchewan History 4, 2(Spring 1951): 68-71.

**4801. Thomas, Theodore Elia** *The Treatment of Male Juvenile Delinquents with Special Reference to Alberta.* Theodore Elia Thomas. Edmonton: University of Alberta, 1951. Thesis (M.A.)–University of Alberta, 1951.

**4802. Thompson, Arthur N.** *"The Wife of the Missionary."* Arthur N. Thompson. Journal of the Canadian Church Historical Society 15, 2(June 1973): 35-44.

**4803. Thompson, Austin Edmund** *Aspirations and Perceptions of Parents and Senior High School Students in an Alberta County System.* Austin Edmund Thompson. Calgary: University of Calgary, 1967. Thesis (M.Ed.)–University of Calgary, 1967.

**4804. Thompson, June Cutt** *"Cree Indians in Northeastern Saskatchewan."* June Cutt Thomson. Saskatchewan History 11, 2(Spring 1958): 41-58.

**4805. Thompson, Ray** *The Queen's Story, 1906-1967: Being a Brief Account of Some Happenings at Queen Alexandra School.* Ray Thompson. Edmonton: Queen Alexandra School, 1967.

**4806. Thompson, Robert H.** *Penny Candy, Bobskates and Frozen Roadapples: Growing Up in the Thirties & Forties.* Robert H. Thompson. Victoria: Orca Book Publishers, c1990.

**4807. Thomson, Colin A.** *Swift Runner.* Colin A. Thomson. Calgary: Detselig Enterprises Ltd., c1984.

**4808. Thomson, Georgina Helen** *Crocus and Meadowlark Country: Recollections of a Happy Childhood and Youth on a Homestead in Southern Alberta.* Georgina Helen Thomson. Edmonton: Institute of Applied Art, 1963.

**4809. Thomson, K.H.** *"Religious Institutions in "Alberta's Public Schools"."* K.H. Thomson. Alberta Journal of Educational Research 13, 1(Mar. 1967): 65-73.

**4810. Thurn, Walter Ralph** *The Famous Bentleys.* Walter Ralph Thurn. [Saskatoon, Sask.: Modern Press], 1947.

**4811. Tierney, Roger J.** *Self-estimate Ability in Relation to Interests and Work Values in Adolescence.* Roger J. Tierney. Calgary: University of Calgary, 1971. (CTM no. 10182)
Thesis (M.Ed.)--University of Calgary, 1971.

**4812. Tiger Hills-Waitville History Group** *The Road From Yesterday to Today: History of Tiger Hills, Waitville and Districts.* Tiger Hills-Waitville History Group. Birch Hills, Sask.: Tiger Hills-Waitville History, 1984.

**4813. Tischler, Kurt** *"The Efforts of the Germans in Saskatchewan to Retain their Language Before 1914."* Kurt Tischler. Toronto: Historical Society of Mecklenburg Upper Canada Inc., 1981. German Canadian Yearbook/Deutschkanadisches Jahrbuch, v.6, pp. 42-61. Edited by Hartmut Froeschle.

**4814. Tkach, Nicholas** *Alberta Catholic Schools: a Social History.* Nicholas Tkach. Edmonton: Faculty of Education, University of Alberta, c1983.

**4815. Toews, Julius G.** *"I Remember: We Spoke English to the Horses But Low German to the Cows."* Julius G. Toews. Winnipeg: Centennial Publications, 1977. In Mennonite Memories: Settling in Western Canada, pp. 98-113. Edited by Lawrence Klippenstein and Julius G. Toews.

**4816. Toews, Julius G.** *"Teach, Learn: a Beginner."* Julius G. Toews. Winnipeg: Centennial Publications, 1977. In Mennonite Memories: Settling in Western Canada, pp. 119-123. Edited by Lawrence Klippenstein and Julius G. Toews.

**4817. Toews, Julius G.** *"Traditional Pastimes."* Julius G. Toews. Winnipeg: Centennial Publications, 1977. In Mennonite Memories: Settling in Western Canada, pp. 300-305. Edited by Lawrence Klippenstein and Julius G. Toews.

**4818. Tolczynski, Borys** *"The Recurrence of Adenoids."* Borys Tolczynski. Canadian Medical Association Journal 72, 9(May 1, 1955): 672-673.

**4819. Tomahawk Trails Book Club** *Tomahawk Trails.* Tomahawk Trails Book Club and Silver Tops Club. Tomahawk, Alta.: Tomahwk Trails Book Club and Silver Tops Club, 1974.

**4820. Tompkins Pioneer History Group** *Tompkins Trials and Triumphs: Tompkins and its Early Trading Area.* Pioneer History Group. Tompkins, Sask.: Pioneer History Group, 1976.

**4821. Torbert, Gerald Mervyn** *A Comparison of Mathematics Achievement after Discovery and Expository Teaching in Grade Eleven.* Gerald Mervyn Torbert. Edmonton: University of Alberta, 1969.
Thesis (M.Ed.)--University of Alberta, 1969.

**4822. Torbit, Gary Edward** *Directed, Nondirected and Prolonged Visual Search of Normal and Retarded Children.* Gary Edward Torbit. Edmonton: University of Albwerta, 1970.
Thesis(M.Ed.)--University of Alberta, 1970.

**4823. Touchette, Pierre Leo** *Language Laboratory Use and Achievement in French Language Study in Alberta.* Pierre Leo Touchette. Edmonton: University of Alberta, 1969.
Thesis (M.Ed.)--University of Alberta, 1969.

**4824. Tovell, Lynn** *"An Evaluation of the Effect of Nursery School Experience in Culturally Disadvantaged Children."* Lynn Tovell. Manitoba Journal of Education 5, 1(Nov. 1969): 15-24.

**4825. Towler, John Orchard** *"Spatial Concepts of Elementary School Children."* J.O. Towler and L.D. Nelson. Alberta Journal of Educational Research 13, 1(Mar. 1967): 34-50.
John Orchard Towler presented a thesis with the same title at the University of Alberta, 1965.

4826. **Towne, Lucille Peskins** *"Preschool Welfare Kindergarten in Saskatoon, Saskatchewan."* Lucille Peskins Towne. Child and Family Welfare 13, 2(July 1937): 61-64.

4827. **Traub, Ross Eugene** *Social Desirability in the Rural High School.* Ross Eugene Traub. Edmonton: University of Alberta, 1961.
   Thesis (M.Ed.)--University of Alberta, 1961.

4828. **Treherne Area History Committee** *Tiger Hills to the Assiniboine: a History of Treherne and Surrounding District.* Treherne Area History Committee. [S.l.]: Treherne Area History Committee, 1976.

4829. **Truax Heritage Club** *Golden Memories of Truax and Districts.* Truax Heritage Club. Truax, Sask.: Truax Heritage Club, 1983.

4830. **Truckey, Lawrence Andrew** *Comparison of Achievement of Grade Nine Students in Selected Single Grade and Multi-grade Classes in Alberta.* Lawrence Andrew Truckey. Edmonton: University of Alberta, 1964.
   Thesis (M.Ed.)--University of Alberta, 1964.

4831. **Truckey, Lawrence Andrew** *"A Comparison of Achievement of Grade Nine Students in Selected Single Grade and Multi-grade Classes in Alberta."* L.A. Truckey and W.D. Knill. Alberta Journal of Educational Research 11, 1(Mar. 1965): 37-44.

4832. **Tsalikis, George** *"The Variability of Preschool Education Programmes in Manitoba."* George Tsalikis. Manitoba Journal of Education 6, 2(June 1971): 48-51.

4833. **Turner, Janice Shirlene** *Day Care and Women's Labour Force Participation: an Historical Study.* Janice Shirlene Turner. Regina: University of Regina, 1981. (CTM no. 50667)
   Thesis (M.A.)--University of Regina, 1981.

4834. **Turner, John Davenall** *Sunfield Painter: the Reminiscences of John Davenall Turner.* John Davenall Turner. Edmonton: University of Alberta Press, 1982.

4835. **Tuxford Heritage Group** *Heritage of the Wheatlands: Tuxford and Area.* Tuxford Heritage Group. Tuxford, Sask.: Tuxford Heritage Group, [1979].

4836. **Twilight Club History Book Committee** *La Glace: Yesterday and Today.* Twilight Club History Book Committee. La Glace, Alta.: Twilight Club History Book Committee, 1981.

4837. **Tymchak, Jo Ann** *"Life in the Brandon Gaol."* Jo Ann Tymchak. Manitoba History 9(Spring 1985): 23.

4838. **Uiskiw, R.** *"Community and Change: the Jewish Experience in Winnipeg's North End, 1900-1914."* R. Uiskiw. Canadian Jewish Historical Society Journal 4, 1(Spring 1980): 71-92.

4839. **Ukrainian Pioneers' Association of Alberta** *Ukrainians in Alberta.* Ukrainian Pioneers' Association of Alberta. Edmonton: The Association, 1975, 1981.
   2 volumes published separately, vol. 1 in 1975 and vol. 2 in 1981.

4840. **University of Alberta. Faculty of Education. Committee on Educational Research** *"A Composition Scale for Alberta Grade Four and Grade Seven Students."* The Committee. Alberta Journal of Educational Research 1, 2(June 1955): 53-61.

4841. **University of Alberta. Institute of Law Research and Reform** *Age of Majority.* The Institute. Edmonton: Institute of Law Research and Reform, 1970.
   Chairman: H.G. Field.

4842. **University of Chicago. Department of Education. Committee on Field Services** *Report of the Directed Self Survey, Winnipeg Public Schools.* University of Chicago. Department of Education. Committee on Field Services. [Winnipeg: Winnipeg Public School Board], 1948.

4843. **Unrau, Henry Harold** *An Experimental Comparison of the Relative Effectiveness of 2 Problem Solving Procedures Taught to EMR Boys.* Henry Harold Unrau. Edmonton: University of Alberta, 1963.
   Thesis (M.Ed.)--University of Alberta, 1963.

4844. **Urdal, Lloyd Bernhard** *An Investigation of the Standard of Achievement at the Lower Limit of the B Group in Grade 10 Physics in June, 1948.* Lloyd Bernhard Urdal. Edmonton: University of Alberta, 1949.
   Thesis (M.Ed.)--University of Alberta, 1949.

**4845. Vanguard Historical Society** *A Place by the Notukeu: Vanguard.* Vanguard Historical Society. Vanguard, Sask.: Vanguard Historical Society, 1984.

**4846. Van Hesteren, Francis Nicholas** *Factors Related to Educational Noncontinuance.* Francis Nicholas Van Hesteren. Edmonton: University of Alberta, 1969.
Thesis (M.Ed.)--University of Alberta, 1969.

**4847. Van Kirk, Sylvia** *""What If Mama Is an Indian?": the Cultural Ambivalence of the Alexander Ross Family."* Sylvia Van Kirk. Edmonton: University of Alberta Press, c1983. In The Developing West: Essays on Canadian History in Honor of Lewis H. Thomas, pp. 125-136. Edited by John E. Foster.
Reprinted in The New Peoples: Being and Becoming Metis in North America, pp. 107-217. Edited by Jacqueline Peterson and Jennifer S.H. Brown.

**4848. Van Kleek, Edith** *Our Trail North: a True Story of Pioneering in the Peace River Country of Northern Alberta.* Edith Van Kleek. Stettler, Alta.: The Author, 1980.

**4849. Vann, Margaret J.** *"Meeting the Challenge of School Lunch Programs for Rural Schools."* Margaret J. Vann. Canadian Journal of Public Health 37, 8(Aug. 1946): 321-324.

**4850. Vargo, James William** *Success-Failure and Retrospective Perception of Task Difficulty.* James William Vargo. Edmonton: University of Alberta, 1970.
Thesis (M.Ed.)--University of Alberta, 1970.

**4851. Vegreville and District Historical Society** *Vegreville in Review: History of Vegreville and Surrounding Area, 1880-1980.* Vegreville and District Historical Society. 2 v. Vegreville, Alta.: Vegreville and District Historical Society, 1980.

**4852. Vella, F.** *"The Electrophoretic Pattern of Hemoglobin in Newborn Babies and Abnormalities of Hemoglobin F Synthesis in Adults."* F. Vella and T.A. Cunningham. Canadian Medical Association Journal/Journal de l'Association medicale canadienne 96, 7(Feb. 18, 1967): 398-401.

**4853. Vidir Ladies Aid** *Beyond the Marsh.* Vidir Ladies Aid. [S.l.: s.n., 1970].

**4854. Vincent, Gordon Bishop** *Vocational and Economic Success of Male High School Dropouts.* Gordon Bishop Vincent. Edmonton: University of Alberta, 1965.
Thesis (M.Ed.)--University of Alberta, 1965.

**4855. Vipond, Jim** *Gordie Howe: Number 9.* Jim Vipond. Rev. ed. Toronto: McGraw-Hill Ryerson, c1971.

**4856. Vogel, Rex William** *The Effect of a Simulation Game on the Attitude of Political Efficiency of Sixth Grade Students.* Rex William Vogel. Edmonton: University of Alberta, 1970.
Thesis (M.Ed.)--University of Alberta, 1970.

**4857. Voisey, Paul** *Vulcan: the Making of a Community.* Paul Voisey. Toronto: University of Toronto Press, 1988.

**4858. Volpe, Richard** *Cognitive and Social Development in Disabled and Non-disabled Children.* Richard Joseph Volpe. Edmonton: University of Alberta, 1970.
Thesis (Ph.D.)--University of Alberta, 1970.

**4859. Vranas, George J.** *"The Eskimos of Churchill, Manitoba."* George J. Vranas and Margaret Stephens. Scarborough, Ont.: Prentice-Hall, 1971. In Native Peoples, pp. 29-54. Edited by Jean Leonard Elliott.

**4860. Wacker, Linda Jean** *Alienation and Anomie in a Detention Home: an Exploratory Study.* Linda Jean Wacker. Calgary: University of Calgary, 1972. (CTM no. 7742)
Thesis (M.S.W.)--University of Calgary, 1972.

**4861. Walker, Bernal Ernest** *A Study of the Reading, Writing, Oral and Aural Skills of French Students in Alberta.* Bernal Ernest Walker. Edmonton: University of Alberta, 1941.
Thesis (M.A.)--University of Alberta, 1941.

**4862. Walter, Cyril Maurice** *Indian Children's Perception of Sex Roles.* Cyril Maurice Walter. Edmonton: University of Alberta, 1970.
Thesis (M.Ed.)--University of Alberta, 1970.

**4863. Walter, Theodore Robert** *A Comparison of Value Orientations of Indian and Non-Indian Schools.* Theodore Robert Walter. Edmonton: University of Alberta, 1971.
Thesis (M.Ed.)--University of Alberta, 1971.

**4864. Wasylyk, Eugene** *The Relation Between Four Selected Teacher Characteristics and Student Achievement in Grade Twelve Mathematics.* Eugene Wasylyk. Edmonton: University of Alberta, 1961.
Thesis (M.Ed.)--University of Alberta, 1961.

**4865. Watkin, J.F.** *Extracurricular Activities in Alberta High Schools.* J.F. Watkin. Edmonton: University of Alberta, 1939.
Thesis (M.A.)--University of Alberta, 1939.

**4866. Watkins, G.M.** *"Hyperchloraemic Uraemia in a Premature Infant on a High Protein Diet."* G.M. Watkins. Canadian Medical Association Journal/Journal de l'Association medicale canadienne 81, 9(Nov. 1, 1959): 736-738.

**4867. Watrous History Book Society** *Prairie Reflections.* Watrous History Book Society. Watrous, Sask.: Watrous History Book Society, 1983.

**4868. Watson, Marg, ed.** *Trails to Little Corner: Namaka and Districts.* Marg Watson, ed. and Namaka Community Historical Committee. Namaka, Alta.: Namaka Community Historical Committee, 1983.

**4869. Watson, Neil B.** *Calgary: a Study of Crime, Offenders and the Police Court, 1924-1934.* Neil B. Watson. Calgary: University of Calgary, 1978. (CTM no. 42101)
Thesis (M.A.)--University of Calgary, 1978.

**4870. Watson, Robert** *"Ojibway Twins."* Robert Watson. Beaver 4, 4(Sept. 1926): 134.

**4871. Watson, William R.** *My Desire.* William R. Watson. Toronto: Macmillan of Canada, 1936.

**4872. Watts, Morrison** *"Character Education in the Secondary Schools of Alberta."* Morrison Watts. Toronto: W.J. Gage, 1959. In Education: a Collection of Essays on Canadian Education, v.2, 1956-1958, pp. [81]-94.

**4873. Webb History Book Committee** *Prairie Memories: Village of Webb.* Webb History Book Committee. Webb, Sask.: Webb History Book Committee, 1982.

**4874. Webb, Jean F.** *"Newborn Infections and Breast Abscesses of Streptococcal Origin."* Jean F. Webb. Canadian Medical Association Journal 70, 4(Apr. 1954): 382-388.

**4875. Webster, Elizabeth E.** *"Balcanes Recollections."* Elizabeth E. Webster. Saskatchewan History 10, 1(Winter 1957): 27-29.

**4876. Weldon and District Historical Society** *Leaves Green and Gold: Weldon, Shannonville, Windermere.* Weldon and District Historical Society. Weldon, Sask.: Weldon and District Historical Society, 1980.

**4877. Welland, Edmund James** *The Effect of Two Density Ratios and Two Background Ratios on the Visual Search Performance of Two Achievement Groups.* Edmund James Welland. Edmonton: University of Alberta, 1969.
Thesis (M.Sc.)--University of Alberta, 1969.

**4878. Wells, Anna E.** *"Little Mothers' Leagues in Manitoba."* Anna E. Wells. Canadian Nurse 22, 3(Mar. 1926): 140-144.

**4879. Wells, Anna E.** *"The Teaching of Health in the Elementary Schools."* A.E. Wells. Canadian Public Health Journal 20, 7(July 1929): 349-354.

**4880. Werner, Walter Harold** *Description of the Verbal Interaction of Grade Eight Social Studies Classes Within the Junior Academic-Vocational High School of Calgary.* Walter Harold Werner. Calgary: University of Calgary, 1971.
Thesis (M.Ed.)--University of Calgary, 1971.

**4881. Wescott, Haze Maclay** *The Use Grade Six Students Make of Small-Scale Maps, Pictures, and Written Material in an Encyclopedia Article.* Haze Maclay Wescott. Calgary: University of Calgary, 1968.
Thesis (M.Ed.)--University of Calgary, 1968.

**4882. Westborne Rural Municipality History Book Committee** *Golden Memories.* History Book Committee, Rural Municipality of Westborne. Winnipeg: Inter-Collegiate Press, 1980.

**4883. Westbury, Ian Douglas** *An Investigation of Some Aspects of Classroom Communication.* Ian Douglas Westbury. Edmonton: University of Alberta, 1968.
Thesis (Ph.D.)--University of Alberta, 1968.

**4884. Westlock History Book Committee** *80 Years of Progress.* Westlock History Book Committee. Westlock, Alta.: Westlock History Book Committee, 1984.

**4885. Wetherell, Donald G.** *"Some Aspects of Technology and Leisure in Alberta 1914-1950."* Donald G. Wetherell. Prairie Forum 11, 1(Spring 1986): 51-67.

**4886. Wetherell, Donald G.** *"Strathcona High School: Beginnings."* Donald G. Wetherell. Alberta History 34, 4(Autumn 1986): 18-23.

**4887. Wetherell, Donald G.** *Useful Pleasures: the Shaping of Leisure in Alberta, 1896-1945.* Donald G. Wetherell with Irene Kmet. Regina: Canadian Plains Research Center, University of Regina, 1990.

**4888. Wheatley, Maisie Violet** *A Study of the Relationship Between Certain Visual Perceptual Abilities and Achievement in First Grade Reading.* Maisie Violet Wheatley. Edmonton: University of Alberta, 1965.
Thesis (M.Ed.)--University of Alberta, 1965.

**4889. White, Clinton O.** *"Education Among German Catholic Settlers in Saskatchewan, 1903-1918: a Reinterpretation."* Clinton O. White. Canadian Ethnic Studies/Etudes ethniques au Canada 16, 1(1984): 78-95.

**4890. Whitecap, Leah** *"The Education of Children in Pre-European Plains America."* Leah Whitecap. Canadian Journal of Native Education 15, 2(Winter 1988): 33-39.

**4891. Whiteford, Jean L., comp.** *Virden Review, 1957-1970.* Jean L. Whiteford, comp. [and] Edith A.M. Moody, comp. Brandon, Man.: Leech Printing, 1970.

**4892. Whitelaw, T.H.** *"Medical Inspection of Schools in Edmonton, Alberta."* T.H. Whitelaw. Public Health Journal 5, 12(Dec. 1914): 714-717.

**4893. Whiteley, A. S.** *"The Peopling of the Prairie Provinces of Canada."* A.S. Whiteley. American Journal of Sociology 38, 2(Sept. 1932): 240-252.

**4894. Whiteside, Ronald Thomas** *Vocational Choice, Attitudes and Self Esteem.* Ronald Thomas Whiteside. Edmonton: University of Alberta, 1969. Thesis (M.Ed.)--University of Alberta, 1969.

**4895. Whitney, Marilyn E.** *An Investigation of the Effects of a Program of Listening Instruction on Reading and Listening Comprehension.* Marilyn E. Whitney. Calgary: University of Calgary, 1970. (CTM no. 7745)
Thesis (M.Ed.)--University of Calgary, 1970.

**4896. Wickstrom, Rod A.** *"Pupil Mobility and School Achievement."* Rod A. Wickstrom. Alberta Journal of Educational Research 13, 4(Dec. 1967): 311-318.

**4897. Wiebe, Gerhard** *Causes and History of the Emigration of the Mennonites from Russia to America.* Gerhard Wiebe; translated by Helen Janzen. Winnipeg: Manitoba Mennonite Historical Society, 1981.
First published in German in 1900 by Druckerei des Nordwestern, Winnipeg.

**4898. Wiebe, Peter T.** *"Learning Was Hard."* Peter T. Wiebe. Winnipeg: Centennial Publications, 1977. In Mennonite Memories: Settling in Western Canada, pp. 128-150. Edited by Lawrence Klippenstein and Julius G. Toews.

**4899. Wilder, Joseph E.** *"An Immigrant Family: from Ploeste to Winnipeg."* Joseph Wilder. Winnipeg: Jewish Historical Society of Western Canada, c1983. In Jewish Life and Times: a Collection of Essays, pp. 169-176.

**4900. Wilder, Joseph E.** *Read All About It: Reminiscences of an Immigrant Newsboy.* Joseph E. Wilder. Winnipeg: Peguis, c1978.

**4901. Williams, Tiger** *Tiger: a Hockey Story.* Tiger Williams with James Lawton. Vancouver: Douglas and McIntyre, c1984.

**4902. Williamson, Norman J.** *"Prospect School, 1876-1880."* Norman J. Williamson. Manitoba Pageant 21, 2(Winter 1976): 13-17.

**4903. Willis, Charles B.** *"The Grading and Promotion of Pupils."* Charles B. Willis. Canadian Journal of Mental Hygiene 3, 4(Jan. 1922): 291-296.

**4904. Willis, Charles B.** *The Practical Application of Mental Tests in the Elementary School.* Charles B. Willis. Toronto: University of Toronto, 1928. Thesis (D.Paed.)--University of Toronto, 1928.

**4905. Willis, Charles B.** *"The Uses of Intelligence Tests in the Schools."* C. Willis. Public Health Journal 15, 2(Feb. 1924): 68-71.

**4906. Willms, A.M.** *"The Brethren Known as Hutterians."* A.M. Willms. Canadian Journal of Economics and Political Science 24, 3(Aug. 1958): 391-405.

**4907. Wilson, Harold Thomas** *Embury House: a Receiving Home for Children.* Harold Thomas Wilson. Vancouver: University of British Columbia, 1950. Thesis (M.S.W.)–University of British Columbia, 1950.

**4908. Wilson, Keith** *The Belgians in Manitoba.* Keith Wilson [and] James B. Wyndels. Winnipeg: Peguis Publishers, 1976.

**4909. Wilson, Keith** *Charles William Gordon.* Keith Wilson. Winnipeg: Peguis Publishers, c1981.

**4910. Wilson, L.J. Roy** *"Agrarian Ideals for Canadian Youth, Alberta 1916-1936: a Case Study."* L.J. Roy Wilson. Toronto: Gage Educational Publishing, 1977. In Canadian Schools and Canadian Identity, pp. 133-149. Edited by Alf Chaiton and Neil McDonald.

**4911. Wilson, L.J. Roy** *"Children, Teachers. and Schools in Early Medicine Hat."* L.J. Roy Wilson. Alberta History 32, 2(Spring 1984): 15-21.

**4912. Wilson, L.J. Roy** *"Cultural Life in Medicine Hat, 1883-1905."* L.J. Roy Wilson. Alberta History 33, 3(Summer 1985): 1-8.

**4913. Wilson, William J.** *The School as Instrument of Urban Reform Education in Winnipeg, 1890-1920.* William J. Wilson. Edmonton: University of Alberta, 1985. Thesis (Ph.D.)--University of Alberta, 1985.

**4914. Wilt, J.C.** *"Aseptic Meningitis in Manitoba, 1957."* J.C. Wilt, H. Medovy, D. Besant and W. Stackiw. Canadian Medical Association Journal 78, 11(June 1, 1958): 839-842.

**4915. Wilt, J.C.** *"Enterovirus Infections in Manitoba, 1959."* J.C. Wilt, W.L. Parker, A.L. Owens and W. Stackiw. Canadian Medical Association Journal/Journal de l'Association medicale canadienne 83, 16(Oct. 15, 1960): 839-843.

**4916. Wilt, J.C.** *"Poliomyelitis Antibodies in Manitoba Children."* J.C. Wilt, D. Grewar and J. Kaminsky. Canadian Medical Association Journal 76, 4(Feb. 15, 1957): 289-292.

**4917. Wilt, J.C.** *"Poliomyelitis in Manitoba, 1958."* J.C. Wilt, R.M. Creighton, A.J.W. Alcock, W. Stackiw and L. Nagel. Canadian Medical Association Journal/Journal de l'Association medicale canadienne 81, 1(July 1, 1959): 1-5.

**4918. Wilton, Keri McCready** *Eye Movements, Surprise Reactions and Conservation in Educable Mentally Retarded and Normal Children.* Keri McCready Wilton. Edmonton: University of Alberta, 1970. Thesis (Ph.D.)–University of Alberta, 1970.

**4919. Wiltshire, E. Bevan** *"Draw-a-man and Raven's Progressive Matrices (1938) Intelligence Test Performance of Reserve Indian Children."* E. Bevan Wiltshire and John E. Gray. Canadian Journal of Behavioural Science/Revue canadienne de sciences du comportement 1, 2(Apr. 1969): 119-122.

**4920. Windthorst History Book Committee** *Windthorst Memories: a History of Windthorst and District.* Windthorst History Book Committee. [Windthorst, Sask.: Windthorst History Book Committee, 1983].

**4921. Winnipeg. Public School Board** *A Visit to Our Schools: a Pictorial Review.* Winnipeg Public School Board. Winnipeg: Bulman Bros., 1945.

**4922. Wiseman, Adele** *Memoirs of a Book Molesting Childhood and Other Essays.* Adele Wiseman. Toronto: Oxford University Press, c1987.

**4923. Wiseton Historical Society** *Wiseton: 1905-1980.* Wiseton Historical Society. [Wiseton, Sask.: Wiseton Historical Society, 1980].

**4924. Wishart-Bankend Historical Society** *Emerald's Past in Prose, Poetry and Pictures.* Wishart-Bankend Historical Society. [S.l.]: Wishart-Bankend Historical Society, 1980.

**4925. Wolseley and District History Book Committee** *Bridging the Past: Wolseley and District, 1880-1980.* Wolseley and District History Book Committee. Wolseley, Sask.: Wolseley and District History Book Committee, 1981.

**4926. Wong, Chak-Sin Julia** *Assimilation and Education: a Study of Postwar Immigrants in Edmonton and Calgary.* Chak-Sin Julia Wong. Edmonton: University of Alberta, 1972. Thesis (M.Ed.)–University of Alberta, 1972.

**4927. Wong, L.C.** *"Visceral Larva Migrans."* L.C. Wong and O.E. Laxdal. Canadian Medical Association Journal 78, 9(May 1, 1958): 695-699.

**4928. Wood River Historical Society**
*Golden Memories of the Wood River Pioneers.* Wood River Historical Society. Lafleche, Sask.: Wood River Historical Society, 1981.

**4929. Woodcock, George** *"The Family Bush: a Pre-autobiographical Exercise."* George Woodcock. Queen's Quarterly 89, 2(Summer 1982): 376-385.

**4930. Woodcock, George** *Gabriel Dumont.* George Woodcock. Don Mills: Fitzhenry and Whiteside Ltd., c1978.

**4931. Woods, Betty** *"Red River School Day, 1871."* Betty Woods. Manitoba Pageant 6, 2(Jan. 1961): 4-5.

**4932. Woods, David Scott** *Education in Manitoba: a Preliminary Report.* David Scott Woods. Winnipeg: Economic Survey Board, 1938.

**4933. Worth, Walter** *Before Six: a Report on the Alberta Early Childhood Education Study.* Walter Worth. Edmonton: Alberta School Trustees' Association, 1966.

**4934. Worth, Walter** *"Promotion vs Nonpromotion I: the Earlier Research Evidence."* Walter H. Worth. Alberta Journal of Educational Research 5, 1(Mar. 1959): 77-86.

**4935. Worth, Walter** *"Promotion vs Nonpromotion II: the Edmonton Study."* Walter H. Worth. Alberta Journal of Educational Research 5, 3(Sept. 1959): 191-203.

**4936. Woycenko, Ol'ha** *The Ukrainians in Canada.* Ol'ha Woycenko. Winnipeg: Trident Press Ltd., 1967.

**4937. Woywitka, Anne B.** *"Homesteader's Woman."* Anne B. Woywitka. Alberta History 24, 2(Spring 1976): 20-24.

**4938. Wrentham Historical Society**
*Homestead Country: Wrentham and Area.* Wrentham Historical Society. Wrentham, Alta.: Wrentham Historical Society, 1980.

**4939. Wright, Doris** *"My Best Christmas."* Doris Wright. Saskatoon: Western Producer Prairie Books, c1982. In Christmas in the West, pp. 111-112. Edited by Hugh A. Dempsey.

**4940. Wright, John Robert** *A Survey and Analysis of Local Home and School Activities in the Edmonton Area.* John Robert Wright. Edmonton: University of Alberta, 1964.
Thesis (M.Ed.)--University of Alberta, 1964.

**4941. Wynn, Glyn Neil** *Teacher and Student Opinions of the Semester System in Edmonton.* Glyn Neil Wynn. Edmonton: University of Alberta, 1971.
Thesis (M.Ed.)--University of Alberta, 1971.

**4942. Yedlin, Tova, ed.** *Alberta's Pioneers From Eastern Europe: Reminiscences.* Tova Yedlin, ed. [and] Joanna Matejko, ed. 2 v. [Edmonton]: Division of East European Studies, University of Alberta, 1978.

**4943. Yellow Creek History Committee**
*Our Pride and Heritage: History of Yellow Creek and the Surrounding School Districts.* Yellow Creek History Committee and "Silver Halos". Yellow Creek, Sask.: Yellow Creek History Committee, 1982.

**4944. Yellow Grass Heritage Committee**
*Yellow Grass: Our Prairie Community.* Yellow Grass Heritage Committee. Yellow Grass, Sask.: Yellow Grass Heritage Committee, 1981.

**4945. Yellow Lake History Group**
*Treasured Memories: Yellow Lake and District.* Yellow Lake History Group. Yellow Lake, Sask.: Yellow Lake History Group, 1982.

**4946. Yeo, W.B.** *"Making Banff a Year-round Park."* W.B. Yeo. Calgary: Historical Society of Alberta, 1990. In Winter Sports in the West, pp. [87]-98. Edited by Elise A. Corbet and Anthony W. Rasporich.

**4947. Yeudall, Lorette Kathleen** *Response Patterns of Institutional and Normal Girls on Problem Checklists.* Lorette Kathleen Yeudall. Edmonton: University of Alberta, 1964.
Thesis (M.A.)--University of Alberta, 1964.

**4948. Young Celebration Committee**
*Footsteps to Follow: a History of Young, Zelma and Districts.* Young Celebration Committee. Young, Sask.: Young Celebration Committee, 1981.

**4949. Young, Egerton R.** *Indian Life in the Great North-west.* Egerton R. Young. Toronto: Musson Book Company Ltd., [189-?].

**4950. Young, Jean Ashmore** *An Objective Comparison of Achievement in the Basic Subjects for Matched Groups of Children in Manchester, England and Edmonton, Alberta.* Jean Ashmore Young. Edmonton: University of Alberta, 1963.
Thesis (M.Ed.)--University of Alberta, 1963.

**4951.** *Young People of All Ages.* Accounts by Calgary authors. [Calgary]: Century Calgary Publications, 1975.

**4952. Youngstown and District Historical Society** *Youngstown Memories Across the Years, 1909-1983.* Youngstown and District Historical Society. [Youngstown, Alta.]: Youngstown and District Historical Society, 1984.

**4953. Younoszai. M.K.** *"Cigarette Smoking During Pregnancy: the Effect Upon the Hematocrit and Acid-base Balance of the Newborn Infant."* M.K. Younoszai and J.C. Haworth. Canadian Medical Association Journal/Journal de l'Association medicale canadienne 99, 5(Aug. 3, 1968): 197-200.

**4954. Zacharias, Peter D.** *Reinland: an Experience in Community.* Peter D. Zacharias [and] Reinland Centennial Committee. [S.l.]: Reinland Centennial Committee, 1976.

**4955. Zado, Phyllis, ed.** *Furrows and Faith: a History of Lake Johnston and Sutton R.M.'s.* Phyllis Zado,. ed. and Lake Johnston-Sutton Historical Society. Mossbank, Sask.: Lake Johnston-Sutton Historical Society, 1980.

**4956. Zak, W.** *"A Study of Attitudes of Indian and Metis Students Towards Euro-Canadians in Northern Manitoba."* W. Zak. Manitoba Journal of Education 7, 1(Nov. 1971): 67-80.

**4957. Zasadny. Norma Jean** *An Investigation of the Ability of Grade One Readers to Make Auditory and Visual Discriminations and Auditory-Visual Correspondences.* Norma Jean Zasadny. Edmonton: University of Alberta, 1971.
Thesis (M.Ed.)--University of Alberta, 1971.

**4958. Zeilig, Ken** *Ste. Madeleine, Community Without a Town: Metis Elders in Interview.* Ken Zeilig and Victoria Zeilig. Winnipeg: Pemmican Publications Inc., 1987.

**4959. Zentner, Henry** *"Cultural Assimilation Between Indians and Non-Indians in Southern Alberta."* Henry Zentner. Alberta Journal of Educational Research 9, 2(June 1963): 79-86.

**4960. Zentner, Henry** *"Parental Behaviour and Student Attitudes Towards Further Training Among Indians and Non-Indian Students in Oregon and Alberta."* Henry Zentner. Alberta Journal of Educational Research 9, 1(Mar. 1963): 22-30.

**4961. Zentner, Henry** *"Parental Behaviour and Student Attitudes Towards High School Graduation Among Indian and Non-Indian Students in Oregon and Alberta."* Henry Zentner. Alberta Journal of Educational Research 8, 4(Dec. 1962): 211-219.

**4962. Zentner, Henry** *"Reference Group Behavior Among High School Students."* Henry Zentner. Alberta Journal of Educational Research 10, 3(Sept. 1964): 142-152.

**4963. Zentner, Henry** *"Religious Affiliation, Social Class, and the Achievement-aspiration Relationship Among Male High School Students."* Henry Zentner. Alberta Journal of Educational Research 11, 4(Dec. 1965): 233-248.

**4964. Zentner, Henry** *"Social Status in the High School: an Analysis of Some Related Variables."* Henry Zentner and Arnold R. Parr. Alberta Journal of Educational Research 14, 4(Dec. 1968): 253-264.

**4965. Zentner, Henry** *"Value Congruence Among Indian and Non-Indian High School Students in Southern Alberta."* Henry Zentner. Alberta Journal of Educational Research 9, 3(Sept. 1963): 168-178.

**4966. Zielinski, Wasyl Gregory** *Achievement of Grade 7 Compound and Coordinate Cree and English Speaking Bilinguals in Northland School, Division 61.* Wasyl Gregory Zielinski. Missoula, Mt.: Montana University, c1971.
Thesis (Ph.D.)--Montana University, 1971.

**4967. Zingle, Harvey W.** *A Rational Therapy Approach to Counselling Underachievers.* Harvey W. Zingle. Edmonton: University of Alberta, 1965.
Thesis (Ph.D.)--University of Alberta, 1965.

# Central Canada

**4968. Abate, Abata Wori** *Iroquois · Control of Iroquois Education: a Case Study of the Iroquois of the Grand River Valley in Ontario, Canada.* Abata Wori Abate. Toronto: University of Toronto, 1984.
Thesis (Ph.D.)–University of Toronto, 1984.

**4969. Abbott, John** *"Hostile Landscapes and the Spectre of Illiteracy: Devising Retrieval Systems for "Sequested" Children in Northern Ontario, 1875-1930."* John Abbott. Vancouver: CSCI, 1984. In An Imperfect Past: Education and Society in Canadian History, pp. 181-194. Edited by J. Donald Wilson.

**4970. Abeele, Cynthia C.** *""The Mothers of the Land Must Suffer": Child and Maternal Welfare in Rural and Outpost Ontario, 1918-1940."* Cynthia Comacchio Abeele. Ontario History 80, 3(Sept. 1988): 183-205.

**4971. Abeele, Cynthia C.** *Nations Are Built of Babies: Maternal and Child Welfare in Ontario.* Cynthia C. Abeele. Guelph: University of Guelph, 1987.
Thesis (Ph.D.)–University of Guelph, 1987.

**4972. Acal, Alice** *A Study of Mutual Attitudes of English (Speaking) Canadian Children and French (Speaking) Canadian Children in Two Elementary Schools, and the Relation of the Attitudes of These Children to Sociometric Status.* Alice Acal. Toronto: University of Toronto, 1949.
Thesis (M.A.)–University of Toronto, 1949.

**4973. Acker, Charles Wilfred** *The Effect of Aggressive Movie Content on Pain-producing Responses of Adults and Adolescents.* Charles Wilfred Acker. Toronto: University of Toronto, 1962.
Thesis (M.A.)–University of Toronto, 1962.

**4974. Adams, F.** *"Immunization Against Diphtheria."* F. Adams. Public Health Journal 19, 2(Feb. 1928): 51-56.

**4975. Adams, Howard** *The Education of Canadians 1800-1867: the Roots of Separatism.* Howard Adams. Montreal: Harvest House Limited, c1968.

**4976. Adams, John Coldwell** *Seated With the Almighty: a Biography of Sir Gilbert Parker.* John Coldwell Adams. Ottawa: Borealis Press, c1979.

**4977. Adams, Leyland** *"Hypertension and Unilateral Kidney Disease: Late Results of Nephrectomy in Seven Patients."* Leyland Adams. Canadian Medical Association Journal 73, 10(Nov. 15, 1955): 800-804.

**4978. Adanovics, Inta** *The Impact of a Mentally Retarded Child on the Family Unit.* Inta Adanovics, Frances Frei, Pauline Leagare, D. McIntosh and P. Robin. Montreal: McGill University, 1960.
Thesis (M.S.W.)–McGill University, 1960.

**4979. Adelman, Sheila** *The Relationship of Mental Age to Children's Concept of Causality.* Sheila Adelman. Toronto: University of Toronto, 1953.
Thesis (M.A.)–University of Toronto, 1953.

**4980. Adi, Rachel V. Nwamaka** *The Self Concept of B Stream Pupils as Related to Streaming on the Basis of Ability and Attainment.* Rachel V. Nwamaka Adi. Montreal: McGill University, 1967. Thesis (M.A.)--McGill University, 1967.

**4981. Aellen, Carol** *"Ethnic Identification and Personality Adjustments of Canadian Adolescents of Mixed English-French Parentage."* Carol Aellen and Wallace E. Lambert. Canadian Journal of Behavioural Science/Revue canadienne de sciences du comportement 1, 2(Apr. 1969): 69-86.

**4982. Agee, Vicki** *"Treating the Violent Juvenile Offender."* Vicki Agee. Ottawa: John Howard Society of Canada, c1987. In Insights into Violence in Contemporary Canadian Society, pp. 298-304. Edited by James M. MacLatchie.

**4983. Aitken, Kate** *Never a Day So Bright.* Kate Scott Aitken. Toronto: Longmans Green, 1956.

**4984. Albani, Emma** *Forty Years of Song.* Emma Albani. London: Mills & Boon, 1911. Republished in 1977 by Arno Press.

**4985. Alderdice, E.T.** *The Relation of Self-recognition to Age, Intelligence, and Perceptual Ability.* E.T. Alderdice. Toronto: University of Toronto, 1955. Thesis (Ph.D.)--University of Toronto, 1955.

**4986. Alderton, Harvey R.** *"A Comparison of the Follow-up Status of Children's Aid Society Wards and Non-Wards Treated in a Children's Psychiatric Hospital."* Harvey R. Alderton. Canadian Medical Association Journal/Journal de l'Association medicale canadienne 100, 22(June 14, 1969): 1035-1042.

**4987. Alexander, C.C.** *"Medical Inspection of Schools in Brantford."* Dr. C.C. Alexander. Public Health Journal 18, 9(Sept. 1927): 417-419.

**4988. Allan, Andrew** *Andrew Allan: a Self-portrait.* Andrew Allan. Toronto: MacMillan of Canada, c1974.

**4989. Allan, Barbara Munroe** *Parental Problems in the Treatment of Children with Cerebral Palsy.* Barbara Munroe Allan. Montreal: McGill University, 1951. Thesis (M.S.W.)--McGill University, 1951.

**4990. Allan, Mona** *The Need for School Social Work in Elementary Schools.* Mona Allan, Ellen Botto and Lydia Keitner. Montreal: McGill University, 1965. Thesis (M.S.W.)--McGill University, 1965.

**4991. Allard, Charles A.** *"Complete Duplication of the Large Bowel Treated by Subtotal Colectomy."* Charles A. Allard, Dudley E. Ross and J.K. Hopkirk. Canadian Medical Association Journal 60, 2(Feb. 1949): 165-167.

**4992. Allen, Isabel H.** *"Sunnyside Children's Centre, Kingston."* Isabel H. Allen. Canadian Welfare 33, 5(Dec. 1957): 204-210.

**4993. Allen Robert Thomas** *My Childhood and Yours: Happy Memories of Growing Up.* Robert Thomas Allen. Toronto: MacMillan of Canada, 1977.

**4994. Allen, Robert Thomas** *When Toronto was for Kids.* Robert Thomas Allen. Toronto: McClelland and Stewart Ltd., 1961.

**4995. Allin, A.E.** *"Meningitis of the Newborn Due to Pseudomonas Aeruginara."* A.E. Allin. Canadian Medical Association Journal 44, 3(Mar. 1941): 288-289.

**4996. Allison, William Talbot** *The Bilingual Schools of Ontario: Summary of Conditions.* W.T. Allison. Toronto: Sentinel Publishing Company, 1910.

**4997. Allison, William Talbot** *This for Remembrance.* W.T. Allison. Toronto: Ryerson Press, c1949.

**4998. Althouse, J.G.** *"Significant Trends in Education in Ontario."* J.G. Althouse. University of Toronto Quarterly 25, 3(Apr. 1956): 232-241.

**4999. Ames, Herbert Brown** *The City Below the Hill: a Sociological Study of a Portion of the City of Montreal, Canada.* Herbert Brown Ames. Montreal: Bishop Engraving and Printing Co., 1897. Republished by University of Toronto Press, 1972.

**5000. Amey, Lorne James** *The Effects of Frequent Changes of School Upon Junior High School Students.* Lorne James Amey. New Brunswick: University of New Brunswick, 1965. Thesis (M.Ed.)--University of New Brunswick, 1965.

**5001. Amiel, Barbara** *Confessions.* Barbara Amiel. Toronto: Macmillan of Canada, c1980.

**5002. Amoss, Harry** *Elementary Science in the Secondary Schools of Ontario.* H.E. Amoss. Toronto: University of Toronto Press, [1916]. Thesis (D.Paed.)--University of Toronto, 1916.

**5003. Amoss, Harry** *Training Handicapped Children.* Harry Amoss and L. Helen DeLaporte. Toronto: Ryerson Press, 1933.

**5004. Anant, Santokh S.** *"Relative Effectiveness of Aptitude Tests."* Santokh S. Anant. Alberta Journal of Educational Research 14, 1(Mar. 1968): 43-47.

**5005. Anderson, Allan** *Remembering Leacock: an Oral History.* Allan Anderson. Ottawa: Deneau, c1983.

**5006. Anderson, Barry D.** *Bureaucratization and Alienation: an Empirical Study in Secondary Schools.* Barry Douglas Anderson. Toronto: University of Toronto, 1970. Thesis (Ph.D.)--University of Toronto, 1970.

**5007. Anderson, G.W.** *"A Group of Auto Theft Cases."* G.W. Anderson and K.H. Rogers. Child and Family Welfare 12, 3(Sept. 1936): 39-45.

**5008. Anderson, John Alexander** *An Ontario Secondary School Student Information System.* John Alexander Anderson. Toronto: University of Toronto, 1968. Thesis (M.A.)--University of Toronto, 1968.

**5009. Anderson, Ursula M.** *"Infant Survival Differentials in the City of Toronto: a Challenge to Health and Planning Research."* Ursula M. Anderson. Canadian Family Physician 16, 9(Sept. 1970): 45-50.

**5010. Anglin, Crawford S.** *"Acute Purulent Meningitis in Childhood."* C.S. Anglin, G.A. McNaughton and N. Silverthorne. Canadian Medical Association Journal 66, 5(May 1952): 435-439.

**5011. Anonymous** *"Child Welfare in Ontario."* Public Health Journal 11, 7(July 1920): 336-337.

**5012. Anonymous** *"The Health of Women and Children."* Public Health Journal 9, 3(Mar. 1918): 137-139.

**5013. Anonymous** *Historical Sketch of the Montreal Protestant Orphan Asylum From Its Foundation on the 16th February 1822 to the Present Day Compiled From Its Minutes and Annual Reports.* [Montreal?: s.n.], 1860.

**5014. Anonymous** *"Infant Mortality."* Public Health Journal 2(1911): 220.

**5015. Anonymous** *"Medical Inspection of Schools."* Public Health Journal 4, 9(Sept. 1913): 516-517.

**5016. Anonymous** *"Medical Inspection of Schools in Ontario."* Public Health Journal 5, 3(Mar. 1914): 158-162.

**5017. Anonymous** *"Medical Inspection of Schools in Quebec."* Public Health Journal 5, 3(Mar. 1914): 155-157.

**5018. Anonymous** *On Both Sides of the Sea, or, Mrs. Birt's Little Emigrants.* [Knowlton, Que.?: Children's Distributing Home?, 188-].

**5019. Anonymous** *"Our Second Son."* Canadian Welfare 32, 4(Nov. 1956): 160-164.

**5020. Anonymous** *"Progress of Fort William's Campaign Against Infant Mortality."* Public Health Journal 2, 9(Sept. 1911): 439.

**5021. Apramian, Jack** *"The Georgetown Boys."* Jack Apramian. Polyphony 4, 2(Fall-Winter 1982): 43-52.

**5022. Archibald, David** *Report on the Treatment of Neglected Children in Toronto.* David Archibald. Toronto: Arcade Printing Co. for Toronto Police Force, 1907.

**5023. Armstrong, A.R.** *"An Unusual Case of Tuberculous Meningitis."* A.R. Armstrong. Canadian Medical Association Journal 72, 7(Apr. 1, 1955): 517-520.

**5024. Armstrong, F.H.** *"John Strachan, Schoolmaster, and the Evolution of the Elite in Upper Canada/Ontario."* F.H. Armstrong. Vancouver: CSCI Publications, 1981. In An Imperfect Past: Education and Society in Canadian History, pp. 154-169. Edited by J. Donald Wilson.

**5025. Armstrong, Harvey** *"Seizures in Canadian Indian Children: Individual, Family, and Community Approach."* Harvey Armstrong and Paul Patterson. Canadian Psychiatric Association Journal/Revue de l'Association canadienne de psychiatrie 20, 4(June 1975): 247-255.

**5026. Armstrong, J.G.** *"Methaemoglobinaemia in Infancy: Two Case Reports, One of the Congenital Kind and One of the Acquired Variety of Methaemoglobinaemia."* J.G. Armstrong, J.B.J. McKendry and K.W. Slemon. Canadian Medical Association Journal 79, 5(Sept. 1, 1958): 392-395.

5027. **Ashby, Gail** *"The Child I Was."* Gail Ashby. Toronto: McClelland and Stewart Ltd., c1972. In Making It: the Canadian Dream, pp. 2-11. Edited by Bryan Finnigan and Cy Gonick.

5028. **Ashgold, Cecile** *Families with Problems: an Exploratory Study of Three-generation Families Known to a Family Service Agency in Montreal, 1913-1963.* Cecile Ashgold, Irene Gordon, Aline Gubbay and Lynda Southam. Montreal: McGill University, 1965. Thesis (M.S.W.)-McGill University, 1965.

5029. **Association Canadienne des Educatuers de Langue Francaise** *Facets of French Canada.* The Association. Ottawa: The Association, c1967.

5030. **Atherton, William H.** *"Child Welfare and the City."* Wm. H. Atherton. Public Health Journal 2, 10(Oct. 1911): 461-466.

5031. **Atkinson, C.J.** *"The Boy Problem."* A.C. Atkinson.

5032. **Atkinson, Doris E.** *Sexual Delinquencies in Juvenile Girls.* Doris E. Atkinson. Toronto: University of Toronto, 1947. Thesis (M.S.W.)-University of Toronto, 1947.

5033. **Atkinson, Elizabeth** *A Study of Agency Services on Adoption and Relinquishment.* Elizabeth Atkinson, E. Burnell, J.N. Burnell, S.C. Martz and E.A. Elliot. Montreal: McGill University, 1953. Thesis (M.S.W.)-McGill University, 1953.

5034. **Audet, Jacques** *"A Case of Ocular Torticollis."* Jacques Audet. Canadian Medical Association Journal 71, 1(July 1954): 60-62.

5035. **Audet, Louis-Philippe** *"Attempts to Develop a School System for Lower Canada: 1760-1840."* Louis-Philippe Audet. In Canadian Education: a History, pp. 145-166. Edited by J. Donald Wilson, Robert M. Stamp and Louis-Philippe Audet.

5036. **Audet, Louis-Philippe** *"Education."* Louis-Philippe Audet. Ottawa: L'Association canadienne des educateurs de langue francaise, c1967. In Facets of French Canada, pp. 53-107.

5037. **Audet, Louis-Philippe** *"Education in Canada East and Quebec: 1840-1875."* Louis-Philippe Audet. In Canadian Education: a History, pp. 167-189. Edited by J. Donald Wilson, Robert M. Stamp and Louis-Philippe Audet.

5038. **Audet, Louis-Philippe** *"Educational Development in French-Canada After 1875."* Louis-Philippe Audet. In Canadian Education: a History, pp. 337-359. Edited by J. Donald Wilson, Robert M. Stamp and Louis-Philippe Audet.

5039. **Audet, Louis-Philippe** *"Society and Education in New France."* Louis-Philippe Audet. In Canadian Education: a History, pp. 70-85. Edited by J. Donald Wilson, Robert M. Stamp and Louis-Philippe Audet.

5040. **Audet, Pierre H.** *Apprenticeship in Early Nineteenth Century Montreal 1790-1812.* Pierre H. Audet. Montreal: Concordia University, 1975. (CTM no. 24173) Thesis (M.A.)-Concordia University, 1975.

5041. **Austin, O.L.** *"The Voluntary Case Work Agency and Juvenile Rehabilitation."* O.L. Austin and K.H. Rogers. Child and Family Welfare 11, 2(July 1935): 35-42.

5042. **Avison, Douglas B.** *"An Epidemic of Mumps in Peterborough, Ont."* Douglas B. Avison. Canadian Public Health Journal 33, 11(Nov. 1941): 548-551.

5043. **Avital, Shmuel M.** *Higher Level Thinking in Secondary School Students' Attainment in Mathematics.* Shmuel M. Avital. Toronto: University of Toronto, 1967. Thesis (Ed.D.)-University of Toronto, 1967.

5044. **Awad, George A.** *"The Process of Psychiatric Work with the Juvenile Courts."* George Awad and Clive Chamberlain. Canadian Journal of Family Law/Revue canadienne de droit familial 1, 3(July 1978): 363-374.

5045. **Axmith, Gail** *Sexually Promiscuous Juvenile Girls in Galt Training School.* Gail Axmith. Toronto: University of Toronto, 1963. Thesis (M.S.W.)-University of Toronto, 1963.

5046. **Aylesworth, Vicki** *The Inmate Social System in Guelph Reformatory.* Vicki Aylesworth. Toronto: University of Toronto, 1966. Thesis (M.S.W.)-University of Toronto, 1966.

5047. **Bacal, H.L.** *"Aminophylline Poisoning in Children."* H.L. Bacal, K. Linegar, R.L. Denton and R. Jourdeau. Canadian Medical Association Journal 80, 1(Jan. 1, 1959): 6-9.

**5048. Baehre, Rainer** *"Pauper Emigration to Upper Canada in the 1830's."* Rainer Baehre. Histoire sociale/Social History 14, 28(Nov. 1981): 339-367.

**5049. Baehre, Rainer** *"Paupers and Poor Relief in Upper Canada."* Rainer Baehre. Canadian Historical Association, Historical Papers/Communications historiques (1981): 57-80.

**5050. Bailey, Nora** *An Analysis of Camp Records.* Nora Bailey. Toronto: University of Toronto, 1938.
Thesis (M.A.)--University of Toronto, 1938.
No bibliography.

**5051. Bain, Harry W.** *"Galactosaemia."* Harry W. Bain, Drummond H. Bowden, A. Lawrence Chute, Sanford H. Jackson, Andrew Sass-Kortsak and Norma Ford Walker. Canadian Medical Association Journal 76, 4(Feb. 15, 1957): 278-285.

**5052. Bain, Ian** *The Role of J.J. Kelso in the Launching of the Child Welfare Movement in Ontario.* Ian Bain. Toronto: University of Toronto, 1955. (CTM no. 25456)
Thesis (M.S.W.)--University of Toronto, 1955.

**5053. Bainbridge, Eleanor J.** *Punishment in Ontario Reformatories: a Study of the Relationship Between the Types of Offence and Punishment Received Within the Institution.* Eleanor J. Bainbridge. Toronto: University of Toronto, 1966.
Thesis (M.S.W.)--University of Toronto, 1966.

**5054. Baker, Sylvia Kathleen** *Integration of Jewish Immigrants from Morocco Into the Toronto Community: a Comment on the Relationship Between Integration and Disciplinary Problems With Their Children Experienced By Parents from Morocco.* Sylvia Kathleen Baker. Toronto: University of Toronto, 1965.
Thesis (M.S.W.)--University of Toronto, 1965.

**5055. Baker, Walter** *"John Joseph Kelso."* Walter Baker. Canadian Welfare 42, 6(Nov.-Dec. 1966): 250-255.

**5056. Ball, Rosemary R.** *""A Perfect Farmer's Wife": Women in 19th Century Rural Ontario."* Rosemary R. Ball. Canada: An Historical Magazine 3, 2(Dec. 1975): 2-21.

**5057. Balliet, Thomas M.** *"Point of Attack in Sex Education."* Thomas M. Balliet. Public Health Journal 4, 12(Dec. 1913): 684-686.

**5058. Ballon, David H.** *"Review of Foreign Body Endoscopy Over a Period of Thirty Years."* David H. Ballon. Canadian Medical Association Journal 74, 2(Jan. 15, 1956): 139-143.

**5059. Bamman, Haley P.** *"Patterns of School Attendance in Toronto, 1844-1878: Some Spatial Considerations."* Haley P. Bamman. History of Education Quarterly 12, 3(Fall 1972): 381-410.
Reprinted in Education and Social Change: Themes from Ontario's Past, pp. 217-245. Edited by Michael B. Katz and Paul H. Mattingly.

**5060. Bancroft, Catherine M.** *Adoption as Seen by Adoptive Parents: a Follow-up Study of 25 Children, Legally Adopted 10 or More Years Ago, with Particular Attention to the Parents' Current Feelings About the Adoption.* Catherine M. Bancroft. Montreal: McGill University, 1953.
Thesis (M.S.W.)--McGill University, 1953.

**5061. Banfield, Paul Anthony** *The Well-regulated Family: John Strachan and the Role of the Family in Early Upper Canada 1800-1812.* Paul Anthony Banfield. Kingston: Queen's University, 1986. (CTM no. 67862)
Thesis (M.A.)--Queen's University, 1986.

**5062. Banister, Philip** *"The Complete Elimination of Retrolental Fibroplasia."* Philip Banister and John C. Locke. Canadian Medical Association Journal 76, 2(Jan. 15, 1957): 81-85.

**5063. Bannerman, Judith Sarah** *A Plan for Family Life Education in the Protestant Schools of Montreal.* Judith Sarah Bannerman. Montreal: McGill University, 1967.
Thesis (M.A.)--McGill University, 1967.

**5064. Bannister, J.A.** *Early Educational History of Norfolk County.* J.A. Bannister. Toronto: University of Toronto Press, 1926.
Text is the published version of the author's D.Paed. dissertation presented at the University of Toronto in 1926.

**5065. Barber, Marilyn** *"Below Stairs: the Domestic Servant."* Marilyn Barber. Material History Bulletin/Bulletin d'histoire de la culture materielle 19(Spring 1984): 37-46.

**5066. Barber, Marilyn** *"The Ontario Bilingual Schools Issue: Sources of Conflict."* Marilyn Barber. Canadian Historical Review 47, 3(Sept. 1966): 227-248.

**5067. Barber, Marilyn** *"The Women Ontario Welcomed: Immigrant Domestics for Ontario Homes, 1870-1930."* Marilyn Barber. Ontario History 72, 3(Sept. 1980): 148-172.

**5068. Barker, Lillian** *The Dionne Legend: Quintuplets in Captivity.* Lillian Barker. Garden City, N.Y.: Doubleday & Co. Ltd., c1951.

**5069. Barkin, Risa** *"Death in Victorian Toronto, 1850-1899."* Risa Barkin and Ian Gentles. Urban History Review/Revue d'histoire urbaine 29, 1(June 1990): 14-29.

**5070. Barnes, A.S.L.** *Requirements for the Boy Scout Forester's Badge With Answers, With Special Reference to Ontario.* A.S.L. Barnes. Toronto: Ontario Department of Planning and Development, 1953.
1955 edition published by the Boy Scouts Association, Provincial Council for Ontario.

**5071. Barr, Robin** *"Reye's Syndrome: Massive Fatty Metamorphosis of the Liver With Acute Encephalopathy."* Robin Barr, Irving H.G. Glass and Gurbachan S. Chawla. Canadian Medical Association Journal/Journal de l'Association medicale canadienne 98, 22(June 1, 1968): 1038-1044.

**5072. Barrados, Maria** *The Influence of School Personnel on Adolescents.* Maria Barrados. Montreal: McGill University, 1970.
Thesis (M.A.)--McGill University, 1970.

**5073. Barrass, Dorothy F.** *A Study of Thirty-three Delinquent Girls.* Dorothy F. Barrass. Toronto: University of Toronto, 1948.
Thesis (M.S.W.)--University of Toronto, 1948.

**5074. Barrett, Harry O.** *An Examination of Certain Standardized Art Tests to Determine Their Relation to Classroom Achievement and to Intelligence.* Harry O. Barrett. Toronto: University of Toronto, 1948.
Thesis (D.Paed.)--University of Toronto, 1948.

**5075. Barrett, Thomas** *A Study of Drop-in Centres for Teenagers in Metropolitan Toronto with Special Reference to Formal and Informal Rules and Sanctions.* Thomas Barrett. Toronto: University of Toronto, 1967.
Thesis (M.S.W.)--University of Toronto, 1967.

**5076. Bartlett, Rose** *An Analysis of the Daily Home Activities of Preschool Children.* Rose Bartlett. Toronto: University of Toronto, 1934.
Thesis (M.A.)--University of Toronto, 1934.

**5077. Bass, Marian Helen** *"Early Development of Interpersonal Distance in Children."* Marian H. Bass and Malcolm S. Weinstein. Canadian Journal of Behavioural Science/Revue canadienne de sciences du comportement 3, 4(Oct. 1971): 368-376.

**5078. Bass, Marian Helen** *Personal Space in Children: a Developmental Study.* Marian Helen Bass. Toronto: York University, 1970.
Thesis (M.A.)--York University, 1970.

**5079. Bassett, Eva** *Social Problems Dealt with by the Guidance Programme in a Secondary School.* Eva Bassett. Toronto: University of Toronto, 1954.
Thesis (M.S.W.)--University of Toronto, 1954.

**5080. Bastedo, D.L.A.** *"Acute Fulminating Myasthenia Gravis in Children."* D.L.A. Bastedo. Canadian Medical Association Journal 63, 4(Oct. 1950): 388-389.

**5081. Bastedo, George McClelland** *"Solitary Eosinophilic Granuloma of Skull (1950), Osteochondritis Dissecans of Knee."* George McClelland Bastedo. Canadian Medical Association Journal 76, 12(June 15, 1957): 1054-1056.

**5082. Bateman, Ingrid** *A Study to Determine Differential Levels of Intellectual Functioning as Manifested in the Development of Children's Vocabulary Definitions with a Qualitative Appraisal of Vocabulary Responses.* Ingrid Bateman. Toronto: University of Toronto, 1952.
Thesis (M.A.)--University of Toronto, 1952.

**5083. Bates, Gordon** *"Hereditary Syphillis: its Prevalence, Results and Means for Controlling."* Gordon Bates. In Proceedings and Papers Fourth Annual Canadian Conference on Child Welfare 1923, pp. 91-96.

**5084. Bates, Gordon** *"A Survey of the Incidence of Venereal Diseases in Toronto in 1937."* Gordon Bates. Canadian Public Health Journal 28, 12(Dec. 1937): 575-581.

**5085. Bates, Gordon** *"The Venereal Disease Clinic."* Gordon Bates. Public Health Journal 19, 10(Oct. 1928): 466-472.

**5086. Bator, Paul Adolphus** "*The Health Reformers Versus the Common Canadian: the Controversy Over Compulsory Vaccination Against Smallpox in Toronto and Ontario, 1900-1920.*" Paul Adolphus Bator. Ontario History 75, 4(Dec. 1983): 348-371.

**5087. Bator, Paul Adolphus** "*Saving Lives on the Wholesale Plan*": *Public Health Reform in the City of Toronto, 1900 to 1930.* Paul Adolphus Bator. Toronto: University of Toronto, 1979.
Thesis (Ph.D.)--University of Toronto, 1979, Volumes 1 and 2.

**5088. Baudouin, J.A.** "*Montreal Anti-Tuberculosis and General Health League.*" J.A. Baudouin. Public Health Journal 19, 7(July 1928): 317-328.

**5089. Bawtinhimer, R.E.** "*The Development of an Ontario Tory: Young George Drew.*" R.E. Bawtinhimer. Ontario History 69, 1(Mar. 1977): 55-75.

**5090. Beale, A.J.** "*Value of Newer Tissue Culture Methods in Epidemiological Inquiries: an Illustrative Outbreak of Poliomyelitis.*" A.J. Beale, M.W. Fujiwara, W. Stackiw, Norma Davis and A.J. Rhodes. Canadian Medical Association Journal 74, 5(Mar. 1, 1956): 337-342.

**5091. Beall, Arthur** *The Living Temple: a Manual of Eugenics for Parents and Teachers.* Arthur Beall. [Ontario]: A.B. Penhale Publishing, 1933.

**5092. Bean, Raymond E.** *An Exploratory Comparison of Indian and Non-Indian Secondary School Students' Attitudes.* Raymond E. Bean. Edmonton: University of Alberta, 1966.
Thesis (M.Ed.)--University of Alberta, 1966.

**5093. Beattie, Earle J.** "*Reformatory "Wheel".*" Earle Beattie and W.E. Mann. In Deviant Behaviour in Canada pp. 55-74. Edited by W.E. Mann.

**5094. Beattie, Jessie L.** *Walk Through Yesterday: Memoirs of Jessie L. Beattie.* Jessie L. Beattie: Dictated to Jean T. Thomson. Toronto: McClelland and Stewart, c1976.

**5095. Beattie, Mac** *This Ottawa Valley of Mine.* Mac Beattie. Arnprior: Beattie Music, 1982.

**5096. Beatty, Joyce** *Social and Emotional Problems of Rheumatic Fever in Children.* Joyce Beatty. Montreal: McGill University, 1951.
Thesis (M.S.W.)--McGill University, 1951.

**5097. Beauchamp, Helene** "*Theatre for Children in Quebec: Complicity, Achievement and Adventure.*" Helene Beauchamp. Canadian Theatre Review 41(Winter 1984): 17-24.

**5098. Beauchamp, L.E.** "*Cerebrospinal Fluid Rhinorrhoea and Recurrent Purulent Meningitis.*" L.E. Beauchamp and Ben Benjamin. Canadian Medical Association Journal 65, 4(Oct. 1951): 372-375.

**5099. Beddoes, Dick** *Pal Hal: an Uninhibited, No-hold-barred Account of the Life and Times of Harold Ballard.* Dick Beddoes. Toronto: MacMillan of Canada, 1989.

**5100. Beech, C. Allen** *Identification, Guilt Control and Dependency Anxiety in Delinquent and Non-delinquent Boys.* C. Allen Beech. Toronto: University of Toronto, 1960.
Thesis (M.A.)--University of Toronto, 1960.

**5101. Beirness, John** *Compulsory Schooling and Child Labour: Related Opposites 1871-1910.* John Beirness. Toronto: University of Toronto, 1986.
Thesis (M.A.)--Ontario Institute for Studies in Education, 1986.

**5102. Belanger, Yves** "*Physical Education in Quebec.*" Yves Belanger. Canadian Education and Research Digest 2, 1(Mar. 1962): 29-36.

**5103. Belford, Joan Elizabeth** *A Study of the Factors Affecting the Use of Community Services by Jewish Youth in North York.* Joan Elizabeth Belford. Toronto: University of Toronto, 1968.
Thesis (M.S.W.)--University of Toronto, 1968.

**5104. Bell, W.J.** "*A Health Week in Lambton County by the Department of Public Health, Ontario.*" W.J. Bell. Canadian Medical Association Journal 15, 6(June 1925): 621-623.

**5105. Bell, Walter N.** *The Development of the Ontario High School.* Walter N. Bell. [Toronto]: University of Toronto Press, c1918.

**5106. Bell, Walter N.** *The Development of the Ontario High School.* Walter N. Bell. Toronto: University of Toronto Press, 1918.
Thesis (D.Paed.)--University of Toronto, 1918.

**5107. Bellamy, Shirley J.** *The Predictive Value of Developmental and Intelligence Tests for Infants and Young Children.* Shirley J. Bellamy. Toronto: University of Toronto, 1958.
Thesis (M.A.)–University of Toronto, 1958.

**5108. Belzer, Judith** *The Unmarried Mother Who Keeps Her Child: a Descriptive-Diagnostic Study of the Characteristics and Experiences of the Unmarried Mother Who Keeps Child, and of Her Use of Resources in the Community, April, 1971.* Judith Belzer, B.E. Shenker and A.D. Yufe. Montreal: McGill University, 1971.
Thesis (M.S.W.)–McGill University, 1971.

**5109. Benaroya, Sigmund** *A Cognitive Approach for Assessment and Evaluation of Some Aspects of Severe Psycho-pathology of Childhood.* Sigmund Benaroya. Montreal: University of Monteal, 1971.
Thesis (Ph.D.)–University of Montreal, 1971.

**5110. Bench, P.J.** *"Children as Wards."* P.J. Bench. Public Health Journal 9, 6(June 1918): 286-287.

**5111. Bench, P.J.** *"Social Background: the Child of the Unmarried Mother."* P.J. Bench. Public Health Journal 11, 6(June 1920): 282-285.

**5112. Bender, Urie A.** *Four Earthen Vessels: Biographical Profiles of Oscar Burkholder, Samuel F. Coffman, Clayton F. Derstine, and John B. Martin.* Urie A. Bender. Kitchener, Ont.: Herald Press, c1982.

**5113. Benjamin, Ben** *"Congenital Toxoplasmosis in Twins."* Ben Benjamin, Helen F. Brickman and Arcadie Neaga. Canadian Medical Association Journal/Journal de l'Association medicale canadienne 80, 8(Apr. 15, 1959): 639-643.

**5114. Bennett, Paul W.** *"Taming "Bad Boys" of the "Dangerous Classes": Child Rescue and Restraint at the Victoria Industrial School 1887-1935."* Paul W. Bennett. Histoire sociale/Social History 21, 41(May 1988): 71-96.

**5115. Bennett, Paul W.** *"Turning "Bad Boys" into "Good Citizens": the Reforming Impulse of Toronto's Industrial Schools Movement, 1883 to the 1920's."* Paul W. Bennett. Ontario History 78, 3(Sept. 1986): 209-232.

**5116. Bennett, W.G.** *An Experimental Investigation into the Influence of Various Factors on Book-keeping Prognosis.* W.G. Bennett. Toronto: University of Toronto, 1930.
Thesis (D.Paed.)–University of Toronto, 1930.

**5117. Bensen, Margaret** *An Analysis of the Imitative Behaviour of Thirty Preschool Children.* Margaret Bensen. Toronto: University of Toronto, 1938.
Thesis (M.A.)–University of Toronto, 1938.

**5118. Benson, Lillian Rea** *"O.A.S Student in the 1880's."* Lillian Rea Benson and Edward Ffolkes. Ontario History 42, 2(Apr. 1950): 67-80.

**5119. Berdnikoff, George** *"Fourteen Personal Cases of Pneumocystis Carinii Pneumonia."* George Berdnikoff. Canadian Medical Association Journal 80, 1(Jan. 1, 1959): 1-5.

**5120. Bereiter, Carl** *"An Experimental Class."* Carl Bereiter. Bulletin of the Institute of Child Study 30, 1(Spring 1968): 38.

**5121. Berg, J.M.** *"Observations on Community School Facilities for the Mentally Retarded and Admissions to Institutions in Ontario, 1954-63."* J.M. Berg and John B. Fotheringham. Canadian Medical Association Journal/Journal de l'Association medicale canadienne 92, 9(Feb. 27, 1965): 465-468.

**5122. Bergeron, J.A.** *"Multiple Twin Births."* Jos. A. Bergeron. Canadian Medical Association Journal 70, 4(Apr. 1954): 447.

**5123. Berlyne, D.E.** *"Some Determinants of the Incidence and Content of Children's Questions."* D.E. Berlyne and Frances D. Frommer. Child Development 37, 1(Mar. 1966): 177-189.

**5124. Bernhardt, Karl S.** *An Analysis of the Social Contacts of Pre-school Children with the Aid of Motion Pictures.* Karl S. Bernhardt, Dorothy A. Millichamp, Marion W. Charles and Mary P. McFarland. Toronto: University of Toronto Press, 1937.

**5125. Bernhardt, Karl S.** *"Dr. Blatz and The Institute of Child Study."* Karl S. Bernhardt. Bulletin of the Institute of Child Study 23, 1(Mar. 1961): 1-4.

**5126. Bernhardt, Karl S.** *Twenty-five Years of Child Study: the Development of the Programme and Review of the Research.* Karl S. Bernhardt, Margaret I. Fletcher, Frances L. Johnson, Dorothy A. Millichamp, and Mary L. Northway. Toronto: University of Toronto Press, 1951.

**5127. Bernier, Bernard** *Memorials Respecting the Working of the Laws Governing Reformatory and Industrial Schools: Submitted to the Executive of the Province of Quebec at Its Sitting of the 29th of March 1892 in the Name of the Hospice Saint-Charles de Quebec.* Bernard Bernier and J.A. Charlebois. [Quebec: s.n., 1893?].

**5128. Berry, A.E.** *"Summer Camp Sanitation."* A.E. Berry. Public Health Journal 19, 6(June 1928): 251-254.

**5129. Berry, Gerald** *"Quebec Legislates on Child Protection."* Gerald Berry. Canadian Welfare 20, 2(June 1944): 7-11.

**5130. Berson, Seemah Cathline** *The Immigrant Experience: Personal Recollections of Jewish Garment Workers in Canada, 1900-1930.* Seemah Cathline Berson. Vancouver: University of British Columbia, 1980.
Thesis (M.A.)--University of British Columbia, 1980.

**5131. Bertley, June** *The Role of the Black Community in Educating Blacks in Montreal from 1910 to 1940, with Special Reference to Reverend Dr. Charles Humphrey Este.* June Bertley. Montreal: McGill University, 1982.
Thesis (M.A.)--McGill University, 1982.

**5132. Berton, Pierre** *The Dionne Years.* Pierre Berton. Toronto: McClelland and Stewart Ltd., c1977.

**5133. Bertram, Virginia** *A Study of Affective Behaviour in Eight Preschool Children.* Virginia Bertram. Toronto: University of Toronto, 1939.
Thesis (M.A.)--University of Toronto, 1939.

**5134. Berzonsky, Michael** *Factors Influencing Children's Casual Reasoning.* Michael Berzonsky. Toronto: University of Toronto, 1969.
Thesis (Ph.D.)--University of Toronto, 1969.

**5135. Berzonsky, Michael** *"The Role of Familiarity in Children's Explorations of Physical Causality."* Michael D. Berzonsky. Child Development 42, 3(Sept. 1971): 705-715.

**5136. Bigras, Julien** *"On the Depressive Illnesses in Childhood Suicidal Attempts in Adolescent Girls: a Preliminary Study."* Julien Bigras, Yvon Gauthier, Colette Bouchard and Yoland Tasse. Canadian Psychiatric Association Journal/Revue de l'Association canadienne de psychiatrie 11, Supplement(1966): s275-s282.

**5137. Bilbrough, Ellen Agnes** *British Children in Canadian Homes.* Ellen Agnes Bilbrough. Belleville, Ontario: [s.n.], 1879.

**5138. Binns, Margaret** *Cultural Pluralism in Canada: an Exploratory Study of the Italians and Ukrainians in London, Ontario.* Margaret Binns. London, Ont.: University of Western Ontario, 1971.
Thesis (M.A.)--University of Western Ontario, 1971.

**5139. Birchard, Isaac James** *"Flashback."* Isaac James Birchard. Toronto: W.J. Gage Ltd., c1967. In Education: a Collection of Essays on Canadian Education, v.6, 1964-1967, pp. 93-99.

**5140. Birks, W.H.** *"The Medical Officer of Health and School Health in a Small Urban Municipality."* W.H. Birks. Canadian Public Health Journal 25, 11(Nov. 1935): 548-551.

**5141. Birnzweig, Olga** *Familial Environment and Asthmatic Child's Response to Treatment.* Olga Birnzweig, Gabriella Kiwih and Irene Paulsen. Montreal: McGill University, 1961.
Thesis (M.S.W.)--McGill University, 1961.

**5142. Bissell, Muriel D.** *Group Intervention in Family Relationships as Exemplified By the Children's Aid Society of Guelph and Wellington County.* Muriel D. Bissell. Toronto: University of Toronto, 1938.
Thesis (M.A.)--University of Toronto, 1938.

**5143. Blackwell, Mary E.** *"Auxillary Classes in the Public Schools."* Mary E. Blackwell. Public Health Journal 6, 12(Dec. 1915): 622-626.

**5144. Blain, Robert** *A Comparison Between French and English Canadian Students.* Robert Blain. Montreal: Universite de Montreal, 1960.
Thesis (Ph.D.) --Universite de Montreal, 1960.

**5145. Blais, Suzanne** *Parent, Child, and Television: Interaction in Communication.* Suzanne Blais. Montreal: McGill University, 1962.
Thesis (M.A.)--McGill University, 1962.

**5146. Blake, Catherine Hume** *"Edward Blake: a Portrait of his Childhood."* Catherine Hume Blake, edited, and with an introduction, by Margaret A. Banks. Ontario History 59, 4(Dec. 1967): 92-96. This issue is alternately known as Centennial Issue: Portrait of a Province.

**5147. Blatz, Margery W.** *The Law of Adoption.* Margery W. Blatz. Toronto: University of Toronto, 1931. Thesis (M.A.)–University of Toronto, 1931.

**5148. Blatz, William E.** *The Development of Emotion in the Infant.* William E. Blatz and Dorothy A. Millichamp. Toronto: University of Toronto Press, 1935.

**5149. Blatz, William E.** *An Evaluation of the Case Histories of a Group of Pre-School Children.* William Emet Blatz and J.D.M. Griffin. Toronto: University of Toronto Press, 1936.

**5150. Blatz, William E.** *The Five Sisters: a Study of Child Psychology.* William E. Blatz. Toronto: McClelland & Stewart Ltd., c1938.

**5151. Blatz, William E.** *"Studies in Mental Hygiene of Children: 1. Behavior of Public School Children: a Description of Method."* William E. Blatz and Helen A. Bott. Pediatric Seminar and Journal of Genetic Psychology 34(1927): 552-582.

**5152. Blatz, William E.** *A Study of Laughter in the Nursery School Child.* William E. Blatz, Kathleen Drew Allin and Dorothy A. Millichamp. [Toronto]: University of Toronto Press, 1936.

**5153. Blatz, William E.** *A Study of Tics in Preschool Children.* William Emit Blatz and Mabel Crews Ringland. Toronto: University of Toronto, 1935.

**5154. Blezard, Ruth J.** *Referrals of Emotionally Disturbed Children to the Child Guidance Clinic, Kingston.* Ruth J. Blezard. Toronto: University of Toronto, 1956. Thesis (M.S.W.)–University of Toronto, 1956.

**5155. Bliss, Michael** *A Canadian Millionaire: the Life and Business Times of Sir Joseph Flavelle, Bart., 1858-1939.* Michael Bliss. Toronto: Macmillan of Canada, c1978.

**5156. Blum, Frank J.** *Further Investigation of Extraversion-Intraversion and Subsequent Recidivism for a Selected Group of Young Adult Offenders.* Frank J. Blum. Ottawa: University of Ottawa, 1965. Thesis (Ph.D.)–University of Ottawa, 1965.

**5157. Blum, Mary H.** *Security of Adolescents in Their Use of Money.* Mary H. Blum. Toronto: University of Toronto, 1950. Thesis (M.A.)–University of Toronto, 1950.

**5158. Blumenthal, Sadie** *An Analysis of the Learning Capacity of Young Children to Reproduce Notes.* Sadie Blumenthal. Toronto: University of Toronto, 1934. Thesis (M.A.)–University of Toronto, 1934.

**5159. Bock, Carson** *The Attitudes of Delinquent and Non-delinquent Boys to Their Parents as Indicated by the Thematic Apperception Test.* Carson Bock. Toronto: University of Toronto, 1949. Thesis (M.A.)–University of Toronto, 1949.

**5160. Bockus, E.C.** *The Common Schools of Upper Canada, 1786-1840.* E.C. Bockus. Montreal: McGill University, 1967. Thesis (M.A.)–McGill University, 1967.

**5161. Boes, Lillian F.** *The Ontario Charitable Institutions Act and Regulations as They Affected Children's Institutions in 1949-1950.* Lillian F. Boes. Toronto: University of Toronto, 1950. Thesis (M.S.W.)–University of Toronto, 1950.

**5162. Bolton, Elda** *"Musical Experiences with Cerebral Palsied Children."* Elda Bolton. Bulletin of the Institute of Child Study 18, 1(Mar. 1956): 27-31.

**5163. Bolton, Elda** *"Parents and Nursery Schools."* Elda Bolton. Bulletin of the Institute of Child Study 29, 3(Fall 1967): 12-16.

**5164. Bolus, C. Robert** *A Proposed Model Treatment Programme for the Province of Ontario Based Upon a Study of Maryvale, a Treatment Center for Emotionally Disturbed Adolescent Girls.* C. Robert Bolus. Detroit: Wayne State University, 1975. Thesis (Ed.D.)–Wayne State University, 1975.

**5165. Bombardier, J.P.** *"Resorption Atelectaris with Hyaline-Like Membrane."* J.P. Bombardier. Canadian Medical Association Journal 73, 6(Sept. 15, 1955): 469-472.

**5166. Boot, Ralph S.** *"Police Interest in Juvenile Delinquency."* Ralph S. Boot. Canadian Journal of Corrections/Revue canadienne de criminology 6, 1(Jan. 1964): 50-57.

5167. **Borenstein, Sam** *Sam Borenstein.*
Sam Borenstein. Toronto: McClelland and
Stewart, 1978.

5168. **Borrow, Claire** *Parental Behaviour*
*and Boys' Academic Performance: a Study*
*of Boys' Perceptions of Parental Child*
*Rearing Behaviour and Academic*
*Underachievement and Achievement.* Claire
Borrow and Philip Borrow. Montreal:
McGill University, 1969.
    Thesis (M.S.W.)--McGill University, 1969.

5169. **Borthwick, Burton** *The Evolution of*
*Special Education Programs and Services*
*for Orthopaedic Children 1911-1974.*
Burton L. Borthwick. Ottawa: University
of Ottawa, 1979. (CTM no. 43971)
    Thesis (Ph.D.)--University of Ottawa,
1979.

5170. **Bosher, John F.** *"The Family in*
*New France."* John F. Bosher. Waterloo:
Wilfrid Laurier University Press, c1975.
In In Search of the Visible Past: History
Lectures at Wilfrid Laurier University,
1973-1974, pp. 1-13. Edited by Barry M.
Gough.

5171. **Bossy, Mike** *Boss: the Mike Bossy*
*Story.* Mike Bossy and Barry Meisel.
Scarborough, Ont.: McGraw Hill Ryerson,
1988.

5172. **Boswell, Hazel** *Town House, Country*
*House: Recollections of a Quebec*
*Childhood.* Hazel Boswell; edited by R.H.
Hubbard. Montreal: McGill-Queen's
University Press, 1990.

5173. **Bott, E.A.** *Studies In Industrial*
*Psychology: Juvenile Employment in*
*Relation to Public Schools and Industries*
*in Toronto.* E.A. Bott. Toronto: The
University of Toronto Press, 1920.

5174. **Bott, Helen** *Adult Attitudes to*
*Children's Misdemeanors.* Helen Bott.
Toronto: University of Toronto Press,
c1937.

5175. **Bott, Helen** *Method in Social Studies*
*of Young Children.* Helen McM. Bott.
[Toronto]: University of Toronto Press,
1933.

5176. **Bott, Helen** *Personality Development*
*in Young Children.* Helen McM. Bott.
Toronto: University of Toronto Press,
1934.

5177. **Botteas, Evelyn** *"Toronto Greek*
*Communal School, 1930-33."* Evelyn
Botteas. Polyphony 6, 1(Spring-Summer
1984): 234-235.

5178. **Bouchard, Gerard** *"Family Structure*
*and Geographic Mobility at Laterriere,*
*1851-1935."* Gerard Bouchard. Journal of
Family History 2, 4(Winter 1977):
350-369.

5179. **Boudin, H.** *"Reading and Disturbed*
*Adolescent: an Individualized Reality-based*
*Approach."* H. Boudin. Canadian
Psychologist/Psychologie canadienne 9,
2(Apr. 1968): 201-210.

5180. **Boulanger, J.B.** *"Group Analytic*
*Psychodrama in Child Psychiatry."* J.B.
Boulanger. Canadian Psychiatric
Association Journal/Revue de l'Association
canadienne de psychiatrie 10, 5(Oct.
1965): 427-432.

5181. **Bourassa, Charles** *Their First Years*
*in Canada: an Exploratory Study of the*
*Living Experiences of Fifty Immigrant*
*Families During their First Years in*
*Montreal.* Charles Bourassa, P. Lobley, L.
Marcus, J. Meislova and R. Morganstern.
Montreal: McGill University, 1955.
    Thesis (M.S.W.)--McGill University, 1955.

5182. **Bourdon, C.A.** *"The Diphtheria*
*Situation in Montreal and Immunization."*
C.A. Bourdon. Canadian Journal of Public
Health 36, 8(Aug. 1945): 305-311.

5183. **Bourgeois, Charles E.** *The*
*Protection of Children in the Province of*
*Quebec.* Charles E. Bourgeois.
Troi-Rivieres, Quebec: [s.n.], 1948.
    Text is a published version of the
author's doctoral thesis presented at the
University of Ottawa in 1946.

5184. **Bourneuf, Roland** *Antoine Dumas.*
Roland Bourneuf. Montreal: Stanke, 1983.

5185. **Bowden, D.H.** *"Observations on*
*Neonatal Mortality."* D.H. Bowden, A.M.
Goodfellow and C.E. Snelling. Canadian
Medical Association Journal 75, 12(Dec.
15, 1956): 1000-1006.

5186. **Bowden, Elsie** *"The Volunteer and*
*Social Service Exchange of Montreal."* Elsie
Bowden. Child and Family Welfare 10,
1(May 1934): 36-37.

5187. **Bowers, Henry** *Transfer Values of*
*Secondary School Science.* Henry Bowers.
Toronto: University of Toronto, 1927.
    Thesis (D.Paed.)--University of Toronto,
[1930].

5188. **Bowers, Joan E.** *The Difficulty of*
*One-step Arithmetical Problems in Relation*
*to the Type of Fundamental Number*
*Operation Involved.* Joan E. Bowers.
Toronto: University of Toronto, 1955.
    Thesis (Ed.D.)--University of Toronto,
1955.

**5189. Bowers, Joan E.** *"A Study of Children With Unusual Difficulty in Reading."* Joan E. Bowers. Canadian Education and Research Digest 4, 4(Dec. 1964): 273-278. ·

**5190. Bowie, William** *"Recreation for Youth."* William Bowie. Child and Family Welfare 12, 6(Mar. 1937): 45-46.

**5191. Box, Colin Edward** *Drug Education in Ontario, Canada Secondary Public Schools.* Colin Edward Box. Bloomington: Indiana University, 1970.
Thesis (Ph.D.)–Indiana University, 1970.

**5192. Boyce, Murray** *"Therapeutic Abortion in a Canadian City."* R.M. Boyce and R.W. Osborn. Canadian Medical Association Journal/Journal de l'Association medicale canadienne 103, 5(Sept. 12, 1970): 461-466.
Reprinted in Critical Issues in Canadian Society, pp. 39-48. Edited by Craig L. Boydell, Carl F. Grindstaff and Paul C. Whitehead.

**5193. Boyd, B.A.** *"A Normal Child Following Insulin Coma Therapy in Early Pregnancy."* B.A. Boyd. Canadian Medical Association Journal 77, 3(Aug. 1, 1957): 227.

**5194. Boyd, Gladys** *"Diabetic Clinic, Hospital for Sick Children, Toronto."* Gladys Boyd. Canadian Nurse 20, 10(Oct. 1924): 624.

**5195. Boyd, Gladys** *"Streptomycin in Childhood Tuberculosis."* Gladys L. Boyd. Canadian Medical Association Journal 60, 5(May 1949): 476-480.

**5196. Boyd, Neil** *The Release of Children from Ontario Training Schools: a Critical Analysis.* Neil Boyd. Toronto: York University, 1978.
Thesis (LL.M.)–York University, 1978.

**5197. Boyle, Harry J.** *"Am I Really as Celtic as They Say?"* Harry J. Boyle. Toronto: Celtic Arts of Canada, 1988. In The Untold Story: the Irish in Canada, v.2, pp. 729-732. Edited by Robert O'Driscoll and Lorna Reynolds.

**5198. Brebeuf, Jean de** *Travels and Explorations of the Jesuit Missionaries in New France, 1610-1791: Hurons, 1636.* Jean de Brebeuf, Paul Le Jeune [and] Reuben Gold Thwaites, ed. Cleveland, Ohio: Burrows Brothers Co., 1897.

**5199. Bradbrook, Adrian J.** *"An Empirical Study of the Attitudes of the Judges of the Supreme Court of Ontario Regarding the Workings of the Present Child Custody Adjudication Laws."* Adrian J. Bradbrook. Canadian Bar Review/Revue

du Barreau Canadien 49, 4(Dec. 1971): 557-576.

**5200. Bradbrook, Adrian J.** *"The Role of Judicial Discretion in Child Custody Adjudication in Ontario."* Adrien J. Bradbrook. University of Toronto Law Journal 21, 3(1971): 402-408.

**5201. Bradbury, Bettina** *"The Family Economy and Work in an Industrializing City: Montreal in the 1870's."* Bettina Bradbury. Canadian Historical Association, Historical Papers/Communications historiques (1979): 71-96.

**5202. Bradbury, Bettina** *"The Fragmented Family: Family Strategies in the Face of Death, Illness, and Poverty, Montreal, 1860-1885."* Bettina Bradbury. Toronto: McClelland and Stewart, c1982. In Childhood and Family in Canadian History, pp. 109-128. Edited by Joy Parr.

**5203. Bradbury, Bettina** *"Women and Wage Labour in a Period of Transition: Montreal, 1861-1881."* Bettina Bradbury. Histoire sociale/Social History 17, 33(May 1984): 115-131.

**5204. Bradbury, Bettina** *The Working Class Family Economy: Montreal, 1861-1881.* Bettina Bradbury. Montreal: Concordia University, 1984. (CTM no. 30657)
Thesis (Ph.D.)–Concordia University, 1984.

**5205. Braddon, Russell** *Roy Thomson of Fleet Street.* Russell Braddon. Toronto: Collins, 1965.

**5206. Bradford, Marjorie** *"The Council of Social Agencies in the Community."* Marjorie Bradford. Child and Family Welfare 6, 2(May 1930): 10-13.

**5207. Bradley, L. Winnifred** *"Canada's First Youth Employment Centre."* L. Winnifred Bradley. Canadian Welfare 22, 4(Sept. 1946): 27-31.

**5208. Brailsford, Eugene Gerald** *An Investigation Into the Topology of Exogenous Feeble Minded Children.* Eugene Gerald Brailsford. Ottawa: University of Ottawa, 1965.
Thesis (Ph.D.)–University of Ottawa, 1965.

**5209. Brandino, Diana** *The Italians of Hamilton, 1921 to 1945.* Diana Brandino. London, Ont.: University of Western Ontario, 1977. (CTM no. 31558)
Thesis (M.A.) – University of Western Ontario, 1977.
Bibliography leaves 152-156.

5210. Brandon, K.F. *"Erythema Nodosum and Tuberculosis."* K.F. Brandon, R.P. Hardman and W.H. Birks. Canadian Public Health Journal 29, 11(Nov. 1938): 533-541.

5211. Brandt, Gail Cuthbert *"Industry's Handmaidens: Women in the Quebec Cotton Industry."* Gail Cuthbert Brandt. Canadian Women's Studies 3, 1(Autumn 1981): 79-82.

5212. Brandt, Gail Cuthbert *""Weaving It Together": Life Cycle and the Industrial Experience of Female Cotton Workers in Quebec, 1910-1950."* Gail Cuthbert Brandt. Labour/Le Travailleur 7(Spring 1981): 113-126.

5213. Braverman, Shirley *The Father's Role in a Child Guidance Clinic.* Shirley Braverman. Montreal: McGill University, 1952.
Thesis (M.S.W.)--McGill University, 1952.

5214. Breault, Henri J. *"The Prevention of Acetylsalicylic Acid Poisonings."* Henri J. Breault. Canadian Medical Association Journal 79, 10(Nov. 15, 1958): 825-827.

5215. Brehaut, Willard *"Trends in the History of Ontario Education."* Willard Brehaut. Toronto: OISE, 1984. In The House That Ryerson Built: Essays in Education to Mark Ontario's Bicentennial, pp. 7-17. Edited by Hugh Oliver, Mark Holmes and Ian Winchester.

5216. Breithaupt, Kirby Eric *The Effects of Immediate Visual Knowledge of Results Upon the Learning of a Selected Track and Field Skill by Grade Seven Boys.* Kirby Eric Breithaupt Montreal: McGill University, 1970.
Thesis (M.A.)--McGill University, 1970.

5217. Brett, Fred W. *A History of Big Brother Movement of Toronto, Incorporated 1912-1939.* Fred W. Brett. Toronto: University of Toronto, 1953.
Thesis (M.S.W.)--University of Toronto, 1953.

5218. Brewin, Margaret Judith *The Establishment of an Industrial Education System in Ontario.* Margaret Judith Brewin. Toronto: University of Toronto, 1967.
Thesis (M.A.)--University of Toronto, 1967.

5219. Bridges, Katherine M. Banham *The Social and Emotional Development of the Preschool Child.* Katherine M. Banham Bridges. London, Eng.: Kegan Paul, Trench Trubner & Co. Ltd., c1931.

5220. Brigel, Faith W. *The Stereotype of Social Work as Seen by Elementary School Children.* Faith W. Brigel and Stephen Wohl. Montreal: McGill University, 1971.
Thesis (M.S.W.)--McGill University, 1971.

5221. Brighty, Isabel McComb *The Diamond Jubilee History of the Protestant Home of St. Catharines 1874-1934.* Isabel McComb Brighty. St. Catherines: [s.n.], 1934.

5222. Brillinger, H. Roy *"The Judge and the Psychiatrist: Toward Mutual Understanding."* H. Roy Brillinger. Canadian Journal of Corrections/Revue canadienne de criminologie 1, 2(Apr. 1958): 1-9.

5223. Broadfoot, Barbara Valerie Richmond *Analysis of the Diets of 28 Low Income Families in Toronto.* Barbara Valerie Richmond Broadfoot. Toronto: University of Toronto, 1942.
Thesis (M.A.)--University of Toronto, 1942.

5224. Broadfoot, Barbara Valerie Richmond *"Vitamin D Intakes of Ontario Children."* B.V.R. Broadfoot, M.L. Trenholme, E.P. McClinton, S.H. Thompson and E.J. Cowan. Canadian Medical Association Journal/Journal de l'Association medicale canadienne 94, 7(Feb. 12, 1966): 332-340.

5225. Brock, Margaret *"A Hospital's Adoption Policy."* Margaret Brock. Canadian Welfare 33, 3(Sept. 1957): 126-129.

5226. Brock, Peter Jeffry *William Rees Brock, 1836-1917: Paradise Regained: an Odyssey in Canadian Business.* Peter Jeffry Brock. Toronto: National Press, 1984, c1983.

5227. Brodie, Hugh R. *"Immunization With Live Measles Virus Vaccine."* Hugh R. Brodie. Canadian Medical Association Journal/Journal de l'Association medicale canadienne 89, 11(Sept. 14, 1963): 533-536.

5228. Brookes, Alan A. *""Working Away" from the the Farm: the Young Women of North Huron, 1910-1930."* Alan A. Brookes and Catherine A. Wilson. Ontario History 77, 4(Dec. 1985): 281-300.

5229. Brooks, Elizabeth E. *A Study of Male Maladjusted Youth and Their Need for Alternative Living Accommodation.* Elizabeth E, Frances Anne Humphreys, Barbara Ann Glendinning and Dorothy Richards. Brooks. Toronto: University of Toronto, 1966.
Thesis (M.S.W.)--University of Toronto, 1966.

5230. **Broomes, Desmond** *Psychological and Sociological Correlates of Mathematical Achievement and Ability Among Grade 9 Students.* Desmond Broomes. Toronto: Unversity of Toronto, 1971.
Thesis (Ph.D.)–University of Toronto, 1971.

5231. **Brough, James** *"We Were Five": the Dionne Quintuplets' Story From Birth Through Girlhood to Womanhood.* James Brough, Annette Dionne, Cecile Dionne, Marie Dionne and Yvonne Dionne. New York: Simon and Schuster, c1963, 1965.

5232. **Brown, Alan** *"Ante-serum Treatment of Chorea."* Alan Brown and George E. Smith. Canadian Medical Association Journal 9, 1(Jan. 1919): 52-62.

5233. **Brown, Alan** *"Blood Transfusion in Hemorrhage of the Newborn."* Alan Brown. Canadian Medical Association Journal 6, 8(Aug. 1915): 716-723.

5234. **Brown, Alan** *"Certain Features of Child Welfare Not Sufficiently Emphasized."* Alan Brown. Public Health Journal 14, 6(June 1923): 243-249.

5235. **Brown, Alan** *"Child Health."* Alan Brown. Public Health Journal 11, 2(Feb. 1920): 49-53.

5236. **Brown, Alan** *"Duodenal Ulcers in Infancy."* Alan Brown. Canadian Medical Association Journal 7, 4(Apr. 1917): 320-323.

5237. **Brown, Alan** *"Essential Features Concerning the Proper Nutrition of the Infant and Child."* Alan Brown and Elizabeth Chant Robertson. Canadian Medical Association Journal 48, 4(Apr. 1943): 297-302.

5238. **Brown, Alan** *"Infant and Child Welfare Work."* Alan Brown. Public Health Journal 9, 4(Apr. 1918): 145-162.

5239. **Brown, Alan** *"The Prevalence of Malnutrition in the Public School Children of Ontario."* Alan Brown and G. Albert Davis. Public Health Journal 12, 2(Feb. 1921): 66-72.

5240. **Brown, Alan** *"The Prevalence of Malnutrition in the Public School Children of Toronto."* Alan Brown and Albert G. Davis. Canadian Medical Association Journal 11, 12(Dec. 1921): 124-126.

5241. **Brown, Alan** *"Problems of the Rural Mother in the Feeding of Her Children."* Alan Brown. Public Health Journal 9, 7(July 1918): 297-301.

5242. **Brown, Alan** *"Protein Milk: Its Composition, Preparation and Application in the Treatment of Digestive Disturbances."* Alan Brown, Howard Spohn and Ida F. MacLachlan. Canadian Medical Association Journal 8, 6(June 1918): 510-522.

5243. **Brown, Alan** *"Protein Milk Powder."* Alan Brown and Ida F. MacLachlan. Canadian Medical Association Journal 22, 6(June 1930): 528-537.

5244. **Brown, Arthur E.** *Negative Feedback and Visual-motor Coordination.* Arthur E. Brown. Toronto: University of Toronto, 1970.
Thesis (Ed.D.)--University of Toronto, 1970.

5245. **Brown, C.A.** *"The Educator Views the Health Needs of the Elementary School."* C.A. Brown. Canadian Public Health Journal 31, 7(July 1940): 331-335.

5246. **Brown, Evelyn M.** *"Family and Feminine Education in Quebec."* Evelyn M. Brown. Canadian Education 11, 1(Dec. 1955): 59-65.

5247. **Brown, Helen C.** *An Analysis of the Technique for Training Preschool Children in Eating Habits in the St. George's School for Child Study.* Helen C. Brown. Toronto: University of Toronto, 1935.
Thesis (M.A.)–University of Toronto, 1935.

5248. **Brown, Jennifer S.H.** *"Diverging Identities: the Presbyterian Metis of St. Gabriel St., Montreal."* Jennifer S.H. Brown. Winnipeg: University of Manitoba Press, c1985. In The New Peoples: Being and Becoming Metis in North America, pp. 197-206. Edited by Jacqueline Peterson and Jennifer S.H. Brown.

5249. **Brown, Murray** *Training in Play as an Antecedent of Interpersonal Aggression.* Murray Brown. Toronto: University of Toronto, 1962.
Thesis (M.A.)–University of Toronto, 1962.

5250. **Brown, W.G.** *"Three Years' Experience with Poliomyelitis Vaccine: Ontario, 1955-1957."* W.G. Brown, G.K. Martin, Beverley Hannah, A.J. Rhodes and N.A. Labzoffsky. Canadian Medical Association Journal 79, 3(Aug. 1, 1958): 155-162.

5251. **Browne, Helen** *The Emotional Problems Arising from the Presence of a Cerebral Palsied Child in the Home: a Study of the Families of the Twenty-five Children Attending the Junior League Nursery Clinic in Toronto.* Helen Browne. Toronto: University of Toronto, 1950.

Thesis (M.S.W.)--University of Toronto, 1950.

**5252. Brubacher, Albert** *"The Unaffluent Society."* Albert Brubacher. Waterloo Historical Society Annual Report 57(1969): 61-62.

**5253. Bruce, Roberta M.** *Parent-Child Relationships of 23 Delinquent Adolescent Girls: a Study of the Emotional Factors in Parent-Child Relationships which Contributed to the Development Behaviour of 23 Adolescent Girls Referred to the Mental Hygiene Institute, and of the Role of the Social Worker in the Treatment Plan.* Roberta M. Bruce. Montreal: McGill University, 1953.
Thesis (M.S.W.)--McGill University, 1953.

**5254. Bruck, Margaret** *Memory and Production of Passive Sentences in Children.* Margaret Ellen Bruck. Montreal: McGill University, 1969.
Thesis (M.A.)--McGill University, 1969.

**5255. Bruegernan, Vera** *"With the Babies' Dispensary."* Vera Bruegernan. Canadian Nurse 22, 5(May 1926): 256.

**5256. Brunelle, Paul** *"The Toxic Effect of Kanamycin on the Inner Ear: Report of a Case."* Paul Brunelle. Canadian Medical Association Journal/Journal de l'Association medicale canadienne 81, 5(Sept. 1, 1959): 381-382.

**5257. Bryce, Peter H.** *"The Work of Bureaus of Child Hygiene and of Medical Inspection in Schools."* Peter H. Bryce. Public Health Journal 7, 2(Feb. 1916): 59-62.

**5258. Bryers, John A.** *A Study of Drop-in Centres in Metropolitan Toronto with Special Reference to the Teenage Respondents' Pattern of Participation in Community Sponsored Youth Services and Their Perception of Drop-in Centre Program and Staff.* John A. Bryers. Toronto: University of Toronto, 1967.
Thesis (M.S.W.)--University of Toronto, 1967.

**5259. Buck, Carol W.** *"Exposure to Virus Diseases in Early Pregnancy and Congenital Malformations."* Carol Buck. Canadian Medical Association Journal 72, 10(May 15, 1955): 744-746.

**5260. Buitenhuis, Elspeth** *Robertson Davies.* Elspeth Buitenhuis. Toronto: Forum House, c1972.

**5261. Bull, Betty** *"Assessment of Intelligence of Cerebral Palsied Children in Windsor and Essex County, Ontario."* Betty Bull. Canadian Medical Association Journal/Journal de l'Association medicale canadienne 95, 24(Dec. 10, 1966): 1241.

**5262. Bullen, John** *Children of the Industrial Age: Children, Work and Welfare in Late Nineteenth Century Ontario.* John Bullen. Ottawa: University of Ottawa, 1989.
Thesis (Ph.D.)--University of Ottawa, 1989.

**5263. Bullen, John** *"Hidden Workers: Child Labour and the Family Economy in Late Nineteenth Century Urban Ontario."* John Bullen. Labour/Le Travail 18(Fall 1986): 163-187.

**5264. Bullen, John** *"J.J. Kelso and the "New" Child-savers: the Genesis of the Children's Aid Movement in Ontario."* John Bullen. Ontario History 82, 2(June 1990): 107-128.

**5265. Bullock, Anne** *Community Care of Severely Handicapped Children at Home: a Movement in the Organization of Women's Work.* Anne Bullock. Ottawa: Carleton University, c1986. (CTM no. 33370)
Thesis (M.S.W.)--Carleton University, 1986.

**5266. Burchard, Marshall** *Sports Hero: Bobby Orr.* Marshall and Sue Burchard. Toronto: Longman Canada, c1973.

**5267. Burgess, Joanne** *"The Growth of a Craft Labour Force: Montreal Leather Artisans, 1815-1831."* Joanne Burgess. Canadian Historical Association, Historical Papers/Communications historiques (1988): 48-62.

**5268. Burgess, Joanne** *Work, Family and Community: Montreal Leather Craftsmen, 1790-1831.* Joanne Burgess. Montreal: University of Quebec at Montreal, 1986.
Thesis (Ph.D.)--University of Quebec at Montreal, 1986.

**5269. Burgess, Marjorie** *Characteristics of Good and Poor Readers in the Primary Grades.* Marjorie Burgess. Toronto: University of Toronto, 1939.
Thesis (M.A.)--University of Toronto, 1939.

**5270. Burgoyne, Lola Martin** *A History of the Home and School Movement in Ontario.* Lola Martin Burgoyne. [Toronto]: Charters Publishing Company, [1935].

5271. **Burke, F.S.** *"Forest Schools as an Adjunct to School Health."* F.S. Burke. Public Health Journal 19, 1(Jan. 1928): 9-19.

5272. **Burke, F.S.** *"The Preschool Child and School Medical Inspection."* F.S. Burke. Canadian Public Health Journal 24, 4(Apr. 1933): 170-176.

5273. **Burke, F.S.** *"A System of School Medical Inspection."* F.S. Burke. Canadian Public Health Journal 20, 1(Jan. 1929): 6-16.

5274. **Burkhardt, Alice** *"Play While You Nurse."* Alice Burkhardt. Canadian Nurse 33, 12(Dec. 1937): 591-595.

5275. **Burley, Kevin** *"Occupational Structure and Ethnicity in London, Ontario, 1871."* Kevin Burley. Histoire sociale/Social History 9, 22(Nov. 1978): 390-410.

5276. **Burnaby, Barbara** *Languages and Their Role in Educating Native Children.* Barbara Burnaby. Toronto: Ontario Institute for Studies in Education Press, c1980.

5277. **Burnham, B.** *A Day in the Life: Case Studies of Pupils in Open Plan Schools.* B. Burnham. Aurora, Ont.: York County Board of Education, 1970.

5278. **Burns, E.** *"The Toronto Juvenile Court."* E. Burns. University of Toronto Faculty of Law Review 8, 1(Spring 1949): 4-8.

5279. **Burns, Neal** *"Age Differences in Empathetic Ability Among Children."* Neal Burns and Lorna Cavey. Canadian Journal of Psychology 11, 4(Dec. 1957): 227-230.

5280. **Burwash, Nathanael** *The Makers of Canada: Egerton Ryerson.* Nathanael Burwash. v. 13. Toronto: Morang & Co., Ltd., 1910.

5281. **Butler, Bernice M.** *An Investigation of the Ability of Public School Teachers to Empathize with Pupils.* Bernice M. Butler. Toronto: University of Toronto, 1951. Thesis (M.A.)–University of Toronto, 1951.

5282. **Butler, Elizabeth F.** *The Life of Venerable Marguerite Bourgeoys.* Elizabeth F. Butler. New York: P.J. Kenedy & Sons, c1932.

5283. **Byles, John A.** *Alienation, Deviance and Social Control: a Study of Adolescents in Metropolitan Toronto.* John A. Byles. Toronto: Interim Research Project on Unreached Youth, 1969.

5284. **Byrne, Niall** *Political Orientations of Canadian Urban Elementary, Junior and High School Students.* Niall Byrne. Toronto: University of Toronto, 1970. Thesis (M.A.)–University of Toronto, 1970.

5285. **Cameron, Christina** *Charles Baillairge: Architect and Engineer.* Christina Cameron. Montreal; Kingston: McGill-Queen's University Press, 1989.

5286. **Cameron, E.** *An Exploratory Study of Two Generation Cases Serviced by Two Children's Aid Societies in Metropolitan Toronto.* E. Cameron, P. Chatterjee, E. Edmison, J. Robinson and M. Sharpe. Toronto: University of Toronto, 1962. Thesis (M.S.W.)–University of Toronto, 1962.

5287. **Cameron, Elspeth** *Irving Layton: a Portrait.* Elspeth Cameron. Don Mills: Stoddart, c1985.

5288. **Cameron, Malcolm H.V.** *"Cystic Hygroma in an Infant."* Malcolm H.V. Cameron. Canadian Medical Association Journal 6, 2(Feb. 1916): 137-138.

5289. **Cameron, Maxwell A.** *The Financing of Education in Ontario.* Maxwell A. Cameron. Toronto: University of Toronto, 1935. Thesis (Ph.D.)–University of Toronto, 1935.

5290. **Cameron, May** *"School is a School, is a School."* May Cameron. Canadian Nurse 53, 6(June 1957): 525-527.

5291. **Camp, M.C.** *A Study of Emotionally Disturbed Children of Preschool Age: an Analysis of the Child and of the Family Structure, with Implications for Needed Treatment Facilities.* M.C. Camp. Montreal: McGill University, 1954. Thesis (M.S.W.)–McGill University, 1954.

5292. **Campbell, D. Roy** *Level of Aspiration of Cerebral Palsied Children.* D. Roy Campbell. Toronto: University of Toronto, 1958. Thesis (M.A.)–University of Toronto, 1958.

5293. **Campbell, Edgar H.** *Racial Awareness and Color Preference in White Children.* Edgar H. Campbell. Toronto: University of Toronto, 1952. Thesis (M.A.)–University of Toronto, 1952.

**5294. Campbell, Eleanor M.** *A Study of Differences in Interaction Patterns of Pairs of Children Chosen According to Sociometric Relationships.* Eleanor M. Campbell. Toronto: University of Toronto, 1951.
Thesis (M.A.)–University of Toronto, 1951.

**5295. Campbell, Hugh A.** *Life and Adventure of a Pioneer.* Hugh A. Campbell. Newmarket, Ont.: Northland Printers Ltd., 1970.

**5296. Campbell, J.A.** *"Vitamin B12 and the Growth of Children: a Review."* J.A. Campbell and J.M. McLaughlan. Canadian Medical Association Journal 72, 4(Feb. 15, 1955): 259-263.

**5297. Campbell, J.D.** *The Arithmetic of the Elementary Schools in Ontario.* J.D. Campbell. Toronto: University of Toronto, 1943.
Thesis (D.Paed)–University of Toronto, 1943.

**5298. Campbell, Marjorie Freeman** *A Mountain and a City: the Story of Hamilton.* Marjorie Freeman Campbell. Toronto: McClelland and Stewart Ltd., 1966.

**5299. Campbell, Susan B.** *Cognitive Styles in Normal and Hyperactive Children.* Susan Campbell. Montreal: McGill University, 1969.
Thesis (Ph.D.)--McGill University, 1969.

**5300. Campeau, Claire** *"How to Reach Indifferent Mothers."* Claire Campeau. Canadian Nurse 18, 3(Mar. 1922): 155-156.

**5301. Canada. Commission to Investigate Whether and If So, To What Extent, the Sweating System is Practised in the Various Industrial Centres of the Dominion** *Report.* The Commission. Toronto: [s.n.], 1896.
Commissioner: Alexander Whyte Wright.

**5302. Canada. Department of Labour. Vocational Training Branch** *The Quebec Answer to the Problem of Apprenticeship.* The Branch. Ottawa: Queen's Printer, 1956.

**5303. Canada. Royal Commission Regarding the Dispute Respecting Hours of Employment Between the Bell Telephone Co. of Canada Limited and Operators at Toronto, Ontario** *Report.* The Commission. Ottawa: Government Printing Bureau, 1907.
Chairman: William Lyon MacKenzie King.

**5304. Canada. Royal Commission to Inquire into Industrial Disputes in the Cotton Factories of the Province of Quebec** *Report.* The Commission. Ottawa: King's Printer, 1909.
Commissioner: William Lyon MacKenzie King.

**5305. Canadian Council on Child and Family Welfare** *"Ambitious Community Survey Completed in Montreal."* Canadian Council on Child and Family Welfare. Child and Family Welfare 11, 3(Sept. 1935): 30-37.

**5306. Canadian Council on Child and Family Welfare** *"Boys Will Be Boys."* Canadian Council on Child and Family Welfare. Child and Family Welfare 10, 4(Nov. 1934): 20-23.

**5307. Canadian Council on Child and Family Welfare** *"Child Placing Versus Institutional Costs."* Canadian Council on Child and Family Welfare. Child and Family Welfare 7, 4(Nov. 1931): 43-45.

**5308. Canadian Council on Child and Family Welfare** *"Child Protection and Family Welfare Services Proposed for the City of Kingston, Ontario, 1931."* Canadian Council on Child and Family Welfare. Child and Family Welfare 7, 4(Nov. 1931): 22-33.

**5309. Canadian Council on Child and Family Welfare** *"Child Protection in Ontario."* Canadian Council on Child and Family Welfare. Child and Family Welfare 6, 3(July 1930): 22-28.

**5310. Canadian Council on Child and Family Welfare** *"Child Welfare Studies in Hamilton."* Canadian Council on Child and Family Welfare. Child and Family Welfare 8, 5(Jan. 1933): 45.

**5311. Canadian Council on Child and Family Welfare** *"The Child With Physical Handicap."* Canadian Council on Child and Family Welfare. Child and Family Welfare 7, 4(Nov. 1931): 53-54.

**5312. Canadian Council on Child and Family Welfare** *"The Children's Aid Society of Toronto."* Canadian Council on Child and Family Welfare. Child and Family Welfare 8, 1(May 1932): 22-23.

**5313. Canadian Council on Child and Family Welfare** *"City of Toronto Maternal Welfare Services."* Canadian Council on Child and Family Welfare. Child and Family Welfare 10, 1(May 1934): 20-21.

**5314. Canadian Council on Child and Family Welfare** *"The Commission on Public Welfare."* Canadian Council on Child and Family Welfare. Child and Family Welfare 6, 4(Sept. 1930): 18-35.

**5315. Canadian Council on Child and Family Welfare** *"Fiftieth Annual Report of the Society for the Protection of Women and Children, Montreal."* Canadian Council on Child and Family Welfare. Child and Family Welfare 6, 7(Mar. 1931): 56-57.

**5316. Canadian Council on Child and Family Welfare** *"Growth of Kindergarten in Toronto Public Schools."* Canadian Council on Child and Family Welfare. Child and Family Welfare 11, 3(Sept. 1935): 58-60.

**5317. Canadian Council on Child and Family Welfare** *"Growth of Nursery School Education in Toronto."* Canadian Council on Child and Family Welfare. Child and Family Welfare 11, 3(Sept. 1935): 57-58.

**5318. Canadian Council on Child and Family Welfare** *"The Hamilton C.A.S. "Blossoms Out"."* Canadian Council on Child and Family Welfare. Child and Family Welfare 10, 6(Mar. 1935): 40-41.

**5319. Canadian Council on Child and Family Welfare** *"Intelligence Quotients of Juvenile Delinquents."* Canadian Council on Child and Family Welfare. Child and Family Welfare 10, 6(Mar. 1935): 51-52.

**5320. Canadian Council on Child and Family Welfare** *"Kingston Has Crusade For Children."* Canadian Council on Child and Family Welfare. Child and Family Welfare 13, 5(Jan. 1938): 28.

**5321. Canadian Council on Child and Family Welfare** *"Montreal Boys' Demonstration Farm."* Canadian Council on Child and Family Welfare. Child and Family Welfare 9, 2(July 1933): 64.

**5322. Canadian Council on Child and Family Welfare** *"The Montreal Training Scheme for Unemployed Girls."* Canadian Council on Child and Family Welfare. Child and Family Welfare 9, 3(Sept. 1933): 26-27.

**5323. Canadian Council on Child and Family Welfare** *"New Children's Aid Standards in Ontario."* Canadian Council on Child and Family Welfare. Child and Family Welfare 10, 5(Jan. 1935): 11-14.

**5324. Canadian Council on Child and Family Welfare** *"Ontario Society for Crippled Children."* Canadian Council on Child and Family Welfare. Child and Family Welfare 6, 3(July 1930): 29.

**5325. Canadian Council on Child and Family Welfare** *"The Ontario Society for Crippled Children."* Canadian Council on Child and Family Welfare. Child and Family Welfare 8, 1(May 1932): 32.

**5326. Canadian Council on Child and Family Welfare** *"The Ontario Society for Crippled Children."* Canadian Council on Child and Family Welfare. Child and Family Welfare 8, 6(Mar. 1933): 47-48.

**5327. Canadian Council on Child and Family Welfare** *"A Plea for the Deaf Child."* Canadian Council on Child and Family Welfare. Child and Family Welfare 10, 6(Mar. 1935): 37-38.

**5328. Canadian Council on Child and Family Welfare** *"Predelinquent Work: Toronto Big Brother Movement."* Canadian Council on Child and Family Welfare. Child and Family Welfare 6, 3(July 1930): 32.

**5329. Canadian Council on Child and Family Welfare** *"Quebec Passes Mothers' Allowance Act."* Canadian Council on Child and Family Welfare. Child and Family Welfare 13, 1(May 1937): 24-25.

**5330. Canadian Council on Child and Family Welfare** *"Report of the Montreal Parks and Playgrounds Association, for the Summer Season, 1930."* Canadian Council on Child and Family Welfare. Child and Family Welfare 6, 7(Mar. 1931): 55-56.

**5331. Canadian Council on Child and Family Welfare** *"Rules and Regulations in Divorce Trials, Ontario."* Canadian Council on Child and Family Welfare. Child and Family Welfare 6, 7(Mar. 1931): 48-50.

**5332. Canadian Council on Child and Family Welfare** *"Social Welfare Recommendations in Quebec."* Canadian Council on Child and Family Welfare. Child and Family Welfare 7, 6(Mar. 1932): 23-30.

**5333. Canadian Council on Child and Family Welfare** *"Step-parents as Liable Guardians."* Canadian Council on Child and Family Welfare. Child and Family Welfare 10, 2(July 1934): 21-22.

5334. **Canadian Council on Child and Family Welfare** "A Thousand Babies a Year and Never an Institutional Bed." Canadian Council on Child and Family Welfare. Child and Family Welfare 10, 4(Nov. 1934): 6-10.

5335. **Canadian Council on Child and Family Welfare** "Three Years of the Groncher System." Canadian Council on Child and Family Welfare. Child and Family Welfare 9, 6(Mar. 1934): 59-61, 64.

5336. **Canadian Council on Child and Family Welfare** "The Toronto Big Sister Association." Canadian Council on Child and Family Welfare. Child and Family Welfare 8, 1(May 1932): 31.

5337. **Canadian Council on Child and Family Welfare** "Toronto Children's Theatre." Canadian Council on Child and Family Welfare. Child and Family Welfare 11, 4(Nov. 1935): 54-55.

5338. **Canadian Council on Child and Family Welfare** "Training Handicapped Children." Canadian Council on Child and Family Welfare. Child and Family Welfare 8, 6(Mar. 1933): 19.

5339. **Canadian Council on Child and Family Welfare** "Trends in Child Labour, 1921-1931." Canadian Council on Child and Family Welfare. Child and Family Welfare 9, 6(Mar. 1934): 24-25.

5340. **Canadian Council on Child and Family Welfare** "Two Important Judgements Re Contributing to Delinquency, Section 215, Criminal Code of Canada." Canadian Council on Child and Family Welfare. Child and Family Welfare 7, 6(Mar. 1932): 41-49.

5341. **Canadian Council on Child and Family Welfare** "Whither Bound?" Canadian Council on Child and Family Welfare. Child and Family Welfare 7, 6(Mar. 1932): 37-39.

5342. **Canadian Council on Child Welfare** "Bowmanville Boys' School." Canadian Council on Child Welfare. Child Welfare News 6, 1(Feb. 1930): 45.

5343. **Canadian Council on Child Welfare** "The Children's Bureau, Ottawa." Canadian Council on Child Welfare. Canadian Child Welfare News 4, 3(Aug. 15, 1928): 4-5.

5344. **Canadian Council on Child Welfare** Fifth Annual Canadian Conference on Child Welfare. Canadian Council on Child Welfare. Ottawa: Department of Labour, 1925.

5345. **Canadian Council on Child Welfare** "Maintenance Payments, Children's Aid Society, Toronto." Canadian Council on Child Welfare. Child Welfare News 5, 2(May 1929): 27-29.

5346. **Canadian Council on Child Welfare** "The Montreal Health Survey." Canadian Council on Child Welfare. Child Welfare News 5, 1(Feb. 1929): 11-29.

5347. **Canadian Council on Child Welfare** "Montreal's Child Welfare Work." Canadian Council on Child Welfare. Canadian Child Welfare News 4, 3(Aug. 15, 1928): 56-66.

5348. **Canadian Council on Child Welfare** "The Ontario Home for Girls at Georgetown." Canadian Council on Child Welfare. Child Welfare News 5, 1(Feb. 1929): 52.

5349. **Canadian Council on Child Welfare** "The Ottawa Children's Bureau Completes First Year." Canadian Council on Child Welfare. Canadian Child Welfare News 4, 1(Feb. 15, 1928): 48.

5350. **Canadian Council on Child Welfare** "Parental Education." Canadian Council on Child Welfare. Child Welfare News 6, 1(Feb. 1930): 50.

5351. **Canadian Council on Child Welfare** "Separate Dominion Institutions for Youthful Convicts." Canadian Council on Child Welfare. Child Welfare News 6, 1(Feb. 1930): 44.

5352. **Canadian Council on Child Welfare** "Shernfold School, Ottawa." Canadian Council on Child Welfare. Canadian Child Welfare News 4, 3(Aug. 15, 1928): 2-4.

5353. **Canadian Council on Child Welfare** The Spiritual and Ethical Development of the Child. Canadian Council of Child Welfare. Ottawa: The Council, 1922.

5354. **Canadian Council on Child Welfare** "Too Few Workers." Canadian Council on Child Welfare. Canadian Child Welfare News 4, 2(May 15, 1928): 47-48.

5355. **Canadian Council on Child Welfare** "Toronto Children's Aid Visits The Archives." Canadian Council on Child Welfare. Child Welfare News 5, 1(Feb. 1929): 37-39.

5356. **Canadian Council on Child Welfare** "Vocational Training and Social Failure." Canadian Council on Child Welfare. Child Welfare News 6, 1(Feb. 1930): 48-49.

**5357. Canadian Council on Child Welfare** *"Welfare Work in Montreal."* Canadian Council on Child Welfare. Canadian Child Welfare News 4, 1(Feb. 15, 1928): 32-36.

**5358. Canadian Medical Association. Special Committee on Medical Inspection of Schools** *"Medical Inspection of Schools."* Canadian Medical Association. Special Committee on Medical Inspection of Schools. Canadian Medical Association Journal 2, 6(June 1912): 513-514.

**5359. Canadian National Committee for Mental Hygiene** *"Mental Hygiene for Normal Children: Account of Experiment Conducted by the Canadian National Committee for Mental Hygiene and the Toronto Kiwanis Club."* Canadian National Committee for Mental Hygiene. Public Health Journal 14, 10(Oct. 1923): 470-473.

**5360. Canadian National Committee for Mental Hygiene** *"Survey of Guelph Public Schools."* Canadian National Committee for Mental Hygiene. Canadian Journal of Mental Hygiene 1, 4(Jan. 1920): 342-346.

**5361. Canadian Tuberculosis Association. Provincial Survey Committee** *Report of an Ontario Survey of Schools and Pre-school Children ... Town of Dundas and the Township of West Flamboro in the County of Wentworth.* Local Survey Committee of the Canadian Tuberculosis Association and the Hamilton Medical Society. [S.l.]: Ontario Department of Health, 1925.

**5362. Canadian Welfare Council** *"Across Canada: Ontario Child Welfare Act."* Canadian Welfare Council. Canadian Welfare 30, 8(Mar. 1955): 39-40.

**5363. Canadian Welfare Council** *"Across Canada: Ottawa Child Guidance."* Canadian Welfare Council. Canadian Welfare 30, 8(Mar. 1955): 40-41.

**5364. Canadian Welfare Council** *"Adoption and the Courts."* Canadian Welfare Council. Canadian Welfare 25, 7(Jan. 1950): 2-4.

**5365. Canadian Welfare Council** *"Care of Children."* Canadian Welfare Council. Canadian Welfare 32, 5(Dec. 1956): 210-211.

**5366. Canadian Welfare Council** *"Children of Divorce."* Canadian Welfare Council. Canadian Welfare 26, 1(Apr. 1950): 36.

**5367. Canadian Welfare Council** *"Consultation on Unreached Youth."* Canadian Welfare Council. Canadian Welfare 40, 4(July-Aug. 1964): 186.

**5368. Canadian Welfare Council** *"Day Nursery Developments in Ontario."* Canadian Welfare Council. Canadian Welfare 18, 5(Oct. 1942): 14-16.

**5369. Canadian Welfare Council** *"Democracy and Patriotism in the Kindergarten."* Canadian Welfare Council. Canadian Welfare 17, 2(May 1941): 34-35.

**5370. Canadian Welfare Council** *"Hamilton Considers Delinquency."* Canadian Welfare Council. Canadian Welfare 21, 5(Oct. 1945): 30-31.

**5371. Canadian Welfare Council** *"Is This Necessary?"* Canadian Welfare Council. Canadian Welfare 17, 2(May 1941): 24-25.

**5372. Canadian Welfare Council** *"Lessons from Whytehover."* Canadian Welfare Council. Canadian Welfare 35, 5(Sept. 1959): 194-195.

**5373. Canadian Welfare Council** *"Ontario Child Welfare Act."* Canadian Welfare Council. Canadian Welfare 30, 1(May 1954): 3.

**5374. Canadian Welfare Council** *"Ontario Child Welfare Report."* Canadian Welfare Council. Canadian Welfare 41, 2(Mar.-Apr. 1965): 78-79.

**5375. Canadian Welfare Council** *"Project on Adoption of Negro Children."* Canadian Welfare Council. Canadian Welfare 38, 4(July-Aug. 1962): 186.

**5376. Canadian Welfare Council** *"Protestant Children's Homes, Toronto, 1851-1951."* Canadian Welfare Council. Canadian Welfare 27, 1(Apr. 1951): 25-27.

**5377. Canadian Welfare Council** *"Shawbridge School."* Canadian Welfare Council. Canadian Welfare 20, 2(June 1944): 11.

**5378. Canadian Welfare Council** *"The Times Test the Children's Aid."* Canadian Welfare Council. Canadian Welfare 17, 3(July 1941): 6-8.

**5379. Canadian Welfare Council** *To Years of Discretion: a Series of Six Letters to Canadian Parents on Child Development Between the Ages of Thirteen and Seventeen Years.* Canadian Welfare Council. Ottawa: Division on Maternal and Child Hygiene, Canadian Council House, 1942.

First edition issued in 1939.

**5380. Caplan, Usher** *Like One That Dreamed: a Portrait of A.M. Klein.* Usher Caplan. Toronto: McGraw-Hill Ryerson, c1982.

**5381. Cappon, Daniel** *"Clinical Manifestations of Autism and Schizophrenia in Childhood."* Daniel Cappon. Canadian Medical Association Journal 69, 1(July 1953): 44-49.

**5382. Cardozo, Mary B.** *"Speech Problems of the Growing Child."* Mary B. Cardozo. Canadian Nurse 44, 7(July 1948): 547-552.

**5383. Carisse, Colette** *"The Family: the Issue of Change."* Colette Carisse. Scarborough: Prentice-Hall of Canada Ltd., c1975. In Issues in Canadian Society: an Introduction to Sociology, pp. 260-302. Edited by Dennis Forcese and Stephen Richer.

**5384. Carlson, Kenneth Allen** *A Multivariate Classification of Reformatory Inmates.* Kenneth Allen Carlson. London, Ont.: University of Western Ontario, 1970. (CTM no. 7598)
Thesis (Ph.D.)--University of Western Ontario, 1970.

**5385. Carlton, Richard A.** *Differential Educational Achievement in a Bilingual Community.* Richard A. Carlton. Toronto: University of Toronto, 1967.
Thesis (Ph.D.)--University of Toronto, 1967.

**5386. Carpenter, Helen M.** *"An Analysis of Home Visits to Newborn Infants Made by the Public Health Nurses in the East York-Leaside Health Unit, Ontario."* Helen M. Carpenter. Canadian Nurse 55, 9(Sept. 1959): 809-825.

**5387. Carpenter, Philip P.** *On Some of the Causes of the Excessive Mortality of Young Children in the City of Montreal.* Philip P. Carpenter. [S.l: s.n., 1869?]. Originally published in Canadian Naturalist and Quarterly Journal of Science (June 1869).

**5388. Carroll, Jock** *The Life and Times of Greg Clark: Canada's Favorite Storyteller.* Jock Carroll. 1st. ed. Toronto: Doubleday Canada, c1981.

**5389. Carruthers, Russell Garfield** *Social and Economic Aspects of Family Life, in a Selected Area in Ontario.* Russell Garfield Carruthers. Toronto: University of Toronto, 1925.
Thesis (M.A.)--University of Toronto, 1925.

**5390. Carson, Kenneth Oliver** *An Evaluation of Segregation in the Programme for Gifted Children in the Kingston Public Schools.* Kenneth Oliver Carson. Toronto: University of Toronto, 1963.
Thesis (M.Ed.)--University of Toronto. 1963.

**5391. Carson, Marjorie E.C.** *An Investigation of the Predictive Value of Intelligence Tests of Preschool Children in Foster Homes.* Marjorie E.C. Carson. Toronto: University of Toronto, 1938.
Thesis (M.A.)--University of Toronto, 1938.

**5392. Carter, Brenda** *"Trends in Pediatric Nursing."* Brenda Carter, Nancy Franklin and Betty Woolner. Canadian Nurse 48, 9(Sept. 1952): 701-704.

**5393. Carter, F.G.** *"Adoption, Guardianship, Education and Religious Training."* F.G. Carter. Western Law Review 5(1966): 160-169.

**5394. Cartwright, Glenn F.** *Personality Orientation Along the Instrumental-Expressive Continuum Preferred by Adolescents in their Educational and Occupational Advisors.* Glenn F. Cartwright. Montreal: McGill University, 1970.
Thesis (M.A.)--McGill University, 1970.

**5395. Case, Robbie** *Information Processing, Social Class, and Instruction: a Developmental Investigation.* Robbie Case. Toronto: University of Toronto, 1970.
Thesis (Ph.D.)--University of Toronto, 1970.

**5396. Cassidy, Deborrah H.** *Family Life Education and the Role of the Father as a Nurturing Figure in the Dynamic of Family Functioning.* Deborrah H. Cassidy. Montreal: McGill University, 1975.
Thesis (M.S.W.)--McGill University, 1975.

**5397. Cates, Tannis** *A Study of the Dominative and Submissive Behaviour of Eight Preschool Children.* Tannis Cates. Toronto: University of Toronto, 1939.
Thesis (M.A.)--University of Toronto, 1939.

**5398. Caverhill, Austin** *A History of St. John's School and Lower Canada College.* Austin Caverhill. Montreal: McGill University, 1961.
Thesis (M.A.)--McGill University, 1961.

**5399. Caverzan, Raymond Cornelius** *An Experimental Language Program for Non-verbal Emotionally Disturbed Children.* Raymond C. Caverzan. Toronto: University of Toronto, 1971. (CTM no. 17758)
Thesis (Ph.D.)--University of Toronto,

1971.

**5400. Chadwick, Ethel** *Social Memoirs of Montreal.* Ethel Chadwick. [S.l: s.n., 193-].

**5401. Chalmers, Floyd S.** *Both Sides of the Street: One Man's Life in Business and the Arts in Canada.* Floyd S. Chalmers. Toronto: MacMillan of Canada, c1983.

**5402. Chalmers, Floyd S.** *A Gentleman of the Press.* Floyd S. Chalmers. Toronto: Doubleday Canada, c1969.

**5403. Chamberlain, A.F.** *"Folk-lore of Canadian Children."* A.F. Chamberlain. Journal of American Folklore 8, 30(July-Sept. 1895): 252-255.

**5404. Chamberlain, Florence A.** *"School Work in the Hospital for Sick Children, Toronto."* Florence A. Chamberlain. Canadian Nurse 21, 1(Jan. 1925): 20.

**5405. Chamberland, J.M.** *"Congenital Anomalies of the Digestive Tract: Report of Two Cases."* J.M. Chamberland, Richard Fortin and Jules Lavoie. Canadian Medical Association Journal 75, 10(Nov. 15, 1956): 837-838.

**5406. Champagne, Louise** *Soothing Effects on Infants Produced by Vertical and Horizontal Rocking.* Louise Champagne. London, Ont.: University of Western Ontario, c1969.
Thesis (M.A.)--University of Western Ontario, 1969.
National Library of Canada MIC TC-5026.

**5407. Champagne, Mireille** *Children's Racial Attitudes: a Cross-Cultural and Historical Analysis.* Mireille Chamagne. Toronto: York University, 1984.
Thesis (Ph.D.)--York University, 1984.

**5408. Chan, Esther Mai-Nin** *A Study of Allancroft, a Children's Institute: a Study of 126 Children in the Care of the Children's Service Centre, Montreal, Who Were Admitted to Allancroft within the Period from July 1, 1953 to June 30, 1956.* Esther Mai-Nin Chan. Montreal: McGill University, 1957.
Thesis (M.S.W.)--McGill University, 1957.

**5409. Chan, Sup Mei** *Cognitive Behavioural Products of the Structure of Intellect Model: Some Preliminary Considerations.* Sup Mei Chan. Montreal: McGill University, 1968.
Thesis (M.A.)--McGill University, 1968.

**5410. Chandler, Margaret Ross** *A Century of Challenge: the History of the Ontario School for the Blind.* Margaret Ross Chandler. Belleville: Mika Pub. Co., 1980.

**5411. Chang, Mary Ann Yee-Sum** *Female-headed Single Parent Families: an Examination of Four Structural Areas of Family Functioning.* Mary Ann Yee-Sum Chang and Margot E. Smith. Montreal: McGill University, 1970.
Thesis (M.S.W.)--McGill University, 1970.

**5412. Charles, Frederick** *The Judgement of Teachers and Examination Records Compared with the Terman Intelligence Tests.* Frederick Charles. Toronto: University of Toronto, 1919.
Thesis (M.A.)--University of Toronto, 1919.

**5413. Charles, Marion W.** *Motion Pictures Versus Direct Observation: a Study of Method in Social Analysis.* Marion Charles. Toronto: University of Toronto, 1937.
Thesis (M.A.)--University of Toronto, 1937.

**5414. Charlesworth, Hector** *Candid Chronicles: Leaves from the Note Book of a Canadian Journalist.* Hector Charlesworth. Toronto: Macmillan Company of Canada, 1925.

**5415. Charon, Milly** *"Appreciation: from an Interview with Lillian Sultaneanu."* Milly Charon. Toronto: Quadrant Editions, 1983. In Between Two Worlds: the Canadian Immigrant Experience, pp. 228-238. Edited by Milly Charon.

**5416. Charon, Milly** *"The Cultural Transition: from an Interview with Frank Cerulli."* Milly Charon. Toronto: Quandrant Editions, 1983. In Between Two Worlds: the Canadian Immigrant Experience, pp. 258-267. Edited by Milly Charon.

**5417. Chawla, Saroj** *Indian Children in Toronto: a Study in Socialization.* Saroj Chawla. Toronto: York University, 1971. (CTM no. 9343)
Thesis (M.A.)--York University, 1971.

**5418. Chemerys, B.S.** *"The Home Care Project."* B.S. Chemerys. Bulletin of the Institute of Child Study 30, 2(Summer 1968): 21-23.

**5419. Cheow, J.** *The Values of the Multi-problem Family.* J. Cheow, P. Gendron, B. Horsham and B. Veitch. Toronto: University of Toronto, 1962.
Thesis (M.S.W.)--University of Toronto, 1962.

**5420. Chicanot, Dustan P.** *Factors Associated with the Selection or Rejection of Teaching by English Speaking Grade Eleven Students in the Province of Quebec.* Dustan P. Chicanot. Montreal: McGill University, 1967.
Thesis (M.A.)--McGill University, 1967.

**5421. Child, Philip** *"Pierre Esprit Radisson and the Race of Coureurs de Bois."* Philip Child. University of Toronto Quarterly 9, 4(July 1940): 407-428.

**5422. Child Welfare Exhibition (1st: 1912: Montreal)** *Souvenir Handbook.* [Montreal: The Exhibition, 1912].

**5423. Children's Aid Society of Toronto** *Constitution and By-laws Together With Rules and Regulations for the Shelter of the Children's Aid Society of Toronto.* The Society. [Toronto: The Society, 1900].

**5424. Children's Fresh Air Fund** *Christmas Eve Entertainment for Poor Children Under the Auspices of the Children's Fresh Air Fund: Over Twelve Hundred Children Will be Given a Free Entertainment Consisting of Music, Refreshments and a Panoramic Exhibition, on Tuesday Evening, December 24, 1889, in Shaftesbury Hall...* Children's Fresh Air Fund. [S.l.: s.n., 1889?].

**5425. Childs, Rosemary Ann** *Verbal Correlates of Discrimination Learning and Transfer in Normal and Retarded Children.* Rosemary Ann Childs. London, Ont.: University of Western Ontario, c1970.
Thesis (M.A.)--University of Western Ontario, 1970.
National Library of Canada MIC TC-6152.

**5426. Choi, Sun I.** *"Idiopathic Thrombocytopenic Purpura in Childhood."* Sun I. Choi and P.D. McClure. Canadian Medical Association Journal/Journal de l'Association medicale canadienne 97, 11(Sept. 9, 1967): 562-568.

**5427. Choquette, P.A.** *"The Juvenile Court in Quebec."* P.A. Choquette. In Proceedings of Sixth Annual Canadian Conference on Child Welfare 1927, pp. 109-110.

**5428. Chouquet, Judge** *"The Juvenile Court."* Judge Choquet. Toronto: Social Services Congress, 1914. In Social Services Congress, Ottawa, 1914: Report of Addresses and Proceedings, pp. 102-106.

**5429. Chown, Alice Amelia** *The Stairway.* Alice A. Chown, with an introduction by Diana Chown. Toronto: University of Toronto Press, c1988.
First published in Boston by Cornhill in 1921.

**5430. Chun, Theresa** *"Chromosomal Studies in Children with Mumps, Chickenpox, Measles and Measles Vaccination."* Theresa Chun, D.S. Alexander, Alex M. Bryans and M. Daria Haust. Canadian Medical Association Journal/Journal de l'Association medicale canadienne 94, 3(Jan. 15, 1966): 126-129.

**5431. Chunn, Dorothy E.** *From Punishment to Doing Good: the Origins and Impact of Family Courts in Ontario, 1888-1942.* Dorothy E. Chunn. Toronto: University of Toronto, 1986.
Thesis (Ph.D.)--University of Toronto, 1986.

**5432. Churchill, Stacy** *"Computer Education in Ontario Secondary Schools."* Stacy Churchill and Norman Williams. Education Canada 10, 3(Sept. 1970): 42-50.

**5433. Churchill, Stacy** *"Franco-Ontarian Education: From Persecuted Minority to Tolerated Nuisance."* Stacy Churchill. Toronto: OISE, 1984. In The House That Ryerson Built: Essays in Education to Mark Ontario's Bicentennial, pp. 74-87. Edited by Hugh Oliver, Mark Holmes and Ian Winchester.

**5434. Chute, A.L.** *"Experiences with Oral Sulfonamide (BZ-55) in the Management of Juvenile Diabetes."* A.L. Chute and H.W. Bain. Canadian Medical Association Journal 74, 12(June 15, 1956): 994-996.

**5435. Clark, C.S.** *Of Toronto the Good: a Social Study: the Queen City of Canada as It Is.* C.S. Clark. Montreal: Toronto Publishing Co., 1898.

**5436. Clark, William Lund** *What is Associated Youth of Canada?: Leamington, Ontario, Canada, W.L. Clark, Founder and Organizer.* William Lund Clarke. [Leamington, Ont.?: s.n., 1898?].

**5437. Clarke, Barrie A.** *My Search for Catherine Anne: One Man's Story of an Adoption Reunion.* Barrie A. Clarke. Toronto: James Lorimer and Co. Publishers, c1989.

**5438. Clarke, C.K.** *"A Study of 5,600 Cases Passing Through the Psychiatric Clinic of the Toronto General Hospital: a Special Study of 188 Clinic Cases, also a Survey of 767 Cases of Illegitimacy."* C.K. Clarke. Canadian Journal of Mental Hygiene 3, 2(July 1921): 11-24.

**5439. Clarke, Eric Kent** *"The Role of the Department of Public Health in the Education of the Adolescent Mentally Defective Child."* Eric Kent Clarke. Public Health Journal 16, 9(Sept. 1925): 436-438.

**5440. Clarke, Eric Kent** *"Survey of the Toronto Public Schools."* Eric Kent Clarke. Canadian Journal of Mental Hygiene 2, 2(July 1920): 182-185.

**5441. Clarke, F.R.C.** *Healey Willan: Life and Music.* F.R.C. Clarke. Toronto: University of Toronto Press, 1983.

**5442. Clarke, Mairin** *"Seasonal Aseptic Meningitis Caused by Coxsackie and Echo Viruses, Toronto, 1957."* Mairin Clarke, Margaret Hunter, G.A. McNaughton, Dietlind Von Seydlitz and A.J. Rhodes. Canadian Medical Association Journal/Journal de l'Association medicale canadienne 81, 1(July 1, 1959): 5-8.

**5443. Clayton, Deidra** *The Eagle: the Life and Times of R. Alan Eagleson.* Deidra Clayton. Toronto: Lester and Orpen Dennys, c1982.

**5444. Clegg, William Crispin** *A Comparative Study of the Use of Colour in the Drawings of Poorly Adjusted and Well Adjusted Children.* William Crispin Clegg. London: University of Western Ontario, 1951.
    Thesis (M.A.)--University of Western Ontario, 1951.

**5445. Cleghorn, Joan** *"Tetanus."* Joan Cleghorn. Canadian Nurse 51, 6(June 1955): 461.

**5446. Clyke, Emily** *Parental and Other Influence in the Adjustment of the Mentally Retarded Child.* Emily Clyke. Montreal: McGill University, 1960.
    Thesis (M.S.W.)--McGill University, 1960.

**5447. Coady, Henry** *Behavioral Correlates of Moral Judgement.* Henry Coady. Ottawa: University of Ottawa, 1971.
    Thesis (Ph.D.)--University of Ottawa, 1971.

**5448. Cochrane, E. George** *The Development of the Curriculum of the Protestant Elementary Schools of Montreal.* E. George Cochrane. Toronto: University of Toronto, 1968.
    Thesis (Ed.D.)--University of Toronto, 1968.

**5449. Cochrane, Jean** *"The Ontario School House."* Jean Cochrane. Toronto: OISE, 1984. In The House That Ryerson Built: Essays in Education to Mark Ontario's Bicentenniel, pp. 18-29. Edited by Hugh Oliver, Mark Holmes and Ian Winchester.

**5450. Coggin, C.J.** *"Natural History of Isolated Patent Ductus Arteriosus and the Effect of Surgical Correction: Twenty Years' Experience at the Hospital for Sick Children, Toronto."* C.J. Coggin, K. Ross Parker and J.D. Keith. Canadian Medical Association Journal/Journal de l'Association medicale canadienne 102, 7(Apr. 12, 1970): 718-720.

**5451. Cohen, Marjorie Griffin** *The Razor's Edge Invisible: Women, Markets and Economic Development in Ontario, 1800-1911.* Marjorie Griffin Cohen. Toronto: York University, 1985.
    Thesis (Ph.D.)--York University, 1985.

**5452. Cohen, Marjorie Griffin** *Women's Work, Markets, and Economic Development in Nineteenth Century Ontario.* Marjorie Griffin Cohen. Toronto: University of Toronto Press, 1988.

**5453. Cohen, Marvin H.** *A Comparative Study of Adolescent Social Patterns in Chomedey.* Marvin H. Cohen and Dagmar R. Hiffeler. Montreal: McGill University, 1969.
    Thesis (M.S.W.)--McGill University, 1969.

**5454. Cohen, Nancy** *Psychophysiological Concomitants of Attention in Hyperactive Children.* Nancy Jane Cohen. Montreal: McGill University, 1970.
    Thesis (Ph.D.)--McGill University, 1970.

**5455. Cohen, Sharon** *The Influence of Competition on Children's Response to Success and Failure.* Sharon Cohen. London, Ont.: University of Western Ontario, c1969.
    Thesis (M.A.)--University of Western Ontario, 1969.
    References leaves 34-36.
    National Library of Canada MIC TC-5308.

**5456. Cohen, Stanley** *"Religious Education in the Public Schools of Ontario."* Stanley Cohen and Ian H. Pitfield. University of Toronto Faculty of Law Review 25(May 1967): 87-102.

**5457. Cohen, Zvi** *"Emancipation, But Not Equal Rights."* Zvi Cohen. Toronto: Canadian Jewish Historical Publishing Co., 1933. In Canadian Jewry: Prominent Jews of Canada, pp. 25-27. Edited by Zvi Cohen.

**5458. Coleclough, A.** *"Marijuana Users of Toronto."* A. Coleclough and Lloyd C. Hanley. Toronto: Social Science Publishers, c1968. In Deviant Behaviour in Canada, pp. 257-291. Edited by W.E. Mann.

**5459. Collins, Maynard** *Lightfoot: If You Could Read His Mind: a Biography.* Maynard Collins. Toronto: Deneau, 1988.

**5460. Collins, Michael** *"Sister Aimee: a Canadian Evangelist Took the Roaring 20's by Storm."* Michael Collins. Beaver 69, 3(June–July 1989): 28-32.

**5461. Collins-Williams, C.** *"Allergy in Children Versus Allergy in Adults."* C. Collins-Williams. Canadian Medical Association Journal 78, 4(Feb. 15, 1958): 276-279.

**5462. Collins-Williams, C.** *"Penicillin Sensitivity."* C. Collins-Williams and J.E. Vincent. Canadian Medical Association Journal 70, 4(Apr. 1954): 388-391.

**5463. Collins-Williams, C.** *"The Use of ACTH and Cortisone in Childhood Allergies."* C. Collins-Williams. Canadian Medical Association Journal 72, 10(May 15, 1955): 776-777.

**5464. Colombo, John Robert** *Years of Light: a Celebration of Leslie A. Croutch.* John Robert Colombo. Toronto: Hounslow Press, c1982.

**5465. Commission on Emotional and Learning Disorders in Children** *The Report of the Ontario Committee of the Commission on Emotional and Learning Disorders in Children: a Supplementary Publication to One Million Children, the CELDIC Report.* The Commission. Toronto: [Canadian Council on Children and Youth], 1970.
Chairman: R.E. Jones.

**5466. Committee for Survey of Hospital Needs in Metropolitan Toronto** *Hospital Accommodation and Facilities for Children in Metropolitan Toronto: Part Six of a Study By the Committee for Survey of Hospital Needs in Metropolitan Toronto.* Committee for Survey of Hospital Needs in Metropolitan Toronto. Toronto: The Committee, 1962.

**5467. Conboy, E.J.** *"Care of the Feeble-minded."* E.J. Conboy. Public Health Journal 7, 12(Dec. 1916): 505-507.

**5468. Condon, Thomas Francis** *Biculturalism and Adolescent Aspirations: a Comparison of English and French-speaking Canadians' Family Size Expectations.* Thomas Francis Condon. Duluth, Min.: University of Minnesota, c1971.
Thesis (Ph.D.)–University of Minnesota, 1971.

**5469. Conference on Problems of Teaching Young Children (1968: Toronto)** *Problems in the Teaching of Young Children: a Report of the Conference on Problems of Teaching Young Children, Toronto, Canada, March 12-13, 1968.* Andrew Biemiller, ed. Toronto: OISE, c1970.

**5470. Connor, Carl Yoder** *Archibald Lampman: Canadian Poet of Nature.* Carl Y. Connor. 2nd ed. Ottawa: Borealis Press, c1977.
First published in 1929 in New York and Montreal by Carrier.

**5471. Conron, Brandon** *Morley Callaghan.* Brandon Conron. New York: Twayne, c1966.

**5472. Conron, Caroline L.** *Merrymount Children's Home, 1874-1974: a Century in Retrospect.* Caroline L. Conron. London, Ont.: Merrymount Children's Centre, 1974.

**5473. Consultation for Action on Unreached Youth (1964: Geneva Park-Lake Couchiching)** *Report and Recommendation of the Consultation for Action on Unreached Youth.* The Consultation. Toronto: Social Planning Committee of Metropolitan Toronto, 1964.

**5474. Conway, Clifford B.** *The Hearing Abilities of Children in Toronto Public Schools.* Clifford B. Conway. Toronto: University of Toronto, 1937.
Thesis (D.Paed.)–University of Toronto, 1937.

**5475. Cook, Harold Sterling** *Improving Educational Opportunity for Quebec Youth.* Harold Sterling Cook. New York: Columbia University, 1951.
Thesis (Ph.D.) – Teachers' College, Columbia University, 1951.

**5476. Cook, Mary** *One for Sorrow, Two for Joy.* Mary Cook. Ottawa: Deneau, c1984.

**5477. Cook, Sharon Anne** *"A Helping Hand and Shelter": Anglo-Protestant Social Service Agencies in Ottawa 1880-1910.* Sharon Anne Cook. Ottawa: Carleton University, 1987.
Thesis (M.A.)–Carleton University, 1987.

**5478. Cooke, Ethel B.** *"Nutrition of Infants."* Ethel B. Cooke. Canadian Nurse 51, 5(May 1955): 381-382.

**5479. Cooper, Barry** *"Valliere's Confusion."* Barry Cooper. Journal of Canadian Studies/Revue d'etudes canadiennes 6, 2(May 1971): 3-17.

5480. Cooper, Deborah, L. *The Effects of Instructions and the Correction Procedure on Cultural Discrimination Learning in Preschool Children.* Deborah L. Cooper. Toronto: University of Toronto, 1970.
Thesis (M.A.)–University of Toronto, 1970.

5481. Cooper, John Irwin *"The Canadian Education and Home Missionary Society."* John Irwin Cooper. Canadian Historical Review 26, 1(Mar. 1945): 42-47.

5482. Copp, J. Terry *The Anatomy of Poverty: the Condition of the Working Class in Montreal 1897-1929.* Terry Copp. Toronto: McClelland and Stewart, 1974.

5483. Copp, J. Terry *"The Conditions of the Working Class in Montreal, 1897-1920."* J. Terry Copp. Canadian Historical Association, Historical Papers/Communications historiques (1972): 157-180.
Reprinted in Studies in Canadian Social History, pp. 189-212. Edited by Michiel Horn and Ronald Sabourin.

5484. Copp, Marion L. *"A Wee Scrap of Humanity."* Marion L. Copp. Canadian Nurse 53, 1(Jan. 1957): 53-55.

5485. Corbett, Barbara E. *The Public School Kindergarten in Ontario 1883-1967: a Study of the Froebelian Origins, History, and Educational Theory and Practice of the Kindergarten in Ontario.* Barbara E. Corbett. Toronto: University of Toronto, 1968.
Thesis (Ed.D.)–University of Toronto, 1968.

5486. Corbett, Hildegard *Two Effects of Verbal Stimulus Familiarization on an Associative Test Task in Children.* Hildegard Corbett. Ottawa: Carleton University, c1969.
Thesis (Ph.D.)–Carleton University, 1969. National Library of Canada MIC TC-3916.

5487. Cork, R. Margaret *The Forgotten Children: a Study of Children with Alcoholic Parents.* R. Margaret Cork. Toronto: PaperJacks Ltd., c1969.
"Who Are They" reprinted in Deviant Behaviour and Societal Reaction, pp. 275-285. Edited by Craig L. Boydell, Carl F. Grindstaff and Paul C. Whitehead.

5488. Cormier, Bruno M. *"The Persistent Offender and His Family."* Bruno M. Cormier, Lydia Keitner and Miriam Kennedy. McGill Law Journal 13. 4(1967): 601-613.

5489. Corry, J.A. *My Life and Work, a Happy Partnership: Memoirs of J.A. Corry.* J.A. Corry. Kingston: Queen's University, 1981.

5490. Couch, Hazel *Some Phases of Child Welfare Work in the City of London.* Hazel Couch. London, Ont.: University of Western Ontario, 1915.
Thesis (M.A.)–University of Western Ontario, 1915.

5491. Coupland, Ronald Fraser *A Study of Sectarian Communal and Religious Organizations with Special Reference to their Function as "Circulation Enabling" and "Match-making" Institutions for Jewish Youth.* Ronald Fraser Coupland. Toronto: University of Toronto, 1968.
Thesis (M.S.W.)–University of Toronto, 1968.

5492. Coutu, Anne *Use of Discriminant Analysis for Selecting Students for Ninth Grade Algebra or General Mathematics.* Anne Coutu. Montreal: McGill University, 1970.
Thesis (M.A.)–McGill University, 1970.

5493. Covernton, C.F. *"Melaena."* C.F. Covernton. Canadian Medical Association Journal 2, 2(Feb. 1912): 128-131.

5494. Cowan, Philip A. *"Compliance and Resistance in the Conditioning of Autistic Children: an Exploratory Study."* Philip A. Cowan, B.A. Hoddinott and Barbara Anne Wright. Child Development 36, 4(Dec. 1965): 913-923.

5495. Cowan, Philip A. *"Mean Length of Spoken Response as a Function of Stimulus, Experimenter, and Subject."* Philip A. Cowan, J. Weber, B.A. Hoddinott and J. Klein. Child Development 38, 1(Mar. 1967): 191-203.

5496. Cowan, Philip A. *"Studies of Reinforcement of Aggression: 1. Effects of Schooling."* Philip A. Cowan and Richard H. Walters. Child Development 34, 3(Sept. 1963): 543-551.

5497. Cowles, J.P. *The Juvenile Employment System of Ontario.* J.P. Cowles. Ottawa: Canadian Council on Child Welfare, 1923.

5498. Cowley, R.H. *"Mentally Defective Pupils in the Public Schools of Toronto."* R.H. Cowley. Public Health Journal 5, 4(Apr. 1914): 223-224.

5499. Cowper, Thomas *A Study of Factors Underlying Recidivism in a Group of Juvenile Delinquents.* Thomas Cowper. Toronto: University of Toronto, 1945.
Thesis (M.A.)–University of Toronto, 1945.

5500. **Cragg, Catherine E.** *"The Child With Leukemia."* Catherine E. Cragg. Canadian Nurse 65, 10(Oct. 1969): 30-34.

5501. **Craig, Gibson E.** *"Larva Migrans in Children Returning From Florida."* Gibson E. Craig. Canadian Medical Association Journal/Journal de l'Association medicale canadienne 80, 10(May 15, 1959): 828.

5502. **Craig, Grace Morris** *But This Is Our War.* Grace Morris Craig. Toronto: University of Toronto Press, c1981.

5503. **Cram, John M.** *Student Self-prediction of High School Marks as an Aid to Guidance Counsellors.* John Murray Cram. Fredericton: University of New Brunswick, 1965.
Thesis (M.Ed.)--University of New Brunswick, 1965, c1966.

5504. **Cram, John M.** *"Student Self-prediction of High School Marks as an Aid to Guidance Counsellors."* John M. Cram. Canadian Education and Research Digest 6, 3(Sept. 1966): 209-218.

5505. **Cranston, J.H.** *Ink on my Fingers.* J.H. Cranston. Toronto: Ryerson Press, c1953.

5506. **Craven, Paul** *"The Law of Master and Servant in Mid-nineteenth Century Ontario."* Paul Craven. Toronto: For Osgoode Society by University of Toronto Press, c1981. In Essays in the History of Canadian Law, v.1, pp. 175-211. Edited by David H. Flaherty.

5507. **Crawford, A.W.** *"The Education and Adjustment of Juvenile Industrial Workers."* A.W. Crawford. In Proceedings and Papers Fourth Annual Canadian Conference on Child Welfare 1923, pp. 109-115.

5508. **Crawford, Douglas G.** *Family Interaction, Achievement Values and Motivation as Related to School Dropouts.* Douglas G. Crawford. Toronto: University of Toronto, 1969.
Thesis (Ph.D.)--University of Toronto, 1969.

5509. **Crawford, Patricia J.** *The Effects of High-rise Living on School Behaviour.* Patricia J. Crawford and Albert E. Virgin. North York, Ont.: Department of Educational Research Services, 1971.

5510. **Crawford, Patricia J.** *School Achievement: a Preliminary Look at the Effects of the Home.* Patricia J. Crawford and Gary Eason. [Toronto: Research Department, Board of Education], 1970.

5511. **Crawford, Ruth Virtue** *"Nutritional Aspects of the Hartman Jones Memorial School Health Study: 1. Preliminary Examination."* Ruth Crawford, Jean Leeson, E.W. McHenry and W. Mosley. Canadian Journal of Public Health 37, 9(Sept. 1946): 351-355.

5512. **Creighton, Donald** *Harold Adams Innis: Portrait of a Scholar.* Donald Creighton. Toronto: University of Toronto Press, 1978.

5513. **Critchley, David** *The Impact of the Community Services Upon a Youth Group.* David M. Critchley. Toronto: University of Toronto, 1949.
Thesis (M.S.W.)--University of Toronto, 1949.

5514. **Crofts, Irene** *Child-parent Identification and Reading Achievement.* Irene Crofts. Toronto: University of Toronto, 1959.
Thesis (M.A.)--University of Toronto, 1959.

5515. **Crombie, D.W.** *"The Present Anti-Tuberculosis Program in Ontario."* D.W. Crombie. Canadian Public Health Journal 26, 10(Oct. 1935): 486-493.

5516. **Cross, D. Suzanne** *"The Neglected Majority: the Changing Role of Women in 19th Century Montreal."* Suzanne D. Cross. Histoire sociale/Social History 6, 12(Nov. 1973): 202-223.
Reprinted in The Canadian City: Essays in Urban History pp. 255-281 and in The Canadian City: Essays in Urban and Social History 304-397. Edited by Gilbert A. Stelter and Alan F.J. Artibise. Also reprinted in The Neglected Majority: Essays in Canadian Women's History, pp. 66-86. Edited by Susan Mann Trofimenkoff and Alison Prentice.

5517. **Cross, Harold C.** *One Hundred Years of Service with Youth: the Story of the Montreal YMCA, 1851-1951.* Harold C. Cross. Montreal: Southam Press, 1951.

5518. **Cruikshank, G.R.** *"Can We Keep Tonsils and Adenoids from Becoming Diseased?"* G.R. Cruikshank. Canadian Medical Association Journal 6, 8(Aug. 1916): 739-742.

5519. **Cruikshank, H.C.** *"Prematurity as a Factor in Infant Mortality."* H.C. Cruikshank. Public Health Journal 15, 1(Jan. 1925): 22-24.

**5520. Cruikshank, H.C.** *"The Problem of Tuberculosis Among Toronto Children."* H.C. Cruikshank. Public Health Journal 16, 2(Feb. 1925): 71-75.

**5521. Cryderman, Ethel** *"Prenatal Work."* Ethel Cryderman. Canadian Nurse 23, 10(Oct. 1927): 536-541.

**5522. Crysdale, Stewart** *"Workers' Families and Education in a Downtown Community."* Stewart Crysdale. Toronto: Holt, Rinehart and Winston of Canada Ltd., 1971. In The Canadian Family, pp. 265-281. Edited by K. Ishwaran. Reprinted in The Canadian Family Revised, pp. 324-340. Edited by K. Ishwaran.

**5523. Csank, J.Z.** *"Developmental Norms on Four Psychophysiological Measures for Use in the Evaluation of Psychotic Disorders."* J.Z. Csank and H.E. Lehmann. Canadian Journal of Psychology 12, 2(June 1958): 127-133.

**5524. Cudmore, Sedley Anthony** *Historical Statistical Survey of Education in Canada.* Sedley Anthony Cudmore and M.C. MacLean. Ottawa: King's Printer, 1921.

**5525. Culham, Lottie J.** *Wards of a Children's Aid Society: a Study of Twenty-nine Case Records of Permanent Wards of the Toronto Children's Aid Society with a View to Determining Their Pattern of Adjustment.* Lottie J. Culham. Toronto: University of Toronto, 1953. Thesis (M.S.W.)--University of Toronto, 1953.

**5526. Cunningham, A.I.** *"Evaluation of a Tuberculosis Mass Survey Conducted in the City of Chatham and in Kent County, Ontario, in 1963."* A.I. Cunningham. Canadian Medical Association Journal/Journal de l'Association medicale canadienne 93, 21(Nov. 20, 1965): 1105-1109.

**5527. Cupchik, Zelda** *A Study of Growth of Intellectually Retarded Dependent Children.* Zelda Cupchik. Montreal: McGill University, 1953. Thesis (M.S.W.)--McGill University, 1953.

**5528. Curran, J.J., ed.** *Golden Jubilee of St. Patrick's Orphan Asylum.* J.J. Curran. Montreal: Catholic Institution for Deaf Mutes, 1902.

**5529. Currey, D.V.** *"An Epidemic of Milk-borne Paratyphoid Fever: 2. Clinical Aspects."* D.V. Currey. Canadian Public Health Journal 23, 7(July 1932): 306-308.

**5530. Currie, A.B.** *The Modern Elementary School.* A.B. Currie. Toronto: Ryerson, 1942.

**5531. Currie, Arthur W.** *"Montreal Anti-Tuberculosis and General Health League."* Arthur W. Currie. Public Health Journal 18, 3(Mar. 1927): 101-114.

**5532. Curry, Ralph Leighton** *Stephen Leacock: Humorist and Humanist.* Ralph Leighton Curry. Garden City, N.Y.: Doubleday, c1959.

**5533. Curry, Ralph Leighton** *Stephen Leacock and His Works.* Ralph Curry. Toronto: ECW Press, [1988].

**5534. Curtis, Bruce** *Building the Educational State: Canada West, 1836-1871.* Bruce Curtis. London, Ont.: Althouse Press, c1988.

**5535. Curtis, Bruce** *""Illicit" Sexuality and Public Education in Ontario, 1840-1907."* Bruce Curtis. Historical Studies in Education/Revue d'histoire de l'education 1, 1(Spring 1989): 73-94.

**5536. Curtis, Bruce** *"The Playground in Nineteenth Century Ontario: Theory and Practice."* Bruce Curtis. Material History Bulletin/Bulletin d'histoire de la culture materielle 22(Fall 1985): 21-29.

**5537. Curtis, Bruce** *The Political Economy of Elementary Educational Development: Comparative Perspectives on State Schooling in Upper Canada.* Bruce Curtis. Toronto: University of Toronto, 1980. Thesis (Ph.D.)--University of Toronto, 1980.

**5538. Curtis, Bruce** *"Schoolbooks and the Myth of Curricular Republicanism: the State and the Curriculum in Canada West, 1820-1850."* Bruce Curtis. Histoire sociale/Social History 16, 32(Nov. 1983): 305-329.

**5539. Cushing, H.B.** *"Treatment of Diphtheria at the Alexandra Hospital, Montreal."* H.B. Cushing. Canadian Medical Association Journal 6, 9(Sept. 1916): 817-822.

**5540. Cushing, Harvey** *The Life of Sir William Osler.* Harvey Cushing. New York: Oxford University Press, 1940.

**5541. D'Oyley, Vincent R.** *Education and Society: Six Studies.* Vincent Roy D'Oyley. Toronto: University of Toronto, 1970.

**5542. D'Oyley, Vincent R.** *Testing: the First Two Years of the Carnegie Study, 1959-1961, Analysis of Scores by Course, Sex and Size of Municipality.* Vincent Roy D'Oyley. [Toronto]: Department of Educational Research, University of Toronto, 1964.

**5543. Dale-Harris, Mary** *A Study of the Form and Context of Earliest Memories.* Mary Dale-Harris. Toronto: University of Toronto, 1937.
Thesis (M.A.)–University of Toronto, 1937.

**5544. Dalzell, Isabel J.** *"Psychiatric Social Work with Recessive Adolescents."* Isabel J. Dalzell. Canadian Public Health Journal 31, 6(June 1940): 280-286.

**5545. Dalzell, Isabel J.** *"Psychiatric Social Work With the Maladjusted Child of Normal Intelligence."* Isabel J. Dalzell. Canadian Public Health Journal 25, 11(Nov. 1934): 602-604.

**5546. Danylewycz, Marta** *"Changing Relationships: Nuns and Feminists in Montreal, 1890-1925."* Marta Danylewycz. Histoire sociale/Social History 14, 28(Nov. 1981): 413-434.

**5547. Danylewycz, Marta** *Taking the Veil: an Alternative to Marriage, Motherhood and Spinsterhood in Quebec, 1840-1920.* Marta Danylewycz. Toronto: McClelland and Stewart, 1987.

**5548. Danziger, Kurt** *The Socialization of Immigrant Children.* Kurt Danziger. Toronto: York University Institute for Behavioural Research, 1971.

**5549. Darbis, Doreen** *Perceptual Performance of Cerebral Palsied Children.* Doreen Darbis. Toronto: University of Toronto, 1959.
Thesis (M.A.)–University of Toronto, 1959.

**5550. Davenport, Harold T.** *"Blood Loss During Pediatric Operations."* Harold T. Davenport and Margaret N. Barr. Canadian Medical Association Journal/Journal de l'Association medicale canadienne 89, 26(Dec. 28, 1963): 1309-1313.

**5551. Davenport, Harold T.** *"Methoxyflurance Anesthesia in Pediatrics: a Clinical Report."* Harold T. Davenport and Paul Quan. Canadian Medical Association Journal/Journal de l'Association medicale canadienne 91, 25(Dec. 19, 1964): 1291-1294.

**5552. Davey, Ian E.** *Educational Reform and the Working Class: School Attendance in Hamilton, Ontario, 1851-1891.* Ian Elliot Davey. Toronto: University of Toronto, 1975. (CTM no. 31193)
Thesis (Ph.D.)–University of Toronto, 1975.

**5553. Davey, Ian E.** *"Patterns of Inequality: School Attendance and Social Structure in the Nineteenth Century, Canada and Australia."* Ian Davey. Leicester, Eng.: History of Education Society, 1981. In Childhood, Youth and Education in the Late Nineteenth Century, pp. 1-30. Edited by John Hurt.

**5554. Davey, Ian E.** *"The Rhythm of Work and the Rhythm of School."* Ian E. Davey. Toronto: MacMillan Company of Canada Limited, c1978. In Egerton Ryerson and His Times, pp. 221-253. Edited by Neil McDonald and Alf Chaiton.

**5555. Davey, Ian E.** *School Reform and School Attendance: the Hamilton Central School, 1853-1861.* Ian E. Davey. Toronto: University of Toronto, 1972. (CTM no. 20552)
Thesis (M.A.)–University of Toronto, 1972.

**5556. Davey, Ian E.** *"School Reform and School Attendance: the Hamilton Central School, 1853-1861."* Ian E. Davey. New York: New York University Press, c1975. In Education and Social Change: Themes from Ontario's Past, pp. 294-314. Edited by Michael B. Katz and Paul H. Mattingly.

**5557. Davey, Ian E.** *"Trends in Female School Attendance in Mid-nineteenth Century Ontario."* Ian E. Davey. Histoire sociale/Social History 8, 16(Nov.-Dec. 1975): 238-254.

**5558. Davey, J.E.** *"Some Observations on Health Supervision in Secondary Schools."* J.E. Davey. Canadian Public Health Journal 20, 10(Oct. 1929): 489-493.

**5559. Davey, R. Barrie** *The Value of School Records in Interpreting the Present Standing of Pupils.* R. Barrie Davey. Toronto: University of Toronto, 1934.
Thesis (M.A.)–University of Toronto, 1934.

**5560. David, Renee** *Emotional Problems of Children with Poliomyelitis: During the Period of Readjustment to Home and Community after Prolonged Hospitalization.* Renee David. Toronto: University of Toronto, 1953.
Thesis (M.S.W.)–University of Toronto, 1953.

**5561. Davidson, Emily Delatre** *Stories My Mother Told Me, and Memories of My Own.* Emily Delatre Davidson. [Toronto: s.n., 1967].

**5562. Davidson, Marsh** *Schizophrenic Performance on the Standard Revision of the Binet-Simon Test.* Marsh Davidson. Toronto: University of Toronto, 1935. Thesis (M.A.)--University of Toronto, 1935.

**5563. Davies, Robertson** *Stephen Leacock.* Robertson Davies. Toronto: McClelland and Stewart, c1970.

**5564. Davignon, Andre** *"Standardization of Cardiopulmonary Roentgenograms in Infants and Children."* Andre Davignon, Micheline Ste.-Marie, George Mairet and Martine Ethier. Canadian Medical Association Journal/Journal de l'Association medicale canadienne 95, 7(Aug. 13, 1966): 295-299.

**5565. Davine, M.** *"The Perception of Phonema Sequences by Monolingual and Bilingual Elementary School Children."* M. Davine, G.R. Tucker and Wallace E. Lambert. Canadian Journal of Behavioural Science/Revue canadienne de sciences du comportement 3, 1(Jan. 1971): 72-76.

**5566. Davis, Carroll** *Room to Grow: a Study of Parent-Child Relations.* Carroll Davis. Toronto: University of Toronto Press, c1966.

**5567. Davis, Inez Adeline** *A Study of the Adjustment of Children of the Same Families in Certain Routine Situations.* Inez Adeline Davis. Toronto: University of Toronto, 1950. Thesis (M.A.)--University of Toronto, 1950.

**5568. Davis, Margaret A.** *An Evaluation of the Criteria for Selecting a Good Foster Home.* Margaret A. Davis. Toronto: University of Toronto, 1930. Thesis (M.A.)--University of Toronto, 1930.

**5569. Dawe, Jane-Alice Kathleen** *The Impact of Social Change on the Development of Welfare Services in Ontario, 1891-1921: an Historical Study of the Transition from Institutional to Foster Care for Children in Ontario, 1891-1921.* Jane-Alice Kathleen Dawe. Toronto: University of Toronto, 1966. Thesis (M.S.W.) --University of Toronto, 1966.

**5570. Dawes, C.H.** *Just Being Around: Reminiscences of a Small Town United Church Minister.* C.H. Dawes. Edmonton: West Wind Press, c1988.

**5571. Dawson, Helen P.** *Adoption Consideration for the Young Child: a Study of Fifty Permanent Wards of the Children's Aid Society of Toronto, with Special Reference to the Fact that They Were Not Placed for Adoption.* Helen P. Dawson. Toronto: University of Toronto, 1953. Thesis (M.S.W.)--University of Toronto, 1953.

**5572. De Avila, Edward A.** *"A Group Measure of the Piagetian Concepts of Conservation and Egocentricity."* Edward A. De Avila, David L. Randall and Joseph A. Struthers. Canadian Journal of Behavioural Science/Revue canadienne de sciences du comportement 1, 4(Oct. 1969): 263-272.

**5573. de Boissiere, Vernon** *"The Treatment of Chronic Sinusitis in Children."* Vernon de Boissiere. Canadian Medical Association Journal 60, 1(Jan. 1949): 14-17.

**5574. de Bruyn, Max R.** *"A Search for Identity."* Max R. de Bruyn. Toronto: Quadrant Editions, 1983. In Between Two Worlds: the Canadian Immigrant Experience, pp. 202-227. Edited by Milly Charon.

**5575. de Gaspe, Philippe-Joseph Aubert** *A Man of Sentiment: the Memoirs of Philippe-Joseph Aubert de Gaspe.* Philippe-Joseph Aubert de Gaspe. Montreal: Vehicule Press, c1988.

**5576. de la Roche, Mazo** *Ringing the Changes: an Autobiography.* Mazo de la Roche. Toronto: MacMillan, c1957.

**5577. De Roux, Margery** *"Writing is Fun."* Margery De Roux. Bulletin of the Institute of Child Study 29, 3(Fall 1967): 46-49.

**5578. de Sainte Croix, Josephine Holmes** *Glimpses of the Monastery: a Brief Sketch of the History of the Ursulines of Quebec, During Two Hundred Years. From 1639 to 1672: Parts I-III.* Josephine Holmes de Sainte Croix. Quebec: C. Darveau, 1875.

**5579. Delagrau, W.R.** *"Juvenile Delinquency."* W.R. Delagrau. Canadian Journal of Corrections/Revue canadienne de criminologie 7, 1(Jan. 1965): 117-121.

**5580. Delta, B.G.** *"Transient Idiopathic Hypoproteinaemia Associated with Oedema and Hypochromic Anaemia."* B.G. Delta. Canadian Medical Association Journal 79, 10(Nov. 15, 1958): 833-836.

**5581. Denison, George T.** *Recollections of a Police Magistrate.* George T. Denison. Toronto: Musson Book Company, 1920.

**5582. Denison, John M.** *"An Unusual Social Experiment to Help Youth in Crisis (Ankh)."* John M. Denison. Canadian Medical Association Journal/Journal de l'Association medicale canadienne 104, 1(Jan. 9, 1971): 15-19.

**5583. Denne, Lexa** *"The Visiting Housekeeper."* Lexa Denne. Canadian Nurse 23, 1(Jan. 1927): 19-20.

**5584. Dennick, Joan** *A Study of Familial Attitudes Towards the Handicapped Child.* Joan Dennick, A. Horvath, J. Prince, W. Rempel and E. Roch. Montreal: McGill University, 1967.
Thesis (M.S.W.)--McGill University, 1967.

**5585. Dennis, Lloyd A.** *Marching Orders: a Memoir.* Lloyd Dennis. Markham; Fitzhenry & Whiteside, 1988.

**5586. Dennison, Robert George** *The Child in the Toronto Daily Press, 1919-1929.* Robert George Dennison. Toronto: University of Toronto, 1988.
Thesis (Ph.D.)--University of Toronto, 1988.

**5587. Denton, Frank T.** *"An Exploratory Statistical Analysis of Some Socioeconomic Characteristics of Families in Hamilton Ontario 1871."* Frank T. Denton and Peter J. George. Histoire sociale/Social History 5(Apr. 1970): 16-44.

**5588. Denton, Frank T.** *Unemployment and Labour Force Behavior of Young People: Evidence from Canada and Ontario.* Frank T. Denton, A. Leslie Robb and Byron G. Spencer. Toronto: University of Toronto Press, 1980.

**5589. Des Roches, Helen** *"Early School Leavers."* Helen Des Roches. Canadian Welfare 38, 5(Sept.-Oct. 1962): 217-218.

**5590. Desbarats, Peter** *Rene: a Canadian in Search of a Country.* Peter Desbarats. Toronto: McClelland and Stewart, 1976.

**5591. Devorski, Lorraine** *Pauline: the Indian Poet.* Lorraine Devorski. Ottawa: Canadian Library Association, c1986.

**5592. Devorski, Lorraine** *Tom Thomson: the Man and His Legend.* Lorraine Devorski. Ottawa: Canadian Library Association, 1986.

**5593. Dewan, John G.** *The Incidence of (a) Schizophrenia (b) Mental Deficiency with Reference to Birth Order.* John G. Dewan. Toronto: University of Toronto, 1935.
Thesis (M.A.)--University of Toronto, 1935.

**5594. Dewar, John** *"The Contributions of James Naismith to Sport in Canada."* John Dewar. Ottawa: Fitness and Amateur Sport Directorate, Department of National Health and Welfare, 1970. In Proceedings of the First Canadian Symposium on the History of Sport and Physical Education, pp. 433-450.

**5595. di Michele, Mary** *"Writers From Invisible Cities."* Mary di Michele. Canadian Woman Studies/Cahiers de la femme 8, 2(Summer 1987): 37-38.

**5596. Dickie, James T.** *Counsellor Characteristics Affecting the Ability of Students to Seek Help with Personal Problems.* James T. Dickie Montreal: McGill University, 1968.
Thesis (M.A.)--McGill University, 1968.

**5597. Dickinson, Clarence Heber** *Lorne Pierce: a Profile.* Clarence Heber Dickinson. Toronto - Ryerson Press, c1965.

**5598. Dickson, Jean** *"Tenth Anniversary of N.E.A.D."* Jean Dickson. Bulletin of the Institute of Child Study 23, 3-4(Sept.-Dec. 1961): 2-3.

**5599. Dilling, Harold John** *Educational Achievement and Social Acceptance of Indian Pupils Integrated in Non-Indian Schools of Southern Ontario.* Harold John Dilling. Toronto: University of Toronto, 1965.
Thesis (Ed.D.)--University of Toronto, 1965.

**5600. Dilling, Harold John** *Integration of the Indian Canadian in and through Schools, with Emphasis on the St. Clair Reserve in Sarnia.* Harold John Dilling. Toronto: University of Toronto, 1961.
Thesis (M.Ed.)--University of Toronto, 1961.

**5601. Dimock, Hedley** *Camping and Character: a Camp Experiment in Character Education.* Hedley Dimock, Charles E. Hendry [and] foreword by William H. Kilpatrick. 2nd ed. New York: Association Press, 1949.
First edition published in 1929.

**5602. Dimock, Hedley** *"Play, a Basic Approach to Pediatric Nursing."* Hedley Dimock. Canadian Nurse 50, 4(Apr. 1954): 259-261.

**5603. Dimock, Hedley** *Talks to Counsellors: as Given to Counsellors at Camp Ahmek for Boys and Wapomeo for Girls.* Hedley Dimock [and] Taylor Statten. New York: Association Press, 1943.

**5604. Dingwall, Nancy E.** *The Problem of Runaway and Non-Runaway Foster Children.* Nancy E. Dingwall. Montreal: McGill University, 1966.
Thesis (M.S.W.)–McGill University, 1966.

**5605. Disbrowe, Harold B.** *A Schoolman's Odyssey.* Harold B. Disbrowe. London: Faculty of Education, the University of Western Ontario, 1984.

**5606. Dixon, Robert Grieves** *A Comparison of Two Junior High Schools, One in Ohio and One in Ontario.* Robert Grieves Dixon. Toronto: University of Toronto, 1958.
Thesis (M.Ed.)–University of Toronto, 1958.

**5607. Djwa, Sandra** *The Politics of the Imagination: a Life of F.R. Scott.* Sandra Djwa. Toronto: McClelland and Stewart, c1987.

**5608. Doan, A.W.R.** *The Evaluation of Elementary School Buildings and Grounds.* A.W.R. Doan. Toronto: University of Toronto, 1932.
Thesis (D. Paed.)–University of Toronto, 1932.

**5609. Doan, A.W.R.** *The Public School Buildings of Toronto.* A.W.R. Doan. Toronto: University of Toronto, 1921.
Thesis (M.A.)–University of Toronto, 1921.
No bibliography.

**5610. Doan, Helen McKinnon** *Conditional Discrimination and the Effective Cues in Children's Discrimination Learning.* Helen McKinnon Doan. Kingston: Queen's University, 1966.
Thesis (Ph.D.)–Queen's University, 1966.

**5611. Dodwell, Peter C.** *"Children's Understanding of Number and Related Concepts."* Peter C. Dodwell. Canadian Journal of Psychology 14, 3(Sept. 1960): 191-205.
Reprinted in Intellectual Development, pp. 205-219. Edited by Pauline S. Sears.

**5612. Dodwell, Peter C.** *"Children's Understanding of Number Concepts: Characteristics of an Individual and of a Group Test."* Peter C. Dodwell. Canadian Journal of Psychology 15, 1(Mar. 1961): 29-36.

**5613. Dodwell, Peter C.** *"Children's Understanding of Spatial Concepts."* Peter C. Dodwell. Canadian Journal of Psychology 17, 1(Mar. 1963): 141-161.

**5614. Dodwell, Peter C.** *"Relations Between the Understanding of the Logic of Classes and of Cardinal Number in Children."* Peter C. Dodwell. Canadian Journal of Psychology 16, 2(June 1962): 152-160.

**5615. Doherty, Gillian** *The Effects of Specific Perceptual-Motor Training on the Physical Fitness, Perceptual-Motor Skills, Academic Readiness, and Academic Functioning of Educable Mentally Retarded Children.* Gillian Doherty. Toronto: York University, 1971. (CTM no. 9089)
Thesis (Ph.D.)–York University, 1971.

**5616. Dohoo, Dudley T.** *Maternal Attitudes: Their Effect on Children in Public School.* Dudley T. Dohoo. Toronto: University of Toronto, 1968.
Thesis (M.S.W.)–University of Toronto, 1968.

**5617. Dolenz, John Joseph** *Reading and Its Relationship to Self-descriptions and Measures of Paternal Identification of Freshmen for Catholic High Schools.* John Joseph Dolenz. Ottawa: University of Ottawa, 1970.
Thesis (Ph.D.)–University of Ottawa, 1970.

**5618. Donald, Janet G.** *Concept Identification: Structuring Responses to Verbal and Pictorial Material.* Janet G. Donald. Toronto: University of Toronto, 1968.
Thesis (Ph.D.)–University of Toronto, 1968.

**5619. Donald, Marjorie N.** *"Concomitants of Smoking Among High School Students."* Marjorie N. Donald. Medical Services Journal of Canada 23, 12(Dec. 1967): 1416-1435.

**5620. Donaldson, Gerald** *Gilles Villeneuve: the Life of the Legendary Racing Driver.* Gerald Donaldson. Toronto: McClelland, Stewart, 1988.

**5621. Donnelly, Grace C.** *"Hydramnios."* Grace C. Donnelly. Canadian Medical Association Journal 78, 2(Jan. 15, 1958): 117-119.

**5622. Donnelly, John F.** *"Tracks in the Snow: Growing Up in Northern Ontario."* John F. Donnelly. Queen's Quarterly 79, 1(Spring 1972): 60-66.

**5623. Donnelly, Murray Samuel** *Dafoe of the Free Press.* Murray Donnelly. Toronto: MacMillan of Canada, c1968.

**5624. Dorland, Arthur Garratt** *Along the Trail of Life: a Quaker Retrospect.* Arthur Garratt Dorland. Belleville, Ont.: Mika Publishing Co., c1979.

**5625. Dorland, Arthur Garratt** *"A Hundred Years of Quaker Education in Canada: the Centenary of Pickering College."* A.G. Dorland. Royal Society of Canada Proceedings and Transactions Series 3, 36, 2(May 1942): 51-91.

**5626. Douglas, Muriel H.** *History of the Society for the Protection of Women and Children from 1882 to 1966.* Muriel H. Douglas. Montreal: McGill University, 1967.
Thesis (M.S.W.)–McGill University, 1967.

**5627. Douglas, Virginia I.** *"Children's Responses to Frustration: a Developmental Study."* Virginia I. Douglas. Canadian Journal of Psychology/Revue canadienne de psychologie 19, 2(June 1965): 161-171.

**5628. Dove, Anna G.** *"Forest Schools in Toronto."* Anna G. Dove. Canadian Nurse 21, 10(Oct. 1925): 524-525.

**5629. Dower, Lola** *A Study of Pupils Considered Dull by Their Teachers.* Lola Dower. Toronto: University of Toronto, 1947.
Thesis (M.A.)–University of Toronto, 1947.

**5630. Downe, William N.** *"Delinquent Boys: a Treatment Classification and Approach."* William N. Downe. Canadian Journal of Corrections/Revue canadienne de criminologie 10, 1(Jan. 1968): 346-351.

**5631. Doyle, James** *Annie Howells and Achille Frechette.* James Doyle. Toronto: University of Toronto Press, c1979.

**5632. Doyle, M. Elizabeth** *"A Streptococcal Epidemic in a Children's Surgical Ward."* M. Elizabeth Doyle and Elizabeth Chant Robertson. Canadian Journal of Public Health 35, 8(Aug. 1944): 302-310.

**5633. Doyle, St.Ignatius** *Margaret Bourgeoys and Her Congregation.* Sister St.Ignatius Doyle. Gardenvale, Que.: Garden City Press, c1940.

**5634. Drolet, Jean-Yves** *A Study of the Impact of Demographic and Socioeconomic Factors on School Attendance Rates in the Province of Quebec from 1901 to 1951.* Jean-Yves Drolet. Edmonton: University of Alberta, 1961.
Thesis (Ph.D.)--University of Alberta, 1961.

**5635. Drummond. Anne** *From Autonomous Academy to Public "High School": Quebec English Protestant Education, 1829-1889.* Anne Drummond. Montreal: McGill University, 1986.
Thesis (M.A.)--McGill University, 1986.

**5636. Drummond, D.S.** *"Fat Embolism in Children: Its Frequency and Relationship to Collagen Disease."* D.S. Drummond, R.b. Salter and J. Boone. Canadian Medical Association Journal/Journal de l'Association medicale canadienne 101, 4(Aug. 23, 1969): 200-203.

**5637. Drummond, Margaret Mary** *The Life and Times of Margaret Bourgeoys (the Venerable).* Margaret Mary Drummond. Boston: Angel Guardian Press, c1907.

**5638. Dryden, Ken** *The Game: a Thoughtful and Provocative Look at a Life in Hockey.* Ken Dryden. Toronto: MacMillan of Canada, c1983.

**5639. Dryden, Murray** *Playing the Shots at Both Ends: the Story of Ken and Dave Dryden.* Murray Dryden with Jim Hunt. Toronto: McGraw-Hill Ryerson, c1972.

**5640. Dubignon, Judith** *"The Relation Between Laboratory Measures of Sucking, Food Intake, and Perinatal Factors During the Newborn Period."* J. Dubignon, D. Campbell, M. Curtis and M.W. Partington. Child Development 40, 4(Dec. 1969): 1107-1120.

**5641. Dubsky, Frederick** *"Congenital Tuberculosis."* Frederick Dubsky. Canadian Medical Association Journal 73, 8(Oct. 15, 1955): 662-665.

**5642. Duffy, Eileen** *The Problem of Foster Home Replacements.* Eileen Duffy. Toronto: University of Toronto, 1948.
Thesis (M.S.W.)--University of Toronto, 1948.

**5643. Dukhan, Hamlyn** *The Development of the Junior High School and the Senior School in Metropolitan Toronto.* Hamlyn Dukhan. Toronto: University of Toronto, 1959.
Thesis (M.Ed.)--University of Toronto, 1959.

**5644. Dunlop, Florence S.** *"Analysis of Data Obtained from Ten Years of Intelligence Testing in the Ottawa Public Schools."* Florence S. Dunlop. Canadian Journal of Psychology 1, 1(Mar. 1947): 87-91.

**5645. Dunlop, Florence S.** *Subsequent Careers of Non-academic Boys.* Florence S. Dunlop. New York: Teachers College, Columbia University, c1935.
Thesis (Ph.D.)–Teachers College, Columbia University, 1935.

**5646. Dunlop, Jean** *The Effects of Replacement on Children Aged Three to Four Years: a Study of the Wards of the Toronto Children's Aid Society Transferred from the Infants' Homes of Toronto in the Year 1944.* Jean Dunlop. Toronto: University of Toronto, 1952.
Thesis (M.S.W.)–University of Toronto, 1952.

**5647. Dunlop, Marilyn** *Bill Mustard, Surgical Pioneer.* Marilyn Dunlop. Toronto: Dundurn Press, 1989.

**5648. Dupuis, Joseph Rosaire Philippe** *A Study of the Changes in the French Catholic System of Education in Quebec from September 1959 to June 1963.* Joseph Rosaire Philippe Dupuis. Edmonton: University of Alberta, 1965.
Thesis (M.Ed.)–University of Alberta, 1965.

**5649. Dybwad, Gunnar** *A Report on Mental Retardation in Montreal: the Miriam Home for the Exceptional, Montreal, 1963.* Gunnar Dybwad. [Montreal: s.n., 1963].

**5650. Dyke, Eunice H.** *"Health Service in Schools."* Eunice H. Dyke. Public Health Journal 12, 2(Feb. 1921): 49-58.

**5651. Dymond, Allan M.** *The Laws of Ontario Relating to Women and Children.* Allan M. Dymond. Toronto: Clarkson W. James, 1923.

**5652. Eames, Frank** *"Gananoque's First Public School, 1816."* Frank Eames. Ontario Historical Society, Papers and Records 17(1919): 90-105.

**5653. Early, L.R.** *Archibald Lampman.* L.R. Early. Boston: Twayne, c1986.

**5654. Early, L.R.** *Archibald Lampman and His Works.* L.R. Early. [Downsview]: ECW Press, [1983].

**5655. Easson, Mrs. McGregor** *The Intermediate School in Ottawa.* Mrs. McGregor Easson. Toronto: University of Toronto, 1934.
Thesis (D.Paed.)–University of Toronto, 1934.

**5656. Eaton, Flora McCrea** *Memory's Wall: the Autobiography of Flora Eaton McCrea.* Flora Eaton McCrea. Toronto: Clarke, Irwin and Company, c1956.

**5657. Ebbs, J.H.** *"Coeliac Disease."* J.H. Ebbs. Canadian Medical Association Journal 75, 11(Dec. 1, 1956): 885-893.

**5658. Ebbs, J.H.** *"Nutrition and Public Health."* J.H. Ebbs. Canadian Medical Association Journal 69, 1(July 1953): 61-63.

**5659. Edgar, Mrs. E.** *"Public Relations and Inter-racial Adoption."* Mrs. E. Edgar. Montreal: The Open Door Society, 1970. In Mixed Race Adoptions, pp. 37-40. Edited by The Open Door Society.

**5660. Edgington, Marion F.** *Measured Personality Characteristics of Spastic and Non-spastic Feeble-minded Children.* Marion F. Edgington. Toronto: University of Toronto, 1949.
Thesis (M.A.)–University of Toronto, 1949.

**5661. Edmund, Joseph** *"Juvenile Diabetes."* Joseph Edmund. Canadian Nurse 47, 1(Jan. 1951): 20-22.

**5662. Edwards, H.E.** *"Aspects of Perennial Allergic Rhinitis and Asthma in Childhood."* H.E. Edwards. Canadian Medical Association Journal 61, 1(July 1949): 36-38.

**5663. Edwards, H.E.** *"The Fatigue Syndrome in School Children."* H.E. Edwards and W.J. Tamblyn. Canadian Public Health Journal 32, 10(Oct. 1941): 518-523.

**5664. Egan, Maurice** *"Changing Concepts in Working With the Pre-delinquent."* Maurice Egan. Canadian Journal of Corrections/Revue canadienne de criminologie 3, 4(Oct. 1961): 271-277.

**5665. Egan, Maurice** *Economic and Social Adjustment of a Group of Mentally Deficient Adolescents: a Study of 34 Mentally Deficient Permanent Wards of the Children's Aid Society of the United Counties of Stormont, Dundas and Glengary, and the City of Cornwall, Who are Between 17 and 21 Years of Age on December 31, 1954.* Maurice F. Egan. Montreal: McGill University, 1956.
Thesis (M.S.W.)–McGill University, 1956.

**5666. Ehrlich, Robert M.** *"Influence of Steroid Therapy on the Nephrotic Syndrome in Children."* R.M. Ehrlich, C.P. Rance and R.J. Slater. Canadian Medical Association Journal/Journal de l'Association medicale canadienne 80, 6(Mar. 15, 1959): 430-432.

**5667. Ehrlich, Robert M.** *"A Neurological Complication in Children on Phenothiazine Tranquillizers."* Robert M. Erhlich. Canadian Medical Association Journal/Journal de l'Association medicale canadienne 81, 4(Aug. 15, 1959): 241-243.

**5668. Eisenberg, Mildred** *Factors Associated with School Performance in the Senior Class of a Large Suburban High School.* Mildred Eisenberg. Montreal: McGill University, 1968.
Thesis (M.A.)--McGill University, 1968.

**5669. Elizabeth, Mary** *"Foreign Body in the Respiratory Tract."* Mary Elizabeth. Canadian Nurse 54, 7(July 1958): 640-645.

**5670. Elliott, Bruce S.** *""The Famous Township of Hull": Image and Aspirations of a Pioneer Quebec Community."* Bruce S. Elliott. Histoire sociale/Social History 12, 24(Nov. 1979): 339-367.

**5671. Ellis, Barbara L.** *A Comparative Study of Delinquent Girls: a Study Based on the Material Found in Fifty Files of Girls Committed to the Ontario Training School, Galt, Twenty-five of Whom Were Later Transferred to the Ontario Training School, Mercer Reformatory, Toronto.* Barbara L. Ellis. Toronto: University of Toronto, 1953
Thesis (M.S.W.)--University of Toronto, 1953.

**5672. Ellis, Dormer** *"The Schooling of Girls."* Dormer Ellis. Toronto: OISE, 1984. In The House That Ryerson Built: Essays in Education to Mark Ontario's Bicentennial, pp. 88-101. Edited by Hugh Oliver, Mark Holmes and Ian Winchester.

**5673. Ellis, M.E. Dormer** *A Study of Age-Grade Statistics in Metropolitan Toronto.* Maxyne Evelyn Dormer Ellis and A.J. Zimmerman. Toronto: Metropolitan Toronto Educational Research Council, 1968.

**5674. Ellis, M.E. Dormer** *A Study of Personal Characteristics, Family Background and School Factors Associated with the Patterns of Progress through the Grades of Grade 13 Students in Metropolitan Toronto.* M.E. Dormer Ellis. Toronto: University of Toronto, 1968.
Thesis (Ed.D.)--University of Toronto, 1968.

**5675. Emery, George** *"Ontario's Civil Registration of Vital Statistics, 1869-1926: the Evolution of an Administrative System."* George Emery. Canadian Historical Review 64, 4(Dec. 1983): 468-493.

**5676. Emery, Winston G.** *Slow Learning Children: a Situational Approach.* Winston G. Emery. Montreal: McGill University, 1967.
Thesis (M.A.)--McGill University, 1967.

**5677. Endicott, Shirley Jane** *Facing the Tiger: Confronting and Conquering One's Hidden Fears, a Book for All Women and Men.* Shirley Jane Endicott. Winfield, B.C.: Wood Lake Books, [1987].

**5678. English, John** *Shadow of Heaven: the Life of Lester Pearson.* John English. vol. 1. Toronto: Lester & Orpen Denys, 1989.

**5679. Erb, I.H.** *"Blood Groups in Poliomyelitis."* I.H. Erb, H.S. Doyle and F.C. Heal. Canadian Public Health Journal 29, 9(Sept. 1938): 441-442.

**5680. Erb, I.H.** *"Congenital Anomalies of the Urinary Tract in Children and Infants and Their Relation to Chronic Pyuria."* I.H. Erb. Canadian Medical Association Journal 44, 1(Jan. 1941): 14-20.

**5681. Esler, E.M.** *"A Nutrition Project to Assess the Efficiency of Classroom Teaching."* E.M. Esler and E.W. McHenry. Canadian Journal of Public Health 40, 3(Feb. 1949): 104-108.

**5682. Etheridge, Kenneth** *Personal, Situational and Socio-Cultural Factors Associated with the Educational Wishes and Expectations of High School Students and Some Probable Consequences of High Discrepancies Between Wishes to Attend College and Expectations to Attend College.* Kenneth Etheridge. Montreal: McGill University, 1968.
Thesis (M.A.)--McGill University, 1968.

**5683. Evans, D.T.** *"Second Annual Meeting of the Child Welfare Section, Canadian Public Health Association, Toronto, 1919."* D.T. Evans, (chairman). Public Health Journal 11, 2(Feb. 1920): 66-78.

**5684. Even, Alexander** *Patterns of Academic Achievement in Grade 12 Chemistry and Their Relationship to Personal, Attitudinal and Environmental Factors.* Alexander Even. Toronto: University of Toronto, 1968. (CTM no. 3895)
Thesis (Ph.D.) -- University of Toronto, 1968.

**5685. Ewald, F.E.A.** *"Acceptance of Staff Values in Ontario Training Schools."* F.E.A. Ewald. Canadian Journal of Corrections/Revûe canadienne de criminologie 6, 1(Jan. 1964): 148-159.

**5686. Ewald, F.E.A.** *A Study of Values in Ontario Training Schools.* F.E.A. Ewald. Toronto: University of Toronto, 1962. Thesis (M.S.W.)--University of Toronto, 1962.

**5687. Fair, Myrtle** *I Remember the One Room School.* Myrtle Fair. Cheltham, Ont.: Boston Mills Press, c1979.

**5688. Family Service Centre of Ottawa** *After-four Project: a Research Study to Evaluate the Adjustment of the Families Involved in a Multi-service Demonstration Project of the Family Service Centre of Ottawa.* Family Service Centre of Ottawa. [Ottawa: s.n.], 1968.

**5689. Fanjoy, R.W.** *"The Future of the Deaf Child."* R.W. Fanjoy. Canadian Medical Association Journal 74, 7(Apr. 1, 1956): 533-538.

**5690. Farina, Margaret Radcliffe** *The Relationship of the State to the Family in Ontario: State Intervention in the Family on Behalf of Children.* Margaret Radcliffe Farina. Toronto: University of Toronto, 1982. (CTM no. 58318) Thesis (Ed.D.)--University of Toronto, 1982.

**5691. Farmer, A.W.** *"Congenital Arteriovenous Fistula of the Ear."* A.W. Farmer and A.M. Cloutier. Canadian Medical Association Journal 75, 1(July 1, 1956): 36-37.

**5692. Farmer, Florence A.** *"A Nutrition Survey in Ste. Anne de Bellevue, Quebec."* Florence A. Farmer and Margaret S. McCready. Canadian Journal of Public Health 36, 7(July 1945): 276-284.

**5693. Farmiloe, Dorothy** *Isabella Valancy Crawford: the Life and the Legends.* Dorothy Farmiloe. Ottawa: Tecumseh Press, c1983.

**5694. Farquharson, C.D.** *"Report of an Epidemic of Diphtheria in Scarborough Township."* C.D. Farqharson. Public Health Journal 17, 6(July 1926): 343-344.

**5695. Farquharson, C.D.** *"The Responsibility of the Part-Time Medical Officer with Regard to Schools."* C.D. Farquharson. Canadian Public Health Journal 31, 7(July 1940): 336-338.

**5696. Farrell, Mona** *An Exploratory Study of Some Possible Antecedents and Possible Consequences of I.Q. Changes in an Inner-city Elementary School Population.* Mona Farrell. Montreal: McGill University, 1970. Thesis (M.A.)--McGill University, 1970.

**5697. Feldbrill, Zelda** *The Adjustment of European Youth in the Toronto Jewish Community: a Study of Some of the Problems in the Socio-psychological Adjustment of Twenty-four European Youths from the Ages of Sixteen to Eighteen, Who Came to Toronto Starting October 1947 Under the Auspices of the Canadian Jewish Congress, as Part of the Canadian Government Plan.* Zelda Feldbrill. Toronto: University of Toronto, 1952. Thesis (M.S.W.)--University of Toronto, 1952.

**5698. Feldman, William** *"Severe Metabolic Acidemia in Infants: Clinical and Therapeutic Aspects."* William Feldman, Donald G.H. Stevens and Pierre H. Beaudry. Canadian Medical Association Journal/Journal de l'Association medicale canadienne 94, 7(Feb. 12, 1966): 328-331.

**5699. Felstiner, James P.** *Detached Work: a Report of the First Stage of the University Settlement Project.* James P. Felstiner. Toronto: University of Toronto Press, 1965.

**5700. Felstiner, James P.** *Youth in Need: a Report of the Second Stage of the University Settlement Project.* James P. Felstiner, et al. Toronto: University of Toronto Press, 1966.

**5701. Fenton, Edith** *"Survey of Preschool Children for the Province of Ontario."* Edith Fenton. Canadian Nurse 20, 5(May 1924): 282-286.

**5702. Ferguson, Edith** *Newcomers and New Learning:* Edith Ferguson. [Toronto: International Institute of Metropolitan Toronto, 1966].

**5703. Ferguson, Edith** *Newcomers in Transition.* Edith Ferguson. Toronto: International Institute of Metropolitan Toronto, [1962-1964].

**5704. Ferguson, Helen P.** *"A Nutrition Survey in East York Township: 3. Repetition of Dietary Studies after Two Years."* Helen P. Ferguson and E.W. McHenry. Canadian Journal of Public Health 35, 6(Jun. 1944): 241-248.

**5705. Ferguson, Helen P.** *"A Nutrition Survey in East York Township: 2. The Influence of the Choice of Dietary Standards upon Interpretation of Data."* Helen P. Ferguson, H. Jean Leeson and E.W. McHenry. Canadian Journal of Public Health 35, 2(Feb. 1944): 66-70.

**5706. Ferns, John** *A.J.M. Smith.* John Ferns. Boston: Twayne, c1979.

**5707. Fetherling, Doug** *Hugh Garner.* Doug Fetherling. Toronto: Forum House, c1972.

**5708. Field, G. Rayworth** *Some Relationship Between Variability in School Achievement.* G. Rayworth Field. Toronto: University of Toronto, 1935.
Thesis (M.A.)--University of Toronto, 1935.

**5709. Findlay, Ian I.** *"The Changing Pattern of Rheumatic Fever in Childhood."* Ian I. Findlay and Rodney S. Fowler. Canadian Medical Association Journal/Journal de l'Association medicale canadienne 94, 20(May 14, 1966): 1027-1034.

**5710. Fine, Charles** *"Forty-six Autobiographies of Juvenile Delinquents: a Content Analysis of Themes."* Charles Fine. Canadian Journal of Corrections/Revue canadienne de criminologie 5, 3(July 1963): 163-175.

**5711. Finkelman, Sandra** *Consequences of Teenage Motherhood.* Sandra Finkelman. [Toronto]: Child in the City Programme and the Centre for Urban and Community Studies, University of Toronto, 1982.

**5712. Finlay, Donald G.** *The Mother-Child Relationship after Treatment at a Child Guidance Clinic.* Donald G. Finlay. Toronto: University of Toronto, 1956.
Thesis (M.S.W.)--University of Toronto, 1956.

**5713. Finlay, Douglas** *"Children Without Families."* Douglas Finlay. Canadian Welfare 31, 3(Sept. 1955): 136-141.

**5714. Finnigan, Joan, ed.** *Legacies, Legends and Lies.* Joan Finnigan, ed. Toronto: Deneau, 1985.

**5715. Firth, Edith G., ed.** *The Town of York, 1815-1834: a Further Collection of Documents of Early Toronto.* Edith G. Firth, ed. Toronto: The Champlain Society, 1966.

**5716. Fischler, Stan** *Stan Mikita: the Turbulent Career of a Hockey Superstar.* Stan Fischler. 1st ed. Toronto: General Publishing, c1969.

**5717. Fiser, Vladimir** *The Development of Services for the Juvenile Delinquent in Ontario, 1891-1921.* Vladimir Fiser. Toronto: University of Toronto, 1966. (CTM no. 21388)
Thesis (M.S.W.)--University of Toronto, 1966.

**5718. Fisher, A.D.** *"Social Background: Standards of Child Placing."* A.D. Fisher. Public Health Journal 11, 5(May 1920): 226-230.

**5719. Fisher, John H.** *"Primary Endocardial Fibrioelastosis: a Review of 15 Cases."* John H. Fisher. Canadian Medical Association Journal/Journal de l'Association medicale canadienne 87, 3(July 21, 1962): 105-109.

**5720. Fisher, John H.** *"Spontaneous Pulmonic Interstitial and Mediastinal Emphysema in an Infant."* John H. Fisher. Canadian Medical Association Journal 44, 1(Jan. 1941): 27-29.

**5721. Fitzgerald, Doris** *"Young Diabetics Enjoy Camp, Too."* Doris Fitzgerald. Canadian Nurse 67, 5(May 1971): 51-53.

**5722. Fitzgerald, J.B.** *"The Curative Value of Tetanus Antitoxin With Case Reports."* J.B. Fitzgerald, G.W. Ross and E.Z. Stirrett. Canadian Medical Association Journal 5, 4(Apr. 1915): 308-312.

**5723. Fitzgerald, J.G.** *"An Analysis of Diphtheria Deaths in Ontario."* J.G. Fitzgerald. Public Health Journal 11, 11(Nov. 1920): 485-502.

**5724. Fitzgerald, Pauline** *Feminism and Self Concept in Working Class Adolescent Girls: an Exploration of the Association Between Self-Concept, Delinquency and Perception of the Feminine Role in Working Class Adolescent Girls.* Pauline Fitzgerald and Cerise Morris. Montreal: McGill University, 1971.
Thesis (M.S.W.)--McGill University, 1971.

**5725. Flannery, Regina** *"Witiko Accounts from the James Bay Cree."* Regina Flannery, Mary Elizabeth Chambers and Patricia A. Jelie. Arctic Anthropology 13, 1(1978): 57-77.

**5726. Fleming, A. Grant** *"Child Hygiene."* A. Grant Fleming. Public Health Journal 14, 7(July 1923): 291-301.

**5727. Fleming, A. Grant** *"Montreal Anti-Tuberculosis and General Health League: Report of the Managing Director, Annual Meeting, 1926."* A. Grant Flemming. Public Health Journal 17, 5(May 1926): 205-221.

**5728. Fleming, A. Grant** *"Montreal Anti-Tuberculosis and General Health League."* A. Grant Fleming. Public Health Journal 18, 4(Apr. 1927): 156-170.

**5729. Fleming, A. Grant** *"Study of Infant Deaths in Toronto During the Summer of 1921."* A. Grant Fleming. Public Health Journal 13, 5(May 1922): 199-203.

**5730. Fleming, Mae** *A Method of Evaluating the Home Discipline of the Preschool Child.* Mae Fleming. Toronto: University of Toronto, 1931.
Thesis (M.A.)--University of Toronto, 1931.

**5731. Fleming, Margaret** *A Study of the Reliability and Validity of a Special Test of "Intelligence".* Margaret Fleming. Toronto: University of Toronto, 1936.
Thesis (M.A.)--University of Toronto, 1936.

**5732. Fleming, W.G.** *Education: Ontario's Preoccupation.* W.G. Fleming. Toronto: University of Toronto Press, c1972.

**5733. Fleming, W.G.** *The Expansion of the Educational System.* W.G. Fleming. Toronto: University of Toronto Press, c1971.

**5734. Fleming, W.G.** *Ontario Grade 13 Students: Who Are They and What Happens to Them?* W.G. Fleming. Toronto: Department of Educational Research, Ontario College of Education, 1957.

**5735. Fleming, W.G.** *Ontario Grade 13 Students: Their Aptitude, Achievement and Immediate Destination.* W.G. Fleming. Toronto: Department of Educational Research, Ontario College of Education, 1958.

**5736. Fleming, W.G.** *Schools, Pupils and Teachers.* W.G. Fleming. Toronto: University of Toronto Press, c1971.

**5737. Fletcher, Margaret I.** *The Adult and the Nursery School Child.* Margaret I. Fletcher. Toronto: University of Toronto Press, 1958.

**5738. Flint, Betty M.** *"Babies that Live in Institutions."* Betty Flint. Bulletin of the Institute of Child Study 19, 3(Sept. 1957): 6-9.

**5739. Flint, Betty M.** *The Child and the Institution: a Study of Deprivation and Recovery.* Betty Margaret Flint. [Toronto]: University of Toronto Press, [1966]. Catholic Children's Aid Society of Toronto

**5740. Flint, Betty M.** *"Need Kindergarten Be Too Late?"* Betty Flint. Educational Theory 20, 4(Fall 1970): 399-405, 425.

**5741. Flint, Betty M.** *New Hope for Deprived Children.* Betty Margaret Flint. Toronto: University of Toronto Press, c1978.

**5742. Floch, W.J.** *An Investigation into the Effects of Three Different Training Schedules on the Attainment of the Concept of Conservation of Substance in Kindergarten Children.* W.J. Floch. Toronto: University of Toronto, 1967.
Thesis (Ed.D.)--University of Toronto, 1967.

**5743. Flores, Miguela Bustos** *Some Differences in Cognitive Abilities Between Canadian and Filipino Students.* Miguela Bustos Flores. Toronto: University of Toronto, 1969.
Thesis (Ph.D.)--University of Toronto, 1969.

**5744. Flowers, John Franklin** *Some Aspects of the Kuder Preference Record-personal as an Instrument for Prediction and Guidance in Ontario Secondary Schools.* John Franklin Flowers. Toronto: University of Toronto, 1957.
Thesis (M.Ed.)--University of Toronto, 1957.

**5745. Flowers, John Franklin** *The Viewpoints of Ontario Grade Twelve Students Toward Themselves and Americans.* John F. Flowers. Toronto: University of Toronto, 1958.
Thesis (Ed.D.)--University of Toronto, 1958.

**5746. Flynn, L.J.** *At School in Kingston, 1850-1973: the Story of Catholic Education in Kingston and District.* L.J. Flynn. Kingston, Ont.: Frontenac, Lennox and Addington County Roman Catholic Separate School Board, c1973.

**5747. Foley, A.R.** *"The 1932 Epidemic of Poliomyelitis in Quebec."* A.R. Foley. Canadian Public Health Journal 25, 6(June 1933): 260-274.

**5748. Foley, A.R.** *"An Epidemic of Bacillary Dysentry in Matane, Quebec."* A.R. Foley. Canadian Public Health Journal 27, 3(Mar. 1936): 113-117.

**5749. Foley, A.R.** *"An Outbreak of Paratyphoid B Fever in a Nursery of a Small Hospital."* A.R. Foley. Canadian Journal of Public Health 38, 2(Feb. 1947): 73-75.

**5750. Foley, A.R.** *"A Three-Year Experiment with Combined Diphtheria Toxoid-Pertussis Vaccine."* A.R. Foley. Canadian Journal of Public Health 37, 7(July 1946): 259-267.

**5751. Foote, Anne** *Some Determinants of Reinforcer Effectiveness for Children.* Anne Foote. Toronto: University of Toronto, 1961.
Thesis (M.A.)--University of Toronto, 1961.

**5752. Forrester, Maureen** *Out of Character: a Memoir.* Maureen Forrester and Marci MacDonald. Toronto: McClelland and Stewart, 1986.

**5753. Forsythe, Enid M.** *"Child Welfare Clinics."* Enid M. Forsythe. Public Health Journal 9, 4(Apr. 1918): 169-170.

**5754. Fortier, de la Broquerie** *"Chlorquinaldol (Sterosan)-Hydrocortisone in Skin Disorders of Infants."* de la Broquerie Fortier and Roch Simard. Canadian Medical Association Journal/Journal de l'Association medicale canadienne 81, 12(Dec. 15, 1959): 996-999.

**5755. Fortier, de la Broquerie** *"Clinical Evaluation of Sterosan in Infantile Eczema."* de la Broquerie Fortier and Yves Gregoire. Canadian Medical Association Journal 77, 11(Dec. 1, 1957): 1035-1036.

**5756. Foster, Mrs. W. Garland** *The Mohawk Princess: Being Some Account of the Life of Tekahion-Wake (E. Pauline Johnson).* Mrs. W. Garland Foster. Vancouver: Lions' Gate Publishing, c1931.

**5757. Fotheringham, John Brooks** *Legal Aspects of Mental Retardation.* John B. Fotheringham, H.C. Hutchison, J.W. Mohr, K.G. Gray, V. Hartman, M.D. Tuchtie and R.E. Turner. [Toronto: Toronto Psychiatric Hospital, 1965.]

**5758. Fotheringham, John Brooks** *The Retarded Child and His Family: the Effects of Home and Institution.* John B. Fotheringham, Mora Skelton and Bernard Hoddinott. Toronto: OISE, c1971.

**5759. Foucar, H.O.** *"Rutin in Hydrocele and Oedema."* H.O. Foucar. Canadian Medical Association Journal 60, 4(Apr. 1949): 402-403.

**5760. Foulche-Delbosc, Isabel** *"Women of New France (Three Rivers: 1651-63)."* Isabel Foulche-Delbosc. Canadian Historical Review 21, 2(June 1940): 132-149.

**5761. Fowler, Marion** *Redney: a Life of Sara Jeannette Duncan.* Marion Fowler. Toronto: House of Anansi, c1983.

**5762. Fowler, Rodney S.** *"Accidents in Childhood: a Survey of 150 Cases in Private Paediatric Practice."* Rodney S. Fowler. Canadian Medical Association Journal 79, 4(Aug. 15, 1958): 241-246.

**5763. Fowler, Rodney S.** *"Cat Scratch Disease in Childhood."* R.S. Fowler and J.D. Bailey. Canadian Medical Association Journal/Journal de l'Association medicale canadienne 84, 24(June 17, 1961): 1365-1368.

**5764. Fox, Nora M.** *"New Policies in Child Welfare."* Nora M. Fox Canadian Welfare 32, 2(June 1956): 60-64.

**5765. Fox, William Sherwood** *"School Readers as an 'Educational Force: a Study of a Century of Upper Canada."* William Sherwood Fox. Queen's Quarterly 39, 4(Nov. 1932): 688-703.

**5766. Francey, Ruth E.** *"Psychological Test Changes in Mentally Retarded Children During Training."* Ruth E. Francey. Canadian Journal of Public Health 51, 2(Feb. 1960): 69-74.

**5767. Francis, R.P.** *"The Training Schools Act, 1965 (Ontario)."* R.P. Francis. Saskatchewan Bar Review 31, 2(June 1966): 117-123.

**5768. Francis, S.A.** *The Canadian Home Boy.* S.A. Francis. 2nd ed. London: H. Williams, 1913.

**5769. Francis, Wynne** *Irving Layton and His Works.* Wynne Francis. Toronto: ECW Press, [1984].

**5770. Frankel, Esther B.** *A Study of Methods of Measuring, and Factors Associated with the Social Relationships of Nursery School Children.* Esther B. Frankel. Toronto: University of Toronto, 1944.
Thesis (M.A.)--University of Toronto, 1944.

**5771. Frankling, S.R.** *"A Study of Reading Difficulties in Toronto School Children."* S.R. Frankling. Canadian Medical Association Journal/Journal de l'Association medicale canadienne 85, 5(July 29, 1961): 237-239.

**5772. Frappier, Armand** *"BCG Vaccination and Pulmonary Tuberculosis in Quebec."* Armand Frappier, Marcel Cantin, Lise Davignon, Jacques St. Pierre, Pierre Robillard and Therese Gauthier. Canadian Medical Association Journal/Journal de l'Association medicale canadienne 105, 7(Oct. 9, 1971): 707-710.

**5773. Frappier-Davignon, Lise** *"Staphylococcal Infection in Hospital Nurseries: Influence of Three Different Nursing Techniques."* L. Frappier-Davignon, A. Frappier and J. St. Pierre. Canadian Medical Association Journal/Journal de l'Association medicale canadienne 81, 7(Oct. 1, 1959): 531-536.

**5774. Fraser, Brian J.** *Education for Neighbourhood and Nation: the Educational Work of St. Christopher House, Toronto, 1912-1918.* Brian J. Fraser. Toronto: University of Toronto, 1975.
Thesis (M.A.)--University of Toronto, 1975.

**5775. Fraser, D.T.** *"Duration of Schick Immunity."* D.T. Fraser and K.F. Brandon. Canadian Public Health Journal 27, 12(Dec. 1936): 597-599.

**5776. Fraser, G. Murray** *"Scarlet Fever Immunization."* G. Murray Fraser. Canadian Public Health Journal 29, 11(Nov. 1938): 545-549.

**5777. Fraser, Mary Constance** *The Convalescent Care of Children in Montreal.* Mary Constance Fraser. Montreal: McGill University, 1951.
Thesis (M.S.W.)--McGill University, 1951.

**5778. Fraser, Sylvia** *My Father's House: a Memoir of Incest and Healing.* Sylvia Fraser. 1st ed. Toronto: Doubleday Canada, c1987.

**5779. Fraskel, Sally** *A Study of Movement in Foster Home Care: a Study of One Hundred Children in the Care of the Children's Service Centre Who Were Replaced within a Period from April 1 to September 30 1954.* Sally Fraskel, D. Sexsmith, C. Balch, M. Goodman and M. Zakus. Montreal: McGill University, 1955.
Thesis (M.Sc.)--McGill University, 1955.

**5780. Fred, Beatrice V.** *A Study of Companionship Among Preschool Children.* Beatrice V. Fred. Toronto: University of Toronto, 1933.
Thesis (M.A.)--University of Toronto, 1933.

**5781. Freiman, Lawrence** *Don't Fall Off the Rocking Horse: an Autobiography.* Lawrence Freiman. Toronto: McClelland and Stewart, 1978.

**5782. French, Maida Parlow** *Kathleen Parlow: a Portrait.* Maida Parlow French. Toronto: Ryerson Press, 1967.

**5783. Frender, Robert** *"The Role of Speech Characteristics in Scholastic Success."* Robert Frender, Bruce Brown and Wallace E. Lambert. Canadian Journal of Behavioural Science/Revue canadienne de sciences du comportement 2, 4(Oct. 1970): 299-306.

**5784. Frey, Kenneth D.** *Comparative Occupational Aspirations of Old Order Mennonite and Non-old Order Mennonite Farm Youth.* Kenneth D. Frey. Guelph: University of Guelph, 1971.
Thesis (M.Sc.)--University of Guelph, 1971.

**5785. Friedrich, Otto** *Glenn Gould: a Life and Variations.* Otto Friedrich. Toronto: Lester and Orpen Dennys, 1989.

**5786. Fuhrer, Charlotte** *The Mysteries of Montreal: Memoirs of a Midwife.* Charlotte Fuhrer, edited by W. Peter Ward. Vancouver: University of British Columbia Press, 1984.
Original edition published in 1881.

**5787. Fulford, Robert** *Best Seat in the House: Memoirs of a Lucky Man.* Robert Fulford. Toronto: W. Collins and Sons Canada, c1988.

**5788. Furesz, J.** *"Vaccination of School Children With Live Mumps Virus Vaccine."* J. Furesz and F.P. Nagler. Canadian Medical Association Journal/Journal de l'Association medicale canadienne 102, 11(May 30, 1970): 1153-1155.

**5789. Futcher, Wilfred G.A.** *Scoring for Partial Knowledge in Mathematics Testing: a Study of a Modification and an Extension of Multiple-choice Items Applied to the Testing of Achievement in Mathematics.* Wilfred G.A. Futcher. Toronto: University of Toronto, 1969.
Thesis (Ph.D.)--University of Toronto, 1969.

**5790. Gaffield, Chad** *"Canadian Families in Cultural Context: Hypotheses from the Mid-nineteenth Century."* Chad Gaffield. Canadian Historical Association, Historical Papers/Communications historiques (1979): 48-70.

**5791. Gaffield, Chad** *Cultural Challenge in Eastern Ontario: Land, Family and Education in the Nineteenth Century.* Charles M. Gaffield. Toronto: University of Toronto, 1978. (CTM no. 38721)
Thesis (Ph.D.)--University of Toronto, 1978.

**5792. Gaffield, Chad** *"Dependency and Adolescence on the Canadian Frontier: Orillia, Ontario in the Mid-19th Century."* Chad Gaffield and David Levine. History of Education Quarterly 18, 1(Spring 1978): 35-48.

**5793. Gaffield, Chad** *"Schooling, the Economy and Rural Society in Nineteenth Century Ontario."* Chad Gaffield. Toronto: McClelland and Stewart, c1982. In Childhood and Family in Canadian History, pp. 69-92. Edited by Joy Parr.

**5794. Gagan, David** *Hopeful Travellers: Families, Land, and Social Change in Mid-Victorian Peel County, Canada West.* David Gagan. Toronto: University of Toronto Press, 1981.

**5795. Gagan, David** *""The Prose of Life": Literary Reflections of the Family, Individual Experience, and Social Structure in Nineteenth Century Canada."* David Gagan. Journal of Social History 9, 3(Spring 1976): 367-381.

**5796. Gagan, R.R.** *Disease, Mortality and the Public Health Movement in Hamilton, 1880-1940.* R.R. Gagan. Hamilton: McMaster University, 1981. (CTM no. 52237)
Thesis (M.A.)--McMaster University, 1967.

**5797. Gage, Beatrice** *A Method for Investigating the Moral Judgment of the Young Child.* Beatrice Gage. Toronto: University of Toronto, 1933.
Thesis (M.A.)--University of Toronto, 1933.

**5798. Gagne, Francois** *"Interstitial Plasmacellular (Parasitic) Pneumonia in Infants."* Francois Gagne and Fernand Hould. Canadian Medical Association Journal 74, 8(Apr. 15, 1956): 620-624.

**5799. Gagnon, Eugene** *"Twenty Years' Progress in the Sanitary Conditions of Montreal."* Eugene Gagnon. Canadian Public Health Journal 27, 4(Apr. 1936): 160-164.

**5800. Gairey, Harry** *"A Black Man's Toronto."* Harry Gairey. Polyphony 6, 1(Spring-Summer 1984): 237-239.

**5801. Gaite, Andrew J.H.** *A Study of Retroactive Inhibition and Facilitation in Meaningful Verbal Learning.* Andrew J.H. Gaite. Toronto: University of Toronto, 1968.
Thesis (Ph.D.)--University of Toronto. 1968.

**5802. Gaite, Andrew J.H.** *A Study of the Outcome of Grade Repetition in the Protestant High Schools of Montreal.* Andrew J.H. Gaite. Montreal: McGill University, 1966.
Thesis (M.A.)--McGill University, 1966.

**5803. Gaitskell, Charles Dudley** *Art Education During Adolescence.* Charles D. Gaitskell and Margaret R. Gaitskell. Toronto: Ryerson Press, 1964.

**5804. Gaitskell, Charles Dudley** *Art Education for Slow Learners.* Charles D. Gaitskell and Margaret R. Gaitskell. Toronto: Ryerson Press, c1953, 1955.

**5805. Gaitskell, Charles Dudley** *Art Education in the Kindergarten.* Charles D. Gaitskell and Margaret R. Gaitskell. Toronto: Ryerson Press, c1952.

**5806. Gaitskell, Charles Dudley** *Art Education in the Province of Ontario.* Charles Dudley Gaitskell. Toronto: University of Toronto, 1947.
Thesis (D.Paed.)--University of Toronto, 1947.

**5807. Gaitskell, Charles Dudley** *Arts and Crafts in Our Schools.* C.D. Gaitskell. Toronto: Ryerson Press, c1949, 1961.

**5808. Gaitskell, Charles Dudley** *Children and Their Pictures.* Charles D. Gaitskell. Toronto: Ryerson Press, c1951, 1961.

**5809. Galarneau, Claude** *"Employment Opportunities for Children in Quebec from the 17th to the 19th Centuries."* Claude Galarneau. Montreal: Societe de publication Critere Inc., 1979. In The Professions: Their Growth and Decline, pp. 223-230. Edited by Jacques Dufresne, Yves Mongeau, Jean Proulx and Roger Sylvestre.

**5810. Galilee, Dorothy** *"A Free Day in Grade 3."* Dorothy Galilee. Bulletin of the Institute of Child Study 24, 2(June 1962): 10-12.

**5811. Gallie, J.G.** *"Antenatal Work and Stillbirths."* J.G. Gallie. Public Health Journal 11, 2(Feb. 1920): 62-65.

**5812. Gallie, W.E.** *"Pyloric Stenosis in Infants."* W.E. Gallie and L. Bruce Robertson. Canadian Medical Association Journal 7, 1(Jan. 1917): 1-9.

**5813. Gandy, John M.** *"The Exercise of Discretion by the Police as a Decision-Making Process in the Disposition of Juvenile Offenders."* John M. Gandy. Osgoode Hall Law Journal 8, 1(1970): 329-344.

**5814. Gandy, John M.** *The Exercise of Discretion by the Police in the Handling of Juveniles.* John M. Gandy. Toronto: University of Toronto, 1967.
Thesis (D.S.W.)–University of Toronto, 1967.

**5815. Gardener, Paul A.** *"What it Takes to Crash Tin Pan Alley at Fifteen."* Paul A. Gardener. Toronto: Macmillan of Canada, c1978. In Canada from the Newstands, pp. 101-110. Edited by Val Clery.

**5816. Gardiner, Judith A.** *Sexually Assaulted Children: an Assessment of the Need for Social Work Intervention.* Judith A. Gardiner and Esther R. Hockenstein. Montreal: McGill University, 1969.
Thesis (M.S.W.)–McGill University, 1969.

**5817. Gardner, Robert C.** *"Motivational Variables in Second-language Acquisition."* Robert C. Gardner and Wallace E. Lambert. Canadian Journal of Psychology 13, 4(Dec. 1959): 266-272.

**5818. Garebian, Keith** *William Hutt: a Theatre Portrait.* Keith Garebian. Oakville: Mosaic Press, c1988.

**5819. Garigue, Philippe** *"Family Life."* Philippe Garigue. Ottawa: L'Association canadienne des educateurs de langue francaise, c1967. In Facets of French Canada, pp. 335-355.

**5820. Garigue, Philippe** *"The French-Canadian Family."* Philippe Garigue. Toronto: University of Toronto Press, 1960. In Canadian Dualism: Studies of French-English Relations, pp. 181-200. Edited by Mason Wade.

**5821. Garigue, Philippe** *"The French-Canadian Family."* Philippe Garigue. In La Vie familiale des Canadiens francais, pp. 29-50. By Philippe Garigue.
Reprinted in Canadian Society: Sociological Perspectives, 3rd ed., 1968, pp. 151-166 and abr. 3rd ed., 1971, pp. 126-141. Edited by Bernard R. Blishen, Frank E. Jones, Kasper D. Naegele and John Porter.

**5822. Garner, Hugh** *One Damn Thing After Another.* Hugh Garner. Toronto: McGraw-Hill Ryerson, c1973.

**5823. Garr, G.C.L.** *"A Comparison of Dark Adaptation (Biophatometer) Tests on French and English School Children in a Quebec Community."* G.C.L. Garr and Florence A. Farmer. Canadian Medical Association Journal 44, 1(Jan. 1944): 30-33.

**5824. Garry, C.** *"Gambling in a Lower Class Area: a Preliminary Exploration."* C. Garry and J. Sangster. Toronto: Social Science Publishers, c1968. In Deviant Behaviour in Canada pp. 102-120. Edited by W.E. Mann.

**5825. Gartshore, William M.** *"London Social Services Council Report of Public Health Committee on Infant Mortality."* Lt.-Col. Wm. M. Gartshore and committee. Public Health Journal 12, 10(Oct. 1921): 438-444.

**5826. Gatch, Helen L.** *A Comparison of Learning in a Museum with Learning in a School.* Helen L. Gatch. Toronto: University of Toronto, 1947.
Thesis (M.A.)–University of Toronto, 1947.

**5827. Gauthier, Jacques** *"A Cheese-borne Epidemic of Typhoid Fever."* Jacques Gauthier and A.R. Foley. Canadian Public Health Journal 34, 12(Dec. 1943): 543-556.

**5828. Gauvreau, Leo** *"Purulent Meningitis Due to Bacterium Paratyphosum B Type 3a, in a Newborn."* Leo Gauvreau and J.-Edouard Morin. Canadian Medical Association Journal 60, 2(Feb. 1949): 169-171.

**5829. Geddes, Aubrey K.** *"Myasthenia Gravis Neonatorum."* Aubrey K. Geddes. Canadian Medical Association Journal 72, 10(May 15, 1955): 772-773.

**5830. George, P.M.** *"Social Factors and Educational Aspirations of Canadian High School Students."* P.M. George and H.Y. Kim. Toronto: Holt, Rinehart and Winston, 1971. In Social Process and Institution: the Canadian Case, pp. 352-363. Edited by James E. Gallagher.

**5831. George, Peter J.** *"Socioeconomic Influences on School Attendance: a Study of a Canadian County in 1871."* Peter J. George and Frank T. Denton. History of Education Quarterly 14, 2(Summer 1974): 223-232.

**5832. George, Ruggles** *"Diphtheria Mortality."* Ruggles George. Public Health Journal 14, 8(Aug. 1923): 450-463.

**5833. George, Ruggles** *"Immunization Against Scarlet Fever."* Ruggles George. Public Health Journal 17, 3(Mar. 1926): 101-105.

**5834. Gerin, M. Leon** *"The French Canadian Family: Its Strengths and Weaknesses."* Leon Gerin. Toronto: McClelland and Stewart Ltd., c1964. In French Canadian Society v.1: Sociological Studies, pp. 32-57. Edited by Marcel Rioux and Yves Martin.

**5835. Germain, Georges-Hebert** *Overtime: the Legend of Guy Lafleur.* Georges-Hebert Germain. Markham, Ont.: Viking Press, 1990.

**5836. Gerrish, Ann** *"Dystonia Musculorum Deformans."* Ann Gerrish. Canadian Nurse 48, 7(July 1952): 563-566.

**5837. Gerstein, Reva Appleby** *An Analysis of Infant Behavioral Development.* Reva Appleby Gerstein. Toronto: University of Toronto, 1945.
Thesis (Ph.D.)–University of Toronto, 1945.
Author published article with same title in Bulletin of the Canadian Psychological Association 5, 3(Oct. 1945): 73-75.

**5838. Gibson, Barbara** *Twenty-nine Delinquent Children.* Barbara Gibson. Toronto: University of Toronto, 1955.
Thesis (M.S.W.)–University of Toronto, 1955.

**5839. Gibson, David** *Intellectual Status and the Cardinal Stigmata of Mongolism: a Study in the Dimensions of Mongolism.* David Gibson. Toronto: University of Toronto, 1960.
Thesis (Ph.D.)–University of Toronto, 1960.

**5840. Gidney, R.D.** *"Egerton Ryerson and the Origins of the Ontario Secondary School."* R.D. Gidney and D.A. Lawr. Canadian Historical Review 60, 4(Dec. 1979): 442-465.

**5841. Gidney, R.D.** *"Elementary Education in Upper Canada: a Reassessment."* R.D. Gidney. New York: New York University Press, 1975. In Education and Social Change: Themes from Ontario's Past, pp. 2-26. Edited by Machael B. Katz and Paul H. Mattingly.

**5842. Gidney, R.D.** *"From Voluntarism to State Schooling: the Creation of the Public School System in Ontario."* R.D. Gidney and W.P.J. Millar. Canadian Historical Review 66, 4(Dec. 1985): 443-473.

**5843. Giles, Harry W.** *"The Toronto French School."* H.W. Giles. Bulletin of the Institute of Child Study 30, 1(Spring 1968): 36-37.

**5844. Giles, Harvey A.** *Counseling Services for Young People: a Study of the Counseling Services for Young People Provided by Some Agencies in the Area of Metropolitan Toronto.* Harvey A. Giles. Toronto: University of Toronto, 1948.
Thesis (M.S.W.)–University of Toronto, 1948.

**5845. Gilkison, Augusta J.G.** *"The Six Nations Indians."* Augusta J.G. Gilkison. Ontario Historical Society, Papers and Records 17(1919): 30-32.

**5846. Gill, Mohindra P.** *Pattern of Achievement in Relation to Self Concept and Self Ideal Congruence of Grade 9 Students.* Mohindra P. Gill. Toronto: University of Toronto, 1967.
Thesis (Ed.D.)–University of Toronto, 1967.

**5847. Gillespie, A. Grant** *"One Board's Approach to Teaching French in Elementary Grades."* A. Grant Gillespie. Education Canada 10, 4(Dec. 1970): 62-63.

**5848. Gillett, Margaret** *We Walked Very Warily: a History of Women at McGill.* Margaret Gillett. Montreal: Eden Press Women's Publications, 1981.

**5849. Gingras, G.** *"A Clinical and Statistical Study in Cerebral Palsy Rehabilitation."* G. Gingras, V. Susset, R.R. Lemieux, J.M. Chevrier, G. Huot, R. Voyer, G. Skuhrovsky and C. Quirion. Canadian Medical Association Journal/Journal de l'Association medicale canadienne 80, 5(Mar. 1, 1959): 342-346.

**5850. Gingras, G.** *"Congenital Anomalies of the Limbs: Part 2. Psychological and Educational Aspects."* G. Gingras, M. Mongeau, P. Moreault, M. Dupuis, B. Hebert and C. Corriveau. Canadian Medical Association Journal/Journal de l'Association medicale canadienne 91, 3(July 18, 1964): 115-119.

**5851. Gingras, G.** *Feet Was I to the Lame.* G. Gingras; translated by Joan Chapman. London: Souvenir Press Ltd, 1977.

**5852. Giop, Norma** *The Relationship between Parent-Adolescent Conflict and the Integration of Immigrants.* Norma Giop. Toronto: University of Toronto, 1966.
Thesis (M.S.W.)--University of Toronto, 1966.

**5853. Giraux, Jean** *Significant Factors in the Family Situations of Children Who Came to the Attention of a Child Guidance Service.* Jean Giraux. Toronto: University of Toronto, 1961.
Thesis (M.S.W.)--University of Toronto, 1961.

**5854. Givner, Joan** *Mazo de la Roche: the Hidden Life.* Joan Givner. Toronto: Oxford University Press, c1989.

**5855. Glassco, Leon H.** *Meeting the Needs of Dull Normal Delinquent Boys.* Leon H. Glassco. Toronto: University of Toronto, 1956.
Thesis (M.S.W.)--University of Toronto, 1956.

**5856. Glazebrook, George Parkin** *Life in Ontario: a Social History.* George Parkin Glazebrook. Toronto: University of Toronto Press, c1968.

**5857. Gleason, Aileen May** *A Study of the Relationships that Exist Between the Deceleration in Academic Achievement of Indian Children Integrated in the Separate School of Fort Frances, Ontario, and Their Social Acceptance and Personality Structure.* Aileen May Gleason. Winnipeg: University of Manitoba, 1970. (CTM no. 7440)
Thesis (M.Ed.)--University of Manitoba, 1970.

**5858. Gledhill, Robert B.** *"Transient Synovitis and Legg-Calve-Perthes Disease: a Comparative Study."* Robert. B. Gledhill and J. Murray McIntyre. Canadian Medical Association Journal/Journal de l'Association medicale canadienne 100, 7(Feb. 15, 1969): 311-320.

**5859. Glen, J. Stanley** *The Relationship between the Intelligence and the Achievement of Elementary School Children.* J. Stanley Glen. Toronto: University of Toronto, 1933.
Thesis (M.A.)--University of Toronto, 1933.

**5860. Glick, Barbara Quatsel** *A Comparison Study: Differences in Students' Reactions to Teachers and Teaching over a Six-Year Period (1960-1966).* Barbara Quatsel Glick. Montreal: McGill University, 1969.
Thesis (M.A.)--McGill University, 1969.

**5861. Glynn, Edward L.** *Self-determined and Externally-determined Token Reinforcement in Classroom Learning.* Edward L. Glynn. Toronto: University of Toronto, 1969.
Thesis (Ph.D.)--University of Toronto, 1969.

**5862. Godfrey, Marvin Julian** *A Study of the Academic Achievement and Personal and Social Adjustment of Jewish Moroccan Immigrant Students in the English High Schools of Montreal.* Marvin Julian Godfrey. Montreal: McGill University, 1970. (CTM no. 7049)

**5863. Goldberg, Benjamin** *"Childhood Psychosis or Mental Retardation: a Diagnostic Dilemma. 1. Psychiatric and Psychological Aspects."* Benjamin Goldberg and H.H. Soper. Canadian Medical Association Journal/Journal de l'Association medicale canadienne 89, 20(Nov. 16, 1963): 1015-1019.

**5864. Goldberg, Benjamin** *"Postnatal Psychological Causes of Mental Retardation."* Benjamin Goldberg and Paul Max. Canadian Medical Association Journal/Journal de l'Association medicale canadienne 87, 9(Sept. 1, 1962): 507-510.

**5865. Goldenberg, Susan** *The Thomson Empire.* Susan Goldenberg. Toronto: Methuen, c1984.

**5866. Goldenson, Karen** *Cognitive Development of Indian Elementary School Children on a Southern Ontario Reserve.* Karen Goldenson. Toronto: University of Toronto, 1970.
Thesis (M.A.)--University of Toronto, 1970.

**5867. Goldie, Terry** *Louis Dudek and His Works.* Terry Goldie. Toronto: ECW Press, [1984].

**5868. Goldman, S.E.** *"Massive Haemorrhage from Gastro-Intestinal Tract Following a Compound Fracture."* S.E. Goldman and J. Wener. Canadian Medical Association Journal 60, 1(Jan. 1949): 67-68.

**5869. Goldring, Cecil Charles** *The Intelligence of Children Measured by the Binet-Simon Tests, Compared With Teachers' Estimates and Examination Records of the Same Children.* Cecil Charles Goldring. Toronto: University of Toronto, 1920.
Thesis (M.A.)--University of Toronto, 1920.
No bibliography.

**5870. Goldring, Cecil Charles** *Intelligence Testing in a Toronto Public School.* Cecil Charles Goldring. Toronto: University of Toronto, 1924.
Thesis (D.Paed.)–University of Toronto, 1924.

**5871. Goldring, L.W.** *The Effect of Tonsillar Defects Upon the Attendance, Intelligence and Progress of School Children.* L.W. Goldring. Toronto: University of Toronto, 1939.
Thesis (D.Paed.)–University of Toronto, 1939.

**5872. Goldstick, Isidore** *Modern Languages in the Ontario High School: a Historical Study.* Isidore Goldstick. Toronto: University of Toronto Press, 1928.
Thesis (D.Paed.)–University of Toronto, 1928.

**5873. Goodeve, Mildred D.** *"The Contribution of the Nutritionist to the Health of the Preschool Child."* Mildred D. Goodeve. Canadian Public Health Journal 26, 9(Sept. 1935): 434-439.

**5874. Goodfellow, Allan W.** *Autobiography.* Allan W. Goodfellow. Grand Falls, N.B.: Merritt Printing, 1981.

**5875. Gordon, David Alexander** *Foster Care for Children Coming Into Care as Adolescents: a Follow-up Study in 1950 of a Group of Children Admitted to Care of the Children's Aid Society of Toronto, Aged 11-15 Inclusive at the Time of the First Admission in 1942.* David Alexander Gordon. Toronto: University of Toronto, 1952.
Thesis (M.S.W.)–University of Toronto, 1952.

**5876. Gordon, Gretta H.** *The Adjustment of Two-year-old Children into the Nursery School Situation.* Gretta H. Gordon. Toronto: University of Toronto, 1930.
Thesis (M.A.)–University of Toronto, 1930.

**5877. Gorrie, Kathleen** *"Placement Opportunities for the Exceptional and Problem Child."* Kathleen Gorrie. Child and Family Welfare 13, 3(Sept. 1937): 21-29.

**5878. Gossage, John D.** *"Acute Purulent Meningitis in Children: Experience at the Hospital for Sick Children, Toronto."* John D. Gossage. Canadian Medical Association Journal/Journal de l'Association medicale canadienne 90, 10(Mar. 7, 1964): 615-617.

**5879. Gossage, Peter** *Abandoned Children in Nineteenth Century Montreal.* Peter Gossage. Montreal: McGill University, 1983. (CTM no. 27465)
Thesis (M.A.)–McGill University, 1983.

**5880. Gottschalk, Judith** *"Spatial Organization of Children's Responses to a Pictorial Display."* Judith Gottschalk, M.P. Bryden and M. Sam Rabinovitch. Child Development 35, 3(Sept. 1964): 811-815.

**5881. Gough, William F.** *"A New Approach to Infant Feeding."* Wm. F. Gough. Canadian Medical Association Journal 68, 6(June 1953): 544-545.

**5882. Gouin, Serge** *The Teenage Market in Canada: a Study of High School Students in London, Ontario, and Chicoutimi, Quebec.* Serge Gouin, Bernard Portis and Brian Campbell. London, Ont.: University of Western Ontario, School of Business Administration, 1967.

**5883. Goulding, Arthur M.** *"The Possibilities of a Heart Clinic in a Children's Hospital."* Arthur M. Goulding. Public Health Journal 13, 1(Jan. 1922): 13-19.

**5884. Goulding, Arthur M.** *"A Toronto Experiment."* A.M. Goulding. Public Health Journal 12, 10(Oct. 1921): 445-450.

**5885. Goulet, Y.** *"Gonadal Dysgenesis with Female Habitus: Report of Two Cases."* Y. Goulet, B. LeBoeuf, J. Grignon and C.E. Grignon. Canadian Medical Association Journal/Journal de l'Association medicale canadienne 81, 8(Oct. 15, 1959): 645-648.

**5886. Gourley, I.M.** *"Amaurotic Familial Idiocy (Tay-Sachs Disease) in Non-Hebrew Siblings."* I.M. Gourley and F.W. Wiglesworth. Canadian Medical Association Journal 72, 7(Apr. 1, 1955): 521-524.

**5887. Graff, Harvey J.** *"Literacy and Social Structure in Elgin County, Canada West, 1861."* Harvey J. Graff. Histoire sociale/Social History 6, 11(Apr. 1973): 25-48.

**5888. Graff, Harvey J.** *Literacy and Social Structure in Elgin County, Canada West, 1861.* Harvey J. Graff. Toronto: University of Toronto, 1975.
Thesis (Ph.D.)–University of Toronto, 1975.

**5889. Graff, Harvey J.** *Literacy and Social Structure in the Nineteenth Century City.* Harvey J. Graff. Toronto: University of Toronto, 1975. (CTM no. 26056)
Thesis (Ph.D.)–University of Toronto, 1975.

**5890. Graff, Harvey J.** *The Literacy Myth: Literacy and Social Structure in the Nineteenth-Century City.* Harvey J. Graff. New York: Academic Press, c1979.

**5891. Graff, Harvey J.** *"The Reality Behind the Rhetoric: the Social and Economic Meanings of Literacy in the Mid-nineteenth Century: the Example of Literacy and Criminality."* Harvey J. Graff. Toronto: Macmillan Company of Canada Limited, c1978. In Egerton Ryerson and His Times, pp. 187-220. Edited by Neil McDonald and Alf Chaiton.

**5892. Graff, Harvey J.** *Towards a Meaning of Literacy: Literacy and Social Structure in Hamilton, Ontario 1861.* Harvey J. Graff. Toronto: University of Toronto, 1971.
Thesis (M.A.)--University of Toronto, 1971.

**5893. Graff, Harvey J.** *"Towards a Meaning of Literacy: Literacy and Social Structure in Hamilton, Ontario, 1861."* Harvey J. Graff. New York: New York University Press, 1975. In Education and Social Change: Themes From Ontario's Past, pp. 246-270. Edited by Michael B. Katz and Paul H. Mattingly.

**5894. Graham, A.H.** *"The Dick Test."* A.H. Graham. Public Health Journal 16, 1(Jan. 1925): 7-12.

**5895. Graham, Carol Ann** *Yorkville: an Exploratory Study of the Attitudes of Yorkville Youth towards the Educational System.* Carol Ann Graham. Toronto: University of Toronto, 1968.
Thesis (M.S.W.)--University of Toronto, 1968.

**5896. Graham, David Murray** *Acquisition of an Instrumental Response in Young Children Under Various Conditions of Reinforcement.* David Murray Graham. Toronto: University of Toronto, 1969.
Thesis (Ph.D.)--University of Toronto, 1969.

**5897. Graham, Elizabeth** *Medicine Man to Missionary: Missionaries as Agents of Change Among the Indians of Southern Ontario, 1784-1867.* Elizabeth Graham. Toronto: Peter Martin Associates Limited, c1975.

**5898. Graham, Howard** *Citizen and Soldier: the Memoirs of Lieutenant-General Howard Graham.* Howard Graham. Toronto: McClelland and Stewart, c1987.

**5899. Graham, Joyce R. Pratt** *A Study of Laughter as a Form of Interaction Between Children of Defined Sociometric Relationships.* Joyce R. Pratt Graham. Toronto: University of Toronto, 1951.
Thesis (M.A.)--University of Toronto, 1951.

**5900. Graham, Mary B.** *Interests of Five-, Six- and Seven-year-old Children.* Mary B. Graham. Toronto: University of Toronto, 1945.
Thesis (M.A.)--University of Toronto, 1945.

**5901. Grainger, Allendale** *Charges Made Against Miss M. Rye: Before the Poor Law Board at Islington and Her Reply Thereto.* Allendale Grainger. [S.l.: s.n., 1874?].

**5902. Grant, Gordon Hunter** *Musings on Medicine.* Gordon Hunter Grant. Portland, Or.: Metropolitan Press, 1984.

**5903. Grant, Ian** *"The "Incorrigible" Juvenile: History and Prerequisites of Reform in Ontario."* Ian Grant. Canadian Journal of Family Law/Revue canadienne de droit familial 4, 3(Nov. 1984): 293-318.

**5904. Grant, John Webster** *George Pidgeon: a Biography.* John Webster Grant. Toronto: Ryerson Press, c1962.

**5905. Grant, Judith Skelton** *Robertson Davies.* Judith Skelton Grant. Toronto: McClelland and Stewart, c1978.

**5906. Grapko, Michael F.** *"The Significance of Social Expectancy and Achievement in the Development of Security in School Age Children."* Michael F. Grapko. Bulletin of the Institute of Child Study 22, 3(Sept. 1950): 7-11.

**5907. Gravel, J.A.** *"Surgical Treatment of Aortic Insufficiency."* J.A. Gravel. Canadian Medical Association Journal 72, 8(Apr. 15, 1955): 599-600.

**5908. Gray, Ann Margaret** *Continuity or Change: the Effects on Girls of Coeducational Secondary Schooling in Ontario, 1860-1910.* Ann Margaret Gray. Toronto: University of Toronto, 1979.
Thesis (M.A.)--University of Toronto, 1979.

**5909. Gray, Margaret** *Carl Schaefer.* Margaret Gray, Margaret Rand and Lois Steen. Agincourt, Ont.: Gage Publishing, 1977.

**5910. Greber, Dave** *Rising to Power: Paul Desmarais and Power Corporation.* Dave Greber. Toronto: Methuen, c1987.

**5911. Green, Bernard** *"The Ontario Legitimacy Act, 1961-62."* Bernard Green and B.I. Winter. University of Toronto Law Journal 16, 1(1965-1966): 181-184.

**5912. Green, Bernard** *"Re Mugford: a Case Study in the Interaction of Child-care Agency, Court and Legislature."* Bernard Green. Reports of Family Law 1(1971): 1-18.

**5913. Green, Bernard** *"Trumpets, Justice and Federalism."* Bernard Green. Canadian Journal of Corrections/Revue canadienne de criminologie 8, 4(Oct. 1966): 246-261.

**5914. Green, Elaine Barbara** *A Study of the Factors Influencing the Use of Community Services by Jewish Youth in North York.* Elaine Barbara Green. Toronto: University of Toronto, 1968. Thesis (M.S.W.)--University of Toronto, 1968.

**5915. Green, Gavin Hamilton** *The Old Log School and Huron Old Boys in Pioneer Days.* Gavin Hamilton Green. Goderich, Ont.: Signal-Star Press, 1939.

**5916. Green, Leanne** *"Foster Care and After."* Leanne Greene. Canadian Women Studies/Les cahiers de la femme 10, 2 & 3(Summer/Fall 1989): 41-43.

**5917. Green, Walter H.H.** *The Development of the Vocational School to Meet Community Needs.* Walter H.H. Green. Toronto: University of Toronto, 1941. Thesis (D.Paed.)--University of Toronto, 1941.

**5918. Greene, Alma** *Forbidden Voice: Reflections of a Mohawk Indian.* Alma Greene. Toronto: Hamlyn, [1971].

**5919. Greenglass, Esther R.** *"A Cross-cultural Comparison of Maternal Communication."* Esther R. Greenglass. Child Development 42, 3(Sept. 1971): 685-692.

**5920. Greenhill, Pauline Jane** *So We Can Remember: Showing Family Photographs.* Pauline Jane Greenhill. Ottawa: National Museums of Canada, 1981.

**5921. Greenland, Cyril** *"Services for the Mentally Retarded in Ontario: 1870-1930."* Cyril Greenland. Ontario History 54, 4(Dec. 1962): 267-274.

**5922. Greenwood, Barbara** *Her Special Vision: a Biography of Jean Little.* Barbara Greenwood and Audrey McKim. Toronto: Irwin, c1987.

**5923. Greer, Allan** *"The Pattern of Literacy in Quebec 1745-1899."* A. Greer. Histoire sociale/Social History 11, 22(Nov. 1978): 293-335.

**5924. Greer, Allan** *"The Sunday Schools of Upper Canada."* Allan Greer. Ontario History 67, 3(Sept. 1975): 169-181.

**5925. Gregory, Marion** *A Study of Children's Behaviour with Chosen Companions in an Experimental Play Setting.* Marion Gregory. Toronto: University of Toronto, 1943. Thesis (M.A.)--University of Toronto, 1943.

**5926. Griffin, John D.** *"Education for Mental Health: an Experiment."* John D. Griffin and John R. Seeley. Canadian Education 7, 3(June 1952): 15-25.

**5927. Griffin, John D.** *"Institutional Care of the Mentally Disordered in Canada: a 17th Century Record."* John D. Griffin and Cyril Greenland. Canadian Journal of Psychiatry/Revue canadienne de psychiatrie 26, 4(June 1981): 274-278.

**5928. Griffith, Idris M.** *"Childhood Asthma and Mental Retardation."* Idris M. Griffith. Canadian Medical Association Journal/Journal de l'Association medicale canadienne 93, 25(Dec. 18, 1965): 1316.

**5929. Griffiths, Margaret** *"Staff Training Program: Youth Protection Services, Quebec."* Margaret Griffiths. Canadian Journal of Corrections/Revue canadienne de criminologie 5, 4(Oct. 1963): 354-364.

**5930. Grignon, Marie-Rose** *"Family Health in Montreal."* Marie-Rose Grignon and Maria Olivier. Canadian Nurse 38, 2(Feb. 1942): 109-112.

**5931. Gross, Dora Pishkes** *A Study of the Ontario Training School for Girls.* Dora Pishkes Gross. Toronto: University of Toronto, 1955. Thesis (M.S.W.)--University of Toronto, 1955.

**5932. Gross, George** *Donald Jackson: King of Blades.* George Gross. Toronto: Queen City, c1977.

**5933. Groves, Mrs. W.E.** *"Special Auxiliary Classes."* Mrs. E.W. Groves. Canadian Journal of Mental Hygiene 1, 2(July 1919): 182-187.

**5934. Grusec, Joan E.** *"Power and the Internalization of Self Denial."* Joan E. Grusec. Child Development 42, 1(Mar. 1971): 93-105.

**5935. Grygier, A.P.** *"The January School."* A.P. Grygier. Bulletin of the Institute of Child Study 30, 1(Spring 1968): 39-40.

**5936. Grygier, Tadeusz** *"Juvenile Delinquents or Child Offenders: Some Comments on the First Discussion Draft of an Act Respecting Children and Young Persons."* Tadeusz Grygier. Canadian Journal of Corrections/Revue canadienne de criminologie 10, 3(July 1968): 458-469.

**5937. Grygier, Tadeusz** *"A Minor Note on the Trumpet."* Tadeusz Grygier. Canadian Journal of Corrections/Revue canadienne de criminologie 8, 4(Oct. 1966): 262-267.

**5938. Guest, D.B.** *"Traumatic Chylothorax."* D.B. Guest. Canadian Medical Association Journal 73, 6(Sept. 15, 1955): 476-477.

**5939. Guest, L. Haden** *"The School Clinic."* L. Haden Guest. Public Health Journal 2(1911): 62-64.

**5940. Guest, L. Haden** *"School Clinics."* L. Haden Guest. Public Health Journal 4, 5(May 1913): 272-277.

**5941. Guillet, Edwin Clarence** *Pioneer Life.* Edwin Clarence Guillet. Toronto: Ontario Publishing Co., 1938.

**5942. Guirgis, Samura S.** *Cohesiveness of Groups and Behaviour Patterns: a Study of Training Schools in Ontario.* Samura S. Guirgis. Toronto: University of Toronto, 1964.
Thesis (M.S.W.)--University of Toronto, 1964.

**5943. Gunning, Doris L.** *Girls in Trouble Again: a Study of Care Records of Thirty-six Unmarried Mothers Who Have Had Two or More Pregnancies Out-of-wedlock.* Doris L. Gunning. Toronto: University of Toronto, 1947.
Thesis (M.S.W.)--University of Toronto, 1947.

**5944. Gurney, Helen** *Girls' Sports: a Century of Progress in Ontario High Schools.* Helen Gurney. Don Mills: Ofsaa Publication, [1979?].

**5945. Guy, Hamidol, R.** *The Identity of the Black Child Adopted by White Parents.* Hamidol R. Guy and Jeanette S. Lewis. Montreal: McGill University, 1971.
Thesis (M.S.W.)--McGill University, 1971.

**5946. Hacker, Carlotta** *E. Cora Hind.* Carlotta Hacker. Don Mills: Fitzhenry and Whiteside, c1979.

**5947. Hackett, G.T.** *The History of Public Education for Mentally Retarded Children in the Province of Ontario 1867-1964.* G.T. Hackett. Toronto: University of Toronto, 1969.
Thesis (Ed.D.)--University of Toronto, 1969.

**5948. Haddad, Jane** *"The Construction of Gender Roles in Social Policy: Mothers' Allowances and Day Care in Ontario Before World War II."* Jane Haddad and Stephen Milton. Canadian Woman Studies/Cahiers de la femme 7, 4(Winter 1986): 68-70.

**5949. Haddad, Jane** *Women and the Welfare State: the Introduction of Mothers' Allowances in Toronto in the 1920's.* Jane Haddad. Toronto: University of Toronto, 1986.
Thesis (M.A.)--University of Toronto, 1986.

**5950. Haddad, John N.** *Teenage Canteens In Toronto.* John N. Haddad. Toronto: University of Toronto, 1948.
Thesis (M.S.W.)--University of Toronto, 1948.

**5951. Haig, Kennethe M.** *Brave Harvest: the Life Story of E. Cora Hind.* Kennethe M. Haig. Toronto: Thos. Allen, 1945.

**5952. Hale, Katherine** *Isabella Valancy Crawford.* Katherine Hale. Toronto: Ryerson Press, c1923.

**5953. Haley, Joseph** *"Handicapped Children."* Joseph Haley. In Proceedings and Papers Fourth Annual Canadian Conference on Child Welfare 1923, pp. 171-177.

**5954. Hall, Oswald** *Basic Skills at School and Work: the Study of Albertown, an Ontario Community.* Oswald Hall and Richard Carlton with the assistance of David Donnelly and Steve Elson. Toronto: Ontario Economic Council, c1977.

**5955. Hambleton, Ronald** *Mazo de la Roche of Jalna.* Ronald Hambleton. Toronto: General Publishing, c1966.

**5956. Hamilton, Gladys A.** *An Exploration of Teacher Opinion on What Constitutes Acceptable Writing at the Grade Eleven Level in High School.* Gladys A. Hamilton. Montreal: McGill University, 1966.
Thesis (M.A.)--McGill University, 1966.

**5957. Hamilton, W.D.** *Charles Sangster.* W.D. Hamilton. New York: Twayne, c1971.

**5958. Hamilton, W.D.** *Charles Sangster and His Works.* W.D. Hamilton. Toronto: ECW Press, [1985].

**5959. Hanley, W.B.** *"Neonatal Respiratory Distress: Experience at the Hospital for Sick Children, Toronto, 1960-61."* W.B. Hanley, M. Braudo and P.R. Swyer. Canadian Medical Association Journal/Journal de l'Association medicale canadienne 89, 9(Aug. 31, 1963): 375-381.

**5960. Hanley, W.B.** *"The Newborn Phenylketonuria Screening Program in Ontario."* W.B. Hanley, M.W. Partington, J.C. Rathburn, C.R. Amies, Jean F. Webb and J. Ellis Moore. Canadian Medical Association Journal/Journal de l'Association medicale canadienne 101, 4(Aug. 23, 1969): 185-190.

**5961. Hannah, Beverley** *"The Prevention of Scarlet Fever in a Children's Hospital."* Beverley Hannah. Canadian Public Health Journal 25, 11(Nov. 1934): 587-591.

**5962. Hannah, Beverley** *"The Schick Reaction in the Control of Diphtheria."* Beverley Hannah. Public Health Journal 12, 6(June 1921): 250-253.

**5963. Hanrahan, James Patrick** *Effects of Early School Entrance on Intelligence.* James Patrick Hanrahan. Montreal: McGill University, 1970. Thesis (M.A.)--McGill University, 1970.

**5964. Harding, E.S.** *"Notes on the Outdoor School, Royal Edward Institute."* E.S. Harding. In Proceedings and Papers Fifth Annual Canadian Conference on Child Welfare 1925, pp. 116-121,

**5965. Hardman, R.P.** *"The Enteric Disease Problem in Ontario."* R.P. Hardman. Canadian Public Health Journal 27, 12(Dec. 1936): 600-605.

**5966. Hardman, R.P.** *"A Food Poisoning Epidemic Probably Due to Cheese."* R.P. Hardman and N.E. McKinnon. Canadian Public Health Journal 21, 8(Aug. 1930): 387-393.

**5967. Hardman, R.P.** *"Poliomyelitis in Ontario, 1929."* R.P. Hardman and A.L. McKay. Canadian Public Health Journal 21, 2(Feb. 1930): 76-90.

**5968. Hardy, Madeline I.** *Clinical Follow-up Study of Disabled Readers.* Madeline I. Hardy. Toronto: University of Toronto, 1968. Thesis (Ed.D.)--University of Toronto, 1968.

**5969. Hardy, Madeline I.** *"Disabled Readers: What Happens to Them After Elementary School."* Madeline I. Hardy. Canadian Education and Research Digest 8, 4(Dec. 1968): 338-346.

**5970. Harkness, Ross** *J.E. Atkinson of the Star.* Ross Harkness. Toronto: University of Toronto Press, c1963.

**5971. Harney, Robert F.** *Immigrants: a Portrait of the Urban Experience, 1890-1930.* Robert F. Harney and Harold Troper. Toronto: Van Nostrand Reinhold Ltd., c1975.

**5972. Harney, Robert F., ed.** *Gathering Place: Peoples and Neighbourhoods of Toronto, 1834-1945.* Robert F. Harney, ed. Toronto: Multicultural History Society of Ontario, c1985.

**5973. Harold, Elsie Freeman** *An Analysis of the Success of Methods of Initiating Social Contacts by Young Children.* Elsie Freeman Harold. Toronto: University of Toronto, 1942. Thesis (M.A.)--University of Toronto, 1942.

**5974. Harris, B.E.** *"Prenatal Education in the Home."* B.E. Harris. Canadian Nurse 20, 6(June 1924): 338-342.

**5975. Harris, C. Bryan** *Significant Factors in the Family Situation of Children Who Came to the Attention of a Child Guidance Service.* C. Bryan Harris. Toronto: University of Toronto, 1963. Thesis (M.S.W.)--University of Toronto, 1963.

**5976. Harris, Donald** *Complaints in Families Known to a Child Guidance Clinic.* Donald Harris. Montreal: McGill University, 1953. Thesis (M.S.W.)--McGill Univerity, 1953.

**5977. Harris, L.J.** *"The Effect of Nystatin (Mycostatin) on Neonatal Candidiasis (Thrush): a Method of Eradicating Thrush From Hospital Nurseries."* L.J. Harris, H.G. Pritzker, B. Laski, A. Eisen, J.W. Steiner and L. Stack. Canadian Medical Association Journal 79, 11(Dec. 1, 1958): 891-896.

**5978. Harris, Robin S.** *Quiet Revolution: a Study of the Educational System of Ontario.* Robin S. Harris. [Toronto]: University of Toronto Press, c1967.

**5979. Harris, Shirley** *"Renal Transplant, Nursing Care."* Shirley Harris and John Dossetor. Canadian Nurse 55, 6(June 1959): 508-512.

**5980. Harris, W. Robert** *"The Early Diagnosis of Slipped Femoral Epiphysis."* W. Robert Harris. Canadian Medical Association Journal 72, 11(June 1, 1955): 835-837.

**5981. Harrison, Constance M.** *Foster Homefinding: a Study of Effective Ways of Increasing the Number of Foster Homes Available for Children.* Constance M. Harrison. Toronto: University of Toronto, 1948.
Thesis (M.S.W.)--University of Toronto, 1948. .

**5982. Harrison, Phyllis** *Never Enough: 75 Years With the Children's Aid Society of Ottawa.* Phyllis Harrison. Ottawa: [s.n.], 1968.

**5983. Harron, Martha** *Don Harron: a Parent Contradiction: a Biography.* Martha Harron. 1st. ed. Toronto: W. Collins and Sons Canada, c1988.

**5984. Hart, I.R.** *"Serum Protein-bound Iodine Levels in Adolescents."* I.R. Hart and J.B.J. McKendry. Canadian Medical Association Journal/Journal de l'Association medicale canadienne 97, 10(Sept. 2, 1967): 516-521.

**5985. Hartley, Lucie** *Pauline Johnson: the Story of an American Indian.* Lucie Hartley. Minneapolis: Dillon Press, c1978.

**5986. Harvey, Edward** *"Adolescence, Social Class and Occupational Expectations."* Edward Harvey. Canadian Review of Sociology and Anthropology/Revue canadienne de sociologie et d'anthropologie 7, 2(Apr. 1970): 138-147.

**5987. Harvey, Fernand** *"Children of the Industrial Revolution in Quebec."* Fernand Harvey. Montreal: Societe de publication Critere Inc., 1979. In The Professions: Their Growth and Decline, pp. 251-263. Edited by Jacques Dufresne, Yves Mongeau, Jean Proulx and Roger Sylvestre.
Reprinted in Readings in Canadian History: Post Confederation, pp. 195-204, edited by R. Douglas Francis and Donald B. Smith.

**5988. Harvey, Janice** *Upper Class Reaction to Poverty in Mid-nineteenth Century Montreal: a Protestant Example.* Janice Harvey. Montreal: McGill University, 1978. (CTM no. 39687)
Thesis (M.A.)--McGill University, 1978.

**5989. Harvie, Katharine** *A Comparative Study of Bright and Dull Children of Equal Mental Age.* Katharine Harvie. Toronto: University of Toronto, 1940.
Thesis (M.A.)--University of Toronto, 1940.

**5990. Hawke, William A.** *"Further Considerations Upon the Treatment of Convulsions by Dilantin Sodium."* William A. Hawke. Canadian Medical Association Journal 45, 3(Sept. 1941): 234-236.

**5991. Haworth, Lorne Helen** *A History of Makay School for the Deaf.* Lorne Helen Howarth. Montreal: McGill University, 1960.
Thesis (M.A.)--McGill University, 1960.

**5992. Hawthorne, Allan B.** *"Congenital Anomolies of the Urinary Tract: the Underlying Cause in Many Urinary Infections in Children."* Allan B. Hawthorne. Canadian Medical Association Journal 44, 2(Feb. 1941): 152-154.

**5993. Hawthorne, Allan B.** *"Renal Tuberculosis in Children."* A.B. Hawthorne and M. Siminovich. Canadian Medical Association Journal 60, 3(Mar. 1949): 276-279.

**5994. Hay, J.** *"Cat Scratch Fever: Non-Bacterial Regional Lymphadenitis."* J. Hay. Canadian Medical Association Journal 77, 3(Aug. 1, 1957): 224-225.

**5995. Heagerty, J.J.** *"Relative Value of Sex Education."* J.J. Heagerty. Public Health Journal 15, 6(June 1924): 258-262.

**5996. Heller, Anita Fochs** *Differences Between a French and an English High School, and Between the Educational and Occupational Aspirations of Their Working-Class Students.* Anita Fochs Heller. Montreal: McGill University, 1970. Thesis (M.A.)--McGill University, 1970.

**5997. Henderson, Elmes** *"Reminiscences of Upper Canada College from 1854 to 1857."* Elmes Henderson. Ontario Historical Society, Papers and Records 26(1930): 457-460.

**5998. Henderson, Nora-Francis** *"Child Welfare in Ontario."* Nora-Francis Henderson. Canadian Welfare 20, 3(July 1944): 28-29.

**5999. Hendrick, George** *Mazo de la Roche.* George Hendrick. New York: Twayne, c1970.

**6000. Hennessey, G. Roland** *A Policy Context for the Welfare of Tomorrow's Children in Quebec.* G. Roland Hennessey. Quebec City: Government of Quebec, Commission of Inquiry on Health and Social Welfare, 1970.

**6001. Henripin, Jacques** *"Population and Ecology: From Acceptance of Nature to Control: the Demography of the French Canadians Since the Seventeenth Century."* Jacques Henripin. Toronto: McClelland and Stewart Ltd., c1964. In French Canadian Society, v.1, pp. 204-216. Edited by Marcel Rioux and Yves Martin.
Reprinted from the Canadian Journal of Economics and Political Science 23, (Feb. 1957): 10-19.

**6002. Henry, Franklin J.** *"University Influence on Student Opinion."* Franklin J. Henry. Canadian Review of Sociology and Anthropology/Revue canadienne de sociologie et d'anthropologie 8, 1(Jan. 1971): 18-31.

**6003. Henshaw, J. Jean** *"Ottawa's Garland House."* J. Jean Henshaw. Canadian Welfare 19, 5(Oct. 1943): 21-23.

**6004. Henshaw, Margaret** *"Our Adopted Children."* Margaret Henshaw and Don Henshaw. Canadian Welfare 31, 6(Feb. 1959): 282-286.

**6005. Hepworth, H. Philip** *"Children in Trouble."* H. Philip Hepworth. Canadian Welfare 46, 2(Mar.-Apr. 1970): 12-13.

**6006. Herman, Fredrick Douglas Grant** *The Proximity of Personality and Cognitive Factors in Indian Students.* F. Douglas Herman. Toronto: University of Toronto, 1971. (CTM no. 11583)
Thesis (Ph.D.)--University of Toronto, 1971.

**6007. Herman, Gloria Nanette** *A Comparison of the Thematic Apperception Test Stories of Preadolescent School Children Differing in Social Acceptance.* Gloria Nanette Herman. Toronto: University of Toronto, 1952.
Thesis (M.A.)--University of Toronto, 1952.

**6008. Hermant, Mrs. Percy** *"The Jewish Girls' Club of Toronto."* Mrs. Percy Hermant. Child and Family Welfare 9, 6(Mar. 1934): 50-52.

**6009. Heron, W. Craig** *Working Class Hamilton, 1895-1930.* W. Craig Heron. Halifax: Dalhousie University, 1981. (CTM no. 53699)
Thesis (Ph.D.)--Dalhousie University, 1981.

**6010. Hersak, Zora** *An Analysis of Formal Punishment in Guelph Reformatory.* Zora Hersak. Toronto: University of Toronto, 1966.
Thesis (M.S.W.)--University of Toronto, 1966.

**6011. Hewitt, Foster** *Foster Hewitt: His Own Story.* Foster Hewitt. Toronto: Ryerson Press, c1967.

**6012. Heyman, Richard D.** *Studies in Educational Change.* Richard D. Heyman, Robert F. Lawson and Robert M. Stamp. Toronto: Holt, Rinehart and Winston of Canada, Limited, c1972.

**6013. Hiess, A.** *St. Jean, Quebec, 1871: a Socioeconomic Profile.* A. Hiess. (CTM no. 25335)
Thesis (M.A.)--Concordia University, 1975.

**6014. Hill, C.E.** *"Typhoid Fever in North York Township."* C.E. Hill. Canadian Public Health Journal 24, 1(Jan. 1933): 44-45.

**6015. Hill, Fred** *Migration in the Toronto-Centred (MTARTS) Region.* Frederick Hill. [Toronto]: Centre for Urban and Community Studies, University of Toronto, 1971.

**6016. Hill, Grace** *"Wanted: Boarding Homes for Babies."* Grace Hill. Canadian Welfare 20, 5(Oct. 1944): 24-25.

**6017. Hill, H.W.** *"The Social Service Council of London: Report of the Public Health Committee on the Reduction of Infant Mortality in London."* H.W. Hill. Public Health Journal 14, 12(Dec. 1923): 542-556.

**6018. Hills, Ken** *"The Operation of a Multicultural School."* Ken Hills. Toronto: Urban Alliance on Race Relations, 1977. In The Impact of Multi-ethnicity on Canadian Education, pp. 121-128. Edited by Vincent R. D'Oyley.

**6019. Hincks, C.M.** *"Mentally Deficient Children."* Clarence M. Hincks. Public Health Journal 9, 3(Mar. 1918): 102-105.

**6020. Hindley, Joyce D.** *Treatment Methods and Philosophy of Sunnyside Children's Centre.* Joyce D. Hindley. Toronto: University of Toronto, 1954.
Thesis (M.S.W.)--University of Toronto, 1954.

**6021. Hinton, George C.** *"Childhood Psychosis or Mental Retardation: a Diagnostic Dilemma. 2. Pediatric and Neurological Aspects."* G.C. Hinton. Canadian Medical Association Journal/Journal de l'Association medicale canadienne 89, 20(Nov. 16, 1963): 1020-1024.

**6022. Hinton, George C.** *"Postnatal Organic Causes of Mental Retardation."* G.C. Hinton. Canadian Medical Association Journal/Journal de l'Association medicale canadienne 87, 9(Sept. 1, 1962): 501-507.

**6023. Hinton, Norman A.** *"A Study of Infections Due to Pathogenic Serogroups of Escherichia Coli."* Norman A. Hinton and R.R. MacGregor. Canadian Medical Association Journal 79, 5(Sept. 1, 1958): 359-364.

**6024. Hobbs, Margaret** *"Dead Horses"* and *"Muffled Voices": Protective Legislation, Education and the Minimum Wage for Women in Ontario.* Margaret Hobbs. Toronto: University of Toronto, 1985. Thesis (M.A.)--University of Toronto, 1985.

**6025. Hodgetts, Charles A.** *"Statistics and Publicity in Child Welfare Work."* Chas. A Hodgetts. Public Health Journal 12, 3(Mar. 1921): 107-113.

**6026. Hodgins, Frank Egerton** *"The Mentally Deficient in Ontario: Mr. Justice Hodgin's Recommendations."* Justice Hodgins. Public Health Journal 11, 3(Mar. 1920): 126-134.

**6027. Hodgins, J. George** *The Establishment of Schools and Colleges in Ontario, 1792-1910.* J. George Hodgins. 3 v. Toronto: L.K. Cameron, King's Printer, 1910.

**6028. Hodgins, J. George** *Historical and Other Papers and Documents Illustrative of the Educational System of Ontario, 1853-1868, Volume 3.* J. George Hodgins. Toronto: L.K. Cameron, King's Printer, 1911.

**6029. Hodgson, J.A.** *"Protestant Foster Home Centre."* J.A. Hodgson. Canadian Welfare Summary 15, 1(May 1939): 37-39.

**6030. Hofferd, George W.** *A Study of the Content and Methodology of Ontario Lower School Biology.* George W. Hofferd. Toronto: University of Toronto, 1932. Thesis (D.Paed.)--University of Toronto, 1932.

**6031. Hoffman, I.J.** *An Analysis of Questionnaire, Intelligence Test and Academic Achievement Data for Students at Lawrence Park Collegiate, Toronto, to Determine the Extent of Their Need for Vocational Guidance.* I.J. Hoffman. Toronto: University of Toronto, 1946. Thesis (M.A.)--University of Toronto, 1946.

**6032. Hogan, Timothy** *Second Language Acquisition and Maternal Language Reading Achievement in Grades 4, 5, 6.* Timothy Hogan. Ottawa: University of Ottawa, 1966. Thesis (Ph.D.)--University of Ottawa, 1966.

**6033. Holbrook, J.H.** *"Prevention of Tuberculosis in School Age."* J.H. Holbrook. Public Health Journal 14, 1(Jan. 1923): 19-26.

**6034. Holmes, Alfred** *Voluntary Reading of Toronto Public School Pupils: a Quantitative and Qualitative Study.* Alfred Holmes. Toronto: University of Toronto, 1932. Thesis (D.Paed.)--University of Toronto, 1932.

**6035. Holmes, Rosalie** *Factors Related to Outcome of Treatment in Child Guidance.* Rosalie Holmes. Toronto: University of Toronto, 1957. Thesis (M.S.W.)--University of Toronto, 1957.

**6036. Holt, C.E.** *An Autobiographical Sketch of a Teacher's Life: Including a Residence in the Northern and Southern States, California, Cuba and Peru.* Miss Holt. [Quebec?: s.n.], 1875.

**6037. Homel, Gene Howard** *"Denison's Law: Criminal Justice and the Police Court in Toronto, 1887-1921."* Gene Howard Homel. Ontario History 73, 3(Sept. 1981): 171-186.

**6038. Hoodless, Adelaide** *Report to the Minister of Education, Ontario, on Trade Schools in Relation to Elementary Education.* Adelaide Hoodless. Toronto: King's Printer, 1909.

**6039. Hooper, H.M.** *"The Brampton Story."* H.M. Hooper, S. Keane, A.S. Agar, R. Brayshaw, V.C. Gunn, F. Blum, C.J.Warden, W. Robertson and T.J.B. Anderson. Canadian Journal of Corrections/Revue canadienne de criminologie 4, 3(July 1962): 221-246.

**6040. Hopmans, C.C.** *"Acute Cholecystitis in Children."* C.C. Hopmans. Canadian Medical Association Journal 72, 2(Jan. 15, 1955): 127.

**6041. Hops, Hyman** *Anxiety, Isolation and Aggression in Young Children.* Hyman Hops. Toronto: University of Toronto, 1962. Thesis (M.A.)--University of Toronto, 1962.

**6042. Hops, Hyman** *"Studies of Reinforcement of Aggression: 2. Effects of Emotionally-Arousing Antecedent Conditions."* Hyman Hops and Richard H. Walters. Child Development 34, 3(Sept. 1963): 553-562.

**6043. Horne, Kathryn Anne** *English as a Second Language in Metropolitan Toronto.* Kathryn Anne Horne. Toronto: University of Toronto, 1969.
Thesis (M.A.)--University of Toronto, 1969.

**6044. Horowitz, I.** *"Anencephaly and Spina Bifida in the Province of Quebec."* I. Horowitz and A.D. McDonald. Canadian Medical Association Journal/Journal de l'Association medicale canadienne 100, 16(Apr. 26, 1969): 748-755.

**6045. Hosking, R.S.** *The Family Court: a Short Description of the Toronto Experiment.* R.S. Hosking. Ottawa: Canadian Council on Child and Family Welfare, 1930.

**6046. Houde, Laurent** *"Combined Treatment for Children with Learning Disorders."* Laurent Houde. Canadian Psychologist/Psychologie canadienne 9, 2(Apr. 1968): 174-186.

**6047. Houston, Susan E.** *Impetus to Reform: Urban Crime, Poverty and Ignorance in Ontario, 1850-1875.* Susan E. Houston. Toronto: University of Toronto, 1974. (CTM no. 27954)
Thesis (Ph.D.)--University of Toronto, 1974.

**6048. Houston, Susan E.** *"Late Victorian Juvenile Reform: a Contribution to the Study of Educational History."* Susan E. Houston. Winnipeg: University of Manitoba, 1981. In Approaches to Educational History, pp. 7-23. Edited by David C. Jones, Nancy M. Sheehan, Robert M. Stamp and Neil G. McDonald.

**6049. Houston, Susan E.** *"Politics, Schools and Social Change in Upper Canada."* Susan E. Houston. Canadian Historical Review 53, 3(Sept. 1972): 249-271.
Reprinted in Education and Social Change: Themes from Ontario's Past, pp. 28-56. Edited by Michael B. Katz and Paul H. Mattingly.
Reprinted in Pre-industrial Canada 1760-1849, pp. 161-188. Edited by Michael S. Cross and Gregory Kealey.

**6050. Houston, Susan E.** *Politics, Schools and Social Change in Upper Canada Between 1836 and 1846.* Susan E. Houston. Toronto: University of Toronto, 1967.
Thesis (M.A.)--University of Toronto, 1967.

**6051. Houston, Susan E.** *"School Reform and Education: the Issue of Compulsory Schooling, Toronto, 1851-71."* Susan E. Houston. Toronto: MacMillan Company of Canada Limited, c1978. In Egerton Ryerson and His Times, pp. 254-276. Edited by Neil McDonald and Alf Chaiton.

**6052. Houston, Susan E.** *Schooling and Scholars in Nineteenth-century Ontario.* Susan E. Houston and Alison Prentice. Toronto: University of Toronto Press, c1988.

**6053. Houston, Susan E.** *"Victorian Origins of Juvenile Delinquency: a Canadian Experience."* Susan E. Houston. History of Education Quarterly 12, 3(Fall 1972): 254-280.
Reprinted in Education and Social Change: Themes from Ontario's Past, pp. 83-109. Edited by Michael B. Katz and Paul H. Mattingly.

**6054. Houston, Susan E.** *"The "Waifs and Strays" of a Late Victorian City: Juvenile Delinquents in Toronto."* Susan E. Houston. Toronto: McClelland and Srewart, c1982. In Childhood and Family in Canadian History, pp. 129-142. Edited by Joy Parr.

**6055. Howard, David James** *The True Life Story of David James Howard.* David James Howard. 2d ed. [Thornhill, Ont.: York Printing House Ltd., 1972].

**6056. Howard, R. Palmer** *The Chief: Doctor William Osler.* R. Palmer Howard. Canton Mass.: Science History Publications, 1983.

**6057. Howe, Margaret G.** *"Mental Health Problems Associated with the Only Child."* Margaret G. Howe and Maribeth E. Madgeet. Canadian Psychiatric Association Journal/Revue de l'Association canadienne de psychiatrie 20, 3(Apr. 1975): 189-194.

**6058. Howie, John** *"Scarlet Fever Immunization in Windsor, Ont."* John Howie. Canadian Public Health Journal 33, 10(Oct. 1941): 471-479.

**6059. Hoy, Claire** *Bill Davis: a Biography.* Claire Hoy. Toronto: Methuen, c1985.

**6060. Hoy, Elizabeth A.** *Programming, Labelling and Concept Learning in Retarded Children.* Elizabeth A. Hoy. Montreal: McGill University, 1969.
Thesis (Ph.D.)--McGill University.

**6061. Huestis, Mrs. Archibald M.**
*"Mothers' Pension vs. Provincial Aid for Children."* Mrs. Archibald M. Huestis. Public Health Journal 9, 4(Apr. 1918): 163-168.

**6062. Hughes, Athol** *The Effect of Educational Films on School Children's Learning.* Athol Hughes. Toronto: University of Toronto, 1947.
Thesis (M.A.)—University of Toronto, 1947.

**6063. Hughes, David Richard** *Migration of Young Adults from Frontenac County, Ontario, 1961-1971.* David Richard Hughes. London, Ont.: University of Western Ontario, 1971. (CTM no. 8945)
Thesis (M.A.)—University of Western Ontario, 1971.

**6064. Hughes, Harley J.** *"Evaluation of Nisentil as an Analgesic Agent in Labour."* Harley J. Hughes and Newell W. Philpott. Canadian Medical Association Journal 71, 1(July 1954): 6-8.

**6065. Hughes, James L.** *"National and Ethical Value of Cadet Training."* James L. Hughes and D.J. Goggin, ed. Toronto: Warwick Brothers and Rutter, 1913. In Empire Club of Canada: Addresses Delivered to the Members During the Session of 1911-12, pp. 104-111. Edited by D.J. Goggin.

**6066. Hulet, Marion** *"Blair Athol."* Marion Hulet and K. Hubblethwaite. Waterloo Historical Society Annual Report 54(1966): 33-35.

**6067. Humphrey, A.** *"Abnormalities of the Urinary Tract in Association With Congenital Cardiovascular Disease."* A. Humphry and J.D. Munn. Canadian Medical Association Journal/Journal de l'Association medicale canadienne 95, 4(July 23, 1966): 143-145.

**6068. Humphreys, Edward H.** *Schools in Change: a Comparative Survey of Elementary School Services, Facilities, and Personnel, 1965-1969.* Edward H. Humphreys. Toronto: Ontario Institute for Studies in Education, 1970.

**6069. Humphries, Michael** *"Performance on Several Control-display Arrangements as a Function of Age."* Michael Humphries and Alfred H. Shephard. Canadian Journal of Psychology 9, 4(Dec. 1955): 231-238.

**6070. Hunt, Gail B.** *The Attitudes of the Westmount Community Towards "4424" Drop-in Centre and Youth Clinic.* Gail B. Hunt and Harriet Kolomeir. Montreal: McGill University, 1971.
Thesis (M.S.W.)—McGill University, 1971.

**6071. Hunter, E.A.** *"Water: a Study in Nine-year-olds."* E.A. Hunter and D. Medhurst. Bulletin of the Institute of Child Study 28, 1(Spring 1966): 24-27.

**6072. Hurl, Lorna F.** *"Overcoming the Inevitable: Restricting Child Factory Labour in Late Nineteenth Century Ontario."* Lorna F. Hurl. Labour/Le Travail 21(Spring 1988): 87-121.

**6073. Hurley, G.A.P.** *"Right-Sided Diaphragmatic Hernia."* G.A.P. Hurley. Canadian Medical Association Journal 60, 6(June 1949): 614-615.

**6074. Hurst, Clara E.** *"Citizenship in the Kindergarten."* Clara E. Hurst. Canadian Welfare 17, 1(Apr. 1941): 34-36.

**6075. Husband, Margaret L.** *The Food Preferences of Nursery School Children.* Margaret L. Husband. Toronto: University of Toronto, 1933.
Thesis (M.A.)—University of Toronto, 1933.

**6076. Hutchinson, Felicia D.**
*"Nontuberculous Spinal Epidural Abcess."* Felicia D. Hutchinson. Canadian Medical Association Journal 72, 3(Feb. 1, 1955): 208-210.

**6077. Hutson, R. Leighton** *An Exploratory Study of the Parent-Child Relationship and Academic Achievement.* R. Leighton Hutson. Montreal: University of Montreal, 1969.
Thesis (Ph.D.)--University of Montreal, 1969.

**6078. Hutton, W.L.** *"Epidemic Cerebr-Spinal Meningitis, Brantford, Ontario."* W.L. Hutton. Canadian Public Health Journal 22, 3(Mar. 1931): 135-137.

**6079. Ibe, Milagros D.** *The Effects of Using Estimation in Learning a Unit of Sixth Grade Mathematics.* Milagros D. Ibe. Toronto: University of Toronto, 1971.
Thesis (Ph.D.)—University of Toronto, 1971.

**6080. Inglis, James** *"Age Differences in Successive Responses to Simultaneous Stimulation."* James Inglis and W.K. Caird. Canadian Journal of Psychology 17, 1(Mar. 1963): 98-105.

**6081. Institute of Child Study**
*"Concerning the Institute: the Nursery School."* Institute of Child Study. Bulletin of the Institute of Child Study 21, 2(June 1959): 1-10.

**6082. Irvin, Dick** *Now Back to You, Dick: a Lifetime in Hockey.* Toronto: McClelland and Steward, 1988.

**6083. Irvine, Lucille** *Personality Structures of Truant and Delinquent Boys.* Lucille Irvine. Montreal: McGill University, 1948. Thesis (M.A.)--McGill University, 1948.

**6084. Irwin, Grace** *Three Lives in Mine.* Grace Irwin. Toronto: Irwin, c1986

**6085. Irwin, Joyce** *"The Underprivileged Child at Camp."* Joyce Irwin. Canadian Nurse 64, 9(Sept. 1968): 47-49.

**6086. Isbister, Ruth** *"The Preschool Parent Centre of Ottawa."* Ruth Isbister. Bulletin of the Institute of Child Study 30, 1(Spring 1968): 30-31.

**6087. Ishwaran, K.** *"Calvinism and Social Behavior in a Dutch Canadian Community."* K. Ishwaran. Toronto: Holt, Rinehart and Winston of Canada Ltd., c1971. In The Canadian Family, pp. 297-314. Edited by K. Ishwaran. Reprinted in The Canadian Family Revised as "Family, Church and School in a Dutch Canadian Community", pp. 356-373.

**6088. Italiano, Carlo** *The Sleighs of My Childhood.* Carlo Italiano. Montreal: Tundra Books, c1974.

**6089. Izraeli, Nundi** *The Image of the Recreational and Informal Education Agency in the Minds of a Sample of Juvenile Delinquents.* Nundi Izraeli. Montreal: McGill University, 1961. Thesis (M.S.W.)--McGill University, 1961.

**6090. Jackson, J.R.** *"Mucormycosis of the Central Nervous System."* J.R. Jackson and P.N. Karnauchow. Canadian Medical Association Journal 76, 2(Jan. 15, 1957): 130-133.

**6091. Jackson, R.W.B.** *The Atkinson Study of Utilization of Student Resources in Ontario.* R.W.B. Jackson. Toronto: Department of Educational Research, Ontario College of Education, c1958.

**6092. Jackson, W.O.** *"Report on Poliomyelitis from Hamilton General Hospital."* W.O. Jackson. Canadian Medical Association Journal 74, 3(Feb. 1, 1956): 207-208.

**6093. Jacob, Alice** *Let the Past Go: a Life History.* Alice Jacob and Sarah Preston. Ottawa: National Museums of Canada, 1986.

**6094. Jaenen, Cornelius J.** *"Education for Francization: the Case of New France in the Seventeenth Century."* Cornelius J. Jaenen. Vancouver: University of British Columbia Press, 1986. In Indian Education in Canada, Volume 1: the Legacy, pp. 45-63. Edited by Jean Barman, Yvonne Hebert and Don McCaskill.

**6095. Jaenen, Cornelius J.** *The Role of the Church in New France.* Cornelius J. Jaenen. Toronto: McGraw-Hill Ryerson Ltd., c1976.

**6096. Jaenen, Cornelius J.** *The Role of the Church in New France.* Cornelius J. Jaenen. Ottawa: Canadian Historical Association, c1985.

**6097. Jain, Nilima P.** *Aspects of Juvenile Justice in Toronto.* Nilima P. Jain. Toronto: York University, 1974. (CTM no. 21548) Thesis (LL.M.)--York University, 1974.

**6098. James, Helen D.** *The Scarborough Branch of the Children's Aid Society of Metropolitan Toronto, 1958-1966.* Helen D. James. Toronto: University of Toronto, 1967. Thesis (M.S.W.)--University of Toronto, 1967.

**6099. James, William C.** *A Fur Trader's Photographs: A.A. Chesterfield in the District of Ungava, 1901-1904.* William C. James. Kingston: McGill-Queen's University Press, c1985.

**6100. Jamieson, Elmer** *The Mental Capacity of Southern Ontario Indians.* Elmer Jamieson. Toronto: University of Toronto, 1928. Thesis (D.Paed.)--University of Toronto, [1928].

**6101. Jarvis, Donald L.** *Common Psycho-social Patterns Presented by a Group of Young Boys in a Special Education Setting.* Donald L. Jarvis. Toronto: University of Toronto, 1960. Thesis (M.S.W.)--University of Toronto, 1960.

**6102. Jarvis, George K.** *"The Ecological Analysis of Juvenile Delinquency in a Canadian City."* George K. Jarvis. Toronto: Holt, Rinehart and Winston of Canada, c1972. In Deviant Behaviour and Societal Reaction, pp. 195-211. Edited by Craig L. Boydell, Carl F. Grindstaff and Paul C. Whitehead.

**6103. Jarvis, Julia** *"The Founding of the Girl Guide Movement in Canada, 1910."* Julia Jarvis. Ontario History 62, 4(Dec. 1970): 213-219.

**6104. Jeffrey, Lois** *"Diabetes."* Lois Jeffrey. Canadian Nurse 48, 4(Apr. 1952): 307-308.

**6105. Jelinek Jr., Henry** *On Thin Ice.* Henry Jelinek Jr. and Ann Pinchot. Englewood Cliffs, New Jersey: Prentice-Hall, c1965.

**6106. Jenkin, R.D.T.** *"Medulloblastoma in Children: Radiation Therapy."* R.D.T. Jenkin. Canadian Medical Association Journal/Journal de l'Association medicale canadienne 100, 2(Jan. 11, 1969): 51-53

**6107. Jenkin, R.D.T.** *"Wilms' Tumour: Treatment of 113 Patients From 1960-1971."* R.D.T. Jenkin, J.M.M. Darte, R.D. Jeffs, C.A. Stephens and M.J. Sonley. Canadian Medical Association Journal/Journal de l'Association medicale canadienne 112, 3(Feb. 8, 1975): 308-313.

**6108. Jensen, Peter Kenneth** *The Attitudes Towards Physical Ability and Game Preference of a Selected Group of French and English Canadian Secondary Schools.* Peter Kenneth Jensen. Edmonton: University of Alberta, 1971.
Thesis (M.A.)–University of Alberta, 1971.

**6109. Jephcott, C.M.** *"Lead in Certain Coloured Chalks and the Danger to Children."* C.M. Jephcott. Canadian Public Health Journal 28, 8(Aug. 1937): 391-393.

**6110. Jerome, Laurence** *"Overrepresentation of Adopted Children Attending a Children's Mental Health Clinic."* Laurence Jerome. Canadian Journal of Psychiatry/Revue canadienne de psychiatrie 31, 6(Aug. 1986): 526-531.

**6111. Jewell, Cedric Beresford** *A Reading Comprehension Test for Senior High School Students in Large Urban Areas in Alberta, Canada.* Cedric Beresford Jewell. Eugene, Or.: Oregon University, c1969.
Thesis (Ph.D.)–Oregon University, 1969.

**6112. Joblin, Elgie Ellingham Miller** *The Education of the Indians of Western Ontario.* Elgie Ellingham Miller Joblin. Toronto: University of Toronto, 1946.
Thesis (M.A.)–University of Toronto, 1946.

**6113. Johnson, Evelyn H.C.** *"Chief John Smoke Johnson."* Evelyn H.C. Johnson. Ontario Historical Society, Papers and Records 12(1914): 102-113.

**6114. Johnson, Frances L.** *A Genetic Study of Distraction in Preschool Children.* Frances Lily Johnson. Toronto: University of Toronto, 1930.
Thesis (M.A.)–University of Toronto, 1930.

**6115. Johnson, Judith A.** *The Relationship Between Social Status and Punishments within Three Ontario Reformatories.* Judith A. Johnson. Toronto: University of Toronto, 1965.
Thesis (M.S.W.)–University of Toronto, 1965.

**6116. Johnson, Ross** *"Central Nervous System Manifestations of Chickenpox."* Ross Johnson and Pauline E. Milbourn. Canadian Medical Association Journal/Journal de l'Association medicale canadienne 102, 8(Apr. 25, 1970): 831-834.

**6117. Johnston, Agnes** *Maternal Attitudes and Behaviour in Relation to Children Born Prematurely: a Comparison of Mother-Child Relationships with Respect to Fifty Boys Born Prematurely and Mother-Child Relationships with Respect to Fifty Boys Born at Full Term.* Agnes Johnston. Montreal: McGill University, 1962.
Thesis (M.S.W.)–McGill University, 1962.

**6118. Johnston, Basil H.** *Indian School Days.* Basil H. Johnston. Toronto: Key Porter Books, c1988.

**6119. Johnston, Gordon** *Duncan Campbell Scott and His Works.* Gordon Johnston. [S.l.]: ECW Press, [1983].

**6120. Johnston, Jean** *"Ancestry and Descendants of Molly Brant."* Jean Johnston. Ontario History 63, 2(June 1971): 87-92.

**6121. Johnston, Jean** *"Molly Brant: Mohawk Matron."* Jean Johnston. Ontario History 56, 2(June 1964): 105-124.

**6122. Johnston, Marion Campbell** *The Development of Special Class Programmes for Gifted Children in the Elementary Schools of Ontario from 1910 to 1962.* Marion Campbell Johnston. Toronto: University of Toronto, 1964.
Thesis (Ph.D.)–University of Toronto, 1964.

**6123. Johnston, Marion M.** *"Further Studies of the Etiology of Acute Intestinal Intoxication in Infants and Children."* Marion M. Johnston, Alan Brown and Mildred Kaake. Canadian Public Health Journal 22, 9(Sept. 1931): 441-453.

**6124. Johnston, Nancy Mary Elizabeth** *An Experimental Investigation into the Role of Language in Discrimination Memory and Transfer in Preschool Children.* Nancy Mary Elizabeth Johnston. Toronto: University of Toronto, 1969.
Thesis (Ph.D.)–University of Toronto, 1969.

**6125. Johnston, Robert S.** *Truancy in Children Referred to a Child Guidance Clinic.* Robert S. Johnston. Montreal: McGill University, 1952.
Thesis (M.S.W.)–McGill University, 1952.

**6126. Johnston, W.H.** *"Septicaemia of the Newborn Due to Listeria Monocytogenes."* W.H. Johnston, S.A. Morton, M.H. Wong and T.E. Roy. Canadian Medical Association Journal 73, 5(Sept. 1, 1955): 402-405.

**6127. Johnston, Wendy** *"Keeping Children in School: the Response of the Montreal Roman Catholic School Commission to the Depression of the 1930s."* Wendy Johnston. Canadian Historical Association, Historical Papers/Communications historiques (1985): 193-221.

**6128. Jolliffe, Russell** *The History of the Children's Aid Society of Toronto, 1891-1947.* Russell Jolliffe. Toronto: University of Toronto, 1952.
Thesis (M.S.W.)–University of Toronto, 1952.

**6129. Joly, J.M.** *"Recent Educational Developments in Quebec."* J.M. Joly. Canadian Education and Research Digest 1, 4(Dec. 1961): 21-39.

**6130. Jonas, Holly C.** *Little Burgandy Dropouts from the High School of Montreal.* Holly C. Jonas. Montreal: McGill University, 1971.
Thesis (M.S.W.)–McGill University, 1971.

**6131. Joncas, J.** *"Incidence of Adenovirus Infection: a Family Study."* J. Joncas, A. Moisan and V. Pavilanis. Canadian Medical Association Journal/Journal de l'Association medicale canadienne 87, 2(July 14, 1962): 52-58.

**6132. Joncas, J.** *"Schlerema Neonatorum: Report of an Unusual Case."* J. Joncas. Canadian Medical Association Journal/Journal de l'Association medicale canadienne 80, 5(Mar. 1, 1959): 365-368.

**6133. Jones, Andrew** *"Closing Penetanguishene Reformatory: an Attempt to Deinstitutionalize Treatment of Juveniles Offenders in Early Twentieth Century Ontario."* Andrew Jones. Ontario History 70, 4(Dec. 1978): 227-244.

**6134. Jones, Andrew** *In the Children's Aid: J.J. Kelso and Child Welfare in Ontario.* Andrew Jones and Leonard Rutman. Toronto: University of Toronto Press, c1981.

**6135. Judd, Fernand J.** *The Sentencing Policy of the Juvenile Court of Hamilton.* Fernand J. Judd. Toronto: University of Toronto, 1961.
Thesis (M.S.W.)--University of Toronto, 1961.

**6136. Julian, Marilyn** *"A Season for Sharks."* Marilyn Julian. Branching Out 3, 2(Apr.-June 1976): 25-29, 48.

**6137. Jung, John** *"Modeling Effects in Children on a Successive Word Association Test."* John Jung. Canadian Journal of Psychology/Revue canadienne de psychologie 24, 6(Dec. 1970): 381-388.

**6138. Junger, Paul W.** *"Interstitial Plasma-Cell Pneumonia: Report of a Case Diagnosed During Life."* Paul W. Junger and John Wyllie. Canadian Medical Association Journal 80, 1(Jan. 1, 1959): 35-38.

**6139. Junger, Paul W.** *"An Unusual Case of Infectious Mononucleosis."* Paul W. Junger. Canadian Medical Association Journal/Journal de l'Association medicale canadienne 81, 11(Dec. 1, 1959): 926-929.

**6140. Kabayama, Joan Eleanor** *Educational Retardation Among Non-Catholic Indians at Oka.* Joan Eleanor Kabayama. Montreal: McGill University, 1958.
Thesis (M.A.)–McGill University, 1958.

**6141. Kage, Joseph** *"The Education of a Minority: Jewish Children in Greater Montreal."* Joseph Kage. Toronto: Peter Martin Associates, 1975. In Sounds Canadian: Languages and Cultures in Multi-Ethnic Society, pp. 93-104. Edited by Paul M. Migus.

**6142. Kahn, Annie** *Intake Decisions in Relation to Families with Children: a Study of the Differential Use of Homemaker and Foster Care Services.* Annie Kahn, Nancy Fuller and Adrienne Carter. Montreal: McGill University, 1971. Thesis (M.S.W.)–McGill University, 1971.

**6143. Kalz, Frederick** *"The External Use of Sulfanomides in Dermatology."* Frederick Kalz and Martin V.H. Prinz. Canadian Medical Association Journal 46, 4(Apr. 1942): 457-463.

**6144. Kamin, Leon J.** *"The Taylor Scale: Hunger and Verbal Learning."* Leon J. Kamin and Olga Fedorchak. Canadian Journal of Psychology 11, 4(Dec. 1957): 212-218.

**6145. Kandel, Patricia F.** *"Continuous Epidural Analgesia for Labour and Delivery: Review of 1000 Cases."* Patricia F. Kandel, W.E. Spoerel and R.A.H. Kinch. Canadian Medical Association Journal/Journal de l'Association medicale canadienne 95, 19(Nov. 5, 1966): 947-953.

**6146. Kaplan, Elsie** *The Existence, Measurement and Significance of a Speed Factor in the Abilities of Public School Children.* Elsie Kaplan. Toronto: University of Toronto, 1932.
Thesis (M.A.)–University of Toronto, 1932.

**6147. Kaprielian, Isabel** *"Armenian Supplementary Schools in Southern Ontario."* Isabel Kaprielian. Polyphony 4, 2(Fall-Winter 1982): 67-73.

**6148. Kaprielian, Isabel** *"Creating and Sustaining an Ethnocultural Heritage in Ontario: the Case of Armenian Women Refugees."* Isabel Kaprielian. Toronto: Multicultural History Society of Ontario, c1986. In Looking into My Sister's Eyes: an Exploration in Women's History, pp. 139-153. Edited by Jean Burnet.

**6149. Karagianis, Leslie D.** *Language as a Mediational Variable in Hearing and Deaf Children.* Leslie D. Karagianis. Toronto: University of Toronto, 1968.
Thesis (Ed.D.)–University of Toronto, 1968.

**6150. Karal, Pearl** *An Analysis of the Social Activities of Children Studied Developmentally.* Pearl Karal. Toronto: University of Toronto, 1949.
Thesis (M.A.)–University of Toronto, 1949.

**6151. Katadotis, Peter** *Guidance in a Boys' Club: a Community Organization Approach.* Peter Katadotis. Montreal: McGill University, 1964.
Thesis (M.S.W.)–McGill University, 1964.

**6152. Katz, Michael B.** *"The People of a Canadian City 1851-1852."* Michael B. Katz. Canadian Historical Review 53, 4(Dec. 1972): 402-426.
Reprinted in The Canadian City: Essays in Urban History, pp. 224-248 and The Canadian City: Essays in Urban and Social History, pp. 227-254. Edited by Gilbert A. Stelter and Alan F.J. Artibise.

**6153. Katz, Michael B.** *The People of Hamilton, Canada West: Family and Class in a Mid-nineteenth Century City.* Michael B. Katz. Cambridge: Harvard University Press, 1975.

**6154. Katz, Michael B.** *"Social Structure in Hamilton, Ontario."* Michael B. Katz. New Haven: Yale University Press, 1969. In Nineteenth-century Cities: Essays in the New Urban History, pp. 209-224. Edited by Stephan Thernstrom and Richard Sennett.
Reprinted in Studies in Canadian Social History, pp. 164-188. Edited by Michael Horn and Ronald Sabourin.

**6155. Katz, Michael B.** *"Who Went to School?"* Michael B. Katz. History of Education Quarterly 12, 3(Fall 1972): 432-454.
Reprinted in Education and Social Change: Themes from Ontario's Past, pp. 271-293. Edited by Michael B. Katz and Paul H. Mattingly.

**6156. Katz, Michael B.** *"Youth and Early Industrialization in a Canadian City."* Michael B. Katz and Ian E. Davey. Chicago: University of Chicago Press, 1978. In Turning Points: Historical and Sociological Essays on the Family, pp. S81-S119. Edited by John Demos and Sarane Spence Boocock.
This item is a supplement to the American Journal of Sociology v.84 (1978).

**6157. Katz, Michael B., ed.** *Education and Social Change: Themes from Ontario's Past.* Michael B. Katz and Paul H. Mattingly, eds. New York: New York University Press, c1975.

**6158. Kay, Guy Gavriel** *"Truscott: the Children's Hour: the Darkest Hour."* Guy Gavriel Kay. Toronto: Lester & Orpen Dennys, 1986. In The Scales of Justice, v.2, pp. 1-61. Edited by George Jonas.

**6159. Kay, Marion** *"Toward an Understanding of the Troubled and Troublesome Adolescent."* Marion Kay. Canadian Journal of Corrections/Revue canadienne de criminologie 1, 4(Oct. 1959): 6-11.

**6160. Kazdan, Jerome J.** *"Uveitis in Children."* Jerome J. Kazdan, J. Clement McCulloch and John S. Crawford. Canadian Medical Association Journal/Journal de l'Association medicale canadienne 96, 7(Feb. 18, 1967): 385-391.

**6161. Kealey, Gregory S.** *Hogtown: Working Class Toronto at the Turn of the Century.* Gregory S. Kealey. Toronto: New Hogtown Press, 1974.
Reprinted in Canadian History: Post Confederation, pp. 175-195. Edited by R. Douglas Francis and Donald B. Smith.

**6162. Keddy, J. Arthur** *"Accidents in Childhood: a Report on 17,141 Accidents."* J. Arthur Keddy. Canadian Medical Association Journal/Journal de l'Association medicale canadienne 91, 13(Sept. 26, 1964): 675-680.

**6163. Keech, James** *"Changing Delinquent Behaviour."* James Keech, Frank Bilodeau and Maurice Egan. Canadian Journal of Corrections/Revue canadienne de criminologie 10, 1(Jan. 1968): 311-320.

**6164. Keegan, Gerald** *"Black '47: a Summer of Sorrow."* Gerald Keegan. Toronto: Celtic Arts of Canada, 1988. In The Untold Story: the Irish in Canada, v. 1, pp. 103-153. Edited by Robert O'Driscoll and Lorna Reynolds.

**6165. Keith, A. Murdock** *"Facts About Unmarried Parenthood."* A. Murdock Keith. Canadian Welfare 18, 3(July 1942): 15-16, 40.

**6166. Kelen, A.E.** *"Aseptic Meningitis Due to Frater Type Virus in Ontario."* A. Kelen, J. Lesiak and N.A. Labzoffsky. Canadian Medical Association Journal/Journal de l'Association medicale canadienne 89, 1(July 6, 1963): 29-30.

**6167. Kelen, A.E.** *"An Outbreak of Aseptic Meningitis Due to ECHO 25 Virus."* A.E. Kelen, J.M. Lesiak and N.A. Labzoffsky. Canadian Medical Association Journal/Journal de l'Association medicale canadienne 90, 24(June 13, 1964): 1349-1351.

**6168. Keller, Betty** *Black Wolf: the Life of Ernest Thompson Seton.* Betty Keller. Vancouver: Douglas & McIntyre, c1984.

**6169. Keller, Betty** *Pauline: a Biography of Pauline Johnson.* Betty Keller. Vancouver: Douglas and McIntyre, c1981.

**6170. Kelly, E. Brian** *A History of the Holy Cross Boys' Club.* E. Brian Kelly. Montreal: McGill University, 1967.
Thesis (M.S.W.)--McGill University, 1967.

**6171. Kelly, Gerald O.** *Effects of Praise and Reproof Upon the Muscular Performance of Boys of Different Socioeconomic Status.* Gerald O. Kelly. Montreal: McGill University, 1968.
Thesis (M.A.)--McGill University, 1968.

**6172. Kelso, J.J.** *"Children: Their Care, Training and Happiness as Future Citizens."* J.J. Kelso. Women's Institutes Bulletin 186(Dec. 1910): 9-20.

**6173. Kelso, J.J.** *The Children's Court: an Outline of the Work It Is Intended to Accomplish...* J.J. Kelso. [Toronto?: s.n., 1893?].

**6174. Kelso, J.J.** *Early History of the Humane and Children's Aid Movement in Ontario, 1886-1893.* J.J. Kelso. Toronto: King's Printer, 1911.
Cover title: Protection of Children; Early History of the Humane and Children's Aid Movement in Ontario, 1886-1893.

**6175. Kelso, J.J.** *"Helping Children to Good Citizenship."* J.J. Kelso. Public Health Journal 4, 6(June 1913): 359.

**6176. Kelso, J.J.** *History of the Humane and Children's Aid Movement in Ontario, 1886-1910.* J.J. Kelso. Toronto: William Briggs, 1911.

**6177. Kelso, J.J.** *Neglected and Dependent Children, Ontario: During the Year 1905.* J.J. Kelso. Toronto: Warwick Bros. and Rutter, 1905.

**6178. Kelso, J.J.** *Revival of the Curfew Law.* J.J. Kelso. Toronto: Warwick Bros. and Rutter, 1896.

**6179. Kelso, J.J.** *Social Laws of Canada and Ontario Summarized for the Use of Children's Aid Societies and Social Workers.* J.J. Kelso. [Toronto: s.n., 1914].

**6180. Kelso, J.J.** *Special Report on the Immigration of British Children.* J.J. Kelso. Toronto: King's Printer, 1898.

**6181. Kelso, J.J.** *Thoughts on Child Saving.* J.J. Kelso. Toronto: Warwick Brothers and Rutter, [1898].

**6182. Kendall, Richard V.** *A Study of the Play Activities of Public School Children.* Richard V. Kendall. Toronto: University of Toronto, 1932.
Thesis (M.A.)--University of Toronto, 1932.

**6183. Kerr, James E.** *"The Public Schools of Galt."* James E. Kerr. Waterloo Historical Society Annual Report 14(1926): 186-189.

**6184. Kerr, James E.** *"Recollections of My Schooldays at Tassie's."* James E. Kerr. Waterloo Historical Society Annual Report 3(1915): 20-23.

**6185. Kerr, Mrs. M.H.** *"Defective Children."* Mrs. M.H. Kerr. Public Health Journal 6, 12(Dec. 1915): 620-622.

**6186. Kershner, John R.** *Children's Spatial Representation of Directional Movement and Figure Orientations Along Horizontal and Vertical Dimensions.* John R. Kershner. Toronto: University of Toronto, 1969.
Thesis (Ph.D.)--University of Toronto, 1969.

**6187. Keschner, Dorothee Anna** *Dependence and Independence in Primary School Children.* Dorothee Anna Keschner. Toronto: University of Toronto, 1957.
Thesis (Ph.D.)--University of Toronto, 1957.

**6188. Keschner, Dorothee Anna** *A Study of the Relationship Between Vocabulary Scores and Sociometric Status.* Dorothee Anna Keschner. Toronto: University of Toronto, 1948.
Thesis (M.A.)--University of Toronto, 1948.

**6189. Ketchum, J. Anthony C.** *"The Most Perfect System": Official Policy in the First Century of Ontario's Government Secondary Schools and Its Impact on Students Between 1871 and 1910.* J. Anthony C. Ketchum. Toronto: University of Toronto, 1979.
Thesis (Ed.D.)--University of Toronto, 1979.

**6190. Keys, Erskine** *"Graduating Children from Boarding Homes."* Erskine Keys. Child and Family Welfare 11, 4(Nov. 1935): 18-28.

**6191. Kieran, Sheila** *The Family Matters: Two Centuries of Family Law and Life in Ontario.* Sheila Kieran. Toronto: Key Porter Books, c1986.

**6192. Kilbourn, William** *Toronto Remembered: a Celebration of the City.* William Kilbourn. Toronto: Stoddart, c1984.

**6193. Kileeg, John** *The Family Life and Home Environment of Disturbed Children: a Study Based on the Case Records of the Big Brother Movement and the Big Sister Association of March, 1950, with Particular Reference to the Family Backgrounds and Home Environments of the Children and Adolescents Concerned.* John Kileeg. Toronto: University of Toronto, 1950.
Thesis (M.S.W.)--University of Toronto, 1950.

**6194. Kilgour, Mary** *"A Program for "Institutionally Damaged" Children."* Mary Kilgour. Canadian Welfare 37, 4(July 1961): 171-175.

**6195. Killan, Gerald** *David Boyle: From Artisan to Archeologist.* Gerald Killan. Toronto: Published in association with the Ontario Heritage Foundation by the University of Toronto Press, c1983.

**6196. King, Alan J.C.** *"Ethnicity and School Adjustment."* A.J.C. King. Canadian Review of Sociology and Anthropology/Revue canadienne de sociologie et d'anthropologie 5, 2(May 1968): 84-91.

**6197. King, Alan J.C.** *Social Class in a Secondary School Setting.* Alan John Campbell King. Toronto: University of Toronto, 1964.
Thesis (Ed.D.)--University of Toronto, 1964.

**6198. King, Audrey J.** *"Stress, Cigarette Smoking and Snacking Behaviour in Adolescent Males."* Audrey J. King. Canadian Journal of Public Health 62, 4(July-Aug. 1971): 297-302.

**6199. Kipkie, G.F.** *"Malignant Mesenchymoma (Haemangioblastomyxomatous Variety) in a Five-year-old Boy."* G.F. Kipkie and M. Daria Haust. Canadian Medical Association Journal/Journal de l'Association medicale canadienne 81, 3(Aug. 1, 1959): 179-182.

**6200. Kirck, Harvey** *Nobody Calls Me Mr. Kirck.* Harvey Kirck. Toronto: Collins Publishers, c1985.

**6201. Kirk, W.R.J.** *A Study of the Application of a Battery of Tests in a Reformatory Training School.* W.R.J. Kirk. Toronto: University of Toronto, 1949.
Thesis (M.A.)--University of Toronto, 1949.

**6202. Klein, Isobel M.** *Recidivism Among Juvenile Delinquents: a Study of the Factors Associated with One Hundred and Forty Juvenile Recidivists Who Were First Examined in the Psychiatric Department of the Toronto Family Court in 1940.* Isobel M. Klein. Toronto: University of Toronto, 1949.
Thesis (M.S.W.)--University of Toronto, 1949.

**6203. Klein, Joel Perry** *A Comparison of Methods for Decreasing the Fear Response to a Stressful Film.* Joel P. Klein. Toronto: University of Toronto, 1971.
Thesis (Ph.D.)--University of Toronto, 1971.

**6204. Klotz, Max O.** *"A Report of Two Cases of Spina Bifida."* Max O. Klotz. Canadian Medical Association Journal 9, 4(Apr. 1919): 329-332.

**6205. Klotz, Otto** *"Preston Reminiscences."* Otto Klotz. Waterloo Historical Society Annual Report 8(1920): 171-182.

**6206. Knight, A.P.** *"Medical Inspection of Schools."* A.P. Knight. Queen's Quarterly 15, 2(Oct.-Dec. 1907): 138-146.

**6207. Knowles, Margaret** *Beyond Domesticity: a Study of Female Employment in Paris, Ontario 1881-1891.* Margaret Knowles. Kingston: Queen's University, 1987. (CTM no. 40365)
Thesis (M.A.)--Queen's University, 1987.

**6208. Knowles, Valerie** *First Person: a Biography of Cairine Wilson, Canada's First Woman Senator.* Valerie Knowles. Toronto: Dundurn Press, c1988.

**6209. Knox, Carol Margaret** *Cerebral Lateralization of Function as Reflected in Auditory-perceptual Asymmetries.* Carol Margaret Knox. London, Ont.: University of Western Ontario, c1968.
Thesis (M.A.)--University of Western Ontario, 1968.
National Library of Canada MIC TC-2725.

**6210. Knox, Peggie Harris** *Lawren S. Harris, the Beginning of Vision: Personal Reminiscences.* Peggis Harris Knox. Toronto: Mira Godard Edition, 1982.

**6211. Kobayashi, Jean H.** *A Descriptive Study of Children in the Residence of the Metropolitan Toronto Association for Retarded Children.* Jean H. Kobayashi. Toronto: University of Toronto, 1962.
Thesis (M.S.W.)--University of Toronto, 1962.

**6212. Kodikara, Ananda** *Schooling, Politics and the State: the Pattern of Post Secondary Schooling Changes in Ontario from Post-World War Two (1945) Up to the Bovey Commission (1985).* Ananda Kodikara. Toronto: University of Toronto, 1986.
Thesis (Ph.D.)--University of Toronto, 1986.

**6213. Koerber, Walter F.** *An Evaluation of Some Methods and Procedures in the Teaching of Reading to Non-academic Adolescent Boys.* Walter F. Koerber. Toronto: University of Toronto, 1947.

**6214. Kojder, Apolonja** *"Polish Schools in Toronto."* Apolonja Kojder. Polyphony 6, 2(Fall-Winter 1984): 41-46.
Longer version published in A Community in Transition: the Polish Group in Canada, pp. 7-41.

**6215. Kojder, Apolonja** *"Women and the Polish Alliance of Canada."* Apolonja Kojder. Toronto: Canadian Polish Research Institute, 1985. In A Community in Transition: the Polish Group in Canada, pp. 119-204. Edited by Benedykt Heydenkorn.

**6216. Konada, Lakshmi K.** *Suicidal Behaviour in Children.* Lakshmi K. Konada. Montreal: McGill University, 1969.
Thesis (M.S.W.)--McGill University, 1969.

**6217. Kornbluth, Roslyn** *Some Aspects of What is Important to Adoptive Parents.* Roslyn Kornbluth. Montreal: McGill University, 1957.
Thesis (M.S.W.)--McGill University, 1957.

**6218. Korolewich, Olga S.** *An Evaluation of the Pintner-Cunningham Primary Test in the Toronto Public School Setting.* Olga S. Korolewich. Toronto: University of Toronto, 1950.
Thesis (M.A.)--University of Toronto, 1950.

**6219. Kovaloff, Alexander A.** *An Updated Survey of Career Opportunities for Four Year High School and Community College Graduates.* Alexander A. Kovaloff. Toronto: Ontario Educational Research Council, 1970.

**6220. Kravitz, Henry** *"Unwed Mothers."* Henry Kravitz, Bernard Trossman and R.B. Feldman. Canadian Psychiatric Association Journal/Revue de l'Association canadienne de psychiatrie 11, 6(Dec. 1966): 456-464.

**6221. Kreisel, Henry** *""Has Anyone Here Heard of Marjorie Pickthall?": Discovering the Canadian Literary Landscape."* Henry Kreisel. Edmonton: NeWest Press, c1985 In Another Country: Writings By and About Henry Kreisel, pp. 109-118. Edited by Shirley Neuman.

**6222. Kuitunen-Ekbaum, E.** *"A Case of Dipylidium Caninum in a Child."* E. Kuitunen-Ekbaum. Canadian Journal of Public Health 40, 3(Mar. 1949): 115-116.

**6223. Kuitunen-Ekbaum, E.** *"The Incidence of Enterobiasis."* E. Kuitunen-Ekbaum. Canadian Medical Association Journal 48, 3(Mar. 1943): 229-231.

**6224. Kuitunen-Ekbaum, E.** *"The Incidence of Entrobiasis in Children in a Convalescent Home in Toronto."* E. Kuitunun-Ekbaum. Canadian Public Health Journal 31, 6(June 1940): 287-290.

**6225. Kuitunen-Ekbaum, E.** *"The Occurrence of Enterobius Vermicularis in the Appendix."* E. Kuitunen-Ekbaum and E.M. Morgan. Canadian Public Health Journal 33, 7(July 1942): 340-343.

**6226. Kuitunen-Ekbaum, E.** *"Phenothiazine in the Treatment of Enterobiasis (II)."* E. Kuitunen-Ekbaum. Canadian Journal of Public Health 37, 3(Mar. 1946): 103-113.

**6227. Kurokawa, Minako** *"Acculturation and Mental Health of Mennonite Children."* Minako Kurokawa. Child Development 40, 3(Sept. 1969): 689-705.
Author later named Minako Kurokawa Maykovich.

**6228. Kurokawa, Minako** *"Beyond Integration and Stability: Mental Health of Mennonite Children."* Minako Kurokawa. British Journal of Social Psychiatry 3(1970): 215-226.
Author later named Minako Kurokawa Maykovich.

**6229. Kurokawa, Minako** *"Psychosocial Roles of Mennonite Children in a Changing Society."* Minako Kurokawa. Canadian Review of Sociology and Anthropology/Revue canadienne de sociologie et d'anthropologie 6, 1(Feb. 1969): 15-35.
Author later named Minako Kurokawa Maykovich.

**6230. Levesque, Rene** *Memoirs.* Rene Levesque. Toronto: McClelland and Stewart, c1986.

**6231. L'Esperance, Aileen** *"The Schools of Hemmingford."* Aileen L'Esperance. Chateauguay Valley Historical Society Annual Journal/Journal annuel de la Socieete historique de la Vallee de la Chateauguay 10(1977): 21-26.

**6232. LaBarge, Claire Munroe** *Jewish Youth in the Community: Jewish Identity and Its Relationship to Choices of Friends and Use of Services.* Claire Munroe LaBarge. Toronto: University of Toronto, 1968.
Thesis (M.S.W.)--University of Toronto, 1968.

**6233. Laberge, C.** *"Genetic Aspects of Tyrosinemia in the Chicoutimi Region."* C. Laberge and L. Dallaire. Canadian Medical Association Journal/Journal de l'Association medicale canadienne 97, 18(Oct. 28, 1967): 1099-1100.

**6234. Labzoffsky, N.A.** *"A Survey of Toxoplasmosis among Mentally Retarded Children."* N.A. Labzoffsky, N.A. Fish, E. Gyulai and F. Roughly. Canadian Medical Association Journal/Journal de l'Association medicale canadienne 92, 19(May 8, 1965): 1026-1028.

**6235. Laferriere, Michel** *"The Education of Black Students in Montreal Schools: an Emerging Anglophone Problem, a Non-Existent Francophone Preoccupation."* Michel Laferriere. Regina: Canadian Plains Research Center, 1978. In Ethnic Canadians: Culture and Education, pp. 243-255. Edited by Martin L. Kovacs.

**6236. LaFleur, Mary Ann** *Seventeenth Century New England and New France in Comparative Perspective: Notre Dame des Anges, a Case Study.* Mary Ann LaFleur. Ann Arbor, Mich.: University Micofilms International, c1988.
Thesis (Ph.D.)--University of New Hampshire, 1987.

**6237. Lafleur, Violette C.** *"Utilizing Voluntary Aid."* Violette Lafleur. In Proceedings and Papers Fifth Annual Canadian Conference on Child Welfare 1925, pp. 149-153.

**6238. LaForest, R.A.** *"Outbreak of Aseptic Meningitis (Meningo-Encephalitis) with Rubelliform Rash: Toronto, 1956."* R.A. LaForest, G.A. McNaughton, A.J. Beale, Mairin Clarke, Norma Davis, I. Sultanian and A.J. Rhodes. Canadian Medical Association Journal 77, 1(July 1, 1957): 1-4.

**6239. Laforest, Thomas J.** *Our French-Canadian Ancestors.* Thomas J. Laforest. Palm Harbor, Fla.: LISI Press, c1983.

**6240. Lajeunesse, E.J.** *"The Coming of the First Nun to Upper Canada."* E.J. Lajeuesse. Canadian Catholic Historical Association Report (1955): 27-37.

**6241. Laliberte, Jean** *"Student Social Action."* Jean Laliberte. Our Generation 4, 3(Nov. 1966): 32-39.

**6242. Lambert, Wallace E.** *"A Note on the Relationship of Bilingualism and Intelligence."* Wallace E. Lambert and Elizabeth Anisfield. Canadian Journal of Behavioural Science/Revue canadienne de sciences du comportement 1, 2(Apr. 1969): 123-128.

**6243. Lambert, Wallace E.** *"What Are They Like, These Canadians?: a Social-Psychological Analysis."* Wallace E. Lambert. Canadian Psychologist/Psychologie canadienne 11, 4(Oct. 1970): 303-333.
Reprinted in abridged form in Readings

in Social Psychology: Focus on Canada, pp. 30-48. Edited by David Koulak and Daniel Perlman.

**6244. Lamon, Helen** *A Study of the Colour Selection of Young Children.* Helen Lamon. Toronto: University of Toronto, 1938.
  Thesis (M.A.)–University of Toronto, 1938.

**6245. Lamontagne, Leopold** *"Ontario: the Two Races."* Leopold Lamontagne. Toronto: University of Toronto Press, 1960. In Canadian Dualism: Studies of French-English Relations, pp. 351-373. Edited by Mason Wade.

**6246. Lamy, Paul** *A Study of the Social and Political Orientations of a Sample of Quebec French-speaking and Ontario English-speaking School Children.* Paul Gerard Lamy. Hamilton: McMaster University, 1969.
  Thesis (M.A.)--McMaster University, 1969.

**6247. Landry, Yves** *"The Life Course of Seventeenth Century Immigrants to Canada."* Yves Landry and Jacques Legan. Journal of Family History 12, 1-3(July 1987): 201-212.

**6248. Langevin, Ron** *"Is Curiosity a Unitary Construct?"* Ron Langevin. Canadian Journal of Psychology/Revue canadienne de psychologie 24, 4(Dec. 1971): 360-374.

**6249. Langevin, Ron** *A Study of Curiosity, Intelligence and Creativity.* Ronald Lindsay Andre Langevin. Toronto: University of Toronto, 1970.
  Thesis (Ph.D.)–University of Toronto, 1970.

**6250. Langton, H.H.** *James Douglas: a Memoir.* H.H. Langton. Toronto: University of Toronto Press, 1940.

**6251. Lank, David M.** *Paintings from the Wild: the Art and Life of George McLean.* David M. Lank. Toronto: Brownstone Press, 1981.

**6252. Lapointe, Jean-L.** *"Reorganization of Services in a Large Institution for Mentally Retarded Children."* Jean-L. Lapointe. Canadian Psychiatric Association Journal/Revue de l'Association canadienne de psychiatrie 10, 5(Oct. 1965): 372-376.

**6253. Larke, R.P.B.** *"Interferon in the Cerebrospinal Fluid of Children With Central Nervous System Disorders."* R.P.B. Larke. Canadian Medical Association Journal/Journal de l'Association medicale canadienne 96, 1(Jan. 7, 1967): 21-32.

**6254. Larochelle, J.** *"Experience With 37 Infants With Tryosinemia."* J. Larochelle, A. Mortezai, M. Belanger, M. Tremblay, J.C. Claveau and G. Aubin. Canadian Medical Association Journal/Journal de l'Association medicale canadienne 97, 18(Oct. 28, 1967): 1051-1054.

**6255. Larson, Lyle E.** *"The Family in Contemporary Society and Emerging Family Patterns."* Lyle E. Larson. Ottawa: Vanier Institute of the Family, 1970. In Day Care, a Resource for the Contemporary Family, pp. 25-41. Edited by Roslyn Burshtyn.

**6256. Latimer, Elspeth A.** *Methods of Child Care as Reflected in the Infants' Homes of Toronto.* Elspeth A. Latimer. Toronto: University of Toronto, 1953.
  Thesis (M.S.W.)–University of Toronto, 1953.

**6257. Latzer, Beth Good** *Myrtleville: a Canadian Farm and Family, 1837-1967.* Beth Good Latzer. Carbondale, Ill.: Southern Illinois University Press, c1976.

**6258. Laurendeau, Monique** *Causal Thinking in the Child: a Genetic and Experimental Approach.* Monique Laurendeau and Adrien Pinard. Montreal: Institute of Psychological Research, 1962.

**6259. Laurin, Carroll A.** *"Rheumatoid Disease in Children."* Carroll A. Laurin and J.C. Favreau. Canadian Medical Association Journal/Journal de l'Association medicale canadienne 89, 7(Aug. 17, 1963): 288-300.

**6260. Lavell, W. Stewart** *"New Theories at Work in Canadian Schools."* W. Stewart Lavell. Queen's Quarterly 46, 3(Autumn 1939): 312-219.

**6261. Lavoie-Roux, Therese** *"A Program for Action in Disadvantaged Areas."* Therese Lavoie-Roux. Education Canada 11, 4(Dec. 1971): 65-68.

**6262. Lawr, Douglas A.** *Development of Agricultural Education in Ontario, 1870-1910.* Douglas A. Lawr. Toronto: University of Toronto, 1972.
  Thesis (Ph.D.)–University of Toronto, 1972.

**6263. Lawrence, I. Lillian** *"Child Guidance Clinic."* I. Lillian Lawrence. Canadian Nurse 20, 2(Feb. 1924): 87-92.

**6264. Lawrence, I. Lillian** *"Mental Hygiene From the Standpoint of a Social Nurse."* I. Lillian Lawrence. Canadian Nurse 19, 4(Apr. 1923): 220-226.

**6265. Lawrence, Leonard G.** *"Organization of a Crime Prevention and Juvenile Bureau."* Leonard G. Lawrence. Canadian Journal of Corrections/Revue canadienne de criminologie 4, 3(July 1962): 212-215.

**6266. Layton, Irving** *Waiting for the Messiah: a Memoir.* Irving Layton with David O'Rourke. Toronto: McClelland and Stewart, c1985.

**6267. Le Bourdais, Isabel** *The Trial of Steven Truscott.* I. Le Bourdais. Toronto: McClelland and Stewart, [c1966].

**6268. Le Jeune, Paul** *Travels and Explorations of the Jesuit Missionaries in New France, 1610-1791: Quebec, 1636.* Paul Le Jeune [and] Reuben Gold Thwaites, ed. Cleveland, Ohio: Burrows Brothers Co., 1897.

**6269. Le Jeune, Paul** *Travels and Explorations of the Jesuit Missionaries in New France, 1610-1791: Quebec, 1632-1633.* Paul Le Jeune [and] Reuben Gold Thwaites, ed. Cleveland, Ohio: Burrows Brothers Co., 1898.

**6270. Le Jeune, Paul** *Travels and Explorations of the Jesuit Missionaries in New France, 1610-1791: Hurons and Quebec, 1636-1637.* Paul Le Jeune, Jean de Brebeuf [and] Reuben Gold Thwaites, ed. Cleveland, Ohio: Burrows Brothers Co., 1898.

**6271. Le Jeune, Paul** *Travels and Explorations of the Jesuit Missionaries in New France, 1610-1791: Quebec, 1637.* Paul Le Jeune [and] Reuben Gold Thwaites, ed. Cleveland, Ohio: Burrows Brothers Co., 1898.

**6272. Le Jeune, Paul** *Travels and Explorations of the Jesuit Missionaries in New France, 1610-1791: Hurons and Quebec, 1637-1638.* Paul Le Jeune, Francois Joseph Le Mercier [and] Reuben Gold Thwaites, ed. Cleveland, Ohio: Burrows Brothers Co., 1898.

**6273. Le Jeune, Paul** *Travels and Explorations of the Jesuit Missionaries in New France, 1610-1791: Quebec and Hurons, 1639.* Paul Le Jeune, Hierosme Lalement [and] Reuben Gold Thwaites, ed. Cleveland, Ohio: Burrows Brothers Co., 1898.

**6274. Le Jeune, Paul** *Travels and Explorations of the Jesuit Missionaries in New France, 1610-1791: Quebec and Hurons, 1640.* Paul Le Jeune, Jerome Lalement [and] Reuben Gold Thwaites, ed. Cleveland, Ohio: Burrows Brothers Co., 1898.

**6275. Le Mercier, Francois** *Travels and Explorations of the Jesuit Missionaries in New France, 1610-1791: Lower Canada, Iroquois, Ottawas, 1667-1669.* Francois Le Mercier, Francois de Laval, Marie de S. Bonnaventure [and] Reuben Gold Thwaites, ed. Cleveland, Ohio: Burrows Brothers Co., 1899.

**6276. Lea, Nora** *"The Protection of Our Children."* Nora Lea. Canadian Welfare 17, 7(Jan. 1942): 47-50.

**6277. Leacock, Stephen** *The Boy I Left Behind Me.* Stephen Leacock. Garden City, N.Y.: Doubleday, c1946.

**6278. Leake, Albert H.** *The Vocational Education of Girls and Women.* Albert H. Leake. Toronto: MacMillan, c1918.

**6279. Leat, Marion** *Effects of Consequences to Film-mediated Model on Children's Resistance to Temptation.* Marion Leat. Toronto: University of Toronto, 1962. Thesis (M.A.)–University of Toronto, 1962.

**6280. Lebeaux, Charles N.** *Maladjusted Children in Grades Three Through Eight of the Schools of Windsor: a Report to the Sub-committee on Children and Youth with Emotional and Behavior Problems, of the Community Welfare Council of Windsor.* Charles N. Lebeaux. [Windsor: s.n.], 1958.

**6281. LeClair, Maurice** *"A Case of Fatal Cyclic Vomiting."* Maurice LeClair. Canadian Medical Association Journal 74, 8(Apr. 15, 1956): 641-642.

**6282. Leclerc, Aurelien** *Claude Ryan, a Biography.* Aurelien Leclerc, translated by Colleen Kurtz. Toronto: NC Press Limited, 1980.

**6283. Lee, Jean E.** *Drop-in Centres of Metropolitan Toronto: a Descriptive Study of the Families of the Teens in Attendance.* Jean E. Lee. Toronto: University of Toronto, 1967. · Thesis (M.S.W.)–University of Toronto, 1967.

**6284. Lee, Marjorie Ann** *A Study of Decision-making in Families Who Foster Children: an Overall View of the Project.* Marjorie Ann Lee. Toronto: University of Toronto, 1967. Thesis (M.S.W.)–University of Toronto, 1967.

**6285. Leeder, Frederick S.** *"An Outbreak of Milk-Borne Typhoid Fever."* Frederick S. Leeder. Canadian Public Health Journal 23, 11(Nov. 1932): 503-506.

6286. Leers, W.D. *"A Survey of Reovirus Antibodies in Sera of Urban Children."* W.D. Leers and K.R. Rozee. Canadian Medical Association Journal/Journal de l'Association medicale canadienne 94, 20(May 14, 1966): 1040-1042.

6287. Leeson, H. Jean *"Nutrition Problems of Preschool Children."* H. Jean Leeson. Canadian Journal of Public Health 37, 7(July 1946): 279-283.

6288. Leeson, H. Jean *"A Study of Nutritional Conditions in a Group of Urban Children."* H.J. Leeson, R. Virtue Crawford, J.F. Webb, F. Swan, J.E. Davey, L.A. Clarke and E.W. McHenry. Canadian Journal of Public Health 37, 3(Mar. 1946): 97-102.

6289. Leeson, H. Jean *"The Value of the Wetzel Grid in the Examination of School Children."* H. Jean Leeson, E.W. McHenry and W. Mosiey. Canadian Journal of Public Health 38, 10(Oct. 1947): 491-195.

6290. Legate, David M. *Stephen Leacock: a Biography.* David M. Legate. Toronto: Doubleday Canada, c1970.

6291. Leighton, Margaret *"Handmaids' Tales: Family Benefits Assistance and the Single-mother-led Family."* Margaret Leighton. University of Toronto Faculty of Law Review 45, 2(Fall 1987): 324-354.

6292. Leithwood, K.A. *Complex Gross Motor Learning and its Influence on Personal and Social Adjustment in Four-year-old Children.* K.A. Leithwood. Toronto: University of Toronto, 1969. Thesis (Ph.D.)--University of Toronto, 1969.

6293. Leithwood, K.A. *"Complex Motor Learning in Four-year-olds."* K.A. Leithwood and W. Fowler. Child Development 42, 3(Sept. 1971): 781-792.

6294. Lemmon, Walter *The Use of Group Work Methods in the Boy Scouts Association.* Walter Lemmon. Toronto: University of Toronto, 1948. Thesis (M.S.W.)--University of Toronto, 1948.

6295. Lemon, Eleanor *"Achieving Adoption Through Publicity."* Eleanor Lemon. Canadian Welfare 32, 3(Sept. 1956): 120-125.

6296. Lenskyj, Helen *"Femininity First: Sport and Physical Education for Ontario Girls, 1890-1930."* Helen Lenskyj. Canadian Journal of History of Sport/Revue canadienne de l'histoire des sports 13, 2(Dec. 1982): 4-17.

6297. Lenskyj, Helen *The Role of Physical Education in the Socialization of Girls in Ontario, 1890-1930.* Helen Lenskyj. Toronto: University of Toronto, 1983. (CTM no. 59828) Thesis (Ph.D.)--University of Toronto, 1983.

6298. Lenskyj, Helen *"Training for "True Womanhood": Physical Education for Girls in Ontario Schools, 1890-1920."* Helen Lenskyj. Historical Studies in Education/Revue d'histoire de l'education 2, 2(Fall 1990): 205-223.

6299. Lenskyj, Helen *"We Want to Play, ... Will Play: Women in Sport in the Twenties and Thirties."* Helen Lenskyj. Canadian Woman Studies/Cahiers de la femme 4, 3(Spring 1983): 15-18.

6300. Leonard, Alvin Kiel *Over-agedness and Under-agedness in the Elementary School of Ontario.* Alvin Kiel Leonard. Toronto: University of Toronto, 1926. Thesis (M.A.)--University of Toronto, 1926.

6301. Leslie, Baily *A Social Analysis of Juvenile Delinquents.* Baily Leslie. Toronto: University of Toronto, 1929. Thesis (M.A.)--University of Toronto, 1929.

6302. Lessard, Alphonse *"The County Health Unit as a Solution to the Problem of Infant Health in Rural Districts."* Alphonse Lessard. Canadian Public Health Journal 22, 4(Apr. 1931): 174-177.

6303. Levesque, Andree *"Deviant Anonymous: Single Mothers at the Hospital de la Misericorde in Montreal, 1929-1939."* Andree Levesque. Canadian Historical Association, Historical Papers/Communications historiques (1983): 168-184.

6304. Levine, Paul *A Follow-up Study of the Social Adjustment of Children's Aid Society Wards and Non-wards Discharged from Thistletown Hospital.* Paul Levine. Toronto: University of Toronto, 1966. Thesis (M.S.W.)--University of Toronto, 1966.

6305. Lewis, E.P. *"Some Mental Abnormalities of Childhood."* E.P. Lewis. Public Health Journal 19, 12(Dec. 1928): 559-562.

6306. Lewis, Elmer N. *Memory: Learning, Retention, and Forgetting of Public School Pupils.* Elmer N. Lewis. Toronto: University of Toronto, 1934. Thesis (D.Paed.)--University of Toronto, 1934.

**6307. Lewis, Jane** *"Motherhood Issues During the Late Nineteenth and Early Twentieth Centuries: Some Recent Viewpoints."* Jane Lewis. Ontario History 75, 1(Mar. 1983): 4-20.

**6308. Lewis, Jane** *"The Prevention of Diphtheria in Canada and Britain 1914-1945."* Jane Lewis. Journal of Social History 20, 1(Fall 1986): 163-176.

**6309. Lewis, Ralph H.** *Guidance in the Secondary Schools.* Ralph H. Lewis. Toronto: Ryerson, 1946.

**6310. Lewis, Ruth** *"Speech and the Cleft Palate Child."* Ruth Lewis. Canadian Medical Association Journal 71, 6(Dec. 1954): 600-603.

**6311. Lewis, Ruth** *A Study in Training Children of Very Low Mentality in Eliminative Control.* Ruth Lewis. Toronto: University of Toronto, 1930.
Thesis (M.A.)--University of Toronto, 1930.

**6312. Libby, Bill** *Phil Esposito: Hockey's Greatest Scorer.* Bill Libby. Toronto: Longman Press, c1975.

**6313. Light, Beth** *"Mothers and Children in Canadian History."* Beth Light. Canadian Women's Studies 2, 1(Autumn 1980): 102.

**6314. Light, Beth** *"Women in Toronto."* Beth Light. Canadian Women's Studies 3, 1(Autumn 1981): 90-91.

**6315. Lindsay, Lionel M.** *"A Case of Rheumatic Fever with Purpura Adema of the Glottis, etc."* Lionel M. Lindsay. Canadian Medical Association Journal 8, 4(Apr. 1918): 352-354.

**6316. Lindsay, Lionel M.** *"Diabetes Mellitus in a Child of Three."* Lionel M. Lindsay. Canadian Medical Association Journal 7, 2(Feb. 1917): 133-135.

**6317. Lindsay, Lionel M.** *"Infantile Eczema and Status Lymphaticus."* Lionel M. Lindsay. Canadian Medical Association Journal 7, 2(Feb. 1917): 135-136.

**6318. Lindsay, Lionel M.** *"Purpuric Measles."* Lionel M. Lindsay. Canadian Medical Association Journal 8, 1(Jan. 1918): 49.

**6319. Line, S. William** *"World Mental Health."* S. William Line. Bulletin of the Institute of Child Study 23, 3-4(Sept.-Dec. 1961): 23-24.

**6320. Linn, J.R.** *The Influence of Theme Environment on Grade 1 Reading Achievement.* J.R. Linn. Toronto: University of Toronto, 1955.
Thesis (D.Paed.)--University of Toronto, 1955.

**6321. Linsao, L.S.** *"Negative Pressure Artificial Respiration: Use in Treatment of Respiratory Distress Syndrome of the Newborn."* L.S. Linsao, A. Aharon, H. Levison and P.R. Swyer. Canadian Medical Association Journal/Journal de l'Association medicale canadienne 102, 6(Mar. 28, 1970): 602-606.

**6322. Lipman, Marvin H.** *Relocation and Family Life: a Study of the Social and Psychological Consequences of Urban Renewal.* Marvin H. Lipman. Toronto: University of Toronto, 1968.
Thesis (D.S.W.)--University of Toronto, 1968.

**6323. Lipsky, Marlene** *Social Role and Role Perception Among Inmates in Guelph Reformatory.* Marlene Lipsky. Toronto: University of Toronto, 1966.
Thesis (M.S.W.)--University of Toronto, 1966.

**6324. Little, Jean** *Little by Little: a Writer's Education.* Jean Little. Markham: Penguin, c1987.

**6325. Little, William T.** *"A Guarantee of the Legal Rights of Children Through Legal Aid."* William T. Little. Law Society Gazette 4, 4(Dec. 1970): 217-228.

**6326. Little, William T.** *"Some Dynamics in Open Type Correctional Institutions."* William T. Little. Canadian Journal of Corrections/Revue canadienne de criminologie 1, 2(Apr. 1958): 27-29.

**6327. Livesay, Dorothy** *Right Hand, Left Hand.* Dorothy Livesay. Erin: Press Porcepic, c1977.

**6328. Lloyd, David** *"Drug Misuse in Teenagers."* David Lloyd. Canadian Nurse 66, 9(Sept. 1970): 46-51.

**6329. Loeb, Nora** *The Educational and Psychological Significance of Social Acceptability and Its Appraisal in an Elementary School Setting.* Nora Loeb. Toronto: University of Toronto, 1941.
Thesis (M.A.)--University of Toronto, 1941.

**6330. Logan, Lillian M.** *Design for Creative Teaching.* Lillian M. Logan and Virgil G. Logan. Toronto: Mcgraw-Hill Co. of Canada, 1971.

**6331. Logan, M. Anne** *School's Out: a Pictorial History of Ontario's Converted Schoolhouses.* Anne M. Logan. Ontario: Boston Mills Press, 1987.

**6332. Lomer, T.A.** *"Report of an Epidemic of Poliomyelitis in Ottawa, 1929."* T.A. Lomer and W.T. Shirreff. Canadian Public Health Journal 21, 2(Feb. 1930): 53-67..

**6333. London Child Welfare Association. Supervising Nurse** *"The Well-baby Clinics in London, Canada: January 1st to December 31st, 1924."* Supervising Nurse of the London Child Welfare Association. Public Health Journal 16, 5(May 1925): 201-204.

**6334. Long, Janet** *"Observations in a Bilingual Agency."* Janet Long. Child and Family Welfare 11, 3(Sept. 1935): 10-12.

**6335. Loranger, Phil** *Cowboy on Ice: the Howie Young Story.* Phil Loranger. Winnipeg: Gateway Publishing, c1975.

**6336. Lorimer, James** *Working People: Life in a Downtown Neighbourhood.* James Lorimer and Myfanwy Phillips. Toronto: James Lewis and Samuel Ltd. Publishers, c1971.

**6337. Lorimer, Rowland M.** *The Acquisition of Moral Judgments in Adolescence: the Effects of an Exposition of Basic Concepts Versus Exposure to and Discussion of a Filmed Dramatic Example.* Rowland M. Lorimer. Toronto: University of Toronto, 1968. (CTM no. 5232)
    Thesis (Ph.D.)--University of Toronto, 1968.

**6338. Lorimer, Rowland M.** *"Changes in the Development of Moral Judgements in Adolescence: the Effect of a Structured Exposition vs. a Film and Discussion."* Rowland Lorimer. Canadian Journal of Behavioural Science/Revue canadienne de sciences du comportement 3, 1(Jan. 1971): 1-10.

**6339. Lowenstein, Louis** *"Haemolytic Disease of the Newborn Due to Rh Isoimmunization: a Ten-Year Review with Emphasis on Exchange Transfusion."* Louis Lowenstein and Morris Sabin. Canadian Medical Association Journal 77, 8(Oct. 15, 1957): 807-814.

**6340. Lutes, Jack R.** *Social and Economic Differences Between Public Assistance Families and Self Supporting Families in Regent Park (South).* Jack R. Lutes. Toronto: University of Toronto, 1954.
    Thesis (M.S.W.)--University of Toronto, 1954.

**6341. McBurney, Margaret** *Homesteads.* Margaret McBurney and Mary Byers. Toronto: University of Toronto Press, 1979.

**6342. McCaffery, Dan** *Billy Bishop, Canadian Hero.* Dan McCaffery. Toronto: J. Lorimer, 1988.

**6343. McCallum, J.W.** *The Effect of Activity Group Experience on Social and Emotional Adjustment of Mentally Defective Boys.* J.W. McCallum. Toronto: University of Toronto, 1954.
    Thesis (M.A.)--University of Toronto, 1954.

**6344. McCarthy, Bill** *"Gender, Delinquency and the Great Depression: a Test of Power-Control Theory."* Bill McCarthy and John Hagan. Canadian Review of Sociology and Anthropology/Revue canadienne de sociologie et d'anthropologie 24, 2(May 1987): 153-177.

**6345. McCaw, William Ralph** *Non-institutional Training of Retarded Children in Ontario.* William Ralph McCaw. Evanston, Illinois: Northwestern University, 1956.
    Thesis (Ph.D.)--Northwestern University, 1956.

**6346. McClelland, Harold** *"Results of a Series of Schick Tests."* Harold McClelland. Public Health Journal 16, 2(Feb. 1925): 66-70.

**6347. McClinton, James B.** *"Obstructive Goitre in a Deaf Mute."* James B. McClinton. Canadian Medical Association Journal 48, 2(Feb. 1943): 135-136.

**6348. McClure, Kathryn H.** *Services Given by the Children's Aid and Infant's Homes of Toronto as Seen by a Group of Ex-wards of this Agency.* Kathryn H. McClure. Toronto: University of Toronto, 1956.
    Thesis (M.S.W.)--University of Toronto, 1956.

**6349. McClure, Wallace B.** *"A Severe Nursery Epidemic of Diarrhoea Associated with Esch. Coli Type 111 B4."* Wallace B. McClure. Canadian Medical Association Journal 72, 2(Jan. 15, 1955): 83-85.

**6350. McColl, Peter** *A Study of Value Systems as Related to Punishment in Ontario Reformatories.* Peter McColl. Toronto: University of Toronto, 1966.
    Thesis (M.S.W.)--University of Toronto, 1966.

**6351. McCollum, Edith M.** *A Study of Male Juvenile Delinquency in the City of Toronto.* Edith M. McCollum. Toronto: University of Toronto, 1932.
Thesis (M.A.)–University of Toronto, 1932.

**6352. McConnachie, Kathleen** *"Methodology in the Study of Women in History: a Case Study of Helen MacMurchy, M.D."* Kathleen McConnachie. Ontario History 75, 1(Mar. 1983): 61-70.

**6353. McConney, Florence S.** *"Renal Dwarfism."* Florence S. McConney, Jessie McGeachy and Anna Gelber. Canadian Medical Association Journal 49, 5(Nov. 1943): 415-417.

**6354. McCook, Edith** *"Citizens' Committee on Children."* Edith McCook. Canadian Welfare 32, 2(June 1956): 69-72.

**6355. McCorkell, Evelyn** *The Request for Adoption Placement of Legitimate Children.* Evelyn McCorkell. Toronto: University of Toronto, 1957.
Thesis (M.S.W.)–University of Toronto, 1957.

**6356. McCorriston, Lila Redmond** *"Hydrocortisone (Compound F) Acetate Ointment in Eczema of Infants and Children."* Lila Redmond McCorriston. Canadian Medical Association Journal 70, 1(Jan. 1954): 59-62.

**6357. McCrae, John** *"A Study of Eight Hundred and Fifty Cases of Scarlet Fever with a More Particular Consideration of Seventy-one Fatal Cases: Part I."* John McCrae. Canadian Medical Association Journal 1, 4(Apr. 1911): 293-310.

**6358. McCrae, John** *"A Study of Eight Hundred and Fifty Cases of Scarlet Fever with a More Particular Consideration of Seventy-one Fatal Cases: Part II."* John McCrae. Canadian Medical Association Journal 1, 5(May 1911): 389-403.

**6359. McCullough, George D.** *Moral Developmental Profile Variability: its Relationship to Choice of Preferred Stage of Moral Reasoning and to Rokeach's Open-Closed Belief System.* George D. McCullough. Toronto: University of Toronto, 1969.
Thesis (Ph.D.)–University of Toronto, 1969.

**6360. McCutcheon, J.M.** *Public Education in Ontario.* J.M. McCutcheon. Toronto: [s.n.], 1941.

**6361. McDiarmid, Garnet Leo** *The Challenge of a Differential Curriculum: Ontario's Indian Children.* Garnet Leo McDiarmid. Toronto: Ontario Institute for Studies in Education, [196.

**6362. Macdonald, Cathy** *"The Best Canadian Female Athlete of 1936."* Cathy Macdonald. Canadian Woman Studies/Cahiers de la femme 4, 3(Spring 1983): 20-21.

**6363. MacDonald, Cheryl** *Adelaide Hoodless: Domestic Crusader.* Cheryl MacDonald. Toronto: Durdurn Press Ltd., c1986.

**6364. MacDonald, Cheryl** *Emma Albani: Victorian Diva.* Cheryl MacDonald. Toronto: Dundurn Press, 1984.

**6365. MacDonald, D.S.** *An Interest Questionnaire for Secondary School Boys.* D.S. MacDonald. Toronto: University of Toronto, 1939.
Thesis (M.A.)–University of Toronto, 1939.

**6366. MacDonald, Donald D.** *Sight-saving Classes in the Public Schools.* Donald D. MacDonald. Toronto: University of Toronto, [1923].
Thesis (D.Paed.)–University of Toronto, [1923].

**6367. MacDonald, E. Mae** *"Parents Participate in the Care of the Hospitalized Child."* E. Mae MacDonald. Canadian Nurse 65, 12(Dec. 1969): 37-39.

**6368. McDonald, Frances S.** *A Study of the Development of Empathy on a Group of Primary School Children.* Frances S. McDonald. Toronto: University of Toronto, 1953.
Thesis (M.A.)–University of Toronto, 1953.

**6369. MacDonald, Gayle Michelle** *Incest and the Law: the Legislation Pertaining to Children.* Gayle Michelle MacDonald. Ottawa: University of Ottawa, 1984. (CTM no. 67547)
Thesis (M.A.)–University of Ottawa, 1984.

**6370. MacDonald, George** *Uniformity in the Academic Subjects of the Industrial Course.* George MacDonald. Toronto: University of Toronto, 1952.
Thesis (D.Paed.)–University of Toronto, 1952.

**6371. MacDonald, I.L.** *The Status of Women in the Province of Quebec.* I.L. MacDonald. Montreal: Canadian Reconstruction Association, 1920.
Thesis (M.A.)–McGill University, 1920.
Published version of the thesis.

6372. **MacDonald, J.A.** *"Meconium Ileus: an Eleven-Year Review at the Hospital For Sick Children, Toronto."* J.A. MacDonald and G.A. Trusler. Canadian Medical Association Journal/Journal de l'Association medicale canadienne 83, 17(Oct. 22, 1960): 881-885.

6373. **MacDonald, James C.** *Provisional Memorandum on the Juvenile Court of the Family Court of Metropolitan Toronto.* James C. MacDonald. [Toronto: Cronish], 1967.

6374. **MacDonald, Maggie** *The Violent Years of Maggie MacDonald: an Autobiography.* Maggie MacDonald with Allan Gould. Scarborough: Prentice-Hall Canada Inc., c1987.

6375. **McDonald, Neil G.** *Forming the National Character: Political Socialization in Ontario Schools, 1867-1914.* Neil G. McDonald. Toronto: University of Toronto, 1980.
Thesis (Ph.D.)–University of Toronto, 1980.

6376. **McDonald, Neil G.** *"Political Socialization Research, the School and the Educational Historian."* Neil G. McDonald. Winnipeg: University of Manitoba, 1981. In Approaches to Educational History, pp. 65-84. Edited by David C. Jones, Nancy M. Sheehan, Robert M. Stamp and Neil G. McDonald.

6377. **MacDonald, Thoreau** *Notebooks.* Thoreau MacDonald. Moonbeam, Ont.: Penumbra Press, 1980.

6378. **MacDonald, V.M.** *"Child Welfare Work in Montreal."* V.M. MacDonald. Canadian Nurse 19, 11(Nov. 1923): 663-665.

6379. **Macdonell, Margaret E.** *The "Advantaged" High School Dropout.* Margaret E. Macdonell. Montreal: McGill University, 1970.
Thesis (M.S.W.)–McGill University, 1970.

6380. **McDougall, Bruce** *Charles Mair.* Bruce McDougall. Don Mills: Fitzhenry and Whiteside, c1978.

6381. **MacDougall, Charles S.** *"Malnutrition in Children of School Age."* Charles S. MacDougall. Public Health Journal 16, 1(Jan. 1925): 25-35.

6382. **MacDougall, James Colin** *Early Auditory Deprivation and Visual Behaviour.* James Colin MacDougall. Montreal: McGill University, 1969.
Thesis (Ph.D.)–McGill University, 1969.

6383. **McDougall, Ruth** *"Traffic Accidents to Children."* Ruth McDougall. Canadian Medical Association Journal/Journal de l'Association medicale canadienne 82, 2(Jan. 9, 1960): 61-65.

6384. **McFadden, Fred** *Abby Hoffman.* Fred McFadden. Don Mills: Fitzhenry and Whiteside, c1978.

6385. **McFarland, Elda** *An Analysis of the Paintings of Preschool Children.* Elda McFarland. Toronto: University of Toronto, 1932.
Thesis (M.A.)–University of Toronto, 1932.

6386. **McFarland, Mary P.** *An Analysis of the Social Contacts of Fifteen Preschool Children.* Mary McFarland. Toronto: University of Toronto, 1937.
Thesis (M.A.)–University of Toronto, 1937.

6387. **MacFarlane, Eleanor** *The Relationship between Social Acceptance and Academic Achievement in Elementary School Children.* Eleanor MacFarlane. Toronto: University of Toronto, 1956.
Thesis (M.A.)–University of Toronto, 1956.

6388. **McFarlane, George G.** *The Probation Officer's Study and Treatment of Delinquent Youth.* George G. McFarlane. [Toronto]: Department of the Attorney General, Probation Services Branch, 1967.

6389. **MacFarlane, Margaret Ann** *The Efficacy of the Group Work Method with Youth Groups, in Achieving the Objectives of a Religious Agency: a Study of a Girls' Auxiliary Group, of the Church of England, in Toronto, Ontario, 1950.* Margaret Ann MacFarlane. Toronto: University of Toronto, 1950.
Thesis (M.S.W.)–University of Toronto, 1950.

6390. **Macfie, John** *Parry Sound: Logging Days.* John Macfie. Erin, Ont.: Boston Mills Press, 1987.

6391. **McGill, Jean S.** *Edmund Morris, Frontier Artist.* Jean S. McGill. Toronto: Dundurn Press, 1984.

6392. **McGill, Jean S.** *The Joy of Effort: a Biography of R. Tait McKenzie.* Jean McGill. Bewdley, Ont.: Distributed by Clay Publishing Company, c1980.

6393. **McGillivray, Robert Hilker** *Differences in Home Background Between High and Low Achieving Gifted Children.* Robert Hilker McGillivray. Toronto: University of Toronto, 1963.
Thesis (Ed.D.)–University of Toronto, 1963.

**6394. McGowan, Mark George** *"We Are All Canadians": a Social, Religious and Cultural Portrait of Toronto's English-speaking Roman Catholics, 1890-1920.* Mark George McGowan. Toronto: University of Toronto, 1988. Thesis (Ph.D.)--University of Toronto, 1988.

**6395. McGreal, Douglas A.** *"Brain Abscess in Children."* Douglas A. McGreal. Canadian Medical Association Journal/Journal de l'Association medicale canadienne 86, 6(Feb. 10, 1962): 261-268.

**6396. McGreal, Douglas A.** *"A Survey of Cerebral Palsy in Windsor and Essex County, Ontario."* Douglas A. McGreal. Canadian Medical Association Journal/Journal de l'Association medicale canadienne 95, 24(Dec. 10, 1966): 1237-1240.

**6397. MacGregor, R.R.** *"Naphthalene Poisoning from the Ingestion of Mothballs."* R.R. MacGregor. Canadian Medical Association Journal 70, 3(Mar. 1954): 313-314.

**6398. MacGregor, Roy** *Chief: the Fearless Vision of Billy Diamond.* Roy MacGregor. Markham, Ontario: Viking, 1989.

**6399. MacHaffie, Lloyd P.** *"Ringworm of the Scalp in Ottawa School Children, 1946-1947."* L.P. MacHaffie, S.F. Penny and E.C. Beck. Canadian Journal of Public Health 38, 3(Mar. 1948): 89-94.

**6400. MacHaffie, Lloyd P.** *"School Health Problems."* Lloyd P. MacHaffie. Canadian Medical Association Journal 44, 5(May 1941): 501-503.

**6401. McHenry, E.W.** *"Confusion and Stupidity in Nutrition Education."* E.W. McHenry. Canadian Journal of Public Health 40, 6(June 1949): 270-274.

**6402. McHenry, E.W.** *"Nutrition in Toronto."* E.W. Henry. Canadian Public Health Journal 29, 1(Jan. 1938): 4-13.

**6403. McHenry, E.W.** *A Report on Food Allowances for Relief Recipients in the Province of Ontario, 1945.* E.W. McHenry and Associates, Department of Nutrition, University of Toronto. Toronto: Department of Public Welfare, 1945.

**6404. McInnes, R.M.** *"Childbearing and Land Availability: Some Evidence from Individual Household Data."* R.M. McInnes. New York: Academic Press, c1977. In Population Patterns in the Past, pp. 201-227. Edited by Ronald Demos Lee.

**6405. McIntosh, Barbara Anne** *Family Life and Sex Education for Five-and Six-Year-olds: Reproduction Information.* Barbara Anne McIntosh. Montreal: Sir George Williams University, 1971. Thesis (M.A.)--Sir George Williams University, 1971.

**6406. McIntosh, Dave** *The Season's of My Youth.* Dave McIntosh. Toronto: General Publishing, c1984.

**6407. McIntosh, Margaret** *"Poliomyelitis."* Margaret McIntosh. Canadian Nurse 43, 10(Oct. 1947): 779-782.

**6408. McIntosh, W. John** *A Study in Shop Guidance at Jarvis School for Boys, Toronto.* W. John McIntosh. Toronto: University of Toronto, 1946. Thesis (D.Paed.)--University of Toronto, 1946.

**6409. McIntyre, Edith** *"Red Letter Days for the Hospital for Sick Children. Toronto."* Edith McIntyre. Canadian Nurse 22, 1(Jan. 1926): 15-17.

**6410. MacIntyre, Robert B.** *"Special Education."* Robert MacIntyre. Toronto: OISE, 1984. In The House That Ryerson Built: Essays in Education to Mark Ontario's Bicentennial, pp. 102-113. Edited by Hugh Oliver, Mark Holmes and Ian Winchester.

**6411. McKay, A.L.** *"The Control of Measles and Whooping Cough."* A.L. McKay. Canadian Public Health Journal 22, 7(July 1931): 351-354.

**6412. McKay, A.L.** *"An Epidemic of Milk-borne Paratyphoid Fever: 1. Epidemiological Features."* A.L. McKay. Canadian Public Health Journal 23, 7(July 1932): 303-306.

**6413. McKay, A.L.** *"A Septic Sore Throat Epidemic: Part 1: Epidemiological Study."* A.L. McKay and R.P. Hardman. Canadian Public Health Journal 22, 5(May 1931): 224-234.

**6414. MacKay, Caroline** *A Study of the Understanding of Arbitrary Consequences by Preschool Children.* Caroline MacKay. Toronto: University of Toronto, 1940. Thesis (M.A.)--University of Toronto, 1940.

**6415. Mackay, Corday** *"Children of the Pioneers."* Corday Mackay. Beaver 279, 2(Sept. 1948): 14-17.

**6416. MacKay, E.N.** *"A Statistical Survey of Leukemia in Ontario and at the Ontario Cancer Foundation Clinics, 1938-1958."* E.N. MacKay and A.H. Sellers. Canadian Medical Association Journal/Journal de l'Association medicale canadienne 96, 25(June 24, 1967): 1626-1635.

**6417. MacKay, Malcolm** *"Pleurisy in Children."* Malcolm Mackay. Canadian Medical Association Journal 2, 7(July 1912): 666-669.

**6418. McKay, Sandy** *The Attitudes of Toronto Students Towards the Canadian Indians.* Sandy McKay. Toronto: Indian-Eskimo Association of Toronto, 1971.

**6419. McKee, Leila Gay Mitchell** *Voluntary Youth Organizations in Toronto, 1880-1930.* Leila Gay Mitchell McKee. Toronto: York University, 1983. (CTM no. 56573)
Thesis (Ph.D.)--York University, 1983.

**6420. McKendry, James B.J.** *"A Study of Enuresis."* J.B.J. McKendry, L. LaForest, H.A. Williams and Eleanor Davidson. Canadian Medical Association Journal 79, 11(Dec. 1, 1958): 899-902.

**6421. McKenzie, B.E.** *"The Psycho-neurosis: Observations Based Upon One Hundred Strongly Marked Cases Seen in Orthopedic Practice."* B.E. McKenzie. Canadian Medical Association Journal 6, 2(Feb. 1916): 118-136.

**6422. McKenzie, Betty Ann** *Care of the Poor in Toronto.* Betty Ann McKenzie. Toronto: University of Toronto, 1966. (CTM no. 22340)
Thesis (M.S.W.)--University of Toronto, 1966.

**6423. MacKenzie, D.A.** *"Treatment of Staphylococcal Empyema in Children."* D.A. MacKenzie and J.S. McKim. Canadian Medical Association Journal 75, 11(Dec. 1, 1956): 914-917.

**6424. McKenzie, Dorothy** *Patterns of Problem-solving of the Preschool Child and the Influence of Instruction on these Patterns.* Dorothy McKenzie. Toronto: University of Toronto, 1946.
Thesis (M.A.)--University of Toronto, 1946.

**6425. McKenzie, Mary** *When I Was Thirteen.* Mary McKenzie. Aylmer: Aylmer Express, [1979].
Mary McKenzie is the pseudonym of Christina Young.
Diary written in 1897-1898.

**6426. McKenzie, T.R.** *The Past and Present Status of the Teaching of English to Non-English Speaking Immigrants to Canada, with Special Reference to Ontario.* T.R. McKenzie. Toronto: University of Toronto, 1954.
Thesis (Ed.D.)--University of Toronto, 1954.

**6427. McKeown, Edward Nugent** *A Comparison of the Teaching of Arithmetic in Grade Four by Teaching Machine, Programmed Booklet and Traditional Methods.* Edward Nugent McKeown. Toronto: University of Toronto, 1964.
Thesis (Ed.D.)--University of Toronto, 1964.

**6428. Mackie, J.** *"The Shortage of Mechanics and the Cure."* J. Mackie. In Proceedings and Papers Fourth Annual Canadian Conference on Child Welfare 1923, pp. 101-109.

**6429. Mackie, Lily C.** *"The Hard-of-hearing Child."* Lily C. Mackie. Canadian Nurse 47, 3(Mar. 1951): 177-179.

**6430. McKinney, Wayne R.** *"The Sioux Lookout Medical Program."* Wayne R. McKinney. Beaver 303, 4(Spring 1973): 52-57.

**6431. MacKinnon, Archibald Roderick** *A Study of the Effects of Group Formation on Primary Reading Standards.* Archibald Roderick MacKinnon. Kingston: Queen's University, 1952.
Thesis (M.A.)--Queen's University, 1952.

**6432. MacKinnon, Kenneth J.** *"Renal Transplantation in Identical Twins."* Kenneth J. MacKinnon. Canadian Nurse 55, 6(June 1959): 506-507.

**6433. MacKinnon, Lilian** *""Miss, It's a Boy"."* Lilian MacKinnon. Canadian Nurse 41, 6(June 1945): 443-445.

**6434. McKinnon, N.E.** *"Mortality Reduction in Ontario, 1900-1942: Tuberculosis"* N.E. McKinnon. Canadian Journal of Public Health 36, 11(Nov. 1945): 423-429.

**6435. McKinnon, N.E.** *"Mortality Reduction in Ontario, 1900-1945: Measles and Whooping Cough."* N.E. McKinnon. Canadian Journal of Public Health 38, 3(Mar. 1948): 95-98.

**6436. McKinnon, N.E.** *"Mortality Reductions in Ontario, 1900-1942."* N.E. McKinnon. Canadian Journal of Public Health 35, 12(Dec. 1944): 481-484.

**6437. McKinnon, N.E.** *"Mortality Reductions in Ontario, 1900-1942."* N.E. McKinnon. Canadian Journal of Public Health 36, 7(July 1945): 285-298.

**6438. McKinnon, N.E.** *"Mortality Reductions in Ontario, 1900-1945."* N.E. McKinnon. Canadian Journal of Public Health 38, 10(Oct. 1948): 417-421.

**6439. McKinnon, N.E.** *"Problem of Diarrhoea and Enuritis, Under Two Years of Age."* N.E. McKinnon. Canadian Public Health Journal 24, 2(Feb. 1933): 53-56.

**6440. McKinnon, N.E.** *"Reduction in Diphtheria in 36,000 Toronto School Children as a Result of an Immunization Campaign."* N.E. McKinnon, Mary A. Ross and R.D. DeFries. Canadian Public Health Journal 22, 5(May 1931): 217-223.

**6441. McKinnon, N.E.** *"Whooping Cough: the Public Health Problem."* N.E. McKinnon and Mary A. Ross. Canadian Public Health Journal 25, 11(Nov. 1934): 533-537.

**6442. McLean, D.M.** *"Enteroviral and Mumps Meningitis in Toronto, 1963."* D.M. McLean, E. Joan Quantz, Ruth D. Bach, B. Mae Pevzner, R.P.B. Larke and G.A. McNaughton. Canadian Medical Association Journal/Journal de l'Association medicale canadienne 90, 25(June 20, 1964): 1390-1393.

**6443. McLean, D.M.** *"Enteroviral Syndromes in Toronto, 1964."* D.M. McLean, R.P.B. Larke, G.A. McNaughton, Jennifer M. Best and Patricia Smith. Canadian Medical Association Journal/Journal de l'Association medicale canadienne 92, 13(Mar. 27, 1965): 658-661.

**6444. McLean, D.M.** *"Enterovirus Infections in Toronto, 1959."* D.M. McLean, Selma J. Walker and G.A. McNaughton. Canadian Medical Association Journal/Journal de l'Association medicale canadienne 82, 13(Mar. 26, 1960): 661-665.

**6445. McLean, D.M.** *"Enterovirus Infections in Toronto During 1962."* D.M. McLean, Ruth D. Bach, E. Joan Quantz and G.A. McNaughton. Canadian Medical Association Journal/Journal de l'Association medicale canadienne 89, 1(July 6, 1963): 16-19.

**6446. McLean, D.M.** *"Infantile Gastroenteritis: Further Viral Investigations."* D.M. McLean, G.A. McNaughton and J.C. Wyllie. Canadian Medical Association Journal/Journal de l'Association medicale canadienne 85, 9(Aug. 26, 1961): 496-497.

**6447. McLean, D.M.** *"Infections of the Central Nervous System With Mumps and Enteroviruses in Toronto, 1960."* D.M. McLean, Selma J. Walker, J.C. Wyllie, E. Joan McQueen and G.A. McNaughton. Canadian Medical Association Journal/Journal de l'Association medicale canadienne 84, 17(Apr. 29, 1961): 941-944.

**6448. McLean, D.M.** *"Infections with Enteroviruses in Toronto, 1961."* D.M. McLean, E. Joan McQueen and G.A. McNaughton. Canadian Medical Association Journal/Journal de l'Association medicale canadienne 86, 8(Feb. 24, 1962): 359-362.

**6449. McLean, D.M.** *"Mumps and Enteroviral Meningitis in Toronto, 1966."* D.M. McLean, R.P.B. Larke, Cathron Cobb, Elizabeth D. Griffis and Suzanne M.R. Hackett. Canadian Medical Association Journal/Journal de l'Association medicale canadienne 96, 20(May 20, 1967): 1355-1361.

**6450. McLean, D.M.** *"Mumps Meningoencephalitis: a Virological and Clinical Study."* D.M. McLean, Selma J. Walker and G.A. McNaughton. Canadian Medical Association Journal/Journal de l'Association medicale canadienne 83, 4(July 23, 1960): 148-151.

**6451. McLean, D.M.** *"Mumps Meningoencephalitis, Toronto, 1963."* D.M. McLean, Ruth D. Bach, R.P.B. Larke and G.A. McNaughton. Canadian Medical Association Journal/Journal de l'Association medicale canadienne 90, 7(Feb. 15, 1964): 458-462.

**6452. McLean, D.M.** *"Myxovirus Dissemination by Air."* D.M. McLean, R.M. Bannatyne and Kathleen F. Givan. Canadian Medical Association Journal/Journal de l'Association medicale canadienne 96, 22(June 3, 1967): 1449-1453.

**6453. McLean, D.M.** *"Myxovirus Infections in Acute Laryngotracheobronchitis, Toronto, 1961-62."* D.M. McLean, H.E. Edwards, E. Joan McQueen and H. Elizabeth Petite. Canadian Medical Association Journal/Journal de l'Association medicale canadienne 87, 19(Nov. 10, 1962): 998-1001.

**6454. McLean, D.M.** *"Myxoviruses Associated With Acute Larynogtracheobronchitis in Toronto, 1962-63."* D.M. McLean, Ruth D. Bach, R.P.B. Larke and G.A. McNaughton. Canadian Medical Association Journal/Journal de l'Association medicale canadienne 89, 25(Dec. 21, 1963): 1257-1259.

**6455. McLean, D.M.** *"Parainfluenza Viruses in Association with Acute Laryngotracheobronchitis, Toronto, 1960-61."* D.M. McLean, T.E. Roy, M.J. O'Brien, J.C. Wyllie and E. Joan McQueen. Canadian Medical Association Journal/Journal de l'Association medicale canadienne 85, 6(Aug. 5, 1961): 290-294.

**6456. McLean, D.M.** *"Powassan Virus: Isolation of Virus From a Fatal Case of Encephalitis."* D.M. McLean and W.L. Donohue. Canadian Medical Association Journal/Journal de l'Association medicale canadienne 80, 9(May 1, 1959): 708-711.

**6457. McLean, D.M.** *"Rubella Virus Infections During Pregnancy, Toronto, 1963-66."* D.M. McLean, G.A. McNaughton, Kathleen F. Givan, Jennifer M. Best, Patricia A. Smith and Marjorie A. Coleman. Canadian Medical Association Journal/Journal de l'Association medicale canadienne 95, 23(Dec. 3, 1966): 1174-1178.

**6458. McLean, D.M.** *"Viral Infections of Toronto Children During 1965: 2. Measles Encephalitis and Other Complications."* D.M. McLean, Jennifer M. Best, Patricia A. Smith, R.P.B. Larke and G.A. McNaughton. Canadian Medical Association Journal/Journal de l'Association medicale canadienne 94, 17(Apr. 23, 1966): 905-910.

**6459. McLean, D.M.** *"Viral Infections of Toronto Children During 1965: 1. Enteroviral Disease."* D.M. McLean, Marjorie A. Coleman, R.P.B. Larke and G.A. McNaughton. Canadian Medical Association Journal/Journal de l'Association medicale canadienne 94, 16(Apr. 16, 1966): 839-843.

**6460. McLeish, Minnie Buchanan** *They Also Lived: a Personal Memoir.* Minnie (Buchanan) McLeish. Ottawa: Runge Press, [1962].

**6461. MacLennan, Anne** *"Charity and Change: Montreal English Protestant Charity Faces the Crisis of Depression."* Anne MacLennan. Urban History Review/Revue d'histoire urbaine 26, 1(June 1987): 1-16.

**6462. MacLeod, Adrienne** *"Telling a Child About His Adoption."* Adrienne MacLeod. Canadian Welfare 35, 3(May 1959): 100-104.

**6463. MacLeod, Betty** *The Development of Improved Bases for Forecasting School Age Population Throughout Ontario: a Study of Demographic Components.* Betty MacLeod, prinicipal investigator, G. Sabir Shaheel, William A. Postl and Richard G. Wolfe. Toronto: Ontario Institute for Studies in Education, c1978.

**6464. MacLeod, Betty, ed.** *Demography and Educational Planning.* Betty MacLeod, ed. Toronto: Ontario Institute for Studies in Education, 1970.

**6465. McLeod, Gordon D.** *Essentially Canadian: the Life and Fiction of Alan Sullivan, 1868-1947.* Gordon D. McLeod. Waterloo: Wilfrid Laurier University Press, c1982.

**6466. McLeod, H.N.** *A Rorschach Study with Preschool Children.* H.N. McLeod. Toronto: University of Toronto, 1948. Thesis (M.A.)--University of Toronto, 1948.

**6467. McLeod, Norman R.** *Need, Culture and Curriculum: Educating Immigrants and Ethnic Minorities.* Norman R. McLeod. Toronto: Research Department, Board of Education, 1968.

**6468. McMillan, Eldon Wayne** *A Comparison of the Motor Skill Learning Abilities of Normal and Emotionally Disturbed Children.* Eldon Wayne McMillan. London: University of Western Ontario, 1970. Thesis (M.A.)--University of Western Ontario, 1970.

**6469. McMillan, George** *The Agricultural High School in Ontario.* George McMillan. Toronto: University of Toronto Press, 1924. Thesis (D.Paed.)--University of Toronto, 1924.

**6470. MacMurchy, Helen** *"The Baby's Father."* Helen MacMurchy. Public Health Journal 9, 7(July 1918): 315-319.

**6471. MacMurchy, Helen** *Infant Mortality: Special Report by Dr. Helen MacMurchy.* Prepared for the Ontario Department of the Provincial Secretary. Toronto: King's Printer, 1910.

**6472. MacMurchy, Helen** *Infant Mortality: Second Special Report Prepared by Dr. Helen MacMurchy.* Prepared for the Ontario Department of the Provincial Secretary. Toronto: King's Printer, 1911.

**6473. MacMurchy, Helen** *Infant Mortality: Third Report by Dr. Helen MacMurchy.* Prepared for the Ontario Department of the Provincial Secretary. Toronto: King's Printer, 1912.

**6474. MacMurchy, Helen** *"The Mentally Defective Child."* Helen MacMurchy. Public Health Journal 6, 2(Feb. 1915): 85-86.

**6475. McMurray, John Grant** *A Study of Factors Contributing to Poor Drawing Performance in Exogenous as Compared with Endrogenous Feebleminded Children.* John Grant McMurray. London, Ont.: University of Western Ontario, 1952.
Thesis (M.A.)--University of Western Ontario, 1952.

**6476. MacNab, Sophia** *The Diary of Sophia MacNab.* Charles Ambrose Carter and Thomas Melville, eds. Rev. ed. Hamilton: W.L. Griffin, 1968, 1974.
Diary of daily experiences in 1846.

**6477. McNabb, A.L.** *"Undulant Fever in Ontario."* A.L. McNabb. Canadian Public Health Journal 25, 1(Jan. 1934): 10-12.

**6478. MacNamara, Jean G.** *A Preliminary Analysis of the Results at the Rorschach Test.* Jean G. MacNamara. Toronto: University of Toronto, 1932.
Thesis (M.A.)--University of Toronto, 1932.

**6479. McNichol Vera Ernst** *Smiling Through Tears.* Vera Ernst McNichol. Bloomindale: One M Printing Co., c1970.

**6480. McNulty, John A.** *"Emotional Arousal, Conflict and Susceptibility to Social Influence."* John A. McNulty and Richard H. Walters. Canadian Journal of Psychology 16, 3(Sept. 1962): 211-220.

**6481. Macoun, John** *Autobiography of John Macoun, Canadian Explorer and Naturalist, 1831-1920.* John Macoun. 2nd ed. Ottawa: Ottawa Field-Naturalists' Club, c1979.
Reprint of the 1922 edition with editorial notes by W.A. Waiser, pp. 307-328.

**6482. MacPherson, Ian** *Matters of Loyality: the Buells of Brockville, 1830-1850.* Ian MacPherson. Belleville, Ont.: Mika Publishing Co., 1981.

**6483. MacRae, Masie Grace** *The Impact of the Teacher on the Vocational Aspirations of Adolescents.* Masie Grace MacRae. Montreal: McGill University, 1969.
Thesis (M.A.)--McGill University, 1969.

**6484. McRaye, Walter** *Pauline Johnson and her Friends.* Walter McRaye. Toronto: Ryerson Press, c1947.

**6485. MacTavish, Donald A.** *The Construction and Application of a Scale to Measure World-mindedness at the Grade 8 Elementary School Level.* Donald A. MacTavish. Toronto: University of Toronto, 1953.
Thesis (M.A.)--University of Toronto, 1953.

**6486. McVie, William Douglas** *The Use of Motion Pictures, Film-strips, and the Delineascope in the Montreal Protestant Schools.* William Douglas McVie. Toronto: University of Toronto, 1950.
Thesis (M.A.)--University of Toronto, 1950.

**6487. Madill, Alonzo James** *History of Agricultural Education in Ontario.* Alonzo James Madill. Toronto: University of Toronto Press, c1930.

**6488. Magder, Beatrice** *An Examination of the Extent to Which the Group Work Method Can Be Used with Two Groups of Six and Seven Year Olds.* Beatrice Magder. Toronto: University of Toronto, 1952.
Thesis (M.S.W.)--University of Toronto, 1952.

**6489. Mahoney, Denis** *Marie of the Incarnation.* Mother Denis Mahoney. Garden City, N.Y.: Doubleday & Company, Inc., c1964.

**6490. Maidman, Frank Victor** *Family Openness and Patterns of Adolescent Social Engagement.* Frank Victor Maidman. Toronto: University of Toronto, 1971. (CTM no. 13062)
Thesis (Ph.D.)--University of Toronto, 1971.

**6491. Main, Mary G.** *Group Interviewing as a Research Instrument in a Study of Disciplinary Measures Among Inmates at Guelph Reformatory.* Mary G. Main. Toronto: University of Toronto, 1966.
Thesis (M.S.W.)--University of Toronto, 1966.

**6492. Mair, Nathan H.** *Protestant Education in Quebec: Notes on the History of Education in the Protestant Public Schools of Quebec.* Nathan H. Mair. Quebec: Conseil superior de l'education, 1981.

**6493. Malarek, Victor** *Hey Malarek: the True Story of a Street Kid Who Made It.* Victor Malarek. Halifax: Goodread Biographies, c1984, 1985.

**6494. Malcolm, Bernice de Pencier** *"Montreal's Youth Centre."* Bernice de Pencier Malcolm. Canadian Welfare 21, 1(Apr. 1945): 19-20.

**6495. Malcolmson, Patricia E.** *"The Poor in Kingston, 1815-1850."* Patricia E. Malcolmson. Montreal: McGill-Queen's University Press, c1976. In To Preserve and Defend: Essays on Kingston in the Ninetenth Century, pp. 281-297. Edited by Gerald Tulchinsky.

**6496. Mallinson, Thomas John** *An Experimental Investigation of Group-directed Discussion in the Classroom.* Thomas John Mallinson. Toronto: University of Toronto, 1954. (CTM no. 31276)
Thesis (Ph.D.)--University of Toronto, 1954.

**6497. Maloney, Timothy Lawrence** *Attitudes Toward Playing a Game and the Sport Involvement of School Age Adolescents.* Timothy Lawrence Maloney. London, Ont.: University of Western Ontario, 1970.
Thesis (M.A.)--University of Western Ontario, 1970.

**6498. Maltby, Lila F.** *The Foster Child of Preschool Age.* Lila F. Maltby. Toronto: University of Toronto, 1929.
Thesis (M.A.)--University of Toronto, 1929.

**6499. Mandel, Eli** *Irving Layton.* Eli Mandel. Toronto: Forum House, c1969.

**6500. Mann, William Edward** *"Deviant Behaviour in a Reformatory."* W.E. Mann. Toronto: Social Science Publishers, c1968. In Deviant Behaviour in Canada, pp. 75-101. Edited by W.E. Mann.

**6501. Manson, Freda** *"The Ontario Child Welfare Act of 1965."* Freda Manson. University of Toronto Law Journal 17, 1(1967): 207-217.

**6502. Marcellus, Dorothy** *"Survey of Attitudes of Parents and Children With Cerebral Palsy in Windsor and Essex County, Ontario."* Dorothy Marcellus and William A. Hawke. Canadian Medical Association Journal/Journal de l'Association medicale canadienne 95, 24(Dec. 10, 1966): 1242-1244.

**6503. Marchessault, J.H. Victor** *"An Epidemic of Aseptic Meningitis Caused by Coxsackie B Type 2 Virus."* V. Marchessault, V. Pavilanis, M.O. Podoski and M. Clode. Canadian Medical Association Journal/Journal de l'Association medicale canadienne 85, 3(July 15, 1961): 123-126.

**6504. Margolis, Eva** *A Comparison Between the Achievement of Pupils in a Progressive School and That of a Similar Group of Pupils in a Public School.* Eva Margolis. Toronto: University of Toronto, 1935.
Thesis (M.A.)--University of Toronto, 1935.

**6505. Marjoribanks, Kevin M.** *Ethnic and Environmental Influences on Levels and Profiles of Mental Abilities.* Kevin McLeod Marjoribanks. Toronto: University of Toronto, 1970.
Thesis (Ph.D.)--University of Toronto, 1970.

**6506. Mark, C.E.** *The Public Schools of Ottawa: a Survey.* C.E. Mark. Toronto: University of Toronto, 1919.
Thesis (D.Paed.)--University of Toronto, 1919.

**6507. Marks, Lynne** *"Kale Meydelach or Shulamith Girls: Harbord Collegiate Institute."* Lynne Marks. Canadian Women Studies/Cahiers de la femme 7, 3(Fall 1986): 85-89.

**6508. Marks, M.I.** *"Fatal Hepatitis in Siblings: Isolation of Coxsackievirus B5 and Herpes Simplex Virus."* M.I. Marks, J.H. Joncas and S.M. Mauer. Canadian Medical Association Journal/Journal de l'Association medicale canadienne 102, 13(June 20, 1970): 1391-1393.

**6509. Martin, Robert A.** *Selected Aspects of Elementary School Structure and Students' Acceptance of the Norm of Universalism.* Robert A. Martin. Toronto: University of Toronto, 1971.
Thesis (Ph.D.)--University of Toronto, 1971.

**6510. Marwood, Betty M.** *The Functions of a Receiving Home in Child Placement: a Study of the Use Made of the Receiving Home of the Children's Aid Society of Montreal in 1950.* Betty M. Marwood. Montreal: McGill University, 1953.
Thesis (M.S.W.)--McGill University, 1953.

**6511. Massey, Raymond** *When I was Young.* Raymond Massey. Toronto: McClelland and Stewart, c1976.

**6512. Mathieson, Kate** *"Reports of Nursing in Hospitals: Diphtheria."* K. Mathieson. Canadian Nurse 2, 2(June 1906): 36-37.

**6513. Mathur, Kusum** *Extracurricular Activities: Some Points of Comparison Between the Montreal Protestant High Schools and the High Schools of Pilani, India.* Kusum Mathur. Montreal: McGill Univesity, 1970.
Thesis (M.A.)--McGill University, 1970.

**6514. Matthews, W.D. Edison** *The History of the Religious Factor in Ontario Elemetary Education.* W.D. Edison Matthews. Toronto: University of Toronto, 1950.
Thesis (D.Paed.)--University of Toronto, 1950.

**6515. Maxwell, Mary Percival** *Social Structure, Socialization and Social Class in a Canadian Private School for Girls.* Mary Percival Maxwell. Ithaca, N.Y.: Cornell University, 1970.
Thesis (Ph.D.)--Cornell University, 1970.

**6516. Maxwell, Mary Percival** *"Women and the Elite: Educational and Occupational Aspirations of Private School Females 1966/67."* Mary Percival Maxwell and James D. Maxwell. Canadian Review of Sociology and Anthropology/Revue canadienne de sociologie et d'anthropologie 21, 4(Nov. 1984): 371-394.

**6517. May, John** *"Bush Life in the Ottawa Valley, 80 Years Ago."* John May. Ontario Historical Society, Papers and Records 12(1914): 153-163.

**6518. Maykovich, Minako Kurokawa** *"Alienation and Mental Health of Mennonites in Waterloo County."* Minako Kurokawa Maykovich. Toronto: Holt, Rinehart and Winston of Canada, c1971. In The Canadian Family, pp. 487-500. Edited by K. Ishwaran.
Reprinted in The Canadian Family Revised, pp. 600-613. Edited by K. Ishwaran.

**6519. Maykovich, Minako Kurokawa** *"The Japanese Family, Tradition and Change."* Minako Kurokawa Maykovich. Toronto: Holt, Rinehart and Winston of Canada, c1971. In The Canadian Family, pp. 111-125. Edited by K. Ishwaran.
Reprinted in The Canadian Family Revised pp. 162-176.

**6520. Mayou, Edith** *"Reports of Nursing in Hospitals: Scarlet Fever Complicated with Adenitis, Ostitis, Media Nephritis and Pemphigus Vulgaris."* Edith Mayou. Canadian Nurse 2, 1(Mar. 1906): 35-36.

**6521. Mazur, W.P.** *"Gilles de la Tourette's Syndrome."* W.P. Mazur. Canadian Medical Association Journal 69, 5(Nov. 1953): 520-522.

**6522. Melady, Thomas S.** *"A Distinguished Son of Huron County: the Reverend Stephen Eckert, O.M. Cap."* Thomas S. Melady. Canadian Catholic Historical Association Report (1940-1941): 95-100.

**6523. Melicherick, John** *"Child Welfare in Ontario."* John Melicherick. 1st ed. Waterloo: Wilfrid Laurier University Press, c1978. In Canadian Social Policy, pp. 187-206. Edited by Shankar A. Yelaja.

**6524. Melnyk, Iryna** *Ukrainian Bilingual Education in the Montreal Public School System.* Iryna Melnyk. Montreal: McGill University, 1987.
Thesis (M.A.)--McGill University, 1987.

**6525. Melvin, W.J.S.** *"Forearm Fractures in Childhood."* W.J.S. Melvin. Canadian Medical Association Journal 70, 3(Mar. 1954): 263-267.

**6526. Mendelsohn, Lillian E.** *History of the Montreal Juvenile Court: an Historical-Descriptive Study of the Development of the Montreal Juvenile Court, Later Known as the Social Welfare Court.* Lillian E. Mendelsohn and Shawn Ronald. Montreal: McGill University, 1969.
Thesis (M.S.W.)--McGill University, 1969.

**6527. Merchant, F.W.** *The Ontario Examination Systems.* F.W. Merchant. London, Ontario: The London Printing and Lithograph Company, 1903.
Thesis (D.Paed.)--University of Toronto, 1903.
Thesis published as monograph.

**6528. Merrill, Geoffrey Hunter** *The Role of Sex Education in the Schools.* Geoffrey Hunter Merrill. Montreal: McGill University, 1966.
Thesis (M.A.)--McGill University, 1966.

**6529. Mestel, A.L.** *"Pneumoperitoneum in the Newborn."* A.L. Mestel, G.A. Trusler, R.P. Humphreys and J.S. Simpson. Canadian Medical Association Journal/Journal de l'Association medicale canadienne 95, 5(July 30, 1966): 201-204.

**6530. Metcalfe, Alan** *"The Evolution of Organized Physical Recreation in Montreal, 1840-1895."* Alan Metcalfe. Histoire sociale/Social History 11, 21(May 1978): 144-166.

**6531. Metropolitan Toronto. School Board. Research Department** *A Survey of Outdoor Education in Metropolitan Toronto: Attitudes, Activities and Facilities.* The Department. [Toronto: The Board], 1970.

**6532. Michael, Darren** *"Interfaith Adoption: a Symposium."* Darren Michael, Patricia M. Chaikoff, W. Ward Markle and Barbi Gunther Plaut. Osgoode Hall Law Journal 3, 1(Apr. 1964): 14-35.

**6533. Michell, W.R.** *"The Evolution of Health Service Work, Medical, Dental and Nursing in Schools on Toronto, with a Detailed Account of its Growth and Present Status."* W.R. Michell. Public Health Journal 15, 12(Dec. 1924): 541-556.

**6534. Miezitis, Solveiga** *An Exploratory Study of Divergent Production in Preschoolers.* Solveiga Ausma Miezitis. Toronto: University of Toronto, 1968. Thesis (Ph.D.)–University of Toronto, 1968.

**6535. Millar, John** *The Educational System of the Province of Ontario, Canada.* John Millar. Toronto: Warwick and Sons, 1893.

**6536. Millar, W.P.J.** *"The Remarkable Rev. Thaddeus Osgood: a Study in the Evangelical Spirit of the Canadas."* W.P.J. Millar. Histoire sociale/Social History 9, 19(May 1977): 59-76.

**6537. Miller, Albert Herman** *The Theory and Practice of Education in Ontario in the 1860's.* Albert Herman Miller. Vancouver: University of British Columbia, 1968. Thesis (D.Ed.)–University of British Columbia, 1968.

**6538. Miller, Barbara** *"Busy Hands, Better Health."* Barbara Miller. Canadian Nurse 42, 10(Oct. 1946): 866-869.

**6539. Miller, Billie** *A Book About Billie.* Billie Miller and David Helwig. Ottawa: Oberron, 1972.

**6540. Miller, Charlotte H.** *A Study of the Social Interaction of Preschool Children Paired According to Sociometric Ratings.* Charlotte H. Miller. Toronto: University of Toronto, 1951. Thesis (M.A.)–University of Toronto, 1951.

**6541. Miller, J.C.** *"The Education of Abnormal Children."* J.C. Miller and Alphonse Pelletier. Canadian Medical Association Journal 22, 4(Apr. 1930): 512-515.

**6542. Miller, James** *"Scarlet Fever Immunization: Further Experience in the City of Kingston."* James Miller. Public Health Journal 17, 7(July 1926): 345-346.

**6543. Miller, Lorne Samuel** *Social Patterns of Gay Adults: an Exploratory Study Survey of Patterns of Group Affiliation and Use of Leisure Time Activities of Young Adults in a Middle Class Area of Montreal.* Lorne Samuel Miller. Montreal: McGill University, 1965. Thesis (M.S.W.)–McGill University, 1965.

**6544. Miller, Max J.** *"Studies on Pinworm Infections: 3. Tests with Phenothiazine in the Treatment of Pinworm Infections."* Max J. Miller and Della Allen. Canadian Medical Association Journal 46, 2(Feb. 1942): 111-115.

**6545. Miller, Orlo** *The Donnellys Must Die.* Orlo Miller. Toronto: Macmillan of Canada, [1967].

**6546. Milley, Chesley Boyd** *The Education of Non-Catholic English-speaking Physically Handicapped Children in Montreal.* Chesley Boyd Milley. Montreal: McGill University, 1957. Thesis (M.A.)–McGill University, 1957.

**6547. Millichamp, Dorothy A.** *"Early Foundations for Mental Health."* Dorothy Millichamp. Bulletin of the Institute of Child Study 23, 3-4(Sept.-Dec. 1961): 3-9.

**6548. Millichamp, Dorothy A.** *The Genetic Development of Emotion in the Infant.* Dorothy A. Millichamp. Toronto: University of Toronto, 1932. Thesis (M.A.)–University of Toronto, 1932.

**6549. Millichamp, Dorothy A.** *"Nursery School and Kindergarten at the Dafoe Hospital."* Dorothy A. Millichamp. Canadian Welfare Summary 14, 3(Sept. 1938): 67-72.

**6550. Mills, Robert E.** *"Birth Registration and Infant Welfare."* Robert E. Mills. Public Health Journal 9, 4(Apr. 1918): 171-172.

**6551. Mills, Robert E.** *"Foster Parent Training."* Robert E. Mills. Child and Family Welfare 11, 2(July 1935): 6.

**6552. Mills, Robert E.** *"Recent Development of Family Care for Dependent Children in Toronto."* Robert E. Mills. In Proceedings and Papers Fifth Annual Canadian Conference on Child Welfare 1925, pp. 147-149.

**6553. Mills, Robert E.** *"Utilization of Provincial Legislation in Connection With Child Placing."* Robert E. Mills. In Proceedings and Papers Fifth Annual Canadian Conference on Child Welfare 1925, pp. 144-146.

**6554. Milne, H.** *"Hemoglobin Levels and Iron Intakes of Infants Attending Selected Child Health Centres in the City of Toronto."* H. Milne, G.H. Beaton, L.M. Latchford, M. Vaughan and G.W.O. Moss. Canadian Medical Association Journal/Journal de l'Association medicale canadienne 105, 3(Aug. 7, 1971): 279-282.

**6555. Milne, H.** *"Studies of Teenage Eating in Ontario."* H. Milne, C. Kerr, M. Trenholme and G.H. Beaton. Canadian Journal of Public Health 54, 10(Oct. 1963): 463-470.

**6556. Milnes, Herbert** *Settlers' Traditions.* Herbert Milnes. Cheltenham, Ont.: Boston Mills Press, c1980.

**6557. Minden, Harold A.** *The Effect of Perceptual-motor Training in Intellectual and Academic Functioning.* Harold A. Minden. Toronto: York University, 1969. Thesis (Ph.D.)–York University, 1969.

**6558. Miner, Jack** *Jack Miner: His Life and Religion.* Jack Miner. Kingsville, Ont.: Jack Miner Migratory Bird Foundation , c1969.

**6559. Minnes, R.S.** *"Two Cases of Sinus Thrombosis and Jugular Resection."* R.S. Minnes. Canadian Medical Association Journal 8, 4(Apr. 1918): 336-342.

**6560. Minns, F.S.** *"The Method of Dealing With Tuberculosis in the Public Schools of Toronto."* F.S. Minns. Public Health Journal 7, 3(Mar. 1916): 145-148.

**6561. Minns, F.S.** *"The Method of Dealing with Tuberculosis in the Public Schools of Toronto, Canada."* F.S. Minns. Canadian Medical Association Journal 5, 10(Oct. 1915): 902-908.

**6562. Minville, Esdras** *Labour Legislation and Social Services of the Province of Quebec: a Study Prepared for the Royal Commission on Dominion-Provincial Relations.* Esdras Minville. Ottawa: King's Printer, 1939.

**6563. Mitchell, Gayle** *"A Child's Response to Consistent Care."* Gayle Mitchell. Canadian Nurse 64, 3(Mar. 1968): 47-48.

**6564. Mitchell, Harriet** *"Thumbsucking: a Practical Appraisal from the Mental Hygiene and Orthodontic Points of View."* Harriet Mitchell. Canadian Medical Association Journal 44, 5(May 1941): 612-617.

**6565. Mitchell, Mary Verity** *Mental Development as Related to Institutional and Foster Home Placement.* Mary Verity Mitchell. Montreal: McGill University, 1942.
  Thesis (M.Sc.) – McGill University, 1942.

**6566. Mitchell, Sheila C.** *"The Finding of Genital Lesions in a Case of Coxsackie Virus Infection."* Sheila C. Mitchell and George Dempster. Canadian Medical Association Journal 72, 2(Jan. 15, 1955): 117-119.

**6567. Mock, Karen R.** *The Effects of Frustration and Failure on Subsequent Behaviour.* Karen R. Mock. Toronto: University of Toronto, 1970. Thesis (M.A.)–University of Toronto, 1970.

**6568. Moffat, John Lynn** *Building the Timburk High School: a Model Developed to Practice Non-programmed Decision Making Through Game Simulation, 1970.* John Lynn Moffat. Calgary: University of Calgary, 1970. Thesis (M.Ed.)–University of Calgary, 1970.

**6569. Moffat, M.D.** *A Study of Spontaneous Changes of Social Status of Grade School Groups.* M.D. Moffat. Toronto: University of Toronto, 1946. Thesis (M.A.)–University of Toronto, 1946.

**6570. Mohr, Emily N.** *"The Child and the Community."* Emily N. Mohr. Public Health Journal 9, 9(Sept. 1918): 427-428.

**6571. Mohr, Johann W.** *Pedophilia and Exhibitionism: a Handbook.* J.W. Mohr, R.E. Turner and M.B. Jerry. Toronto: University of Toronto Press, c1964.

**6572. Mongeau, M.** *"Medical and Psychosocial Aspects of the Habilitation of Thalidomide Children."* M. Mongeau, G. Gingras, E.D. Sherman, B. Hebert, J. Hutchison and C. Corriveau. Canadian Medical Association Journal/Journal de l'Association medicale canadienne 95, 9(Aug. 27, 1966): 390-395.

**6573. Montreal Junior Board of Trade. Committee on the Protestant School Situation in Montreal** *Report of the Committee on the Protestant School Situation in Montreal.* The Committee. Montreal: [The Board], 1936.

**6574. Montreal Rotary Club. Mental Health Committee** *Proceedings of the Institute on the Prevention and Treatment of Juvenile Delinquency.* Mental Health Committee of the Rotary Club of Montreal and the Montreal Council of Social Agencies. Montreal: Montreal Council of Social Agencies, 1953.

**6575. Montreuil, Fernand** *"Congenital Cysts and Fistulae of the Neck."* Fernand Montreuil. Canadian Medical Association Journal 73, 11(Dec. 1, 1955): 883-886.

**6576. Moogk, Peter N.** *"Apprenticeship Indentures: a Key to Artisan Life in New France."* Peter N. Moogk. Canadian Historical Association, Historical Papers/Communications historiques (1971): 65-83.

**6577. Moogk, Peter N.** "Apprenticeship of Edward Davis, an Abandoned Child, by the Town Wardens of Waterloo to Christian Schwartzentruber, a Farmer of Wilmot Township, 1 June 1839." Peter Moogk. Waterloo Historical Society Annual Report 57(1969): 80-84.

**6578. Moogk, Peter N.** "Manual Education and Economic Life in New France." Peter N. Moogk. Studies on Voltaire and the Eighteenth Century 167(1977): 125-168.

**6579. Moogk, Peter N.** "Les Petits sauvages: the Children of Eighteenth Century New France." Peter N. Moogk. Toronto: McClelland and Stewart, c1982. In Childhood and Family in Canadian History, pp. 17-43. Edited by Joy Parr.

**6580. Mooney, Craig M.** "Age in the Development of Closure Ability in Children." Craig M. Mooney. Canadian Journal of Psychology 11, 4(Dec. 1957): 210-226.

**6581. Moore, Sue** "A Step Forward at Thistletown." Sue Moore. Canadian Nurse 56, 2(Feb. 1960): 160-166.

**6582. Moreux, Colette** "The French Canadian Family." Colette Moreux. Toronto: Holt, Rinehart and Winston of Canada Ltd., c1971. In The Canadian Family, pp. 126-147. Edited by K. Ishwaran.

**6583. Morgan, A. Lloyd** "Plastic Repair of Deformities of the Eyelids." A. Lloyd Morgan. Canadian Medical Association Journal 44, 6(June 1941): 560-562.

**6584. Morgan, Barbara** Relationships between Degree of Handedness, Right Left Discrimination, and Age on Normal Right Handed and Left Handed Children. Barbara Morgan. Toronto: University of Toronto, 1960.
Thesis (M.A.)--University of Toronto, 1960.

**6585. Morgan, E.A.** "Penicillin in the Treatment of Pre-natal Syphilis." E.A. Morgan. Canadian Medical Association Journal 61, 3(Sept. 1949): 275-278.

**6586. Morgan, E.A.** "Syphilis: Its Relation to Infant Mortality and Child Welfare, With a Discussion of Present Day Methods for Its Control." E.A. Morgan. Canadian Medical Association Journal 11, 11(Nov. 1921): 849-852.
Author published article with the same title in Public Health Journal 12, 11(Nov. 1921): 500-506.

**6587. Moritz, Albert** Leacock: a Biography. Albert and Theresa Moritz. Don Mills: Stoddart, c1985.

**6588. Morphy, A.G.** "Mental Hygiene Survey of Montreal Protestant Schools." A.G. Morphy and William D. Tait. Canadian Journal of Mental Hygiene 3, 1(Apr. 1921): 49-94.

**6589. Morrison, Terrence** The Child and Urban Social Reform in Late Nineteenth Century Ontario. Terrence Robert Morrison. Toronto: University of Toronto, 1970. (CTM no. 27928)
Thesis (Ph.D.)--University of Toronto, 1970.

**6590. Morrison, Terrence** "Reform as Social Tracking: the Case of Industrial Education in Ontario." T.R. Morrison. Journal of Educational Thought 8, 2(Aug. 1974): 87-110.

**6591. Morrison, Terrence** ""Their Proper Sphere.": Feminism, the Family, and Child-centered Social Reform in Ontario, 1875-1900: Parts I and II." T.R. Morrison. Ontario History 68, 1(Mar. 1976): 45-64 and 68, 2(June 1976): 65-74.

**6592. Morrow, Don** "The Strathcona Trust in Ontario 1911-1939." Don Morrow. Canadian Journal of History of Sport and Physical Education 8, 1(May 1977): 12-19.

**6593. Morrow, Leslie Donald** Selected Topics in the History of Physical Education in Ontario: from Dr. Egerton Ryerson to the Strathcona Trust 1844-1939. Leslie Donald Morrow. Edmonton: University of Alberta, 1975. (CTM no. 26853)
Thesis (Ph.D.)--University of Alberta, 1975.

**6594. Morton, David** The Development of the Private English Academic Secondary Schools of Quebec, from 1965 to 1975. David Morton. Montreal: McGill University, 1977.
Thesis (M.A.)--McGill University, 1977.

**6595. Mosley, James Lawrence** The Influence of Social Reinforcement on the Rectilinear Dot Progression Task Performance of Normal and Retarded Subjects. James Lawrence Mosley. London, Ont.: University of Western Ontario, 1970. (CTM no. 6170)
Thesis (Ph.D.)--University of Western Ontario, 1970.

**6596. Moss, John George** Bellrock. John Moss. Toronto: NC Press, c1983.

**6597. Mott, H.S.** *"Some Amendments to the Juvenile Delinquent's Act."* H.S. Mott. In Proceedings and Papers Fourth Annual Canadian Conference on Child Welfare 1923, pp. 165-167.

**6598. Mullin, J. Heurner** *"History of the Organization of the Babies' Dispensary Guild, Hamilton, Inc."* J. Heurner Mullen. Public Health Journal 6, 11(Nov. 1915): 542-543.

**6599. Mullinger, Margaret** *"Cretinism."* Margaret Mullinger, John Munn, and A.L. Chute. Canadian Medical Association Journal 66, 6(June, 1952): 560-562.

**6600. Multari, G.** *"Stealing as a Symptom in Children Seen in a Mental Health Clinic."* G. Multari and F.K. Boden. Canadian Journal of Corrections/Revue canadienne de criminologie 6, 1(Jan. 1964): 95-105.

**6601. Multimer, Brian Thomas Paul** *Attitudes Towards Physical Activity of Grade Twelve Boys in Two London High Schools.* Brian T.P. Multimer. London, Ont.: University of Western Ontario, 1969. Thesis (M.A.)–University of Western Ontario, 1969.

**6602. Muncaster, Eric** *"Rosemount, Montreal Shows One Way Out."* Eric Muncaster. Child and Family Welfare 9, 2(July 1933): 50-54.

**6603. Mundie, Gordon S.** *"The Child Guidance Clinic: For Vocational and Educational Guidance and the Prevention of Mental Disease and Juvenile Delinquency."* G.S. Mundie and Barruch Silverman. Public Health Journal 15, 10(Oct. 1924): 441-451.

**6604. Mundie, Gordon S.** *"Juvenile Delinquency."* Gordon S. Mundie. Canadian Medical Association Journal 5, 5(May 1915): 405-410.

**6605. Mundie, Gordon S.** *"The Out-patient Psychiatric Clinic."* Gordon S. Mundie. Canadian Journal of Mental Hygiene 3, 3(Oct. 1921): 297-313.

**6606. Munro, Donald Richard** *The Care of the Dependent Poor, 1891-1921.* Donald Richard Munro. Toronto: University of Toronto, 1966. (CTM no. 31294) Thesis (M.S.W.)–University of Toronto, 1966.

**6607. Munro, I.R.** *"An Analysis of Burns in Children."* I.R. Munro, A.W. Farmer, A. Csima and W.K. Lindsay. Canadian Medical Association Journal/Journal de l'Association medicale canadienne 97, 9(Aug. 26, 1967): 459-463.

**6608. Munro, P.F.** *An Experimental Investigation of the Mentality of the Jew in Ryerson Public School Toronto.* P.F. Munro. Toronto: University of Toronto Press, 1926. Thesis (D.Paed.)–University of Toronto, 1926.

**6609. Munro, W. Bennett** *High School Cadet Drill Manual.* W. Bennett Munro. Toronto: Copp, Clark Company Limited, 1898.

**6610. Munroe, Alex Wood** *An Evaluation of a Method of Teaching Human Relations in Secondary Schools.* Alex Wood Munroe. Toronto: University of Toronto, 1949. Thesis (M.A.)–University of Toronto, 1949.

**6611. Murdoch, Louise Helen** *A Study of the Hopes, Aspirations and Attitudes of the Traditional Rural Disadvantaged Families Which May Be Used By the Helping Professions to Motivate These Families to Upgrade Themselves.* Louise Helen Murdoch. Toronto: University of Toronto, 1968. Thesis (M.S.W.)–University of Toronto, 1968.

**6612. Murdock, William L.** *The Service Structures and Administrative Implications Involved in Meeting a Need for Alternative Living Accommodation for Youths in the City of London, Ontario.* William L. Murdock. Toronto: University of Toronto, 1969. Thesis (M.S.W.)–University of Toronto, 1969.

**6613. Murphy, Arthur G.** *An Industrial School for Epileptics and Feebleminded.* Arthur G. Murphy. Montreal: [s.n.], 1921.

**6614. Murray, Joan** *The Last Buffalo: the Story of Frederick Arthur Verner, Painter of the Canadian West.* Joan Murray. Toronto: Pagurian Press, 1984.

**6615. Murray, Judith Margaret** *A Study of Perceived Decision-making in Families Who Foster Infants.* Judith Margaret Murray. Toronto: University of Toronto, 1967. Thesis (M.S.W.)–University of Toronto, 1967.

**6616. Murray, L.M.** *"The Dick Test."* L.M. Murray. Public Health Journal 17, 4(Apr. 1926): 157-164.

**6617. Murray, N.** *The Experience of an Old Country Pedler (sic) Among the Montreal Servant Girls and Their Mistresses.* N. Murray. 2nd ed. [Montreal?: s.n., 1887?].

**6618. Mustard, W.T.** *"Mediastinal Vascular Anomalies Causing Tracheal and Esophageal Compression and Obstruction in Childhood."* W.T. Mustard, A.W. Trimble and G.A. Trusler. Canadian Medical Association Journal/Journal de l'Association medicale canadienne 87, 25(Dec. 22, 1962): 1301-1305.

**6619. Mustard, W.T.** *"Mortality in Congenital Cardiovascular Surgery."* W.T. Mustard. Canadian Medical Association Journal 72, 10(May 15, 1955): 740-744.

**6620. Mustard, W.T.** *"The Operative Approach to Congenital Aortic Stenosis in Childhood."* W.T. Mustard, G.A. Trusler and J. Yao. Canadian Medical Association Journal/Journal de l'Association medicale canadienne 89, 21(Nov. 23, 1963): 1068-1071.

**6621. Myers, C. Roger** *An Application of the Control Group Method to the Problem of the Etiology of Mongolism.* C. Roger Myers. Toronto: University of Toronto, 1936.
Thesis (Ph.D.)--University of Toronto, 1936.

**6622. Myers, C. Roger** *The Child and the Comic.* C. Roger Myers. Toronto: University of Toronto, 1929.
Thesis (M.A.)--University of Toronto, 1929.

**6623. Nadeau, Emile** *"The Groncher System."* Emile Nadeau. Child and Family Welfare 8, 3(Sept. 1932): 31-35.

**6624. Nadeau, Guy** *"Two Cases of Ethylene Glycol Poisoning."* Guy Nadeau and F.J. Delaney. Canadian Medical Association Journal 70, 1(Jan. 1954): 69-70.

**6625. Nagata, Judith A.** *English Language Classes for Immigrant Women With Pre-school Children.* Judith A. Nagata, Joan Rayfield and Mary Ferraris. [Toronto: s.n.], 1970.

**6626. Nash, Knowlton** *History on the Run: the Trenchcoat Memoirs of a Foreign Correspondent.* Knowlton Nash. Toronto: McClelland and Stewart, c1984.

**6627. Neale, John M.** *"Egocentrism in Institutionalized and Noninstitutionalized Children."* John M. Neale. Child Development 37, 1(Mar. 1966): 97-101.

**6628. Nease, Barbara** *An Ecological Approach to the Measurement of Juvenile Delinquency in Hamilton.* Barbara J.S. Nease. Toronto: University of Toronto, 1965.
Thesis (M.S.W.)--University of Toronto, 1965.

**6629. Nease, Barbara** *"Measuring Juvenile Delinquency in Hamilton."* Barbara Nease. Canadian Journal of Corrections/Revue canadienne de criminologie 8, 2(Apr. 1966): 133-145.
Reprinted in Deviant Behaviour in Canada, pp. 43-54. Edited by W.E. Mann.
Reprinted in Deviant Behaviour and Societal Reaction, pp. 185-195. edited by Craig L. Boyell, Carl F. Grindstaff and Paul C. Whitehead.

**6630. Nelson, Cliff** *"The Vagrancy Dilemma: an Empirical Study."* Cliff Nelson and Ray Steel. Osgoode Hall Law Journal 7, 2(1969): 177-197.

**6631. Nelson, Marian** *The Relation of Early Adolescent Adjustment to Socioeconomic Status.* Marian Nelson. Toronto: University of Toronto, 1957.
Thesis (M.A.)--University of Toronto, 1957.

**6632. Neutel, Clasine Ineke** *A Study of the Epidemiology of Childhood Cancer with Special Emphasis on Smoking During Pregnancy.* Clasine Ineke Neutel. London, Ont.: University of Western Ontario, 1970. (CTM no. 6349)
Thesis (Ph.D.)--University of Western Ontario, 1970.

**6633. Newcombe, Ervin E.** *The Place of Motion Pictures in the Lives of 50 Delinquent and 50 Non-delinquent Boys.* Ervin E. Newcombe. Toronto: University of Toronto, 1945.
Thesis (M.A.)--University of Toronto, 1945.

**6634. Newman, Peter C.** *The Establishment Man: a Portrait of Power.* Peter C. Newman. Toronto: McClelland and Stewart, 1982.

**6635. Newman, Warren Oscar** *A Study of the Relationship Between Time Understanding and Social Studies Achievement in Grade Six Children.* Warren Oscar Newman. Toronto: University of Toronto, 1969.
Thesis (Ph.D.)--University of Toronto, 1969.

**6636. Nicholls, John V.V.** *"A Survey of the Opthalmic Conditions Among Rural School Children."* John V.V. Nicholls. Canadian Medical Association Journal 44, 5(May 1941): 472-473.

**6637. Nichols, M. Doreen** *The Adoption Practices of the Children's Aid Society of Toronto in 1949.* M. Doreen Nichols. Toronto: University of Toronto, 1950.
Thesis (M.S.W.)--University of Toronto, 1950.

**6638. Nicholson, Jean** *The Records of the Institute of Child Study with Special Reference to the "Follow-up" Interview.* Jean Nicholson. Toronto: University of Toronto, 1946. Thesis (M.A.)--University of Toronto, 1946.

**6639. Nicholson, Murray W.** *"Irish Catholic Education in Victorian Toronto: an Ethnic Response to Urban Conformity."* Murray W. Nicholson. Histoire sociale/Social History 17, 34(Nov. 1984): 287-306.

**6640. Nicolson, Murray W.** *"The Education of a Minority: the Irish Family Urbanized."* Murray W. Nicolson. Toronto: Celtic Arts of Canada, 1988. In The Untold Story: the Irish in Canada, v.2, pp. 759-784. Edited by Robert O'Driscoll and Lorna Reynolds.

**6641. Nielsen, Donald** *The Expectations of Grade Twelve Students in Physical Education in Burlington Ontario.* Donald Nielsen. London, Ont.: University of Western Ontario, 1968. Thesis (M.A.)--University of Western Ontario, 1968.

**6642. Nipp, Dora** *""But Women Did Come": Working Chinese Women in the Interwar Years."* Dora Nipp. Toronto: Multicultural History Society of Ontario, c1986. In Looking into My Sister's Eyes: an Exploration in Women's History, pp. 179-194. Edited by Jean Burnet.

**6643. Nock, David A.** *A Victorian Missionary and Canadian Indian Policy: Cultural Synthesis vs Cultural Replacement.* David A. Nock. Waterloo, Ontario: Published for the Canadian Corporation for Studies in Religion by Wilfrid Laurier University Press, 1988.

**6644. Norman, Margaret G.** *"Encephalopathy and Fatty Degeneration of the Viscera in Childhood: 1. Review of Cases at the Hospital for Sick Children, Toronto 1954-1966."* M.G. Norman. Canadian Medical Association Journal/Journal de l'Association medicale canadienne 99, 11(Sept. 21, 1968): 522-526.

**6645. Norris, Darrell A.** *"Household and Transiency in a Loyalist Township: the People of Adolphustown 1784-1822."* Darrell A. Norris. Histoire sociale/Social History 13, 26(Nov. 1980): 399- 415.

**6646. Norris, Darrell A.** *"Migration, Pioneer Settlement and Life Course: the First Families in an Ontario Township."* Darrell A. Norris. Gananoque, Ont.: Langdale Press, c1984. In Canadian Papers in Rural History v.4, pp. 130-152.

Edited by Donald A. Akenson.

**6647. Northway, Mary L.** *"Children's Social Development: a Summary of the Toronto Studies."* Mary L. Northway. Bulletin of the Canadian Psychological Association 3, 1(Feb. 1943): 3-5.

**6648. Northway, Mary L.** *"Introducing Child Study to Education."* Mary L. Northway. Bulletin of the Institute of Child Study 30, 1(Spring 1968): 3-7.

**6649. Northway, Mary L.** *"Social Studies in Progress at the Institute of Child Study."* Mary L. Northway and Marie Milton. Bulletin of the Institute of Child Study 26, 3-4(Winter 1964-1965): 22-31.

**6650. Northway, Mary L.** *"The Sociometry of Society: Some Facts and Fancies."* Mary L. Northway. Canadian Journal of Behavioural Science/Revue canadienne de sciences du comportement 3, 1(Jan. 1971): 18-36.

**6651. Northway, Mary L., ed.** *Charting the Counselor's Course: a Guide for Camp Leaders.* Mary L. Northway, ed. 1st ed.. Toronto: Longmans, Green & Company, 1940.

**6652. Novick, Thelma** *School Referral and Psychiatric Consultation: a Follow-up Study of Thirty-six Children Referred by Five Protestant Elementary Schools in Montreal Between September 1967 and August 1969 to the School Psychiatric Services of the Child and Adolescent Services, a Department of the Allan Memorial Institute.* Thelma Novick and Penelope Winship. Montreal: McGill University, 1971. Thesis (M.S.W.)--McGill University, 1971.

**6653. Nyiti, Raphael Majala** *A Study Comparing Factors Associated with the Selection or Rejection of Teaching by English-Speaking Catholic and Protestant High School Students in the Montreal Area.* Raphael Majala Nyiti. Montreal: McGill University, 1968. Thesis (M.A.)--McGill University, 1968.

**6654. Obodiac, Stan** *Red Kelly.* Stan Obodiac. Toronto: Clarke, Irwin and Company, c1971.

**6655. O'Brien, Andy** *The Jacques Plante Story.* Andy O'Brien with Jacques Plante. Toronto: McGraw-Hill Ryerson, c1972.

**6656. O'Brien, Andy** *Young Hockey Champions.* Andy O'Brien. 1st ed. Toronto: Ryerson Press, c1969.

**6657. O'Brien, John R.** *"Causes of Birth Asphyxia and Trauma."* John R. O'Brien, Robert H. Usher and George B. Maughan. Canadian Medical Association Journal/Journal de l'Association medicale canadienne 94, 21(May 21, 1966): 1077-1085.

**6658. O'Dell, Doris M.** *Launching Loyalist Children: the Stuart Family of Early Kingston.* Doris Mary O'Dell. Kingston: Queen's University, 1984. (CTM no. 25063)
Thesis (M.A.)--Queen's University, 1984.

**6659. O'Gallagher, Marianna** *Grosse Ile: Gateway to Canada, 1832-1937.* Marianna O'Gallagher. Ste-Foy, Quebec: Carraig Books, c1984.

**6660. Ohikhena, Titus Ofuovo** *Values and Perception of Educational Objectives as Factors in Preferential Behavior.* Titus Ofuovo Ohikhena. Toronto: University of Toronto, 1970.
Thesis (Ph.D.)--University of Toronto, 1970.

**6661. Oliver, Hugh, ed.** *The House That Ryerson Built: Essays in Education to Mark Ontario's Bicentennial.* Hugh Oliver, Mark Holmes and Ian Winchester, eds. Toronto: Ontario Institute for Studies in Education, c1984.

**6662. Olson, David R.** *"Conceptual Differences: Quantity and Pouring Time."* David R. Olson and Roland Lorimer. Canadian Journal of Behavioural Science/Revue canadienne de sciences du comportement 1, 4(Oct. 1969): 273-281.

**6663. Olson, Ruth A.** *"Rape: an "Un-Victorian" Aspect of Life in Upper Canada."* Ruth A. Olson. Ontario History 68, 1(Mar. 1976): 75-79.

**6664. Olstead, Margery** *Performance on the Children's Form of the Rosenzweig Picture-frustration Test as Related to Sociometric Status.* Margery Olstead. Toronto: University of Toronto, 1950.
Thesis (M.A.)--University of Toronto, 1950.

**6665. O'Neill, Gail** *"A Special Hemophilia Program."* Gail O'Neill. Canadian Nurse 76, 11(Dec. 1980): 18-19.

**6666. Ontario. Advisory Committee on Wartime Day Nurseries**
*Dominion-Provincial Wartime Day Nurseries.* The Committee. Toronto: The Committee, [194-].

**6667. Ontario. Advisory Committee on Wartime Day Nurseries**
*Dominion-Provincial Wartime Day Nurseries: School Day Care.* The Committee. Toronto: The Committee, 1940.

**6668. Ontario Association for Curriculum Development (7th: 1957: Toronto)** *Basic Problems in Education: Report of the Seventh Annual Conference of the Ontario Association for Curriculum Development.* Ontario Association for Curriculum Development. Toronto: Clarke, Irwin and Company Limited, c1958.

**6669. Ontario Association for Curriculum Development (8th: 1958: Toronto)** *Standards in Education in Ontario Schools: Report of the Eighth Annual Conference of the Ontario Association for Curriculum Development.* Ontario Association for Curriculum Development. Toronto: Copp Clark Publishing Company Limited, c1958.

**6670. Ontario. Commission on Unemployment** *Report.* The Commission. Toronto: King's Printer, 1916.
Chairman: John S. Willison.

**6671. Ontario. Commission to Enquire Into and Report Upon the Workings of the Deaf and Dumb Institute at Belleville** *Report of the Commission to Enquire into and Report Upon the Workings of the Deaf and Dumb Institute at Belleville.* Ontario. Commission to Enquire into and Report Upon the Workings of the Deaf and Dumb Institute at Belleville. [Belleville, Ont.: s.n., 1907].
Commissioner: A.J. Russell Snow.

**6672. Ontario. Commission to Inquire Into the Recent Disturbances of and Among the Prisoners at the Ontario Reformatory at Guelph** *Report of the Commission to Inquire Into the Recent Disturbances of and Among the Prisoners at the Ontario Reformatory at Guelph.* The Commission. [S.l.: s.n., 1937].
Commissioner: James Ernest Madden.

**6673. Ontario. Commission to Investigate the Workings of the Blind Institute at Brantford and the Deaf and Dumb Institute at Belleville** *Report of the Commission to Investigate the Workings of the Blind Institute at Brantford and the Deaf and Dumb Institute at Belleville.* The Commission. [Brantford, Ont.?: s.n., 1907].
Commissioner: A.J. Russell Snow.

**6674. Ontario. Committee on Child Labour, 1907** *"Report of Committee on Child Labour 1907."* The Committee. Toronto: King's Printer, 1907. In Journals of the Legislative Assembly of Ontario 1907, vol.41, Appendix 1.

322HISTORY OF CANADIAN CHILDHOOD AND YOUTH

Chairman: Nelson Monteith.

**6675. Ontario. Committee on Religious Education in the Public Schools of Ontario** *Religious Information and Moral Development.* The Committee. Ontario: Department of Education, 1969.

**6676. Ontario Curriculum Institute. Committee on the Scope and Organization of the Curriculum** *Children, Classrooms, Curriculum, and Change: a Report.* Ontario Curriculum Institute, Committee on the Scope and Organization of the Curriculum. Toronto: Ontario Institute for Studies in Education, 1966.

**6677. Ontario. Department of Education** *Children's Gardening.* Department of Education. Toronto: The Department, 1912.

**6678. Ontario. Department of Health** *The Early Years: a Booklet of Baby and Child Care.* The Department. Toronto: The Department, 1954.

**6679. Ontario. Department of Health** *The Early Years: a Booklet of Baby and Child Care.* The Department. Ontario: Department of Health, 1956.

**6680. Ontario. Department of Labour** *Dominion-Provincial Youth Training Programme, Aircraft Training School Galt: Treatise of Training for Royal Canadian Air Force and Industrial Requirements.* The Department. [Toronto]: The Department, 1941.

**6681. Ontario. Department of Neglected and Dependent Children** *Thirteenth Report: Neglected and Dependent Children, Ontario, 1905.* Department of Neglected and Dependent Children and J.J. Kelso. Toronto: L.K. Cameron, King's Printer, 1906.

**6682. Ontario. Department of Public Welfare** *Program to Place British Children in Ontario Homes for the Duration of the War.* The Department. Toronto: The Department, 1941.

**6683. Ontario. Department of Public Welfare. Committee on Child Care and Adoption Services** *Report to the Minister of the Committee on Child Care and Adoption Services.* The Committee. Toronto: The Committee, 1954.

**6684. Ontario. Department of Reform Institutions** *Information Concerning the Ontario Training School for Boys, Bowmanville, Galt.* The Department. Toronto: The Department, 1940.

**6685. Ontario. Department of the Provincial Secretary** *Official Regulations for the Government of Public and Private Hospitals, Refuges, Orphanages and Infants' Homes.* The Department. Toronto: The Department, 1920.

**6686. Ontario. Department of the Provincial Secretary** *Official Regulations for the Government of Public and Private Hospitals, Refuges, Orphanages and Infant's Homes ... With Suggestions for the Economic Control of Dietaries in Public Institutions.* The Department. Toronto: The Department, 1914.

**6687. Ontario. Department of the Provincial Secretary** *Official Rules and Regulations for the Guidance of Officers and Employees of the Andrew Mercer Reformatory for Female Prisoners.* The Department. Toronto: The Department, 1941.

**6688. Ontario. Department of the Provincial Secretary** *The Ontario Reformatory.* The Department. Toronto: The Department, [191-?].

**6689. Ontario. Department of the Provincial Secretary and Citizenship. Citizenship Division** *The Immigrant Child in the Canadian Community.* The Division. Toronto: The Department, 1965.

**6690. Ontario Economic Council** *Poverty and Institutional Reform: a Report of the Ontario Economic Council.* Ontario Economic Council. [Ontario: s.n., 1969].

**6691. Ontario (Government)** *Services for Children with Mental and Emotional Disorders.* Government of Ontario. Toronto, Ont.: Government of Ontario, 1967.

**6692. Ontario. Interdepartmental Nutrition Committee** *Essentials of Infant Feeding.* The Committee. Toronto: The Committee, 1953.

**6693. Ontario. Interdepartmental Nutrition Committee** *Good Food for Every Child.* The Committee. Toronto: The Committee, 1950.
Reprinted for several years.

**6694. Ontario Law Reform Commission** *Report on the Age of Majority and Related Matters.* The Commission. Toronto: Ontario Law Reform Commission, 1969.
Chairman: H. Allan Leal.

**6695. Ontario. Legislative Assembly. Select Committee on Youth** *Report of the Ontario Legislature's Select Committee on Youth.* The Committee. [Toronto: s.n., 1967].

**6696. Ontario Medical Association. Committee on Child Welfare** *A Program for Handicapped Children.* The Committee. [London, Ont.: s.n., 1962].

**6697. Ontario. Minister's Advisory Committee on Child Welfare** *Report of the Advisory Committee on Child Welfare to the Minister of Public Welfare.* The Committee. [Toronto: s.n., 1964].

**6698. Ontario. Ministry of Community and Social Services** *Three Decades of Change: the Evolution of Residential Care and Community Alternatives in Children's Services.* Ontario. Ministry of Community and Social Services. [Toronto]: The Ministry, [1983].

**6699. Ontario. Physical Fitness Study Committee** *Report of the Ontario Physical Fitness Study Committee.* The Committee. [Toronto]: The Committee, c1961.

**6700. Ontario. Provincial Committee on Aims and Objectives of Education in the Schools of Ontario** *Living and Learning: the Report of the Provincial Committee on Aims and Objectives of Education in the Schools of Ontario.* Ontario. Provincial Committee on Aims and Objectives of Education in the Schools of Ontario. Toronto: Newton Publishing Company, 1968.
Report is also referred to as the Hall-Dennis Report.

**6701. Ontario. Public Welfare Department** *"Report of the Ontario Public Welfare Department."* Ontario Public Welfare Department. Child and Family Welfare 13, 6(Mar. 1938): 62-64.

**6702. Ontario. Royal Commission Appointed to Enquire Into the Prison and Reformatory System** *Report of the Commissioners Appointed To Enquire Into the Prison and Reformatory System of Ontario.* The Commission. Toronto: Warwick & Sons, 1891.
Chairman: J.W. Langmuir.

**6703. Ontario. Royal Commission on Education, 1950** *Report of the Royal Commission on Education in Ontario.* The Commission. Toronto: B. Johnston, King's Printer, 1950.
Chairman: John Andrew Hope.

**6704. Ontario. Royal Commission on Public Welfare** *Report of the Royal Commission on Public Welfare.* The Commission. Toronto: King's Printer, 1930.
Chairman: P.D. Ross.

**6705. Ontario. Royal Commission on the Care and Control of the Mentally Defective and Feeble-minded in Ontario (and the Prevalence of Venereal Disease)** *Report of the Royal Commission on the Care and Control of the Mentally Defective and Feeble-minded in Ontario: (and the Prevalence of Venereal Disease).* The Commission. Toronto: King's Printer, 1919.
Commissioner: Frank Egerton Hodgins.

**6706. Ontario. Royal Commission to Inquire Into the Administration, Management and Welfare of the Ontario School for the Blind** *Report of the Royal Commission to Inquire Into the Administration, Management and Welfare of the Ontario School for the Blind.* The Commission. Toronto: King's Printer, 1917.
Commissioner: Norman Blain Gash.

**6707. Ontario. Royal Commission to Investigate the Victoria Industrial School for Boys, Mimico** *Report of the Royal Commission to Investigate the Victoria Industrial School for Boys, Mimico.* The Commission. Toronto: [s.n.], 1921.
Chairman: John Waugh.

**6708. Oppenheimer, Jo** *"Childbirth in Ontario: the Transition from Home to Hospital in the Early Twentieth Century."* Jo Oppenheimer. Ontario History 75, 1(Mar. 1983): 36-60.

**6709. Ord, Nan** *Play Interests of the Preschool Child.* Nan Ord. Toronto: University of Toronto, 1935.
Thesis (M.A.)--University of Toronto, 1935.

**6710. Ord, Violet** *An Analysis of the Method of Art Instruction Used at the Children's Art Centre, Toronto.* Violet Ord. Toronto: University of Toronto, 1938.
Thesis (M.A.)--University of Toronto, 1938.

**6711. O'Reilly-Hewitt, F.T.** *A Study of the Occupational Choice of Grade Twelve Students in High Schools of Different Social Levels.* F.T. O'Reilly-Hewitt. Toronto: University of Toronto, 1947.
Thesis (M.A.)--University of Toronto, 1947.

**6712. Ormrod, Georgina** *"Individualized Reading."* Georgina Ormrod. Bulletin of the Institute of Child Study 24, 2(June 1962): 7-10.

**6713. Ormsby, H.L.** *"Ophthalmia Neonatorum."* H.L. Ormsby. Canadian Medical Association Journal 72, 8(Apr. 15, 1955): 576-580.

**6714. Orphans' Home and Female Aid Society (Toronto)** *The Orphans' Home and Female Aid Society, Toronto: Incorporated by Act of Parliament, August 2nd, 1851.* Orphans' Home and Female Aid Society (Toronto). [Toronto: s.n.], 1851.

**6715. Orvis, Kenneth** *Over and Under the Table: the Anatomy of an Alcoholic.* Kenneth Orvis. Montreal: Optimum Pub. International, c1985.

**6716. Ostiguy, Jean Rene** *Charles Huot.* Jean Rene Ostinguy. Ottawa: National Gallery of Canada, 1979.

**6717. Pace, James B.** *Operant Conditioning Procedures with Profoundly Retarded Children in the Acquisition of Concepts.* James B. Pace. Ottawa: University of Ottawa, c1971.
Thesis (Ph.D.)--University of Ottawa, 1971.

**6718. Page, Joseph L.** *"Quebec on the Move."* Joseph L. Page. Toronto: W.J. Gage, 1960. In Education: a Collection of Essays on Canadian Education, v.3, 1958-1960, pp. [1]-9.

**6719. Paivio, Allan** *"Childrearing Antecedents of Audience Sensitivity."* Allan Paivio. Child Development 35, 2(June 1964): 397-416.

**6720. Pajonas, Patricia J.** *Obedience and Heterogeneity: Catholic Secondary Schools in Boston and Montreal.* Patricia J. Pajonas. Cambridge, Ma.: Harvard University, c1970.
Thesis (Ph.D.)--Harvard University, 1970.

**6721. Palmer, A. Judith** *"The Junior Kindergarten Experiment."* A. Judith Palmer. Bulletin of the Institute of Child Study 29, 3(Fall 1967): 39-43.

**6722. Palmer, John A.** *"Congenital Malformation of the Anus."* John A. Palmer. Canadian Medical Association Journal 74, 11(June 1, 1956): 882-886.

**6723. Palmer, Judith A.** *Home Environment and Achievement.* Judith A. Palmer. Toronto: Board of Education, Research Department, 1967.

**6724. Pammett, Jon H.** *"The Development of Political Orientations in Canadian School Children."* Jon H. Pammett. Canadian Journal of Political Science 4, 1(Mar. 1971): 132-141.

**6725. Pammett, Jon H.** *Political Orientations in Public and Separate School Children.* Jon H. Pammett. Kingston: Queen's University, 1967.
Thesis (M.A.)--Queen's University, 1967.

**6726. Panabaker, D.N.** *"Pastimes Among the Pennsylvania Dutch in Waterloo."* D.N. Panabaker. Waterloo Historical Society Annual Report 19(1931): 245-249.

**6727. Panabaker, Katherine** *The Story of Girl Guides in Ontario.* Katherine Panabaker. Toronto: Ryerson Press, 1966.

**6728. Pantel, Norman W.** *A Study of Decision-making in Families in a Suburban Area of Metropolitan Toronto: Children's Perception of and Participation in Family Decision-making.* Norman W. Pantel. Toronto: University of Toronto, 1968.
Thesis (M.S.W.)--University of Toronto, 1968.

**6729. Paris, Erna** *Jews: an Account of Their Experience in Canada.* Erna Paris. Toronto: Macmillan of Canada, 1980.

**6730. Park, Edna Wilhelmene** *The Judgement of Teachers and Examination Results Compared with Terman Intelligence Tests.* Edna Wilhelmene Park. Toronto: University of Toronto, 1921.
Thesis (M.A.)--University of Toronto, 1921.

**6731. Parker, Janet A.** *A Comparative Study of Legitimate and Illegitimate Wards.* Janet A. Parker. Toronto: University of Toronto, 1928.
Thesis (M.A.)--University of Toronto, 1928.

**6732. Parker, Stephanie M.** *A Comparison of the Effects of Presentation and Withdrawal of Positive Reinforcement on Discrimination Learning, Perceptual-motor Performance and Emotionality in Children.* Stephanie M. Parker. Toronto: University of Toronto, 1960.
Thesis (M.A.)--University of Toronto, 1960.

**6733. Parks, F. Elizabeth** *Camp Amy Molson: a Discussion of the Need and Potential for Diagnosis and Treatment in a Summer Camp for Underprivileged Children.* F. Elizabeth Parks. Montreal: McGill University, 1971.
Thesis (M.S.W.)--McGill University, 1971.

**6734. Parmelee, G.W.** *Education in the Province of Quebec.* G.W. Parmelee and J.C. Sutherland. Quebec: Department of Public Instruction, c1914.

**6735. Parmenter, Morgan D.** *The "Ambitions" of Public School Children.* Morgan D. Parmenter. Toronto: University of Toronto, 1935.
Thesis (M.A.)–University of Toronto, 1935.

**6736. Parnall, Maxwell Bennett** *A Study of the Senior Public Schools and the Neighbourhood Schools of Guelph.* Maxwell Bennett Parnall. Toronto: University of Toronto, 1958.
Thesis (M.Ed.)–University of Toronto, 1958.

**6737. Parreno, Marietta** *A Descriptive Study of the Deviant Role of the "Rat" in Guelph Reformatory.* Marietta Parreno. Toronto: University of Toronto, 1967.
Thesis (M.S.W.)–University of Toronto, 1967.

**6738. Parsons, Allan F.** *Voluntary Social Maintenance in the Child Welfare Field in Toronto.* Allan F. Parsons. Toronto: University of Toronto, 1949.
Thesis (M.S.W.)–University of Toronto, 1949.

**6739. Partington, M.W.** *"The Heights and Weights of Indian and Eskimo School Children on James Bay and Hudson Bay."* M.W. Partington and Norma Roberts. Canadian Medical Association Journal/Journal de l'Association medicale canadienne 100, 11(Mar. 15, 1969): 502-509.

**6740. Partington, M.W.** *"Paediatric Admissions to Kingston General Hospital, Kingston, Ontario (1889-1901)."* M.W. Partington. Families 22, 1(1983): 33-46.

**6741. Partington, M.W.** *"Variations in Intelligence in Phenylketonuria."* M.W. Partington. Canadian Medical Association Journal/Journal de l'Association medicale canadienne 86, 16(Apr. 21, 1962): 736-743.

**6742. Partington, M.W.** *"Waardenburg's Syndrome and Heterochromia Iridum in a Deaf School Population."* M.W. Partington. Canadian Medical Association Journal/Journal de l'Association medicale canadienne 90, 17(Apr. 25, 1964): 1008-1017.

**6743. Partlow, Hugh R.** *Arithmetic and Reading, Yesterday and Today: a Comparison of St. Catharines Public School Standards 1933-38 and 1952-54.* Hugh R. Partlow. Toronto: Copp Clark Company Limited, 1955.

**6744. Partlow, Hugh R.** *A Comparison of St. Catharines' Public School Standards in Arithmetic and Reading, 1933-38 and 1952-54.* Hugh R. Partlow. Toronto: University of Toronto, 1955.
Thesis (D.Paed.)–University of Toronto, 1955.

**6745. Partridge, Ruth C.** *"Daylight Glare in School Rooms."* Ruth C. Partridge and D.L. MacLean. Canadian Public Health Journal 26, 3(Mar. 1935): 127-129.

**6746. Partridge, Ruth C.** *"A Method of Determining the Blackboard Visibility in a School."* Ruth C. Partridge and D.L. MacLean. Canadian Public Health Journal 26, 2(Feb. 1935): 70-72.

**6747. Partridge, Ruth C.** *"A Survey of Hearing in School Children."* Ruth C. Partridge and D.L. MacLean. Canadian Public Health Journal 24, 11(Nov. 1933): 524-529.

**6748. Pascoe, M. Gilbert** *"Acute Suppurative Parotitis Secondary to a Foreign Body (Feather)."* M. Gilbert Pascoe. Canadian Medical Association Journal 72, 1(Jan. 1, 1955): 35-36.

**6749. Patel, Hawa** *"The Problem of Routine Circumcision."* Hawa Patel. Canadian Medical Association Journal/Journal de l'Association medicale canadienne 95, 11(Sept. 10, 1966): 576-581.

**6750. Paterson, W.P.E.** *"Malignant Thymoma."* W.P.E. Paterson. Canadian Medical Association Journal 71, 3(Sept. 1954): 276-277.

**6751. Paton, Richard Thurston** *The Influence of Three Reinforcement Modifications on Perseveration in Psychotic Children.* Richard Thurston Paton. Kingston: Queen's University, 1969.
Thesis (Ph.D.)–Queen's University, 1969. Author published an article with the same title in Canadian Psychologist/Psychologie canadienne 11, 3(July 1970): 261-268.

**6752. Patrias, Carmela** *"Passages From the Life...: an Italian Woman in Welland, Ontario."* Carmela Patrias. Canadian Woman Studies/Cahiers de la femme 8, 2(Summer 1987): 69-73.

**6753. Pattee, C.J.** *"Female Pseudohermaphroditism Treated with Oral Cortisone."* J.C. Pattee, D.M. Wise and R. Palmer Howard. Canadian Medical Association Journal 71, 4(Oct. 1954): 385-386.

**6754. Pattee, C.J.** *"Sexual Precocity: Report of an Ovarian Tumour in a Girl of 19 Months."* C.J. Pattee, F.J. Tweedie and A.K. Geddes. Canadian Medical Association Journal 76, 7(Apr. 1, 1957): 573-576.

**6755. Patterson, G.J.** *"The Unit Promotion System in the Hamilton Public Schools."* G.J. Patterson. Canadian Education and Research Digest 3, 1(Mar. 1963): 48-53.

**6756. Patterson, Jean M.** *"A Dietaty Investigation in Toronto Families Having Annual Incomes Between $1,500-$2,400."* Jean M. Patterson and E.W. McHenry. Canadian Public Health Journal 32, 5(May 1941): 251-258.

**6757. Patterson, Nancy Lou** *"Mennonite Folk Art of Waterloo County."* Nancy Lou Patterson. Ontario History 60, 3(Sept. 1968)): 81-104.

**6758. Paul, E.M.** *"School Nursing."* E.M. Paul. Canadian Nurse 10, 10(Oct. 1914): 586-593.

**6759. Paulsen, Ann Karen** *A Study of 50 Youths Known to Some Particular Social Agency in the City of London During January-December, 1965: Including Characteristics of the Youth, Peer Relationships, Spare-time Activities, and Need for Alternative Living Accommodation.* Ann Karen Paulsen. Toronto: University of Toronto, 1966.
Thesis (M.S.W.)--University of Toronto, 1966.

**6760. Pavalko, Ronald M.** *"Peer Influence on College Plans of Canadian High School Students."* Ronald M. Pavalko and David R. Bishop. Canadian Review of Sociology and Anthropology/Revue canadienne de sociologie et d'anthropologie 3, 2(May 1966): 191-200.

**6761. Pavilanis, V.** *"Western Equine Encephalomylitis: Report of a Case in Montreal."* V. Pavilanis, Isobel L. Wright and M. Silverberg. Canadian Medical Association Journal 77, 2(July 15, 1957): 128-130.

**6762. Pavilanis, V.** *"A Winter Epidemic of Poliomyelitis in Saint-Augustin, Que.: 3. Laboratory Studies."* V. Pavilanis and A. Frappier. Canadian Medical Association Journal 79, 1(July 1, 1958): 11-14.

**6763. Pawlicki, Robert Edward** *The Influence of Contingent and Noncontingent Social Reinforcement upon Internal and External Controlling Children in a Simple Operant Task.* Robert Edward Pawlicki. Toronto: York University, 1970. (CTM no. 6780)
Thesis (Ph.D.)--York University, 1970.

**6764. Payne, Julien D.** *"The Deserted Wives and Children's Maintenance Act, RSO 1960 Ch. 105 Proposal for Reform."* Julien D. Payne. Western Ontario Law Review 8(1969): 67-121.

**6765. Pearlman, L.N.** *"Acute Myelitis Following Measles."* L.N. Pearlman and W.T. Shirreff. Canadian Medical Association Journal 50, 1(Jan. 1944): 50-51.

**6766. Pearlman, L.N.** *"Goitre in a Premature Infant."* L.N. Pearlman. Canadian Medical Association Journal 70, 3(Mar. 1954): 317-318.

**6767. Pearlman, L.N.** *"Salmonella Newport Meningitis."* L.N. Pearlman and A.S.P. Gordon. Canadian Medical Association Journal 60, 5(May 1949): 483-486.

**6768. Peate, Mary** *Girl in a Red River Coat.* Mary Peate. Toronto: Clarke, Irwin and Company, c1970.

**6769. Pedersen, Diana L.** *"The Scientific Training of Mothers: the Campaign for Domestic Science in Ontario Schools, 1890-1913."* Diana Pedersen. Thornhill: HSTC Publications, c1983. In Critical Issues in the History of Canadian Science, Technology and Medicine = Problemes cruciaux de l'histoire de la science, de la technologie et de la medecine au Canada, pp. 178-194. Edited by Richard A. Jarrell and Arnold E. Roos.

**6770. Pedersen, Eigil** *"Measured I.Q. Related to Teacher-estimated Intelligence: an Exploration in Bias."* Eigil Pedersen. McGill Journal of Education 3, 1(Spring 1968): 12-23.

**6771. Pedersen, Eigil** *"A New Perspective on the Effects of First-grade Teachers on Children's Subsequent Adult Status."* Eigil Pedersen, Therese Annette Faucher and William W. Eaton. Harvard Educational Review 48, 4(1978): 1-31.

**6772. Pelletier, Alphonse J.** *"Movements in the Development of the Canadian Family: Statistical Studies."* A.J. Pelletier. Canadian Public Health Journal 25, 10(Oct. 1934): 466-475.

**6773. Pelletier, Wilfred** *No Foreign Land: the Biography of a North American Indian.* Wilfred Pelletier and Ted Poole. New York: Pantheon Books, c1973.

**6774. Pennacchio, Luigi G.** *"The Defence of Identity: Ida Siegel and the Jews of Toronto versus the Assimilation Attempts of the Public School and its Allies, 1900-1920."* Luigi G. Pennacchio. Canadian Jewish Historical Society

Journal 9, 1(Spring 1985): 41-60.

**6775. Pennacchio, Luigi G.** *"Toronto's Public Schools and the Assimilation of Foreign Students, 1900-1920."* Luigi G. Pennacchio. Journal of Educational Thought/Revue de la pensee educative 20, 1(Apr. 1986): 37-48.

**6776. Pennington, Doris** *Agnes Macphail, Reformer: Canada's First Female M.P.* Doris Pennington. Toronto: Simon and Pierre, 1989.

**6777. Pepson, Elsie** *"The Suzuki Approach to Violin Playing."* Elsie Pepson. McGill Journal of Education 3, 1(Spring 1968): 71-78.

**6778. Pequegnat, L.A.** *"The Present Problem in Infant Mortality."* L.A. Pequegnat. Canadian Public Health Journal 29, 10(Oct. 1938): 477-483.

**6779. Percival, Walter Pilling** *Across the Years: a Century of Education in the Province of Quebec.* Walter Pilling Percival. Montreal: Gazette Printing Company Limited, 1946.

**6780. Percival, Walter Pilling** *Life in School: an Explanation of the Protestant School System of the Province of Quebec.* Walter Pilling Percival. Montreal: [The Herald Press, 1941].
Originally published in 1940. Reprinted in 1941.

**6781. Percival, Walter Pilling** *Should We All Think Alike?: Differentiating Characteristics of French Canadian Education in Quebec.* W.P. Percival. Toronto: W.J. Gage and Company Limited, 1951.

**6782. Percival, Walter Pilling** *Why Educate?* Walter Pilling Percival. Toronto: J.M. Dent and Sons, 1935.

**6783. Perley-Robertson, Alex, comp.** *One Hundred Years 1864-1964, Protestant Children's Village Ottawa, Canada.* Alex Perley-Robertson, [comp.]. Ottawa: [s.n.], 1964.

**6784. Perron, Rheal Rolland** *A Study of the Non-repeating Grade 9 Bilingual Pupils of Sudbury in the Private and Public Secondary Schools.* Rheal Rolland Perron. Toronto: University of Toronto, 1965.
Thesis (M.Ed.)–University of Toronto, 1965.

**6785. Peterman, Michael** *Robertson Davies.* Michael Peterman. Boston: Twayne, c1986.

**6786. Peters, M.I.** *"The Post-natal Visit: Its Opportunities."* M.I. Peters. Canadian Nurse 23, 3(Mar. 1927): 127-128.

**6787. Peterson, Robert James** *Apprenticeship in Ontario, 1911-1965.* Robert James Peterson. Toronto: University of Toronto, 1971.
Thesis (M.A.)–University of Toronto, 1971.

**6788. Phair, J.T.** *"An Experiment in Health Teaching in Ontario."* J.T. Phair. Canadian Public Health Journal 28, 4(Apr. 1937): 166-178.

**6789. Phair, J.T.** *"Incidence of Disease in School Age Children."* J.T. Phair. Canadian Public Health Journal 24, 8(Aug. 1933): 373-376.

**6790. Phair, J.T.** *"Survey of Health Habits Among School Age Children."* J.T. Phair. Canadian Public Health Journal 25, 8(Aug. 1933): 380-386.

**6791. Phelps, David C.** *A Study of Drop-in Centres for Teenagers in Metropolitan Toronto with Special Emphasis on the Alienation of Youth Using the Centres.* David C. Phelps. Toronto: University of Toronto, 1967.
Thesis (M.S.W.)–University of Toronto, 1967.

**6792. Philanthropy** *Care of Our Destitute and Criminal Population: a Series of Letters Published in the Montreal Gazette.* Philanthropy. [Montreal: s.n.], 1857.

**6793. Philip, B. Roger** *"An Objective Evaluation of Brief Group Psychotherapy on Delinquent Boys."* B. Roger Philip and Helen E. Peixotto. Canadian Journal of Psychology 13, 4(Dec. 1959): 273-280.
B. Roger Philip published an article with the same title in Canadian Journal of Corrections/Revue canadienne de criminologie 3, 4(Oct. 1961): 463-466. Helen Peixotto was not listed as a joint author on the 1961 article.

**6794. Philippe, Marilyn** *"Hurler's Disease."* Marilyn Philippe. Canadian Nurse 55, 12(Dec. 1959): 1122-1126.

**6795. Phillips, A.J.** *Discovery, Identification and Remedial Treatment of Difficulties in the Fundamental Operations in Elementary School Arithmetic.* Alexander J. Phillips. Toronto: University of Toronto, 1945.
Thesis (Ph.D.)–University of Toronto, 1945.

**6796. Phillips, A.J.** *Relative Difficulties of the Fundamental Facts in Arithmetic Based on a Study of Errors Made by Ontario Children.* A.J. Phillips and H.M. Fowler. [Toronto]: Department of Educational Research, University of Toronto, 1946.

**6797. Phillips, Bluebell Stewart** *"Portrait of Margaret."* Bluebell Stewart Phillips. Dalhousie Review 29, 2(July 1949-1950): 157-165.

**6798. Phillips, Charles E.** *"The Schools of Quebec."* Charles E. Phillips. Canadian Education 1, 1(Dec. 1945): 45-80.

**6799. Phillips, Charles E.** *The Teaching of English in Ontario, 1800-1900.* C.E. Phillips. Toronto: University of Toronto, [1935].
Thesis (D.Paed.)--University of Toronto, [1935].

**6800. Phillips, Kenneth G.** *"Factors Affecting the Prognosis for Survival in Prematurely Born Infants."* K.G. Phillips, J.G. Armstrong and B.G. Delta. Canadian Medical Association Journal/Journal de l'Association medicale canadienne 80, 10(May 15, 1959): 800-802.

**6801. Phillips, Kenneth G.** *"Incidence of Hypoglycemia in the Low-birth-weight Neonate."* Kenneth G. Phillips and James Graham. Canadian Medical Association Journal/Journal de l'Association medicale canadienne 102, 4(Feb. 28, 1970): 386-387.

**6802. Picard, Marilen Joy** *Intersensory Integration and Reading Ability in Children.* Marilen Joy Picard. London, Ont.: University of Western Ontario, 1967.
Thesis (M.A.)--University of Western Ontario, 1967.

**6803. Pierce, Lorne** *Marjorie Pickthall: a Book of Remembrance.* Lorne Pierce. Toronto: Ryerson Press, c1925.

**6804. Pimm, June B.** *Children's Motor Skills and the Partial Reinforcement Acquisition Effect.* June B. Pimm. Ottawa: Carleton University, 1968.
Thesis (Ph.D.)--Carleton University, 1968.

**6805. Pimm, June B.** *"The Effects of Early Childhood Experience."* June B. Pimm. Ottawa: The Vanier Institute of the Family, 1970. In Day Care, a Resource for the Contemporary Family, pp. 42-55. Edited by Roslyn Burshtyn.

**6806. Pitsula, James M.** *"The Emergence of Social Work in Toronto."* James Pitsula. Journal of Canadian Studies/Revue d'etudes canadiennes 14, 1(Spring 1979): 35-42.

**6807. Pitsula, James M.** *The Relief of Poverty in Toronto 1880-1930.* James Michael Pitsula. (CTM no. 41010) Thesis (Ph.D.)--York University, 1979.

**6808. Pitts, Ruth Ann** *"Low Francophone Male Social Mobility in Quebec Before 1976: Cultural Explanations Revisited."* Ruth Ann Pitts. Canadian Ethnic Studies/Etudes ethniques au Canada 17, 3(1985): 17-36.

**6809. Piva, Michael J.** *The Condition of the Working Class in Toronto, 1900-1921.* Michael J. Piva. Ottawa: University of Ottawa Press, 1979.
Revision of the author's Ph.D. thesis, presented at Concordia University, 1975.

**6810. Plewes, Burns** *"Multiple Glomus Tumours: Four in One Finger Tip."* Burns Plewes. Canadian Medical Association Journal 44, 4(Apr. 1941): 364-365.

**6811. Plumptre, Adelaide M.** *The Nonacademic Child: a Reprint of Two Papers.* Adelaide M. Plumptre and E.P. Lewis. Ottawa: Canadian Council on Child and Family Welfare, 1931.

**6812. Podmore, Christopher John** *Private Schooling in English Canada.* Christopher John Podmore. Hamilton: McMaster University, 1976. (CTM no. 38014) Thesis (Ph.D.)--McMaster University, 1976.

**6813. Poirier, Paul** *"Acne and its Treatment."* Paul Poirier. Canadian Medical Association Journal 77, 9(Nov. 1, 1957): 866-870.

**6814. Poldon, Amelia** *"Women in Pioneer Life."* Amelia Poldon. Ontario Historical Society, Papers and Records 17(1919): 25-29.

**6815. Pollock, Sheila Joy** *A Study of the Impact of Social Change on Developments in the Philosophy of Child Welfare in Ontario Between 1891-1921.* Sheila Joy Pollock. Toronto: University of Toronto, 1966.
Thesis (M.S.W.)--University of Toronto, 1966.

**6816. Pond, Kathleen M.** *The Home of the Female Juvenile Delinquent.* Kathleen M. Pond. Toronto: University of Toronto, 1951.
Thesis (M.A.)--University of Toronto, 1951.

6817. **Porter, George D.** *"Health Work Among Students."* Geo. D. Porter. Public Health Journal 14, 6(June 1923): 261-271.
Article deals with male university students whose average age is 19 years.

6818. **Porter, John A.** *Stations and Callings: Making it Through the School System.* John Porter, Marion Porter and Bernard Blishen with Maria Barrados, Sid Gilbert, Hugh A. McRoberts and Susan Russell. Toronto: Methuen, c1982.

6819. **Posen, Minda M.** *A Study of Adopted Children.* Minda M. Posen. Toronto: University of Toronto, 1948.
Thesis (M.S.W.)--University of Toronto, 1948.

6820. **Potashin, Reva** *An Examination of "Withdrawing" as a Personality Characteristic of Pre-adolescent Children.* Reva Potashin. Toronto: University of Toronto, 1951.
Thesis (Ph.D.)--University of Toronto, 1951.

6821. **Potashin, Reva** *A Study of Social Relationships of Grade-school Children: Friends and Non-friends.* Reva Potashin. Toronto: University of Toronto, 1944.
Thesis (M.A.)--University of Toronto, 1944.

6822. **Pottle, Herbert L.** *An Analysis of Childrens' Lies with Particular Reference to a School Situation.* Herbert L. Pottle. Toronto: University of Toronto, 1934.
Thesis (M.A.)--University of Toronto, 1934.

6823. **Pottle, Herbert L.** *An Analysis of Errors Made in Arithmetical Addition.* Herbert L. Pottle. Toronto: University of Toronto, 1937.
Thesis (Ph.D.)--University of Toronto, 1937.

6824. **Potts, Florence** *"Report of Nursing in Hospitals: a Case of Psoriasis Complicated by Chicken Pox."* Florence Potts. Canadian Nurse 2, 3(Sept. 1906): 24.

6825. **Poulton, Ron** *The Paper Tyrant: John Ross Robertson of the Toronto Telegram.* Ron Poulton. Toronto: Clarke, Irwin and Company, c1971.

6826. **Power, Mary** *"The Management of a Child Welfare Week in Small Cities and Towns with Results."* Mary Power. Public Health Journal 9, 8(Aug. 1918): 362-363.

6827. **Power, Michael** *A Documentary History of Assumption College.* Michael Power. Leamington: The Author, 1984.

6828. **Pozsonyi, Joseph** *"Skeletal Age in Subjects With Mental Retardation."* Joseph Pozsonyi and Donald E. Zarfas. Canadian Medical Association Journal/Journal de l'Association medicale canadienne 89, 20(Nov. 16, 1963): 1038-1039.

6829. **Prang, Margaret** *"Clerics, Politicians, and the Bilingual Schools Issue in Ontario, 1910-1917."* Margaret Prang. Canadian Historical Review 41, 4(Dec. 1960): 281-307.

6830. **Pratt, David** *An Instrument for Measuring Evaluative Assertions Concerning Minority Groups and its Application or an Analysis of History Textbooks Approved for Ontario Schools.* David Pratt. Toronto: University of Toronto, 1969.
Thesis (Ph.D.)--University of Toronto, 1969.

6831. **Pratt, E.J.** *"The Application of the Binet-Simon Tests (Stanford Revision) to a Toronto Public School."* E.J. Pratt. Canadian Journal of Mental Hygiene 3, 1(Apr. 1921): 95-116.

6832. **Pratt, E.J.** *"Mental Measurement as Applied to a Toronto School."* E.J. Pratt. Public Health Journal 12, 4(Apr. 1921): 149-155.

6833. **Precious, Carole** *J. Armand Bombardier.* Carole Precious. Markam, Ont.: Fitzhenry & Whiteside, 1984.

6834. **Prentice, Alison** *"Education and the Metaphor of the Family: the Upper Canadian Experience."* Alison Prentice. History of Education Quarterly 12, 3(Fall 1972): 281-303.
Reprinted in Education and Social Change: Themes from Ontario's Past, pp. 110-132. Edited by Michael B. Katz and Paul H. Mattingly.

6835. **Prentice, Alison** *The School Promoters: Education and Social Class in Mid-nineteenth Century Upper Canada.* Alison L. Prentice. Toronto: University of Toronto, 1974. (CTM no. 31306)

6836. **Prentice, Alison** *The School Promoters: Education and Social Class in Mid-nineteenth Century Upper Canada.* Alison L. Prentice. Toronto: McClelland and Stewart Limited, c1977.

6837. **Preston, Charles F.** *The Development of Moral Judgement in Young People.* Charles Franklyn Preston. Toronto: University of Toronto, 1962.
Thesis (Ph.D.)--University of Toronto, 1962.

6838. **Price, R.M.** *"Bovine Tuberculosis in Children."* R.M. Price. Canadian Public Health Journal 29, 6(June 1938): 251-254.

6839. **Price, R.M.** *"The Incidence of Bovine Tuberculosis in Children."* R.M. Price. Canadian Public Health Journal 20, 7(July 1929): 323-330.

6840. **Prichard, John Stobo** *"Abdominal Pain of Cerebral Origin in Children."* John Stobo Prichard. Canadian Medical Association Journal 78, 9(May 1, 1958): 665-667.

6841. **Prichard, John Stobo** *"Celontin in the Treatment of Petit Mal in Children."* John Stobo Prichard, E.G. Murphy and Florencio E. Escardo. Canadian Medical Association Journal 76, 9(May 1, 1957): 770-771.

6842. **Prince, John Stevens** *Attitude Toward Physical Education: a Comparative Study of First and Fourth Year Secondary School Boys and Girls.* John Stevens Prince. London, Ont.: University of Western Ontario, 1969. (CTM no. 4272) Thesis (M.A.)--University of Western Ontario, 1969.

6843. **Prisoner's Aid Association of Canada** *Prison Reform.* [The Association?]. [Toronto?: s.n., 1889?].
At head of title: With the Compliments of the Prisoner's Aid Association of Canada.

6844. **Prisoners' Aid Association of Canada** *Prison Reform.* [The Association?]. [Toronto?: s.n., 189-?].

6845. **Prissick, F.H.** *"Cervical Lymphadenitis in Children Caused by Mycobacteria."* F.H. Prissick and A.M. Masson. Canadian Medical Association Journal 75, 10(Nov. 15, 1956): 798-803.

6846. **Pritchard, James S.** *"For the Glory of God: the Quinte Mission, 1668-1680."* James S. Pritchard. Ontario History 65, 3(Sept. 1973): 133-148.

6847. **Proulx, Louis** *Asylum of the Sisters of Charity at Quebec.* Louis Proulx. [Quebec: s.n.], 1851.

6848. **Proyer, Valene Antoinette** *The Effects of a Programme of Educational Gymnastics and a Programme of Perceptual Motor Training on the Behavioural and Psychological Traits of Trainable Retarded Children.* Valene Antoinette Proyer. Montreal: McGill University, 1970. Thesis (M.A.)--McGill University, 1970.

6849. **Prueter, H.J.** *Care and Education of Crippled Children in Ontario.* H.J. Prueter. Toronto: University of Toronto, 1936. Thesis (D.Paed.)--University of Toronto, 1936.

6850. **Pullan, Vivian** *A Longtitudinal Study of Absenteeism Among School Children and Its Relation to Their Present Adjustment.* Vivian Pullan. Toronto: University of Toronto, 1950. Thesis (M.A.)--University of Toronto, 1950.

6851. **Pullen, Harry** *A Study of Secondary School Curriculum Change in Canada with Special Emphasis on an Ontario Experiment.* Harry Pullen. Toronto: University of Toronto, 1955. Thesis (Ed.D.)--University of Toronto, 1955.

6852. **Purdy, Al** *Morning and It's Summer: a Memoir.* Al Purdy. Dunvegan: Quadrant Editions, c1983.

6853. **Purdy, Judson D.** *"The English Public School Tradition in Nineteenth Century Ontario."* J.D. Purdy. Toronto: University of Toronto Press, 1974. In Aspects of Nineteenth Century Ontario, pp. 237-252. Edited by F.H. Armstrong, H.A. Stevenson, and J.D. Wilson.

6854. **Purdy, Judson D.** *John Strachan and Education in Canada, 1800-1851.* Judson D. Purdy. Toronto: University of Toronto, 1962. Thesis (Ph.D.)--University of Toronto, 1962.

6855. **Purdy, Ruth E.** *"A New Approach to Reading."* Ruth E. Purdy. Toronto: W.J. Gage, 1960. In Education: a Collection of Essays on Canadian Education, v.3, 1958-1960, pp. [121]-125.

6856. **Putman, J.H.** *Egerton Ryerson and Education in Upper Canada.* J. Harold Putman. Toronto: William Briggs, 1912.

6857. **Puxley, Evelyn** *Poverty in Montreal.* Evelyn Puxley. Montreal: Dawson College Press, c1971.

6858. **Quebec. Royal Commission of Inquiry on Education, 1963-1966** *Report of the Royal Commission of Inquiry on Education in the Province of Quebec: Part One, The Structure of the Educational System at the Provincial Level.* The Commission. Montreal: Pierre desMarais, 1963.
Chairman: Alphonse-Marie Parent.

**6859. Quebec. Royal Commission of
Inquiry on Education, 1963-1966** *Report
of the Royal Commission of Inquiry on
Education in the Province of Quebec: Part
Two, the Pedagogical Structures of the
Educational System: A - The Structures
and the Levels of Education.* The
Commission. Montreal: Pierre desMarais,
1965.
Chairman: Alphonse-Marie Parent.

**6860. Quebec. Royal Commission of
Inquiry on Education, 1963-1966** *Report
of the Royal Commission of Inquiry on
Education in the Province of Quebec: Part
Two, the Pedagogical Structures of the
Educational System: B - The Programmes
of Study and the Educational Services.*
The Commission. Montreal: Pierre
desMarais, 1965.
Chairman: Alphonse-Marie Parent.

**6861. Quebec. Royal Commission of
Inquiry on Education, 1963-1966** *Report
of the Royal Commission of Inquiry on
Education in the Province of Quebec: Part
Three, Educational Administration: B -
Finances, C - Participants in Education.*
The Commission. Montreal: Pierre
desMarais, 1966.
Chairman: Alphonse-Marie Parent.

**6862. Quebec. Royal Commission of
Inquiry on Education, 1963-1966** *Report
of the Royal Commission of Inquiry on
Education in the Province of Quebec: Part
Three, Educational Administration: A -
Religious and Cultural Diversity Within a
Unified Administration.* The Commission.
Montreal: Pierre desMarais, 1966.
Chairman: Alphonse-Marie Parent.

**6863. Quebec. Royal Commission of
Inquiry on the Position of the French
Language and on Language Rights in
Quebec** *"Education for Immigrants."* The
Commission. Quebec: Official Editor of
Quebec, 1972. In Report of the Royal
Commission of Inquiry on the Position of
the French Language and on Language
Rights in Quebec, v.1, pp. 193-279.

**6864. Quiney, Linda Joan** *A Canadian
Orphanage in the Nineteenth Century: the
Orphan's Home of the City of Ottawa,
1864-1893.* Linda Joan Quiney. Toronto:
University of Toronto, 1982.
Thesis (M.A.)--University of Toronto,
1982.

**6865. Quinlan, Frank** *"Infant's Ability to
Learn."* Frank Quinlan. Ontario Education
1, 6(Nov.-Dec. 1969): 20-21, 31-32.

**6866. Quinlivan, W.L.G.** *"Compound
Presentation."* W.L.G. Quinlivan. Canadian
Medical Association Journal 76, 8(Apr.
15, 1957): 633-635.

**6867. Quinn, George** *Impact of European
Immigration upon the Elementary Schools
of Central Toronto, 1815-1915.* George
Quinn. Toronto: University of Toronto,
1968.
Thesis (M.A.)--University of Toronto,
1968.

**6868. Quinn, William J.** *""I Have Seen
Great Things Happen...""* William J.
Quinn. Education Canada 10, 4(Dec.
1970): 42-49.

**6869. Quirk, Eve-Lyn** *The Reliability and
Validity of the H-T-P as a Measure of
Intelligence in Adolescents.* Eve-Lyn Quirk.
Toronto: University of Toronto, 1955.
Thesis (M.A.)--University of Toronto,
1955.

**6870. Rabinowitch, I.M.** *"Juvenile
Diabetes."* I.M. Rabinowitch. Canadian
Nurse 27, 3(Mar. 1931): 124-129.

**6871. Race, Joseph** *"Milk Supply in
Relation to Tuberculosis in Ontario."*
Joseph Race. Public Health Journal 6,
8(Aug. 1915): 378-383.

**6872. Radcliffe, S.J.** *Retardation in the
Schools of Ontario.* S.J. Radcliffe. Toronto:
University of Toronto, [1922].
Thesis (D.Paed.)--University of Toronto,
[1922].

**6873. Radford, Peter F.** *Undergraduate
Physical Education Students: a Preliminary
Study.* Peter F. Radford and Geoff R.
Gowan. Hamilton: McMaster University,
1969.

**6874. Radin, Paul** *"Introductive Enquiry in
the Study of Ojibwa Religion."* Paul Radin.
Ontario Historical Society, Papers and
Records 12(1914): 210-220.

**6875. Ramraj, Victor** *Mordecai Richler.*
Victor Ramraj. Boston: Twayne, c1983.

**6876. Ramsden, Peter** *"Andaskwe: Part
1."* Peter Ramsden. Journal of
Anthropology at McMaster 3, 1(Winter
1977): 79-90.

**6877. Ramsden, Peter** *"Andaskwe: Part
2."* Peter Ramsden. Journal of
Anthropology at McMaster 4, 1(Winter
1978): 104-118.

**6878. Ramsey, C.A.** *Non-Canadian Born Students: Their Placement in Grade Nine Programmes and Its Relationship to Other Factors.* C.A. Ramsey and E.N. Wright. Toronto: Board of Education, Research Department, 1969.

**6879. Ramsey, C.A.** *Students of Non-Canadian Origin: a Descriptive Report of Students in Toronto Schools.* C.A. Ramsey and E.N. Wright. Toronto: Board of Education, 1969.

**6880. Ramsey, C.A.** *Students of Non-Canadian Origin: the Relation of Language and Rural Urban Background to Academic Achievement and Ability.* C.A. Ramsey and E.N. Wright. Toronto: Board of Education, Research Department, 1969.

**6881. Ramsey, Dean P.** *The Development of Child Welfare Legislation in Ontario: a History of Child Welfare Legislation in Ontario With Particular Reference to the Children's Protection Act, the Adoption Act, and the Children of Unmarried Parents Act, and Subsequent Amendments of These Acts.* Dean P. Ramsey. Toronto: University of Toronto, 1949. (CTM no. 31315)
Thesis (M.S.W.)--University of Toronto, 1949.

**6882. Rance, C.P.** *"Treatment of the Nephrotic Syndrome in Children."* C.P. Rance and A.L. Chute. Canadian Medical Association Journal 73, 12(Dec. 15, 1955): 959-964.

**6883. Randhawa, Bikkar S.** *Information Processing: a Developmental Study.* Bikkar S. Randhawa. Toronto: University of Toronto, 1969.
Thesis (Ph.D.)--University of Toronto, 1969.

**6884. Rasky, Frank** *Just a Simple Pharmacist: the Story of Murray Koffler, Builder of the Shoppers Drug Mart Empire.* Frank Rasky. Toronto: McClelland and Stewart, 1988.

**6885. Rathbun, J.C.** *"Idiopathic Galactose Intolerance in a Premature Infant."* John C. Rathbun. Canadian Medical Association Journal 72, 12(June 15, 1955): 923-925.

**6886. Rathbun, J.C.** *"Rectal Suppositories for Infants and Children."* J.C. Rathbun. Canadian Medical Association Journal 72, 1(Jan. 1, 1955): 37.

**6887. Ray, Edward** *The Effects of Anxiety and Social Isolation on the Effectiveness of Social Reinforcers in the Conditioning of Young Children.* Edward Ray. Toronto: University of Toronto, 1960.
Thesis (M.A.)--University of Toronto, 1960.

**6888. Ray, Janet** *Emily Stowe.* Janet Ray. Don Mills, Ont.: Fitzhenry & Whiteside, 1978.

**6889. Raynsford, William** *Silent Casualties: Veterans' Families in the Aftermath of the Great War.* William Raynsford and Jeannette Raynsford. Madoc, Ont.: Merribrae Press, c1986.

**6890. Rea, Jocelyn** *A Systematic Evaluation of the Content of Preschool Stories in Terms of Children's Recalls.* Jocelyn Rea. Toronto: University of Toronto, 1940.
Thesis (M.A.)--University of Toronto, 1940.

**6891. Read, John H.** *"Medical Education and the Native Canadian: an Example of Mutual Symbiosis."* John H. Read and Frances L. Strick. Canadian Medical Association Journal/Journal de l'Association medicale canadienne 100, 11(Mar. 15, 1969): 515-520.

**6892. Reade, Terry** *"Home Care of Children With Inborn Errors of Metabolism."* Terry Reade and Caroline Clow. Canadian Nurse 66, 10(Oct. 1970): 41-43.

**6893. Rean, Margery L.** *Factors Related to the Occupational Preferences of High School Boys.* Margery L. Rean. Toronto: University of Toronto, 1936.
Thesis (M.A.)--University of Toronto, 1936.

**6894. Rebhan, Augusta W.** *"An Outbreak of Asian Influenza at a Girl's Camp."* Augusta W. Rebhan. Canadian Medical Association Journal 77, 8(Oct. 15, 1957): 797-799.

**6895. Rebhan, Augusta W.** *"Staphylococcal Pneumonia: a Review of 329 Cases."* A.W. Rebhan and H.E. Edwards. Canadian Medical Association Journal/Journal de l'Association medicale canadienne 82, 10(Mar. 5, 1960): 513-517.

**6896. Record, Maurice Adrian** *A Study of Mathematical Achievement of Controlled Groups of Fourth Year Students in New York and Ontario High Schools.* M.A. Record. Toronto: University of Toronto, 1949.
Thesis (M.A.)--University of Toronto, 1949.

**6897. Redekop, Magdalene** *Ernest Thompson Seton.* Magdalene Redekop. Don Mills, Ont.: Fitzhenry & Whiteside, c1979.

**6898. Reesor, Eleanor** *"The St. Christopher House."* Eleanor Reesor. Canadian Welfare 41, 1(Jan.-Feb. 1965): 16-20.

**6899. Reich, Carol** *Follow Up of the Montessori Programme.* Carol Reich. Toronto: Board of Education, 1974.

**6900. Reid, Edith Gittings** *The Great Physician: Sir William Osler.* Edith Gittings Reid. New York: Oxford University Press, c1931.

**6901. Reid, John** *"Suicide in Slow Motion."* John Reid. Canadian Welfare 45, 5(Sept.-Oct. 1969): 11-12, 16.

**6902. Reitsma-Street, Marge** *A Feminist Analysis of Ontario Laws for Delinquency and Neglect: More Control than Care.* Marge Reitsma-Street. [Toronto]: Faculty of Social Work, University of Toronto, 1986.

**6903. Renaud, Andre** *Indian Education Today.* Andre Renaud. [Ottawa: Indian Eskimo and Welfare Oblate Commission, 1958].

**6904. Repo, Satu** *"CEGPS, Charlebois, Chartrand: the Quebec Revolution Now."* Satu Repo interviewing Dimitri Rousoppoulos. Vancouver, Copp Clark Publishing Co., c1970. In Social and Cultural Change in Canada v.2, pp. 200-210. Edited by W.E. Mann.

**6905. Repplier, Agnes** *Mere Marie of the Ursulines: a Study in Adventure.* Agnes Repplier. 1st ed. Garden City, N.Y.: Doubleday, Doran & Company, Inc., 1931.

**6906. Rexford, Elson Irving** *Our Educational Problem: the Jewish Population and the Protestant Schools.* Elson I. Rexford. Montreal: Renouf Publishing Company, [1920?].

**6907. Richardson, D.W.** *"Transient Tachypnea of the Newborn Associated With Hypervolemia."* D.W. Richardson. Canadian Medical Association Journal/Journal de l'Association medicale canadienne 103, 1(July 4, 1970): 70-71.

**6908. Richardson, Margaret Reid** *A Study of Sibling I.Q.s.* Margaret Reid Richardson. Toronto: University of Toronto, 1939.
Thesis (M.A.)--University of Toronto, 1939.

**6909. Richardson, Wayne** *The Effects of Tokens, Praise and Tangibles on Academic and Conduct Behaviours.* Wayne Richardson. Toronto: York University, 1971.
Thesis (Ph.D.)--York University, 1971.

**6910. Richardson, Wayne** *A Modified Pursuit Rotor to Obtain a More Accurate Measure of Eye-hand Coordination of Emotionally Disturbed Children.* Wayne Richardson. Toronto: York University, 1970.
Thesis (M.A.)--York University, 1970.

**6911. Richer, Andre** *The Relation Between the Attitude of the Teacher and Success in Learning a Second Language.* Andre Richer. Montreal: McGill University, 1969.
Thesis (M.A.)--McGill University, 1969.

**6912. Richler, Mordecai** *The Street.* Mordecai Richler. Toronto: McClelland and Stewart, c1969.

**6913. Richmond, Anthony H.** *Immigrants and Ethnic Groups in Metropolitan Toronto.* Anthony H. Richmond. Toronto: Institute for Behavioural Research, York University, 1967.

**6914. Riis, Jacob A.** *"The Value of Playgrounds to the Community."* Jacob A. Riis. Public Health Journal 4, 5(May 1913): 267.

**6915. Rintoul, Dorothy F.** *An Experimental Study of Laughter and Smiling in Preschool Children.* Dorothy F. Rintoul. Toronto: University of Toronto, 1938.
Thesis (M.A.)--University of Toronto, 1938.

**6916. Risk, Jacob** *Towards a Descriptive Definition of Adolescence: Some Preliminary Steps in the Evolution of a Research Design.* Jacob Risk, C. Anastasiadis and J. Dade-Morkpli. Montreal: McGill University, 1956.
Thesis (M.S.W.)--McGill University, 1956.

**6917. Risteen, Frank B.** *"Children of Sir John Johnson and Lady Mary Polly Johnson, Married at New York June 30, 1773."* Frank B. Risteen. Ontario History 63, 2(June 1971): 93-102.

**6918. Robb, Preston** *"Quackery in the Treatment of the Brain-injured Child."* Preston Robb. Canadian Medical Association Journal 72, 9(May 1, 1955): 660-663.

**6919. Robbins, John E.** *"The Home and Family Background of Ottawa Public School Children in Relation to their IQs."* John E. Robbins. Canadian Journal of Psychology 2, 1(Mar. 1948): 254-267.

**6920. Robert, Guy** *Lemieux.* Guy Robert, translated by John David Allan. Agincourt, Ont.: Gage Publications, 1978.

**6921. Robert, Jean-Claude** *"The City of Wealth and Death: Urban Mortality in Montreal, 1821-1871."* Jean-Claude Robert. Toronto: McClelland and Stewart, 1988. In Essays in the History of Canadian Medicine, pp. 18-38. Edited by Wendy Mitchinson and Janice Dickin McGinnis.

**6922. Roberts, F. Barry** *"The Prognosis of Henoch-Schonlein Nephritis."* F. Barry Roberts, R.J. Slater and Bernard Laski. Canadian Medical Association Journal/Journal de l'Association medicale canadienne 87, 2(July 14, 1962): 49-51.

**6923. Roberts, James** *"The Schick Test and Active Immunization Against Diphtheria."* Dr. James Roberts. Public Health Journal 14, 8(Aug. 1923): 347-355.

**6924. Roberts, James** *"Tuberculosis in Hamilton."* James Roberts. Canadian Public Health Journal 22, 12(Dec. 1932): 600-605.

**6925. Roberts, Jean** *Characteristics of the Abused Child and His Family: an Agency Study.* Jean Roberts. Vancouver: University of British Columbia, 1968. Thesis (M.S.W.)--University of British Columbia, 1968.

**6926. Robertson, Edwin M.** *"Fatal Duodenal Haemorrhage in the Newborn."* Edwin M. Robertson and W.D. Stevens. Canadian Medical Association Journal 70, 3(Mar. 1954): 294-298.

**6927. Robertson, Elizabeth Chant** *"Vitamin C Content of Diets of Lower Income Toronto Families."* Elizabeth Chant Robertson and Margaret E. Galloway. Canadian Medical Association Journal 59, 3(Sept. 1948): 236-240.

**6928. Robertson, J.K.** *"Further Sketches of Tayville: I. A Blacksmith and a Blacksmith Shop: II The Relief of Ladysmith."* J.K. Robertson. Queen's Quarterly 38, 4(Autumn 1931): 666-677.

**6929. Robertson, J.K.** *"Tayville:"* J.K. Robertson. Queen's Quarterly 37, 4(Autumn 1930): 711-723.

**6930. Robertson, L. Bruce** *"Blood Transfusions in Infants and Young Children."* L. Bruce Robertson and Alan Brown. Canadian Medical Association Journal 5, 4(Apr. 1915): 298-305.

**6931. Robertson, R.S.** *"Juvenile Delinquency."* R.S. Robertson. Canadian Bar Review 21, 8(Oct. 1943): 601-604.

**6932. Robilliard, J.A.** *"The Legislation of Quebec."* J.A. Robilliard. Child and Family Welfare 8, 3(Sept. 1932): 1-5.

**6933. Robinson, C.R.** *"Report of an Outbreak of Febrile Illness with Pharyngeal Lesions and Exanthem: Toronto, Summer 1957, Isolation of Group A Coxsackie Virus."* C.R. Robinson, Frances W. Doane and A.J. Rhodes. Canadian Medical Association Journal 79, 8(Oct. 15, 1958): 615-621.

**6934. Robinson, Dean** *Howie Morenz: Hockey's First Superstar.* Dean Robinson. Erin: Boston Mills Press, c1982.

**6935. Robinson, George Carlton** *A Historical and Critical Account of Public Secondary Education in the Province of Ontario, Canada, 1792-1916.* George Carlton Robinson. Cambridge, Mass.: Harvard University, 1918. Thesis (D. Ed.)--Harvard University, 1918.

**6936. Robinson, Gilbert de B.** *Percy James Robinson, 1873-1953: Classicist, Artist, Teacher, Historian.* Gilbert de B. Robinson. [Toronto; University of Toronto Press], 1981.

**6937. Robinson, Helen Caister** *Decades of Caring: the Big Sister Story.* Helen Caister Robinson. Toronto: Dundurn Press, c1979.

**6938. Robinson, Marina** *The Child, the Family and Society in Ontario 1850-1900, According to Four Educational Journals.* Marina Robinson. Thunder Bay: Lakehead University, c1978. (CTM no. 34742) Thesis (M.A.)--Lakehead University, 1978.

**6939. Robinson, Marion L.** *"Case Study in Paediatrics."* Marion L. Robinson. Canadian Nurse 27, 4(Apr. 1931): 198-199.

**6940. Robinson, Mona** *A Study of Re-opened Protection Cases in the Children's Aid and Infants' Homes of Toronto in 1953.* Mona Robinson. Toronto: University of Toronto, 1957. Thesis (M.S.W.)--University of Toronto, 1957.

**6941. Robinson, Ruth B.** *Truant-delinquents: a Study Based on the Records of the Toronto Juvenile Court Clinic for the Years 1946-1947.* Ruth B. Robinson. Toronto: University of Toronto, 1948. Thesis (M.S.W.)--University of Toronto, 1948.

**6942. Robinson, Winifred** *The Effect of Interest on Comprehension and Retention.* Winifred Robinson. Toronto: University of Toronto, 1946.
Thesis (M.A.)--University of Toronto, 1946.

**6943. Robson, Albert Henry** *Clarence A. Gagnon.* Albert Henry Robson. Toronto: The Ryerson Press, 1938.

**6944. Rochester, R.B.** *A Preliminary Exploratory Study in a Secondary Boys Boarding College.* R.B. Rochester. Toronto: University of Toronto, 1933.
Thesis (M.A.)--University of Toronto, 1933.

**6945. Rodgers, C.L.** *"Leukaemia in Children."* C.L. Rodgers, W.L. Donohue and C.E. Snelling. Canadian Medical Association Journal 65, 6(Dec. 1951): 548-552.

**6946. Rodgers, Denis Cyril** *An Investigation of the Auditory Memory Abilities of Grade 2 Retarded-underachieving Readers and Competent-achieving Readers Under Conditions of Reinforcement and Non-reinforcement.* Denis Cyril Rodgers. Toronto: University of Toronto, 1969.
Thesis (Ph.D.)--University of Toronto, 1969.

**6947. Roe, Henry** *"Reminiscences of the Earliest Days."* Henry Roe and T.R. Millman. Journal of the Canadian Church Historical Society 13, 3(Sept. 1971): 38-43.

**6948. Rogers, Kenneth H.** *"Camp for Emotionally Disturbed Boys."* Kenneth H. Rogers. Canadian Welfare 24, 6(Dec. 1948): 18-19.

**6949. Rogers, Kenneth H.** *"Intelligence" and "Perseveration" Related to School Achievement.* Kenneth H. Rogers. Toronto: University of Toronto, 1933.
Thesis (Ph.D.)--University of Toronto, 1933.

**6950. Rogers, Kenneth H.** *"Social Work with Boys."* Kenneth H. Rogers. Canadian Public Health Journal 31, 8(Aug. 1940): 381-386.

**6951. Rogers, Kenneth H.** *Street Gangs in Toronto: a Study of the Forgotten Boy.* Kenneth H. Rogers. Toronto: Ryerson Press, c1945.

**6952. Rogers, Kenneth H.** *"Toward Mental and Social Stability."* Kenneth H. Rogers. Child and Family Welfare 11, 5(Jan. 1936): 26-32.

**6953. Rogers, Lina L.** *"The School Nurse."* Lina L. Rogers. Canadian Nurse 7, 7(July 1910): 354-355.

**6954. Rogers, R. S.** *Who Leaves and Why?: Pupil Attrition in Toronto Public Schools: Selected Statistics from the Study of Achievement.* R.S. Rogers. Toronto: Research Department, Board of Education for the City of Toronto, 1969.
References p. 14.

**6955. Rohmer, Richard** *E.P. Taylor: the Biography of Edward Plunket Taylor.* Richard Rohmer. Toronto: McClelland and Stewart, 1978.

**6956. Roland, Charles G.** *"Health and Disease Among Early Loyalists in Upper Canada."* Charles G. Roland. Canadian Medical Association Journal/Journal de l'Association medicale canadienne 128, 5(Mar. 1, 1983): 587-595.

**6957. Rome, D.** *"Inventory of Documents on the Jewish School Question, 1903-1932."* D. Rome. Canadian Jewish Archives, New Series 2(1975): 1-105.

**6958. Rome, D.** *On the Jewish School Question in Montreal, 1903-1931.* David Rome. Montreal: Canadian Jewish Congress, 1975.

**6959. Romkey, Lillian** *The Disposition of Children of Unmarried Mothers with Limited Intelligence.* Lillian Romkey. Toronto: University of Toronto, 1951.
Thesis (M.S.W.)--University of Toronto, 1951.

**6960. Roos, Robert C.** *Guidance in Elementary Education with Special Reference to the Interests of Grade 8 Pupils.* Robert C. Roos. Toronto: University of Toronto, 1947.
Thesis (M.A.)--University of Toronto, 1947.

**6961. Roquebrune, Robert de** *Testament of My Childhood.* Robert de Roquebrune [pseud.], translated by Felix Walter. [Toronto]: University of Toronto Press, 1964.

**6962. Rose, John** *Reflections of a Country Corner: the Story of Schooldays and the Glencoe Corner Neighborhood During the Early Years of the Century.* John Rose. [S.l: s.n., 197-].

**6963. Rose, Vera** *"Incidence of Heart Disease in Children in the City of Toronto."* Vera Rose, A.R.J. Boyd and T.E. Ashton. Canadian Medical Association Journal/Journal de l'Association medicale canadienne 91, 3(July 18, 1964): 95-100.

**6964. Rose, Vera** *"Infants of Diabetic Mothers: Clinical and Pathological Features in a Series of 25 Cases."* Vera Rose. Canadian Medical Association Journal/Journal de l'Association medicale canadienne 82, 6(Feb. 6, 1960): 306-310.

**6965. Rose, Vera** *"The Prevalence of Ventricular Septal Defect in Elementary School Children in the City of Toronto."* Vera Rose and John D. Keith. Canadian Medical Association Journal/Journal de l'Association medicale canadienne 95, 22(Nov. 26, 1966): 1132-1134.

**6966. Rosenberg, Jerome H.** *Margaret Atwood.* Jerome H. Rosenberg. Boston: Twayne, c1984.

**6967. Rosenberg, Leah** *The Errand Runner: Reflections of a Rabbi's Daughter.* Leah Rosenberg. Toronto: J. Wiley & Sons Canada, c1981.

**6968. Rosenberg, Louis** *Jewish Children in the Protestant Schools of Greater Montreal in the Period From 1878 to 1958.* Louis Rosenberg. Montreal: Canadian Jewish Congress, 1959.

**6969. Rosenberg, Louis** *Jewish Children in the Protestant Schools of Greater Montreal in the Period From 1878 to 1962.* Louis Rosenberg. Montreal: Canadian Jewish Congress, 1962.

**6970. Rosenberg, Louis** *Population Characteristics (Distribution by Age and Sex) of the Jewish Community of Montreal.* Louis Rosenberg. Montreal: Canadian Jewish Congress, [1955].

**6971. Rosenberg, Louis** *Population Characteristics of the Jewish Community of Toronto.* Louis Rosenberg. Montreal: Canadian Jewish Congress, 1955.

**6972. Rosenberg, Louis** *Population of the Jewish Community of Montreal.* Louis Rosenberg. Montreal: Canadian Jewish Congress, 1956.

**6973. Rosenberg, Louis** *A Statistical Study of the Number and Percentage of Jewish Children in the Protestant Schools of Greater Montreal and the Suburb of Chomedey as at April 30, 1964.* Louis Rosenberg Montreal: Canadian Jewish Congress, 1964.

**6974. Rosenberg, Louis** *A Statistical Study of the Number and Percentage of Jewish Children in the Protestant Schools of Greater Montreal and the Suburb of Greater St. Martin (Chomedey), in the Period From 1878 to 1968.* Louis Rosenberg. Montreal: Canadian Jewish Congress, 1969.

**6975. Rosenblatt, Joe** *Escape From the Glue Factory: a Memoir of a Paranormal Toronto Childhood in the Late Forties.* Joe Rosenblatt. Toronto: Exile Editions, c1985.

**6976. Rosenfeld, Mark** *""It Was a Hard Life": Class and Gender in the Work and Family Rhythms of a Railway Town, 1920-1950."* Mark Rosenfeld. Canadian Historical Association. Historical Papers/Communications historiques (1988): 237-279.

**6977. Ross, Barbara A.** *"Distribution of Milk in Toronto Schools."* B.A. Ross. Canadian Nurse 18, 4(Apr. 1922): 219-221.

**6978. Ross, Barbara A.** *"Health Teaching in Elementary Schools."* B.A. Ross. Canadian Nurse 19, 9(Sept. 1923): 535-539.

**6979. Ross, Barbara A.** *The Value of Health Teaching in the School.* Barbara A. Ross. Public Health Journal 17, 8(Aug. 1926): 388-393.

**6980. Ross, Dudley** *"Phrenic Crush as an Aid in the Repair of Omphalocoeles."* Dudley Ross and Herbert F. Owen. Canadian Medical Association Journal 70, 4(Apr. 1954): 421-424.

**6981. Ross, George W.** *The School System of Ontario: Its History and Distinctive Features.* George W. Ross. New York: D. Appleton and Company, c1896.

**6982. Ross, Gretta M.** *"Camping for Crippled Children."* Gretta M. Ross. Canadian Nurse 46, 7(July 1950): 543-547.

**6983. Ross, Harold** *The Jew in the Educational System of the Province of Quebec.* Harold Ross. Montreal: McGill University, 1947.
Thesis (M.A.)--McGill University, 1947.

**6984. Ross, John R.** *"Poisonings Common in Children."* John R. Ross and Alan Brown. Canadian Medical Association Journal 64, 4(Apr. 1951): 285-289.

**6985. Ross, John R.** *"Symposium on Common Poisonings."* John R. Ross and Alan Brown. Canadian Public Health Journal 26, 5(May 1935): 225-243.

**6986. Ross, Marvin** *"Economic Conditions and Crime, Metropolitan Toronto 1965-1972."* Marvin Ross. Criminology Made in Canada 2, 2(July 1974): 27-41.

**6987. Ross, Mary A.** *"The Efficiency of Toxoid in Controlling Diphtheria: Toronto, 1926-1930."* Mary A. Ross and Neil E. McKinnon. Canadian Public Health Journal 22, 7(July 1931): 333-341.

**6988. Ross, Mary A.** *"Mortality From Respiritory Diseases Excluding Tuberculosis."* Mary A. Ross. Canadian Public Health Journal 25, 11(Nov. 1935): 552-565.

**6989. Ross, Mary A.** *"The Mortality in Ontario of Four Communicable Diseases of Childhood."* Mary A. Ross. Canadian Public Health Journal 23, 7(July 1932): 331-341.

**6990. Ross, Mary A.** *A Survey of Mortality of Diphtheria, Scarlet Fever, Whooping Cough, Measles, Tuberculosis, Typhoid Fever, Influenza, and Other Respiratory Diseases, and Diabetes for Fifty Years in Ontario and an Analysis of the Results of the Use of Toxoid in the Prevention of Diptheria in Toronto School Children, 1926-1930.* Mary Alexandra Ross. Toronto: University of Toronto, 1934.
Thesis (Ph.D.)--University of Toronto, 1934.

**6991. Ross, Mary A.** *"Typhoid Fever Mortality in Ontario, 1880-1931."* Mary A. Ross. Canadian Public Health Journal 26, 2(Feb. 1935): 73-84.

**6992. Ross, Murray G.** *Toronto Y.M.C.A. in a Changing Community.* Murray G. Ross. [Toronto]: University of Toronto, 1947.
Thesis (M.A)--University of Toronto, 1947.

**6993. Rosset, M.** *"Epidermolysis Bullosa of the Newborn."* M. Rosset. Canadian Medical Association Journal 75, 6(Sept. 15, 1956): 507-509.

**6994. Rossiter, Amy B.** *From Private to Public: a Feminist Exploration of Early Mothering.* Amy B. Rossiter. Toronto: Women's Press, 1988.

**6995. Rousmaniere, Kate Bodine** *To Prepare the Ideal Woman: Private Denominational Girls' Schooling in Late Nineteenth Century Ontario.* Kate Bodine Rousmaniere. Toronto: University of Toronto, 1984.
Thesis (M.A.)--University of Toronto, 1984.

**6996. Rowan-Legg, C.K.** *"Self-demand Feeding of Infants."* C.K. Rowan-Legg. Canadian Medical Association Journal 60, 4(Apr. 1949): 388-391.

**6997. Rowe, Richard D.** *"Congenital Cardiac Malformation in the Newborn Period: Frequency in a Children's Hospital."* Richard D. Rowe and T. Emmett Cleary. Canadian Medical Association Journal/Journal de l'Association medicale canadienne 83, 7(Aug. 13, 1960): 299-302.

**6998. Rowe, Richard D.** *"Experiences with 180 Cases of Tetralogy of Fallot in Infants and Children."* Richard D. Rowe, Peter Vlad and John D. Keith. Canadian Medical Association Journal 73, 1(July 1, 1955): 23-30.

**6999. Rowe, Richard D.** *"Severe Valvular Pulmonary Stenosis with Normal Aortic Root: Immediate Results of Transarterial Valvotomy, with Notes on the Clinical Assessment of Patients Before and After Operation."* Richard D. Rowe, S.C. Mitchell, John D. Keith, W.T. Mustard and W.T. Barnes. Canadian Medical Association Journal 78, 5(Mar. 1, 1958): 311-317.

**7000. Royce, Marion V.** *"Arguments Over the Education of Girls, Their Admission to Grammar Schools in This Province."* Marion V. Royce. Ontario History 67, 1(Mar. 1975): 1-13.

**7001. Royce, Marion V.** *"Education for Girls in Quaker Schools in Ontario."* Marion V. Royce. Atlantis 3, 1(Fall 1977): 181-192.

**7002. Royce, Marion V.** *"A Landmark in Victorian Education for Young Ladies."* Marion V. Royce. Improving College and University Teaching 22, 4(Winter 1975): 9-11.

**7003. Royce, Marion V.** *"Methodism and the Education of Women in Nineteenth Century Ontario."* Marion V. Royce. Atlantis 3, 2(Spring 1978): 131-143.

**7004. Royce, Marion V.** *The Methodists Enter the Field of Education.* Marion V. Royce. Toronto: Women in Canadian History Project, Ontario Institute for Studies in Education, 1976.

**7005. Royce, Marion V.** *Notes on Schooling for Girls in Upper Canada from the Pre-conquest Period Until the Mid-nineteenth Century.* Marion V. Royce. Toronto: Women in Canadian History Project, Ontario Institute for Studies in Education, 1978.

**7006. Ruddell, David Terence** *Apprenticeship in Early Nineteenth Century Quebec, 1793-1815.* David Terence Ruddell. Montreal: Laval University, 1969.
Thesis (M.A.)--Laval University, 1969.

**7007. Rudney, Bernice D.** *The Treatment of Child Behaviour Problems in the Foster Home.* Bernice D. Rudney. Toronto: University of Toronto, 1949.
Thesis (M.S.W.)--University of Toronto, 1949.
No bibliography.

**7008. Rudolf, Robert Dawson** *"Low Percentages in Infant Feeding."* Robert Dawson Rudolph. Canadian Medical Association Journal 2, 3(Mar. 1912): 173-180.

**7009. Rudski, Ephraim** *Adolescent Awakenings: an Exploration in Adolescence through Material Probed by Adolescents.* Ephraim Rudski. Montreal: McGill University, 1971.
Thesis (M.S.W.)--McGill University, 1971.

**7010. Russell, Edmund Thomas Pete** *A Glance Back.* Edmund Thomas Pete Russell. Battleford, Sask.: Turner-Warwick Publications, c1984.

**7011. Russell, H. Howard** *An Intensive Study of Some Gifted Students Who Participate in a Partial-segregation Program.* H. Howard Russell. Toronto: University of Toronto, 1959.
Thesis (M.A.)--University of Toronto, 1959.

**7012. Russell, H. Howard** *Measurement of Reasoning Abilities in Adolescents.* H. Howard Russell. Toronto: University of Toronto, 1962.
Thesis (Ed.D.)--University of Toronto, 1962.

**7013. Rutherford, William Herbert** *The Industrial Worker in Ontario.* William Herbert Rutherford. Toronto: University of Toronto, 1914.
Thesis (D.Paed.)--University of Toronto, 1914.

**7014. Ryan, Thomas J.** *"Response Speed as a Function of Age, Incentive Value, and Reinforcement Schedule."* Thomas J. Ryan and Alan R. Moffitt. Child Development 37, 1(Mar. 1966): 103-113.

**7015. Sabia, Laura** *""You Are Not One of Us": the Roots of My Militant Feminism."* Laura Sabia. Canadian Woman Studies/Cahiers de la femme 8, 2(Summer 1987): 32-36.

**7016. Sabin, Morris** *"Haemolytic Disease of the Newborn due to ABO Isoimmunization."* Morris Sabin and Louis Lowenstein. Canadian Medical Association Journal 77, 2(July 15, 1957): 92-97.

**7017. Saint-Pierre, W.** *"School Savings Banks in the Province of Quebec."* W. Saint-Pierre. Canadian Education 12, 4(Sept. 1956): 52-59.

**7018. Sajid, Muhammad S.** *The Effect of Remedial Instruction on Achievement in Seventh Grade Algebraic Linear Equations.* Sajid S. Muhammad. Toronto: University of Toronto, 1959.
Thesis (Ed.D.)--University of Toronto, 1959.

**7019. Sande Van De, Adje** *Native Child Welfare in Ontario: Historical Background and Annotated Bibliography.* Adje Van De Sande. Waterloo: Wilfrid Laurier University, 1987.

**7020. Sandham, A.** *History of the Montreal Young Men's Christian Association, the First Formed on the Continent: Also, an Account of the Origin of Young Men's Christian Associations and Subsequent Progress of the Work in America.* A. Sandham. Montreal: D. Bentley, 1873.

**7021. Sandiford, Peter** *The Mental and Physical Life of School Children.* Peter Sandiford. London: Longman's, Green and Co., 1913.

**7022. Satanove, Sora M.** *The Relationship Between Child Adjustment and the Integration of Immigrant Parents.* Sora M. Satanove. Toronto: University of Toronto, 1963.
Thesis (M.S.W.)--University of Toronto, 1963.

**7023. Savage, H.W.** *The Manifestation and Prediction of Authoritarianism in Classroom Control.* H.W. Savage. Toronto: University of Toronto, 1960.
Thesis (Ed.D.)--University of Toronto, 1960.

**7024. Savard, E.N.A.** *"Infant Mortality."* E.N.A. Savard. Public Health Journal 14, 11(Nov. 1923): 489-500.

**7025. Sax, Judith Paula** *Effects of Disability on Altruism in Children.* Judith Paula Sax. Toronto: York University, 1970.
Thesis (M.A.)--York University, 1970.

**7026. Saxe, Mary Solace** *Our Little Quebec Cousin.* Mary Solace Saxe. Boston: The Page Co., 1919.

**7027. Scarlett, Glenn L., Mrs.** *"A Nursery School Project at St. Thomas, Ontario."* Mrs. Glen L. Scarlett. Child and Family Welfare 12, 3(Sept. 1936): 49.

**7028. Schab, Fred** *"Honor and Dishonor in the Secondary Schools of Three Cultures."* Fred Schab. Adolescence 6, 22(Summer 1971): 145-154.

**7029. Schalburg, Annette** *School Leaving at Fifteen: a Study of Work Permits Issued by the Toronto Board of Education.* Annette Schalburg. Toronto: University of Toronto, 1948.
Thesis (M.S.W.)–University of Toronto, 1948.

**7030. Scheffe, Norman, ed.** *Issues for the Seventies: Youth Today.* Norman Scheffe, ed. Toronto: McGraw-Hill Co. of Canada Ltd., c1970.

**7031. Schmalz, Peter Stanley** *The Ojibwa of Southern Ontario.* Peter Stanley Schmalz. Waterloo: University of Waterloo, 1985. (CTM no. 20658)
Thesis (Ph.D.)–University of Waterloo, 1985.

**7032. Schneider, Aili Gronlund** *The Finnish Baker's Daughters.* Aili Gronlund Schneider. [Toronto]: Multicultural History Society of Ontario, c1986.

**7033. Schreiber, Jan Edward** *In The Course of Discovery: West Indian Immigrants in Toronto Schools.* Jan Schreiber. [Toronto]: Board of Education for the City of Toronto, 1970.

**7034. Schuessler, Karl** *School on Wheels: Reaching and Teaching the Isolated Children of the North.* Karl Schuessler and Mary Schuessler. Erin, Ont.: Boston Mills Press, c1986.

**7035. Schull, Joseph** *The Great Scot: a Biography of Donald Gordon.* Joseph Schull. Montreal: McGill-Queen's University Press, c1979.

**7036. Schwalbe, A. Lenore** *Negro and Partly Negro Wards of the Children's Aid Society of Metropolitan Toronto.* A. Lenore Schwalbe. Toronto: University of Toronto, 1958.
Thesis (M.S.W.)–University of Toronto, 1958.

**7037. Scott, Duncan Campbell** *The Makers of Canada: John Graves Simcoe.* Duncan Campbell Scott. v. 7. Toronto: Morang & Co., Ltd., 1910.

**7038. Scott, Frances** *Adult-Child Relationship in a Nursery School Setting.* Frances Scott. Toronto: University of Toronto, 1939.
Thesis (M.A.)–University of Toronto, 1939.

**7039. Scott, J.** *Twenty-one Problem Boys in the Training School Setting.* J. Scott. Toronto: University of Toronto, 1957.
Thesis (M.S.W.)–University of Toronto, 1957.

**7040. Scott, Jean Thompson** *The Conditions of Female Labour in Ontario.* Jean Thompson Scott. Toronto: University of Toronto, 1892.

**7041. Scott, Wilfrid George** *Certain Factors Connected with Successful Placement of Children in Adoptive Foster Homes.* Wilfrid George Scott. Toronto: University of Toronto, 1944.
Thesis (Ph.D.)–University of Toronto, 1944.

**7042. Scriver, Charles R.** *"A Commentary on Multiple Screening for Aminoacidopathies in the Newborn Infant."* Charles R. Scriver, Carol Clow, Eluned Davies, Angeles Ramos and Leo Stern. Canadian Medical Association Journal/Journal de l'Association medicale canadienne 92, 26(June 26, 1965): 1331-1333.

**7043. Scriver, Jessie Boyd** *The Montreal Children's Hospital: Years of Growth.* Jessie Boyd Scriver. Montreal: McGill-Queen's University Press, 1979.

**7044. Scriver, Walter deM.** *"The Diabetic and His Disease."* Walter deM. Scriver and Jean Trenholme. Canadian Medical Association Journal 69, 5(Nov. 1953): 477-480.

**7045. Seabrook, Karen Scott** *The Results of Motivating Performance on a Non-verbal Discrimination Task with Autistic and Control Children.* Karen Scott Seabrook. Toronto: University of Toronto, 1970.
Thesis (M.A.)–University of Toronto, 1970.

**7046. Seaton, E.T.** *Practice in Arithmetic.* E.T. Seaton. Toronto: University of Toronto Press, 1924.
Thesis (D.Paed.)–University of Toronto, 1924.

**7047. Sedal, Virve S.** *The Stanford-Binet with Nine- to Ten-year-old Children Whose Knowledge of English is Inadequate.* Virve S. Sedal. Toronto: University of Toronto, 1956.
Thesis (M.A.)–University of Toronto, 1956.

**7048. Sedgewick, Mildred S.** *A Study of Unlawful Non-attendance (Truancy) in the City of Toronto.* Mildred S. Sedgewick. Toronto: University of Toronto, 1939.
Thesis (M.A.)–University of Toronto, 1939.

**7049. Segall, Harold N.** *"Auricular Paroxysmal Tachycardia in Infancy (First Year)."* Harold N. Segall and Alton Goldbloom. Canadian Medical Association Journal 45, 1(July 1941): 64-68.

**7050. Segall, Harold N.** *"Rehabilitation of the Cardiac Patient in Industry and in the Home."* Harold N. Segall. Canadian Medical Association Journal 72, 7(Apr. 1, 1955): 492-499.

**7051. Sellers, A. Hardisty** *"The Classification·of the Causes of Foetal Death."* A. Hardisty Sellers. Canadian Public Health Journal 28, 6(June 1937): 282-290.

**7052. Sellers, A. Hardisty** *"Pneumonia in Ontario."* A. Hardisty Sellers. Canadian Public Health Journal 30, 2(Feb. 1939): 73-81

**7053. Sellers, A. Hardisty** *"A Study of Foetal Mortality in Ontario."* A. Hardisty Sellers. Canadian Public Health Journal 28, 1(Jan. 1937): 22-31.

**7054. Sellery, E. Mildred** *"Foster Family Care for Children."* Mildred E. Sellery. Child and Family Welfare 12, 3(Sept. 1936): 12-18.

**7055. Selye, Hans** *The Stress of My Life: a Scientist's Memoirs.* Hans Selye. Toronto: McClelland and Stewart, 1977.

**7056. Semple, S.W.** *A Survey of French in the Elementary Grades in Metropolitan Toronto: Part I - Public Schools.* S.W. Semple. Toronto: Metropolitan Toronto Educational Research Council, 1965.

**7057. Sepp, A.H.** *"Listeria Monocytogenes Infections in Metropolitan Toronto: a Clinicopathological Study."* A.H. Sepp and T.E. Roy. Canadian Medical Association Journal/Journal de l'Association medicale canadienne 88, 11(Mar. 16, 1963): 549-561.

**7058. Sereny, G.** *"An Unusual Case of Tuberculous Meningitis."* G. Sereny, H.W. Fletcher and C.A. Cline. Canadian Medical Association Journal 71, 5(Nov. 1954): 486-489.

**7059. Seton, Julia M.** *By a Thousand Fires: Nature Notes and Extracts from the Life and Unpublished Journals of Ernest Thompson Seton.* Julia M. Seton. Garden City: Doubleday & Co. Inc., c1967.

**7060. Setterington, Ronald G.** *"Effects of Concurrent Delays of Material Rewards and Punishments on Problem-solving in Children."* Ronald G. Setterington and Richard H. Walters. Child Development 35, 1(Mar. 1964): 275-280.

**7061. Sexton, George B.** *"Thomson's Syndrome."* George B. Sexton. Canadian Medical Association Journal 70, 6(June 1954): 662-665.

**7062. Shackleton, Doris** *"The Mayor's Committee."* Doris Shackleton. Canadian Welfare 45, 5(Sept.-Oct. 1969): 15.

**7063. Shamai, Shmuel Jacob** *Ethnic and National Identity Among Jewish Students in Toronto.* Shmuel Jacob Shamai. Toronto: University of Toronto, 1986. Thesis (Ph.D.)–University of Toronto, 1986.

**7064. Shardt, Anthony** *"Notes on Neonatal Thrush and its Epidemiology."* Anthony Shardt and T.E. Roy. Canadian Medical Association Journal 76, 12(June 15, 1957): 1029-1032.

**7065. Shaw, Arthur Richard** *Some Possible Effects of an Inflexible School Entrance Policy upon Achievement in the Elementary School.* Arthur Richard Shaw. Montreal: McGill University, 1970. Thesis (M.A.)–McGill University, 1970.

**7066. Shaw, Bertha Mary Constance** *Broken Threads: Memories of a Northern Ontario School Teacher.* Bertha Mary Constance Shaw. New York: Exposition Press, 1955.

**7067. Shaw, Margaret Mason** *Frederick Banting.* Margaret Mason Shaw. Don Mills, Ont.: Fitzhenry & Whiteside, 1976.

**7068. Shea, M.** *"Traumatic Hyphaema in Children."* M. Shea. Canadian Medical Association Journal 76, 6(Mar. 15, 1957): 466-469.

**7069. Sheikh, Anees A.** *"Response Speed as a Function of Different Reinforcement· Conditions and a Ready Signal."* Anees A. Sheikh. Child Development 38, 3(Sept. 1967): 857-867.

**7070. Shephard, David A.E.** *Norman Bethune: His Times and His Legacy.* David A.E. Shephard and Andree Levesque. Ottawa: Canadian Public Health Association, 1982.

**7071. Shephard, Roy J.** *"The Working Capacity of Toronto School Children: Part 2."* R.J. Shephard, C. Allen, O. Bar-Or, C.T.M. Davies, S. Degre, R. Hedman, K. Ishii, M. Kaneko, J.R. LaCour, P.E. di Prampero and V. Seliger. Canadian Medical Association Journal/Journal de l'Association medicale canadienne 100, 15(Apr. 19, 1969): 705-714.

**7072. Shepherd, William G.** *A Follow-up Study of the School Adjustment of Wards and Non-wards Discharged from Thistletown Hospital.* William G. Shepherd. Toronto: University of Toronto, 1966. Thesis (M.S.W.)–University of Toronto, 1966.

**7073. Shiff, Murray** *The Youth Program of the Canadian Jewish Congress in Ontario.* Murray Shiff. Toronto: University of Toronto, 1952. Thesis (M.S.W.)–University of Toronto, 1952.

**7074. Shipley, Vivian Helen** *Conformity to Sex Role Among Adolescents: Social Background and Educational Consequences.* Vivian Helen Shipley. Montreal: McGill University, 1969. Thesis (M.A.)--McGill University, 1969.

**7075. Shirai, Tsune** *Developmental Variation in the Visual Discrimination of Cube Size by Children 2 to 13 Years of Age.* Tsune Shirai. Toronto: University of Toronto, 1951. Thesis (M.A.)--University of Toronto, 1951.

**7076. Shirreff, W.T.** *"Meningococcus Meningitis in Ottawa, 1940-41."* W.T. Shirreff, L.N. Pearlman, T.A. Lomer and Diane Croll. Canadian Public Health Journal 32, 11(Nov. 1941): 551-558.

**7077. Shortt, Adam** *"Early Records of Ontario."* Adam Shortt. Queen's Quarterly 7, 2(Oct. 1899): 137-152.

**7078. Shouldice, D.** *"Mumps, in Utero."* D. Shouldice and S. Minty. Canadian Nurse 51, 6(June 1955): 454-455.

**7079. Shrum, Gordon** *Gordon Shrum: an Autobiography.* Gordon Shrum with Peter Stursberg, and Clive Cocking, ed. Vancouver, University of British Columbia Press, 1986.

**7080. Shute, Evan** *The Vitamin E Story: the Medical Memoirs of Evan Shute.* Evan Shute. Burlington, Ont.: Welch Pub., c1985.

**7081. Silcox, C.E.** *The Hope Report on Education: a Brief Critique of the Report of the Royal Commission on Education in Ontario.* Claris Edwin Silcox. Toronto: The Ryerson Press, c1952.

**7082. Silverman, Irwin William** *"Mediational Performances as Affected by Overt Verbalization During Training and Testing."* Irwin William Silverman and James G. Craig. Child Development 40, 1(Mar. 1969): 295-305.

**7083. Silverman, Irwin William** *"Test Anxiety and the Effectiveness of Social and Nonsocial Reinforcement in Children."* Irwin William Silverman and S.V. Waite. Child Development 40, 1(Mar. 1969): 307-314.

**7084. Silverthorne, Nelles** *"Nonparalytic Poliomyelitis: Some Observations on Differential Diagnosis."* Nelles Silverthorne, Alice M. Goodfellow, Crawford Anglin, A.J. Rhodes, T.E. Roy and C.E. Snelling. Canadian Medical Association Journal 60, 4(Apr. 1949): 356-359.

**7085. Silverthorne, Nelles** *"Pneumonia in Infancy and Childhood."* Nelles Silverthorne, Alan Brown and W.J. Auger. Canadian Medical Association Journal 44, 5(May 1941): 496-498.

**7086. Silverthorne, Nelles** *"Studies on Poliomyelitis in Ontario: 1. Observations of the Apparent Infectiousness of the Acute Case."* Nelles Silverthorne, M. Patricia Armstrong, F.H. Wilson, W.L. Donohue, Alice M. Goodfellow, T.E. Roy, L. McClelland, Eina M. Clark, A.J. Rhodes, J.W. Leach, C.I. Scott, R.N. Kyles, E.G. Johnson, W.J. McLean and W. Berwick. Canadian Medical Association Journal 61, 3(Sept. 1949): 241-250.

**7087. Simcoe, Elizabeth** *Mrs. Simcoe's Diary.* Elizabeth Posthuma (Gwillim) Simcoe. Toronto: Macmillan of Canada, 1978, c1965.

**7088. Simmons, Harvey G.** *From Asylum to Welfare.* Harvey G. Simmons. Toronto: National Institute on Mental Retardation, c1982.

**7089. Sinclair, Donald** *"A Modern Security Institution for Delinquent Boys."* D. Sinclair. Canadian Journal of Corrections/Revue canadienne de criminologie 1, 1(Jan. 1958): 21-25.

**7090. Sinclair, Elizabeth** *The Problem of Referring the Hospitalized Child to a Psychiatrist.* Elizabeth Sinclair. Toronto: University of Toronto, 1955. Thesis (M.S.W.)–University of Toronto, 1955.

**7091. Sinclair, Gordon** *Will the Real Gordon Sinclair Please Stand Up.* Gordon Sinclair. Toronto: McClelland and Stewart, c1966.

**7092. Sinclair, Samuel Bower** *"Special Classes for Children Requiring Special Training."* S.B. Sinclair. In Proceedings of Sixth Annual Canadian Conference on Child Welfare 1927, pp. 63-67.

7093. **Sinclair, Samuel Bower** *Special Training for School-age Children in Need of Special Care: Ontario Auxiliary Classes.* Samuel Bower Sinclair. Ottawa: The Council, 1928.

7094. **Singer, Carolyn B.** *Intake at the Jewish Family and Child Service.* Carolyn B. Singer. Toronto: University of Toronto, 1954.
Thesis (M.S.W.)–University of Toronto, 1954.

7095. **Singh, Balwant** *The Development and Analysis of Objective Group Tests Based on Piaget Tasks.* Balwant Singh. Toronto: University of Toronto, 1968.
Thesis (Ed.D.)–University of Toronto, 1968.

7096. **Sirkis, Rubin** *How Well do French Canadian Students Know English?* Rubin Sirkis.

7097. **Sissons, C.B.** *Nil Alienum: the Memoirs of C.B. Sissons.* C.B. Sissons. Toronto: University of Toronto Press, 1964.

7098. **Skelton, Isabel** *The Backwoodswoman: a Chronicle of Pioneer Home Life in Upper and Lower Canada.* Isabel Skelton. Toronto: Ryerson Press, 1924.

7099. **Sketch, Ralph** *Equestrian Sculpture.* Ralph Sketch. Toronto: NC Press, 1986.

7100. **Skinner, Myrl E.** *"Scoliosis."* Myrl E. Skinner. Canadian Nurse 49, 5(May 1953): 369-372.

7101. **Slater, R.J.** *"Hypertension in Children."* R.J. Slater, D.W. Geiger, P. Azzopardi and B.W. Webb. Canadian Medical Association Journal/Journal de l'Association medicale canadienne 81, 2(July 15, 1959): 71-77.

7102. **Sliter, Dorothy Murray** *Memoirs.* Dorothy Murray Sliter. Kingston: Brown and Martin, 1980.

7103. **Smallman, Marjory Maude** *Foster Homefinding: a Comparative Study of the Old and New Methods of Homefinding Employed by the Infants' Homes of Toronto.* Marjory Maude Smallman. Toronto: University of Toronto, 1952.
Thesis (M.S.W.)–University of Toronto, 1952.

7104. **Smart, Reginald G.** *The Extent of Drug Use in Metropolitan Schools: a Study of Changes from 1968 to 1970.* Reginald George Smart, Dianne Fejer and Jim White. Toronto: Addiction Research Foundation, 1970.

7105. **Smart, Reginald G.** *"Some Current Studies of Psychoactive and Hallucinogenic Drug Use."* Reginald G. Smart. Canadian Journal of Behavioural Science/Revue canadienne de sciences du comportement 2, 3(July 1970): 232-245.
Reprinted in Readings in Social Psychology: Focus on Canada, pp. 162-174. Edited by David Koulak and Daniel Perlman.

7106. **Smart, Reginald G.** *Trends in Drug Use Among Metropolitan Toronto High School Students 1968-1974.* Reginald G. Smart, Dianne Fejer, D. Smith and W. J. White. Toronto: Addiction Research Foundation of Ontario, 1975.

7107. **Smart, Reginald G.** *The Yorkville Subculture: a Study of the Life Styles and Interactions of Hippies and Non-hippies.* Reginald G. Smart and David Jackson. Toronto: Addiction Research Foundation, 1969.

7108. **Smith, Donald R.** *"The Life of George Copway or Kah-ge-gah-bowh (1818-1869): and a Review of His Writings."* Donald R. Smith. Journal of Canadian Studies/Revue d'etudes canadiennes 23, 3(Fall 1988): 5-37.

7109. **Smith, Elizabeth** *A Woman With a Purpose: the Diaries of Elizabeth Smith 1872-1884.* Elizabeth Smith; Veronica Strong-Boag, ed. Toronto: University of Toronto Press, 1980.

7110. **Smith, Gary J.** *"Recent Changes in Ontario Adoption Legislation."* Gary J. Smith and Alfred W. J. Dick. Osgoode Hall Law Journal 2, 1(Apr. 1960): 130-139.

7111. **Smith, George E.** *"The Prevention of Infection in Early Infancy."* George Smith. Public Health Journal 17, 8(Aug. 1926): 405-409.

7112. **Smith, George E.** *"The Result of Three Years' Work in The Department of Child Hygiene, Toronto."* George Smith. Public Health Journal 9, 7(July 1918): 310-314.

7113. **Smith, George E.** *"The Treatment and Management of Congenital Syphilis."* George E. Smith. Canadian Medical Association Journal 7, 1(Jan. 1917): 27-30.

7114. **Smith, Harley** *"Institutions for Children."* Harley Smith. Public Health Journal 6, 2(Feb. 1915): 82-84.

**7115. Smith, Helen** *"The Possibilities of Women's Work in Relation to the Babies Dispensary, Hamilton."* Helen Smith. Public Health Journal 6, 11(Nov. 1915): 548-549.

**7116. Smith, James K.** *Alexander MacKenzie.* James K. Smith. Don Mills: Fitzhenry and Whiteside, c1976.

**7117. Smith, Shirley F.** *A Comparison of Separate and Combined Playgrounds for Juniors and Seniors in Nursery Schools.* Shirley F. Smith. Toronto: University of Toronto, 1945.
  Thesis (M.A.)–University of Toronto, 1945.

**7118. Smylie, Clifford Hugh** *Northern Doctor: Memoirs of Clifford Hugh Smylie M.D.* Clifford Hugh Smylie. Cobalt, Ont.: Highway Book Shop, 1979.

**7119. Smythe, Conn** *Conn Smythe: If You Can't Beat 'Em in the Alley.* Conn Smythe with Scott Young. Toronto: McClelland and Stewart, c1981.

**7120. Snelling, Charles E.** *"Medullary Sponge Kidney in a Child."* Charles E. Snelling, N.M. Brown and C.A. Smythe. Canadian Medical Association Journal/Journal de l'Association medicale canadienne 102, 5(Mar. 14, 1970): 518-519.

**7121. Snelling, Charles E.** *"The Use of Evaporated Half-skimmed Milk in Infant Feeding."* Charles E. Shelling. Canadian Medical Association Journal 48, 1(Jan. 1943): 32-33.

**7122. Snow, Catherine Elizabeth** *Conjunctive and Disjunctive Thinking in Children.* Catherine Elizabeth Snow. Montreal: McGill University, 1967. (CTM no. 2247)
  Thesis (M.A.)--McGill University, 1967.

**7123. Social Planning Council of Metropolitan Toronto** *The Adoption of Negro Children.* Social Planning Council of Metropolitan Toronto. Toronto: The Council, 1966.

**7124. Social Planning Council of Metropolitan Toronto** *Report on Family Day Care of Children.* The Council. Toronto: The Council, 1966.

**7125. Social Planning Council of Metropolitan Toronto** *A Report on School Drop-outs.* The Council. Toronto: The Council, 1961.

**7126. Social Planning Council of Metropolitan Toronto** *A Report on the Needs of the Retarded in Metropolitan Toronto.* The Council. [Toronto: The Council, 1961].
  Chairman: J.O. Klaehn.

**7127. Social Planning Council of Metropolitan Toronto. Committee on Day Care of Children** *Day Care for Children in Metropolitan Toronto: a Report.* The Committee. [Toronto: The Council], 1968.

**7128. Society for Emotionally Disturbed Children (Montreal)** *Report to the Canadian Conference on Children.* Society for Emotionally Disturbed Children, Montreal. [S.l: s.n., 1960].

**7129. Society for the Protection of Women and Children (Montreal)** *A History of Seventy-five Years Operation in the Service of the Community.* Society for the Protection of Women and Children. Montreal: The Society, 1956.

**7130. Soles, L.** *Needs and Resources Study: Effects of Ethnicity and Social Class on Parents' Aspirations for and Awareness of Their Children's Education.* L. Soles. Toronto: University of Toronto, 1968. (CTM no. 17810)
  Thesis (M.S.W.)–University of Toronto, 1968.

**7131. Solway, Maurice** *Recollections of a Violinist.* Maurice Solway. Toronto: Mosaic Press, 1984.

**7132. Somwaru, Jwalla P.** *Cognitive Patterns Found Among Children from Different Occupational Backgrounds.* Jwalla P. Somwaru. Toronto: University of Toronto, 1967.
  Thesis (Ed.D.)--University of Toronto, 1967.

**7133. Somwaru, Jwalla P.** *"A School Board Consults Its Consumers."* Jwalla P. Somwaru. Education Canada 11, 3(Sept. 1971): 20-25.

**7134. Soren, Paul Victor** *A Study of Individual and Group Decision-making in Eight Drop-in Centres Serving Teenage Youth in Metropolitan Toronto.* Paul Victor Soren. Toronto: University of Toronto, 1967.
  Thesis (M.S.W.)–University of Toronto, 1967.

**7135. Sorensen, C.** *"Primary Agammaglobulinaemia as a Cause of Repeated Infection in Childhood."* C. Sorensen and C.N. Partington. Canadian Medical Association Journal 75, 7(Oct. 1, 1956): 579-581.

**7136. Sourial, Nabil** *"Testosterone Treatment of an XXYY Male Presenting with Aggression: a Case Report."* Nabil Sourial and Fred Fenton. Canadian Journal of Psychiatry/Revue canadienne de psychiatrie 33, 9(Dec. 1988): 847-850.

**7137. Southam, H.D.** *The Validation of an Objective Measurement in Geography.* H.D. Southam. Toronto: University of Toronto, 1933.
Thesis (D.Paed.)--University of Toronto, 1933.

**7138. Sparling, Margaret** *Variation and Predictive Value of the Intelligence Quotients of Preschool Children.* Margaret Sparling. Toronto: University of Toronto, 1938.
Thesis (M.A.)--University of Toronto, 1938.

**7139. Speare, Allan D.** *Student Mobility and Academic Achievement.* Allan D. Speare. Toronto: University of Toronto, 1971.
Thesis (Ed.D.)--University of Toronto, 1971.

**7140. Speers, A.H.** *"High School Medical Inspection in Burlington Ontario."* A.H. Speers. Canadian Public Health Journal 32, 12(Dec. 1941): 608-611.

**7141. Speisman, Stephen A.** *The Jews of Toronto: a History to 1937.* Stephen A. Speisman. Toronto: McClelland and Stewart, 1979.

**7142. Spence, C. Graeme** *A Descriptive Study of the Adjustment and Social Competency of Adolescents of Borderline Mentality Living in Foster Homes.* C. Graeme Spence. Ottawa: University of Ottawa, 1958.
Thesis (Ph.D.)--University of Ottawa, 1958.

**7143. Spence, Ruth Elizabeth** *Education as Growth: Its Significance for the Secondary Schools of Ontario.* Ruth Elizabeth Spence. New York: Columbia University, 1925.
Thesis (Ph.D.)--Columbia University, 1925.

**7144. Spencer, John C.** *"Juvenile Delinquency and the City."* John C. Spencer. Canadian Journal of Corrections/Revue canadienne de criminologie 3, 2(Apr. 1961): 115-127.

**7145. Spettigue, Charles Owen** *An Historical Review of Ontario Legislation on Child Welfare.* Charles Owen Spettigue. Toronto: Ontario, Department of Public Welfare, 1958.

**7146. Splane, Richard B.** *The Administration of the Children of Unmarried Parents Act of the Province of Ontario.* Richard B. Splane. Toronto: University of Toronto, 1951.
Thesis (M.S.W.)--University of Toronto, 1951.

**7147. Splane, Richard B.** *The Development of Social Welfare in Ontario, 1791 to 1893: the Role of the Province.* Richard B. Splane. 2 vol. Toronto: University of Toronto, 1961.
Thesis (D.S.W.)--University of Toronto, 1961.

**7148. Splane, Richard B.** *Social Welfare in Ontario, 1791-1893: a Study of Public Welfare Administration.* Richard B. Splane. Toronto: University of Toronto Press, 1965.

**7149. Spragge, George W.** *"Cornwall Grammar School Under John Strachan, 1803-1812."* George W. Spragge. Ontario Historical Society, Papers and Records 34(1942): 63-84.

**7150. Spragge, George W.** *"Joseph Lancaster in Montreal."* George W. Spragge. Canadian Historical Review 22, 1(Mar. 1941): 35-41.

**7151. St. John, J. Bascom** *"The School, the Home, the Child."* J. Bascom St. John. Ontario Education 1, 1(Jan.-Feb. 1969): 5-6, 20.

**7152. St. Pierre, Arthur** *"Child Labour and the Nation."* Arthur Saint Pierre. In Proceedings and Papers Fourth Annual Canadian Conference on Child Welfare 1923, pp. 121-124.

**7153. Stacey, Cooper H.** *"Acute Rheumatic Fever with Associated Meningitis."* Cooper H. Stacey and Michael Kaye. Canadian Medical Association Journal 71, 6(Dec. 1954): 607-609.

**7154. Stachan, J. Grant** *"Mastoiditis Complicating Scarlet Fever."* J. Grant Stachan. Public Health Journal 19, 10(Oct. 1928): 473-476.

**7155. Stamp, Robert M.** *The Campaign for Technical Education in Ontario 1876-1914.* Robert Stamp. London, Ont.: University of Western Ontario, 1970.
Thesis (Ph.D.)--University of Western Ontario, 1970.

**7156. Stamp, Robert M.** *"Empire Day in the Schools of Ontario: the Training of Young Imperialists."* Robert M. Stamp. Journal of Canadian Studies/Revue d'etudes canadiennes 8, 3(Aug. 1973): 32-42.
Reprinted in Canadian Schools and

Canadian Identity, pp. 100-115. Edited by Alf Chaiton and Neil McDonald.

**7157. Stamp, Robert M.** *The Schools of Ontario, 1876-1976.* Robert M. Stamp. Toronto: Toronto University Press, c1982.

**7158. Stamp, Robert M.** *"Schools on Wheels: the Railway Car Schools of Northern Ontario."* Robert M. Stamp. Canada: An Historical Magazine 1, 3(Spring 1974): 34-42.

**7159. Stanley, J.R.** *Our St. Mary's Schools: an Historical Sketch.* J.R. Stanley. [St. Mary's, Ont.]: St. Mary's Journal, [1909].

**7160. Stapleford, E.N.** *"Camping for Handicapped Children: an Experiment at Illshee Lodge."* E.N. Stapleford. Canadian Welfare 25, 7(Jan. 1950): 22-25.

**7161. Stapleford, Elsie Maude** *A Study of Resistance in Preschool Children.* Elsie Maude Stapleford. Toronto: University of Toronto, 1932.
Thesis (M.A.)--University of Toronto, 1932.

**7162. Stapleford, M. Elsie** *"Licensing in Ontario."* M. Elsie Stapleford. Bulletin of the Institute of Child Study 29, 3(Fall 1967): 58-63.

**7163. Staples, Lindsay** *Wilderness and Storytelling.* Lindsay Staples. Ottawa: National Museums of Canada, 1981.

**7164. Starr, Alida** *Emotional Episodes in Nursery-school Children.* Alida Starr. Toronto: University of Toronto, 1930.
Thesis (M.A.)--University of Toronto, 1930.

**7165. Starr, Clarence L.** *"Congenital Dislocation of the Hip."* Clarence L. Starr. Canadian Medical Association Journal 5, 1(Jan. 1915): 26-31.

**7166. Statten, Taylor** *"The Genesis of Work with Boys in Canada."* Taylor Statten. Canadian Welfare 16, 2(May 1940): 15-18.

**7167. Statten, Taylor** *"The Psychiatrist and the Child."* Taylor Statten. Canadian Nurse 55, 7(July 1959): 620-622.

**7168. Ste. Mechtilde, Soeur** *"The Unmarried Mother."* Soeur Ste. Mechtilde. Medical Services Journal of Canada 23, 4(Apr. 1967): 522-527.

**7169. Stee, Marjorie J.** *An Investigation of Self and Family Identification by Preschool Children.* Marjorie J. Stee. Toronto: University of Toronto, 1949.
Thesis (M.A.)--University of Toronto, 1949.

**7170. Steele, Robert** *"The Relationship of Antenatal and Postnatal Factors to Sudden Unexpected Death in Infancy."* Robert Steele and Jane T. Langworth. Canadian Medical Association Journal/Journal de l'Association medicale canadienne 94, 22(May 28, 1966): 1165-1171.

**7171. Steele, Robert** *"Sudden Unexpected Death in Infancy: a Reassessment."* Robert Steele. Canadian Medical Association Journal/Journal de l'Association medicale canadienne 92, 11(Mar. 13, 1965): 554-556.

**7172. Steer, H.O.** *An Investigation of the Concept of Self-definition.* H.O. Steer. Toronto: University of Toronto, 1951.
Thesis (Ph.D.)--University of Toronto, 1951.

**7173. Steinhauer, Paul D.** *"Where Have All The Children Gone?: Child Psychiatric Emergencies in a Metropolitan Area."* Paul D. Steinhauer. Canadian Psychiatric Association Journal/Revue de l'Association canadienne de psychiatrie 16, 2(Apr. 1971): 121-127.

**7174. Steinmatz, Geraldine** *"The Clean Milk Campaign in Hamilton."* Geraldine Steinmatz. American Journal of Public Hygiene 6, 10(Oct. 1909): 98-101.

**7175. Stern, Leo** *"Negative Pressure Artificial Respiration: Use in Treatment of Respiratory Failure of the Newborn."* Leo Stern, Angeles D. Ramos, Eugene W. Outerbridge and Pierre H. Beaudry. Canadian Medical Association Journal/Journal de l'Association medicale canadienne 102, 6(Mar. 28, 1970): 595-601.

**7176. Sternberg, Joseph** *"Serum Proteins in Parturient Mother and Newborn: an Electrophoretic Study."* J. Sternberg, P. Dagenais-Perusse and M. Dreyfuss. Canadian Medical Association Journal 74, 1(Jan. 1, 1956): 49-58.

**7177. Stevens, Ethel** *"Metropolitan Toronto Nursery and Day Care Centres."* Ethel Stevens. Bulletin of the Institute of Child Study 30, 1(Spring 1968): 25-26.

**7178. Stevens, Peter** *Miriam Waddington and Her Works.* Peter Stevens. Toronto: ECW Press, 1984.

**7179. Stevens, W.J.** *"A Review of Obstetrics."* W.J. Stevens. Canadian Nurse 23, 9(Sept. 1927): 461-465.

**7180. Stewart, D.A.** *"Diagnosis and Treatment of Throat Infections in Children."* D.A. Stewart and H. Moghadam. Canadian Medical Association Journal/Journal de l'Association medicale canadienne 105, 1(July 10, 1971): 69-71.

**7181. Stewart, Flora F.** *"Teaching Public Health to Groups of Mothers."* Flora F. Stewart. Canadian Nurse 24, 10(Oct. 1928): 546-550.

**7182. Stewart, Kate Lillico** *The Problem of Vocabulary Ability and School Studies.* Kate Lillico Stewart. Toronto: University of Toronto, 1922.
    Thesis (M.A.)--University of Toronto, 1922.
    No bibliography.

**7183. Stewart, Margaret C.** *The Application of a Theory of Discipline in a Private Home Setting.* Margaret C. Stewart. Toronto: University of Toronto, 1938.
    Thesis (M.A.)--University of Toronto, 1938.

**7184. Stewart, R.A.D.** *An Examination of the Predictive Value of the Toronto Medical Aptitude Test and Senior Matriculation Grades.* R.A.D. Stewart. Toronto: University of Toronto, 1947.
    Thesis (M.A.)--University of Toronto, 1947.

**7185. Stewart, Roderick** *Norman Bethune.* Roderick Stewart. Don Mills, Ontario: Fitzhenry & Whiteside, 1974.

**7186. Stewart, V. Lorne** *"Family Breakdown."* V. Lorne Stewart. Canadian Welfare 33, 2(June 1957): 59-64.

**7187. Stewart, V. Lorne** *A Follow-up Study of a Group of 161 Juvenile Delinquents.* V. Lorne Stewart. Toronto: University of Toronto, 1939.
    Thesis (M.A.)--University of Toronto, 1939.

**7188. Stirling, Margaret E.** *An Analysis of the Questions Asked by a Group of Preschool Children in a Controlled Setting.* Margaret E. Stirling. Toronto: University of Toronto, 1937.
    Thesis (M.A.)--University of Toronto, 1937.

**7189. Stitt, Jack M.** *"Correction Facilities for the Juvenile Offender: a Comparison of Ontario and the U.K."* Jack M. Stitt. Osgoode Hall Law Journal 2, 3(Apr. 1962): 356-369.

**7190. Stoddart, Jennifer** *"Quebec's Legal Elite Looks at Women's Rights: the Dorion Commission 1929-31."* Jennifer Stoddart. Toronto: the Osgoode Society by University of Toronto Press, c1981. In Essays in the History of Canadian Law, v.1, pp. 323-357. Edited by David H. Flaherty.

**7191. Stoddart, William B.** *A Critical Analysis of the Provisions for the Gifted Child in the Forest Hill School System: a Case Study.* William B. Stoddart. Toronto: University of Toronto, 1965.
    Thesis (Ed.D.)--University of Toronto, 1965.

**7192. Stone-Blackburn, Susan** *Robertson Davies, Playwright: a Search for the Self on the Canadian Stage.* Susan Stone-Blackburn. Vancouver: University of British Columbia Press, c1985.

**7193. Strachan, J. Grant** *"Atrophic Rhinitis or Ozaena in Children."* J. Grant Strachan. Canadian Medical Association Journal 44, 2(Feb. 1941): 158-161.

**7194. Strahm, Helen** *"Stepping Stones."* Helen Strahm. Canadian Welfare 28, 8(Mar. 1953): 14-16.

**7195. Stratton, Taylor** *"Fear of School."* Taylor Stratton. Canadian Psychiatric Association Journal/Revue de l'Association canadienne de psychiatrie 11, Supplement(1966): s306.

**7196. Strean, George J.** *"Maternal-Fetal Relationships: Placental Transmission of Poliomyelitis Antibodies in Newborn."* George J. Strean, Morrie M. Gelfand, Vytautas Pavilanis and Joseph Sternberg. Canadian Medical Association Journal 77, 4(Aug. 15, 1957): 315-323.

**7197. Strean, L.P.** *"Clinical Studies in Immunity to Pertussis with the Use of Pertussis Skin Testing Toxin and Antiendotoxin."* L.P. Strean. Canadian Medical Association Journal 45, 4(Oct. 1941): 326-331.

**7198. Stromberg-Stein, Susan** *Louis Dudek: a Biographical Introduction to his Poetry.* Susan Stromberg-Stein. Ottawa: Golden Dog Press, c1983.

**7199. Strong-Boag, Veronica** *"Intruders in the Nursery: Childcare Professionals Reshape the Years One to Five, 1920-1940."* Veronica Strong-Boag. Toronto: McClelland and Stewart, c1982. In Childhood and Family in Canadian History, pp. 160-178. Edited by Joy Parr.

**7200. Struthers, R.R.** *"Treatment of Pneumonia in Children."* R.R. Struthers. Canadian Medical Association Journal 44, 3(Mar. 1941): 271-275.

**7201. Struthers, W.E.** *"Medical Inspection of Schools in Toronto."* W.E. Struthers. Public Health Journal 5, 2(Feb. 1914): 67-78.

**7202. Stuart, Meryn Elizabeth** *"Let Not the People Perish for Lack of Knowledge": Public Health Nursing and the Ontario Child Welfare Project, 1916-1930 (Canada).* Meryn Elizabeth Stuart. Ann Arbor, Mi.: University Microfilms International, c1988. Thesis (Ph.D.)--University of Pennsylvania, 1987. Chapter notes include bibliographical references, leaves 181-222.

**7203. Stuewe, Paul** *Hugh Garner and His Works.* Paul Stuewe. Toronto: ECW Press, [1984].

**7204. Stuhr, Christian A.** *"Marks and Patterns of Parental Mobility in a Downtown School."* Christian A. Stuhr and E.N. Wright. Alberta Journal of Educational Research 16, 1(Mar. 1970): 47-55.

**7205. Sturino, Franc** *"A Case Study of a South Italian Family in Toronto, 1935-1960."* Franc Sturino. Urban History Review/Revue d'histoire urbaine 2(Oct. 1978): 38-57.

**7206. Stursberg, Peter** *Mister Broadcasting: the Ernie Bushnell Story.* Peter Stursberg. Toronto: Peter Martin Associates, c1971.

**7207. Stutt, Howard A.** *"The Education of Exceptional Children in Montreal."* Howard A. Stutt. McGill Journal of Education 2, 2(Fall 1967): 99-107.

**7208. Suddon, Florence** *Perceptual Closure in Children.* Florence Suddon. Toronto: University of Toronto, 1961. Thesis (M.A.)--University of Toronto, 1961.

**7209. Sullivan, Edmund V.** *"The Development of Canadian Students' Political Conceptions: Theoretical and Methodological Considerations for an Initial Inquiry."* Edmund V. Sullivan, Niall Byrne and Mary Stager. Interchange 1, 3(1970): 56-67.

**7210. Sumagaysay, Lourdes S.** *The Effects of Varying Practice Exercises and Relating Methods of Solution in Mathematics Problem Solving.* Lourdes S. Sumagaysay. Toronto: University of Toronto, 1970. Thesis (Ph.D.)--University of Toronto, 1970.

**7211. Summers, Georgina M.** *A Study of the Sacred Heart Orphanage.* Georgina M. Summers. Toronto: University of Toronto, 1951. Thesis (M.S.W.)--University of Toronto, 1951.

**7212. Sutherland de Merlis, Doris** *The Effect of Phonetic Kinesthetic Training on the Measurable Reading Performance of Primary Pupils with Reversal and Inversion Difficulties.* Doris Sutherland de Merlis. Ottawa: University of Ottawa, 1959. Thesis (Ph.D.)--University of Ottawa, 1959.

**7213. Sutton, Robert E.** *"Tolerance of Young Children With Severe Gastroenteritis to Dietary Lactose: a Controlled Study."* Robert E. Sutton and J.R. Hamilton. Canadian Medical Association Journal/Journal de l'Association medicale canadienne 99, 20(Nov. 23, 1968): 980-982.

**7214. Swackhamer, J.W.** *"Custody and Maintenance."* J.W. Swackhamer. Western Law Review 5(1966): 126-135.

**7215. Swain, John Gwynn** *Letters to His Mother, Written on His Entrance Into Life, Aged Seventeen, Giving a Description of His Voyage to Canada and Adventures at Lake Superior.* John Gwynn Swain. Edinburgh: [Turnbull and Spears], 1869.

**7216. Swain, Merrill, ed.** *Bilingual Schooling: Some Experiences in Canada and the United States.* Merrill Swain, ed. Toronto: Ontario Institute for Studies in Education, c1972.

**7217. Swainson, Donald** *"Schuyler Shibley and the Underside of Victorian Ontario."* Donald Swainson. Ontario History 65, 1(Mar. 1973): 51-60.

**7218. Swanson, Norrie** *"The Prevention and Correction of Deformity in Rheumatoid Arthritis."* Norrie Swanson. Canadian Medical Association Journal 75, 4(Aug. 15, 1956): 257-261.

**7219. Swartz, D.P.** *"Preventable Perinatal Loss."* D.P. Swartz, J.C. Rathburn, J.H. Walters and R.A.H. Kinch. Canadian Medical Association Journal/Journal de l'Association medicale canadienne 86, 20(May 19, 1962): 927-930.

**7220. Swartz, Faye M.** *I.Q., Divergent Thinking Ability and School Achievement in Tenth Grade Boys.* Faye M. Swartz. Toronto: University of Toronto, 1968. Thesis (M.A.)--University of Toronto, 1968.

7221. **Sweezey, Gilmour G.** *"Free Speech and the Student's Right to Govern His Personal Appearance."* Gilmour G. Sweezey. Osgoode Hall Law Journal 7, 3(1969): 293-310.

7222. **Swyer, Paul R.** *"The Control of Supplemental Oxygen by Oximetry."* Paul R. Swyer and John Wright. Canadian Medical Association Journal 78, 4(Feb. 15, 1958): 231-235.

7223. **Swyer, Paul R.** *"The Physiological Basis for Supplemental Oxygen in the Newborn."* Paul R. Swyer. Canadian Medical Association Journal 78, 4(Feb. 15, 1958): 236-240.

7224. **Swyripa, Frances** *"Outside the Bloc Settlement: Ukrainian Women in Ontario during the Formative Years of Community Consciousness."* Frances Swyripa. Toronto: Multicultural History Society of Ontario, c1986. In Looking into My Sister's Eyes: an Exploration in Women's History, pp. 155-178. Edited by Jean Burnet.

7225. **Sykes, Donald** *Sustained Attention in Hyperactive Children.* Donald Sykes. Montreal: McGill University, 1969. Thesis (Ph.D.)--McGill University, 1969.

7226. **Synge, Jane** *"The Transition from School to Work: Growing Up Working Class in Early 20th Century Hamilton, Ontario."* Jane Synge. Toronto: McGraw-Hill Ryerson, c1979. In Childhood and Adolescence in Canada, pp. 249-269. Edited by K. Ishwaran.

7227. **Tait, George E.** *A History of Art Education in the Elementary Schools of Ontario.* George E. Tait. Toronto: University of Toronto, 1957. Thesis (Ed.D.)--University of Toronto, 1957.

7228. **Talbot, Betty M.** *A Longitudinal Study of Attentive Behaviour of a Group of Preschool Children.* Betty M. Talbot. Toronto: University of Toronto, 1948. Thesis (M.A.)--University of Toronto, 1948.

7229. **Talbot, Carol** *Growing Up Black in Canada.* Carol Talbot. Toronto: Williams-Wallace, 1984.

7230. **Tanser, H.A.** *Settlement of Negroes in Kent County, Ontario, and a Study of the Mental Capacity of Their Descendants.* H.A. Tanser. Toronto: University of Toronto, [1939]. Thesis (D.Paed.)--University of Toronto, [1939].

7231. **Tate, Douglas Lloyd** *The Influence of Percentage of Reward Shifts on Children's Response Speeds.* Douglas Lloyd Tate. London, Ont.: University of Western Ontario, 1968. Thesis (M.A.)--University of Western Ontario, 1968.

7232. **Taylor, George** *A Descriptive Study of Dropouts: a Study of Employment, Future Planning and the Four Major Areas of Socialization i.e. Family, School, Peer Group and Mass Media as They Pertain to a Group of English Speaking Catholic High School Dropouts from a Middle Class Area of Montreal.* George Taylor. Montreal: McGill University, 1970. Thesis (M.S.W.)--McGill University, 1970.

7233. **Taylor, Lyra B.** *"The Churches and Social Work: an Interesting Effect in Montreal."* Lyra B. Taylor. Child and Family Welfare 10, 1(May 1934): 60-63.

7234. **Taylor, Ryan, trans.** *Pioneer Families: Their Odyssey, Their Settlement.* Ryan Taylor, trans. [Sudbury]: Sudbury Public Library, 1980. First published in French, 1944.

7235. **Teasdall, Ethel** *"Education of the Crippled Child."* Ethel Teasdall. Canadian Nurse 25, 4(Apr. 1929): 171-175.

7236. **Teghsoonian, Okser** *"Armenians in Toronto: the Early Years."* Okser Teghsoonian. Polyphony 6, 1(Spring-Summer 1984): 232.

7237. **Tessaro, Angelo Fortunato** *The Juvenile Male Sex Offender.* Angelo Fortunato Tessaro. Toronto: University of Toronto, 1956. Thesis (M.S.W.)--University of Toronto, 1956.

7238. **Thirlaway, Jean** *"The New Look in Typhoid Fever."* Jean Thirlaway. Canadian Nurse 46, 9(Sept. 1950): 729-730.

7239. **Thomas, Charles** *"Reminiscences of First Settlers in County of Brant."* Charles Thomas and James C. Thomas. Ontario Historical Society, Papers and Records 12(1914): 58-71.

7240. **Thomas, Clara** *William Arthur Deacon: a Canadian Literary Life.* Clara Thomas. Toronto: University of Toronto Press, c1982.

7241. **Thompson, G.F.** *"A Child Placing Programme in a Rural Setting."* G.F. Thompson. Child and Family Welfare 13, 2(July 1937): 24-27.

**7242. Thompson, Lee Briscoe** *Dorothy Livesay.* Lee Briscoe Thompson. Boston: Twayne, c1987.

**7243. Thompson, Nina M.** *Investigation of the Change in I.Q. Occurring with Age Increase.* Nina M. Thompson. Toronto: University of Toronto, 1948.
Thesis (M.A.)--University of Toronto, 1948.

**7244. Thomson, Dale C.** *"Louis Stephen St. Laurent: Eastern Townships Boy."* Dale C. Thomson. Journal of Canadian Studies/Revue d'etudes canadiennes 1, 3(Nov. 1966): 31-39.

**7245. Thomson, Mary** *An Analysis of the Sociometric Ratings of Groups of Children from Three to Eight Years of Age.* Mary Thomson. Toronto: University of Toronto, 1948.
Thesis (M.A.)--University of Toronto, 1948.

**7246. Thomson, P.G.** *"The Subnormal Child."* P.G. Thomson. Canadian Medical Association Journal 76, 6(Mar. 15, 1957): 506-510.

**7247. Thornback, P.** *"Sudden Unexpected Death in Children With Congenital Heart Disease."* P. Thornback and R.S. Fowler. Canadian Medical Association Journal/Journal de l'Association medicale canadienne 113, 8(Oct. 18, 1975): 745-748.

**7248. Thornhill, Mary Elizabeth** *Between Friends.* Mary Elizabeth Thornhill. Toronto: Reginald Saunders, 1935.

**7249. Tisdall, F.F.** *"The Canadian Red Cross School Meal Study."* Frederick F. Tisdall, Elizabeth C. Robertson, S.H. Jackson, H.M. Fowler, J.A. Long, Lucien Brouha, R.G. Ellis, A.J. Phillips, and Rosamund Stevenson Rogers. Canadian Medical Association Journal 64, 6(June 1951): 477-489.

**7250. Tisdall, F.F.** *"Deficiency Diseases of Childhood."* F.F. Tisdall. Canadian Nurse 24, 10(Oct. 1928): 515-518.

**7251. Tisdall, F.F.** *"Zinc-Sulphate Nasal Spray in the Prophylaxis of Poliomyelitis: Observation of a Group of 4,713 Children, Age 3-10 Years, During an Epidemic in Toronto, Canada."* F.F Tisdall, Alan Brown, R.D. Defries, M.A. Ross and A. Hardisty Sellers. Canadian Public Health Journal 28, 11(Nov. 1937): 493-497.

**7252. Tomes, Nigel** *"Childlessness in Canada 1971."* Nigel Tomes. Canadian Journal of Sociology/Cahiers canadien de sociologie 10, 1(Winter 1985): 37-68.

**7253. Tomev, Foto S.** *"A Macedonian Memoir."* Foto S. Tomev. Polyphony 6, 1(Spring-Summer 1984): 226-227.

**7254. Tomic-Trumper, Patricia** *The Care of Unwed Mothers and Illegitimate Children in Toronto, 1867-1920: a Study in Social Administration.* Patricia Tomic-Trumper. Toronto: University of Toronto, 1986. (CTM no. 31493)
Thesis (Ph.D.)--University of Toronto, 1986.

**7255. Tomlinson, Peter D.** *"Differential Effects of Role-example Order as a Function of Learner Conceptual Level."* Peter D. Tomlinson and David E. Hunt. Canadian Journal of Behavioural Science/Revue canadienne de sciences du comportement 3, 3(July 1971): 237-245.

**7256. Tomlinson, Peter D.** *An Investigation into the Development of Short-term Retention Capacity in Children as a Function of Age and Item Familiarity.* Peter D. Tomlinson. Toronto: University of Toronto, 1971. (CTM no. 12229)
Thesis (M.A.)--University of Toronto, 1971.

**7257. Torgov, Morley** *A Good Place to Come From.* Morley Torgov. Toronto: Lester & Orpen Ltd., 1974.

**7258. Toronto. Board of Education. Research Department** *Immigrants and Their Education.* The Department. Toronto: The Department, 1965.

**7259. Toronto Boys Home** *125 Years of Caring: the Boys' Home 1859-1984.* Toronto Boys Home. Toronto: The Home, 1984.

**7260. Toronto. Department of Public Health** *"Height and Weight Tables of Toronto School Children."* Prepared by the Department of Public Health, Toronto, Canada. Public Health Journal 15, 9(Sep 1924): 391-403.

**7261. Toronto. Department of Public Health. Supervisor of Homes** *"What a Good Foster Mother Did for a Puny Baby."* Supervisor of Homes, Department of Public Health, Toronto. Canadian Nurse 13, 10(Oct. 1917): 637.

7262. **Toronto General Hospital. Ophthalmological Department** *The Cross-Eyed or Squinting Child Needs Prompt Corrective Treatment.* Toronto General Hospital, Ophthalmological Department. Ottawa: Canadian Welfare Council, 1935.

7263. **Toronto Humane Society** *Aims and Objects of the Toronto Humane Society.* J. George Hodgins, ed. Toronto: William Briggs, 1888.

7264. **Toronto Humane Society** *What Has Been Accomplished During Five Years by the Toronto Humane Society Including an Annual Report of the Society for the Year 1891-92.* J. George Hodgins, ed. [and] Toronto Humane Society. Toronto: Massey Press, 1892.

7265. **Toronto Psychiatric Hospital** *Miscellaneous Papers.* Toronto Psychiatric Hospital. Toronto: [The Hospital, 1960-64].

7266. **Toronto School Board. Association of Heads of Guidance Departments** *Gifted Students in the Toronto Secondary Schools.* Association of Heads of Guidance Departments, Toronto Schools. Toronto: [s.n.], 1958.

7267. **Traill, Catherine Parr** *The Backwoods of Canada: Being Letters From the Wife of an Emigrant Officer.* Catherine Parr Traill. 4th ed. London, Eng.: Nattali and Bond, 1839.

7268. **Travis, Keith I.** *The Effects of Modifying Interruptions of Organized Behavioral and Cognitive Sequences.* Keith I. Travis. Toronto: University of Toronto, 1970.
Thesis (Ph.D.)--University of Toronto, 1970.

7269. **Trent, Bill** *Who Killed Lynne Harper?* Bill Trent and Steven Truscott. Montreal: Optimum Pub., c1979.

7270. **Trowsdale, George Campbell** *A History of Public School Music in Ontario.* George Campbell Trowsdale. 2 v. Toronto: University of Toronto, 1962.
Thesis (Ed.D.)--University of Toronto, 1962.

7271. **Trumble, David** *When I Was a Boy.* David Trumble; edited by Glen Ellis. Don Mills, Ont.: J.M. Dent and Sons, 1976.

7272. **Truscott, Steven** *The Steven Truscott Story.* Steven Truscott as told to Bill Trent. Markham, Ont.: PaperJacks, 1979, c1971.

7273. **Trusler, G.A.** *"Intravenous Polyethylene Catheter Successfully Removed from the Heart."* G.A. Trusler and W.T. Mustard. Canadian Medical Association Journal 79, 7(Oct. 1, 1958): 558-559.

7274. **Trusler, G.A.** *"Operative Closure of Isolated Patent Ductus Arteriosus in the First Two Years of Life."* G.A. Trusler, P. Arayangkoon and W.T. Mustard. Canadian Medical Association Journal/Journal de l'Association medicale canadienne 99, 18(Nov. 9, 1968): 879-881.

7275. **Tsao, Fei** *Age and Grade as Functions of Variability.* Fei Tsao. Toronto: University of Toronto, 1942.
Thesis (Ph.D.)--University of Toronto, 1942.

7276. **Tuck, James A.** *Aspiration for Academic Success Among High School Boys and Girls.* James A. Tuck. Toronto: University of Toronto, 1956.
Thesis (Ph.D.)--University of Toronto, 1956.

7277. **Turk, James Leonard** *The Measurement of Intra-familial Power.* James Leonard Turk. Toronto: University of Toronto, 1970. (CTM no. 10600)
Thesis (Ph.D.)--University of Toronto, 1970.

7278. **Turnbull, William A.** *"Is War Affecting Delinquency?"* William A. Turnbull. Canadian Welfare 17, 6(Nov. 1941): 17-18.

7279. **Turner, G.H.** *"The Scholastic Aptitude of the Indian Children of the Caradoc Reserve."* G.H. Turner and D.J. Penfold. Canadian Journal of Psychology 6, 1(Mar. 1952): 31-44.

7280. **Turner, J.A.** *"Present Day Aspects of Acute Laryngotracheitis."* J.A. Turner. Canadian Medical Association Journal 70, 4(Apr. 1954): 401-404.

7281. **Turner, J.A.** *"The Protean Manifestations of Mycoplasma Infections in Childhood."* J.A. Peter Turner, Edward C. Burchak, Robert M. Bannatyne and Peter C. Fleming. Canadian Medical Association Journal/Journal de l'Association medicale canadienne 99, 13(Oct. 5, 1968): 633-637.

7282. **Turner, Wesley B.** *Life in Upper Canada.* Wesley B. Turner. Toronto: Grolier Ltd., c1980.

7283. **Turner, Wesley B.** *"Miss Rye's Children and the Ontario Press, 1875."* Wesley B. Turner. Ontario History 68, 3(Sept. 1976): 169-200.

**7284. Tweddell, T.N.** "A 90% Burn with Recovery." T.N. Tweddell. Canadian Medical Association Journal 71, 6(Dec. 1954): 604-605.

**7285. Tymchuk, Alexander J.** "Neuropsychological Test Results of Children with Brain Lesions, Abnormal EEGs and Normal EEGs." Alexander J. Tymchuk, Robert M. Knights and George C. Hinton. Canadian Journal of Behavioural Science/Revue canadienne de sciences du comportement 2, 4(Oct. 1970): 322-332.

**7286. United Community Services of Greater London** Family Centred Project of London, Ontario. United Community Services of Greater London. [London: s.n.], 1967.

**7287. University of Toronto. Institute for Child Study** Outlines for Parent Education Groups: Pre-school Learning. The Institute. [Toronto]: University of Toronto Press, [1935?].

**7288. University of Toronto. Institute for Child Study** Outlines for Parent Education Groups: Discipline. The Institute. [Toronto]: University of Toronto Press, [1939].

**7289. Urquhart, Germaine M.** A Study of Negative Behaviour in Infants. Germaine M. Urquhart. Toronto: University of Toronto, 1950.
Thesis (M.A.)–University of Toronto, 1950.

**7290. Usher, Saul J.** "The Etiology of Sydenham's Chorea: Electroencephalographic Studies." Saul J. Usher and Herbert H. Jasper. Canadian Medical Association Journal 44, 4(Apr. 1941): 365-371.

**7291. Valentine, G.H.** "Exchange Transfusion in the Newborn Using Heparinized Blood." G.H. Valentine. Canadian Medical Association Journal 78, 12(June 15, 1958): 927-931.

**7292. Valin, Claire** A Survey of a Shut-in Population of Dependent Girls. Claire Valin. Ottawa: University of Ottawa, 1950.
Thesis (M.A.)–University of Ottawa, 1950.

**7293. Valisno, Mona Dumalao** The Relationship Between Aptitudes and Vocabulary Learning at Different Stages of Practice. Mona D. Valisno. Toronto: University of Toronto, 1969.
Thesis (Ph.D.)--University of Toronto, 1969.

**7294. Vallieres, Pierre** White Niggers of America. Pierre Vallieres. Toronto: McClelland and Steward, 1971.

**7295. Vandenhazel, Bessel J.** "Communicable Diseases and Ontario Schools." Bessel J. Vandenhazel. Ontario Education 18, 2(Mar.-Apr. 1986): 3-6.

**7296. Vanderburgh, R.M.** I Am Nokomis. Too: the Biography of Verna Patronella Johnston. R.M. Vanderburgh. Don Mills: General Publishing Company Limited, c1977.

**7297. Van Horson, Jan E.** Sacred Heart Children's Village, the Development of a Residential Treatment Centre. Jan E. Van Horson. Toronto: University of Toronto, 1967.
Thesis (M.S.W.)–University of Toronto, 1967.

**7298. Vanier Institute of the Family** Day Care, a Resource for the Contemporary Family: Papers and Proceedings of a Seminar, Ottawa, September 1969. The Institute. Ottawa: The Institute, 1970.

**7299. VanLoon, John W.** "Unit Promotion: Each at His Own Pace." John W. VanLoon. Journal of Education of the Faculty and College of Education: Vancouver and Victoria 6(Dec. 1961): 101-112.

**7300. Vermette, Luce** Domestic Life at Les Forges du Saint-Maurice. Luce Vermette. Ottawa: Parks Canada, 1982.

**7301. Vigod, Bernard L.** Quebec Before Duplessis: the Political Career of Louis-Alexandre Taschereau. Bernard L. Vigod. Kingston: McGill-Queen's University Press, 1986.

**7302. Vimont, Barthelemy** Travels and Explorations of the Jesuit Missionaries in New France, 1610-1791: Quebec and Hurons, 1642. Barthelemy Vimont, Hierosme Lalement [and] Reuben Gold Thwaites, ed. Cleveland, Ohio: Burrows Brothers Co., 1898.

**7303. Vimont, Barthelemy** Travels and Explorations of the Jesuit Missionaries in New France, 1610-1791: Iroquois, Hurons, Quebec, 1642-1644. Barthelemy Vimont [and] Reuben Gold Thwaites, ed. Cleveland, Ohio: Burrows Brothers Co., 1898.

**7304. Vince, Dennis J.** "Nodular Panniculitis After Massive Predrisone Therapy." Dennis J. Vince. Canadian Medical Association Journal 79, 10(Nov. 15, 1958): 840-841.

**7305. Vincent, Patrick** *The Assimilation Process: With Special Reference to Italian Children in the Hamilton School System.* Patrick Vincent. Hamilton: McMaster University, 1968.
Thesis (M.A.)--McMaster University, 1968.

**7306. Virgin, A.R.** *"The Bowmanville Boys' School, Ontario."* A.R. Virgin. Child and Family Welfare 9, 6(Mar. 1934): 46-49.

**7307. Virtue, Ruth** *"Comparison of Observed Intakes and Recommended Allowances of Calories."* Ruth Virtue and E.W. McHenry. Canadian Journal of Public Health 36, 6(June 1945): 240-244.

**7308. Vivian, R.P.** *"The Nutrition and Health of the James Bay Indian."* R.P. Vivian, Charles McMillan, P.E. Moore, E. Chant Robertson, W.H. Sebrell, F.F. Tisdall and W.G. McIntosh. Canadian Medical Association Journal 59, 6(Dec. 1948): 505-518.

**7309. Von Eberts, E.M.** *"Living Case: Congential Pyloric Stenosis."* E.M. Von Eberts. Canadian Medical Association Journal 6, 7(July 1916): 605-606 and 662-664.

**7310. Wade, Mason** *The French-Canadian Outlook: a Brief Account of the Unknown North Americans.* Mason Wade. New York: Viking Press, 1946.

**7311. Wagman, Barbara Ann** *Preschool and Childhood Cognitive Development of Indians at Curve Lake Reserve.* Barbara Ann Wagman. Toronto: University of Toronto, 1970.
Thesis (M.A.)--University of Toronto, 1970.

**7312. Wagner, Edith M.** *Education as Revealed in Family Papers, Ontario 1800-1900.* Edith M. Wagner. Toronto: University of Toronto, 1954.
Thesis (M.A.)--University of Toronto, 1954.

**7313. Walden, Keith** *"Hazes, Hustles, Scraps and Stunts: Initiations at the University of Toronto, 1880-1925."* Keith Walden. Kingston: McGill-Queen's University Press, 1989. In Youth, University and Canadian Society: Essays in the Social History of Higher Education, pp. 94-121. Edited by Paul Axelrod and John G. Reid.

**7314. Walker, C. Jean** *"The Social Problems of School Children."* C. Jean Walker. Canadian Nurse 23, 7(July 1927): 358-363.

**7315. Walker, Elsie M.H.** *Trends in Companionships of Public School Children.* Elsie M.H. Walker. Toronto: University of Toronto, 1935.
Thesis (M.A.)--University of Toronto, 1935.

**7316. Wallace, W.G.** *""A Tassie Boy": Fragment of an Autobiographical Sketch."* W.G. Wallace. Ontario History 46, 3(Summer 1954): 169-178.

**7317. Wallace, W. Stewart** *"The Story of Charlotte and Cornelia de Grassi."* W. Stewart Wallace. Royal Society of Canada Proceedings and Transactions Series 3, .35, 2(May 1941): 147-153.

**7318. Wallerstein, Harvey** *"An Electromyographic Study of Attentive Listening."* Harvey Wallerstein. Canadian Journal of Psychology 8, 4(Dec. 1954): 228-238.

**7319. Walters, Chester S.** *"The Duty of the City to the Child: What Can be Accomplished by a Baby Week."* Chester S. Walters. Public Health Journal 6, 11(Nov. 1915): 540-541.

**7320. Walters, Richard H.** *"Enhancement of Punitiveness by Visual and Audio Visual Displays."* Richard H. Walters and Edward Llewellyn Thomas. Canadian Journal of Psychology 17, 2(June 1963): 244-255.

**7321. Walters, Richard H.** *"Imitative Behavior of Disturbed and Nondisturbed Children Following Exposure to Aggressive and Nonaggressive Models."* Richard H. Walters and Donna C. Willows. Child Development 39, 1(Mar. 1968): 79-89.

**7322. Walters, Richard H.** *"Inhibition and Disinhibition of Responses Through Empathetic Learning."* Richard H. Walters, Marion Leat and Louis Mezei. Canadian Journal of Psychology 17, 2(June 1963): 235-243.

**7323. Walters, Richard H.** *"Social Isolation, Effect of Instructions and Verbal Behaviour."* Richard H. Walters and G. Bruce Henning. Canadian Journal of Psychology 16, 3(Sept. 1962): 202-210.

**7324. Walters, Richard H.** *"Studies of Reinforcement of Aggression: 3. Transfer of Responses to an Interpersonal Situation."* Richard H. Walters and Murray Brown. Child Development 34, 3(Sept. 1963): 563-571.

**7325. Walters, Richard H.** *"Timing of Punishment as a Determinant of Response Inhibition."* Richard H. Walters and Lillian Demkow. Child Development 34, 1(Mar. 1963): 207-214.

**7326. Ward, Patricia C.** *"Infant Birth Weight and Nutrition in Industrializing Montreal."* Patricia C. Ward and W. Peter Ward. American Historical Review 89, 2(Apr. 1984): 324-345.

**7327. Ward, W. Peter** *"Family Papers and the New Social History."* W. Peter Ward. Archivaria 14(Summer 1982): 63-74.

**7328. Ward, W. Peter** *"Unwed Motherhood in Nineteenth Century English Canada."* W. Peter Ward. Canadian Historical Association, Historical Papers/Communications historiques (1981): 34-56.

**7329. Wargny, Nancy Jean** *Meaningfulness, Structure, and the Recall of Verbal Material by Children.* Nancy Jean Wargny. Montreal: McGill University, 1969.
Thesis (M.A.)--McGill University, 1969.

**7330. Wass, D. Keith** *A Children's Aid Society and Wards over Sixteen Years of Age.* D. Keith Wass. Toronto: University of Toronto, 1949.
Thesis (M.S.W.)--University of Toronto, 1949.

**7331. Wasteneys, Hortense Catherine Fardell** *The Adequacy of the Social Services Made Available to Displaced Families in Toronto.* Hortense Catherine Fardell Wasteneys. Toronto: University of Toronto, 1950.
Thesis (M.S.W.)--University of Toronto, 1950.

**7332. Watson, Cicely** *Ontario Grade 13: Three Studies.* Cicely Watson and Patricia M. Lyle. Toronto: Ontario Institute for Studies in Education, c1965.

**7333. Watson, Geoffrey G.** *Sport and Games in Ontario Private Schools, 1830-1930.* Geoffrey G. Watson. Edmonton: University of Alberta, 1970.
Thesis (M.A.)--University of Alberta, 1970.

**7334. Watson, Peter** *Effects of Reward Schedule, Type of Reward, and Isolation Condition on Children's Lever-pulling Performance.* Peter Watson. London, Ont.: University of Western Ontario, 1967. (CTM no. 1626)
Thesis (Ph.D.)--University of Western Ontario, 1967.

**7335. Weaver, John C.** *"Order and Efficiency: Samuel Morley Wickett and the Urban Progressive Movement in Toronto, 1900-1915."* Weaver, John C. Ontario History 69, 4(Dec. 1977): 218-234.

**7336. Webber, Marlene** *Square John: a True Story.* Marlene Webber and Tony McGilvary. Toronto: University of Toronto Press, c1988.

**7337. Webster, Edward** *Vocational Guidance in Relation to School Training and the Distribution of Mental Abilities.* Edward Webster. Montreal: McGill University, 1936.
Thesis (Ph.D.)--McGill University, 1936.

**7338. Webster, Loyola Cathleen** *Parental Expectations of the Jewish Child in School Achievement, Extra Curricular Activities and Peer Relationships.* Loyola Cathleen Webster. Toronto: University of Toronto, 1964.
Thesis (M.S.W.)--University of Toronto, 1964.

**7339. Weiner, Judith** *"Serial Order Ability in Good and Poor Readers."* Judith Weiner, Roger H. Barnsley and M. Sam Rabinovitch. Canadian Journal of Behavioural Science/Revue canadienne de sciences du comportement 2, 2(Apr. 1970): 116-123.

**7340. Weinzweig, Paul Alan** *Socialization and Subculture in Elite Education: a Study of a Canadian Boys' Private School.* Paul Alan Weinzweig. Toronto: University of Toronto, 1970. (CTM no. 28015)
Thesis (Ph.D.)--University of Toronto, 1970.

**7341. Weiss, Gabrielle** *"Comparison of the Effects of Chlorpromazine, Dextroamphetamine and Methylphenidate on the Behaviour and Intellectual Functioning of Hyperactive Children."* Gabrielle Weiss, Klaus Minde, Virginia Douglas, John Werry and Donald Sykes. Canadian Medical Association Journal/Journal de l'Association medicale canadienne 104, 1(Jan. 9, 1971): 20-25.

**7342. Welfare Council of Toronto and District** *A Study of the Adjustment of Teen Children Born Out of Wedlock Who Remained in the Custody of their Mothers and Relatives.* Welfare Council of Toronto and District. Toronto: Subcommittee of Unmarried Parenthood Committee, 1943.

**7343. Werry, John W.** *"Studies on the Hyperactive Child I: Some Preliminary Findings."* J.W. Werry, Gabrielle Weiss and V. Douglas. Canadian Psychiatric Association Journal/Revue de l'Association canadienne de psychiatrie 9, 2(Apr. 1964): 120-130.

**7344. Westley, William A.** *"The Protective Environment and Adolescent Socialization."* William A. Westley and Frederick Elkin. New York: Harper and Row Pub., c1967. In Middle Class Juvenile Delinquency, pp. 9-22. Edited by Edmund W. Vaz.
Reprinted from Social Forces 35(Mar. 1957): 243-249.

**7345. Whatmough, K.D.** *The Championships of School Children.* K.D. Whatmough. Toronto: University of Toronto, 1934.
Thesis (M.A.)–University of Toronto, 1934.

**7346. Whelan, Eugene** *Whelan: the Man in the Green Stetson.* Eugene Whelan with Rick Archibald. Toronto: Irwin, 1986.

**7347. Whelen, Warren S.** *"The Rising Incidence of Scurvy in Infants."* Warren S. Whelen, Donald Fraser, Elizabeth Chant Robertson and Hedy Tomczak. Canadian Medical Association Journal 78, 3(Feb. 1, 1958): 177-181.

**7348. Whitaker, Muriel** *"Great Aunt Jennie's Fourth Ontario Reader."* Muriel Whitaker. Ontario Education 10, 5(Nov.-Dec. 1978): 18-21.

**7349. White, C.C.** *"Spinal Anaesthesia in Obstetrics."* C.C. White. Canadian Medical Association Journal 69, 5(Nov. 1953): 488-491.

**7350. White, Catherine** *"Reminiscence of Mrs. White of White's Mills, near Coburg, Upper Canada, Fomerly Miss Catherine Chrysler of Sydney, near Belleville, Aged 79 Years."* Catherine White. Ontario Historical Society, Papers and Records 7(1906): 153-157.

**7351. White, George E.** *"Sensitivity to Sulfathiazole."* George E. White. Canadian Medical Association Journal 49, 4(Oct. 1943): 317-318.

**7352. Whitehead, Eric** *Cyclone Taylor: a Hockey Legend.* Eric Whitehead. 1st ed. Toronto: Doubleday Canada, c1977.

**7353. Whitehead, Eric** *The Patricks: Hockey's Royal Family.* Eric Whitehead. Toronto: Doubleday Canada, c1980.

**7354. Whitney, William Bruce** *Jewish Youth and the Community: the Relationship between Behavior and Participation in Organized Community Activities.* William Bruce Whitney. Toronto: University of Toronto, 1969.
Thesis (M.S.W.)–University of Toronto, 1969.

**7355. Whitton, Charlotte** *"The Questioning of Jurisdiction in Certain Social Causes."* Charlotte Whitton. Child and Family Welfare 13, 6(Mar. 1938): 1-11.

**7356. Whyte, D.W.** *"Special Indications for Rectal Pentothal in Children."* D.W. Whyte. Canadian Medical Association Journal 64, 6(June 1951): 525-528.

**7357. Wideman, Harley R.** *An Exploratory Study of the Relationship of Mental Ability and School Achievement in Grade One.* Harley R. Wideman. Toronto: University of Toronto, 1949.
Thesis (M.A.)–University of Toronto, 1949.

**7358. Widows and Orphans' Asylum (Toronto)** *Report of the Managing Commitee of the Widows and Orphans' Asylum for the Care and Maintenance of the Destitute Widows and Orphans of Emigrants of 1847.* Managing Commitee of the Widows and Orphans' Asylum. [Toronto?: s.n.], 1848.

**7359. Wild, Marjorie** *Elizabeth Bagshaw.* Marjorie Wild. Markam, Ont.: Fitzhenry & Whiteside, 1984.

**7360. Wilensky, Dora** *"From Juvenile Immigrant to Canadian Citizen."* Dora Wilensky. Canadian Welfare 26, 6(Dec. 1950): 17-22.

**7361. Wilkey, John R.** *"A Tuberculosis Fact-finding Study in the London Secondary Schools."* John R. Wilkey. Canadian Public Health Journal 34, 1(Jan. 1943): 22-25.

**7362. Willebrands, Elsa Magdalena** *Health Care Services In and Through the Toronto School System from 1910 to 1980.* Elsa Magdalena Willebrands. Toronto: University of Toronto, 1988.
Thesis (Ed.D.)–University of Toronto, 1988.

**7363. Williams, Alice L.** *A Study of Religious Attitudes and Activities in a Group of Adolescent Boys.* Alice L. Williams. Toronto: University of Toronto, 1934.
Thesis (M.A.)–University of Toronto, 1934.

**7364. Williams, D.C.** *Factors Related to Reading Achievement.* D.C. Williams. Toronto: University of Toronto, 1940.
Thesis (Ph.D.)–University of Toronto, 1940.

**7365. Williams, J. Ivan** *"Diet in the Management of Hyperkinesis: a Review of the Tests of Feingold's Hypothesis."* J. Ivan Williams and Douglas M. Cram. Canadian Psychiatric Association Journal/Revue de l'Association canadienne de psychiatrie 23, 4(June 1978): 241-248.

**7366. Willis, Edith B.** *Factors Relating to Teacher-Child Contacts in Preschool Education.* Edith B. Willis. Montreal: McGill University, 1948.
Thesis (M.A.)--McGill University, 1948.

**7367. Willis, Hal L.** *"A Survey of How Students Perceive Their High Schools."* Hal L. Willis and Gerald Halpern. Education Canada 10, 2(June 1970): 29-33.

**7368. Willis, Jane** *Geniesh: an Indian Girlhood.* Jane Willis. Toronto: New Press, 1973.

**7369. Willis, Kenneth Richard** *Pupil Participation in the Activities of the Secondary School: an Analysis of Supporting Thought With a Subsidiary Examination of Actual Practice.* Kenneth Richard Willis. Toronto: University of Toronto, 1950.
Thesis (Ph.D.)--University of Toronto, 1950.

**7370. Willoughby, Brenda** *Pauline Johnson.* Brenda Willoughby. Toronto: Grolier, c1988.

**7371. Wilson, J. Donald** *"Education in Upper Canada: Sixty Years of Change."* J. Donald Wilson. Scarborough: Prentice-Hall of Canada, c1970. In Canadian Education: a History, pp. 190-213. Edited by J. Donald Wilson, Robert M. Stamp and Louis-Philippe Audet.

**7372. Wilson, J. Donald** *""No Blanket to be Worn in School": the Education of Indians in Early Nineteenth Century Ontario."* J. Donald Wilson. Histoire sociale/Social History 7, 14(Nov. 1974): 293-305.
Updated and revised version reprinted in Jean Barman, Yvonne Hebert and Don McCaskill, ed. Indian Education in Canada, vol. 1 Legacy (Vancouver: University of British Columbia Press, 1985): 64-87.

**7373. Wilson, J. Donald** *"A Note on the Shingwauk Industrial Home for Indians."* J. Donald Wilson. Canadian Church Historical Society Journal 14, 4(Dec. 1974): 66-71.

**7374. Wilson, J. Donald** *"The Ryerson Years in Canada West."* J. Donald Wilson. Scarborough: Prentice-Hall of Canada, c1970. In Canadian Education: a History, pp. 214-240. Edited by J. Donald Wilson, Robert M. Stamp and Louis-Philippe Audet.

**7375. Wilson, Mary Carol** *Marion Hilliard.* Mary Carol Wilson. Don Mills, Ont.: Fitzhenry & Whiteside, 1977.

**7376. Wilson, Mrs.** *"Medical Inspection in Rural Schools."* Mrs. Wilson. Canadian Nurse 10, 1(Jan. 1914): 84-87.

**7377. Wilson, Nora R.** *A Study of the Victor Home for Unmarried Mothers.* Nora R. Wilson. Toronto: University of Toronto, 1961.
Thesis (M.S.W.)--University of Toronto, 1961.

**7378. Wilson, Reginald** *"Diphtheria and Tetanus Toxoids Combined with Pertussis and Poliomyelitis Vaccine: Clinical Trial of a Quadruple Antigen."* R.J. Wilson, G.W.O. Moss, F.C. Potter and D.R.E. MacLeod. Canadian Medical Association Journal/Journal de l'Association medicale canadienne 81, 6(Sept. 15, 1959): 450-453.

**7379. Wilson, W.M.G.** *"Congenital Blindness (Pseudoglioma) Occurring as a Sex-linked Developmental Anomaly."* W.M.G. Wilson. Canadian Medical Association Journal 60, 6(June 1949): 580-584.

**7380. Winchester, Ian** *"Review of Peel County History Project and the Saguenay Project."* Ian Winchester. Histoire sociale/Social History 13, 25(May 1980): 195-205.

**7381. Wingfield, Alex H.** *Twins and Orphans: the Inheritance of Intelligence.* Alex H. Wingfield. London, Eng.: J.M. Dent and Sons, 1928.
Thesis (Ph.D.)--University of Toronto, [1928].
Thesis published as a monograph.

**7382. Wintrob, Ronald M.** *"Rapid Socio-cultural Change and Student Mental Health."* Ronald M. Wintrob. McGill Journal of Education 4, 2(Fall 1969): 174-183.

**7383. Winzer, Margaret** *An Examination of Some Selected Factors that Affected the Education and Socialization of the Deaf in Ontario, 1870-1900.* Margaret Ann Winzer. Toronto: University of Toronto, 1981.
Thesis (Ed.D.)--University of Toronto, 1981.

7384. Wise, S.F. "Sport and Class Values in Old Ontario and Quebec." S.F. Wise. Montreal: McGill-Queen's University Press, 1974. In His Own Man: Essays in Honour of Arthur Reginald Marsden Lower, pp. 93-117. Edited by W.H. Heick and Roger Graham.

7385. Wismer, Ruth E. A Survey of Individual Differences in the Paintings of Preschool Children. Ruth E. Wismer. Toronto: University of Toronto, 1950. Thesis (M.A.)–University of Toronto, 1950.

7386. Wittkower, E.D. "Psychological Aspects of Atopic Dermatitis in Children." E.D. Wittkower and B.R. Hunt. Canadian Medical Association Journal 79, 10(Nov. 15, 1958): 810-817.

7387. Wodehouse, Robert E. "Municipal Health Work Pertaining to Infant Welfare." Robert E. Wodehouse. Canadian Medical Association Journal 3, 3(Mar. 1913): 186-190.

7388. Wodehouse, Robert E. "Public Health Information Bearing Upon Prenatal Subjects." Robt. E. Wodehouse. Public Health Journal 11, 5(May 1920): 211-215.

7389. Wolfish, Martin G. "Birth Control Counselling in an Adolescent Clinic." Martin G. Wolfish. Canadian Medical Association Journal/Journal de l'Association medicale canadienne 105, 7(Oct. 9, 1971): 750-753.
Reprinted in Family Planning in Canada: a Sourcebook, pp. 183-186. Edited by Benjamin Schlesinger.

7390. Wolinsky, Paul I. A Study of Recidivist and Non-recidivist Delinquents in the City of Toronto. Paul I. Wolinsky. Toronto: University of Toronto, 1933. Thesis (M.A.)–University of Toronto, 1933.

7391. Wong, M.H. "Multiple Infestation with Dipylidium Caninum in an Infant." M.H. Wong. Canadian Medical Association Journal 72, 6(Mar. 15, 1955): 453-455.

7392. Woodcock, George Mordecai Richler. George Woodcock. Toronto: McLelland and Stewart, c1971.

7393. Woodill, Gary An Examination of Preschool Special Education in Ontario: a Critical Perspective. Gary Woodill. Toronto: University of Toronto, 1984. (CTM no. 66004)
Thesis (Ed.D.)–University of Toronto, 1984.

7394. Woodliffe, Helen M. A Study of Change in the Creative Thinking Ability of Grade 5 Children. Helen M. Woodliffe. Toronto: University of Toronto, 1970. Thesis (Ed.D.)–University of Toronto, 1970.

7395. Woodman, Ross James Reaney. Ross Woodman. Toronto: McClelland and Stewart, c1971.

7396. Woods, Shirley E. The Molson Saga, 1763-1983. Shirley E. Woods. Toronto: Doubleday Canada, 1983.

7397. Worden, O.O. A Comparative Experimental Study of Two Similar Groups of Super-Normal Elementary School Children. O.O. Worden. Toronto: University of Toronto, 1936. Thesis (D.Paed.)–University of Toronto, 1936.

7398. Wright, E.N. Learning English as a Second Language: a Summary of Research Department Studies. E.N. Wright. Toronto: Board of Education, Research Department, 1970.

7399. Wright, E.N. Parents' Occupations, Students' Mother Tongue and Immigrant Status: Further Analysis of the Every Student Survey Data. E.N. Wright. Toronto: Board of Education, Research Department, 1971.

7400. Wright, E.N. Programme Placement Related to Selected Countries of Birth and Selected Languages. E.N. Wright. Toronto: Board of Education, Research Department, 1971.

7401. Wright, E.N. Student's Background and Its Relationship to Class and Programme in School: the Every Student Survey. E.N. Wright. Toronto: Board of Education, Research Department, 1970.

7402. Wright, E.N. Students of Non-Canadian Origin: Age on Arrival, Academic Achievement and Ability. E.N. Wright and C.A. Ramsey. Toronto: Board of Education, Research Department, 1970.

7403. Wright, Glenn "Railway School Cars and Education in North Ontario." Glenn Wright. Archivist/Archiviste 12, 3(May–June 1985): 3-4.

7404. Wright, H.E. ""Five-Score and Seventeen Years Ago": the High School of Montreal 1843-1959." H.E. Wright. Journal of Education of the Faculty and College of Education: Vancouver and Victoria 4(Mar. 1960): 12-20.

**7405. Wright, H.P.** *"A Simple Method of Artificial Feeding in Infancy."* H.P. Wright and A.K. Geddes. Canadian Nurse 27, 4(Apr. 1931): 187-189.

**7406. Wright, Mary J.** *A Follow-up Study of Superior Children from Special Classes: an Investigation at the Secondary School Level of the Effects upon Superior Children of an Enriched Curriculum and Special Class Placement During Four Elementary School Grades.* Mary J. Wright. Toronto: University of Toronto, 1949.
Thesis (Ph.D.)--University of Toronto, 1949.

**7407. Wright, W.G.** *"Treatment Program at the Reception, Diagnostic and Treatment Centre, Grandview School, Galt, Ontario."* W.G. Wright. Canadian Journal of Corrections/Revue canadienne de criminologie 10, 1(Jan. 1968): 337-345.

**7408. Wrigley, F.R.H.** *"The Hazards and Principles of Anaesthesia for Tonsillectomy and Adenoidectomy in Children."* F.R.H. Wrigley. Canadian Medical Association Journal 79, 6(Sept. 15, 1958): 459-463.

**7409. Wuerscher, Rose** *Problems with the Legislative Base for Native Child Welfare Services.* Rose Wuerscher. Ottawa: Research Branch, Policy, Research and Evaluation, Indian and Inuit Affairs Program, Department of Indian and Northern Affairs, 1979.

**7410. Wyllie, John C.** *"Facial Paralysis in Relation to Poliomyelitis: a Study of a Family Outbreak."* J. Wyllie. Canadian Journal of Public Health 35, 2(Feb. 1944): 71-79.

**7411. Wyllie, John C.** *"A Family Outbreak of Lead Poisoning from the Burning of Storage Battery Casings."* J. Wyllie. Canadian Medical Association Journal 70, 3(Mar. 1954): 287-290.

**7412. Yackley, Andrew** *"Interethnic Group Competition and Levels of Aspiration."* Andrew Yackley and Wallace E. Lambert. Canadian Journal of Behavioural Science/Revue canadienne de sciences du comportement 3, 2(Apr. 1971): 135-147.

**7413. Yelin, Shulamis** *Shulamis: Stories from a Montreal Childhood.* Shulamis Yelin. Montreal: Vehicule Press, 1983.

**7414. Yiu, E.K.Y.** *Youth in Need: a Study of the Need for After-school Programs Geared to the Acculturation of Chinese Immigrant Youth from Downtown Toronto.* E.K.Y. Yiu. Toronto: University of Toronto, 1968.
Thesis (M.S.W.)--University of Toronto, 1968.

**7415. Young, Jim** *Dirty 30.* Jim Young with Jim Taylor. Toronto: Methuen, c1974.

**7416. Young, John E.M.** *"A Study in the Measurement of the Expressed Attitude of Canadian High School Seniors Towards Americans."* J.E.M. Young. Canadian Education 7, 4(Sept. 1952): 43-58.

**7417. Young Men's Conference of the Young Men's Christian Association in Canada (2nd: 1943: Toronto)** *Young Canada Confers: the Report of the Second National Young Men's Conference of the YMCA's in Canada, Hart House, University of Toronto, April 23, 24, 25, 1943.* The Association, Joseph McCulley, Murray G. Ross and Gregory Vlastos. Toronto: Ryerson Press, 1943.

**7418. Young, Scott** *100 Years of Dropping the Puck: a History of the OHA.* Scott Young. Toronto: McClelland and Stewart, 1989.

**7419. Yule, D.L.G.** *A Study of the Relationship Between Reading Ability and Performance on the Dominion Group Test of Learning Capacity.* D.L.G. Yule. Toronto: University of Toronto, 1950.
Thesis (M.A.)--University of Toronto, 1950.

**7420. Zaidi, Zafar H.** *"Hula-hoop Syndrome."* Zafar H. Zaidi. Canadian Medical Association Journal/Journal de l'Association medicale canadienne 80, 9(May 1, 1959): 715-716.

**7421. Zeibots, Barbara** *"Montessori: a Teacher's Viewpoint."* Barbara Zeibots. Bulletin of the Institute of Child Study 30, 1(Spring 1968): 27-29.

**7422. Zelikovitz, Laura** *School Experience, Occupational Success and Satisfaction.* Laura Zelikovitz. Montreal: McGill University, 1969.
Thesis (M.A.)--McGill University, 1969.

**7423. Ziemann, Anna M.** *The Changing Emphasis on the Use of Clause 3 of the Children's Protection Act at the Children's Aid Society of Toronto, 1951: a Comparative Study of the Use of the Clause for the Two Time Periods 1930-1931 and 1950.* Anna M. Ziemann. Toronto: University of Toronto, 1951.
Thesis (M.S.W.)--University of Toronto, 1951.

**7424. Zola, Meguido** *Karen Kain: Born to Dance.* Meguido Zola. Toronto: Grolier, c1983.

7425. **Zucchi, John Emilio** *Paesani in a Toronto Neighbourhood: the Italian Immigrant of the "Ward", 1870-1940.* John Emilio Zucchi. Toronto: University of Toronto, 1979.
  Thesis (M.A.)—University of Toronto, 1979.

# Atlantic Canada

**7426. Adams, John Coldwell** *Sir Charles God Damn: the Life of Sir Charles G.D. Roberts.* John Coldwell Adams Toronto: University of Toronto Press, c1986.

**7427. Adamson, J.D.** *"Medical Survey of Nutrition in Newfoundland."* J.D. Adamson, N. Jolliffe, H.D. Kruse, O.H. Lowry, P.E. Moore, B.S. Platt, W.H. Sebrell, J.W. Tice, F.F. Tisdall, R.M. Wilder, P.C. Zamecnik. Canadian Medical Association Journal 52, 3(Mar. 1945): 227-250.

**7428. Aiton, Grace** *"The Selling of Paupers By Public Auction in Sussex Parish."* Grace Aiton. New Brunswick Historical Society Collections 16(1961): 93-110.

**7429. Allen, Kenneth Edgar** *A Review of Education in New Brunswick from Earliest Times to the Present Day with Special Attention to the Development of Vocational Education.* Kenneth Edgar Allen. Edmonton: University of Alberta, 1952. Thesis (M.Ed.)–University of Alberta, 1952.

**7430. Alphonsus, Mary** *"Life on Baccalieu: the Reminiscences of the Last Teacher There, (Miss) Margaret Noonan now Sister Mary Alphonsus R.S.M. St. Patrick's Convent, Bay Bulls."* Mary Alphonsus. Newfoundland Quarterly 75, 3(Christmas 1979): 10-12.

**7431. Anderson, George M.** *Vocational Education in Newfoundland: a Brief History.* George M. Anderson. Edmonton: University of Alberta, 1979. Thesis (M.Ed.)--University of Alberta.

**7432. Anonymous** *"Medical Inspection of Schools in Nova Scotia."* Public Health Journal 5, 1(Jan. 1914): 96-99.

**7433. Anonymous** *"Report on the Home for Young Women Seeking Employment, Halifax, 1870."* Atlantis 5, 2(Spring 1980): 196-199.

**7434. Anonymous** *"Saving Babies in Halifax."* Public Health Journal 11, 2(Feb. 1920): 84-87.

**7435. Armstrong, Alvin** *Flora MacDonald.* Alvin Armstrong. Don Mills, Ont: J.M. Dent and Sons (Canada) Ltd., 1976.

**7436. Arseneau, Marcel** *A Study of Ninety Wards in Child Caring Institutions in Halifax.* Marcel Arseneau. Halifax: Maritime School of Social Work, c1960. Thesis (M.S.W.)–Maritime School of Social Work, 1960.

**7437. Arseneau, Mona** *Mothers of One-parent Families.* Mona Arseneau, Judy Nymar, Marie Murphy and Jacques Senechal. Halifax: Dalhousie University, c1971. Thesis (M.S.W.)–Dalhousie University, 1971.

**7438. Atlee, H.B.** *"The First Ten Minutes."* H.B. Atlee. Canadian Medical Association Journal 71, 3(Sept. 1954): 227-233.

**7439. Axelrod. Paul** *"Moulding the Middle Class: Student Life at Dalhousie University in the 1930s."* Paul Axelrod. Acadiensis 15, 1(Autumn 1985): 84-122.

**7440. Aykroyd, W.R.** *"Medical Resurvey of Nutrition in Newfoundland 1948."* W.R. Aykroyd,, N. Joliffe, O.H. Lowry, P.E. Moore, W.H. Sebrell, R.E. Shank, F.F. Tisdall, R.M. Wilder, and P.C. Zamecnik. Canadian Medical Association Journal 60, 4(Apr. 1949): 329-352

**7441. Babcock, Robert H.** *"A Jewish Immigrant in the Maritimes: the Memoirs of Max Vanger."* Robert H. Babcock. Acadiensis 16, 1(Autumn 1986): 136-148.

**7442. Barss, Peter** *Images of Lunenburg County.* Peter Barss. Toronto: McClelland and Stewart, c1978.

**7443. Barter, Geraldine** *"The Folktale and Children in the Tradition of French Newfoundlanders."* Geraldine barter. Canadian Folklore canadien 1, 1(1979): 5-11.

**7444. Battiste, Marie** *"Mi'Kmaq Linguistic Integrity: a Case Study of Mi'Kmawey School."* Marie Battiste. Vancouver: University of British Columbia Press, 1987. In Indian Education in Canada, Volume 2: the Challenge, pp. 107-125. Edited by Jean Barman, Yvonne Hebert and Don McCaskill.

**7445. Beaton, Sarah Margaret** *Effects of Relocation: a Study of Ten Families Relocated from Africville.* Sarah Margaret Beaton. Halifax: Maritime School of Social Work, c1969.
Thesis (M.S.W.)--Maritime School of Social Work, 1969.

**7446. Beck, J. Murray** *Joseph Howe: Conservative Reformer 1804-1848.* J. Murray Beck. vol. 1. Kingston: McGill-Queen's University Press, 1982.

**7447. Beckwith, C.J.W.** *"Administration of Toxoid and Results of Shick Testing in Glace Bay, Nova Scotia, 1938-1939."* C.J.W. Beckwith. Canadian Public Health Journal 32, 3(Mar. 1941): 103-112.

**7448. Beckwith, C.J.W.** *"The Tuberculosis Control Program in Halifax."* C.J.W. Beckwith. Canadian Journal of Public Health 37, 12(Dec. 1946): 481-487.

**7449. Bell, Winthrop** *"A Halifax Boyhood of One Hundred and Twenty Years Ago."* Winthrop Bell. Collections of the Nova Scotia Historical Society 28(1949): 106-132.

**7450. Berard, Robert Nicholas** *"Moral Education in Nova Scotia, 1880-1920."* Robert Nicholas Berard. Acadiensis 14, 1(Autumn 1984): 49-63.

**7451. Bird, Lilah Smith** *"My Island Home."* Lilah Smith Bird. Nova Scotia Historical Quarterly 5, 4(Dec. 1975): 323-352.

**7452. Blakeley, Phyllis R.** *"Margaret Marshall Saunders: the Author of "Beautiful Joe"."* Phyllis J. Blakeley. Nova Scotia Historical Quarterly 1, 3(Sept. 1971): 225-246.

**7453. Blois, Ernest H.** *"Placing Neglected and Dependent Children in Rural Areas."* Ernest H. Blois. In Proceedings and Papers Fifth Annual Canadian Conference on Child Welfare 1925, pp. 162-168.

**7454. Bolger, Francis W.P.** *The Years Before "Anne".* Francis W.P. Bolger. [S.l.]: Prince Edward Island Heritage Foundation, c1974.

**7455. Bond, Courtney C.J.** *An Iron in Many a Fire.* Courtney C.J. Bond. Ottawa: University of Ottawa Press, 1982.

**7456. Boucher, Jacqueline Delia** *A Study of Student Drop-Outs, Grades 5 to 12 in the New Brunswick Public Schools 1959-1960.* Jacqueline Delia Boucher. Fredericton: University of New Brunswick, 1962.
Thesis (M.Ed.)--University of New Brunswick, 1962.

**7457. Bowers, Gregory Martin** *Juvenile Correctional Services in Nova Scotia.* Gregory Martin Bowers. Halifax: Maritime School of Social Work, Saint Mary's University, c1971.
Thesis (M.S.W.)--Maritime School of Social Work, Saint Mary's University, 1971.

**7458. Boyd, Vaughan** *Religion, Occupation, School Attendance and Literacy in Newfoundland, 1901-1921.* Vaughan Boyd. St. John's: Memorial University of Newfoundland, 1978. (CTM no. 40829) Thesis (M.Ed.)--Memorial University of Newfoundland, 1978.

**7459. Brett, Betty Marion** *A Survey of the Leisure Reading of Grade 9 Students in Central High Schools of Newfoundland.* Betty Marion Brett. Edmonton: University of Alberta, 1964.
Thesis (M.Ed.)--University of Alberta, 1964.

**7460. Brookes, Alan A.** *"Family, Youth and Leaving Home in Late Nineteenth Century Rural Nova Scotia: Canning and the Exodus, 1868-1893."* Alan A. Brookes. Toronto: McClelland and Stewart, c1982. In Childhood and Family in Canadian History, pp. 93-108. Edited by Joy Parr.

**7461. Browne, William J.** *And Now, Eighty-seven Years a Newfoundlander: Memoirs of William J. Brown, P.C., Q.C., LL.D.* William J. Browne. vol. 2. St. John's: The Author, 1984.

**7462. Browne, William J.** *Eighty-four Years a Newfoundlander: Memoirs of William J. Browne, P.C., Q.C., LL.D.* William J. Browne. vol. 1. St. John's: The Author, 1981.

**7463. Brownrigg, G.M.** *"Staphylococcal Empyema."* G.M. Brownrigg. Canadian Medical Association Journal 73, 10(Nov. 15, 1955): 787-789.

**7464. Bruce, Harry** *Down Home: Notes of a Maritime Son.* Harry Bruce. Toronto: Key Porter Books Ltd., c1988.

**7465. Buitenhuis, Peter** *Hugh MacLennan.* Peter Buitenhuis. Toronto: Forum House, c1969.
Reprinted under same title by Coles, 1974.

**7466. Bumsted, J.M.** *Henry Aline: 1748-1784.* J.M. Bumsted. [Toronto]: University of Toronto Press, [1971].

**7467. Burns, Helen** *The Positive and Negative Aspects of Institutional Care.* Helen Burns, Pat Callaghan, Mary Pothier, Niery St. Amand and Philip Thompson. Halifax: Dalhousie University, c1971.
Thesis (M.S.W.)--Dalhousie University, 1971.

**7468. Burns, Kevin** *The Social Worker and the Delinquent.* Kevin C. Burns. Halifax: Maritime School of Social Work, c1961.
Thesis (M.S.W.)--Maritime School of Social Work, 1961.

**7469. Burpee, Lawrence** *"At Home on the Fundy Shore."* Lawrence Burpee. Dalhousie Review 23, 2(July 1944): 311-316.

**7470. Burris, M.G.** *"Pseudo-Muscular Hypertrophy."* M.G. Burris. Canadian Medical Association Journal 2, 1(Jan. 1912): 15-19.

**7471. Burroughs, Judith** *The Anglican Design in Loyalist Nova Scotia 1783-1816.* Judith Burroughs. London, Eng.: Society for Promoting Christian Knowledge, 1972.

**7472. Burton, Barbara** *Wardship: a Study of Factors Leading to Foster Care.* Barbara Burton. Halifax: Maritime School of Social Work, c1963.
Thesis (M.S.W.)--Maritime School of Social Work, 1963.

**7473. Butler, Victor** *The Little Nord Easter: Reminiscences of a Placentia Bayman.* Victor Butler. St. John's: Breakwater, 1980.

**7474. Cahill, Helen F.** *"Through the Eyes of a Boy."* Helen F. Cahill. Canadian Nurse 35, 8(Aug. 1939): 440-442.

**7475. Caldwell, George** *Inverness County--Part 2 of Rural Need in Canada, 1965: a Case Report on the Problems of Families in Four Provinces.* George Caldwell. Ottawa: Canadian Welfare Council, 1965.

**7476. Cameron, Elspeth** *Hugh MacLennan: a Writer's Life.* Elspeth Cameron. Toronto: University of Toronto Press, c1981.

**7477. Campbell, A.D.** *"What Can We Do About the Truant?"* A.D. Campbell. Child and Family Welfare 12, 1(May 1936): 34-37.

**7478. Campbell, Bertha J.** *"Springhill's First Doctor."* Bertha J. Campbell. Nova Scotia Historical Quarterly 9, 4(Dec. 1979): 297-312.

**7479. Campbell, D.** *Beyond the Atlantic Roar: a Study of the Nova Scotia Scots.* D. Campbell and R.A. MacLean. Toronto: McClelland and Stewart, c1974.

**7480. Campbell, G.G.** *"Susan Dunlap: Her Diary."* G.G. Campbell. Dalhousie Review 46, 2(July 1966): 215-222.

**7481. Campbell, I.L.** *"The Mount Allison Family and Group Experience Inventory: a Preliminary Report Based on Small Samples."* I.L. Campbell. Canadian Journal of Corrections/Revue canadienne de criminologie 3, 4(Oct. 1961): 467-473.

**7482. Campbell, J.G.D.** *"Is the Medical Supervision of Institutional Children of Any Importance?"* J.G.D. Campbell. Canadian Child Welfare News 4, 1(Feb. 1928): 40-42.

7483. Campbell, Lydia *"Sketches of a Labrador Life."* Lydia Campbell. Canadian Women's Studies 3, 1(Autumn 1981): 4-9.

7484. Canadian Council on Child and Family Welfare *"Child Protection."* Canadian Council on Child and Family Welfare. Child and Family Welfare 10, 6(Mar. 1935): 44.

7485. Canadian Council on Child and Family Welfare *"Child Protection in Nova Scotia."* Canadian Council on Child and Family Welfare. Child and Family Welfare 8, 1(May 1932): 26-27.

7486. Canadian Council on Child and Family Welfare *"Children's Aid Society of Saint John."* Canadian Council on Child and Family Welfare. Child and Family Welfare 8, 1(May 1932): 25-26.

7487. Canadian Council on Child and Family Welfare *"Delinquency Services in the Maritime Provinces."* Canadian Council on Child and Family Welfare. Child and Family Welfare 6, 6(Jan. 1931): 31-41.

7488. Canadian Council on Child and Family Welfare *"Five Years in Delinquency Statistics."* Canadian Council on Child and Family Welfare. Child and Family Welfare 10, 6(Mar. 1935): 50-51.

7489. Canadian Council on Child and Family Welfare *"New Brunswick Boys' Industrial School."* Canadian Council on Child and Family Welfare. Child and Family Welfare 8, 1(May 1932): 29-30.

7490. Canadian Council on Child and Family Welfare *"The New Brunswick Children's Protection Act, 1930."* Canadian Council on Child and Family Welfare. Child and Family Welfare 6, 2(May 1930): 23-25.

7491. Canadian Council on Child and Family Welfare *"News for Prince Edward Island."* Canadian Council on Child and Family Welfare. Child and Family Welfare 10, 1(May 1934): 19-20.

7492. Canadian Council on Child and Family Welfare *"Nova Scotia Mothers' Allowance Act."* Canadian Council on Child and Family Welfare. Child and Family Welfare 6, 2(May 1930): 22-23.

7493. Canadian Council on Child Welfare *"Child Welfare in Nova Scotia."* Canadian Council on Child Welfare. Canadian Child Welfare News 4, 3(Aug. 15, 1928): 66-67.

7494. Canadian Council on Child Welfare *"Child Welfare in Nova Scotia."* Canadian Council on Child Welfare. Child Welfare News 5, 2(May 1929): 29-30.

7495. Canadian Council on Child Welfare *"The Halifax Children's Aid Society."* Canadian Council on Child Welfare. Canadian Child Welfare News 4, 1(Feb. 15, 1928): 47.

7496. Canadian Council on Child Welfare *"The Halifax Children's Aid Society."* Canadian Council on Child Welfare. Child Welfare News 5, 2(May 1929): 30-31.

7497. Canadian Council on Child Welfare *"News from the Front: St. John."* Canadian Council on Child Welfare. Child Welfare News 6, 1(Feb. 1930): 10-12.

7498. Canadian Council on Child Welfare *"The Nova Scotia Home for Coloured Children."* Canadian Council on Child Welfare. Child Welfare News 5, 2(May 1929): 31.

7499. Canadian Council on Child Welfare *"Nova Scotia Training School for the Feebleminded."* Canadian Council on Child Welfare. Child Welfare News 5, 2(May 1929): 32.

7500. Canadian Council on Child Welfare *Report of the New Brunswick Child Welfare Survey, Financed by the Kiwanis Club of St. John City, 1928-29.* Canadian Council on Child Welfare. [Ottawa]: The Council, [1929].

7501. Canadian National Committee for Mental Hygiene *"Nova Scotia Survey."* Canadian National Committee for Mental Hygiene. Canadian Journal of Mental Hygiene 3, 1(Apr. 1921): 3-48.

7502. Canadian Welfare Council *"Across Canada: Child Welfare in New Brunswick."* Canadian Welfare Council. Canadian Welfare 24, 2(June 1948): 33.

7503. Cappon, James *Bliss Carman and the Literary Currents and Infuences of his Time.* James Cappon. Toronto: Ryerson Press, c1930.

7504. Cappon, James *Charles G.D. Roberts.* James Cappon. Toronto: Ryerson Press, c[1925].

7505. Carter, Jeff *Robert Meade - and So Did I: the Biography of a Newfoundlander.* Jeff Carter. St. John's: Creative Printers and Publishers, 1986.

**7506. Chandler, Helen Joan** *A Psychosocial Study of Delinquent Girls.* Helen Joan Chandler. Halifax: Maritime School of Social Work, c1961. Thesis (M.S.W.)--Maritime School of Social Work, 1961.

**7507. Cheong, George S.C.** *"Acquisition of Experimental Attitude by Young Children."* George S.C. Cheong. Alberta Journal of Educational Research 16, 3(Sept. 1970): 157-163.

**7508. Chiasson, R.J.** *"Bilingualism in the Schools of Eastern Nova Scotia."* R.J. Chiasson. Canadian Education 15, 2(Mar. 1960): 24-27.

**7509. Christine, Reverend Sister** *"The Health of Children in Institutions."* Reverend Sister Christine. Canadian Child Welfare News 4, 1(Feb. 15, 1928): 42-45.

**7510. Clark, S. Barbara** *"The Brunswick Cornwallis Pre-school: a Programme for Disadvantaged White and Negro Children."* S. Barbara Clark. Bulletin of the Institute of Child Study 29, 3(Fall 1967): 17-27.

**7511. Cochrane, W.A.** *"The Battered Child Syndrome."* W.A. Cochrane. Canadian Journal of Public Health 56, 5(May 1965): 193-6.

**7512. Cochrane, W.A.** *"Intravenous Therapy in Infants and Children."* W.A. Cochrane. Canadian Medical Association Journal/Journal de l'Association medicale canadienne 80, 6(Mar. 15, 1959): 471-474.

**7513. Coffey, J.E.** *"Trichinosis in Canadian Eskimos."* J.E. Coffey and F.W. Wiglesworth. Canadian Medical Association Journal 75, 4(Aug 15, 1956): 295-299.

**7514. Cogswell, Fred** *Charles G.D. Roberts and His Works.* Fred Cogswell. [S.l.]: ECW Press, [1983].

**7515. Cole, I.N.** *"Mental Hygiene and the Baby Welfare Exhibit at Halifax."* I.N. Cole. Canadian Journal of Mental Hygiene 1, 4(Jan. 1920): 347-349.

**7516. Coleman, C.M.** *"School in Newfoundland."* C.M. Coleman. Empire Review and Magazine 73, 480(Jan. 1941): 43.

**7517. Conner, Desmond M.** *The Role of Education in Rural Development, Musquodoboit Valley.* Desmond M. Conner and Dennis W. Magill. Ottawa: The Queen's Printer, 1965.

**7518. Cousins, Leone B.** *"The Life and Times of James Barclay Hall, Ph.D."* Leone B. Cousins. Nova Scotia Historical Quarterly 10, 1(Mar. 1980): 59-87.

**7519. Crandall, Joseph** *"The Autobiography of Joseph Crandall."* Joseph Crandall and J.M. Bumstead. Acadiensis 3, 1(Autumn 1973): 79-85.

**7520. Critchley, David** *"OFY as Seen from the East."* David Critchley. Canadian Welfare 47, 6(Nov.-Dec. 1971): 17.

**7521. Crocker, Oswald Kitchener** *The Leisure Reading of High School Students in Newfoundland, Library Facilities in the Schools, and Home Background as Related to Reading.* Oswald Kitchener Crocker. Bloomington: Indiana University, 1967. Thesis (Ph.D.)--Indiana University, 1967.

**7522. Crockett, John Everett** *Origin and Establishment of Free Schools in Nova Scotia.* John Everett Crockett. Halifax: Dalhousie University, 1940. Thesis (M.A.)--Dalhousie University, 1940.

**7523. Cusack, Ruby M.** *The Maggie Vail Story.* Ruby M. Cusack. [Saint John]: Yesteryear, [1987].

**7524. Daniel, J.W.** *"Presidential Address, Delivered Before the Canadian Association for the Prevention of Tuberculosis."* J.W. Daniel. Canadian Medical Association Journal 6, 10(Oct. 1916): 865-871.

**7525. Davies, J.W.** *"Epidemic Virus Meningitis Due to Echo 9 Virus in Newfoundland."* J.W. Davies, A. McDermott and D. Severs. Canadian Medical Association Journal 79, 3(Aug. 1, 1958): 162-167.

**7526. Davies, J.W.** *"Epidemiological Features of the 1959 Newfoundland Epidemic of Type 1 Poliomyelitis."* J.W. Davies, D. Severs and T. Williams. Canadian Medical Association Journal/Journal de l'Association medicale canadienne 87, 12(Sept. 22, 1962): 646-655.

**7527. Davis, Dona** *"The Family and Social Change in the Newfoundland Outpost."* Dona Davis. Culture 3, 1(1983): 19-32.

**7528. Davis, M.M.** *"Heroin, Demerol, and Hyoscine in Labour."* M.M. Davis and W.R.C. Tupper. Canadian Medical Association Journal 60, 2(Feb. 1949): 113-119.

7529. **Davis, Nanciellen** *"Patriarchy from the Grave: Family Relations in 19th Century New Brunswick Wills."* Nanciellen Davis. Acadiensis 13, 2(Spring 1984): 91-100.

7530. **Dawson, A.B.** *"Recreation as a Public Health Measure."* A.B. Dawson. Public Health Journal 11, 3(Mar. 1920): 119-127.

7531. **Dayton, Mary Elizabeth** *An Investigation of the Relationship Between Reading Level and Academic Achievement at the Grade Ten Level.* Mary Elizabeth Dayton. Fredericton: University of New Brunswick, c1969.
  Thesis (M.Ed.)--University of New Brunswick, 1969.
  National Library of Canada MIC TC-5648.

7532. **Demerson, George Alexander** *The Values of Correlations Between Marks in the Elementary School and Marks in the High School.* George Alexander Demerson. Fredericton: University of New Brunswick, c1968.
  Thesis (M.Ed.)--University of New Brunswick, 1968.
  National Library of Canada MIC TC-3624.

7533. **Dewar, Lloyd George** *A History of My Family and the Family Farm at New Perth Prince Edward Island: and a Short History of New Perth.* Lloyd George Dewar. [Summerside: Williams and Crue Ltd.], 1975.

7534. **DeWitt, George E.** *"A Few Hints to the Medical Profession in Relation to Public Health Work."* George E. DeWitt. Public Health Journal 7, 2(Feb. 1916): 63-68.

7535. **Dickinson, Joyce Marie** *An Investigation of Acceleration at the Junior High School Level and Adjustment to the Senior High School Situation.* Joyce Marie Dickinson. Fredericton: University of New Brunswick, c1969.
  Thesis (M.Ed.)--University of New Brunswick, 1969.
  National Library of Canada MIC TC-5650.

7536. **Dodge, Helen** *My Childhood in the Canadian Wilderness.* Helen Carmichael Dodge. New York: Vantage Press, 1961.

7537. **Donnelly, F.K.** *"British Protestants and French Catholics: a Study of Two New Brunswick Fishing Settlements."* F.K. Donnelly. Saint John: University of New Brunswick, 1986. In The Family and Household in Mid-nineteenth Century New Brunswick, pp. 13-29. Edited by F.K. Donnelly.

7538. **Donovan, Kenneth** *"Tattered Clothes and Powdered Wigs: Case Studies of the Poor and Well-to-do in Eighteenth Century Louisbourg."* Kenneth Donovan. Sydney: University of Cape Breton Press, c1985. In Cape Breton at 200: Historical Essays in Honour of the Island's Bicentennial 1785-1985, pp. 1-20. Edited by Kenneth Donovan.

7539. **Doucet, Clive** *My Grandfather's Cape Breton.* Clive Doucet. Toronto: McGraw-Hill Ryerson, c1980.

7540. **Doyle, Arthur T.** *The Premiers of New Brunswick.* Arthur T. Doyle. Fredericton: Brunswick Press, c1983.

7541. **Doyle, Robert Urban** *The Community and the Delinquent: a Study of Some Community Institutions and Attitudes in Relation to the Juvenile Delinquent.* Robert Urban Doyle. Halifax: Maritime School of Social Work, c1961.
  Thesis (M.S.W.)--Maritime School of Social Work, 1961.

7542. **Drent, Janice** *Foster Care: a Study of Differing Needs of the Children in Care.* Janice Drent. Halifax: Maritime School of Social Work, c1963.
  Thesis (M.S.W.)--Maritime School of Social Work, 1963.

7543. **Drummie, Mary A.** *Research Report on New Brunswick School Drop-outs.* Mary A. Drummie. Fredricton: New Brunswick Department of Youth and Welfare, 1965.

7544. **Dwight, Mary Lane** *Children of Labrador.* Mary Lane Dwight. London: Oliphants, 1913.

7545. **Dykeman, Huilota S.** *"Billy and His Family."* Huilota S. Dykeman. Canadian Nurse 34, 11(Nov. 1938): 645-647.

7546. **Dykeman, Huilota S.** *"Fighting Diphtheria in New Brunswick."* Huilota Dykeman. Canadian Nurse 25, 3(Mar. 1929): 143-144.

7547. **Eastman, Wayne David** *A Historical Analysis of Physical Education in Newfoundland, Canada.* Wayne David Eastman. Ann Arbor, Michigan: University Microfilms International, 1987.
  Thesis (Ed.D.)--Boston University, 1987.

7548. **Eastman, Wayne David** *"Religion and Sport, the Denominational Colleges, the Genesis of Physical Education in Newfoundland."* Wayne Eastman. Canadian Journal of History of Sport/Revue canadienne de l'histoire des sports 19, 2(Dec. 1988): 30-49.

**7549. Edwards, John** *The Aspirations of High School Students.* John Edwards. Fredericton: University of New Brunswick, 1969.
Thesis (M.Ed.)--University of New Brunswick, 1969.
National Library of Canada MIC TC-5652.

**7550. Elwood, Marie** *"Halifax Cabinet-makers, 1837-1875: Apprenticeships."* Marie Elwood. Material History Bulletin/Bulletin d'histoire de la culture materielle 15(Summer 1982): 67-71.

**7551. Ewing, Russell M.** *The Standardization of the Chicago Non-verbal Examination on English Speaking School Children in Nova Scotia.* Russell M. Ewing. Wolfville: Acadia University, 1950.
Thesis (M.A.)--Acadia University, 1950.

**7552. Fairfax, Donald E.** *"The Black Church and Youth."* Donald E. Fairfax. Halifax: International Education Centre, Saint Mary's University, 1979. In Canadian Black Studies, pp. 224-227. Edited by Bridglal Pachai.

**7553. Faulkner, Ruth S.** *"Virus Meningitis: Seven Cases in One Family."* Ruth S. Faulkner, Alan J. MacLeod and C.E. van Rooyen. Canadian Medical Association Journal 77, 5(Sept. 1, 1957): 439-444.

**7554. Feavyour, Herman E.** *Problem Solving Ability in Arithmetic.* Herman E. Feavyour. 2 vol. Toronto: University of Toronto, 1956.
Thesis (Ed.D.)--University of Toronto, 1956.

**7555. Feder, Alison** *Margaret Duley, Newfoundland Novelist: a Biographical and Critical Study.* Alison Feder. St. John's: H. Cuff Publications, c1983.

**7556. Feehan, John A.** *An Island Family: the Feehans.* John A. Feehan. Hantsport, N.S.: Lancelot Press, 1986.

**7557. Fekete, John F.** *"Severe Brain Injury and Death Following Minor Hockey Accidents: the Effectiveness of "Safety Helmets" of Amateur Hockey Players."* John F. Fekete. Canadian Medical Association Journal/Journal de l'Association medicale canadienne 99, 25(Dec. 28, 1968): 1234-1239.

**7558. Ferguson, D.** *"The Preachers and Teachers of the Old Days."* D. Ferguson. Prince Edward Island Magazine 1, 3(May 1899): 91-93.

**7559. Fingard, Judith** *"Attitudes Towards the Education of the Poor in Colonial Halifax."* Judith Fingard. Acadiensis 2, 2(Spring 1973): 15-42.

**7560. Fingard, Judith** *"College, Career and Community: Dalhousie Coeds, 1881-1921."* Judith Fingard. Kingston: McGill-Queen's University Press, 1989. In Youth, University and Canadian Society: Essays in the Social History of Higher Education, pp. 26-50. Edited by Paul Axelrod and John G. Reid.

**7561. Fingard, Judith** *The Dark Side of Life in Victorian Halifax.* Judith Fingard. Porter's Lake, N.S.: Pottersfield, 1989.

**7562. Fingard, Judith** *"The Relief of the Unemployed Poor in Saint John, Halifax and St. John's, 1815-1860."* Judith Fingard. Acadiensis 5, 1(Autumn 1975): 32-54.

**7563. Fitch, J.H.** *A Century of Educational Progress in New Brunswick, 1800-1900.* J.H. Fitch. Toronto: University of Toronto, [1930].
Thesis (D.Paed.)--University of Toronto, [1930].

**7564. Fitzgerald, Jack** *Rogues and Branding Irons.* Jack Fitzgerald. St. John's: Jesperson Press, 1987.

**7565. Flanagan, Patrick** *Schooling, Souls and Social Class: the Labrador Inuit.* Patrick Flanagan. Fredricton: University of New Brunswick, 1984. (CTM no. 25238)
Thesis (M.A.)--University of New Brunswick, 1984.
No bibliography.

**7566. Fletcher, J.H.** *"Old Time Charivari."* J.H. Fletcher. Prince Edward Island Magazine 4, 9(Nov. 1902): 307-314.

**7567. Flewwelling, Susan** *"The Diary of Mary Ann Norris, 1818-1832."* Susan Flewwelling. Dalhousie Review 29, 4(Jan. 1950): 439-450.

**7568. Flewwelling, Susan** *"The Diary of Mary Ann Norris, 1818-1838: Section 5, Religion; Section 6, Transportation; Section 7, Events of Interest; Section 8, Recreation and Amusements."* Susan Flewwelling. Dalhousie Review 30, 1(Apr. 1950): 90-103.

**7569. Forsyth, Victoria** *The Doctor: Hector J. Pothier.* Victoria Forsyth. Hantsport, N.S.: Lancelot Press, 1982.

**7570. Fraser, Sarah** *Spruce Pasture.* Sarah Fraser. Halifax: Petheric Press, 1971. Cover subtitle: A Story of Rural Life in Nova Scotia at the Turn of the Century.

**7571. Frecker, G.A.** *Education in the Atlantic Provinces.* G.A. Frecker. Toronto: W.J. Gage and Company Limited, [1956].

**7572. Fullerton, Jessie R.** *"Child Welfare on "The Island"."* Jessie R. Fullerton. Canadian Welfare 17, 6(Nov. 1941): 25-27.

**7573. Gallant, Lawrence R.** *Juvenile Delinquency and the Working Mother.* Lawrence R. Gallant. Halifax: Maritime School of Social Work, c1962. Thesis (M.S.W.)--Maritime School of Social Work, 1962.

**7574. Gathercole, Frederick J., ed.** *Secondary Education in Canada.* Frederick J. Gathercole, ed. Toronto: The Ryerson Press, c1963.

**7575. Gibbons, R.J.** *"Diphtheria Among Schick-negative Persons in Halifax, Nova Scotia."* R.J. Gibbons. Canadian Journal of Public Health 36, 9(Sept. 1945): 341-348.

**7576. Gillen, Mollie** *Lucy Maud Montgomery.* Mollie Gillen. Don Mills: Fitzhenry and Whiteside, c1978.

**7577. Gillen, Mollie** *The Wheel of Things: a Biography of L.M. Montgomery, Author of Anne of Green Gables.* Mollie Gillen. Don Mills: Fitzhenry and Whiteside, c1975. Bibliography pp. 193-195.

**7578. Gillis, D.A.** *"Papillary Tumours of the Choroid Plexus."* D.A. Gillis and C.R.F. di Profio. Canadian Medical Association Journal 74, 5(Mar. 1, 1956): 361-363.

**7579. Gillis, James D.** *The Cape Breton Giant: a Truthful Memoir.* Jas. D. Gillis. Halifax: T.C. Allen & Company, 1919.

**7580. Gillis, John** *"Some Personality Factors of Matched Groups of New Brunswick Blacks and Whites."* John S. Gillis and Noel A. Kinsella. Canadian Journal of Behavioural Science/Revue canadienne de sciences du comportement 3, 1(Jan. 1971): 66-71.

**7581. Gillis, John** *The Well-being of Foster Children Related to Agency Services.* John Gillis, Paul Green, Paul Leger, Stephen McQuaid and Phyllis Parker. Halifax: Dalhousie University, c1971. Thesis (M.S.W.)--Dalhousie University, 1971.

**7582. Girl Guides of Canada. New Brunswick Council** *Girl Guides of New Brunswick, 1867-1985.* The Council. Saint John: The Council, 1985.

**7583. Goldsmith, Oliver** *Autobiography of Oliver Goldsmith: a Chapter in Canada's Literary History.* Oliver Goldsmith. 2nd ed. Hantsport: Lancelot Press, 1985.

**7584. Goudie, Elizabeth** *Woman of Labrador.* Elizabeth Goudie [and] David Zimmerly, ed. Toronto: Peter Martin Associates Ltd., 1973.

**7585. Gouett, Paul M.** *"The Halifax Orphan House 1752-1787."* Paul M. Gouett. Nova Scotia Historical Quarterly 6, 3(Sept. 1976): 281-291.

**7586. Grant, B.J.** *Six for the Hangman.* Barry J. Grant. Fredericton: Fiddlehead Poetry Books & Goose Lane Editions, c1983, 1984.

**7587. Grant, Francis W.** *"George Woodland, Master Builder."* Francis W. Grant. Nova Scotia Historical Quarterly 7, 1(Mar. 1977): 55-67.

**7588. Green, Leo** *"An Unusual Case of Infectious Mononucleosis."* Leo Green. Canadian Medical Association Journal 72, 1(Jan. 1, 1955): 36-37.

**7589. Griffiths, Naomi** *The Acadians: Creation of a People.* Naomi Griffiths. Toronto: McGraw-Hill Ryerson Ltd., 1973.

**7590. Griffiths, Naomi** *"Petitions of Acadian Exiles, 1755-1785: a Neglected Source."* N.E.S. Griffiths. Histoire sociale/Social History 11, 21(May 1978): 215-223.

**7591. Gunn, C.R.** *"Nova Scotians at School in 1867."* C.R. Gunn. Journal of Education, Series 5, 17, 1(Oct. 1967): 31-34.

**7592. Haliburton, Robert Grant** *"A Sketch of the Life and Times of Judge Haliburton."* Robert Grant Haliburton. Toronto: William Briggs, 1897. In Haliburton: a Centenary Chaplet, pp. 13-40. Edited by A.B. De Mille

**7593. Halifax. Metropolitan Area Planning Committee** *A Community Profile: Demographic Characteristics and the Incidence of Social Problems in the Halifax-Dartmouth Metropolitan Region.* Metropolitan Area Planning Committee. Halifax: [s.n.], 1971.

**7594. Halifax Welfare Council** *The Child and Welfare Services Study, 1961.* Halifax Welfare Council. [Halifax: The Council, 1961?].

**7595. Hamilton, W.D.** *The Federal Indian Day Schools of the Maritimes.* W.D. Hamilton. Fredericton, N.B.: MicMac-Maliseet Institute, University of New Brunswick, 1986.

**7596. Hamilton, W.D., ed.** *Memories of a Micmac Life: J. Richard McEwan.* W.D. Hamilton. Fredericton: Micmac-Maliseet Institute, University of New Brunswick, c1988.

**7597. Hamilton, William B.** *"Society and Education in Newfoundland."* William B. Hamilton. Scarborough: Prentice-Hall of Canada, c1970. In Canadian Education: a History, pp. 126-144. Edited by J. Donald Wilson, Robert M. Stamp and Louis-Philippe Audet.

**7598. Hamilton, William B.** *"Society and Schools in New Brunswick and Prince Edward Island."* William B. Hamilton. Scarborough: Prentice-Hall of Canada, c1970. In Canadian Education: a History, pp. 106-125. Edited by J. Donald Wilson, Robert M. Stamp and Louis-Philippe Audet.

**7599. Hamilton, William B.** *"Society and Schools in Nova Scotia."* William B. Hamilton. Scarborough: Prentice-Hall of Canada, c1970. In Canadian Education: a History, pp. 86-105. Edited by J. Donald Wilson, Robert M. Stamp and Louis-Philippe Audet.

**7600. Handforth, C.P.** *"Cardiovascular Manifestations of Rheumatoid Arthritis."* C.P. Handforth and J.F.L. Woodbury. Canadian Medical Association Journal 80, 2(Jan. 15, 1959): 86-90.

**7601. Handforth, C.P.** *"Sudden Unexpected Death in Infants."* C.P. Handforth. Canadian Medical Association Journal/Journal de l'Association medicale canadienne 80, 11(June 1, 1959): 872-873.

**7602. Harris, Michael** *Unholy Orders: Tragedy at Mount Cashel.* Michael Harris. Markham, Ont.: Viking, 1990.

**7603. Hart, George E.** *"The Halifax Poor Man's Friend Society, 1820-27: an Early Social Experiment."* George E. Hart. Canadian Historical Review 34, 2(June 1953): 109-123.

**7604. Harvey, D.C.** *"Pre-Agricola John Young: or a Compact Family in Search of Fortune."* D.C. Harvey. Collections of the Nova Scotia Historical Association 32(1959): 125-159.

**7605. Harvey, Robert** *"From Pulpit to Platform: Alexander Forrester."* Robert Harvey. Nova Scotia Historical Quarterly 2, 4(Dec. 1972): 349-366.

**7606. Hatt, Herbert** *Alive to All True Values, My Ninety Years Experience.* Herbert Hatt. Hantsport: Lancelot, 1988.

**7607. Hichens, Walter W.** *Back to My Father and Home: Memories of Barrington Passage, Nova Scotia and One of Its Most Beloved Citizens of Early 1900s.* Walter W. Hichens. Hantsport, N.S.: Lancelot Press, 1987.

**7608. Hill, Kathleen L.** *Joe Howe: the Man Who Was Nova Scotia.* Kay Hill. Toronto: McClelland and Stewart, 1980.

**7609. Hincks, C.M.** *"A Study of Mental Deficiency in a Canadian Province."* C.M. Hincks. Journal of Psycho-Asthenics 32(1927): 69-74.

**7610. Hirsch, Solomon** *"Observations on Illegitimacy."* Solomon Hirsch. Canadian Psychiatric Association Journal/Revue de l'Association canadienne de psychiatrie 5, 1(Jan. 1960): 37-41.

**7611. Hirsch, Solomon** *"Suicidal Behaviour in Halifax, Nova Scotia."* Solomon Hirsch, Margaret Lowman and Roland Perry. Canadian Psychiatric Association Journal/Revue de l'Association canadienne de psychiatrie 23, 5(Aug. 1976): 309-316.

**7612. Hoar, William S.** *Branches of a Family Tree: the Hoar Ancestry.* William S. Hoar. Vancouver: Tangled Roots, 1986.

**7613. Hoar, William S.** *Steeves and Colpitts: Pioneers of the Upper Petitcodiac.* William S. Hoar. Vancouver: Tangled Roots Press, 1988.

**7614. Hody, Maud Hazel** *The Development of the Bilingual Schools of New Brunswick, 1784-1960.* Maud Hazel Hody. Toronto: University of Toronto, 1964. Thesis (Ed.D.)--University of Toronto, 1964.

**7615. Hollohan, Francis G.** *Albert Perlin: a Biography.* Francis G. Hollohan. St. John's: Jesperson Press, c1985.

**7616. Horsley, Frederick Richard**
*Attitudes of Institutionalized Juvenile Delinquents: a Study to Develop a Method for Modifying Attitudes and to Examine the Effects of Attitude to the Training School on Behaviour Within the Training School.* Frederick Richard Horsley. Fredericton, University of New Brunswick, c1968.
  Thesis (M.A.)–University of New Brunswick, 1968.
  National Library of Canada MIC TC-3637.

**7617. How, Douglas** *A Very Private Person: the Story of Izaak Walton Killam, and His Wife Dorothy.* Douglas How. [Nova Scotia]: Dalhousie Graphics, 1976.

**7618. Howley, M.F.** *Ecclesiastical History of Newfoundland.* The Very Reverend M.F. Howley. Rpt. ed. Belleville, Ont.: Mika Publishing Company, 1979.
  Originally published under the same title in 1888 by Doyle & Whittle, Boston.

**7619. Hudson, Elliott** *"Youth at the Crossroads."* Elliott Hudson. Canadian Welfare 17, 7(Jan. 1942): 51-53.

**7620. Hutchins, Nancy Bowden** *Guides, All Guides: a History of Girl Guiding in Nova Scotia, 1911-1977.* Nancy Bowden Hutchins. Halifax: McCurdy Printing Co. Ltd., c1977.

**7621. Infant School Society of Halifax**
*Rules and Regulations of the Infant School Society Constituted in May, 1883.* Infant School Society of Halifax. [S.l.: s.n., 1883?].

**7622. Irvin, John** *"History of Bridgetown."* John Irvin. Collections of the Nova Scotia Historical Society 19(1918): 39-42.

**7623. J., J.** *"School Days at Long River."* J.J. Prince Edward Island Magazine 3, 5(July 1901): 172-176.

**7624. Jackson, Joyce Ernestine** *A Development of Transposition: Relative Versus Absolute Response as a Function of Test Content and Verbalization.* Joyce Ernestine Jackson. Fredericton: University of New Brunswick, 1965.
  Thesis (M.A.)–University of New Brunswick, 1965.

**7625. Janes, Percy** *House of Hate.* Percy Janes. Toronto: McClelland and Stewart, c1970.

**7626. Jessamine, A.G.** *"A Peculiar Pulmonary Foreign Body."* A.G. Jessamine. Canadian Medical Association Journal 79, 4(Aug. 15, 1958): 272-273.

**7627. Johnston, A.J.B.** *"Education and Female Literacy at Eighteenth Century Louisbourg: the Work of the Soeurs de la Congregation de Notre-Dame."* A.J.B. Johnston. Vancouver: CSCI Publications, 1981. In An Imperfect Past: Education and Society in Canadian History, pp. 48-61. Edited by J. Donald Wilson.

**7628. Johnston, A.J.B.** *"The Men of the Garrison: Soldiers and Their Punishments at Louisbourg 1751-53."* A.J.B. Johnston. Nova Scotia Historical Review 10, 2(1990): 45-62.

**7629. Johnston, A.J.B.** *Religion in Life at Louisbourg 1713-1758.* A.J.B. Johnston. Montreal: McGill-Queen's University Press, c1984.

**7630. Johnston, Martha V.** *That the Past May Live: Tales of My Childhood and Youth in Stanley, N.B.* Martha V. Johnston. Stanley, N.B.: Upper Nashwaak Bicentennial Committee, Stanley, N.B., c1978.

**7631. Johnston, Michael K.** *A Study of Municipal Welfare and Its Contribution to the Phenomenon of Generation to Generation Dependency on Social Assistance.* Michael K. Johnston. Halifax: Dalhousie University, c1968.
  Thesis (M.S.W.)--Dalhousie University, 1968.

**7632. Jones, Orlo, ed.** *An Island Refuge: Loyalists and Disbanded Troops on the Island of Saint John.* Orlo Jones and Doris Haslam, editors. Charlottetown: Abegweit Branch of the United Empire. Loyalist Association of Canada, 1983.

**7633. Jones, Ted** *All the Days of His Life: a Biography of Archdeacon H.A. Cody.* Ted Jones. Saint John: New Brunswick Museum, c1981.

**7634. Josephson, J.E.** *"Report of a Fatal Case of Listeriosis Meningitis in a Seven-day-old Infant."* J.E. Josephson, R.W. Butler and C.J. Hutton. Canadian Medical Association Journal 78, 4(Feb. 15, 1958): 262-264.

**7635. Jost, A.C.** *"Epidemiology and Vital Statistics."* A.C. Jost and Neil E. McKinnon. Public Health Journal 19, 8(Aug. 1928): 385-388.

**7636. Jost, A.C.** *"Standardizing the Provincial Death Rates."* A.C. Jost. Public Health Journal 16, 12(Dec. 1925): 578-581.

**7637. Kahn, Alison Joanne** *The Jews of St. John's Newfoundland: a Rhetorical Approach to a Community Autobiography.* Alison Joanne Kahn. St. John's: Memorial University, 1983. (CTM no. 24374) Thesis (M.A.)–Memorial University, 1983.

**7638. Kanigsberg, Robert Abe** *Trials and Tribulations of a Bluenose Barrister.* Robert Abe Kanigsberg. 1st ed. Halifax: Petheric Press, c1977.

**7639. Kanungo, Rabindra N.** *"Differential Roles of Frequency and Meaningfulness in Free Recall."* Rabindia N. Kanungo and Gour S. Mohanty. Canadian Journal of Psychology/Revue canadienne de psychologie 24, 3(June 1970): 161-168.

**7640. Keene, Roger** *Conversations With W.A.C. Bennett.* Roger Keene. Toronto: Methuen, 1980.

**7641. Keith, William John** *Charles G.D. Roberts.* William John Keith. [Toronto]: Copp Clark, c1969.

**7642. Kerenyi, N.** *"Herpes Simplex Encephalitis: a Fatal Case."* N. Kerenyi, Ruth Faulkner and Elizabeth Petite. Canadian Medical Association Journal/Journal de l'Association medicale canadienne 81, 12(Dec. 15, 1959): 1011-1014.

**7643. Keyes, Mary E.** *"A Canadian Physical Educator: John Howard Crocker LL.D."* Mary E. Keyes. Ottawa: Fitness and Amateur Sport Directorate, Department of National Health and Welfare, 1970. In Proceedings of the First Canadian Symposium on the History of Sport and Physical Education, pp. 453-466.

**7644. King, William L.** *"Rule Learning and Transfer as a Function of Age and Stimulus Structure."* William L. King. Child Development 39, 1(Mar. 1968): 311-324.

**7645. Kitchen, Hubert William** *Relationships Between the Value Orientations of Grade Nine Pupils in Newfoundland and the Characteristics of Their Primary and Secondary Groups.* Hubert William Kitchen. Edmonton: University of Alberta, 1966. Thesis (Ph.D.)–University of Alberta, 1966.

**7646. Knockwood, William** *"Early Memories of a Micmac Boy."* William Knockwood. Tawow 5, 2(1976): 31-32.

**7647. Kozma, Albert** *"Instructional and Isolation Effects on Susceptibility to Social Reinforcement."* Albert Kozma. Canadian Journal of Behavioural Science/Revue canadienne de sciences du comportement 3, 4(Oct. 1971): 388-392.

**7648. Kreisel, Henry** *"From a Letter to Robert Weaver."* Henry Kreisel. Edmonton: NeWest Press, c1985. In Another Country: Writings By and About Henry Kreisel, pp. 45-49. Edited by Shirley Neuman.

**7649. LaFosse, Thomas J.** *The Degree of Implementation of Certain Recommendations of the Newfoundland Royal Commission on Education and Youth.* Thomas J. LaFosse. Edmonton: University of Alberta, 1971. Thesis (M.Ed.)–University of Alberta, 1971.

**7650. Lajoie, Cyr Raymond** *Educating the Mentally Retarded in New Brunswick: a Survey of the Educational Services for the Trainable Mentally Retarded Children.* Cyr Lajoie. Fredericton: University of New Brunswick, 1969. Thesis (M.Ed.)–University of New Brunswick, 1969.

**7651. Lawton, R.L.** *"Duplication of the Intestinal Tract."* R.L. Lawton and Edwin F. Ross. Canadian Medical Association Journal 75, 1(July 1, 1956): 38-40.

**7652. Le Calir, Edmond Charles** *A Study of Juvenile Delinquents in After Care.* Edmond Charles Le Clair. Halifax: Maritime School of Social Work, c1962. Thesis (M.S.W.)–Maritime School of Social Work, 1962.

**7653. Lee, H.D.C.** *Bliss Carman: a Study in Canadian Poetry.* H.D.C. Lee. [S.l.]: Buxton, [1912].

**7654. Leith, G.O.M.** *"The Place of Review in Meaningful Verbal Learning Sequences."* G.O.M. Leith, L.A. Biran and J.A. Opollot. Canadian Journal of Behavioural Science/Revue canadienne de sciences du comportement 1, 2(Apr. 1969): 113-118.

**7655. Loiselle, Patricia** *"Scaling Drug Use: an Examination of the Popular Wisdom."* Patricia Loiselle and Paul C. Whitehead. Canadian Journal of Behavioural Science/Revue canadienne de sciences du comportement 2, 4(Oct. 1971): 347-356. Reprinted in Readings in Social Psychology: Focus on Canada, pp. 174-184. Edited by David Koulak and Daniel Perlman.

**7656. Lord, Margaret Gray** *One Woman's Charlottetown: Diaries of Margaret Gray Lord 1863, 1876, 1890.* Margaret Gray Lord and Evelyn J. MacLeod. Ottawa: Canadian Museum of Civilization, 1988.

**7657. Lowe, Frank** *I Beg to Differ: a Collection.* Frank Lowe. Montreal: Infocor, c1973

**7658. Lucas, Alec** *Hugh MacLennan.* Alec Lucas. Toronto: McClelland and Stewart, c1970.

**7659. Lunn, C.W.** *"From Trapper Boy to General Manager: a Story of Brotherly Love and Perseverance."* C.W. Lunn and Ian McKay, intro. Labour/Le Travailleur 4(1979): 211-240.

**7660. Lye, William Frank** *"Growing Up in the Dockyard: Memories of a Boyhood in Early Halifax, Part One."* William Frank Lye. Journal of Education, Series 5, 22, 4(Spring 1973): 31-39.
Author's name misspelled as Pye.

**7661. Lye, William Frank** *"Growing Up in the Dockyard: Memories of a Boyhood in Early Halifax, Part Two."* William Frank Lye. Journal of Education, Series 6, 1, 1(Fall 1973): 24-30.

**7662. Lynch, Charles** *You Can't Print That!: Memoirs of a Political Voyeur.* Charles Lynch. Edmonton: Hurtig, c1983.

**7663. M., J.** *"The Golden Age."* J. M. Prince Edward Island Magazine 2, 10(Dec. 1900): 307-309.
Author identified only by initials.

**7664. McAllister, Emily** *Effects of Reading Training in Treatment of Delinquents.* Emily McAllister. Fredericton: University of New Brunswick, 1969.
Thesis (M.A.)—University of New Brunswick, 1969.

**7665. MacArthur, Harvey** *"History of the Colchester Children's Aid Society."* Harvey MacArthur. Social Service News 25(Christmas 1975): 6-12.

**7666. McCann, Phillip** *"Class, Gender and Religion in Newfoundland Education, 1836-1901."* Phillip McCann. Historical Studies in Education/Revue d'histoire de l'education 1, 2(Fall 1989): 179-200.

**7667. McCann, Phillip** *"Denominational Education in the Twentieth Century in Newfoundland."* Phillip McCann. St. John's, Nfld.: Breakwater Books, 1988. In The Vexed Question: Denominational Education in a Secular Age, pp. 60-79. Edited by William A. McKim.

**7668. McCann, Phillip** *"The Politics of Denominational Education in the Nineteenth Century in Newfoundland."* Phillip McCann. St. John's, Nfld.: Breakwater Books, 1988. In The Vexed Question: Denominational Education in a Secular Age, pp. 30-59. Edited by William A. McKim.

**7669. McCann, Phillip, ed.** *Blackboards and Briefcases: Personal Stories by Newfoundland Teachers, Educators and Administrators.* Edited by Phillip McCann. St. John's: Jesperson Press, c1982.

**7670. McCullogh, Harold** *A Century of Caring: the Story of the New Brunswick Protestant Orphans' Home.* Harold McCullogh. St. Stephen, N.B.: Print 'N Press, 1986.

**7671. MacDonald, Dan J.** *"Farewell to Coal: into the Mines as a Child."* Dan J. MacDonald and Ed Payne. Atlantic Advocate 57, 12(Aug. 1967): 21-23.

**7672. MacDonald, M.R.** *"The Diphtheria Situation in Cape Breton Island, Nova Scotia, Over a Two-year Period."* M.R. MacDonald. Canadian Journal of Public Health 37, 10(Oct. 1947): 391-398.

**7673. MacEachern, George** *George MacEachern: an Autobiography, the Story of a Cape Breton Labour Radical.* George MacEachern Nova Scotia: University College of Cape Breton Press, 1987.

**7674. McFarland, Charles Jerome** *The Relationship of the Minnesota Counselling Inventory with Academic Achievement and Mental Ability in High School.* C. Jerome McFarland. Fredericton: University of New Brunswick, 1969.
Thesis (M.Ed.)—University of New Brunswick, 1969.

**7675. McGahan, Peter** *Crime and Policing in Maritime Canada: Chapters from the Urban Records.* Peter McGahan. Fredericton: Goose Lane Editions, 1988.

**7676. McIntosh, John** *A Brief Memoir of the Last Few Weeks of Anne McIntosh: Daughter of John and Marion McIntosh, Earltown.* John McIntosh. 2nd ed. [Pictou, N.S.: s.n.], 1876.

**7677. McIntosh, Robert** *"The Boys in the Nova Scotian Coal Mines: 1873 to 1923."* Robert McIntosh. Acadiensis 16, 2(Spring 1987): 35-50.

**7678. McIntosh, Robert** *""Grotesque Faces and Figures": Child Labourers and Coal Mining Technology in Victorian Nova Scotia."* Robert McIntosh. Scientia Canadensis 12, 2(Fall/Winter 1988): 97-112.

7679. McIvor, Desmond Joseph *A Study of Juvenile Delinquents Under Twelve Years of Age*. Desmond Joseph McIvor. Halifax: Maritime School of Social Work, c1961.
Thesis (M.S.W.)--Maritime School of Social Work, 1961.

7680. MacKay, A.H. *"The Teaching of Hygiene."* A.H. MacKay. Canadian Medical Association Journal 8, 4(Apr. 1918): 424-426.

7681. McKay, Ian *"The Realm of Uncertainty: the Experience of Work in the Cumberland Coal Mines 1873-1927."* Ian McKay. Acadiensis 16, 1(Autumn 1986): 3-57.

7682. MacKenzie, Margaret *"Sydney Kiwanis Health Camp."* Margaret MacKenzie. Canadian Public Health Journal 20, 7(July 1929): 344-348.

7683. McKenzie, Vera Annie *The Implementation of Continuous Progress in Montgomery Street School: a Case Study.* Vera Annie McKenzie. Fredericton: University of New Brunswick, 1969.
Thesis (M.Ed.)--University of New Brunswick, 1969.

7684. McKinley, Edgar E. *"The Memoirs of Robert Kent of Kent's Island (now Pleasant Point), Halifax County, 1813-1840: an Extract."* Edgar E. McKinley. Collections of the Nova Scotia Historical Society 30(1954): 121-129.

7685. Mackinnon, F.R. *"Public Welfare Costs in Nova Scotia."* F.R. Mackinnon. Canadian Welfare Summary 15, 6(Mar. 1940): 32-39.

7686. MacKinnon, Loretta *St. Vincent's High School: a History of Adaptation.* Sister Loretta MacKinnon. St. John: University of New Brunswick, c1985. (CTM no. 21015)
Thesis (M.Ed.)--University of New Brunswick, 1985.

7687. McLaren, Katherine I. *"The Proper Education For All Classes": Compulsory Schooling and Reform in Nova Scotia, 1890-1930.* Katherine I. McLaren. Halifax: Dalhousie University, 1984. (CTM no. 24458)
Thesis (M.Ed.)--Dalhousie University, 1984.

7688. Macleod, Donald *"Practicality Ascendant: the Origins and Establishment of Technical Education in Nova Scotia."* Donald Macleod. Acadiensis 15, 2(Spring 1986): 53-92.

7689. MacLeod, Malcolm *"Parade Street Parade: the Student Body at Memorial University College, 1925-49."* Malcolm MacLeod. Kingston: McGill-Queen's University Press, 1989. In Youth, University and Canadian Society: Essays in the Social History of Higher Education, pp. 51-71. Edited by Paul Axelrod and John G. Reid.

7690. McLeod, Scott H. *Nova Scotia Farm Boy to Alberta M.D.* Scott H. McLeod. Calgary: The Author, 1968.

7691. MacLulich, T.D. *Hugh MacLennan.* T.D. MacLulich. Boston: Twayne, c1983.

7692. MacMahon, Amy E. *"Child Welfare in Prince Edward Island."* Amy E. MacMahon. Public Health Journal 14, 2(Feb. 1923): 57-61.

7693. MacMahon, Amy E. *"Pioneer Public Health Nursing in Prince Edward Island."* A.E. MacMahon. Canadian Nurse 19, 9(Sept. 1923): 539-542.

7694. MacNaughton, Katherine F.C. *The Development of the Theory and Practice of Education in New Brunswick 1784-1900: a Study in Historical Background.* Katherine F.C. MacNaughton. Fredericton: University of New Brunswick, c1946.

7695. MacNeil, Joe Neil *Tales Until Dawn: the World of a Cape Breton Gaelic Story-teller.* Joe Neil MacNeil, translated and edited by John Shaw. Kingston: McGill-Queen's University Press, c1987.

7696. MacNeil, Robert *Wordstruck: a Memoir.* Robert MacNeil. New York: Viking, 1989.

7697. Maddison, Janis M. *"The Improvement of Reading: an Experimental Study."* Janis M. Maddison and Gerald T. Rimmington. Canadian Education and Research Digest 6, 3(Sept. 1966): 188-190.

7698. Majury, Ernest *Report of a Survey of Child Welfare Services in Nova Scotia.* Ernest Majury. [Halifax: s.n.], 1964.

7699. Manos, James *A Semantic Differential Study of Some White and Negro Adolescent Attitudes.* James Manos. Calgary: University of Calgary, 1970.
Thesis (M.Ed.)--University of Calgary, 1970.

7700. Marble, Allan E. *"Epidemics and Mortality in Nova Scotia, 1749-1799."* Allan E. Marble. Nova Scotia Historical Review 8, 2(1988): 72-93.

**7701. Marshall, Mortimer W.** *"The Makings of a School Museum."* Mortimer W. Marshall. Nova Scotia Historical Quarterly 1, 4(Dec. 1971): 287-306.

**7702. Marshall, Vera G.** *"Great Grandmother Isabel: a Story of the Turn of the Century."* Vera G. Marshall. Nova Scotia Historical Quarterly 6, 2(Mar. 1976): 57-68.

**7703. Martell, Jean** *"Chorea."* Jean Martell. Canadian Nurse 50, 8(Aug. 1954): 659-662.

**7704. Martin, George Ernest** *A Survey of Factors Related to Dropouts in Canada in Newfoundland Central High Schools in 1961-62.* George Ernest Martin. Edmonton: University of Alberta, 1964.
Thesis (M.Ed.)–University of Alberta, 1964.

**7705. Martin, Jed** *"Convict Transportation to Newfoundland in 1789."* Jed Martin. Acadiensis 5, 1(Autumn 1975): 84-99.

**7706. Mason, Edward Charles** *A Study of Preschool Children in Institutions.* Edward Charles Mason. Halifax: Maritime School of Social Work, c1960.
Thesis (M.S.W.)–Maritime School of Social Work, 1960.

**7707. Matheson, Wayne Elmer** *Personality Characteristics of Underachievers in a Prince Edward Island High School.* Wayne Elmer Matheson. Edmonton: University of Alberta, 1969.
Thesis (M.Ed.)–University of Alberta, 1969.

**7708. Matthews, Ralph** *"There's No Better Place Than Here": Social Change in Three Newfoundland Communities.* Ralph Matthews. Toronto: Peter Martin Associates Ltd., c1976.

**7709. Mayers, C.P.** *"Manifestations of Pinworms."* C.P. Mayers and R.J. Purvis. Canadian Medical Association Journal/Journal de l'Association medicale canadienne 103, 5(Sept. 12, 1970): 489-493.

**7710. Maynard, Steven J.** *On the Market's Edge: Family, the Productive Household and the Capitalist Transformation of the Maritime Countryside, Hopewell, Nova Scotia, 1870-1890.* Steven J. Maynard. Kingston: Queen's University, 1987. (CTM no. 40492)
Thesis (M.A.)–Queen's University, 1987.

**7711. Medjuck, Sheva** *Jews of Atlantic Canada.* Sheva Medjuck. St. John's: Breakwater Books Ltd., 1986.

**7712. Merritt, John W.** *"Intrathoracic Leiomyosarcoma."* John W. Merritt and K. Ross Parker. Canadian Medical Association Journal 77, 11(Dec. 1, 1957): 1031-1033.

**7713. Millar, Ann** *Narration and Life History of a Newfoundland Woman.* Ann Millar. Hamilton: McMaster University, 1981. (CTM no. 54184)
Thesis (M.A.)–McMaster University, 1981.

**7714. Miller, Muriel** *Bliss Carman: a Portrait.* Muriel Miller. Toronto: Ryerson Press, c1935.

**7715. Miller, Muriel** *Bliss Carman: Quest and Revolt.* Muriel Miller St. John's: Jesperson Press, c1985.

**7716. Mitchell, David Joseph** *W.A.C.: Bennett and the Rise of British Columbia.* David Joseph Mitchell. Vancouver: Douglas and MacItyre, c1983.

**7717. Montgomery, Lucy Maud** *The Alpine Path: the Story of My Career.* L.M. Montgomery. Don Mills: Fitzhenry and Whiteside, c1917.

**7718. Montgomery, Lucy Maud** *The Selected Journals of L.M. Montgomery.* L.M. Montgomery, edited by Mary Rubio and Elizabeth Waterston. Toronto: Oxford University Press, c1985.

**7719. Moore, Christopher** *Louisbourg Portraits: Life in an Eighteenth-Century Garrison Town.* Christopher Moore. Toronto: Macmillan of Canada, 1982.

**7720. Moore, Tom** *Wilfred Grenfell.* Tom Moore. Don Mills: Fitzhenry and Whiteside, 1980.

**7721. Morton, Sydney** *"Sydney Morton's Diary."* Sydney Morton and John Leefe. Acadiensis 4, 1(Autumn 1974): 121-129. Introduction by John Leefe.

**7722. Mowat, Alex S.** *"Problems of High School Education in Nova Scotia."* Alex S. Mowat. Public Affairs 2(Aug. 1940): 28-31.

**7723. Mulcahy, Mary Nolasco** *"The St. John's Schools of Industry."* Mary Nolasco Mulcahy. Newfoundland Quarterly 78, 4(Spring 1983): 17-23.

7724. **Murphy, George** *"My Educational Memories."* George Murphy. Dalhousie Review 20, 3(Oct. 1940): 319-334.

7725. **Murray, E.M.** *"Saving Babies in Halifax."* E.M. Murray. Canadian Nurse 15, 12(Dec. 1919): 2171-2174.

7726. **Murray, Hilda E.L.** *More Than Fifty Percent: Woman's Life in a Newfoundland Outport, 1900-1950.* Hilda Chaulk Murray. [St. John's]: Breakwater Books Limited, c1979.

7727. **Murray, Hilda E.L.** *The Traditional Role of Women in a Newfoundland Fishing Community.* Hilda E.L. Murray. St. John's: Memorial University, 1972.
Thesis (M.A.)--Memorial University, 1972. Bibiliography leaves 314-319.

7728. **New Brunswick. Commission Appointed to Consider the Payment of Mothers' Allowance** *Report of the Commission Appointed to Consider the Payment of Mothers' Allowance.* The Commission. [Fredricton: The Commission, 1930].
Chairman: W.C.H. Grimmer.

7729. **New Brunswick. Department of Health and Social Services** *A Health Survey in a New Brunswick Rural School.* The Department. Fredricton: Department of Health Services, Maternal and Child Health Division, 1959.

7730. **Newfoundland Family Law Study** *Family Law in Newfoundland.* Newfoundland Family Law Study, R. Gushue and David Daig. St. John's: Government of Newfoundland, 1973.

7731. **Newfoundland. Royal Commission on Education and Youth** *Report.* The Commission. Newfoundland. Royal Commission on Education and Youth, 1967.

7732. **Nichols, E.W.** *"The Little White Schoolhouse."* E.W. Nichols. Dalhousie Review 5, 3(Oct. 1925): 311-323.

7733. **Norman, Jane Margaret** *Loran Arthur de Wolfe and Rural Educational Reform in Nova Scotia.* Jane Margaret Norman. Calgary: University of Calgary, 1970. (CTM no. 6129)
Thesis (Ph.D)--University of Calgary, 1970.

7734. **Nova Scotia. Commission of Hours of Labour (Eight Hour Day Commission)** *"Report of the Commission of Hours of Labour (Eight Hour Day Commission)."* The Commission. [Halifax: s.n.], 1910. In Journal and Proceedings of the Nova Scotia House of Assembly, 1910, Appendix 26.

Chairman: Henry MacDonald.

7735. **Nova Scotia. Commission on Mother's Allowances** *"Report of the Commission on Mothers' Allowances."* The Commission. Halifax: Weeks Printing Co. Ltd., 1921.
Chairman: J. McKeen.

7736. **Nova Scotia. Commission Respecting Feeble Minded in Nova Scotia** *"Report of the Commission Respecting Feeble Minded in Nova Scotia."* The Commission. Halifax: Commission of Public Works and Mines, King's Printer, 1918. In Journal and Proceedings, Part 2, of the Nova Scotia House of Assembly, 1917, Appendix 33.

7737. **Nova Scotia. Department of Public Health** *Social Services for Children in Nova Scotia.* Department of Public Health. [Halifax]: The Department, 1940.

7738. **Nova Scotia. Department of Public Welfare** *An Abridgement of the Report of a Survey of Child Welfare Services in Nova Scotia and Recommendations.* The Department. Halifax: [s.n.], 1964.

7739. **Nova Scotia. Department of Public Welfare** *Children With Special Needs: a Report to the Minister of the Department of Public Welfare of the Province Regarding Possible Future Programs of Five Voluntary Child Caring Institutions.* Department of Public Welfare. Halifax: [s.n.], 1970.

7740. **Nova Scotia. Department of Public Welfare** *The Development of Social Welfare in Nova Scotia.* Department of Public Welfare. Halifax: s.n., 1967.

7741. **Nova Scotia. Department of Public Welfare** *The Nova Scotia Association and Children's Aid Societies 1926-1956 [Part 1] [and] The Nova Scotia Association of Child Caring Institutions 1948-1956 [Part 2].* Department of Public Welfare. [Halifax: s.n., 1972].

7742. **Nova Scotia. Department of Public Welfare** *Report of the Gordon-Crook Commission on Homes for the Disabled in Nova Scotia.* Department of Public Welfare. Halifax: [s.n.], 1970.

7743. **Nova Scotia. Department of Public Welfare** *Social Welfare in Nova Scotia: a Summary of Historical Material.* Department of Public Welfare. Halifax: [s.n.], 1968.

7744. Nova Scotia. Department of Public Welfare *Social Welfare Pioneers in Nova Scotia.* Department of Public Welfare. Halifax: [s.n.], 1972.

7745. Nova Scotia. Department of Public Welfare. Family and Child Welfare Division *Child Care Institutions: Nova Scotia Youth Training Centre, Nova Scotia School for Girls, Nova Scotia School for Boys, Children's Homes.* Department of Public Welfare, Family and Child Welfare Division. Halifax: [s.n.], 1973.

7746. Nova Scotia. Department of Public Welfare. Family and Child Welfare Division *The Extra Burden: a Study of Foster Care in Three Counties of the Province of Nova Scotia.* Department of Public Welfare, Family and Child Welfare Division. Halifax: [s.n.], 1971.

7747. Nova Scotia. Department of Public Welfare. Minister's Advisory Committee on Day Care Services *Brief from the Minister's Advisory Committee on Day Care Services.* Minister's Advisory Committee on Day Care Services. Halifax: [s.n.], 1967.

7748. Nova Scotia. Joint Committee on Public Attitudes Towards Our Schools *Nova Scotia Looks at its Schools: a Survey Project of the Joint Committee on Public Attitudes Towards Our Schools.* Nova Scotia. Joint Committee on Public Attitudes Towards Our Schools. [S.l.: s.n.], 1952.

7749. Nova Scotia. Royal Commission Concerning Mentally Deficient Persons in Nova Scotia *Report.* The Commission. Halifax: [s.n.], 1927.
Chairman: W.L. Hall.

7750. Nova Scotia. Royal Commission in the Matter of Certain Charges Affecting the Treatment of the Poor in the County of Digby *Report of the Royal Commission in the Matter of Certain Charges Affecting the Treatment of the Poor in the County of Digby.* The Commission. Halifax: Commissioner of Public Works and Mines, 1886.
Commissioner: Francis H. Bell.

7751. Nova Scotia. Royal Commission on the Safe Transportation of School Pupils *Report of the Royal Commission on the Safe Transportation of School Pupils.* The Commission. Yarmouth, N.S.: [s.n.], 1964.
Commissioner: C. Roger Rand.
Also known as The School Bus Inquiry.

7752. O'Flaherty, Patrick *"Growing Up Irish in a Newfoundland Outport."* Patrick O'Flaherty. Toronto: Celtic Arts of Canada, 1988. In The Untold Story: the Irish in Canada, v.2, pp. 723-728. Edited by Robert O'Driscoll and Lorna Reynolds.

7753. O'Hanlon, Betty *Finding a Familiar Stranger.* Betty O'Hanlon. Edmonton: Plains Pub., 1988.

7754. O'Hearn, Marilyn Elaine *Canadian Native Education Policy: a Case Study of the Residential School at Shubenacadie, Nova Scotia.* Marilyn Elaine O'Hearn. Halifax: St. Mary's University, 1989. (CTM no. 50920)
Thesis (M.A.)–St. Mary's University, 1989.

7755. Oldershaw, Marion Donkin *"William Donkin, Northumbrian, and His Nova Scotia Descendants."* Marion Donkin Oldershaw. Nova Scotia Historical Review 10, 1(1990).

7756. O'Rafferty, Ann *"Acute Laryngotracheo Bronchitis."* Ann O'Rafferty. Canadian Nurse 51, 8(Aug. 1955): 621-624.

7757. Ozere, R.L. *"A Survey of Poliovirus Neutralizing Antibody in Newfoundland, 1959-1960."* R.L. Ozere and K.R. Rozee. Canadian Medical Association Journal/Journal de l'Association medicale canadienne 85, 2(July 8, 1961): 63-67.

7758. Paradis, Roger *"Henriette, la capuche: the Portrait of a Frontier Midwife."* Roger Paradis. Canadian Folklore canadien 3, 2(1981): 110-126.

7759. Peach, Earle *Memories of a Cape Breton Childhood.* Earle Peach. Halifax: Nimbus, 1990.

7760. Penney, Sheila M. *Tuberculosis in Nova Scotia, 1882-1914.* Sheila M. Penney. Halifax: Dalhousie University, 1986. (CTM no. 29731)
Thesis (M.A.)--Dalhousie University, 1985.

7761. Perry, Beulah Gullison *"Remembering: Growing Up as a Sea-Captain's Daughter."* Beulah Gullison Perry. Nova Scotia Historical Review 7, 2(1987): 31-34.

7762. Pett, L.B. *"A Nutrition Survey on a Nova Scotia Island."* L.B. Pett and F.W. Hanley. Canadian Medical Association Journal 59, 3(Sept. 1948); 230-236.

7763. **Pitt, David G.** *E.J. Pratt: the Truant Years, 1882-1927.* David G. Pitt. Toronto: University of Toronto Press, c1984.

7764. **Poirier, Leonie Comeau** *My Acadian Heritage.* Leonie Comeau Poirier. Hantsport: Lancelot Press, 1985.

7765. **Pomeroy, E.M.** *Sir Charles G.D. Roberts: a Biography.* E.M. Pomeroy. Toronto: Ryerson Press, c1943.

7766. **Poole, Cyril F.** *The Time of My Life.* Cyril F. Poole. St. John's: Harry Cuff Publications, 1983.

7767. **Porter, Helen** *Below the Bridge: Memories of the South Side of St. John's.* Helen Porter. [St. John's]: Breakwater, 1979.

7768. **Porter, Marilyn** *"Mothers and Daughters: Linking Women's Life Histories in Grand Bank, Newfoundland, Canada."* Marilyn Porter. Women's Studies International Forum 11, 6(1988): 545-558.

7769. **Powell, Ben W.** *Labrador by Choice.* Ben Powell. St. John's: Jesperson Press, 1984.

7770. **Pratt, E.J.** *E.J. Pratt on his Life and Poetry.* E.J. Pratt. Toronto: University of Toronto Press, c1983.

7771. **Prince Edward Island. Commission on Education in Prince Edward Island** *Report of the Commission on Education in Prince Edward Island.* The Commission. Charlottetown: King's Printer, 1910.
Chairman: D.C. McLeod.

7772. **Prince Edward Island. Royal Commission on Education in the Province of Prince Edward Island** *Report of the Royal Commission on Education in Prince Edward Island.* The Commission. Charlottetown: Patriot Job Print, 1930.
Chairman: C. MacMillan.

7773. **Pryke, Kenneth** *"Poor Relief and Health Care in Halifax, 1827-1849."* Kenneth Pryke. Toronto: McClelland and Stewart, 1988. In Essays in the History of Canadian Medicine, pp. 39-61. Edited by Wendy Mitchinson and Janice Dickin McGinnis.

7774. **Purdy, Reginald C.** *Probation as a Treatment Process in Juvenile Delinquency.* Reginald C. Purdy. Halifax: Maritime School of Social Work, c1961.
Thesis (M.S.W.)--Maritime School of Social Work, 1961.

7775. **Quinlan, J.J.** *"Lung Resection for Tuberculosis in Children."* J.J. Quinlan, V.D. Schaffner and J.E. Hiltz. Canadian Medical Association Journal/Journal de l'Association medicale canadienne 87, 26(Dec. 29, 1962): 1362-1366.

7776. **Rawlyk, George A.** *Acadian Education in Nova Scotia: an Historical Survey.* George Rawlyk and Ruth Hafter.

7777. **Rawlyk, George A.** *"New Lights, Baptists and Religious Awakenings in Nova Scotia: a Preliminary Probe."* George A. Rawlyk. Journal of the Canadian Church Historical Society 25, 2(June 1981): 64-67.

7778. **Read, Winifred** *"School Nursing."* Winifred Read. Public Health Journal 9, 9(Sept. 1918): 431-433.

7779. **Reay, Phyllis M.** *"Royal Canadian Naval Well Baby Health Service."* Phyllis M. Reay. Canadian Nurse 40, 7(July 1944): 469-472.

7780. **Reed, R.W.** *"Listeriosis in Man."* R.W. Reed, W.F. Gavin, Joan Crosby and Phyllis Dobson. Canadian Medical Association Journal 73, 5(Sept. 1, 1955): 400-402.

7781. **Reid, Joanne** *"Witches, Whores and Waifs: Judicial Treatment of Deviant Women in Pre-confederation New Brunswick: Selected Examples."* Joanne Reid. [Ottawa: Carleton University, 1987]. In Papers Presented at the 1987 Canadian Law in History Conference, vol. 1, pp. 108-133.

7782. **Richards, James** *The Sea in My Blood: the Life and Times of Captain Andy Publicover.* James and Marlene Richards with Eric Hustvedt. Hansport: Lancelot, c1987.

7783. **Richardson, Evelyn** *"The Halifax Explosion, 1917."* Evelyn M. Richardson. Nova Scotia Historical Quarterly 7, 4(Dec. 1977): 305-330.

7784. **Richardson, Evelyn** *My Other Islands.* Evelyn May Fox Richardson. Toronto: Ryerson Press, 1960.

7785. **Ridley, Hilda M.** *The Story of L.M. Montgomery.* Hilda M. Ridley. Toronto: Ryerson Press, c1956.

7786. **Ritchie, Charles** *My Grandfather's House: Scenes of Childhood and Youth.* Charles Ritchie. Toronto: Macmillan of Canada, 1987.

**7787. Roberts, Charles G.D.** *"Bliss Carman."* Charles G.D. Roberts. Dalhousie Review 9, 4(Jan. 1930): 409-417.

**7788. Roberts, Maureen H.** *"Tetanus Neonatorum."* Maureen H. Roberts. Canadian Medical Association Journal 78, 12(June 15, 1958): 922-924.

**7789. Robertson, J.S.** *"A Tuberculosis Survey in Bridgetown, Nova Scotia."* J.S. Robertson. Canadian Public Health Journal 31, 4(Apr. 1940): 194-197.

**7790. Robinson, Charlotte Gourlay** *Pioneer Profiles of New Brunswick Settlers.* Charlotte Gourlay Robinson. Belleville: Mika Publishing Company, 1980.

**7791. Rockwood, Walter G.** *"Social Welfare in Northern Labrador."* Walter G. Rockwood. Canadian Welfare 30, 7(Feb. 1955): 21-25.

**7792. Rooke, Patricia T.** *"Guttersnipes and Charity Children: Nineteenth Century Child Rescue in the Atlantic Provinces."* Patricia T. Rooke and R.L. Schnell. Calgary: Detselig Enterprises Ltd., 1982. In Studies in Childhood History: a Canadian Perspective, pp. 82-104. Edited by Patricia T. Rooke and R.L. Schnell.

**7793. Ross, Winifred Mary** *Child Rescue and the Nova Scotia Society for the Prevention of Cruelty, 1880-1920.* Winifred Mary Ross. Halifax: Dalhousie University, c1975. (CTM no. 28947) Thesis (M.A.)--Dalhousie University, 1975.

**7794. Rowe, Frederick W.** *The Development of Education in Newfoundland.* Frederick W. Rowe. Toronto: The Ryerson Press, c1964. Text is a revised version of the original study by the author entitled The History of Education in Newfoundland (Toronto: The Ryerson Press, 1952).

**7795. Rowe, Frederick W.** *History of Education in Newfoundland.* Fred W. Rowe. Toronto: University of Toronto, 1951. Thesis (D.Paed.)--University of Toronto, 1951.

**7796. Rowe, Frederick W.** *The Smallwood Era.* Frederick W. Rowe. Toronto: McGraw-Hill Ryerson, 1985.

**7797. Russell, Christian Annabel** *Child Welfare Problems in the Coloured Community.* Christian Annabel Russell. Halifax: Maritime School of Social Work, c1961. Thesis (M.S.W.)--Maritime School of Social Work, 1961.

**7798. Ryan, James Joseph** *Disciplining the Inuit: Social Form and Control in Bush, Community and School.* James J. Ryan. Toronto: University of Toronto, 1988. Thesis (Ph.D.)--University of Toronto, 1988.

**7799. Ryan, Jim** *My Friend, W.A.C. Bennett.* Jim Ryan. Victoria: The Author, 1980.

**7800. Rye, Maria** *Further Letters Furnished to the Department of Agriculture by Miss Rye, in Rebuttal of Mr. Doyle's Report.* Maria Rye. [S.l.: s.n., 1875?].

**7801. Saarnit, Joann** *"Voyage to Freedom."* Joann Saarnit. Toronto: Quadrant Editions, 1983. In Between Two Worlds: the Canadian Immigrant Experience, pp. 16-26. Edited by Milly Charon.

**7802. Salsman, Lillian V.** *Homeland: Country Harbour, Nova Scotia, 1783-1983.* Lillian V. Salsman. Hantsport: Lancelot Press, 1984.

**7803. Saunders, Catherine Estelle** *Social Conditions and Legislation in Nova Scotia (1815-1851).* Catherine Estelle Saunders. Halifax: Dalhousie University, 1949. Thesis (M.A.)--Dalhousie University, 1949.

**7804. Saunders, Christopher** *"The Making of an Historian: the Early Years of George McCall Theal."* Christopher Saunders. South Africa Historical Journal 13(Nov. 1981): 3-11.

**7805. Saunders, Doris** *"A Daughter of Labrador."* Doris Saunders. Canadian Women's Studies 2, 1(Autumn 1980): 105.

**7806. Schoel, Gerald** *A Comparison of the Amount of Change Brought About by Short Term Counselling in Grade Nine Students.* Gerald Schoel. Fredericton: University of New Brunswick, 1970. (CTM no. 5704) Thesis (M.Ed.)--University of New Brunswick, 1969.

**7807. Scobie, Kathleen** *"Studies of Nutrition in Newfoundland Children."* Kathleen Scobie, Bertha S. Burke and Harold C. Stuart. Canadian Medical Association Journal 60, 3(Mar. 1949): 233-241.

**7808. Scotland, James** *"Education in Old and New Scotland."* James Scotland. Nova Scotia Historical Quarterly 4, 4(Dec. 1974): 355-372.

**7809. Severs, D.** *"Epidemic Gastroenteritis in Newfoundland During 1963 Associated With E. Coli 0111 B4."* D. Severs, P. Fardy, S. Acres and J.W. Davies. Canadian Medical Association Journal/Journal de l'Association medicale canadienne 94, 8(Feb. 19, 1966): 373-378.

**7810. Sexton, F.H.** *"Training the Unemployed: Unemployed Youth Training in Nova Scotia."* F.H. Sexton. Public Affairs 2, 2(Dec. 1938): 69-74.

**7811. Shaw, Blair** *How We See Them: an Analysis of Selected Psycho-Social Educational Factors Relevant to the Problem of Disadvantage.* Blair Shaw. Yarmouth, N.S.: [Nova Scotia NewStart Inc.], 1971.

**7812. Sheehan, Nancy M.** *"National Pressure Groups and Provincial Curriculum Policy: Temperance in Nova Scotia Schools, 1880-1930."* Nancy M. Sheehan. Canadian Journal of Education 9, 1(Winter 1984): 73-88.

**7813. Sheldon, Mary** *The Establishment of the Denominational School System in Newfoundland With Particular Reference to the Role of the Anglican Church 1836-1876.* Mary Sheldon. Toronto: University of Toronto, 1972.
Thesis (M.A.)–University of Toronto, 1972.

**7814. Shepard, Odell** *Bliss Carman.* Odell Shepard. Toronto: McClelland and Stewart, c1923.

**7815. Sherwood, Roland H.** *Jotham Blanchard: the Forgotten Patriot of Pictou.* Roland H. Sherwood. Hantsport, N.S.: Lancelot Press, 1982.

**7816. Sider, Gerald M.** *"Family Fun in Stave Harbour: Custom, History and Confrontation in Village Newfoundland."* Gerald M. Sider. In Interest and Emotion: Essays in the Study of Family Kinship, pp. 340-370. Edited by Hans Medick and David Warren Sabean.

**7817. Simmons, Christina** *""Helping the Poor Sisters": the Women of the Jost Mission, Halifax 1905-1945."* Christina Simmons. Acadiensis 14, 1(Autumn 1984): 3-27.

**7818. Skinner, George F.** *"Ganglioneuroma of the Mediastinum."* George F. Skinner. Canadian Medical Association Journal 49, 5(Nov. 1943): 397-399.

**7819. Smallwood, Joseph R.** *I Chose Canada: the Memoirs of the Honourable Joseph R. "Joey" Smallwood.* Joseph R. Smallwood. Toronto: MacMillan of Canada, 1973.

**7820. Smallwood, Joseph R., ed.** *Book of Newfoundland.* J.R. Smallwood, ed. 4 v. St. John's: Newfoundland Book Publishers, 1937.
Reprinted 1968.

**7821. Smart, Elizabeth** *"Scenes One Never Forgets."* Elizabeth Smart. Ottawa: Deneau, c1984. In In the Meantime, pp. 5-21.

**7822. Smith, Barbara** *The Historical Development of Child Welfare Legislation in Newfoundland, 1832-1949.* Barbara Smith. St. John's: Memorial University, 1971. Thesis (M.S.W.)–Memorial University, 1971.

**7823. Smith, Eleanor** *"The Descendants of Jasper and Elizabeth (Hanson) Harding."* Eleanor Smith. Nova Scotia Historical Review 9, 1(1989): 94-119.

**7824. Smith, G.M.** *"An Outbreak of Pulmonary Tuberculosis in a Public School."* G.M. Smith, Maude MdLellan and J.E. Hiltz. Canadian Journal of Public Health 41, 2(Feb. 1950): 60-65.

**7825. Smith, Michael** *"Graceful Athleticism or Robust Womanhood: the Sporting Culture of Women in Victorian Nova Scotia, 1870-1914."* Michael Smith. Journal of Canadian Studies/Revue d'etudes canadiennes 23, 1 & 2(Spring-Summer 1988): 120-137.

**7826. Smith, Rankine M.** *The History of Basketball in New Brunswick, Canada (1892-1985).* Rankine M. Smith. Sussex, N.B.: [s.n.], 1986.

**7827. Sorg, Marcella H.** *"Patterns of Infant Mortality in the Upper St. John Valley French Population, 1791-1838."* Marcella H. Sorg and Beatrice C. Craig. Human Biology 55, 1(Feb. 1983): 100-113.

**7828. Stanley, Della Margaret M.** *Louis Robichaud: a Decade of Power.* Della M.M. Stanley. Halifax: Nimbus Publishing Ltd., 1984.

**7829. Stansford, Joshua** *Fifty Years of My Life.* Joshua Stansford. Ilfracombe: Arthur H. Stockwell, [1950].

**7830. Stephens, Donald** *Bliss Carman.* Donald Stephens. New York: Twayne, c1966.

**7831. Stevenson, Margaret** *Emotional Problems of Orphanage Children.* Margaret Stevenson. Halifax: Dalhousie University, 1951.
  Thesis (M.A.)–Dalhousie University, 1951.

**7832. Stevenson, Margaret** *"Some Emotional Problems of Orphanage Children."* Margaret Stevenson. Canadian Journal of Psychology 6, 4(Dec. 1952): 179-182.

**7833. Stirling, Emma M.** *Our Children in Old Scotland and Nova Scotia: Being a History of Her Work.* Emma M. Stirling. London: J. Haddon, [1892?].

**7834. Stirling, Emma M.** *Our Children in Old Scotland and Nova Scotia: With Sequel Being a History of Her Work.* Emma M. Stirling. Coatesville, Pa.: C.N. Speakman, [1898?].

**7835. Strong, Cyril W.** *My Life as a Newfoundland Union Organizer: the Memoirs of Cyril W. Strong 1912-1987.* Cyril W. Strong and Gregory S. Kealey, ed. St. John's: Memorial University of Newfoundland, 1987.

**7836. Sturtevant, W.C.** *"The First Inuit Depiction by Europeans."* W.C. Sturtevant. Etudes Inuit Studies 4, 1 and 2(1980): 47-49.

**7837. Sutherland, Neil** *"Albert School, Saint John, New Brunswick: a Case Study of Urban Schooling in the 1890's."* Neil Sutherland. Journal of Education of the Faculty of Education, Vancouver 19(Spring 1973): 63-73.

**7838. Swan, Florence B.** *"Problems Encountered in a Rural School Lunch Program."* Florence B. Swan. Canadian Journal of Public Health 40, 12(Dec. 1949): 491-496.

**7839. Swan, Florence B.** *"Rural School Lunch Program."* Florence Swan. Canadian Nurse 49, 9(Sept. 1953): 703-705.

**7840. Swingle, Paul G.** *"Social Class, Age, and the Nature of the Incentive in Children's Lever-pressing Performance."* Paul G. Swingle and Henry V. Coady. Canadian Journal of Psychology/Revue canadienne de psychologie 23, 1(Feb. 1969): 41-48.

**7841. Tanzman, Helene Isabel** *Recidivism in Relation to the School and to Employment.* Helene Isabel Tanzman. Halifax: Maritime School of Social Work, c1962.
  Thesis (M.S.W.)–Maritime School of Social Work, 1962.

**7842. Taylor, Charles E.** *"The Unique Position of Newfoundland in the Case of the Mentally Retarded Child."* Charles E. Taylor and Patrick Flynn. Canadian Psychiatric Association Journal/Revue de l'Association canadienne de psychiatrie 8, 5(Oct. 1963): 344-348.

**7843. Terasita, M.** *A Comparison of Two Phonetic Methods, Symbolic and Analytic, in the Teaching of Reading to Grade One Beginners.* Sister M. Terasita. Fredericton: University of New Brunswick, 1965, c1966.
  Thesis (M.Ed.)–University of New Brunswck, 1965.

**7844. Theal, George McCall** *"Schooldays, Schooldays ...: Cocagne Academy in the 1840s."* George McCall Theal. Acadiensis 5, 2(Spring 1975): 132-137.

**7845. Thompson, Harold R.** *"Training the Mentally Deficient."* Harold R. Thompson. Canadian Welfare 27, 7(Feb. 1952): 10-12.

**7846. Thomson, Colin A.** *Born With a Call: a Biography of Dr. William Pearly Oliver, C.M.* Colin A. Thomson. Dartmouth: Black Cultural Centre for Nova Scota, 1986.

**7847. Tingley, Anna L.** *Effect of Organizational Change on Foster Home Programs.* Anna L. Tingley. Halifax: Maritime School of Social Work, c1967.
  Thesis (M.S.W.)–Maritime School of Social Work, 1967.

**7848. Tizzard, Aubrey Malcolm** *On Sloping Ground: Reminiscences of Outport Life on Notre Dame Bay, Newfoundland.* Audbrey Malcolm Tizzard, edited with an introduction by J.D.A. Widdowson. St. John's: Breakwater Books, 1984.

**7849. Tomkinson, Grace** *"My Two Worlds."* Grace Tomkinson. Dalhousie Review 38, 1(Apr. 1959): 65-76.

**7850. Tompkins, M. Gregory** *"Experience in a Maternal Mortality Study in Nova Scotia."* M.G. Tompkins. Canadian Medical Association Journal/Journal de l'Association medicale canadienne 88, 17(Apr. 27, 1963): 887-891.

**7851. Toward, L.M.** *A Case For a Family Court in Nova Scotia.* L.M. Toward. Halifax: Dalhousie University, c1958.
  Thesis (LL.M.)–Dalhousie University, 1958.

**7852. Treen, Arthur** *Over Ninety Years of Reminiscences.* Arthur Treen. Hantsport, N.S.: Lancelot Press, 1985.

**7853. Tretheway, Eric** *"Marginal Lessons: a Memoir."* Eric Tretheway. Dalhousie Review 62, 3(Autumn 1982): 397-412.

**7854. Trueman, Stuart** *Don't Let Them Smell the Lobsters Cooking: the Lighter Side of Growing Up in the Maritimes a Long Time Ago.* Stuart Trueman. Toronto: McClelland and Stewart, c1982.

**7855. Tuck, Robert C.** *"The Charlottetown Boyhood of Robert Harris."* Robert C. Tuck. Island Magazine 3(Fall-Winter 1977): 7-12.

**7856. Tuck, Robert C.** *Gothic Dreams: the Life and Times of a Canadian Architect, William Critchlow Harris, 1854-1913.* Robert C. Tuck. Toronto: Dundurn Press, c1978.

**7857. Tuck, Robert C., ed.** *The Island Family Harris: Letters of an Immigrant Family in British North America, 1856-1866.* Robert Critchlow Tuck, ed. Charlottetown: Ragweed Press, 1983.

**7858. Tupper, Carl** *"The Problem of Prematurity."* Carl Tupper. Canadian Medical Association Journal/Journal de l'Association medicale canadienne 83, 2(July 9, 1960): 51-53.

**7859. Tweedie, Robert A.** *On With the Dance: a New Brunswick Memoir 1935-1960.* R.A. Tweedie. [Fredericton]: New Ireland Press, 1986.

**7860. Uniacke, Richard John** *"Fatherly Advice in Post-Loyalist Nova Scotia: Richard John Uniake to His Son Norman."* Richard John Uniacke and C.B. Cuthbertson, ed. Acadiensis 9, 2(Spring 1980): 78-91.

**7861. Veinott, Rebecca** *"Child Custody and Divorce: a Nova Scotia Study, 1866-1910."* Rebecca Veinott. Toronto: University of Toronto, 1990. In Essays in the History of Canadian Law, v.3 Nova Scotia, pp. 273-302. Edited by Philip Girard and Jim Phillips.

**7862. Vogt, Mary Isobel** *The Juvenile Delinquent and His Offence.* Mary Isobel Vogt. Halifax: Maritime School of Social Work, c1963.
Thesis (M.S.W.)--Maritime School of Social Work, 1963.

**7863. Waite, P.B.** *Lord of Point Grey: Larry MacKenzie of U.B.C.* P.B. Waite. Vancouver: University of British Columbia Press, 1987.

**7864. Wallis, W.D.** *The Micmac Indians of Eastern Canada.* W.D. Wallis and Ruth S. Wallis. Minneapolis: University of Minnesota Press, 1955.

**7865. Waterston, Elizabeth** *"Lucy Maud Montgomery: 1874-1942."* Elizabeth Waterston. Guelph: Canadian Children's Press, c1976. In L.M. Montgomery: an Assessment, pp. 9-26. Edited by John R. Sorfleet.

**7866. Weale, David** *"The Emigrant: Beginnings in Scotland, 1."* David Weale. Island Magazine 16(Fall/Winter 1984): 15-22.

**7867. Webb, Jean F.** *"Infant and Preschool Health."* Jean F. Webb. Canadian Journal of Public Health 38, 12(Dec. 1948): 486-489.

**7868. Webb, Jean F.** *"Nutritional Aspects of a School Health Study in Marysville, New Brunswick."* Jean F. Webb and Florence B. Swan. Canadian Journal of Public Health 37, 10(Oct. 1946): 399-406.

**7869. Webster, John Clarence** *The Distressed Maritimes: a Study of Educational and Cultural Conditions in Canada.* John Clarence Webster. Toronto: Ryerson Press, 1926.

**7870. Welch, J.P.** *"The Distribution of Height and Weight and the Influence of Socioeconomic Factors, in a Sample of Eastern Canadian Urban School Children."* J.P. Welch, E.J. Winsor and S.M. Mackintosh. Canadian Journal of Public Health 62, 5(Sept.-Oct. 1971): 373-381.

**7871. Whalen, James M.** *""Almost as Bad as Ireland": the Experience of the Irish Famine Immigrant in Canada, Saint John, 1847."* James M. Whalen. Toronto: Celtic Arts of Canada, 1988. In The Untold Story: the Irish in Canada, v.1, pp. 154-168. Edited by Robert O'Driscoll and Lorna Reynolds.

**7872. Whalen, James M.** *"The Nineteenth Century Almshouse System in Saint John County."* James M. Whalen. Histoire sociale/Social History 7(Apr. 1971): 5-27.

**7873. Whalen, James M.** *"Social Welfare in New Brunswick, 1784-1900."* James. M. Whalen. Acadiensis 2, 1(Autumn 1972): 54-64.
Introduction by Brian D. Tennyson.

**7874. White, George M.** *"A Case of Cyclops."* Geo. M. White and Thomas A. Foster. Canadian Medical Association Journal 72, 3(Feb. 1, 1955): 213-214.

**7875. Whitebone, Russ** *Showman: the Russ Whitebone Story.* Russ Whitebone. Fredericton: Fiddlehead Poetry Books and Goose Lane Editions, c1986.

**7876. Whitehead, Paul C.** *Drug Use Among Adolescent Students in Halifax.* Paul C. Whitehead. Rev ed. [Halifax?]: Youth Agency, Province of Nova Scotia, 1970.

**7877. Whitehead, Paul C.** *"The Epidemiology of Drug Use in a Canadian City at Two Points in Time: Halifax, 1969-1970."* Paul C. Whitehead. Toronto: Holt, Rinehart and Winston of Canada, [1971]. In Critical Issues in Canadian Society, pp. 520-533. Edited by Craig L. Boydell, Carl F. Grindstaff and Paul C. Whitehead.

**7878. Whitehead, Paul C.** *"Head or Brain? Drug Use and Academic Performance."* Paul C. Whitehead. Toronto: Holt, Rinehart and Winston, 1971. In Social Process and Institution: the Canadian Case, pp. 352-363. Edited by James E. Gallagher.

**7879. Widdowson, John David Allison** *Aspects of Traditional Verbal Control: Threats and Threatening Figures in Newfoundland Folklore.* John David Allison Widdowson. St. John's: Memorial University, 1972. (CTM no. 43193) Thesis (Ph.D.)--Memorial University, 1972.

**7880. Widdowson, John David Allison** *"The Function of Threats in Newfoundland Folklore."* J.D.A. Widdowson. Toronto: McClelland and Stewart Ltd., 1985. In Explorations in Canadian Folklore, pp. 277-288. Edited by Edith Fowke and Carole H. Carpenter.

**7881. Widdowson, John David Allison** *If You Don't Be Good: Verbal Social Control in Newfoundland.* J.D.A. Widdowson. St. John's: Institute of Social and Economic Research, Memorial University of Newfoundland, 1977.

**7882. Williams, Eugene Edward** *Nova Scotia Association for the Advancement of Coloured People: a Historical Review of the Organization and Its Role in the Area of Education.* Eugene Edward Williams. Halifax: Dalhousie University, c1969. Thesis (M.S.W.)--Dalhousie University, 1969.

**7883. Williams, Relief** *"Poor Relief and Medicine in Nova Scotia, 1749-1783."* Relief Williams. Collections of the Nova Scotia Historical Society 24(1938): 40-45.

**7884. Williams, Relief** *"Poor Relief and Medicine in Nova Scotia, 1749-1783 (Part I)."* Relief Williams. Canadian Welfare Summary 15, 2(July 1939): 22-30.

**7885. Williams, Relief** *"Poor Relief and Medicine in Nova Scotia, 1749-1783 (Part II)."* Relief Williams. Canadian Welfare Summary 15, 3(Sept. 1939): 23-30.

**7886. Williamson, Moncrieff** *Island Painter: the Life of Robert Harris.* Moncrieff Williamson. Charlottetown: Ragweed Press, 1983.

**7887. Williamson, Moncrieff** *Robert Harris, 1849-1919: an Unconventional Biography.* Moncrieff Williamson. Toronto: McClelland and Stewart, 1972.

**7888. Wilson, Myron** *"The New Brunswick Slave Trade."* Myron Wilson. Weekend Magazine (June 8, 1974): 8-10.

**7889. Wood, Earle William Harold** *The Taylor-Spence Drive Theory on a Competitive Versus Non-competitive Paired-associate Learning Task.* Earle William Harold Wood. Vancouver: University of British Columbia, 1970. Thesis (M.A.)--University of British Columbia, 1970.

**7890. Woodcock, George** *Hugh MacLennan.* George Woodcock. Toronto: Copp Clark, c1969.

**7891. Worthen, Robert H., ed.** *For the Love of the Sea: the Autobiography of Captain Robert H. Worthon.* Robert H. Worthen and Marion L. Worthen, eds. Hantsport, N.S.: Lancelot Press, 1987.

**7892. Wright, Esther Clark** *Grandmother's Child: the Life of Harriet H.R. Clark.* Esther Clark Wright. [Ottawa]: The Author, c1959.

**7893. Wright, Mary Ellen** *"Unnatural Mothers: Infanticide in Halifax, 1850-1875."* Mary Ellen Wright. Nova Scotia Historical Review 7, 2(1987): 13-29.

**7894. Young, Alan R.** *Ernest Buckler.* Alan R. Young. Toronto: McClelland and Stewart, c1976.

**7895. Young, E. Gordon** *"Boric Acid as a Poison: Report of Six Accidental Deaths in Infants."* E. Gordon Young, R.P. Smith and O.C. MacIntosh. Canadian Medical Association Journal 61, 5(Nov. 1949): 447-450.

7896. Young. R.C. *"Familial Adrenal Phaeochromocytoma with Sustained Hypertension."* R.C. Young and W.A. Murray. Canadian Medical Association Journal 72, 7(Apr. 1, 1955): 503-509.

7897. Young, R.C. *"Post-traumatic Streptococcus Viridans Meningitis."* R.C. Young and W.A. Murray. Canadian Medical Association Journal 77, 3(Aug. 1, 1957): 223-224.

# Northern Canada

7898. Acheson, Ann W. *"The Kutchin Family: Past and Present."* Ann W. Acheson. Toronto: McGraw-Hill Ryerson Ltd., c1980. In Canadian Families: Ethnic Variations, pp. 241-265. Edited by K. Ishwaran.

7899. Adamson, J.D. *"Poliomyelitis in the Arctic."* J.D. Adamson, J.P. Moody, A.F.W. Peart, R.A. Smillie, J.C. Wilt and W.J. Wood. Canadian Medical Association Journal 61, 4(Oct. 1949): 339-348.

7900. Beamish, W.E. *"Laurence-Moon-Biedl Syndrome in Eskimos."* W.E. Beamish. Canadian Medical Association Journal/Journal de l'Association medicale canadienne 81, 9(Nov. 1, 1959): 734-736.

7901. Berton, Pierre *Starting Out, 1920-1947.* Pierre Berton. Toronto: McClelland and Stewart, 1987.

7902. Black, L. *"Morbidity, Mortality and Medical Care in the Keewatin Area of the Central Arctic, 1967."* L. Black. Canadian Medical Association Journal/Journal de l'Association medicale canadienne 101, 10(Nov. 15, 1969): 577-581.

7903. Bork, Egon *"Children in the North."* Egon Bork et al. Beaver 293, 3(Winter 1962): 40-47.

7904. Brant, Charles S. *"Education for Canadian Eskimos."* Charles S. Brant. Toronto: Gage Educational Publishing, 1977. In Education, Change and Society: a Sociology of Canadian Education, pp. 173-182. Edited by Richard A. Carlton, Louise A. Colley and Neil J. MacKinnon.

7905. Briggs, Jean L. *Never in Anger: Portrait of an Eskimo Family.* Jean L. Briggs. Cambridge, Mass.: Harvard University Press, 1970.

7906. Brown, Jennifer S.H. *"A Colony of Very Useful Hands."* Jennifer S.H. Brown. Beaver 307, 4(Spring 1977): 39-45.

7907. Bruemmer, Fred *Children of the North.* Fred Bruemmer. Montreal: Optimum Publishing Company, c1979.

7908. Bullen, Edward Lester *An Historical Study of the Education of the Indians of Teslin, Yukon Territory.* Edward Lester Bullen. Edmonton: University of Alberta, 1968.
Thesis (M.Ed.)--University of Alberta, 1968.

7909. Burch Jr., Ernest S. *Authority, Aid and Affection: the Structure of Eskimo Kin Relationships.* Ernest S. Burch Jr. Chicago: University of Chicago, 1966.
Thesis (Ph.D.)--University of Chicago, 1966.

7910. Camsell, Charles *Son of the North.* Charles Camsell. Toronto: Ryerson Press, 1954.

7911. Canadian Association of School Superintendents and Inspectors *Education North of 60.* The Association. Toronto: The Ryerson Press, c1965.

7912. **Canadian Welfare Council** *"Across Canada: First Eskimo Day School."* Canadian Welfare Council. Canadian Welfare 24, 4(Sept. 1948): 34.

7913. **Christian, Edgar** *Death in the Barren Ground.* Edgar Christian with George Whalley, ed. [Ottawa?]: Oberon Press, 1980.
    Originally published in 1937 as Unflinching: a Diary of Tragic Adventure.

7914. **Coates, Kenneth Stephen** *""Betwixt and Between": the Anglican Church and the Children of the Carcross (Chooutla) Residential School, 1911-1954."* Kenneth Coates. BC Studies 64(Winter 1984-1985): 27-47.

7915. **Coates, Kenneth Stephen** *"A Very Imperfect Means of Education: Indian Day Schools in the Yukon Territory, 1890-1955."* Ken Coates. Vancouver: University of British Columbia Press, 1986. In Indian Education in Canada, Volume 1: the Legacy, pp. 132-149. Edited by Jean Barman, Yvonne Hebert and Don McCaskill.

7916. **Cram, John M.** *"Native Education Programs in the Canadian North."* J.M. Cram. Journal of Canadian Studies/Revue d'etudes canadiennes 21, 2(Dec. 1986): 47-56.

7917. **Cruikshank, Julie** *Athapaskan Women: Lives and Legends.* Julie Cruikshank. Ottawa: National Museums of Canada, 1979.

7918. **Cruikshank, Julie** *"Becoming a Woman in Athapaskan Society: Changing Traditions on the Upper Yukon River."* Julie Cruikshank. Western Canadian Journal of Anthropology 5, 2(1975): 1-14.

7919. **Cruikshank, Julie** *Life Lived Like a Story: Cultural Constructions of Life History by Tagish and Tutchone Women.* Julia Margaret Cruikshank. Vancouver: University of British Columbia, 1987. Thesis (Ph.D.)--University of British Columbia, 1987.

7920. **de Caraffe, Marc** *Teaching in Mission Country: the Schools of the Northwest Territories and the Yukon Prior to 1930.* Marc de Caraffe. Ottawa: Parks Canada, 1983.

7921. **Douglas, W.O.** *"Last Resort."* W.O. Douglas. Beaver 303, 1(Summer 1972): 52-55.

7922. **Dunn, Willie** *"Northern "Justice"."* Willie Dunn. Western Canadian Journal of Anthropology 1, 1(1969): 119-120.

7923. **Fainberg, L.** *"On the Question of the Eskimo Kinship System."* L. Fainberg. Arctic Anthropology 4, 1(1967): 244-256.

7924. **Forsyth, Robert** *"Homesteading on the Carrot River."* Robert Forsyth. Beaver 302, 1(Summer 1971): 53-57.

7925. **Franklyn, G.J.** *A Comparative Empirical Study of the Relationship Between Alienation from School and Academic Achievement.* Gaston J. Franklyn. Ottawa: University of Ottawa. 1971.
    Thesis (Ph.D.)--University of Ottawa, 1971.

7926. **Freeman, Milton M.R.** *"Social and Ecological Analysis of Systematic Female Infanticide Among the Netsilik Eskimo."* Milton M.R. Freeman. American Anthropologist 73(1971): 1011-1018.

7927. **Freeman, Minnie Aodla** *Life Among the Qallunaat.* Minnie Aodla Freeman. Edmonton: Hurtig Publishers, c1978.

7928. **French, Alice** *"My Name is Masak."* Alice French. Beaver 307, 2(Autumn 1976): 28-31.

7929. **Frideres, James S.** *"Culture, Education and Ethnicity: a Case Study of the Canadian North."* James S. Frideres. Regina: Canadian Plains Research Center, 1978. In Ethnic Canadians: Culture and Education, pp. 257-268. Edited by Martin L. Kovacs.

7930. **Gimpel, Charles** *"Journey from the Igloo."* Charles Gimpel. Beaver 289, 3(Winter 1958): 12-19.

7931. **Glassford, Robert Gerald** *"Organization of Games and Adaptive Strategies of the Canadian Eskimo."* Robert Gerald Glassford. Champaign, Ill.: Stripes Pub. Co., 1970. In The Cross Cultural Analysis of Sports and Games. Edited by Gunther Luschen.

7932. **Harring, Sidney L.** *"The Rich Men of the Country: Canadian Law in the Land of the Copper Inuit, 1914-1930."* Sidney L. Harring. Ottawa Law Review/Revue de droit d'Ottawa 21, 1(1989): 1-64.

7933. **Harrington, Richard** *The Inuit: Life as it Was.* Richard Harrington. Edmonton: Hurtig Publishers, c1981.

7934. **Helmericks, Constance** *Down The Wild River North.* Constance Helmericks. Boston: Little, Brown and Co., c1968.

7935. **Hinds, Margery** *School House in the Arctic.* Margery Hinds. London, Eng.: Geoffrey Bles, c1958.

7936. **Hinds, Margery** *"School in the High Arctic."* Margery Hinds. Beaver 290, 2(Autumn 1959): 13-17.

7937. **Hoare, Catherine** *"Herschel Island to Aklavik."* Catherine Hoare. Beaver 269, 3(Dec. 1938): 42-45.

7938. **Hobart, Charles W.** *"Eskimo Education, Danish and Canadian: a Comparison."* Charles W. Hobart. Canadian Review of Sociology and Anthropology/Revue canadienne de sociologie et d'anthropologie 3, 1(Jan. 1966): 47-67.

7939. **Hobart, Charles W.** *"Eskimo Education in the Arctic."* Charles W. Hobart. Canadian Review of Sociology and Anthropology/Revue canadienne de sociologie et d'anthropologie 7, 1(Jan. 1970): 49-60.

7940. **Hobart, Charles W.** *"The Influence of the School on Acculturation with Special Reference to Greenland."* Charles W. Hobart. Journal of Educational Thought 2, 1(Apr. 1968): 97-116.

7941. **Hobart, Charles W.** *"Some Consequences of Residential Schooling of Eskimos in the Canadian Arctic."* Charles W. Hobart. Arctic Anthropology 6, 2(1970): 123-135.

7942. **Honigmann, John** *"The Eskimo of Frobisher Bay."* John Honigmann and Irma Honigmann. Scarborough, Ont.: Prentice-Hall, 1971. In Native Peoples, pp. 55-74. Edited by Jean Leonard Elliott.

7943. **Howard, Philip G.** *"History of the Use of Dene Languages in Education in the Northwest Territories."* Philip G. Howard. Canadian Journal of Native Education 10, 2(Winter 1983): 1-18.

7944. **Hunt, L.A.C.O.** *Rebels, Rascals and Royalty: the Colourful North of Laco Hunt.* L.A.C.O. Hunt with Barbara Hunt, ed. Yellowknife, N.W.T.: Outcrop, c1983.

7945. **Ipellie, Alootook** *"Frobisher Bay Childhood."* Alootook Ipellie. Beaver 310, 4(Spring 1980): 4-11.

7946. **Jones, Henry** *"Mackenzie River Days."* Henry Jones. Beaver 276, 4(Mar. 1946): 22-27.

7947. **Jorden, Dennis** *"Survey of Blood Grouping an Rh Factor in the Eskimos of the Eastern Arctic, 1945."* Dennis Jorden. Canadian Medical Association Journal 54, 5(May 1946): 429-434.

7948. **King, Alfred Richard** *A Case Study of an Indian Residential School.* Alfred Richard King. Stanford: Stanford University, 1964. Thesis (Ph.D.)–Stanford University, 1964.

7949. **King, Richard** *The School at Mopass: a Problem of Identity.* A. Richard King. New York: Holt, Rinehart and Winston, c1967.

7950. **Klugie, Garry** *"The Poverty and the Poetry: a Native Indian Woman's Life History."* Gary Klugie. Canadian Woman Studies/Cahiers de la femme 4, 2(Winter 1982): 39-41.

7951. **Lent, D. Geneva** *"Boyhood at Oxford House."* D. Geneva Lent. Beaver 292, 4(Spring 1962): 47-51.

7952. **Lesage, Jean** *"Education of Eskimos."* Jean Lesage. Canadian Education 12, 3(June 1956): 44-48.

7953. **Lewis, Brian Wyndham** *The Teaching of English to Canadian Eskimos.* Brian Wyndham Lewis. Toronto: University of Toronto, 1971. Thesis (M.A.)--University of Toronto, 1971.

7954. **Lubart, Joseph M.** *Psychodynamic Problems of Adaptation, Mackenzie Delta Eskimos: a Preliminary Study.* Joseph M. Lubart. Ottawa: Northern Science Research Group, Department of Indian Affairs and Northern Development, 1969.

7955. **Lyall, Ernie** *An Arctic Man: Sixty-five Years in Canada's North.* Ernie Lyall. Edmonton: Hurtig Publishers, c1979.

7956. **MacArthur, Russell S.** *"Assessing Intellectual Potential of Native Canadian Pupils: a Summary."* R.S. MacArthur. Alberta Journal of Educational Research 14, 2(June 1968): 115-122.

7957. **MacArthur, Russell S.** *"Some Cognitive Abilities of Eskimo, White and Indian-Metis Pupils Aged 9-12 Years."* R.S. MacArthur. Canadian Journal of Behavioural Science/Revue canadienne de sciences du comportement 1, 1(Jan. 1969): 50-59.

**7958. MacArthur, Russell S.** *"Some Differential Abilities of Northern Canadian Native Youth."* Russell S. MacArthur. International Journal of Psychology 3(1968): 43-51.

**7959. Macdonald, Hugh A.** *Programmed Instruction with Teacher Participation: an Experiment in Teaching Fractions to Children Who Reside in the Northwest Territories.* Hugh A. Macdonald. Montreal: McGill University, 1965.
    Thesis (M.A.)–McGill University, 1965.

**7960. McElroy, Ann** *"The Negotiation of Sex-Role Identity in Eastern Arctic Culture Change."* Ann McElroy. Western Canadian Journal of Anthropology 6, 3(1976): 184-200.

**7961. Marriott, Richard** *"Arctic Bay Baby."* Richard Marriott. Beaver 270, 1(June 1939): 46.

**7962. Martin, David Standish** *A Study of Pupil Ethnocentrism Toward Pre-western Eskimo Culture in Relation To Certain Learner Variables and Instructional Materials.* David Standish Martin. Boston, Ma.: Boston College, c1971.
    Thesis (Ph.D.)--Boston College, 1971.

**7963. Mary-Rousseliere, Guy** *"Innurivat."* Guy Mary-Rousseliere. Beaver 289, 4(Spring 1959): 29-36.

**7964. Matas, Matthew** *"Brucellosis in an Eskimo Boy."* Matthew Matas and Cameron Corrigan. Canadian Medical Association Journal 69, 5(Nov. 1953): 531.

**7965. Matthiasson, John S.** *"But Teacher, Why Can't I Be a Hunter: Inuit Adolescence as a Double Bind Situation."* John S. Matthiasson. Toronto: McGraw-Hill Ryerson, c1979. In Childhood and Adolescence in Canada, pp. 72-82. Edited by K. Ishwaran.

**7966. Matthiasson, John S.** *"The Inuit Family: Past, Present and Future."* John S. Matthiasson. Toronto: McGraw-Hill Ryerson Ltd., c1980. In Canadian Families: Ethnic Variations, pp. 266-279. Edited by K. Ishwaran.

**7967. Mead, Margaret** *"The Eskimos."* Margaret Mead. Beaver 290, 2(Autumn 1959): 32-41.

**7968. Money, Anton** *This Was the North.* Anton Money with Ben East. New York: Crown Pub., 1975.

**7969. Musson, Patricia** *"Infant Mortality in Canada."* Patricia Musson. Toronto: Holt, Rinehart and Winston of Canada, c1972. In Critical Issues in Canadian Society, pp. 60-67. Edited by Craig L. Boydell, Carl F. Grindstaff and Paul C. Whitehead.

**7970. Nagler, F.P.** *"An Influenza Virus Epidemic at Victoria Island, N.W.T., Canada."* F.P. Nagler, C.E. van Rooyen and J.H. Sturdy. Canadian Journal of Public Health 40, 11(Nov. 1949): 457-465.

**7971. Norcross, J.W.** *"Children of the Northland."* J.W. Norcross, R.S. Crone, L.A. Learmonth, R.L. Sutton, Harvey Basset and A. Figgures. Beaver 272, 3(Dec. 1941): 14-15.

**7972. Nuligak** *I. Nuligak.* Nuligak, edited and translated by Maurice Metayer. Markham, Ontario: Pocket Books, [1975], c1966.

**7973. Peart, A.F.W.** *"An Outbreak of Poliomyelitis in Canadian Eskimos in Wintertime: Epidemiological Feature."* A.F.W. Peart. Canadian Journal of Public Health 40, 10(Oct. 1949): 405-417.

**7974. Peary, Stafford** *"Child of the Arctic."* Stafford Peary and Marie Ahnighito. Beaver 275, 2(Sept. 1944): 8-13.

**7975. Pitseolak** *Pitseolak: Pictures Out of My Life.* Pitseolak as interviewed by Dorothy Harley Eber. Montreal: Design Collaborative Books in Association with Oxford University Press, Toronto, [1971?].

**7976. Pitseolak, Peter** *People From Our Side.* Peter Pitseolak as interviewed by Dorothy Harley Eber and translated by Ann Meekitjuk Hanson. Edmonton: Hurtig Publishers, 1975.

**7977. Ramsay, A.A.W.** *"Letters from Letitia Hargrave."* A.A.W. Ramsay. Beaver 271, 2(Sept. 1940): 37-39.

**7978. Reich, Lee Campbell** *Equivalence Concepts in Cross-Cultural Perspective: a Developmental Comparison of Eskimo and White Children.* Lee Campbell Reich. Cambridge, Ma.: Harvard University, c1969.
    Thesis (Ph.D.)–Harvard University, 1969.

**7979. Remie, Cornelius H.** *"Flying Like a Butterfly, or Knud Rasmussen Among the Netsilingmuit."* Cornelius H. Remie. Etudes Inuit Studies 12, 1-2(1988): 101-127.

**7980. Remie, Cornelius H.** *"Towards a New Perspective on Netjilik Inuit Female Infanticide."* Cornelius Remie. Etudes Inuit Studies 9, 1(1985): 67-76.

**7981. Schaefer, O.** *"Pre- and Post-Natal Growth Acceleration and Increased Sugar Consumption in Canadian Eskimos."* O. Schaefer. Canadian Medical Association Journal/Journal de l'Association medicale canadienne 103, 10(Nov. 10, 1970): 1059-1068.

**7982. Schrire, Carmel** *"Arctic Infanticide Revisited."* Carmel Schrire and William Lee Steiger. Etudes Inuit Studies 5, 1(1981): 111-117.

**7983. Sellers, F.J.** *"The Incidence of Anaemia in Infancy and Early Childhood Among Central Arctic Eskimos."* F.J. Sellers, W.J. Wood and J.A. Hildes. Canadian Medical Association Journal/Journal de l'Association medicale canadienne 81, 8(Oct. 15, 1959): 656-657.

**7984. Sissons, John Howard** *Judge of the Far North, the Memoirs of Jack Sissons.* John Howard Sissons. Toronto: McClelland and Stewart, c1968.

**7985. Steinmetz, N.** *"Medical Care of Eskimo Children."* N. Steinmetz. Canadian Nurse 63, 3(Mar. 1967): 29-31.

**7986.** *Stories From Pangnirtung.* Edmonton: Hurtig Publishers, c1976.

**7987. Sutton, R.L.** *"Eskimo Children."* R.L. Sutton. Beaver 271, 2(Sept. 1940): 18-19.

**7988. Taylor, Phyllis** *"Tales from the Delta."* Phyllis Taylor. Beaver 284, 1(June 1953): 22-25.

**7989. Tedjuk, Joe** *"Times of Sorrow, Times of Joy."* Joe Tedjuk. Beaver 66, 1(Jan.-Feb. 1986): 28-38.

**7990. Teicher, Morton I.** *"Adoption Practice Among the Eskimos on Southhampton Island."* Morton I. Teicher. Canadian Welfare 29, 2(June 1953): 32-37.

**7991. Thrasher, Anthony Apakark** *Thrasher ... Skid Row Eskimo.* Anthony Apakark Thrasher in collaboration with Gerard Deagle and Alan Mettrick. Toronto: Griffin House, c1976.

**7992. Tompkins, Robert Gilmore** *The Youth of Yellowknife: a Study of the Social Organization of an Adolescent Community.* Robert Gilmore Tompkins. Edmonton: University of Alberta, 1969. Thesis (M.A.)--University of Alberta, 1969.

**7993. Vallee, Frank G.** *"Kabloona and Eskimo: Social Control."* F.G. Vallee. Toronto: Holt, Rinehart and Winston of Canada Ltd., c1971. In Critical Issues in Canadian Society, pp. 238-254. Edited by Craig L. Boydell, Carl F. Grindstaff and Paul C. Whitehead.

**7994. Van Den Steenhoven, Geert** *"Ennadai Lake People, 1955."* Geert Van Den Steenhoven. Beaver 298, 3(Winter 1967): 12-18.

**7995. Webster, J.H.** *"Boy Hero."* J.H. Webster. Beaver 278, 1(June 1947): 37.

**7996. West, Lloyd W.** *Assessing Intellectual Abilities with a Minimum of Cultural Bias for Two Samples of Metis and Inuit Children.* Lloyd Wilbert West. Edmonton: University of Alberta, 1962. Thesis (M.Ed.)--University of Alberta, 1962.

**7997. West, Lloyd W.** *"An Evaluation of Selected Intelligence Tests for Two Samples of Metis and Indian Children."* L.W. West and R.S. MacArthur. Alberta Journal of Educational Research 10, 1(Mar. 1964): 17-27.

**7998. Wilkinson, D.** *Land of the Long Day.* Doug Wilkinson. Toronto: Clarke, Irwin and Company Limited, c1955.

# Subject Index

Biographical Accounts 4045, 4048, 4050, 4051,
4052, 4053, 4064, 4098, 4099, 4103, 4105, 4106,
4107, 4108, 4109, 4111, 4112, 4118, 4119, 4134,
4142, 4144, 4146, 4153, 4156, 4158, 4160, 4162,
4165, 4172, 4181, 4202, 4208, 4210, 4234, 4237,
4257, 4264, 4285, 4288, 4298, 4299, 4302, 4303,
4307, 4308, 4316, 4318, 4324, 4328, 4329, 4330,
4332, 4335, 4336, 4338, 4340, 4348, 4355, 4365,
4372, 4375, 4376, 4377, 4384, 4385, 4394, 4395,
4396, 4403, 4404, 4405, 4408, 4409, 4410, 4411,
4413, 4418, 4419, 4422, 4430, 4436, 4437, 4449,
4452, 4453, 4463, 4464, 4467, 4468, 4476, 4481,
4483, 4485, 4487, 4492, 4493, 4494, 4497, 4498,
4502, 4511, 4512, 4518, 4519, 4522, 4524, 4525,
4528, 4533, 4535, 4539, 4540, 4542, 4545, 4553,
4556, 4557, 4566, 4569, 4570, 4580, 4581, 4588,
4590, 4591, 4592, 4601, 4608, 4627, 4637, 4641,
4642, 4643, 4660, 4661, 4665, 4667, 4678, 4693,
4701, 4702, 4712, 4713, 4714, 4715, 4717, 4718,
4721, 4725, 4726, 4727, 4728, 4729, 4730, 4735,
4737, 4738, 4740, 4749, 4753, 4754, 4759, 4771,
4774, 4775, 4776, 4797, 4798, 4799, 4800, 4812,
4819, 4820, 4828, 4829, 4835, 4836, 4837, 4839,
4845, 4851, 4853, 4855, 4867, 4868, 4873, 4876,
4882, 4884, 4901, 4909, 4920, 4923, 4924, 4925,
4928, 4929, 4930, 4937, 4938, 4942, 4943, 4944,
4945, 4948, 4952, 4955, 4976, 5005, 5089, 5099,
5146, 5155, 5171, 5184, 5205, 5226, 5260, 5266,
5280, 5282, 5287, 5380, 5388, 5402, 5415, 5421,
5437, 5441, 5443, 5459, 5460, 5464, 5470, 5471,
5476, 5479, 5532, 5533, 5540, 5563, 5590, 5591,
5592, 5594, 5597, 5607, 5620, 5623, 5631, 5639,
5647, 5653, 5654, 5678, 5693, 5707, 5714, 5715,
5716, 5756, 5761, 5769, 5782, 5785, 5786, 5787,
5818, 5835, 5848, 5854, 5865, 5867, 5904, 5905,
5909, 5910, 5922, 5932, 5946, 5951, 5952, 5955,
5957, 5958, 5970, 5983, 5985, 5999, 6056, 6059,
6082, 6093, 6103, 6105, 6113, 6119, 6121, 6168,
6169, 6195, 6208, 6250, 6251, 6282, 6290, 6299,
6312, 6335, 6342, 6362, 6363, 6364, 6380, 6384,
6391, 6392, 6398, 6406, 6465, 6482, 6484, 6499,
6522, 6587, 6593, 6614, 6634, 6643, 6654, 6655,
6656, 6658, 6716, 6776, 6785, 6797, 6803, 6825,
6827, 6833, 6875, 6884, 6888, 6897, 6900, 6920,
6928, 6929, 6934, 6936, 6943, 6955, 6966, 6994,
7026, 7035, 7059, 7067, 7070, 7098, 7108, 7109,
7116, 7178, 7185, 7192, 7198, 7203, 7206, 7240,
7244, 7296, 7301, 7317, 7335, 7352, 7353, 7359,
7370, 7375, 7392, 7395, 7396, 7424, 7426, 7435,
7441, 7442, 7446, 7452, 7454, 7465, 7466, 7476,
7478, 7503, 7504, 7505, 7514, 7518, 7533, 7540,
7555, 7564, 7569, 7576, 7577, 7579, 7587, 7592,
7596, 7605, 7607, 7608, 7615, 7617, 7632, 7633,
7640, 7641, 7643, 7653, 7658, 7676, 7691, 7702,
7713, 7714, 7715, 7716, 7719, 7733, 7763, 7765,
7782, 7785, 7787, 7790, 7796, 7799, 7804, 7805,
7814, 7815, 7828, 7830, 7846, 7855, 7856, 7863,
7865, 7866, 7886, 7887, 7890, 7894, 7917, 7924,
7928, 7950, 7968, 7979,
Birchard, Isaac James 5139,
Bird, Henry 7077,
Bird, Lilah Smith 7451,
Birney, Earle 19, 646, 1584, 2994, 3423,
Birt, Louisa 159, 6180,
Birth Control 5, 86, 688, 800, 1023, 1358, 2158,
2821, 3615, 4317, 4677, 5711, 5757, 7389,
Birth Experience 185, 299, 303, 311, 430, 490,
705, 888, 1382, 1523, 1735, 1968, 2197, 2202,
2820, 2832, 3086, 3113, 3227, 3363, 3939, 3966,
4342, 4371, 4560, 4561, 4599, 4677, 5484, 5621,
5786, 6064, 6117, 6138, 6145, 6657, 6679, 6708,
6800, 6866, 6994, 7064, 7170, 7219, 7349, 7438,
7528, 7726, 7727,
Birth Order 115, 1877, 4123, 5593,
Birt's Distributing Home of Knowlton,
Quebec 159, 5018, 6180,
Bishop, Billy 6342,
Bishop Pinkham College of Calgary 3621,
Bishop's College 5607, 6947,

Bissett, Bill 1720,
Bitney Family 4545,
Black, Conrad 6634,
Blackfoot 2289, 3513, 3562, 3845, 4090, 4178,
4438, 4706, 4710, 4868, 4959,
Blacks 68, 182, 622, 738, 822, 1000, 1056, 1067,
1068, 1260, 2064, 2147, 2148, 2483, 2628, 2724,
2983, 3222, 3641, 4662, 5131, 5293, 5375, 5407,
5659, 5800, 5945, 6235, 7036, 7123, 7229, 7445,
7469, 7496, 7498, 7510, 7552, 7580, 7699, 7706,
7739, 7797, 7846, 7882,
Blaise, Clark 1720,
Blake, Edward 5146,
Blanchard, Jotham 7815,
Blatzian Theory 171, 5125, 5148, 5151, 5152,
7199,
Blood 3687, 3845, 4090, 4150, 4178, 4362, 4959,
Blye, Allan 3902,
Boarding Schools 106, 207, 243, 244, 775, 1449,
1755, 2239, 2240, 2241, 2243, 2245, 2246, 2265,
2404, 2489, 2584, 2585, 2818, 2825, 2897, 2964,
3097, 3262, 3832, 4155, 4489, 4511, 4839, 4859,
5210, 5540, 5692, 6094, 6184, 6515, 6834, 6900,
6944, 6995, 7565, 7991,
Bombardier, J. Armand 6833,
Bond, Cortney C.J. 7455,
Bonding 142, 614, 643, 905, 1293, 1348, 2267,
6996,
Borenstein, Sam 5167,
Bossy, Mike 5171,
Boswell, Helen 5172,
Bourgeoys, Marguerite 5282,
Bowmanville Boys' School 5093, 5342, 6684,
7306,
Boy Scouts 113, 201, 202, 203, 204, 671, 746,
1288, 1687, 1991, 2018, 2698, 3083, 3264, 3266,
3270, 3273, 3274, 3285, 3286, 3287, 3292, 3304,
3316, 3327, 3369, 3382, 3384, 3413, 3448, 3472,
3504, 3551, 3602, 3604, 3605, 3619, 3625, 3661,
3675, 3680, 3684, 3686, 3701, 3720, 3723, 3732,
3762, 3763, 3797, 3799, 3803, 3805, 3834, 3856,
3858, 3872, 3877, 3904, 3910, 3930, 3934, 3938,
3955, 3968, 4004, 4045, 4048, 4052, 4053, 4098,
4101, 4105, 4107, 4108, 4118, 4142, 4144, 4153,
4158, 4160, 4165, 4172, 4202, 4288, 4298, 4299,
4316, 4329, 4332, 4335, 4348, 4376, 4377, 4384,
4396, 4403, 4405, 4413, 4419, 4422, 4423, 4430,
4436, 4452, 4464, 4467, 4493, 4511, 4512, 4517,
4518, 4519, 4522, 4524, 4533, 4535, 4540, 4553,
4557, 4580, 4581, 4592, 4643, 4660, 4702, 4717,
4721, 4728, 4735, 4771, 4820, 4829, 4835, 4851,
4867, 4868, 4876, 4891, 4900, 4923, 4938, 4944,
4951, 4955, 5070, 5490, 6294, 6419,
Boyd, Denny 2292,
Boyd, Helen 3457,
Boyer, Cedric M. 2293,
Boyle, David 6195,
Boyle, Harry J. 207,
Boys' and Girls' Clubs 3284, 3285, 3427, 4044,
4101, 4118, 4396, 4868,
Boys' and Girls' Clubs of Alberta 3605,
Boys' and Girls' Clubs of Manitoba 3858,
4303, 4384, 4413, 4557,
Boys' and Girls' Clubs of Winnipeg 360,
Boys' Clubs of Canada 991, 2164, 2826, 6151,
6170,
Boys' Farm and Training School
(Shawbridge) 6083,
Brander, Lorraine 2295,
Brant Family 6120, 6121,
British North America Act, 1867 (U.K.)
3355,
Brock, David 2322, 2708,
Brock, William Rees 5226,
Bronchitis 2236, 2372, 5358, 7756,
Brooks, Allan 1184,
Brooks, Martha 3475,
Brown, Annora 3479,
Brown, Irene 2323,

# Name Index

Chown, Diana 5429,
Christensen, Rolf Buschardt 2390,
Christian, Edgar 7913,
Christine, Reverend Sister 7509,
Chun, Theresa 5430,
Chunn, Dorothy E. 548, 5431,
Church, E.J.M. 549, 550,
Churchbridge History Committee 4775,
Churchill, Stacy 5432, 5433,
Chute, A.L. 5051, 5434, 6599, 6882,
Cipywnyk, Sonia 551, 3613,
Claman, A. David 2391, 2820, 3227,
Clark, C.S. 5435,
Clark, Cecil 2392,
Clark, Donna 552,
Clark, Earl Arthur 553,
Clark, Eina M. 7086,
Clark, James Boyd 3614,
Clark, James W. 554, 1118,
Clark, Mary Nora 2230,
Clark, Ronald B. 1935,
Clark, Ruth 555,
Clark, S. Barbara 7510,
Clark, Samuel Delbert 556,
Clark, William Lund 5436,
Clarke, Barrie A. 5437,
Clarke, C.K. 557, 558, 5438,
Clarke, C.W. 4312,
Clarke, David A. 2978,
Clarke, Emma deV. 559, 560,
Clarke, Eric Kent 5439, 5440,
Clarke, F.R.C. 5441,
Clarke, G.B. 3615,
Clarke, L.A. 6288,
Clarke, Mairin 5442, 6238,
Clarke, S.C.T. 561, 3616,
Clarke, Sandra 562,
Claxton, M. 2393, 2394, 2395,
Clayton, Deidra 5443,
Cleary, T. Emmett 6997,
Cleaveau, J.C. 6254,
Clegg, William Crispin 5444,
Cleghorn, I.M. 39,
Cleghorn, Joan 5445,
Cleland, C.A. 563,
Clement, Josie 197,
Clerk, Gabrielle 564,
Clery, Val, ed. 2668, 5815,
Clifford, Howard 565, 566, 567,
Clifton, Rodney A. 3617,
Climenhaga, Clarence Eugena 3618,
Cline, C.A. 7058,
Clode, M. 6503,
Cloutier, A.M. 5691,
Clow, Caroline 6892, 7042,
Clyke, Emily 5446,
Clyne, Dorothy 2396,
Coady, C.J. 2900, 3050,
Coady, Henry 5447, 7840,
Coady, Mary Frances 568,
Coaldale Historical Society 3619,
Coalhurst History Society 3620,
Coates, Kenneth Stephen 7914, 7915,
Coats, Douglas 3621,
Cobb, Cathron 6449,
Cobbin, Jack Macdonald 2397,
Coburn, John 569,
Cochrane, E. George 5448,
Cochrane, Jean 570, 5449,
Cochrane, Jessie 571,
Cochrane, W.A. 572, 670, 7511, 7512,
Cocking, Clive, ed. 7079,
Cocks, A.W. 2398,
Coffey, J.E. 7513,
Coggin, C.J. 5450,
Cogswell, Fred 7514,
Cohen, J.L. 573,
Cohen, Marjorie Griffin 5451, 5452,
Cohen, Marvin H. 5453,

Cohen, Nancy 5454,
Cohen, Sharon 5455,
Cohen, Stanley 5456,
Cohen, Zvi 574, 5457,
Cohen, Zvi, ed. 575, 1278,
Cohn, Jeri 576,
Colbeck, J.C. 3622,
Coldwell, G.R., chairman 4282,
Cole, Douglas 2399,
Cole, I.N. 7515,
Cole, P.J.E. 3623,
Coleclough, A. 5458,
Coleman, C.M. 7516,
Coleman, H.T.J. 577,
Coleman, Marjorie A. 6457, 6459,
Colley, Louise A. ed. 7904,
Collier, Eric 2400,
Collier, H.W. 2401,
Collinge, F.B. 3012,
Collins, David L. 2402,
Collins, Joan Manon 2403,
Collins, Maynard 5459,
Collins, Michael 5460,
Collins, Robert 3624,
Collins-Williams, C. 578, 579, 5461, 5462,
   5463,
Colman, Mary Elizabeth 2404,
Colombo, John Robert 5464,
Colonsay History Book Committee 3625,
Colpitts, Grant 4253,
Commission on Emotional and Learning
   Disorders in Children 580, 5465,
Committee for Survey of Hospital Needs in
   Metropolitan Toronto 5466,
Common, W.B. 1283,
Community Centres Conference (1946:
   Vancouver) 2405,
Community Chest and Council of Greater
   Vancouver. Family and Child Welfare
   Division. Working Boys' Home
   Committee 2406,
Community Chest and Councils of the
   Greater Vancouver Area. Social
   Planning Section 3199, 3200,
Community Chest and Councils of the
   Greater Vancouver Area. Welfare and
   Recreation Council 2407,
Community Chest and Councils of the
   Greater Vancouver Area. Welfare and
   Recreation Council. Committee to Study
   Day Care Needs in the Greater
   Vancouver Area 2408,
Comparative and International Education
   Society of Canada (1969: Toronto) 581,
Con, Harry 2119,
Con, Ronald J. 2119,
Conboy, E.J. 5467,
Condon, Thomas Francis 5468,
Conference on Problems of Teaching
   Young Children (1968: Toronto) 5469,
Conference on the Canadian High School
   (1st: 1963: Banff) 582,
Conference on the Canadian High School
   (2nd: 1964: Banff) 583, 3238,
Conklin, Rodney Craig 584,
Conn, Gertrude Mary 3626,
Conner, Desmond M. 7517,
Connor, Carl Yoder 5470,
Conquest, George Rionzi 3627,
Conrad, R. 585,
Conron, Brandon 5471,
Conron, Caroline L. 5472,
Conroy, J.J. 2409,
Consultation for Action on Unreached
   Youth (1964: Geneva Park-Lake
   Couchiching) 5473,
Conway, Clifford B. 2410, 5474,
Cook, Dean 3628,
Cook, E.B. 4370,

Ontario. Committee on Religious
Education in the Public Schools of
Ontario 6675,
Ontario Curriculum Institute. Committee
on the Scope and Organization of the
Curriculum 6676,
Ontario. Department of Education 6028,
6677,
Ontario. Department of Health 6678, 6679,
Ontario. Department of Labour 1946, 6680,
Ontario. Department of Neglected and
Dependent Children 6681,
Ontario. Department of Public Welfare
6403, 6682,
Ontario. Department of Public Welfare.
Committee on Child Care and Adoption
Services 6683,
Ontario. Department of Reform
Institutions 6684,
Ontario. Department of the Provincial
Secretary 1831, 6471, 6472, 6473, 6685, 6686,
6687, 6688,
Ontario. Department of the Provincial
Secretary and Citizenship. Citizenship
Division 6689,
Ontario Economic Council 6690,
Ontario (Government) 6691,
Ontario Institute for Studies in Education
7332,
Ontario. Interdepartmental Nutrition
Committee 6692, 6693,
Ontario Law Reform Commission 6694,
Ontario. Legislative Assembly. Select
Committee on Youth 6695,
Ontario Medical Association. Committee
on Child Welfare 6696,
Ontario. Minister's Advisory Committee
on Child Welfare 6697,
Ontario. Ministry of Community and
Social Services 6698,
Ontario. Physical Fitness Study
Committee 6699,
Ontario. Provincial Committee on Aims
and Objectives of Education in the
Schools of Ontario 6700,
Ontario. Public Welfare Department 6701,
Ontario. Royal Commission Appointed to
Enquire Into the Prison and Reformatory
System 6702,
Ontario. Royal Commission on Education,
1950 6703, 7081,
Ontario. Royal Commission on Public
Welfare 6704,
Ontario. Royal Commission on the Care
and Control of the Mentally Defective and
Feeble-minded in Ontario (and the
Prevalence of Venereal Disease) 6705,
Ontario. Royal Commission to Inquire
Into the Administration, Management
and Welfare of the Ontario School for the
Blind 6706,
Ontario. Royal Commission to Investigate
the Victoria Industrial School for Boys,
Mimico 6707,
Ontario. Superintendent of Neglected and
Dependent Children 6180,
Opdecam, Nancy E. 105,
Open Door Society 1056,
Open Door Society, ed. 1260, 5659,
Opollot, J.A. 7654,
Oppenheimer, Jo 6708,
O'Rafferty, Ann 7756,
Orange Benevolent Society of
Saskatchewan 4431, 4432,
Orchard, Imbert, ed. 2935, 2936,
Orcutt, E. Roy 4433,
Ord, Nan 6709,
Ord, Violet 6710,
O'Reilly-Hewitt, F.T. 6711,

Orlikow, Lionel 1578,
Ormrod, Georgina 6712,
Ormsby, H.L. 6713,
Ormsby, Margaret A. 1579,
Ormsby, Margaret A., ed. 2196,
Orn, Donald Elroy 4434,
Ornstein, Michael D. 644, 645,
O'Rourke, David 6266.
Orphans' Home and Female Aid Society
(Toronto) 6714,
Orvis, Kenneth 6715,
Osborn, R.W. 5192,
Osborne, Robert F. 1580, 2937,
Osmond, Humphry 3387,
Ostiguy, Jean Rene 6716,
Ostry, Ethel 1581,
Ostry, Sylvia 673,
Ottewell, A.E. 4435,
Ouellet, Francoise Miller 1582,
Oughton, Libby 1583,
Outerbridge, Eugene W. 7175,
Owen, Herbert F. 6980,
Owen, Wendy 264,
Owens, A.L. 4915,
Oxbox-Glen Ewen History Book Committee
4436,
Oyen and District Historical Society 4437,
Ozere, R.L. 7757,
Pepin, Jean-Luc, ed. 1709,
Pace, James B. 6717,
Pacey, Desmond 1584,
Pachai, Bridglal, ed. 7552,
Pacific Northwest Conference on Family
Relations (8th: 1946: Vancouver) 3187,
Packford, B. Levitz 2938,
Pady, Cecil A. 1585,
Page, Joseph L. 6718,
Page, Shirley 2939,
Paget, A.P. 1586, 1839,
Paivio, Allan 6719,
Pajonas, Patricia J. 6720,
Pakes, Fraser 4438,
Palate, Elizabeth Leon 4439, 4440,
Palmer, A. Judith 6721,
Palmer, Gwen 4441,
Palmer, Howard 268, 4442,
Palmer, Howard, ed. 2033, 3669, 3746, 3806,
4204, 4444, 4697, 4698,
Palmer, Hugh 2940,
Palmer, John A. 6722,
Palmer, Judith A. 6723,
Palmer, Tamara, ed. 4204, 4697, 4698,
Pammett, Jon H. 6724, 6725,
Pammett, Jon H., ed. 1709,
Panabaken, Harold Edward 4443,
Panabaker, D.N. 6726,
Panabaker, Katherine 6727,
Pannekoek, Frits 1587, 4444,
Pantel, Norman W. 6728,
Paradis-Richard, Rachel 190,
Paradis, Roger 7758,
Parent, Alphonse-Marie, chairman 6858,
6859, 6860, 6861, 6862,
Paris, Erna 6729,
Paris, R.P. 2827,
Park, E. Louise 1588,
Park, Edna Wilhelmene 6730,
Park, Edwards A. 1589,
Parker, Alfred J. 1590,
Parker, Edwin B. 1591, 1592,
Parker, Graham 1593, 1594, 1595,
Parker, Janet A. 6731,
Parker, K. Ross 5450, 7712,
Parker, Margaret 1596,
Parker, Mrs. G. Cameron 2941,
Parker, Phyllis 7581,
Parker, Stephanie M. 6732,
Parker, William L. 2146, 4445, 4915,
Parks, F. Elizabeth 6733,

## About the Compilers

NEIL SUTHERLAND is professor in the Department of Social and Educational Studies at the University of British Columbia and the author of *Children in English Canadian Society: Framing the Twentieth Century Consensus* (1976).

JEAN BARMAN is associate professor in the Department of Social and Educational Studies at the University of British Columbia. Her most recent book is *The West beyond the West: A History of British Columbia* (1991).

LINDA L. HALE is an instructor in the history department at Douglas College, British Columbia. She and Jean Barman are co-compilers of *British Columbia Local Histories: A Bibliography* (1991).